DICTIONARY OF
American History
Third Edition

EDITORIAL BOARD

DICTIONARY OF
American History

Third Edition

Stanley I. Kutler, *Editor in Chief*

Volume 3
Denomination to Ginseng

CHARLES SCRIBNER'S SONS®

THOMSON
GALE™

New York • Detroit • San Diego • San Francisco • Cleveland • New Haven, Conn. • Waterville, Maine • London • Munich

THOMSON
GALE

Dictionary of American History, Third Edition

Stanley I. Kutler, *Editor*

For more information, contact
Charles Scribner's Sons
An imprint of the Gale Group
300 Park Avenue South
New York, NY 10010

LIBRARY OF CONGRESS CATALOGING-IN-PUBLICATION DATA

Dictionary of American history / Stanley I. Kutler.—3rd ed.
p. cm.
Includes bibliographical references and index.
ISBN 0-684-80533-2 (set : alk. paper)
1. United States—History—Dictionaries. I. Kutler, Stanley I.
E174 .D52 2003
973'.03—dc21

Printed in United States of America
10 9 8 7 6 5 4 3 2 1

CONTENTS

DICTIONARY OF
American History

Third Edition

D

(Continued)

DENOMINATIONALISM. Religion scholars developed this term to account for the variety of faiths in the United States. Because of its associations with religious pluralism, denominationalism also implies ecclesiastical disestablishment and religious freedom, in the sense that no particular religious body receives the endorsement of nor financial support from the government. Prior to the last quarter of the twentieth century, the concept was usually a Protestant term that referred to a cooperative spirit among the largest Protestant denominations in the United States. But after 1970, as those denominations lost members and influence, and as public institutions began to reflect the United States' religious diversity, denominationalism expanded to include all faiths, even those for whom the idea may be foreign.

Origins

In sociological theory, "denomination" is a category that stands midway on the spectrum of ecclesiastical structure, with "church" at one end and "sect" at the other. Max Weber was one of the first sociologists of religion to develop the dichotomy between church and sect. According to him, a sect is primarily a voluntary association of adults who affiliated on the basis of a shared religious ideal, while the church, in contrast, is an inclusive arrangement with less stringent demands for conformity and self-consciousness. Weber's student Ernst Troeltsch, a theological ethicist, however, popularized the term for many Protestants in the United States with his book *The Social Teaching of the Christian Churches* (1912). He used the concept more prescriptively than had Weber. Troeltsch elevated churches above sects because the former are capable of ministering to society's needs, while the latter are socially withdrawn and reinforce among their adherents a sense of religious purity.

Although denominationalism has been a construct used throughout the twentieth century to understand PROTESTANTISM, the idea first gained currency several centuries earlier. During the English Civil War of the 1640s, when Parliament called the Westminster Assembly to set the theological and liturgical direction for the Church of England, the Independents were the most vigorous advocates of the idea that the true church could not be confined to any particular ecclesiastical institution, whether the Church of Rome, the Church of England, or the Scottish Kirk. Instead, Independents argued that believers should be free to assemble without fear of coercion from the state or its established religious body. Although such a view would have meant religious disestablishment—something contrary to the very purpose for which Parliament had called the Westminster Assembly—the Westminster Confession of Faith reflects the influence of Independents and hints at the idea of denominationalism in its chapter on the church: "The catholick church hath been sometimes more, sometimes less visible. And particular churches, which are members thereof, are more or less pure, according as the doctrine of the gospel is taught and embraced, ordinances administered, and publick worship performed more or less purely in them." Crucial to the notion of denominationalism here was the idea that several churches, despite disunity, were part of the true church.

This was the outlook that the earliest Protestants took to the British colonies in North America. In fact, Protestantism in the United States was largely comprised of groups who were religious dissenters in England. The British context for the emergence of religious disestablishment in effect gave denominationalism plausibility. The churches in the United States would not attempt to set themselves up as the only church with legitimacy, as the Church of England had. Instead, they agreed to recognize each other as sharing a common mission, even if holding to different creeds or forms of worship. In the United States, the Presbyterian Church's 1787 revision of the Westminster Confession demonstrates exactly the spirit that the Independents had expressed in the seventeenth century, and how the word "denomination" would become the primary means for tolerating diversity. The church revised the chapter on the civil magistrate to say that "the duty of civil magistrates to protect the church of our common Lord, without giving the preference to any denomination of Christians above the rest, in such a manner that all ecclesiastical persons whatever shall enjoy the full, free, and unquestioned liberty of discharging every part of their sacred functions, without violence or danger." In effect, the word "denomination" was a glorified way of speaking about bodies that in England would have been regarded as dissenting or, worse, sectarian.

The diversity of churches encouraged by religious disestablishment proved to be baffling to observers of religious life in the United States. Throughout the nineteenth century, foreign visitors to the new nation commented regularly on the array of religious practices among Americans, but they used "sect" and "denomination" interchangeably. Achille Murat, for example, a son of French nobility and living in exile, wrote in 1832 that he believed it would be impossible even to catalogue "all the dogmas of the thousand and one sects which divide the people of the United States." When writing of government assistance for religious bodies, however, Murat noted that public lands had been set aside for a "school and a church, of any denomination whatever." Similarly, Frances Trollope, an Englishwoman who resided briefly in Cincinnati, observed in her book *The Domestic Manners of the Americans* (1832) that, "besides the broad and well-known distinctions of Episcopalian, Roman Catholic, Presbyterian, Calvinist, Baptist, Quaker, Swedenborgian, Universalist, Dunker, &c. &c. &c., there are innumerable others springing out of these." This "queer variety," as she called it, suggested that denominationalism was little more than a form of sectarianism, where each group has "a church government of its own," headed by "the most intriguing and factious individual." Although denominations in the early United States may have looked sectarian from a European perspective, most visitors agreed with the English reformer, Harriet Martineau, who attributed American religious pluralism to the "Voluntary Principle" of "professing to leave religion free."

Only a few Protestant churchmen in the United States tried to give order to this diversity. Robert Baird, a Presbyterian whose *Religion in the United States of America* (1844) was the first religious history of the United States, followed Martineau in locating the nation's religious diversity in its decision to make belief a voluntary and private matter. Yet, despite the number of denominations, Baird believed far more unity existed than was commonly acknowledged. He offered two interpretive schemes. One was to divide the denominations theologically between the Calvinists and the Arminians. The other was to notice differences in church polity with three large groupings: Episcopalian, Presbyterian, and Congregationalist. Otherwise, religion in America was generally homogenous, except for such "unevangelical" denominations as Unitarians, Roman Catholics, Mormons, Jews, and atheists. Philip Schaff, a German American theologian, was less optimistic than Baird about the unity of American religion. In lectures he gave to German audiences and published as *America: A Sketch of its Political, Social, and Religious Character* (1854), Schaff praised the voluntaristic impulse running through American Christianity: "It is truly wonderful what a multitude of churches, ministers, colleges, theological seminaries, and benevolent institutions are there founded and maintained entirely by free-will offerings." But he feared that such religious freedom also nurtured the Protestant tendency toward sectarianism, thus preventing the harmony Christianity required.

Denominationalism and Post-Denominationalism

In Baird and Schaff's books, a new understanding of denominationalism was beginning to emerge. It was no longer simply a way of recognizing all British Protestant dissenters as members of a true church that transcended ecclesiastical particularities. Instead, denominationalism was becoming a way of forming a quasi-religious establishment, where the Protestants who joined the ecumenical enterprise were regarded as a denomination of the true church, and those who resisted cooperation were deemed sectarian. In other words, from the late nineteenth century until the 1960s, denominationalism lost its association with religious dissent and functioned as a form of ecclesiastical establishment.

The impetus for this new meaning was a concerted effort among Anglo American Protestant leaders after the Civil War to make common cause against infidelity and preserve Christian civilization in the United States. The culmination of these endeavors was the founding in 1908 of the Federal Council of Churches (FCC), renamed the National Council of Churches in 1951. The aim of the organization was to "manifest the essential oneness of the Christian churches of America" and to "secure a larger combined influence . . . in all matters affecting the moral and social condition of the people." Although the intentions of the FCC's organizers were to be as broad as possible (while excluding Roman Catholics and Unitarians, for instance), over time the Federal Council emerged as the glue of mainstream American Protestantism, with member denominations constituting the denominational ideal and dissenting groups manifesting a sectarian spirit. Not only was this outlook reflected in books justifying Protestant ecumenism, such as Samuel McCrea Cavert's *The American Churches in the Ecumenical Movement, 1900–1968* (1968), which argues that competition among churches was analogous to the divisions caused by race and class; it also proved to be a unifying perspective for historians of religion in the United States, whose narratives focused on the ecumenical Protestant denominations.

By 1970, however, the Protestant mainstream was no longer synonymous with American religion, and denominationalism began to return to its earlier designation as a form of religious, as opposed to Protestant, pluralism. Some sociologists of religion attribute the decline of denominationalism to the Protestant mainline's inability to retain members and recruit new ones, as well as the concomitant rise of special-purpose religious organizations that replaced the services of ecumenical Protestantism. Another factor has been the shift since the 1960s from the ideal of assimilating the diversity of American culture into a common whole to one that relishes ethnic and cultural particularity. Because the impulse behind Protestant ecumenism was largely assimilative, when cultural diversity replaced the melting pot as the preferred way to understand variety in the United States, the idea of denominationalism also shifted from one that set boundaries between cooperative and sectarian faiths to one where all religions were equal and, so, transcended distinctions among church, sect, or denomination. The historian R. Laurence Moore exemplified this changed outlook and argued, as did nineteenth-century observers of American religion, that division and the creation of new religions—not interdenominational cooperation—is the religious "mainstream" in the United States, precisely because of the nation's tradition of religious freedom and faith's capacity to give identity to people living in society without clear structures and delineated social roles. As Moore writes, "The American religious system may be said to be 'working' only when it is creating cracks within denominations, when it is producing novelty, even when it is fueling antagonisms."

The recognition that diversity and change are at the heart of religious life in the United States has returned denominationalism to earliest usage in the nation's history. In handbooks and directories on churches and religion in America, denominationalism lacks a sense that some religious bodies are denominations of one whole, say, Protestant or mainline. Instead, denominationalism has become a way to affirm that each faith (whether Methodism, Hinduism, or Eastern Rite Catholicism) constitutes but one particular expression of generic religion. Because of its Christian and Protestant origins, denominationalism may not be the most felicitous way of describing religious diversity in the United States. But, as a term that is bound up with the nation's tradition of religious freedom and ecclesiastical disestablishment, the term "denominationalism" possesses advantages that may account for its ongoing usage.

BIBLIOGRAPHY

Baird, Robert. *Religion in the United States of America.* New York: Arno Press, 1969.

Cavert, Samuel McCrea. *The American Churches in the Ecumenical Movement, 1900–1968.* New York: Association Press, 1968.

Greeley, Andrew M. *The Denominational Society: A Sociological Approach to Religion in America.* Glenview, Ill.: Scott, Foresman, 1972.

Moore, R. Laurence. *Religious Outsiders and the Making of Americans.* New York: Oxford University Press, 1986.

Mullin, Robert Bruce, and Russell E. Richey, eds. *Reimagining Denominationalism: Interpretive Essays.* New York: Oxford University Press, 1994.

Niebuhr, H. Richard. *The Social Sources of Denominationalism.* New York: Meridian Books, 1957.

Powell, Milton, ed. *The Voluntary Church: American Religious Life, 1740–1865, Seen Through the Eyes of European Visitors.* New York: Macmillan, 1967.

Richey, Russell E., ed. *Denominationalism.* Nashville, Tenn.: Abingdon, 1977.

Wuthnow, Robert. *The Restructuring of American Religion: Society and Faith since World War II.* Princeton, N.J.: Princeton University Press, 1988.

D. G. Hart

See also **Religion and Religious Affiliation.**

DENTISTRY. In the eighteenth century, the practice of dentistry was primarily concerned with extracting diseased teeth, not protecting healthy ones. When George Washington was inaugurated in 1789 at the age of 57, he had only one natural tooth left. State-of-the-art dental care in his day consisted of yanking out rotten teeth without benefit of painkillers and crafting awkward dentures from elk and cow teeth, and from the ivory tusks of elephants, hippopotami, and walruses. (Washington owned several pairs of such dentures, though none made of wood, despite the myth.) Dr. A. A. Plantou, a Frenchman who had emigrated to Philadelphia, introduced porcelain teeth to the United States in 1817. (France was the center of dentistry in the eighteenth century; American dominance in the field began in the nineteenth century.) In the 1850s, Nelson Goodyear's invention of Vulcanite—an inexpensive hard rubber that could be molded to the shape of the jaw and fitted with porcelain teeth—finally made false teeth affordable for the average person.

The introduction of nitrous oxide ("laughing gas") in the early 1830s made extraction less painful, but correct dosages were hard to determine. Ether was first used in surgery in 1842 by Dr. Crawford W. Long (though the patent went to Drs. William Thomas Green Morton and Charles Thomas Jackson in 1846). Chloroform, discovered in the early 1830s by doctors in several countries, also began to be used as an anesthetic in dentistry. In 1884, Dr. William Stuart Halsted reported that morphine injected into the lower jaw resulted in complete numbness in six minutes. However, the drug was addictive and could cause localized tissue death (necrosis). It wasn't until 1905 and the invention of the first non-addictive anesthetic, novocaine ("new cocaine"), that dental work could be both safe and painless.

In 1855, Dr. Robert Arthur introduced a cohesive gold foil filling for teeth, produced by heating and cooling the metal to make it stronger. The first crowns were developed in 1880 by Dr. Cassius M. Richmond, who patented a porcelain tooth soldered to a gold body. The invention of the electric furnace (in 1894) and low-fusing porcelain (in 1898) made possible the first strong porcelain "jacket" crown, introduced in 1903.

The first dental school, the Baltimore College of Dental Surgery, was founded in 1840 in Maryland. For decades, however, dentists were not required to pass a test or obtain a license in order to practice. It took nearly one hundred years for dental education to develop its present form: three or four years of undergraduate study and four years of dental school, with a curriculum including medical science, technical training, and clinical practice.

The Mercury Controversy

Mercury compounds introduced to the United States in 1832 as a filling for the cavities left after dental caries are removed provoked a controversy that continues to the present day. Because the injurious effects of mercury poisoning—ranging from muscle tremors to hallucinations—

were well known in the nineteenth century, many were fearful of the new treatment. Mercury still accounts for 50 percent of modern silver amalgam fillings, developed in 1895 by Dr. G. V. Black (known as "the father of scientific dentistry"). The other components are: 35 percent silver, about 15 percent tin (or tin and copper, for added strength), and a trace of zinc. In the late 1980s it was discovered that minute amounts of mercury vapor are released in chewing. A few years later researchers demonstrated the ill effects of silver amalgam in sheep (the mercury caused kidney malfunction) and human fetuses (mercury from mothers with silver fillings was found in the brain tissue of stillborn babies). Some worried patients have had all their amalgam fillings removed and replaced with porcelain inlays (developed in the late 1890s) or composite resin fillings (invented in the late 1930s). On the other hand, considering the long and widespread use of amalgam fillings—contained in the teeth of more than 100 million living Americans, and handled constantly by dentists—many experts believe such findings to be inconclusive. The American Dental Association (ADA) not only affirms the safety of dental amalgam but also claims that it is unethical for dentists to recommend removal of amalgam fillings from a patient's teeth "for the alleged purpose of removing toxic substances from the body." The ADA cites other studies, of dentists as well as patients, that show no correlation between amalgam fillings and kidney disease or nervous disorders.

Treating Tooth Decay

In the early nineteenth century, it was believed that decay (dental caries) originated on the surface of the tooth. In 1890, American dentist Willoughby D. Miller's groundbreaking work, *The Micro-organisms of the Human Mouth*, revealed that acids from dissolved sugars in foods decalcify tooth enamel, followed by bacterial action that destroys the bone-like dentin underneath that surrounds living tissue. This discovery led dentists to place more emphasis on oral prophylaxis—disease-preventive measures—as well as on proper sterilization of dental tools. Yet dental health nationwide remained less than optimum. During World War II, the Selective Service initially required each new armed forces recruit to have at least twelve teeth, three pairs of matching front teeth (incisors) and three pairs of chewing teeth (molars). When it turned out that one in five of the first two million men didn't qualify, all dental standards were dropped.

The addition of fluoride to city water systems, beginning in 1945 in Michigan and Illinois, sparked a major controversy. In 1942, a U.S. Public Health Service dentist, Dr. H. Trendley Dean, had determined that adding one part fluoride per million of drinking water reduced dental caries. By 1950, more than 50 cities had fluoridated their water supply. Then came the protests, most famously those of the John Birch Society, which believed the program to be a Communist plot to poison Americans. Others, including health food advocates, were concerned about potential poisons. Yet by the 1960s fluoride was in nearly 3,000 water systems serving 83 million people. By the end of the twentieth century, some 155 million Americans—62 percent of the population—had fluoridated water. Fluoride also has been added to many toothpaste and mouthwash brands.

In 1954 a team of scientists at the University of Notre Dame, led by Frank J. Orland, identified Streptococcus mutans as the bacteria that produces the acid that dissolves tooth enamel and dentin. The origin of gum (periodontal) disease was unknown until the mid-1960s, when bacterial plaque was found to be the culprit. Since the 1970s, biotechnology has helped the dental researchers known as oral ecologists to begin to identify some of the more than 400 species of microorganisms (mostly bacteria) that live in the mouth.

Dental Tools

Invented in 1895 in Germany, x-rays were demonstrated for dental use the following year in the United States by Dr. Charles Edmund Kells Jr., who also invented the automatic electric suction pump to drain saliva. (The first tool for saliva control was the rubber dental dam, invented in 1864 by Dr. Sanford C. Barnum.) Commercial x-ray equipment made for dentistry was first used in the United States in 1913. Other features of modern dental offices took many decades to achieve their present form. In 1832 James Snell developed the first dental chair, which included a spirit lamp and mirror to illuminate the patient's mouth. A major breakthrough in chair design occurred in 1954, with Dr. Sanford S. Golden's reclining model. John Naughton's Den-Tal-Ez chair, powered by hydraulic cylinders, was introduced in the 1960s. The first self-cleaning device to receive patients' spit was the Whitcomb Fountain Spittoon, marketed in 1867.

The electric-powered drill was invented in 1868 by George F. Green, a mechanic employed by the S. S. White Company. Inspired by the workings of the Singer sewing machine mass-produced a decade earlier, James Beall Morrison added a foot treadle and pulley system in 1871. But the drill was still very heavy, and dentists' offices were not wired for electricity until the late 1880s, when Dr. Kells first adopted the new technology. In 1953 a team at the National Bureau of Standards, led by Dr. Robert J. Nelson, finally developed a hydraulic-powered turbine drill that could achieve speeds of 61,000 revolutions per minute. (Today, electrically powered drill speeds of 400,000 revolutions per minute or more are common.) Speed is significant because it reduces not only the time it takes to remove caries but also the amount of pressure on the tooth.

Recent Developments

Since the mid-1980s composite resin fillings have grown increasingly popular in the United States as an alternative to amalgam. The first composite filling was developed in 1955 by Michael Buonocore and others, but the acrylic proved too soft for the stress caused by chewing. The addition of microscopic particles of glass or quartz to the plastic resin base in 1967 solved this problem. While composite resin is white—and therefore relatively invisible—it is not as long-lasting as silver amalgam, can be more costly for the patient, and requires greater skill on the dentist's part because it is applied in separate layers that must harden under a strong light.

Numerous advances in dental treatment in the late twentieth century have radically altered the field. Digital imagery of the teeth, transmitted through fiber optics from an x-ray sensor to a computer screen, offers a faster, safer, and more easily readable alternative to x-ray film. This process emits 90 to 95 percent less radiation than ordinary x-rays, and allows the image to be magnified and more easily stored, reproduced, and shared with other doctors. The first laser "drill" was approved by the FDA in 1997. Lasers burn through decay without vibration or pressure on the tooth. Other advances include "invisible" braces that attach to the insides of teeth, dental implants that anchor to the jaw to permanently replace missing teeth, and computer-generated tooth restorations. Cosmetic dentistry, including bonding (using composite resin to improve tooth shape and whiteness) and bleaching, has spawned business franchises devoted exclusively to these services.

BIBLIOGRAPHY

Hoffmann-Axthelm, Walter, trans. H. M. Koehler. *History of Dentistry.* Chicago: Quintessence, 1981.

Jedynakiewicz, Nicolas M. *A Practical Guide to Technology in Dentistry.* London: Wolfe, 1992.

Jong, Anthony W., ed. *Community Dental Health.* St. Louis, Mo.: Mosby, 1988.

Prinz, Hermann. *Dental Chronology: A Record of the More Important Historic Events in the Evolution of Dentistry.* Philadelphia: Lea & Febiger, 1945.

Ring, Malvin E. *Dentistry: An Illustrated History.* New York: Abrams, 1985.

Weinberger, Bernhard W. *An Introduction to the History of Dentistry.* St. Louis, Mo.: Mosby, 1948.

Wynbrandt, James. *The Excruciating History of Dentistry.* New York: St. Martin's Press, 1998.

Cathy Curtis

DENVER. A consolidated city and county and the capital of COLORADO, Denver grew from 467,610 people in 1990 to 554,636 in 2000. In the latter year there were more than two million additional people in the metropolitan area counties of Adams, Arapahoe, Boulder, Douglas, Jefferson, and Weld. Some 32 percent of the core city population is Hispanic, the fastest-growing ethnic group. About 11 percent are African American, 3 percent Asian American, and 1 percent Native American. Denver has elected a Hispanic mayor, Federico F. Pena (1983–1991) and an African American mayor, Wellington E. Webb (1991–). Local lumber being scarce, Denver is characterized by brick buildings. Even in the poorest residential neighborhoods, single-family detached housing prevails, reflecting the western interest in "elbow room" and the city's location on a spacious, flat high-plains site where sprawling growth is unimpeded by any large body of water. Geography makes the Mile High City, at an altitude of 5,280 feet, dry with only fourteen inches of precipitation per year and sunny for about three hundred days a year. It is, however, subject to dramatic temperature changes.

Denver Gateway. The Welcome Arch greets visitors arriving by rail at Union Depot, c. 1908. LIBRARY OF CONGRESS

Denver was founded in 1858 by participants in the first Colorado gold rush and experienced its first significant growth with the development of mining around Idaho Springs and Central City in the adjacent mountains. Town site promoter William Larimer named the city for the governor of Kansas Territory, of which eastern Colorado was then a part. Rivalry with the nearby city of Golden was decided in Denver's favor by virtue of the permanent location of the Colorado capital there and its superior rail connections. Denver's economy surged again with the expansion of silver mining in the Rockies, particularly at Leadville after 1878. Denver was the supply center for the mines and also developed a major smelting industry. The expansion of stock raising and then agriculture on the Colorado plains from the 1870s onward further diversified the city's economy as the capital of the Rocky Mountain Empire. By 1890 Denver had become a city of more than 100,000 residents with a prominent economic elite, a growing middle class, and an active labor movement. During the early decades of the twentieth century, Robert Speer dominated Denver politics as mayor from 1904 to 1912 and again from 1916 to 1918. Speer

Modern Denver. A high-rise hotel, 1961. Library of Congress

brought immigrant neighborhoods, vice interests, and local business leaders together in a powerful political machine but also worked to beautify the city and to modernize municipal services. He was an important impetus behind the development of the Civic Center complex below the state capitol. One of the best examples of City Beautiful planning, the Civic Center has continued to attract public buildings and cultural institutions. Denver's growth slowed in the 1920s and 1930s, but it revived as an important war production center during World War II and benefited from the expansion of federal agencies serving the mountain West.

The 1970s energy boom in the northern Rockies, for which Denver was the business center, produced fifty-story high-rise office towers downtown and a proliferation of suburban subdivisions, shopping malls, and a second office core in the suburban Denver Tech Center. Dependence on nonrenewable natural resources as an underpinning of its economy, however, returned to haunt the city during the 1980s oil bust. When the price of crude oil dropped from thirty-nine dollars to nine dollars a barrel, Denver briefly went into a depression, losing population and experiencing the highest office vacancy rate in the nation. A large federal service center, augmented by state and local government jobs, provided some stability. Mining and agriculture, the traditional local economic base, were replaced by service industries, tourism, and electronic, computer, and cable telecommunications, the latter a boom industry of the 1980s and 1990s. Notable institutions include the Denver Museum of Natural History, the Colorado History Museum, the Denver Art Museum, the Denver Center for the Performing Arts, the Denver Public Library, and a major branch of the U.S. Mint. Denver is also home to major league basketball, football, and baseball teams; Coors Field, home of the Colorado Rockies baseball club since 1995, helped to spark substantial residential and commercial reinvestment in the core districts. Handgun violence and crime, as well as smog and traffic congestion, were among the city's principal problems. As one of the most isolated major cities in the United States, Denver has from its beginnings focused on building—some have said overbuilding—transportation systems. Fear of being bypassed began when railroads and airlines avoided Denver because of the fourteen-thousand-foot Rocky Mountains barrier. In the first half of the 1990s, Denver built an outer ring of freeways, began a light rail system, and opened the fifty-three-square-mile Denver International Airport, the nation's largest airport in terms of area and capacity for growth.

BIBLIOGRAPHY

Abbott, Carl, Stephen J. Leonard, and David McComb. *Colorado: A History of the Centennial State.* Niwot: University Press of Colorado, 1994.

Leonard, Stephen J., and Thomas J. Noel. *Denver: Mining Camp to Metropolis.* Niwot: University Press of Colorado, 1990.

Carl Abbott
Thomas J. Noel

See also **Energy Industry; Gold Mines and Mining; Rocky Mountains; Silver Prospecting and Mining.**

DEPARTMENT STORES have their roots in the New York City business arena of the industrial era. Their success in the mid-nineteenth century created such retailing giants as Macy's, Gimbels, Marshall Field's in Chicago, and Neiman-Marcus in Dallas. Department stores indirectly paved the way for department/mail-order stores, smaller department/chain stores, and late-twentieth-century mass merchandising department/discount stores like Wal-Mart. The story of department store shopping is one that seemingly forever will be bound up in the transportation and travel patterns of Americans. At the beginning of the nineteenth century, subsistence growing and local handwork were the anchors of American buying. The limitations of foot travel or horse-drawn travel necessitated such an economy. Farmers grew what their families needed as well as what they could sell from the back of a wagon to people in nearby towns. In addition, handicraft artisans sold items such as furniture, candles, or tack to locals. Transportation advances began to change that economy. River travel by steamboat became practical after 1810; canal travel after 1825; rail travel after about 1832 in the East and from coast to coast after 1869 when work crews completed the Transcontinental Railroad.

Until the Industrial Revolution, however, production could not effectively utilize the potential of new transportation. Interchangeable parts, assembly line techniques, vertical integration of businesses, and urban industrialized centers made production of virtually all goods quicker and more cost efficient, allowing manufacturers to capitalize on transportation.

Yet merchandising outlets for mass-produced goods lagged behind the capabilities of industrialized production and transportation. Producers discovered that, without sufficient retail outlets, a large percentage of their goods could quickly become surplus, eating away at their bottom line. Industrialization also enabled companies to produce new goods that the buying public had never encountered and for which it had no need or desire. Wholesalers and brokers had already worked the agricultural produce system, taking grain and vegetables from farms to markets and profiting in the process. They were prepared to do the same for manufactured goods, but the cycle begged for some type of marketing or retail system to marry goods to consumers.

A new type of store filled the bill. City stores and shops specialized in specific goods, such as clothing or cookware. General stores had small offerings of a variety of goods, but neither could exploit what industrialized production and transportation could supply. Department stores could. From the beginning, department stores were large. Inside, owners divided them into "departments" which contained similar types of goods.

Although not the most famous of storeowners, Alexander Turney Stewart is the father of the American department store. An immigrant Irish schoolteacher, Stewart opened a small dry-goods store in New York in 1823. He prospered well enough to open a second store, Marble Dry Goods in 1848. In 1862 he built the huge Cast Iron Palace that claimed an entire city block and was the largest retail store in the world at the time.

Aside from creating the department store, Stewart started the practice of "no haggle" shopping. Haggling, the practice of buyers and sellers negotiating a price acceptable to both, was a tradition in American shopping. But Stewart saw that salesmen could conduct more business without the obstacle of haggling, and he also perceived that many shoppers did not like the haggling ritual. Instead, he settled on a price he could accept for every product he sold, then he marked the product with that price. His customers were free to pay the price or shop elsewhere. With little exception, they liked the policy and Stewart made millions of dollars.

The Philadelphia merchant John Wanamaker, as did all other department store pioneers, adopted Stewart's "one-price" policy, but he took it a step farther. Wanamaker, who first partnered with Nathan Brown in 1861, then worked alone after Brown's death in 1868, offered customers a "satisfaction guaranteed" policy that he backed with the promise of exchanges or refunds. While other merchants followed suit, Wanamaker was one of the first merchants to run a full-page ad in newspapers, and his endless advertising associated him most with the satisfaction pledge, something he called "the Golden Rule of business." Wanamaker branched out with stores in Pittsburgh, Memphis, St. Louis, Baltimore, Richmond, and Louisville. Ultimately he expanded into New York City, setting up business in one of Alexander Stewart's old stores.

Today, neither Stewart nor Wanamaker is a household name. R. H. Macy is. Rowland H. Macy founded the famous New York City department store that is known to most Americans as the annual sponsor of the Macy's Thanksgiving Day Parade and also because it is the scene of much of the story in the classic Christmas movie *Miracle on 34th Street.* The Macy's name is synonymous with American department stores.

R. H. Macy opened his first store—a sewing supply store—in Boston in 1844. He followed that with a dry goods store in 1846. Like thousands of other Americans, Macy followed the gold rush to California in 1849–1850. Unlike most of them, however, he did not mine for gold, but instead opened another store. In that Macy showed savvy, for most argonauts remained poor; those who serviced them did markedly better.

By 1851, Macy had returned to Haverhill, Massachusetts, where he opened the Haverhill Cheap Store, advertising a one-price policy. By 1858, Macy had moved to New York City, opening a dry goods store uptown. His business was remarkable, doing more than $85,000 in sales the first year. That same year Macy inaugurated the practice of setting up beautiful, fanciful toy displays in his store windows at Christmas.

Macy started buying up adjacent properties to expand his business. He also leased departments inside his store to outside retailers, which served to increase customer traffic. His sales volume enabled him to undercut other department stores, and he advertised the lowest prices of any store in the city. Macy entered mail-order sales in 1861. He inaugurated the now-traditional policy of clearance sales to liquidate merchandise and bolster cash flow. He also offered free delivery to nearby New York City boroughs.

Macy died in 1877, and management of the store passed through various hands until Isidor and Nathan Straus, friends who had previously leased a china concession inside Macy's, took over the management and ultimately bought controlling stock in Macy's. Later Macy's would become part of the Federated Department Store group.

Gimbel's was another famous New York City department store. Bavarian immigrant Adam Gimbel began his business career on the American frontier, establishing a trading post at Vincennes, Indiana, in 1842. There he brought the one-price policy to westerners. Gimbel prospered and opened stores in Milwaukee and Philadelphia. In 1910, Gimbel's son, Isaac, opened a store in New York City that successfully competed with Macy's. The Gimbel family later acquired the Saks company and, with Horace Saks, opened Saks Fifth Avenue for more affluent customers in 1924.

Department stores with one-price policies and satisfaction guarantees opened in urban areas across the nation. One of the most successful outside of New York City was Marshall Field's in Chicago. Marshall Field was a

Department Store Giant with Modest Beginnings. James Cash Penney, one of the founding fathers of the department store, opened his first dry-goods store in Wyoming in 1902 (shown in the picture Penney is holding). From there, he turned his holdings into more than 1,600 stores nationwide as one of the first retailers to own multiple stores. He also expanded into catalog sales so that people could shop from their homes; by the start of the twenty-first century, J. C. Penney was one of the last department stores to continue issuing a catalog, outlasting early catalog giants Sears and Montgomery Ward. Penney died in 1971. © Archive Photos, Inc.

young businessman working in Chicago in the late 1850s at the same time as businessman Potter Palmer was parlaying a dry goods store into a lucrative business and real-estate holding. In 1865, Palmer took in Field and Field's friend Levi Leiter to form Field, Leiter, and Palmer. By 1868, Field and Leiter bought out Palmer, then rented business space from him on State Street in Chicago. The pair survived the devastating Chicago Fire of 1871, but parted ways a decade later. Field bought out Leiter, and he formed Marshall Field and Company.

Field directed the store to annual profits of more than $4 million. Part of Field's success was that he practiced two policies that became the credo of American businessmen. First, "give the lady what she wants"; second, "the customer is always right." Field brought up John G. Shedd and Harry G. Selfridge, two former stock boys, to help with management. Shedd directed the store's change from a dry goods store to a department store like Macy's in New York. He became president of Marshall Field's after Field's death in 1906.

Department stores have always had to identify their niche with the public. Some, like Macy's, catered to all classes. Others, like Saks Fifth Avenue, appealed to a more elite clientele. One Dallas department store has always catered to customers with exotic tastes. In 1907, Herbert Marcus and his brother-in-law A. L. Neiman opened Neiman-Marcus with the intent of bringing the finest goods to customers in the West. While Neiman-Marcus was in some ways a traditional department store like Macy's, it always had a flair for the flamboyant. Nowhere but Neiman-Marcus could customers buy submarines, robots, or airplanes. Neiman-Marcus established a reputation, as Dallas citizens might say, "as big as Texas."

As the twentieth century progressed, some department stores consolidated into groups or "chains" for buying clout and protection from rival onslaught. Federated Department Stores formed in 1929 as a holding company for several department stores, such as Abraham & Straus and F&R Lazarus. For more than seventy years, Federated has offered the protection of consolidation to family-owned stores. It is one of the largest chains in the nation and includes such standards as Macy's and Bloomingdale's.

In big cities, department stores were seemingly unlimited in the products they could provide customers. But to many Americans—farmers in the Midwest, for example—those stores were out of reach. Some enterprising businessmen decided they would simply take the department store to the customer. While most department stores got into mail order at one time or another, none succeeded like Montgomery Ward, Sears and Roebuck, and J.C. Penney's.

The first man to capitalize on the mail order business was Aaron Montgomery Ward, a former salesman for Marshall Field's. In 1872 he began a mail order business, catering chiefly to Grangers at first. Grangers, or officially the Patrons of Husbandry, were groups of Midwestern farmers organized to protest the exorbitant freight and storage rates of railroads. They also protested the high mark-ups of goods at general stores, which, by location they were almost bound to patronize. Montgomery Ward capitalized on that Granger frustration and devoted itself to serving American agrarians at prices less than the general store. One of Ward's first catalogs, in fact, offered buyers an official Granger hat, a tall-crowned affair made of "all wool" and costing $1.25.

Of course, Wards could not have succeeded without the famous catalog. Its first issues were only four-to-six pages, crowded with pictures and price lists. Later issues were more organized. Ward updated them every year. It may have been to Ward's chagrin, or perhaps to his satisfaction that his business had made it another year, that out-of-date catalogs usually got relegated to the outhouse.

Montgomery Ward drew its chief competition from Sears, Roebuck and Company. By the mid-1890s, Richard W. Sears had teamed with Alva C. Roebuck to create Sears, Roebuck and Co. Sears had begun a career selling watches in 1886, but by 1895 he and Roebuck were making a lucrative living through catalog sales. Through diligent warehouse organization (which Sears hired out) and the establishment of regional fulfillment houses, Sears, Roebuck and Co. could promise quick turnaround on orders.

Perhaps more so than the Wards catalog, the Sears catalog, which by 1897 was running at more than 500 pages, became an American icon. Americans came to know it as the "Wish Book." From its pages customers could buy hammers and nails, dresses, hats, corsets, pots and pans, soaps, rugs. They could even buy—by ordering component parts and assembling them on site—a complete house with indoor plumbing.

Both Sears and Ward fared well through World War I, but the 1920s brought a new phenomenon. Just as Henry Ford's mass production of automobiles revolutionized freeway systems and suburban living, it impacted catalog sales as well. The catalog giants discovered that the automobile freed rural Americans from the nearby country store. On weekends they could drive to cities and partake of the big department stores, which was infinitely more exciting than leafing through catalogs. Almost simultaneously, both Montgomery Ward and Sears, Roebuck decided to get into the retail department store business and attract their share of urban trade. That business served as a complement to continued catalog sales.

Another catalog giant, J.C. Penney, entered mail-order sales in the reverse way. In 1902, with the backing of two silent partners, James Cash Penney opened a dry goods and general store in the mining town of Kemmerer, Wyoming. Penney was the son of a Baptist preacher, and he practiced his religion through business. He called his store the "Golden Rule" store (photos of which grace almost any modern Penney's store), and he offered fair prices, good service, and late store hours. He immediately made a profit, which enabled him to open more stores in the next few years. In actuality, J.C. Penney became one of the first multi-store companies, totaling 1,600 stores by 1950. Larger Penney's department stores became mall anchors, and in the 1960s began to draw fire from such companies as Dillards, Brown-Dunkin, now simply Dillards. J.C. Penney lived until 1971. He saw the company's move into catalog sales in the preceding decades. Ironically, at the turn of the twenty-first century Sears is out of the catalog business and Montgomery Ward is out of business altogether, leaving J.C. Penney as the major American catalog retailer.

Chain stores are the little siblings to big department stores. While in fact they contain departments, they are usually located on one level and are much smaller than urban multi-floor department stores. As such the U.S. Census bureau does not officially recognize them as department stores. Their rise, however, has impacted traditional department stores.

The grandfather of American chain stores was Frank W. Woolworth. In 1878, while clerking in the Watertown, New York, store of Moore and Smith, Woolworth learned the value of selling special goods at five cents or less. With money borrowed from one of his employers, Woolworth opened his own five-cent store, and made more than $200 profit before closing it. He periodically opened and closed stores, amassing a personal wealth of more than $2,000. In the process he realized that customers would also buy "more expensive" items for ten cents. Thus Woolworth created the purely American "five-and-dime" stores.

Chain Stores. Usually on just one floor, chain stores sell far fewer goods than full-fledged department stores and are not recognized as the latter by the U.S. Census. The founder of the "five-and-dime" chain store—where nothing cost more than five or ten cents—was F. W. Woolworth, who founded the Woolworth's chain. Shown here is an early Woolworth's store, c. 1910, in Montpelier, Vermont. © BETTMAN-CORBIS

By 1895, Woolworth had more than twenty-five stores garnering more than $1 million in annual sales. Realizing the potential of five-and-dimes, other stores followed suit: Kress, Kresge, T.G.&Y., and Ben Franklin to name a few. Most of those stores, however, were regional. Only Woolworths had a national base and widespread recognition.

By the 1960s, with suburbia rapidly eclipsing established cities, malls were becoming the fashionable place to shop. And few malls could survive without at least one full-fledged department store, a chain store, and a five-and-dime to anchor them down. But, like early department stores, malls were the provinces of large cities. Retailers soon saw a need for mid-range, hybrid stores that blended the departmentalization and variety of department stores, the accessibility of chain stores, and the relative value of five-and-dimes. Into that void stepped discount stores, direct forerunners of the superstores of the 1990s. Those stores include Kmart, the upscale Target, and Wal-Mart.

Wal-Mart originator Sam Walton got into the retail business in the 1950s, leasing a Ben Franklin store in Arkansas, making it turn a nice profit, then going into business for himself. Based on his experience working in five-and-dimes, Walton was able to negotiate good deals from producers by buying merchandise in bulk, then selling to customers at discount prices. Walton's target competition was Kmart, which had grown from the Kresge five-and-dimes. Walton opened his first Wal-Mart store in Rogers, Arkansas, in 1962. By 1985 he had 859 stores in twenty-two states. By the early 1990s, Wal-Mart was pioneering "supercenters"—extra-large stores that included full-size grocery stores, photography studios, McDonald's franchises, hair salons, and other specialty shops. Sales clerks and shift managers frequently got around the huge stores on in-line skates. In an unusual social phenomenon, Wal-Mart stores, with their toy aisles, arcade rooms, and fast food shops, became substitute amusement parks for millions of kids in rural America.

Walton died in 1992, but his chain continued to grow. By 1998 Wal-Mart boasted more than 3,000 stores in the United States, Canada, South America, and Europe. Wal-Mart critics have charged that the discount/department stores have caused the death of many small downtown areas by attracting business to peripheral locations. Some chambers of commerce have refused to let Wal-Mart open in their town unless it did so in or near downtown. Other critics have charged that Wal-Mart has marketed goods made by child labor in foreign sweatshops, even as the store advertised its "Made in America" campaign.

Author Bob Ortega has said, however, that Wal-Mart's legacy runs deeper than a chamber of commerce fight. By targeting the bottom-line—both his own and the consumer's—Sam Walton revolutionized department/chain-store style shopping. He had done nothing less than Henry Ford had when he married the assembly line with automobile production. Now all types of stores, from booksellers to video-rental stores, practice bulk buying, offering large selections and discount prices, all packaged in attractive, easily accessible stores. Wal-Mart stores have also forced traditional department stores to rethink marketing strategies to keep middle-class shoppers spending money in their stores and not at Wal-Mart.

Nevertheless, discount and discount/department stores have severely cut into the profits of traditional department stores. The fact that they are still centered in urban centers and rarely in the suburbs and even less frequently in rural areas has isolated department stores even in the age of the automobile. When department stores were novel and automobile travel special, a trip to the city was fun. Now, increased traffic in urban areas and consumers having less time to shop has contributed to the decline in the popularity of the department store as a destination. Customers report a preference for specialty stores, like Toys-R-Us or Barnes and Noble, and discount/department stores in strip shopping centers. They prefer to drive to a store, immediately get what they want, and leave, rather than face parking problems or a maze of poorly marked sales areas in department stores.

Department stores are responding, however. Some of the major companies are experimenting with centralized checkouts for customer convenience, better signage, and relocation of popular departments close to entrances. Sears has started focusing more on marketing the sale of tools and appliances, longtime strong sellers for the company, and less on clothes and soft goods. Other department stores have cornered higher-end brand names, especially in clothing, that are unavailable at discount supercenters.

Department stores began in the mid-nineteenth century when transportation enabled wholesalers and retailers to offer a wide variety of goods to urban buyers. Catalog sales did the same thing for isolated rural Americans. When individual transportation became widely available to all Americans in the 1920s, retail stores, even those built on catalog empires, had to find new ways to vie for business. In the 1960s and 1970s, Wal-Mart and Kmart brought a low-end, discount/department store alternative to middle America. Those supercenters offered busy shoppers an effective alternative to driving to department stores.

BIBLIOGRAPHY

Federated Department Stores. Home page at http://www.federated-fds.com.

Groner, Alex, ed., *The American Heritage History of American Business and Industry.* New York: American Heritage, 1972.

Latham, Frank B. *1872–1972: A Century of Serving Consumers; The Story of Montgomery Ward.* Chicago: Montgomery Ward, 1972.

Merrick, Amy, Jeffrey A. Trachtenberg, and Ann Zimmerman. "Are Department Stores Dead?," *The Wall Street Journal Classroom Edition,* May 2002. Available from http://www.wsjclassroomedition.com.

Ortega, Bob. *In Sam We Trust: The Untold Story of Sam Walton and How Wal-Mart Is Devouring America.* New York: Times Business, 1998.

Plunkett-Powell, Karen. *Remembering Woolworth's: A Nostalgic History of the World's Most Famous Five-and-Dime.* New York: St. Martin's Press, 1999.

Trimble, Vance H. *Sam Walton: The Inside Story of America's Richest Man.* New York: Dutton, 1990.

Weil, Gordon L. *Sears, Roebuck, U.S.A.: The Great American Catalog Store and How it Grew.* New York: Stein and Day, 1977.

R. Steven Jones

See also **Chain Stores; Dime Stores; Mail-Order Houses; Malls, Shopping; Retailing Industry.**

DEPLETION ALLOWANCES. The U.S. tax code provides so-called depletion allowances for mineral deposits and standing timber used in the creation of income. These allowances were instituted by the Revenue Act of 1913 and derive from the Sixteenth Amendment, which allows the federal government to tax income, but not capital. The Revenue Act of 1926 allows owners or operators of mineral properties to calculate depletion as a percentage of gross income. As of 2001, the depletion allowance on mineral deposits may be calculated on either a cost or a percentage basis. Since 1975, however, integrated producers have not been allowed to calculate oil and gas depletion on a percentage basis. Timber depletion must be calculated on a cost basis.

BIBLIOGRAPHY

Bradley, Robert L., Jr. *Oil, Gas, and Government: The U.S. Experience.* Lanham, Md.: Rowman and Littlefield, 1995. Comprehensive review of oil and gas regulations at the state and federal level.

Solomon, Jerry R. *The Depletion Allowance: A Summary of Fifty-Eight Years of Congressional Controversy and Change.* Berkeley: University of California Press, 1974.

Michael R. Adamson

DEPORTATION. Deportation, formally known as "removal," is a federal, statutory process by which a noncitizen is compelled to leave the United States. Though antecedents may be traced to colonial times, federal authority was first asserted in the Alien and Sedition Acts of 1798. This legislation empowered the president to deport "alien enemies"—citizens of nations with which the United States was at war—and, more controversially, any resident alien judged to be "dangerous to the peace and safety of the United States." Arguably unconstitutional for many reasons, these laws were never tested in the United States Supreme Court.

The Supreme Court established federal supremacy over state regulation of immigration in the mid-nineteenth century. The major federal laws of that time were "exclusion" statutes—restrictions on entry based upon various factors such as the nature of the contract by which an alien had been recruited abroad or personal characteristics, including physical and mental health, poverty, criminal records, and morality. In the 1880s the federal government also enacted a series of explicitly race-based exclusion laws aimed at Chinese laborers.

Deportation laws developed during this period primarily as an adjunct to the exclusion power. For example, the Act of October 19, 1888, authorized the deportation of an immigrant who had been "allowed to land contrary to the prohibition in the contract labor exclusion laws." This power was expanded by the Act of March 3, 1891, which authorized the deportation of "any alien who shall come into the United States in violation of law."

The Supreme Court upheld federal deportation power against numerous constitutional challenges in *Fong Yue Ting v. United States* (1893), which involved the Act of May 5, 1892, known as "An Act to prohibit the coming of Chinese persons into the United States," which authorized the deportation of any "Chinese alien" unlawfully in the United States and required all Chinese laborers to obtain a certificate of residence by the affidavit of a "credible" white witness. Though the *Fong Yue Ting* decision intimated that the deportation power was "absolute and unqualified," later decisions by the Court imposed important constitutional limitations, particularly as to procedural due process. The Court has, however, held that deportation is for constitutional purposes neither a criminal proceeding nor punishment. The effect of this doctrine is to render inapplicable many constitutional protections such as the ex post facto clause in Article I, sections 9 and 10; the Sixth Amendment right to counsel; the Seventh Amendment right to jury trial; and the Eighth Amendment prohibition on cruel and unusual punishment.

In the early twentieth century deportation laws began to focus increasingly on ideology—especially "subversive" ideas such as anarchism and socialism—and, more generally, on post-entry conduct. Deportation was used as a powerful government tool of social control. The Immigration Act of 1917 authorized deportation for "subversive" advocacy without a time limit after entry. The so-called Palmer Raids, led by Attorney General A. Mitchell Palmer in 1919 and 1920, resulted in the arrest of thousands and the ultimate deportation of some five hundred aliens on political grounds. The number of deportations increased steadily throughout the early twentieth century, from a total of 256 in 1900 to 16,631 in 1930.

The McCarran-Walter Act of 1952, also known as the Immigration and Naturalization Act (INA), was a major recodification of all existing immigration laws. It organized deportation laws into criteria for removal, among them pre-entry conduct; various grounds relating to entry control violations; and post-entry conduct, including criminal conduct, ideological grounds (which included advocacy of certain ideas and membership in proscribed groups), and reliance on public benefits. In addition, the INA was generally retroactive and, with only a few exceptions, lacked any statutes of limitation as to the time between commission of a deportable act and the institution of proceedings. The 1952 law also established a system of discretionary forms of "relief" or "waivers" from deportation for which an alien could apply to the Justice Department. The essential form of this system remained in place into the early twenty-first century.

The Immigration Acts of 1990 and 1991 re-categorized the grounds of deportation and introduced some statutes of limitation. More major changes were made by the Antiterrorism and Effective Death Penalty Act of 1996, which, among other provisions, eliminated judicial review of certain types of deportation orders, limited the scope of discretionary relief from deportation that could be granted by immigration judges, expanded the grounds of deportation, created new "summary exclusion" laws allowing the return of certain asylum-seekers, and created streamlined deportation procedures for those accused of terrorist activity. The even more comprehensive Illegal Immigration Reform and Immigrant Responsibility Act of 1996, among other effects, completely restructured the entire system of judicial review of removal orders, retroactively expanded many grounds of inadmissibility and removal, revised the discretionary waivers of removal, developed a system of mandatory detention, created expedited removal procedures for certain types of cases, and authorized increased state and local law enforcement involvement in removal proceedings. Court challenges to judicial review preclusion, retroactivity, and long-term detention met with some success in lower courts and in the Supreme Court case of *INS v. St. Cyr* (2001) and *Zadvydas v. Davis* (2001). Still, as a result of statutory changes and increased enforcement, the total number of removals increased from approximately 114,000 in 1997 to more than 180,000 in 2000.

BIBLIOGRAPHY

Aleinikoff, T. Alexander, David A. Martin, and Hiroshi Motomura. *Immigration and Citizenship: Process and Policy*. 4th ed. St. Paul, Minn.: West, 1998.

Clark, Jane Perry. *Deportation of Aliens from the United States to Europe*. New York: Columbia University Press, 1931.

Gordon, Charles, Stanley Mailman, and Stephen Yale-Loehr. *Immigration Law and Procedure*. New York: Mathew Bender, 1998 (supplemented through May 2002).

Daniel Kanstroom

See also **Immigration; McCarran-Walter Act; Palmer Raids.**

DEPOSIT ACT OF 1836 provided for the distribution of approximately $30 million of the $35 million U.S. Treasury surplus (from tariff proceeds and public land sales), to state banks on the basis of each state's representation in Congress. The act ended congressional fights over the surplus, thwarted Western hopes for reduced prices for government land, benefited old states more than the new, and diverted attention from Henry Clay's distribution bill that proposed distributing proceeds of federal land sales to the states (which President Andrew Jackson pledged to veto). Deposits were halted when the surplus became a deficit during the panic of 1837.

BIBLIOGRAPHY

Feller, Daniel. *The Public Lands in Jacksonian Politics*. Madison: University of Wisconsin Press, 1984.

Gatell, Frank Otto. "Spoils of the Bank War: Political Bias in the Selection of Pet Banks," *The American Historical Review* 70 (October 1964).

McFaul, John M. *The Politics of Jacksonian Finance*. Ithaca, N.Y.: Cornell University Press, 1972. Originally published as a thesis by the University of California, Berkeley, in 1963.

Paul W. Gates / T. M.

See also **American System; Bank of the United States; Financial Panics; Pet Banks; Surplus, Federal.**

DEPRESSION. *See* **Great Depression.**

DEPRESSION OF 1920. The prosperity generated by WORLD WAR I prevailed into the early part of 1920. Prices began to rise, however, and rumors of a buyers' strike spread. After commodity prices peaked in May, they declined rapidly, precipitating an unprecedented cancellation of orders. Money was extremely tight, although the stringency did not become acute until autumn. A noticeable flight of gold from the country caused a marked advance in money rates, and the end of the year saw a 30 percent decline in industrial stocks. Depression—characterized by inactive industries, business failures, and a severe decline in foreign trade—continued throughout 1921.

BIBLIOGRAPHY

Baumol, William J. *Business Behavior: Value and Growth.* New York: Harcourt, Brace and World, 1967. Original edition: New York: Macmillan, 1959.

Frank Parker / c. w.

See also **Commodity Exchanges; Gold Standard; Stock Market.**

DEREGULATION refers to efforts to reduce government involvement in the day-to-day activities of the private sector. The regulation of business began in the early twentieth century when progressive reformers passed legislation to monitor corporate behavior. Franklin Roosevelt's New Deal programs enormously expanded the realm of government regulations, a trend that continued through the 1960s. By the end of the 1970s, however, the U.S. economy suffered high inflation and high unemployment and underemployment, a phenomenon known as STAGFLATION. Many observers blamed stagflation on government regulation, which critics claimed sapped the entrepreneurial energy of the private sector. To cure this problem, deregulators advocated a sweeping reduction in government rules—the idea being to turn businesses free to operate, letting the market do the regulating.

After the administration of President Jimmy Carter deregulated the airline industry in 1978, the federal regulatory apparatus setting rules for much of industry unraveled. The Reagan Administration accelerated deregulatory policies begun under Carter and implemented the most comprehensive rollback of government regulations in American history. Deregulation affected the nation's basic industries, including trucking, railroads, buses, oil and gas, local electric and gas utilities, telecommunications, and financial services. Deregulation concentrated on eliminating trade barriers to industries and eliminating price controls. Free-market economic and political theorists fostered much of the deregulation, but so did the federal courts, which broke up the monopoly on telephone service held by the American Telephone and Telegraph Corporation (AT&T).

The results of deregulation were mixed. New airlines appeared, sparking fare wars and cheap flights on the most competitive routes. The AT&T breakup created long-distance telephone companies offering lower rates for calls. Deregulation, however, also produced disasters. A botched deregulation of the savings and loan industry contributed to the failure of thousands of savings and loan companies, forcing an enormous bailout of the industry financed by U.S. taxpayers. Competition in some industries led to workers being laid off or paid less and having benefits such as health insurance reduced or eliminated. As a result, a backlash developed against deregulation in the late 1980s.

After Republican victories in the 1994 midterm congressional elections, however, government regulation of businesses again came under attack. This time deregulators set their sights on environmental regulations, such as the federal Clean Air Act (1990) and the Clean Water Act (1972), as well as entry barriers and price controls. Once again, deregulatory zeal outpaced public support. Pro-regulation Democrats accused antiregulation Republicans of doing big business's bidding and claimed that corporate lobbyists played an unseemly role in deregulatory legislation. The Clinton Administration announced it would oppose deregulation policies that threatened to increase pollution and energy costs. Public opposition grew even stronger when a disastrously inept effort to deregulate the California utilities industry led to widespread power failures on the west coast. In the face of such opposition, Congress abandoned many of its most ambitious deregulatory plans. Thus, by the early twenty-first century, the battle between regulators and deregulators stood at a stalemate.

BIBLIOGRAPHY

Drew, Elizabeth. *Showdown: The Struggle Between the Gingrich Congress and the Clinton White House.* New York: Simon & Schuster, 1996.

Gingrich, Newt. *To Renew America.* New York: HarperCollins, 1995.

Kahn, Alfred E. *The Economics of Regulation: Principles and Institutions.* Cambridge, Mass.: MIT Press, 1988.

Majone, Giandomenico, ed. *Deregulation or Reregulation? Regulatory Reform in Europe and the United States.* New York: St. Martin's Press, 1990.

Nocera, Joseph. *A Piece of the Action: How the Middle Class Joined the Money Class.* New York: Simon & Schuster, 1994.

Noll, Roger. *The Political Economy of Deregulation: Interest Groups in the Regulatory Process.* Washington, D.C.: American Enterprise Institute for Public Policy Research, 1983.

Thomas G. Gress / A. G.

See also **Business, Big; Laffer Curve Theory; Laissez-Faire; Price and Wage Controls; Reaganomics; Savings and Loan Associations; Trickle-Down Economics.**

DES ACTION USA. From 1938 to 1971 physicians prescribed diethylstilbestrol (DES) to pregnant women in an attempt to prevent miscarriages. In 1971 rare cancers in young women were linked to DES, and the Food and Drug Administration issued a warning against its use during pregnancy. Later researchers found reproductive problems in the daughters of women who were given

White Resistance. The path toward desegregation was often difficult, especially for pioneers. Dorothy Counts, the first African American to attend Harding High School in Charlotte, N.C., in 1957, is jeered at and spat on by a hostile crowd. The fifteen-year-old's parents later transferred her to a private school in Pennsylvania. ASSOCIATED PRESS/WORLD WIDE PHOTOS

DES during their pregnancy. These women and their children founded DES Action USA, a nonprofit consumer group, in 1977. DES Action provides medical and legal information to those who were exposed to DES. In addition, the organization has educated medical and legal professionals to provide effective services, and it has helped to obtain funding from Congress for continuing research.

BIBLIOGRAPHY

Orenberg, Cynthia Laitman. *DES, the Complete Story.* New York: St. Martin's Press, 1981.

Bonnie L. Ford

See also **Food and Drug Administration; Women's Health.**

DESEGREGATION. Efforts to eliminate the legally required separation of the races in schools, housing, transportation, and other public accommodations began almost as soon as segregation laws were enacted. The Supreme Court upheld a law requiring railroads to provide separate facilities for whites and African Americans in *PLESSY V. FERGUSON* (1896), holding that the Constitution was not violated by laws requiring facilities that, though separate, were equal. In 1915 the Court indicated that it stood ready to enforce the requirement of equality. But *MISSOURI EX REL. GAINES V. CANADA* (1938) was the first case in which a state's segregation law was declared unconstitutional because it failed to ensure that African Americans had access to facilities equal to those available to whites.

In a series of cases involving state universities culminating in *Sweatt v. Painter* (1950), the Supreme Court held that the facilities at issue were not in fact equal. The states could have responded by investing more money in the separate schools to make them equal. But states faced with court orders found the cost of upgrading too high, and they eliminated their rules barring the enrollment of African Americans in their universities.

BROWN V. BOARD OF EDUCATION OF TOPEKA (1954) repudiated the idea that separate facilities, at least in education, could ever be equal. The Court's 1955 decision on the appropriate remedy in *Brown* blurred the distinction between desegregation, meaning the elimination of laws requiring the separation of the races, and integration, meaning a state of affairs in which all races were in fact present in every school or public accommodation. Laws requiring segregation could have been replaced by rules assigning students to schools without regard to race, for example, by assigning all students to their neighborhood schools. The Court, however, required that desegregation occur "with all deliberate speed," suggesting that the goal was integration, a far more difficult accomplishment.

Brown and the emerging civil rights movement extended the challenge to legally required segregation beyond the schools to the South's entire Jim Crow system. The Montgomery bus boycott of 1955 and 1956 was aimed at desegregating the city's bus system, whose rules required African Americans to sit in the back of the bus and give up their seats when whites demanded them. The Supreme Court repeatedly held that all forms of segregation were unconstitutional, usually in short opinions that simply referred to *Brown*.

Southern resistance to desegregation persisted, and civil rights activists shifted their attention from the courts to the streets. In February 1960 four students in Greensboro, North Carolina, went to the food counter of their local Woolworth's department store and requested service. Remaining after service was denied, they sparked a series of sit-ins at other segregated public accommodations. The CONGRESS OF RACIAL EQUALITY (CORE) sponsored Freedom Rides, in which African Americans boarded interstate buses in the North and refused to comply with segregation laws when the buses crossed into the South. Civil rights activism prompted violent responses from southern defenders of segregation. Freedom Riders were beaten in bus stations while local police officers watched.

The civil rights mobilization of the early 1960s prodded Congress to enact the CIVIL RIGHTS ACT OF 1964. Relying on congressional power to regulate interstate commerce, the Civil Rights Act required nondiscrimination in all places of public accommodation, which in-

Desegregated. Black and white girls take recess together at McDonogh 11 Public School, New Orleans, 1961. ASSOCIATED PRESS/ WORLD WIDE PHOTOS cluded essentially all the nation's restaurants, hotels, and theaters. The act also denied federal funds to school systems that continued to maintain segregated systems. This financial threat led to a rapid increase in the pace of desegregation in the Deep South.

As laws requiring segregated facilities fell, attention turned to de facto segregation, the separation of the races despite the absence of any legal requirement. Schools in the urban North were often segregated in that sense. No state law required separate facilities, but widespread patterns of residential segregation, usually based on historic patterns and differences in the ability of whites and African Americans to afford housing in affluent areas, produced schools that were racially identifiable as white or African American.

In *Green v. School Board of New Kent County* (1968), a case involving a school system that had been segregated by law in 1954, the Supreme Court said the Constitution required neither white schools nor black schools "but just schools." Applied in northern settings, that holding would have required substantial alterations in existing practices. Resistance to expansive efforts to achieve integration grew as the desegregation effort moved north. The Supreme Court never endorsed the idea that the Constitution required the elimination of de facto segregation, although it was creative in finding that some northern districts had actually imposed segregation by law.

Through the 1990s the Supreme Court issued a series of rulings that allowed formerly segregated school systems to remove themselves from judicial supervision. No laws remained that required the separation of the races. The Civil Rights Act and other statutes had effectively eliminated separation in most places of public accommodation, although discrimination persisted. In those senses desegregation had been achieved. The broader goal of integration remained unmet, however.

BIBLIOGRAPHY

Grantham, Dewey W. *The South in Modern America: A Region at Odds.* New York: HarperCollins, 1994.

Patterson, James T. *"Brown v. Board of Education": A Civil Rights Milestone and Its Troubled Legacy.* New York: Oxford University Press, 2001.

Wilkinson, J. Harvie, III. *From Brown to Bakke: The Supreme Court and School Integration, 1954–1978.* New York: Oxford University Press, 1979.

Mark V. Tushnet

See also **Discrimination: Race; Freedom Riders; Integration; Jim Crow Laws; Segregation.**

DESERET. The Mormons in 1849 gave their provisional state the name "Deseret," which came from the Book of Mormon and meant "land of the honeybee." The territory included the vast region between the Sierra Nevadas and the Rocky Mountains. Mormons soon drafted a constitution and made Salt Lake City their capital. They also created counties, established local government, and elected state officers, including Brigham Young as governor. Congress declined to admit Deseret into the union as a state at that time, but it organized the region as the Territory of Utah in 1850. The Mormons accepted their territorial status as a temporary measure and preserved remnants of the Deseret government until they sought statehood in 1883.

BIBLIOGRAPHY

Arrington, Leonard J. *Great Basin Kingdom: An Economic History of the Latter-Day Saints, 1830-1900.* Cambridge, Mass.: Harvard University Press, 1958.

Stegner, Wallace. *Mormon Country.* Lincoln: University of Nebraska Press, 1970.

Effie Mona Mack / S. B.

See also **Latter-Day Saints, Church of Jesus Christ of; Mormon Expedition; Salt Lake City; Utah; West, American; Westward Migration.**

DESERTION from military service has been a continual phenomenon in American history although its extent has varied widely depending upon the circumstances that have confronted soldiers. The armed forces require enlisted men and women to serve tours of duty of specific duration and, unlike commissioned officers, enlisted personnel may not legally resign before the end of that period. Thus desertion—being absent without authorization for over a month—constitutes the enlisted person's repudiation of his or her legal obligation.

In peacetime there has been a direct correlation between desertion rates and the business cycle. When the country has experienced a depression and a labor surplus, fewer soldiers have abandoned the army. By contrast, in an expanding economy, with workers in demand and wage scales increasing, many more servicemen and women have forsaken the high job security but low monetary rewards of the army.

The highest peacetime desertion rates in American history occurred during the periods of economic growth in the 1820s, early 1850s, early 1870s, 1880s, early 1900s, and 1920s, when the flow of deserters averaged between 7 and 15 percent each year. A peak of 32.6 percent was reached in 1871, when 8,800 of the 27,010 enlisted men deserted in protest against a pay cut. Lured by higher civilian wages and prodded by the miserable living conditions of most frontier outposts, a total of 88,475, or one-third of the men recruited by the army, deserted between 1867 and 1891.

During wartime, desertion rates have varied widely but have generally been lower than in peacetime service, a tendency that perhaps reflects the increased numbers of troops, national spirit, and more severe penalties prescribed for combat desertion. A dramatic flight from military duty has generally accompanied the termination of hostilities. After almost every war the desertion rate has doubled temporarily as many servicemen and women have joined other Americans in returning to peacetime pursuits. The variation in wartime desertion rates seems to result from differences in public sentiment and military prospects. Although many factors are involved, generally the more swift and victorious the campaign and the more popular the conflict, the lower the desertion rate. Defeat and disagreement or disillusionment about a war have been accompanied by a higher incidence of desertion.

In the American Revolution, desertion depleted both the state militias and the Continental army after such reverses as the British seizure of New York City; at spring planting or fall harvesting time, when farmer-soldiers returned to their fields; and as veterans deserted in order to reenlist, seeking the increased bounties of cash or land that the states offered for new enlistees. Widespread desertion, even in the midst of battle, plagued the military during the WAR OF 1812. In the MEXICAN-AMERICAN WAR, 6,825 men, or nearly 7 percent of the army, deserted. Moreover, American deserters composed one unit of the Mexican army, the San Patricio Artillery Battalion.

The CIVIL WAR produced the highest American wartime desertion rates because of its bloody battles, new enlistment bounties, and relative ease with which deserters could escape capture in the interior regions. The Union armies recorded 278,644 cases of desertion, representing 11 percent of the troops. As the Confederate military situation deteriorated, desertion reached epidemic proportions. Whole companies and regiments, sometimes with most of their officers, fled together. In all, Confederate deserters numbered 104,428, or 10 percent of the armies of the South.

The SPANISH-AMERICAN WAR resulted in 5,285 desertions, or less than 2 percent of the armed forces in 1898. The rate climbed to 4 percent during the PHILIPPINE INSURRECTION between 1900 and 1902. In WORLD WAR I, because Selective Service regulations classified anyone failing to report for induction at the prescribed time as a deserter, the records of 1917–1918 showed 363,022 deserters who would have been more appropriately designated draft evaders. Traditionally defined deserters amounted to 21,282, or less than 1 percent of the army. In WORLD WAR II desertion rates reached 6.3 percent of the armed forces in 1944 but dropped to 4.5 percent by 1945. The use of short-term service and the rotation system during the KOREAN WAR kept desertion rates down to 1.4 percent of the armed forces in fiscal year 1951 and to 2.2 percent, or 31,041 soldiers, in fiscal year 1953.

The unpopular war in Vietnam generated the highest percentage of wartime desertion since the Civil War. From 13,177 cases, or 1.6 percent of the armed forces, in fiscal year 1965, the annual desertion statistics mounted to 2.9 percent in fiscal year 1968, 4.2 percent in fiscal year 1969, 5.2 percent in fiscal year 1970, and 7.4 percent in fiscal year 1971. Like the draft resisters from this same war, many deserters sought sanctuary in Canada, Mexico, or Sweden. In 1974 the Defense Department reported that there had been 503,926 incidents of desertion between 1 July 1966 and 31 December 1973.

BIBLIOGRAPHY

Higginbotham, Don. *War and Society in Revolutionary America: The Wider Dimensions of Conflict.* Columbia: University of South Carolina Press, 1988.

Jessup, John E., et al., eds. *Encyclopedia of the American Military: Studies of the History, Traditions, Policies, Institutions, and Roles of the Armed Forces in War and Peace.* New York: Scribners; Toronto: Macmillan, 1994.

Weitz, Mark A. *A Higher Duty: Desertion among Georgia Troops During the Civil War.* Lincoln: University of Nebraska Press, 2000.

Whiteclay, John, et al., eds. *The Oxford Companion to American Military History.* New York: Oxford University Press, 1999.

John Whiteclay Chambers/A. E.

See also **Amnesty; Army, Confederate; Army, Union; Bounty Jumper; Confederate States of America; Revolution, American: Military History.**

DESERTS. Definition has been the central problem in the history of the deserts of the United States. The need to ascertain the limits of arability and the difficulty of establishing such boundaries where precipitation fluctuates unpredictably constitute a basic developmental theme for more than half the nation. Archaeological evidences of prehistoric Native American communities indicate that droughts occasioned recurrent disaster to ag-

Monument Valley. This 1947 photograph by Ansel Adams shows the scrub and buttes of this unusual desert landscape in northeastern Arizona and southeastern Utah, made familiar by numerous movies directed by John Ford. © ANSEL ADAMS PUBLISHING RIGHTS TRUST/CORBIS

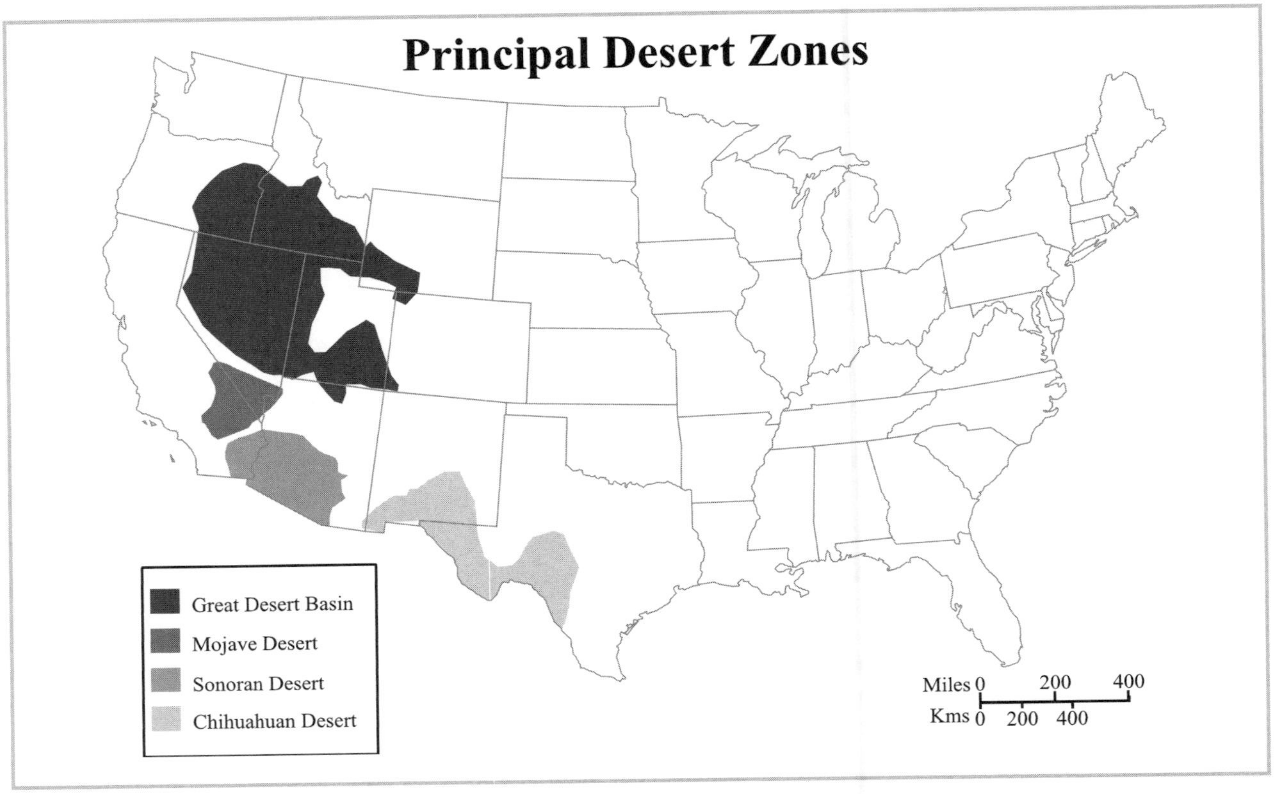

ricultural societies long ago, as now, in border areas. In 1803 President Thomas Jefferson, seeking congressional support for exploration of the upper Missouri River, summarized existing knowledge of newly purchased Louisiana in describing it as a region of "immense and trackless deserts" but also, at its eastern perimeter, as "one immense *prairie*"—a land "too rich for the growth of forest trees." The subsequent expedition of Meriwether Lewis and William Clark (1804–1806) marked the official beginning of American efforts to elaborate the description.

Until the 1860s a conception prevailed that the vast province west from the meridian of Council Bluffs, on the Missouri River, to the Rocky Mountains, between thirty-five and forty-nine degrees north latitude, was a "Great American Desert." The explorations of Lewis and Clark, Zebulon Pike, and Stephen Harriman Long, followed by the experiences of traders to Santa Fe, Rocky Mountain fur trappers, immigrants to Oregon and CALIFORNIA, soldiers along the Gila Trail, surveyors for transcontinental railroads, and prospectors throughout the West confirmed the appellation.

While commentators agreed that agriculture could have no significant role in the region, they did occasionally recognize that the Great Plains, the mountain parks, and the interior valleys of California and the Northwest afforded excellent pasturage. As livestock industry developed in these areas during the period from 1866 to 1886, redefinition of the limits of aridity evolved. Maj. John Wesley Powell's surveys and, notably, his *Report on the Lands of the Arid Region* (1878) expressed the new point of view; agriculture, Powell asserted, could be profitably conducted in many parts of the West, but only as an irrigated enterprise and generally as a supplement to stock growing. The collapse of open-range ranching in the mid-1880s emphasized the need for expanded hay and forage production and gave impetus to development of IRRIGATION programs. But Powell's efforts to classify the public lands and the passage of the Carey Desert Land Grant Act of 1894 raised controversy. States east of the 104th meridian were excluded, at the request of their representatives, from the application of the Carey legislation. Farmers during the 1880s had expanded cultivation without irrigation nearly to that meridian in the Dakotas and even beyond it in the central plains. Many were convinced that "rainfall follows the plow." They saw no need to assume the costs and the managerial innovations of supplemental watering. A new conception of the boundaries of aridity was emerging.

Drought in the mid-1870s had driven a vanguard of settlers eastward from the James River Valley, a prairie zone normally receiving more than twenty inches of annual rainfall. Drought in the period 1889–1894 forced thousands back from the plains farther west, where average precipitation ranges between fifteen and twenty inches annually. As normal conditions returned, however, farmers in the first two decades of the twentieth century expanded cultivation across the plains to the foothills of the Rockies—in Montana, Colorado, and New Mexico—and in many areas beyond—Utah, Idaho, the interior valleys of California, and eastern Oregon and Washington. Irrigation supplied water to only a small portion of these lands. Dry farming—a specialized program that, ideally, combines use of crop varieties adapted to drought resistance, cultivation techniques designed to conserve moisture, and management systems that emphasize large-scale operations—provided a new approach to the problem of aridity. The deserts, promoters claimed, could be made to "blossom like the rose."

When severe droughts again returned from 1919 to 1922, and from 1929 to 1936, assessment of the effectiveness of dry farming raised new concern for defining the limits of aridity—an outlook most strongly expressed in the reports of the National Resources Board of the mid-1930s but one that still permeates the writings of agricultural scientists. Long-term precipitation records, with adjustment for seasonality and rate of variability in rainfall, humidity, temperature, and soil conditions, now afford some guidance to the mapping of cultivable areas.

By established criteria a zone of outright desert (less than five inches average annual precipitation) ranges from southeastern California, northward through the western half of Nevada, nearly to the Oregon border. Because cropping without irrigation is impracticable when rainfall averages less than ten inches annually, climatic pockets found in all states west of the 104th meridian—most prevalently in Arizona, central New Mexico, eastern Nevada, Utah, and the lee side of the Cascades in Oregon and Washington—may also be defined as arid. Semiaridity—an average precipitation of from ten to fifteen inches annually—characterizes the western Dakotas, much of Montana, and large sections of eastern New Mexico, Colorado, Wyoming, Idaho, Oregon, and Washington. There dry farming may be successful but only when management programs include allowances for recurrent drought. Throughout much of the semiarid region livestock production predominates, with cropping to afford feed and forage supplementary to native short-grass pasturage. In many areas, however, the possibility of raising wheat of superior milling quality, which commands premium prices, encourages alternative land utilization. The costs of marginal productivity must be carefully weighed.

Eastward, roughly from the Missouri River to the ninety-eighth meridian and curving to the west through the central and southern plains, is a subhumid zone, in which rainfall averages from fifteen to twenty inches annually, an amount sufficient, if well distributed, to permit cultivation without recourse to specialized programs but so closely correlated to the margin of general farming requirements that a deficiency occasions failure. Almost every spring, alarms are raised that some areas of the vast wheat fields extending from the central Dakotas, through western Kansas and Nebraska and eastern Colorado and New Mexico, into the panhandles of Oklahoma and Texas have suffered serious losses. There the problem of defining limits of arability is yet unresolved; the boundaries of America's deserts and arid regions remain uncertain.

BIBLIOGRAPHY

Fite, Gilbert C. *The Farmers' Frontier, 1865–1900.* New York: Holt, Rinehart and Winston, 1966.

Goetzmann, William H. *Exploration and Empire: The Explorer and the Scientist in the Winning of the American West.* New York: Knopf, 1966.

Hargreaves, Mary W. M. *Dry Farming in the Northern Great Plains, 1900–1925.* Lawrence: University Press of Kansas, 1993.

Limerick, Patricia Nelson. *Desert Passages: Encounters with the American Deserts.* Albuquerque: University of New Mexico, 1985.

Teague, David W. *The Southwest in American Literature and Art: The Rise of a Desert Aesthetic.* Tucson: University of Arizona Press, 1997.

Mary W. M. Hargreaves/A. R.

See also **Agriculture; Death Valley; Great Plains.**

DETROIT, known as the "Automotive Capital of the World," is the largest city in the state of Michigan. The city sits at the heart of an official three-county metropolitan region comprising Wayne, Oakland, and Macomb counties.

French for "by or near the straits," Detroit was founded on 24 July 1701, by Antoine de la Mothe Cadillac, a French military officer and explorer, as a base to block British expansion. The permanent outpost system did not prove successful, particularly after the French and Indian War (also called the Seven Years' War) resulted in the French losing much of their North American empire to the British in 1763. Though the United States gained official control of the region after the American Revolution, the British remained in place until the Jay Treaty of 1794. The first territorial judge, August Woodward, arrived in June 1805 to discover that the primarily French-speaking city had burned to the ground in an accidental fire. He based the new city on Pierre-Charles L'Enfant's design for Washington, D.C., using broad avenues radiating fanlike from large circular centers. The plan was never fully accepted, but the downtown area still retains some of the original Woodward design.

The city served as the territorial capital and then as the state capital from 1805 until 1847, when the capital was moved to Lansing. Industries, including wood finishing, shipbuilding, metal production, steelmaking, and shipping, developed before and after the Civil War. At the time Detroit lacked a full-time police force, and it was not until 1863 that one was organized. The depression of 1893 brought most of Detroit's industries to a halt and placed enormous pressure on the city's charities. Republican Mayor Hazen M. Pingree extended public aid to

Detroit Skyline, c. 1929. LIBRARY OF CONGRESS

workers and made plots of land available for use as vegetable patches. He also expanded the city's government, taking on the management of the city's water, sewage, electric, and public transportation services. Immigration expanded the city's population, as waves of Polish, German, Russian, and Southern European families arrived to work in the growing industries. African Americans, though still a small part of the population, had established a separate community east of downtown, a segregated ghetto that would remain in place until the 1950s.

Detroit became the financial center of Michigan's natural-resource wealth, and lumber baron David M. Whitney and railroad tycoons Frank Hecker and Henry B. Joy continued to look for new investment opportunities. A variety of entrepreneurs and inventors sought backing in the city, including Henry Ford, Horace and John Dodge, and the most successful at the time, Ransom E. Olds. Detroit quickly developed into the center of the automobile industry through a combination of financial resources, location, and luck. The expansion of industry production from 6,000 units in 1903 grew to more than 250,000 for Ford alone in 1915, and the concurrent growth in factories and suppliers transformed Detroit. The city exploded from 465,766 people in 1910 to more than 990,000 in 1920, making it the fourth most populous city in America.

Prohibition brought an increase in violence, and clashes between the United Auto Workers union and auto companies, primarily Ford Motor Company, only added to the problem. A shortage of housing continued to plague the city, as did its racial tensions, which eventually ignited into widespread rioting in June 1943. The success of the "Arsenal of Democracy," as Detroit was known during World War II, did not last as long as the auto industry, and much of the white population moved to the suburbs and open land. Detroit's population hit its high point of 1,848,568 in 1950 and then declined rapidly. Deindustrialization left minorities increasingly isolated in the central city areas. Frustration with this situation and anger at the predominantly white police force sparked another outbreak of violence in July 1967.

This period also saw significant accomplishments by the city's African American citizens. In 1959 Berry Gordy Jr. founded Motown Records in Detroit, which became one of the most influential and successful record companies in the country. By 1973 Detroit had its first African American mayor, Coleman Young, who remained in office through 1993 and battled against the city's declining economy.

During this time, the "Motor City" earned a derisive new moniker—"Murder City"—as crime and poverty peaked from the mid-1970s to the early 1990s. The city's population dropped from the disputed figure of 1,027,974 in 1990 to 951,270 in 2000. Instead of a housing shortage, the city now experienced a housing surplus. The election of a new mayor, Dennis W. Archer, in 1993 coincided with the economic boom of the 1990s and resulted in some new development within the city.

BIBLIOGRAPHY

Darden, Joe T., et al. *Detroit: Race and Uneven Development.* Philadelphia: Temple University, 1987.

Glazer, Sidney. *Detroit: A Study in Urban Development.* Detroit, Mich.: Bookman Associates, 1965.

Levine, David. *Internal Combustion: The Races in Detroit, 1915–1925.* Westport, Conn.: Greenwood, 1976.

Sugrue, Thomas J. *Origins of the Urban Crisis: Race and Inequality in Post-war Detroit.* Princeton, N.J.: Princeton University, 1996.

Zunz, Olivier. *The Changing Face of Inequality: Urbanization, Industrial Development, and Immigrants in Detroit, 1880–1920.* Chicago: University of Chicago Press, 1982.

Matthew L. Daley

See also **Automobile Industry; Ford Motor Company.**

DETROIT, SURRENDER OF (16 August 1812). On the eve of the War of 1812, Gen. William Hull was ordered to Detroit in Michigan Territory. Not knowing that war had been declared, Hull sent his baggage by water. The ship carrying his baggage, the *Cuyahoga*, was captured by the British and with it Hull's military papers. The information thus secured was of valuable assistance to the British in the campaign that followed.

The fortress at Detroit needed repairs, but no improvements were made because the War Department ordered Hull to capture Malden in Canada. Hull crossed into Canada on 11 July and remained there until 7 August. During this time he did not attack Malden, as he did not believe he could carry the place without the heavy artillery. However, the artillery could not be removed from Detroit because they had only rotted gun carriages on which to carry them. After the British captured the American post at Mackinac in July, large numbers of Indians flocked to the British side, and a party of them cut Hull's communications, forcing him to return to America. Hull's troops lost confidence in their commander and plotted to depose him; in turn, Hull lost all confidence in his troops. At this juncture Gen. Isaac Brock, lieutenant-governor of Upper Canada, arrived and demanded the surrender of Detroit. Lacking the supplies to withstand a siege and fearing a massacre if he were starved into a surrender, Hull yielded without resistance on 16 August.

Hull was subsequently court-martialed on charges of treason, cowardice, and neglect of duty. He was found guilty on the latter two charges and sentenced to be executed. President James Madison remanded the execution because of Hull's service during the Revolution.

BIBLIOGRAPHY

Gilpin, Alec Richard. *The War of 1812 in the Old Northwest.* East Lansing: Michigan State University Press, 1958.

Stagg, J. C. A. *Mr. Madison's War.* Princeton, N.J.: Princeton University Press, 1983.

John G. Van Deusen / A. R.

See also **Courts-Martial; Mackinac, Straits of, and Mackinac Island.**

DETROIT RIOTS. Riots in Detroit have occurred over particular issues of justice, economics, and race. The city's first major riot, which took place in March 1863, stemmed from the trial of a black man for rape and was fueled by the local press. The violence resulted in the killing of one black and the burning of thirty homes and buildings. For a long time afterwards, Detroit avoided major civil violence, even into the period following World War I, when riots broke out in many other major cities. Detroit's avoidance of mass social upheaval lasted until June 1943, when poor housing conditions, racial tensions, and a heat wave contributed to making a riot in that city the worst of the year. The violence resulted in the deaths of nine whites and twenty-five blacks along with the destruction of millions of dollars of property. The city responded by creating a committee on racial relations, but worse violence was to come. In July 1967 the increasing economic and social isolation of blacks in the inner city of Detroit contributed to the outbreak of violence that left forty-three dead and thousands injured. The riots shattered Detroit's image as a model city for race relations and deepened the metropolitan region's racial divide into the twenty-first century.

BIBLIOGRAPHY

Capeci, Dominic J. *Layered Violence: The Detroit Rioters of 1943.* Jackson: University of Mississippi, 1991.

Fine, Sidney. *Violence in the Model City: The Cavanagh Administration, Race Relations, and the Detroit Riot of 1967.* Ann Arbor: University of Michigan Press, 1989.

Schneider, John C. *Detroit and the Problem of Order, 1830–1880: A Geography of Crime, Riot, and Policing.* Lincoln: University of Nebraska Press, 1980.

Matthew L. Daley

See also **Michigan; Riots, Urban; Riots, Urban, of 1967;** *and picture (overleaf).*

DEVALUATION, a downward adjustment of the price of a currency in terms of other currencies, in a system in which each currency has a gold par value. The downward adjustment may be achieved through a devaluation of one currency, an upward revaluation of other currencies, or a combination of the two. The U.S. dollar has been devalued several times since the early nineteenth century. The gold content of the U.S. dollar, established at 24.75 grains (2 April 1792), was reduced to 23.2 grains (29 June 1834) and then raised to 23.22 grains (18 January 1837). The 1834 devaluation was intended to attract gold from Eu-

Detroit Riot, 1943. National Guardsmen ride past a damaged store on Hastings Street, 22 June 1943. AP/WIDE WORLD PHOTOS

rope and thereby encourage a shift away from bank notes in domestic transactions. A century later, when the gold content of the dollar was reduced to 13.71 grains (31 January 1934), the aim was to raise dollar prices of U.S. farm products, which had a world market, by reducing the foreign-exchange value of the dollar. Under President Richard M. Nixon, the gold content of the dollar was reduced to 12.63 grains (31 March 1972) and then reduced another 10 percent to 11.368 grains (12 February 1973). For each dollar weight in gold, there is a corresponding price of gold per fine troy ounce of 480 grains (480/11.368 = $42.22). Since convertibility of the dollar into gold was suspended 15 August 1971, the devaluations in terms of gold were pro forma only. The new gold prices were merely devices for measuring the downward adjustment of the U.S. dollar relative to other currencies set by the Smithsonian Accord (17–18 December 1971) to help correct a deficit in the U.S. international payments balance. The Reagan Administration briefly adopted devaluation policies in the 1980s, but abandoned them when they failed to reduce the trade deficit.

BIBLIOGRAPHY

Edwards, Sebastian. *Devaluation Controversies in the Developing Countries: Lessons from the Bretton Woods Era.* Cambridge, Mass.: National Bureau of Economic Research, 1992.

Friedman, Milton. *A Monetary History of the United States, 1867–1960.* Princeton N.J.: Princeton University Press, 1963.

North, Douglass C. *Structure and Change in Economic History.* New York: Norton, 1981.

Samuelson, Robert J. *The Good Life and Its Discontents: America in the Age of Entitlement, 1945–1995.* New York: Times Books, 1995.

Anna J. Schwartz / A. G.

See also **Consumer Purchasing Power; Cost of Living; Financial Panics; Inflation; Keynesianism; Wages and Salaries.**

DICTIONARIES. In the colonial era, Americans used British dictionaries. While dictionaries were published in the colonies during the late eighteenth century, nearly all of them were based on the famous 1755 lexicon compiled by Samuel Johnson in London. Dictionaries of the English language were not widely used until the early nineteenth century, when the expansion of print culture and basic schooling moved the dictionary into countless homes and offices. Dictionaries came in various sizes but most popular was the "school dictionary," a book about as big as a contemporary pocket dictionary. The first dictionary compiled by an American was Samuel Johnson Jr.'s *A School Dictionary*, published in 1798. The author was no relation to the famed British lexicographer.

The first well-known American dictionary was Noah Webster's *An American Dictionary of the English Language*, published in 1828. Webster is often thought of as a linguistic nationalist, but he was actually more of a linguistic reformer. He argued that English, both in Britain and the United States, should follow "rational" rules. He introduced a system to reform English spelling and make it more uniform. He also devised an elaborate etymological system, based on his own research. This etymology won almost no acceptance at the time and remains universally discredited. Webster's faith in the rational reform of language contradicted the traditional commitment of the Anglo-American lexicography to use dictionaries to record refined usage.

Joseph Worcester, a Boston lexicographer, published a competing dictionary in 1846, three years after Webster died. A new edition of Webster's dictionary appeared the next year, published by the Merriam-Webster Company. These publications set off the "dictionary wars" of the 1840s and 1850s. Educators, editors, literary people, and even politicians all took sides, debating linguistics and hurling insults. Webster's publishers won the war in the 1860s by making their dictionary more conventional. The strange spellings and etymologies disappeared—Webster's dictionary now recorded refined contemporary usage.

Dictionary-making took a new turn after the Civil War (1861–1865). Lexicographers started adding thousands of slang and technical terms to major dictionaries as well as recording the history of words. They began to quote from newspapers as well as literature. Current refined usage was no longer the only principle of selection. These lexicographers also started recording national and regional variations of the language. In 1890, the Merriam-Webster Company renamed its flagship text *Webster's International Dictionary.* These dictionaries became huge, the largest of them becoming multivolume. The most famous of these "encyclopedic" dictionaries was British, the *Oxford English Dictionary,* edited by James A. H. Murray. Compilation on that dictionary began in the 1860s. An American text, *The Century Dictionary of the English Language,* edited by the Yale philologist William Dwight Whitney, is unknown today but was a competitor of the Oxford dictionary at the time. Whitney's was the first dictionary in the United States to enthusiastically include slang. Despite some opposition from conservatives opposed to slang and newspaper quotations, the new encyclopedic dictionary quickly became the standard form for the major dictionaries of the English language.

As the comprehensive dictionaries became huge, a new format was needed to accommodate most day-to-day use. In 1898, the Merriam-Webster Company published the first "collegiate" dictionary. Neatly packed into one manageable volume, this became the most popular dictionary of the next century, found as often in the home or office as in a college dorm room. *Webster's Collegiate Dictionary* dominated the first half of the century; Random House's *American College Dictionary,* first published in 1947, was most popular in the second half. In the 1990s, 2 million collegiate dictionaries were sold each year. The only other format that rivaled its popularity was the paperback pocket dictionary, introduced in the 1950s.

The 1961 publication of *Webster's Third New International Dictionary* served as a flash point for new debates about informality and slang. Philip Gove, the editor of the new *Webster's,* streamlined definitions and tried to eliminate overbearing editorializing. Academics, journalists, and literary people all over the country quickly took sides for or against the book. As during the dictionary war of the 1850s, the debate was intense, with linguistics and invective freely mixing. One particularly charged argument was over *Webster's* entry for "ain't." Critics claimed that *Webster's Third* sanctioned its use. Gove countered that the entry reflected the way people really talked. In general, critics argued that the new dictionary abandoned any meaningful effort to distinguish good English from bad English. Dictionaries, defenders argued, were supposed to describe the language, not regulate it.

The early 1960s debate over *Webster's Third* was really part of a larger discussion about the merits or demerits of progressive education. Controversy about progressive methods of schooling became particularly intense in the years after 1957, when the Soviet Union put a satellite in outer space and took the lead—for the moment—in the space race. There was widespread concern that soft, progressive methods in schools had put the United States behind in the Cold War. Critics of *Webster's Third* echoed arguments then being made against "progressive" methods of teaching English.

Despite the criticism, *Webster's Third* was a commercial success. Later in the decade, two other dictionaries appeared that became popular competitors. *The Random House Dictionary of the English Language* (1966) and the *American Heritage Dictionary* (1969) were both conservative alternatives to *Webster's.* The *American Heritage,* a collegiate dictionary, was immediately popular and remained so through the end of the century. It created a "usage panel" of 105 leading writers, editors, and professors to give advice about good and bad English. A number of its members had been vocal critics of *Webster's Third.*

In the 1990s, dictionary makers became preoccupied with going electronic. *The Random House Dictionary* and *Encarta World English Dictionary* were the first to become available on CD-ROM. The *Oxford English Dictionary* started working on an online version in 1994; it became commercially available in 2000, being licensed to libraries for a fee. The electronic emphasis promises to turn future dictionaries into multimedia works, with pronunciations spoken instead of written, routine links to encyclopedia entries, and lexicons updated constantly instead of having a single new edition compiled every generation.

BIBLIOGRAPHY

Cmiel, Kenneth. *Democratic Eloquence: The Fight Over Popular Speech in Nineteenth-Century America.* New York: William Morrow, 1990.

Friend, Joseph. *The Development of American Lexicography, 1798–1864.* The Hague, Paris: Mouton, 1967.

Landau, Sidney. *Dictionaries: The Art and Craft of Lexicography.* 2d ed. Cambridge, U.K.: Cambridge University Press, 2001.

Kenneth Cmiel

See also **English Language; Linguistics.**

DIETS AND DIETING. Although "diet" most broadly refers to the intake of food, "dieting" more commonly implies the manipulation of food and/or dietary supplements to achieve a particular end—for example, weight loss, athletic endurance, disease prevention/mitigation, or religious compliance. The modification of diet for religious purposes can be traced to the earliest tribal cultures and to Judeo-Christian traditions given in the Torah and Bible. The importance of diet in maintaining health and ameliorating illness also dates to antiquity, at least to the fifth-century B.C. Greek physician, Hippocrates.

Whatever their origins, American diet fads have a unique history rooted in popular appeal that has incorporated at one time or another virtually all aspects described above. The first widespread "diet" came from a Presbyterian minister, Sylvester Graham (1794–1851), who in the 1830s and 1840s blended diet and lifestyle into a moralistic campaign against excess of all kinds. A vegetarian, Graham was opposed to alcohol and to what he called "rich foods." His followers, the "Grahamites," found advocates in the revivalist Charles Finney, Transcendentalist Henry David Thoreau, and Mormon founder Joseph Smith. Establishing America's first health food store in New York City, the Grahamites featured their natural whole grain brown flour (later produced commercially as the "graham cracker") as preferable to white, refined flour.

Graham's influence was far reaching and formed the basis for later American health food and dieting regimens such as those promoted by John Harvey Kellogg (1852–1943), who with his brother William created the now-famous corn flake as the dietary centerpiece of his health resort in Battle Creek, Michigan, and Horace Fletcher (1849–1919), called the "Great Masticator," who advocated chewing food to a liquid consistency. All of these early-twentieth-century diet crazes were based more on conviction than on science.

Sounder concepts of dieting developed with the emergence of scientific medicine toward the end of the nineteenth century. One of the most significant works in the emergence of scientific diet therapy was the publication of W. O. Atwater and Charles Dayton Woods's *The Chemical Composition of American Food Materials* in 1896. The real revolution, however, came from Casimir Funk (1884–1967), a Polish-born naturalized citizen. His seminal paper on vitamins as a prevention and cure for a whole range of dietary deficiency diseases in 1912 set the stage for true nutritional science. With the emergence of the trained dietician during World War I (1914–1918) and the increased understanding of the nutritional aspects of diet during the 1930s and 1940s, diet therapy and dieting were finally placed on a more scientific footing.

While health professionals recognize a number of dietary patterns amenable to good health, faddish diets and quick-fix weight loss plans abound in the popular media. As of 2002, there were some 2,000 weight loss books in print, part of a nearly $40 billion industry boosted also by the popularity of the ergogenic diets designed to give athletes a competitive edge. Some have a scientific basis; others are useless or even dangerous; all are best pursued under the advice of a trained health care professional.

BIBLIOGRAPHY

Applegate, Elizabeth A., and Louis E. Grivetti. "Search for the Competitive Edge: A History of Dietary Fads and Supplements." *Journal of Nutrition* 127, Supplement (1997): 869S–873S.

Christen, A. G., and J. A. Christen. "Horace Fletcher (1849–1919): 'The Great Masticator'." *Journal of the History of Dentistry* 45, no. 3 (1997): 95–100.

Haubrich, William S. "Sylvester Graham: Partly Right, Mostly for the Wrong Reasons." *Journal of Medical Biography* 6 (November 1998): 240–243.

Levenstein, Harvey. *Paradox of Plenty: A Social History of Eating in Modern America.* New York: Oxford University Press, 1993.

———. "The Perils of Abundance: Food, Health, and Morality in American History." In *Food: A Culinary History from Antiquity to the Present.* Edited by Jean-Louis Flandrin and Massimo Montanari. New York: Columbia University Press, 1999. A comprehensive resource.

Ohlson, Margaret A. "Diet Therapy in the U.S. in the Past 200 Years." *Journal of the American Dietetic Association* 69 (November 1976): 490–497.

Michael A. Flannery

See also **Health Food Industry; Nutrition and Vitamins; Obesity; Self-Help Movement; Vegetarianism.**

DIGITAL TECHNOLOGY. American engineers began developing digital technology in the mid-twentieth century. Their techniques were based on mathematical concepts suggested by the seventeenth-century German mathematician, Gottfried Wilhelm Leibniz, who proposed a binary computing system. His innovation inspired such numerical codes as American Standard Code for Information Interchange (ASCII) that described objects with digits.

Digital technology is a base two process. Digitized information is recorded in binary code of combinations of the digits 0 and 1, also called bits, which represent words and images. Digital technology enables immense amounts of information to be compressed on small storage devices that can be easily preserved and transported. Digitization also quickens data transmission speeds. Digital technology has transformed how people communicate, learn, and work.

Telecommunications has relied on digital methods to transmit messages. In the early 1980s, enhanced fiber optics enabled the development of digital communication networks. Digital technology replaced analog signals for many telecommunication forms, particularly cellular telephone and cable systems. Analog-to-digital converters utilized pulse code modulation (PCM) to change analog data into digital signals. Compared to analog transmissions, digitized signals were less distorted and could easily be duplicated.

In 1998, commercial digital television broadcasts premiered in the United States. Communication satellites known as direct broadcast satellite (DBS) transmitted compressed digital signals for viewers to receive several hundred television programming choices. Other forms of digital information, including audio programs, were sent to subscribers via satellite. The Federal Communications Commission ordered all American broadcasts to be digital by 2010.

Digital printing with electrophotographic and formatted data technologies have altered how books and magazines are published. The Library of Congress National Digital Library Project has worked to preserve and expand access to rare items. Copyright issues concerning digital technology have addressed the copying of music and videos without performers receiving royalties.

The Electronic Numerical Integrator, and Calculator (ENIAC) was often credited as the first electronic digital computer. A 1973 court ruling on patent infringement declared John V. Atanasoff and Clifford E. Berry were the digital computer's inventors and that the ENIAC had been derived from their design.

In the early 2000s, digital computers ranging from laptops to Internet networks came in many sizes and performed various tasks. Supercomputers performed complex mathematical calculations analyzing vast amounts of data. The Digital Data Broadcast System (DDBS) guided air-traffic control. Digital radiography converted analog signals of x-rays to create digital images. Digital information was stored on plastic disks with pitted patterns of 1s and 0s that lasers translated. By the early 2000s, digital cameras had transformed photography by recording color and light intensities with pixels. Also, digital compression of images and video was achieved by Joint Photographic Experts Group (JPEG) and the Moving Picture Experts Group (MPEG) codes. Animation had often been digitized with some films and cartoons being created entirely with computers.

BIBLIOGRAPHY

Compaine, Benjamin M., ed. *The Digital Divide: Facing a Crisis or Creating a Myth?* Cambridge, Mass.: MIT Press, 2001.

Couch, Leon W., II. *Digital and Analog Communication Systems.* 5th ed. Upper Saddle River, N.J.: Prentice Hall, 1997.

Gordon, David T., ed. *The Digital Classroom: How Technology is Changing the Way We Teach and Learn.* Cambridge, Mass.: Harvard Education Letter, 2000.

Jurgen, Ronald, ed. *Digital Consumer Electronics Handbook.* New York: McGraw-Hill, 1997.

Kiesler, Sara, ed. *Culture of the Internet.* Mahwah, N.J.: Lawrence Erlbaum Associates, Publishers, 1997.

Mansell, Robin, ed. *Inside the Communication Revolution: Evolving Patterns of Social and Technical Interaction.* Oxford and New York: Oxford University Press, 2002.

Mollenhoff, Clark R. *Atanasoff: Forgotten Father of the Computer.* Ames, Iowa: Iowa State University Press, 1988.

Wheeler, Paul. *Digital Cinematography.* Boston: Focal Press, 2001.

Williams, Gerald E. *Digital Technology.* 3rd ed. Chicago: Science Research Associates, 1986.

Elizabeth D. Schafer

See also **Compact Discs; Computers and Computer Industry; DVD; Electricity and Electronics; Fiber Optics, Internet, Telecommunications.**

DIME NOVELS, inexpensive, sensational fiction published roughly from 1840 to 1900, began as fiction supplements to newspapers, such as Park Benjamin's *New World,* that could distribute fiction cheaply under the post office's low newspaper rate. Selling for twelve and one-half cents, Benjamin's "shilling novelettes" declined soon after the post office began to apply the higher book rates to fiction supplements in 1843. In 1845 reduced "book rates" revived cheap fiction, which later claimed national as well as local audiences through the distributor American News Company (1864). The most successful publishers of inexpensive literature, Beadle and Adams, released weekly *Beadle's Dime Novels* beginning in 1860. Competitors included Thomas and Talbot's *Ten Cent Novelettes* (1863), George Munro's *Ten Cent Novels* (1864), and Robert DeWitt's *Ten Cent Romances* (1867). However, dime novels declined in the 1890s due to the panic of 1893; the development of slick, inexpensive magazines; and the copyright agreement of 1891, which curtailed pirating of European fiction. By 1900 the journal *Bookman* could proclaim confidently "the extinction of the dime novel."

Although widely remembered as male-oriented, frontier adventure tales, dime novels also included detective stories, thrilling accounts of urban life, and romances aimed at a female audience. Their authors—often newspaper journalists—worked swiftly under tight deadlines and creative limitations. Sometimes multiple authors used the same well-known pseudonym or popular character, both of which remained the intellectual property of the publisher. Nevertheless, publishers did pirate many stories from British papers, and authors themselves frequently derived their plots from current theater productions and news stories.

Young working men and women—both Yankee and ethnic—composed the bulk of dime-novel readership, and publishers aimed such series as *Ten-Cent Irish Novels* and *Die Deutsche Library* directly at ethnic audiences. Nationwide circulation and popular appeal mark the dime-novel market as a precursor of late-twentieth-century mass culture. Although condemned and even restricted in their day as "immoral" influences on impressionable youth, by the beginning of the twenty-first century dime novels were remembered nostalgically as wholesome and innocent entertainment.

BIBLIOGRAPHY

Denning, Michael. *Mechanic Accents: Dime Novels and Working-Class Culture in America.* New York: Verso, 1987.

Rae Sikula Bielakowski

See also **Literature: Popular.**

DIME STORES, also known as five-and-ten-cent stores and variety stores, began in the late nineteenth century and developed into a major sector of U.S. retailing. However, changes in shopping patterns and new forms of retailing in the 1970s and 1980s caused the virtual demise of dime stores by the early 1990s. The dime store format also provided the impetus for some of the first chain stores and became an important outlet for American mass-manufactured merchandise.

Frank Winfield Woolworth, the father of dime stores, learned the concept while running a five-cent booth in the store of William Moore in Watertown, New York. In 1879, Woolworth opened his first store in Utica, New York. That store failed, but his second store, in Lancaster, Pennsylvania, succeeded, and by 1899 he owned fifty-four stores. Woolworth eliminated the wholesaler and also entered into a buying arrangement with other store operators across the country. After a merger with these chains in 1911, the F. W. Woolworth Company became the dominant variety store chain in the United States and Great Britain.

The five-and-ten-cent stores copied the department store concept of a wide variety of merchandise. The dime stores lowered prices for housewares and other products, so European immigrants and rural Americans, who had moved to the cities, could afford to buy merchandise in incredible volumes. The stores' major merchandise classifications in the early days included toys, notions (sewing supplies), china, glassware, stationery, shoes, and Christmas ornaments. In time, candy and toiletries also became big sellers. The burgeoning U.S. manufacturing industry provided low-price merchandise, and the major variety store chains also sent buyers to scout Europe for distinctive and inexpensive merchandise.

The stores also featured lunch counters that became popular, making Woolworth's the largest seller of restaurant food in the world. The Woolworth lunch counter in Greensboro, North Carolina, became world famous in 1960, when blacks staged a sit-in there to demand service. A part of that counter is in the Smithsonian Museum of American History.

Other early dime store operators included Samuel H. Kress, who opened his first variety store in Memphis in 1896 and in a few years had twelve stores. When Kress died in 1955, his chain had 262 stores with $168 million in sales. Sebastian S. Kresge and J. G. McCrory teamed together to buy a dime store in Memphis in 1897. After the pair opened a second store in Detroit, they parted ways. By 1917, Kresge had over 150 stores, and his operation was second to Woolworth's in size. After experimenting with dollar stores, mail-order, and department stores, the Kresge Company branched into self-service discount stores called Kmart, converting old dime stores into the new format. Fifteen years after the first store opened, Kmart became the second largest retailer in the world. Only Sears, Roebuck and Company had greater sales.

Other major variety store chains included W. T. Grant, H. L. Green, McLellan Stores, G. C. Murphy, Neisner's, and J. J. Newberry. Most chains owned all of their stores. However, Ben Franklin Stores operated as a franchise. Sam Walton started his retail business with a Ben Franklin store in Newport, Arkansas. When he was unable to convince the Ben Franklin management to open discount stores, he opened his own Wal-Mart stores.

The dime stores traded up to higher price points and continued to grow until the early 1970s. Chain store operators controlled over 80 percent of the $8.2 million in sales garnered by 21,582 stores in 1973.

Soon the variety stores' business declined because they lost their advantage in all of the major merchandise classifications they once dominated. Other forms of retailing took away their hegemony as the dime stores failed to compete effectively. They lost the stationery business to the new home office stores. Growing shoe chains, such as Payless, Thom McAn, and Kinney Shoes (owned by Woolworth), grabbed the low-price shoe business. Drug stores, particularly deep-discount drug stores, captured the toiletries business. Discount stores and toy chains, such as Toys 'R' Us and KB Toys, captured the toy business. Grocery stores and drug stores took over the candy business. The notions business went to fabric stores and became a victim of cultural changes.

Woolworth closed its last dime store in 1997. By the early twentieth century, the McCrory Corporation, under the ownership of Meshulam Riklis, owned many of the famous names but operated only 160 stores.

The growth of malls and discount stores and the demise of downtown shopping centers took away the foot traffic that dime stores needed to survive. Inflation took away the five-and-ten-cent prices. The variety stores left to others the concept of dollar stores, which prospered in free-standing, neighborhood locations, while downtown shopping and dime stores faded away. In 2001, Dollar General had 2,734 stores, and Dollar Tree had 1,732 stores. These dollar stores could be considered the dime stores of the twenty-first century, adjusted by inflation to contemporary price levels.

BIBLIOGRAPHY

Lebhar, Godfrey M. *Chain Stores in America, 1859–1962.* New York: Chain Store Publishing, 1963.

Winkler, John K. *Five and Ten: The Fabulous Life of F. W. Woolworth.* New York: R. M. McBride, 1940.

Jerry Brisco

See also **Department Stores; Retailing Industry.**

DIPLOMACY. *See* **Foreign Policy; Foreign Service;** *and individual nations and treaties.*

DIPLOMACY, SECRET. Americans have always been uncomfortable with secret diplomacy and its association with European aristocracies. American leaders have consistently advocated open deliberations and public accountability. These values are embodied in the constitutional provisions for making foreign policy. The U.S. Senate must confirm all high-level diplomatic appointees and ratify, with a two-thirds vote, all foreign treaties. In addition, the right of free speech presumes that journalists and historians will investigate and challenge the government's actions. Time and again, open debate about American diplomacy has forced leaders to change their policies—as in the case of President Richard Nixon's planned escalation of the Vietnam War in October 1969. On other occasions, stubborn figures—particularly President Woodrow Wilson—have watched international agreements disintegrate because they refused to compromise with domestic critics.

This bias toward openness has not prohibited secret diplomacy, especially in the case of foreign negotiations and military maneuvers. Since Benjamin Franklin, Silas Deane, and Arthur Lee negotiated the treaty of alliance with France in 1778, almost every American diplomat sent abroad has relied upon secrecy to influence foreign counterparts and, when necessary, depart from the letter of U.S. government instructions. Diplomacy necessitates flexibility and creativity. It also requires some freedom from day-to-day intrusions by critical on-lookers. The distinction between secret deliberations and open accountability poses a dilemma. Once diplomats have formulated their agreements in privacy, they can often manipulate the domestic political agenda. They can depict their accomplishments—as President George Washington did in the case of the Jay Treaty (1794)—as the only available alternative. They can assert that a rejection of their diplomatic work will bring certain disaster. To some extent, President Franklin Roosevelt followed this tact when he circumvented America's neutrality legislation between 1939 and 1941. Most significantly, leaders can claim that they are acting in the face of an emergency that requires patriotic consent in the name of "national security." Secret diplomacy combined with a call to "rally around the flag" has silenced dissenters in nearly every American war—including the War of 1812, the Mexican-American War, the War of 1898, World War I, and the Korean War.

Since 1945 the rhetoric of openness has remained strong in America, but leaders have made far greater use of secret diplomacy than ever before. Three developments explain this shift in behavior. First, American interests became truly global after 1945. Competing with a perceived communist menace, U.S. leaders believed that they needed to employ subversive means of influence in far-away places. The creation of the Central Intelligence Agency in 1947 and its secret sponsorship of coups in Iran (1953) and Guatemala (1954) reflect this development. Second, the Cold War motivated the U.S. government to classify large quantities of scientific research, strategic analysis, and decision making behind a wall of secrecy. The NATIONAL SECURITY COUNCIL (NSC), formed in 1947, served as a central coordinating body for secret activities in these areas. Congress did not have any oversight for the NSC, which was designed to organize America's capabilities for maximum effect in FOREIGN POLICY. Third, a world with large nuclear arsenals and global subversives required quick and decisive presidential authority. American leaders argued that the pace of war after 1945 necessitated more substantial powers for the executive branch of government. To engage in extended public deliberation would, in the eyes of many, allow America's adversaries to achieve their aims before the U.S. could react. This kind of reasoning contributed to the rise of what some scholars have called the "imperial presidency." The management of the Vietnam War between 1965 and 1975 by presidents Johnson and Nixon is a clear indication of this trend. Nixon, in particular, felt he needed to act in secrecy, because he could not trust the American people to make "realistic" decisions. At the dawn of the twenty-first century, Americans continued to reconcile their democratic values with the growing pressures for secret diplomacy.

BIBLIOGRAPHY

Kissinger, Henry. *Diplomacy.* New York: Simon and Schuster, 1994.

McDougall, Walter A. *Promised Land, Crusader State: The American Encounter with the World Since 1776.* Boston: Houghton Mifflin, 1997.

Perkins, Bradford. *The Creation of a Republican Empire, 1776–1865.* New York: Cambridge University Press, 1993.

Jeremi Suri

DIPLOMATIC MISSIONS. Since the 1770s, U.S. diplomatic missions to foreign countries have grown in number, size, and complexity. Important U.S. diplomatic traditions evolved during the American Revolution. The founders experimented with a variety of foreign policy institutions, including the Committee of Correspondence (established in 1775 and later known as the Committee of Secret Correspondence), the Committee for Foreign Affairs (1777), and the Department of Foreign Affairs (1781). Under these arrangements, Congress assigned diplomats, as individuals and as commissioners, to negotiate with foreign governments. John Jay, secretary of Foreign Affairs from 1784 to 1790, enacted procedures for appointing and recalling diplomats and founded a policymaking process. Once the Constitution was ratified, Congress established the Department of State, under presidential control, to conduct foreign affairs.

U.S. diplomatic missions exhibited several weaknesses through the early nineteenth century. Little coordination occurred between diplomats, who developed political relations with other governments, and consuls, who served the legal and commercial needs of U.S. citizens abroad. Congress perpetually underfunded both types of missions. Most presidents appointed ministers (the highest ranking diplomats) on the basis of nepotism or cronyism rather than merit. Until 1855, most U.S. consuls were foreigners employed by the U.S. government in their native lands. In lieu of receiving salaries, they were authorized to retain the fees they collected for the services they rendered to U.S. citizens.

The number of U.S. diplomatic missions grew modestly before the Civil War. There were six (all in Europe) in 1789 and fifteen (including seven in newly independent countries of Latin America) in 1830. By 1861, thirty-four missions had been established, mostly in Europe and Latin America but also in Hawaii, Japan, China, Turkey, and Egypt. The number of consulates increased from 52 in 1800 to 140 by 1830.

From the 1850s through World War II, diplomatic missions were extensively reformed. In 1855, Congress required that consuls must be American citizens who would earn regular salaries and deposit collected fees in the U.S. Treasury. In 1893, Congress authorized the appointment of envoys at the rank of ambassador in order to bolster the prestige of U.S. missions. President Grover Cleveland established examinations as the means of selecting consular officials, and President Theodore Roosevelt extended basic civil service principles to the consular corps.

The Rogers Act of 1924 overhauled U.S. diplomatic missions. The law combined the diplomatic and consular corps into a single Foreign Service, required entry by competitive examination, established a hierarchy of ranks with promotion based on merit, mandated periodic rotations of personnel from overseas posts to Washington, D.C., and insulated career diplomats from the political whims of presidents. It also increased salaries and benefits so that service became a career option for non-elites. As a result, morale and professionalism soared. By the 1930s, diplomatic missions typically included a chief of mission presiding over a staff organized in political, economic, and consular sections. Missions identified their principal duties as representing the president, negotiating disputes, observing the position of the host government, and recommending policy to Washington.

Diplomatic missions grew in size and reach as the United States broadened its international responsibilities in the twentieth century. The United States had missions in forty-eight countries by 1913 and sixty countries by 1940. The number of consulates increased from 282 in 1860 to 304 in 1910 (although this number declined after the Rogers Act combined the consular and diplomatic corps). In 1893, the United States appointed its first ambassador (to London). Eleven ambassadors served by 1911 and forty-one by 1945. The increasing number of ambassadors reflected America's growing power and its desire to improve relations with certain states.

The growth in U.S. diplomatic missions accelerated after World War II. Between 1945 and 1985, the United States established 125 new missions, most of them embassies. The government even recognized Vatican City (population 1,000) and three other countries with fewer than 50,000 citizens. To meet the growing demand for Foreign Service officers, the Dwight D. Eisenhower administration approved "lateral entry," by which talented individuals joined the Foreign Service at ranks above entry level. The Foreign Service tripled in size in between 1955 and 1970, and several embassies grew to more than 1,000 staff members. In 1999, the government had missions to 189 countries and to more than a dozen international organizations.

As they increased in size and number, U.S. foreign missions also grew more complex. Most embassies were headed by ambassadors, who were advised by a counselor and assisted by first, second, and (in some cases) third secretaries who managed Foreign Service officers assigned to political, economic, administrative, and consular affairs. Embassies were also staffed by officers of State Department agencies such as the Arms Control and Disarmament Agency, Agency for International Development, and United States Information Agency. Foreign Service officers were tasked with such challenges as narcotics control, counter-terrorism, and environmental protection. In many countries, networks of consulates were maintained to deal with commercial and legal issues affecting American citizens.

Embassy staffs also included officers serving agencies other than the State Department. Congress first authorized army and navy attachés in the 1880s, and in following decades the Departments of Commerce, Agriculture, Interior, and Labor dispatched attachés to overseas missions. The Federal Bureau of Investigation and Central Intelligence Agency also assigned personnel, usually undercover, to embassies around the world.

Despite the burgeoning size and reach of missions, the influence of the State Department over foreign policy declined in the late twentieth century. Military officers exerted a strong voice in foreign policymaking during World War II and the Cold War, as the line between policy and strategy blurred and as the Pentagon grew in prestige. After 1947, the National Security Council emerged as a central feature in the foreign policy establishment. Cold War diplomacy was conducted by presidents at summit meetings, by secretaries of state on extensive personal ventures abroad, and through multilateral conferences. As the twentieth century closed, the State Department and the Foreign Service struggled to identify their exact positions in the complex process of making U.S. foreign policy.

BIBLIOGRAPHY

Etzold, Thomas H. *The Conduct of American Foreign Relations: The Other Side of Diplomacy.* New York: Franklin Watts, 1977.

Plischke, Elmer. *U.S. Department of State: A Reference History.* Westport, Conn.: Greenwood Press, 1999.

Peter L. Hahn

See also **Ambassadors; Embassies; Executive Agent; Foreign Service; State, Department of.**

DIRECT MAIL is a MARKETING method for targeting prospective customers or contributors using personalized postal mailings. Like mail order, direct mail entails a two-way exchange: an organization sends a promotional mailing to a recipient who responds with a contribution or an order for products or services. But while the mail-order process generally begins with the mass, anonymous distribution of catalogs, advertisements, coupons, and/or samples of products, users of direct mail carefully choose the recipients of their marketing material, usually on the basis of some characteristic that indicates a high likelihood of interest in the promoter's business or cause. In the 1950s, for example, magazines seeking increased circulation often generated new business by pinpointing people who subscribed to other periodicals on similar topics.

Lillian Vernon. The entrepreneur stands with some of her wide variety of household and other products available by mail. AP/WIDE WORLD PHOTOS

Successful direct-mail campaigns require the composition or acquisition of an initial mailing list and the creation of an overall marketing approach—beginning with a personally addressed envelope and letter—that will arouse the reader's interest and generate a high degree of response. Many users of direct mail consider the method a cost-effective way to do business because buyers or donors can be targeted on the basis of memberships, interests, or previous purchases or donations and addressed with solicitations designed specifically to tap these affinities, often through emotional or psychological appeals. The maintenance and development of the mailing list is vital to continued success in repeat mailings, for new names can be added, unresponsive individuals deleted, and responsive customers and donors "upgraded," or offered new products or tapped for higher sum donations. Since the 1960s, computers and database software have allowed the management of the kinds of information necessary for sophisticated direct-mail targeting, and the development of affordable personal computers since the 1980s has made this marketing method available to the smallest of businesses and organizations. The widespread use of credit cards for payments and donations has also made direct mail more viable.

Direct mail has also become an important fundraising technique for political candidates, advocacy groups, and nonprofit organizations. In the 1960s and 1970s direct mail business owner Richard A. Viguerie was critical in raising money for conservative political causes and candidates, including approximately $7 million for Alabama governor George Wallace's presidential campaigns in the 1970s. The post-Watergate federal election reforms also contributed to the growth of direct-mail political appeals and the professionalization of the direct-mail industry. Candidates often turned to businesses specializing in direct mail appeals in order to reach many donors for relatively small contributions (to the $1,000 legal maximum), while POLITICAL ACTION COMMITTEES and nonprofit organizations similarly used professional direct mail services to solicit unrestricted donations on behalf of particular issues or causes.

Critics charge that direct mail fuels public frustrations with unwanted and wasteful junk mail and that the exchange or sale of mailing lists and customer/donor information raises concerns about privacy. As a marketing method, it also faces increased competition from home-shopping television programs, Internet businesses, and electronic mail.

BIBLIOGRAPHY

Fraser-Robinson, John. *The Secrets of Effective Direct Mail.* New York: McGraw-Hill, 1989.

Hodgson, Richard S. *The Dartnell Direct Mail and Mail Order Handbook.* 3d ed. Chicago: Dartnell, 1980.

Sabato, Larry J. "How Direct Mail Works." In *Campaigns and Elections: A Reader in Modern American Politics.* Glenview, Ill.: Scott, Foresman, 1989.

Jeffrey T. Coster

See also **Advertising; Campaign Financing and Resources; Mail-Order Houses.**

DIRIGIBLES, or motor-driven lighter-than-air craft that can be flown against the wind and steered, were first constructed in America by Caesar Spiegler. His first dirigible made its maiden flight 3 July 1878, with the great American balloonist John Wise as its pilot. Thomas Scott Baldwin built the first dirigible for the government; it was 96 feet long and had a 20-horsepower engine built by Glenn H. Curtiss. Called the *SC-1*, it made its first flight at Fort Myer, Virginia, in August 1908.

When the United States entered World War I, the U.S. Navy ordered sixteen dirigibles of the nonrigid type. Developed from a British model the Royal Navy used for antisubmarine patrols, U.S. Navy personnel who had been positioned in England used the English nickname for the nonrigid airship—"blimp"—and the term subsequently came into common usage in the United States. By the end of the war the navy had twenty "B-type" blimps (77,000–84,000 cubic feet; single engine) and ten "C-type" blimps (182,000 cubic feet; twin engine). In 1919 the navy airship *C-5* failed in its attempt to fly across the Atlantic, but nevertheless set a 1,177-mile nonstop distance record between Montauk, New York, and Saint John's, Newfoundland, where it was destroyed in an accident.

In 1917 an army-navy joint board delegated to the navy the development of the much larger and more complex rigid airship, and in July 1919 Congress authorized the procurement of two rigid airships, one to be built in the United States and the other to be purchased abroad. The army transferred the site of Camp Kendrick, a military facility near Lakehurst, New Jersey, to the navy, which erected a huge hangar, mooring mast, and other facilities there. The Lakehurst Naval Air Station came into commission in 1921, and for the next forty-one years it was the center of American lighter-than-air aeronautics.

As the navy began the development of rigid airships, the army also began to operate dirigibles, concentrating on the semirigid type and blimps. In 1921 the army purchased the Italian semirigid T-34 airship named *Roma*, 412 feet long, having a gas volume of 1.2 million cubic feet, and powered by six 400-horsepower Anasaldo engines. As it had been shipped to the United States disassembled, army engineers erected it at Langley Field, Virginia, where it made its first American flight on 21 November 1921. During a trial flight with new Liberty engines on 21 February 1922 the *Roma* went out of control and flew into a high voltage electrical transmission line. Being inflated with hydrogen, the *Roma* went up in flames and crashed, killing thirty-four of the forty-five men aboard. In 1922 the army airship *C-2* made the first coast-to-coast flight achieved by a lighter-than-air craft. And on 15 December 1924, a Sperry Messenger airplane equipped with a skyhook hooked onto a trapeze hung from the blimp *TC-3*, demonstrated the possibility of the airship's becoming an aircraft carrier. In 1925 the army procured the semirigid *RS-1*, fabricated by the Goodyear-Zeppelin Corporation and erected by the army's center of lighter-than-air aeronautics at Scott Field, Illinois. The *RS-1* made its first flight on 9 January 1926, and although its project engineers hoped to develop it into an airplane carrier, they never conducted appropriate experiments. Shortly after its last flight on 16 October 1928, during which it sustained serious damage, the army dismantled the *RS-1*.

In the meantime the navy had progressed in the development of rigid airships. To begin with, the navy purchased the British airship *R-38*, which became the *ZR-2*. On 24 August 1921, the *ZR-2* suffered a catastrophic structural failure during its flight trials, broke up in the air, and crashed near Hull, England, killing forty-four of the forty-nine men on board. The navy's own first rigid dirigible, the *ZR-1*, was 677 feet long, had a gas volume of 2.235 million cubic feet, and was powered by six 300-horsepower Packard engines. It made its first flight on 4 September 1923, and became the first rigid airship in the world to be inflated with nonflammable helium gas, following the example of the navy blimp *C-7*, which became the first airship of any type to use helium rather than hydrogen on 1 December 1921. (The following year, despite the greater cost of helium and its inferior lift, the navy adopted a policy of using only helium in its dirigibles, rather than highly flammable hydrogen.) On 10 October 1923, the navy formally christened the *ZR-1* the U.S.S. *Shenandoah.* The *Shenandoah* made fifty-seven flights totaling 740 hours, including two coast-to-coast flights in 1924, maneuvers with the Atlantic fleet, and moorings to a floating mooring mast on the stern of the tanker U.S.S. *Patoka.* On 3 September 1925, the *Shenandoah* broke up in a violent thunderstorm and crashed near Ava, Ohio, killing fourteen of the forty-three men on board.

At the end of World War I the navy was to have received two rigid dirigibles, German zeppelins, as spoils of war, but their German crews destroyed them before they could be delivered. In compensation Germany was obliged to build a new zeppelin for the navy. Germany thus constructed the *LZ-126*, the navy's *ZR-3*, best known as the U.S.S. *Los Angeles.* The *Los Angeles* was 658 feet long, had a gas volume of 2.762 million cubic feet, and relied on five 530-horsepower Maybach engines for power. It made its first flight at the Zeppelin factory in Friedrichshafen, Germany, on 27 August 1924; it made its delivery flight to the United States from 12–15 October, a transatlantic passage of eighty-one hours with thirty persons on board, the sixth transatlantic flight made by any type of aircraft. (Charles A. Lindbergh's celebrated transatlantic crossing by airplane was the seventh.) During the next eight years the *Los Angeles* served as a training and experimental airship for the navy, making 331 flights totaling 4,398 hours, which included two flights to Bermuda and two to Panama. The navy decommissioned it on 30 June 1932, but retained it at Lakehurst for various structural tests until scrapping it in 1940.

In 1928 the Goodyear-Zeppelin Corporation started work on two rigid airships for the navy, the *ZRS-4* and *ZRS-5.* They were sister ships, 785 feet long, having a gas volume of 6.850 million cubic feet, and powered by eight 560-horsepower Maybach engines. At that time they were the largest airships in the world, not exceeded in size until 1936, when Germany constructed the airship *Hindenburg.* These airships were unique in that each could carry five Curtiss F-9C fighter planes housed in a hangar within their hulls; the airplanes were equipped with sky-hooks, and the airships could launch and retrieve planes in flight by means of a trapeze lowered from a T-shaped door in their undersides.

The *ZRS-4*, christened *Akron*, made its first flight on 25 September 1931. It made seventy-three flights totaling 1,695 hours, including two coast-to-coast flights and one to Panama. On the night of 4 April 1933, a violent electrical storm over the Atlantic caught and destroyed the *Akron*, which crashed at sea; of the seventy-six men on board, only three survived. The *ZRS-5*, christened *Macon*, made its first flight on 21 April 1933. It made fifty-four flights totaling 1,798 hours, including three coast-to-coast flights, and participated in several war games with the U.S. fleet. While returning from maneuvers on 12 February 1935, it suffered a minor structural failure that became uncontrollable, and the *Macon* crashed in the Pacific. Miraculously, only two of the eighty-three persons were killed in the accident.

The loss of the *Macon* ended the navy's development of the rigid airship, but the blimp remained. On the eve of World War II the navy had only a half-dozen blimps, but during the war the navy expanded its blimp forces to more than 160 airships for antisubmarine patrols. By the end of the war the United States had constructed a network of blimp bases that reached from South Weymouth, Massachusetts, to Key West, Florida, extending across the Caribbean and down the coast of South America to Rio de Janiero. In 1944 the navy flew five airships to French Morocco, where, based at Port Lyautey, they flew a low-altitude antisubmarine barrier over the Strait of Gibraltar.

Dirigible. A U.S. Navy airship accompanies the USS *Casablanca*, a recently constructed escort carrier, in 1943.
National Archives and Records Administration

The basic training airship of the war years was the L-type blimp (146 feet long, 123,000 cubic feet gas volume, two 146-horsepower Warner engines). The backbone of the antisubmarine patrol forces was the K-type blimp (251 feet, 425,000 cubic feet gas volume, two 425-horsepower Pratt & Whitney engines). During the war the United States lost only one airship to enemy action, the *K-74*, on 18 July 1943, after its bombs failed to release in an attack on the German submarine *U-134* in the Caribbean.

After the war the navy continued its blimp development, increasing the size, lift, endurance, and versatility of its airships. In 1954 the ZPG-1-type blimp appeared (324 feet, 875,000 cubic feet, two 800-horsepower engines). The ZPG-1 was unusual in the new configuration of its tail surfaces; formerly all airship tail surfaces had been affixed to the hull at right angles to the vertical, but the ZPG-1, and all navy airships thereafter, had their tail surfaces disposed in an X configuration, 45 degrees to the vertical, which contributed to increased maneuverability.

Dirigibles have never been fast aircraft; what has recommended their use is their great lift relative to the small engine power required, and their great endurance. An airplane can be airborne for only a few hours; an airship can cruise the air for days. In 1954, for example, an American ZPG-2 stayed in the air for 200 hours. And in 1957 a ZPG-2 made a leisurely nonstop circumnavigation of the North Atlantic, 8,216 nautical miles, from South Weymouth, Massachusetts, to Portugal, Morocco, and the Antilles, finally landing at Key West, Florida, after being in the air for 264 hours.

The ZPG-2 that flew this nonstop double crossing of the Atlantic was 342 feet long and had a gas volume of

975,000 cubic feet. Like all other navy blimps, it was an antisubmarine aircraft. In addition, the navy modified five other ZPG-2's into ZPG-2W's that could carry an extraordinarily large air-search radar for airborne early warning duty. In 1956 the navy procured four more ZPG-3W's to carry an even larger radar. With a gas volume of 1.5 million cubic feet, the ZPG-3W was the largest nonrigid airship ever built.

By 1960 high-speed, deep-cruising nuclear submarines were rendering the blimp's antisubmarine capabilities obsolete; in addition, experts had begun to fear an attack by missiles rather than by bombers, which degraded the airship's early-warning mission. In June 1961 the navy decommissioned its blimp squadrons, and on 21 August 1962, terminated all flight operations by airships.

Since the 1920s the Goodyear Tire & Rubber Company has maintained a small fleet of advertising blimps, beginning with the *Pilgrim* of 1925. The Goodyear fleet reached its maximum strength in the 1930s, when it operated six airships, the *Defender*, *Resolute*, *Enterprise*, *Reliance*, *Rainbow*, and *Ranger*, all of which had been turned over to the navy as training ships by 1942. Goodyear revived its fleet after the war, but fear of the competition of television advertising caused the company to cut back its investment in the enterprise. Goodyear had only one blimp remaining when a study revealed what the American public had long known: the blimp was a unique advertising vehicle, and "blimp" had become synonymous with "Goodyear." Since 1969 three Goodyear blimps have been cruising the skies of the United States, the *Columbia*, *Mayflower*, and *America*, while a fourth, the *Europa*, operates in Western Europe. Goodyear's was the only organized airship operation in the world in the 1970s. Since then a number of other companies have built smaller blimps, including MetLife insurance company, which operates the blimps *Snoopy One* and *Snoopy Two* (decorated with images of the dog Snoopy, from the *Peanuts* comic strip). These flying billboards have become common sights at American sporting events, where they often provide aerial shots to television networks in exchange for free advertising.

BIBLIOGRAPHY

Kirschner, Edwin J. *The Zeppelin in the Atomic Age: The Past, Present, and Future of the Rigid Lighter-Than-Air Aircraft.* Urbana: University of Illinois Press, 1957.

Robinson, Douglas H. *Giants in the Sky: A History of the Rigid Airship.* Seattle: University of Washington Press, 1973.

Smith, Richard K. *The Airships Akron & Macon: Flying Aircraft Carriers of the United States Navy.* Annapolis, Md.: U.S. Naval Institute, 1965.

Toland, John. *Ships in the Sky: The Story of the Great Dirigibles.* New York: Holt, 1957.

Richard K. Smith / c. w.

See also **Air Defense; Air Force, United States; Army, United States; Navy, United States.**

DISABILITY RIGHTS MOVEMENT. Comprises a number of related but distinct social movements advocating civil rights for an estimated 53 million U.S. citizens (as of 1997) with physical, sensory, psychological, or cognitive disabilities that affect their daily activities. Emerging after World War II, these movements replaced a medical model of disability with a minority-group model. The medical model defined disability as physical, psychosocial, and vocational limitation resulting from illness or injury. Locating the problem within individuals, it prescribed the solution as treatment to cure or at least to correct individual functioning. The minority model asserted that limitations in social and vocational functioning were not the exclusive and inevitable result of bodily impairment but were also a product of the inadequacies in the architectural and social environment. Thus, for example, paralyzed legs did not inevitably cause limitations in mobility, but the absence of ramps did. The new model saw devaluation of disabled persons as producing socioeconomic discrimination.

The disability rights movements arose in response to a historic legacy of discrimination and segregation. In the late nineteenth and early twentieth centuries, most professionals in medicine, social services, and education increasingly attributed a lack of moral and emotional self-control to the "defective classes," which included virtually anyone with a disability, blaming them for the poverty, vice, crime, and dislocations of the new industrial order. People with mental retardation, epilepsy, or cerebral palsy were often permanently institutionalized as a danger to society. Others with physical disabilities were at times segregated by such ordinances as Chicago's "ugly" law, which prohibited "diseased, maimed, mutilated, or . . . deformed" persons from appearing in public. Reacting to an emerging deaf subculture, an "oralist" movement began in the 1880s to oppose sign language and insist that deaf people learn speech and speechreading. Led by Alexander Graham Bell, it took over much of deaf education and sought to disperse the deaf community. Eugenicists pressed for the sterilization of people with various disabilities, and by 1931 more than half the states had adopted sterilization laws, and thousands of people were sterilized. Meanwhile, contemporary welfare policy defined disability as the incapacity for productive labor and, in effect, incompetency to manage one's life. It thus brought many disabled people under permanent medical and social-service supervision and relegated them to a stigmatized and segregated economic dependency.

Beginning during World War I, some professionals avowed continuing faith in treatment and training. Special education of disabled children and medical-vocational rehabilitation of disabled adults sought to correct the functional limitations that allegedly prevented social integration. People with physical and sensory disabilities were imbued with an ethos of individualistic striving known as "overcoming," with President Franklin D. Roosevelt's life in a wheelchair as the prime example during the 1930s and early 1940s. People with mental handicaps, however, were still often institutionalized or subjected to social control in the community.

After 1945, the disability rights movements developed in opposition to these ideologies and practices. Parents' groups lobbied in state legislatures and in Congress for the right of disabled children to a "free and appropriate" public education in "the least restrictive environment"—or integration to the maximum extent. These principles were embodied in the Education for All Handicapped Children Act of 1975. Other parents' groups and reform-minded professionals promoted deinstitutionalization and community-based group homes for developmentally disabled persons. Beginning in the late 1960s, deaf advocates redefined deafness as a linguistic difference and demanded their rights to sign language and cultural self-determination. Their efforts culminated in the March 1988 "Deaf President Now" campaign at Gallaudet University, when a student strike at that university for deaf people, supported by the deaf community, won its demand for selection of a deaf educator to head the university.

Meanwhile, physically disabled activists launched an independent-living movement for self-directed, community-based living. They also claimed the right of equal access to public transit and public accommodations. Advocacy groups, such as Americans Disabled for Accessible Public Transit (ADAPT), took to the streets—sometimes tying up traffic, construction, and business—as well as to the halls of legislatures to win passage and enforcement of accessibility statutes. The organized blind movement, long the most politically effective disability movement, lobbied successfully for both access (the right to use white canes and guide dogs in public places) and policies to advance economic well-being (through tax exemptions, for example).

All these efforts reflected an emerging minority consciousness documented in a 1986 opinion survey of disabled adults: 54 percent of those aged eighteen to forty-four identified disabled people as a minority group that faced discrimination. The movement thus demanded federal protection against discrimination in education, jobs, public accommodations, and government-funded activities. Antidiscrimination and the right of equal access were the basis of fifty federal laws that began with the Architectural Barriers Act of 1968 and culminated in the Americans with Disabilities Act of 1990. These statutes adopted the disability rights movements' major contribution to U.S. civil rights theory—the concept of equal access. Adaptive devices, assistive services, and architectural modifications (for example, Braille markings, sign-language interpreters, and ramps) had been considered special benefits to those who were fundamentally dependent. Equal access moved beyond such social welfare notions by viewing these provisions as reasonable accommodations for different ways of functioning. Traditional civil rights theory sometimes allowed differential treatment of a minority as a temporary remedy to achieve equality. Disability rights ideology argued that for persons with disabilities, permanent differential treatment in the form of accessibility and reasonable accommodations was legitimate because it was necessary to achieve and maintain equal access and thus equal opportunity for full participation in society.

BIBLIOGRAPHY

Barnartt, Sharon N., and Richard K. Scotch. *Disability Protests: Contentious Politics 1970–1999.* Washington, D.C.: Gallaudet University Press, 2001.

Fleischer, Doris Zames, and Frieda Zames. *The Disability Rights Movement: From Charity to Confrontation.* Philadelphia: Temple University Press, 2001.

Longmore, Paul K., and Lauri Umansky, eds. *The New Disability History: American Perspectives.* New York: New York University Press, 2001.

Scotch, Richard K. *From Good Will to Civil Rights: Transforming Federal Disability Policy.* 2d ed. Philadelphia: Temple University Press, 2001.

Shapiro, Joseph P. *No Pity: People with Disabilities Forging a New Civil Rights Movement.* New York: Times Books, 1993.

Trent, James W., Jr. *Inventing the Feeble Mind: A History of Mental Retardation in the United States.* Berkeley: University of California Press, 1994.

Paul K. Longmore / C. P.

See also **Americans with Disabilities Act; Civil Rights and Liberties; Eugenics; Gallaudet University; Mental Illness; Social Security.**

DISABLED, EDUCATION OF THE. A definition in the 1970s of the educationally handicapped as "persons with difficulties and disadvantages derived primarily from physical causes," as distinguished from "the mentally, emotionally, socially, and economically handicapped," is no longer accurate, as the scope of what is recognized as an educational disability underwent a significant expansion in the next thirty years, along with a broadening of the concept of how these disabilities should be addressed.

There are two distinct periods in the education of the disabled in America: from colonial times until approximately 1970, and from the early 1970s forward, during which time much of what is currently perceived to form the substance and procedure of special education rapidly developed. One representative indication of this explosion in the education of the disabled is the change in terminology from "handicapped" to "disabled," a result of amendments to the federal legislation that has come to define much of special education. This change reflects the belief that "handicapped" has historically been a demeaning term and that "disabled" more precisely identifies the population in question.

The earliest approaches to the education of the disabled in America—during colonial times and for some time thereafter—had little to do with education and more to do with management. Overtly physically or developmentally disabled children were either cared for by individual families or excluded from local society. For example, a 1691 New York act included the mentally challenged among the "Vagabonds and Idle persons" it sought to "discourage." In 1773, New York passed a law permitting the denial of settlement to the mentally ill or retarded or, if they were already residents, compelling their families to see to their care. By the early nineteenth century, institutions for the "feeble-minded" were established, once again more as a segregating social management tool than as a means to educate independent citizens.

From the early nineteenth through the mid-twentieth century, a number of movements arose that offered more educational approaches for specific disability groups, although often in isolated settings. Meaningful deaf education began in 1817, with the founding of Thomas Gallaudet's private school in Hartford, Connecticut, and was extended by the founding of the first state school for the deaf in Kentucky in 1823, and the eventual proliferation of schools throughout the East and Midwest. In 1864 the first higher education institution for the deaf, the National Deaf-Mute College, now Gallaudet, was federally funded. Additional educational services for the hearing-impaired were developed through the much-publicized efforts of Samuel Gridley Howe and Alexander Graham Bell.

Similarly, educational opportunities for the blind and vision-impaired were established throughout the nineteenth century. Howe founded a private school for the blind in Boston in 1832, soon to be followed by others, all residential. Public day programs for the blind were instituted in Chicago in 1900 and New York in 1909. With the services of the American Printing House for the Blind, Congress and the states began funding local facilities for the blind, often library services, as early as 1868.

In somewhat of a contrast, the education of the developmentally delayed or behaviorally impaired was still more a function of social management. Mentally retarded children in Pennsylvania could be removed from their families to private schools pursuant to an 1852 appropriation, and in New York early public school classes for "unruly boys" (begun in 1871) served only to segregate "problem" children from the mainstream and made no attempt to remediate learning difficulties.

By the early twentieth century, more emphasis was placed on effective education for the disabled, as evidenced by the passing of mandatory special education laws in New Jersey, Massachusetts, and New York. In 1915, Minnesota was the first state to enact special education teacher certification requirements, and Pennsylvania and Oregon instituted intrastate cooperative agreements for meeting the needs of educationally exceptional students. However, during the 1930s this trend was significantly curtailed by the Great Depression. It was not until the 1970s that scientific and pedagogical advances and the expansion of civil rights theory combined to literally rewrite the very definition of the education of the disabled.

Building directly on the Supreme Court's 1954 decision *Brown v. Board of Education of Topeka, Kansas*, coalitions of advocacy groups for the disabled turned to the federal courts for recognition and definition of special education rights. They primarily based their claims on the equal protection and due process clauses of the U.S. Constitution, the same legal mandates that had ended "separate but equal" education based on race. In two landmark decisions, *Pennsylvania Association for Retarded Children v. Commonwealth of Pennsylvania* (1971) and *Mills v. Board of Education of the District of Columbia* (1972), the concept of the education of the disabled was redefined. Under the equal protection clause (*Pennsylvania Association*) and the due process clause (*Mills*), the federal courts recognized the fundamental right of each disabled child in America to attend school, to receive individual educational services at least equivalent to those enjoyed by nondisabled students, and to not be denied educational services without the right to contest that action through due process of law.

Those two Court cases led directly to the Education of All Handicapped Children Act in 1975, which eventually was retitled the Individuals with Disabilities Education Act (IDEA). For the first time, the following components were identified nationwide as prerequisites for the appropriate education of the disabled:

1. A broad definition of educational disability. Basing its drafting on the input of current scientific and educational disciplines, the federal government greatly expanded its definition of educational disability. The traditional categories of physical disabilities were retained, but now the great majority of children identified as disabled were those with processing, executive, and affective disorders, such as specific learning disabilities (the category that accounted for nearly half of the six million identified disabled students in 1999); emotional impairment; receptive and expressive language disorders; autism spectrum disorders; and attention deficit disorders.
2. Zero reject. The education of the disabled is premised upon the belief that all students can benefit from education, that none are so disabled that services should not be provided.
3. Free appropriate public education (FAPE). The provision of FAPE to all disabled students is mandated in the IDEA and requires that education and related services (such as speech therapy, occupational therapy, and counseling) be provided at no charge to the parents of the students through public or privately contracted programs implemented by an individualized educational program.
4. The individualized educational program (IEP). Since 1975, IEPs have formed the foundation upon which education is provided to the disabled. A paper program drafted through a cooperative effort of parents

and school staff, the IEP is individualized for the particular special education student and forms a contract between school and family as to the provision of specific services.

5. The least restrictive environment. Founded upon constitutional principles, the education of the disabled is to be provided in the least restrictive environment. Since the goal of the education is for the student to be able to become a productive citizen within the greater society, removal of the student from the mainstream school experience is only to occur if necessary for appropriate instruction.

At the end of the twentieth century, the education of the disabled was a heavily funded ($4.9 billion in 2000) national program, primarily concerned with the recognition of educational disabilities in a broad population of students and with individual programming to remediate or compensate for the impact of those disabilities. In contrast to over two hundred years of segregated programming provided largely for social management purposes, its ultimate goal was to enable the productive inclusion of disabled students in American society.

BIBLIOGRAPHY

Tarver, Sara. "How Special Education Has Changed." In *Changing Perspectives in Special Education.* New York: Charles E. Merrill, 1977.

U.S. Department of Education. "To Assure the Free Appropriate Public Education of All Children with Disabilities." Twenty-second Annual Report to Congress on the Implementation of the Individuals with Disabilities Education Act. Washington, D.C.: Office of Special Education Programs, 2000.

Weintraub, Frederick J., and Joseph Ballard. *Special Education in America: Its Legal and Governmental Foundations.* Council for Exceptional Children, 1982.

Michael J. Eig

See also **Americans with Disabilities Act; Disability Rights Movement; Discrimination: Disabled; Gallaudet University.**

DISASTERS. In the modern world, the traditional view of natural disasters as punishments for human wickedness has given way to the scientific study of the causes of seemingly unpredictable acts of nature. In recent years, however, scholars have placed more emphasis on the roles played by greed and indifference to potential human suffering in many seemingly "natural" disasters. The following is a selective list of natural and man-made disasters that have occurred in the United States. It should be noted that disaster statistics are often approximations, at best. Not only do contemporary news accounts frequently differ, but there are no standards by which to judge whether deaths and injuries were directly caused by a cataclysmic event.

Aviation

17 September 1908. The first airplane crash involving a fatality took place at Fort Myer, Virginia. A plane flown by Orville Wright and Thomas E. Selfridge was thrown out of control when it hit a bracing wire. Wright was badly injured and Selfridge was killed.

2 July 1912. The first U.S. DIRIGIBLE *Akron* blew up over Atlantic City, New Jersey, at an altitude of 2,000 feet; the builder of the *Akron* and four crewmembers were killed.

21 February 1922. The Italian-built hydrogen-filled U.S. dirigible *Roma* exploded in Hampton, Virginia, killing thirty-four of the crew of forty-five. After the disaster, hydrogen—which is much cheaper than helium but highly flammable—was no longer used in U.S. airships.

6 May 1937. The 803-foot-long German dirigible *Hindenburg*—the largest airship ever built—exploded in midair at Lakehurst Naval Air Station in New Jersey, just thirty-two seconds after dropping rope mooring lines to the ground. The airship, filled with highly flammable hydrogen gas, crashed in flames, killing thirteen passengers, twenty-two crewmembers, and one ground handler. The cause of the crash was never determined. Leading theories suggested either an electrical discharge in the atmosphere or sabotage (for which there was no evidence).

28 July 1945. The pilot of a B-25 bomber lost his bearings and crashed into the Empire State Building in New York City between the seventy-eighth and seventy-ninth floors, setting fire to the upper part of the building. The three military men in the plane and eleven people in the building were killed; twenty-six people were injured.

30 June 1956. A TWA Lockheed Super Constellation and a United Airlines DC-7 collided at an estimated angle of thirty degrees over the Grand Canyon, killing all 128 people onboard both planes. The planes had left Los Angeles, California, within minutes of each other and were flying at 300 MPH at 21,000 feet. The captains had chosen to fly in airspace not controlled by Air Route Traffic Control Centers. A result of the crash was the 1958 Federal Aviation Act, establishing an independent FEDERAL AVIATION ADMINISTRATION (FAA) to modernize air traffic control and expand controlled airspace.

16 December 1960. A United Airlines DC-8 jet bound for Idlewild (now Kennedy) Airport with eighty-four passengers and crew, and a TWA Super Constellation bound for La Guardia Airport with forty-four passengers and crew collided in midair over Staten Island, New York, during a snowstorm. The United plane crashed in a Brooklyn tenement district, the TWA plane, in Staten Island harbor. All 128 people in the planes, and six people on the ground, were killed. As a result, the FAA drastically reduced speed limits for aircraft entering terminals and assigned extra traffic controllers to airports with high flight volumes.

1 March 1962. An American Airlines Boeing 707 crashed in Jamaica Bay, New York, shortly after takeoff. All ninety-five people aboard were killed.

3 June 1963. A chartered military airplane vanished near southeast Alaska. Of the 101 people aboard, no survivors were ever found.

4 September 1971. A Boeing 727 carrying 111 persons crashed into a mountainside while approaching the airport at Juneau, Alaska, and fell into a deep gorge; everyone aboard died.

29 December 1972. An Eastern Airlines L-1011 TriStar jumbo jet crashed in the Florida Everglades during its landing approach. Wreckage from the 350,000-pound craft was strewn over a 15,000-foot area. Of the 176 people aboard, 101 died.

24 June 1975. An Eastern Airlines Boeing 727 jetliner crashed in flames at the edge of Kennedy International Airport in New York City while attempting to land during an electrical storm. Of the 124 passengers and crew, 112 died.

25 September 1978. A private plane and jetliner collided near San Diego, California, killing 144 people.

25 May 1979. In one of the worst air disasters in history, a U.S. DC-10 jetliner bound for Los Angeles, California, crashed on takeoff at O'Hare International Airport in Chicago after one engine and its support pylon fell off. All 258 passengers and thirteen crew were killed.

9 July 1982. A Pan American jetliner crashed in Kenner, Louisiana, killing all 146 on board and eight on the ground.

2 August 1985. A Delta jetliner crashed in a storm near the Dallas–Fort Worth Airport, killing 134 people.

16 August 1987. A Northwest Airlines jet bound for Phoenix crashed after takeoff from Detroit, killing 156 people.

11 May 1989. ValuJet Airlines flight 592 crashed in the Florida Everglades, a few minutes after taking off from Miami, killing 110 passengers and the crew. Investigators determined the plane was carrying illegally stored oxygen generators that apparently fanned a fire, causing the crash.

8 September 1994. A USAir Boeing 737 was approaching Pittsburgh when it crashed into the woods northwest of the airport, killing all 132 aboard.

17 July 1996. Trans-World Airlines Flight 800 exploded shortly after takeoff from Kennedy International Airport, killing all 230 passengers and crew. Investigators concluded that air conditioners cooling the plane had turned the fuel in the nearly empty fuel tank into combustible vapors that ignited from a tiny spark in the electrical wiring. (See TWA FLIGHT 800.)

31 October 1999. Cairo-bound Egyptair Flight 990, a Boeing 767-300, left New York with 217 passengers and crew. A half-hour later the plane plunged into the Atlantic off the coast of Massachusetts.

12 November 2001. Minutes after takeoff from Kennedy International Airport, American Airlines Flight 587, bound for the Dominican Republic, crashed into the town of Belle Harbor in Queens, New York, killing all 260 people onboard and five on the ground.

Building and Dam Collapses

31 May 1889. The Conemaugh Lake in Johnstown, Pennsylvania, flooded after a forty-eight-hour storm and burst through South Fork Dam, sending 20 million tons of water into the valley below in less than forty-five minutes. The man-made lake, built as a reservoir, had been purchased in 1852 by a group of industrialists as a private fishing pond. They removed the dam's discharge pipes to keep the water level high and partially blocked the spillways to keep the fish from escaping. These actions had the effect of removing the dam's pressure valve. As many as 3,000 people were killed by the flood or the fire that broke out on a thirty-acre island of floating wreckage blocked by a stone bridge. This was one of the most severe floods in U.S. history (see JOHNSTOWN FLOOD).

28 January 1922. The roof of the 1,800-seat Knickerbocker Theatre in Washington, D.C., collapsed during a performance, killing ninety-five (some accounts say 120) and injuring more than 100.

13 March 1928. The collapse of St. Francis Dam, in San Francisquito Canyon, California, forty-five miles north of Los Angeles, sent billions of gallons of water racing through the sixty-mile-wide floodplain at 500,000 cubic feet per second. The death toll was 350; most of the victims were crushed by boulders and debris.

26 February 1972. A coal-refuse dam in Buffalo Creek, West Virginia, collapsed, spreading water and sludge into the valley below; 118 died and 4,000 were left homeless.

17 July 1981. Two of the three concrete walkways at the Hyatt Regency Hotel in Atlanta collapsed, killing 114 people and injuring nearly 200. An investigation revealed that the wrong configuration of metal rods was used in the construction of the walkways.

Earthquakes and Volcanic Eruptions

15 December 1811. A strong earthquake in New Madrid, Missouri, the first of many over a nearly two-month period, destroyed the town and several others nearby. While few casualties were reported, the earthquakes could be felt over a 1.5-million-square-mile area. They destroyed forests, opened large ravines, and even changed the course of the Mississippi River for several months.

31 August 1886. An earthquake shook the Eastern United States from Boston to Charleston, North Carolina, and from Milwaukee to New Orleans, killing 110 people in Charleston.

18 April 1906. SAN FRANCISCO EARTHQUAKE. One of the most devastating natural disasters in the recorded history of North America, this earthquake and the subsequent fires killed 700 people and ravaged the city.

27 March 1964. One of the most powerful earthquakes to strike anywhere in the world (measuring up to 8.4 on the Richter scale) hit southern Alaska, killing at least 115 and causing over $350 million in damage.

18 May 1980. MOUNT ST. HELENS in southwest Washington erupted in the first of a series of explosions 500 times as powerful as the atomic bomb dropped on Hiroshima. Advance warning and evacuations kept the death toll at sixty-one. The eruption felled 130,000 acres of forest, and buried 150 miles of rivers and twenty-six lakes. Across the Northwest, nearly 6,000 miles of roadway were covered with ash; a cloud of ash 500 miles long and 100 miles wide moved eastward over Montana and Idaho.

17 October 1989. With an epicenter ten miles northeast of Santa Cruz, California, the Loma Prieta earthquake (which measured 7.1 on the Richter scale) was responsible for sixty-three deaths, 3,767 injuries and $6 billion in property damage in the Los Angeles area.

17 January 1994. Measuring 6.7 on the Richter scale, with an epicenter twenty miles northwest of downtown Los Angeles, the Northridge earthquake killed fifty-seven people, severely injured 1,500, and caused an estimated $15 to $30 billion in damage.

Epidemics

Fall 1793. A YELLOW FEVER epidemic killed thousands in Philadelphia.

Mid-August–October 1878. A yellow fever epidemic in Memphis, Tennessee, killed 5,000 residents; 25,000 people fled, spreading the disease elsewhere in the South, increasing the overall death toll to 14,000.

1918–1919. The worldwide INFLUENZA pandemic first appeared in the United States at the Fort Riley and Camp Funston army training camps in Kansas, where forty-six died. At the height of the outbreak, in October 1918, more than 21,000 U.S. deaths were attributed to the disease. Total U.S. fatalities were said to be 550,000, more than ten times the number of American casualties in World War I.

1931. A diphtheria epidemic killed about 17,000 children in the United States.

1981– . A virus believed to have originated in Africa in the 1950s, possibly in monkeys, was first documented in humans in the United States in 1981. The infecting agent of ACQUIRED IMMUNE DEFICIENCY SYNDROME (AIDS) is the human immuno-deficiency virus (HIV), which spreads primarily through sexual contact and injected-drug use. As of mid-2001, AIDS deaths in the United States totaled 457,667; an estimated 800,000–900,000 persons are infected with HIV/AIDS. While new drug formulations have kept HIV-infected individuals alive for increasingly longer periods, and the new AIDS cases and deaths have declined, the rate of HIV infection remains about 40,000 annually.

Fires

16 December 1835. In New York City, 674 buildings burned in a fire.

14 July 1845. A fire that started on a New York City street spread to a building where saltpeter (used in manufacturing gunpowder) was stored. An unknown number of people were killed, and 1,000 buildings were destroyed.

8–9 October 1871. The CHICAGO FIRE left 300 dead and 90,000 homeless, with property loss at $200 million.

8–14 October 1871. After months of drought, hot, dry gale-force winds whipped forest fires into an inferno that destroyed Peshtigo, Wisconsin, killing 1,152 of its citizens as well as about 350 people from neighboring towns. Nearby swamps produced methane gas, which exploded in the intense heat even before the fires reached town. Many sought refuge from the airborne chunks of burning debris on the bridge over the Peshtigo River, which ignited and collapsed. More than 4 million acres of forests and grasslands burned. Yet the fire received minimal news coverage because the Chicago fire, caused by the same dry winds, began on the same day.

5 December 1876. A fire that apparently started when a lamp ignited a backstage curtain in the Brooklyn Theater in Brooklyn, New York, killed 295.

4 June 1892. Flaming oil from a storage tank was carried by rushing floodwaters into Oil City and Titusville, Pennsylvania. Both towns were destroyed; the death toll was 130.

1 September 1894. A forest fire in eastern Minnesota spread to Hinkley (population 1,200), destroying it and more than twelve other neighboring towns. The death toll was more than 600. Hinkley's survivors took refuge in a gravel pit filled with stagnant water or in a lake several miles out of town, where they had fled on a train that caught fire.

30 December 1903. A fire started by a stage light that ignited gauze draperies resulted in tragedy at the new, 1,602-seat Iroquois Theater in Chicago. Stagehands waited too long to lower the fireproof safety curtain, and the fire exits led to only one narrow passageway. Of the 602 deaths, 400 were caused by a massive stampede for the exits. A new fire code for public theaters in Chicago was instituted after the disaster.

7 February 1904. A strong wind turned a fire in a dry goods warehouse in Baltimore into an out-of-control blaze that raged for two days and caused $85 million in property damage, the second worst fire to date in U.S. history. Yet only one person, a fireman, was killed.

4 March 1908. An overheated furnace burst into flame at the Lake View School in Collinwood, Ohio, a suburb of Cleveland, killing 171 of the 360 children and nine teachers.

25 March 1911. TRIANGLE SHIRTWAIST FIRE killed 145, mostly young women, in a garment factory.

12 October 1918. Forest fires near Duluth, Minnesota, and northern Wisconsin destroyed twenty-one towns, killing 800, and leaving 12,000 homeless.

21 April 1930. Fire broke out at a construction site in the Ohio State Penitentiary in Columbus and spread to the tarpaper roof of the prison. Most of the prisoners were kept in their cells until escape from the flames was impossible. The prison, designed to hold 1,500 inmates, had a population of 4,300; 317 died and 231 were injured.

18 March 1937. A gas leak caused a violent explosion near the end of the school day at the schoolhouse in New London, Texas. Parents waiting to collect their children watched in horror as 294 children and teachers were killed by the explosion or crushed under debris.

23 April 1940. A dance hall fire in Natchez, Mississippi, killed 198.

28 November 1942. Lack of exit doors, doors that opened inward, and a great deal of flammable material contributed to the death by fire of 474 people (or 493; accounts differ) at the Cocoanut Grove nightclub in Boston. Fire had broken out in the basement bar and spread quickly up to the dance floor.

6 July 1944. A Ringling Bros. and Barnum & Bailey circus tent, weatherproofed with a highly flammable substance, caught fire and collapsed in Hartford, Connecticut. Blocked exits prevented escape for many of the 7,000 people attending the show. The fatalities numbered at least 163; injury statistics range from 174 to 261.

7 December 1946. Fire broke out early in the morning in a corridor of the fifteen-story Winecoff Hotel in Atlanta, which had been classified as "fireproof" in a safety inspection despite having no sprinkler system or fire escapes. Of the 280 guests, 119 died; those who perished had barricaded themselves in their rooms or could not be reached by firemen, whose ladders extended only to the tenth floor. Ninety other guests suffered serious injuries.

1 December 1958. A fire at Our Lady of the Angels parochial school in Chicago killed 93 children and nuns. The disaster prompted the establishment of new safety regulations, fire drills, and fire fighting equipment in many U.S. schools.

28 May 1977. A supper club fire in Southgate, Kentucky, killed 164.

21 November 1980. A fire that broke out in the kitchen of the twenty-one-story MGM Grand Hotel in Las Vegas, Nevada, killed 85 and injured more than 600, mostly from smoke inhalation. There were no sprinklers on many floors, flammable synthetics were used in building materials, and self-locking doors on stairwells trapped guests. The tragedy accelerated updating of fire codes to emphasize smoke control and provide for the special needs of high-rise buildings.

Industrial: Chemical Spills, Explosions, and Mining

1 May 1900. An underground explosion at a Scofield, Utah, mine killed 201 miners.

19 May 1902. A mine at Coal Creek, Tennessee, exploded, killing 184 workers.

6 December 1907. In two adjoining Monongah, West Virginia, coal mines owned by the Consolidated Coal Company, runaway mining cars filled with coal created an electrical fire (probably by crashing into an electrical line) that ignited highly explosive coal dust. The explosion—the worst U.S. mining disaster ever—killed 362 miners. Only four escaped; recovery of the bodies took more than three weeks.

19 December 1907. An apparent gas explosion at the Darr Coal Mine in Jacob's Creek, Pennsylvania, killed 239 of the 240 miners.

13 November 1909. Bales of hay caught fire near the entrance to a mine at Cherry, Illinois, and spread to the mineshaft, killing 259.

22 October 1913. An explosion caused by a buildup of coal dust in a mine owned by the Stag Canyon Fuel Company in Dawson, New Mexico, filled the mine with deadly gases and sealed off the exits. Only five miners were rescued; 263 died.

18 May 1918. A TNT explosion blew up the Aetna Chemical Company plant in Oakdale, Pennsylvania, killing about 200 people.

17 July 1944. Explosions at two ammunition dumps killed more than 300 in Port Chicago, California.

30 September 1944. Liquid gas tanks exploded in Cleveland, Ohio, setting off a fire that spread over a fifty-block area. Property damage was estimated at $10 million, about 100 people lost their lives, and more than 200 were injured.

20 October 1944. Another liquid gas tank exploded in Cleveland; 121 died and hundreds were left homeless.

19 May 1928. A coal mine explosion at Mather, Pennsylvania, killed 195 miners.

1942–1980. More than 20,000 tons of chemical waste, including dioxin, buried between 1942 and 1953 by the Hooker Electrochemical and Olin corporations in the Love Canal neighborhood of Niagara Falls, New York, began to seep into backyards and basement walls in the mid-1970s. Residents had far greater than normal occurrences of cancer, birth defects, miscarriages, and other serious health problems. Studies helped focus public attention on the problem of toxic waste and led to passage of the Emergency Response (SUPERFUND) Act in 1980, making owners and operators of hazardous waste dumps liable for clean-up costs.

2 May 1972. A fire in the nearly 5,000-foot-deep Sunshine Silver Mine in Kellogg, Idaho, spread flames and carbon monoxide fumes, blocking hoist exits; ninety-one perished. Two miners were found alive after seven days.

5 December 1982. When the Meramec River in TIMES BEACH, Missouri, thirty-five miles southwest of St. Louis, overflowed its banks, it spread oil that had been sprayed on the roads to control dust. The oil contained dioxin, the most toxic chemical known, producing adverse health effects at all tested levels. Virtually the entire town of 300 was evacuated, and more than $33 million was spent on cleanup.

24 March 1989. The tanker *EXXON VALDEZ*, loaded with crude oil, struck Bligh Reef in Prince William Sound, Alaska, spilling 10.8 million gallons over a 500-square-mile area. Cleanup efforts were hampered by frozen ground and the remoteness of the site.

Marine

31 October 1837. The side-wheeler *Monmouth* collided with the *Tremont* on the Mississippi River near Profit Island, killing 300.

13 January 1840. Near Eaton's Neck, New York, the steamboat *Lexington* caught fire, killing 140.

9 August 1841. Containers of turpentine stored near the boilers on the steamboat *Erie* exploded soon after it left Buffalo, New York, for Chicago. The newly painted and varnished ship immediately caught fire, killing 242, many of whom were immigrant passengers trapped in the steerage section.

17 June 1850. A fire aboard the steamer *Griffith* on Lake Erie took the lives of all 300 aboard.

24 December 1853. En route to California, the steamer *San Francisco* foundered off the Mexican coast; of its 700 passengers, 240 drowned.

13 November 1854. The wreck of an immigrant ship, the *New Era*, en route to New York from Bremen, Germany, killed more than 300 off the New Jersey coast.

12 September 1857. The side-wheel steamer *Central America* was bound from Havana, Cuba, to New York City with miners transporting about three tons of gold bars and coins when it was struck by a hurricane and began leaking. As soon as the last lifeboats left with women and children, a giant wave pushed the steamer to the bottom of the ocean, about 160 miles off the South Carolina coast. Only 153 of the 575 passengers and crew were saved. The wreck was finally located in 1987; after three years of litigation, a federal judge awarded the gold to a salvage group.

7–8 September 1860. The steamer *Lady Elgin* collided with the schooner *Augusta* on Lake Michigan; 287 of the 400 passengers and crew drowned.

25 March 1865. The *General Lyon*, a propeller-driven steamship, caught fire and sank off Cape Hatteras, North Carolina, killing some 400 passengers and crew.

27 April 1865. The coal-burning Mississippi steamer *Sultana*, licensed to carry 376 persons, left New Orleans on 21 April en route for Cairo, Illinois. On 23 April, while the ship docked at Vicksburg, Mississippi, for boiler repairs, the roughly 100 passengers and eighty crewmen were joined by 2,134 Union soldiers paroled from Confederate prisons. (The ship's owners stood to earn $5 for each enlisted man and $10 for each officer transported north.) At 2 A.M. on 27 April, less than an hour after sailing from Memphis, the ship's boilers burst, hurling hundreds into the Mississippi. The steam's twin smokestacks collapsed, crushing men underneath. An upper deck fell, spilling passengers into the burning boiler. The fire spread, causing hundreds of soldiers to jump overboard into dangerously crowded waters. Fire ruined the lifeboats or made them impossible to reach. The dead officially numbered 1,547; some estimates put the toll higher. Although this was one of the worst ship disasters of all time, newspaper coverage was minimal because of coverage of the funeral of President Abraham Lincoln, assassinated on 15 April.

3 October 1866. En route to New Orleans from New York City, the steamer *Evening Star* foundered at sea; 250 were lost.

26 November 1898. A rainstorm that swept the New England coast and Long Island, New York, destroyed or damaged 213 vessels. The *Portland*, a side-wheeler, had sailed from Boston before the storm and disappeared the next day, far south of its course. It is believed that the *Portland* collided with another ship near Cape Cod, Massachusetts, and sank.

30 June 1900. A steamship and pier at Hoboken, New Jersey, caught fire, killing 326 persons and causing over $4 million in property damage.

Sinking of the *General Slocum*, off North Brother Island in the East River of New York City. The steamship caught fire just 300 yards from a pier, but Captain William van Schaick refused to turn back, instead forging ahead and fanning the flames. His grave error was compounded by several crew mistakes and faulty safety equipment, including fire hoses that were full of holes and lifeboats tied down with wires. As a result of all the blunders, 1,021 people—approximately half of them children—burned to death, drowned, or were crushed in the ship's giant paddlewheels. © Harper's Weekly

15 June 1904. On the paddle wheel excursion steamer *General Slocum* a paint locker (or a stove in the galley; accounts differ) caught fire just 300 yards from a New York City pier. Yet Captain William van Schaick kept steaming up the East River into a strong northeast wind that fanned the flames and crashed the boat into North Brother Island. Of the 1,500 passengers, mostly parents, teachers, and children, 1,021 burned to death, drowned, or were caught in the churning paddle wheels. The inexperienced crew opened hatchways that allowed the fire to spread to the upper decks. Even worse, lifeboats were tied down with wire, fire hoses were full of holes, and the life preservers had been filled with sawdust and metal rods to bring them up to mandatory weight. Many of those who perished were drowned or caught in the paddle wheels in an attempt to leave the burning ship; more than half the dead were children. This was the worst harbor disaster in U.S. history. Van Schaick was convicted of manslaughter and sentenced to ten years in prison, but President Theodore Roosevelt pardoned him after only two years, citing his age (sixty-three).

11 February 1907. The schooner *Harry Knowlton* crashed into the side-wheel Joy Line steamer *Larchmont*, en route from Providence, Rhode Island, to New York, punching a hole in its port side. The *Larchmont* sank in fifteen minutes. A lifeboat rescued only nine survivors, including the captain. The other 332 passengers and crew drowned in the freezing waters, were fatally scalded by steam from a ruptured steam line, or froze to death on a life raft.

24 July 1915. An excursion steamer, the *Eastland*, capsized while in port in Chicago, killing over 800.

24–25 October 1918. The Canadian-Pacific steamship *Princess Sophia* struck a reef west of Juneau, Alaska, to no apparent ill effect—rescuers responding to distress calls decided evacuation was unnecessary—but a subsequent storm dashed the ship against the reef and killed all 398 aboard, a tragedy witnessed by the powerless men in the rescue boats.

8 September 1934. A fire that broke out in the writing room of the cruise ship *Morro Castle* off the New Jersey coast left 137 (some accounts say 134) dead of the 562 people aboard. The captain had died suddenly the previous evening, and the ship—returning from Havana to New York—was commanded by the chief officer, William Warms. He wasn't informed of the fire until after he steered the ship into a twenty-knot wind, which created a raging inferno. No passenger drills had been held on the ship, and some of the hydrants had been capped to avoid leakage. Of the first ninety-eight people to evacuate in lifeboats, ninety-two were crew. Warms and the chief engineer were found guilty of negligence, and the Cuba Mail Steamship Company received the maximum ($10,000) penalty.

16 April 1947. Fire broke out on the freighter *Grandcamp* at Texas City, Texas, on the Gulf of Mexico. Loaded with highly flammable ammonium nitrate, the freighter blew up and set fifty tankers in the harbor ablaze. The death toll was estimated as at least 500, perhaps as high as 800.

25 July 1956. On a foggy morning off the coast of Massachusetts, the captain of the *Stockholm*, owned by the Swedish–American Line, misinterpreted radar signals and plowed into the Italian Line flagship *Andrea Doria*. Forty-three passengers and crew on the *Doria* died, mostly from the collision (survivors were rescued by nearby ships); three Stockholm crewmembers disappeared and others died later of injuries.

10 April 1963. About 220 miles off Cape Cod, Massachusetts, the U.S.S. *Thresher*, a nuclear-powered submarine, mysteriously sank during a routine dive with 129 aboard (see Thresher Disaster).

29 July 1967. The U.S. aircraft carrier *Forrestal* broke into flames off the coast of North Vietnam following a flight deck explosion; 134 died and 100 others were injured. Sixty planes and helicopters were destroyed or badly damaged. Total damage was estimated at $135 million.

Railroads and Bridges

8 November 1833. The earliest recorded train wreck involving passenger deaths occurred when a Camden and Amboy train derailed and crashed near Hightstown, New Jersey. Two people were killed and twenty-four injured. Former president John Quincy Adams was on the train but escaped unhurt.

29 December 1876. A train bridge spanning a gorge in Ashtabula, Ohio, collapsed in a blizzard. Overturned heating stoves set fire to the passenger cars of the Pacific Express after the train fell into the freezing creek. Ninety-two of the 150 passengers were killed.

10 August 1887. A seventeen-car excursion train packed with about 900 passengers was unable to stop in time to avoid crossing a burning wooden bridge in Chatsworth, Illinois. The dead numbered 82; about 270 were seriously injured.

2 March 1910. An avalanche in Wellington, Washington, threw two trains that had been stranded for a week in a blizzard into a 300-foot canyon; 118 perished.

1 November 1918. A crowded Brighton Beach commuter train operated by an inexperienced motorman crashed into the barrier at the Malbone Street tunnel in Brooklyn, New York; ninety-two died.

6 February 1951. A Pennsylvania Railroad commuter train fell through a temporary overpass at Woodbridge, New Jersey, that had opened only three hours before, killing eighty-five. Injured passengers numbered 330 (or 500, according to other reports). The cause of the wreck was attributed to the motorman, who confessed to speeding across the trestle at 50 mph. The trestle was replaced with a 2,000-ton bridge and automatic speed-control devices were installed on the trains.

15 December 1967. The Silver Bridge over the Ohio River connecting Gallipolis, Ohio, and Point Pleasant, West Virginia, collapsed during the evening rush hour, plunging seventy-five cars and trucks into the river; forty-six people were killed. The Federal Highway Administration found "corrosion fatigue" to be a contributing factor. As a result, new bridge inspection standards were developed, and U.S. bridges were systematically inspected for the first time, resulting in drastic reductions in posted speed and load limits.

Space Exploration

27 January 1967. The pressure-sealed *Apollo 1* spacecraft caught fire doing a routine test at Cape Canaveral, Florida, killing astronauts Virgil I. Grissom, Edward H. White, and Roger B. Chaffee. The tragedy exposed the need for higher design, workmanship, and installation standards at NASA.

28 January 1985. The space shuttle *Challenger* exploded seventy-four seconds after takeoff from Cape Canaveral; all seven crewmembers were killed. It was the worst accident in the history of the U.S. space program. The Rogers Commission study identified two primary causes: faulty design of the rubber O-rings joining sections of the solid-rocket boosters and the unusually cold temperature on the day of the launch (see CHALLENGER DISASTER).

Terrorism

26 February 1993. A bomb in the underground garage of the World Trade Center in New York City killed six people and injured more than 1,000 (see WORLD TRADE CENTER BOMBING, 1993). The explosion tore through steel reinforced floors on three levels and left a crater with a 150-foot diameter. In 1994, four followers of Sheik Omar Abdel Rahman of Egypt were convicted of roles in the bombing. Reported mastermind Ramzi Ahmed Yousef was captured in 1995 and convicted in 1997.

19 April 1995. A bomb in the Alfred P. Murrah Federal Building in Oklahoma City, Oklahoma, killed 169, including children in a day-care center, and injured 500. Timothy McVeigh was convicted of murder and conspiracy in 1997 and sentenced to death. The following year, Terry Nichols received a life sentence for conspiracy and involuntary manslaughter. (See OKLAHOMA CITY BOMBING.)

11 September 2001. Two hijacked planes, American Airlines Flight 11 and United Airlines Flight 175, crashed into the North and South towers of the World Trade Center in New York City at 8:46 A.M. and 9:03 A.M. EST, killing an estimated 2,823 people—including those who perished in the towers, 157 passengers and crew in the planes, and New York City firefighters and other rescue personnel. At 9:41 A.M., a third hijacked plane, American Airlines Flight 77, crashed into the Pentagon in Washington, D.C., killing 189. A scant twenty minutes later, a fourth plane, United Airlines Flight 93, crashed in a field in Somerset County, Pennsylvania, killing all forty-five on board. Both trade center towers collapsed as well as a third trade center building. This was the worst disaster in American history, with a death toll in excess of 3,000. The mastermind of the attacks, carried out by 19 hijackers, is believed to be Khalid Shaikh Mohammed, a lieutenant of Osama bin Laden, head of the Islamic terrorist organization Al Qaeda. (See 9/11 ATTACK.)

Weather: Avalanches, Droughts, Floods, Storms, and Tornadoes

17–21 November 1798. New England houses were buried by massive snowdrifts; hundreds of people died.

19 February 1804. Tornadoes stretching from Illinois to the Gulf of Mexico killed 800.

California Floods. In 1998, the warm weather pattern known as "El Niño" caused torrential rainstorms throughout California; this triggered flooding in many parts of the state and led President Clinton to declare thirty-one California counties disaster areas on 9 February. The Sacramento River region was among the hardest-hit areas, as this aerial photo of Tehuma, Calif., clearly shows. © AP/Wide World Photos

10 September 1811. A tornado flattened much of Charleston, South Carolina. The death toll was not recorded, but estimates run as high as 500 or more.

7 May 1840. Tornadoes whipped through Natchez, Mississippi, capsizing a steamboat, the Natchez ferry, and sixty other flatboats on the Mississippi River. The death toll was 317.

September 1841. A hurricane wiped out Saint Jo, Florida (near today's Apalachicola), killing 4,000.

16 June 1842. Another deadly tornado hit Natchez, Mississippi, killing about 500.

10 August 1856. Île Dernier (Last Island), a popular resort off the southern coast of Louisiana, became a desolate beach after a hurricane that killed more than 250 of the island's 300 inhabitants.

27 August 1881. A hurricane flooded lowlands, knocked down buildings, and killed about 700 people from Florida to the Carolinas.

19 February 1884. A cyclone moving up from the Gulf of Mexico devastated Georgia and the Carolinas, killing about 800 people.

11–13 March 1888. A blizzard immobilized New York City, with snowdrifts up to eighteen feet. About 15,000 people were stranded on elevated trains stopped between stations. The storm lashed the East Coast from Washington, D.C., to Boston. As many as 800 people died, 200 in New York City.

28 August 1893. A hurricane in Georgia and South Carolina wiped out coastal towns from Savannah to Charleston and killed about 1,000 people.

1 October 1893. A hurricane struck the coasts of Louisiana, Mississippi, and Alabama, killing an estimated 2,000 people.

27 May 1896. St. Louis and East St. Louis were struck by a tornado that killed 306, injured 2,500, left 5,000 homeless, and caused damage estimated at $13 million.

26–27 November 1898. A blizzard brought heavy snow and gale-force winds to the East Coast from New York to Maine, wrecking more than 100 ships and killing 455 people.

8 September 1900. Galveston, Texas, hurricane.

31 May 1903. The Kansas, Missouri, and Des Moines rivers overflowed, drowning 200, leaving 8,000 homeless, and causing over $4 million in property damage.

26 May 1917. Tornadoes that swept through Illinois, Indiana, Kansas, Kentucky, Missouri, Tennessee, Alabama, and Arkansas killed 249 and injured more than 1,200.

12–14 September 1919. A hurricane in Florida, Texas, and Louisiana caused 488 to drown at sea; 284 more were killed on land. The devastation included $22 million in property damage.

18 March 1925. Thirty-five towns in Missouri, Illinois, and Alabama were destroyed by a five-hour onslaught of tornadoes, the deadliest tornado attack in U.S. history. As many as 792 died; the injured numbered more than 2,000 (one estimate was as high as 13,000). Property damage estimates ranged as high as $500 million, 15,000 were left homeless.

18 September 1926. Florida's east coast, between Miami and Palm Beach, was hit by a hurricane that killed at least 373, made 40,000 homeless, and caused $165 million damage; the injured numbered as many as 6,000.

Late April 1927. Flooding of the Mississippi River from Cairo, Illinois, southward after a severe rainstorm inundated 26,000 square miles, leaving 313 dead and $300 million in damages. Afterward, a new system of river management was instituted, included large reservoirs and spillway channels.

16–17 September 1928. The Lake Okeechobee area of Florida, near West Palm Beach, was struck by a hurricane on its way from Puerto Rico. Despite timely warnings of the storm's path, 2,500 died. Many were farm workers living in shantytowns. An estimated 350,000 were left homeless. The federal government later sponsored a $5 million flood control program for the area and built an eighty-five-mile-long rock levee to replace the mud dikes that had collapsed.

29 September 1927. In a mere five minutes, a tornado that struck Saint Louis, Missouri, killed eighty-five and injured 1,300, leaving $40 million of property damage in a six-square-mile area.

1932–1937. Drought and poor farming practices in the Great Plains produced huge dust storms; known as the Dust Bowl. The phenomenon forced 500,000 to abandon their homes and farms.

2 September 1935. Florida was struck by a hurricane that killed at least 376 and caused property damage estimated at $6 million, including the railroad from Key West to Florida City.

5–6 April 1936. Tornadoes in five southern states killed 421.

January 1937. Record flooding in Ohio and the mid–Mississippi River valleys killed 137 and caused $418 million in property damage.

21 September 1938. The combined forces of a hurricane, ocean storm, and flooding struck Long Island, New York, and New England, killing 680 and causing an estimated $500 million in damages; nearly 2,000 were injured.

21–22 March 1952. Mississippi, Missouri, Alabama, Arkansas, Kentucky, and Tennessee were hit by tornadoes that killed 239 and injured 1,202.

8 June 1953. Michigan and Ohio were hit by a series of tornadoes that killed 139 and injured nearly 1,000.

12–18 October 1954. Hurricane Hazel began in Haiti, hit North Carolina and moved up the East Coast, hitting New York and Canada; ninety-nine were killed in the United States and over $100 million in damages was reported.

17–19 August 1955. Hurricane Diane struck six northeastern states, causing heavy floods in southern New England; 191 died, nearly 7,000 were injured. Property damage was $457 million.

26–28 June 1957. Hurricane Audrey and a tidal wave hit Texas and Louisiana, wiping out the town of Cameron, Louisiana, leaving 531 dead or missing, and causing $150 million property damage.

11 April 1965. Thirty-seven tornadoes in six Midwestern states left 242 dead and $250 million in damages.

9–10 February 1969. New England, New York, New Jersey, and Pennsylvania were hit by a two-day snowstorm that left more than fifteen inches of snow; 166 died in the storm and loss of business was estimated at $25 million.

17–20 August 1969. Hurricane Camille struck the southern United States, mainly in Louisiana, Mississippi, and Virginia, killing at least 258, leaving nearly 100,000 homeless, and causing $1.5 billion in damages.

12 February 1971. Tornadoes hit Mississippi and Louisiana, killing 115, injuring 500, and causing $7.5 million in damages.

9–10 June 1972. Heavy rains in the Black Hills of South Dakota caused Rapid Creek to flood, killing 235 and knocking out railroads, bridges, roads, and communications. Damages totaled $100 million.

15–25 June 1972. Hurricane Agnes, which began in Cuba, hit Florida and then the rest of the Atlantic coast up to New York with heavy rains. The death toll for Cuba and the United States was 134, with $60 billion in damages to homes and businesses.

3 April 1974. Nearly 100 tornadoes struck eleven southern and Midwestern states and Canada during an eight-hour period, killing more than 324 and causing property damage estimated as high as $1 billion.

31 July 1976. A violent flashflood in Big Thompson River, Colorado, sent fifty tons of water rushing down the canyon at 200 times the normal flow, killing 145 people, and destroying 600 buildings.

29 August–7 September 1979. Hurricane David left at least 1,000 dead in the southeastern United States and Caribbean.

23–25 August 1992. Hurricane Andrew hit southern Florida and Louisiana, and generated rainstorms in the Middle Atlantic states and as far north as Maine. The storm killed 65 people and caused an estimated $20–$30 billion in damages. As many as 250,000 people lost their homes.

12–14 March 1993. A powerful snowstorm hit the East Coast. More than 270 deaths were attributed to the storm; total damage cost exceeded $6 billion.

7–8 January 1996. The "Blizzard of '96" brought record snows to the Northeast, causing more than 100 deaths.

18 April 1997. The Red River broke through its dike and flooded Grand Forks, North Dakota, and its sister city, East Grand Forks, Minnesota. More than 58,000—nearly the entire population—evacuated. No deaths were reported, but damages exceeded $1 billion. More than 11,000 homes and businesses were destroyed.

3 May 1999. In eleven Oklahoma counties more than forty tornadoes—one of which reached 318 mph, a record—raged for five hours, leaving 44 dead and at least 500 injured. More than 3,000 houses and 47 businesses were destroyed. In neighboring Kansas, three died and more than 1,000 buildings were destroyed.

BIBLIOGRAPHY

Alexander, David. *Confronting Catastrophe: New Perspectives on Natural Disasters.* New York: Oxford University Press, 2000.

Barry, John M. *Rising Tide: The Great Mississippi Flood of 1927 and How It Changed America.* New York: Simon and Schuster, 1997.

Flexner, Stuart, and Doris Flexner. *The Pessimist's Guide to History.* New York: Quill, 2000.

Hewitt, Kenneth, ed. *Interpretations of Calamity from the Viewpoint of Human Ecology.* Boston: Allen and Unwin, 1983.

Karplus, Walter J. *The Heavens Are Falling: The Scientific Prediction of Catastrophes in Our Time*. New York: Plenum, 1992.

Platt, Rutherford H. *Disasters and Democracy: The Politics of Extreme Natural Events*. Washington, D.C.: Island Press, 1999.

Ross, Andrew. *Strange Weather: Culture, Science, and Technology in an Age of Limits*. London and New York: Verso, 1991.

Schlager, Neil, ed. *When Technology Fails: Significant Technological Disasters, Accidents, and Failures of the Twentieth Century*. Detroit: Gale, 1994.

Smith, Roger. *Catastrophes and Disasters*. Edinburgh and New York: Chambers, 1992.

Steinberg, Ted. *Acts of God: The Unnatural History of Natural Disaster in America*. New York: Oxford University Press, 2000.

Wade, Nicholas. *The Science Times Book of Natural Disasters*. New York: Lyons, 2000.

Cathy Curtis

See also **Accidents; Blizzards; Centralia Mine Disaster; Earthquakes; Epidemics and Public Health; Floods and Flood Control; Hurricanes; *Princeton*, Explosion on the; Three Mile Island; *Titanic*, Sinking of the; Tornadoes; Volcanoes; Wildfires.**

DISCIPLES OF CHRIST. The Christian Church (Disciples of Christ) and the Churches of Christ both trace their origins to the Appalachian frontier revivals of 1795 through 1810. Early leaders of the Disciples stressed the need for the reunion of divided Christendom, the restoration of the primitive Church described in the New Testament, and the importance of human freedom in the search for truth, unencumbered by denominational creeds or traditions. One early theorist was Barton Stone, a Presbyterian minister, who was the host of Kentucky's Cane Ridge revival of 1801. Stone separated from his Church in 1804 and created an association of churches in Kentucky and Tennessee. He was soon joined by Alexander Campbell, the son of Thomas Campbell, the Presbyterian minister who had authored the "Dedication and Address" of the Christian Association of Washington in 1809. A key text for the Disciples of Christ, the "Dedication and Address" announced, "Where the scriptures speak, we speak; where the scriptures are silent, we are silent."

Alexander Campbell. An engraving of the early leader of what became known as the Disciples of Christ, the author of a key text, and the founder and first president of Bethany College Library of Congress

Under Alexander Campbell, the Restoration Movement in Ohio and Pennsylvania grew rapidly. Although initially operating under the auspices of the Mahonic Baptist Association, the Campbellite churches broke with the Baptists in 1827 and merged with the Stoneite churches in 1832. Both groups shared an aversion to creeds and a desire to convert all people to evangelical Christianity. The new entity laid great stress on education, chartering such institutions as Bethany College in Virginia (now West Virginia) and Franklin College in Tennessee. It also organized church-wide associations such as the American Church Publication Society (1846) and the American Christian Missionary Society (1849), although southern congregations denounced the latter for infringing on their prerogative to evangelize.

Dividing the Movement

In 1861, most Disciples, who resided in the border states and feared the consequences of war, believed that the Bible permitted slavery and refused to participate in the Civil War. Alexander Campbell was critical of slavery, but strongly opposed abolitionism, favoring gradual emancipation and resettlement. In 1863, however, the American Christian Missionary Society passed a resolution condemning Southern secession, an action denounced by southern leaders like Tolbert Fanning. Campbell's death in 1866 removed one potential source of unity. In the next thirty years, other divisions surfaced over full-time paid preachers, the practice of open communion, and the use of instrumental music in church services (all of which were favored by many congregations in the north), which steadily pushed members of the future Churches of Christ away from the Disciples of Christ. Although formal separation was not acknowledged until 1906, actual separation preceded this event by at least ten years.

The Disciples took an activist stance during the nineteenth century, establishing the Christian Women's Board of Missions (1874), which worked in Central and South America and Liberia, erecting a number of new colleges and endowing chairs in biblical studies at several state universities. They also organized the National Benevolent Association (1887) and the Board of Ministerial Relief (1895). Between 1870 and 1900, the movement grew from 330,000 to 1,125,000.

The Modernist Controversy

During the early twentieth century, the Disciples were forced to grapple with modernist theology, which had gained a following in the Campbell Institute at the Disciples Divinity House at the University of Chicago. J. W. McGarvey, President of the College of the Bible in Lexington, Kentucky, launched a series of bitter attacks on modernism, which culminated in a dispute with younger faculty at his own institution in 1917. Equally divisive was the clash over the Federated Church Movement between 1905 and 1914, which aroused hostility because it represented a denial of the Disciples' earlier stance against denominationalism and because of the increasing identification of the Federal Council of Churches with modernism and social justice. A flashpoint on this issue was the Disciples' Monterrey mission in Mexico; many members objected to a 1918 interdenominational agreement that called upon them to surrender this activity to the Methodists. Finally, the questions of open membership and the admission of the unimmersed to full membership drove conservatives to launch a series of efforts in 1918 to defend "orthodoxy," criticizing trends in the newly established United Christian Missionary Society and attempting to pass resolutions that liberals claimed were "creedal."

After 1926, conservative congregations largely abandoned efforts to reform the Church's organizational structure, forming an independent organization and calling themselves Christian Churches or Churches of Christ. Efforts during the 1930s and 1940s to restore unity to the movement by stressing the common theological roots of all the groups came to nothing. In the 1960s, the Disciples of Christ only accentuated division from the independents with its promotion of "Brotherhood Restructure," advocating a repudiation of historic congregationalism in favor of a more structured national church organization with a delegate convention rather than a mass meeting, a move that cost them roughly one-third of their member congregations.

The Disciples in the Early 2000s

The Disciples of Christ have been very active in the ecumenical movement, but participation in the Federal Council of Churches and later in the National and World Council of Churches has always been rejected by the independent Christian Churches and the Churches of Christ. Some Disciples have worked with the National Association of Evangelicals, although uneasy with its creedal basis, and with the Consultation on Church Union. There have also been discussions with the United Church of Christ that have resulted in an "ecumenical partnership." Today, the Christian Church (Disciples of Christ) has a very denominational style. It has welcomed women into the ministry and is sympathetic to biblical criticism. Most congregations practice open membership and favor a mission role that assists national churches to grow rather than aggressive evangelism. It attaches considerable importance to social ministry, but takes a relaxed view on moral questions. All the agencies historically established by the Disciples of Christ are controlled by the Christian Church (Disciples of Christ), which has experienced a considerable decline in membership since 1945.

On their part, the Churches of Christ disdain any sort of extracongregational activity or involvement in social issues. They are opposed to instrumental music in church services and to missionary organizations. They are very conservative, with regard to both the Bible and moral issues, oppose women in the ministry, and are very critical of ecumenism. The growth rate in the Churches of Christ has been declining. In 1999, the Christian Church (Disciples of Christ) had 831,125 members and the Churches of Christ had 1,500,000 members.

BIBLIOGRAPHY

Dunnavant, Anthony L., ed. *Cane Ridge in Context: Perspectives on Barton W. Stone and the Revival.* Nashville, Tenn.: Disciples of Christ Historical Society, 1992.

Dunnavant, Anthony L., Richard T. Hughes, and Paul M. Blowers. *Founding Vocation and Future Vision: The Self-Understanding of the Disciples of Christ and the Churches of Christ.* St. Louis, Mo: Chalice Press, 1999.

Hughes, Richard T. *Restoring the Ancient Faith: The Story of Churches of Christ in America.* Grand Rapids, Mich.: Eerdmans, 1996.

McAllister, Lester G., and William E. Tucker. *Journey in Faith: A History of the Christian Church (Disciples of Christ).* St. Louis, Mo: Bethany Press, 1975.

Webb, Henry E. *In Search of Christian Unity: A History of the Restoration Movement.* Cincinnati, Ohio: Standard Publishing, 1990.

Jeremy Bonner

See also **Christianity; Denominationalism; Protestantism; Religion and Religious Affiliation.**

DISCO refers to both the dance music and the nightclubs that became popular after the 1977 release of the movie *Saturday Night Fever*. The Bee Gees, Village People, Donna Summer, and Gloria Gaynor were among the top music acts whose recordings were danced to in discos (or discothèques). The most important American disco was Studio 54 in New York, which attracted a glamorous clientele that included movie stars, artists, and "Eurotrash" and spawned a generation whose drug of choice was cocaine. Disco also incorporated such fashions as platform shoes and white leisure suits for men.

BIBLIOGRAPHY

Haden-Guest, Anthony. *The Last Party: Studio 54, Disco, and the Culture of the Night.* New York: William Morrow, 1997.

Rebekah Presson Mosby

See also **Music, Popular; Nightclubs.**

DISCOUNT STORES. *See* Retailing Industry.

DISCOVERY, the name given to three historically significant vessels. Two British war vessels during the period of discovery of the northwest coast of America bore this name: a small vessel of 300 tons used as the companion ship to the *Resolution* in Capt. James Cook's third voyage (1776–1780), on which he explored the northwest coast to the Arctic Ocean; and a sloop-of-war of about 400 tons' burden, the chief ship of Capt. George Vancouver's explorations of North America (1792–1794). The third vessel was NASA's SPACE SHUTTLE *Discovery,* the successful maiden voyage of which, on 29 September 1988, restored confidence in a space program nearly decimated by the *CHALLENGER* DISASTER.

BIBLIOGRAPHY

Fisher, Robin. *Vancouver's Voyage: Charting the Northwest Coast, 1791–1795.* Vancouver, Wash.: Douglas and McIntyre, 1992.

Marquardt, Karl H. *The Anatomy of the Ship Captain Cook's Endeavour.* London: Conway Maritime Press, 1995; 2001.

Robert Moulton Gatke / A. R.

See also **Cook, James, Explorations of; Explorations and Expeditions: U.S.; Vancouver Explorations.**

DISCOVERY OF AMERICA. *See* Exploration of America, Early.

DISCRIMINATION

This entry includes 6 subentries:
Age
Disabled
Race
Religion
Sex
Sexual Orientation

AGE

Age discrimination is what occurs when an employer uses age as a determining (and negative) factor in a job-related decision. For example, age discrimination takes place when an employer denies an applicant a job based on age. Similarly, age discrimination occurs any time an employer denies training, promotions, or any other opportunities based on age.

Many factors result in age discrimination, including lack of knowledge, ageist attitudes, and myths and stereotypes about older workers. The most common stereotypes about older workers are that older workers are less productive than younger workers; that older workers are more expensive than younger workers; that older workers are less adaptable and more rigid than younger workers; and that older people want to retire early, that they do not want to work.

The United States enacted legislation, the Age Discrimination in Employment Act (ADEA), in 1967 to prohibit age discrimination in employment. Three years earlier, amendments to add age to Title VII of the CIVIL RIGHTS ACT OF 1964 (which prohibits employment discrimination based on race, gender, religion and national origin) had been rejected. Several reasons have been offered for excluding age from Title VII. First, Congress worried that it lacked the information necessary to enact age discrimination legislation. Second, many legislators feared that adding a prohibition against age discrimination would overload the civil right measure and lead to its defeat. Finally, in 1964 members of Congress simply did not understand or believe the magnitude of the age discrimination problem. As a result of the Civil Rights Act of 1964, however, Congress directed the secretary of labor to "make a full and complete study of the factors which might tend to result in discrimination in employment because of age and of the consequences of such discrimination on the economy and individuals affected."

The secretary of labor's report confirmed that age discrimination in employment was a pervasive and debilitating problem, particularly insofar as hiring practices, which can result in long-term unemployment, and advised Congress that legislation was needed to address the problem.

The federal Age Discrimination in Employment Act (ADEA) of 1967 prohibits age discrimination in all aspects of employment including, hiring, termination, benefits, training, and promotions. As originally enacted, the ADEA protected employees aged forty to sixty-five. In 1978, Congress raised the upper age limit to 70. In 1986, Congress eliminated the upper age limit on the ADEA's protections. As a result, with very few and narrow exceptions, there is no mandatory retirement in the United States. Groups who are still subject to mandatory retirement include federal, state, and local firefighters and law enforcement personnel, air traffic controllers, and bona fide executives and high policy makers.

The ADEA applies to employers with twenty or more employees including employers in federal, state, and local governments. The ADEA also commands that labor organizations with twenty or more members may not exclude or expel members or refuse to refer members for hire based on age. Employment agencies may not fail or refuse to refer an applicant based on age. In addition, employment agencies may be covered as "employers" under the ADEA if they have the requisite twenty employees.

The United States also has fifty state laws that address age discrimination in employment. While the national statute protects individuals age forty and older, many of the state laws prohibit discrimination at any age. The majority of these laws cover employers with fewer than twenty employees. In addition, many provide broader relief than the ADEA, including allowing a victim to recover compensatory and punitive damages. Legal challenges to age discrimination in employment must commence with a timely charge filed with the Equal Employment Opportunity Commission (EEOC). However, given the fact that the EEOC files suit in less than one half of one percent of the charges it receives, enforcement of the ADEA is left largely in the hands of individuals. For example, in 2001, the EEOC received 17,405 charges but only filed suit or intervened in thirty-four age discrimination lawsuits. Because of the high cost of litigating an age discrimination lawsuit—in terms of time, money, and emotion—and the increasingly higher evidentiary burdens imposed by the courts on age bias victims, much age discrimination goes unchallenged.

While the ADEA may have raised societal awareness regarding age discrimination and eliminated the most blatant forms of it, such discrimination continues to plague the U.S. workforce. One explanation is that historically, Congress, the courts, and society have viewed age discrimination as less malevolent than race or sex discrimination and have treated freedom from age discrimination as something less than a civil right. Stereotypes about age and ability persist, in part, because of society's failure to fully attack and condemn ageist policies and practices.

BIBLIOGRAPHY

Butler, Robert N. *Why Survive?: Being Old in America.* New York: Harper and Row, 1975.

Eglit, Howard C. *Age Discrimination.* 3 vols. Colorado Springs, Colo.: Shepard's/McGraw Hill, 1994.

Gregory, Raymond F. *Age Discrimination in the American Workplace: Old at a Young Age.* New Brunswick, N.J.: Rutgers University Press, 2001.

Munk, Nina. "Finished at Forty." *Fortune* 139, no. 2 (1 February 1999): 50–66.

Palmore, Erdman B. *Ageism: Negative and Positive.* New York: Springer, 1990.

Platt, L. Steven, and Cathy Ventrell-Monsees. *Age Discrimination Litigation.* Costa Mesa, Calif.: James Publishing, 2000.

Simon, Ruth. "Too Damn Old." *Money* (July 1996): 118–120.

Worsnop, Richard I. "Age Discrimination: Does Federal Law Protect Older Workers' Job Rights?" *CQ Researcher* 7, no. 29 (1 August 1997): 675–695.

Laurie McCann

See also **Old Age.**

Disabled

The U.S. Congress noted when enacting the 1990 Americans with Disabilities Act (ADA) that the country's 43 million disabled citizens have been "subjected to a history of purposeful unequal treatment" and politically disempowered because of "stereotypic assumptions not truly indicative" of their individual abilities "to participate in, and contribute to, society." Highly illustrative of this situation was Congress's citation of survey data which indicated that two-thirds of working age individuals with disabilities were unemployed, while two-thirds of nonworking disabled individuals wanted to work. Largely in response to this figure (census data was relatively more sanguine, reporting that "only" about half of working age disabled individuals were then unemployed), Congress promulgated Title I of the ADA in an effort to increase labor market participation among workers with disabilities.

Title I covers entities employing more than fifteen workers, prohibits their discriminating against "qualified individuals with disabilities" in all aspects of the employment relationship, and requires them to provide those individuals with "reasonable accommodations." These include making existing facilities physically accessible, job restructuring or modification, and reassignments. Accommodations which cause "undue hardship" to their putative providers are exempted from compliance, as is the hiring or retention of disabled individuals who pose a "direct threat" to public health or safety. To assert a Title I claim, disabled workers must first demonstrate that they are "qualified" individuals with disabilities. This requires workers not only to satisfy the ADA's definition of who is disabled, but also to establish the ability to "perform the essential functions" of a given job either with or without the assistance of a reasonable accommodation.

Although the determination of which accommodations are reasonable, and what job functions are essential, in any given dispute may seem at first blush the proper province for a jury, a vast majority of courts have instead deferred to employers' assertions of feasibility and essentiality, and have thus ruled as a matter of law that plaintiffs were unqualified for their positions. As a result, only some 5 percent of Title I plaintiffs prevailed in their federal trials during the period between 1992 and 1997.

As of 2002, the overall unemployment statistics of disabled workers remained essentially unchanged, while their employment rate relative to that of nondisabled workers had moderately decreased, leading some economists to assert that the ADA is actually harmful to the group it is intended to assist. Although issue can be taken with many of the assumptions underlying these analyses, including the metrics utilized, the picture painted remains dismal and should provoke concern and examination. Several factors have contributed to these negative post-ADA employment effects.

First is the unique civil rights chronicle of people with disabilities who, unlike other marginalized minority group members, were empowered by legislation prior to a general elevation of social consciousness about their circumstances and capabilities. Thus, popular opinions about people with disabilities, especially misperceptions regarding their capabilities, do not yet conform to the spirit of the ADA's legislative findings nor to the letter of assertions made by disability rights advocates.

Second, although a great deal of rhetoric has surrounded the costs of accommodations, the practical consequences of Title I have been the subject of surprisingly little research. The few empirical studies that have been conducted, however, indicate that many of the accommodation costs engendered by Title I are generally nonexistent or minimal. In fact, they suggest that certain economic benefits, such as increased retention rates and concurrently reduced worker replacement costs, can make many accommodations cost effective for the providing employers.

A third factor is that, until 2000, national policymakers overlooked the impact of environmental factors exogenous to the ADA, including the availability of health care and accessibility of public transportation, on increasing disabled workers' labor market participation. Only a decade after the ADA's enactment were a series of policy initiatives passed to allow people with disabilities receiving social security disability-related benefits to earn more income without losing their cash or health benefits.

BIBLIOGRAPHY

Americans with Disabilities Act (1990), 42 U.S.C. § 12,101 et seq.

Stein, M. A. "Empirical Implications of Title I." *Iowa Law Review* 85 (2000): 1671–1690.

———. "Employing People with Disabilities: Some Cautionary Thoughts for a Second Generation Civil Rights Statute." In *Employment, Disability, and the Americans with Disabilities Act: Issues in Law, Public Policy, and Research.* Edited by P. D. Blanck. Evanston, Ill.: Northwestern University Press, 51–67. (2000).

———. "Labor Markets, Rationality, and Workers with Disabilities." *Berkeley Journal of Employment and Labor Law* 21 (2000): 314–334.

Michael Stein

See also **Deaf in America; Disability Rights Movement.**

RACE

Racial discrimination, a long-standing issue in American society, has taken many forms and been "more than black and white" in terms of whom it has affected. At various times and to varying degrees, African Americans, Asian Americans, Latinos, Native Americans, and other Americans of color have experienced racial discrimination, as have ethnic groups that in the past were regarded by many as a separate "race," such as Jews. The type and degree of racial discrimination have also varied in different regions of the country, although historically some of the most egregious discrimination has taken place in the American South.

Causes and Effects

Immigration has affected racial discrimination in a number of ways. In each wave of immigration, the newest groups to America's shores have often taken or been shunted into the least desirable, lowest-paying jobs. Some immigrant groups went into certain industries for cultural or social reasons, such as Chinese launderers and Jewish garment workers. For the most part, though, these new immigrants were at the mercy not only of "native" Americans but also of earlier immigrant groups. In the workplace, immigrants were often pitted against one another by employers and labor unions alike. While employers exploited them for cheap labor and sought to prevent them from becoming a united working class, organized labor unions fanned the flames of prejudice to protect their hard-won gains by limiting entrance to the crafts they represented. The oppressed immigrant groups themselves rarely remained solely victims. As they became more established in American society, they sometimes discriminated against newer groups in order to distance themselves from their own sense of "otherness." Moreover, for white European immigrants, racial discrimination served as a way to become part of white America and therefore superior to more visible minorities, especially (though not exclusively) African Americans.

Discrimination in the workplace has had the most profound and lasting impact on the groups it has affected. At the most basic level, it has limited minority groups to low-paying, menial jobs that offered no potential for advancement and were at times even hazardous. In the past, minority groups were restricted from the skilled trades and occupations, which have been more apt to provide union protection and opportunities for advancement than unskilled jobs. At the professional level, minorities have had to struggle on two fronts: first for admission to the educational programs necessary to pursue a profession such as law or medicine, and then for hiring and advancement within the profession. Even those who have succeeded in obtaining satisfying work have likely suffered from subtler forms of job discrimination, whether in lower wages, lack of advancement, or poor work environment. Women in minority groups, furthermore, have had to struggle against both racial and sexual discrimination.

Combating Discrimination

Throughout American history, African Americans and other minority groups, with and without white allies, have combated racial discrimination using a variety of tactics. These have included public protests, such as street picketing and riots; organized publicity campaigns; educational efforts; and litigation. They have also included efforts at economic self-help through voluntary organizations such as the National Urban League. For example, in New York City during the Great Depression, the League sponsored the "Don't Buy Where You Can't Work Campaign," picketing and boycotting white-owned businesses that had primarily black customers but discriminated against blacks in employment. These protests spread to other cities, and in 1937 the Supreme Court upheld the protesters' right to peacefully picket.

Political efforts to end racial discrimination were first undertaken in a serious way in 1941. The African American labor leader A. Philip Randolph threatened to organize a march on Washington to protest racial discrimination, especially in the then-booming military and World War II defense industries. In response, President Franklin D. Roosevelt issued Executive Order 8802 in June 1941, creating the Fair Employment Practices Committee (FEPC). Although at first the FEPC's powers of enforcement were limited and therefore its accomplishments were few, it was the first step in the federal government's role in stamping out racial discrimination in the workplace. Following World War II, President Harry S. Truman issued two executive orders: one that desegregated the U.S. armed forces, and one that eliminated discrimination on the basis of race or religion in federal employment and established a Fair Employment Board as part of the Civil Service Commission. In 1955 President Dwight D. Eisenhower issued executive orders affirming antidiscrimination as a federal government policy and creating the President's Committee on Government Employment Policy to administer it. It was President John F. Kennedy, however, who used the creation of the President's Committee on Equal Employment Opportunity (which also required nondiscriminatory employment practices of government contractors) to send a message to the southern-dominated Congress as he prepared what would under President Lyndon B. Johnson become the Civil Rights Act of 1964. In 1965, a permanent Equal Employment Opportunity Commission was established, with much greater powers of enforcement than its predecessors.

By the time of President Richard M. Nixon's administration, with the passage of the Equal Employment Opportunity Act in 1972, affirmative action, as the policy came to be known, evolved in theory and policy from merely hiring on an equitable basis to actively seeking minorities in order to achieve racial balance in the workplace (and in higher education). Affirmative action subsequently courted new controversy, and in 1978 the Supreme Court rejected the active seeking of hiring quotas but permitted race to be a factor in employment decisions in the landmark case *Regents of the University of California v. Bakke.*

Race and Organized Labor

Racial discrimination became an issue for organized labor long before it did for the U.S. government. Organized labor was, for much of its history, more a part of the problem than a part of the solution. Beyond the attitudes of organized workers, racial discrimination was, beginning in the nineteenth century, the established policy of many of the craft unions affiliated with the American Federation of Labor (AFL), as well as the policy of the independent railroad unions. These policies effectively restricted many blacks to menial, unskilled labor. The AFL craft unions, which also supported the anti-Oriental movement and its official manifestation, the Chinese Exclusion Act of 1882, were motivated partly by simple racism and partly by their desire to restrict the labor supply and ensure that their services would remain in demand. Those craft unions that did admit black workers generally organized them in segregated locals. African Americans as well as nonwhite immigrants, therefore, were often used as strikebreakers by employers.

The labor organizations that seemed most committed to organizing on an inclusive, rather than exclusive, basis—the Knights of Labor and the Industrial Workers of the World—unfortunately also proved to have the least staying power on the American labor scene. Not until the rise of the industrial unions, and with them the Congress of Industrial Organization (CIO), in the mid-1930s did organized labor make a serious effort to eliminate racial discrimination as an official policy. The CIO unions were not perfect either; even without official segregation in union ranks, contracts often allowed for wage discrimination, and people of color were largely kept out of leadership positions. The unions that proved to be notable exceptions to this rule, such as the United Packinghouse Workers of America, were generally leftist in orientation, making them targets for the McCarthy-era onslaught against organized labor as a source of communist subversion. Even then, by the postwar years, many industrial unions were (at least on paper) emphasizing solidarity among workers across racial lines. Unions that did not move toward equality voluntarily were increasingly forced to do so by state and federal regulations. For example, the Italian Locals of the International Ladies Garment Workers Union, once evidence of the union's commitment to diversity, were by the 1960s an embarrassing source of discrimination when they refused to admit black and Puerto Rican workers. The changing demographics of the workforce eventually forced a reassessment of labor's stance on issues of race, in matters of organizing and leadership alike. In 1995 the AFL-CIO elected Linda Chavez-Thompson as its first Latina executive vice president. And the AFL-CIO's drive to organize the unorganized was increasingly conducted with a recognition and even a celebration of the diversity of the American workforce.

Yet from the beginning, organized labor had to deal with both the popular prejudices of the day and the needs of its predominantly white male constituency. For example, before the Civil War the northern working class opposed the expansion of slavery not so much out of humanitarian concern as concern over its effect on wage labor. African Americans and other minority groups saw little reason to support the craft unions that excluded them, and their role as strikebreakers created a vicious cycle. Even when unions were willing to actively organize black workers, they undercut their own effectiveness by trying to honor local (usually southern) prejudices. This is what ultimately led to the demise of the effort by the Textile Workers Union of America to organize southern workers during Operation Dixie in 1946. In the 1960s the drive to organize the J.P. Stevens textile mills (made famous by the 1979 movie *Norma Rae*) was complicated by the union's effort to recruit white workers without alienating black workers, who were joining out of proportion to their numbers in the industry. McCarthyism also forced many unions to moderate antiracist rhetoric for fear of being thought communist. Finally, employers would often use race as a wedge against organizing, or use worker prejudices (perceived or actual) as an excuse to delay integrating the workplace.

Minorities Organize

Despite labor's checkered history in matters of racial discrimination, minority workers struggled to carve out a place for themselves in organized labor almost from its beginnings. Starting in the mid-nineteenth century, before the Civil War, African Americans formed their own labor unions in a number of trades. The best known was the Brotherhood of Sleeping Car Porters. In the late twentieth century the United Farm Workers built upon a Latino self-help movement, the Community Service Organization, to end the exploitation of migrant farm workers in the American Southwest. Minorities have also formed organizations to work for equality within the structure of organized labor. Among the more radical efforts to eradicate racism in organized labor and ultimately build interracial solidarity was the League of Revolutionary Black Workers, which flourished briefly in Detroit in the late 1960s and early 1970s. Although the League did not last, it helped raise general consciousness among black workers and strengthened mainstream efforts towards greater inclusiveness. The most successful organization, the Coalition of Black Trade Unionists, was founded in 1972 and continues to work with both labor and civil rights organizations to achieve African American equality in organized labor, the workplace, and beyond.

Race Discrimination in History

The long history of oppression of nonwhites goes back to America's founding, beginning with the systematic destruction of Native Americans and the importation of Africans for slave labor. Although African American men practiced a variety of crafts and trades during the early decades of the republic, by the time of the Civil War, slavery had become deeply entrenched in the American South, and most were restricted to agricultural labor. Following the Civil War and Emancipation, the Reconstruction did not deliver on most of its promises to freed slaves. The sharecropping system and the black codes kept most southern blacks working in slavery-like conditions. The men were rarely able to get more than agricultural work and the women, domestic work. Also during the late nineteenth century, the American West was built in large part with the labor of immigrants from China, Japan, Mexico, and the Philippines, who were paid low wages for backbreaking work. These immigrants were largely reviled by the AFL unions, which viewed them as a threat to white workers.

In the opening decades of the twentieth century black migration took many African Americans to northern cities to seek better work and better lives. In the North, these migrants found discrimination and strenuous, low-paying jobs, for which they competed with a rising number of immigrants from various countries who also suffered discrimination and exploitation. Although during the early twentieth century a number of black business owners and professionals emerged, most African Americans remained part of the economic underclass, as did other peoples of color. Even so, for African Americans the industrial opportunities in the North were a marked improvement over conditions in the South, where industry lagged and the destruction of crops caused by the boll weevil sharply reduced the amount of agricultural work.

When the Great Depression hit, American minorities suffered disproportionately. Those who had previously been the "last hired" were now the "first fired," as whites often took over what had been "black" jobs. Drought and economic hardship, for example, pushed white farm workers off midwestern farms to compete with nonwhite migrant farm workers in the fields of California. After 1932 most black voters switched from the Republican to the Democratic Party because of Franklin D. Roosevelt, but the New Deal had a mixed record for minorities, who still suffered discrimination in obtaining federal jobs and unemployment benefits. World War II revived the economy to a degree the New Deal had not. However, the FEPC failed to eradicate racial discrimination in wartime industry. Its main problems were spotty enforcement and a failure to address the kinds of workplace discrimination that went beyond the hiring process, such as workplace segregation. At the same time, desegregation of the United States Armed Forces, the other reason Randolph threatened to march on Washington, was only accomplished after World War II.

Although the civil rights movement of the 1950s and 1960s is primarily remembered for gaining voting rights for African Americans and ending legal segregation in the South, its role in ending workplace discrimination with the passage of Title VII should not be underestimated. Although the mainstream civil rights movement ultimately failed to tackle the economic aspects of discrimination, the failure was not for lack of interest among its leaders. Prior to his assassination in 1968, Martin Luther King Jr. had announced the formation of a "Poor Peoples' Campaign" to address economic injustices against people of all races. In fact, on the night of his assassination, he was making a public appearance in support of striking garbage workers.

Into the Twenty-First Century

Toward the end of the twentieth century, the rising tide of conservatism and complaints about political correctness threatened the gains made in eradicating discrimination. Affirmation action came increasingly under attack, both in the courts and in public opinion, with both its efficacy and its fairness questioned. Many opponents of affirmative action raised the possibility that it perpetuates the very discriminatory attitudes it was designed to eradicate, arguing that when any nonwhite employee is hired, particularly at a higher level, suspicion is aroused that he or she obtained the position unfairly through racial preferences (even if the employee's job qualifications clearly indicate otherwise). Additionally, opponents of affirmative action have argued that the system, designed to correct for past inequities of race (and gender), does not address issues of class, since many of the program's beneficiaries belong to the middle class, with all its educational and economic advantages. Proponents of affirmative action counter that affirmative action, while not eradicating racial discrimination in the workplace, has made enough of a difference in the hiring and promotion of minorities that these small losses to non-favored groups are justified. At the same time, the fact that discrimination in the workplace has not yet been eliminated has been a key argument that affirmative action is still a necessary tool to promote a more just society in an increasingly diverse America.

BIBLIOGRAPHY

Burstein, Paul. *Discrimination, Jobs and Politics: The Struggle for Equal Employment Opportunity in the United States since the New Deal.* Chicago: University of Chicago Press, 1985.

Edley, Christopher, Jr. *Not All Black and White: Affirmative Action, Race, and American Values.* New York: Hill and Wang, 1996.

Edmondson, Munro S. "Industry and Race in the Southern United States." In *Industrialisation and Race Relations: A Symposium.* Edited by Guy Hunter. London: Oxford University Press, 1965.

Ferriss, Susan, and Ricardo Sandoval. *The Fight in the Fields: Cesar Chavez and the Farmworkers Movement.* Edited by Diana Hembree. New York: Harcourt, 1997.

Georgakas, Dan, and Marvin Surkin. *Detroit: I Do Mind Dying.* Cambridge, Mass.: South End Press, 1998. Updated edition on the Dodge Main Revolutionary Union Movement (DRUM).

Honey, Michael K. *Southern Labor and Black Civil Rights: Organizing Memphis Workers.* Urbana: University of Illinois Press, 1993.

Horowitz, Roger. *"Negro and White, Unite and Fight!": A Social History of Industrial Unionism in Meatpacking, 1930–90.* Urbana: University of Illinois Press, 1997.

Kushner, Sam. *Long Road to Delano.* New York: International Publishers, 1975.

Marable, Manning. *How Capitalism Underdeveloped Black America: Problems in Race, Political Economy, and Society.* Boston: South End Press, 1983.

Mills, Nicolaus, ed. *Debating Affirmative Action: Race, Gender, Ethnicity, and the Politics of Inclusion.* New York: Dell Publishing, 1994. Covers various contemporary views.

Minchin, Timothy J. *Hiring the Black Worker: The Racial Integration of the Southern Textile Industry, 1960–1980.* Chapel Hill: University of North Carolina Press, 1999.

Steinberg, Stephen. *Turning Back: The Retreat from Racial Justice in American Thought and Policy.* Boston: Beacon Press, 2001.

Susan Roth Breitzer

See also **Affirmative Action; Immigration; Labor; Trade Unions;** *and vol. 9:* **Pachucos in the Making.**

RELIGION

Religious discrimination involves the persecution or harassment of a person because of his or her religious beliefs or practices. Throughout history, many people have been victims of religious discrimination. A primary reason that the Puritans and other groups left Europe and came to America was to escape religious persecution.

Freedom of religion—the right to believe in and practice whatever faith a person chooses as well as the right to have no religious beliefs at all—became a defining tenet of the young United States. On 15 December 1791, ten amendments to the U.S. Constitution known as the Bill of Rights became law. The first of these specifically states that "Congress shall make no law respecting an establishment of religion, or prohibiting the free exercise thereof. . . ."

Several court rulings have interpreted this to mean that the government may not give special treatment or promote any religion. For example, it has been ruled unconstitutional for the government to give financial aid to religious schools and for public schools to teach religious texts, such as the Bible, or to recite prayers. However, the First Amendment was meant to protect religious groups from unfair treatment by the federal government.

It would take about 175 years for the United States to pass laws dealing with religious discrimination in the private sector, specifically labor.

The Civil Rights Act of 1964

The CIVIL RIGHTS ACT OF 1964 greatly expanded the rights of minorities in key areas, such as employment, education, voting, and the use of public facilities. It was intended to end discrimination in these areas based on race, color, religion, or national origin. Many consider it to be the most important U.S. law on civil rights since Reconstruction (1865–77). Like most major legislation, the Civil Rights Act of 1964 occurred as a result of great social pressure.

After World War II, minority groups, specifically African Americans, grew increasingly vocal in their demands for civil rights. Many white Americans from various walks of life also began to see the need for civil rights laws. The U.S. courts reflected these changes in attitude by protecting the civil rights of minorities in various circumstances, particularly by making it possible for African Americans to participate in some activities on an equal basis with whites.

The executive branch of government, by presidential order, followed suit in the 1940s by legally ending discrimination in the nation's military forces, in federal employment, and in government contract work. Other bills, introduced in Congress regarding employment policy, brought the issue of civil rights to the forefront of legislators' agendas. Along with this push for racial equality came demands for equal rights for all minorities, including religious minorities.

By the 1960s, the federal government, responding to intense pressure, sought to pass a comprehensive civil rights law. Although President John F. Kennedy was unable to secure passage of such a bill in Congress, a stronger version was eventually passed with the support of his successor, President Lyndon B. Johnson. After one of the longest debates in Senate history, Johnson signed the bill into law on 2 July 1964.

Despite strong support for the measure, there were also determined critics who immediately challenged the constitutionality of the law. Not only did the Supreme Court uphold the law (in the test case *Heart of Atlanta Motel v. U.S.*), but the law itself gave federal law enforcement agencies the power to prevent discrimination in employment, voting, and the use of public facilities.

Title VII

One section of the Civil Rights Act of 1964—Title VII—specifically targets discrimination based on race, sex, color, religion, and national origin in the area of employment. The Act covers nearly every aspect of employment—recruitment, hiring, wages, assignment, promotions, benefits, discipline, discharge, and layoffs. It applies to private employers of fifteen or more persons, as well as labor unions and employment agencies.

Title VII also created the U.S. EQUAL EMPLOYMENT OPPORTUNITY COMMISSION (EEOC), which was given the mission of enforcing the law against discrimination in the workplace. The five members of the commission, no more than three of whom may be from the same political party, serve five-year terms. They are appointed by the president and confirmed by the Senate.

The EEOC began operating on 2 July 1965, one year after Title VII became law. To those who had been fired or denied promotion because of their religious beliefs or endured other forms of religious-based discrimination in the workplace, the EEOC became a valuable ally in their fight for justice.

Claiming Religious Discrimination

Once a person or group files a charge of religious discrimination to the EEOC, the commission will determine the validity of the claim. If a case is proven, a monetary benefit is often awarded to the claimant.

Companies can often avoid a charge of religious discrimination by making reasonable accommodations for the religious needs of their employees and prospective employees. Such accommodations include giving time off for the Sabbath or holy days, except in an emergency, and allowing employees who don't come to work for religious reasons to take leave without pay, or to make up the time, or to charge the time against any other leave with pay, except sick pay. However, employers may not be required to give time off to employees who work in vital health and safety occupations or to any employee whose presence is critical to the company on any given day.

Employers also cannot schedule examinations or other important activities at times that conflict with an employee's religious needs. Nor can employers insist on a dress code that interferes with a person's religious dress.

An employee whose religious practices prohibit payment of dues to a labor organization will not be required to pay the dues. However, he or she will often be required to pay an equal amount to a charitable organization.

Training programs, designed to improve employee motivation or productivity through meditation, yoga, biofeedback, or other practices, may also conflict with the non-discriminatory provisions of Title VII of the 1964 Civil Rights Act. If so, employers must accommodate such employees.

Two Key Amendments to Title VII

In 1972, an amendment to Title VII of the Civil Rights Act of 1964 created a loophole for employers: They would not be charged with religious discrimination if they could prove that accommodating the religious practices and beliefs of their employees would cause "undue hardship." An example of undue hardship would be if accommodating an employee's religious practices would require more than customary administrative costs. This might happen if an employer incurs overtime costs to replace an employee who will not work on Saturday. Undue hardship also may be claimed if accommodating an employee's religious practices denies another employee a job or shift preference guaranteed by the seniority system.

What constitutes undue hardship varies on a case-by-case basis. The court weighs the facts to determine whether the employer offered a reasonable accommodation or that undue hardship existed. The plaintiff will attempt to show that the hardship was not severe or that the accommodation offered was not reasonable.

Another amendment, passed in 1991, allows claimants of the Civil Rights Act to request a jury trial and to sue for compensatory and punitive damages. Compensatory damages cover the actual losses incurred as a result of the discriminatory act. Punitive damages are sought strictly to punish wrongdoers for their discriminatory act. Forcing a business or company to pay punitive damages is meant to discourage them from discriminating again in the future.

A Look at EEOC Statistics

The statistics complied by the EEOC show an upward trend in the number of charges of religious discrimination. Records also show a corresponding increase in the monetary benefits awarded claimants.

In 1992, there were 1,388 claims filed charging religious-based discrimination. In 1996, there were 1,564 claims, and in 2001, the number had climbed to 2,127. In many cases, the EEOC found no "reasonable cause" for the claim. Despite that, in 1992 $1.4 million were awarded to claimants, $1.8 million in 1996, and $14.1 million in 2001. (These figures do not include monetary benefits obtained through litigation.)

The United States is one of the most religiously diverse countries in the world, and its citizens enjoy great religious liberty. Such freedom from religious discrimination, however, obviously requires vigilance to maintain.

BIBLIOGRAPHY

Bernbach, Jeffrey M. *Job Discrimination II: How to Fight—How to Win.* Rev. ed. Englewood Cliffs, N.J.: Voir Dire Press, 1998.

Perlmutter, Philip. *Legacy of Hate: A Short History of Ethnic, Religious, and Racial Prejudice in America.* Armonk, N.Y.: M.E. Sharpe, 1999.

Repa, Barbara Kate. *Your Rights in the Workplace.* 5th ed., edited by Amy Delpo. Berkeley, Calif.: Nolo, 2000.

The United States Commission on Civil Rights. *Religious Discrimination: A Neglected Issue.* Washington, D.C.: 1980.

U.S. Equal Employment Opportunity Commission. Home page at http://www.eeoc.gov.

Lynda DeWitt

See also **Anti-Catholicism; Anti-Semitism; First Amendment; Religion and Religious Affiliation.**

SEX

Sex discrimination refers to differential treatment based on sex. Gender, the meaning attached to being male or female, carries different connotations of value in different cultures. Traditionally in American culture a higher value has been given to whatever is defined as male. Anglo colonists brought with them the ancient English custom of coverture, by which a married woman's civil identity was "covered by" or absorbed into her husband's for virtually all purposes except crime. Therefore, all of the personal property she brought to the marriage became her husband's as well as any earnings or income thereafter. Unable to sign a legal contract, she had to be a widow in order to make a will. With voting rights initially tied to property ownership, blocking women's access to economic resources also meant denying their political rights.

The Gendering of Work and Wages and the Devaluation of Work Done in the Home

The advent of industrial capitalism in the nineteenth century brought new economic opportunities for men but closed options for women. As the gendered work that men and women performed within the household economy was transferred to mill and factory, jobs were gendered. Little value and low pay was attached to tasks usually performed by women. For minority women, sex discrimination in employment compounded racial and ethnic discrimination, relegating them to jobs at the very bottom of the economic scale. Occupational segregation and lower wages, as well as unrecognized, uncompensated labor for those doing housework, left most women economically dependent on men. As a result, the feminization of poverty long predated the twentieth century. Those women who remained in the home performed work central to the history of U.S. labor. But because the home came to be seen as a place of refuge from work, women's labor there went unacknowledged and, was never assigned monetary value. In 2002, the U.S. Gross Domestic Product, the measure of the nation's total output, still did not include an estimate for the value of household work.

Although some women found new employment opportunities during the nineteenth century as secretaries, librarians, and school teachers, feminization of jobs once held by men resulted in a decline in pay and prestige. For those educated women seeking advanced training that could provide them entrée into better paying, male-dominated professions, universities served as gate keepers, barring their entry. Harvard Law School, for example, did not open its doors to female students until 1950.

Strategies For Improvement

Workers attempting to improve their position through protest and ultimately unionization found ready adherents among working-class women. Women weavers in Pawtucket, Rhode Island, who walked off work in 1824 were among the first American workers to strike against low wages and long hours. Yet for several reasons male union leaders were often reluctant to include women in organizing efforts. Men held the highly skilled jobs that carried greater leverage in the event of strikes. Women workers, who were for the most part young and single, were considered temporary members of the labor force. With marriage they were expected to return to their proper sphere, the home, where they could remain if male workers received the "family wage" unions sought. The assumption that women workers were neither interested in unionizing nor effective organizers was put to rest in the early years of the twentieth century by organizers such as Rose Schneiderman, Fannia Cohn, Pauline Newman, Clara Lemlich, and Lenora O'Reilly. Still in their teens and early twenties, these young women were successful in bringing half of all female garment work into trade unions by 1919. Nonetheless, women workers and their middle- and upper-class allies for the most part turned to government rather than unions for protection from exploitation.

The young female textile workers at Massachusetts' Lowell Mills were the first industrial workers in the nation to demand state regulation of the length of the workday. As more of the country industrialized, these demands were heeded. State legislators limited the workday to ten hours. In the late nineteenth and early twentieth century, the Supreme Court held that such statutes interfered with the right and liberty of the individual to contract his labor. Women reformers successfully argued that an exception should be made for laws limiting women's hours of labor on the basis of their physical vulnerability, especially during pregnancy. In the landmark case *MULLER V. OREGON* (1908), the Court upheld Oregon's ten-hour law for women on the basis of their role as child bearers. Yet without comparable legislation establishing a minimum wage, minimum hours legislation disadvantaged those women living at the margin of subsistence, who needed to work more hours to make a sufficient income. When minimum hours legislation was supplemented by laws preventing women from performing night work or "heavy" work, the restrictions were used to designate some better-paying skilled jobs as male. Minimum wage legislation did not follow until the New Deal.

While the FAIR LABOR STANDARDS ACT (1938) established a minimum wage for both men and women, it too proved a mixed blessing. Many women covered by the act were paid less than men for the same jobs, while others, such as domestics, were simply not included. Efforts to equalize wages for men and women gained momentum after World War II amidst popular sentiment that the nation was indebted to the large numbers of women who flooded factories and ship yards to meet the wartime need for armaments. Passage of the EQUAL PAY ACT did not occur until 1963, in part because the legislation acknowledged women as workers in their own right, not just as temporary earners contributing to the family economy. Even some male union leaders supporting the legislation may have done so not out of a fundamental belief in gender equity but rather because they anticipated that equal pay legislation would play upon employers' gender bias, prompting them to hire male workers at the expense of female workers.

The new statute prohibited different pay for men and women when their jobs required equal skill, effort, and responsibility and were performed under similar work conditions. However, since occupational segregation resulted in so few jobs in which men and women performed the same tasks, foes of sex discrimination sought in the 1970s to enlarge what constitutes equal skill, effort, and responsibility by advocating equal pay for jobs of "comparable worth."

Some state and local governments reevaluated state and municipal jobs in an effort to see whether nurses, for example, were performing work that represented the same level of training, stress, and difficult working conditions as that performed by sanitation workers so that pay scales for undervalued jobs, usually those held by women, could be adjusted. This form of pay equity encountered fierce opposition from those who feared that widespread re-evaluation of work done by government employees could impact salaries in the private sector. Some feminists also opposed the policy of equal pay through comparable worth, arguing that the wage gap between fully employed men and women could best be closed by attacking job segregation.

An important start had been made with congressional passage of the CIVIL RIGHTS ACT in 1964. Title VII prohibited sex- as well as race-based discrimination in employment, pay, and promotion and called for the establishment of an EQUAL EMPLOYMENT OPPORTUNITY COMMISSION (EEOC) to monitor compliance with the law on the part of employers and labor unions. In addition, the federal government was obliged to undertake an affirmative action program that would provide equal employment opportunities to job applicants and employees. As later amended, the Civil Rights Act also barred discriminatory treatment of pregnant employees, who were often forced to resign as soon as they learned they were pregnant, thereby jeopardizing both their jobs and seniority. In 1978, an executive order amended the Civil Rights Act to set goals and a timetable for promoting women's access to jobs in construction, an industry in which electricians, plumbers, machinists, welders, and carpenters were almost 100 percent male and 100 percent white. Accompanied by additional legislation mandating equal educational opportunities, women in the 1970s had a far better chance of obtaining the specialized training that provided access to better paying blue-collar jobs as well as positions in professions traditionally monopolized by men.

Inequities also existed for women in the labor force with respect to benefits. SOCIAL SECURITY provisions enacted in the 1930s reflected an era when many women were not in the labor force and most were presumed to be economically dependent on male wage earners who paid into Social Security. Consequently, wives meeting certain criteria upon the death of a spouse could collect small sums intended to allow them to stay at home and care for dependent children. Yet as more women moved into the workforce, it became clear that what they paid into Social Security did not entitle their spouse and children to the same benefits. The case of *Weinberger v. Wisenfeld* (1975) concerned a widower who, after his wife died in childbirth, was denied Social Security benefits that would allow him to stay home and care for his infant son. This case demonstrated that sex discrimination could cut both ways: when the law discounted women as workers it could result in inequity for male as well as female plaintiffs.

SEXUAL HARASSMENT was a term first used in the mid-1970s. For decades working women had endured covert or explicit sexual advances from supervisors and employers, sexual innuendos, derogatory references to their sexual activities or body parts, and unwelcome "flirting" and fondling by coworkers. *MERITOR SAVINGS BANK V. MECHELLE VINSON* (1986) was the first in a series of decisions that defined this type of sex discrimination. Feminist legal scholar Catharine MacKinnon, one of the attorneys for Vinson, who claimed to be a victim of sexual harassment, named two forms of such behavior for the Supreme

Court: 1) "quid pro quo": when sexual submission to a supervisor becomes, either implicitly or explicitly, a condition for employment; and (2) "offensive working environment": when the conduct of a supervisor, coworker, or client unreasonably interferes with an individual's work or creates an intimidating and hostile workplace. In a unanimous opinion, the Court found for Vinson, declaring that the intent of Congress in Title VII of the Civil Rights Act was "to strike at the entire spectrum of disparate treatment of men and women" in employment.

Later Gains and Persistent Problems

As the result of such policies and, not least, women's own determination to break down gender barriers, sex discrimination in the workplace decreased during the late twentieth century. Yet it by no means disappeared. Earnings differentials, while narrowing, especially for younger women, persisted. In 2000, full-time female workers earned 76 cents for every dollar earned by males. The difference was due to the fact that 80 percent of working women held gender-segregated positions where wages were artificially low. Women made up two-thirds of all minimum-wage workers in the United States, and as a consequence, women also make up two-thirds of poor Americans. Even in higher paying positions where equally credentialed young men and women start out with the same pay, differentials tended to increase over time for a variety of reasons. Barriers to upward mobility and higher pay sometimes came in the form of a "GLASS CEILING," which women had difficulty breaking through because of subtle but lingering gender bias. Other barriers arose from the fact that the workplace, designed originally for males, only slowly accommodated to women who usually bore the greater responsibility for care work, even in dual income families.

Major companies with highly skilled employees whom they wish to retain instituted family-friendly policies such as flexible time schedules, maternity leave, and child care facilities. But many small businesses, especially those employing less skilled workers, offered little to employees, some of whom were already working two jobs, to help offset the burden of wage work, care work, and house work. For the increasing number of women who were their families' sole breadwinner the burden was especially heavy.

At a time when women now constitute 46 percent of the labor force and 64.5 percent of all mothers with children under six work outside the home, a fundamental rethinking of both work and family are needed to minimize the gender disparities that have historically inhibited the achievement of economic parity between the sexes. Necessary too is an extension of family-friendly government policies. Passage of the 1993 FAMILY AND MEDICAL LEAVE ACT was a start, albeit a problematic one. In the early 2000s women constituted 46 percent of the labor force and 65 percent of all mothers with children under six worked outside the home. The 1993 Family and Medical Leave Act acknowledged the need for family-friendly government policies. The statute required employers of over fifty persons to grant up to twelve weeks of unpaid leave annually to all full-time employees who had been on the payroll for a year for family or personal medical emergencies, childbirth, or adoption. However most Americans could not afford three months without income. Unlike Japan and Western European countries that allowed for longer leaves and, more important, paid leaves, the United States was the only industrialized nation that did not provide paid maternity leave.

The fight against gender discrimination faced obstacles in the late twentieth century. Beginning with the Reagan Administration in 1981, measures instituted in the 1960s and 1970s that were intended to promoted gender equity were eroded through the appointment process, cuts in funding, and other measures. The EEOC, which once had the power to institute legal proceeding against companies where a pattern of sex-based discrimination could be determined statistically, was no longer the effective monitor of the workplace Congress originally intended. The controversial welfare laws of the 1990s required benefits recipients to make the transition to employment without providing the necessary supports of a living wage, child care, and health care.

In sum, the policies of the second half of the twentieth century eroded gender barriers, lessening the impact of sex discrimination. Women made significant inroads in traditionally male professions such as engineering and law. More women owned their own businesses and earned better wages—by 2002 one in five American women earned more than her husband. Yet in a highly stratified labor market, discrimination based on sex and compounded by race and ethnicity continued, though often in subtler forms than in the past. Occupational segregation, while weakened in some areas, remained intact in others. Nurses and secretarial workers were still over 90 percent female, while the work force in the construction industry remained 98 percent male. The feminization of poverty continued. In an era when the number of female-headed households continued to rise, those penalized were not just women but their children. Gender equity in the work place remained an elusive and essential goal.

BIBLIOGRAPHY

Baron, Ava, ed. *Work Engendered: Towards a New History of American Labor.* Ithaca, N.Y.: Cornell University Press, 1991.

Boydston, Jeanne. *Home and Work: Housework, Wages, and the Ideology of Labor in the Early Republic.* New York: Oxford University Press, 1990.

Goldin, Claudia. *Understanding the Gender Gap: An Economic History of American Women.* New York: Oxford University Press, 1989.

Jones, Jacqueline. *Labor of Love, Labor of Sorrow: Black Women, Work, and the Family From Slavery to the Present.* New York: Basic Books, 1985.

Kessler-Harris, Alice. *Out to Work: A History of Wage-Earning Women in the United States.* New York: Oxford University Press, 1982.

———. *A Woman's Wage: Historical Meanings and Social Consequences.* Lexington: University Press of Kentucky, 1990.

———. *In Pursuit of Equity: Women, Men, and the Quest for Economic Citizenship in Twentieth Century America.* New York: Oxford University Press, 2001.

Orleck, Annelise. *Common Sense and a Little Fire: Women and Working-Class Politics in the United States, 1900–1965.* Chapel Hill: University of North Carolina Press, 1995.

Ruiz, Vicki L. *From Out of the Shadows: Mexican Women in Twentieth Century America.* New York: Oxford University Press, 1995.

Salmon, Marylynn. *Women and the Law of Property in Early America.* Chapel Hill: University of North Carolina Press, 1986.

White, Deborah. *Ar'n't I a Woman?: Female Slaves in the Plantation South.* New York: Norton, 1985.

Jane Sherron De Hart

See also **Civil Rights and Liberties; Gender and Gender Roles; Minimum-Wage Legislation; Women in Public Life, Business, and Professions;** *and vol. 9:* **Letter to President Franklin D. Roosevelt on Job Discrimination; NOW Statement of Purpose.**

Sexual Orientation

This refers to the treatment of individuals based on their sexual orientation by other individuals and public or private institutions. People whose sexual orientation places them in minority categories, such as lesbians, homosexuals, and bisexuals, have sought legal protection from this type of discrimination. The political and legal fight against this discrimination has been the general aim of the gay rights movement, which established its presence in American society and politics with the 1969 Stonewall Riots in New York City.

Federal, state, and local civil rights legislation, as well as private corporate employment policy, is used to remedy this type of discrimination. In 1982, Wisconsin became the first state to legally ban discrimination based on sexual orientation in private and public sector employment. At the end of 2001, ten other states (California, Connecticut, Hawaii, Massachusetts, Minnesota, Nevada, New Hampshire, New Jersey, Rhode Island, and Vermont), the District of Columbia, and 122 counties and cities had a similar ban in place. Public-sector employees in an additional ten states (Colorado, Delaware, Illinois, Indiana, Maryland, Montana, New Mexico, New York, Pennsylvania, and Washington), as well as in 106 cities and counties, have legal protection against this type of sexual discrimination. More than half of the Fortune 500 companies and 2,000 other corporate entities have policies banning discrimination based on sexual orientation.

On 28 May 1998 President William J. Clinton signed an executive order banning this type of discrimination against all civilian federal employees. This executive order affords protection to all civilians employed by all federal departments, including the Department of Defense. At the beginning of the first term of his presidency, Clinton sought to overturn the Department of Defense's policy of discharging gay and lesbian noncivilians. This action marked the first controversy of his administration, and resulted in the Department of Defense's 1993 policy that became known as "Don't Ask, Don't Tell." Still enforced in 2002, this policy prohibits military officers and other enlisted personnel from asking fellow noncivilians about their sexual orientation. It was implemented as an attempt to end the military's practice of discharging noncivilians from service because of their sexual orientation, but it did not end the practice. In fact, it apparently had the opposite effect: by 2001 the number of such discharges increased 73 percent from 1993, the year when the policy was implemented.

There have been other attempts at the federal level to ban this type of discrimination. First introduced in the U.S. Congress in 1994, the Employment Anti-Discrimination Act (ENDA) seeks to ban discrimination based on sexual orientation in private and public employment in the thirty-nine states that have not enacted this law. In 1996, the bill was narrowly defeated in the Senate by one vote. It was reintroduced in 2001 to the 107th Congress, but it still lacked a majority vote needed for passage. Despite the anti-discrimination bill's failure to gain passage in Congress, a 1999 Gallup poll showed that 89 percent of Americans favored banning workplace discrimination based on sexual orientation.

Legislation protecting against discrimination based on sexual orientation has sustained scrutiny by the U.S. Supreme Court. In the early 1990s, several cities and towns in Colorado enacted such anti-discrimination laws. These laws were overturned in 1992 when Coloradans approved Amendment 2, which outlawed throughout the state any legal protection against discrimination afforded to gays and lesbians. The constitutionality of Amendment 2 was tested in the case *Romer v. Evans*, which came before the Supreme Court in 1995. In 1996, a majority of Supreme Court justices ruled that Amendment 2 violated the equal protection clause in the Fourteenth Amendment to the U.S. Constitution. In 1998, however, the U.S. Supreme Court appeared to contradict its ruling when it refused to hear a challenge to Cincinnati's Issue 3. Issue 3 stated that the city could never pass any legislation remedying discrimination based on sexual orientation. Justices Stevens, Souter, and Bader Ginsburg noted that the Court's refusal to hear the case neither set new law nor precedent, and that the Court's decision was based upon uncertainty concerning Issue 3's legal scope and effect.

The issue of discrimination based on sexual orientation is a controversial one. In 2001, for example, the Maryland legislature passed a law banning such discrimination in the public and private sector. Subsequently, citizens in the state drew up a petition to subject the ban to a statewide referendum to be held the following year. By placing the ban on a referendum, the law's detractors were able to suspend its enforcement for a year until the vote on the referendum could take place. Nevertheless, despite the controversy, the movement to ban sexual discrimination continues to grow. The Human Rights Campaign Foundation reported that in 2002, 161 employers, including state and local governments, unions, colleges and universities, and private corporations, enacted for the first time policies that ban this type of discrimination.

BIBLIOGRAPHY

D' Emilio, John, William B. Turner, and Vaid Urvashi, eds. *Creating Change: Sexuality, Public Policy, and Civil Rights.* New York: St. Martin's Press, 2000.

State of the Workplace for Lesbian, Gay, Bisexual, and Transgendered Americans 2001. Washington, D.C.: The Human Rights Campaign Foundation, 2001.

State of the Workplace for Lesbian, Gay, Bisexual, and Transgendered Americans: A Semiannual Snapshot. Washington, D.C.: The Human Rights Campaign Foundation, 2002.

William B. Turner

See also **Defense of Marriage Act; Gay and Lesbian Movement; Military Service and Minorities; Homosexuals; Sexual Orientation.**

DISFRANCHISEMENT is a denial of the right to vote. Before 1776, a higher proportion of Americans could vote than in any other country. Still, the vast majority of women and free persons of color were voteless, and white men who owned less than a certain amount of property, such as forty acres of land, or land or housing that would rent for forty British shillings per year, were also disfranchised. Property qualifications, which primarily affected younger men, were considerably loosened even before 1800 and were generally abolished in the 1820s and 1830s. By the Civil War, America enjoyed nearly universal white male adult citizen suffrage, and during the nineteenth century, twenty-two states enfranchised male immigrants who had indicated their intention to become citizens. But African American males could vote only in New England and, for those who owned substantial property, in New York State. No females could vote.

Although voters rejected universal black male suffrage in twelve of fifteen referenda in northern states from 1846 to 1869, Republicans extended the vote to southern black males by congressional act in 1867 and to all black males through the Fifteenth Amendment to the U.S. Constitution in 1870. Efforts to include women in the Fifteenth Amendment failed, and the movement for female suffrage took another fifty years, slowly but gradually winning support at the local and state levels until it developed sufficient strength to win passage of the Nineteenth Amendment.

By the time most white women won the vote, nearly all southern black men and many southern white men had lost it. Their disfranchisement came about gradually, through a sequence of actions motivated by inseparably intertwined racial and partisan interests. The process began when the Ku Klux Klan wing of the Democratic Party attacked its white and African American opponents. Violence and intimidation allowed Democrats to conquer the polls, stuff ballot boxes, and count in more Democrats. Democratic state legislators passed laws that, for instance, gerrymandered districts to make it harder for blacks and Republicans to win, and they restricted the rights of individuals to vote by requiring them to register long before elections or pay high poll taxes. They also mandated secret ballots or required voters to deposit ballots for different offices into separate ballot boxes, both of which served as de facto literacy tests.

To secure white Democratic supremacy permanently, upper-class southern leaders beginning in 1890 engineered the passage of state constitutional provisions that required voters to pay poll taxes and pass literacy or property tests administered by racist, partisan registrars. Disfranchisement transformed a southern political system with fairly vigorous party competition, solid voter turnout, and somewhat egalitarian governmental policy to one with no parties, shrunken participation, few policy benefits for poorer whites, and almost no role for African Americans.

Only with the passage of the Voting Rights Act of 1965 were such laws overturned and a free, competitive political system restored to the South. Even today, state laws that disfranchise felons and former felons, particularly in the South, deny the vote to 4.7 million U.S. citizens, 36 percent of whom are black. In ten states, such laws disfranchise a quarter or more of black adult males.

BIBLIOGRAPHY

Keyssar, Alexander. *The Right to Vote: The Contested History of Democracy in the United States.* New York: Basic Books, 2000.

Kousser, J. Morgan. *Colorblind Injustice: Minority Voting Rights and the Undoing of the Second Reconstruction.* Chapel Hill: University of North Carolina Press, 1999.

Perman, Michael. *Struggle for Mastery: Disfranchisement in the South, 1888–1908.* Chapel Hill: University of North Carolina Press, 2001.

J. Morgan Kousser

See also **Poll Tax; Suffrage; Voting.**

DISMAL SWAMP, an immense wetland in North Carolina and Virginia covering about 750 square miles. In the center of the swampland is circular Lake Drummond, 3.5 miles in diameter. The swamp was named by a wealthy Virginia land speculator, William Byrd, in 1728, and four thousand acres of it were owned by George Washington. During the eighteenth century the area was the subject of land speculation by wealthy easterners. It was immortalized by Henry Wadsworth Longfellow in

Henry Wadsworth Longfellow. The poet's works include "The Slave in the Dismal Swamp" (1842), an antislavery hymn to a runaway. AP/WIDE WORLD PHOTOS

"The Slave in the Dismal Swamp." In the 1970s a controversial drainage and agricultural development program aroused conservationists. Although today it is a National Wildlife Refuge, water is drained from the swamp to help maintain water levels in the nearby Intracoastal Waterway.

BIBLIOGRAPHY

Royster, Charles. *The Fabulous History of the Dismal Swamp Company: A Story of George Washington's Times.* New York: Borzoi Books, 1999.

James Elliott Walmsley / H. S.

See also **Wetlands.**

DISNEY CORPORATION. The Walt Disney Company was incorporated by Walt and Roy Disney in 1923, first as the Disney Brothers Cartoon Studio, then as the Walt Disney Studio. Based in Los Angeles, California, the company produced short animated films that were distributed by other film companies and appeared before feature-length films in movie theaters around the world.

Never one of the major studios, the company grew gradually, always with financial difficulties, and established itself as an independent production company in Hollywood. The Disney brothers built a reputation for quality animation, utilizing cutting-edge technological developments such as sound and color, and producing feature-length animated films. The popularity of Disney's products, which included merchandise based on their animated characters, such as Mickey Mouse, Donald Duck, and Snow White, was instantaneous and unmistakable, not only in the United States but in other countries.

Setting the foundations for the diversification that emerged in the ensuing decades, during the 1950s Disney expanded to include television production and live-action feature films. In 1953 the company opened Disneyland, the first of many theme parks. During this period, the company also started distributing its own films. By the mid-1970s, however, the company appeared to be stagnating until a management and ownership shuffle rejuvenated its established businesses and developed new investments.

At the end of the twentieth century, the Walt Disney Company was the second largest media conglomerate in the world (behind AOL Time Warner), with a wide array of domestic and international investments. The company's revenues for 2000 were over $25 billion. Disney owned the American Broadcasting Company (ABC) television network, broadcast TV stations, and radio stations and networks, and maintained partial ownership of several cable networks, including 80 percent of ESPN and 38 percent of A&E and Lifetime. Walt Disney Studios pro-

Walt Disney. The man who gave the world Mickey Mouse, Disneyland, and decades of innovative animation and entertainment. LIBRARY OF CONGRESS

duced films under the Touchstone, Hollywood Pictures, and Miramax labels. In addition, the company was also involved in home video, recorded music, theatrical productions, and consumer products, which were sold at over 600 Disney Stores around the world.

Disney's theme parks and resorts division encompassed six major theme parks in the United States, including Disneyland in Anaheim, California, and the Walt Disney World Resort in Florida (EPCOT, The Animal Kingdom, Disney-MGM Studios). Other theme park sites were Tokyo Disney, Disneyland Paris, and, by 2003, Hong Kong Disneyland. The company also owned extensive hotel and resort properties, a variety of regional entertainment centers, a cruise line, sports investments, and a planned community in Florida called Celebration. The Walt Disney Internet Group included sites such as ABC.com, Disney Online, and ESPN.com.

BIBLIOGRAPHY

Smoodin, Eric, ed. *Disney Discourse: Producing the Magic Kingdom.* New York: Routledge, 1994.

Wasko, Janet. *Understanding Disney: The Manufacture of Fantasy.* Malden, Mass.: Blackwell, 2001.

Janet Wasko

See also **Cartoons; Film; Mass Media.**

DISPLACED HOMEMAKERS SELF-SUFFICIENCY ASSISTANCE ACT. The act was adopted in 1990 with the intention of assisting women who had been homemakers to advance in the labor market. A displaced homemaker was defined as "an individual who has been providing unpaid services to family members in the home and who—(A) has been dependent either—(i) on public assistance and whose youngest child is within two years of losing eligibility under part A of title IV of the Social Security Act, or (ii) on the income of another family member but is no longer supported by that income, and (B) is unemployed or underemployed and is experiencing difficulty in obtaining or upgrading employment." The act was repealed in 1998.

Carol Weisbrod

DISQUISITION ON GOVERNMENT. *See* ***South Carolina Exposition and Protest.***

DISSENTERS, the name commonly applied in America to those who disagreed with the doctrines of the religious establishments, particularly the Church of England in Massachusetts. Dissenting bodies, or "nonconformists," splintered from established churches with increasing frequency in the late eighteenth and early nineteenth centuries. The most important dissenters were the Congregationalists, Baptists, Quakers, Presbyterians, and Wesleyans, or Methodists. Once the legal separation of church and state ended the Anglican and Congregational franchises, the ranks of the dissenters grew rapidly. Organized collectively in evangelical groups, these congregations would dominate social reform and force political realignments during the antebellum era.

BIBLIOGRAPHY

Gaustad, Edwin S. *Faith of our Fathers: Religion and the New Nation.* San Francisco: Harper and Row, 1987.

Hatch, Nathan O. *The Democratization of American Christianity.* New Haven, Conn.: Yale University Press, 1989.

Robert Fortenbaugh / A. R.

See also **Baptist Churches; Church of England in the Colonies; Congregationalism; Methodism; Presbyterianism; Quakers; Religion and Religious Affiliation; Religious Liberty.**

DISTILLING. It did not take long for the colonists to begin producing alcoholic beverages from fruit and grain. Settlers on Roanoke Island (Virginia) brewed crude ale from maize, and New Englanders made wine from wild grapes. Distilling more potent liquor required little more than a fire, a large kettle, and a blanket stretched to absorb the vapors of the heated wine or brew.

Commercial distilleries, with more sophisticated distilling techniques, were operating in New Amsterdam as early as 1640 and shortly thereafter in Boston (1654) and in Charleston, South Carolina (1682). Rum distilled from West Indian sugar was an important colonial industry and, along with the import of slaves from Africa, a significant component in the commerce of the British Empire.

Yet, as the nation began to expand and distance impeded access to imports, Americans developed a taste for whiskey distilled from locally grown corn, rye, and barley. Besides being a popular beverage, frontier whiskey served as a medicine, a commodity, and a cash crop more easily transported than whole grain.

By 1791, Kentuckians already had enough interest in whiskey to warrant a convention opposing an excise tax on it levied by the federal government. As only spirits distilled from American-grown produce were taxed, rum distillers were exempt. This led to the Whiskey Rebellion in 1794.

But the federal government eventually proved to be at least as good a customer as it was a taxing agent: the army, until 1832, and the navy, until 1862, provided enlisted personnel with a liquor ration, and government purchases of whiskey ran as high as 120,000 gallons annually.

Even George Washington himself had advocated for the liquid fortification of his revolutionary warriors. In 1777, Washington wrote, "It is necessary there should be a sufficient quantity of spirits with the Army to furnish moderate supplies to the troops."

Distilling. A man fills kegs in an industrial brewery. GETTY IMAGES

Washington did more than supply his troops with liquor. In his final years, he also helped supply the nation with whiskey. He opened a distillery near the gristmill of his Mt. Vernon, Virginia, plantation in 1798. The following year, the distillery produced some 11,000 gallons of corn and rye whiskey, netting around $7,500—making it one of the nation's largest whiskey producers. Washington died later that year, however, and his distillery was shut down. In December 2000, the Distilled Spirits Council of the United States (DISCUS) announced a $1.2 million donation to help reconstruct the Mt. Vernon distillery as an historic landmark.

It could not have hurt that such an eminent American spent his final years in the distilling business. The homegrown industry was further strengthened by events in the early nineteenth century that weakened American reliance on imports for liquor. The Embargo Act of 1807 and the War of 1812 meant that rum distilleries were blockaded from their sources of cane sugar and molasses; and rum drinkers, unable to obtain the country's traditionally favorite liquor, were forced to develop a taste for whiskey, especially Kentucky whiskey, also known as bourbon.

The greatest threat to the distilling industry in America began in the late nineteenth century with the increasingly vigorous efforts of temperance organizations such as the Women's Christian Temperance Foundation (founded in Cleveland in 1874) and the Anti-Saloon League of America (also formed in Ohio, in 1893). Among the early triumphs of the temperance movement was a program known as Scientific Temperance Instruction, a highly successful anti-alcohol education program that taught American schoolchildren the dangers of drinking.

The temperance movement had its share of visible supporters, among them the adventure novelist Jack London, whose book *John Barleycorn* (1913) preached the virtues of alcohol abstinence. Meanwhile, any candidate running for national office made a point of stumping at temperance organization rallies, to prove his moral worthiness for public service. The Prohibition Party, founded in 1869 in Chicago, devoted its entire political platform to ending alcohol trafficking and consumption in America.

By 1916, nearly half of the states had passed "anti-saloon" legislation; and in 1919, the states ratified the 18th Amendment to the U.S. Constitution, officially putting a cork in America's drinking habit with the advent of Prohibition.

Prohibition is credited with giving America many things, among them, the first solid foundation upon which organized crime flourished. Al Capone made millions smuggling liquor and the associated businesses of speakeasies and prostitution. The popularity of the cocktail suddenly soared as drinkers used flavored mixers to mask the unpleasant taste of bathtub gin. The devil-may-care culture of the Roaring Twenties was partly a by-product of Prohibition, which turned even normally law-abiding citizens into minor criminals in order to enjoy alcoholic beverages.

The repeal of Prohibition in 1933 with the passing of the Twenty-first Amendment concluded America's "noble experiment," but most of the small distillers had shut down during Prohibition. Others had switched to the manufacture of chemicals; a handful had continued operations by distilling medicinal alcohol (which had not been banned by Prohibition). As the economy sank into the Great Depression, few distillers possessed either the necessary capital or the marketing capabilities to resume operations.

The remainder of the twentieth century saw a steady return to business for distillers, despite battles over advertising placement, the drinking age, and increased public awareness of the dangers of alcoholism and of driving while intoxicated.

As the twenty-first century began, the distilled spirits industry was generating some $95 billion annually (according to DISCUS). With about 1.3 million people in America employed in the manufacture, distribution, or sales of distilled spirits, distilling remains a significant American industry.

Major mergers and acquisitions in the industry, including the 2001 acquisition of Seagrams by Pernod Ricard (makers of Wild Turkey) and Diageo (owners of such brands as Johnny Walker, Baileys, and Tanqueray), have left once-rival brands living under the same corporate roof. Even as these industry giants combined forces, small-batch makers are once again on the rise with a revival of the old-fashioned distilleries that once dominated the industry.

BIBLIOGRAPHY

Barr, Andrew. *Drink: A Social History of America.* New York: Carroll & Graf, 1999.

Carson, Gerald. *The Social History of Bourbon: An Unhurried Account of our Star-Spangled American Drink.* Lexington: University Press of Kentucky, 1984.

Downard, William. *Dictionary of the History of the American Brewing and Distilling Industries.* Westport, Conn.: Greenwood Press, 1981.

Kyvig, David E. *Repealing National Prohibition.* 2nd ed. Kent, Ohio: Kent State University Press, 2000

Lender, Mark E. *Dictionary of American Temperance Biography: From Temperance Reform to Alcohol Research, the 1600s to the 1980s.* Westport, Conn.: Greenwood Press, 1984.

Miron, Jeffrey A. *The Effect of Alcohol Prohibition on Alcohol Consumption.* Cambridge, Mass.: National Bureau of Economic Research, 1999.

Walker, Stanley. *The Night Club Era.* Baltimore: Johns Hopkins University Press, 1999. The original was published in 1933.

Zimmerman, Jonathon. *Distilling Democracy: Alcohol Education in America's Public Schools, 1880–1925.* Lawrence: The University of Kansas Press, 1999.

Laura A. Bergheim
David C. Roller

See also **Alcohol, Regulation of; Moonshine; Prohibition; Rum Trade; Temperance Movement; Whiskey; Whiskey Rebellion.**

DISTRIBUTION OF GOODS AND SERVICES.

It is not unreasonable to wonder why all products are not sold directly from producer to final consumer. The simple answer is that distributors lower the costs of market transactions in a specialized economy. First, distributors lower the costs of market transactions by taking advantage of economies of scale and scope. For example, retail stores typically offer many varieties of goods. It would be very costly for consumers to purchase every item directly from producers. Second, distributors reduce the information costs of market transactions. Wholesale merchants traditionally, and retail merchants more recently, lower the costs of trade by lowering the costs of discovering supply and demand conditions. Third, distributors also lower the cost of trade by solving the asymmetric information problem. This problem typically arises when consumers cannot easily discern the quality of a product sold in the market place. Historically, the wholesale merchants solved this problem by organizing exchanges that inspected quality and standardized grades. The traditional local retail merchants often solved this problem by developing a reputation for honesty. Over time, as market transactions became increasingly anonymous, multi-unit chain retail stores and multi-unit manufacturing firms used advertising and branding as a solution to the asymmetric information problem.

Changing Patterns of Distribution

The nature of production and of the distribution of goods and services has changed greatly over the course of American history. As the basis of the U.S. economy shifted from agriculture to manufacturing, and then, more recently, to service industries, distribution's role in the economy changed along with the nature of the goods produced and sold in the market.

The market economy of colonial America in the seventeenth and eighteenth centuries was dominated by agriculture, fisheries, and the other extractive industries. For those goods produced for the market, the general merchant was the key distributor. The merchant bought goods of all types and was the ship owner, exporter, importer, banker, insurer, wholesaler, and retailer. The merchant's role, however, was often limited to the distribution of goods and services intended for the very wealthy. Most households manufactured their own clothing, farm implements, candles, and so on, and performed many household services themselves.

In the early nineteenth century, revolutions in transportation and communications increased the size of domestic markets, which led in turn to significant organizational changes in the production and distribution of goods and services. Although households continued to produce many of their own services such as cooking, laundering, and cleaning, the production and distribution of goods that were part of the market economy became more extensive and specialized. As the United States became an industrial nation, manufacturing firms that specialized in a single product line began to proliferate. In response, the general merchant gave way to distributors who specialized in one or two product lines, such as cotton, provisions, wheat, dry goods, hardware, or drugs. As new products were introduced, wholesale merchants specializing in these products also emerged.

The first census of distribution, taken in 1929, provides a picture of the flow of goods (especially manufactured goods) from producer to consumer. Manufacturers ultimately sell their goods to two distinct markets: industry and the home consumer. The census data shows that manufacturers sold 31 percent of their goods directly to final industrial consumers and 2.5 percent to final home consumers. The rest was sold to distributors such as wholesalers, manufacturers' own sales branches, and retailers. These distributors then resold their products to final industrial consumers or to retailers. The retailers in turn resold their products to final home consumers. In total, 169,702 wholesale establishments distributed $69 billion worth of goods. Manufacturing goods constituted 81 percent, farm products 13 percent, and the remainder, from other extractive industries, 6 percent. These goods were distributed by different types of wholesalers. Merchant wholesalers, agents, and brokers distributed 79 percent of the goods, whereas manufacturer's sales branches accounted for 21 percent. Some 1,476,365 retail establishments distributed $48.3 million worth of goods to final consumers.

The emergence of a national domestic market in the twentieth century transformed the organization of production and distribution once again. In the early twentieth century, mass retail distributors and chains replaced many local store merchants. These multi-unit retail firms often purchased their products directly from manufacturers. Moreover, as the twentieth century progressed, wholesale merchants were squeezed from the other direction. Many large multi-unit manufacturing firms began to market their products directly to consumers and retailers. Yet, despite these trends, the traditional wholesale merchants continued to play a significant role in the American economy.

BIBLIOGRAPHY

Chandler, Alfred, Jr. *The Visible Hand: The Managerial Revolution in American Business.* Cambridge, Mass.: Harvard University Press, 1977.

Kim, Sukkoo. "Markets and Multiunit Firms from an American Historical Perspective." In *Multiunit Organization and Multimarket Strategy.* Edited by Joel A. C. Baum and Heinrich R. Greve. *Advances in Strategic Management* 18 (June 2001), 305–326.

Sukkoo Kim

See also **Retailing Industry.**

DISTRICT, CONGRESSIONAL. Members of the U.S. House of Representatives are selected to represent a congressional district by the citizens living in the geographic region that comprises the district.

Under the Constitution each state is entitled to at least one representative, serving a two-year term. Congress determines the size of the House of Representatives, which in 2001had 435 members. A state's population determines the number of congressional seats apportioned to it. Although in early American history some states frequently elected congressmen-at-large, the single-member district has generally prevailed since the 1840s. Early districts varied widely in terms of population, but the U.S. Supreme Court decided in *Baker v. Carr* (1962) that unequally populated districts violated the equal protection clause of the Constitution. Since this decision districts within a state each have approximately the same population.

Following each decennial census, the federal government reapportions congressional districts for all the states. Each state government then redraws its district boundaries to reflect changes in the population. Districts are generally expected to be compact and contiguous, but as states redraw their district maps, "gerrymandering," the drawing of district lines to maximize political advantage, is the norm.

Partisan gerrymandering is perhaps the most common; this is done when the party currently in control of the state government redraws district lines to their own advantage. Drawing lines to protect the incumbents of all parties is also common, resulting in a few districts that are very competitive and many where incumbents are routinely reelected with high margins.

Historically, greater political conflict has occurred over the practice of racial gerrymandering; this is when boundaries are drawn to benefit one race over another in representation. Many states routinely have their redistricting maps challenged for racial gerrymandering on the grounds that such maps violate the equal protection clause of the Constitution. The U.S. Supreme Court, in its 1993 *Shaw v. Reno*, decision, signaled that racial gerrymandering designed solely to increase minority representation in Congress is unconstitutional, but in 2001 the Court decided in *Easley v. Cromartie* that creation of majority-minority districts is acceptable so long as the boundary criteria are based on voting behavior rather than merely race.

The relationship between representatives and their districts is generally close. Advances in travel and communication have allowed them to visit with constituents in their districts more frequently, and many members travel home to their districts as often as once a week. Representatives also generally try to vote in the manner approved by the majority in their districts in order to enhance their chances of reelection. The Constitution requires a member of Congress to reside in the state, but not necessarily the district, from which he or she is elected. Nevertheless, except in large metropolitan areas or in districts with rapidly expanding populations, local residency for representatives has been an unwritten rule of American politics.

BIBLIOGRAPHY

Davidson, Chandler, ed. *Minority Vote Dilution.* Washington, D.C.: Howard University Press, 1984.

Davidson, Roger H., and Walter J. Oleszek. *Congress and Its Members.* Washington, D.C.: Congressional Quarterly Press, 1996.

Brian D. Posler

See also **Congress, United States; Gerrymander.**

DISTRICT OF COLUMBIA. *See* **Washington, D.C.**

Cotton Mather. A religious and political leader during early colonial times, Mather was born a Calvinist, but later authored the *Christian Philosopher*, in which he supported the shift toward deism and the growing use of scientific inquiry.

DIVINE PROVIDENCES. In early colonial New England events that came to pass through the agency of natural causes and yet appeared to be specifically ordained by the will of God were construed as divine providences. Theologians believed that the age of miracles had passed, but that God still achieved his desired ends, not by reversing or suspending the laws of nature, but rather by guiding the laws according to their proper natures. As the Rev. James Fitch expressed it, God in working them does not refuse to attend to the order of things, but voluntarily submits himself to it. Thus the doctrine permitted perfect freedom for scientific inquiry, but at the same time preserved a basically religious and teleological concept of nature. Storms, earthquakes, sudden deaths from heart failure, comets, eclipses, or any natural phenomena, if they could be improved to point a theological or ethical moral, were to be regarded as divine providences.

BIBLIOGRAPHY

Hall, David D. *Worlds of Wonder, Days of Judgment: Popular Religious Belief in Early New England.* New York: Knopf, 1989.

Perry Miller/A. R.

See also **Mysticism; Naturalism; "New England Way"; Puritans and Puritanism; Religion and Religious Affiliation; Religious Thought and Writings.**

DIVORCE AND MARITAL SEPARATION. It was once difficult, perhaps impossible, to obtain a divorce, even when couples found themselves to be incompatible, even when one found the other detestable. Many individuals, apparently locked in unhappy marriages, found ways to leave or separate from spouses and to make new marriages, but only very few could obtain divorces. Since the late nineteenth century, however, there has been a huge increase in the number of marriages ended by formal divorce. Eventually, Americans of all religious faiths and cultural traditions came to understand that there existed an inherent legal right to end marriages whenever it suited them, for reasons good or ill. Since the 1980s, roughly 50 percent of all American marriages end in divorce.

Legislative History

As a legislative matter, the story of American divorce can be told in three chapters or stages. During the first stage, in colonial New England, the law of marriage differed sharply from legal practices in England, where marriage was understood as an indissoluble religious sacrament. English church courts could, however, order separations without right of remarriage and, by the eighteenth century, it was possible for a few very rich men to obtain private legislative acts authorizing their divorces, once they had proved their wives' adultery in civil judicial actions. In New England, by contrast, marriage was a civil contract, and divorces were granted after a judicial proceeding when a wife's or husband's misconduct was proved. Divorces were occasionally granted elsewhere in colonial North America, but other colonial legislatures did not pass laws allowing divorce.

After the American Revolution, a great change occurred, which introduced the second chapter in the history of American divorce. By the early years of the nineteenth century, every new American state except South Carolina had enacted laws authorizing divorce under limited circumstances. In every state, again excepting South Carolina, a full divorce with right of remarriage for the "innocent" party could be granted if the adultery of the "guilty" spouse were proved. In some states (for example, in New Hampshire), a variety of other grounds, including incest, bigamy, abandonment for three years, and extreme cruelty, would also justify a divorce decree. In many states, only the innocent party was set free from the "bonds of matrimony." That meant the guilty party was, at least in theory, forbidden to remarry during the lifetime of the innocent party and also that the innocent spouse might retain a right to inherit land or other property from the guilty one. In most of the new states, particular courts were designated to hear such cases, but in a few states, Maryland for one, a divorce was understood as an exceptional act requiring a private bill of divorce by the state legislature.

By the second third of the nineteenth century, the many varieties of divorce available in America had become a matter of amazed comment by European travelers and others, although the actual number of divorces granted remained minuscule by early twenty-first-century standards. As everyone noted, some legislatures (Connecticut first, then a series of midwestern jurisdictions, most notoriously Indiana) had begun to experiment with divorce rules that were radically "liberal," both in terms of the multiplicity of fault grounds (and the ease with which "fault" could be proved) and in ease of proving state residence. These transformative jurisdictional changes enabled wives to establish independent residences in a state and to file for divorce in that state, a radical break with the inherited English and early American law that held that a wife, even an abandoned wife, had no right to a settlement or to a legal residence independent of her husband. Why legislatures instituted these liberal "reforms" remains mysterious. In some cases, the change can be identified with liberal or anti-Calvinist Protestant beliefs or with anti-Catholicism. Part of the explanation lies in the enormous faith in contractual freedom characteristic of nineteenth-century America. But another part of the story was the competitive position of these new states within the American federal polity. All states competed with each other for new residents, and legislators in many of the newer western and midwestern states perceived a particular "need" for white women willing to settle and marry or remarry.

Through the first half of the nineteenth century, the dominant American understanding of divorce was as a form of punishment for misconduct by the occasional miscreant who had behaved so criminally that his or her spouse was morally obliged to separate and seek a judicial remedy. All the varied divorce regimes in all the states were premised on the notion that a divorce was awarded to one party because of the fault of another party and because of the wrong done to the innocent party. A divorce case bore similarities to a criminal case, and many of the practices of the case law are understandable only if one recognizes that judges worried about tarring a wife or husband with a quasi-criminal label—as an adulterer or a deserter or someone guilty of "extreme cruelty" (which at first denoted physical abuse). A few divorces did not implicate the meaning of marriage, and the resulting judicial processes were designed not to uncover the foundations of marital breakdown but to ensure that the guilty were properly identified and that the rights of the innocent party were protected, since it was assumed that the consequence of divorce was dishonor.

Eventually, divorce became a wronged wife's remedy. Judges worried about the coercions of husbands and about husbands' desires to toss away wives when they came upon younger or wealthier possibilities. Increasingly, men became the wrongdoers in the legal imagination, and wives became victims. Legislators added "causes" for divorce, particularly the omnibus category of "cruelty" (widened to include many forms of emotional harm) that almost always implied what a man had done to his wife. Meanwhile, divorce practice evolved to focus less on dishonor and crime and more on the forms of compensation former wives could receive from their former husbands and on the new question of under what circumstances a separated or divorced wife could be awarded the custody of her children. In Michael Grossberg's image, judges became "judicial patriarchs," replacing the husband-patriarch in his home.

Nineteenth-century changes in divorce law have played a surprisingly important role in the constitutional history of American federalism. For every Indiana, where in 1851 divorces could be granted for reasons large and small and where a short six-month stay was sufficient to establish residence entitling one to the jurisdiction of the divorce court, there was a New York, which only allowed a divorce for proven "criminal" adultery (a limitation on divorce that would not be changed until the 1960s). Both New York and Indiana, it should be noted, justified their rules as protective of vulnerable women. On the one hand, Indiana legislators imagined a wife enchained to a drunken and abusive man and thus fashioned legislative tools to free her. Horace Greeley, on the other hand, who defended New York's law in a series of debates that he printed in his *New York Tribune*, regarded a rigid divorce law as the only protection for dependent wives, who would otherwise be left helpless by men using a liberal divorce law to escape from financial and moral obligations. (Woman's rights advocates lined up on both sides of the question.) Both New York and Indiana were clearly constitutionally entitled to enact their own distinctive divorce regimes. On the other hand, nothing kept married people in one state (perhaps a state like New York, where divorce was difficult) from divorcing in another (where divorce was easier), remarrying in a third, and settling (and perhaps divorcing again) in a fourth or, even more problematically, returning to the first state. Given the variety of rules in the various states, it became possible to imagine men and women who were legally married in one state and fornicators or criminal bigamists in another. This imagined result produced a great deal of constitutional conflict, as state and federal courts tried to find a way to balance the "Full Faith and Credit" clause of the U.S. Constitution (Article IV, section 1), which requires courts in each state to recognize the valid acts (including divorces) enacted in other states, including the particular political and moral interests of individual states regarding divorce. Only in the midst of World War II did the U.S. Supreme Court chart a way out of the dilemma (in *Williams v. North Carolina*). In so doing, it destroyed the capacity of conservative jurisdictions to keep residents from using the liberal divorce laws of other states. (By then, Nevada had become the twentieth-century paradigm of a liberal divorce jurisdiction.)

Beginning early in the nineteenth century, judges and legal commentators warned about the evil of a "collusive divorce." Standard legal lore stated that if both parties wanted a divorce, neither would be entitled to one, and yet couples, even in conservative divorce jurisdictions, manipulated the rules to end their marriages. They used lawyers and others to reproduce the circumstances that entitled them to divorce. For example, in New York a man would travel to New Jersey, where he would be photographed by a detective while sitting on a bed in the company of a prostitute. Or, alternatively, men would fund their wives' travel to liberal jurisdictions (Indiana or South Dakota in the nineteenth century, Nevada or the Virgin Islands in the twentieth), where they could be divorced. By the early twentieth century, collusive divorce had become ordinary legal practice across America, a cultural symbol depicted in novels and movies and *New Yorker* cartoons.

In post–World War II America, first in California (1969) and soon everywhere else, a new generation of reformers, influenced by feminism, used anxiety over the collusive divorce as a reason to remake divorce law (and to produce the third stage in the legislative history of American divorces). Whatever one thought of the moral foundation for the fault grounds that littered the divorce statutes across America, those grounds had by then been so subverted by divorce practices that divorce law was a laughingstock. Respect for the legal system required eliminating fault grounds from divorce law. "No fault divorce" thus became the new rule, and by 1980, it was available in almost every U.S. jurisdiction. "No fault" meant a divorce at will, a right that belonged to both wife and husband during their marriage, a divorce that the state facilitated rather than a divorce that was granted after a long and exhaustive trial. Fault grounds have remained on the statute books, and there are particular strategic reasons why lawyers still sometimes advise their clients to use those archaic procedures. No fault divorce, however, has become the norm and has been transported around the world as a distinctively American export.

Cultural Implications

What of the quantitative growth in the rate of divorce, a growth that in the early 1930s was already labeled as the "galloping increase" in the American rate of divorce? There was probably a steady secular increase in the divorce rate from 1860 to 1980, punctuated by a decline during the Great Depression, a jump after World War II, and perhaps a decline during the 1950s. Although divorce would seem to be the one familial act for which we should have reliable statistics, in fact pre–World War II statistics are extremely unreliable. The divorce rate reported in the decennial federal censuses after 1860 depended on the uncertain capacity of states to enumerate the divorces granted by their local courts and on a generally unknown rate of marriage. Meanwhile, underlying the progression from rare to frequent divorce lies deep uncertainty about the significance of divorce as a legal mechanism to end existing marriages before death. The apparent increase in the rate of divorce over the past two centuries of American history tells us little about the rate of change in marital dissolution, since it tells us nothing about the less formal means that Americans have used to escape unhappy marriages. For example, serial bigamy was a form of marital refashioning that served Americans during much of the era between the beginnings of colonial settlement and the early twentieth century. Many second or third or fourth marriages were not preceded by divorce. A divorce became necessary only when there was a significant amount of property to be divided. Because of its criminal connotations, a divorce sometimes offered a useful mechanism for allowing the "innocent" victim of the guilty spouse to reclaim honor and an identity within an established community. For middle-class women, divorce (and judicially imposed separations) offered the possibility of a maintenance or alimony award (although throughout American history, men have been remarkably successful in escaping even legally imposed awards). The availability of a divorce action was often an important negotiating tool in the zero-sum games of ending a marriage. The characteristic forms of marital escape, however, were abandonment and desertion—unsullied by any public state action. A husband or, less often, a wife would leave and go elsewhere, probably to remarry in a place where no one knew of a previous marriage. This strategy left later generations of demographers, sociologists, historians, and census gatherers without a way to measure what they most wanted to know: How many marriages would end before the death of either wife or husband? Only in post–World War II America, where for the first time most employed men and women paid federal income taxes and could be tracked by means of a social security card, were women and men unable simply to disappear from unhappy marriages, leaving no trail.

As a result, it is easy to diminish the significance of divorce as an aspect of American social history, and yet, for an enormous number of polemicists on all sides in many cultural conflicts throughout American history, divorce has served as a lens through which to understand the marital and moral health of the republic.

In the seventeenth century, there were radical Protestant voices—John Milton's being the most famous of these—that advocated divorce as a remedy for marital misery. There were also powerfully articulated utilitarian justifications for not permitting divorce. In the eighteenth century, David Hume argued that unhappy couples became friends when they knew they could not escape from the relationship. In addition, there was a longstanding Christian understanding of marriage as an inescapable sacrament.

By the late 1860s and 1870s, conservative religious polemicists had begun to describe easy divorce as a symptom of moral breakdown and as destructive of marital and social stability. Forms of that critique continue to the present. Inherent in the arguments of the conservatives, as well as those of feminists like Elizabeth Cady Stanton, was an understanding that modern divorce was becoming a means of voluntary exit from unhappy unions, not a punishment for crime. For polemicists on both sides, the conditions of exit from marriage determined the conditions of life within that institution. To Stanton, that meant that men who depended on their wives would treat their wives with greater care and with greater equality if they knew that wives could leave. She also believed that divorce as a continuing potentiality was a necessary precondition for continuing love between spouses. To the conservatives, on the other hand, easy divorce transformed marriage into a scene of ongoing bargaining and threats, a merely strategic arrangement that had lost its sacred character and undermined the authority of the husband.

For Stanton, divorce offered women a form of self-emancipation and also created the possibility of a reconfigured marriage. For religious conservatives, likewise, divorce recreated those joined together in matrimony into selfish, merely "emancipated" individuals. On the other hand, if one asks why wives and husbands actually divorced throughout the nineteenth and most of the twentieth centuries, the answer is clear: in order to remarry. Divorce was almost always the precondition to remarriage after the first marriage had already fallen apart. Until recently, being married was central to the identity of an adult man or woman. In addition, marriage provided the necessary labor and care of another adult. Women in particular depended on the income provided by a husband. In the early years of the twenty-first century, in a world where women and men can survive, perhaps even flourish, without a spouse, divorce no longer implied remarriage. Some critics saw divorce as a cause of female impoverishment and victimization. Others blamed the self-emancipation of divorce, leading predictably to child rearing in single-parent (typically mother-headed) households, for a variety of general social ills and particular harms to vulnerable children. Debates over divorce and its significance in American society and human relationships continued, even as divorce had become a right available to all.

BIBLIOGRAPHY

Basch, Norma. *Framing American Divorce: From the Revolutionary Generation to the Victorians.* Berkeley: University of California Press, 1999.

Brown, Kathleen M. *Good Wives, Nasty Wenches, and Anxious Patriarchs: Gender, Race, and Power in Colonial Virginia.* Published for the Institute for Early American History and Culture, Williamsburg, Va. Chapel Hill: University of North Carolina Press, 1996.

Caldwell, Kathleen L. "Not Ozzie and Harriet: Postwar Divorce and the American Liberal Welfare State." *Law and Social Inquiry* 23, no. 1 (Winter 1998): 1–54.

Clark, Elizabeth Battelle. "Matrimonial Bonds: Slavery and Divorce in Nineteenth-Century America." *Law and History Review* 8, no. 1 (Spring 1990): 25–54.

Cott, Nancy. "Divorce and the Changing Status of Women in Eighteenth-Century Massachusetts." *William and Mary Quarterly*, 3d. Ser., 33, no. 4. (October 1976): 586–614.

———. *Public Vows: A History of Marriage and the Nation.* Cambridge, Mass.: Harvard University Press, 2000.

Friedman, Lawrence. "Rights of Passage: Divorce Law in Historical Perspective." *Oregon Law Review* 63 (1984): 649–669.

Grossberg, Michael. *Governing the Hearth: Law and the Family in Nineteenth-Century America.* Chapel Hill: University of North Carolina Press, 1985.

Hartog, Hendrik. *Man and Wife in America, a History.* Cambridge, Mass.: Harvard University Press, 2000.

May, Elaine Tyler. *Great Expectations: Marriage and Divorce in Post-Victorian America.* Chicago: University of Chicago Press, 1980.

O'Neill, William L. *Divorce in the Progressive Era.* New Haven, Conn.: Yale University Press, 1967.

Phillips, Roderick. *Putting Asunder: A History of Divorce in Western Society.* New York: Cambridge University Press, 1988.

Stanley, Amy Dru. *From Bondage to Contract: Wage Labor, Marriage, and the Market in the Age of Slave Emancipation.* New York: Cambridge University Press, 1998.

Stone, Lawrence. *Road to Divorce: England 1530–1987.* New York: Oxford University Press, 1990.

Hendrik Hartog

See also **Family; Marriage.**

"DIXIE." The song "Dixie" traditionally is attributed to the white minstrel violinist Daniel Decatur Emmett. An immediate popular hit in 1859, "Dixie" was adopted—with new lyrics by General Albert Pike—as the Confederate anthem during the Civil War. A century later "Dixie" became inextricable from the massive resistance of white southerners to the civil rights movement. However, historical affiliations of "Dixie" with blackface minstrelsy and white southern racism have been complicated by late-twentieth-century scholarship associating the song with African American neighbors of Emmett in Mount Vernon, Ohio.

The standard account is that Emmett wrote "Dixie"—originally entitled "I Wish I Was in Dixie's Land"—for Bryant's Minstrels, who with Emmett himself on violin, premiered the song on Broadway on 4 April 1859. The etymology of the word "Dixie" is highly debatable: it has been traced to a slaveholder named Dixey; to "dix," a ten-dollar note issued in Louisiana; and to the Mason-Dixon Line. Emmett himself commented that "Dixie" was a showman's term for the black South. Hence, many scholars have interpreted Emmett's song as an inauthentic and racist product of northern minstrelsy. By contrast, critics interrogating Emmett's authorship of "Dixie" have usually questioned how a man from Ohio could have come into contact with the southern black culture evoked in the song. However, Howard and Judith Sacks have demonstrated, in *Way up North in Dixie: A Black Family's Claim to the Confederate Anthem* (1993), that Emmett could have learned "Dixie" from the Snowdens, an African American family of musicians resident in Emmett's hometown, Mount Vernon. Their book further argues that the original lyrics of "Dixie" may be the semi-autobiographical account of Ellen Snowden, formerly a slave in Maryland.

BIBLIOGRAPHY

Nathan, Hans. *Dan Emmett and the Rise of Early Negro Minstrelsy.* Norman: University of Oklahoma Press, 1962.

Sacks, Howard L., and Judith Rose Sacks. *Way up North in Dixie: A Black Family's Claim to the Confederate Anthem.* Washington, D.C.: Smithsonian Institution Press, 1993.

Martyn Bone

See also **Minstrel Shows.**

DNA (deoxyribonucleic acid) is a nucleic acid that carries genetic information. The study of DNA launched the science of MOLECULAR BIOLOGY, transformed the study of genetics, and led to the cracking of the biochemical code of life. Understanding DNA has facilitated GENETIC ENGINEERING, the genetic manipulation of various organisms; has enabled cloning, the asexual reproduction of identical copies of genes and organisms; has allowed for genetic fingerprinting, the identification of an individual by the distinctive patterns of his or her DNA; and made possible the use of GENETICS to predict, diagnose, prevent, and treat disease.

Discovering DNA

In the late nineteenth century, biologists noticed structural differences between the two main cellular regions, the nucleus and the cytoplasm. The nucleus attracted attention because short, stringy objects appeared, doubled, then disappeared during the process of cell division. Scientists began to suspect that these objects, dubbed chromosomes, might govern heredity. To understand the operation of the nucleus and the chromosomes, scientists needed to determine their chemical composition.

Swiss physiologist Friedrich Miescher first isolated "nuclein"—DNA—from the nuclei of human pus cells in 1869. Although he recognized nuclein as distinct from other well-known organic compounds like fats, proteins, and carbohydrates, Miescher remained unsure about its hereditary potential. Nuclein was renamed nucleic acid in 1889, and for the next forty years, biologists debated the purpose of the compound.

In 1929, Phoebus Aaron Levene, working with yeast at New York's Rockefeller Institute, described the basic chemistry of DNA. Levene noted that phosphorus bonded to a sugar (either ribose or deoxyribose, giving rise to the two major nucleic acids, RNA and DNA), and supported one of four chemical "bases" in a structure he called a nucleotide. Levene insisted that nucleotides only joined in four-unit-long chains, molecules too simple to transmit hereditary information.

Levene's conclusions remained axiomatic until 1944, when Oswald Avery, a scientist at the Rockefeller Institute, laid the groundwork for the field of molecular genetics. Avery continued the 1920s-era research of British biologist Fred Griffiths, who worked with pneumococci, the bacteria responsible for pneumonia. Griffiths had found that pneumococci occurred in two forms, the disease-causing S-pneumococci, and the harmless R-pneumococci. Griffiths mixed dead S-type bacteria with live R-type bacteria. When rats were inoculated with the mixture, they developed pneumonia. Apparently, Griffiths concluded, something had transformed the harmless R-type bacteria into their virulent cousin. Avery surmised that the transforming agent must be a molecule that contained genetic information. Avery shocked himself, and the scientific community, when he isolated the transforming agent and found that it was DNA, thereby establishing the molecular basis of heredity.

DNA's Molecular Structure

Erwin Chargaff, a biochemist at Columbia University, confirmed and refined Avery's conclusion that DNA was complex enough to carry genetic information. In 1950, Chargaff reported that DNA exhibited a phenomenon he dubbed a complementary relationship. The four DNA bases—adenine, cytosine, guanine, and thymine (A, C, G, T, identified earlier by Levene)—appeared to be paired. That is, any given sample of DNA contained equal amounts of G and C, and equal amounts of A and T; guanine was the complement to cytosine, as adenine was to thymine. Chargaff also discovered that the ratio of GC to AT differed widely among different organisms. Rather than Levene's short molecules, DNA could now be reconceived as a gigantic macromolecule, composed of varying ratios of the base complements strung together. Thus, the length of DNA differed between organisms.

Even as biochemists described DNA's chemistry, molecular physicists attempted to determine DNA's shape. Using a process called X-ray crystallography, chemist Rosalind Franklin and physicist Maurice Wilkins, working together at King's College London in the early 1950s, debated whether DNA had a helical shape. Initial measurements indicated a single helix, but later experiments left Franklin and Wilkins undecided between a double and a triple helix. Both Chargaff and Franklin were one step away from solving the riddle of DNA's structure. Chargaff understood base complementarity but not its relation to molecular structure; Franklin understood general structure but not how complementarity necessitated a double helix.

In 1952, an iconoclastic research team composed of an American geneticist, James Watson, and a British physicist, Francis Crick, resolved the debate and unlocked DNA's secret. The men used scale-model atoms to construct a model of the DNA molecule. Watson and Crick initially posited a helical structure, but with the bases radiating outward from a dense central helix. After meeting with Chargaff, Watson and Crick learned that the GC and AT ratios could indicate chemical bonds; hydrogen atoms could bond the guanine and cytosine, but could not

James Watson. The recipient of the 1962 Nobel Prize in physiology or medicine—along with British colleague Francis Crick and physicist Maurice Wilkins—and a model of the double-helix structure of DNA, which Watson and Crick discovered a decade earlier. © UPI/CORBIS-BETTMANN

bond either base to adenine or thymine. The inverse also proved true, since hydrogen could bond adenine to thymine. Watson and Crick assumed these weak chemical links and made models of the nucleotide base pairs GC and AT. They then stacked the base-pair models one atop the other, and saw that the phosphate and sugar components of each nucleotide bonded to form two chains with one chain spinning "up" the molecule, the other spinning "down" the opposite side. The resulting DNA model resembled a spiral staircase—the famous double helix.

Watson and Crick described their findings in an epochal 1953 paper published in the journal *Nature.* Watson and Crick had actually solved two knotty problems simultaneously: the structure of DNA and how DNA replicated itself in cell division—an idea they elaborated in a second pathbreaking paper in *Nature.* If one split the long DNA molecule at the hydrogen bonds between the bases, then each half provided a framework for assembling its counterpart, creating two complete molecules—the doubling of chromosomes during cell division. Although it would take another thirty years for crystallographic confirmation of the double helix, Crick, Watson, and Rosalind Franklin's collaborator Maurice Wilkins shared the 1962 Nobel Prize in physiology or medicine (Franklin had died in 1958). The study of molecular genetics exploded in the wake of Watson and Crick's discovery.

Once scientists understood the structure of DNA molecules, they focused on decoding the DNA in chromosomes—determining which base combinations created structural genes (those genes responsible for manufacturing amino acids, the building blocks of life) and which combinations created regulator genes (those that trigger the operation of structural genes). Between 1961 and 1966, Marshall Nirenberg and Heinrich Matthaei, working at the National Institutes of Health, cracked the genetic code. By 1967, scientists had a complete listing of the sixty-four three-base variations that controlled the production of life's essential twenty amino acids. Researchers, however, still lacked a genetic map precisely locating specific genes on individual chromosomes. Using enzymes to break apart or splice together nucleic acids, American scientists, like David Baltimore, helped develop recombinant DNA or genetic engineering technology in the 1970s and 1980s.

Genetic engineering paved the way for genetic mapping and increased genetic control, raising a host of political and ethical concerns. The contours of this debate have shifted with the expansion of genetic knowledge. In the 1970s, activists protested genetic engineering and scientists decried for-profit science; thirty years later, protesters organized to fight the marketing of genetically modified foods as scientists bickered over the ethics of cloning humans. Further knowledge about DNA offers both promises and problems that will only be resolved by the cooperative effort of people in many fields—medicine, law, ethics, social policy, and the humanities—not just molecular biology.

DNA and American Culture

Like atomic technology, increased understanding of DNA and genetics has had both intended and unintended consequences, and it has captured the public imagination. The popular media readily communicated the simplicity and elegance of DNA's structure and action to nonscientists. Unfortunately, media coverage of advances in DNA technology has often obscured the biological complexity of these developments. Oversimplifications in the media, left uncorrected by scientists, have allowed DNA to be invoked as a symbol for everything from inanimate objects to the absolute essence of human potential.

DNA's biological power has translated into great cultural power as the image of the double helix entered the iconography of America after 1953. As Dorothy Nellkin and M. Susan Lindee have shown, references to DNA and the power of genetics are ubiquitous in modern culture. Inanimate objects like cars are advertised as having "a genetic advantage." Movies and television dramas have plots that revolve around DNA, genetic technology, and the power of genetics to shape lives. Humorists use DNA as the punch line of jokes to explain the source of human foibles. Consumer and popular culture's appropriation of DNA to signify fine or poor quality has merged with media oversimplifications to give rise to a new wave of hereditarian thinking in American culture.

The DNA technology that revolutionized criminology, genealogy, and medicine convinced many Americans that DNA governed not only people's physical development, but also their psychological and social behavior. Genetic "fingerprints" that allow forensics experts to discern identity from genetic traces left at a crime scene, or that determine ancestral ties by sampling tissue from long-dead individuals, have been erroneously touted as foolproof and seem to equate peoples' identities and behavior with their DNA. Genomic research allows scientists to identify genetic markers that indicate increased risk for certain diseases. This development offers hope for preventive medicine, even as it raises the specter of genetic discrimination and renewed attempts to engineer a eugenic master race. In the beginning of the twenty-first century, more scientists began to remind Americans that DNA operates within a nested series of environments—nuclear, cellular, organismic, ecological, and social—and these conditions affect DNA's operation and its expression. While DNA remains a powerful cultural symbol, people invoke it in increasingly complex ways that more accurately reflect how DNA actually influences life.

Without question, in the 131 years spanning Miescher's isolation of nuclein, Crick and Watson's discovery of DNA's structure, and the completion of the human genome, biologists have revolutionized humanity's understanding of, and control over, life itself. American contributions to molecular biology rank with the harnessing of atomic fission and the landing of men on the moon as signal scientific and technological achievements.

BIBLIOGRAPHY

Chargaff, Erwin. *Heraclitean Fire?: Sketches from a Life before Nature.* New York: Rockefeller University Press, 1978. Bitter but provocative.

Judson, Horace Freeland. *The Eighth Day of Creation: Makers of the Revolution in Biology.* New York: Simon and Schuster, 1979. Readable history of molecular biology.

Kay, Lily E. *Who Wrote the Book of Life?: A History of the Genetic Code.* Stanford, Calif.: Stanford University Press, 2000.

Kevles, Daniel J., and Leroy Hood, eds. *The Code of Codes: Scientific and Social Issues in the Human Genome Project.* Cambridge, Mass.: Harvard University Press, 1992.

Lagerkvist, Ulf. *DNA Pioneers and Their Legacy.* New Haven, Conn.: Yale University Press, 1998.

Nelkin, Dorothy, and M. Susan Lindee. *The DNA Mystique: The Gene as Cultural Icon.* New York: W. H. Freeman, 1995. Excellent cultural interpretation of DNA in the 1990s.

Watson, James D. *The Double-Helix.* New York: Atheneum, 1968. Crotchety account of discovery.

Watson, James D., and F. H. C. Crick. "Molecular Structure of Nucleic Acid: A Structure for Deoxyribonucleic Acid." *Nature* 171 (1953): 737–738.

Gregory Michael Dorr

See also **Biochemistry; Eugenics; Human Genome Project.**

DODGE CITY. Located on the Arkansas River in southwestern Kansas, Dodge City owes its location and much of its initial economic activity to its position as a "break in transport" where different forms of transportation meet. In September 1872, when the Santa Fe Railroad reached a point five miles east of Fort Dodge, a settlement originally known as Buffalo City emerged. For several years, hunters hauled bison hides by the cartload to Dodge City. By the late 1870s, ranchers were driving their cattle to Dodge City, whence they were shipped to feed lots and markets in the East. In 2000, Dodge City remained a regional center of the trade in livestock and other agricultural products, and its population was 25,176.

BIBLIOGRAPHY

Haywood, C. Robert. *The Merchant Prince of Dodge City: The Life and Times of Robert M. Wright.* Norman: University of Oklahoma Press, 1998.

Andrew C. Isenberg

See also **Arkansas River; Cattle Drives; Cowboys; Kansas;** *and picture (overleaf).*

DODGE CITY TRAIL was one of the famous cattle trails from west Texas to the railway terminal in Kansas. Herds of cattle were gathered along the trail at such Texas points as Mason, Brady, Coleman, and Fort Griffin. Crossing the Red River at Doan's Store near Vernon, the moving herds continued through Fort Supply in western Oklahoma to Dodge City. Texas cattle and cattlemen became the foundations of Dodge City's economy and rough culture. During the decade 1875–1885 the number of cattle driven up this trail amounted to several hundred thousand head. Local farmers eventually closed the trail to cattle drives in 1885.

BIBLIOGRAPHY

Haywood, C. Robert. *Trails South: The Wagon-Road Economy in the Dodge City–Panhandle Region.* Norman: University of Oklahoma Press. 1986.

Jordan, Terry G. *Trails to Texas: Southern Roots of Western Cattle Ranching,* Lincoln: University of Nebraska Press, 1981.

Lamar, Howard R. *Texas Crossings: The Lone Star State and the American Far West, 1836–1986.* Austin: University of Texas Press, 1991.

L. W. Newton/H. S.

See also **Abilene Trail; Cattle Drives.**

"Dodge City Peace Commission." This version of a famous 1883 photograph (another includes an eighth man), published in the *National Police Gazette* with this mock title, shows the legendary Wyatt Earp (*seated second from left*) and Bat Masterson (*standing at right*) back in the booming cow town to help their friend Luke Short (*standing, center*) keep his saloon.

DOLLAR DIPLOMACY involved arrangements by which insolvent foreign governments gained access to U.S. private bank loans in return for direct U.S. financial supervision or for acting as part of an economic consortium of great powers. Often U.S. financial experts tied to the loan process assumed the tasks of fiscal reorganization and administrative management within the client country, while U.S. government emissaries orchestrated the arrangements. Imposed fiscal reforms included adoption of the gold standard, "scientific" tax reform, and administrative rationalization.

The phrase is a loose one, indiscriminately applied to decades of economic policies ranking from trade with British and Spanish colonies to penetration by multinational corporations. In its most conventional sense, it focuses on the presidency of William Howard Taft. In his first annual message, dated 7 December 1909, Taft said, "Today, more than ever before, American capital is seeking investment in foreign countries." In his final annual message, dated 3 December 1912, he boasted that his administration was characterized as "substituting dollars for bullets." Secretary of State Philander Knox, an avid promoter of dollar diplomacy, well articulated such goals on 15 June 1910: "The problem of good government is inextricably interwoven with that of economic prosperity and sound finance." According to Taft-Knox tenets, loans from U.S. business, or at least from multinational groups in which U.S. business participated, could expedite the repayment of crippling debts while launching prosperity. In the eyes of their framers, who envisioned "every diplomat a salesman," the loans-for-supervision arrangements would aid the U.S. economy by alleviating overproduction, supplying needed manufactured goods to underdeveloped nations, and offering monopolized spheres for

American investors. Eventually, economic progress, political stability, and the spread of Western, indeed U.S., "civilization" would result. Of necessity, the policy often involved U.S. competition with Europe and Japan in the developing countries, centering on such matters as buying bonds, floating loans, building railroads, and establishing banks. When the contemporary press first used the term "dollar diplomacy," Taft took umbrage, saying the label entirely ignored "a most useful office to be performed by a government in its dealing with foreign governments."

Caribbean

The Caribbean served as a major focal point, for there the United States had its eye on strategic as well as commercial interests, particularly in light of the ongoing construction of the Panama Canal. Knox remarked that in the Caribbean "the malady of revolutions and financial collapse is most acute precisely . . . where it is most dangerous to us."

Soon after he assumed office in 1909, Knox wanted American bankers to assume the debt Honduras owed to British investors. In 1911, he signed a treaty with the Honduran minister allowing American bankers to refund that nation's foreign debt and establish an American customs receivership. The Honduran government, however, refused to ratify the convention. Knox was more successful in Haiti in 1910, persuading four New York banking firms to invest in Haiti's national bank to aid in currency stabilization.

Nicaragua, however, remained the classic case of dollar diplomacy. In 1909, the United States supported a rebellion against the dictator José Santos Zelaya and his successor José Madriz, sending marines to the Nicaraguan city of Bluefields to protect foreign nationals and property. In 1911, because of U.S. backing, Adolfo Díaz, the former secretary of the United States–Nicaragua concession, became Nicaragua's president. On 6 June 1911, Knox signed a treaty with the Nicaraguan minister establishing a U.S. customs receivership and enabling two New York banking firms to refund Nicaragua's foreign debt. Democrats in the U.S. Senate, however, blocked ratification of the Knox-Castrillo Treaty. While the Senate was debating the matter, American bankers began to rehabilitate Nicaraguan finances. At the State Department's request, New York bankers advanced $1.5 million, receiving in return majority control of the state railways and the National Bank of Nicaragua. Later in the same year, the banking houses appointed an American receiver-general, who was approved by both governments.

Díaz, however, lacked popular support. In 1912, Zelaya and his Liberal Party launched a revolt. Amid widespread disorder, insurgents seized U.S. properties, and thirty-three Americans and more than a thousand Nicaraguans were killed. Zelaya would have succeeded had Taft not sent 2,700 marines and several warships to suppress the uprising. These marines remained for many years, intensifying anti-U.S. feelings in Latin America.

East Asia

The objectives of dollar diplomacy in East Asia were nearly as ambitious as those in Central America. In Asia, Willard Straight, a former U.S. diplomat who represented various banking groups in China, was highly influential in pressing for a more active American role. In 1909, because of the crucial role played by railroads in China's economic development, Straight and Knox demanded that American financiers be allowed to join a major British-French-German consortium. The group had contracted with the Chinese government to build a network of railroads, including a route between Beijing and Guangzhou (Canton). Despite the hostility of the European powers, Knox got his way, and an American banking syndicate formed by J. P. Morgan and Company was admitted. The entire project, however, eventually was aborted. Knox also proposed a multilateral loan aimed at currency reform, but the overthrow of the Manchu government in 1911 terminated the scheme.

The efforts of Straight and Knox to neutralize Manchuria in 1909 and to open it to the commerce of all nations also were unsuccessful. The two Americans sought to form a consortium of American, European, and Japanese bankers who would lend China sufficient funds to purchase the Chinese Eastern Railroad, owned by Russia, and the South Manchurian Railroad, owned by Japan. In January 1910, however, Russia and Japan vetoed the plan. The British also opposed the plan, as they were encouraging Japanese expansion in Manchuria to keep Japan safely away from their own sphere of influence.

Dollar diplomacy had few successes. As seen in Honduras, Nicaragua, and China, it gained none of its objectives. At the same time, it deepened the antagonism of both the Latin Americans and the Japanese.

BIBLIOGRAPHY

Munro, Dana Gardner. *Intervention and Dollar Diplomacy in the Caribbean, 1900–1921.* Princeton, N.J.: Princeton University Press, 1964.

Rosenberg, Emily S. "Revisiting Dollar Diplomacy: Narratives of Money and Manliness." *Diplomatic History* 22, no. 2 (spring 1998): 155–176.

Scholes, Walter V., and Marie V. Scholes. *The Foreign Policies of the Taft Administration.* Columbia: University of Missouri Press, 1970.

Trani, Eugene P. "Dollar Diplomacy." In *Encyclopedia of American Foreign Policy: Studies of the Principal Movements and Ideas.* Vol. 2. Rev. ed. Edited by Alexander DeConde et al. New York: Scribners, 2002.

Justus D. Doenecke

See also **China, Relations with; Foreign Policy; Haiti, Relations with; Latin America, Relations with; Nicaragua, Relations with.**

DOLLAR SIGN. Popular belief often ascribes the origin of the dollar sign ($) to a mark on government mail-bags standing for U.S., or Uncle Sam. Another common story claims that the symbol represents the pillars of Hercules on the Spanish dollar. A third explanation for its origin identifies it as a conversion of the old Spanish symbol for the Spanish dollar. Most probably, however, the dollar sign is a conventionalized combination of the letters *p* and *s* for pesos. As early as 1788, a government clerk used such a mark, and the present symbol came into general use shortly after that time.

Neil Carothers / A. E.

See also **Currency and Coinage; Money; Treasury, Department of the.**

DOLLAR-A-YEAR MAN. When the United States entered World War I in 1917, the moral fervor of the American commitment, inspired by President Woodrow Wilson's ringing call for a "war to end all wars," motivated a large number of prominent merchants, manufacturers, bankers, professional men, and others to enter the service of the government as executives in departments in which they were expert. For their service they accepted only a token salary of one dollar per year, plus their necessary expenses. These federal appointees, and others who later followed their example, served primarily in times of national emergency, such as during the world wars.

BIBLIOGRAPHY

Walter, David O. *American Government at War.* Chicago: R. D. Irwin, 1942.

Alvin F. Harlow / C. W.

See also **Volunteerism; World War I, Economic Mobilization for.**

DOMESTIC VIOLENCE encompasses a range of actions, including assault, battery, rape, and murder, committed by someone to whom the victim is intimately related. Intimate relations include spouses, sexual partners, parents, children, siblings, extended family members, and dating relationships. Although victims of domestic violence include both men and women, females are affected disproportionately. According to the surgeon general, domestic violence is the leading cause of injury to women in the United States.

Historically, social and cultural responses to domestic violence have been complex. Americans have differed over what behaviors constitute abuse, to whom responsibility should be assigned, and what relief victims should receive. The evolution of legal doctrines concerning domestic violence has been predicated on the question of whether abuse committed by intimate relations constitutes a matter of private or public concern. A movement to define protection from domestic violence as a civil right entitled to constitutional protection emerged at the end of the twentieth century.

Common Law

Anglo-American common law tradition held that the male head of household possessed the authority to act as both disciplinarian and protector of all those who were dependent on him. The concept of the household was broader than that of the nuclear family for it included extended kin, servants, apprentices, and slaves in addition to wife and children. In the agrarian societies of England and colonial America, members of a household worked together as an economic unit; therefore the law also treated the household as a single entity and granted full legal status only to its male head. The household head acted as the unit's representative; individual members did not usually enjoy legal recognition as separate persons. Under the category of laws known as coverture, a married woman's identity merged with that of her husband. As an individual she could not own property, vote, sign contracts, or keep wages earned by employment outside the household.

Common law allowed the male head considerable discretion in controlling the behavior of the members of his household. In certain cases husbands might even be held liable for failing to control the actions of their dependents. In the American colonies the law defined extreme acts of violence or cruelty as crimes, but local community standards were the most important yardsticks by which domestic violence was defined and dealt with. In the seventeenth-century Puritan communities of New England, for example, a husband had a legal right to "use" his wife's body, but "excessive" use could be subject to prosecution. Puritan parents felt a strong sense of duty to discipline their children, whom they believed to be born naturally depraved, to save them from eternal damnation. While Puritan society tolerated a high degree of physicality in parental discipline, the community drew a line at which it regarded parental behavior as abuse rather than acceptable discipline. Those who crossed the line were brought before the courts.

The law of slavery in the United States granted the master virtually complete authority in punishing his chattel property. Although every slave state defined killing a slave as murder, the historical record amply demonstrates that extreme violence by masters against their slaves was common. Because slave populations greatly outnumbered whites in many communities, whites may have regarded strict control over slaves as necessary to the preservation of the social order. Again, local community standards played a significant role in drawing the boundaries between acceptable and unacceptable levels of violence within a slave-owning household.

The Nineteenth Century

A number of social changes during the nineteenth century altered the public perception of domestic violence, and these changes were reflected in the law as well. The twin forces of industrialization and urbanization loosened the community ties that had traditionally served as important regulators of domestic behavior, and over time victims of domestic violence became more dependent on the police and courts for protection, although not always with positive results. A case brought before the North Carolina Supreme Court in 1864, *State v. Jesse Black*, illustrates the trend. Jesse Black had been found guilty of assault and battery in criminal court for seizing his estranged wife by the hair, pinning her to the ground and holding her there, and severely injuring her throat. The state supreme court, in reversing Black's conviction, held that while the abuse could be considered severe by local standards, the wife had provoked the quarrel, therefore Black was simply controlling her outburst in a manner allowable under the law. As this case demonstrates, in the mid-nineteenth century women could turn to the law for protection from domestic violence, but the common law tradition allowing men wide discretionary authority in controlling their wives retained its influence in the reasoning of the courts.

Even when the law did find in their favor, women and children who were victims of abuse lacked the legal standing and economic power necessary to survive outside of the household, and so they often gained no actual relief. Early women's rights advocates redefined women's legal dependency on men as an injustice rather than merely an accepted social convention and worked to reform property and child custody laws to allow women greater control over their lives. The first conference devoted to the topic of women's rights, held in 1848 in Seneca Falls, New York, produced a declaration that in part criticized the law for granting husbands the power to "administer chastisement" to their wives.

By midcentury commercial capitalism had created a large middle class whose attitudes and values exerted considerable influence over American society as a whole. The new middle-class view regarded mothers and children less as productive members of the household and more as fulfillers of the family's spiritual and emotional needs. While violence within middle-class households remained largely hidden from public view, some reformers working in private charitable organizations began efforts to ameliorate the problem as they observed it among poor and working-class families. The WOMAN'S CHRISTIAN TEMPERANCE UNION (WCTU), the single largest women's organization of the nineteenth century, focused on domestic violence as the most serious consequence of alcohol consumption. The WCTU invariably portrayed women as the helpless victims of male drunkenness, rarely publicly recognizing women as either alcoholics or abusers.

Most nineteenth-century reformers, however, viewed children as the primary victims of domestic violence. In actuality the majority of cases brought to their attention constituted child neglect rather than physical abuse. They exhibited little sympathy, however, for mothers who, because of the urgent need to earn family income, failed to meet middle-class expectations for the proper education, hygiene, and supervision of children. Abused women, to access the protective services they needed for themselves, commonly claimed that male members of the household were injuring the children. These services tended to be quite informal and highly personalized interactions between agency workers and their clients.

The Progressive Era

A change in American social welfare practices occurred in the last quarter of the nineteenth century. Social reformers of the Progressive Era (c. 1890–1920) believed problems such as chronic poverty, poor health, and domestic violence among poor and working-class Americans to be the result of larger systemic forces rather than the particularized problems of individuals. They worked to create a more efficient system for addressing domestic violence. Protective services became the province of professionals trained in the social sciences or the law rather than philanthropists, and both private and public relief organizations developed into more bureaucratized and rational, although also more impersonal, agencies. In addition Progressives urged that solving the problem required more active involvement on the part of the state.

By the early twentieth century the increasing social recognition of adolescence as a distinct stage of human development became an important dimension of efforts to address domestic violence. Largely influenced by the work of the psychologist G. Stanley Hall, Progressive reformers extended the chronological boundaries of childhood into the midteens and sought laws mandating that children stay in school and out of the workforce. Reformers also worked for the establishment of a juvenile justice system that would allow judges to consider the special psychological needs of adolescents and keep them separated from adult criminals in order to protect them from harmful influences. Consequently juvenile courts began to play a central role in adjudicating cases of domestic violence.

Individual states began to allow women more control over property and child custody, and in 1920 the Nineteenth Amendment prohibited states from denying women the vote. But while they had gained a measure of legal equality, most women still lacked sufficient economic and social resources to escape abuse in their households.

Although it is unlikely that its incidence actually decreased over the following decades, domestic violence as a social rather than a private concern retreated from its Progressive Era prominence. When abuse was addressed in popular media, such as magazines, films, and television, it was interpreted as the result of individuals' psychological weaknesses rather than as a systemic problem integrally tied to lingering social, political, and economic inequalities among the members of a household. Often these popular portrayals indicted mothers for being either too permissive or too demanding in raising their sons.

Thus women were commonly identified as the responsible agents in perpetuating domestic violence rather than its disadvantaged victims. Such an unfavorable cultural climate obscured the social and economic roots of the problem and was a barrier to individuals bringing their claims to the courts for redress.

Civil Rights

A sea change occurred in the 1960s as the product of two powerful and related forces, the civil rights movement and the emergence of modern feminism. The long crusade to bring full citizenship rights to African Americans engendered new movements to empower the poor and the disenfranchised. Campaigns for safe and adequate housing, equal opportunity in employment and education, and welfare rights redefined the many benefits of America's prosperous postwar years as entitlements for all citizens rather than privileges for a few. At the same time feminist legal scholars and political activists identified lingering manifestations of women's traditional social, economic, and legal subordination to men as severe impediments to full equality. Women's rights activists reclaimed domestic violence as a problem worthy of legal and social redress rather than merely an unfortunate dimension of intimate relations between men and women. Shelters for battered women proliferated as a response to this change.

In the 1960s the liberal Warren Court rendered a series of opinions that greatly expanded the protections the Constitution offered for citizens' rights. These interpretations were founded in the Fourteenth Amendment's guarantee that "no state shall deprive any person of life, liberty, or property without due process of law; nor deny to any person within its jurisdiction the equal protection of the laws." The Court's expansive reading of the amendment defined new rights of citizenship. In 1964 Congress passed a landmark Civil Rights Act that protected citizens against discrimination in housing, employment, and education based on race or gender. Within this renewed climate of civil rights activism, advocates for domestic violence victims sought to add protection against abuse to the growing list of citizens' constitutional protections.

In 1989 the Rehnquist Court heard the case *DeShaney v. Winnebago County Department of Social Services.* The case originated in an incident in which a custodial father had beaten his four-year-old son so badly that the child's brain was severely damaged. Emergency surgery revealed several previous brain injuries. Wisconsin law defined the father's actions as a crime, and he was sentenced to two years in prison. But the boy's noncustodial mother sued the Winnebago County Department of Social Services, claiming that caseworkers had been negligent in failing to intervene to help the child despite repeated reports by hospital staff of suspected abuse. Her claim rested in the Fourteenth Amendment, asserting that the state's failure to help her son amounted to a violation of his civil rights. The U.S. Supreme Court, however, ruled that the Fourteenth Amendment protects citizens' civil rights from violations arising from actions taken by the state, not from actions the state may fail to take. In other words, individuals do not enjoy an affirmative right to protection by the state from violence committed by a family member in the privacy of the home.

Critics of the *DeShaney* decision worked to reform the law to make protection against domestic violence a matter of civil rights. Feminists argued that, because the majority of abuse victims are women, domestic violence constitutes not solely a private wrong but a form of gender discrimination. The ever-present threat of violence, they asserted, prevents women from realizing their full potential in employment, in education, and in exercising the privileges of citizenship. In the early 1990s the states formed gender bias task force commissions, twenty-one of which reported that a number of pervasive practices in their legal systems resulted in discrimination against women. For example, they documented that crimes disproportionately affecting women tended to be treated much less seriously by law enforcement and the courts than comparable crimes in which the victims were men. In response Congress enacted the 1994 VIOLENCE AGAINST WOMEN ACT (VAWA), the first federal legislation to provide legal remedies for domestic violence. The act's provisions required states to give full faith and credit to protection orders issued in other states; directed federal funding to increase the effectiveness of law enforcement and to support shelters for battered women; and amended the Federal Rules of Evidence to increase protections for rape victims. Most significantly the act established protection from gender-motivated violence as a civil right and allowed women to bring civil lawsuits to redress violations.

In 2000 the U.S. Supreme Court struck down the civil rights provisions of the VAWA. A university student in Virginia had been raped in her dormitory room by three assailants who had also verbally indicated their disdain for her as a female both during and after the rape. She subsequently filed suit against her attackers. In *United States v. Morrison* (2000) the Court ruled that Congress did not have the power to legislate the civil rights remedies contained in the VAWA. In providing them Congress relied on its constitutional authority over interstate commerce and its power to enforce the provisions of the Fourteenth Amendment safeguarding individual rights against infringement by the states. But the Court found that congressional powers under the commerce clause did not extend to regulating this area of law in the states. Further, because the civil rights remedies in the VAWA pertained to the actions of private individuals rather than the states, they did not have a basis in the Fourteenth Amendment. The Court's decision in *United States v. Morrison* has been both affirmed and criticized by legal scholars and the public. Disputes over the private and public dimensions of domestic violence therefore continued into the twenty-first century.

BIBLIOGRAPHY

Gordon, Linda. *Heroes of Their Own Lives: The Politics and History of Family Violence: Boston, 1880–1960.* New York: Viking, 1988.

MacKinnon, Catharine A. *Sex Equality.* New York: Foundation Press, 2001.

Taylor, Betty, Sharon Rush, and Robert J. Munro, eds. *Feminist Jurisprudence, Women, and the Law: Critical Essays, Research Agenda, and Bibliography.* Littleton, Colo.: F. B. Rothman, 1999.

Wallace, Harvey. *Family Violence: Legal, Medical, and Social Perspectives.* Boston: Allyn and Bacon, 1996.

Lynne Curry

See also **Child Abuse; Civil Rights and Liberties; Common Law; Marriage; Rape; Slavery; Violence; Women's Rights Movement.**

DOMINICAN REPUBLIC, RELATIONS WITH.

Since the mid-nineteenth century, diplomatic relations between the United States and the Dominican Republic have generally been guided by the strategic and economic interests of the United States. Those interests often strained relations between the two governments, and on more than one occasion, the United States resorted to military force to implement its policies in the Caribbean nation.

The United States did not establish official diplomatic relations with the Dominican Republic until 1866, over two decades after Dominican independence from neighboring Haiti in 1844. The delay in recognition was attributable to a number of factors. That the Dominican Republic had been controlled by Haiti—the so-called "negro republic"—for over twenty years certainly worked against relations with the United States. Stalwart U.S. southern congressmen blocked any efforts at recognition of Haiti, and after 1844, the new nation of the Dominican Republic. While publicly they argued that no white nation should ever have official relations with "colored" nations, privately they also worried about the effect recognition of independent "black" republics would have on the nearly four million slaves in the South. During the Civil War, diplomatic relations were finally established with Haiti, but by that time, the Dominican Republic had been re-annexed by Spain. Recognition was delayed until after the Spanish departed in 1865.

The delay in official relations, however, did not indicate a lack of interest on the part of the United States. The Dominican Republic's declaration of independence in 1844 coincided with the development of "manifest destiny" in America—an expansionist philosophy that combined economic, political, social, and even religious elements into a popular cry for U.S. dominance on the North American continent and beyond. With its strategic location on Caribbean shipping lanes and its rich natural resources, the Dominican Republic was a tempting target. In 1854, journalist Jane McManus Storms Cazneau and her husband, the wealthy Texan William Cazneau, were able to secure government appointments to study the economic possibilities in the Dominican Republic. They produced a report extolling the island nation's treasure trove of resources. Surprisingly, considering the United States did not even have diplomatic relations with the Dominican Republic, they also managed to secure a treaty granting America the right to construct a naval base at Samaná Bay. The British and French already had powerful economic presences in the Dominican Republic; they were horrified by the treaty and their pressure eventually quashed the agreement before it was submitted to the U.S. Senate.

The Cazneaus proved to be prescient in one sense, however. When it became clear the United States was not going to pursue the issue further, they predicted the Dominican government, strapped for funds, would turn to Spain or another European nation for assistance. In March 1861, as America's attention focused on the rapidly approaching Civil War, Spain announced that, with the acquiescence of the Dominican government, it was re-annexing its former colony. The U.S. response was that Spain's action violated the Monroe Doctrine and issued some threatening statements. One month later, the Civil War erupted and any U.S. action toward Spain became highly unlikely. However, both the Spanish and Dominican governments had badly miscalculated. The Dominicans quickly found that Spanish rule was corrupt and harsh. Very soon, the Spanish found themselves confronted with a full-fledged revolution. The Dominican Republic became a graveyard for Spanish troops ravaged by malaria and yellow fever, and a drain on the Spanish treasury. In 1865, as the Civil War in America drew to a close, the Spanish government decided it had had enough and announced it was abandoning its Dominican protectorate. One year later, the United States formally recognized the Dominican Republic.

In the years after the Civil War, U.S. interest in the Dominican Republic continued. President Ulysses S. Grant made several attempts in 1869 and 1870 to secure American annexation of the island nation. Partisan politics, and racial fears concerning the absorption of the Dominican people into the American republic, worked to derail these plans. Despite this setback, U.S. economic relations with the Dominican Republic increased dramatically during the latter part of the nineteenth century. The growing presence of the United States pushed Germany, Great Britain, and France to take more aggressive stances toward the issue of debt collection from the perennially bankrupt Dominican government. In 1900 and again in 1903, the Europeans dispatched naval vessels to collect debts. President Theodore Roosevelt responded to these European actions by declaring the Roosevelt Corollary to the Monroe Doctrine, in which he suggested that the "chronic wrongdoing" of nations such as the Dominican Republic would force the United States to exercise an "international police power." Roosevelt ordered the sei-

Rafael Leónidas Trujillo Molina. The head of the Dominican National Army, and the generally pro-American dictator of the Dominican Republic for over thirty years. LIBRARY OF CONGRESS

zure of the customs houses in the Dominican Republic. Although the U.S. Senate refused to approve the President's actions, Roosevelt used the power of an executive agreement to secure a virtual American protectorate.

The U.S. presence did not bring the desired stability, however. In 1916, President Woodrow Wilson ordered American troops into the Dominican Republic, beginning an eight-year occupation of the nation. The occupation accelerated U.S. economic penetration of the Dominican Republic and led to the development of an American-trained and supplied national army. Conflict between the Dominicans and the occupying forces was frequent and sometimes bloody. Controversy raged over the actions of U.S. forces in the nation, and charges of torture were leveled at congressional hearings in 1921. Faced with these problems, the United States formally ended its occupation in 1924. Within six years, the head of the Dominican National Army, Rafael Leónidas Trujillo Molina, rose to assume complete control of the nation through a combination of bribery, force, and fraud.

For over three decades, Trujillo exerted his brutal rule over the Dominican Republic. Violent, corrupt, and manipulative, Trujillo nevertheless managed to maintain good relations with the United States. His dictatorial rule provided a stable climate for American investment, and during World War II, he was a willing American ally. In the postwar years, Trujillo trumpeted his anticommunism, which was enough to cement positive relations with America. By the 1950s, however, the aging despot was becoming a liability. The overthrow of another pro-American dictator in Cuba in 1959, and the rise of the leftist Fidel Castro, led American policymakers to conclude that Trujillo had outlived his usefulness. In May 1961, Trujillo was assassinated. Although there were rumors of U.S. complicity in the murder, no solid evidence emerged.

The death of Trujillo created a political vacuum in the Dominican Republic. In 1962, elections resulted in the victory of Juan Bosch. His term was short lived, however. His policies of land redistribution, agrarian reform, and his refusal to maintain Trujillo's stringent anticommunist foreign policy made him immediately suspect in American eyes. Less than two years after taking office, Bosch was forced out by a coup. Again, U.S. covert involvement was suspected. A shaky triumvirate of Dominican business leaders and military officers assumed control, but was itself faced with a countercoup in 1965. President Lyndon Johnson, claiming—wrongly—that communists were behind the insurrection, ordered American troops into the Dominican Republic. In short order, more than 20,000 U.S. troops had occupied the nation. Elections, monitored closely by the United States, took place in 1966 and resulted in the selection of Joaquin Balaguer. Balaguer's right-of-middle politics generally pleased U.S. officials, and his rule continued until 1978.

In the decades after Balaguer left office in 1978, U.S.-Dominican relations were generally friendly. The United States has kept a careful eye on Dominican elections, often eliciting cries of fraud and intimidation from the losing parties; the Dominican military always looms large in these contests. America accounts for nearly two-thirds of all Dominican imports and exports, and U.S. companies play a dominant role in the Dominican economy. The two governments have cooperated in a well-publicized attack on the drug trade and in efforts to stem the flow of illegal immigrants from the Dominican Republic into the United States.

BIBLIOGRAPHY

Atkins, G. Pope, and Larman C. Wilson. *The Dominican Republic and the United States: From Imperialism to Transnationalism.* Athens: University of Georgia Press, 1998.

Calder, Bruce J. *The Impact of Intervention: The Dominican Republic During the U.S. Occupation of 1916–1924.* Austin: University of Texas Press, 1984.

Logan, Rayford W. *Haiti and the Dominican Republic.* New York: Oxford University Press, 1968.

Roorda, Eric P. *The Dictator Next Door: The Good Neighbor Policy and the Trujillo Regime in the Dominican Republic, 1930–1945.* Durham, N.C.: Duke University Press, 1998.

Michael L. Krenn

See also **Imperialism; Latin America, Relations with; Roosevelt Corollary.**

DOMINICANS, or Order of Preachers, are part of a worldwide Roman Catholic religious community of friars founded in 1216 by Saint Dominic. The Dominicans arrived in America with the Spanish explorers. Although the first two Catholic bishops of New York—Richard L. Concanen (1808) and John Connolly (1815)—were Dominicans, the first community (organized with a democratic constitution) was established at Saint Rose in Springfield, Kentucky, in 1806. Its founder, Edward Dominic Fenwick, also established the first Catholic school for boys west of the Alleghenies (1806) and the first Catholic church in Ohio—at Somerset in 1818. In California, community life was established by José Sadoc Alemany, who was appointed bishop of Monterey (1851) and later the first archbishop of San Francisco (1853). About the same time, the Dominicans established themselves in Washington, D.C. (1852) and New York (1867).

By the 1990s, there were three Dominican provinces in the United States, with more than 1,000 priests, brothers, and sisters engaged chiefly in parochial, educational, and missionary apostates. Dominicans staff Providence College in Rhode Island and teach at many other universities, some high schools, and their own seminaries. In 1909, they organized the Holy Name Society, which, by mid-century, had a membership of over 5 million and joined an expanding list of Dominican lay organizations, including the international Dominican Youth Movement. The Dominicans publish scholarly periodicals (*The Thomist* and *Cross and Crown*) and critical editions of the writings of Saint Thomas Aquinas. Significant foreign missionary work has been done by American Dominicans in Pakistan, Peru, Chile, China, Kenya, Bolivia, Nigeria, Ghana, and the Philippines.

BIBLIOGRAPHY

Woods, Richard. *Mysticism and Prophecy: The Dominican Tradition.* Maryknoll, N.Y.: Orbis; London: DLT, 1998.

Cornelius P. Forster, O.P. / A. R.

See also **Catholicism; Franciscans; Jesuits; Missions, Foreign.**

DOMINION OF NEW ENGLAND. After Charles II (1660–1685) was restored to the English throne in 1660, the Crown took steps to limit the independence of localities within England and the American colonies. Various measures were taken to ensure that the colonies remained loyal and subordinate to Britain. The Navigation Acts restricted colonial trade in favor of English commercial interests, and in 1675 colonial policy was placed under the Lords of Trade and Plantations, a subcommittee of the king's own Privy Council. Bitter land disputes, restrictions placed on Church of England members by the Puritan government, conflict with the Indians (particularly King Philip's War), and especially mass evasion of the Navigation Acts drew the Crown's attention toward Massachusetts and New England.

Until its charter was revoked in 1684 the fiercely independent Massachusetts colony had never had a royal governor. In May 1686, however, King James II (1685–1688) carried forward plans initiated under Charles II to place the New England colonies directly under Crown control. James named Edmund Andros, a soldier and former New York governor, "Captain General and Governor in Chief of Our Territory and Dominion of New England" on 3 June 1686. Andros had jurisdiction over Massachusetts, Maine, New Hampshire, the disputed Narragansett territory, Rhode Island, and Connecticut. New York and New Jersey were added in 1688.

The Dominion government, headquartered in Boston, was modeled on the Spanish viceroyalty system, in which the Spanish crown ruled directly through appointed officials and councils. Governor Andros arrived in December 1686 with a force of sixty English soldiers and quickly moved to establish a viceregal government, consisting of the appointed governor and council but no representative assembly. The governor's appointees replaced local elected officials. Rights to jury trial and bail were restricted, the press was censored, and freedom to leave the Dominion was limited. Church of England members were favored for appointments, as Andros actively promoted the Church and dislodged Massachusetts Puritans from their formerly exclusive hold on government power. Andros even forced Puritan congregations to allow Church of England services in their meetinghouses. Though not all were sorry to see Puritan power broken, colonists united in opposition to Andros's tax and land policies. In March 1687 Andros imposed new direct and indirect taxes without any legislative consent. He infuriated colonists with his land distribution policies, especially when the Dominion government claimed title to all undistributed land that had formerly been held in common by individual towns.

By the summer of 1688 the Dominion government had completely alienated Puritan and non-Puritan colonists alike. Then in early 1689 reports arrived that William of Orange had, by invitation of parliamentary leaders, invaded England with his Dutch army and ousted James II from power. Spurred on by the still unofficial news, an uprising began in Boston on 18 April 1689. Andros was arrested after a brief siege and the colonies' former governments restored. Though Massachusetts absorbed Plymouth Colony and was placed under a royal governor in 1691, the new king, William III (1669–1702), made no renewed attempt to impose direct royal power upon the colonies.

BIBLIOGRAPHY

Johnson, Richard R. *Adjustment to Empire: The New England Colonies, 1675–1715.* New Brunswick, N.J.: Rutgers University Press, 1981.

Lovejoy, David S. *The Glorious Revolution in America.* New York: Harper and Row, 1972.

McFarlane, Anthony. *The British in the Americas: 1480–1815.* New York: Longman, 1994.

Sosin, J. M. *English America and the Revolution of 1688: Royal Administration and the Structure of Provincial Government.* Lincoln: University of Nebraska Press, 1982.

Speck, W. A. *Reluctant Revolutionaries: Englishmen and the Revolution of 1688.* Oxford: Oxford University Press, 1988.

Aaron J. Palmer

See also **Lords of Trade and Plantation; Navigation Acts; New England Colonies.**

DOMINO THEORY. For many years the domino theory was a key ideological component of America's Cold War foreign policy. The theory was first advanced during Harry S. Truman's presidency to justify an American aid package to Greece and Turkey, and President Dwight Eisenhower later applied it to Vietnam in 1954. Worried about the consequences of a communist victory there, Eisenhower said: "You have a row of dominoes set up, you knock over the first one, and what will happen to the last one is the certainty that it will go over very quickly. So you could have a beginning of a disintegration that would have the most profound influences."

Policymakers in the John F. Kennedy and Lyndon B. Johnson administrations added another dimension to the domino theory that embraced the notion of credibility. From their perspective the need to contain communist expansion in Vietnam had taken on a symbolic and global dimension in the fight against wars of national liberation. Thus the domino theory had been incorporated into a more sweeping doctrine, shaped by the need to appear strong and resolute in the face of any possible Chinese or Russian geopolitical challenge to American global interests.

BIBLIOGRAPHY

Herring, George. *America's Longest War: The United States and Vietnam, 1950–1975.* 3d ed. New York: McGraw-Hill, 1996.

Hess, Gary R. *Presidential Decisions for War: Korea, Vietnam, and the Persian Gulf.* Baltimore, Md.: Johns Hopkins University Press, 2001.

William C. Berman

See also **Cold War.**

"DON'T ASK, DON'T TELL, Don't Pursue" refers to the policy, begun in 1993, regarding lesbians and gay men in the U.S. military. Service personnel may be discharged for homosexual conduct but not simply for being gay. Therefore, military commanders do not ask military personnel about their sexual orientations or begin an investigation except upon the receipt of "credible information" of homosexual conduct. If a person acknowledges his or her homosexuality publicly, military commanders presume that he or she intends to engage in homosexual conduct. The policy was a compromise between President Bill Clinton, who sought to repeal the military's ban on gay personnel, and the opponents of that repeal in Congress and among the Joint Chiefs of Staff. Professor Charles Moskos of Northwestern University developed the policy's framework, and Senator Sam Nunn of Georgia brokered the compromise. According to those monitoring its implementation, the policy has failed to meet Clinton's goals of decreasing discharges for homosexuality and reducing harassment of lesbian and gay military personnel.

BIBLIOGRAPHY

Frank, Nathaniel. "What's Love Got to Do with It? The Real Story of Military Sociology and 'Don't Ask, Don't Tell.'" *Lingua Franca* (October 2000): 71–81.

Halley, Janet E. *Don't: A Reader's Guide to the Military's Anti-Gay Policy.* Durham, N.C.: Duke University Press, 1999.

Shawver, Lois. *And the Flag Was Still There: Straight People, Gay People, and Sexuality in the U.S. Military.* New York: Haworth Press, 1995.

Cynthia R. Poe

See also **Discrimination: Sexual Orientation; Gay and Lesbian Movement; Military Service and Minorities: Homosexuals.**

"DON'T FIRE UNTIL YOU SEE THE WHITE OF THEIR EYES." The origin of this alleged command to the American patriots at Bunker Hill on 17 June 1775 may have been Col. William Prescott's order to reserve fire and aim low because powder was scarce. Reputedly Israel Putnam passed on the order in these words: "Men, you are all marksmen—don't one of you fire until you see the white of their eyes." The British won the battle, but the patriots' stubborn resistance at Bunker Hill became a symbol of American resolve.

BIBLIOGRAPHY

Fleming, Thomas J. *Now We Are Enemies: The Story of Bunker Hill.* New York: St. Martin's Press, 1960.

Ketchum, Richard M. *Decisive Day: The Battle for Bunker Hill.* Garden City, N.Y.: Doubleday, 1974.

Charles K. Bolton / A. G.

See also **Boston, Siege of; Bunker Hill; Bunker Hill Monument; Revere's Ride.**

"DON'T GIVE UP THE SHIP," the words spoken by James Lawrence, commander of the American frigate

Chesapeake, after he fell fatally wounded in the engagement with the British frigate Shannon, thirty miles off of Boston harbor, on 1 June 1813. Despite Lawrence's brave words, the British captured the Chesapeake, and Lawrence died four days later. When Commodore Oliver Hazard Perry won his famous victory over the British on Lake Erie on 10 September 1813, he flew at the mainmast of his flagship a blue battleflag inscribed with Capt. Lawrence's dying words.

BIBLIOGRAPHY

Peabody Museum of Salem. *"Don't Give Up the Ship."* Salem: Peabody Museum, 1942.

Roosevelt, Theodore. *Naval War of 1812.* New York: G. P. Putnam's Sons, 1902

Louis H. Bolander / c. w.

See also **Great Lakes Naval Campaigns of 1812; Navy, United States; War of 1812.**

DONELSON, FORT, CAPTURE OF. In January 1862, the Confederate line of defense in the West extended from the CUMBERLAND GAP westward to Columbus, Ohio. After the capture of Fort Henry, in February 1862, Fort Donelson, twenty miles west on the CUMBERLAND RIVER, was the only remaining obstacle to a Union advance. On 13 February, Grant's troops assaulted Fort Donelson unsuccessfully. The following day the river gunboats bombarded the fort but were driven off. The next morning the Confederates counterattacked without success. During the night of 15 February the fort and more than 14,000 men were surrendered.

BIBLIOGRAPHY

Ambrose, Stephen. "The Union Command System and the Donelson Campaign." *Military Affairs* 24, no. 2 (Summer 1960): 78–86.

Cooling, Benjamin F. *Forts Henry and Donelson—The Key to the Confederate Heatland.* Knoxville: University of Tennessee Press, 1987.

Hamilton, James J. *The Battle of Fort Donelson.* South Brunswick, N.J.: T. Yoseloff, 1968.

Thomas Robson Hay / A. R.

See also **Civil War; Henry, Fort; Unconditional Surrender.**

DONGAN CHARTERS. Thomas Dongan, as governor of New York (1682–1688), oversaw the adoption of several city charters, the most significant of which were granted to New York City and Albany. New York City had already received a charter providing for city government from Sir Richard Nicolls in 1665. Dongan, however, created a more formal government with his 1684 charter, which divided the city into the five inner wards of South, Dock, East, West, and North, and an outer ward. Each ward had the privilege of electing assessors and constables, as well as an assistant and an alderman. The assistants, aldermen, city recorder, and mayor formed the common council, which had the power to make and enforce laws but not to tax. In 1686 Dongan approved a charter of incorporation for Albany, providing for a city government similar to that of New York City. The royal governor appointed mayors in both New York and Albany.

New York City's privileges as a corporation were reconfirmed in 1731 with the Montgomerie Charter, but were lost with the British occupation in 1776 when a military government was established. After the war, charter government resumed in New York City and Albany, with only property-owning freeholders and freemen permitted to vote for members of the common council. This policy persisted until 1804, when the state legislature passed a reform bill that extended the vote for common council members to people who paid rent. The direct election of mayors was instituted in 1833.

BIBLIOGRAPHY

Kammen, Michael. *Colonial New York: A History.* 2d ed. New York and Oxford: Oxford University Press, 1996. The original edition was published in 1975.

Kim, Sung Bok. *Landlord and Tenant in Colonial New York: Manorial Society, 1664–1775.* Chapel Hill: University of North Carolina Press, 1978.

Ritchie, Robert C. *The Duke's Province: A Study of New York Politics and Society, 1664–1691.* Chapel Hill: University of North Carolina Press, 1977.

Smith, William, Jr. *The History of the Province of New York.* 2 vols. Reprint, edited by Michael Kammen. Cambridge, Mass.: Belknap Press, 1972. The original edition was published in 1757.

Mary Lou Lustig

See also **Colonial Charters.**

DONNER PARTY. The Donner party, setting out from Illinois, was among the thousands of people who attempted to cross the plains to California and Oregon in 1846. Half of the eighty-seven members of the Donner party were women and children. Poorly led, they dawdled along the way, quarreled viciously, and refused to help one another. Worse, they chose a supposed shortcut through Utah that held them up for a month. By the time they reached the Sierra it was late November and snow was already falling.

When a blizzard stopped them just short of the summit, they threw up hasty shelters of wood and hides. Several attempts to force the pass failed. Finally, fifteen men and women trudged off on improvised snowshoes to bring help. Most starved to death, and their companions ate their bodies to survive. The campers on the crest of the Sierra also ate the bodies of the dead. One man finally reached a settlement in California. Heavy snow hampered rescue efforts; when the last of the Donner party was brought down from the summit in April, forty were dead. The San Francisco press sensationalized the tragedy, which passed into American myth.

BIBLIOGRAPHY

Mullen, Frank. *The Donner Party Chronicles: A Day-by-Day Account of a Doomed Wagon Train, 1846–1847.* Reno: Nevada Humanities Committee, 1997.

Stewart, George Rippey. *Ordeal By Hunger: The Story of the Donner Party.* New York: Holt, 1936. Reissue. Boston: Houghton Mifflin, 1992.

Cecelia Holland

See also **Westward Migration.**

DORCHESTER COMPANY. Certain English merchants, having ships sailing from Weymouth to fish off the banks of Newfoundland, decided in 1622 that a settlement on the coast of New England would be to their advantage because they had to double-man their ships to have, besides the crews, enough men for the fishing. With a settlement, the men needed for fishing could be left onshore with sufficient provisions for the winter and employ their time until the fishing fleet returned in building, curing fish, trapping fur-bearing animals, and planting corn.

The Reverend John White, rector of Holy Trinity, Dorchester, England, was a prime mover in this enterprise. While at Oxford, he imbibed the principles of the early Puritans, who believed the Church could be purified from within, and therefore had little sympathy with Plymouth Colony's rigid separatism. Not only could a clergyman of his persuasion reside on this new plantation to attend to the spiritual welfare of the settlers, but here would be a refuge for those likely to suffer from the strict religious discipline of Plymouth Colony as well.

The merchants, represented by Richard Bushrod and his associates, obtained a fishing license from the Council for New England on 20 February 1622, which entitled them to search for a colony site. A year later, on 18 February 1623, the council granted a patent to Sir Walter Earle. The promoters, led by Earle and White, met in March 1624 at Dorchester to formally organize the venture. They formed a company of associates, consisting of 119 stockholders paying £25 per share. Altogether, the company's initial fund came to more than £3,000. Even before that meeting, the new "Dorchester Company" purchased a ship—the *Fellowship*—that set out for New England in the summer of 1623. It arrived too late for productive fishing and left fourteen men and provisions to occupy Cape Ann. Two additional voyages, in 1624 and 1625, also failed as fishing expeditions. The latter had to be financed on borrowed funds, resulting in great loss to the company. Sinking into debt with no obvious way to turn a profit quickly, the company folded in 1626.

By that time about fifty men had been left at Cape Ann, and some men from Plymouth Colony who disliked Separatist rule (including John Lyford and Roger Conant) joined them. Their experience as colonists was useful to the plantation, yet the undertaking did not flourish. Cape Ann was twenty miles from the best fishing waters and had little agriculturally productive land. The site being unsuitable, Roger Conant advised all who wished to remain in New England to transfer to Nahum Keike, afterward named Salem. Despite the Dorchester Company's bankruptcy, John White undertook to provide the necessary supplies for the Nahum Keike colonists.

White still desired to establish a successful colony in New England, especially one that would serve as a refuge for non-Separatist dissenters. He hoped Nahum Keike could become such a colony and worked to attract new investors. A second joint-stock company—the New England Company—formed as a result, enabling John Endicott and about forty other colonists to ship for Nahum Keike on 20 June 1628. The New England Company, organized by patent from the Council for New England, was an unincorporated joint-stock company of ninety members. Its business concluded when it was merged into the Massachusetts Bay Company by royal charter in 1629.

BIBLIOGRAPHY

Andrews, Charles McLean. *The Colonial Period of American History.* 4 vols. New Haven, Conn.: Yale University Press, 1934.

Andrews, Kenneth R. *Trade, Plunder, and Settlement: Maritime Enterprise and the Genesis of the British Empire, 1480–1630.* Cambridge, U.K.: Cambridge University Press, 1984.

Labaree, Benjamin W. *Colonial Massachusetts: A History.* Milwood, N.Y.: KTO Press, 1979.

Rabb, Theodore K. *Enterprise and Empire: Merchant and Gentry Investment in the Expansion of England, 1575–1630.* Cambridge, Mass.: Harvard University Press, 1967.

Rose-Troup, Frances. *John White: The Patriarch of Dorchester (Dorset) and the Founder of Massachusetts, 1575–1648.* New York: G. P. Putnam's Sons, 1930.

———. *The Massachusetts Bay Company and Its Predecessors.* New York: Grafton, 1930.

Aaron J. Palmer
Frances Rose-Troup

See also **Council for New England; Massachusetts Bay Colony; New England Company; Plymouth Colony; Salem.**

DORR'S REBELLION. Dorr's Rebellion of 1842 was an extralegal attempt to achieve suffrage reform and create a new state constitution for Rhode Island. It was suppressed by force, but a new state constitution corrected the problems of disfranchisement and malapportionment that had provoked the uprising.

Dorr's Rebellion Aftermath. A vituperative political broadside, based on a July 1845 letter by Whig John Whipple, attacks Democrats trying to free the imprisoned Thomas Wilson Dorr. Dorr's head appears on a cow behind Cerberus, the hound of Hades; other allusions are to Satan and Benedict Arnold. LIBRARY OF CONGRESS

By 1841 Rhode Island was experiencing severe disfranchisement because suffrage under the state constitution (still the 1663 royal charter) was limited to male freeholders owning at least $134 of real property and their eldest sons. Industrialization in the northeastern part of the state had concurrently resulted in gross malapportionment in the General Assembly under the fixed apportionment scheme of the charter. The extant government, beneficiary of both evils, refused to concede reform.

In 1841 a radicalized reformist group, the Rhode Island Suffrage Association, drew up a new state constitution, called the People's Constitution, that meliorated both problems. The association then submitted it for ratification to the entire male electorate, the disfranchised as well as freeholders. Suffragists relied on the principles of the Declaration of Independence, especially its ideal of popular sovereignty. Concurrently, the so-called Freeholders government drafted its own reformed constitution but submitted it only to freeholders for ratification.

The People's Constitution was overwhelmingly (but extralegally) ratified, while voters rejected the Freeholders' document. The suffragists then held elections for a new state government, in which Thomas Wilson Dorr was elected governor. They installed a state legislature and hoped that the Freeholders government would dissolve itself. Instead, it enacted repressive legislation and declared martial law to suppress what it considered an insurrection. President John Tyler declined to assist the Dorr government and covertly promised to back the Freeholders government. The Freeholders crushed a minor effort to defend the Dorr government by force. Dorr himself was convicted of treason and sentenced to life imprisonment but was later pardoned. The victorious Freeholders then adopted a new constitution that conceded most of what the suffragists had demanded.

In *Luther v. Borden* (1849) the U.S. Supreme Court refused to endorse suffragist theories of popular sovereignty. Chief Justice Roger B. Taney declared such matters to be political questions committed by the U.S. Constitution to the political branches of government (Congress and the president) for resolution.

BIBLIOGRAPHY

Dennison, George M. *The Dorr War: Republicanism on Trial, 1831–1861.* Lexington: University Press of Kentucky, 1976.

Gettleman, Marvin E. *The Dorr Rebellion: A Study in American Radicalism, 1833–1849.* New York: Random House, 1973.

William M. Wiecek

See also **Apportionment; Rhode Island; Suffrage.**

DOT-COM. *See* **Electronic Commerce.**

DOUBLOON was a Spanish gold piece, so called because its value was double that of a pistole (the vernacular term for the Spanish gold coin, equal to two escudos). Its value varied from $8.25 in the period 1730–1772, $8.00 during the American Revolution, and later to about $7.84 from 1786 to 1848. It was freely used in the West Indies and South American trade, and southerners in the colonial period often had their cash assets in Spanish gold.

BIBLIOGRAPHY

Brock, Leslie V. *The Currency of the American Colonies, 1700–1764: A Study in Colonial Finance and Imperial Relations.* New York: Arno Press, 1975.

Carl L. Cannon/A. R.

See also **Currency and Coinage; Money; Pieces of Eight.**

DOUGHBOY. Word that was universally used in the U.S. Army to mean an infantryman, and specifically an American infantryman, up until World War II, when it was replaced with "GI." When it was first used is uncertain, but it can be traced as far back as 1854, when it was already in use on the Texas border, and it was especially popular in World War I. The explanation then was that the infantrymen wore white belts and had to clean them with "dough" made of pipe clay. Originally a term of ridicule used by the mounted service, it was adopted by the infantry itself and used with great pride.

BIBLIOGRAPHY

Kennedy, David M. *Over Here: The First World War and American Society.* New York: Oxford University Press, 1980.

Oliver Lyman Spaulding/D. B.

See also **Slang; Uniforms, Military.**

DOUGHFACES were northerners who, before the Civil War, supported southern policies relative to territorial expansion and slavery. The word was coined in 1819 by John Randolph of Virginia as a term of contempt for members of the House of Representatives from the North who voted against the amendment to prevent the further introduction of slavery into Missouri proposed by Rep. James Tallmadge of New York. Under the terms of the Missouri Compromise of 1820, Missouri entered the Union as a slave state, whereas Maine entered the Union as a free state.

BIBLIOGRAPHY

Moore, Glover. *The Missouri Controversy, 1819–1821.* Lexington: University of Kentucky Press, 1953.

Potter, David M. *The Impending Crisis, 1848–1861.* New York: Harper and Row, 1976.

C. H. Hamlin/A. R.

See also **Barnburners; Era of Good Feeling; House Divided; Hunkers.**

DOVES AND HAWKS are terms applied to people based upon their views about a military conflict. A dove is someone who opposes the use of military pressure to resolve a dispute; a hawk favors entry into war. The terms came into widespread use during the Vietnam War, but their roots are much older than that conflict. The association of doves with peace is rooted in the biblical story of the Great Flood: the dove that Noah released after the rains had stopped returned with an olive branch, the symbol of peace and a sign that the waters had receded from the ground. "War hawk" was applied to advocates of war in the United States as early as 1798 when Thomas Jefferson used it to describe Federalists ready to declare war on France.

The juxtaposition of the two terms originates in a 1962 account of the Kennedy administration's decision-making process during the Cuban missile crisis. The hawk-dove antithesis quickly became a popular way of labeling partisans in the Vietnam debate. But it also oversimplified their differences. The term "dove" was applied both to those who supported U.S. intervention to stop the spread of communism, but who opposed military means, and to those who opposed U.S. intervention altogether. The latter were also sometimes called other names such as "peaceniks."

Use of the terms declined in the post-Vietnam years, but reappeared in the 1990s during debates over U.S. policy in the Balkans, Afghanistan, and Iraq.

BIBLIOGRAPHY

Anderson, David L., ed. *Shadow on the White House: Presidents and the Vietnam War, 1945–1975*. Lawrence: University Press of Kansas, 1993.

Egan, Clifford L. "The Path to War in 1812 through the Eyes of a New Hampshire 'War Hawk'." *Historical New Hampshire* 30, no. 3 (Fall 1975): 147–177.

Gerster, Friedrich Wilhelm. "Linguistic Aspects of the Vietnam War." *Amerikastudien/American Studies* 20, no. 2 (1975): 307–319.

Jacob E. Cooke
Cynthia R. Poe/H. S.

See also **War Hawks; War of 1812.**

DOW JONES & Company, Incorporated, founded by Charles Henry Dow, Edward Davis Jones, and Charles M. Bergstresser in 1882, originally hand-delivered news about bonds and stock transactions to Wall Street subscribers on "flimsies," copies of one- or two-sentence notes handwritten on slips of tissue paper layered between carbons. By 1883, the company printed a summary of each day's trades, the *Customers' Afternoon Letter.* Six years later, this daily evolved into *The Wall Street Journal.* In 1893, Jones sold his share to his two partners, who, by 1902, sold the firm to Clarence Barron. Nineteen years later, the company introduced *Barron's National Business and Financial Weekly.* Hand-delivered bulletins were discontinued in 1948, but by then *The Wall Street Journal* had become the mainstay of Wall Street.

In 1896, Dow introduced two averages, one of industrial companies' stocks and another of railroad stocks, as indexes of the whole stock market. More than 100 years later, the Dow Jones Industrial Average (DJIA) is the most universally recognized barometer of U.S. stock price behavior, comprises the stocks of thirty large industrial companies, and is quoted in points, not dollars. This price-weighted average is adjusted periodically to reflect splits in those stocks.

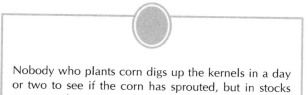

> Nobody who plants corn digs up the kernels in a day or two to see if the corn has sprouted, but in stocks most people want to open an account at noon and get their profit before night.
>
> *Charles Henry Dow*
>
> SOURCE: Rosenberg, Jerry M. *Inside The Wall Street Journal: The History and the Power of Dow Jones & Company and America's Most Influential Newspaper.* New York: Macmillan Publishing Co., Inc., 1982.

BIBLIOGRAPHY

Downes, John, Elliot Goodman, and Jordan Elliot Goodman. *Dictionary of Finance and Investment Terms*. 4th ed. New York: Barron's, 2001.

Gordon, John Steele. *The Great Game: The Emergence of Wall Street As a World Power 1653–2000*. New York: Scribner, 1999.

Rosenberg, Jerry M. *Inside The Wall Street Journal: The History and the Power of Dow Jones & Company and America's Most Influential Newspaper.* New York: Macmillan Publishing Co., Inc., 1982.

Sutton, George, ed. *Hoover's Handbook of American Business 2002.* Austin, Tex.: Hoover's Business Press, 2001.

Mary Lawrence Wathen

DOWNSIZING is the act of reducing the number of employees within a company in order to decrease costs and increase efficiency, with the ultimate goal of greater profitability. Downsized companies either continue the same work functions with fewer employees or they decrease the scope of companywide activities.

More than 85 percent of Fortune 1000 corporations downsized professional staff between 1987 and 1991, and analysts have suggested that the rise of automation is causing the loss of jobs, both in manual labor and service industries. In 1996, the *New York Times* wrote that, because of downsizing, the workplace is changing as greatly as it did during the industrial revolution.

Advocates applaud streamlining, believing that downsizing reduces bureaucracy and leads to greater productivity. Critics, however, cite a 1991 Wyatt Company survey of 1,005 downsized businesses, which found that fewer than one-third of the companies experienced projected profitability, 46 percent discovered that expenses did not decrease as expected, and only 22 percent encountered satisfactorily increased productivity. Downsizing also eliminates employees with vital skills, leading to disruption of productivity, and employees who remain often experience reduced morale.

BIBLIOGRAPHY

New York Times. *The Downsizing of America*. New York: Times Books, 1996.

Kelly Boyer Sagert

See also **Corporations.**

DRAFT. *See* **Conscription and Recruitment.**

DRAFT RIOTS. One of the bloodiest riots in American history, the New York City Draft Riots erupted on 13 July 1863 and lasted until 16 July 1863. The Draft Riots broke out when officials attempted to enforce the first federally enacted draft. As the Civil War dragged on and troops dwindled, the Union hoped to increase its ranks through a draft that called upon all white men between 20 and 35 and all unmarried white men between 35 and 45. The Conscription Act excluded African American men, who were not considered citizens, and also released men capable of paying $300 to obtain a waiver.

The draft lottery was held at the office located on Third Avenue and Forty-sixth Street, and officials picked more than 1,200 names on the first draft day held 11 July 1863. The next one was scheduled for Monday 13 July 1863. Shortly after dawn that Monday morning, working-class white men protested the draft by going on a looting spree throughout the city. Mobs first attacked the conscription office, protesting the draft law. Then the rioters targeted Republican sympathizers, conscription personnel, and abolitionists who supported the Union cause. They also set fire to buildings like the Brooks Brothers store as well as the offices of the *New York Tribune*. Within hours of the outbreak of violence, the mobs sought out African Americans, attacking their places of work, institutions, homes, and blacks themselves. For the next four days, white mobs beat blacks, ransacked their homes, set fire to their buildings, and leveled their community institutions like the Colored Orphan Asylum. Rioters injured over thirty African Americans and murdered at least eleven.

The riots had a sweeping effect on New York City's African American population, driving nearly 5,000 blacks from the city. Eight hundred members of the metropolitan police could not quell the riot, so city officials called Union troops back from a battle at Gettysburg, Pennsylvania, and the soldiers restored order on 16 July 1863. William M. "Boss" Tweed and Tammany Hall held the next draft in August 1863. Over 100 black men from the city enlisted in the United States Colored Infantry in order to demonstrate their support for the Union troops.

BIBLIOGRAPHY

Bernstein, Iver. *The New York City Draft Riots: Their Significance for American Society and Politics in the Age of the Civil War.* New York: Oxford University Press, 1990.

Jane E. Dabel

See also **Civil War; Riots.**

DRAPER'S MEADOWS, the first settlement west of the great Allegheny divide, on the present site of Blacksburg, Virginia, was founded in 1748 in the New River section by John Draper, Thomas Ingles, and other Scottish and Irish immigrants from Pennsylvania. On 8 July 1755, the settlement was destroyed by a party of SHAWNEE Indians. Mrs. William Ingles was carried into captivity on the lower Ohio River but made her escape and returned more than 700 miles on foot.

BIBLIOGRAPHY

Tillson, Albert H., Jr. "The Localist Roots of Backcountry Loyalism." *The Journal of Southern History* 54 (August 1988): 387–404.

James Elliott Walmsley / A. R.

See also **Captivity Narratives; Virginia; Westward Migration.**

DREADNOUGHT, a type of battleship that derived its name from the British warship *Dreadnought*, launched in 1906. This ship, which marked a new era in naval construction and made obsolete every battleship afloat, bettered its predecessors in displacement, speed, armor, and firepower. It had a displacement of 17,900 tons, a speed of 21.6 knots, a cruising radius of 5,800 sea miles, and was protected by armor eleven inches thick. It was the first battleship to be driven by turbines. Its main battery consisted of ten twelve-inch guns, making it the first all-big gun ship in the world. After its launching and until WORLD WAR I, every battleship built with a main armament entirely of big guns all of one caliber was considered to be in the Dreadnought class.

The *Dreadnought* inaugurated a race in building battleships of this type between Great Britain, the United States, and other naval powers. In the United States, two ships of this type were designed and authorized in 1905 but were not launched until 1908. They were the *South Carolina* and *Michigan*, each with a 16,000-ton displace-

HMS *Dreadnought*. The British warship, seen here in 1909, began an international arms race to build well-armored battleships of this specific type, designed for speed and armed entirely with big guns. ARCHIVE PHOTOS, INC.

ment and armed with eight twelve-inch guns. The United States built fifteen other ships of this type before the outbreak of World War I, all of greater tonnage than the *Michigan* and *South Carolina.* On 29 August 1916, Congress authorized a building program that included ten Dreadnoughts. During the war, this program was discontinued in favor of building destroyers for overseas duty but was resumed after the armistice. It was finally halted by the Washington Conference of 1922.

BIBLIOGRAPHY

Hough, Richard A. *Dreadnought: A History of the Modern Battleship.* New York, Macmillan, 1964.

Massie, Robert K. *Dreadnought: Britain, Germany, and the Coming of the Great War.* New York: Random House, 1991; New York: Ballantine, 1992.

Louis H. Bolander / A. R.

See also **Warships; Washington Naval Conference; World War I, Navy in.**

DRED SCOTT CASE (*Dred Scott v. Sandford,* 60 U.S. 393, 1857). In 1846, the slave Dred Scott and his wife, Harriet, sued Irene Emerson, the widow of Scott's former owner, Dr. John Emerson, a surgeon in the U.S. Army. Scott claimed he was free because Dr. Emerson had taken him from the slave state of Missouri to Fort Snelling in the Wisconsin Territory (present-day Minnesota), where Congress had prohibited slavery under the Missouri Compromise of 1820. Scott also claimed to be free because Emerson had taken him to the free state of Illinois.

In 1850, a Missouri trial court declared Scott a free man based on the theory that he had become free while living at Fort Snelling and in Illinois, and that he had the right to continue being free. However, in 1852, the Missouri Supreme Court overturned Scott's victory. In 1854, Scott sued his new owner, John F. A. Sanford, in federal court (Sanford's name is misspelled as Sandford in the official report of the case). Scott sued under a clause in Article III of the U.S. Constitution, which states that a citizen of one state may sue a citizen of another state in federal court. Scott argued that if he were free under the MISSOURI COMPROMISE, he was a citizen of Missouri and could sue Sanford, a citizen of New York, in federal court. Sanford responded that Scott could never be considered a citizen "because he is a negro of African descent; his ancestors were of pure African blood, and were brought into this country and sold as negro slaves."

U.S. District Judge Robert W. Wells rejected this argument, concluding that if Dred Scott were free, then he could sue in federal court as a citizen of Missouri. But Scott lost at trial and appealed to the U.S. Supreme Court. In 1857, by a vote of 7–2, the Court held that the Missouri Compromise, under which Scott claimed to be free, was unconstitutional. In a bitterly proslavery opinion, Chief Justice Roger B. Taney held that Congress lacked the power to ban slavery in the territories. This decision shocked and angered most northerners, who had long seen the Missouri Compromise as a central piece of legislation for organizing the settlement of the West and for accommodating differing sectional interests.

Dred Scott. A portrait of the man whose long, unsuccessful legal attempt to gain his freedom culminated in a polarizing U.S. Supreme Court decision, widely considered one of the worst in the Court's history and a major indirect cause of the Civil War four years later. By then, ironically, Scott had been freed anyway but died of tuberculosis not long after. LIBRARY OF CONGRESS

Ignoring the fact that free black men in most of the northern states, as well as in North Carolina, could vote at the time of the ratification of the Constitution, Taney declared that African Americans could never be citizens of the United States. He wrote that blacks "are not included, and were not intended to be included, under the word 'citizens' in the U.S. Constitution, and can therefore claim none of the rights and privileges which the instrument provides and secures to citizens of the United States. On the contrary, they were at that time [1787–88] considered as a subordinate and inferior class of beings who had been subjugated by the dominant race, and, whether emancipated or not, yet remained subject to their authority, and had no rights or privileges but such as those who held the power and Government might choose to grant them." According to Taney, blacks were "so far inferior, that they had no rights which the white man was bound to respect."

Taney's opinion outraged most northerners. Abraham Lincoln attacked the decision in his debates with Stephen A. Douglas in 1858, and again during the presidential campaign of 1860. The Supreme Court decision forced Republicans to take a firm stand in favor of black citizenship and fundamental rights for blacks.

Although the Dred Scott decision denied civil rights to blacks, the Civil War era (1861–1865) federal government ignored it; during the conflict, Congress banned slavery in all the western territories, despite Taney's assertion that such an act was unconstitutional. In 1866, Congress sent the Fourteenth Amendment to the states, declaring that all persons born in the nation are citizens of the United States and of the state in which they live. The ratification of this amendment, in 1868, made the civil rights aspects of Dred Scott a dead letter. The decision nevertheless remains a potent symbol of the denial of civil rights and the constitutionalization of racism.

BIBLIOGRAPHY

Fehrenbacher, Don Edward. *The Dred Scott Case: Its Significance in American Law and Politics.* New York: Oxford University Press, 1981.

Finkelman, Paul. *Dred Scott v. Sandford: A Brief History With Documents.* Boston: Bedford Books, 1997.

Paul Finkelman

See also **Slavery;** *and vol. 9:* **A House Divided.**

DRESS. *See* **Clothing.**

DROGHER TRADE was a type of shipping carried on from about 1825 to 1834, between American firms, mostly in Boston, and Spaniards in California. This trade consisted largely of New England manufactures exchanged for cattle hides. The term "drogher" is a West Indian word applied to slow and clumsy coast vessels. The route of the drogher trade extended from New England, around Cape Horn at the southernmost point of South America, and up the coast of California. The ships stopped in numerous ports along the way up the coast, to trade American-made goods for hides in the ports of San Pedro, San Diego, Santa Barbara, Santa Cruz, and along the hide-curing beaches surrounding these ports. This shipping became immortalized in Richard Henry Dana's *Two Years before the Mast*, a memoir of Dana's employment on a drogher vessel that was published in 1840. Based on a diary he kept during his employment on a drogher, Dana's work describes the commercial life of the California coast, and Americans' involvement in the region a decade before the Gold Rush. Dana's work discussed the details of the drogher trade along the coast of Spanish California, and provided detailed accounts of the lives of those involved in the many aspects of the drogher trade, including Hispanic, Native American, and European participants.

BIBLIOGRAPHY

Francis, Jessie Davies. *An Economic and Social History of Mexican California, 1822–1846: Volume I, Chiefly Economic.* New York: Arno Press, 1976.

Shapiro, Samuel. *Richard Henry Dana Jr., 1815–1882.* East Lansing: Michigan State University Press, 1961.

Carl L. Cannon/H. S.

See also **Coasting Trade; San Diego.**

DRUG ADDICTION. *See* **Substance Abuse.**

DRUG TRAFFICKING, ILLEGAL. The black market for illegal drugs accounts for 8 percent of the world's trade revenue, according to United Nations estimates. Enormous profits can be had for those who successfully smuggle narcotics from Latin America, Southeast Asia, and other parts of the globe into the world's largest black market for illegal drugs: the United States. Successfully smuggling cocaine into the United States in the 1990s brought profits between 700 to 900 percent over original product costs. Drug Enforcement Agency (DEA) officials estimate that a drug organization could have 70 to 80 percent of its product confiscated before sale and still turn a profit. Because of the economics of the black market, efforts to stanch the flow of illegal drugs have mostly been frustrated. Best estimates conclude that government interdiction captures one-third of the illegal drugs that smugglers try to bring into the United States; the two-thirds of the narcotics that do cross U.S. borders supplied an estimated $60-billion-a-year retail market in 2000.

From the passage of the first major piece of federal drug control legislation, the Harrison Act, in 1914, until the late 1960s, efforts to interdict illegal drugs were organized by drug enforcement divisions within the Treasury Department. During the same period most of the drug trade was controlled by U.S.-based Mafia organizations. The rise in drug use in the late 1960s prompted President Richard Nixon to declare a "War on Drugs," and efforts to stop smuggling were stepped up. In 1973 the DEA was created as part of the Justice Department to coordinate drug interdiction and drug trafficking intelligence gathering among federal agencies. Other agencies involved in stopping drug trafficking include the State Department, the Department of Defense, the U.S. Coast Guard, the U.S. Customs Service, and the Federal Bureau of Investigation. The federal government spent approximately $1.5 billion on drug interdiction efforts in 1997.

Among the more prominent operations to stop drug traffic into the United States occurred in the 1970s with the breakup of the "French Connection," the name given to a heroin-smuggling route that began in Turkey, passed through the port of Marseilles, and ended up in New York. The 1980s and 1990s saw further major operations resulting in the destruction of leading international drug traffic organizations, such as the Medellin and Cali cartels in Latin America. In 2000 U.S. Customs seized 1.3 million pounds of marijuana, 150,000 pounds of cocaine, and 2,550 pounds of heroin. Important single-case seizures include the capture of 1,071 pounds of heroin on the cargo ship *President Truman* in 1991 and the capture of 13 tons of cocaine from the cargo ship *Svesda Maru* in 2001. Both ship seizures took place off the coast of California.

BIBLIOGRAPHY

Bertram, Eva, et al. *Drug War Politics: The Price of Denial.* Berkeley: University of California Press, 1996.

Meier, Kenneth J. *The Politics of Sin: Drugs, Alcohol, and Public Policy.* Armonk, N.Y.: M. E. Sharpe, 1994.

Musto, David. *The American Disease: Origins of Narcotic Control.* 3d ed. New York: Oxford University Press, 1999.

Richard M. Flanagan

See also **Crime, Organized; Narcotics Trade and Legislation; Substance Abuse.**

DRY DOCKS. Employed by the Greeks and Romans for construction and repair of war galleys, dry docks have constituted the foundations of naval architecture. Like the great dock house at Delos, which accommodated vessels up to twenty-eight feet wide, dry docks were typically, until the late Renaissance, erected on an inclined plane to facilitate launchings. Although such ship houses survived into nineteenth-century America, they were superseded in sixteenth-century Europe by open masonry basins erected below water level by means of cofferdams and fitted with watertight gates whose closure, upon entrance of a vessel, permitted the dock to be pumped dry. Henry VII ordered the construction of England's first dry dock—a wood and stone construction enclosed by walls of wood, stone, and earth—at Portsmouth in 1496. Under Henry VIII, dockyards at Woolwich and Deptford inaugurated major warship construction, spurring the building of dry docks elsewhere in Europe and opening three centuries of naval rivalry with Spain, the Netherlands, and France.

Construction features of those European establishments were embodied in the first federal dry dock erected in the United States, a 253-foot graving dock completed at Boston in 1833. Equipped with both copper-sheathed turning gates and a caisson (floating gate), this early work had substantial pump wells, pumping machines, discharge culverts, capstans, and the customary stock of keel blocking. The New York Navy Yard's 307-foot dock, opened in 1851, boasted the world's first all-metal cofferdam, with a sixty-eight-foot entrance and a maximum depth of twenty-six feet, completely adequate for the repair, construction, or routine bottom cleaning of the largest warships.

After floating dry docks were introduced in European and North American shipyards, the U.S. Navy decided to construct such "balance" docks at Portsmouth, New Hampshire (1800) and Pensacola, Florida, and to fabricate a floating sectional dry dock at Mare Island (1853). The advent of steel construction and the rapid increase in warship dimensions necessitated larger all-masonry docks and placed a severe strain on existing facilities. Following the Spanish-American War, 740-foot graving docks were constructed at Portsmouth, Boston, Philadelphia, and Mare Island. Increasing overseas responsibilities subsequently persuaded the navy to establish dry docks at Puget Sound and Pearl Harbor. During World War I, 1,000-foot dry docks equipped with massive traveling cranes and typically committed to Dreadnought construction were built at Norfolk, Philadelphia, and San Francisco.

On the eve of World War II, naval graving docks with reinforced concrete walls more than twenty feet thick were under construction at Norfolk and Philadelphia, designed to accommodate warships 1,100 feet long and 150 feet wide. The rapid strategic movement contemplated for American naval forces in the Pacific dictated that the floating dry dock join the U.S. Fleet's mobile service force. From 1942 to 1945, twenty-seven 457-foot landing ship docks (LSDs) were launched, many joining the Pacific fleet as combined dry docks and landing craft carriers. Capable of steaming into landing areas with their well decks filled with combat-loaded landing craft mechanized (LCMs), these amphibious mother ships discharged their craft through stern gates for direct beachhead assault.

BIBLIOGRAPHY

Mazurkiewicz, B. K. *Design and Construction of Dry Docks.* Rockport, Mass.: Trans Tech, 1980.

Du-Plat-Taylor, Francis M. G. *The Design, Construction and Maintenance of Docks, Wharves and Piers.* London: Benn, 1928; 1934; London: Eyre and Spottiswoode, 1949.

Stuart, Charles B. *The Naval Dry Docks of the United States.* New York: Norton, 1852; New York: Van Nostrand; London: Trubner, 1870.

Philip K. Lundeberg/A. R.

See also **Colonial Ships; Shipbuilding; World War I, Navy in; World War II, Navy in.**

DRY FARMING refers to agricultural operations without irrigation in a climate with a moisture deficiency, usually places with an annual rainfall of less than 20 inches. It involves raising drought-resistant or drought-evasive crops (that is, crops that mature in late spring or fall) and makes the best use of a limited water supply by maintaining good surface conditions—loosening the soil so that water may enter easily and weeding so that the moisture is better utilized.

In the United States, dry-farming techniques evolved through experiments conducted more or less independently where settlements were established in locations with little precipitation. During the early part of the 1850s, for example, Americans in California began to raise crops such as winter WHEAT, whose principal growing season coincided with the winter rainfall season. By 1863, settlers in Utah extensively and successfully practiced dry farming techniques. In some interior valleys of the PACIFIC NORTHWEST, dry farming was reported before 1880. In the GREAT PLAINS, with its summer rainfall season, adaptation to dry farming methods accompanied the small-farmer invasion of the late 1880s and later. Experimental work for the Kansas Pacific Railroad had begun near the ninety-eighth meridian by R. S. Elliott between 1870 and 1873.

On the northern Great Plains, H. W. Campbell carried on private experiments that attracted the attention and support of railroad interests, resulting in the formulation of much of his system of dry farming by 1895. The state agricultural experiment stations of the Great Plains inaugurated experimental activities under government auspices soon after their foundation, and the federal Department of Agriculture created the Office of Dry Land Agriculture in 1905. Once inaugurated, development of dry farming was continuous in the Great Plains proper, but the drought cycles of the 1930s intensified experimental work and the invention of machinery for special soil-culture processes both in the Plains and in the transitional subhumid country where it was neglected during wet periods.

The net income result per hour of labor in dry farming is high, but so are the fixed costs (because of special implements required). In addition, the risk of failure is higher than in traditional farming.

BIBLIOGRAPHY

Hargreaves, Mary Wilma M. *Dry Farming in the Northern Great Plains, 1900–1925.* Cambridge, Mass.: Harvard University Press, 1957.

———. *Dry Farming in the Northern Great Plains, 1920–1990: Years of Readjustment.* Lawrence: University of Kansas Press, 1993.

Wessel, Thomas R., ed. *Agriculture in the Great Plains.* Washington, D.C.: Agricultural History Society, 1977.

Widtsoe, John A. *Dry Farming.* New York: Macmillan, 1911.

James C. Malin / C. W.

See also **Agricultural Machinery; Agriculture; Climate; Irrigation.**

DUCKING STOOL, an armchair used for punishing certain offenders, including witches, scolds, and prostitutes. The offender was strapped into a sturdy chair, which was fastened to a long wooden beam fixed as a seesaw on the edge of a pond or stream, where the offender was immersed. This form of public humiliation prevailed in England and America from the early seventeenth century through the early nineteenth century, when reformers called for more humane punishments. Still, judges in many states continued to sentence lesser offenders to ducking as late as the 1820s. Many of these sentences, however, either were not carried out or were reduced to fines.

BIBLIOGRAPHY

Pestritto, Ronald J. *Founding the Criminal Law: Punishment and Political Thought in the Origins of America.* DeKalb: Northern Illinois University Press, 2000.

Fred B. Joyner / S. B.

See also **Crime; Pillory; Punishment; Stocks.**

DUE PROCESS OF LAW encompasses several doctrines of U.S. Constitutional law protecting important liberties from limitation and requiring that citizens only be deprived of rights or property through valid and fair procedures.

These doctrines are rooted in the common law, state constitutions, the Bill of Rights, and the Fifth and Fourteenth Amendments. The Fifth Amendment limits the national government: "No person shall . . . be deprived of life, liberty, or property, without due process of law." Section one of the Fourteenth Amendment correspondingly binds the states. Constitutions in the fifty states incorporate similar requirements.

Due process of law has many sources. It is a descendent of the Aristotelian idea of the rule of law, that the best state is one governed by laws rather than by men. It is rooted in a requirement of Magna Carta, accepted by King John in 1215 and finally confirmed in 1297 by Edward I. Chapter 29 (chapter 39 in 1215) states,

> "No Freeman shall be taken, or imprisoned, or be disseised [dispossessed] of his Freehold, or Liberties, or free Customs, or be outlawed, or exiled, or any otherwise destroyed; nor will we pass upon him, nor condemn him, but by lawful Judgment of his Peers, or by the Law of the Land. We will sell to no man, we will not deny or defer to any man either Justice or Right."

This formula was restated in a statute of 1354, which declared "no man . . . shall be put out of his lands or tenements nor taken, nor disinherited, nor put to death, without he be brought to answer by due process of law." The influence of Magna Carta in English law, however, was not great during the later feudal age.

The influence of Magna Carta and chapter 39 revived in England just before the founding of the English colonies in America. In a series of opinions from the bench, English judges—particularly Sir Edward Coke, Chief

Justice under James I—argued according to Magna Carta and "the ancient constitution" it enshrined that law must be based in courts alone, that judges must be independent from executive influence, and that neither King, Church, nor sheriffs could enter houses without warrants, raise taxes without Parliament, or make arrests not according to the law. These arguments were printed in Sir Edward Coke's *Reports of Cases*, in his *Second Institute of the Laws of England*, and in the Petition of Right, which he wrote and which passed Parliament in 1628. Coke's *Reports* and *Institutes* were the standard books for students and lawyers in the American colonies and early republic. In his *Second Institute* commentary on Magna Carta, Coke equated the "law of the land" with "due process of law," and so due process was made to encompass the broadest meaning of the common law, a meaning accepted both by Sir William Blackstone in his *Commentaries* and by the lawyers of colonial and early federal America. Perhaps more importantly, the Petition of Right was reaffirmed in the English Bill of Rights of 1689, which became a model for colonists who wrote similar provisions into colonial charters and for Americans seeking a Bill of Rights.

Thomas Jefferson's Lockean understanding of the state was a further influence. In 1690 John Locke wrote his *Second Treatise*, which much impressed the founding generation. Man in a state of nature, Locke argued, was free "to preserve his property—that is, his life, liberty, and estate," from the deprivations of others, judging them as he sees fit. But man in political society must cede this power to the community. The community's legislature was limited only by an obligation that Locke derived from natural law, although it echoed the common-law maxim, *salus populi suprema lex* ("the welfare of the people is the highest law"): "Their power in the utmost bounds of it is limited to the public good of the society." Such sentiments reverberated in Baron de Montesquieu's *Spirit of the Laws* (1748). It was this philosophical tradition that informed Thomas Jefferson's assertion in the Declaration of Independence that "all men are created equal, that they are endowed by their Creator with certain unalienable Rights, that among these are Life, Liberty, and the pursuit of Happiness. That to secure these rights, Governments are instituted among Men, deriving their just powers from the consent of the governed." The first abuse of the Crown Jefferson listed to justify rebellion was that the king had "refused his Assent to Laws, the most wholesome and necessary for the public good."

These two strains of thought—the revived Magna Carta and a belief in "the rule of law to the good of the people"—influenced the early constitutions of the independent American states. For example, the Connecticut Constitutional Ordinance of 1776 required,

> "That no Man's Life shall be taken away: No Man's Honor or good Name shall be stained: No Man's Person shall be arrested, restrained, banished, dismembered, nor any Ways punished, No Man shall be deprived of his Wife or Children: No Man's Goods or Estate shall be taken away from him nor any Ways indamaged under the Colour of Law, or Countenance of Authority; unless they be clearly warranted by the Laws of this State."

Virginia's Declaration of Rights required that "no man be deprived of his liberty except by the law of the land, or the judgment of his peers."

During the ratification debates of the 1780s, the agreement famously reached among sponsors and critics of the proposed constitution was struck following ratification of a bill of individual rights. When James Madison introduced the Bill of Rights, he drew its provisions primarily from proposals by the various states, four of which—New York, North Carolina, Virginia, and Pennsylvania—had proposed that no person be deprived of liberty except according to the law of the land or according to due process of law. Madison included a "due process of law" provision, based on New York's submission and reflecting its constitution. The Fifth Amendment was adopted and ratified with little debate.

Cases in the Supreme Court under the Due Process Clause were rare and initially limiting of its scope. In *The Schooner Betsy*, 8 US 443 (1807), Chief Justice Marshall ruled that the seizure of a vessel did not require a jury trial to ensure due process, because such cases are considered in admiralty court, which does not require a jury. In *United States v. Bryan and Woodcock*, 13 US 374 (1815), the Court rejected an argument that due process was violated by federal claims against the estate of a dead bankrupt. The most important limit to the amendment, however, was the Court's rebuff of attempts to bind the states to its terms (see BARRON V. BALTIMORE, 32 US 243 [1833]; *Withers v. Buckley*, 61 US 84 [1857]).

The first constructive applications of due process in the Court were a passing comment by Justice William Johnson that Magna Carta was "intended to secure the individual from the arbitrary exercise of the powers of government, unrestrained by the established principles of private rights and distributive justice" (*Bank of Columbia v. Okely*, 17 US 235 [1819]), and a reference by Justice Joseph Story to arguments that the state could limit the privileges of a college with a royal charter only pursuant to due process of law. In the latter case, *Trustees of Dartmouth College v. Woodward*, 17 US 518 (1819), Story agreed with the argument of Daniel Webster, who had argued that due process, or law of the land, is "the general law; a law which hears before it condemns; which proceeds upon inquiry, and renders judgment only after trial. The meaning is that every citizen shall hold his life, liberty, property, and immunities, under the protection of the general rules which govern society." This definition was widely accepted. (See Thomas M. Cooley's *Constitutional Limitations*, 1868.)

The earliest cases in which the Fifth Amendment limited Congressional action involved attempts to enforce the rights of slaveholders. Justice Baldwin, dissenting in a case construing state slavery laws, noted that state laws define what is property, even including slaves, so that "under the fifth amendment of the Constitution, these rights do not consist merely in ownership; the right of disposing of property of all kinds, is incident to it, which Congress cannot touch" (*Groves v. Slaughter*, 40 US 449 [1841]). This view that due process limited not only how a right may be lost but also what rights can be taken through legislation was widely held among state courts (see *Wynehamer v. People*, 13 NY 378 [1855]). Thus when in *Dred Scott v. Sanford*, 60 US 393 (1857), the Supreme Court finally confronted the question of whether Congress could limit slavery, with dreadful predictability the Court held that under the Fifth Amendment, Congress could not limit the property rights of slaveholders entering federal territories. The *Dred Scott* case was a severe blow to the Court's prestige, and in later years its memory would underscore arguments to limit the application of due process over the substance of laws.

During Reconstruction, Congress passed and the states ratified, the Southern states under compulsion, the Fourteenth Amendment. Section one of that amendment provides, "No State shall . . . deprive any person of life, liberty, or property, without due process of law; nor deny to any person within its jurisdiction the equal protection of the laws." This latter clause, intended to ensure that no state discriminated against groups, such as the freedmen of the South or the Germans of the North, made specific an idea that once had been only implicitly within the scope of due process. (See EQUAL PROTECTION OF THE LAW.) The drafters of the Fourteenth Amendment made a further distinction, between "law" and "the laws." One reading of this difference is that "the laws" are those actually passed by legislatures, while "law" remains the ideal of the common law.

In the late nineteenth century, the Court employed due process among several tools curbing Congressional and state power to regulate labor and commerce. In the *Slaughterhouse Cases,* 83 US 36 (1873), Justices Bradley and Swayne argued, in dissent, that a state law granting a monopoly deprived the people of liberty and property in their choice of employment. The right of choice in adopting lawful employments is, "a portion of their liberty: their occupation is their property." This view, quickly adopted by state courts, was later accepted by the Court's majority and applied in a series of cases ruling that the Due Process Clause and the Contracts Clause forbade statutes limiting child labor, wage and hour laws, and laws requiring safe or sanitary working conditions (for example, *Allgeyer v. Louisiana*, 165 US 578 [1897]; *Lochner v. New York,* 198 US 45 [1905]). The seeds of doubt had been sown, however, and Oliver Wendell Holmes argued in an influential dissent in Lochner that due process did not enshrine one economic theory of the law.

The pressures of the Great Depression, the influence on judges of progressivism and legal realism, and the drumbeat of legislation from the states and the Congress led the Court to severely limit its broad use of due process to evaluate legislation. (See POLICE POWER.) In *National Labor Relations Board v. Jones and Laughlin* (1937), the Court ruled that it would defer to Congress and to agencies in regulating commerce, interfering only if the statute or action was unreasonable. Similar deference was extended to labor and property regulation. "Reasonableness review" is not utterly empty, and the Court has continued to assert that due process requires every statute to pursue a legitimate governmental purpose through reasonable means.

Due process since the New Deal era has followed distinct lines of argument, based on procedure, the incorporation of liberties into the Bill of Rights, limits on laws that are vague, limits on laws that burden excluded classes, and the protection of ordered liberty.

"Procedural due process" is the twentieth-century term for the traditional concern that no one lose life, liberty, or property without proper adjudication. It appears to have first been used in 1934 by Justice Roberts, dissenting in *Snyder v. Massachusetts*, 291 US 97: "Procedural due process has to do with the manner of the trial; dictates that in the conduct of judicial inquiry certain fundamental rules of fairness be observed; forbids the disregard of those rules, and is not satisfied, though the result is just, if the hearing was unfair." This element of due process most importantly requires that any permanent loss of property be preceded by a fair proceeding by a court with jurisdiction over the matter, and that the person defending there have adequate notice and a fair opportunity to defend the case before an impartial judge (see *Rees v. City of Watertown*, 86 US 107 [1873]; *Hurtado v. California,* 110 US 516 [1884]). The extent of the process required has, since *Mathews v. Eldridge*, 424 US 319 (1976), varied according to the interest at risk: if the interest to the individual is more important, and additional procedures would likely diminish factual mistakes and are not too expensive, it is more likely the procedures will be required.

The most critical question of procedural due process is what interests it protects. The nineteenth- and early twentieth-century view was to distinguish protected rights from unprotected interests. Thus, when Justice Holmes said, "there is no right to be a policeman," it followed that denying certain liberties to a policeman on the job did not give rise to due process requirements (*McAuliffe v. Mayor of New Bedford*, 155 Mass. 216 [1892]). In the last third of the twentieth century, this distinction dissolved, and the Court recognized due process guarantees against the loss of government-created entitlements (*Goldberg v. Kelly*, 397 US 254 [1970]), finding in *Board of Regents v. Roth*, 408 US 564 (1972) that due process rights apply to job termination if a reasonable expectation of continued government employment gives rise to a property interest. *Paul v. Davis*, 424 US 693 (1976) recognized similar protections for a liberty interest. (See also *Morrissey v. Brewer*, 408 US 471 [1972], in reference to prisoner parole hearings; and *Goss v. Lopez*, 419 US 565 [1975], concerning public education.)

The closing decades of the twentieth century saw some retreat from broad applications of procedural due process. Acting often on arguments to reassert the "original intent" of the framers, the Court also limited the requirements of notice, as when a prior conviction serves as notice for all postconviction harms by state officials (*Parratt v. Taylor*, 451 US 527 [1981]), or the definition of liberty is narrowed to exclude the civil commitment to prison (*Kansas v. Hendricks*, 521 US 346 [1997]).

Although review of economic legislation has diminished, it has yet to die. The potential for the Court to strike down state economic regulations persists, although it is unclear how willing the Court is to act on such grounds alone, and much of the scrutiny of state regulations once done as a matter of due process was done in the 1980s and 1990s as review of limitations on property rights under the takings clause (see *Eastern Enterprises v. Apfel*, 524 US 498 [1998]).

The Court has continued to apply due process to protect individual liberties, interpreting it to incorporate the restrictions of the Bill of Rights. In *Twining v. New Jersey*, 211 US 78 (1908), the Court suggested the possibility, manifested in Justice Cardozo's opinion in *Palko v. Connecticut*, 302 US 319 (1937), that some limits on the central government in the first eight amendments are "incorporated" into the due process clause of the Fourteenth Amendment and so binding on the states. Since then, the Court has incorporated into due process the First Amendment's guarantees of speech, religion, and association (*West Virginia v. Barnette*, 319 US 624 [1943]; *Everson v. Board of Education*, 330 US 1 [1947]; *Edwards v. South Carolina*, 372 US 229 [1963]); the Fourth Amendment's warrants and search clauses (*Mapp v. Ohio*, 367 US 643 [1961]; *Ker v. California*, 374 US 23 [1963]); the Fifth Amendment's bars of double jeopardy, self-incrimination, and takings of property without just compensation (*Palko* [1937]; *Malloy v. Hogan*, 378 US 1 [1964]; *Penn Central v. New York City*, 438 US 104 [1978]); the Sixth Amendment's guarantees of a speedy and public jury trial, with notice of the charge, and of the right to confront witnesses, who must appear, and the right to counsel (*Klopfer v. North Carolina*, 386 US 213 [1967]; *In re Oliver*, 333 US 257 [1948]; *Duncan v. Louisiana*, 391 US 145 [1968]; *Cole v. Arkansas*, 333 US 196 [1948]; *Pointer v. Texas*, 380 US 400 [1965]; *Washington v. Texas*, 388 US 56 [1967]; *GIDEON V. WAINWRIGHT*, 372 US 335 [1963]); and the Eighth Amendment's bars on excessive bail and on cruel and unusual punishment (*Schilb v. Kuebel*, 404 US 357 [1971]; *Robinson v. California*, 370 US 660 [1962]).

Vagueness has been a due-process standard for criminal law since *Stromberg v. California*, 283 US 359 (1931), in which Chief Justice Hughes wrote that a statute so vague as to allow the punishment of speech protected under the First Amendment would violate the Fourteenth Amendment. This idea was expanded in 1948 into a general standard of definiteness, which requires that crimes be defined with appropriate definiteness so that anyone with common intelligence can determine what conduct is punishable (*Winters v. New York*, 333 US 507). (See also *Papachristou v. City of Jacksonville*, 405 US 156 [1972], invalidating a vagrancy law, and *Chicago v. Morales*, 527 US 41 [1999], invalidating a gang-member loitering law.)

Some federal due-process cases examine laws more strictly than merely assuring they are reasonable. If a law burdens a fundamental interest in liberty or creates a burden that falls particularly on a discreet and insular minority group that has been denied access to the legislative process, the degree of judicial scrutiny rises, and such laws will only be upheld if they pursue compelling state interests by the most narrowly tailored means possible. This idea, announced in a footnote in Justice Stone's opinion in *United States v. Carolene Products*, 304 US 144 (1938), has been the basis of the development of civil rights doctrines of equal protection. It has also been the basis for several cases that suggest the continuing vitality of general, substantive due process review, as one justification both for decisions protecting a right to privacy and guaranteeing rights to medical procedures (see *PLANNED PARENTHOOD OF SOUTHEASTERN PENNSYLVANIA V. CASEY*, 505 US 833 [1992]; *WASHINGTON V. GLUCKSBERG*, 521 US 702 [1997]).

One important application of this approach has been to read the Fifth Amendment's due-process limits on Congress as including an assurance of equal protection. Signaling such a change in the Japanese internment cases, the Court announced in *Hirabayashi v. United States*, 320 US 81 (1943), that the Fifth Amendment may restrain "such discriminatory legislation by Congress as amounts to a denial of due process" and in *Korematsu v. United States*, 323 US 214 (1944), that "all legal restrictions which curtail the civil rights of a single racial group are immediately suspect" and to be reviewed with "the most rigid scrutiny." Thus in *Bolling v. Sharpe*, 347 US 497 (1954), the Court struck down District of Columbia school-segregation laws under the Fifth Amendment.

Lastly, the states remain important sources for the expansion of due process laws. State courts have the final authority to determine the meaning of state constitutions, and the due process clauses of state law have often been interpreted to encompass broader protections of individual rights than have been found in the Fifth and Fourteenth Amendments.

BIBLIOGRAPHY

Aynes, Richard L. "On Misreading John Bingham and the Fourteenth Amendment." *Yale Law Journal* 103 (October 1993): 57–104.

Ely, James W., Jr. "The Oxymoron Reconsidered: Myth and Reality in the Origins of Substantive Due Process." *Constitutional Commentary* 16 (Summer 1999): 315–345.

Mott, Rodney. *Due Process of Law: A Historical and Analytical Treatise*. Indianapolis, Ind.: Bobbs-Merrill, 1926.

Nelson, William E. *The Fourteenth Amendment: From Political Principle to Judicial Doctrine*. Cambridge, Mass.: Harvard University Press, 1988.

The Burr-Hamilton Duel. This print depicts the common account of the moment Vice President Aaron Burr *(right)* fatally wounded the Federalist Party leader Alexander Hamilton, his archenemy, at Weehawken, N.J., on 11 July 1804. LIBRARY OF CONGRESS

Perry, Michael J. *We the People: The Fourteenth Amendment and the Supreme Court.* New York: Oxford University Press, 1999.

Schwartz, Bernard, ed. *The Fourteenth Amendment: Centennial Volume.* New York: New York University Press, 1970.

Ten Broek, Jacobus. *Equal under Law.* New York: Collier Books, 1965.

Steve Sheppard

See also **Bill of Rights in U.S. Constitution; Constitution of the United States;** *and vol. 9:* **Congress Debates the Fourteenth Amendment.**

DUELING. The practice of dueling dates back to the Middle Ages as a method of settling a point of honor between two men or families. Dueling in the United States fell out of favor by the 1880s but remains a popular and romanticized act of American culture. It arrived in the United States with the first settlers, and the earliest recorded duel in the colonies took place in Plymouth in 1621. Dueling was never very popular in the North and lost favor and legal status there after the American Revolution. In the South, the aristocracy that developed within the planter class embraced dueling as a method of settling disputes of honor. Duels in the South continued through the Civil War, with recorded duels as late as 1901.

Life in the Deep South was isolated and rural, with definitive class and racial distinctions. The solitary life demanded a code of conduct that centered on one's personal honor, as well as family honor, in order to protect the female members of the family. The southern man was raised to defend his community, his state, and his honor, with his life. Early settlers brought the act of dueling from England, Ireland, and Scotland, and American dueling rules were based on English and Irish codes of conduct. Dueling and honor in some parts of the Deep South were influenced by French and Spanish culture as well. Various geographic regions spurred their own codes, and the most popular printed codes were those of South Carolina, New Orleans, and the English code.

For a man to have grounds for challenging an opponent to a duel, he would have to have incurred some form of insult. The code of honor among Southerners strictly prohibited questioning a man's word. To charge him with "giving a lie" was to question his reputation. Without truth in his word, a man had nothing in society and could not be trusted as a business partner or friend. Calling a man a liar was the most common way to bring on a dueling challenge. Other grounds included disputes over gambling, debts, or drunkenness. Contrary to common belief, women were rarely the cause of duels.

After the challenge, the process of dueling required each opponent to choose a second, normally a relative or close friend, and all arrangements for the duel were handled by the seconds. The man challenged had the choice of weapons, normally pistols. Once the arrangements were made, the opponents met on an arranged dueling ground, where the rules were reviewed and the weapons provided. The duel took place at ten to thirty paces, and if no one was hurt on the first shot, the seconds would meet and decide if an additional shot would be taken. Unlike Europeans, Americans gradually developed a preference for dueling to the death as opposed to simply satisfying honor.

A number of duels are known to history, most famously that of Aaron Burr and Alexander Hamilton in 1804. Others include Andrew Jackson and Charles Dickinson in 1817 and John Randolph and Henry Clay in 1826. Though most states had laws against dueling by 1820, the practice continued, usually late at night or at dawn, in open spaces such as fields, racetracks, or small islands near shore. George Washington, Thomas Jefferson, and other political icons supported laws prohibiting dueling, but the practice would not die until the planter class of the antebellum South passed into history at the turn of the twentieth century.

BIBLIOGRAPHY

Greenberg, Kenneth S. *Honor and Slavery.* Princeton, N.J.: Princeton University Press, 1996.

Stowe, Steven M. *Intimacy and Power in the Old South: Ritual in the Lives of the Planters.* Baltimore: Johns Hopkins University Press, 1987.

Wyatt-Brown, Bertram. *Honor and Violence in the Old South.* New York: Oxford University Press, 1986.

Karen Rae Mehaffey

See also **Burr-Hamilton Duel; South, the: The Antebellum South.**

DUGOUT, a temporary home of the prairie settlers. Lumber was scarce and expensive for settlers moving out to the plains in the late nineteenth century, so they erected these structures to provide immediate shelter for themselves and their families. Built into the side of a hill or ravine, a dugout was constructed of sod bricks, a wooden door and window frames, and a roof of brush. They were generally built into hills facing south or east, away from the harshest winter winds. A dugout was usually replaced after some time by a SOD HOUSE as a settler's abode.

BIBLIOGRAPHY

Dickenson, James R. *Home on the Range: A Century on the High Plains.* New York: Scribners, 1995.

Rogers, Mondel. *Old Ranches of the Texas Plains: Paintings.* College Station: Texas A&M University Press, 1976.

Eli Moses Diner

See also **Westward Migration.**

DUKE OF YORK'S LAWS, a legal code drawn up in 1665 by Gov. Richard Nicolls in order to bring a more uniform system of government to the newly created shire of Yorkshire. Nicolls drew largely from the existing codes of Massachusetts and New Haven and negotiated with representatives in the assembly to produce the final version. He established a civil and criminal code with provisions for local governments, provincial courts, and a militia, as well as regulations for Indian affairs, ecclesiastical establishments, social and domestic regulations, standards for weights and measures, and legal methods for recordkeeping. Gradually, the code was extended to apply to the whole province of New York.

BIBLIOGRAPHY

Merwick, Donna. *Possessing Albany, 1630–1710. The Dutch and English Experiences.* Cambridge, U.K.; New York: Cambridge University Press, 1990.

Rink, Oliver A. *Holland on the Hudson: An Economic and Social History of Dutch New York.* Ithaca, N.Y.: Cornell University Press; Cooperstown, N.Y.: New York State Historical Association, 1986.

A. C. Flick/Shelby Balik

See also **Colonial Policy, British; Colonial Settlements; New Netherland; New York Colony.**

DUKE OF YORK'S PROPRIETARY had its origin in the new nationalism of the Restoration period in England. King Charles II decided to conquer NEW NETHERLAND and to bestow it on his brother, James Stuart, Duke of York. After purchasing the claims to Long Island and northern Maine, in March 1664—several months before the conquest of New Netherland—the king conveyed to the duke a proprietary stretching from the Connecticut River to the Delaware River and Delaware Bay, including the nearby islands of Martha's Vineyard, Nantucket, and Long Island, and the part of Maine north of Sir Ferdinando Gorges's grant situated between the St. Croix and the Pemaquid.

The duke's charter granted him unchecked authority to rule his province. Holding all legislative, executive, and judicial power subject only to appeal to the king, he delegated this authority to governors, whom he carefully instructed about policy. Regions preponderantly English, such as Long Island, were governed by laws of neighboring colonies. Liberty of conscience (the idea that a person's thoughts cannot be legislated) prevailed throughout the province. Two features, however, grated on the duke's subjects: his inordinate interest in revenue and the absence of a representative assembly. Although he at first denied petitions for representation, he later instructed his governor, Sir Edmund Andros, to call an assembly, which met for a few sessions in 1683–1685 and adopted the CHARTER OF LIBERTIES. However, it came to an abrupt end with the creation of the DOMINION OF NEW ENGLAND.

Rival claims and limited vision resulted in periodic dismemberment of the duke's domain. Even before the conquest of New Netherland, he had leased the rich farmlands of the Jerseys. In 1664, another piece went to Connecticut, whose charter of 1662 overlapped the duke's grant. Long Island was also included in both grants, although a commission headed by Colonel Richard Nicolls, the governor of New York, settled the dispute in 1667 by assigning Long Island to New York, and land west of the Connecticut River to within twenty miles of the Hudson River, to Connecticut.

The duke granted his possessions on the west bank of Delaware Bay to William Penn in 1682, probably in deference to the duke's regard for Penn's father, Admiral William Penn. Penn was afraid his proprietary of Pennsylvania might be shut out from the ocean by the possessor of the territory to the south, along the west shore of the river and bay. In 1682, York executed two leases, although he had no strict legal title to these lands that he claimed only by right of conquest. The duke made an effort, perhaps at Penn's instigation, to obtain a royal grant, but its dubious validity prompted the duke, after his accession to the throne as James II in 1685, to plan to grant Penn a royal charter. His abdication in 1688, however, disrupted this plan.

The last sizable outlying section of the duke's proprietary to go was Pemaquid, which became part of the Dominion of New England in June 1686. James, having become king, apparently had no further interest in keeping the scattered pieces of his proprietary intact and turned his attention to experimenting with dominion rule throughout the English provinces. After the overthrow of the dominion in 1689 by revolutions in Boston and New York City, New York became a royal province with representative government.

BIBLIOGRAPHY

Kammen, Michael, ed. *Colonial New York: A History.* New York: Scribners, 1975.

Viola F. Barnes / C. W.

See also **Colonial Charters; New York Colony; Western Lands.**

DULL KNIFE CAMPAIGN (1878–1879). After the Battle of Little Bighorn, hundreds of Northern Cheyenne were forcibly relocated to a reservation at Darlington, in the Indian Territory, where dozens perished from sickness. On 9 September 1878 the survivors started for their home in Montana, led by Chief Dull Knife and Chief Little Wolf. Fighting off pursuing troops in several skirmishes, they crossed the Kansas border, killing cowmen and hunters as they progressed. The band contained 89 warriors and 246 women and children. Although large forces of troops were sent to head them off, the Cheyenne eluded or defeated every detachment, killing Lt. Col. William H. Lewis at Punished Women's Fork on 28 September and slaying 18 settlers at Sappa Creek, Kansas, on 30 September.

In October the Cheyenne crossed the South Platte River, and the camps of Little Wolf and Dull Knife separated. Dull Knife's people were captured on 23 October by Col. J. B. Johnson and placed in empty barracks at Fort Robinson, Nebraska. Capt. Henry W. Wessells, commandant, received orders on 5 January 1879, to transport the Indians back to Oklahoma, but they refused to go. When, five days later, Wessells arrested the chiefs Wild Hog and Crow, the remainder of the band broke out of the barracks and made a dash for freedom. Troops pursued, but it was not until 22 January that the last of the Indians were killed or captured. Dull Knife escaped to the Sioux. Little Wolf's band, induced to surrender by Lt. W. P. Clark at Boxelder Creek on 25 March, was permitted to remain in Montana.

BIBLIOGRAPHY

Boye, Alan. *Holding Stone Hands: On the Trail of the Cheyenne Exodus.* Lincoln: University of Nebraska Press, 1999.

Sandoz, Mari. *Cheyenne Autumn.* Lincoln: University of Nebraska Press, 1992

Paul I. Wellman / A. R.

See also **Indian Removal; Indian Reservations; Indian Territory; Little Bighorn, Battle of; Scouting on the Plains.**

DUMBARTON OAKS CONFERENCE was held from 21 August to 7 October 1944 at an estate in the Georgetown area of Washington, D.C. Four powers participated: the United States, Great Britain, the Soviet Union, and China. Because of Soviet neutrality in the Asian conflict, China only attended beginning 29 September, the day the Russians departed. The conference had the task of preparing a charter for a "general international organization," as stipulated in the Moscow Declaration of 30 October 1943. The conference chose the name of the wartime alliance, the United Nations (UN), for the new body. In imitation of the League of Nations, the new UN would possess a Security Council, a General Assembly, a Secretariat, and an International Court of Justice. To avoid, however, the pitfalls of the League of Nations, the conferees concluded that unanimous votes should not be mandatory to reach decisions in the Security Council or the General Assembly; all signatories must agree in advance to act on the Security Council's findings; contingents of the armed forces of member states must be at Security Council disposal; and that the creation of an Economic and Social Council was necessary. Certain crucial matters were deferred to such meetings as Yalta (February 1945) and San Francisco (April–June 1945). The most important deferred decision concerned the use of the veto in the Security Council. All participants at Dumbarton Oaks agreed on the right of the permanent Security Council members to exercise the veto to prevent the UN from taking any action against themselves. They nonetheless deferred for future consideration the stage at which they might interpose their vetoes. Other matters postponed for further consideration included voting procedures in the Security Council, admission to the new body, the jurisdiction of the International Court, and the former German islands in the Pacific that had been mandated to Japan.

BIBLIOGRAPHY

Hilderbrand, Robert C. *Dumbarton Oaks: The Origins of the United Nations and the Search for Postwar Security.* Chapel Hill: University of North Carolina Press, 1990.

Schild, Georg. *Bretton Woods and Dumbarton Oaks: American Economic and Political Postwar Planning in the Summer of 1944.* New York: St. Martin's Press, 1995.

Justus D. Doenecke

See also **League of Nations; United Nations; Yalta Conference.**

DUNMORE'S WAR (1774) resulted from competion between American Indians and white colonists for control of the trans-Ohio region. Tensions between Virginians and Pennsylvanians, who vied for possession of the fort at Pittsburgh, exacerbated the conflicts. Early in 1774 an agent of the royal governor of Virginia, the Earl of Dunmore, took possession of Fort Pitt, renamed it Fort Dunmore, and initiated attacks against local Indian settlements. The Delawares, under the influence of Moravian missionaries, kept the peace, but the Shawnees pressed for war. On 10 June the governor called out the militia of southwest Virginia, which, under Gen. Andrew Lewis, prepared for an expedition to the Shawnee towns beyond the Ohio.

Early in August the militia of Frederick County, Virginia, raided the Wapatomica towns on the Muskingum River. Dunmore advanced in person to Fort Dunmore, where he called on the neighboring militia to join in an expedition against the Shawnees. Before he could join Lewis, Shawnee warriors attacked Lewis's division on 10 October. After an all-day battle at Point Pleasant, Lewis won a decisive victory. The Shawnees fled to their Ohio towns, and the chiefs sought Dunmore's camp and offered peace. Dunmore marched to the Pickaway Plains, where he established Camp Charlotte and made a treaty, which was sealed by the delivery of hostages. For the colonists who participated, this victory provided valuable military experience that would benefit the soldiers during the Revolutionary War. For the American Indian groups, defeat intensified resentment over white encroachment and heightened the stakes in competition for the Ohio Valley.

BIBLIOGRAPHY

Calloway, Colin. *The American Revolution in Indian Country: Crisis and Diversity in Native American Communities.* Cambridge, U.K.: Cambridge University Press, 1995.

Dowd, Gregory Evans. *A Spirited Resistance: The North American Indian Struggle for Unity, 1745–1815.* Baltimore: Johns Hopkins University Press, 1992.

Merrell, James H. *Into the American Woods: Negotiators on the Pennsylvania Frontier.* New York: W. W. Norton, 1999.

Louise Phelps Kellogg / s. b.

See also **Frontier; Frontier Defense; Indian Treaties; Ohio Wars; Shawnee;** *and vol. 9:* **Logan's Speech.**

DUQUESNE, FORT, a French stronghold at the confluence of the Allegheny and Monongahela Rivers, at Pittsburgh, Pennsylvania. In 1753, the Marquis Duquesne de Menneville, governor of New France, moved to seize the Ohio Valley from the British. On the route from Lake Erie to the Allegheny River, forts were erected at Presque Isle, Le Boeuf, and Venango. In the same year, Robert Dinwiddie, British lieutenant-governor, sent George Washington to warn the French to cease encroaching on the Ohio Valley. The French refused to back down. In February 1754, an expedition of 800 Frenchmen left Montreal, and, on 17 April, took possession of the fort being built by the Ohio Company at the confluence of the Ohio River. The French destroyed this work and constructed Fort Duquesne on the site. The rivers protected two sides of the triangle; walls of squared logs and earth twelve feet thick protected its base. Outside the walls was a deep ditch and beyond that a log stockade.

Troops left Fort Duquesne to defeat Washington at Great Meadows in 1754 and to rout Gen. Edward Braddock's expedition in 1755. After Braddock's defeat, the French held undisputed possession of the Ohio Valley for three years, administering their military occupation from Fort Duquesne and stimulating Indian raids on the frontiers of Pennsylvania, Virginia, and the Carolinas. Finally, on 24 November 1758, when Gen. John Forbes's expedition neared the forks of the Ohio, the French destroyed Fort Duquesne and retreated. The English rebuilt the fort and renamed it Fort Pitt; the protection provided by Fort Pitt allowed Pittsburgh to develop as a city.

BIBLIOGRAPHY

O'Meara, Walter. *Guns at the Forks.* Englewood Cliffs, N.J.: Prentice-Hall, 1965; Pittsburgh, Pa.: University of Pittsburgh Press, 1979.

Solon J. Buck / a. r.

See also **Braddock's Expedition; French and Indian War; Monongahela River; Pennsylvania.**

DUST BOWL, a 97-million-acre section of southeastern Colorado, northeastern New Mexico, western Kansas, and the panhandles of Texas and Oklahoma, that in the Depression-torn 1930s was devastated by dust storms, resulting in the one of the greatest agroecological disasters in American history. Already suffering from one

Dust Bowl. Covering their mouths against the ever-present dust, two females seek water from a pump. AP/WIDE WORLD PHOTOS

of the worst droughts in recent history and with eastern markets insisting upon the adoption of unsustainable agricultural practices to maximize production, the region was hit by strong winds that lifted the dry topsoil from fields, creating clouds of dust that, at their worst, plunged communities into total darkness sometimes for hours at a time. As a result of economic and agricultural depression, many small farmers were forced to foreclose and leave the region.

BIBLIOGRAPHY

Bonnifield, Mathew Paul. *The Dust Bowl: Men, Dirt, and Depression.* Albuquerque: University of New Mexico Press, 1979.

Gregory, James N. *American Exodus: The Dust Bowl Migration and Okie Culture in California.* New York: Oxford University Press, 1989.

Hurt, R. Douglas. *The Dust Bowl: An Agricultural and Social History.* Chicago: Nelson-Hall, 1981.

Worster, Donald. *Dust Bowl: The Southern Plains in the 1930s.* New York: Oxford University Press, 1979.

Michael Egan

See also **Great Depression.**

DUTCH BANKERS' LOANS. The financial independence of the United States was assured when John Adams, minister to the Hague, secured in June 1782 the flotation of a $2 million loan through Amsterdam banking houses. The loan secured for the American government badly needed foreign exchange and tacitly recognized the enlarged commercial role played by the United States, whose trade with Holland and France had developed considerably since 1775. It also foreshadowed the interest of the Dutch in American commercial, security, land, bank, and canal enterprises over the next twenty years.

BIBLIOGRAPHY

Bemis, Samuel Flagg. *The Diplomacy of the American Revolution.* Bloomington: Indiana University Press, 1957.

Ellis, Joseph. *Passionate Sage: The Character and Legacy of John Adams.* New York: Norton, 1993.

Robert A. East / A. G.

See also **Debt and Investment, Foreign; Debts, Colonial and Continental; Trade, Foreign.**

DUTCH WEST INDIA COMPANY. The Dutch West India Company was organized by Dutch merchants and chartered by the States General on 3 June 1621. The charter conferred considerable political and commercial powers on the company, including monopolistic trading privileges in parts of Africa, the West Indies, America, and Australia, as well as the rights to make alliances with the natives, build forts, and plant colonies. The company planted settlements at Fort Orange (1624) and Manhattan

Island (1625), forming the colony of New Netherland. The director and council of New Netherland acted on the company's instructions and required strict obedience from all colonists. The colony's welfare suffered from this continued despotic control and the company's neglect of colonization efforts in order to focus on trade.

BIBLIOGRAPHY

Merwick, Donna. *Possessing Albany, 1630–1710: The Dutch and English Experiences.* New York: Cambridge University Press, 1990.

Rink, Oliver A. *Holland on the Hudson: An Economic and Social History of Dutch New York.* Ithaca, N.Y.: Cornell University Press, 1986.

A.C. Flick / S. B.

See also **Colonial Settlements; New Amsterdam; New Netherland; New York Colony; Petition and Remonstrance of New Netherland.**

DUTIES, AD VALOREM AND SPECIFIC. Duties are levied upon imports, ad valorem as a percentage of their price and specific as a fixed amount per unit. Both are a source of revenue for the government. Ad valorem duties provide the least protection when imports are inexpensive; conversely, protection is greatest when imports are expensive and therefore fall in volume. Specific duties prevent a reduction in revenue when prices fall so they were often favored for commodities which have unstable prices. Customs administrators generally prefer specific rather than ad valorem duties, in particular because of the difficulty in determining the correct value of the latter. Ad valorem duties are also much easier to evade.

The first United States tariff act, passed in 1789, used both ad valorem and specific duties, but they were mostly low. The tariff act of 1816 was more explicitly protectionist and extended the range of specific duties. The rates in the Walker Tariff Act of 1846 and The Tariff Act of 1857 were entirely ad valorem. The Morrill Tariff Act of 1861 restored many specific duties and in the long era of protectionism that ensued, they were largely retained.

The framers of the Wilson Tariff Act of 1894 unsuccessfully attempted to substitute ad valorem rates for many of the specific duties. In the Dingley Tariff Act of 1897 and The Payne-Aldrich Tariff Act Of 1909 there was a clear trend toward more numerous and more detailed specific duties. The tariff act of 1897 adopted the former practice of combining specific compensatory duties and ad valorem protective duties. Under this act commodity duties were raised to the highest average level of the nineteenth century. Specific compensatory duties are intended to compensate manufacturers for the higher cost of raw materials, insofar as such higher cost is caused directly by the tariff.

The tariff act of 1909 replaced many ad valorem with specific duties. Changes from specific to ad valorem rates, however, were a characteristic of the Underwood Tariff Act of 1913. In the Emergency Tariff Act of 1921 the duties were specific, with the exception of ad valorem duties on cattle, prepared or preserved meat, wheat flour and semolina, and cheese. A significant characteristic of the Fordney-McCumber Tariff Act of 1922 was the frequency of the compound duty, a combination of specific and ad valorem duties.

In the Smoot-Hawley Tariff Act of 1930, most duties were specific. Under the act duties reached a historic equivalent average ad valorem peak of 41 percent. The Roosevelt administration believed that the Smoot-Hawley tariff was exacerbating the Great Depression. The Trade Agreements Act of 1934 empowered the president to negotiate reductions in duties.

After World War II the United States used the General Agreement on Tariffs and Trade (GATT), created in 1947, to persuade the rest of the world to liberalize trade. At home, the trade acts of 1962, 1974, 1984, and 1988 resulted in substantial tariff rate reductions and movement to an equal balance between specific and ad valorem duties. In the international agreement of 1994 to replace GATT with the World Trade Organization, the United States agreed to further trade liberalization. However, that has not prevented the occasional use of ad valorem anti-dumping duties against particular imports.

BIBLIOGRAPHY

Ratner, Sidney. *The Tariff in American History.* New York: Van Nostrand, 1972.

Salvatore, Dominick. *International Economics.* 7th ed.. New York: Wiley, 2001.

Taussig, F. W. *The Tariff History of the United States.* 8th ed. New York: Putnam's, 1931.

Richard A. Hawkins

See also **General Agreement on Tariffs and Trade; Tariff.**

DVD. The Digital Versatile Disc (DVD) is an optical information storage technology with multiple applications. Lasers read pitted digital patterns stamped on DVDs. American, Dutch, and Japanese manufacturers, specifically Philips Electronics, Sony Corporation, Matsushita Electric Industrial Company, and Toshiba Corporation, innovated DVDs simultaneously to surpass compact disc (CD) memory capabilities. Industrial DVD standards were released in 1995 after producers of rival formats, Super Density and Multi Media Compact Disc agreed to coordinate efforts which resulted in the creation of DVDs.

DVDs consist of two extremely thin, round plastic discs known as substrates, which are sealed together. Each DVD can store 4.7 gigabytes of compressed information per side, enough to hold a two-hour movie. If the sides are double-layered, a DVD can contain 17 gigabytes.

American manufacturers first distributed DVD players and introduced DVD-Video for movie storage in

1997. Starting that year, people could also access computer programs stored on DVD-Read-Only Memory (DVD-ROM). In 1998, DVD-Random-Access Memory (DVD-RAM) enabled users to record data on DVDs. By 2000, DVD-Audio provided an alternative to CD players and acoustically supplemented DVD-Video. Consumers eagerly bought several million units of DVD products making them the most quickly adopted technology in the history of electronics.

Most computers manufactured since the late 1990s have incorporated DVD drives. In the early 2000s, engineers had refined DVD technology, issuing new types of recording players and disc polymers. Electronics companies continued to secure patents for innovative DVD designs.

BIBLIOGRAPHY

De Lancie, Philip, and Mark Ely. *DVD Production.* Boston: Focal Press, 2000.

Purcell, Lee. *CD-R/DVD: Disc Recording Demystified.* New York: McGraw-Hill, 2000.

Taylor, Jim. *DVD Demystified.* 2nd ed. New York: McGraw-Hill, 2001.

Elizabeth D. Schafer

See also **Computers and Computer Industry; Electricity and Electronics.**

E

"E PLURIBUS UNUM" (Out of many, one), motto featured on the Great Seal of the United States. After declaring independence, the CONTINENTAL CONGRESS appointed Benjamin Franklin, John Adams, and Thomas Jefferson to devise a seal. In consultation with Swiss-born artist Pierre Eugène du Simitière, they selected E Pluribus Unum, motto of the popular London-based anthology, *Gentleman's Magazine*, to emblematize the diversity of the American people. Scholars have not located the exact phrase in classical literature, but Virgil's *Moretum* contains a similar expression. Subsequent committees kept this motto, but substituted an eagle for the proposed heraldic shield. Adopted by Congress on 20 June 1782, the Great Seal appears on numerous currencies, seals, and flags.

BIBLIOGRAPHY

McDonald, Forrest. *E Pluribus Unum: The Formation of the American Republic, 1776–1790.* Boston: Houghton Mifflin, 1976. A history of the critical period taking E Pluribus Unum as its theme.

Patterson, Richard S., and Richardson Dougall. *The Eagle and the Shield: A History of the Great Seal of the United States.* Washington, D.C.: Office of the Historian, Bureau of Public Affairs, Department of State, under the Auspices of the American Revolution Bicentennial Administration, 1976. The most thorough history of the Great Seal, its origins, components, and official uses.

Benjamin H. Irvin

See also **Seal of the United States.**

EADS BRIDGE, the first bridge across the MISSISSIPPI RIVER, constructed 1868–1874 at Saint Louis, Missouri. Engineer James B. Eads, designer of IRONCLAD WARSHIPS for the Union navy, spent part of his youth in Saint Louis and was active in raising funds for the bridge project. He spanned the river with three arches of steel ribs and iron girders. The central span measures 520 feet and the two side spans 502 feet each—the longest arches in existence at the time it was constructed. For many years, the bridge was the only one crossing the river that far south and still serves as a major vehicular artery across the Mississippi.

Eads Bridge. A view of the long arches of the first bridge across the Mississippi River. LIBRARY OF CONGRESS

BIBLIOGRAPHY

Dorsey, Florence L. *Road to the Sea: The Story of James B. Eads and the Mississippi River.* New York: Rinehart, 1947.

Petroski, Henry. *Engineers of Dreams: Great Bridge Builders and the Spanning of America.* New York: Knopf, 1995.

Scott, Quinta. *The Eads Bridge.* Columbia: University of Missouri Press, 1979.

Alvin F. Harlow / A. R.

See also **Bridges; Railroads; Saint Louis.**

EAGLE, AMERICAN. The American bald eagle *(Haliaeetus leucocephalus)* was chosen in 1782 by a committee of the Continental Congress consisting of Arthur Middleton and John Rutledge of South Carolina, Elias Boudinot of New Jersey, and Arthur Lee of Virginia to represent the infant nation on an official seal. The Continental Congress had put aside the matter of the seal in 1776, returning to it in May 1782, when shown a sketch of a bald eagle drawn by the brother of a Philadelphia naturalist, who argued that the raptor represents "supreme power and authority." An informal heraldic seal bore the eagle, along with other symbols of the new nation, until Charles Thomson of Philadelphia devised a

American Eagle. Marcus W. Baldwin's drawing from 1898—the year of the Spanish-American War—shows a bald eagle resting on an American flag, its talons grasping war arrows and an olive branch of peace. LIBRARY OF CONGRESS

new seal that was officially adopted as the emblem of the United States in 1787 and is still in use today. It has since appeared on coinage. The species is protected under the National Emblem Act of 1940.

BIBLIOGRAPHY

Herrick, Francis Hobart. *The American Eagle: A Study in Natural and Civil History.* New York: D. Appleton-Century, 1934.

Stalmaster, Mark V. *The Bald Eagle.* New York: Universe Books, 1987.

Alvin F. Harlow
John Howard Smith

See also **Continental Congress; Currency and Coinage; Seal of the United States.**

EAGLETON AFFAIR. Senator George McGovern of South Dakota, the Democratic Party's nominee for president in 1972, selected Missouri Senator Thomas Eagleton to be his vice-presidential running mate. Eagleton, a fellow liberal and Vietnam dove, appeared to be a good choice. But after news sources revealed that he had undergone shock therapy and hospitalization several times in the past, many Democrats feared that his continuing presence would hurt the ticket in November. Although McGovern initially declared that he supported Eagleton "1,000 percent," he soon replaced the Missourian with Sargent Shriver, the husband of John F. Kennedy's sister. As a result of the Eagleton affair, McGovern's campaign for the presidency was seriously damaged, and he never recovered from it.

BIBLIOGRAPHY

White, Theodore. *The Making of the President, 1972.* New York: Atheneum, 1973.

William C. Berman

See also **Elections, Presidential.**

EARTH DAY. Following an idea pioneered by the Democratic senator Gaylord Nelson of Wisconsin, the first nationwide Earth Day was celebrated on 22 April 1970. (A month earlier, San Francisco had organized its own Earth Day celebration at the instigation of the social activist John McConnell.) Concerned by the dark side of economic progress and inspired by the protest movements of the 1960s, twenty million Americans took to the streets to demonstrate for a cleaner environment. In its aftermath, President Richard M. Nixon proposed the creation of the Environmental Protection Agency in July 1970 and Congress passed the Clean Air (1970), Clean Water (1972), and Endangered Species (1973) Acts. In 1990, Earth Day, held every year since 1970 on 22 April, became a worldwide celebration.

BIBLIOGRAPHY

Hayes, Denis. *The Official Earth Day Guide to Planet Repair.* Washington, D.C.: Island Press, 2000.

Philippe R. Girard

See also **Conservation; Environmental Protection Agency.**

EARTHQUAKES occur when the lithospheric plates that compose the surface of the earth shift in relation to one another. Earthquakes are happening constantly all over the world, but major quakes seem to occur only once every two or three years. The size of an earthquake is generally described in terms of intensity and magnitude. The Modified Mercalli scale gauges earthquake intensity by assessing the effect of the quake on the inhabitants of an area. Intensity assessments do not depend on seismographic instruments, but are subjective appraisals of (1) human and animal reaction to shaking and, (2) damage to structures of human origin and to the ground surface. Seismologists use the scale to assign to each earthquake an intensity ranking from I (felt by only a few people under favorable conditions) to XII (total damage).

Magnitude of energy released by an earthquake at its point of origin is a strictly quantitative measure based upon data from seismographs that record maximum wave amplitude (the extreme range of vibrations—or shock waves—caused by the sudden movement of the earth's crust). Charles Richter developed the first magnitude scale in 1935, but a variety of magnitude scales are used today. The Richter magnitude scale has no upper or lower numerical limits; some very small earthquakes are actually given negative numbers. The scale is logarithmic, meaning that each increase of one Richter number represents

Earthquakes. Large cracks split the ground after an earthquake in Alaska. JLM VISUALS

a tenfold increase in the magnitude of the earthquake. An earthquake of magnitude 5 releases energy equivalent to that released by 1,000 tons of TNT. Recently, seismologists and earthquake engineers have begun to use a measure called "seismic moment" to estimate the size of seismic sources. Moment magnitude measures the leverage of the forces (couples) across the whole area of the fault slip rather than just wave motion, which is affected by fracture and friction in the rocks.

Scientists have used intensity and magnitude data to prepare seismic risk maps of the United States. One map places locales in one of four zones: Zone 0, such as Florida, is an area where no damage is expected; Zone 3 is one in which a quake intensity of VIII and higher is expected, as in parts of CALIFORNIA. The western United States exhibits the greatest seismic activity in the country—especially Alaska, California, Nevada, Utah, and Montana—although the upper part of the Mississippi embayment, southwest Kentucky, southern Illinois, and southeastern Missouri are also seismically active.

The historical record of earthquakes in the United States goes back to 1638 in NEW ENGLAND and to about 1800 in California. One of the earliest major earthquakes to affect the colonies occurred in the Three Rivers area north of Quebec, along the lower SAINT LAWRENCE RIVER, on 5 February 1663. It caused chimneys to break as far away as Massachusetts Bay. In the early nineteenth century, the Midwest was hit with a series of earthquakes that began in New Madrid, Missouri. The largest of the shocks from these quakes, which occurred in 1811 and 1812, were felt over an area of about 950,250 square miles. Nor has the southern part of the United States been spared. An unpredicted earthquake occurred near Charleston, South Carolina, on 31 August 1886 that did considerable damage in Charleston (much of which was built on filled land) and killed, by some estimates, more than one hundred people. It was the largest seismic event in recorded history on the eastern seaboard. Tremors were felt as far away as New York, Boston, Cuba, and Bermuda. The most notorious earthquake in U.S. history was the one that hit SAN FRANCISCO on 18 April 1906. It was associated with a rupture of the San Andreas fault from the vicinity of Point Delgada to a point in San Benito County near San Juan, a distance of more than 250 miles. The shock hit at 5 A.M. and, almost instantly, building after building crumbled to the ground. Thousands of fires ignited and burned out of control for three days fed by severed electrical wires, overturned coal burners, ruptured gas mains, broken water lines that prevented fighting the fires, and bungled efforts of troops trying to create backfires with

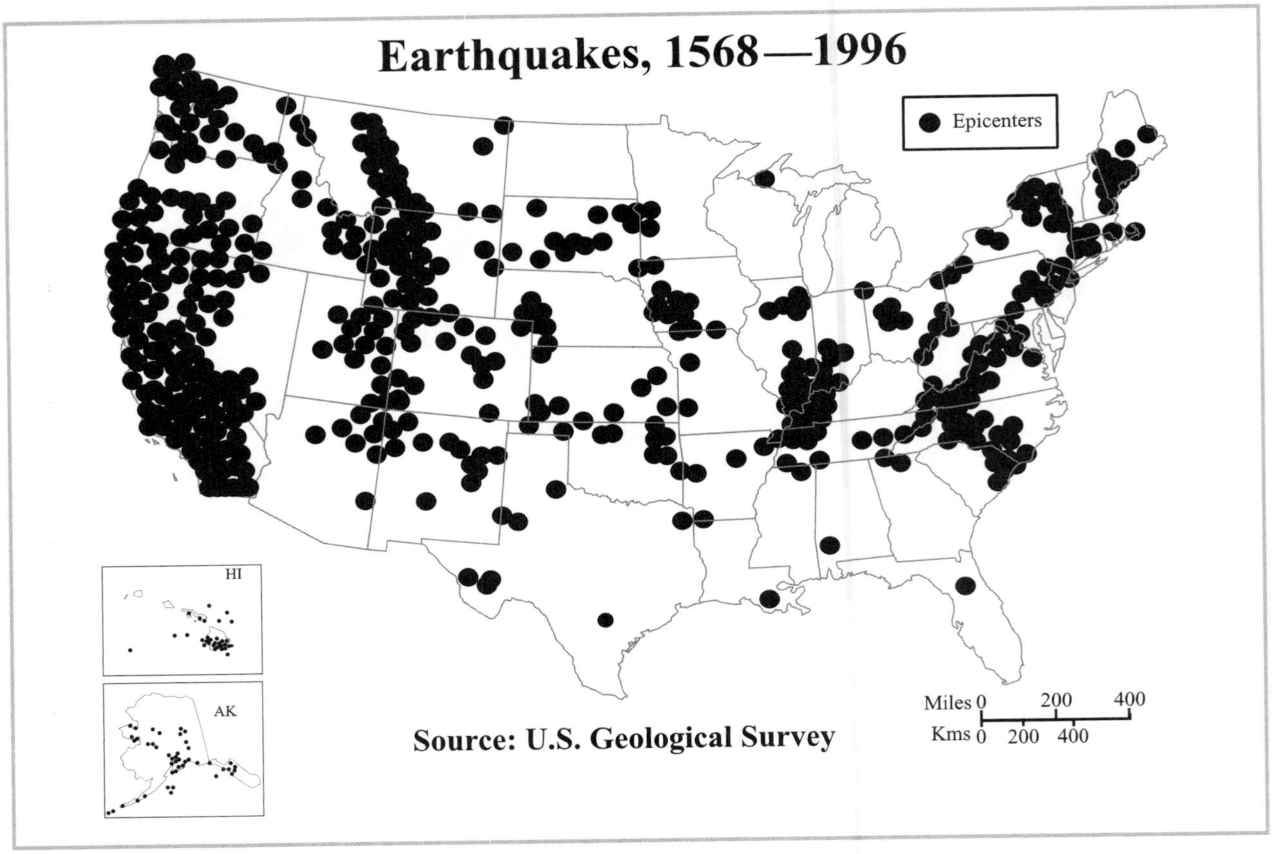

dynamite. The earthquake and fire caused extensive damage throughout northern California, but in San Francisco it obliterated 500 city blocks, caused nearly $500 million in damages, and killed more than 3,000 people.

California was hit again by major earthquakes in 1925 and 1933, but it was almost sixty years before the United States experienced another quake of the magnitude of the 1906 San Francisco earthquake. That event occurred during the late afternoon of 27 March 1964, at 5:36 P.M. local time. An earthquake of magnitude 8.6 on the Richter scale occurred in the sparsely inhabited mountainous area of northern Prince William Sound in south central ALASKA. It caused serious damage within an area of approximately 7,500 square miles, creating large changes in land levels and vertical displacements of nearly thirty-six feet in places along the continental margin. Three hundred people were killed, some from the effects of the quake itself and others by drowning in the seismic seawave (tsunami, or tidal wave) caused by the quake.

During the last third of the twentieth century, California again rocked from seismic activity. On 9 February 1971, an earthquake of magnitude 6.5 on the Richter scale struck the San Fernando Valley. This earthquake demonstrated the extent of damage that can occur from a moderate shock centered in a large metropolitan area (the Los Angeles Basin, with a population of 5 million). It caused sixty-five deaths, and damage was estimated to exceed $500 million. Southern California experienced an earthquake measuring 6.4 on the Richter scale in 1979. Eight years later, another quake in the area measured 5.9. In October 1989, the Loma Prieta earthquake struck the San Francisco Bay area, killing at least sixty-three people and collapsing several elevated highways, including a section of the bridge between San Francisco and Oakland. Damages from this earthquake, that registered 7.1 on the Richter scale, reached $6–7 billion. In 1992, a quake measuring 7.4 on the Richter scale struck the desert east of LOS ANGELES, with one fatality. That same year, a quake of 6.9 struck northern California, with no fatalities. And in 1994, a major quake struck the Los Angeles area, with its epicenter in the city's Northridge section. This quake, measuring 6.6 on the Richter scale, damaged many structures in the city, including freeways, and killed at least fifty-one people. Property losses exceeded $4 billion. Scientists have not yet determined how to predict the precise onset of an earthquake; however, since the 1960s, engineers have developed earthquake-resistant building techniques that can reduce the impact of ground shaking. Regardless, public acceptance of earthquake probability estimates and mandated hazard abatement measures often has been slow.

BIBLIOGRAPHY

Bolt, Bruce A. *Earthquakes.* New York: Freeman, 1999.

Bolt, Bruce A. *Earthquakes and Geological Discovery.* New York: Scientific American Library, 1993.

Coffman, Jerry L., and Carl A. von Hake, eds. *Earthquake History of the United States.* Boulder, Colo.: Environmental Data Service, 1973.

Geschwind, Carl-Henry. *California Earthquakes: Science, Risk, and the Politics of Hazard Mitigation.* Baltimore: Johns Hopkins University Press, 2001.

Hansen, Gladys C., and Emmet Condon. *Denial of Disaster: The Untold Story and Photographs of the San Francisco Earthquake and Fire of 1906.* San Francisco: Cameron, 1989; 1990.

Steinberg, Theodore. *Acts of God: The Unnatural History of Natural Disaster in America.* New York: Oxford University Press, 2000.

Bruce A. Bolt
Nancy M. Gordon / C. P.

See also **Charleston; Disasters; Geological Survey, U.S.; San Francisco Earthquakes.**

EAST INDIA COMPANY, ENGLISH. The English East India Company (1600–1874) was one of the longest-lived and richest trading companies. It exercised a pervasive influence on British colonial policy from early in its history because of its wealth and power both in England and in the rest of the commercial world. Nevertheless, not until the era of the American Revolution did the company figure in American affairs. At that time it was expanding its activities in the East, particularly in China, and in order to strengthen its rather precarious foothold at Canton, the company purchased increasing amounts of tea. Soon, with its warehouses overflowing and a financial crisis looming, the company surrendered part of its political power for the exclusive right to export tea directly to America under Lord North's Regulating Act (1773).

This development coincided with and influenced the outbreak of disputes between Great Britain and its American colonies. After Britain imposed the tea tax in 1767, American boycotts reduced colonial tea consumption from 900,000 pounds in 1769 to 237,000 pounds in 1772. The Regulating Act allowed the East India Company to ship huge quantities of tea to America duty-free. Although this act allowed Americans to purchase tea at a discounted rate (even accounting for the tea tax), it also enabled the East India Company to undersell colonial smugglers who had benefited from tea boycotts. When Boston importers resisted Patriot pressure to refuse tea shipments, proponents of the tea boycott organized anti-British activities, which culminated in the Boston Tea Party (1773). After the Revolution the company had little or no contact with America.

BIBLIOGRAPHY

Keay, John. *The Honourable Company: A History of the English East India Company.* New York: Macmillan, 1994.

Lawson, Philip. *The East India Company: A History.* New York: Longman, 1993.

Charles F. Mullett / S. B.

See also **Boston Tea Party; Coercive Acts; East Indies Trade; Intolerable Acts; Smuggling, Colonial; Tea, Duty on.**

EAST INDIES TRADE. During the late eighteenth and early nineteenth centuries, East Indies commerce spanned the Atlantic and Indian oceans, including such points of trade as Salem, Massachsuetts; the Cape of Good Hope; Mauritius; Madras; Bombay; Calcutta; and Canton. Ships traveling between these ports carried provisions such as wine, tea, cotton, iron, ginseng, furs, naval supplies, and specie. The end of the East India Company's monopoly in 1813 and the end of the Napoleonic wars in 1814 increased competition until it was sometimes cheaper to buy Indian goods in London. By 1840 American merchants were importing Calcutta goods from Manchester, England, and shipping cloth from Lowell, Massachusetts, to India.

BIBLIOGRAPHY

Keay, John. *The Honourable Company: A History of the English East India Company.* New York: MacMillan, 1994.

Kenneth Wiggins Porter / S. B.

See also **Colonial Commerce; Dutch West India Company; East India Company, English; Trade, Foreign; Trading Companies.**

EAST JERSEY. East Jersey was incorporated as a proprietary holding within the colony of New Jersey after the English conquest of 1664. From its inception it fell victim to conflicting claims. George Carteret was the original proprietor designated by the Crown; he and his heirs added others, so that by the Revolution, the Board of East Jersey Proprietors centered on Perth Amboy numbered twenty-four shareholders. Meanwhile, late in the seventeenth century the king granted some of the same land to the Puritan-dominated Elizabethtown patentees, who settled the towns of Newark and Elizabeth and their environs as tenants and freemen. These conflicting tenant and proprietary claims exacerbated the already-great social, ethnic, religious, and economic tensions that persisted beyond American independence.

In 1743 a definitive dividing line was finally accepted by the Crown, severing conflicting Quaker claims by placing all Jersey Quaker communities in West Jersey. But the proprietary-patentee conflict continued unabated. The dividing line demarking East Jersey ran southeast from Sussex County's Delaware River border diagonally across New Jersey to Tuckerton in what is now Ocean County. East Jersey then encompassed rural, mostly English Sussex and Morris Counties; Dutch-dominated Bergen and Somerset Counties; the Puritan-settled towns of

Newark and Elizabeth in populous Essex County; and the mixed populations of the original Middlesex and Monmouth Counties to the south.

Tenant-proprietary conflict kept East Jersey in turmoil. "Rent riots" were at the center of the disturbances, involving as they did unpaid tenant obligations to the Board of Proprietors. The board was made up of elite, largely Anglican merchants and men of property who dominated the Council, or upper house of the colonial legislature. The tenants, inheritors of patent rights, were mostly farmers and artisans of average means, Congregational and Presbyterian successors to Puritan settlers in Essex County. The Dutch in Bergen and Somerset and the large number of free people of color in Monmouth only added to the volatile population mix of East Jersey in the eighteenth century.

New Jersey was the epicenter of the Revolution from 1776 to 1783, and many internecine East Jersey scores were settled during that time. Essex County was Whig (Patriot), while Dutch Bergen and Somerset Counties remained Loyalist; where proprietors held sway—as, for example, in, Perth Amboy in Middlesex County and among elite landowners everywhere—economic interests dictated their loyalty to the Crown as well. Monmouth County, with its racial mix, remained a battleground too. So in East Jersey, internal conflict was the rule in the greater struggle for independence.

The geographic designation "East Jersey" ended with the war; most proprietors went into exile. The culture wars of colonial East Jersey, however, informed the politics of the new state. These culture wars included class hostility between middling farmers and well-to-do merchants and landowners: conflicts played out during the 1780s when the revolutionary government parceled out the former proprietor lands in the form of smaller holdings and were evident too in the party politics of the Confederation era and the 1790s (see ANTIFEDERALISTS; CONFEDERATION). It took the completion of the Revolution in the generation after the war to introduce into old East Jersey a distinctly American national identity that somewhat ameliorated the former ethnic, religious, political, and economic animosities in perhaps the most diverse population area in all the original American states.

BIBLIOGRAPHY

Hodges, Graham R. *Root and Branch: African Americans in New York and East Jersey, 1613–1863.* Chapel Hill: University of North Carolina Press, 1999.

McCormick, Richard P. *New Jersey from Colony to State, 1609–1789.* Rev. ed. Newark: New Jersey Historical Society, 1981. The original edition was published in 1964.

Prince, Carl E., et al. *The Papers of William Livingston.* 5 vols. New Brunswick, N.J.: Rutgers University Press, 1979–1988.

Carl E. Prince

See also **Loyalists; New Jersey.**

EASTERN EUROPE. *See* **Central Europe, Relations with.**

EATING DISORDERS are a group of psychological ailments characterized by intense fear of becoming obese, distorted body image, and prolonged food refusal (anorexia nervosa) and/or binge eating followed by purging through induced vomiting, heavy exercise, or use of laxatives (bulimia). The first American description of eating disorders appeared in 1859, when the asylum physician William Stout Chipley published a paper on "sitomania," a type of insanity consisting of an intense dread or loathing of food. Clinical research in Great Britain and France during the 1860s and 1870s replaced sitomania with the term "anorexia nervosa" and distinguished the disorder from other mental illnesses in which appetite loss was a secondary symptom and from physical "wasting" diseases, such as tuberculosis, diabetes, and cancer.

Eating disorders were extremely rare until the late twentieth century. Publication of Hilde Bruch's *The Golden Cage* (1978) led to increased awareness of anorexia nervosa, bulimia, and other eating disorders. At the same time, a large market for products related to dieting and exercise emerged, and popular culture and the mass media celebrated youthful, thin, muscular bodies as signs of status and popularity. These developments corresponded with an alarming increase in the incidence of eating disorders. Historically, most patients diagnosed with eating disorders have been white, adolescent females from middle- and upper-class backgrounds. This phenomenon suggests that eating disorders are closely linked with cultural expectations about young women in early twenty-first century American society.

BIBLIOGRAPHY

Brumberg, Joan Jacobs. *Fasting Girls: The Emergence of Anorexia Nervosa as a Modern Disease.* Cambridge, Mass: Harvard University Press, 1988.

Vandereycken, Walter, and Ron van Deth. *From Fasting Saints to Anorexic Girls: The History of Self-Starvation.* Washington Square: New York University Press, 1994.

Heather Munro Prescott/C. W.

See also **Diets and Dieting; Mental Illness; Women's Health.**

EATON AFFAIR. In April 1828 John B. Timberlake, a U.S. Navy purser, committed suicide at sea. Rumors quickly spread that he had done so because his wife, Margaret, was having an affair with Senator John Henry Eaton, a boarder at her father's Washington, D.C., inn. When Margaret Timberlake and Senator Eaton married on 1 January 1829, the new Mrs. Eaton, long an accused violator of society's norms because of her outspokenness and forward behavior, came under new attacks for not observing the required mourning period after her husband's death.

John Eaton was a close friend of President-elect Andrew Jackson, whose own wife had been the subject of gossip during the 1828 presidential campaign. Jackson blamed the death of his wife in December 1828 on the viciousness of his political opponents. When he appointed John Eaton secretary of war, most of the cabinet wives joined Washington society women in ostracizing Margaret Eaton, and Jackson was furious. He saw Mrs. Eaton, like his recently deceased wife, as unfairly wronged and defended her vociferously.

Jackson made the Eaton affair a major issue in his administration. Vice President John C. Calhoun and his wife supported Washington society, while Secretary of State Martin Van Buren, a widower, befriended Margaret Eaton. In April 1831 Jackson forced his cabinet's resignation over the dispute, and the controversy was among the major reasons why Van Buren replaced Calhoun as vice president in 1832. In reality, however, the Eaton affair was a battle over women's proper place in society.

BIBLIOGRAPHY

Allgor, Catherine. *Parlor Politics: In Which the Ladies of Washington Help Build a City and a Government.* Charlottesville: University Press of Virginia, 2000.

Marszalek, John F. "The Eaton Affair: Society and Politics." *Tennessee Historical Quarterly* 55 (Spring 1996): 6–19.

———. *The Petticoat Affair: Manners, Mutiny, and Sex in Andrew Jackson's White House.* New York: Free Press, 1997.

Wood, Kirstin E. "'One Woman So Dangerous to Public Morals': Gender and Power in the Eaton Affair." *Journal of the Early Republic* 17 (1997): 237–275.

John F. Marszalek

See also **Jacksonian Democracy.**

ECOLOGY. *See* **Conservation; Environmental Movement.**

E-COMMERCE. *See* **Electronic Commerce.**

ECONOMIC INDICATORS. The indexes of leading economic indicators are statistical measures applied to evaluate the performance of the American economy. Also known as "business indicators," they are used to analyze business and economic trends with the aim of predicting, anticipating, and adjusting to the future. The index is made up of three composite indexes of economic activity that change in advance of the economy as a whole. The index is thus capable of forecasting economic downturns as much as 8 to 20 months in advance, and economic recoveries from between 1 and 10 months in advance. The economic indicators are not foolproof, however, and have on occasion suggested the opposite of what actually came to pass.

The Historical Background

In one form or another, economic indicators, however crude, have been in use since World War I. Until the Great Depression of the 1930s, economists devoted little effort to measuring and predicting economic trends, other than perhaps to compile statistical information on annual employment. With the onset of the depression, the importance of economic indicators grew, as the crisis made evident the need for businessmen and politicians to have detailed knowledge of the economy. As a result of the depression, business and government alike clamored for a more accurate measurement of economic performance.

A group of economists at Rutgers University in New Brunswick, New Jersey, developed the first official national economic indicators in 1948. Since then, the indicators have evolved into the composite index of economic indicators in use as of the early 2000s. The list of economic indicators was first published by the U.S. Department of Commerce, Bureau of Economic Analysis (BEA). Overall, the department has a noteworthy record: since 1948 the BEA has accurately predicted every downturn and upswing in the American economy.

Although economists are divided on the value of the index in predicting trends, businesspeople and the American public consider it the leading gauge of economic performance. Although the list of economic indicators has been revised many times to reflect the changes in the American economy, within a few years of its inception reporters began regularly citing information from the index in their writing about the American economy. In an effort to improve the accuracy of reporting on the economy, the BEA began issuing explanatory press releases during the 1970s. Considered crude gauges compared to the more complicated econometric models that have since been developed, the indexes of the BEA are still referred to by economists, the business community, and others interested in economic conditions and tendencies in the United States.

The Evolution of the Economic Indicator Index

After years of analyzing business cycles, the National Bureau of Economic Research created a number of indicators to measure economic activity, categorized into three general composite indexes. The first group is known as the leading indicators because its numbers change months in advance of a transformation in the general level of economic activity. The National Bureau of Economic Research uses ten leading economic indicators, which represent a broad spectrum of economic activity. These indicators include the average number of weekly hours of workers in manufacturing, the average initial weekly claims for unemployment insurance and state programs, new orders for manufacturers of consumer goods that have been adjusted for inflation, vendor performance, manufacturers' new orders for nondefense capital goods also adjusted for inflation, and new private housing units that indicate the future volume of the housing market and construction. Included also are the stock prices of 500 common stocks based on Standard and Poor's 500 Index, the M-2 money supply, which consists of all cash, checking, and savings deposits, interest rates along with ten-year Treasury bonds, and consumer expectations as researched by the University of Michigan.

Using this cluster of indicators, the Bureau predicts the national economic performance in the coming months based on a "diffusion index," or DI. The DI number at any given time is the percentage of the ten leading indicators that have risen since the previous calculation. A DI number greater than fifty indicates an expanding economy; the larger the DI number, the stronger the basis for predicting economic growth.

The remaining two indexes that are also consulted include the composite index of coincident indicators and the lagging index. The composite index of coincident indicators measures the current economy based on the number of employees on nonagricultural payrolls, personal income, industrial production, and manufacturing and trade sales. This index moves more in line with the overall economy. The lagging index does not react until a change has already occurred in the economy. This index consists of the average duration of unemployment, the ratio of manufacturing and trade inventories to sales, changes in the index of labor costs per unit of output, the average prime rate, outstanding commercial and industrial loans, the ratio of outstanding consumer installment credit to personal income, and any changes in the Consumer Price Index. Economists generally believe that lagging indicators are useless for prediction. The value of construction completed, for example, is an outdated indicator, for the main economic effect of the construction occurred earlier when the plans were made and construction actually carried out.

Other Economic Indicators

In addition to the composite indexes, there are other indicators that economists use to study the American economy. *The Survey of Current Business*, published by the U.S. Department of Commerce, is a quarterly volume addressing national production and the patterns of economic fluctuation and growth. The monthly *Federal Reserve Bulletin* provides measures of the national productive activity based on data from 207 industries. Also included are separate production indexes for three market groups: consumer goods, equipment, and materials, and for three industry groups, manufacturing, mining, and utilities.

Detailed statistics on the state of labor in the United States are contained in the *Monthly Labor Review*, which is published by the U.S. Bureau of Labor Statistics. Analysts and policymakers use the indicators of population, labor force size, and the number of employed workers to interpret the growth of national productive capacity. The index also provides the number and percentage of unemployed workers, the average number of hours worked, and the average earnings, all of which prove invaluable during periods of recession.

Other economic indicators include the monthly Consumer Price Index, which measures the general price level and prices charged by certain industries. Stock price averages are also evaluated. These consist of the four Dow Jones averages, which are calculated from the trading prices of 30 industrial stocks, 20 transportation stocks, 15 utility stocks, and a composite average of 65 other stocks. The Standard and Poor's composite index of 500 stocks serves as a leading economic indicator, as do the stocks traded on the New York Stock Exchange. The Federal Reserve supplies the additional indicators of money and credit conditions in the United States, covering the money supply, the amount of currency in circulation, checking account deposits, outstanding credit, interest rates, and bank reserves.

The Effectiveness of Economic Indicators

Over time, economic indicators have greatly increased the level of sophistication in economic forecasting and the analysis of business performance. The usefulness of these indicators, however, depends as much on the user's knowledge of their limitations as on the indicators themselves. Indicators provide only averages, and as such record past performance. As some economists have pointed out, applying indicators to predict future developments requires an understanding that history never repeats itself exactly.

Skeptical economists have warned that each new release of the leading economic indicators can trigger an unwarranted reaction in the stock and bond markets. They believe that the so-called flash statistics, as the monthly release of the leading economic indicators is known, are almost worthless. In many cases, the indicator figures are revised substantially for weeks and months after their initial release, as more information becomes available. As a result, the first readings of the economy that these indicators provide are unreliable.

One oft-cited example is the abandonment of the stock market that occurred during the final weeks of 1984. Initial statistics based on the leading indicators showed that the economy was slowing down; the Gross National Product (GNP) was predicted to rise only 1.5 percent. Further, statistics pointed to a worse showing for the following year. Certain that a recession was imminent, investors bailed out of the stock market in late December. In the following months, revised figures showed that the GNP had actually gained 3.5 percent, almost triple the initial prediction, an announcement that sent the stock market soaring.

The impact of current events can also play an important and unpredictable role in determining the leading economic indicators. In the aftermath of the terrorist attacks on New York and Washington, D.C., which took place on 11 September 2001, the leading indicators showed an unemployment rate of 5.4 percent, the biggest increase in twenty years. Included in that were 415,000 agricultural jobs that were lost during September, which was double the number analysts expected. The jobless rate also included 88,000 jobs lost in the airline and hotel industries, as well as 107,000 temporary jobs in the service sector. An additional 220,000 jobs were lost in unrelated businesses, pointing to an economy in distress.

BIBLIOGRAPHY

Carnes, W. Stansbury, and Stephen D. Slifer. *The Atlas of Economic Indicators: A Visual Guide to Market Forces and the Federal Reserve.* New York: HarperBusiness, 1991.

Dreman, David. "Dangerous to your investment health; here are some good reasons you should stay clear of 'flash' economic indicators." *Forbes* 135 (April 8, 1985): 186–187.

The Economist Guide to Economic Indicators: Making Sense of Economics. New York: John Wiley & Sons, 1997.

Lahiri, Kajal, and Geoffrey H. Moore, eds. *Leading Economic Indicators: New Approaches and Forecasting Records.* New York: Cambridge University Press, 1991.

"Lengthening shadows; The economy." *The Economist* (November 10, 2001): n. p.

Rogers, R. Mark. *Handbook of Key Economic Indicators.* New York: McGraw-Hill, 1998.

Meg Greene Malvasi

See also **Business Cycles; Productivity, Concept of.**

ECONOMIC ROYALISTS. President Franklin D. Roosevelt, in his speech accepting the Democratic nomination for a second term, delivered at Philadelphia on 27 June 1936, said, "The economic royalists complain that we seek to overthrow the institutions of America. What they really complain of is that we seek to take away their power. Our allegiance to American institutions requires the overthrow of this kind of power." He was referring to persons prominent in finance and industry who in general opposed his tendency to centralize the government and to put it into competition with private enterprise. The phrase was repeated many times thereafter.

BIBLIOGRAPHY

Kennedy, David M. *Freedom from Fear.* New York: Oxford University Press, 1999.

Alvin F. Harlow / c. w.

See also **Elections, Presidential; Government Regulation of Business; New Deal.**

ECONOMICS

General Characteristics

Economics studies human welfare in terms of the production, distribution, and consumption of goods and services. While there is a considerable body of ancient and medieval thought on economic questions, the discipline of political economy only took shape in the early modern period. Some prominent schools of the seventeenth and eighteenth centuries were Cameralism (Germany), Mercantilism (Britain), and Physiocracy (France). Classical political economy, launched by Adam Smith's *Wealth of Nations* (1776), dominated the discipline for more than one hundred years. American economics drew on all of these sources, but it did not forge its own identity until the end of the nineteenth century, and it did not attain its current global hegemony until after World War II. This was as much due to the sheer number of active economists as to the brilliance of Paul Samuelson, Milton Friedman, and Kenneth Arrow, among others. Prior to 1900, the American community of economists had largely been perceived, both from within and from abroad, as a relative backwater. The United States did not produce a theorist to rival the likes of Adam Smith (1723–1790), David Ricardo (1772–1823), or Karl Marx (1818–1883).

Several factors in American economic and intellectual history help explain this fact. First, the presence of a large slave economy before the Civil War resulted in a concentrated effort to weigh the arguments for and against free labor. The landmark study in American economic history of the last century, Robert Fogel and Stanley Engerman's *Time on the Cross* (1974), speaks to this unfortunate legacy. Second, the belated onset of industrialization (in 1860, 80 percent of the population was still rural), and the founding of many land-grant colleges with the Morrill Act of 1862 resulted in the emergence of a field of specialization that endures to this day: agricultural or land economics. Even in the interwar years, the Bureau of Agricultural Economics was a major center of research in the field. Third, American federalism, by decentralizing the management of money and credit, had direct and arguably dire consequences for the development of banking and capital accumulation. Persistent debates on the merits of paper currency can be traced from the latter half of the eighteenth century right up to 1971, when American fiat money replaced the gold standard once and for all.

The relatively high standard of living and the massive wave of immigration during the latter part of the nineteenth century might also have played a part in the diminished role of socialist thinking. A liberal ideology coupled with the absence of an aristocracy meant that socialism never became as rooted in America as in Europe. In the few instances that it did, it tended to be of the more innocuous variety, such as Robert Owen's (1771–1858) 1825 settlement of New Harmony, Indiana, or Richard T. Ely's (1854–1943) Christian socialism. The most popular reform movement in late-nineteenth-century economics was inspired by Henry George's (1839–1897) *Progress and Poverty* (1879), which argued for a single tax on land. Economic theory tended then as now toward liberalism if not libertarianism, with its deeply entrenched respect for individual rights, market forces, and the diminished role of the government.

What probably most explains the form and content of American economics is its resistance to the influence of other disciplines. Because of the sheer size of the economics profession (there are some 22,000 registered members of the American Economic Association, and that by no means exhausts the number), it tends to be very inward-looking. Not since before World War II have economists eagerly borrowed from the other sciences. Even prewar economists were more likely to assimilate concepts and methods from physics and biology than from sociology or psychology. Instead, "economic imperialists" such as Gary Becker take topics that have traditionally been in other social sciences, such as voting, crime, marriage, and the family, and model them in terms of utility maximization.

The Colonial and Antebellum Period

In colonial America, most contributors to economics, such as Thomas Pownall (1722–1805), governor of Massachusetts, and Samuel Gale (1747–1826) were inspired by the British economists John Locke (1632–1704), David Hume (1711–1776), and Adam Smith. Benjamin Franklin (1706–1790) befriended both the British and French political economists of the time. Because of the shortage of American money, Franklin advocated the circulation of paper money as a stimulus to trade, and he even convinced Hume and Smith of the relative soundness of paper issue in Pennsylvania. Although Franklin wrote on the importance of the development of manufacturing for the American economy, he believed, as would Thomas Paine (1737–1809) and Thomas Jefferson (1743–1826), that the true destiny for America lay with agriculture.

The American republic called for concrete measures on money and banking, as well as policies on trade and manufacturing. In the early years of the new regime, Jefferson and Alexander Hamilton (1757–1804) loomed large as forgers of economic ideas and policy. Jefferson was a friend of Pierre Samuel du Pont de Nemours (1739–1817), Destutt de Tracy (1754–1836), and Jean-Baptiste Say (1767–1832), and he supervised the translation of Tracy's *Treatise on Political Economy* (1817). In a series of tracts, he argued that commerce ought to remain a handmaiden to agriculture, and he took seriously Hume's caveats about public debt. Hamilton, by contrast, advocated the growth of commerce and manufacturing. He sought means to improve the mobility of capital as a stimulus to trade, and with his *National Bank Act and Report on Manufactures* (1791), he went very much against Jefferson's policies.

In antebellum United States we find dozens of contributors to political economy, notably Jacob Cardozo (1786–1873), Daniel Raymond (1786–1849), Francis Wayland (1790–1865), Henry C. Carey (1793–1879), Amasa Walker (1799–1875), and Charles Dunbar (1830–1900). Many of these tailored their analyses to the American context of unlimited land and scarcity of labor. Malthusian scenarios held little sway. The two most prominent European writers in America, both adherents to Smith, were Say, whose *Treatise on Political Economy* was widely read and circulated after its first translation in 1821, and John Ramsey McCulloch (1789–1864). Jane Marcet's (1769–1858) *Conversations on Political Economy* (1816) sold in the thousands, thereby disseminating some of the more central principles of British and French political economy to the inquiring American. The prominent German economist of the period, Friedrich List (1789–1846), first made his name while living in the United States; his *Outlines of American Political Economy* (1827) helped sustain the enthusiasm for protective tariffs. Carey is usually viewed as the most original American-born thinker of the period, and the first to gain an international reputation. His three-volume *Principles of Political Economy* (1837) did much to challenge Ricardo's doctrine of rent, as well as propel him into a significant role as economic advisor to the government in Washington.

The Gilded Age (1870–1914)

Homegrown economic theorists became much more common in this period, spurred into controversies over banking and trade and the onset of large monopolies. The most prominent measure taken in this period, the SHERMAN ANTITRUST ACT (1890), was not received enthusiastically by the more conservative economists such as Arthur Hadley (1856–1930) because it violated the central principle of laissez-faire. But others, such as Ely, saw the Act as a necessary measure.

Steps were also taken to professionalize, with the formation of the American Economics Association (1885) and the *Quarterly Journal of Economics* (1887). Two more journals of high quality were formed in this period, the *Journal of Political Economy* (1892) and the *American Economic Review* (1911). Economics also made its way into the universities. Before the Civil War, numerous colleges taught the subject under the more general rubric of moral philosophy, or even theology. But explicit recognition first came with the appointment of Charles Dunbar to the chair of political economy at Harvard in 1871. The prolific economist and son of Amasa, Francis A. Walker (1840–1897) gained a chair at Yale in 1872 and then served as president of MIT in the 1880s and 1890s. By 1900, hundreds of institutions were offering graduate degrees in economics, though the majority of doctorates came from a small set of universities, notably Chicago, Columbia, California, Harvard, and Johns Hopkins. The expansion of institutions of higher learning in this period served to reinforce the propensity to specialize within the field. While the economics profession mostly honors its contributors to pure theory, the majority of doctorates in American economics are and have been granted in applied fields, notably labor, land, business, and industrial economics.

In the area of theoretical economics, the names of Simon Newcomb (1835–1909), Irving Fisher (1867–1947), and John Bates Clark stand out. Newcomb was better known for his work in astronomy and coastal surveying, but his *Principles of Political Economy* (1886) did much to endorse the advent of mathematical methods. Fisher was without question the most renowned and brilliant of his generation of economic theorists. As a doctoral student at Yale, Fisher worked with the eminent physicist J. Willard Gibbs (1839–1903) and the social Darwinist William Graham Sumner (1840–1910). His first book, *Mathematical Investigations in the Theory of Value and Prices* (1892), was a significant landmark in the rise of mathematical economics, and it treated the utility calculus in terms of thermodynamics. His later efforts, *The Purchasing Power of Money* (1911) and *The Theory of Interest* (1930) became two of the most significant works of the twentieth century. The Fisher Equation is still taken to be the best rendition of the quantity theory of money, noted for its efforts to distinguish different kinds of liquidity and to measure the velocity of money.

Clark reigned at Columbia for much of his career, and he is most noted for his analysis of the concept of marginal productivity as an explanation of factor prices, wages, interest, and rent. His *Philosophy of Wealth* (1886) and *Distribution of Wealth* (1899) blended the new marginalism with sociological and ethical concerns. Clark earned international renown for his concept of marginal productivity and helped inspire the next generation of American marginalists, notably Frank Taussig (1859–1940) at Harvard, Frank Fetter (1863–1949) at Princeton, and Laurence Laughlin (1871–1933) at Chicago.

Although the contributions of Fisher and Clark were more enduring, the school that was most distinctively American from approximately 1890 to 1940 was the one known during the interwar years as Institutionalism. The most prominent founders were Ely, Veblen, Mitchell, and John R. Commons (1862–1945). Later contributors included the son of John Bates, John Maurice Clark (1884–1963), and Clarence E. Ayres (1891–1972), but there were many more foot soldiers marching to the cause. Inspired by evolutionary biology, the Institutionalists took a historical, antiformalist approach to the study of economic phenomena. Veblen's *Theory of the Leisure Class* (1899), the most enduring text of this group, examines consumption patterns in terms of biological traits, evolving in step with other institutions—political and pecuniary. Commons focused on labor economics and helped devise many of the measures, such as workmen's compensation, public utility regulations, and unemployment insurance, that resulted in the social security legislation of the 1930s.

Interwar years 1919–1939

American economics was invigorated by the war and benefited enormously from a wave of immigration from Europe's intellegentsia. Of the three most prominent grand theorists of the period, and arguably of the entire century, namely John Maynard Keynes (1883–1946), Joseph Schumpeter (1883–1950), and Friedrich Hayek (1899–1992), the latter two came and settled in the United States: Schumpeter to Harvard (1932–1950), and Hayek to New York (1923–1924) and later to Chicago (1950–1962). Both did most of their critical work while in Europe, but were part of a larger migration of the Austrian school of economics, notably Ludwig von Mises (1881–1973), Fritz Machlup (1902–1983), and Karl Menger (1902–1985). Other prominent immigrants from Europe were Abraham Wald (1902–1950), John Harsanyi (1920–2000), Tjalling Koopmans (1910–1985), Oskar Lange (1904–1965), Wassily Leontief (1906–1999), Jacob Marschak (1898–1977), John von Neumann (1903–1957), Oskar Morgenstern (1902–1977), Franco Modigliani, Ronald Coase, and Kenneth Boulding (1910–1993).

Notwithstanding the inestimable stimulation of foreign-trained economists, the most prominent figures of this period were American born and educated, notably Fisher, Mitchell, Frank Knight (1885–1972), Henry Ludwell Moore (1869–1958), and Edward Chamberlain (1899–1967). Chamberlain's landmark study, *The Theory of Monopolistic Competition* (1933), contributed to the recognition of the mixed economy of mature capitalism. Fisher's *The Making of Index Numbers* (1922) made important headway on the measurement of key economic indicators. Mitchell stood out as the one who blended a still vibrant community of Institutionalism with the more ascendant neoclassicism. He and Moore's studies of business cycles helped foster the growth of econometrics, resulting in the formation of the National Bureau of Economic Research (1920) and the Cowles Commission (1932), which proved to be an important spawning ground for econometrics and, more generally, mathematical economics. Some leading economists associated with the Cowles Commision are Fisher, Koopmans, Marschak, Lange, Arrow, Gérard Debreu, James Tobin (1918–2002), and Simon Kuznets (1901–1985).

Knight's *Risk, Uncertainty and Profit* (1921) remains a classic in the study of capital theory and the role of the entrepreneur. Together with Currie, Jacob Viner (1892–1970), and Henry Simons (1899–1946), Knight helped to push the economics department of the University of Chicago into the top rank. With the subsequent contributions of George Stigler (1911–1991), Hayek, and Friedman, Chicago became the leading voice of the status quo. Among Nobel prizewinners in economics, roughly one-half have at some point in their career been associated with the "Chicago School."

Postwar Era

Here we see the clear ascendancy of mathematical economics as the dominant professional orientation. Economists shifted away from the literary pursuit of laws and general principles that characterized nineteenth-century political economy, in favor of models and econometric tests disseminated in the periodical literature. The number of U.S. journals began to surge in the postwar years to 300 by the year 2002, and the number of articles has grown almost exponentially.

No one stands out more prominently in the 1950s to 1960s than Paul Samuelson, not least because of his best-selling textbook, *Principles of Economics* (1948). His precocity for mathematics resulted in a series of papers, which were immediately acclaimed for their brilliance. Published as *The Foundations of Economic Analysis* (1947),

Samuelson's opus contributed to almost every branch of microeconomics. He devised a solution to the longstanding problem of price dynamics and formulated the axiom of revealed preference, which stands at the very core of neoclassical theory.

Other major contributors to mathematical economics, starting from the interwar period, were Wald on decision theory, Koopmans on linear programming, Leontief on input-output analysis, L. J. Savage (1917–1971) on mathematical statistics, and Harold Hotelling (1895–1973) and Henry Schultz (1893–1938) on demand theory. Arrow and Debreu, who moved to the States in 1949, devised through a series of papers in the 1950s an axiomatic rendition of the general theory of equilibrium—the doctrine by which prices bring about market clearance. In many respects, this put a capstone on the neoclassical theory that had commenced in the 1870s.

Arrow also made significant contributions to welfare economics with his *Social Choice and Individual Values* (1951). His book targeted the role of strategizing in economics, an idea that was of parallel importance to game theory.

The landmark works in the field of game theory came out of Princeton during and immediately after the war—namely, von Neumann and Morgenstern's *Theory of Games and Economic Behavior* (1944) and two seminal papers by the mathematician John Nash (1950, 1952). Strategic thinking also fostered the pursuit of Operations Research at the RAND Corporation in Santa Monica (founded in 1946). The World War II and the Cold War had much to do with the funding of these new fields, with Thomas Schelling's *Strategey of Conflict* (1960) as one of the best-known results. Related investigations are Rational Choice Theory, associated most closely with James Buchanan, and experimental economics, launched by Vernon Smith and Charles Plott. Herbert Simon's (1916–2001) concept of satisficing has also linked up with the emphasis in Game Theory on suboptimal behavior. In a nutshell, neither utility nor social welfare are maximized because information and cooperation prove to be too costly.

Keynes had traveled to the United States during and after World War II both to advise the American government and to help launch the International Monetary Fund that came out of the famous Bretton Woods gathering of 1944. Keynes's *General Theory of Employment, Interest, and Money* (1936) is widely viewed to this day as the single most influential book of the last century, and his ideas were widely disseminated by Alvin Hansen (1887–1975), Lauchlin Currie (1902–1993), Lawrence R. Klein, Tobin, Galbraith, and Samuelson. Nevertheless, KEYNESIANISM was superceded in the 1950s by Friedman's monetarism—and then in the 1970s by the New Classicism of John Muth, Neil Wallace, Thomas Sargent, and Robert Lucas. McCarthyism may have also reinforced this shift since it became expedient for survival to avoid any controversial political issues that might stem from economic analysis. While Keynes was not a socialist, his inclinations toward a planned economy and his skepticism about market forces were seen as suspect.

Two other areas of specialization to which Americans made considerable postwar contributions are consumption theory and economic development. Of the first field, the names of Samuelson, Friedman, Modigliani, Hyman Minsky (1919–1997), James Duesenberry, and William Vickery (1914–1996) belong in the front rank. Of the second field, Kuznets, W. Arthur Lewis (the first major African American economist, originally from St. Lucia), Theodore W. Shultz (1902–1998), Robert Solow, and Albert O. Hirschman are noteworthy. Almost all of these men garnered the Alfred Nobel Memorial Prize in Economic Science, which commenced in 1969.

Until the latter part of the twentieth century, women had been grossly under-represented in American economics, but from those decades forward they have included roughly 25 percent of the profession. More women entered the profession in the interwar years, so that by 1920, 19 percent of Ph.D.'s went to women, though this figure dropped dramatically after World War II. Three who made important insights in consumption theory during the 1940s were Dorothy Brady (1903–1977), Margaret Reid (1895–1991), and Rose Friedman. Both Rose Friedman and Anna J. Schwartz have coauthored major works with the more famous Milton Friedman, making them the most widely read of contemporary American women economists. Many of the economists listed in this article advised the government—particularly on money, banking, and trade. Significant guidance from economists was widely acknowledged during the Great Depression with Franklin Roosevelt's New Deal. But it was in the postwar period that economists were extensively instituted into the government rather than brought in on an ad hoc basis. The Council of Economic Advisors, established in 1946, oversaw the fiscal reforms of the Kennedy era and took credit for the subsequent economic growth. The American government is replete with committees forging economic policy on virtually every applied field in the discipline. The chairman of the Federal Reserve Board, founded in 1914, is often taken from academic ranks and now stands out as the most powerful player in the American economy. Keynes once remarked of economists that "the world is ruled by little else." For better or for worse, the power that economists now hold in the American government epitomizes the triumph of the economics profession and the widespread view that the economy—and hence human well-being—is within our control.

BIBLIOGRAPHY

Allen, William R. "Economics, Economists, and Economic Policy: Modern American Experiences." *History of Political Economy* 9, no. 1 (1977): 48–88.

Barber, William J. *From New Era to New Deal: Herbert Hoover, the Economists, and American Economic Policy, 1921–1933.* New York: Cambridge University Press, 1985.

Barber, William J., ed. *Breaking the Academic Mould: Economists and American Higher Learning in the Nineteenth Century.* Middletown: Wesleyan University Press, 1988.

Carver, Earlene, and Axel Leijonhufvud. "Economics in America: the Continental Influence." *History of Political Economy* 19, no. 2 (1987): 173–182.

Coats, A.W. *On the History of Economic Thought: British and American Economic Essays.* Volume 1. London and New York: Routledge, 1992.

Conkin, Paul. *Prophets of Prosperity: America's First Political Economists.* Bloomington: Indiana University Press, 1980.

Dorfman, Joseph. *The Economic Mind in American Civilization.* 5 volumes. New York: Viking, 1946–1959.

Goodwin, Craufurd D. "Marginalism Moves to the New World." *History of Political Economy* 4, no. 2 (1972): 551–570.

Hirsch, Abraham, and Neil De Marchi. *Milton Friedman: Economics in Theory and Practice.* Ann Arbor: University of Michigan Press, 1990.

Mehrling, Perry. *The Money Interest and the Public Interest: The Development of American Monetary Thought, 1920–1970.* Cambridge, Mass.: Harvard University Press, 1997.

Mirowski, Philip. *Machine Dreams: Economics Becomes a Cyborg Science.* New York: Cambridge University Press, 2002.

Morgan, Mary S., and Malcolm Rutherford, eds. *From Interwar Pluralism to Postwar Neoclassicism.* Durham: Duke Unviersity Press, 1998.

Rutherford, Malcolm. *Institutions in Economics: The Old and the New Institutionalism.* New York: Cambridge University Press, 1996.

———, ed. *The Economic Mind in America: Essays in the History of American Economics.* London and New York: Routledge, 1998.

Ross, Dorothy. *The Origins of American Social Science.* New York and Cambridge: Cambridge University Press, 1991.

Vaughn, Karen I. *Austrian Economics in America: The Migration of a Tradition.* New York and Cambridge: Cambridge University Press, 1994.

Yonay, Yuval P. *The Struggle over the Soul of Economics: Institutionalist and Neoclassical Economists in America Between the Wars.* Princeton: Princeton University Press, 1998.

Margaret Schabas

EDUCATION. Americans have long invested importance in education as a means of social improvement and individual fulfillment. Education has entailed both formal instruction in schools, universities, and other institutions, and informal learning in a variety of settings. Schools were respected institutions early in American history, and their significance has grown with time. Education and schooling have also been at the center of social and political conflict, often over issues of status and inequality. Schools eventually became instruments of government social policy, utilized to offset historic inequities and to help achieve social justice. Education also contributed human capital to the nation's economy. In the nineteenth century, reformers focused on training reliable workers; in the twentieth century, schools prepared men and women for office and professional employment. At the same time, education has been a vital element of social and economic mobility for generations of Americans.

Historically, the primary schools were the objects of the nation's first great era of education reform. Next came secondary schools, which grew most rapidly during the early twentieth century, and colleges and universities expanded notably in the years following World War II. Schools at all levels have been indispensable to the formation of a national identity for Americans throughout history. From the very earliest stages of the new republic, schools have helped to foster loyalty to the principles of democratic governance, and to the particular tenets of American nationalism. They also have served as a forum for debate over the evolution of these principles.

Education in the Colonial and Revolutionary Periods

The cultivation of skills and the transmission of culture were major concerns of English settlers in North America, evident almost immediately upon their arrival. This was apparent in New England, where early laws called for establishing schools and for educating young men—and eventually young women too. But schools were established elsewhere, along with colleges, to provide avenues of formal education. Schools were fragile institutions in the colonial world, existing alongside older and more familiar agencies of education, the family and the church. Even though there was a high level of rhetorical commitment to formal education in certain colonies, only a minority of youth were "educated" by today's standards.

New England's colonists placed special value on the necessity of moral and religious leadership, and preparing a cadre of educated leaders was considered essential. An early sign of this was the decision to establish Boston Latin School in 1635 and Harvard College a year later. In the wake of religious debates and schisms, other colleges were started in nearby Connecticut (Yale, 1701), Rhode Island (Brown, 1764), and New Hampshire (Dartmouth, 1769). These were small institutions, enrolling fewer than a hundred students, and hardly represented a well-developed education system.

In 1647, Massachusetts enacted a law requiring towns of fifty families to establish a school, to confound the "Old Deluder Satan" in his never-ending quest to lead Christians astray. Connecticut enacted a similar law just a few years later and eventually other New England colonies did as well, with the exception of Rhode Island. It is unlikely, however, that most towns large enough to be covered by these measures complied immediately, especially if there was not a large number of families interested in establishing a school. Only eleven known schools existed in Massachusetts in 1650, serving some 2,339 households (or one for every 212); by 1689, the number of schools had grown to 23 and households to 8,088 (one for every 352). Even if the quantity of schools increased significantly in the eighteenth century, many children probably attended only briefly, if at all.

In other colonies, schools were even fewer. In 1689, Virginia had only eight schools for more than seven thousand households (or about one for every nine hundred); and New York had eleven for about 2200 families (one for every two hundred). Virginia's William and Mary (1693) was the only southern college of the colonial era. Others appeared in the middle colonies, reflecting the region's religious and cultural diversity. The College of New Jersey (today Princeton) was established in 1746, New York's Kings College (Columbia) in 1754, the College of Philadelphia (University of Pennsylvania) in 1755, and New Jersey's Queens College (Rutgers) in 1766.

While the appearance of such institutions was notable, there also was considerable indifference or even hostility to formal education, especially in the South. In 1671, Lord Berkeley of Virginia made this famous statement: "I thank God that there are no free schools nor printing, and I hope that we shall not have these [for a] hundred years." Berkeley, who was governor at the time, echoed the view of many aristocrats and wealthy planters that "learning has brought disobedience, and heresy, and sects into the world." Attitudes such as these no doubt accounted for some of the regional disparities in colonial education.

Schools typically were run by a single teacher, or "master." Outside of Boston, New York or Philadelphia, schools rarely were larger than a single classroom, with perhaps several dozen students. For most colonists, schooling lasted less than seven or eight years, with only four or five months in each term. Students read the Bible, along with spellers, prayer books, catechisms, and other religious materials. The famous *New England Primer*, first published before 1690, was the best known of a wide range of reading materials used to impart lessons in spelling and grammar, along with morality and virtue. While there were a few legendary teachers, such as Ezekial Cheever of the Boston Latin School, many were college students or recent graduates waiting to be called to a pulpit. Yet other teachers were men of modest education, ill suited for other lines of work, managing schools for lack of better employment. In certain New England towns "dame schools" were run by women, offering classes for young children of both sexes. As a rule, teaching was a relatively low status occupation, even when schools were few and education was considered at least nominally important.

Statistics on literacy seem to confirm the general regional distribution of schools, although it is not clear that reading was always linked to formal education. New England exhibited the highest rates of literacy, as measured by counting signatures on wills. About three-quarters of the male population was literate in the mid-eighteenth century, and nearly 90 percent by the time of the revolution. Literacy rates appear to have been lower in the middle colonies, New York and Pennsylvania, and were the lowest in the South. The male literacy rate in Virginia was about 70 percent by the end of the eighteenth century, comparable to England. The female literacy rate was lower than men's everywhere, although in New England the gap appears to have narrowed by the end of the eighteenth century.

Much of life in colonial society revolved around the family, the central unit of productive activities and a key site of informal education. Families were large and children were expected to contribute to the welfare of each household. Relevant skills and bodies of knowledge, ranging from farming, carpentry, husbandry, and hunting to food preservation, soap making, cooking, and sewing were imparted informally, along with basic literacy. Popular books praised the independence of children, and the virtue of lessons learned away from parents and family. Many families sent older children to board with neighbors or relatives, as a form of apprenticeship and a means of discipline. There also were traditional apprenticeships for young men interested in learning a trade, a practice with deep European roots, observed widely in the colonies. In most cases, formal contracts were drawn up, periods of service were outlined, and lessons were agreed upon. The host household typically provided food, lodging, and other necessities of support in exchange for work, training, and education as specified by the contract. Occasionally there were complaints about cruel or unfair masters who did not abide by such agreements.

A limited number of schools were established to educate Native Americans and Blacks, the principal non-European groups in colonial society. Dartmouth College included a provision for American Indians in its original charter, although this idea was short lived. The Anglican Society for the Propagation of the Gospel in Foreign Parts, or SPG, aimed to convert non-Christian residents of the colonies, particularly Native Americans and Africans. Starting in the early eighteenth century, the SPG dispatched hundreds of ministers and teachers to the New World, opening a number of schools, most of them transitory. It was more effective at printing Bibles and religious tracts that circulated widely in colonial society.

The American Revolution was a watershed event in the early history of American education. The war disrupted many institutions, forcing students to suspend studies and teachers to consider joining one side or the other. More importantly, the revolution led to a new republican sensibility in the former colonies, articulated by a generation of enlightened leaders who believed that education was essential to the new political order. Citizens of a representative democracy, they reasoned, had to be well informed and prepared to critically assess the arguments and opinions of the day.

Education and schooling became topics of discussion and debate, the subject of speeches, addresses, articles, and pamphlets. Thomas Jefferson proposed publicly supported schools throughout Virginia, in a "Bill for the More General Diffusion of Knowledge," before the revolution ended in 1779. He believed that free schooling would lead to a "natural aristocracy" of talent and accomplishment, leaders for the new nation. Jefferson's plan was never adopted, but it reflected the new significance attached to education. Benjamin Rush advocated making American children into "republican machines" through improved systems of schooling. Noah Webster advocated universal free education to foster national unity. Webster called for schools to establish "an inviolable attachment to their country" in the minds of children, and urged Americans to "begin with the infant in the cradle; let the first word he lisps be Washington." Early federal legislation for the distribution of public lands, passed in 1785 and 1787, called for a portion of the proceeds to be used for establishing state education systems, including universities. Seven of the new state constitutions also made reference to education, reflecting these concerns.

Among the most important effects of the American Revolution was its impact on the lives of colonial women. Benjamin Rush probably was the best-known proponent of women's education in the years immediately following the revolution. The reasoning was plain: if children needed to be trained in the virtues of republican government, the task of early education would fall to their mothers. Consequently, American women had to be educated, at least enough to read, write, and teach their children moral precepts and principles of republicanism. Historians have labeled this view "republican motherhood," and it contributed to increased interest in women's education during the latter decades of the eighteenth century.

While the colonial era saw limited development in education, the closing decades of the eighteenth century were marked by considerable ferment about it. Revolutionary ideas about state-sponsored systems of schooling, republican socialization, and women's education marked the dawn of a new era. It would take time, and the efforts of another generation of reformers, for these notions to affect the schooling of most Americans.

Education in the Nineteenth Century

The nineteenth century was a time of rapid economic growth and urbanization, an era of institution building, and education was shaped by these developments. Schools became instruments of reform, intended to help redress pressing social problems. State and city systems of schooling came into view, although local prerogatives continued to dictate most educational practices. It was a time when schools and education gradually assumed greater importance, and came to reflect prevailing social divisions and patterns of inequality in American life.

The nation's total investment in education grew dramatically, as more people attended school for greater lengths of time. In 1800, the average American received about 210 days of formal education in a lifetime. By 1850, that figure had more than doubled and by 1900, it had jumped to 1050 days, about half of what it would be in 2000. In the course of these changes, formal education began to assume the familiar dimensions of modern school experiences. Schooling became associated with the cultivation of proper "habits" of industriousness and responsibility, along with essential skills of literacy, numerical calculation, and knowledge of history, geography, and other subjects.

Education in the countryside evolved slowly, but schools developed more rapidly in the cities. Education was linked to questions of poverty and destitution, crime and social conflict. The earliest publicly supported urban institutions were called "charity schools," and were designated for the children of the poor. Started by civic-minded members of the urban middle and upper classes, they imparted proper norms of behavior along with basic lessons in literacy, mathematics, geography, and other subjects. Monitorial schools, modeled on the ideas of English educator Joseph Lancaster, featured a single teacher managing hundreds of children by using older students as "monitors." These and other schools reflected prevailing norms of strict discipline and order. Urban reformers struggled to improve attendance and introduce uniformity into lessons, at the same time that city growth created rising demand for schooling.

Industrialization posed challenges to education. With the advent of child labor, the factory became a school by default, although its lessons were usually quite harsh. While some states passed laws requiring factory owners to arrange for teaching child employees, such measures often were honored in the breach. Some reformers rejected the idea of industry altogether and attempted to establish ideal agrarian societies in isolated communities dotting the countryside. The best known of these communal experiments was Robert Owen's socialist cooperative in Indiana, called New Harmony. Established on principles of shared work and property, and an education system predicated on performing useful tasks without the imposition of discipline, New Harmony was a challenge to long-standing conventions. Although other communal experiments persisted considerably longer than Owen's, their collective influence on the educational system was limited.

Schools in the countryside were isolated and small; classes were conducted for relatively short periods and taught by itinerant masters with little formal training. A typical district school served an area of two to four square miles, populated by twenty to fifty families. These institutions helped to enhance basic literacy skills, but they built on a foundation established by local households. By the early nineteenth century, they literally dotted the countryside in most northern states, serving millions of children. Overall, levels of enrollment were quite high, over 70 percent for children aged nine to thirteen in 1830. Only Germany had higher rates, and by 1880, the U.S. led the world. These figures reflect girls attending along with boys, at least in the Northeastern states and the upper Midwest, another unique feature of American education.

Enrollments notwithstanding, the length of school terms varied, and day-to-day attendance often was inconsistent. There was scarcely any advanced training, as most teachers knew little beyond the "three Rs" and seldom remained in any one place longer than a year or two. Schools generally were ungraded, with children of all ages in the same room and enduring the discomforts of poor ventilation and threadbare accommodations. Discipline was emphasized, with rules enforced by harsh physical punishments. The chief instructional technique was recitation, requiring students to repeat portions of text they had memorized. Schools also conveyed basic mathematical and computational principles, along with a smattering of history, geography, and "moral philosophy." Contests and games, such as spelling bees or multiplication tournaments, helped break the monotony, and storytelling imparted history and geography lessons.

Early reformers were troubled by the variability that existed in the rural schools. They fretted over the haphazard training of teachers, the short terms squeezed between harvest and planting seasons, and the chance provision of such basic school supplies as books and firewood. Reformers also worried about the growing diversity of American society and the possibility of social conflict in the absence of common values and a shared identity. In light of these concerns, and the reforms they inspired, historians have referred to this period as the "age of the common school."

The best-known proponent of common school reform was Horace Mann, an indefatigable lawyer and state legislator who accepted the newly created post of Secretary of the State Board of Education in Massachusetts in 1837. Like other reformers, Mann worked with a modest salary and little formal authority, traveling widely to proclaim the virtues of common schools. His annual reports, published by the state, became influential statements of educational reform. Mann battled over issues of religious sectarianism in instruction, property taxes for education, longer school terms, and systematic examinations and training requirements for teachers. In particular, he succeeded in persuading the Massachusetts legislature to establish the nation's first publicly supported teacher-training institution, called a normal school, derived from the French word *normale*, in Lexington in 1838.

Mann and other reformers thought that women had a special role to play as teachers. Many believed women naturally suited for this role, due to their supposed maternal characteristics of patience and affection toward small children. Women teachers also cost less than men, even when professionally trained, so their employment could help restrain the expense of reforms. Feminization of teaching had occurred earlier in New England, but proceeded rapidly elsewhere, and by the time of the Civil War a majority of teachers in most northern states were women.

Henry Barnard was a famous contemporary of Mann who held similar appointments in Connecticut and Rhode Island and served as the first U.S. Commissioner of Education from 1867 to 1870. Other leading reformers included John Pierce in Michigan and Calvin Stowe in Ohio. This generation shared a similar set of values and assumptions about schooling and its purposes, much of it derived from their Protestant upbringing and nationalist ardor. Influential textbooks transmitted these values to generations of students, especially the popular McGuffey readers first published in 1836. These reforms found support in the fervent language regarding education in new state constitutions, particularly in the northern tier extending west from New England and the Middle Atlantic States.

Larger cities became sites of battles over the control and content of public schooling. Immigrant religious groups objected to the inveiglement of Protestant precepts and values in most curricula and textbooks, and they demanded support for parochial schools. The best-known conflict occurred in 1842, when New York's Bishop John Hughes challenged local charity school groups, prompting creation of a public board of education. Eventually, parochial schools became quite numerous in many northern cities, enrolling thousands of children and providing an important alternative to public schools.

Another aspect of reform concerned secondary or high schools, which became popular institutions in the nineteenth century. There had been little public demand for secondary schools until after the revolution, as private tutoring and tuition-based academies prepared young men for college and few occupations required advanced schooling. Beginning in 1821, with the establishment of the first public high school, Boston's English High School, American secondary schools, as distinct from a classical grammar school or academy, prepared students for a host of practical purposes. By the end of the nineteenth century, they existed in one form or another in nearly every type of city or large town in the country, enrolling nearly a half million students. The high school had become pervasive, even though it served less than 10 percent of the nation's teenage population.

High schools also featured instruction in some classical subjects, especially Latin, long considered a sign of achievement and status. Most larger public high schools admitted students by examination, and many prospective scholars were turned away. These tax-supported institutions often were quite costly, occupying palatial buildings erected at great expense and with considerable fanfare. This, along with their exclusivity, led to attacks, culminating in a landmark 1874 decision in Kalamazoo, Michigan, upholding the right of school boards to levy taxes to support such institutions. High schools in the United States also generally were coeducational. Advances in women's secondary education were envisioned by such pioneering educators as Emma Willard, Mary Lyon, and Catharine Beecher. While these reformers' influence was limited, and conservatives attacked the idea of coeducation, public support for women's education was high. By the end of the nineteenth century, female students outnumbered males in high schools across the country.

Education in the South lagged behind other regions. This was partly due to the plantation elite, which viewed popular education with suspicion. It also was linked to the legacy of slavery, and concerns with keeping the black population in a condition of servitude. Informal forms of education abounded, from tutoring to apprenticeship and other forms of vocational training. Despite their exclusion from formal education, slave families imparted lessons from one generation to another, transmitting a rich cultural tradition that left an indelible imprint on the region.

Free blacks established schools for their struggling communities, or modified those founded by philanthropic whites. This was true in northern cities before the Civil War, and throughout the South after. The Freedman's Bureau supported thousands of schools in the war's aftermath, providing critical skills and training. Black literacy rates began to improve significantly, and by 1890, nearly two-thirds could read. Even so, inequities abounded. Term lengths in southern black schools stagnated, while those in the white schools began to increase, even approaching the standard of the northern states by the 1890s. Black teachers were paid less than their white counterparts, and were allotted meager sums for textbooks and other supplies. Legal challenges to this were denied in the U.S. Supreme Court case *Cumming v. School Board of Education of Richmond County, Georgia* (1899). Where there had been some measure of parity during Reconstruction, southern school districts eventually spent as little on black students as a fifth of that expended for whites.

Native American education in the nineteenth century featured a deliberate crusade to alter an indigenous way of life. American Indians had long practiced their own forms of education, a process of acculturation that varied from one tribal group to another. Early schools for Native Americans were established by religious missionaries, intent on evangelizing and introducing basic literacy skills. The Bureau of Indian Affairs (BIA), established as part of the War Department in 1824, supervised dozens of schools by 1850, reaching a small fraction of the population. In 1870, programs were run by both the BIA and missionaries, as part of the federal government's "Peace Policy," although government schools eventually predominated. In 1877, there were 150 BIA schools enrolling several thousand students, and by 1900, the number of institutions had more than doubled and enrollments exceeded twenty thousand, representing half the school age population. Certain schools boarded students, the most famous being the Carlisle School, founded in 1879 by Captain Richard Henry Pratt. These institutions attempted aggressive assimilation of American Indian students, but rarely succeeded. Despite these efforts, and an extensive network of BIA schools, Native Americans remained isolated on reservations, and outside the nation's social and economic mainstream.

The nineteenth century is also referred to as the "age of the college." While only a handful of higher education institutions existed in 1800, several hundred others were founded in the next fifty years. Leading state universities were established and other institutions were sponsored by religious denominations. Most fought for survival, competing for students and financial support. The *Dartmouth College* case, settled in 1819, granted private institutions autonomy from the state legislatures that chartered them. Many colleges offered few advanced courses, however, the rest being "prepatory" classes equivalent to those in academies or high schools. Through much of the nineteenth century, American collegiate institutions were dominated by a classical curriculum and an academic culture shaped by traditions handed down from the colonial period. Latin and Greek represented the core of the curriculum and most classes were conducted by recitation. There were efforts to introduce more scientific, historical, and literary studies. Francis Wayland advocated such innovations as president at Brown, but the Yale Report of 1828, a faculty document defending classical studies, helped to slow widespread change during the antebellum period. Tradition held the classical emphasis to be indispensable; without it, no course of study could represent collegiate standards.

Change was evident, however, in the latter decades of the century. The first Land Grant College Act in 1862, drafted by Vermont congressman Justin Smith Morrill, established support for institutions devoted to practical and scientific study. A second Morrill act in 1890 provided even more support for these state universities. Meanwhile, visionary leaders such as Harvard's Charles Eliot broke the stranglehold of tradition in the collegiate curriculum, introducing a liberal elective system that allowed students to choose courses freely. Scientific research institutes had been opened at Harvard, Yale, and other institutions even before Eliot's reforms, and new research-oriented universities were established afterward, with Cornell (1868), Johns Hopkins (1876), and Chicago (1890) leading the way. These institutions were influenced by the German model of higher education, which emphasized research-based learning instead of classical training. Flagship state universities, such as Michigan, Wisconsin, and California, also exhibited German influences and attracted professors dedicated to scholarship and research.

Adult education found expression in the lyceum movement, which began in 1826 and within a decade had established more than three thousand local forums for lectures and debates. After the Civil War, the Chautauqua movement sponsored traveling and local exhibitions and lectures, eventually embracing hundreds of local associations. These forms of popular learning continued into the early twentieth century, when their roles were increasingly filled by universities, museums, libraries, and other institutions.

By 1900, the basic elements of a modern education system were in place. Common school reform had established a network of primary schools, public high schools existed in towns and cities across the country, and colleges and universities were widely accessible. Americans attended school at higher rates than in any other nation and engaged in a variety of other educational activities. This keen interest in education would continue in the years ahead.

Reforming Education in the Early Twentieth Century

Education reform appeared in many guises in the opening decades of the twentieth century. Progressive education was identified with such renowned reform figures as John Dewey, Francis W. Parker, and William Wirt, and influenced a small but highly visible cadre of educational reformers. Other school reformers were less idealistic by temperament and more concerned with issues of efficiency and carefully aligning the purposes of schooling with the needs of the economy. High schools expanded rapidly, and colleges and universities also grew.

Progressive educators represented the legacy of such well-known European thinkers as Frederck Froebel, Henrich Pestalozzi, and Johann Herbart. They also were influenced the experiential psychology of William James and the work of Edward Sheldon, principal of the Oswego, New York Normal School. Dewey was the most famous of progressive educators, well known for his work with the University of Chicago Laboratory School, which he founded upon joining the university's faculty in 1894. A leading academic and popular philosopher, Dewey's best-known work on schooling was *Democracy and Education* (1916). Chicago had become a center for these ideas after Francis Parker arrived in 1883 to head the Cook County Normal School, one of the city's teacher-training institutions. William Wirt introduced "platoon schools" in nearby Gary, Indiana, in 1908.

Women were especially prominent in reform, founding progressive schools and occasionally providing leadership to school districts. Caroline Pratt, Marietta Johnson, and Flora Cook were leaders of innovative private institutions, and Chicago's Ella Flagg Young was among the nation's most important progressive superintendents. Their efforts met resistance, as many educators complained experiential methods did not impart academic skills. Other critics lampooned progressive education as a trendy fad among the social and intellectual elite.

Additional reformers in this period contributed to the emergence of new, centralized, and efficient city school systems between 1890 and 1920. This was a part of a sweeping reform campaign in municipal government, one that attacked the corruption associated with ward-based political regimes. Hundreds of municipalities changed from ward-level school boards and city councils to centralized and bureaucratic forms of governance and administration. Urban school systems came to be run by boards elected from across a community or municipality, and administered by superintendents selected for their experience and professional competence. This gave rise to new bureaucratic forms of school management and control. New organizational forms were adopted, the most important being the kindergarten and junior high schools.

A corollary to this was the development of standardized or mental testing, and school personnel trained in the new subfield of psychological measurement. French researchers Alfred Binet and Théodore Simon devised the first general test of mental aptitude in 1908; Lewis Terman of Stanford University and Edward Thorndike of Columbia University were among the chief American proponents of these techniques. By the latter 1920s, thousands of school districts employed standardized tests to judge student abilities, to justify curricular decisions, or simply to inform teachers and parents.

The rise of the mental testing movement was especially important for children with special needs or learning difficulties. Blind, deaf, or speech-impaired students had been educated in special schools since the mid-nineteenth century. As urban school systems grew, particular courses were established for such students. In 1879, for instance, Cleveland created a class for "feebleminded" children; Boston followed suit in 1898, as did other cities. Eventually, public fears were raised about these children intermingling with the "normal" population, sentiments fueled by pseudoscientific advocates of "mental hygiene" and "eugenics," a term for human perfectibility. Zealous proponents of these ideas issued racist bromides against immigration and the assimilation of minority groups, and even urged the sterilization of "feebleminded" couples.

This also was a time of rapid expansion for the American high school. Enrollments stood at about 300,000 in 1890 (public and private schools combined), and by 1930, the number had increased to nearly 5 million, almost half of the nation's eligible teenage population. Much of this was due to the growing number of institutions: on average, a new secondary school was established every day. The regions leading this expansion were the northern, midwestern, and western states, especially areas with high levels of income and little inequality. Enrollments tended to be higher in communities with fewer manufacturing jobs and smaller numbers of immigrants. On average, high school graduates earned higher wages, an indication of their contributions to the economy.

The general bearing and purpose of secondary education was framed by the "Report of the Committee of Ten," published in 1893. Comprised of university representatives and national education leaders, this group was chaired by Harvard's Charles Eliot, and included William Torrey Harris, U.S. Commissioner of Education. Its purpose was to establish order and uniformity in a secondary education system that included public high schools, academies, private and religious schools, and various other institutions. Twenty-five years later, a second national report was issued by the Commission on the Reorganization of Secondary Education of the National Education Association, chaired by Clarence Kingsley. Widely known as the "Cardinal Principles Report," this document outlined a broad range of social and academic purposes for the high school. It provided a vision of the "comprehensive high school," embracing vocational and academic curricula and uniting students in a common commitment to democratic citizenship. This would serve as an important American ideal for decades to come.

Specialized secondary curricula were developed for women and blacks. Ellen Richards, a chemist and the Massachusetts Institute of Technology's first female faculty member, helped to launch a distinctive academic field called "home economics." In high schools home economics became a way of defining women's roles through training in "domestic science" and socialization in prescribed standards of conduct. At the same time, commercial education, training in stenography, typing and bookkeeping, became popular among women interested in office employment.

Due to limited opportunities, fewer than 5 percent of eligible black students were enrolled at the secondary level at this time, most of them in private schools supported by tuition, local donations, and northern philanthropy. Public high schools were established throughout the south for whites. Between 1905 and 1920 more than five hundred were established, making secondary schooling accessible across the region. By contrast, in 1916 only fifty-eight public high schools for African Americans existed in fourteen southern states, just twenty-five in the former Confederate states. Many of these schools featured a curriculum focused on manual trades and domestic science, reflecting the influence of Booker T. Washington, the period's most famous black educator. W. E. B. Du Bois was an outspoken critic of Washington, advocating high academic standards for a "talented tenth" of black students.

Nationally, post-secondary education continued to expand. Overall enrollment climbed from about a quarter million in 1900 to more than a million in 1930, representing more than 10 percent of the age group. The number of female students grew even faster, from less than 40 percent of the student body in the 1890s to almost half by the twenties. These developments infused new verve into campus life. Fraternities, sororities, and dating became popular, especially after 1920, along with spectator sports such as football.

There was a decided shift in the university curriculum, and a new utilitarian disposition was signaled by the appearance of professional schools and institutes. Nineteenth-century legal and medical training had been conducted by private schools or individuals; after 1900 universities began acquiring these institutions, or developing their own, and awarding degrees to their graduates. Similar arrangements were made for the preparation of engineers, social workers, and other professionals. The first university programs to provide training for business also appeared, offering courses in accounting, finance, management, marketing, and similar subjects.

The growth of higher education also led to new types of institutions. Among the most important was the junior college, a two-year school intended to offer preparation for higher study, later called community colleges. These schools first appeared in the West and the Midwest, numbering some two hundred by the 1920s, but enrolling less than a tenth of all undergraduates. Other more popular forms of higher education also flourished, among them municipal colleges in the larger cities and private urban universities, many of them religious. State-sponsored normal schools gradually expanded their purview, and began to evolve into state colleges and universities. These institutions served local students, providing baccalaureate education along with a variety of professional programs. Altogether, the range of higher education alternatives expanded appreciably, accounting for much of the increase in enrollments.

By the close of this period, much of the creative energy of progressive education had dissipated. Due to the Great Depression, the 1930s were years of fiscal distress for many school districts, particularly those in larger cities. Programs were cut, especially extracurricular activities and such "frills" as music and art. At the same time, high school and college enrollments increased as youth employment opportunities disappeared. World War II, on the other hand, pulled students away from the schools to serve in the military or work in war industries. Neither episode provided an environment for educational reform. Many of the developments of earlier decades remained in place, such as standardized testing, the comprehensive high school and the new research-based and utilitarian university. Yet, the impact of other reform ideals, particularly those of Dewey and his progressive allies, was less enduring.

Education in Postwar America

Among the most striking features of the latter twentieth century was the growing importance attached to formal education, both as a matter of public policy and as a private concern. The federal government became a source of funding, and education developed into a major issue in national politics. At the same time, more Americans attended school, as enrollments climbed at all levels of the educational system, but especially in the nation's high schools and colleges.

In the 1950s schools expanded rapidly, straining resources with the postwar "baby boom." A number of prominent academics and journalists criticized progressive education, linking it in the public mind with failure in the schools. This was partly due to the climate of the Cold War and suspicions that progressive educators were "soft headed" or left-leaning. It also reflected perceptions of a lack of discipline in American children, particularly teenagers. When the Russian Sputnik spacecraft was launched in 1957, many attributed American failures in the "space race" to shortcomings in the schools. This led to passage of the National Defense Education Act in 1958, boosting federal support for instruction in science and mathematics.

The major events in postwar education, however, revolved around questions of race and inequality. The 1954 Supreme Court decision in *Brown v. Board of Education*, declaring segregated schools to be inherently unequal, was a milestone of national educational policy and in popular thinking about social justice. The decision was the culmination of a series of legal challenges to segregated education undertaken by the NAACP in the 1930s, 1940s, and 1950s. It immediately led to vows of non-compliance by southern politicians and educators. Consequently, desegregation proceeded slowly but gained speed in the following decade, when compliance was linked to federal school funding. Civil rights activists waged local battles against segregation and educational inequality, first in the South and later in the North, where de facto segregation was widespread. De jure policies of separate schooling ended, but overall patterns of segregation proved much harder to change.

The changing racial and ethnic composition of the nation's principal metropolitan areas exacerbated these issues. With the migration of millions of blacks after World War II, big city public schools systems became divided along racial lines. Despite the principles of integration and equity embodied in the "Brown" decision and the efforts of liberal-minded educators, growing inequalities in education came to characterize metropolitan life. Because of residential segregation, school resources were also spatially distributed, a point that eventually became contentious. Schools in black neighborhoods tended to be overcrowded, with larger classes and fewer experienced teachers than schools in white areas. Migration to the suburbs, widely known as "white flight," also made it difficult to desegregate city schools. Between 1960 and 1980, the country's suburban population nearly doubled in size, making urban desegregation an elusive goal.

Civil rights organizations issued legal challenges to de facto patterns of school segregation, charging school districts with upholding segregation to avoid aggravating whites. A series of federal court decisions in the latter 1960s and early 1970s articulated a new legal doctrine requiring the active pursuit of integrated schools. In the landmark case of *Swan v. Charlotte-Mecklenburg* (1971), a federal district court established mandatory bussing of students as a remedy to residential segregation. In subsequent years, desegregation plans requiring bussing were implemented in scores of cities, most of them by order of federal or state authorities. These decisions were supported by research, particularly a national survey undertaken in 1966 by sociologist James Coleman, finding that integrated schooling produced high achievement levels in minority students. The Supreme Court's 1974 *Miliken v. Bradley* decision, however, limited the impact of desegregation plans by prohibiting bussing across district lines, effectively exempting most suburban communities.

Meanwhile, education became an integral part of Lyndon Johnson's "War on Poverty." In 1965, he sponsored the Elementary and Secondary Education Act (ESEA), dramatically expanding federal assistance to schools. Title 1 of this legislation provided resources to schools with high numbers of poor students, to address inequities. Other educational initiatives begun under the Johnson administration included Head Start, a preschool program aimed at children from poor families. By 1972, more than a million children were enrolled in the program and studies showed that it boosted academic achievement.

Legislation addressing inequality and discrimination extended to other groups of students. The Bilingual Education Act of 1968 provided funding to schools serving the nation's 3 million students who did not speak English as a primary language. In 1970 the Office of Civil Rights issued guidelines requiring districts where such students constituted more than 5 percent of the population to take "affirmative steps" to meet their needs. At about the same time a series of court cases challenged the principle of separate classes for special education students, a group that had grown rapidly in the postwar period. In 1975, the Education for All Handicapped Children Act was signed into law by President Gerald Ford. With this measure, the federal government required school districts to provide these students with free and equitable schooling in the least restrictive environment possible. Similarly, the National Organization of Women (NOW) included a provision in its 1967 Women's Bill of Rights calling for "equal and unsegregated education." Five years later, Title IX was included in ESEA, declaring "no person . . . shall, on the basis of sex, be excluded from participation in, be denied the benefits of, or be subjected to discrimination under any education program or activity receiving federal financial assistance." School districts responded most visibly in the area of women's athletics. The 1970s witnessed a five-fold increase in female participation in competitive sports, although change in other areas was much slower.

The post-World War II period also witnessed significant change in higher education. An influential Harvard faculty report in 1945 advocated flexible curricula under the heading "general education," and a presidential commission on higher education in 1949 presciently argued the need for greater capacity. By 1970, enrollments had quadrupled to more than 8 million. Early growth was due to the GI Bill, which provided tuition benefits to veterans, but the major source of new students was the affluent postwar "baby-boom" generation, a third of whom eventually enrolled in college. The number of institutions did not increase significantly, but the size of campuses grew dramatically. Colleges dropped any pretense of governing the daily living habits of students, even those residing on campus, creating a fertile field for alternative lifestyles and cultural practices. It also opened the door to widespread sexual freedom. The Supreme Court decision in *Tinker v. Des Moines Independent School District* (1969), limiting the ability of schools to control student self-expression, extended many of the same freedoms to secondary students.

Perhaps more important, the large concentrations of young people with little supervision abetted the development of political organizations, and students became conspicuous participants in both the civil rights and antiwar movements. The latter was based largely on campuses, and came to a head in the spring of 1970, when four students were killed by national guardsmen at Kent State University. Yet other protests focused on curricular issues, leading to a number of new courses, departments, and programs. The most important of these were African American (or Black) Studies and Women's Studies programs, but there were others as well.

All of these developments helped to make education a contentious national political issue. Bussing plans produced heated reactions from white urbanites. Others believed the schools had drifted away from their academic mission, and that the universities cultivated protestors. The Supreme Court's 1978 *Bakke* decision, barring quotas but allowing race to be considered in university admissions, further polarized public opinion. In 1980, promising to end federal involvement in education, presidential candidate Ronald Reagan vowed to remove the U.S. Department of Education as a cabinet position. It was a promise that remained unfulfilled, however. A national commission's 1983 report on the schools, "A Nation at Risk," further galvanized support for federal leadership in strengthening the education system. These concerns led George H. Bush to campaign as the "education president," even though he proposed little change in policy.

In the closing decades of the twentieth century, American interest in formal education reached historic highs. With public expenditures on education (in constant dollars) more than doubling since 1960, by 1990 there was growing interest in student performance on tests of scholastic achievement. As the economy shifted away from manufacturing, rates of college enrollment among secondary graduates increased from less than 50 percent in 1980 to nearly two-thirds in 2000. Spurred by the women's movement and growing employment options, the number of female students increased even more rapidly, after lagging in earlier decades. At the same time, vocational education programs considered integral to the comprehensive high school were increasingly seen as irrelevant.

Growing disquiet about the quality of public education contributed to movements to create "charter schools," publicly supported institutions operating outside traditional school systems, and "voucher" programs offering enrollment in private institutions at public expense. These and other "choice" or "market-based" alternatives to the public schools were supported by Republicans, keen to challenge existing systems and to undermine Democratic teacher's unions. By 2000, there were more than two thousand charter schools in communities across the country, with states such as Arizona and Michigan leading the movement. Voucher experiments in Milwaukee, Cleveland, and a few other cities have not produced decisive results.

In the 2000 presidential election, candidates Albert Gore and George W. Bush both placed education policy initiatives in the forefront of their campaigns. This was a historic first and an indication of the heightened significance of education in the public mind. Bush's narrow victory in the election was at least partly due to his calls for greater accountability in schooling at all levels. Passage of federal legislation re-authorizing ESEA, popularly known as "Leave No Child Behind Act," established testing programs as a requirement for receiving federal assistance. Even though this was a natural extension of the "systemic reform" initiatives undertaken by the Clinton Administration, encouraging state testing regimes, it marked a new level of federal involvement in the nation's school system.

Conclusion

American education has changed a great deal since 1647, when Massachusetts passed its first school law. The reforms of the nineteenth and twentieth centuries helped to establish a comprehensive education system extending from the primary school to the university. The ferment of the postwar period revolved around issues of equity and excellence, as ever more Americans attended some form of school. Much has been accomplished, however. Many of the most abhorrent inequities have been narrowed considerably. As a result of past struggles there is considerable parity in black and white education, despite persistent segregation and achievement gaps. Gender differences have diminished even more dramatically. This is not to say that problems do not exist. The United States is host to a new generation of immigrants, and battles have been waged over bilingual education and other cultural issues; but the outlook is bright, as Americans still exhibit a firm commitment to education as a means of providing opportunity. That, more than anything else, is the principal legacy of American education, and its great hope for the future.

BIBLIOGRAPHY

Adams, David Wallace. *Education for Extinction: American Indians and the Boarding School Experience, 1875–1928.* Lawrence: University Press of Kansas, 1995.

Anderson, James D. *The Education of Blacks in the South, 1860–1935.* Chapel Hill: University of North Carolina Press, 1988.

Angus, David L., and Jeffrey E. Mirel. *The Failed Promise of the American High School, 1890–1995.* New York: Teachers College Press, 1999.

Axtell, James. *The School upon a Hill: Education and Society in Colonial New England.* New Haven, Conn.: Yale University Press, 1974.

Cremin, Lawrence Arthur. *American Education; the Colonial Experience, 1607–1783.* New York, Harper and Row, 1970.

———. *American Education, the Metropolitan Experience, 1876–1980.* New York: Harper and Row, 1988.

———. *American Education, the National Experience, 1783–1876.* New York: Harper and Row, 1980.

———. *The Transformation of the School: Progressivism in American Education, 1876–1957.* New York: Knopf, 1961.

Kaestle, Carl F. *Pillars of the Republic: Common Schools and American Society, 1780–1860.* New York: Hill and Wang, 1983.

Levine, David O. *The American College and the Culture of Aspiration, 1915–1940.* Ithaca, N.Y.: Cornell University Press, 1986.

Lockridge, Kenneth A. *Literacy in Colonial New England: An Enquiry into the Social Context of Literacy in the Early Modern West.* New York: Norton, 1974.

Ravitch, Diane. *The Troubled Crusade: American Education, 1945–1980.* New York: Basic Books, 1983.

Reese, William J. *The Origins of the American High School.* New Haven, Conn.: Yale University Press, 1995.

Rury, John L. *Education and Social Change: Themes in the History of American Schooling.* Mahwah, N.J.: Lawrence Erlbaum Associates, 2002.

Tyack, David B., and Elisabeth Hansot. *Learning Together: A History of Coeducation in American Schools.* New Haven, Conn.: Yale University Press, 1990.

———. *Managers of Virtue: Public School Leadership in America, 1820–1980.* New York: Basic Books, 1982.

Tyack, David B; Thomas James; and Aaron Benavot. *Law and the Shaping of Public Education, 1785–1954.* Madison: University of Wisconsin Press, 1987.

Veysey, Laurence R. *The Emergence of the American University.* Chicago, University of Chicago Press, 1965.

John Rury

See also **Carlisle Indian Industrial School; Charity Schools; Chautauqua Movement; Dame School; Dartmouth College Case; Indian Boarding Schools; McGuffey's Readers; *New England Primer;*** *and vol. 9:* **Massachusetts School Law.**

EDUCATION, AFRICAN AMERICAN. Whites have traditionally determined the type and extent of education for African Americans in the United States; these educational policies have largely reflected the prevailing white culture's ideas about the role of blacks in society, especially their relations with nonblacks. Thus, public activity in this area has mirrored closely the general attitudes of the white majority toward the black minority. Both whites and blacks have recognized the relationship between education and control, so policies related to the education of African Americans have extended from prohibition to encouragement.

The education of blacks began with religious instruction, for some justified slavery as part of a divine plan for the conversion of heathen Africans to Christianity. The Quakers in Philadelphia were leaders in providing education for African Americans, having initiated elementary schools for them as early as 1745. Various churches established special missions to bring the gospel to plantation slaves, and masters were under church injunction to provide for the religious instruction of their slaves when no regular white pastor or missionary was available. Clandestine schools existed in various southern cities, often in violation of legal prohibitions in local black codes. Prohibitions of this nature date back to legislation passed in South Carolina in 1740. The conflict between the desire to teach religion and the opposition to the education of slaves led to efforts to promote religious instruction without letters; blacks learned Christian doctrine, but very few learned to read or write.

A violent reaction against any form of education for slaves set in after any slave plot or uprising involving literate blacks. When Nat Turner, a literate black preacher who drew his inspiration from reading the Bible, led an insurrection in Southampton County, Virginia, in 1831, the reaction spread across the South. Stern penalties punished anyone who taught blacks to read and write, and conviction and punishment were frequent. Nevertheless, a number of slaves learned from owners or members of owners' families, who taught them either out of kindness or for the advantages a literate slave provided. A survey of the biographies of blacks who reached adulthood as slaves and attained prominence after empancipation reflects both the extent of such clandestine teaching and learning and the importance placed on education by blacks seeking to break the bonds of slavery.

During this first phase of black education, extending up to the Civil War, states with the largest numbers of African Americans maintained the most stringent prohibitions against their education, but some slaves were nevertheless able to circumvent such laws. At emancipation, more than 95 percent of blacks were illiterate. During the second, very brief phase, covering the period from the start of Reconstruction to the 1890s, blacks and white allies feverishly attempted to overcome the past effects of slavery through education. Immediately after the Civil War, agencies of northern church missionary societies set up numerous schools for empancipated slaves in the South. The Freedmen's Bureau materially aided these early foundations. Titled "colleges" and "universities" by optimistic founders, these institutions had to begin on the lowest level. New England "schoolmarms" carried on a large part of the instruction. With a clientele dazzled by the promise of learning, they were strikingly effective.

Public education in the South had its origin, legally, in systems patterned after midwestern prototypes and enacted by combinations of African American carpetbaggers and poor white members of Reconstruction governments, the latter known as "scalawags." The destitution of the South prevented any considerable development of the ambitious schemes devised, and the effect of the attitudes reflected in *Plessy v. Ferguson* (1896) and later Supreme Court decisions undermined public efforts in support of African American education. Nevertheless, between the time of emancipation and 1900, black literacy increased from less than 5 percent to more than 50 percent.

During the third phase, which extended from the 1890s to 1954, black education was hampered by legal racial segregation in southern states, by local de facto segregation in border and northern states, and by preponderantly inferior financial support for black schools. The "equal" aspect of the "separate but equal" doctrine of *Plessy* never materialized, although some small effort was made in that direction before 1954.

Local school districts diverted state education funds to the support of schools for white children. In some southern counties with high percentages of African Americans, per capita distribution of school funds reached the proportion of $40 to $1 spent, respectively, on the white child and on the black child. With growing prosperity in the South and a smaller proportion of African American children in the population, the vast differences began to decrease in the 1920s, but they remained substantial. By 1934 there were only fifty-nine accredited high schools for blacks in the South, and twenty of these were private. Of the thirty-nine public institutions, ten were located in North Carolina. Mississippi had none, South Carolina had one, and Alabama and Florida had two each.

Attacks on legal segregation in education, first successful in the 1930s, continued until the 1954 decision in *Brown v. Board of Education of Topeka* declared segregated education by race to be unconstitutional. By that time, the issue of education for African Americans was shifting from rural to urban areas, where a majority of the African American population had moved. Since 1954 trends in African American education have included the following: (1) slow and modest integration of public schools in the South and in small towns throughout the nation; (2) increasing segregation in education by race in those urban areas where blacks concentrate in central cities and whites have moved to suburbs; (3) concern on the part of African Americans about the content of the curriculum and the degree to which it supports racial bias; and (4) efforts by urban African Americans to gain greater influence in the schools their children attend through the movement for community control.

Higher Education

The higher education of blacks in the United States dates back to an occasional student at a northern college during the eighteenth century. After several unsuccessful efforts to establish a college for blacks, in 1854 supporters of the African colonization movement founded the Ashmun Institute, later called Lincoln University. In the South the end of the Civil War encouraged the founding of numerous colleges for former slaves. Some have ceased to exist, but in 1970 there were more than fifty fully accredited private institutions, some of which also enrolled white students. In the years prior to World War II, most African Americans receiving college degrees graduated from these institutions.

State-supported institutions of higher education were slower to emerge and, like public schools for blacks, were not well financed. Support improved after World War II, but, without exception, these institutions were receiving less financial support than their white counterparts when the Supreme Court announced the *Brown* decision.

College attendance among African Americans has increased since the *Brown* decision, and the percentage attending all-black institutions has declined significantly. Despite severe financial difficulties, the traditionally black private institutions continue to provide education for a sizable portion of the African American student population. The formerly all-black state institutions remain largely black but are legally open to all. Nonetheless, blacks continue to attend college at lower levels than do whites.

BIBLIOGRAPHY

Anderson, Eric, and Alfred A. Moss, Jr. *Dangerous Donations: Northern Philanthropy and Southern Black Education, 1902–1930.* Columbia: University of Missouri Press, 1999.

Anderson, James D. *The Education of Blacks in the South, 1860–1935.* Chapel Hill: University of North Carolina Press, 1988.

Fairclough, Adam. *Teaching Equality: Black Schools in the Age of Jim Crow.* Athens: University of Georgia Press, 2001.

Lomotey, Kofi, ed. *Going to School: The African-American Experience.* Albany: State University of New York Press, 1990.

Lomotey, Kofi, ed. *Sailing against the Wind: African Americans and Women in U.S. Education.* Albany: State University of New York Press, 1997.

Henry N. Drewry / A. E.

See also **African Americans; *Brown v. Board of Education of Topeka*; Desegregation; Education, Higher: African American Colleges; *Plessy v. Ferguson*.**

EDUCATION, BILINGUAL. Bilingual education refers to an educational program in which both a native language and a second language are taught as subject matter and used as media of instruction for academic subjects. In the United States the tradition of public bilingual education began during the 1840s as a response to the many children who spoke German, Dutch, French, Spanish, Swedish, and other languages. As a result of the nativism of World War I and the adverse popular reaction to the large number of non-English-speaking immigrants entering the country in the late nineteenth and early twentieth centuries, restrictive laws prohibiting instruction in languages other than English brought this educational practice to a halt.

Renewed interest developed, however, with the civil rights movement of the 1960s. In 1968 Congress provided funding for bilingual programs in Title VII of the

Elementary and Secondary Education Act, also known as the Bilingual Education Act. In *Lau v. Nichols* (1974) the U.S. Supreme Court ruled that eighteen hundred Chinese students in the San Francisco School District were being denied a "meaningful education" when they received English-only instruction and that public schools had to provide special programs for students who spoke little or no English. The number of students fitting this description increased dramatically toward the end of the twentieth century. Since 1989, for example, they went from 2,030,451 to 4,148,997 at the end of the century, representing an increase from 5 percent to almost 9 percent of the school-age population. These children come from more than one hundred language groups. Of those served by special language programs, almost half are enrolled in bilingual education programs; the others are served by English-as-a-second-language or regular education programs. In the 1990s an increasing number of English-speaking children sought to learn a second language by enrolling in enrichment bilingual education programs. Title VII appropriation for special language programs for both minority language and mainstream groups rose from $7.5 million in 1969 to $117 million in 1995.

The effectiveness of such programs has been much debated. Opponents have claimed that promoting languages other than English would result in national disunity, inhibit children's social mobility, and work against the rise of English as a world language. Advocates propose that language is central to the intellectual and emotional growth of children. Rather than permitting children to languish in classrooms while developing their English, proponents claim that a more powerful long-term strategy consists of parallel development of intellectual and academic skills in the native language and the learning of English as a second language. Proponents also argue that immigrants and other non-English-speaking students have valuable resources to offer this multicultural nation and the polyglot world. While in 1999 forty-three states and the District of Columbia had legislative provisions for bilingual and English-as-a-second-language programs, the citizens of California and Arizona voted to restrict the use of languages other than English for instruction. The growing anti-bilingual-education movement had similar proposals on the ballot in other states at the beginning of the twenty-first century.

BIBLIOGRAPHY

August, Diane, and Kenji Hakuta. *Education of Language-minority Children*. Washington, D.C.: National Academy Press, 1998.

Baker, Colin, and Sylvia Prys Jones. *Encyclopedia of Bilingualism and Bilingual Education*. Clevedon, U.K.: Multilingual Matters, 1998.

Brisk, Maria Estela. *Bilingual Education: From Compensatory to Quality Schooling*. 2d ed. Mahwah, N.J.: Erlbaum, 2001.

Maria Emilia Torres-Guzman

See also **Spanish Language.**

EDUCATION, COOPERATIVE, is a program that integrates classroom studies with paid, real-life work experience in a related field. As a result, students receive an academic degree and practical work experience.

Originally designed for college-level students working toward a bachelor's degree, these programs received a considerable amount of interest in the 1970s. In the 1980s, "co-op" programs declined due to increased academic requirements and budget cutbacks.

Since the early 1990s, there has been a resurgence of interest. Presently, they are offered at numerous two-year and four-year institutions. Similar programs offering classroom studies and time on the job have become popular in both vocational and traditional high schools. These provide students not bound for college with a smooth transition from school to work.

The federal government has had an impact in this area. As part of former Vice President Al Gore's "Staffing Reinvention Program," the Office of Personnel Management has consolidated thirteen programs, including Cooperative Education, into the Student Education Employment Program. This program serves as a bridge between classroom instruction and on-the-job training and at the same time introduces talented students to public service. Positions are available to students pursuing a high school diploma, a vocational or technical degree, an associate degree, a bachelor's degree, or a postgraduate degree.

The popularity of employing co-op students has also increased with employers in the private sector. According to the National Commission for Cooperative Education, more than 80 percent of the top 100 companies in the Fortune 500 employ students through college co-op programs.

College students in these programs working toward a bachelor's degree characteristically commit to a period of study that goes beyond the standard four-year timeframe. They alternate between their traditional studies and related on-the-job experience. Started in 1909, the co-op program at Boston's Northeastern University, an often copied example, offers students a practice-oriented education that blends the strengths of a traditional liberal arts and sciences curriculum with an emphasis on professionally focused practical skills.

Values of the co-op system include the increased visibility and abilities of the student entering the job market, the easing of the student's college financial burden due to compensation for work, and the ability to comprehend learning on a more concrete level due to the exposure to the work environment. Values to the employer include the opportunity to view potential employees as they work in the co-op programs and the establishment of connections with colleges whose students will seek employment upon graduation.

One drawback of the co-op system is the fragmentation of liberal arts studies due to interruptions as the student goes to work. Less opportunity for continuity in extracurricular activities and college social life are also seen as negatives for the student. For the employer, drawbacks include the expense of training students who would not return after the co-op experience had been completed and the disruptions caused by the continual changing of members within the workforce.

Other related programs include summer internships, apprenticeships, and independent-study courses based on on-the-job experience.

BIBLIOGRAPHY

College Cooperative Education: The National Commission's Site: http://www.co-op.edu.

Hoberman, Solomon. "Time-Honored or Time Worn? Cooperative Education in the 1990s." *Vocational Education Journal* (March 1994).

Northeastern University's Division of Cooperative Education: http://www.coop.neu.edu.

Re, Joseph M. *Earn & Learn: An Introduction to Cooperative Education.* Alexandria, Va.: Octameron Associates, 1997.

Dawn Duquès

See also **Apprenticeship; Free Universities.**

EDUCATION, DEPARTMENT OF. Public Law 96-98, known as the Department of Education Organization Act, established the U.S. Department of Education (DOE) on 4 May 1980. It was established to increase the commitment of the federal government to assuring equal access to educational opportunity; improving the quality of education; encouraging greater involvement of parents, students, and the public in federal education programs; promoting federally supported research, evaluation, and sharing of information; enhancing the coordination of federal education programs; improving the management of federal education activities; and increasing the accountability of federal education programs to the public, Congress, and the president. The department was the first cabinet-level education agency of the U.S. government. It superseded the U.S. Office of Education, established in 1867, and replaced the National Institute of Education, established in 1972.

The Federal Role in Education

There are several organizations within the DOE. They include the Office of Educational Research and Improvement, the National Center for Education Statistics, the Planning and Evaluation Service, the National Assessment of Educational Progress, the Fund for the Improvement of Postsecondary Education, the National Institute on Disability and Rehabilitation Research, the Office of Special Education Programs, and the National Research and Dissemination Centers for Career and Technical Education.

In the United States, state and local governments decide most education policy. The role of the federal government is restricted by the Tenth Amendment to that of guarding the right of its citizens to equal access to public institutions and equal opportunity within them. Additionally, through the funding of research, financial aid to students, and the dissemination of information, the federal government is involved in improving the quality of education. The federal government also funds and administers elementary and secondary schools for dependents of civilian and military personnel abroad, operated by the Department of Defense, and has some control over postsecondary institutions that prepare students for military careers. Otherwise, it is not involved directly in postsecondary educational institutions except for certain responsibilities delineated in the Civil Rights Act of 1864. Education funding comes primarily from state, local, and federal taxes.

Programs of the Department

The DOE has undertaken programs in elementary, secondary, postsecondary, vocational, bilingual, and special education, and has fulfilled specified responsibilities for four federally supported institutions: the American Printing House for the Blind; Gallaudet University; Howard University; and the National Technical Institute for the Deaf. The department coordinates its efforts with the cabinet departments of defense, commerce, health and human services, and labor; the National Science Foundation; the National Endowment for the Humanities; and other federal agencies with education-related assignments. The department works primarily to ensure both equal access (for such groups as the disadvantaged, racial and religious minorities, the disabled, women, and at-risk children) and educational excellence in terms of measurable performance.

National Goals

In 1981, Secretary of Education Terrel H. Bell created a National Commission on Excellence in Education, whose report, *A Nation at Risk: The Imperative for Educational Reform* (1983), called for widespread, systemic reform, including stronger graduation requirements, more rigorous and measurable standards, more time in school, and significantly improved teaching. A national debate ensued, and throughout the 1980s and into the 1990s, the department remained at the forefront of campaigns to introduce national curriculum and assessment standards to hold students, teachers, and schools accountable for higher levels of achievement.

Following President George Bush's Education Summit in 1990, the nation's governors adopted six National Education Goals to enable the country to develop standards of performance for all schools and to measure progress toward the achievement of these standards. The original goals, intended to be met by the year 2000, follow: first, all children will start school ready to learn; second, the high school graduation rate will increase to at least 90 percent; third, American students will leave grades four, eight, and twelve having demonstrated competency in challenging subject matter including English, mathematics, science, history, and geography, with every school in America ensuring that all students learn to use their minds well, so they may be prepared for responsible citizenship, further learning, and productive employment in a modern economy; fourth, U.S. students will lead the world in science and mathematics achievement; fifth, every adult American will be literate and will possess the ability to compete in a global economy and exercise the rights and responsibilities of citizenship; and sixth, every school will be free of drugs and violence and will offer a disciplined environment conducive to learning.

Federal Legislation

Between 1990 and 1994, a number of new laws were enacted that changed the American education system: the National Literacy Act (1991); the Education Council Act (1991); the Reauthorization of the Higher Education Act of 1965 (1992); the Education of the Deaf Act Amendments (1992); the Rehabilitation Act Amendments (1992); the Student Loan Reform Act (1993); the Rehabilitation Act and Education of the Deaf Act Technical Amendments (1993); the Migrant Student Record Transfer System Act (1993); the Higher Education Technical Amendments Act (1993); the National Service Trust Act (1993); the Goals 2000: Educate America Act (1994); the School-to-Work Opportunities Act (1994); the Safe Schools Act (1994); the Educational Research, Development, Dissemination, and Improvement Act (1994); the Student Loan Default Exemption Extension Act (1994); the Improving America's Schools Act (1994); and the National Education Statistics Act (1994).

Reform at the federal level, stemming from the America 2000 Excellence in Education Act, called for funding for Presidential Merit Schools (rewards to schools that make progress in raising achievement, fighting drugs, and reducing the dropout rate); Presidential Awards for Excellence in Education ($5,000 awards to teachers who meet the highest standards of excellence); National Science Scholarships (annual scholarships for high school seniors to encourage them to take more science and math courses); and Magnet Schools of Excellence (competitive grants awarded to local districts to support magnet schools for purposes other than desegregation).

On 8 January 2002, President George W. Bush signed into law the No Child Left Behind Act of 2001, which mandated that states and school districts develop strong systems of accountability based on student performance. The act also enabled federal Title I funds to be used for supplemental education services, such as tutoring, after-school services, and summer programs, tripled the federal funding investment in reading through the Reading First program, and provided almost $3 billion during the first year to improve teacher quality.

BIBLIOGRAPHY

Bloom, Allan. *The Closing of the American Mind: How Higher Education Has Failed Democracy and Impoverished the Souls of Today's Students.* New York: Simon and Schuster, 1988.

"Department of Education." Available from http://www.ed.gov.

Hacsi, Timothy A. *Children as Pawns: The Politics of Educational Reform.* Cambridge, Mass.: Harvard University Press, 2002.

Ladd, Helen F., and Janet S. Hansen, eds. *Making Money Matter: Financing America's Schools.* Washington, D.C.: National Academy Press, 1999.

Rochester, J. Martin. *Class Warfare: What's Wrong with American Education.* 2002.

Toch, Thomas. *In the Name of Excellence: The Struggle to Reform the Nation's Schools, Why It's Failing, and What Should Be Done.* Bridgewater, N.J.: Replica Books, 1991, 2000.

Veith, Gene Edward, Jr., and Andrew Kern. *Classical Education: The Movement Sweeping America.* Washington, D.C.: Capital Research Center, 2001.

Christine E. Hoffman

EDUCATION, EXPERIMENTAL, encompasses nontraditional methods, curricula, and classroom management. The experimental learning movement departs from competition-based classroom learning by using team assignments and grading procedures that give students a part in each other's progress. Prominent among experimental curricula are Mortimer Adler's Paideia proposal and Theodore Sizer's Coalition for Essential Schools—both of which eliminate electives and vocational programs—and a program based on the theories of psychologist Howard Gardner.

The Paideia proposal focuses on the Socratic method of teaching and three modes of learning—knowledge, skills, and understanding. The foundations of the program are critical thinking, weekly seminars, and scheduling of all three learning modes. Teachers in Essential Schools act as coaches for the study of a few essential subjects using interdisciplinary courses and themes. Rather than assign grades based on objective testing, teachers assess students based on demonstrations of accomplishments through exhibits and learning portfolios. Gardner encourages theme-based courses designed around seven types of intelligence that include linguistic, logical-mathematical, bodily kinesthetic functions, and interpersonal relations.

The experimental educational movement has proved controversial. In reaction to public perception of the failure of the public education system, schools have tried using site-based management, altered school schedules, flexible classrooms, and private management. These methods of school management have come under fire by critics who question whether nontraditional administration has in fact improved education. In another example, multimedia technology and telecommunications predominate, including individual instruction via computers, television, and satellites. Critics fear that the high costs of this technology will create additional unequal educational opportunities among the nation's primary and secondary school systems.

BIBLIOGRAPHY

Adler, Mortimer J. *The Paideia Proposal: An Educational Manifesto.* New York: Macmillan, 1982.

Centron, Marvin, and Margaret Gayle. *Educational Renaissance: Our Schools at the Turn of the Century.* New York: St. Martin's Press, 1991.

Fiske, Edward B. *Smart Schools, Smart Kids: Why Do Some Schools Work?* New York: Simon and Schuster, 1991.

Sizer, Theodore R. *Horace's Hope: What Works for the American High School.* Boston: Houghton Mifflin, 1996.

Myrna W. Merron/Shelby Balik

See also **Curriculum; Magnet Schools; Schools, For-Profit; Schools, Private.**

EDUCATION, HIGHER

This entry includes 4 subentries:
African American Colleges
Colleges and Universities
Denominational Colleges
Women's Colleges

African American Colleges

The institutions of higher education currently referred to as the historically black colleges originated in the mid-nineteenth century as a result of the enslavement of African Americans. Because of the numerous slave revolts by literate slaves, literacy was denied most slaves in the South and formal education was prohibited. Throughout the North, free African Americans prior to and after the Civil War had limited opportunities for collegiate education. With the exception of Oberlin College in Ohio, which began admitting blacks in the 1830s, African Americans only sporadically attended a small number of white colleges. Often, blacks who attended white institutions during this period were light in complexion and not always known to be of African descent. As the push for emancipation of slaves became more pronounced in the 1850s and 1860s, several colleges were established to prepare the freed blacks of the North for leadership in the black communities. As with the history of white institutions of higher education, the earliest black colleges maintained preparatory departments and were often colleges in name only for decades.

Northern Black Colleges

Three institutions of higher education were established for black students prior to the Civil War. Each was established by a religious denomination. The Institute for Colored Youth in Philadelphia was established in 1837 at the behest of a Quaker, Richard Humphreys. Established originally as a school for boys, by the 1850s it had become a prominent coeducational private primary and high school. It moved to Cheyney, Pennsylvania, at the turn of the century and became Cheyney State College by the 1920s.

Lincoln University was also established in Pennsylvania prior to the end of the Civil War. Established by the Presbyterian Church as the Ashmun Institute for black males in 1854, this institution obtained collegiate status before any other founded for black students. The primary mission of Lincoln was to educate ministers to evangelize in Africa and to provide religious leadership to blacks in the United States. In an attempt to produce black leaders and professionals after emancipation, Lincoln established a law school and medical school. However, both closed in 1873. In 1953, the institution became coeducational.

Wilberforce University was established in 1856 by the African Methodist Episcopal Church in Ohio shortly after the founding of Lincoln University. While institutions of education founded for blacks by whites were overwhelmingly single-sex, African Americans believed education important for both men and women and established coeducational institutions. In addition, black-founded colleges employed black faculty and staff of both sexes. For example, Wilberforce employed the well-known Oberlin graduate Mary Church Terrell in 1884 as well as the young Harvard- and German-trained W. E. B. Du Bois in his first faculty position in 1894. These institutions offered liberal-arts and professional courses as well as teacher training.

A Federal University

After the legal abolishment of slavery, the federal government through the Bureau of Refugees, Freedmen, and Abandoned Lands established thousands of schools throughout the South for the newly freed blacks. In addition, in an act of Congress, Howard University was established in 1867 in the nation's capital for the education of youth in the "liberal arts and sciences." The institution was named for General Oliver O. Howard, a Civil War hero and commissioner of the Freedmen's Bureau. In addition to the collegiate department, the university also had a normal department for the training of teachers as well as medical, law, and theology departments. Although identified as a black college, Howard was opened to students regardless of race and nationality. There were white students at the institution from its inception. Throughout its history, Howard University was viewed as the preeminent black institution due to its diverse student body and distinguished faculty and the aforementioned curricular offerings (later to include a school of dentistry as well as Ph.D. programs).

Private Black Colleges

Private black colleges proliferated after the Civil War. Founded primarily by black and white missionary organizations, these institutions varied greatly in quality and size. Those institutions established by the American Missionary Association (AMA), such as Fisk, Tougaloo, Talladega, Dilliard, and Atlanta University, offered the classical liberal arts degrees as well as teacher training and were among the leading institutions of higher education for blacks in the Deep South. The all-male Morehouse College (1867) and female Spelman College (1881) in Atlanta were both founded by the American Baptist Home Mission Society and were leading examples of distinguished single-sex institutions. These institutions, established by New England missionaries, reflected the culture and curriculum of the colleges of that region—classical education and liberal culture.

Hampton Normal and Agricultural Institute (1868) and TUSKEGEE Institute (1881) were made famous by Booker T. Washington. He was a graduate of the former institution and founder of the latter. Washington ignited a heated debate within the black community at the end of the nineteenth century and in the first decade of the twentieth century over the prominence of classical versus industrial education within the curriculum of black colleges. Although both Hampton Institute in Virginia and Tuskegee in Alabama were the preeminent industrial and manual training schools among black colleges, their primary mission was the training of teachers for the common schools of the South.

Private philanthropy played an important role in the shaping of private black colleges and was instrumental in the growth and success of Hampton and Tuskegee Institutes. White and black religious denominations were key in establishing black colleges, but by the dawn of the twentieth century, many industrial philanthropists contributed to black higher education that stressed industrial education, which they believed more practical for the descendants of slaves. Among these supporters were the General Education Board, Anna T. Jeanes Foundation, Phelps-Stokes Fund, Carnegie Foundation, Julius Rosenwald Foundation, and the Laura Spelman Rockefeller Foundation.

Land Grant Colleges

The Morrill Act of the United States Congress in 1862 provided for use of public taxes to establish public state institutions for each state's agricultural and industrial training but not at the expense of the liberal arts. As a result of segregation in the southern and border states, only three southern states provided for black colleges from this fund. Consequently, Congress passed a second Morrill Act in 1890 that prohibited discrimination with these funds. Thus, to comply with this new act, southern and border states established separate black land grant institutions that stressed vocational rather than academic courses. Seventeen black land grant institutions were established in the southern and border states. These institutions were colleges in name only until well into the twentieth century. A study of black higher education in 1917 noted that only one black land grant college offered college courses at that time. According to James Anderson, the bulk of black higher education was in the black private colleges. He noted that in 1926–1927, some 75 percent of all black college students were enrolled in private institutions.

Conclusion

Because slaves had been denied the right to an education, the building of a school system in the South was of paramount importance. As a result, most black colleges initially stressed teacher training in their curriculum. The preparation of ministers was also an important mission of the black private colleges, as it was for the earliest white colleges. More than 200 institutions were established for the higher education of black people beginning in the mid-nineteenth century, although most of the institutions did not function as true colleges until the illiterate freedmen could obtain a primary education. By the 1940s, only 117 black colleges survived. These primarily private colleges also offered professional education: by the end of World War II, they included two medical schools, three law schools, two schools of social work, two dental schools, two pharmacy schools, one school of journalism, one school of veterinary medicine, two library science schools, and nine schools of nursing.

The federal abolishment of legal segregation in education as a result of major Supreme Court rulings and acts of Congress from the 1950s and 1960s has resulted in black colleges being referred to as "historically" black colleges to reflect the desire to abolish the notion of racially segregated institutions. Due to a court order, black land grant colleges have been required to aggressively recruit white students and provide them with financial incentives to attend historically black public institutions. While nearly three-quarters of all black college students attend predominantly white institutions today, until the later twentieth century the historically black college produced generations of the nation's black leadership, including W. E. B. Du Bois (Fisk University), Mary McLeod Bethune (Scotia Seminary, now Barber-Scotia College), Thurgood Marshall (Lincoln University of Pennsylvania), and Martin Luther King Jr. (Morehouse College). Black college graduates were also the backbone of the segregated schools in the South. While current black college students have many options in terms of higher education, the historically black college's mission to train the leaders of the black community remains one of its central goals.

BIBLIOGRAPHY

Anderson, James D. *The Education of Blacks in the South, 1860–1935.* Chapel Hill: University of North Carolina Press, 1988.

Bond, Horace Mann. *Education for Freedom: A History of Lincoln University, Pennsylvania.* Lincoln University, Pa.: Lincoln University Press, 1976.

Logan, Rayford W. *Howard University: The First Hundred Years, 1867–1967.* New York: New York University Press, 1969.

Payne, Bishop Daniel A. "The History of the Origin and Development of Wilberforce University." Wilberforce University Archives, circa 1877–1878.

Perkins, Linda M. *Fanny Jackson Coppin and the Institute for Colored Youth, 1865–1902.* New York: Garland, 1987.

Work, Monroe N. *Negro Yearbook and Annual Encyclopedia of the Negro, 1941–46.* Tuskegee, Ala.: Tuskegee Institute, 1946.

Linda M. Perkins

Colleges and Universities

The widespread system of American colleges and universities began modestly in 1636 with the founding of Harvard College (now Harvard University), which began classroom instruction in 1638. The other colonial colleges were the College of William and Mary, which was chartered in 1693 but began classes only in 1729; the Collegiate School (Yale University), founded in 1701; the College of New Jersey (Princeton University), chartered in 1746, with instruction in 1747; King's College (Columbia University), founded in 1754; the College, Academy, and Charitable School of Philadelphia (University of Pennsylvania), chartered in 1755 after collegiate classes began in 1754; the College of Rhode Island (Brown University), chartered in 1764, with instruction a year later; Queen's College (Rutgers—the State University), chartered in 1766, with instruction in 1771; and Dartmouth College, chartered in 1769, with classes beginning in 1770. Religious groups and their leaders generally controlled college administration and instruction. At first, the colleges had a Protestant Christian character, but with the advent of the Enlightenment the classical-religious curriculum expanded to include medicine, law, the sciences, and modern languages. The influence of Benjamin Franklin, Thomas Jefferson, and others helped bring secularism and modernism into the American academy.

American usage of the term "university" dates from 1779, with the rechartering of the College of Philadelphia as the University of the State of Pennsylvania without loss of private status. State-controlled colleges and universities appeared in Georgia, North Carolina, and Tennessee by 1800. Other major developments prior to the Civil War included the growth of state and municipal colleges, coeducational collegiate facilities, professional education in dentistry and engineering, and military colleges. The Dartmouth College decision (1819) by the U.S. Supreme Court, a ruling barring state interference, became the Magna Charta of private and denominational colleges. Also significant were the increase of foreign study by Americans and the early provisions for graduate work. In the first half of the ninteenth century, colleges and universities sprang up all over the country, with the College (now University) of California chartered as a private institution in 1855. The federal government authorized land grants for colleges and universities in the Morrill Act (1862), enabling agricultural and engineering colleges that developed later into state universities to open. Students, too, actively shaped college and university life, often supplementing the limited official curriculum with literary societies, secret societies, and fraternities—organizations that exposed them to public speaking and current events.

After the Civil War, the number of colleges and universities continued to increase. In 1842, there were 101 colleges; in 1869, 563; and in 1900, 977. New institutions opened for women, African Americans, American Indians, and members of various faiths. Normal schools were upgraded to collegiate level. Many colleges added graduate and professional schools and became universities. The opening of the Johns Hopkins University (1876) brought German standards of research and scholarship to American higher education. Other changes included Harvard's institution of the undergraduate elective system; introduction of such new subjects as psychology, sociology, and anthropology; the extension of studies in the sciences and mathematics, history, economics, and modern languages; and the granting of funds under the second Morrill Act (1890) for instruction in agricultural and engineering colleges. Although this post-Civil War expansion of the curriculum incorporated most students' career needs, many students still focused their energies outside the classroom, especially on fraternities or sororities, athletics, and in "coffeehouse" organizations.

During the twentieth century, enrollment in colleges and universities climbed sharply upward, from 237,592 (1899–1900) to 8.1 million (1971–1972) to 14.5 million (1992–1993), although the number fell slightly in the mid-1990s to 14.3 million (1995–1996). The percentage of college students in the 18–21 age group rose from 4.01 (1899–1900) to over 50 percent by the 1970–1971 school year. By 1999, 25 percent of the American population over 25 years old had completed four or more years of college. (Roughly 8 percent held a master's degree or higher.) The number of women students and faculty members also increased perceptibly, as did the number of members of minority racial and ethnic groups and students with foreign citizenship.

Among the major developments of the twentieth century have been the growth of junior or community colleges, the proliferation of professional courses in all fields, the trend toward coeducation, the impact of the College Entrance Examination Board and the accrediting associations on admissions and standards, the federal government's contributions through such legislation as the Servicemen's Readjustment Act (GI Bill of Rights) of 1944 and the National Defense Education Act of 1958, the eruption of student dissent and violence in the 1960s, the unionization of faculties, and the introduction of open-admission plans and external degrees. In the 1960s the curriculum expanded with such innovations as black, women's, and ethnic studies; the financial crisis of the early 1970s made many colleges and universities, especially the private and denominational institutions, insecure; and in the 1980s and 1990s critics of affirmative action and "political correctness" brought the debate over curricular changes into the mainstream of debate.

Dartmouth College. This engraving depicts the campus of the New Hampshire college, founded in 1769. GETTY IMAGES

During the 1960s protesting students not only forced university administrations to abolish *in loco parentis* rules but helped bring about the diversity that has become a hallmark of higher education. Student ranks expanded to include more members of minority groups and nontraditional students, such as men and women past the age of twenty-two, who often work at least part-time and may raise families while attending college. Diversification has brought a wider array of needs to the attention of campus administrators. Special offices, centers, and advocacy groups for women and minority students were created in attempt to meet their unique needs, but not without controversy. Complaints of favoritism and voluntary resegregation by minority groups occasionally accompanied such centers.

By the 1970s, 44 percent of the 2,600 colleges and universities were under governmental (mostly state) control and had 75 percent of the total enrollment. The remaining 56 percent of schools comprised institutions under denominational direction and those under the governance of self-perpetuating secular boards of trustees. A number of denominational colleges, though, have secularized the composition of their boards of trustees so as to qualify for much needed public funds. Financial pressures in the 1970s also forced private institutions to expand enrollments, raise tuition rates, and curtail some services. Many students relied on scholarships and grants from public and private sources to attend.

Colleges and universities also faced other new difficulties. One serious issue, especially for the junior faculty during the period of widespread protest in the 1960s and 1970s, was that of academic freedom and tenure. Pressures to limit or abolish tenure came from within and outside higher education. To some extent, criticism of faculty derived from the activism of some professors and from the prevalence of collective bargaining in some areas. The question of equal opportunity and affirmative action programs proved to be equally perplexing and controversial. Although accessibility barriers to higher education for racial and ethnic minorities and for women fell, some forms of discrimination continued. One source of dissatisfaction was the feeling that growing attention to the financial and other needs of the low-income groups was accompanied by difficulties for students from middle-income groups.

Mirroring the increasing diversity of student bodies, the professoriate likewise expanded somewhat to better reflect the makeup of the U.S. population. In part because of affirmative action initiatives by colleges and universities, the numbers of female, African American, Hispanic, Asian American, and Native American professors increased through the 1980s and 1990s, although not at the rate desired by many advocates. The numbers of women studying in such nontraditional fields as law and medicine have not been matched by proportionate numbers of tenured female professors in these fields. At the end of the twentieth century, more part-time faculty members, and many women and members of minority groups, fell into this category of low-paid instructors.

During the last quarter of the twentieth century, curricular offerings and types of higher-education institutions diversified as well. Partly a result of student protests during the 1960s, colleges and universities expanded offerings in such subjects as the history, music, and religions of non-Western cultures and literature by women and members of minority groups. The number of such academic departments as women's studies and African American studies increased, and some colleges and universities introduced racial or ethnic studies requirements to guarantee students the exposure to ideas outside the traditional white male European heritage. Critics dubbed this new wave of interests "political correctness" and argued that it inhibited dialogue, that the expanded curriculum was less rigorous than the traditional curriculum and therefore poorly served students and intellectual life. Best-selling books expanded the discussion beyond academe.

Beginning in the mid-1970s there was also a diversification of institutional structures. Community colleges expanded and many public institutions and some private colleges offered evening and weekend classes and courses via cable television and, in the late 1990s, via the Internet. More institutions took their courses to the students, offering courses in prisons, on military bases, and at community centers. At the same time, more colleges distinguished themselves from the mainstream. Historically black colleges and a few remaining women's colleges clarified their missions, advertising racial or single-sex atmospheres that fostered more success among minorities and women than racially mixed and coeducational schools. Similarly, new tribal colleges served Native American students.

At the end of the century, public universities continued their missions of teaching, research, and service to society, with research receiving much attention. As federal expenditures for research increased, the popular press criticized universities for spending research money unwisely and professors for spending more time on research than teaching. As a result, more stringent teaching requirements, downsizing, more efficient business practices to lower tuitions, and elimination of academic tenure were some of the solutions proposed by state legislatures and some university administrations. Along with diversification of colleges and universities came inflation of grades and educational credentials, making some bachelors' and graduate degrees of questionable value. At the same time employers required more and more extensive educational backgrounds. All of these factors guaranteed that colleges and universities would be important, and contested, territory for years to come, as the United States adjusted to post-Cold War educational and economic conditions.

BIBLIOGRAPHY

Brickman, William W., and Stanley Lehrer, eds. *A Century of Higher Education.* New York: Society for the Advancement of Education, 1962.

Brubacher, John S., and Willis Rudy. *Higher Education in Transition: A History of American Colleges and Universities, 1636–1968.* New York: Harper and Row, 1968.

Chamberlain, Mariam K., ed. *Women in Academe: Progress and Prospects.* New York: Russell Sage Foundation, 1988.

Horowitz, Helen Lefkowitz. *Campus Life: Undergraduate Cultures from the End of the Eighteenth Century to the Present.* New York: Knopf, 1987.

Jencks, Christopher, and David Riesman, *The Academic Revolution.* Garden City, N.Y.: Anchor Books, 1969.

Kerr, Clark. *The Great Transformation in Higher Education, 1960–1980.* Albany: State University of New York Press, 1991.

Parsons, Talcott, and Gerald M. Platt. *The American University.* Cambridge, Mass.: Harvard University Press, 1973.

Riesman, David and Verne A. Stadtman, eds. *Academic Transformation: Seventeen Institutions Under Pressure.* New York: McGraw-Hill, 1973.

Rudolph, Frederick. *The American College and University: A History.* New York: Knopf, 1962.

William W. Brickman
Christine A. Ogren / c. w.

See also **Curriculum; Education; Education, Higher: African American Colleges; Education, Higher: Denominational Colleges; Education, Higher: Women's Colleges; Intelligence Tests; Multiculturalism; Pluralism; Schools, Single-Sex.**

DENOMINATIONAL COLLEGES

The establishment of institutions of higher learning in America was fostered by the central assertion of Puritanism that laity should possess the ability to read the Bible and understand theology. This principle made New England one of the most literate societies in the world during the seventeenth century; and it was upon this premise that Harvard College, the first denominational college in the English colonies, was established in 1636. A little more than thirty years later, Anglicans established the College of William and Mary in Virginia in order to educate the laity—male laity—to carry out their errand in the New World. Similar denominational institutions of faith and learning soon followed with the establishment of Yale, Princeton, Brown, Pennsylvania, and King's College (now Columbia) early in the eighteenth century. In 1789, largely through the efforts of Bishop John Carroll, Roman Catholics established their own institution of higher learning with the founding of Georgetown College. Other Catholic institutions such as St. Joseph's College and St. Louis College soon followed. By 1830, American Catholics had founded fourteen colleges. The curriculum in both Protestant and Catholic colleges mirrored the medieval educational model with students studying the Bible as well as ancient languages and the classics.

During the course of the next two hundred years, approximately nine hundred colleges were founded throughout the nation with heavy concentrations in the northeast and midwestern states. With the advent of the Civil War, however, few of these institutions of higher learning remained operable. Of the one hundred and eighty-two colleges that remained, some one hundred and sixty of them were denominationally related institutions. In part, this growth was attributable to the decentralized ecclesiastical structures of Protestant denominations that encouraged lay participation, a concern for educated leadership, and fund-raising. Not only were the percentages of denominational colleges growing during this era, but their curriculums and student populations were expanding as well.

The year 1828 saw the publication of "Original Papers in Relation to a Course of Liberal Education," in which the Yale report recommended that the curriculum of colleges should be extended beyond educating the nation's male citizenry in Christianity, the classics, and republicanism. At the same time, European schools of thought began to take hold in America. Scottish common sense realism, a philosophy widely espoused at colleges such as Princeton, held great sway in schools during this era, but so did the teachings of the Enlightenment and German idealism. Further efforts to educate the populace were taken in 1843 with the establishment of the interdenominational Society for the Promotion of Collegiate and Theological Education at the West. Ordained clergy often presided over these institutions, which came to reflect and articulate the ideals of the Protestant establishment.

Other religious institutions, such as Oberlin College, resisted some of the social conventions of the day. Founded in 1833, Oberlin soon gained the support of the popular revivalist Charles Grandison Finney and attracted students charged with being bound together in a "solemn covenant" and pledged to "the plainest living and highest thinking." Oberlin's admission policies were remarkably progressive for their time. The first class consisted of twenty-nine male and fifteen female students. In 1841, the college conferred bachelor's degrees upon three female students, making it the nation's first institution of higher education to do so. Such egalitarian measures were extended to people of color as well. By the mid-1830s Oberlin was advertising the admission of any youth "irrespective of color." Over time these efforts were a great success as nearly one-third of the college's graduates by the turn of the century were African American.

Several social currents contributed to the proliferation of denominational colleges in the late nineteenth century. Foremost were the country's industrial development and its geographical expansion. This growth, albeit modest at first, resulted in the expansion of the upper class, many of whom regarded higher education as a symbol of status. A result of these class assumptions was the increased numerical demands on the nation's institutions. But these market forces also helped to modernize the nation, consequently increasing its need for so-called "human capital formation." As the nation's need for professional workers increased, so did the demand for and opportunities of an educated middle class. Yet in the post–Civil War decade, only five hundred colleges were still solvent.

To stem the emerging demand for education, Congress passed the Morrill Land Grant Act of 1862 that helped establish more than seventy land-grant colleges. While seemingly inconsequential to the life of denominational colleges, the passage of this act helped to break the monopoly held by churches in higher education. Further loosening this stronghold was the growing internal bureaucracy found within denominations. With this latter development came two important changes. First, the creation of internal bureaucracies tended to distance educational institutions from their sponsoring denominations. This increased distance affected the shape of the curriculum and the way the mission of the school was carried out. Second, as these structures grew more complex internally, there tended to be less interdenominational cooperation. The balkanization of education agendas unwittingly served to severely undermine the cultural dominance several mainline Protestant denominations had attained.

At the same time, societal demands for an educated class were rapidly changing; this led to the development of an appreciable gap between both Catholic and Protestant curriculums and the needs of an industrializing nation. The long-standing "classical" curriculums of Latin, Greek, ethics, and rhetoric offered by these institutions did not meet the demands of the new economy. While the curriculums of a number of Protestant institutions gradually changed to meet these demands, Catholic institutions were slower to change. Their resistance was due in part to structural issues. Unlike Protestant institutions, Catholic colleges in America remained modeled on a European Jesuit system of instruction that combined secondary and collegiate education into a seven-year program. It would take several decades before the educational programs of Catholic colleges had adjusted to the prevailing patterns of American secondary education and economic change.

Protestant denominational colleges underwent a period of consolidation in the early twentieth century. Typically, the educational mission of schools fell under the auspices of appointed boards whose ideas of a religious-based education were often more broadly construed than those of the respective churches. Although some boards produced specific guidelines in determining the character or definition of church-related schools, among them Presbyterians, others simply sought to develop "Christian gentlemen" among their students. Protestant colleges were increasingly divesting themselves of their specific Christian heritage in order to serve the public at large. Further distancing church-related institutions from their historic roots was the emergence of philanthropic foundations whose terms often precluded funding colleges falling under sectarian controls. Faced with the mounting costs of running such institutions, many schools redefined their relationships with their denominations in order to qualify for funding.

Church-related institutions went through a difficult period between the 1960s and the 1980s. Skepticism among the nation's student population toward organized religion coupled with mounting costs and increased competition by tax-supported schools forced several colleges to either sever ties with their respective denominations or close altogether. In the midst of these changes, conservative evangelicals and fundamentalists from various denominations stepped in to fill what they perceived to be a void in American higher education. Establishing their own institutions of higher learning, such as Oral Roberts

University, with decidedly faith-based curriculums, evangelicals were widely successful in attracting prospective students seemingly alienated by the concessions traditional religious institutions had made to American culture. While many publications and leading spokespersons predicted the not-too-distant end of denominational colleges, a great many remain viable centers of higher education.

BIBLIOGRAPHY

Axtell, James. *The School upon a Hill: Education and Society in Colonial New England.* New Haven, Conn.: Yale University Press, 1974.

Marsden, George M. *The Soul of the American University: From Protestant Establishment to Established Nonbelief.* New York: Oxford University Press, 1994.

Parsonage, Robert R., ed. *Church Related Higher Education: Perceptions and Perspectives.* Valley Forge, Pa.: Judson Press, 1978.

Power, Edward J. *A History of Catholic Higher Education in the United States.* Milwaukee, Wis.: Bruce Publishing, 1958.

Pattillo Jr., Manning M., and Donald M. MacKenzie. *Church-Sponsored Higher Education in the United States.* Washington, D.C.: American Council on Education, 1966.

Tewksbury, Donald G. *The Founding of American Colleges and Universities before the Civil War.* New York: Arno Press, 1969. Original edition published in 1932.

Kent A. McConnell

See also **Brown University; Harvard University; Land Grants: Land Grants for Education; Morrill Act; Oberlin College; Princeton University; University of Pennsylvania; William and Mary, College of; Yale University.**

Women's Colleges

Once the only option available to women wanting to pursue higher education, women's colleges have become victims of their own success. With more American women than men enrolled in college during 2000–2001, many educators questioned whether all-female colleges have outlived their purpose.

Beginnings

Colleges for women grew from the female seminaries of the early nineteenth century. Based upon principles of "republican motherhood" and imbued with religiosity, Emma Willard's Troy Seminary (Troy, New York, 1821) and Catharine Beecher's Hartford Female Seminary (Hartford, Connecticut, 1824), among others, educated young women to be intelligent wives and mothers who would rear literate and moral sons capable of governing the new nation. Some of these institutions, such as Mount Holyoke (South Hadley, Massachusetts, 1837), adopted the vocational mission of training women to teach. With a curriculum for educating teachers and an endowment supporting lower-income students, Mount Holyoke rose to the forefront of the female academies.

Although labeled "seminaries" rather than "colleges" and open to girls as young as twelve, many early female schools offered curricula comparable to those of men's liberal arts colleges. Seminary students took Greek, Latin, French, botany, geology, chemistry, physics, mathematics, geography, American history, and physiology, in addition to "traditionally feminine" studies in fine arts, music, and dancing. Between 1830 and 1870, the 107 female seminaries and academies covered most subjects addressed in the upper levels of men's colleges. In this way, the largely northeastern female academies of the era combined concern with "female qualities" like piety, purity, and domesticity with mastery of subjects considered off-limits for women. They thus expanded but left intact the boundaries of conventional womanhood.

The Development of Women's Higher Education

In the 1850s, as the common-school movement developed across the United States, a widespread need for teachers prompted the formation of "normal schools." Considered the more "nurturing" of the sexes, women were welcomed into schools as teachers. The Civil War with its casualties heightened demand for nurses. Women answered the call, increasing demands for their advanced training. Most of those (58.9 percent) who pursued higher education in America at this time did so at single-sex institutions.

By the 1860s, a growing push toward coeducation brought the issue of women's training to the forefront. In the wake of the Civil War, many previously all-male colleges wrestled with the question of coeducation. By 1889–1890, 39,500 women, or 70.1 percent of American female collegians, attended coeducational schools. Women's schools—many of them the former seminaries such as Mount Holyoke, now renamed as colleges—claimed the rest, a decline in the percentage of those choosing women-only, but still a massive increase in number: 16,800 students, up from 6,500 in 1869–1870.

Resistance to women's higher education remained, however. Dr. Edward Clarke's widely read *Sex in Education* (1873) argued that higher education was unnatural and harmful to women. Schools such as Stanford, University of Chicago, and University of Wisconsin, alarmed by growing female enrollments, introduced curbs, in the form of quotas and segregated classes. In the Northeast and South, some of the oldest and most prestigious colleges and universities steadfastly refused coeducation. Rather than opening their doors to women, some schools chose to form "coordinate" institutions. In Cambridge, Massachusetts, Harvard's stance prompted the founding of Radcliffe College (1894), while in New York City, Barnard College (1889) served as Columbia's "female annex."

In response to the continued exclusion of women from many institutions, several new and independent female colleges opened their doors: Elmira College (Elmira, New York) in 1855, Vassar (Poughkeepsie, New York) in 1865, Wellesley (Wellesley, Massachusetts) and Smith (Northampton, Massachusetts) in 1875, and Bryn Mawr (Bryn Mawr, Pennsylvania) in 1885.

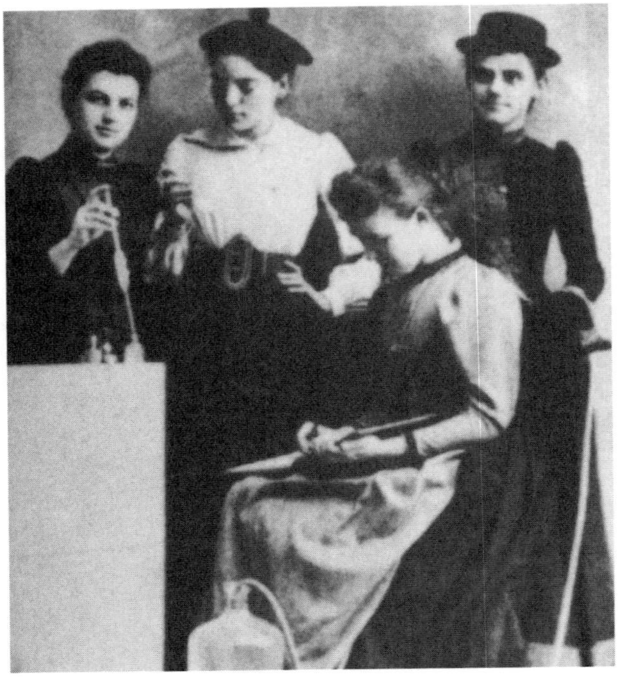

Wellesley College. Four women in a science laboratory at the first women's college to have such labs.

Coming into Their Own

In the 1890s, following a national trend, many women's colleges shed their preparatory departments and recruited elite faculty, both male and female, to enhance their prestige. The institutions later known as the "Seven Sister Schools" came into their own academically, strengthening their curricula and instituting student governments as well as intercollegiate athletics and debate teams. Although Vassar College led the others in attaining national recognition, all took on serious roles in educating women not only for motherhood and womanhood but for careers in the public and private sectors as well. In the South, the still largely ornamental and wholly white "ladies seminaries" also became increasingly academic. Still, they continued to exhibit the conservative thinking of their environs by displaying greater reluctance to embrace women's expanding opportunities than did their northern predecessors.

Prior to the 1920s, most collegiate women were Protestant, white, and middle or upper middle class. Whereas coeducational state colleges attracted farmers' daughters and other members of the working classes, the women's colleges of the South and Northeast, with their high tuitions, residence fees, and limited financial aid, attracted the wealthier offspring of professional families. These schools offered an education that would not jeopardize their students' femininity. Students lived and studied under faculty supervision. Prohibitions against dancing and other "suspect activities" were common.

Many early female college graduates eschewed or delayed traditional patterns of marriage and childbearing, instead continuing their education or pursuing careers. Some enrolled in graduate programs ranging from science and medicine to English and music. Others taught or pursued paid or unpaid employment on academic and professional boards, in charities and other reform-oriented societies. As careers grew more common, many colleges altered their curricula. Rather than offering only liberal arts courses, many added instruction in education, home economics, and other social sciences.

In the 1910s and 1920s, greater numbers of Jewish, Catholic, and African American women, as well as recent immigrants, began to seek higher education. When they did, they often found the doors of select women's colleges closed. Tacit as well as explicitly articulated policies barred the admission, in particular, of qualified African American and Jewish students. In other instances, while enrollment may have been permitted, the nonwhite and non-Protestant students, often poorer, found tuition too steep and scholarship money too limited.

Some all-women's schools in urban areas enrolled greater numbers of religious, ethnic, and racial minorities. At Radcliffe in 1936–1937, for example, 24.8 percent of the women enrolled were Jewish, whereas at Mount Holyoke and Wellesley, that percentage stood at 6.5 and 9.0, respectively. Discrimination, however, prompted African Americans and Catholics to open their own women's schools. Bennett College (1926) in Greensboro, North Carolina, joined Spelman (1924), the former Atlanta seminary, as a leading educator of African American women. For Catholics, Trinity College of Washington, D.C. (1897), and the College of Notre Dame in Maryland (1896) increased their enrollments and liberalized their curricula.

Steps Forward—and Back

The World War II era changed American higher education. Shortages of male workers paved the way for the entry of women into new fields like engineering, while decreased enrollments forced many all-male schools to relax prohibitions against females. In 1943, Harvard opened its classrooms to women through the "Harvard-Radcliffe agreement." Other bastions of male scholarship also admitted women to their law, medical, and professional graduate programs.

At the war's end, however, the trends largely reversed, as troops came home and the GI Bill encouraged male enrollment. The percentage of women enrolled in higher education dropped to its lowest point in the twentieth century. Schools such as Vassar saw a 50 percent drop in the percentage of women pursuing chemistry and physics degrees between 1945 and 1955. The percentage of female doctorates in the sciences declined, while the percentages of those opting for marriage over careers increased.

At the women's colleges of the 1950s, many administrators began to reinvoke the language of republican motherhood in discussions of female higher education. At Radcliffe, President W. K. Jordan welcomed incoming classes by assuring them that their "education would prepare them to be splendid wives and mothers." Mills College (1852) in California inserted cooking, home decorating, and flower arranging into its curriculum. Across the women's colleges of the country, and the coeducational schools as well, engagement, rather than a professional degree or satisfying career, marked the ultimate in female collegiate fulfillment.

Women's Colleges in the New Century: Challenges and Possibilities

The women's movement of the 1960s and 1970s radically altered American higher education. As most all-male colleges opened to women, many of the all-women's colleges decided to open to men, citing, among other reasons, declining interest in single-sex education and decreased need, due to societal changes, for the separate education of the sexes. Vassar College became coeducational, while Wellesley, Bryn Mawr, and Mills affiliated with coeducational colleges, sometimes against students' wishes. As the twentieth century drew to a close, Radcliffe merged entirely with Harvard. Whereas one hundred years before, women's colleges had educated almost 29 percent of the female college population, at the end of the 1990s, only 1.3 percent of female collegians earned their degrees from a single-sex school.

Although increasingly challenged to justify their place and purpose, women's colleges still claimed support. A study of women executives in Fortune 500 companies found a disproportionately high number of female college attendees. Likewise, examinations of *Who's Who* and other female achievement catalogs have found higher than proportional numbers of women's college graduates among their ranks.

BIBLIOGRAPHY

Butcher, Patricia Smith. *Education for Equality: Women's Rights Periodicals and Women's Higher Education, 1849–1920.* New York: Greenwood Press, 1989.

Chamberlain, Miriam K., ed. *Women in Academe: Progress and Prospects.* New York: Russell Sage Foundation, 1988.

Eschbach, Elizabeth Seymour. *The Higher Education of Women in England and America, 1865–1920.* New York and London: Garland, 1993.

Faragher, John Mack, and Florence Howe, eds. *Women and Higher Education in American History: Essays from the Mount Holyoke College Sesquicentennial Symposium.* New York: Norton, 1988.

Frankfort, Roberta. *Collegiate Women: Domesticity and Career in Turn-of-the-Century America.* New York: New York University Press, 1977.

Gordon, Lynn D. *Gender and Higher Education in the Progressive Era.* New Haven, Conn.: Yale University Press, 1990.

Horowitz, Helen Lefkowitz. *Alma Mater: Design and Experience in the Women's Colleges from Their Nineteenth-Century Beginnings to the 1930s.* New York: Knopf, 1984.

Komarovsky, Mirra. *Women in College: Shaping New Feminine Identities.* New York: Basic Books, 1985.

Minnich, Elizabeth, Jean O'Barr, and Rachel Rosenfeld. *Reconstructing the Academy: Women's Education and Women's Studies.* Chicago: University of Chicago Press, 1988.

Newcomer, Mabel. *A Century of Higher Education for American Women.* New York: Harper, 1959.

Solomon, Barbara Miller. *In the Company of Educated Women: A History of Women and Higher Education in America.* New Haven, Conn.: Yale University Press, 1985.

Woody, Thomas. *A History of Women's Education in the United States.* 2 vols. 1929. Reprint, New York: Octagon Books, 1980.

Diana B. Turk

See also **Mount Holyoke College; Schools, Single-Sex; Seven Sisters Colleges.**

EDUCATION, INDIAN.

For generations, Native Americans educated their children through ceremony, storytelling, and observation, teaching them about their cultural heritage and a spiritual relationship with the earth and all beings. Then came the *suyapo* (the Yakama word for "white man"), whose education centered on one God, the written word, and a materialistic relationship with the earth. Colonial, and later U.S, educators thrust these values upon Indian children, but Native families also participated in schooling decisions. From the sixteenth through the early twentieth centuries, parents and communities sent selected youth to school to learn about the other culture, thereby empowering them as cultural intermediaries to serve their nations.

From the Colonial Era through the Nineteenth Century

Each of the European colonial powers offered some form of education to Native people. The Spanish Franciscans in the Southwest and the French Jesuit missions in the Great Lakes region promoted basic literacy. In the British colonies Roman Catholic and Protestant religious leaders introduced a more ambitious program of European education to children of Eastern Woodlands nations. From the awkward efforts of early tidewater Virginia to the sophisticated fund-raising network of Eleazar Wheelock, a Congregational minister who founded a coeducational boarding school in eighteenth-century Connecticut, colonial schoolmasters influenced hundreds of Native children.

The reputation of colonial educators overshadows that of Native schoolmasters of this era. Among the Iroquois and southern New England Algonquins, many Indian students emerged as teachers within their own communities or among neighboring tribes. As educational intermediaries, these Indian schoolmasters reinforced cross-cultural awareness. Echoing their ancestors, who traded extensively with other Native groups, they interpreted Euro-American culture to their people. Foremost among these Native educators, Samson Occom, a Mohegan Presbyterian minister, served Native groups of New England and New York. In the 1760s, Occom earned an international reputation when he preached in England, Wales, and Scotland, while raising thousands of pounds for Wheelock's school and his new venture, Dartmouth College. Purportedly founded for Indian students, Dartmouth catered largely to European Americans. Like its predecessors, Harvard and Princeton, Dartmouth graduated a handful of Indians who had survived disease and the foreign environment of the institution. Two centuries later, Dartmouth retrieved its legacy by reviving its Indian enrollment. In the colonial era, the College of William and Mary enrolled the greatest number of Indians, but their studies were limited to literacy and rudimentary arithmetic.

During the nineteenth century, thousands of Native people endured the traumas of warfare, disease, and removal. Nonetheless, small groups, both Indian and European American, remained committed to the education introduced by the outsiders. In the young Republic, the Christian denominations reached an agreement with Congress that was formalized in 1819 in the Indian Civilization Fund Act. In effect from 1819 to 1873, this measure promised an Indian education partnership between the federal government and "benevolent societies" (church-related groups), ironically violating the constitutional mandate for separation of church and state.

Although the Civilization Act stipulated a federal contribution of $10,000 per annum, in reality the federal portion remained below 10 percent. While the denominational groups raised additional funds, the Indian nations absorbed the greatest expense for their children's schooling because tribal leaders appropriated funds designated by educational provisions in their treaties. More than one-fourth of the almost four hundred treaties ne-

Athletes. This 1909 photograph by William J. Boag shows the football team at the Osage Indian School in Pawhuska, Okla. Library of Congress

Students. Young Sioux boys line up outside the Government School at the Yankton Agency in South Dakota. NORTH WIND PICTURE ARCHIVES

gotiated between Indian nations and the United States contained federal promises of education.

Most of the early Indian schools opened in the Southeast, serving the Cherokees, Choctaws, Creeks, and Chickasaws. Initiated by the founding of Brainerd School among the Cherokees (1817) and the Choctaw Academy (1825), these schools reflected the willingness of portions of the southern Indian nations to welcome certain Protestant denominations who sought to open missions and schools within the nations' lands. These short-lived experiments were interrupted by the removal of eastern Indian nations to Indian Territory in the 1830s.

Following the wrenching removals, the relocated Indian nations established national school systems in their new lands in Indian Territory. The schools and seminaries of the five southern tribes (including the Seminoles) exemplified educational self-determination in Indian Territory until 1907, when the federal government unilaterally closed them as it created the state of Oklahoma.

In 1879, Richard Henry Pratt opened the Indian Industrial Training School in an abandoned army barracks in Carlisle, Pennsylvania. This event marked the beginning of federal Indian schooling. Pratt was a public-relations wizard who persuaded private donors and federal agencies to acknowledge Carlisle as the premier off-reservation Indian boarding school. Pratt believed in the potential of Indian youth to emulate their European American counterparts through what he dubbed "total immersion" education. During his twenty-five-year tenure at Carlisle, he supervised over five thousand Indian students from numerous tribes.

Pratt also crafted widely adopted boarding school patterns, including half-day vocational training, half-day academic curriculum, uniforms and military discipline, mandatory church attendance, and the "outing system," whereby students lived among farming families in nearby communities. Pratt's ideas were the blueprint for other off-reservation boarding schools like Phoenix (Arizona), Chemawa (Oregon), and Chilocco (Oklahoma).

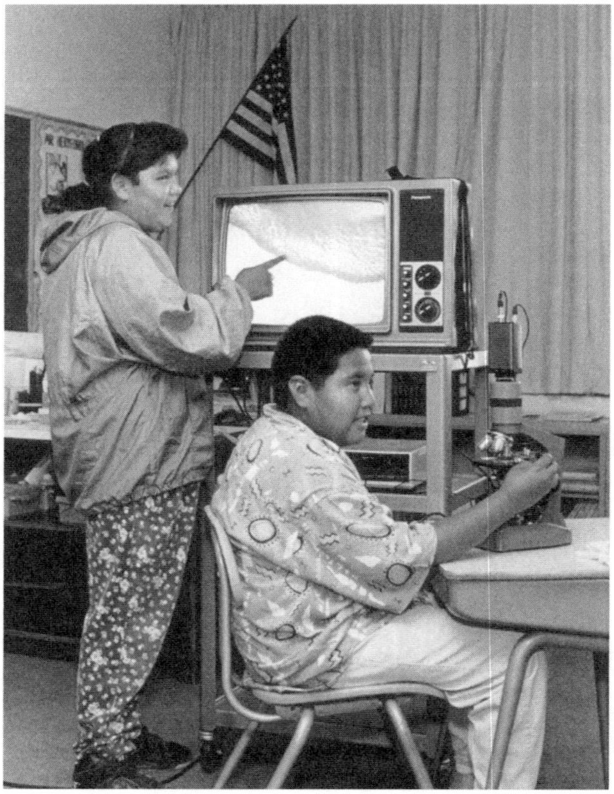

Gifted and Talented Program. Two students demonstrate how a television monitor displays the image from an electronic video microscope. McClure Photography and Media Works

The Twentieth Century

The early twentieth century saw the dramatic rise of Indian enrollment in public schools, but popular perception focused on the notorious schools operated by the Bureau of Indian Affairs (BIA). During the 1920s, reformers lambasted the federal boarding schools for their severe discipline, overcrowding and widespread disease, meager diet, and zealous assimilation tactics that demanded uniformity of language (English only) and appearance. Less well known is the fact that Indian students also molded these institutions. Developing initiatives that escaped contemporary observers, students, who came from many tribal backgrounds, used English as a lingua franca to form pan-Indian alliances and other secret networks that eluded the authorities and persisted well into their postschooling lives.

In the wake of growing criticism, Congress authorized an extensive study of federal Indian policy. The Meriam Report, published in 1928, confirmed that the government's critics had been correct. As a consequence, the educational reformers W. Carson Ryan and Willard W. Beatty, successive directors of BIA education (1930–1952), broadened the curriculum of BIA schools to include Native cultures. During the Indian New Deal, the commissioner of Indian Affairs John Collier (1933–1945) depended on a remarkable group of Indian leaders, including the Winnebago educator Henry Roe Cloud and BIA troubleshooters Ruth Muskrat Bronson (Cherokee) and D'Arcy McNickle (Metis/Flathead). But innovative changes were eclipsed by World War II, and bilingual texts, inclusion of Native art in schools, and summer institutes for BIA teachers quickly lost ground. By 1945 the postwar mood that spawned federal programs known as "termination" (of federal services to tribes) and "relocation" (of Indians to urban areas) persuaded Beatty to refocus BIA school curriculum on education for urban life.

In the 1950s, however, the lack of schooling for thousands of Indians motivated the Navajo Nation, with 14,000 youth in this category, to challenge the BIA to address this need. Special programs, transfer to distant boarding schools, federal Indian-school construction, and further public schooling aided Navajo, Alaska Native, and Choctaw youth, and brought national Indian-school enrollment to over 90 percent by the mid-1960s.

By the 1970s, Indian leaders, tested on the battlefields of World War II, Korea, and Vietnam, and in the fight against termination, were addressing issues of self-determination in Indian education. Galvanized by the Red Power insurgency of that decade, Native people stood ready to assume the direction of their children's education. Following the Kennedy Report (1969), a stinging congressional indictment of Indian education, Indian leaders worked with empathetic members of Congress to craft legislation that would enable Native Americans to shape the educational programs in their communities. During this pathbreaking decade, Congress enacted more legislation on Indian education than at any other moment in its history. Keynote measures began with the Indian Education Act (1972), which belatedly addressed the needs of Indians in public school—the vast majority of Indian children—by opening the Office of Indian Education within the U.S. Office (now Department) of Education. The Indian Self-Determination and Education Assistance Act (1975) provided the foundation for contracting. It enabled tribes and other Indian groups to contract with the federal government to provide specific services to tribal members, including health care and education. Directly after its passage, the All Indian Pueblo Council contracted to supervise the Santa Fe Indian School, the first of numerous such contracts.

Capping this legislative marathon, Congress also passed the Tribally Controlled Community College Assistance Act (1978), which provided funding for tribal colleges. Over thirty colleges were opened, beginning in 1969 with Navajo Community College (later Dine College), and including Haskell Indian Nations University in Lawrence, Kansas, and the Institute of American Indian Arts in Santa Fe. They have earned a significant place in American and Canadian Indian education and provide an alternative for the growing numbers of Indians earning undergraduate and graduate degrees at mainstream colleges and universities.

Although the administration of President Ronald Reagan attempted to modify these measures, the 1990s returned to a policy that celebrated the Indian voice. Native leadership directed the decade's national studies of Indian education, and Native communities—from grassroots groups to organizations like the National Indian Education Association—crafted a blueprint for Indian education in the twenty-first century, coordinating their efforts with Bill Clinton's administration. The executive order "American Indian and Alaska Native Education," issued on 6 August 1998, reflected the tone of cooperation between Natives and the federal government. It opened with a frank, though often ignored, acknowledgment: "The Federal Government has a special, historic responsibility for the education of American Indian and Alaska Native students." As the new millennium opened, this promise emerged as a new reality, one that suggested strong Native leadership in Indian education.

BIBLIOGRAPHY

Adams, David Wallace. *Education for Extinction: American Indians and the Boarding School Experience, 1875–1928.* Lawrence: University Press of Kansas, 1995.

Child, Brenda J. *Boarding School Seasons: American Indian Families, 1900–1940.* Lincoln: University of Nebraska Press, 1998.

Coleman, Michael C. *American Indian Children at School, 1850–1930.* Jackson: University Press of Mississippi, 1993.

Szasz, Margaret Connell. *Indian Education in the American Colonies, 1607–1783.* Albuquerque: University of New Mexico Press, 1988.

———. "Education." In *Encyclopedia of North American Indians.* Edited by Frederick E. Hoxie. Boston and New York: Houghton Mifflin, 1996.

———. *Education and the American Indian: The Road to Self-Determination since 1928.* 3d ed. Albuquerque: University of New Mexico Press, 1999.

Margaret Connell-Szasz

See also **Indian Boarding Schools; Indian Policy, U.S.; Tribal Colleges;** *and vol. 9:* **Land of the Spotted Eagle.**

EDUCATION, PARENTAL CHOICE IN. A wide-ranging reform movement intended to infuse competitive forces into elementary and secondary schooling, parental choice in education has always had a limited existence in the United States. Since the early 1800s, state and local governments have generally supported only government-run schools. This has given parents the choice between tuition-free public schools and private schools that charge tuition. In general, only the wealthy and those with strong religious convictions have chosen privately run schools.

At a minimum, parental choice means giving parents the right to choose the specific public schools their children attend, rather than having them assigned to the school based on place of residence. In its more far-reaching form, however, the movement has called for a complete restructuring of the educational system. It has proposed that governments give money to parents in the form of vouchers or tax credits, which they can use to enroll their children at public or private schools of their choice. In all its forms, the movement has sought to increase parental involvement in education and to improve schools by forcing them to compete for students and resources.

The modern school choice movement originated with ideas proposed in a 1955 article by the libertarian economist (and later, Nobel laureate) Milton Friedman. This prompted Virgil Blum, a Jesuit priest and political scientist at Marquette University, to found, in 1957, the advocacy group Citizens for Educational Freedom to lobby for vouchers.

A 1966 article, "Are Public Schools Obsolete?," by the liberal Harvard sociologist, Christopher Jencks, prompted the federal Office of Economic Opportunity to offer grants to test the voucher concept. Because of local opposition, only one test occurred—from 1972 to 1976 in the Alum Rock school district near San Jose, California—and it drew only limited attention. Interest in school choice became stronger in the 1980s due to growing perceptions of the educational system's failures. As nationally recognized academic barometers—such as Scholastic Aptitude Test scores—showed declining student performance, and as behavioral problems and dropout rates in urban schools soared, the 1983 Department of Education report, *A Nation at Risk*, cautioned that American students were falling behind students in other countries. However, throughout the 1980s, little action was taken. Congress rejected Reagan administration proposals for tuition tax credits, and the school choice movement was confined mostly to libertarians and conservatives.

In 1990, the tide began to turn in favor of school choice. The liberal-leaning Brookings Institution published *Politics, Markets and America's Schools* by John Chubb and Terry Moe, which provided statistical evidence that over-regulated public schools were outperformed by private schools. It called for public school bureaucracies to be replaced by "choice offices" and a voucher system. In the same year, Wisconsin's legislature approved a program to provide vouchers to low-income students in Milwaukee for use at nonreligious schools. This legislation grew out of the efforts of state representative Annette "Polly" Williams (a Democrat), who was prompted by the frustrations of her inner-city constituents and aided by the state's Republican leadership. The Milwaukee experiment received immense national attention. Analysis of the program immediately showed that parents preferred being able to choose schools, while evidence on academic achievement was more hotly debated. Some studies found no measurable academic gains, but most concluded that the program modestly boosted test scores, even though per-pupil expenditures at these schools were less than half those in the public schools. The state legislature expanded the program significantly in 1995, allowing parochial schools to participate, and the Wisconsin Supreme Court upheld the voucher program's constitutionality in 1998.

School choice became the most hotly debated educational reform of the 1990s. Choice sprouted up within many public schools systems, which increasingly used magnet and charter schools. Following Milwaukee's lead, Cleveland adopted a tuition voucher system in 1995. By the 2001–2002 school year, more than ten thousand Milwaukee students and four thousand Cleveland students, all from poor families, used publicly funded vouchers to attend private schools. In 1999, Florida approved the first statewide voucher program, providing stipends to students at schools that received "failing" grades for performance and did not improve within one year. In 1991, J. Patrick Rooney, chairman of Golden Rule Insurance, created the first privately funded voucher program. By 2001 private voucher plans covered nearly 100,000 students, with scholarships averaging a little over $1,000. Arizona and Illinois adopted state income tax credits for taxpayers who contributed to private scholarship organizations that distributed the funds to families choosing private schools.

School choice was especially popular among families within poorly performing public school systems. It was seen by many Republicans as a way to increase support among minorities and religious conservatives (especially Catholics), while pushing free-market principles. In 1996, Robert Dole became the first major-party candidate to endorse school vouchers. Gallup Polls showed rising support for school vouchers, with fifty-four percent backing school vouchers in 2001. However, when faced with sweeping school choice proposals not tailored to failing school systems and poor families, voters were not generally supportive. From 1970 to 2000, twelve out of twelve statewide referenda failed that would have granted school vouchers or tuition tax credits. In 1993, for example, California voters defeated Proposition 174 by a seven-to-three margin. Voucher opponents, funded mostly by teachers' unions, outspent opponents by ten-to-one.

Opponents warned that vouchers would siphon support and funding away from public schools. Ironically, in Milwaukee, local politicians of all political stripes eventually supported school vouchers, and funding for public schools rose substantially. The school system responded to the voucher threat by granting parents an increasing array of choices within the public school system and by allocating resources only to schools that attracted students. In addition, public school achievement scores began to rise.

Opponents also warned of excessive religious influence in education and complained that vouchers would breach constitutional strictures against establishment of religion. In the 1973 case *Committee for Public Education v. Nyquist*, the Supreme Court struck down a New York law granting reimbursements and tax credits to parents for private school tuition, saying that it effectively subsidized religious education. The Court seemed to back away from this in later rulings, allowing an increasing flow of government resources to religious schools. In 1999, a federal judge ruled Cleveland's voucher program unconstitutional on church-state–separation grounds. However, in 2002, the Supreme Court heard arguments in the widely watched *Zelman v. Simmons-Harris* case, and, on 27 June 2002, upheld the constitutionality of Cleveland's school choice program by a five to four vote.

BIBLIOGRAPHY

Chubb, John E. and Terry M. Moe. *Politics, Markets, and America's Schools*. Washington, D.C.: Brookings Institution, 1990.

Jost, Kenneth. "School Vouchers Showdown: How Will the Supreme Court Rule?" *CQ Researcher* 12, no. 6 (2002): 121–144.

Masci, David, "School Choice Debate," *CQ Researcher* 7, no. 27 (1997): 625–648.

Milton and Rose Friedman Foundation. http://www.friedmanfoundation.org/.

Ravitch, Diane and Maris A. Vinvskis, eds. *Learning from the Past: What History Teaches Us about School Reform*. Baltimore: Johns Hopkins University Press, 1995.

Robert Whaples

See also **Charter Schools; Education; Home Schooling; Magnet Schools; School Vouchers; Schools, For-Profit; Schools, Private.**

EDUCATION, SPECIAL. *See* **Disabled, Education of the.**

EDUCATION, UNITED STATES OFFICE OF.

The United States Office of Education was established by Congress on 2 March 1867 as a division within the cabinet-level Department of Health, Education, and Welfare. Designated at the time as an independent, subcabinet Department of Education and placed under the direction of scholar-statesman Henry Barnard, this unit functioned as an advisory council, a school advocate, and an information clearinghouse.

The name of the division changed to the Office of Education in 1869 when it was placed in the Department of the Interior. From 1870 to 1929, it was known as the Bureau of Education. From 1939 to 1953 it was located in the Federal Security Agency, and on 11 April 1953, it became a constituent division within the Department of Health, Education, and Welfare.

In 1896 the department added to its annual reports on education in the United States and other countries bulletins and studies of educational developments. The combined publishing activity of the bureau and the Office of Education earned the widespread respect and admiration of the European education ministries, some of which—the British, for example—established similar bodies.

The Office of Education now administers federal participation in vocational education, grants and loans to state and local programs, and aid for the education of the disabled, among other functions, and its size and budget have grown along with its responsibilities. The independent National Institute of Education, established in 1972 within the Department of Health, Education, and Welfare, assumed the research functions of the office.

BIBLIOGRAPHY

Kursh, Harry. *The United States Office of Education: A Century of Service.* Philadelphia: Chilton Books, 1965.

Warren, Donald R. *To Enforce Education: A History of the Founding Years of the United States Office of Education.* New York: Greenwood Press, 1985.

William W. Brickman / C. W.

See also **Disabled, Education of the; Education, Department of; Education; Interior, Department of the.**

EDUCATIONAL AND INTELLIGENCE TESTING. *See* **Intelligence Tests.**

EDUCATIONAL TECHNOLOGY. Since 1990, educational technology has undergone rapid changes, with a significant impact on historical research and learning. For example, CD-ROM (compact disc-read only memory) systems and historical databases have altered the storage and use of information in classrooms. CD-ROM technology allows the compilation of immense amounts of text, illustrations, audio, and video on interactive videodiscs. The centerpiece is a laser-based device similar to a compact disc player that plays back information stored on the videodiscs, which look just like the music CDs that have been popular for years. The videodiscs themselves can record sound and store texts, still photographs, and video programs. Each disc holds as many as 108,000 distinct pictures, half an hour of film, or literally hundreds of thousands of pages of text. The content of these videodiscs, which may include an encyclopedia or audiovisual display, are displayed on a television monitor or computer screen. Users can move in almost infinite ways through menus, tables of contents, and detailed, cross-referenced indexes. CD-ROM technology has profound implications for data storage and general use as a reference tool for scholars and students.

With equally important implications for education and research, computers now provide access to complex linkages that broaden the reach for information and library resources. Indeed, between 1994 and 2000, the percentage of public schools in the United States connected to the INTERNET rose from 35 percent to 98 percent. On-line services, specialized databases with sophisticated search capacities, and electronic transfers (including ELECTRONIC MAIL, or e-mail), provide new reference tools and capabilities. News and media file libraries, pictorial and documentary sources, and study statistics are now available through computer networks that again can be displayed on computer screens or television monitors, thus radically changing and enlarging research horizons.

Nevertheless, new technology such as CD-ROM and on-line services will not prove a panacea for all that ails American education. For instance, like all information systems, the quality of data input on a CD-ROM determines the quality of the disc. Critics argue that it is difficult for a CD-ROM, even if well-constructed, to act as a textbook. They maintain that the medium cannot present sequential text, study exercises, and comprehensive lesson plans in portable form (the spread of laptop computers and small personal data assistants in the early 2000s may solve the portability dilemma). Furthermore, the educational value of any new technology hinges on the ability of teachers to use it effectively. At present, many teachers still lack necessary training. Student use of the Internet also raises questions about how to prevent access to inappropriate materials. The United States Department of Education's Office of Educational Technology (OET) creates and carries out policies to counter such difficulties and, more generally, to promote the overall use of new technology in the classroom.

BIBLIOGRAPHY

Baier, John L., and Thomas S. Strong, eds. *Technology in Student Affairs: Issues, Applications, and Trends.* Lanham, Md.: University Press of America, 1994.

Cummins, Jim, and Dennis Sayers. *Brave New Schools: Challenging Cultural Illiteracy Through Global Learning Networks.* New York: St. Martin's Press, 1995.

De Vaney, Ann, ed. *Watching Channel One: The Convergence of Students, Technology, and Private Business.* Albany: State University of New York Press, 1994.

Jones, Byrd L., and Robert W. Maloy. *Schools for an Information Age: Reconstructing Foundations for Learning and Teaching.* Westport, Conn.: Praeger, 1996.

Gilbert T. Sewall / A. E.

See also **Compact Discs; Computers and Computer Industry; Curriculum; Education, Department of; Textbooks.**

EDUCATIONAL TESTING SERVICE. The Educational Testing Service (ETS) is a nonprofit testing and measurement organization founded in 1947 and headquartered in Princeton, New Jersey. ETS administers more than 12 million tests annually, including the SAT (formerly called the Scholastic Aptitude Test), Graduate Record Exam (GRE), Graduate Management Admissions Test (GMAT), Test of English as a Foreign Language (TOEFL), and Praxis Series (Professional Assessments for Beginning Teachers) examinations. These tests are used to help evaluate candidates for admission to undergraduate- and graduate-level institutions of higher learning. The organization is expressly dedicated to helping advance quality and equity in education by providing fair and valid assessments, research, and related services. ETS conceived and developed standardized testing as a tool for measuring aptitude and merit in an objective and fair way that would counter the self-perpetuating elite favoritism characteristic of American higher education into the 1960s. Toward the end of the twentieth century, these same tests became the object of some skepticism and charges of racial and gender bias.

ETS was founded to serve three organizations: the American Council on Education, the Carnegie Foundation for the Advancement of Teaching, and the College Entrance Examination Board, all of which needed skilled staff to assist in their test development and operational processing initiatives. Once established, the Educational Testing Service became the world's largest private educational testing and measurement organization and a leader in educational research that generates annual revenue of more than $600 million.

Standardized testing requires three sound practices: development, measurement, and administration. Test questions or items are prepared according to a specified methodology that ensures accuracy, fairness, and the meeting of exact specifications and standards. Test measurement is accomplished through the application of statistical models. ETS's distinguished research staff has long been on the forefront of psychometric (pertaining to the measure of intelligence) theories and practices used to measure skills, knowledge, and performance. Once a test is developed, it must be administered in a secure testing environment and scored according to precise, detailed procedures, ensuring the accuracy and validity of the results.

The largest client for whom ETS does work is the College Board, a national, nonprofit membership association of more than forty-two hundred schools, colleges, universities, and other educational organizations whose primary mission is to assist students in their preparation for admission to colleges and universities. ETS's mandate to provide standardized tests to support educational goals including equity and fairness extends beyond college admissions: it operates as an agent for an assortment of principals. Some are external boards: GRE is sponsored by a board of seventeen members and is affiliated with the Association of Graduate Schools and the Council of Graduate Schools. TOEFL has a fifteen-member board whose expertise and affiliations include the College Board, the GRE Board, undergraduate and graduate schools, and specialists in English as a foreign or second language. Others, like the College Board, are external organizations with independent administrative offices. These include the Graduate Management Admission Council and the National Board for Professional Teaching Standards.

ETS's work flourished most successfully in the years during which "merit" and "objectivity" were considered relatively unproblematic concepts. Beginning in the 1980s, concern for diversity and multiculturalism produced a more sophisticated but less secure sense of aptitude and achievement as well as their measurement.

BIBLIOGRAPHY

Cameron, Robert G. *The Common Yardstick: A Case for the SAT.* New York: College Entrance Examination Board, 1989.

Lemann, Nicholas. *The Big Test: The Secret History of the American Meritocracy.* New York: Farrar, Straus and Giroux, 1999.

Sandra Schwartz Abraham

See also **Education, Higher: Colleges and Universities; Intelligence Tests; SAT.**

EDWARDSEAN THEOLOGY is the designation applied to the variety of Calvinism enunciated by the eighteenth-century New England theologian Jonathan Edwards. This system rested upon Edwards's vision of the absolute glory of God and humanity's complete dependence upon the deity. Edwards held that God acted for reasons of his own glory and that his complete sovereignty best served that glory. True virtue consisted of an assent to the beauty and excellence of this arrangement. In his work *Freedom of the Will* (1754) Edwards further proposed that humans depended entirely upon God to achieve true virtue. People were free only to follow those volitions that God predetermined for the purposes of his own glory.

Often remembered for his fiery denunciations of sinners, Edwards displayed a remarkable ability to blend the metaphysics of the Enlightenment with his vision of God's absolute glory. Although Edwards's preaching constituted an important component of the Great Awakening of the late 1730s and early 1740s, he should not be considered the sole spokesperson for the Awakening. Following his death Edwards's theology was perpetuated by theologians such as Samuel Hopkins, who tried to preserve his metaphysics but who lacked the visionary quality of his work.

BIBLIOGRAPHY

Edwards, Jonathan. *Representative Selections.* Edited by Clarence H. Faust and Thomas H. Johnson. New York: Hill and Wang, 1962.

Hatch, Nathan O., and Harry S. Stout, eds. *Jonathan Edwards and the American Experience.* New York: Oxford University Press, 1988.

Holbrook, Clyde A. *The Ethics of Jonathan Edwards: Morality and Aesthetics.* Ann Arbor: University of Michigan Press, 1973.

Miller, Perry. *Jonathan Edwards.* New York: W. Sloan Associates, 1949.

Leo P. Hirrel

See also **Calvinism; Great Awakening.**

EGYPT, RELATIONS WITH. When John Ledyard (1751–1789) traveled to Egypt in the late eighteenth century, he had little enthusiasm for Egypt, stating that

Alexandria was merely "a small town built on the ruins of antiquity." This first contact between Egypt and the United States illustrates the incidental, and somewhat disappointing, encounters that the new empire would experience until the twentieth century, when the United States adopted a pivotal role in the Middle East.

In general, the nineteenth century presented a wide spectrum of U.S. encounters with Egypt that were not motivated by diplomatic or economic concerns. Americans traveled to Egypt to tour the Holy Land and to study Egyptology and archaeology. Missionaries, such as the Presbyterians, considered the country a worthwhile field for Christian evangelism and mission work. The philanthropic effort of these missionaries to build over one hundred nonsectarian, Arabic schools for both men and women was welcomed more than any other U.S. policy in the nineteenth century.

The first U.S.-born consul to Egypt assumed his post in 1848, only to write several complaints that the United States had little political influence compared to the more established European consulates. One of the U.S. consul's central concerns was to encourage commercial activity in the Mediterranean, although this would not be actively explored until the outbreak of the Civil War, when the United States realized that demands for cotton could be met by Egyptian imports. The success of this Civil War trade was short-lived. When the cotton markets stabilized in the United States, trade with the Egyptian market was no longer necessary.

Despite the few Union and Confederate soldiers who found work in Egypt as advisors after the Civil War, early U.S.–Egyptian relations were minimal and lacked any clear objectives. Any U.S. presence or influence was quickly overshadowed by the British occupation of the region in 1882. The inclusion of Egypt under Britain's domain effectively eliminated Egypt from U.S. foreign policy until the twentieth century, when World War II, the Cold War, and the search for peace in the Middle East challenged Western interests.

The United States's first sustained diplomatic involvement with Egypt came after World War II, although the nature of the interactions was mixed due to U.S. support for Israel and Egypt's desire to end the shadow of British imperialism. Although the United States wanted to participate in the affairs of the Middle East, it was more concerned with the Cold War and specifically with methods for preventing Soviet expansion into the Middle East. In order to protect the Suez from the Soviets, the United States sought to alleviate tensions between Britain and Egypt while simultaneously maintaining positive relations with both parties.

With the success of the Free Officers's coup in 1952, Egypt established its true independence as a republic in 1953, and Jamal 'Abd al-Nasir (1918–1970) began a campaign to revitalize Egypt's economy through increased agriculture. Nasir looked to Western nations, especially the United States, for funds to build the Aswan High Dam, but the United States hesitated to offer the type of assistance Nasir wanted. Frustrated with the delayed response for arms and economic aid, Nasir created his own funds by nationalizing the privately owned Suez Canal Company. Such a bold action was applauded by Arab states, but it also propelled Egypt into direct military conflict with Britain and France, the two nations most involved with the Suez Company, as well as Israel, which felt the need to protect itself against Egyptian aggression. The Suez Crisis of 1956 brought an end to British imperialism in Egypt and also was a turning point for U.S.–Egyptian relations in which the United States finally committed itself to an active presence in the Middle East. U.S. policies, however, were not always considered positive and were often in conflict with the goals of Arab nationalism.

The presidency of Anwar al-Sadat (1970–1981) marked a significant transition in U.S.–Egyptian relations as Egypt shifted from instigating confrontations with Israel to seeking diplomatic alternatives for coexistence. In 1979, the Carter administration's commitment to find solutions to the Arab-Israeli conflict was finally realized when Sadat and Israel's Prime Minister Menachem Begin signed a peace agreement. The success of the Camp David Accords provided Egypt with much needed economic aid, but the financial benefits did not outweigh the political costs for Sadat and his relationship with other Arab states. Egypt was banned from the Arab League between 1979 and 1989, and Sadat's cooperation with the United States fueled animosity toward his presidency that ultimately led to his assassination in 1981.

President Hosni Mubarak (1981–) extended the policies of Sadat by further cultivating positive U.S.–Egyptian relations and ensuring continued economic aid from the United States. With Mubarak's efforts, the United States received international support for the Gulf War (1990–1991), and Egypt provided military troops for both the Gulf War and UN peacekeeping missions. The United States also relied on Mubarak to sponsor summits for negotiations between the Palestinians and Israelis when U.S. talks have faltered. After the hijackings of 11 September 2001, Egypt offered diplomatic support for the U.S.'s War on Terrorism against Osama bin Laden, Al Qaeda, and the Taliban. With renewed fighting between the Palestinians and Israelis, however, it could not be determined if Egypt could continue to maintain U.S. interests in the region and how U.S.–Egyptian relations would be ultimately affected by the tragic events of 11 September.

BIBLIOGRAPHY

el-Calamawy, Sahair. "The American Influence on Education in Egypt." *In For Better or Worse.* Edited by Allen F. Davis. Westport, Conn.: Greenwood Press, 1981. 137–144.

Field, James A. *America and the Mediterranean World 1776–1882.* Princeton: Princeton University Press, 1969.

Finnie, David H. *Pioneers East: The Early American Experience in the Middle East.* Cambridge, Mass.: Harvard University Press, 1967.

Hahn, Peter L. *The United States, Great Britain, and Egypt 1945–1956.* Chapel Hill: University of North Carolina Press, 1991.

Owen, Roger, and Şevket Pamuk. *A History of Middle East Economies in the Twentieth Century.* Cambridge, Mass.: Harvard University Press, 1998.

Thomas, Nancy, ed. *The American Discovery of Ancient Egypt.* Los Angeles: Los Angeles County Art Museum, 1995.

Darlene L. Brooks Hedstrom

See also **Arab Nations, Relations with.**

EISENHOWER DOCTRINE. Following the Suez Crisis and the decline of British influence in the Middle East, President Dwight D. Eisenhower and Secretary of State John Foster Dulles believed that Soviet assertiveness and growing Arab nationalism, especially that of Egypt's Gamal Abdel Nasser, posed a threat to vital U.S. interests. On 5 January 1957, Eisenhower announced that the United States would use military force to defend the independence and territorial integrity of Middle Eastern states against communist aggression. Congress voted its approval two months later.

The Eisenhower Doctrine defined itself as a defensive move to contain Soviet expansionism, but response from the governments of the Middle East was mixed. Jordan and Lebanon welcomed the declaration. Egypt and Syria denounced it as a threat to their security. Israel responded skeptically and Iraq and Saudi Arabia opposed a U.S. military role in the region.

Eisenhower did not invoke the doctrine in 1958, when he ordered troops to Lebanon to thwart an uprising by Muslim rebels, because there was no evidence of communist involvement. In late 1958 Eisenhower replaced the activist principles of his doctrine with a new policy of seeking accommodation with Arab nationalists to preserve U.S. influence in the Middle East. The Carter Doctrine of 1980 revived the military emphasis in U.S. policy toward the region.

BIBLIOGRAPHY

Ashton, Nigel John. *Eisenhower, Macmillan, and the Problem of Nasser: Anglo-American Relations and Arab Nationalism, 1955–59.* New York: St. Martin's Press, 1996.

Brands, H. W. *The Specter of Neutralism: The United States and the Emergence of the Third World.* New York: Columbia University Press, 1989.

Takeyh, Ray. *The Origins of the Eisenhower Doctrine: The US, Britain, and Nasser's Egypt, 1953–57.* New York: St. Martin's Press, 2000.

Max Paul Friedman

See also **Carter Doctrine; Egypt, Relations with; Israel, Relations with; Lebanon, U.S. Landing in.**

EL PASO, a city in west Texas, is located on the Rio Grande. The city's history and development are linked to that of its sister city, Ciudad Juárez, Mexico (originally named El Paso del Norte). El Paso has been a principal entry point for immigrants from Mexico as well as other countries since 1900. Indigenous people first inhabited the area ten thousand years ago. In the 1500s, several Spanish explorers passed through the region. The first Spanish settlement gained its name, Paso del Norte, because it was a natural passageway across the river on the way north. In 1659, Franciscans established a mission, Nuestra Señora de Guadalupe, on what is now the Mexican side of the river. Following the Mexican-American War (1846–1848), the new border between Mexico and the United States divided the settlement. In 1873, the American settlement of El Paso was incorporated as a city. Following the coming of the railroads in 1881, the economy developed quickly. Agriculture, mining, and manufacturing formed the foundation of the economy. In the twentieth century, El Paso became an important manufacturing and commercial center. Following the creation of the maquiladora (twin plant) industry in 1965 and the North American Free Trade Agreement in 1994, El Paso's economic ties to Mexico grew. In 2000, 24 percent of border trade to Mexico, representing over $17 billion, passed through El Paso. The population of El Paso increased from 428 in 1860 to 563,662 in 2001. Seventy-seven percent of the population was Latino, 63 percent of Mexican descent. The total metro population, including Ciudad Juárez, was 1,897,440 in 2001.

BIBLIOGRAPHY

Garcia, Mario T. *Desert Immigrants: The Mexicans of El Paso, 1880–1920.* New Haven, Conn.: Yale University Press, 1981.

Martinez, Oscar J. *Border Boom Town: Ciudad Juárez since 1848.* Austin: University of Texas Press, 1978.

Timmons, W. H. *El Paso: A Borderlands History.* El Paso: University of Texas at El Paso, 1990.

Yolanda Chávez Leyva

See also **Mexico, Relations with; North American Free Trade Agreement; Texas.**

EL SALVADOR, RELATIONS WITH. The smallest nation in Central America, El Salvador was slow in gaining its independence from Spain (1821), Mexico (1823), and the United Provinces of Central America. When it achieved full independence in 1841, the political and economic elite guarded their virtual fiefdom from foreign interventions. Until 1979, Salvadoran leaders achieved stability and autonomy through military rule and sensitivity to U.S. interests. The parameters of local social structures and politics, however, were established by the United States and the international economic system.

Beginning in the 1880s, coffee replaced indigo as the main Salvadoran export. Laws promoting large-scale coffee production forced peasants from communal lands and consolidated vast estates into elite hands, eventually resulting in 2 percent of the population controlling 60 percent of the land. The so-called Fourteen Families entrusted the military with the power to preserve an orderly labor force and plantation economy and formed an aristocracy controlling commerce, banking, transportation, and infrastructure.

The international economic system's collapse in 1929 sparked the country's first modern peasant rebellion, foreshadowing the 1980s civil war. The depression crushed coffee prices and market demand, leading to reduced wages, high unemployment, and labor unrest. On May Day 1930, eighty thousand people marched on the capital of San Salvador, demanding government action. The government responded by imprisoning hundreds of opposition leaders and suppressing civil liberties. Agustin Farabundo Marti and other radical leaders continued to organize, but Marti's arrest and execution in January 1932 ignited a peasant uprising. General Maximiliano Hernandez Martinez led the brutal *matanza* (massacre) to eradicate suspected rebels, killing thirty thousand peasants and beginning forty-seven years of military rule.

The military provided stability and order, which, following World War II, helped fuel modest industrial gains, urbanization, and the development of a small middle class. Eager to enter politics, the middle class backed reformist parties, the most important being the Christian Democratic Party (PDC), founded in 1960. Most Salvadorans, however, did not benefit from the improved economy and remained among the most malnourished peoples in the world. El Salvador was reliant on U.S. trade for basic foodstuffs and goods, and through John F. Kennedy administration's Alliance for Progress, its dependence increased when the United States became the leading foreign investor. Closer U.S. relations brought Peace Corps volunteers, military assistance, hundreds of new light industries, and one of the highest economic growth rates in the hemisphere. However, the maldistribution of wealth and power persisted. Some Salvadorans felt compelled to take up arms in the 1960s to break the status quo. Escalating government repression caused greater polarization. The number of radicals and desperate workers increased following the brief 1969 "Soccer War" with Honduras, when one hundred thousand repatriated Salvadorans fueled demands for land reform. Jose Napoleon Duarte, the PDC candidate in 1972, was about to reap the political benefits of widespread discontent when the army resorted to blatant electoral fraud. The army sent Duarte into exile and set about destroying the PDC and its sympathizers.

On 15 October 1979, moderate military officers staged a coup, hoping to forestall revolution. Despite U.S. support, the reformers were without domestic allies, the army having eliminated the political center—notably the middle class and the Roman Catholic Church. The remaining opposition consisted of revolutionary groups determined to overthrow the system, the most important being the Farabundo Marti National Liberation Front. Paramilitary death squads targeted labor leaders, teachers, priests, students, and other presumed subversives. The

Oscar Romero. The archbishop, whose 1980 murder helped to focus international attention on El Salvador's civil conflict. Catholic News Service

military reformers, unable to deliver land reform or liberalization, could not stop right-wing death squads and leftist guerrillas from escalating the violence. Within five months, conservative officers toppled the government. Without any viable moderate elements, the United States grudgingly supported the status quo. U.S. aid continued, notwithstanding the 24 March 1980 murder of Archbishop Oscar Romero by individuals associated with the government and the brutal murder of three North American nuns and a lay worker later that year. The Jimmy Carter administration quietly sent the Salvadoran army military advisers. Between 1979 and 1985, more than fifty thousand civilians were killed or "disappeared" in the conflict.

In 1981, the Ronald Reagan administration attempted to curtail "outside interference" and prevent another enemy beachhead in Central America by escalating U.S. aid. Although most informed observers recognized the conflict's indigenous origins, the Reagan administration maintained that the Soviet Union, along with local proxies Cuba and Nicaragua, was responsible. Military aid mushroomed from $82 million in 1982 to $196 million in 1984—with total U.S. aid reaching $2 million per day—while Reagan officials assured Americans of limited involvement. In 1982 and 1984, the Central Intelligence Agency channeled funds to "moderate" presidential candidate Duarte in hopes of finding the middle ground. The left boycotted the 1982 contest, and Roberto D'Aubuisson, the far-right candidate, prevailed in fraudulent elections supervised by the military. Two years later, the CIA succeeded in electing Duarte, but as president he could not control the military or implement necessary reforms. At decade's end, despite almost total U.S. subsidization, Salvadoran exports and per capita income were nearly half the 1979 levels, and maldistribution of land prevailed. The murders continued; particularly shocking was the November 1989 assassination of six Jesuit priests, their housekeeper, and her daughter by Salvadoran soldiers. In 1992, locked in a stalemated war, Salvadoran military and rebel leaders agreed to a settlement brokered by the United Nations, restoring order, but not justice, to the troubled land.

BIBLIOGRAPHY

Arnson, Cynthia. *El Salvador: Revolution Confronts the United States.* Washington, D.C.: Institute for Policy Studies, 1982.

Bonner, Raymond. *Weakness and Deceit: U.S. Policy and El Salvador.* New York: Times Books, 1984.

LaFeber, Walter. *Inevitable Revolutions: The United States in Central America.* 2d ed. New York: Norton, 1993.

Leonard, Thomas M. *Central America and the United States: The Search for Stability.* Athens: University of Georgia Press, 1991.

Montgomery, Tommie Sue. *Revolution in El Salvador: From Civil Strife to Civil Peace.* 2d ed. Boulder, Colo.: Westview Press, 1995.

Dominic Cerri

See also **Alliance For Progress.**

ELBE RIVER. The Elbe and a tributary, the Mulde, served as a dividing line between Soviet and Allied forces when World War II ended in Europe. Ceding the honor of liberating Berlin to the Soviets, the Allied high command used the rivers as readily discernible terrain features to avoid inadvertent clashes between converging Allied and Soviet troops. A patrol of the Sixty-ninth Infantry Division under First Lieutenant Albert L. Kotzebue established contact with the Soviets late on the morning of 25 April but radioed the wrong map coordinates, so that credit went instead to a patrol from the same division, under Second Lieutenant William D. Robertson, which in midafternoon of the same day met the Soviets at Torgau.

BIBLIOGRAPHY

Ambrose, Stephen. *Eisenhower and Berlin, 1945: The Decision to Halt at the Elbe.* New York: Norton, 1967.

Toland, John. *The Last 100 Days.* New York: Bantam Books, 1966.

Charles B. MacDonald / A. R.

See also **Russia, Relations with; World War II.**

ELECTION LAWS. Election laws regulate who votes, when and how they vote, for whom they can vote, how campaigns are conducted, and how votes are recorded, counted, and allocated. The Fifteenth Amendment to the U.S. Constitution (1870) prohibits discrimination on the basis of race and the Nineteenth (1920) on the basis of gender. Congress has set uniform dates for congressional, senatorial, and presidential elections, and it requires all members of Congress to be elected from contiguous, single-member districts. In three major federal laws, the Tillman Act (1907), the Federal Election Campaign Act (1971, 1974), and the McCain-Feingold Act (2002), Congress sought to reduce fraud and curb the influence of rich interest groups. Loopholes in these laws, often created or widened by court decisions, have diminished their effectiveness. By contrast, the VOTING RIGHTS ACT OF 1965, inspired by the civil rights movement and pushed through Congress by President Lyndon B. Johnson, quickly eliminated remaining racial discrimination in voting qualifications and gradually reduced discrimination in electoral practices such as redistricting. Decisions of the Supreme Court in the 1990s, however, severely undercut the act and threatened its constitutionality.

Most elections take place at the state and local levels, and most election laws are passed by state and local governments. Americans elect more officials, at more different times, in more overlapping districts, and with more complicated ballots, than citizens of any other country. For a century, most municipal officials have run in nonpartisan contests held at times different from those of national elections to draw attention to local issues. States and municipalities regulate campaign finances with widely varying expenditure and contribution limits and publicity requirements, and some provide public subsidies to campaigns. Parties choose candidates in conventions or closed primaries, where only registered party members may vote, or in open primaries, where any citizen can choose a party's nominees. Since 1990, many state and local governments have adopted limits of two or three terms as the maximum anyone can serve in a particular office. In many states, particularly in the West, citizens began in the early twentieth century to vote directly on issues through initiatives or referenda.

In the November 2000 presidential election, confusing ballot forms, physically faulty ballots, and vague recount laws in Florida, as well as the unprecedented intervention by a 5–4 majority of the U.S. Supreme Court, cost the popular vote winner, Al Gore, the presidency and reminded the nation of just how important nuances of election law are.

BIBLIOGRAPHY

Issacharoff, Samuel, Pamela S. Karlan, and Richard H. Pildes. *The Law of Democracy: Legal Structure of the Political Process.* Westbury, N.Y.: Foundation Press, 1998.

Lowenstein, Daniel Hays, and Richard L. Hasen. *Election Law: Cases and Materials.* 2d ed. Durham, N.C.: Carolina Academic Press, 2001.

J. Morgan Kousser

See also **Campaign Financing and Resources.**

ELECTIONS. An election is a process by which qualified individuals choose a candidate or set of candidates to represent them in office. Elections may involve a selection by a very restricted group, such as a legislature, or it may be broadly extended to universal adult suffrage. The process of election is linked, however, to choices of candidates rather than issues. Thus referenda, ballot propositions, state constitutions, charters, or amendments put before the voters do not constitute elections in the strictest sense. Since direct democracies involve decision making by the entire body politic, the system of elections is nearly unnecessary. Election, therefore, is a republican rather than a purely democratic institution.

Election systems play a vital part in representative democracy, however. The possibility of free unconstrained choice is a vital component in determining how democratic a country may be. In addition, the limitations on the voting franchise also limit the extent of true representation of the population. While both the British constitution and the American Declaration of Independence recognize the people's right to overthrow a tyrannical government, the system of free elections makes revolutions unnecessary, so long as the will of the people is accurately reflected and carried out. The American system of elections evolved out of the parliamentary system of polling for members of Parliament. In the Middle Ages, the right to vote for members of Parliament was spread rather broadly throughout the freehold population. In the towns, or boroughs, the vote was sometimes extended to all adult males. These were known as "potwalloper" boroughs, because the only criterion that an adult free male needed to meet in order to vote was possession of a pot.

Elections in the American Colonies

By the late seventeenth century in England, and in the English colonies, restrictive property qualifications were the norm. In Virginia, for example, property qualifications were sufficiently restrictive that less than one-quarter of the free white male population could vote. In Massachusetts and Pennsylvania, the voting universe was somewhat larger, perhaps one-third of the free adult white male population. This demographic was a function of the more even distribution of wealth in the northern colonies. In no colony before the American Revolution was a majority of adult white males allowed to vote.

In southern American colonies and states like Virginia and South Carolina, polling took place over several days in the county seat, usually in the square in front of the courthouse. This practice continued well into the nineteenth century. In the southern colonies, before the polling actually took place, the candidates would usually provide refreshment for their neighbors, which included rum toddies and a "bull roast." Since only the gentry could afford such an expense, this custom ensured that in colonial elections only the wealthiest members of the gentry could afford to run for office. Once the polling began, the candidate might "spout" or give a speech, usually not related to politics. When the polling began, the eligible freeholders would stand up and announce their votes in front of their neighbors. After each vote, the candidate would personally thank the voter for this "honor." This public announcement meant that the community could exert a kind of coercive force on the voters. Since each vote was recorded by name, voters were usually very deferential in their behavior at the time they exercised their vote. They could, however, heckle the candidates in a good-natured sort of way, and sometimes this threat of humiliation was enough to keep well-qualified candidates from running for office. James Madison, who had helped draft the U.S. Constitution and the Federalist Papers, was very reluctant to run for office in the first congressional election of 1788. As a very short man with an insecure ego, Madison required a lot of persuasion from his friends to brave the humiliation.

Elections before the U.S. Civil War

After the American Revolution, the extension of voting rights to a wider group of men took nearly two decades. Only after the turn of the nineteenth century, beginning with the election that Thomas Jefferson called "the Revolution of 1800," did men with little or no property begin to vote. Then, between 1800 and 1816, voter turnout widened dramatically. In those years voter turnout in New Hampshire, Massachusetts, and North Carolina rose to over 60 percent of the adult white male population. In the New England states and in Pennsylvania, as African American slaves were emancipated, African American adult males were also permitted to vote. African Americans in this first flush of enfranchisement were often given equal opportunity to vote with whites in the North. By the 1840s property restrictions on adult white male voters had been almost entirely eliminated, except in the state of South Carolina. Ironically, however, increased property restrictions were imposed on free African American males in both New York and Pennsylvania in this so-called "Age of the Common Man."

Perhaps because of their service in the American Revolution, or perhaps by oversight, New Jersey legislators permitted female heads of household possessing more than £50 of property to vote. Women heads of household possessed the vote in New Jersey until 1807. In that year the state legislature repealed the vote for women, perhaps because women tended to vote Federalist and the state for the first time in 1807 came under the control of the Democratic Republicans.

Beginning in the nineteenth century, voice voting gave way to ballot voting. In the Old South this did not occur without some protest. Many politicians of the older generation feared their loss of control of the election process. They complained that voice voting ensured against corruption: a vote accounted for at the time it was delivered could not be stolen. Ballot boxes could be stuffed and voting rolls could be padded, and they frequently were. Voice voting, however, did not ensure against corruption. It only ensured against voter autonomy. Kentucky, which had been one of the first states to institute ballot voting, from 1792 to 1799, reinstituted voice voting and was the last state to abandon it before the Civil War.

By the 1840s political parties developed into nationally competitive organizations, and new election rituals connected the voters to the political parties. In the month leading up to an election, voters would assemble in mass rallies. In the large cities, several thousand people at a time might gather at one of these rallies. In the "Log Cabin" campaign of 1840, for example, voters in Boston, New York, Philadelphia, and smaller cities across the Union gathered in the city centers to show their support for "Old Tippecanoe," William Henry Harrison, who allegedly lived in a log cabin beside the Ohio River and drank hard cider. Actually, Harrison was the son of a signer of the Declaration of Independence and came from one of the most prominent families in Virginia. He lived in a very grand house and drank Kentucky bourbon but that did not stop the mass rallies around replicas of his log cabin that were set up in every city of any size. The Whigs, who sponsored Harrison's campaign, called for ball-rolling rallies during the Log Cabin campaign. Young boys were set to work rolling an enormous ball through the cities and towns to demonstrate the popular momentum of "Old Tip."

Not to be outdone, the Democrats centered their campaign on Martin Van Buren, whom the party nicknamed "Old Kinderhook," or "O.K." Like "Old Hickory" before him (Andrew Jackson), O.K. was supposed to be a man of the people living simply on his farm in upstate New York. Although Van Buren and the Democrats lost the campaign of 1840, Van Buren's nickname became so ubiquitous in the American language in the late 1830s and early 1840s that anything that had popular approval came to be "O.K." in the American idiom. This is a remarkable testament to how prevalent electioneering language became in American speech.

Election newspapers began to appear with great frequency in the 1840s. Both the Democratic Republicans and the Federalists had supported electioneering newspapers for a short period leading up to an election in the early part of the century. By the 1840s these electioneering newspapers had become important in themselves. The most famous of these electioneering newspapers was the *New York Log Cabin*, which was edited by an ambitious young editor newly emigrated from New Hampshire named Horace Greeley. Greeley's experience on the *Log Cabin* led to his editorship of the *New York Tribune*. Not only Whigs like Greeley, but also Democrats like Duff Green and Isaac Hill, had electioneering experience. Hill and another editor, Francis P. Blair, were among the most important members of Andrew Jackson's Kitchen Cabinet.

Election Frauds and "Reforms"

In the era of the Civil War, elections took on a more militaristic quality. Voters were urged into "battle." They drilled in military formations. Over and over, voters were reminded to "Vote as you shot!" In these late-nineteenth-century elections, American adult men reached the highest levels of participation ever recorded in the United States. Typically in the North and Midwest, a presidential election year might see a turnout of 70 to 80 percent of all adult male voters. There were few restrictions on voting and in many urban areas where large numbers of immigrants lived the urban machines enlisted votes even before they were formally qualified as citizens.

The late-nineteenth-century elections relied on ethnocultural dissonance to sustain voters' loyalties at the polls. Republicans were more likely to be northern European, Protestant, Union Civil War veterans, middle class, and in favor of protectionism. For the Republicans, African Americans in the South were the most reliable ethnic cohorts. Democrats were more likely to be southern or eastern European, Catholic, Confederate Civil War veterans, working class, and in favor of free trade. For the Democrats, southern whites and Irish Catholics constituted the most reliable blocs of voters.

Beginning in the 1870s and accelerating in the 1890s, the American voting universe began to shrink, thanks to many of the reforms instituted to protect elections from "voter fraud." After 1877, with the withdrawal of federal troops from the South, African Americans were gradually systematically excluded from voting. By the 1890s the African American vote in the South was negligible, thanks to outright intimidation, poll taxes, and highly subjective "literacy tests." This was defended by some in the South as a necessary "reform" to end political "corruption." In the northern cities, voter registration laws allowed for a much more stringent inspection of immigrants' claims of citizenship. Residency requirements, waiting periods, and literacy in English all helped reduce the immigrant vote and the power of the urban machines.

Ironically, one of the most important reforms that reduced the power of the political parties was the introduction of the Australian ballot, beginning in the United States in 1888. The Australian ballot, which had been in use in that country for thirty years, listed all candidates for all offices on a single sheet of paper. Reformers hailed this victory for individual autonomy over the coercion of political party machines. The benefits were not so clear, however. Many voters were confused by the way the lists of candidates were presented on these "secret" ballots.

Many times they voted for someone they had not intended to choose, or they abandoned voting for candidates "down the list": for those minor offices where name recognition did not aid them in making a choice.

With the introduction of the Australian ballot, the primary election became increasingly important in determining which candidate would be the party's "nominee." Before the Australian ballot, the nomination function had been the prerogative of the political parties. At the end of the nineteenth century, Minnesota instituted a mandatory state primary system and by the 1920s this became the favored means of selecting candidates for state and local offices.

In the South, however, the primary became a means of circumventing African American participation in elections even if they could gain the right to vote. In many southern states, winning the Democratic primary election was tantamount to winning office. Beginning in the 1920s, some southern states instituted a "whites only" clause in the primary election, stipulating that only whites could be "members" of the Democratic Party and only "members" of the party could vote. The U.S. Supreme Court outlawed this practice as a violation of the Fifteenth Amendment in a Texas case in 1944, *Smith v. Allwright*.

After World War I the Nineteenth Amendment to the Constitution was ratified, and in 1920 for the first time women across the nation were permitted to vote in all elections. In addition to New Jersey's brief experiment with woman suffrage, Wyoming had allowed women to vote since 1869 and western states generally were more favorable in extending full equality to women than the states in the East. Although women in the late twentieth century were more likely to vote than men, in the 1920s many women were discouraged from voting. Women have been blamed for the low turnout in the 1920 and 1924 elections, when voter turnout in the presidential race plummeted in 1916 from 61.6 percent of all eligible adults (including women in some states) to 49.2 and 48.9 percent, respectively. While some research indicates women voted in lower numbers in those years, other factors, including conflicted sympathy, may have depressed turnout generally, as it did in elections in the 1990s. In any event turnout rose dramatically during the Great Depression and, by 1936, 61.6 percent of all adult men and women were voting.

Elections in the Late Twentieth Century

In the 1950s the political scientist V. O. Key produced an influential study in which he argued that certain "critical" elections produced fundamental realignments of American voters. "Critical" elections showed higher turnout and changes in key blocs or generational cohorts of voters in favor of one party. The elections of 1800, 1828, 1860, 1896, and 1932 were the elections Key identified. Each one of these elections ushered in a new political "party system," with different ideologies and voter loyalties.

In a series of studies commenced at the University of Michigan in the 1950s, and continuing through the election of 2000, survey researchers began examining how voters made choices in elections. The results caused serious concerns for political scientists and citizens alike. Voters increasingly drew upon information from television in making up their minds before election day. Party preference played an increasingly limited role in determining how voters chose a candidate. Voters indicated that personality and single issues often determined which candidate they would vote for.

In the age of television, as political scientists and citizens' groups pointed out, a candidate who was relatively untested in office and unknown by his party could be elected to office on the basis of his or her good looks, winning personality, or position on a single issue that might be irrelevant to other important issues before the public. As the twentieth century wore on, electronic media became increasingly expensive and the political parties were faced with the necessity of full-time fundraising in order to get their message before the public.

Campaign finance reform was attempted in the aftermath of the Watergate scandal but, like all previous election reforms, the Watergate financing laws had unintended consequences. By allowing for "soft money" (contributions of large sums of money by special interest groups and individuals to political parties ostensibly for "party building" purposes that are unrelated to influencing federal elections), campaign finance reform created a loophole in regulating political campaign financing that has made oversight difficult, if not nearly impossible. Campaign finance reform was sponsored by a group of liberal Democrats and conservative Republicans at the turn of the twenty-first century because both parties and all politicians were spending too much time raising money to do their jobs effectively. As the result of an uncertain presidential election outcome in 2000, both parties declared the need for clearer, less ambiguous ballots and for an overhaul of voting machines. Reversing the trend of the early twentieth century, twenty-first-century reformers urged legislators to reform the ballot process by protecting against confusion rather than fraud.

BIBLIOGRAPHY

Baker, Jean H. *Affairs of Party: The Political Culture of Northern Democrats in the Mid-Nineteenth Century*. Ithaca, N.Y.: Cornell University Press, 1983.

Benson, Lee. *The Concept of Jacksonian Democracy: New York as a Test Case*. Princeton, N.J.: Princeton University Press, 1961.

Burnham, Walter Dean. *Critical Elections and the Mainsprings of American Politics*. New York: Norton, 1970.

Chambers, William Nisbet, and Walter Dean Burnham. *The American Party Systems: Stages of Political Development*. New York: Oxford University Press, 1967.

Clubb, Jerome M. *Electoral Change and Stability in American Political History*. New York: Free Press, 1971.

Jordan, Daniel P. *Political Leadership in Jefferson's Virginia*. Charlottesville: University Press of Virginia Press, 1983.

Key, V. O. *The Responsible Electorate: Rationality in Presidential Voting, 1936–1960.* Cambridge, Mass.: Harvard University Press, 1966.

McWilliams, Wilson Cary. *Beyond the Politics of Disappointment? American Elections, 1980–1998.* New York: Chatham House, 2000.

Nie, Norman H., Sidney Verba, and John R. Petrocik. *The Changing American Voter.* Cambridge, Mass.: Harvard University Press, 1976.

Sydnor, Charles. *Gentlemen Freeholders: Political Practices in Washington's Virginia.* Chapel Hill: University of North Carolina Press, 1952.

Andrew W. Robertson

See also **Ballot; Suffrage; Voting.**

ELECTIONS, CONTESTED. A contested election is an election in which the results are challenged. Challenges may come from one or more candidates in an election for public office, or in response to the declared result of a question voted on in the election, from petitioners, voters or designated election officials. Grounds for contesting include any canvassing or counting irregularities, deliberate violations of election laws, and the ineligibility of a candidate who is declared elected. Primarily a legal matter, contests are generally settled in civil court or by a legislative body, depending on state law. Election laws in the United States are not uniform, however, and rules for proceeding with a legal challenge vary.

Once the proceeding is initiated, either the contestant or the contestee may investigate any aspect of the election night process, including the inspection or recount of ballots. This may involve repeating parts of the election process to gather evidence for trial. The contest is judged by whichever authority is empowered to declare a winner. For most state and local offices, election contests are judged by regular civil courts. For some municipal, state, and federal legislative offices, the legislature judges the qualifications of its own members. In the U.S. House of Representatives, for example, the House has the final word on elections, including determining the eligibility of the declared winner—a provision reaffirmed by court cases in the 1970s. Congress has also decided contested presidential elections: in 1800 the House chose Thomas Jefferson over Aaron Burr, and in 1876 a House-approved panel chose Rutherford B. Hayes over Samuel J. Tilden. In the 2000 election, however, it was the U.S. Supreme Court that determined the outcome when they upheld a deadline that ended Al Gore's recount of Florida ballots in several contested precincts. Gore conceded to George W. Bush the next day, thirty-six days after the election.

BIBLIOGRAPHY

Butler, Anne M., et al. *United States Senate Election, Expulsion and Censure Cases, 1793–1990.* Washington, D.C.: Government Printing Office, 1995.

Dershowitz, Alan M. *Supreme Injustice: How the High Court Hijacked Election 2000.* New York: Oxford University Press, 2001.

Sammon, Bill. *At Any Cost: How Al Gore Tried to Steal the Election.* Washington, D.C.: Regnery, 2001.

Paul Hehn

See also ***Bush v. Gore.***

ELECTIONS, PRESIDENTIAL

This entry contains 48 subentries, comprising an overview and brief accounts of each election from 1789 to 2000.

Overview

Presidential elections have taken place in the United States quadrennially, beginning in 1789. They include both the process of candidate nomination and the subsequent campaign for election. Since the 1830s, nomination has centered on national party conventions called to choose individuals to run for president and vice president and to adopt the party's platform. Delegate selection for these conventions was for a long time wholly extralegal and determined by local party traditions. Early in the twentieth century, some states set up presidential primaries to choose delegates and record voter preferences among the aspiring candidates. In the late 1960s, a further reform movement began to broaden the ability of party members to participate in delegate selection and to reduce the influence of party organizations. By the end of the twentieth century the party primary system dominated the nominating process, with party conventions reduced to a merely symbolic role.

An incumbent president who desires renomination usually obtains it without a serious primary challenge. If a president does not want it or has already served two terms, the convention makes the final choice, sometimes only after a lengthy and bitter struggle. Beginning in the late 1950s, rapid modes of transportation and ease of communication usually enabled one candidate to build up a strong lead prior to the convention and to win on the first ballot. Thus, the preconvention campaign has become the decisive part of the nominating process. Since 1972, the primaries have determined every major party nominee. Broadening public participation has reduced the role of state party leaders and hence also reduced past practices of convention bargaining among politicians who control blocs of delegates.

Candidates for president were often chosen from among successful governors, especially the governors of key states like Ohio and New York, which have large blocs of electoral votes. By the late twentieth century, Texas, California, and the deep South emerged as major breeding grounds for presidential nominees. In the nineteenth century, generals frequently won presidential nominations, but none has since 1956. After World War II the trend seemed to move away from governors in favor of U.S. senators because of greatly increased American concern with foreign relations and the greater national "visibility" senators can acquire. The trend reversed itself in the 1970s, as governors won every presidential election between 1976 and 2000, with the sole exception of 1988.

Once chosen, the presidential candidate selects a new national party chairman and sets up his own campaign organization. In the nineteenth century the nominee himself did little stumping and conducted instead a "front porch" campaign, but the twentieth century saw increased candidate involvement, often reaching a frantic pace after the middle of the century. From the 1920s on, radio figured prominently in getting the candidates' messages disseminated; since the 1952 campaign, television has been the key medium, although the Internet shows promise of playing a growing role in future campaigns. Generally the media increased in importance as grass-roots party organization declined in vigor and usefulness. Public relations experts and opinion pollsters also came to occupy crucial roles in campaign management.

Little has changed overall in the extent to which presidential campaigns emphasize general appeals and slogans rather than focus on clear-cut issues. With communications improvements, these appeals are more often carefully designed for national audiences instead of being tailored to each local group encountered on a campaign tour. Nevertheless, the New Deal era and the elections of 1964 and 1972 did see issues posed more sharply than usual.

The seven presidential campaigns between 1976 and 2000 represent a period of change in American politics, including new rules for campaigns, challenges to the two-party system, and altered electoral coalitions. The 1976 campaign was the first conducted under new rules for selecting convention delegates and new campaign finance regulations, and by 1992 these changes had been fully assimilated by both the Democratic and Republican parties. Extending the turmoil of the 1960s, these campaigns witnessed regular challenges to the two-party system by divisive primaries and significant independent candidacies. In addition, the dissension associated with the Vietnam War protests and the WATERGATE scandal of 1972–1974 developed into a persistent "anti-Washington" theme in presidential campaigns. During this period there were significant changes in the major parties' electoral coalitions as well, with southerners and religious conservatives shifting from the Democratic to the Republican camp in the 1970s and 1980s.

Conversely, suburbanites, Californians, and northeasterners shifted from the Republican camp to the Democratic in the 1990s. These shifting political alliances resulted in an extremely closely divided electoral map, as revealed by the 2000 presidential campaign. In the closest presidential election in modern history, Al Gore, the Democratic candidate, carried the popular vote by 650,000 votes, and George W. Bush, the Republican candidate, carried the electoral college by four votes. As the twenty-first century unfolded, no party seemed likely to create a national mandate anytime soon. Instead, divided government and close elections were likely to be the dominant features of American presidential politics for some time to come.

BIBLIOGRAPHY

Asher, Herbert B. *Presidential Elections and American Politics: Voters, Candidates, and Campaigns Since 1952.* 4th ed. Chicago: Dorsey Press, 1988.

Brinkley, Alan, and Davis Dyer. *The Reader's Companion to the American Presidency.* Boston: Houghton Mifflin, 2000.

Congressional Quarterly. *Presidential Elections Since 1789.* 5th ed. Washington, D.C.: Congressional Quarterly, 1991.

Dallek, Robert. *Hail to the Chief: The Making and Unmaking of American Presidents.* New York: Hyperion, 1996.

DeGregorio, William A. *The Complete Book of U.S. Presidents.* New York: Wings Books, 1993.

Dover, E. D. *Presidential Elections in the Television Age, 1960–1992.* Westport, Conn.: Praeger, 1994.

Graff, Henry E. *The Presidents: A Reference History.* New York: Simon & Schuster, 1997.

Heale, M. G. *The Presidential Quest: Candidates and Images in America Political Culture, 1787–1852.* New York: Longman, 1982.

Hofstadter, Richard. *The American Political Tradition.* New York: Knopf, 1948.

Leuchtenburg, William E. *In the Shadow of FDR: From Harry Truman to Ronald Reagan.* Ithaca, N.Y.: Cornell University Press, 1983.

Levy, Leonard W., and Louis Fisher. *Encyclopedia of the American Presidency.* 4 vols. New York: Simon & Schuster, 1994.

Lorant, Stefan. *The Presidency: A Pictorial History of Presidential Elections from Washington to Truman.* New York: Macmillan, 1951.

Milkis, Sidney M. *The Presidents and the Parties: The Transformation of the American Party System Since the New Deal.* New York: Oxford University Press, 1993.

Nelson, Michael, ed. *Congressional Quarterly's Guide to the Presidency.* 2 vols. Washington, D.C.: Congressional Quarterly, 1996.

Polsby, Nelson W., and Aaron Wildavsky. *Presidential Elections: Strategies and Structures of American Politics.* New York: Chatham House, 2000.

Pomper, Gerald M. *Nominating the President: The Politics of Convention Choice.* New York: Norton, 1966.

Rosebloom, Eugene H. *A History of Presidential Elections.* 3rd ed. New York: Macmillan, 1970.

Wright, Russell O. *Presidential Elections in the United States: A Statistical History, 1860–1992.* Jefferson, N.C.: McFarland, 1995.

Elmer E. Cornwell Jr. / A. G.

See also **Campaign Financing and Resources; Campaign Songs; Conventions, Party Nominating; Democratic**

Party; Governors; Inauguration, Presidential; Platform, Party; Popular Sovereignty; President, U.S.; Primary, Direct; Radio; Republican Party; Television: Programming and Influence; Two-Party System; Vice President, U.S.; Voting.

1789 AND 1792

These first two campaigns had no formal nominations, only one presidential candidate, and little opposition to the second choice. The Constitution ratified, the Continental Congress delayed three months before fixing the first Wednesday in January 1789 for choosing electors, the first Wednesday in February for their voting, and the first Wednesday in March for starting the new government. Pennsylvania, Maryland, and Virginia elected electors; the Massachusetts legislature chose from elected electors; New Hampshire's election failed and its legislature appointed electors, as did those of the remaining states. Thirteen states could cast ninety-one votes; two states had not ratified, and one (New York) failed to elect or appoint electors; four electors failed to vote. George Washington received sixty-nine votes, one of the two votes of every elector. John Adams received thirty-four of the second votes, and the other thirty-five were scattered among ten different candidates (John Jay, Robert Harrison, John Rutledge, John Hancock, George Clinton, Samuel Huntington, John Milton, James Armstrong, Edward Telfair, and Benjamin Lincoln).

In 1792 fifteen states could cast 132 electoral votes. Alexander Hamilton's financial measures and the consolidation of national power roused an opposition (Jeffersonian Antifederalists), which centered its efforts on the defeat of Adams by the Antifederalist George Clinton, since to defeat Washington was seen to be futile. The attempt failed. Washington's vote was again unanimous, and Adams defeated Clinton by seventy-seven votes to fifty.

BIBLIOGRAPHY

Elkins, Stanley M., and Eric McKitrick. *The Age of Federalism: The Early American Republic, 1788–1800.* New York: Oxford University Press, 1993.

McDonald, Forrest. *The Presidency of George Washington.* Lawrence: University of Kansas Press, 1974.

John C. Fitzpatrick / A. G.

See also **Federalist Party.**

1796

For the first time the national election was contested by political parties. The French Revolution, the Genêt affair, and JAY'S TREATY resulted in bitter partisanship. Without the modern machinery of nomination, the Federalists informally agreed on John Adams as Washington's successor; with him they chose Thomas Pinckney as the vice presidential nominee. With more enthusiasm the Democratic-Republicans chose their leaders, Thomas Jefferson and Aaron Burr. Electors were chosen in sixteen states—by popular vote in six and by the legislature in ten. Of the total electoral votes, Adams secured seventy-one, Jefferson sixty-eight, Pinckney fifty-nine, and Burr thirty; the remaining forty-eight were divided among nine others.

BIBLIOGRAPHY

Brown, Ralph Adams. *The Presidency of John Adams.* Lawrence: University Press of Kansas, 1975.

Miller, John C. *The Federalist Era: 1789–1801.* New York: Harper & Row, 1960.

Sharp, James Roger. *American Politics in the Early Republic: The New Nation in Crisis.* New Haven, Conn.: Yale University Press, 1993.

Frank Monaghan / A. G.

See also **Republicans, Jeffersonian.**

1800 AND 1804

The election of 1800 marks a turning point in American political history. Its preliminaries were expressed in the Virginia and Kentucky Resolutions proffered by Thomas Jefferson and James Madison as a party platform. Its party machinery, still more essential to success, was directed by Aaron Burr, with supplemental support in Pennsylvania and South Carolina.

Burr had already established the nucleus of a political machine that was later to develop into TAMMANY HALL. With this organization, he swept New York City with an outstanding legislative ticket, gained control of the state assembly, and secured the electoral votes of New York for the Democratic-Republicans. He had already secured a pledge from the Democratic-Republican members of Congress to support him equally with Jefferson. Hence the tie vote (seventy-three each) that gave him a dubious chance for the presidency. The Federalist candidates were John Adams, sixty-five votes, and Charles Cotesworth Pinckney, sixty-four votes.

Publicly disclaiming any intent to secure the presidency, Burr was, nevertheless, put forward by the Federalists in order to defeat Jefferson and bring about another election. A slight majority in the House of Representatives enabled them to rally six states to Burr and divide the vote of two others, thus neutralizing the vote of the eight states that supported Jefferson. The contest was prolonged through thirty-five fruitless ballots; on the thirty-sixth, by prearrangement, a sufficient number of Federalists cast blank ballots to give Jefferson ten states and the presidency.

This narrow escape from frustrating the popular will led the incoming administration to pass the Twelfth Amendment to the Constitution, separating the balloting for president and vice president, in time for the 1804 election. Jefferson covertly helped eliminate Burr in New York, and the party caucus brought George Clinton forward as candidate for the vice presidency. Burr, already divining his political ostracism, attempted to recover ground as an independent candidate for governor of New York. Representative Federalists of New England sought his support in their plans for disunion, but he refused to commit himself to such a program. The Federalists selected Pinckney as their presidential candidate, and chose Rufus King for the vice presidency. Jefferson, preeminently successful in the more important measures of his administration, was triumphantly reelected in 1804 as president with Clinton as vice president.

BIBLIOGRAPHY

Ellis, Joseph J. *American Sphinx: The Character of Thomas Jefferson.* New York: Knopf, 1996.

Malone, Dumas. *Jefferson the President.* Boston: Little, Brown, 1970.

McDonald, Forrest. *The Presidency of Thomas Jefferson.* Lawrence: University Press of Kansas, 1976.

Peterson, Merrill D. *Thomas Jefferson and the New Nation.* New York: Oxford University Press, 1970.

Weisberger, Bernard A. *America Afire: Jefferson, Adams, and the Revolutionary Election of 1800.* New York: William Morrow, 2000.

Isaac J. Cox/A. G.

See also **Constitution of the United States; Federalist Party; Jefferson-Burr Election Dispute; Republicans, Jeffersonian.**

1808 AND 1812

The field of candidates for the Democratic-Republican nomination in 1808 included James Madison, the choice of Thomas Jefferson; James Monroe, somewhat tainted by affiliation with John Randolph and the QUIDS, who were anathema to the outgoing administration; and George Clinton, a New Yorker not favored by the VIRGINIA DYNASTY. Jefferson's own refusal to consider a third term confirmed the two-term tradition for a president. At the party caucus Madison received eighty-three votes; his rivals, three each.

The Federalist opposition was led by Charles Pinckney and Rufus King, but the chief obstacle to the Madison slate came from his own party, notably in Virginia and Pennsylvania, where William Duane, a powerful journalist, was unreconcilable. The malcontents finally voted the party ticket, and in the electoral college Madison obtained 122 out of 176 votes. Clinton ran far behind on the presidential ticket but became vice president by a wide margin. Defeated for the presidency, the Federalists nevertheless made serious inroads upon the Republican majority in the House of Representatives.

In 1812 Madison secured his renomination by a tacit rather than a formal yielding to the demands of Henry Clay and the war hawks. With Clinton having died in office, the vice presidential nomination, tendered first to John Langdon of New Hampshire, went to Elbridge Gerry of Massachusetts. Opposition to the party slate was led by DeWitt Clinton of New York, who finally accepted nomination from the prowar Republicans, with the endorsement of the Federalists. Jared Ingersoll of Pennsylvania was nominated as his running mate. The electoral college gave Madison 128 votes, against 89 for Clinton. Vermont and Pennsylvania stood by Madison, but New York was led by Martin Van Buren into the Clinton column. Gerry and the ticket could not carry the candidate's own state of Massachusetts, notwithstanding his recent election as governor. Thus, at the beginning of the WAR OF 1812, the Republican party was seriously divided.

BIBLIOGRAPHY

Ketcham, Ralph. *James Madison.* New York: Macmillan, 1971.

Rutland, Robert A. *The Presidency of James Madison.* Lawrence: University Press of Kansas, 1990.

Louis Martin Sears/A. G.

See also **Doves and Hawks.**

1816 AND 1820

There was no campaign by parties in 1816 worth the name, none at all in 1820. President James Madison's choice was James Monroe, old Jeffersonian protégé, secretary of state and war. Some Democratic-Republicans favored Gov. Daniel D. Tompkins of New York. Younger Republicans, interested in nationalist measures following the War of 1812, including a bank, protective tariffs, and internal improvements to speed the development of the West, preferred William H. Crawford, secretary of the treasury and citizen of Georgia. They gave him fifty-four votes in the congressional caucus to sixty-five for Monroe. In the electoral college, Monroe overwhelmed Rufus King, signer of the Constitution and statesman of note, but a Federalist whose party now was thoroughly discredited by the Hartford Convention. Monroe was given 183 votes to 34 for King.

Newer sectional conflicts and rivalry among the younger leaders embittered the ERA OF GOOD FEELING, but President Monroe was secure. He was reelected in 1820, with only one dissenting electoral vote (cast by William Plummer of New Hampshire for John Quincy Adams). Federalists saw a greater menace to their propertied interests rising with the democracy of the West; it was to dethrone "King Caucus" (the congressional caucus nominating system) and the Virginia dynasty in the free-for-all campaign of 1824.

BIBLIOGRAPHY

Ammon, Harry. *James Monroe: The Quest for National Identity.* New York: McGraw-Hill, 1971.

Cunningham, Noble E., Jr. *The Presidency of James Monroe.* Lawrence: University Press of Kansas, 1996.

Dangerfield, George. *The Awakening of American Nationalism, 1815–1828.* New York: Harper & Row, 1965.

Arthur B. Darling/A. G.

1824

With the second inauguration of James Monroe in 1820, preparations began for the next campaign, which was to mark the beginning of the transition from federalism to democracy, with resulting voter realignment under new party emblems. The five candidates were prominent in national affairs and represented sections or factions rather than parties. In general, the politicians supported William H. Crawford; John Quincy Adams represented business; John C. Calhoun, the South and the rising slavocracy; Henry Clay, the expanding West; and Andrew Jackson, the people everywhere. The first three were cabinet members, Clay was speaker of the House, and Jackson was the country's most popular military figure.

Crawford was virtually eliminated by a paralytic stroke; Jackson was brought in late by his friends; Clay's support was never impressive; and Calhoun withdrew and became candidate for vice president on both the Adams and Jackson tickets. No candidate received a majority electoral vote. Jackson secured the greatest number, 99; Adams, 84; Crawford, 41; and Clay, 37. The House of Representatives made a selection and chose Adams. Jackson's supporters charged that a "corrupt bargain" had been made when it was learned that Clay threw his support to Adams in exchange for the position of secretary of state. The effect of Jackson's complaint was that he immediately began campaigning for the election of 1828.

BIBLIOGRAPHY

Dangerfield, George. *The Awakening of American Nationalism, 1815–1828.* New York: Harper & Row, 1965.

Hargreaves, Mary W.M. *The Presidency of John Quincy Adams.* Lawrence: University Press of Kansas, 1985.

Nagel, Paul. *John Quincy Adams: A Public Life, A Private Life.* New York: Knopf, 1997.

Thomas Robson Hay / A. G.

1828 AND 1832

In 1828 President John Quincy Adams stood for reelection on the National Republican ticket and Andrew Jackson of Tennessee made his second campaign for the presidency, his supporters now being called Democrats. Designated the people's candidate by the action of friends in the legislature of his own state, Jackson won and held the necessary support of influential leaders in New York, Pennsylvania, and South Carolina. The campaign was waged throughout the administration of Adams. It was not marked by any clear-cut declaration of political principle or program, and Jackson came to think of it as a personal vindication.

Of the twenty-four states, Delaware and South Carolina still expressed their choice by vote of the legislature. In twenty-two states the elections were held in the period from late October to early December. There was a great increase in the popular vote cast, and both candidates shared in the increase: 647,286 being cast for Jackson and 508,064 for Adams. The electoral vote stood 178 for Jackson to 83 for Adams. John C. Calhoun of South Carolina was again elected vice president. In many parts of the nation there was evidence of a more effective organization of the vote than in any previous contest, yet over and above all considerations in this election was the appeal that the frontier hero made to an increasing body of democratically minded voters. Jackson himself was the cause of an alignment of public opinion in the years that followed. Jackson men controlled the Congress, and platforms and programs were supported by leaders and sections and groups, but not by clearly defined political parties.

Naturally, Jackson stood for re-election in 1832, although he had spoken in favor of a single term, and the campaign to renominate him began at once. After December 1831, when Henry Clay returned to the Senate, he, rather than Adams, received the support of most of those who were opposed to Jackson. This did not include Calhoun, who in 1830 had broken with Jackson. Clay was formally presented by a national convention that met in December 1831. He was endorsed by a national convention of young men, which prepared a platform in a meeting held in May of 1832. In that month a national convention of Jackson supporters nominated Martin Van Buren of New York for the vice presidency. The newly formed Anti-Masonic party supported William Wirt of Maryland.

The campaign not only witnessed the general use of the national party convention, but platforms were presented and cartoons freely used, and there was a concentration of popular attention upon the pageantry of parades. Aside from the personal contest between Jackson and Clay, the issues centered on Jackson's attack on the Bank of the United States and particularly his veto of the bill for the recharter of the bank, a bill that had the backing of Clay supporters in both houses of Congress. Twenty-four states participated in this election, and all except South Carolina provided a popular vote. The electorate endorsed Jackson's administration, for the distribution of the vote in twenty-three states gave Jackson, 687,502 votes; Clay, 530,189; and Wirt, 101,051. In the electoral college the vote stood Jackson, 219; Clay, 49; and Wirt, 7; with the 11 votes representing South Carolina cast for John Floyd of Virginia.

BIBLIOGRAPHY

Cole, Donald B. *The Presidency of Andrew Jackson.* Lawrence: University Press of Kansas, 1993.

Dangerfield, George. *The Awakening of American Nationalism, 1815–1828.* New York: Harper & Row, 1965.

Remini, Robert V. *Andrew Jackson and the Course of American Freedom, 1822–1832.* New York: Harper & Row, 1981.

Edgar Eugene Robinson / A. G.

See also **Anti-Masonic Movements; Conventions, Party Nominating; Jacksonian Democracy.**

1836

Made up chiefly of Anti-Masons, National Republicans, and anti-Jackson Democrats, the Whig party, formed in

1834, lacked unity. Because of this, the Whig leaders decided to put forward several sectional candidates in the 1836 presidential campaign. Accordingly, Judge Hugh L. White was entered in the race through nomination by legislative caucuses in Tennessee and Alabama, held in January 1835. At about the same time, Judge John McLean was nominated by a legislative caucus in Ohio, but he withdrew from the race in the following August. Sen. Daniel Webster was nominated by a Massachusetts legislative caucus, also in January 1835. Still another candidate of the Whigs was Gen. William H. Harrison, who was formally nominated by both Anti-Masonic and Whig state conventions in Pennsylvania in December 1835.

Meanwhile, at the Democratic National Convention held in Baltimore on 21–22 May 1835, Martin Van Buren, who was President Andrew Jackson's personal choice, had been unanimously nominated for the presidency. No platform was adopted by the convention, but a committee was authorized to draw up an address. Published in the party organ, the Washington *Globe*, on 26 August 1835, this address presented Van Buren as one who would, if elected, continue "that wise course of national policy pursued by Gen. Jackson." For all practical purposes, this address may be regarded as the first platform ever issued by the Democratic party.

When the election returns were finally in, Van Buren had won the presidency with 170 electoral votes and a popular vote of 765,483 to 739,795 for his opponents. White received 26 electoral votes, Webster 14, and Harrison 73, while South Carolina bestowed its 11 votes on W. P. Mangum. No candidate for the vice presidency received a majority of the electoral vote, so on 8 February 1837, the Senate chose the Democratic candidate Richard M. Johnson over his leading rival, Francis Granger.

BIBLIOGRAPHY

Niven, John. *Martin Van Buren: The Romantic Age of American Politics.* New York: Oxford University Press, 1983.

Remini, Robert V. *Martin Van Buren and the Making of the Democratic Party.* New York: Columbia University Press, 1959.

Wilson, Major L. *The Presidency of Martin Van Buren.* Lawrence: University Press of Kansas, 1984.

Erik McKinley Eriksson/A. G.

1840

Distinctive in American history as the first national victory of the Whig party, the campaign of 1840 was unique for its popular and emotional appeal, organized on an unprecedented scale. To the Whigs belongs the credit of introducing into a presidential battle every political device calculated to sway the "common man." The Whig convention, assembled at Harrisburg, Pennsylvania, on 2 December 1839, nominated Gen. William Henry Harrison of Indiana for president and John Tyler of Virginia for vice president. No attempt was made to frame a platform; indeed, the only bond uniting the various groups under the Whig banner was a determination to defeat the Democrats. The Democratic convention, held at Baltimore on 5 May 1840, was united behind Martin Van Buren for president, but the choice of a vice president was left to the state electors. A platform on strict construction lines was adopted.

The Whigs conducted their campaign at a rollicking pitch. Harrison was adroitly celebrated as the "Hard Cider and Log Cabin" candidate, a phrase the Democrats had used in contempt. Popular meetings, "log cabin raisin's," oratory, invective against Van Buren the aristocrat, songs, and slogans ("TIPPECANOE AND TYLER Too") swamped the country. In the election Harrison polled an electoral vote of 234, a popular vote of 1,274,624; Van Buren received 60 electoral votes and 1,127,781 popular votes. A minor feature in the campaign was the appearance of an abolition (the Liberty) party, whose candidate, James G. Birney, received 7,069 votes. Although the causes for Van Buren's defeat should be traced back to his opposition to Jackson, the Panic of 1837, the unpopular SEMINOLE WARS, and the campaign methods employed by the Whigs contributed largely to Harrison's success.

BIBLIOGRAPHY

Gunderson, Robert Gray. *The Log-Cabin Campaign.* Lexington: University of Kentucky Press, 1957.

Peterson, Norma L. *The Presidencies of William Henry Harrison and John Tyler.* Lawrence: University Press of Kansas, 1989.

Dorothy Burne Goebel/A. G.

See also **Antislavery; Campaign Songs; Financial Panics; Liberty Party.**

1844

No outstanding Democratic candidate could muster the necessary two-thirds vote in the 1844 convention, so James K. Polk of Tennessee, the first "DARK HORSE" (compromise candidate), was nominated with George M. Dallas of Pennsylvania as running mate, on a platform demanding "the re-annexation of Texas and the re-occupation of Oregon" and in favor of tariff reform. The Whigs nominated Henry Clay of Kentucky and Theodore Frelinghuysen of New Jersey on a platform favoring protective tariffs and a national bank, but quibbling on the Texas annexation issue, which alienated some of the Whigs. The Liberty party unanimously selected James G. Birney as its presidential candidate. Polk carried New York by a small popular majority and was elected with 170 electoral votes to 105 for Clay. The popular vote was Polk, 1,338,464; Clay, 1,300,097; and Birney, 62,300.

BIBLIOGRAPHY

Bergeron, Paul H. *The Presidency of James K. Polk.* Lawrence: University Press of Kansas, 1987.

McCoy, Charles A. *Polk and the Presidency.* Austin: University of Texas Press, 1960.

Walter Prichard/A. G.

1848

The Whig nominee, Zachary Taylor, who sidestepped the burning issue of SLAVERY extension, coasted to victory on his military reputation with Millard Fillmore as his vice president. His Democratic opponent, Gen. Lewis Cass of Michigan, straddled the slavery extension question by advocating state sovereignty. The new FREE SOIL PARTY, specifically opposed to extension and headed by Martin Van Buren, split the Democratic vote in New York and thus contributed materially to Taylor's triumph. (Gerrit Smith, the National Liberty party candidate and staunch abolitionist, advised those who would not vote for an abolitionist to vote for Van Buren, rather than Cass.) Taylor carried half the states: eight in the South and seven in the North. The popular vote was Taylor, 1,360,967; Cass, 1,222,342; Van Buren, 291,263; Smith 2,733. The electoral vote was Taylor, 163; Cass, 127.

BIBLIOGRAPHY

Hamilton, Holman. *Zachary Taylor: Soldier in the White House.* Indianapolis, Ind.: Bobbs-Merrill, 1951.

Rayback, Robert J. *Millard Fillmore: Biography of a President.* Buffalo, N.Y.: American Political Biography Press, 1959.

Smith, Elbert B. *The Presidencies of Zachary Taylor and Millard Fillmore.* Lawrence: University Press of Kansas, 1988.

Holman Hamilton / A. G.

1852

The Whig party, suffering from apathy and demoralized by the slavery issue, entered the 1852 campaign in dangerously weak condition. Democratic victory seemed almost certain, but the question of who would serve on the Democratic ticket remained open. After many ballots, the leading Democrats, Lewis Cass, James Buchanan, and Stephen Douglas, fell out of the running and a dark horse, Franklin Pierce of New Hampshire, was nominated with William R. King of Alabama. The Whigs nominated the military hero Gen. Winfield Scott; the Free Soilers nominated the antislavery leader John P. Hale of New Hampshire. Both major parties endorsed the COMPROMISE OF 1850, so there were no issues and little contest. Pierce carried all states save Massachusetts, Vermont, Kentucky, and Tennessee. The popular vote was Pierce, 1,601,117; Scott, 1,385,453; and Hale, 155,825. The electoral vote was Pierce, 254; Scott, 42.

BIBLIOGRAPHY

Gara, Larry. *The Presidency of Franklin Pierce.* Lawrence: University Press of Kansas, 1991.

Nichols, Roy F. *Franklin Pierce: Young Hickory of the Granite Hills.* Philadelphia: University of Pennsylvania Press, 1931.

Roy F. Nichols / A. G.

1856

In its first presidential campaign, the Republican party nominated John C. Frémont of California. Its platform opposed slavery expansion and condemned slavery and Mormonism as twin relics of barbarism. The American, or Know-Nothing, party nominated Millard Fillmore, who had succeeded to the presidency following the death of Zachary Taylor. The Democrats nominated James Buchanan, selecting John C. Breckinridge as his running mate. Their conservative platform stressed STATES' RIGHTS, opposed sectionalism, and favored a somewhat ambiguous plank that gave popular sovereignty to the territories. The electoral vote was Buchanan, 174; Frémont, 114; and Fillmore, 8. The popular vote was Buchanan, 1,832,955; Frémont, 1,339,932; and Fillmore, 871,731. The Republicans rejoiced at their showing, having won the votes of eleven free states, while the Democrats congratulated themselves for saving the Union.

BIBLIOGRAPHY

Klein, Philip S. *President James Buchanan: A Biography.* University Park: Penn State University Press, 1962.

Smith, Elbert B. *The Presidency of James Buchanan.* Lawrence: University Press of Kansas, 1975.

Philip G. Auchampaugh / A. G.

See also **Know-Nothing Party; Latter-Day Saints, Church of Jesus Christ of.**

1860

The Democratic National Convention met amid great excitement and bitterness over the slavery issue, at Charleston, South Carolina, on 23 April 1860. The delegates from the eight states of the far South (Southern Democrats) demanded the inclusion of a plank in the platform providing that Congress should guarantee slave property in the territories. This was refused, and after several days of useless wrangling and failure to unite the convention upon a candidate, adjournment was taken to Baltimore on 18 June. At this meeting the convention nominated Stephen A. Douglas of Illinois for president, and later the national committee nominated Herschel V. Johnson of Georgia for vice president. The platform pledged the party to stand by the Dred Scott decision or any future Supreme Court decision that dealt with the rights of property in the various states and territories.

Southern Democrat delegates met separately at Baltimore on 28 June and nominated John C. Breckinridge of Kentucky for president and Joseph Lane of Oregon for vice president. The platform reaffirmed the extreme Southern view regarding slavery. Meanwhile, the remains of the old-line Whig and American (Know-Nothing) parties had met in a convention in Baltimore on 9 May and adopted the name of the CONSTITUTIONAL UNION PARTY and a seemingly simple platform: "the Constitution of the country, the Union of the States and the enforcement of the laws." They nominated John Bell of Tennessee for president and Edward Everett of Massachusetts for vice president and attempted to ignore slavery and other sectional issues, with a plea for the preservation of the Union.

The Republican National Convention met in Chicago on 16 May. By means of the platform issues of nonextension of slavery, homestead law, and advocacy of a protective tariff, the agricultural elements of the Northern and Western parts of the country and the industrial elements of Pennsylvania, New England, and other Northern and Eastern sections of the country were united. At first it seemed that the convention would nominate either William H. Seward of New York or Salmon P. Chase of Ohio, but when a deadlock between their respective supporters seemed imminent, the convention instead nominated Abraham Lincoln of Illinois on the third ballot. Hannibal Hamlin of Maine received the nomination for vice president on the second ballot. The split in the Democratic party made possible Lincoln's election. He received 180 electoral votes against 72 for Breckinridge, who carried the extreme Southern states, and 39 for Bell, who carried the border states. Douglas received but 12 electoral votes—9 from Missouri and 3 of the 7 from New Jersey. The popular vote totaled 1,865,593 for Lincoln, 1,382,713 for Douglas, 848,356 for Breckinridge, and 592,906 for Bell. The combined opponents thus received 958,382 votes more than Lincoln, who was a minority president during his first administration.

BIBLIOGRAPHY

Donald, David H. *Lincoln.* New York: Simon & Schuster, 1995.

Oates, Stephen B. *With Malice Toward None: The Life of Abraham Lincoln.* New York: Harper & Row, 1977.

Paludan, Philip S. *The Presidency of Abraham Lincoln.* Lawrence: University Press of Kansas, 1994.

William Starr Myers/A. G.

See also **Dred Scott Case; Slave Trade.**

1864

A national convention was called in the name of "the executive committee created by the national convention held in Chicago on the sixteenth day of May 1860." The use of the name Republican was carefully avoided. The convention met in Baltimore on 7 June 1864 and named itself the National Union (Arm-in-Arm) Convention. The Republican leaders wanted to appeal to Union sentiment and eliminate partisan influence as much as possible. The platform, which was unanimously adopted, was a statement of "unconditional Union" principles and pledged the convention to put down rebellion by force of arms. Abraham Lincoln was nominated for a second term by the vote of every delegate except those from Missouri, who had been instructed to vote for Gen. Ulysses S. Grant. The nomination then was made unanimous. Andrew Johnson of Tennessee, a leading Southern Democrat who had been staunch in his loyalty to the Union, was nominated for vice president. The Democratic party met in convention on 29 August, also in Chicago. Its platform declared the war a failure and advocated the immediate cessation of hostilities and the restoration of the Union by peaceable means. The convention nominated Gen. George B. McClellan for president and George H. Pendleton for vice president. McClellan accepted the nomination but at the same time virtually repudiated the platform out of fear that it would alienate the Northern electorate.

At first it appeared that the Democrats might defeat Lincoln, but the victories of the Union army in the field—particularly the capture of Atlanta in September—proved that the war was not a failure and rallied the people to support Lincoln and Johnson and the Union cause. The election took place on 8 November. For the first time in U.S. history certain states—those of the South—deliberately declined to choose the electors whose job it was to select the president. Lincoln carried every state that took part in the election except New Jersey, Delaware, and Kentucky. He received 212 electoral votes, while McClellan received 21. Lincoln was given a popular majority of only 403,151 votes out of a total of 4,010,725 cast. This election was one of the most vital in the history of the country because the very survival of the national Union may have depended upon the outcome.

BIBLIOGRAPHY

Castel, Albert E. *The Presidency of Andrew Johnson.* Lawrence: Regents Press of Kansas, 1979.

Donald, David H. *Lincoln.* New York: Simon & Schuster, 1995.

Oates, Stephen B. *With Malice Toward None: The Life of Abraham Lincoln.* New York: Harper & Row, 1977.

Paludan, Philip S. *The Presidency of Abraham Lincoln.* Lawrence: University Press of Kansas, 1994.

William Starr Myers/A. G.

See also **Assassinations, Presidential; Civil War; Slave Trade; Slavery.**

1868 and 1872

The issues in 1868 were southern Reconstruction and the "Ohio Idea" (payment of the national debt in greenbacks). Horatio Seymour of New York and Frank Blair of Missouri, the Democratic nominees, ran on a platform calling for a restoration of the rights of the southern states and payment of the war bonds in greenbacks. Alarmed by Democratic victories in 1867, the Republicans nominated the war hero, Ulysses S. Grant, and Schuyler Colfax of Indiana. Their platform acclaimed the success of Reconstruction and denounced as repudiation the payment of the bonds in greenbacks. Personal attacks on the candidates and Republican "waving the bloody shirt" were campaign features. An effort to replace the Democratic nominees in October failed but foreshadowed defeat. Grant received 214 electoral votes to Seymour's 80, and nearly 53 percent of the popular vote, receiving 3,013,421 votes to 2,706,829 for Seymour. Seymour carried eight states. The result was a personal victory for Grant rather than for Republican policies.

Dissatisfaction with the Reconstruction policy and a desire for reform led to a Liberal Republican organization, supported by tariff and civil-service reformers, independent editors, and disgruntled politicians. The new party nominated Horace Greeley, with B. Gratz Brown of Missouri as vice president, to oppose Grant's reelection in 1872. (Grant's running mate in this campaign was Henry Wilson of Massachusetts.) Its platform demanded civil-service reform, universal amnesty, and specie payment. The tariff issue was straddled to please Greeley, a protectionist. The Democrats accepted the Liberal Republican platform and nominees. The Greeley campaign lacked enthusiasm, and he was mercilessly lampooned. Grant received 286 electoral votes to Greeley's 66 and over 55 percent of the popular vote, receiving 3,596,745 votes to 2,843,446 for Greeley. Greeley died shortly after the election and before the electoral college met. His electoral votes were scattered among four other candidates.

BIBLIOGRAPHY

McFeely, William S. *Grant: A Biography.* New York: Norton, 1981.

Perret, Geoffrey. *Ulysses S. Grant: Soldier and President.* New York: Random House, 1997.

Simpson, Brooks D. *The Reconstruction Presidents.* Lawrence: University Press of Kansas, 1998.

Charles H. Coleman/A. G.

See also **Bloody Shirt; Civil War; Greenbacks; Liberal Republican Party; Reconstruction Finance Corporation.**

1876

This campaign is especially notable because it resulted in the famous disputed presidential election. The leading aspirant for the Republican nomination was James G. Blaine of Maine. His name was presented to the national convention at Cincinnati by Robert G. Ingersoll in a striking speech in which he dubbed Blaine "the Plumed Knight." Among the other candidates were Benjamin H. Bristow of Kentucky, Roscoe Conkling of New York, Oliver P. Morton of Indiana, and Rutherford B. Hayes of Ohio. For six ballots Blaine led the field, but his involvement in a scandal brought to light a few weeks before the Republican convention caused a stampede to Hayes on the seventh ballot, resulting in his nomination. William A. Wheeler of New York was named as his running mate. The platform endorsed the Resumption Act and eulogized the Republican party for its work during the Civil War and Reconstruction.

Thomas F. Bayard of Delaware, Allen G. Thurman of Ohio, Winfield Scott Hancock of Pennsylvania, and Thomas A. Hendricks of Indiana sought the Democratic nomination, but the leading contender was Gov. Samuel J. Tilden of New York, who was named on the first ballot. Hendricks was then nominated for the vice presidency. The scandals of the Grant administration were denounced in unsparing terms and "reform" was declared to be the paramount issue. Repeal of the clause of the act of 1875 providing for the resumption of specie payments was advocated, but Tilden personally was known to be a sound-money man rather than a Greenbacker. The platform also declared in favor of civil-service reform.

During the campaign, the Democratic speakers dwelt heavily upon the scandals under Republican rule and contended that only through a change of men and parties could there be any real reform. Republican orators resorted to "bloody shirt" tactics (that is, revived the Civil War issues), questioned Tilden's loyalty during that conflict, and praised Hayes's military record—four honorable wounds and a brevet major generalcy. In the North the campaign was a quiet one, but in some of the southern states, attempts to intimidate African American voters produced violent outbursts and considerable bloodshed.

Early returns on election night indicated Tilden's election, but quickly it became obvious that the result would be in doubt. When the electoral college met and voted, Tilden received 184 unquestioned votes, Hayes, 165. The 4 votes of Florida, Louisiana's 8 votes, South Carolina's 7 votes, and Oregon's 1 vote were claimed by both parties. After a protracted, bitter dispute, Congress created an electoral commission of five senators, five representatives, and five Supreme Court judges to help decide the result. Of the senators, three were to be Republicans and two Democrats; of the representatives, three were to be Democrats and two Republicans; four of the judges, two Republicans and two Democrats, were designated by their districts, and together they were to choose the fifth judge. It was expected that the fifth judge would be David Davis, but his election to the Senate by the Democrats in the Illinois legislature gave him an excuse to decline the thankless task. The choice then fell upon Joseph P. Bradley, who had been appointed to the bench as a Republican but then made several decisions that made him acceptable, temporarily, to the Democrats.

In case the two houses of Congress, voting separately, refused to accept any return, the dispute was to be referred to the commission, whose decision was to be final unless it was rejected by both houses. The two houses, voting separately on strict party lines, did disagree. The decision, therefore, rested with the commission, which, in all cases, by a vote of eight to seven (Bradley voting with the majority), refused to go against the election results as certified by the state authorities (in the case of Oregon by the secretary of state) and declared in favor of the Republican contenders. In each case the Senate accepted this decision, while the House rejected it. All the disputed votes were therefore counted for Hayes and Wheeler, and they were declared elected.

BIBLIOGRAPHY

Hoogenboom, Ari. *Rutherford B. Hayes: Warrior and President.* Lawrence: University Press of Kansas, 1995.

Simpson, Brooks D. *The Reconstruction Presidents.* Lawrence: University Press of Kansas, 1998.

Woodward, C. Vann. *Reunion and Reaction: The Compromise of 1877 and the End of Reconstruction.* Boston: Little, Brown, 1951.

Paul L. Haworth / A. G.

1880

Taking place during a business revival and with no definite issue before the country, the 1880 campaign was routine politics. The Republicans overcame a serious split between groups headed by James G. Blaine and Roscoe Conkling by nominating James A. Garfield, a member of neither faction, over former President Ulysses S. Grant, who had the support of the Conkling wing in seeking a third term in office. The nomination of Chester A. Arthur for the vice presidency appeased the Conkling faction. Against Garfield the Democrats nominated Winfield Scott Hancock, a nonpolitical Civil War general. However, their party had no positive program and was discredited by its factious opposition to the Hayes administration, two factors that led to a narrow defeat. The Republicans carried the "doubtful states" and regained control over Congress. The popular vote was Garfield, 4,453,295; Hancock, 4,414,082. The electoral vote was Garfield, 214; Hancock, 155.

BIBLIOGRAPHY

Doenecke, Justus D. *The Presidencies of James A. Garfield and Chester A. Arthur.* Lawrence: Regents Press of Kansas, 1981.

Peskin, Allan. *Garfield: A Biography.* Kent, Ohio: Kent State University Press, 1978.

Theodore Clark Smith / A. G.

See also **Assassinations, Presidential.**

1884

Fought primarily between Republican James G. Blaine and Democrat Grover Cleveland, the campaign of 1884 was one of the most vicious in American history. There were several reasons why it became relentlessly personal in character. From the moment of Blaine's nomination in Chicago on 6 June, he came under heavy fire from the reform element of all parties. He was believed to be allied with the spoils element in Republican politics; he had an unhappy record for baiting the South; he favored certain big business interests; and his railroad transactions had raised a suspicion that he had used his position as speaker of the House for personal profit. To divert attention from these attacks, certain Republicans published evidence that Cleveland, nominated on 10 July, also in Chicago, was the father of an illegitimate son born in Buffalo some ten years earlier.

There were virtually no serious issues between the two parties—both had good reason not to meddle seriously with the currency question or tariffs, and international affairs attracted little attention. One leading feature of the campaign was the secession of a large body of Republicans who could not stomach Blaine and who became Cleveland Democrats, or MUGWUMPS. Another feature was the open enmity of TAMMANY HALL, under political boss John Kelly, for Cleveland, and the success of it and other malcontents in carrying many Irish voters over to Blaine or to the new Antimonopoly party headed by Benjamin F. Butler. After exchanges that one observer compared to the vulgar battles between quarreling tenement dwellers, the two parties approached election day running neck and neck. Democratic victory was finally decided by the vote of New York state, where three key events unfolded: the Rev. Samuel D. Burchard's "rum, Romanism and rebellion" speech at a reception for Blaine, the "Belshazzar's feast" of Republican millionaires and politicians at Delmonico's just before the election, and Roscoe Conkling's knifing of Blaine; together, the three spelled a narrow defeat for Blain. Cleveland and his running mate, Thomas A. Hendricks, obtained a popular vote of 4,879,507 against Blaine's 4,850,293, and an electoral vote of 219 against Blaine's 182. Butler's popular vote was just over 175,000, and that of John P. St. John, Prohibition candidate, was just over 150,000.

BIBLIOGRAPHY

Summers, Mark Wahlgren. *Rum, Romanism, and Rebellion: The Elections of 1884.* Chapel Hill: University of North Carolina Press, 2000.

Welch, Richard. *The Presidencies of Grover Cleveland.* Lawrence: University Press of Kansas, 1988.

Allan Nevins / A. G.

See also **Antimonopoly Parties; Prohibition Party; Tariff.**

1888

The TARIFF was the chief issue of this campaign, which resulted in the election of Republican candidate Benjamin Harrison over Grover Cleveland by a majority of the electoral college but not of the popular vote. The Republicans had approached the election with scant hope of victory, for Cleveland had proved an admirable president; however, when his annual message of 1887 was devoted entirely to arguments for tariff reform, they gained new hope. The issue was one on which they could rally nearly all manufacturers, most general businesses, and perhaps a majority of workingmen. Benjamin Harrison, who represented extreme high-tariff demands, was nominated by the Republicans at Chicago on 25 June after James G. Blaine withdrew for health reasons and John Sherman and Walter Q. Gresham, whose tariff views were moderate, failed to gain any additional supporters. Levi P. Morton was named Harrison's vice presidential candidate.

Harrison was supported by Blaine, by manufacturing interests who were induced by the Republican chairman (Matthew S. Quay) to make large campaign donations, and by Civil War veterans hungry for pension legislation. With their assistance, Harrison waged an aggressive campaign, during which his speechmaking abilities made a deep impression on the country.

Cleveland, who was renominated by the Democrats at Saint Louis early in June, felt that his presidential office made it improper for him to actively campaign, and his running mate, former Sen. Allen G. Thurman of Ohio, was too old and infirm to be anything but a liability to the party; to make matters worse, campaign funds were slender. However, the worst news for the Democrats involved their national chairman, Sen. Calvin S. Brice of Ohio, who held high-tariff convictions, was allied with big business, and refused to put his heart into the battle. Two weeks before election day, the Republicans published an indiscreet letter by Lord Sackville-West, the U.S. minister to Britain, hinting to a supposed British colleague that Cleveland would probably be more friendly to England than Harrison; and though Cleveland at once had Sackville-West recalled, the incident cost him many Irish-American votes. Cleveland received 5,537,857 popular votes, Harrison 5,447,129; but Cleveland had only 168 electors against Harrison's 233. Clinton B. Fisk of New Jersey, the Prohibition candidate, polled 249,506 votes; Alson J. Streeter of Illinois, the Union Labor nominee, 146,935.

BIBLIOGRAPHY

Sievers, Harry J. *Benjamin Harrison: Hoosier President.* New York: University Publishers, 1968.

Socolofsky, Homer E., and Allan B. Spetter. *The Presidency of Benjamin Harrison.* Lawrence: University Press of Kansas, 1987.

Allan Nevins / A. G.

See also **Pensions, Military and Naval.**

1892

Grover Cleveland was reelected over Benjamin Harrison in 1892 by a majority, the size of which surprised observers of both parties. Cleveland had been named on the first ballot at the Democratic convention in Chicago, although David B. Hill of New York had made a demagogic attempt to displace him. Adlai E. Stevenson was selected for the vice presidency. The incumbent Harrison, who had estranged the professional politicians of his party, who had quarreled with its most popular figure (James G. Blaine), and who had impressed the country as cold and unlikable, was reluctantly accepted by the Republicans at Minneapolis on 10 June. With no other desirable candidate available, the party found it politically unfeasible to repudiate his administration. However, the McKinley Tariff of 1890 had excited widespread discontent, the SHERMAN SILVER PURCHASE ACT of the same year had angered the conservative East, and heavy federal expenditures had caused general uneasiness. Cleveland's firm stand on behalf of the gold standard and low tariffs and his known strength of character commended him to large numbers of independent voters. One factor that hurt the Republicans was the great strength manifested by the Populists, who polled 1,040,000 votes for James B. Weaver of Iowa and James G. Field of Virginia, most from old Republican strongholds in the Middle West. Another factor was the labor war at Homestead, Pennsylvania, which revealed that the highly protected steel industry did not properly pass on its tariff benefits to the worker. Cleveland, with a popular vote of 5,555,426, had 277 electors; Harrison, with a popular vote of 5,182,690, had 145; while Weaver won 22 electoral votes.

BIBLIOGRAPHY

Nevins, Allan. *Grover Cleveland: A Study in Courage.* New York: Dodd, Mead, 1932.

Welch, Richard. *The Presidencies of Grover Cleveland.* Lawrence: University Press of Kansas, 1988.

Allan Nevins / A. G.

See also **Populism.**

1896

This campaign and election marked the end of a twenty-two-year period in which neither major party had been able to control the national government for more than the life of a single Congress; it ushered in a period of Republican domination that lasted until 1911. Favored by Marcus A. Hanna's cannily managed campaign, William McKinley of Ohio was named on the first ballot by the Republican convention meeting at Saint Louis. Garret A. Hobart was selected as the vice presidential candidate. The traditional party platform was adopted with the exception of a declaration for the GOLD STANDARD until BIMETALLISM could be secured by international agreement. A bloc of western delegates bolted and organized the SILVER REPUBLICAN PARTY.

With Cleveland tainted by the sour economy, no candidate had an inside track on the Democratic nomination. The important contest was over the platform. As presented to the delegates, it was an anti-administration document favoring free silver at the sixteen-to-one ratio, criticizing the use of injunctions in labor disputes, and denouncing the overthrow of the federal income tax. In its support William Jennings Bryan delivered his "Cross of Gold" oration and endeared himself to the silver delegates by his effective answers to the criticisms of the administration orators. The enthusiasm growing out of that speech gave impetus to Bryan's candidacy for the presidential nomination. Backing this was also the long campaign he had waged by personal conferences, speeches, and correspondence with the inflationist delegates from the South and West. Another factor was the bolting Republicans and the Populists, who saw themselves being forced to support the Democratic nominee and demanded someone not too closely identified with the regular Democratic party platform. Bryan appealed to the delegates as the Democrat who could unite the silver and agrarian factions. The Populists, Silver Republicans, and National Silver party members joined the Democrats in support of Bryan. The administration Democrats placed a National

Democratic ticket in the field to hold conservative Democratic votes away from him, nominating John M. Palmer of Illinois as their presidential candidate.

The campaign was highly spectacular. The Democrats exploited Bryan's oratory skills by sending him on speaking tours across the country, at which enormous crowds came out to hear him. In sharp contrast, the Republican management kept McKinley at his home in Canton, Ohio, where carefully selected delegations made formal calls and listened to "front porch" speeches by the candidate. More important was the flood of advertising, the funds for building local organizations, and the large group of speakers that campaigned for McKinley, which all were maintained by Hanna's organization. The metropolitan press, like the other business groups—except the silver miners—overwhelmingly opposed Bryan. The results showed a sharp city-versus-rural division, with Bryan carrying the Solid South and most of the trans-Missouri states. The remainder, including California, Oregon, North Dakota, Kentucky, and Maryland, went to McKinley. With him were elected a Republican House and a Senate in which various minor party members held a nominal balance of power. The popular vote was unusually large, each candidate receiving larger totals than any previous candidate of his party, McKinley's vote being 7,102,246 and Bryan's 6,492,559. The electoral vote was 271 and 176, respectively.

BIBLIOGRAPHY

Glad, Paul W. *McKinley, Bryan, and the People.* Philadelphia: Lippincott, 1964.

Gould, Lewis L. *The Presidency of William McKinley.* Lawrence: University Press of Kansas, 1980.

Elmer Ellis / A. G.

See also **Cross of Gold Speech; Free Silver.**

1900

The presidential candidates and most of the issues of the 1896 campaign carried over to the 1900 campaign. With the trend of prices upward, the pressure for inflation had declined, and the expansion of American control over new territories had created the issue of IMPERIALISM. At the Republican convention in Philadelphia, a combination of circumstances forced Marcus A. Hanna and President William McKinley to accept Theodore Roosevelt as the vice presidential candidate. The party's position on the new territories was defined as American retention with "the largest measure of self-government consistent with their welfare and our duties." When the Democrats met at Kansas City, they once again selected William Jennings Bryan as their presidential candidate, but they were unwilling to accept the conservatives' proposal to forget the last platform and make anti-imperialism the only issue. The 1896 platform was reendorsed, an antitrust plank added, and imperialism designated the "paramount issue."

The campaign lacked the fire of 1896. The Republicans emphasized the "FULL DINNER PAIL" and the danger threatening it from the Democratic platform; the Democrats stressed the growth of monopolies under the McKinley administration and the danger of imperialistic government. The result was a more emphatic Republican victory than in 1896, one generally interpreted as an endorsement of both McKinley's domestic and foreign policies. The popular vote was McKinley, 7,218,491; Bryan, 6,356,734. McKinley obtained 292 electoral votes to 155 for Bryan. This election made Roosevelt's elevation to the presidency automatic upon McKinley's death in September 1901.

BIBLIOGRAPHY

Gould, Lewis L. *The Presidency of William McKinley.* Lawrence: Regents Press of Kansas, 1980.

Morgan, Wayne H. *William McKinley and His America.* Syracuse, N.Y.: Syracuse University Press, 1963.

Elmer Ellis / A. G.

See also **Assassinations, Presidential.**

1904

Theodore Roosevelt, who succeeded to the presidency on the death of William McKinley in 1901, ardently hoped to be nominated and elected "in his own right." The death of Marcus A. Hanna of Ohio, whom the big business interests of the country would have preferred, made possible the president's nomination by acclamation when the Republican convention met in Chicago on 21 June. Charles W. Fairbanks of Indiana was chosen for the vice presidency. The Democrats, meeting at Saint Louis on 6 July, pointedly turned their backs upon "Bryanism" by omitting from their platform all reference to the money question. They nominated for president Alton B. Parker, a conservative New York judge, who at once pledged himself to maintain the gold standard, and for vice president, Henry Gassaway Davis, a wealthy West Virginia octogenarian. Business leaders, more afraid of the Democratic party than of Roosevelt, contributed so heavily to the Republican campaign chest that Parker rashly charged "blackmail." He claimed that the Republican party had forced corporations to contribute funds to the campaign, and in return the government pledged to suppress evidence it had against them. Roosevelt, indignantly denying the charge, won by a landslide that reclaimed Missouri from the SOLID SOUTH and gave him 336 electoral votes to Parker's 140 and a popular plurality of 2,544,238. Prohibitionist, Populist, Socialist, and Socialist Labor candidates received only negligible support.

BIBLIOGRAPHY

Brands, H.W. *TR: The Last Romantic.* New York: Basic Books, 1997.

Gould, Lewis L. *The Presidency of Theodore Roosevelt.* Lawrence: University Press of Kansas, 1991.

Morris, Edmund. *Theodore Rex.* New York: Random House, 2001.

Mowry, George E. *The Era of Theodore Roosevelt and the Birth of Modern America, 1900–1912.* New York: Harper & Row, 1958.

John D. Hicks/A. G.

See also **Antimonopoly Parties; Socialist Labor Party; Socialist Movement.**

1908

Theodore Roosevelt, although at the height of his popularity, refused to run for a second elective term in 1908, but swung his support at the Republican convention to William Howard Taft, who was nominated. The convention selected James S. Sherman of New York for the vice presidency. William Jennings Bryan completely dominated the Democratic convention and became its nominee. Party differences on the issues played an insignificant role in the election. After an apathetic campaign Bryan carried only the Solid South, Kansas, Colorado, and Nevada, although he received about 44 percent of the popular vote, securing 6,412,294 to Taft's 7,675,320. Taft's electoral vote was 321; Bryan's, 162. The Republicans won the presidency and both houses of Congress.

1908 Presidential Election. A campaign poster for Democratic candidate William Jennings Bryan—making his third and final bid for president—and his running mate, John W. Kern; they lost to Republican William Howard Taft and vice-presidential nominee James Schoolcraft Sherman.

BIBLIOGRAPHY

Anderson, Donald F. *William Howard Taft: A Conservative's Conception of the Presidency.* Ithaca, N.Y.: Cornell University Press, 1973.

Coletta, Paolo E. *The Presidency of William Howard Taft.* Lawrence: University Press of Kansas, 1973.

Chester Lloyd Jones/A. G.

1912

This campaign marked the culmination of the progressive movement in national politics and resulted in the return of the Democrats after sixteen years of Republican presidents. The struggle for the Republican nomination became a bloody battle between the progressive and conservative wings, aided in each case by personal followings and some division of support from large interests. In the beginning it was the progressive Sen. Robert M. La Follette of Wisconsin against the incumbent, William Howard Taft. But former President Theodore Roosevelt, who had been largely responsible for Taft's nomination in 1908, entered the race to rally behind him Republicans who believed Taft had been too friendly with the conservative Old Guard. The influence in Taft's hands was sufficient to return delegates pledged to him where they were named by conventions, but either Roosevelt or La Follette was successful in states where presidential primaries were held, save one. The conservative-controlled national committee placed Taft delegates on the temporary roll in all contests, and the small majority resulting gave Taft the nomination. Roosevelt was later nominated by the newly organized Progressive (Bull Moose) party, consisting largely of Republican bolters.

The contest for the Democratic nomination was also hard fought with both of the leading candidates accepted as progressives. Beauchamp ("Champ") Clark of Wisconsin led from the beginning and had an actual majority in the convention for a time, but when William Jennings Bryan transferred his support to the second progressive, Woodrow Wilson, a shift began that resulted in the latter's nomination. The choice for vice president was Thomas R. Marshall. All three party platforms adopted planks unusually favorable to progressive policies. Wilson, backed by a united party, won easily, and Roosevelt was second. There was an unusual amount of shifting of party loyalties, although most Democrats voted for Wilson and most Republicans for Roosevelt or Taft. Wilson's popular vote was 6,296,547, Roosevelt's was 4,118,571, and Taft's was 3,486,720. The electoral vote was, respectively, 435, 88, and 8. The Democrats won majorities in both branches of Congress. In spite of the three-way contest, a fourth candidate, Eugene V. Debs, Socialist, secured approximately 900,000 votes.

BIBLIOGRAPHY

Burton, David H. *The Learned Presidency: Theodore Roosevelt, William Howard Taft, and Woodrow Wilson.* Rutherford, N.J.: Fairleigh Dickinson University Press, 1988.

Clements, Kendrick A. *The Presidency of Woodrow Wilson.* Lawrence: University Press of Kansas, 1992.

Cooper, John Milton, Jr. *The Warrior and the Priest: Woodrow Wilson and Theodore Roosevelt.* Cambridge, Mass.: Harvard University Press, 1983.

Link, Arthur S. *Wilson.* Princeton, N.J.: Princeton University Press, 1947.

Mowry, George E. *Theodore Roosevelt and the Progressive Movement.* Madison: University of Wisconsin Press, 1946.

Elmer Ellis / A. G.

See also **Bull Moose Party; Progressive Movement.**

1916

This campaign reunited the Republican party and determined that American foreign policy should be left in Woodrow Wilson's hands. The Republicans reunited when, after the nomination of Charles Evans Hughes, Theodore Roosevelt, already nominated by the rapidly declining Progressive party, announced support of the ticket. There was no opposition to the renomination of President Wilson and Vice President Thomas R. Marshall. The Democrats defended the policies of the administration, especially the Underwood Tariff and the measures for the regulation of business. They also praised the foreign policy as one that had kept the United States out of war and preserved national honor. The Republicans attacked the policies of the administration, promised a stronger foreign policy, and were supported by the more extreme partisans of both alliances in the European war.

The results were in doubt for several days because of the close vote in several states. Wilson won the presidency, carrying Ohio, New Hampshire, the South, and most of the border and trans-Missouri states, including California, with an electoral vote of 277, against 254 for Hughes. The popular vote was Wilson, 9,127,695; Hughes, 8,533,507. Congress remained Democratic only because independent members of the House were friendly.

BIBLIOGRAPHY

Clements, Kendrick A. *The Presidency of Woodrow Wilson.* Lawrence: University Press of Kansas, 1992.

Cooper, John Milton, Jr. *The Warrior and the Priest: Woodrow Wilson and Theodore Roosevelt.* Cambridge, Mass.: Harvard University Press, 1983.

Elmer Ellis / A. G.

See also **World War I.**

1920

The debate on the LEAGUE OF NATIONS determined the alignment of political forces in the spring of 1920. The Republicans were confident: the wounds of the intraparty strife of 1912 had been healed; the mistaken strategy of 1916 admitted; and the conservative mood of the country was easily interpreted. They met in convention in Chicago, could not agree upon any one of the leading preconvention candidates (Frank O. Lowden, Hiram Johnson, or Leonard Wood), and nominated Warren G. Harding, senator from Ohio, on the tenth ballot. Calvin Coolidge, governor of Massachusetts, was nominated for the vice presidency. The Democrats met in San Francisco. None of the discussed candidates, William G. McAdoo, Alfred E. Smith, John W. Davis, A. Mitchell Palmer, or James M. Cox, commanded a great following. Cox, governor of Ohio, was nominated on the forty-fourth ballot, with Franklin D. Roosevelt, thirty-eight-year-old assistant secretary of the navy, as vice presidential nominee. The Socialist party, meeting in May, nominated Eugene Debs for the fifth time. A Farmer-Labor ticket appeared also.

None of the platforms was unexpected or significant on domestic issues. The Republicans attacked the president and opposed American entrance into the League of Nations. The Democratic national committee supported Wilson's appeal for a "solemn referendum" on the covenant of the League; Cox waged a persistent and vigorous campaign. Harding, remaining at his home for the most part, contented himself with vague generalizations. Neither candidate had been nationally known at the outset of the contest, no clear-cut issue developed, and no real contest transpired. The total vote cast was 26,733,905. The Nineteenth Amendment had been proclaimed in August, and in every state women were entitled to vote. Harding won more than 60 percent of the total vote cast. Cox won the electoral vote in only eleven states, receiving 127 electoral votes to Harding's 404. The Socialist vote was 919,799, but the strength of all the third parties totaled only about 5.5 percent.

BIBLIOGRAPHY

Ferrell, Robert H.. *The Strange Deaths of President Harding.* Columbia: University of Missouri Press, 1996.

Trani, Eugene P., and David L. Wilson. *The Presidency of Warren G. Harding.* Lawrence: Regents Press of Kansas, 1977.

Edgar Eugene Robinson / A. G.

See also **Constitution of the United States; Farmer-Labor Party of 1920; Suffrage: Woman's Suffrage.**

1924

As in 1920, the candidates in 1924 were new in a presidential CANVASS. The Republican convention, meeting in Cleveland, with a few scattered votes in dissent, nominated Calvin Coolidge, who as vice president had succeeded to the presidency in August 1923 when President Warren Harding died. The vice presidential nomination, refused by several, was accepted by Charles G. Dawes of Illinois. The platform was marked by extreme conservatism. The Democrats met in New York and were in almost continuous session for two and a half weeks. Not only did serious division exist on the matter of American adherence to the League of Nations and on the proposed denunciation of the Ku Klux Klan, but also upon the choice of the nominee. Each of the two leading candidates, Alfred E. Smith and William G. McAdoo, possessed enough delegates to prevent the nomination of the other, and finally on the 103d ballot the nomination went to John W. Davis of West Virginia. Gov. Charles W. Bryan of Nebraska was nominated for vice president. The platform called for a popular referendum on the League of Nations.

The Conference for Progressive Political Action brought about a series of meetings and eventually a widespread support of Sen. Robert M. La Follette in his independent candidacy, with Burton K. Wheeler as his running mate. La Follette's platform, in which appeared most of the progressive proposals of the previous twenty years, was endorsed by the Socialist party and the officers of the American Federation of Labor. So real did the threat of the third-party candidacy appear to be that much of the attack of the Republicans was on La Follette, who waged an aggressive campaign.

The total vote cast exceeded that of 1920 by 2.36 million, but because of the vote cast for La Follette (nearly 5 million), that cast for Republican and for Democratic tickets was less than four years earlier, Coolidge securing 15,718,211 votes, and Davis 8,385,283. La Follette carried Wisconsin (13 electoral votes). Coolidge topped the poll in thirty-five states, receiving 382 electoral votes, leaving the electoral vote for Davis in only twelve states, or 136 votes.

BIBLIOGRAPHY

Ferrell, Robert H. *The Presidency of Calvin Coolidge.* Lawrence: University Press of Kansas, 1998.

Sobel, Robert. *Coolidge: An American Enigma.* Washington D.C.: Regnery, 1998.

Edgar Eugene Robinson/A. G.

See also **Progressive Party, 1924.**

1928

On 2 August 1927, President Calvin Coolidge announced that he would not run for reelection in 1928. The majority of Republican party leaders was undecided as to which candidate they should support. A popular movement, taking its strength from the rank and file voters, forced the nomination of Secretary of Commerce Herbert Hoover on the first ballot at the Republican National Convention, which met at Kansas City, Missouri, in June. The platform contained strong support of the usual Republican policies, such as a protective tariffs and sound business administration. It advocated the observance and rigorous enforcement of the Eighteenth Amendment. Charles Curtis of Kansas was nominated for vice president. The Democrats met at Houston, Texas, and on 28 June nominated New York Gov. Alfred E. Smith, the first Catholic to be nominated for the presidency. They then nominated Arkansas Sen. Joseph T. Robinson for vice president. The platform did not differ strikingly from that of the Republicans. The contest became one between rival personalities. Smith, an avowed "wet," took a stand in favor of a change in the Prohibition amendment, and advocated that the question of Prohibition and its enforcement be left to the determination of the individual states.

At the election on 6 November, Hoover was overwhelmingly successful. He carried forty states, including five from the Old South, with a total of 444 electoral votes. Smith carried eight states with an electoral vote of 87. The popular plurality of Hoover over Smith was 6,375,824 in a total vote of 36,879,414.

BIBLIOGRAPHY

Burner, David. *Herbert Hoover: A Public Life.* New York: Knopf, 1979.

Fausold, Martin L. *The Presidency of Herbert C. Hoover.* Lawrence: University Press of Kansas, 1985.

Finan, Christopher M. *Alfred E. Smith: The Happy Warrior.* New York: Hill and Wang, 2002.

William Starr Myers/A. G.

See also **Financial Panics; Great Depression; Stock Market.**

1932 and 1936

The presidential campaign of 1932 began in earnest with the holding of the Republican National Convention at Chicago from 14 to 16 June. President Herbert Hoover and Vice President Charles Curtis were renominated on the first ballot. The platform praised the Hoover record, including his program for combating the depression. After a long debate a "wet-dry" plank on Prohibition was adopted, which favored giving the people an opportunity to pass on a repeal amendment. The Democratic National Convention was also held in Chicago, 27 June to 2 July 1932. On the fourth ballot, Gov. Franklin Delano Roosevelt of New York was nominated for the presidency, defeating Alfred E. Smith and ten other candidates. John Nance Garner of Texas was selected as the vice presidential candidate. The platform pledged economy, a sound currency, unemployment relief, old-age and unemployment insurance under state laws, the "restoration of agriculture," and repeal of the Eighteenth Amendment together with immediate legalization of beer.

After a campaign featuring Roosevelt's promise of "a new deal," the elections were held on 5 November. The popular vote for each party was as follows: Democratic, 22,809,638; Republican, 15,758,901; Socialist, 881,951; Socialist-Labor, 33,276; Communist, 102,785; Prohibition, 81,869; Liberty, 53,425; and Farmer-Labor, 7,309. The electoral vote was 472 for the Democrats and 59 for the Republicans.

In 1936 the Republican National Convention was held at Cleveland beginning on 9 June. Gov. Alfred M. Landon of Kansas and Frank Knox, a Chicago publisher, were nominated for the presidency and vice-presidency, respectively. The platform strongly denounced the New Deal administration, from both constitutional and economic viewpoints. It pledged the Republicans "to maintain the American system of constitutional and local self-government" and "to preserve the American system of free enterprise." The Democratic National Convention assembled at Philadelphia on 25 June for what proved to be a ratification meeting for the NEW DEAL. President Roosevelt and Vice President Garner were renominated without opposition. The platform vigorously defended the New Deal and pledged its continuance. When the election was held on 3 November, the Democrats again won an overwhelming victory, carrying every state except Maine and Vermont. The popular vote for each party was as follows: Democratic, 27,752,869; Republican, 16,674,665; Union, 882,479; Socialist, 187,720; Communist, 80,159; Prohibition, 37,847; and Socialist-Labor, 12,777. The Democrats received 523 electoral votes while the Republicans received only 8.

BIBLIOGRAPHY

Burns, James MacGregor. *Roosevelt: The Lion and the Fox.* New York: Harcourt Brace Jovanovich, 1956.

Freidel, Frank. *Franklin D. Roosevelt: A Rendezvous with Destiny.* Boston: Little, Brown, 1990.

Schlesinger, Arthur M., Jr. *The Age of Roosevelt: The Crisis of the Old Order, 1919–1933.* Boston: Houghton Mifflin, 1957.

Erik McKinley Eriksson / A. G.

1940

Although either Robert A. Taft, Arthur H. Vandenberg, or Thomas E. Dewey was expected to be the Republican candidate, the nomination was won by Wendell L. Willkie at Philadelphia, 28 June, on the sixth ballot. As president of a large utilities corporation Willkie had fought the NEW DEAL, but in foreign affairs he was an internationalist, and with Europe at war, this fact commended him to the liberal element of the party, which carried his nomination against the Old Guard. The nomination of a liberal by the Republicans, together with the international crisis, in turn made the nomination of Franklin D. Roosevelt by the Democrats (Chicago, 16 July) a practical certainty, even though his running for a third term was unprecedented. Foreign affairs dominated the campaign. Both candidates promised aid to the Allies; both promised at the same time to keep the United States out of foreign wars. Roosevelt and Henry A. Wallace, secretary of agriculture, received 27,307,819 popular and 449 electoral votes against 22,321,018 popular and 82 electoral votes for Willkie and Charles L. McNary of Oregon.

BIBLIOGRAPHY

Burns, James MacGregor. *Roosevelt: The Soldier of Freedom.* New York: Harcourt Brace Jovanovich, 1970.

Freidel, Frank. *Franklin D. Roosevelt: A Rendezvous with Destiny.* Boston: Little, Brown, 1990.

Christopher Lasch / A. G.

See also **Foreign Aid; Foreign Policy; World War II.**

1944

Thomas E. Dewey, governor of New York, was nominated by the Republican convention in Chicago on 26 June with little opposition. John W. Bricker of Ohio was chosen as his running mate. President Franklin D. Roosevelt, running for a fourth term, encountered even less opposition at the Democratic convention in Chicago. The real struggle revolved around the choice of a vice presidential candidate. With Roosevelt's support, Vice President Henry Wallace could probably have been nominated for another term, but the opposition to Wallace from within the party convinced the president that a compromise candidate had to be found. James F. Byrnes of South Carolina was acceptable to the White House and to the party conservatives, but not to labor, in particular not to Sidney Hillman of the Congress of Industrial Organizations. Accordingly, Sen. Harry S. Truman of Missouri was nominated on the second ballot on 20 July.

In the November election Roosevelt received 25,606,585 popular and 432 electoral votes to Dewey's 22,014,745 popular and 99 electoral votes. The Democrats preserved their control of both houses of Congress.

BIBLIOGRAPHY

Burns, James MacGregor. *Roosevelt: The Soldier of Freedom.* New York: Harcourt Brace Jovanovich, 1970.

Freidel, Frank. *Franklin D. Roosevelt: A Rendezvous with Destiny.* Boston: Little, Brown, 1990.

Goodwin, Doris Kearns. *No Ordinary Time: Franklin and Eleanor Roosevelt: The Home Front in World War II.* New York: Simon & Schuster, 1994.

Christopher Lasch / A. G.

See also **American Federation of Labor–Congress of Industrial Organizations.**

1948

The Republicans, having gained control of Congress in 1946 and confidently expecting to turn the apparently unpopular Truman administration out of power in the autumn elections, for the first time in the party's history renominated a defeated candidate, Thomas E. Dewey, at the convention meeting in Philadelphia on 21 June. The Democrats, on the other hand, suffered from severe internal conflicts. Truman's nomination at Philadelphia on 15 July roused no enthusiasm. Radicals left the party and, meeting in the same city on 22 July, nominated Henry A. Wallace and Sen. Glen Taylor of Idaho as the candidates of the Progressive party. Southerners, offended by the civil rights planks of the Democratic platform, also seceded and in Birmingham, Alabama, on 17 July, formed the States' Rights Democratic Party, with Gov. J. Strom Thurmond of South Carolina and Gov. Fielding L. Wright of Mississippi as their candidates.

Under these circumstances Truman's candidacy appeared to be hopeless. The president, however, proved to be a whistle-stop campaigner of unexpected ability. Moreover, he enjoyed the support not only of organized labor and of African American voters but, as it turned out—to the great surprise of prophets and pollsters—of midwestern farmers as well. The election was close—Truman retired for the evening on election night thinking he had lost. He and Alben W. Barkley of Kentucky polled 24,105,812 popular and 304 electoral votes against 21,970,065 popular and 189 electoral votes for Dewey and Gov. Earl Warren of California. Thurmond polled 1,169,063 popular votes and the 38 electoral votes of South Carolina, Alabama, Mississippi, and Louisiana. Wallace won 1,157,172 popular votes. The Democrats regained control of Congress by small majorities.

BIBLIOGRAPHY

Hamby, Alonzo L. *Man of the People: A Life of Harry S. Truman.* New York: Oxford University Press, 1995.

Karabell, Zachary. *The Last Campaign: How Harry Truman Won the 1948 Election.* New York: Knopf, 2000.

McCullough, David. *Truman.* New York: Simon & Schuster, 1992.

Christopher Lasch / A. G.

1952

After a long and bitter struggle, the internationalist wing of the Republican party succeeded on 11 July in bringing about the nomination of Gen. Dwight D. Eisenhower against the opposition of Sen. Robert A. Taft and his supporters. The Democrats, following the Republicans to Chicago ten days later, turned to Gov. Adlai E. Stevenson of Illinois, who consented to become a candidate only at the last moment. In the campaign that followed Stevenson suffered from revelations of corruption in the Truman administration, from the widespread dissatisfaction with the seemingly inconclusive results of the war in Korea, and from the vague feeling that it was "time for a change." Eisenhower's personal appeal, moreover, was immense. He and Sen. Richard M. Nixon of California polled 33,936,234 votes to 27,314,987 for Stevenson and Sen. John J. Sparkman of Alabama. The Republicans carried the electoral college, 442 to 89. They carried the House of Representatives by a narrow margin and tied the Democrats in the Senate.

BIBLIOGRAPHY

Ambrose, Stephen. *Eisenhower: The Soldier and Candidate, 1890–1952.* New York: Simon & Schuster, 1983.

Cochran, Bert. *Adlai Stevenson: Patrician Among the Politicians.* New York: Funk & Wagnalls, 1969.

Patterson, James T. *Mr. Republican: A Biography of Robert A. Taft.* Boston: Houghton Mifflin, 1972.

Christopher Lasch / A. G.

See also **Korean War.**

1956

Adlai E. Stevenson was renominated on the first ballot by the Democrats at Chicago, with Sen. Estes Kefauver of Tennessee as his running mate. President Dwight D. Eisenhower and Vice President Richard M. Nixon were renominated by the Republicans at San Francisco with equal ease. The campaign, however, was far from a rehash of 1952. Stevenson, having been advised that his serious discussions of issues in 1952 had been over the voters' heads, agreed to pitch his campaign at a somewhat lower level. The results disappointed his more ardent supporters without winning him any votes. The Suez crisis, occurring on the eve of the election, further strengthened the administration's position by creating a national emergency. In the election the president polled 35,590,472 popular and 457 electoral votes to Stevenson's 26,022,752 popular and 73 electoral votes. As in 1952, Eisenhower broke into the Solid South, carrying not only Florida, Virginia, and Tennessee, which he had carried in 1952, but also Texas, Oklahoma, and Louisiana. In spite of his personal triumph, however, the Democrats carried both houses of Congress.

BIBLIOGRAPHY

Ambrose, Stephen. *Eisenhower: The President.* New York: Simon & Schuster, 1984.

Broadwater, Jeff. *Adlai Stevenson and American Politics: The Odyssey of a Cold War Liberal.* New York: Twayne, 1994.

Greenstein, Fred I. *The Hidden-Hand Presidency: Eisenhower as Leader.* New York: Basic Books, 1982.

Christopher Lasch / A. G.

1960

The Democrats nominated Sen. John F. Kennedy of Massachusetts at Los Angeles in July, with Sen. Lyndon B. Johnson of Texas as his running mate. The Republicans, meeting at Chicago two weeks later, nominated Vice President Richard M. Nixon and Henry Cabot Lodge of Massachusetts. The most striking feature of the campaign was a series of televised debates, in which the candidates submitted to questioning by panels of reporters. By sharing a national audience with his lesser-known opponent, Nixon may have injured his own cause. Indeed, the debates, in view of the closeness of the result, may have been the decisive factor in Kennedy's victory. The final vote was not known until weeks after the election. Kennedy received 34,227,096, Nixon 34,108,546, and minor candidates 502,773. Despite the fact that Kennedy won by only 118,550 votes and had only 49.7 percent of the total vote as compared with 49.6 percent for Nixon, the President-elect won 303 electoral votes to Nixon's 219.

At forty-three, Kennedy was the youngest man ever elected to the presidency (although not the youngest to occupy the office). He was also the first Roman Catholic ever to become president.

BIBLIOGRAPHY

Matthews, Christopher. *Kennedy and Nixon: The Rivalry That Shaped Postwar America.* New York: Simon & Schuster, 1996.

Parmet, Herbert S. *JFK: The Presidency of John F. Kennedy.* New York: Dial Press, 1983.

White, Theodore H. *The Making of the President: 1960.* New York: Atheneum, 1962.

Christopher Lasch / A. G.

See also **Assassinations, Presidential; Bay of Pigs Invasion; Catholicism; Cold War; Cuban Missile Crisis.**

1964

Upon assuming office following the assassination of President John F. Kennedy in November 1963, Vice President Lyndon B. Johnson acted quickly to restore public calm and to achieve many of President Kennedy's legislative goals. Johnson was subsequently nominated by acclamation by the Democrats, meeting in Atlantic City, New Jersey. The only uncertainty was the choice of a vice presidential nominee. After Johnson's earlier veto of Attorney General Robert F. Kennedy, brother of the slain president, the choice of Johnson and the party fell to Minnesotan Hubert H. Humphrey, assistant majority leader of the Senate.

Conflict over the presidential nomination centered in the Republican party. New York's Gov. Nelson Rockefeller represented the moderate and liberal factions that had dominated the party since 1940. A new, conservative group was led by Arizona's Sen. Barry M. Goldwater, who offered "a choice, not an echo." Presidential primaries indicated the limited appeal of both candidates, but no viable alternative emerged. Goldwater accumulated large numbers of delegates in the nonprimary states, particularly in the South and West, and sealed his first-ballot victory with a narrow win in the California primary. Rep. William E. Miller of New York was selected as his running mate.

The main issues of the 1964 campaign were presented by Goldwater, who challenged the previous party consensus on a limited welfare state and the emerging Democratic policy of accommodation with the Communist world. The Democrats defended their record as bringing peace and prosperity, while pledging new social legislation to achieve a "Great Society." The armed conflict in Vietnam also drew some attention. In response to an alleged attack on American warships in the Gulf of Tonkin, the president ordered retaliatory bombing of North Vietnam, at the same time pledging "no wider war."

In the balloting, Lyndon Johnson was overwhelmingly elected, gaining 43,129,484 popular votes (61.1 percent) and a majority in forty-four states and the District of Columbia—which was voting for president for the first time—for a total of 486 electoral votes. Goldwater won 27,178,188 votes (38.5 percent) and six states—all but Arizona in the Deep South—for a total of 52 electoral votes. There was a pronounced shift in voting patterns, with the South becoming the strongest Republican area, and the Northeast the firmest Democratic base.

BIBLIOGRAPHY

Dallek, Robert. *Flawed Giant: Lyndon Johnson and His Times, 1961–1973.* New York: Oxford University Press, 1998.

Perlstein, Rick. *Before the Storm: Barry Goldwater and the Unmaking of the American Consensus.* New York: Hill & Wang, 2001.

White, Theodore H. *The Making of the President: 1964.* New York: Atheneum, 1965.

Gerald M. Pomper / A. G.

See also **Civil Disobedience; Civil Rights Movement; Cold War; Student Nonviolent Coordinating Committee; Students for a Democratic Society; Tonkin Gulf Resolution; Vietnam War; Youth Movements.**

1968

The presidential election took place in an atmosphere of increasing American civil disorder, evidenced in protests over the Vietnam War, riots in black urban neighborhoods, and assassinations of political leaders. On 31 March, President Lyndon B. Johnson startled the nation by renouncing his candidacy for re-election. His withdrawal stimulated an intense contest for the Democratic nomination between Minnesota's Sen. Eugene McCarthy, New York's Sen. Robert F. Kennedy, and Vice President Hubert H. Humphrey. Kennedy appeared to have the greatest popular support, his campaign culminating in a narrow victory over McCarthy in the California primary. On the night of this victory, Kennedy was assassinated. Humphrey abstained from the primaries but gathered support from party leaders and from the Johnson administration. At an emotional and contentious convention in Chicago, Humphrey easily won nomination on the first ballot. Maine's Sen. Edmund S. Muskie was selected as the vice presidential candidate.

Former Vice President Richard M. Nixon was the leading candidate for the Republican nomination. He withstood challenges from moderate Gov. Nelson Rockefeller of New York and conservative Gov. Ronald Reagan of California. Gaining a clear majority of delegates on the first ballot at the party's convention in Miami Beach, he then named Gov. Spiro T. Agnew of Maryland as his running mate. A new party, the American Independent Party, was organized by Gov. George C. Wallace of Alabama and able to win a ballot position in every state. Curtis LeMay, former air force general, was selected as the new party's vice presidential candidate. The campaign centered on the record of the Johnson administration. Nixon denounced the conduct of the war and promised both an "honorable peace" and ultimate withdrawal of American troops. He also pledged a vigorous effort to reduce urban crime and to restrict school DESEGREGATION. Wallace denounced both parties, calling for strong action against North Vietnam, criminals, and civil rights protesters. Humphrey largely defended the Democratic record, while also proposing an end to American bombing of North Vietnam.

The balloting brought Nixon a narrow victory. With 31,785,480 votes, he won 43.4 percent of the national total, thirty-two states, and 301 electoral votes. Humphrey won 31,275,166 votes, 42.7 percent of the total, thirteen states and the District of Columbia, and 191 electoral votes. Wallace gained the largest popular vote for a third-party candidate since 1924—9,906,473 votes and 13.5 percent of the popular total. The five southern states he captured, with 46 electoral votes, were too few to accomplish his strategic aim—a deadlock of the electoral college.

BIBLIOGRAPHY

Ambrose, Stephen E. *Nixon: The Triumph of a Politician.* New York: Simon & Schuster, 1987.

Gould, Lewis L. *1968: The Election That Changed America.* Chicago: Ivan R. Dee, 1993.

White, Theodore H. *The Making of the President: 1968.* New York: Atheneum, 1969.

Gerald M. Pomper/A. G.

See also **Assassinations and Political Violence, Other; Riots, Urban; Riots, Urban, of 1967; Vietnam War.**

1972

The Nixon administration provided the campaign setting in 1972 with a series of American policy reversals, including the withdrawal of most American ground forces from Vietnam, the imposition of wage and price controls, and presidential missions to Communist China and the Soviet Union. President Richard M. Nixon's control of the Republican party was undisputed, resulting in a placid party convention in Miami, where he and Vice President Spiro T. Agnew were renominated.

In the Democratic party, major party reform resulted in a more open delegate selection process and increased representation at the convention of women, racial minorities, and persons under the age of thirty. At the same time, a spirited contest was conducted for the presidential nomination. The early favorite, Maine's Sen. Edmund S. Muskie, was eliminated after severe primary defeats. Alabama's Gov. George C. Wallace raised a serious challenge but was eliminated from active campaigning after being seriously injured in an assassination attempt. The contest then became a two-man race between South Dakota's Sen. George S. McGovern and former Vice President Hubert H. Humphrey, the 1968 candidate. A series of upset primary victories and effective organization in local party caucuses culminated in a direct victory for McGovern in the California primary and a first-ballot nomination in Miami, the convention city. The vice presidential Democratic position was awarded to Missouri's Sen. Thomas Eagleton. After the convention adjourned, it was revealed that Eagleton had been hospitalized three times for mental depression. He was persuaded to resign, and the Democratic National Committee then, at McGovern's suggestion, named Sergeant Shriver as his running mate. With Wallace disabled, the American Independent party named Rep. John G. Schmitz of California as its presidential candidate.

The Democrats attempted to focus the campaign on the alleged defects of the administration, including the continuation of the war in Vietnam, electronic eavesdropping by the Republicans on the Democratic national headquarters at Washington's WATERGATE complex, and governmental favors for Republican party contributors. The full extent of these improprieties was not revealed, however, until the following year. Aside from defending the Nixon record, the Republicans attacked the Democratic candidate as advocating radical positions on such issues as amnesty for war resisters, marijuana usage, and abortion, and as inconsistent on other questions. Much attention centered on 25 million newly eligible voters, including the eighteen-year-olds enfranchised by constitutional amendment.

The final result was an overwhelming personal victory for Nixon, who won the highest total and proportion of the popular vote in electoral history. Nixon won 47,169,905 popular votes (60.7 percent) and 521 electoral votes from forty-nine states. McGovern won 29,170,383 popular votes (37.5 percent), but only 17 electoral votes (from Massachusetts and the District of Columbia). Despite this landslide, the Republicans failed to gain control of the House and lost two seats in the Senate.

BIBLIOGRAPHY

Ambrose, Stephen E. *Nixon: The Triumph of a Politician.* New York: Simon & Schuster, 1987.

White, Theodore H. *The Making of the President: 1972.* New York: Atheneum, 1973.

Witker, Kristi. *How to Lose Everything in Politics Except Massachusetts.* New York: Mason & Lipscomb, 1974.

Gerald M. Pomper/A. G.

See also **Assassinations and Political Violence, Other; China, Relations with; Nixon, Resignation of; Nixon Tapes; Russia, Relations with.**

1976

The Democratic nomination attracted hopefuls from across the political spectrum. Former Georgia Gov. James Earl (Jimmy) Carter, an unknown moderate, defeated better-known rivals in a classic campaign. Understanding the new delegate selection rules, Carter first attracted media attention by winning the Iowa caucus and the New Hampshire primary, and then defeated in turn each of his liberal and conservative rivals. The national convention displayed great unity, and Carter picked former Minnesota Sen. Walter F. Mondale as his vice presidential candidate.

The Republican nomination contest was more divisive. Gerald R. Ford, the only president not to have been elected to the office, faced a conservative challenge from former California Gov. Ronald Reagan. After a bitter campaign, Ford prevailed with slightly more than half the delegates, and at a divided national convention replaced Vice President Nelson A. Rockefeller (also appointed to office and not elected) with Kansas Sen. Robert Dole. Ford ran on the record of his brief administration, emphasizing continued restraint on the federal government and détente with the Soviet Union. Carter offered a mix of conservative and liberal critiques of the Nixon-Ford record, including the poor economy and foreign policy controversies. His basic appeal was returning trust and morality to government, promising the voters, "I will never lie to you." Both candidates sought to avoid divisive social issues, such as abortion.

On election day 54 percent of the electorate went to the polls and gave Carter a very narrow victory; he won 50 percent of the popular vote (40,828,929 ballots) and 23 states and the District of Columbia for 297 electoral votes. The key to Carter's success was victory in all but one of the southern states. Ford won 49 percent of the popular vote (39,148,940 ballots) and 27 states for 241 electoral votes. The independent campaign of former Sen. Eugene McCarthy received 1 percent of the vote and influenced the outcome in several states.

BIBLIOGRAPHY

Anderson, Patrick. *Electing Jimmy Carter: The Campaign of 1976.* Baton Rouge: Louisiana State University Press, 1994.

Greene, John Robert. *The Limits of Power: The Nixon and Ford Administrations.* Bloomington: Indiana University Press, 1992.

Kutler, Stanley I. *The Wars of Watergate: The Last Crisis of Richard Nixon.* New York: Knopf, 1990.

Stroud, Kandy. *How Jimmy Won: The Victory Campaign from Plains to the White House.* New York: Morrow, 1977.

John C. Green/A. G.

1980

The 1980 presidential election occurred in an atmosphere of crisis. The taking of American hostages in Iran in 1978 and the invasion of Afghanistan by the Soviet Union in 1979 had produced popular indignation, while the scarcity of oil and a poor economy generated discontent. Tensions mounted with the founding of the MORAL MAJORITY, a religious interest group, and President Jimmy Carter declared the country suffered from a "malaise" and a "crisis of confidence." Under these circumstances, the Republican nomination attracted several candidates. Former California Gov. Ronald Reagan was the early favorite but had to overcome spirited challenges from party moderates, including former Rep. George Bush of Texas and Rep. John Anderson of Illinois. At the national convention, Reagan chose Bush for vice president, but Reagan's conservatism led Anderson to run as an independent in the general election, stressing moderation.

Meanwhile, President Carter faced serious divisions in the Democratic party. His principal challenger was Massachusetts Sen. Edward Kennedy. Although popular with party liberals, questions about Kennedy's character and foreign policy crises undermined his campaign, allowing Carter to score early and decisive primary victories. Kennedy pursued his campaign into a divided convention, where he refused to endorse Carter. The fall campaign produced sharp ideological divisions. Carter ran a liberal campaign based on his comprehensive energy program, plans to manage the economy, the EQUAL RIGHTS AMENDMENT, and human rights in foreign policy. In contrast, Reagan ran a conservative campaign based on free enterprise, reduction of federal spending, traditional moral values, and an anticommunist foreign policy. The climax of the campaign came in the last televised presidential debate, when Reagan asked the voters "Are you better off than you were four years ago?"

On election day, 54 percent of the electorate went to the polls and gave Reagan a decisive victory. He won 51 percent of the popular vote (43,899,248) and 44 states for 489 electoral votes; his victory extended to every region of the country, including the South. Carter won 41 percent of the popular vote (35,481,435) and 6 states and the District of Columbia for 49 electoral votes. Independent Anderson collected 7 percent of the vote but won no states.

BIBLIOGRAPHY

Cannon, Lou. *Reagan.* New York: Putnam, 1982.

Evans, Rowland, and Robert Novak. *The Reagan Revolution.* New York: Dutton, 1981.

Germond, Jack W., and Jules Witcover. *Blue Smoke and Mirrors: How Reagan Won and Why Carter Lost the Election of 1980.* New York: Viking, 1981.

Jordan, Hamilton. *Crisis: The Last Year of the Carter Presidency.* New York: Putnam, 1982.

Kaufman, Burton Ira. *The Presidency of James Earl Carter, Jr.* Lawrence: University Press of Kansas, 1993.

John C. Green/A. G.

See also **Iran Hostage Crisis.**

1984

The 1984 presidential campaign occurred in a climate of peace and prosperity. Anti-Soviet foreign policy produced a sense of security and a strong economy reduced discontent. While the nation faced many problems, the public was tranquil compared to previous elections. President Ronald Reagan enjoyed considerable personal popularity, even with voters who disagreed with him on issues, and was not challenged for the Republican nomination. Although there was some grumbling from the right wing about Vice President George Bush, both he and Reagan were renominated by acclamation, giving the Republicans the luxury of a united party. They also enjoyed the support of a broad conservative coalition, including many southerners and religious conservatives, who came to be known as Reagan Democrats.

Among the Democrats, former Vice President Walter Mondale was the front-runner, but he received a strong challenge from former Colorado Sen. Gary Hart, who won the New Hampshire primary, and the Reverend Jesse Jackson, the first African American candidate to make a serious presidential bid. A divided Democratic National Convention made history by nominating the first female vice presidential candidate, New York Rep. Geraldine Ferraro. During the campaign Reagan ran on the theme of "It's morning in America," stressing national pride and optimism and his defense and economic policies. Mondale offered a liberal alternative, attacking Reagan's aggressive foreign policy and conservative economic program. Mondale received attention for his unpopular promise to raise taxes to reduce the federal budget deficit. The candidates also differed on women's rights and **ABORTION**, and a "gender gap" developed in favor of the Democrats. Reagan ran far ahead for most of the campaign, stumbling briefly when he showed apparent signs of age in a televised debate.

On election day 53 percent of the electorate went to the polls and overwhelmingly reelected Reagan. He won 59 percent of the popular vote (54,281,858 ballots) and 49 states for a record high 525 electoral votes; indeed, he came within some 4,000 votes of being the first president to carry all fifty states. Mondale won 41 percent of the popular vote (37,457,215) and carried only the District of Columbia and his home state of Minnesota, for 13 electoral votes.

BIBLIOGRAPHY

Cannon, Lou. *President Reagan: The Role of a Lifetime.* New York: Simon & Schuster, 1991.

Germond, Jack W., and Jules Witcover. *Wake Us When It's Over: Presidential Politics of 1984.* New York: Macmillan, 1985.

Mayer, Jane, and Doyle McManus. *Landslide: The Unmaking of the President, 1984–1988.* Boston: Houghton Mifflin, 1988.

Wills, Garry. *Reagan's America: Innocents at Home.* New York: Penguin Books, 1988.

John C. Green / A. G.

See also **Reaganomics.**

1988

The selection of candidates for the 1988 campaign began in an atmosphere of uncertainty. President Ronald Reagan could not run for reelection and, although the economy was strong, some of the costs of Reagan's programs caused public concern. In addition, the Iran-Contra scandal had hurt Reagan's foreign policy, and tensions over social issues were increasing. The Democratic nomination attracted a crowded field. Because of his strong showing in 1984, former Colorado Sen. Gary Hart was the favorite but a personal scandal ended his campaign early. Massachusetts Gov. Michael Dukakis became the front-runner because of a well-financed and disciplined campaign. After winning the New Hampshire primary, Dukakis outlasted his rivals, including a strong surge for the Reverend Jesse Jackson, who finished second and hoped for the vice presidential nomination. Instead, Texas Sen. Lloyd Bentsen was chosen in an otherwise united national convention.

Vice President George Bush, the Republican favorite, attracted numerous opponents and was upset in the Iowa caucus by Kansas Sen. Robert Dole and televangelist Marion (Pat) Robertson and his "invisible army" of religious conservatives. Bush rallied to win in New Hampshire and the southern primaries that followed. The unity of the national convention was marred by a controversial vice presidential choice, Indiana Sen. J. Danforth (Dan) Quayle, whom critics accused of lacking the personal and intellectual qualifications necessary for high office.

The fall campaign began with Dukakis enjoying a big lead in the polls, but it collapsed under Republican attacks on his record and liberal views, some of which had racial overtones. The Bush campaign stressed the Reagan record on foreign and economic policy and included the pledge, "Read my lips. No new taxes." Dukakis campaigned on his immigrant roots, fiscal conservatism, and the need for economic growth, calling for "good jobs at good wages."

Fifty percent of the electorate went to the polls and gave Bush a solid victory—54 percent of the popular vote (48,881,221) and 40 states for 426 electoral votes. Dukakis won 46 percent of the popular vote (41,805,422 ballots) and 10 states and the District of Columbia for 112 electoral votes.

BIBLIOGRAPHY

Cramer, Richard Ben. *What It Takes: The Way to the White House.* New York: Random House, 1992.

Germond, Jack W., and Jules Witcover. *Whose Broad Stripes and Bright Stars?: The Trivial Pursuit of the Presidency, 1988.* New York: Warner Books, 1989.

John C. Green / A. G.

See also **Iran-Contra Affair; Religion and Religious Affiliation; Taxation.**

1992

The end of the Cold War in 1990 left the United States in search of a "new world order," while major economic and social transformations suggested the need for a new domestic agenda, and the 1992 campaign occurred in a time of great change. These strains produced high levels of disaffection with politics and government. Republican President George Bush's popularity after the **PERSIAN GULF WAR** reduced the number of contenders for the

Democratic nomination. Arkansas Gov. William J. (Bill) Clinton emerged early as the front-runner, and a unified national convention nominated another southerner, Tennessee Sen. Albert Gore, for the vice presidency.

Bush's early popularity also reduced the number of contenders for the Republican nomination, but a weak economy and his broken pledge not to raise taxes led commentator Patrick Buchanan to enter the race. Although Buchanan won no primaries, he embarrassed Bush and created dissension at the national convention, where Bush and Vice President Dan Quayle were renominated.

The fall campaign began with Bush behind in the polls, but unlike in 1988 he never recovered. Bush campaigned on his foreign policy successes, free enterprise, and conservative social issues and sharply attacked his opponent's character. Clinton offered himself as a "new Democrat" with a moderate message of economic opportunity and personal responsibility and waged a disciplined campaign.

The independent candidacy of Texas billionaire and political newcomer H. Ross Perot complicated the race. He launched his campaign from a television talk show in February but withdrew from the race in July, only to reenter in September. Drawing on voter discontent, Perot offered an attack on politics and government as usual.

On election day 55 percent of the electorate went to the polls and gave Bill Clinton a narrow victory—43 percent of the popular vote (44,908,254 ballots) and 32 states and the District of Columbia for 370 electoral votes. At age forty-six, Clinton was the first baby boomer to win the White House. Bush won 38 percent of the popular vote (39,102,343 ballots) and 18 states for 168 electoral votes. Perot received 19 percent of the popular vote, for the second strongest performance by a twentieth-century independent candidate, but won no states.

BIBLIOGRAPHY

Germond, Jack W., and Jules Witcover. *Mad as Hell: Revolt at the Ballot Box, 1992.* New York: Warner Books, 1993.

Maraniss, David. *First in His Class: A Biography of Bill Clinton.* New York: Simon & Schuster, 1995.

John C. Green/A. G.

See also **Conservatism; Free Trade; Persian Gulf Syndrome.**

1996

The Republican landslide in the 1994 midterm elections set the stage for the presidential election of 1996. Expecting to win handily, the Republicans nominated Senate Majority Leader Robert Dole of Kansas, a seventy-three-year-old pragmatic conservative who was known for his dry wit. Despite his age and dour demeanor, Dole was minimally acceptable to all elements of the Republican coalition. He chose as his running mate Representative Jack Kemp, a former Buffalo Bills quarterback from upstate New York. Fearing a sweeping Republican victory, Democrats united behind President Bill Clinton and Vice President Al Gore, making Clinton the first Democrat nominated without substantial opposition since Franklin Delano Roosevelt in 1944. H. Ross Perot, the Texas billionaire whose third-party candidacy garnered 19 percent of the vote in 1992, entered the race as an independent.

Clinton pursued a strategy of "triangulation," attempting to stake out a position between Republicans and Democratic liberals in Congress. He called for a balanced federal budget, declared that the "era of big government is over," and advocated a welfare reform bill that took away one of the Republicans' key issues. Clinton's candidacy was also buoyed by the wave of prosperity that swept the country during his first term, and by a growing backlash against the Republican Congress and House Speaker Newt Gingrich.

The Republicans ran a lackluster campaign, marked by Dole's clumsy rhetoric. They blamed Clinton for a lack of leadership, character, and trustworthiness, but these charges did not stick with most voters. Dole resigned from the Senate, but could not shake his image as a Washington insider. Desperate, he proposed a tax cut he had once scorned, but this only damaged his credibility. The Republican ticket was also hurt by memories of a partial federal government shutdown in the fall of 1995, which most voters blamed on the Republican Congress. In the end, Clinton won 49 percent of the popular vote to Dole's 41 percent, took every region of the country except the South, and captured a large majority of the electoral college.

BIBLIOGRAPHY

Denton, Robert E., Jr. *The 1996 Presidential Campaign: A Communication Perspective.* Westport, Conn.: Praeger, 1998.

Pomper, Gerald M., et. al. *The Election of 1996: Reports and Interpretations.* Chatham, N.J.: Chatham House, 1997.

Wendy Wall

2000

The conflicted legacy of the Clinton years profoundly shaped the presidential election of 2000, an election that ultimately proved to be the longest, one of the closest, and among the most controversial in history. Ultimately decided by the Supreme Court, the election highlighted serious flaws in the nation's electoral system.

The campaign opened in the midst of the nation's longest economic boom and in the wake of the Monica Lewinsky scandal, which led to President Clinton's impeachment. Vice President Al Gore fended off a primary challenge by New Jersey Senator Bill Bradley to secure the Democratic nomination. A staunch environmentalist and policy enthusiast, Gore had held national elective office from the age of twenty-eight. Though smart and experienced, Gore was widely viewed as wooden, and he was haunted by his ties to the Clinton administration. Nevertheless, in a time of peace and prosperity, most commentators believed the election was Gore's to lose.

The Republicans chose Texas Governor George W. Bush over Arizona Senator John McCain. Son of the forty-first president, Bush had been a heavy drinker and playboy before becoming a born-again Christian at age forty. Affable and self-confident, but widely viewed as both inexperienced and an intellectual lightweight, Bush used his family name and connections to raise a huge campaign war chest. Rejecting the hard-line approach taken by Republican congressional leaders since 1994, Bush ran as a "compassionate conservative" and argued that a limited government could care for those in need by enlisting the private sector.

Two key questions framed the campaign: was Bush competent to be president, and did Gore have the personal integrity required? Both men picked running mates designed to offset these concerns. Bush selected Richard "Dick" Cheney, who had served as his father's secretary of defense during the Gulf War. Gore chose Connecticut Senator Joseph Lieberman, an openly observant Orthodox Jew who had publicly denounced Clinton's sexual conduct. (Lieberman was the first Jew named to the presidential ticket of a major party.) In debates, Bush generally did better than expected, while Gore was caught in several exaggerations and misstatements that hurt his credibility. Nevertheless, as the election neared, dissatisfaction with both candidates prompted some voters to turn to Green Party candidate Ralph Nader, who argued for sweeping reform of the political system.

When the election was held on 7 November Gore won the popular vote by 540,000 votes, a mere five of every 1,000 cast. Meanwhile, Bush appeared to have won the electoral college by 271 to 266 votes, thus becoming the first president since 1892 to be elected without a plurality of the popular vote. The outcome, however, remained uncertain for thirty-six days because of the closeness of the vote in Florida, where only a few hundred votes separated the two candidates. The Democrats protested election irregularities, particularly involving punch-card voting, and demanded a manual recount in certain counties. Eventually, they took their case to the courts. The Florida Supreme Court initially ruled 4 to 3 in favor of allowing such a recount, but its decision was overturned by the U.S. Supreme Court in a controversial 5 to 4 ruling. The justices' decision in *Bush v. Gore* effectively ended the election and delivered the presidency to Bush. The election revealed problems with vote-counting machinery and procedures that disfranchised voters, and prompted some commentators to call for an end to the electoral college system.

BIBLIOGRAPHY

Ceaser, James W., and Andrew E. Busch, *The Perfect Tie: The True Story of the 2000 Presidential Election.* Lanham, Md: Rowman & Littlefield Publishers, Inc., 2001.

Deadlock: The Inside Story of America's Closest Election by the Political Staff of the Washington Post. New York: Public Affairs, Washington Post Co., 2001.

Jamieson, Kathleen Hall, and Paul Waldman, eds. *Electing the President, 2000.* Philadelphia: University of Pennsylvania Press, 2001.

Rakove, Jack, ed. *The Unfinished Election of 2000.* New York: Basic Books, 2001.

Wendy Wall

See also ***Bush v. Gore****; and vol. 9:* **Responses to Supreme Court Decision in *Bush v. Gore*.**

ELECTORAL COLLEGE. Created by the Constitutional Convention of 1787, the electoral college selects individuals for the U.S. presidency and vice presidency. It has been modified both by extra-constitutional developments, like the growth of political parties, and by constitutional amendments.

Origins and Procedures

Delegates to the U.S. Constitutional Convention divided the national government into legislative, executive, and judicial branches. This arrangement seemed incompatible with a system, like that in most parliamentary democracies, in which the majority party or coalition within the legislature selects the chief executive. Convention delegates were especially fearful that the legislature might exert undue influence on individuals who were seeking reelection. Some delegates favored electing the president by direct popular vote, but this was not particularly feasible at a time before computer technology, and delegates feared that many members of the public would not be familiar with candidates from states other than their own.

At the Constitutional Convention proponents of the Virginia Plan argued for a bicameral legislature, in which state representatives in both houses would be elected on the basis of population. Proponents of the New Jersey Plan favored maintaining the system of representation under the Articles of Confederation, in which states were represented equally. Delegates eventually resolved this issue with the Connecticut Compromise (also called the Great Compromise), which apportioned state representation according to population in the House of Representatives but then granted each state two votes in the Senate. This compromise also influenced the construction of the electoral college.

Outlined in Article II, Section 1 of the U.S. Constitution, this plan granted each state a number of electoral votes equal to its combined representation in the House and Senate. Each state would choose this number of electors, who would meet in their respective state capitals (a meeting that now occurs in December), cast two votes (at least one of which had to be for an out-of-state candidate), send the votes to the U.S. Congress, and disband. When the votes were opened in Congress (which now occurs in January), the individual receiving the majority of votes would become president and the runner-up would become vice president. If no individual received a majority—a situation many delegates at the Constitutional Convention thought would be the norm—the House of Representatives would choose the president and vice president from among the top five candidates, with each state delegation receiving a single vote. If the House tied on its choice for vice president, senators would make this selection.

This system worked relatively well in the first election of 1789, when, in an event never again repeated, George Washington was unanimously selected as president and John Adams was selected, over some competition, for vice president. However, the system did not work very well as political parties developed and candidates began running as a team. Thus, in the election of 1796, delegates chose Federalist John Adams as president and Democratic-Republican Thomas Jefferson as vice president. The results of the election of 1800 were even murkier. Although Jefferson beat Adams in the election for president, he tied in the electoral college with his party's putative vice president, Aaron Burr. Lame-duck Federalists had the chance to decide the election. It took thirty-six ballots before some Federalists abstained from voting and thus chose Jefferson as president over Burr, but the election had clearly pointed to a problem.

The Twelfth Amendment and After

To remedy this problem, the Twelfth Amendment (1804) mandated that electors cast separate votes for president and vice president, thus allowing those who voted for a party ticket to do so without worrying about a tie. If no one received a majority of the votes for president, the House, again voting by states, would choose from among the top three candidates. If no one received a majority of votes for the vice presidency, the Senate would choose from among the top two candidates. This has happened only once in U.S. history, when in 1837 the Senate chose Richard M. Johnson of Kentucky.

The revised electoral system did not avert controversy in the presidential election of 1824, which featured four main candidates, none of whom received a majority of electoral votes. Andrew Jackson, the well-liked hero of the War of 1812, received the largest number of popular votes. John Quincy Adams, son of the former president, received the next largest number of votes; Georgia's ailing William Crawford came in third; and Kentucky's Henry Clay was fourth. Clay threw his support in the House to Adams, who won the election and later appointed Clay as secretary of state. Jackson charged that a "corrupt bargain" had been struck and beat Adams in the next presidential election.

The Constitution left states free to select presidential electors as they chose, but over time all decided to choose such electors through popular elections. Voters further came to expect that electors would vote for the candidates to whom they were pledged rather than exercising their own individual judgments. Eventually, all states except for Maine and Nebraska adopted a "winner-take-all" system, whereby the individuals who won a majority of votes within a state received all of the state's electoral votes. This generally magnifies the winning margin, giving successful candidates a higher percentage of the electoral vote than of the popular vote. Such a system also advantages the third-party candidacies of individuals with strong regional appeal, like Strom Thurmond (1948) and George Wallace (1968), over those with broader but more widely diffused support, like Millard Fillmore (1856) and Ross Perot (1992).

On occasion, however, the two votes come into conflict. Republican Rutherford B. Hayes beat Democrat Samuel Tilden in the election of 1876 despite receiving fewer popular votes. Ballots were disputed in three key southern states. An electoral commission created by Congress and composed in part of Supreme Court justices, who, like others on the commission, voted a straight party line, gave all the disputed ballots to Hayes.

Similarly, in the election of 1888 Republican Benjamin Harrison won the electoral votes even though Democratic President Grover Cleveland outpolled him in popular votes. Despite other extremely close elections, in which delegations from one or two states sometimes held the balance, such an event was not repeated until the historic election of 2000. Republican George W. Bush eked out a narrow win in the electoral college over Democrat Albert Gore by claiming a similarly narrow win in the state of Florida, after the U.S. Supreme Court decided in *Bush v. Gore* (2000) that continuing recounts of votes in that state violated the equal protection clause of the Fourteenth Amendment.

Other Amendments

Several constitutional amendments, most notably the Fifteenth (1870), the Nineteenth (1920), and the Twenty-sixth (1971), have increased the number of citizens eligible to vote in presidential elections. By altering the date that new members of Congress are inaugurated, the Twentieth Amendment (1933) ensured that any decisions made by Congress in cases where no candidate receives a majority would be made by newly elected rather than lame-duck members; by moving the presidential inauguration forward, it also gave Congress far less time to resolve disputed elections. The Twenty-third Amendment (1961) further provided that representatives of the District of Columbia, who were previously unrepresented in the electoral college, would have votes equal to that of the smallest states (currently three), raising the total electoral votes to 538, of which 270 constitute a majority. Moreover, the Twenty-fifth Amendment (1967) provided for vice-presidential vacancies by establishing a mechanism whereby a majority vote of both houses of Congress would approve a candidate nominated by the president for such vacancies. To date, the mechanism has been used to appoint two vice presidents, Gerald Ford and Nelson Rockefeller, with Ford becoming the first unelected president in U.S. history when President Richard M. Nixon resigned from office in 1974.

Pros and Cons

Supporters generally praise the electoral college for bolstering the two major political parties. By giving them incentives to "carry" their state, the system forces candidates to pay special attention to populous states with strong two-party competition. Advocates of federalism favor the electoral college system, and some argue that it is easier to resolve close elections on a state-by-state basis than on a national one. Other supporters of the electoral college praise the mechanism for generally magnifying popular margins of support, giving winning candidates clearer mandates.

Critics of the electoral college generally focus on the complexity of what they label an antiquated system that sometimes awards the presidency and vice presidency to individuals who did not win the popular vote. Critics are not as united in their solutions, however. The most obvious and popular solution is direct popular election, with a runoff election if no candidate gets 40 percent or more of the vote. The U.S. House of Representatives proposed such an amendment by a vote of 338 to 70 in 1969, but in part because of concerns over the runoff election, the Senate twice killed it.

Other critics of the electoral college have focused on eliminating the occasional "faithless electors," who vote for individuals other than the ones to whom they are pledged by their state's popular vote. Still others have proposed awarding votes by individual congressional districts (with a state's two additional votes going to the winner of the state) or allocating such votes by percentages. Although presumably they would make the possibility less likely, both such systems could still result in an electoral college winner who did not capture a majority of the popular vote.

BIBLIOGRAPHY

Berns, Walter, ed. *After the People Vote: A Guide to the Electoral College.* Washington, D.C.: AEI Press, 1992.

Best, Judith A. *The Choice of the People? Debating the Electoral College.* Lanham, Md.: Rowman and Littlefield Publishers, 1996.

Dionne, E. J., and William Kristol, eds. *Bush v. Gore: The Court Cases and Commentary.* Washington, D.C.: Brookings Institution, 2001.

Kuroda, Tadahisa. *The Origins of the Twelfth Amendment: The Electoral College in the Early Republic, 1787-1804.* Westport, Conn.: Greenwood Press, 1994.

Longley, Lawrence D., and Neal R. Peirce. *The Electoral College Primer 2000.* New Haven, Conn.: Yale University Press, 1999.

Nelson, Michael, ed. *Guide to the Presidency.* 3d ed., 2 vols. Washington, D.C.: Congressional Quarterly, Inc., 2002.

Vile, John R. *A Companion to the United States Constitution and Its Amendments.* 3d ed. Westport, Conn.: Praeger, 2001.

John R. Vile

See also ***Bush v. Gore*****; Connecticut Compromise; Constitution of the United States; Corrupt Bargain.**

ELECTRIC POWER AND LIGHT INDUSTRY.

The social and economic impact of the electric power and light industry, which began its rapid development during the last quarter of the nineteenth century, has been so great that some refer to the twentieth century as the "Age of Electricity." Not only have such giant companies as General Electric and Westinghouse been associated with the rise of this industry—which has dramatically altered manufacturing methods, transportation, and the domestic environment—but thousands of local, municipal, and regional utility and manufacturing companies have also engaged in generating and distributing electricity, as well as in manufacturing, selling, and servicing electrical apparatus. The success of the electrical industry in supplanting older methods of providing illumination and mechanical power—such as the gaslight and the steam engine—was the result of the ease and economy with which companies could generate and transmit over long distances large quantities of electrical energy and then convert it into heat, light, or motion.

Although the electric power and light industry did not reach a level of commercial importance until near the end of the nineteenth century, there were notable related scientific and technological developments prior to 1875. One of the earliest electric motors developed in America was the "electrical jack," primarily a philosophical toy, described by Benjamin Franklin in 1749. Franklin and other colonial natural philosophers also commonly used triboelectric or frictional electrostatic generators. Following the announcement of the electrochemical battery by Count Alessandro Volta in 1800 and Hans Christian Oersted and André Marie Ampère's discovery in 1820 of the mechanical force that current-carrying conductors would exert on permanent magnets or other conductors, many investigators perceived that electricity might compete with the steam engine as a source of power in manufacturing and transportation. In 1831 the American Joseph Henry devised a small motor that produced a rocking motion and developed powerful electromagnets capable of lifting up to 3,600 pounds. Thomas Davenport, a Vermont blacksmith, built several electric direct-current rotary motors during the 1830s and used them to drive woodworking tools, a printing press, and a small "electric train." Charles G. Page of Washington, D.C., developed motors used to propel an experimental locomotive at speeds up to twenty miles per hour in 1851. Nevertheless, by the 1850s most observers recognized that the electric motor required a more efficient and inexpensive source of electrical energy than the battery before it could threaten the dominance of the steam engine.

An alternative to the voltaic battery as a source of electrical current had been available in principle since Michael Faraday's discovery of electromagnetic induction in 1831. This discovery led to the development of magnetogenerators, which converted mechanical motion into electricity. Joseph Saxton of Washington, D.C., produced an early magnetogenerator that was used in medical experiments and in electroplating during the 1840s. Magnetogenerators began to be used for arc lights in lighthouses after about 1850. Several major changes in the design of the magnetogenerator culminated in the invention of the more efficient self-excited generator, or dynamo, during the 1860s. The first commercially successful dynamo was that of the Belgian Zénobe T. Gramme. Used both as a generator and as a motor, the Philadelphia Centennial Exposition of 1876 prominently featured a Gramme dynamo built by William A. Anthony, a Cornell University professor, probably the first dynamo built in America. In the same year Thomas A. Edison established his famous laboratory at Menlo Park, New Jersey, which became the center for the creation of his incandescent light and power system.

The arc-lighting industry became the first sector of the electric light and power industry to achieve a substantial commercial success, largely replacing the gaslight industry for street lighting in urban areas. Charles F. Brush of Cleveland, Ohio, became the pioneer innovator in arc lighting in America. His first commercial installation was in Philadelphia in 1878, and several other cities, including San Francisco, soon adopted the Brush system. Numerous competitors soon entered the field, including Elihu Thomson's and E. J. Houston's Thomson-Houston Electric Company and Elmer A. Sperry's Sperry Electric Light, Motor and Car Brake Company, both founded in 1883. Thomson pioneered several improvements in arc lighting, including an automatic current regulator and a lightning arrester, and Sperry devised a current regulator and invented an automatic regulator of electrode spacing in the arc light. Sperry was also responsible for a spectacular installation of arc lights (1886) located at the top of a 300-foot tower on the Board of Trade Building in Chicago that could be seen from sixty miles away. The Thomson-Houston Company came to dominate the industry by 1890, with the number of arc lights in use growing to about 300,000 in 1895, by which time incandescent gas and electric lights both provided strong competition.

Edison and his associates at Menlo Park were largely responsible for the introduction of a successful incandescent lighting system. Edison already enjoyed a reputation as an inventor of telegraph instruments when he turned his attention to the problem of indoor electric lighting in 1878. The Edison Light Company attracted substantial financial support from J. P. Morgan and other investment bankers, who spent a half-million dollars before the Edison system achieved commercial success. After a study of the gaslight industry, Edison decided that a high-resistance lamp was necessary for the economical subdivision of electricity generated by a central station. A systematic search for a suitable lamp resulted in the carbon-filament high-vacuum lamp by late 1879. The Menlo Park team also developed a series of dynamos of unprecedented efficiency and power capacity, such as the "Jumbo Dynamo," which provided power for 1,200 lamps. The first public demonstration of the new system was held at Menlo Park on 31 December 1879, and the first commercial central station, located on Pearl Street in New York City, began operation in 1882. Three separate manufacturing companies produced lamps, dynamos, and transmission cables, but were combined in 1889 to form the Edison General Electric Company. The subsequent merger of this company with the Thomson-Houston Company in 1892 resulted in the General Electric Company. By the early 1880s electrical journals, regional and national societies devoted to electrical technology, national and international exhibitions of electrical apparatuses, and new academic programs in electrical science and engineering proliferated in recognition of the new industry's economic potential.

George Westinghouse pioneered the introduction of a competing incandescent lighting system using alternating current, which proved to have decisive advantages over the Edison direct-current system. A key element of the new system was the transformer, which increased a generator's voltage to any desired amount for transmission to remote points, where another transformer then reduced the voltage to a level suitable for lamps. This feature overcame the major limitation of the direct-current distribution system, which could provide energy economically only at distances of a mile or less from the generator. Westinghouse, who had considerable experience in manufacturing railway-signaling devices and in natural-gas distribution, organized the Westinghouse Electric Company in 1886 to begin the manufacture of transformers, alternators, and other alternating-current apparatus. Westinghouse opened the first commercial installation in Buffalo, New York, late in 1886. Shortly thereafter the Thomson-Houston Company entered the field and was Westinghouse's only serious competitor in America until the formation of General Electric. The advent of the Westinghouse alternating-current system precipitated the "battle of the systems," during which spokesmen of the Edison Company argued that alternating current was much more dangerous than direct current and even used Westinghouse generators to electrocute a convicted murderer in 1890. But the economic advantages of alternating current soon settled the matter. By 1892 more than five hundred alternating-current central stations operated in the United States alone, boosting the number of incandescent lamps in use to 18 million by 1902.

During the late 1880s, urban streetcar systems, which had previously depended on horses or cables, began to electrify their operations. Frank J. Sprague, a former Edison employee, organized the Sprague Electric Railway and Motor Company in 1884. Sprague had developed an efficient fifteen-horsepower direct-current motor by 1885 and obtained a contract to build a forty-car system in Richmond, Virginia, in 1887. The Richmond installation, which began operation the following year, became the prototype for the industry, which spread to all major American cities before the end of the century. The Westinghouse Company began to manufacture railway motors in 1890, followed by General Electric in 1892. These two companies soon dominated the field: Westinghouse had produced about twenty thousand railway motors by 1898, and General Electric, about thirty thousand. Sprague continued to improve his system and won the contract for the electrification of the South Side Elevated Railway in Chicago in 1897. His company was purchased by General Electric in 1902.

The next major innovation in electric motors and generators was the introduction of alternating-current machines during the 1890s. The Westinghouse Company acquired the strategic alternating-current motor patents of the Serbian immigrant Nikola Tesla and became the leading American firm in exploiting the new technology. In particular, the company developed practical alternating-current motors for use in interurban railroads and in industry. In 1891 the company installed a single-phase system to supply a hundred-horsepower motor near Telluride, Colorado, and built a large display at the 1893 World's Columbian Exposition in Chicago. In October of the same year, Westinghouse received the contract to construct the generating equipment for the famous Niagara Falls Power project. The project successfully generated an enormous amount of power and transmitted it up to twenty miles from the site, clearly establishing the superiority of alternating current for hydroelectric power and opening the prospect that previously inaccessible sites might be exploited. The availability of cheap electric power at Niagara stimulated the rapid growth of a number of energy-intensive electrochemical industries in the vicinity. The growth of the alternating-current power and lighting industry also stimulated the work of Charles P. Steinmetz, who joined the General Electric Company as an electrical engineer in 1893 and who presented a classic paper on the use of complex algebra in alternating-current analysis at the International Electrical Congress in Chicago the same year. He also formulated a law of magnetic hysteresis that became a basis for the rational design of transformers and alternators.

Sidney B. Paine of General Electric was responsible for the first major use of alternating-current motors in industry. He persuaded the owners of a new textile factory in Columbia, South Carolina, to abandon the traditional system of belting and shafting powered by giant steam engines in favor of textile machines using polyphase induction motors. In this instance the constant speed of the motors was a distinct advantage, and the new system soon spread throughout the industry. Direct-current motors remained in wide use in applications requiring variable speed, such as in steel mills and in machine tooling. By 1909 almost 250,000 industrial motors were being manufactured per year, more than half of the alternating-current type. Nearly every industry in the country had installed electric motors by the beginning of World War I.

One of the most significant events in the history of the electric light and power industry was the introduction of high-speed turboelectric generators in central power stations during the first decade of the twentieth century. By 1900 the unit capacity of alternators driven by the reciprocating steam engine had reached a practical limit of around five thousand kilowatts with giant thirty-foot rotors weighing up to two hundred tons and driven at speeds of around seventy-five revolutions per minute. The new turbogenerators were much more compact for the same capacity and could be built for much greater output power. However, the higher speeds of the turbogenerators (up to two thousand revolutions per minute) necessitated the use of stronger materials, such as nickel-steel alloys, that could withstand the increased mechanical stresses. New rotor designs were also necessary to reduce air resistance and improve ventilation. Both Westinghouse and General Electric decided to manufacture their own turbines based on the patents of C. A. Parsons and G. G. Curtis, respectively. General Electric built the first large commercial installation, a five-thousand-kilowatt unit, for the Commonwealth Edison Company of Chicago in 1903. In 1909 the company replaced it with a twelve-thousand-kilowatt turbogenerator. Of the 1.8 million kilowatts of turbogenerator capacity installed by 1908, 56 percent was manufactured by General Electric, 33 percent by Westinghouse, and 11 percent by the newcomer Allis-Chalmers Company of Milwaukee.

Turboelectric generators made possible significant economies of scale, making it more economical for most consumers to purchase electric power from central generating stations than to install their own isolated generating plants. The history of the turbogenerator since 1910 has been one of steady increase in the maximum size of units and a concomitant reduction in the consumption of fuel per unit of energy generated.

Another "battle of the systems" broke out in the first two decades of the twentieth century—this time between steam and electric locomotives. In this case the older steam technology won out. Most of the electrified interurban transportation operated in areas having high population density or requiring tunnels, where the smoke from steam locomotives presented problems. The mileage of "electrified track" jumped from 250 in 1905 to about 3,000 in 1914. After a fairly rapid growth in track mileage during the period 1904–1908, alternating-current rail systems plateaued until the electrification of the New York–Washington, D.C., line of the Pennsylvania Railroad during the 1930s. In contrast, the steam railroad mileage increased steadily at the rate of about six thousand miles per year from 1900 to the beginning of World War I, reaching a total of about 260,000 miles in 1912. The steam locomotive was supplanted during the period 1930–1960 by the diesel-electric locomotive, in which the power for the electric drive motors was locally generated by diesel-powered electric generators. Developments in power electronics since 1950 have created a renewed interest in electric locomotives powered from remote central stations.

Another major trend in the electric power industry during the twentieth century has been toward higher transmission voltages, which increase the distances over which electrical energy can be transmitted economically. The introduction of the suspension insulator in 1906 soon enabled transmission voltages of the order of 100 kilovolts to become common. The adoption of 345 kilovolts as a standard transmission line voltage in the 1950s made feasible transmission distances of more than three hundred miles. Coincident with the development of techniques that have made possible the production of large quantities of electrical energy at a single location and its efficient transmission over high-voltage lines was a rising concern for the conservation of nonrenewable resources, such as coal. This concern, which crested just prior to World War I, led to the formulation of a policy for the rational development of the nation's hydroelectric power resources. This policy was articulated by conservationists—notably Gifford Pinchot and W. J. McGee—and supported by leading engineers. Numerous privately and publicly owned hydroelectric power projects, especially in the South and West, implemented their program, including the well-known impoundments built by the Tennessee Valley Authority (TVA) beginning during the 1930s.

The growth of hydroelectric generating stations and the realization by Samuel Insull and others in the electric utility industry that even further economies could be achieved through the creation of power "pools" or "superpower systems" led to a consolidation movement beginning around 1910. Insull, who was already president of the Commonwealth Electric Company of Chicago, organized the Middle West Utilities Company as a combination of several smaller plants in 1912. After World War I, Insull established a utilities empire financed by the sale of holding-company stock to the public. By 1930 the Insull-managed power companies had become a giant in the industry with assets of more than $2 billion while producing approximately 10 percent of the nation's electric power. When the stock market crash ruined Insull financially and led to his indictment for mail fraud and embezzlement, it discredited the electric light and power industry and helped provide the rationale for the TVA experiment.

The impact of industrial research laboratories on the power and light industry was especially evident just prior to World War I, when scientists such as W. R. Whitney, W. D. Coolidge, and Irving Langmuir of the General Electric Research Laboratory, which had been organized in 1900, played a leading role. This group was responsible for the development of the famous Mazda series of gas-filled tungsten-filament lamps, which quickly supplanted the carbon-filament vacuum lamps and enabled the production of lamps in a range of sizes with unprecedented efficiency. Lamp production increased enormously following these innovations, and by 1925 more than 14 million residential homes had been wired for electricity. Other domestic uses of electricity developed during the 1920s, including electric stoves, refrigerators, irons, and washing machines. The establishment of the Rural Electrification Administration in the 1930s accelerated the spread of power lines into areas of low population density: the U.S. consumption of electric energy reached 65 billion kilowatt-hours in 1924, approximately equal to that of the rest of the world combined, and the output of the electric power industry doubled each decade through most of the twentieth century. The cost of electrical energy provided for residential purposes declined steadily from an average of 16.2 cents per kilowatt-hour in 1902 to 2.3 cents in 1964.

American energy consumption continued to expand, and prices remained low until 1973, when an oil embargo set off a worldwide energy crisis that sent the cost of energy soaring. The electric utility industry responded by steadily reducing the percentage of oil-fired generators from 16 or 17 percent in the 1960s and early 1970s to only 2 percent in 1997. Retail prices for electricity remained high through the early 1980s, when they began a steady decline (in real dollars) through the next two decades. Gas-fired, coal-fired, and nuclear generators have accounted for the bulk of the difference between declining oil-generated electricity and growing energy consumption.

Nuclear generators had received their start in 1954, when the federal government launched a development program that resulted in an installation located in Shippingport, Pennsylvania, which began generating electric power in 1957. By the beginning of the 1980s, the United States had more than a hundred nuclear power plants in operation—almost exactly the same number as in 1999, and far less than the thousand reactors that some early projections suggested would be needed by the end of the century. The turning point for nuclear energy production came in 1979, when a serious accident at Three Mile Island caused public support for nuclear energy to plummet from 70 percent before the accident to only 43 percent in 1999. Although no new orders for commercial nuclear reactors have been made since the incident at Three Mile Island, existing nuclear generators have greatly improved their output, raising the national capacity factor from under 65 percent through the 1970s and 1980s to 76 percent in 1996.

One of the more significant new chapters in the electric power and light industry opened on 31 March 1998, when California deregulated its electric industry. The experiment, hailed by some as a boon to consumers, sent power prices skyrocketing in 2000, when shortages began to mount, prompting the state to reregulate the industry in 2001. Then, in 2002, following the collapse and bankruptcy of the energy giant Enron, the public was stunned by revelations that its energy traders had used various strategems to create artificial energy shortages to push prices up in California.

BIBLIOGRAPHY

Adams, Stephen B. *Manufacturing the Future.* New York: Cambridge University Press, 1999.

Kranzberg, Melvin, and Carroll W. Pursell, Jr. *Technology in Western Civilization.* New York: Oxford University Press, 1967.

Passer, Harold C. *The Electrical Manufacturers.* Cambridge, Mass.: Harvard University Press, 1953.

Schurr, Sam H., ed. *Electricity in the American Economy.* New York: Greenwood Press, 1990.

Silverberg, Robert. *Light for the World.* Princeton, N.J.: Van Nostrand, 1967.

James E. Brittain / c. w.

See also **Deregulation; Electricity and Electronics; Electrification, Household; Energy Industry; Hydroelectric Power; Industrial Research; Lamp, Incandescent; Lighting; Nuclear Power; Railways, Urban, and Rapid Transit; Steam Power and Engines; Tennessee Valley Authority;** *and vol. 9:* **Power.**

ELECTRICAL WORKERS. The United Electrical, Radio, and Machine Workers of America (UE) began as an outgrowth of an organizational drive among Philadelphia Philco plant workers in July 1933. That year, Philco agreed to a contract with the American Federation of Radio Workers that provided for an eight-hour day, a minimum wage, premium pay for overtime, and a forty-hour workweek. The American Federation of Labor (AFL) shortly thereafter chartered the union as a federal local, and it subsequently expanded its organization to workers in other companies. For the next three years, the federal locals sought to organize workers along industrial lines, an idea that conflicted with AFL craft unionism. In March 1936, union leaders of locals at General Electric (GE), Westinghouse, Philco, RCA, and Delco (the electrical division of the General Motors Corporation) manufacturing plants merged and formed the UE, which the newly founded Congress of Industrial Organizations (CIO) soon chartered.

UE leadership represented three distinct tendencies within the labor movement. Heading the branch of electrical workers principally organized at GE and Westinghouse were Alfred Coulthard and Julius Emspak, both of whom espoused socialism and communism. The radical organizer and New Deal supporter James Matles led machinist locals from the Delco plants into the UE, while James Carey, a Catholic anticommunist, represented the old federal locals of the radio plants of Philco and RCA. And, although Carey became the UE's first president, the union's approach to organizing was inclusive and militant as it sought equal wages for men and women.

By the end of 1941, UE membership had increased to 300,000, despite the persistence of ideological factionalism among its leaders and jurisdictional conflict with the International Brotherhood of Electrical Workers (IBEW). Employers and the AFL-affiliated IBEW collaborated to stop the UE from organizing plants until the UE filed suit against the IBEW under the National Labor Relations Act (NLRA).

While the UE locals held the line on wages during World War II and supported boosts in productivity, the postwar years witnessed a concerted effort by the union to improve wages in the larger plants. By 1946, UE membership had reached 650,000, and the union waged its first national strike against GE, Westinghouse, and Delco. The union's success in obtaining significant wage increases led to corporation and media charges that UE leadership was communist dominated.

The 1947 Taft-Hartley Act escalated the controversy when the CIO and the UE refused to comply with the legislation's section requiring union officers to sign noncommunist affidavits. The charged political atmosphere facilitated constant raiding of the UE by the United Steelworkers of America and the United Auto Workers (UAW). Simultaneously, the CIO refused to grant the UE a no-raiding agreement and acquiesced to signing noncommunist affidavits. When the UE quit paying CIO dues and refused to send delegates to its 1949 convention, the CIO officially expelled the UE for communist domination. In the process, the CIO formed the competing International Union of Electrical, Radio, and Machine Workers (IUE), headed by James Carey. For the remainder of the decade, the IUE, operating within the context of Cold War politics, registered success in raiding dozens of UE locals, especially at the General Motors Delco manufacturing plants.

While UE membership dwindled to near 100,000 as a result of raiding, the McCarthy era heightened the attacks on the UE for alleged communist domination. In 1955 the U.S. Justice Department charged the UE with communist infiltration. After UE elected officials finally agreed to sign noncommunist affidavits, the Justice Department dropped the charges and the courts granted the union's request to prevent charges of communist domination from being brought against the UE in the future.

By the mid-1960s, raiding of the UE by other unions had ceased, largely due to plant shutdowns and the beginnings of what became known as the "rust belt" phenomenon. Within this context, the UE and IUE had no choice but to bury the hatchet and cooperate. Cooperation began in 1966, when the two unions coordinated a strike against GE. In 1969–1970, during another strike against GE, the UE and IUE joined up with the Teamsters to coordinate bargaining, and GE finally agreed to a negotiated settlement, its first in more than twenty years. But multiple plant closings in the 1970s had reduced UE membership in the 1980s to around 80,000.

Since the advent of the North American Free Trade Agreement (NAFTA) in 1994, the UE, in cooperation with the Teamsters, has been a pioneer in cross-border solidarity and organizing with Mexican unions, especially the Frente Auténtico del Trabajo (Authentic Labor Front, or FAT). The cooperation focused on advocacy of labor rights for workers employed in U.S. runaway shops located on the Mexican side of the border. Unlike most American unions, which belonged to the AFL-CIO, the UE remained independent and elected its national union officers by a vote of the full membership. In 2000, the UE's endorsement of Ralph Nader for president reflected its ongoing independent and radical political tradition.

BIBLIOGRAPHY

Hathaway, Dale A. *Allies Across the Border: Mexico's "Authentic Labor Front" and Global Solidarity.* Cambridge, Mass.: South End Press, 2000.

Matles, James J., and James Higgins. *Them and Us: Struggle of a Rank and File Union.* Englewood Cliffs, N.J.: Prentice Hall, 1974.

Schatz, Ronald W. *The Electrical Workers: A History of Labor at General Electric and Westinghouse, 1923–1960.* Urbana: University of Illinois Press, 1983.

Zieger, Robert. *The CIO, 1935–1955.* Chapel Hill: University of North Carolina Press, 1995.

Norman Caulfield

See also **American Federation of Labor–Congress of Industrial Organizations; Taft-Hartley Act.**

ELECTRICITY AND ELECTRONICS. In December 1879 Thomas Alva Edison and his associates invited the public to their work site in Menlo Park, New Jersey. People from New York and elsewhere gathered to see what they had never seen before—buildings and grounds illuminated with about 100 electric incandescent lamps.

By the time of Edison's Menlo Park demonstration, much had already been discovered about electricity. The Italian scientist Alessandro Volta had invented the electric battery, and the English scientist Michael Faraday had created a generator using magnetism to produce electricity. Even the idea of electric lighting was not new.

Various scientists and inventors in different parts of the world were working to develop forms of electric lighting, but until that time nothing had been developed that was practical for home use. Commercial and street lighting were powered by gas and carbon-arc systems. The latter produced an extremely bright light by sending electricity across a gap between two carbon terminals.

By contrast, an incandescent lamp produced a much less intense light by passing electricity through a filament, or wire, which would then glow. But what was the best filament to use? Edison and his associates spent months searching. They first experimented with a platinum filament, but this metal was quick to overheat and burn out. Success finally came when they tested a carbon filament made from burned sewing thread and improved the vacuum inside the bulb. The carbonized sewing thread burned for thirteen and a half hours and was used in their public demonstration. Later, they made bulbs with bamboo filaments, which extended the life of the bulbs even further.

At first, Edison's electric light was a mere novelty because few homes and businesses had electricity. To make his invention practical for everyday use, electricity had to be readily available to customers. Edison spent the next several years creating the electric industry, a system of producing electricity in central power plants and distributing it over wires to homes and businesses. Before long, electrical power would spread around the world.

What Is Electricity?

Electricity, a form of energy, occurs from the flow of electrons, or negatively charged particles. The number of electrons in an atom usually equals the number of protons, or positively charged particles. When this balance is upset, such as when two distinct surfaces are rubbed together, an atom may gain or lose an electron. The resulting free movement of a "lost" electron is what creates an electric current.

The phenomenon of electricity had been observed, though not understood, by ancient Greeks around 600 B.C. They found that by rubbing amber, a fossilized resin, against a fur cloth, they could create a tiny spark. In 1752 Benjamin Franklin proved that electricity is a basic part of nature and that lightning and the spark from amber were one and the same. He did this, in his now famous experiment, by fastening a wire to a silk kite and flying it during a thunderstorm. Franklin held the end of the kite string by an iron key. When a bolt of lightning struck the wire, it traveled down the kite string to the key and caused a spark.

Not only did Franklin prove that lightning was electricity, he theorized that electricity was a type of fluid that attracted or repulsed materials—an idea that continues to help scientists describe and understand the basics of electricity.

Generating Electricity

While electricity is a form of energy, it is not an energy source. It is not harvested or mined; it must be manufactured. Electricity comes from the conversion of other sources of energy, such as coal, natural gas, oil, nuclear power, solar power, and others. And because it is not easily stored in quantity, electricity must be manufactured at or near the time of demand.

In 1881 Edison and his associates moved to New York City to promote the construction of electric power plants in cities. They invested in companies that manufactured products—generators, power cables, electric lamps, and lighting fixtures—that were needed for a com-

Thomas Alva Edison. A portrait of the extraordinary, exceptionally prolific inventor, c. 1904. GETTY IMAGES

mercially successful electric lighting system. They also built the Pearl Street Station, a steam electric power plant near Wall Street. On 4 September 1882, this power plant began providing light and power to customers in a one-square-mile area.

A model of efficiency for its time, Pearl Street used one-third the fuel of its predecessors, burning about ten pounds of coal per kilowatt-hour, a unit of electric power equal to the work done by one kilowatt acting for one hour. Initially the Pearl Street utility served fifty-nine customers for about twenty-four cents per kilowatt-hour.

In the late 1880s power demand for electric motors brought the industry from mainly nighttime lighting to twenty-four-hour service. Soon, small central stations dotted many U.S. cities. However, each was limited to an area of only a few blocks because of transmission inefficiencies of direct current (DC).

A breakthrough came in 1888 when the Serbian-born American Nikola Tesla discovered the principles of alternating current (AC), a type of electric current that reverses direction at regular intervals and uses transformers to transmit large blocks of electrical power at high voltages. (Voltage refers to the pressure or force that causes electrons to move.) Tesla went on to patent a motor that generated AC. Around the turn of the twentieth century, it was clear that the future of electricity in this country and elsewhere lay with AC rather than DC.

The first commercial electric power plant to use AC began operating in the United States in 1893. Built by the Redlands Electric Light and Power Company, the Mill Creek plant in California transmitted power 7.5 miles away to the city of Redlands. The electricity was used for lighting and for running a local ice house.

Two years later, on 26 August 1895, water flowing over Niagara Falls was diverted through two high-speed turbines connected to two 5,000-horsepower AC generators. Initially, local manufacturing plants used most of the electricity. But before long, electricity was being transmitted twenty miles to Buffalo, where it was used for lighting and for streetcars.

This new source of energy had so many practical applications that it greatly changed the way people lived. Inventors and scientists developed electric devices that enabled people to communicate across great distances and to process information quickly. The demand for electric energy grew steadily during the 1900s.

The technical aspects of the generation and transmission of electricity continued to evolve, as did the electric utility industry. Clearly, large-scale power plants and the electricity they produced were major forces that shaped life in twentieth-century America.

Electronics

The world's reliance on electronics is so great that commentators claim people live in an "electronic age." People are surrounded by electronics—televisions, radios, computers, and DVD players, along with products with major electric components, such as microwave ovens, refrigerators, and other kitchen appliances, as well as hearing aids and medical instruments.

A branch of physics, electronics deals with how electrons move to create electricity and how that electric signal is carried in electric products. An electric signal is simply an electric current or voltage modified in some way to represent information, such as sound, pictures, numbers, letters, or computer instructions. Signals can also be used to count objects, to measure time or temperature, or to detect chemicals or radioactive materials.

Electronics depend on certain highly specialized components, such as transistors and integrated circuits, which are part of almost every electronic product. These devices can manipulate signals extremely quickly; some can respond to signals billions of times per second. They are also extremely tiny. Manufacturers create millions of these microscopic electronic components on a piece of material—called a chip or a microchip—that is no larger than a fingernail. Designing and producing microscopic electronic components is often referred to as microelectronics or nanotechnology.

The development, manufacture, and sales of electronic products make up one of the largest and most important industries in the world. The electronics industry is also one of the fastest growing of all industries. The United States and Japan are the world's largest producers of electronic components and products. In the mid-1990s, electronics companies in the United States had sales that totaled more than $250 billion. During the same period, Japanese firms had sales that totaled more than $200 billion in U.S. dollars.

Areas of Impact

Communication. Electronic communication systems connect people around the world. Using telephones and computers, people in different countries communicate almost instantly. Radios transmit sounds and televisions transmit sounds and pictures great distances. Cellular telephones enable a person to call another person while riding in a car, walking down the street, or hiking in the woods. Within seconds, fax machines send and receive copies of documents over telephone lines.

Information processing. Scientists, artists, students, government and business workers, and hobbyists at home all rely on computers to handle huge amounts of information quickly and accurately. Computers solve difficult mathematical problems, maintain vast amounts of data, create complex simulations, and perform a multitude of other tasks that help people in their everyday lives. Many computer users also have instant access to the Internet, which offers a wide variety of information and other features.

Medicine and research. Physicians use a variety of electronic instruments and machines to diagnose and treat disorders. For example, X-ray machines use radiation to take images of bones and internal organs. The radiation is produced in a type of electronic vacuum tube. Radiation therapy, or radiotherapy, uses X-rays and other forms of radiation to fight cancer. Many hearing-impaired people depend on hearing aids to electrically amplify sound waves.

Computers and other electronic instruments provide scientists and other researchers with powerful tools to better understand their area of study. Computers, for example, help scientists design new drug molecules, track weather systems, and test theories about how galaxies and stars develop. Electron microscopes use electrons rather than visible light to magnify specimens 1 million times or more.

Automation. Electronic components enable many common home appliances, such as refrigerators, washing machines, and toasters, to function smoothly and efficiently. People can electronically program coffeemakers, lawn sprinklers, and many other products to turn on and off automatically. Microwave ovens heat food quickly by penetrating it with short radio waves produced by a vacuum tube.

Many automobiles have electronic controls in their engines and fuel systems. Electronic devices also control air bags, which inflate to protect a driver and passengers in a collision.

Lighting—Beyond Edison

Edison's carbonized sewing thread and bamboo filaments were not used in incandescent bulbs for long. Around 1910, chemists at the General Electric Company developed a much improved filament material—tungsten. This metal offered many advantages over its predecessors—a higher melting point, a tensile strength greater than steel, a much brighter light, and it could easily be shaped into coils. So good was tungsten that it is still used in incandescent lightbulbs. But today, incandescent lightbulbs are not the only option for consumers. Other lighting choices include fluorescent and halogen lamps. Fluorescent lamps produce light by passing electricity through mercury vapor, causing the fluorescent coating to glow. This type of light is common outdoors and in industrial and commercial uses. Another type of incandescent lamp, called halogen, produces light using a halogen gas, such as iodine or bromine, that causes the evaporating tungsten to be returned to the filament. Halogen bulbs are often used in desk and reading lamps. They can last up to four times longer than other incandescent bulbs.

BIBLIOGRAPHY

Gibilisco, Stan. *Teach Yourself Electricity and Electronics.* 3rd ed. New York: McGraw-Hill, 2002.

Horowitz, Paul, and Winfield Hill. *The Art of Electronics.* 2nd ed. New York: Cambridge University Press, 1989.

Institute of Electrical and Electronics Engineers, Inc. Home page at http://www.ieee.com.

Kaiser, Joe. *Electrical Power: Motors, Controls, Generators, Transformers.* Tinley Park, Ill.: Goodheart-Willcox, 1998.

Ryan, Charles William. *Basic Electricity: A Self-Teaching Guide.* 2nd ed. New York: Wiley, 1986.

Singer, Bertrand B., Harry Forster, and Mitchell E. Schultz. *Basic Mathematics for Electricity and Electronics.* 8th ed. New York: Glencoe/McGraw-Hill, 2000.

Timp, Gregory, ed. *Nanotechnology.* New York: Springer Verlag, 1999.

United States Navy. *Basic Electricity.* Mineola, N.Y.: Dover, 1975.

Van Valkenburgh, Nooger. *Basic Electricity: Complete Course.* 5 vols. Clifton Park, N.Y.: Delmar, 1995.

Lynda DeWitt

See also **Energy Industry; Lighting.**

ELECTRIFICATION, HOUSEHOLD. The electrification of the American household was a complicated social and technological phenomenon. The basic scientific knowledge dated to the early nineteenth century; but this knowledge could find no practical application until a number of economic, industrial, and social prerequisites

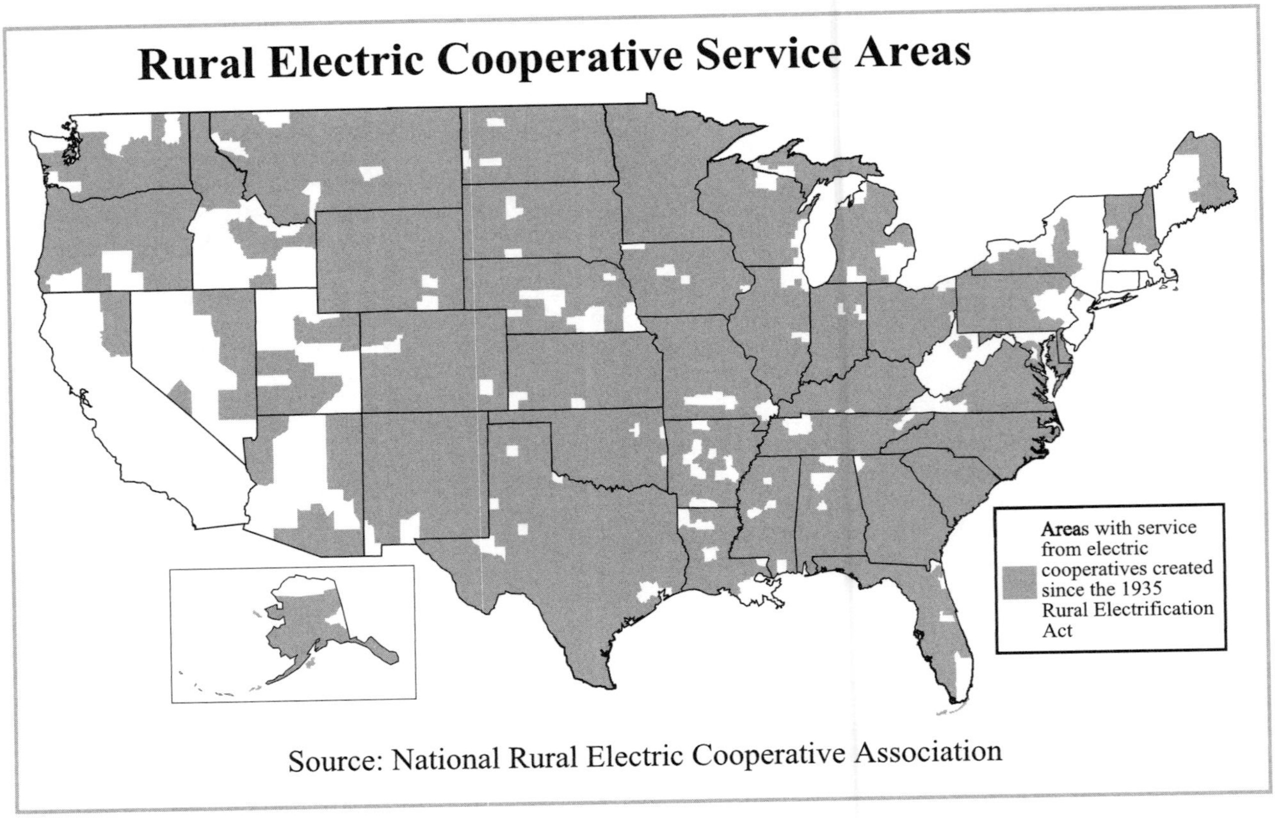

had been established. As early as 1832, an Englishman named William Sturgeon established the principle of converting electric energy into mechanical energy. But no commercial domestic-service motors were available until about 1895, when they first began to appear in fans and sewing machines. Similarly, the scientific principle of converting electricity into heat preceded its practical domestic implementation by more than a hundred years: not until the 1890s did electric irons, coffee makers, and toasters become available. Furthermore, many of the mechanical inventions of the twentieth century, including the washing machine, vacuum cleaner, dishwasher, and the electric range, were actually developed in the 1850s or 1860s.

Electricity became commercially available in America in the 1880s, as incandescent lighting began to brighten homes. The telephone followed, and together they set the stage for the development of electrified housework. However, certain barriers delayed the implementation of the developing technology until about 1920. Utility companies were not ready to make the substantial investments in infrastructure needed to meet the demand for industrial power and domestic lighting. Moreover, many utilities had complementary interests in supplying gas for home cooking and heating; the changeover to electrical heating seemed to threaten previous investments. Only gradually did it become clear to the utilities that the morning and evening power needs of households complemented perfectly the peak loads supplied to industry. The second major obstacle was the conservative attitude of American consumers. Electricity was initially considered "unnatural"; its proponents were obligated to alter the popular imagination through advertising and public relations campaigns. In addition, the first electrical appliances were prohibitively expensive to purchase and operate. For example, the first Frigidaire refrigerator cost $750 in 1920. Finally, the early appliances were unreliable and short-lived. Electric motors in the 1920s had one-tenth the life expectancy of their early twenty-first century counterparts.

The demand for electrical appliances and industrial sales soared after World War I. The remaining technological barriers to mass use gradually disappeared, but there were other factors, both ideological and economic. Middle-class aspirations emerged as a powerful factor in favor of electrical appliances. As far back as the mid-nineteenth century, social commentators like Catharine Esther Beecher and her sister, Harriet Beecher Stowe, championed the ideal of a self-reliant nuclear family structure among the middle and upper middle classes, one that made women the center of the bourgeois home's spiritual and emotional life. Resident domestic servants did not fit well into this scheme. Domestic handbooks counseled women to become more efficient homemakers and thus make domestic servants unnecessary through careful study and application of "domestic science." Household electrification seemed consistent with this emerging ideal of domestic efficiency. Electric doorbells emulated a feature associated with the largest mansions, even without a butler; electric Christmas-tree lights emerged as a safe alternative to candles. Meanwhile, feminists identified the potential of electrified washers and vacuums to free middle-class women from the oppressive drudgery of domestic work. Other critics of the industrial system hoped that household electrification would undermine the hegemony of the factory and return the American economy to an earlier era of home crafts and industries.

More directly than domestic ideals or anti-industrial ideology, the economic and political consequences of America's involvement in World War I accelerated the introduction of electrical appliances into households. Indeed, the War Industries Board recognized the importance of electricity by giving the appliance industry a high priority when it allocated labor and materials. During the war immigration was drastically reduced, and the chief source of cheap domestic labor—European immigrants—was cut off. Then, too, war allocations constrained consumer demand for durable goods; the release of this pent-up demand after the war greatly benefited the appliance industries. In particular housing starts, which increased at record rates after 1918, provided the occasion for modern electrical wiring and up-to-date electrical appliances to be included in mortgage packages. Many of these new houses were located in what historians describe as the "streetcar suburbs," residential subdivisions outside of cities made accessible by the growing network of interurban trains—powered, not coincidentally, by electricity. By World War I, also, the technology of the electric light, the telephone, the telegraph, and the streetcar had developed a large pool of skilled electrical workers in the United States. Thus, all of the factors necessary for the electrification of American households were in balance.

Technological developments brought household appliances within the reach of most middle-class Americans. Two crucial advances came with the invention of a low-cost, nondegradable electrical resistance and the perfection of a high-speed, fractional-horsepower electric motor.

Electric heat had interested scientists for many years before it became commercially practical. Its status began to change from that of a philosophical toy to that of possible practicality during the 1890s, when it became conspicuous at expositions and international trade fairs. Perhaps the first public exhibit of electrical cooking was at the International Exposition in Vienna in 1883, when a spiral of platinum was used to boil water. But probably the most spectacular display was that of an all-electric kitchen—including electric frying pan, coffee percolator, toaster, and dishwasher—at the World's Columbian Exposition in Chicago in 1893.

Platinum resistance was the earliest used in electrical heating appliances. Its high melting point and resistance to chemical degradation from oxidation made platinum ideal for long-term performances; but its price made it impractical for general use. About 1892, nickel-steel alloys began to be used widely. These could endure temperatures greater than a thousand degrees Fahrenheit, but the enamel used to prevent oxidation was fragile and prone to shattering. In 1904 the Simplex Electric Heating Company introduced a patented method of embedding and sealing the heating element into the appliance itself.

Two years later A. L. Marsh patented the Nichrome wire resistor, and this discovery became the foundation of all subsequent electrical heating apparatuses. Marsh's nickel-chromium alloy had a high electrical resistance, a very high melting point, and little susceptibility to oxidation; furthermore, it was economical to produce. George Hughes built the first electric range using the Marsh resistance and demonstrated it at the National Electric Light Association exhibit in Saint Louis in 1910. Hughes made his first sale the following year. By 1914, at least seven major firms were manufacturing cooking and heating appliances under the Marsh patent.

Throughout the 1920s, the Hotpoint Division of General Electric continued to innovate in electric range development. In 1922 it pioneered a process for reducing stress in the metal chassis of electric ranges so that a durable porcelain finish could be applied. In 1926 Hotpoint introduced the Calrod element, which further protected the resistance from chemical degradation and gave it a greater mechanical support. In the late 1920s manufacturers introduced the third wire connection, allowing a more even balance of household loads of voltage and began to increase the wattage of electric ranges to reduce warm-up time.

The second major technological advance was the creation of a practical, high-speed, fractional-horsepower electric motor. Westinghouse built the earliest fractional-horsepower alternating-current motors in the 1890s, based on the engineering designs of Nikola Tesla; but most of these units were dedicated to industrial purposes and lacked sufficient speed. In 1909 C. H. Hamilton designed and began to produce a reliable fractional-horsepower motor that produced eight thousand to ten thousand revolutions per minute, a significant advance. In 1913 General Electric widened the field with a motor especially designed to power washing machines.

In the 1910s and 1920s the dolly agitator emerged as the preferred design for mass-produced electric washing machines. Early dolly agitators consisted of a wooden, stationary tub and an agitator resembling a three-legged stool that thrashed about its axis and moved up and down. In the early 1920s the Maytag Company made a significant advance by giving its agitator a propeller shape. This propeller concept was soon widely imitated within the

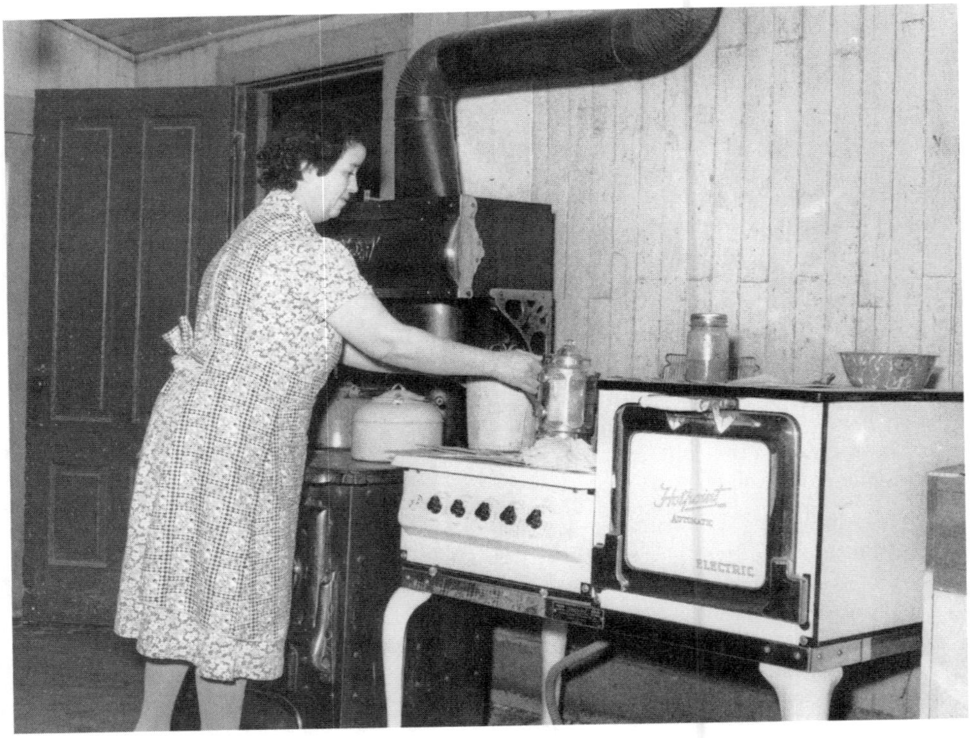

Electrification. Russell Lee's 1940 photograph shows a farmer's wife using an electric stove—but not giving up her older wood- or coal-burning type next to it, common practice where electric rates were high—in her home near Auburn, Calif., west of Lake Tahoe. LIBRARY OF CONGRESS

industry. James B. Kirby, of Cleveland, Ohio, experimented with a centrifugal dryer innovation that quickly displaced the wringer as a permanent fixture of the home laundry. The tub evolved from a basic wooden construction, through galvanized iron, copper, and dark blue cobalt enamels that had a high chemical affinity for the iron tubs, to colored enamels and acrylic finishes by the 1970s. Rex Bassett and John W. Chamberlain invented the automatic washer in 1932. The first Bendix automatic washer appeared five years later; it washed, soaked, rinsed, and spun dry the clothes with only one setting of the controls.

The earliest domestic refrigerator was patented in 1908 by Marcel Audiffron and Henry Stengrum. General Electric bought the patent in 1911, but its development was delayed for six years by technical problems. Fred D. Wolf made an independent start on the design of a smaller, practical domestic refrigerator, and in 1914 sold his first model. The condensation of the ammonia coolant required very high pressure; breaks in the coils were frequent and extremely irritating. Wolf's patents changed hands several times, until they were bought in 1920 by Frigidaire, a subsidiary of General Motors.

E. J. Copeland and A. H. Goss pioneered domestic refrigerator technology. They formed the Electro-Automatic Refrigerator Company in 1914 and built their first model that same year. Two years later, the company reorganized to sell its first sulfur-dioxide refrigerated machine under the name of Kelvinator. For many years Kelvinator specialized in converting iceboxes into electrically refrigerated units by building compressors, condensers, and evaporators into the iceboxes. But sulfur dioxide is extremely irritating to the nose and throat when it is inhaled. This was a serious drawback, since it was impossible to make the pressure-proof connections airtight, especially in the compressor shaft seal, with the rather crude machine tools of the day. In 1935 Kelvinator introduced a hermetically sealed compressor. In 1936, Thomas Midgley, Jr., discovered a new synthetic refrigerant with an almost ideal set of physical properties: Freon was odorless, not toxic, and a very good refrigerant. It soon replaced sulfur dioxide as a coolant.

David D. Kenney patented a vacuum cleaner to clean railroad cars in 1902. All subsequent vacuum cleaners were manufactured under his patent. Kenney's proprietary claim would have been voided if the U.S. Patent Office had researched the 1859 McCarthy patent, which covered all aspects of the modern vacuum cleaner except the electric power source. But it was the great marketing success of W. H. Hoover, beginning in 1907, that made vacuum cleaning widely accepted. Murray Spander designed the rolling vacuum cleaner with its broom handle and dust bag. In 1910 Skinner and Chapman in San Fransisco had added a semiportable tank cleaner, based on the commercial design of a wagon-mounted house-to-house cleaning facility.

The structure of the home appliance industry has altered radically since its beginnings in the 1910s, when many small manufacturers specializing in a specific type of appliance predominated in the industry. During the first half of the 1930s, electric appliance sales were badly depressed. Sales did not climb back to their 1929 level until 1935, when the New Deal's vast electrification projects expanded the market for electrical appliances into rural America. This prolonged depressed market forced many small manufacturers who could not diversify into other product lines out of business. Perhaps even more important in altering the structure of the industry were mass marketing techniques, which were first successfully applied after World War II.

During the 1940s and 1950s, a new industry structure emerged. Consolidations and mergers concentrated industry production in the hands of major full-appliance line manufacturers, such as General Electric, Westinghouse, Philco, RCA, and Frigidaire. Independent distributors became less important as these large producers integrated vertically as well as horizontally. Building contractors became a stronger link in the distribution chains; by the 1950s, they replaced salesmen as the most important distributors. In the late 1950s a swing away from exclusive brand-name retail distribution developed with the proliferation of discount houses, variety stores, and supermarket sales. With a saturation of the market in the 1960s—when electric mixers, toasters, coffeemakers, can openers, knives, and other appliances were common in many households—and the threat of an energy shortage and the rise of the price of electricity in the 1970s, many large manufacturers began to abandon the appliance industry. By the late twentieth century, refrigerators and washing machines no longer inspired utopian visions of social progress, and the fully automated home of science fiction lore had failed to materialize. The focus had shifted from domestic hygiene to the more private frontiers of entertainment, information, and communication. The Internet, in particular, had emerged as the newest expression of a corporate vision of domestic order and efficiency.

BIBLIOGRAPHY

Barrett, John Patrick. *Electricity at the Columbian Exposition.* Chicago: R.R. Donnelley and Sons, 1894.

Giedion, Siegfried. *Mechanization Takes Command: A Contribution to Anonymous History.* New York: Oxford University Press, 1948.

Nye, David E. *Elecrifying America: Social Meanings of a New Technology, 1880–1940.* Cambridge, Mass.: MIT Press, 1990.

Tobey, Ronald C. *Technology as Freedom: The New Deal and the Electrical Modernization of the American Home.* Berkeley: University of California Press, 1996.

Ronald J. Kopicki/A. R.

See also **Family; Lighting; Railways, Urban, and Rapid Transit; Refrigeration;** *and vol. 9:* **Power.**

ELECTRONIC COMMERCE, or e-commerce, is the conduct of business by electronic means. Following this general definition, e-commerce began soon after Samuel Morse sent his first telegraph message in 1844, and it expanded across the sea when another message, containing share price information from the New York stock market, linked Europe and North America in 1858. By 1877, Western Union, the dominant telegraph company, moved $2.5 million worth of transactions annually among businesses and consumers, and news companies led by Reuters sold financial and other information to customers around the world. The telephone permitted electronic voice transactions and greatly extended the reach of retail companies like Sears, whose mail- and telephone-order catalog helped to create genuine national firms.

In the twenty-first century, e-commerce referred more specifically to transactions between businesses (B2B e-commerce) and between businesses and consumers (B2C e-commerce) through the use of computer communication, particularly the Internet. This form of electronic commerce began in 1968, when what was called Electronic Data Interchange permitted companies to carry out electronic transactions. However, it was not until 1984 that a standardized format (known as ASC X12) provided a dependable means to conduct electronic business, and it was not until 1994 that Netscape introduced a browser program whose graphical presentation significantly eased the use of computer communication for all kinds of computer activity, including e-commerce.

To take advantage of the widespread adoption of the personal computer and the graphical browser, Jeff Bezos in 1995 founded Amazon.com to sell books and eventually a full range of consumer items over the Internet. Amazon went public in 1997 and in 2000 earned $2.76 billion in revenue, though its net loss of $417 million troubled investors. Other booksellers followed quickly, notably Barnes and Noble, whose web subsidiary—begun in 1997—also experienced rapid revenue growth and steep losses. One of the most successful e-commerce companies, eBay, departed from traditional retail outlets by serving as an electronic auction site or meeting place for buyers and sellers, thereby avoiding expensive warehousing and shipping costs. Its earnings derive from membership and transaction charges that its participants pay to join the auction. The company's profit of $58.6 million in 2000 made it one of the few to show a positive balance sheet. Other notable consumer e-commerce firms like the "name your own price" company Priceline.com and the online stock trading company E*TRADE suffered significant losses. Despite the backing of the *New York Times,* the financial news site TheStreet.com also failed to live up to expectations and eliminated most of its staff. Others did not manage to survive, notably the online-community

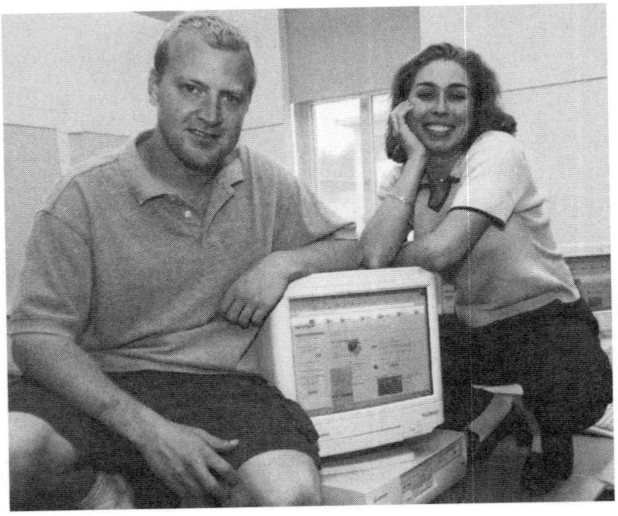

E-Commerce. Students James Walker and Elena Kholodenko, members of the first class to graduate from Carnegie Mellon University with master of science degrees in electronic commerce, show off a Web site that the class developed, 2000. AP/WIDE WORLD PHOTOS

firm theglobe.com, which received strong startup support in 1998, and Value America, which sold discounted general merchandise and enjoyed the backing of Microsoft's cofounder Paul Allen and the FedEx corporation.

The business-to-business form of e-commerce fared better in 2000 and 2001, although a faltering economy lowered expectations. B2B e-commerce evolved with the development of the Internet. One of the leading B2B firms, i2 Technologies, was founded in 1988 as a business software producer to help companies manage inventories electronically. As the Internet expanded, the role of i2 grew to include the procurement and management of all the elements required to produce finished goods. Successful in this endeavor, its revenue grew to $1.1 billion and its profit to $108 billion in 2000. Another form of B2B e-commerce involves managing a market for firms in specific industries. VerticalNet, founded in 1995, links producer goods and services markets, earning money on commissions it receives for deals struck using its electronic marketplace. Other market-creating firms focus on specific products. These include Pantellos in the utilities industry, ChemConnect in chemicals, and Intercontinental Exchange for oil and gas. Concerned about this trend, manufacturers began creating their own electronic purchasing markets, the largest of which, Covisint, was founded in 2000 by General Motors, Ford, and Daimler Chrysler. In its first year of operation, the company managed the purchasing of $129 billion in materials for the automobile industry. Other B2B companies have concentrated on the services sector, with consulting (Sapient) and advertising (DoubleClick) somewhat successful, and health services (Healthion/WebMD) less so.

By 2001, electronic commerce had not grown to levels anticipated in the late 1990s. In addition to a decline in economic growth, there remained uncertainties, particularly in relation to the consumer sector. Buyers were slower than expected to change habits and make the shift from going to a store to shopping on a computer. Concerns about privacy and security remained, although some progress was made in setting national and international regulations. Businesses remained reluctant to guarantee strict privacy protection because selling information about customers was a valuable part of the e-commerce business. Nevertheless, business-to-business sales continued to grow and companies that developed their electronic sales divisions slowly over this period and carefully integrated their e-commerce and conventional business practices appeared to be more successful. Forecasters remained optimistic, anticipating the $657 billion spent worldwide on e-commerce in 2000 to double in 2001 and grow to $6.8 trillion by 2004.

BIBLIOGRAPHY

Frank, Stephen E. *NetWorth: Successful Investing in the Companies that Will Prevail through Internet Booms and Busts.* New York: Simon and Schuster, 2001.

Lessig, Lawrence. *Code and Other Laws of Cyberspace.* New York: Basic, 1999.

Schiller, Dan. *Digital Capitalism: Networking the Global Market System.* Cambridge, Mass.: MIT Press, 1999.

Standage, Tom. *The Victorian Internet: The Remarkable Story of the Telegraph and the Nineteenth Century's Online Pioneers.* New York: Walker, 1998.

Vincent Mosco

See also **Digital Technology; Internet; Telegraph; Telephone.**

ELECTRONIC MAIL. The exact origins of electronic mail (or E-mail) are difficult to pinpoint, since there were many nearly simultaneous inventions, few of which were patented or widely announced. According to the standard account, computer-based messaging systems emerged alongside computer networks of the early 1960s, such as the pioneering "time-sharing" computer system installed on the campus of Massachusetts Institute of Technology (MIT). The MIT system and those that followed were intended to allow multiple users, sometimes spread out in various computer labs around campus, to access a central computer using keyboard and monitor terminals. The geographic dispersion of the terminals led to a desire for a convenient text message service. The resulting service at MIT was called "Mailbox," and may have been the first, but there were many similar programs written at about the same time.

By all accounts the first electronic mail program intended to transmit messages between two computers was written in 1972 by the engineer Ray Tomlinson of the company Bolt, Baranek and Newman [BBN]. MIT and BBN were both involved in the development of Advanced

Research Projects Agency Network (ARPANET), the computer network that became the basis of the current Internet. In modifying Mailbox for this purpose, Tomlinson contributed the now-ubiquitous use of the "@" character to separate one's unique user name from the name of the host computer.

One of the well-known anecdotes of ARPANET lore is the way that the network, intended for research purposes, was regularly used for sending electronic mail messages. Indeed, electronic mail, along with the electronic bulletin board, became by far the most popular applications by the mid-1970s. As the volume of mail grew, programmers at various institutions around the United States and in Europe collaboratively improved the mail system and imposed technical standards to allow universal service.

It was estimated that less than ten thousand electronic mail messages were being transmitted per day in 1976, compared to about 140 million postal messages. By the end of the decade there were an estimated 400,000 unique electronic mailboxes across the country.

The relatively unplanned growth of the Internet (successor to ARPANET) makes it difficult to track the diffusion of electronic mail usage after the 1970s. In addition to the Internet, a host of mutually incompatible "dial-up" networks (such as Compuserve) existed, many of which also fostered the growth of E-mail usage. Many of these services were later absorbed into the Internet.

E-mail gained many new users as universities began making Internet service available to most students, and as corporations such as IBM encouraged its use on private networks by managers and executives. By the 1990s, E-mail came to refer only to electronic messaging via the Internet, which had now linked most of the previously separate computer networks in the United States.

Like the personal computer itself, E-mail usage by businesses became common several years before individuals began using it at home. Yet by the late 1990s, approximately forty percent of all American householders owned a computer, and twenty-six percent of those families had Internet access. An estimated 81 million E-mail users generated 3.4 trillion messages in 1998.

BIBLIOGRAPHY

Abbate, Janet. *Inventing the Internet.* Boston: MIT Press, 1999.

David Morton

See also **Computers and Computer Industry; Internet.**

ELECTRONIC SURVEILLANCE. Court-approved electronic surveillance has become an increasingly important, and controversial, law enforcement tool to fight crime. Its origins date to the simple wiretapping procedure of connecting a listening device to the circuit of a handset telephone, begun in the late 1920s. However, advances in communications during the last decades of the twentieth century have challenged surveillance techniques to become more sophisticated, and in the eyes of some, too intrusive.

Law enforcement's court-approved access to communication, including wiretaps, pen registers, and traps and traces, are neither technically nor legally simple. Intercepting communication information has become further complicated by the changing concept of the "telephone number," which used to represent a physical location. However, technology now often uses such a number merely as the beginning of a communication link that soon loses its identity with an individual as the call becomes routed to others. The shift from analog to digital data, the use of microwave and satellite carriers in the 1960s, and computer-based switching have all changed the nature of surveillance substantially. Additionally, computerized data transfer and mobile communications have made surveillance more costly.

Legally, the Fourth Amendment of the Constitution protects citizens against unlawful, unreasonable search and seizure by the government. Governmental intrusion into the private lives of Americans must fit guidelines outlined by the Constitution and interpreted by the U.S. Supreme Court. But technological changes in communication challenge both the court system and the U.S. Congress to seek a reasonable balance between personal rights and the public interest. In 1928, the Supreme Court ruled in *Olmstead v. the United States* that wiretapping did not violate the Fourth Amendment. Congress responded in 1934 with the Communication Act, which established wiretap statutes to govern the procedure. By 1968, legal interpretations of the Communication Act had become so complex that Congress again clarified guidelines regulating federal wiretap surveillance under Title III of the Omnibus Crime Control and Safe Streets Act. By the end of the twentieth century, thirty-seven states had enacted statutes that parallel the Title III guidelines. The provisions of the 1968 act continue to govern the procedures for legal authority to intercept wire, oral, and electronic communication.

To obtain a court order for surveillance requires evidence of probable cause as well as demonstration that normal investigative techniques cannot yield the same results. Legal permission is normally limited to thirty days and must also record surveillance in such a way that it cannot be altered or edited. Interception has the additional responsibility to minimize data gathering that may not be relevant to investigations.

In a digital age, gathering such information has become costly, and in 1994 Congress passed the Communications Assistance for Law Enforcement Act authorizing $500 million over fiscal years 1995–1998 to upgrade interception technologies. The Act also required service providers to build surveillance needs into the design of their equipment and systems.

In part because of the enhanced sophistication of modern electronic surveillance, the NATIONAL SECURITY

AGENCY (NSA) and other law enforcement organizations came under increasing criticism in the 1990s for unconstitutional spying on its citizens. In April 2000, public sentiment compelled NSA Director Lt. Gen. Michael V. Hayden to appear before the House of Representatives Permanent Select Committee on Intelligence to defend secret electronic intelligence gathering in the interests of national security. American rights organizations such as the American Civil Liberties Union vigorously opposed newly developed Internet spy technologies like "Carnivore," which gave the FBI the ability to intercept and analyze large amounts of e-mail from both suspects and non-suspects alike.

A political shift to support an increase in domestic surveillance began after the 19 April 1995 bombing in Oklahoma City. Following the terrorist attacks on New York City and the Pentagon on 11 September 2001, Congress strengthened federal authority to conduct electronic surveillance coincident with the FBI's 2002 mandate to focus on terrorism.

BIBLIOGRAPHY

Colbridge, Thomas D. "Electronic Surveillance: A Matter of Necessity." *The FBI Law Enforcement Bulletin* (1 February 2000): 1–10.

Lyon, David, and Elia Zureik, ed. *Computers, Surveillance, and Privacy*. Minneapolis: University of Minnesota Press: 1996.

Ray, Diana. "Big Brother Is Watching You (Electronic Surveillance)." *Insight on the News* (23 July 2001): 1–3.

Mark Todd

Safety Elevator. Elisha Otis demonstrates in 1854 that his elevator—an invention that helped to make high-rise buildings practical—is "all safe" even with its cable cut. © CORBIS

ELEVATORS. Primitive elevators were first used in ancient Rome. These grew out of the rope and pulley and used a platform instead of a hook or net to raise cargo. The development of the modern elevator began with the INDUSTRIAL REVOLUTION and the use of the steam engine to power the mills. Steam-powered machines—used for spinning, weaving, or metalworking—were not individually powered. They were driven by a central steam engine through line shafting consisting of long lines of rotating shafts located overhead. At each machine location, a belt and pulley transmitted power to the machine. Most mills at the time were multistoried, requiring a hoisting machine to move material between floors. The central steam engine powered this machine, as it did all other machines in the mill. The operator pulled a rope that controlled the rotation of the hoisting machine, giving the operator control over starting and stopping. Later, when elevators were installed in locations other than mills, it became apparent that a separate steam engine would have to be installed for the elevator.

Almost all hoists or elevators functioned by winding a rope on a drum to raise the platform. Because of the ever-present danger of rope breakage, however, they were not used to carry passengers. Elisha Otis (1811–1861), a mechanic in a mattress factory in Yonkers, New York, pioneered the technology of elevator safety and paved the way for the modern passenger elevator. During the second year of the New York CRYSTAL PALACE EXHIBITION in 1854, he gave dramatic demonstrations of a safety device that would grip the elevator guide rails if the hoist ropes parted. Showman as well as inventor, Otis would have himself raised on the elevator and then direct an assistant to cut the hoist rope with an ax. The safety always worked. In 1857 Otis built the first elevator exclusively for passengers and installed it in a china and glass store in NEW YORK CITY.

Use of the drum machine for elevators was restricted to relatively low-rise buildings because the length and weight of the drum imposed a severe restriction on the building structure and on the height that the elevator could travel. By 1870 a rope-geared hydraulic system was developed whereby a piston acting through a system of sheaves (complex pulleys) raised and lowered the elevator. One foot of motion of the piston could cause the elevator to move two, three, or even ten feet, depending on the alignment of the sheave and rope system. This was a major design improvement and eliminated the winding drum with its inherent limitations.

By 1880, both these systems were in general use. In some locations, they could use city water pressure, obviating the need for a steam engine to drive the necessary water pump. At about this time, engineers also developed a plunger hydraulic elevator, which was practical except in tall buildings, where it suffered from the same drawbacks as the drum machine. This elevator required that a hole be drilled in the ground to the same depth as the height of the building in order to accommodate the hydraulic cylinder. At first, the development of the electric motor had only a minor effect on the operation of elevators when it was used to replace the steam engine that powered the pumps used on hydraulic systems. Otis then designed a drum machine that used an electric motor to drive the drum, and the first such electric-powered elevator was installed (1889) in the Demarest Building in New York City.

The major breakthrough in elevator design and the beginning of the modern high-speed elevator occurred about 1900 with the development of the traction machine. The traction machine depends on friction between the driving sheave or pulley and the hoist ropes (or, more frequently as technology improved, metal cables). With the traction machine, elevators can serve buildings of any height and are limited in speed only by the height of the building. Prior to 1900, all elevator machines, whether steam or electric powered, transmitted the driving power through a train of gears to the driving sheave or drum. This method is suitable for moderate elevator speeds under 500 feet per minute. At higher speeds, gear wear and gear noise make the application impractical. In 1904 the Otis Company installed the first gearless traction machine in Chicago, which was to make high elevator speeds practical. In this machine, the drive sheave is mounted directly on the motor shaft and there are no gears. The result is a quiet and smooth-running elevator, even at speeds of 2,000 feet per minute.

After the gearless traction machine, the major developments in elevator engineering were control refinements in order to provide a smooth ride at high speeds. Further control developments were made during the 1920s and 1930s by Otis, Westinghouse, and other companies to minimize the skills needed by the elevator operator. These systems provided automatic landing of the elevators at floor level and automatic floor selection by pressing buttons for the desired stop. Completely automatic elevators that did not require the presence of an operator were developed in the 1920s, but did not come into general use until 1950. By 1960 the installation of any elevator requiring an operator was a rarity.

BIBLIOGRAPHY

Lampugnani, V. M., and Lutz Hartwig, eds. *Vertical: A Cultural History of Vertical Transport.* Berlin: Ernst & Sohn, 1994.

Strakosch, George R., ed. *The Vertical Transportation Handbook.* New York: Wiley, 1998.

Vogel, Robert M. *Elevator Systems of the Eiffel Tower, 1889.* Washington: Smithsonian Institution, 1961.

Philip L. Fosburg/A. R.

See also **Skyscrapers; Steam Power and Engines.**

ELEVATORS, GRAIN. Unlike most agricultural products, individual grain kernels are not damaged by scooping or pouring. Also, WHEAT and CORN can be safely stored for long periods. The inventor of the grain elevator, Oliver Evans, took advantage of these properties when, in the late eighteenth century, he designed machinery to lift grain into storage bins at the top floor of his flour mills. The machines featured iron buckets attached to a moving belt that was driven by hand, or by horse or waterpower.

For years, large flour mills only operated mechanical grain elevators based on Evans's system. By the early 1840s, however, expanding grain production in the Old Northwest made it difficult to transfer and store grain surpluses by hand. In 1842, a Buffalo, New York, grain merchant, Joseph Dart, built a steam-powered elevating apparatus that unloaded grain from vessels into his waterfront warehouse, reducing unloading time from days to hours. Merchants, warehouse workers, and railroad officials at booming GREAT LAKES ports saw the advantages of this technology and, within years, grain warehouses at these ports featured similar machinery. The devices grew larger, more powerful, and more efficient, and, by the mid-1850s, fused elevating and warehousing functions into a single structure called a "grain elevator."

This technology spread slowly. In the 1870s, it appeared in major MISSISSIPPI RIVER ports and on the eastern seaboard. By the 1880s, railroad feeder lines west of the Mississippi boasted elevators at each station. On the Pacific slope, unique weather and ocean shipping conditions retarded the introduction of grain elevators until after WORLD WAR I. As they spread, grain elevators changed basic marketing methods, introducing standardized grading and futures contracts, and exposed grain producers to the power of large firms with exclusive control of "line" elevators at rural shipping points and warehouses at terminal markets.

Strong reaction against real and imagined abuses—such as fraudulent grading and price-fixing—followed. Backed by the GRANGER MOVEMENT, spokesmen demanded government regulation. In 1871, Illinois passed a Warehouse Act that the Supreme Court upheld in *Munn v. Illinois*. Some farmers also sought relief through cooperative elevators, but most of these failed in the 1870s. Later, the FARMERS' ALLIANCE, Populist, and National NONPARTISAN LEAGUE movements obtained cooperative action, stronger government regulation, and—in places—even state or municipal ownership of elevators, forcing private firms to share market control and conform to government regulation.

Some reductions in abuses resulted; however, twentieth-century grain firms adjusting to abrupt shifts in government regulation and the varying market conditions encountered during wars, depression, and major shifts in world trading patterns, have tended to develop greater centralization and efficiency. Since the interwar period, more grain elevators have come under the control of a few multinational firms, which have responded quickly to shifting grain belt locations, the new importance of soybeans, and flour and feed mill needs. These multinational firms continue to share the building and control of grain elevators with government agencies and farm cooperative organizations and have adopted technical advances in elevator construction—such as pneumatic machinery—to handle grain delivered by trucks. Thus, the innovation of the grain elevator, which helped make the United States a leading producer and exporter of grain crops in the mid-nineteenth century, still serves that function in the early 2000s and continues to evolve.

BIBLIOGRAPHY

Clark, J. G. *The Grain Trade in the Old Northwest.* Urbana: University of Illinois Press, 1966.

Cronon, William. *Nature's Metropolis: Chicago and the Great West.* New York: Norton, 1991; 1992.

Fornari, Harry. *Bread Upon the Waters: A History of United States Grain Exports.* Nashville, Tenn.: Aurora, 1973.

Lee, G. A. "The Historical Significance of the Chicago Grain Elevator System." *Agriculture History* 11 (1937):16–32.

Morton Rothstein / C. W.

See also **Agricultural Machinery; Agriculture; Cereal Grains; Cooperatives, Farmers'; Grain Futures Act; Northwest Territory; Oats; Populism.**

ELIZABETHTOWN ASSOCIATES, the first group of people to be granted permission by the English government to settle in NEW JERSEY. On 30 September 1664, Governor Richard Nicolls consented to a petition from six residents of Jamaica, Long Island, to purchase and settle 400,000 acres of land west of the Arthur Kill in New Jersey. By deed of 28 October, confirmed by patent from Nicolls on 1 December of that year, the associates purchased from the Indians a broad tract extending from the mouth of the Raritan River northward along the Arthur Kill and Newark Bay to the mouth of the Passaic River, and inland some thirty-four miles. The associates, limiting their number to eighty, admitted Governor Philip Carteret when he purchased the rights of a prior associate, and together they founded Elizabethtown (now Elizabeth). The original settlers were Puritans from NEW ENGLAND and LONG ISLAND, but after 1682, immigrants from Scotland arrived. Elizabethtown was the capital of the province until it was divided in 1676, and then the capital of EAST JERSEY until 1686. The first general assembly for New Jersey met in Elizabethtown in May 1668. In the early 1700s, when the proprietors attempted to collect rents, the associates refused to pay, invoking their Indian titles and the Nicolls's patent. On 8 February 1740, King George II granted a charter for the Free Borough and Town of Elizabeth.

BIBLIOGRAPHY

Purvis, Thomas L. "Origins and Patterns of Agrarian Unrest in New Jersey, 1735 to 1754." *William and Mary Quarterly* 39 (October 1982).

C. A. Titus / A. R.

See also **Land Grants; Puritans and Puritanism.**

ELKINS ACT. With this 1903 act Congress sought to strengthen the power of the Interstate Commerce Commission to set maximum railroad freight rates. The act required railroads to hold to their published rates and forbade rate cutting and rebates. Railroads favored the act, because it prevented loss of revenue. The Elkins Act also supplemented the Interstate Commerce Act of 1887 by providing more specific methods of procedure and penalties for nonobservance of its provisions. The law provided for prosecution and punishment of railroad corporations, as well as their agents and officers, for giving or receiving rebates and made it a misdemeanor to deviate from published rates.

BIBLIOGRAPHY

Eisner, Marc Allen. *Regulatory Politics in Transition.* 2d ed. Baltimore: Johns Hopkins University Press, 2000.

Kolko, Gabriel. *Railroads and Regulation, 1877–1916.* Princeton, N.J.: Princeton University Press, 1965.

Sanders, Elizabeth. *Roots of Reform: Farmers, Workers, and the American State, 1877–1917.* Chicago: University of Chicago Press, 1999.

John B. Clark / C. P.

See also **Commerce, Court of; Hepburn Act; Interstate Commerce Commission; Railroad Rate Law.**

ELLIS ISLAND. From 1892 to 1954, Ellis Island was a gateway for more than 12 million immigrants seeking access to the United States' way of life. Because of its historical significance and proximity to the statue, the site was declared part of the Statue of Liberty National Monument in 1965, but the land and its buildings remained in decay and disrepair. After a $1 million cleanup grant by the federal government for the bicentennial in 1976, $165 million was raised in private donations to restore the main building, including the huge Great Hall, which was opened as a museum for visitors in 1990.

The federal government established its first immigration center at the site in 1890, using ballast from incoming ships as landfill to double the island in size. In

Ellis Island. The immigration station where millions of new arrivals to the United States were processed—or, in much smaller numbers, turned away. LIBRARY OF CONGRESS

1892, Annie Moore from Ireland, age 15, was the first immigrant recorded to come through Ellis Island proper (for a few years before this, immigrants were processed at Castle Garden, still considered part of the Ellis Island experience today). In 1897, the original wooden buildings burned to the ground. While some records were lost, none of the ship manifests were lost as they were stored elsewhere. The main building that exists today was opened in 1900, and 389,000 immigrants were processed through it in the first year alone. The record number in one day occurred in 1907, with 11,747. By 1917, Congress required all immigrants over age 16 be literate, and quotas began a few years later.

An estimated forty percent, or over 100 million Americans, can trace their ancestry through at least one man, woman, or child who entered the country through Ellis Island. During the peak years, thousands of immigrants arrived each day. Each immigrant was checked for diseases, disabilities, and legal problems, and each name was recorded. In the confusion and with so many languages entering the country, many of the clerks wrote names based on English phonetic spellings or quick approximations, and many of these names have stayed with families to this day. People in steerage class on the crossing steamships were asked to board ferries that brought them to the Ellis Island facilities. There, they stood for hours in long lines reaching up the long stairs to the Great Hall, complete with children and all the belongings they had brought with them, awaiting inspection and passage through Ellis Island to the trains or boats that would take them to New York City or upstate New York, or on to other areas of the country. About two percent, or 250,000, did not pass the inspections and were turned around to go back to their countries of origin.

The open-door policy of immigration did not always exist at Ellis Island. In the 1920s, quotas were enacted; later, immigration processing was moved overseas. During World War II, the facility was used to house enemy aliens. Finally, the entryway was closed in 1954 and offered for sale as surplus government property, until the National Park Service took it over during the Johnson administration in 1965.

Today, thousands of visitors include a trip to Ellis Island with their visit to the Statue of Liberty. Ferries bring them to the hallowed island, much as they did years ago with their ancestors. A passenger database helps them locate their ancestors' records.

Connie Ann Kirk

See also **Immigration; Immigration Restriction.**

ELMIRA PRISON. In July 1864 the federal government established a Union prison camp at Elmira, New

York, to contain the overflow of captured Confederate enlisted men from the camp at Point Lookout, Maryland. The thirty-acre prison enclosure housed 12,123 captives in barracks and tents. Although the camp was well-equipped and efficiently managed, exceptional hardships marked the prison's history. A stagnant pond used as a sink became, during the summer drought, a fetid and disease-laden cesspool. Scurvy resulted from lack of vegetables in the prisoners' rations. Smallpox spread over the camp. An exceptionally cold winter and inadequate fuel added to the suffering, and, in the spring, melting snows produced a flood. As a result of these conditions, 2,963, or 24 percent, of the prisoners died before the prison closed in the late summer of 1865. This percentage of deaths was the second highest of the twenty-four northern military prisons. Such unfortunate conditions became increasingly common in all Union prison camps as the number of Confederate captives grew, after negotiations to exchange prisoners of war stalled in early 1863.

BIBLIOGRAPHY

Hesseltine, William Best. *Civil War Prisons: A Study in War Psychology.* Columbus: Ohio State University Press, 1930.

Paludan, Phillip S. *Victims: A True Story of the Civil War.* Knoxville: University of Tennessee Press, 1981.

W. B. Hesseltine / A. E.

See also **Atrocities in War; Prisoners of War: Prison Camps, Confederate, Prison Camps, Union.**

E-MAIL. *See* **Electronic Mail.**

EMANCIPATION, COMPENSATED, was a device for eliminating slavery by having the government buy the slaves from their white masters, usually proposed in connection with schemes for colonizing freed slaves. The constitutional convention of Virginia in 1829–30 proposed an amendment to the U.S. CONSTITUTION giving Congress the power to appropriate money to purchase and colonize slaves. Others argued that profits from public lands be used to emancipate and transport slaves. After the decline of the colonization movement, interest in compensated emancipation faded. Strict constructionists believed it to be unconstitutional, and radical abolitionists believed that slaveowners did not deserve compensation.

The Republican Party revived interest in compensated emancipation. The party's 1860 platform recognized it as desirable where slaves were legally held. President Abraham Lincoln believed that it was just, that it distributed fairly the financial burden of emancipation, and that it was cheaper than war. In a special message to Congress, on 6 March 1862, he asked for the adoption of a joint resolution pledging financial aid to any state adopting gradual emancipation. The resolution was passed, and Lincoln tried to persuade the border states to accept the offer, but none of them did. The only successful attempt at compensated emancipation was in the District of Columbia. Lincoln's final effort on behalf of compensated emancipation was his 1 December 1862 proposal to permit the issuance of government bonds to any state adopting gradual emancipation. The Emancipation Proclamation ended all interest in the scheme.

BIBLIOGRAPHY

Cox, LaWanda C. Fenlason. *Lincoln and Black Freedom: A Study in Presidential Leadership.* Columbia: University of South Carolina Press, 1981.

Hallie Farmer / A. R.

See also **Slavery.**

EMANCIPATION PROCLAMATION. President Abraham Lincoln's grant of freedom, on 1 January 1863, was given to slaves in states then in rebellion. In conformity with the preliminary proclamation of 22 September 1862, it declared that all persons held as slaves within the insurgent states—with the exception of Tennessee, southern Louisiana, and parts of Virginia, then within Union lines—"are and henceforth shall be, free." The proclamation was a war measure based on the president's prerogatives as commander in chief in times of armed rebellion. Admonishing the freedmen to abstain from violence, it invited them to join the armed forces of the United States and pledged the government to uphold their new status. Unlike the preliminary proclamation, it contained no references to colonization of the freed slaves "on this continent or elsewhere."

Enshrined in American folklore as the central fact of Lincoln's administration, the actual proclamation was a prosaic document. On the day it was issued, it ended slavery legally and effectively only in limited areas, chiefly along the coast of South Carolina. Eventually, as Union forces captured more and more Southern territory, it automatically extended freedom to the slaves in the newly conquered regions. Moreover, the mere fact of its promulgation ensured the death of slavery in the event of a Northern victory. The Emancipation Proclamation may thus be regarded as a milestone on the road to final freedom as expressed in the Thirteenth Amendment, declared in force on 18 December 1865.

Although Lincoln had always detested the institution of slavery, during the first year of the war, he repeatedly emphasized that the purpose of the conflict was the maintenance of the Union rather than the emancipation of the slaves. Aware of the necessity to retain the support of both the border states and the Northern Democrats, he refrained from pressing the antislavery issue. Thus, he countermanded General John C. Frémont's emancipation order in Missouri and General David Hunter's proclamation in the Department of the South. But Lincoln signed confiscation bills, by which the private property of Southerners was subject to forfeiture, as well as measures freeing the slaves in the District of Columbia and in the

Emancipation Proclamation. President Abraham Lincoln reads the document to his cabinet for the first time on 22 July 1862. Engraving by A. H. Ritchie, c. 1866, from an 1864 painting by Francis B. Carpenter. LIBRARY OF CONGRESS

federal territories. In addition, he urged loyal slave states to accept proposals for compensated emancipation.

These piecemeal measures did not satisfy the radical Republicans. Tirelessly advocating a war for human freedom, they pressured the president to implement their program. Lincoln sought to satisfy his radical Republican supporters and reap the diplomatic rewards of an antislavery policy—foreign powers were reluctant to recognize the slaveholding Confederacy—all without alienating the border states. The peculiar wording of the Emancipation Proclamation shrewdly balanced these conflicting interests.

The president wrote the first draft of the preliminary proclamation during June 1862. On 13 July he revealed his purpose to Secretary of State William H. Seward and Secretary of the Navy Gideon Welles. Nine days later, he read the document to the cabinet but, upon Seward's advice, postponed its publication. To promulgate the proclamation so shortly after General George B. McClellan's early summer failure to take Richmond would have been impolitic. It is also possible that Salmon P. Chase, secretary of the treasury, desiring piecemeal emancipation, persuaded Lincoln to wait a bit longer.

During the following weeks various groups urged Lincoln to adopt an emancipation policy. However, even though he had already decided to comply with their request, Lincoln refused to commit himself and remained silent about the document then in preparation. Even in his celebrated reply to Horace Greeley's "Prayer of Twenty Millions" (22 August 1862), Lincoln emphasized that his paramount objective in the war was to save the Union, not to destroy slavery. Although he conceded that his personal wish had always been that all men everywhere could be free, it was not until after the Battle of Antietam (17 September 1862) that he believed the time had come for the proclamation. Informing his cabinet that his mind was made up, Lincoln accepted a few minor alterations and published the document on 22 September, promising freedom to all persons held as slaves in territories still in rebellion within the period of 100 days.

The reaction to the preliminary proclamation was varied. Denounced in the South as the work of a fiend, in the North it was generally acclaimed by radicals and moderates. Conservatives and Democrats condemned it, while all blacks enthusiastically hailed it as a herald of freedom.

During the 100-day interval between the two proclamations, some observers questioned Lincoln's firmness of purpose. Republican reversals in the election of 1862, the president's proposal in December for gradual compensated emancipation, and the revolutionary nature of the scheme led many to believe that he might reconsider. But, in spite of the conservatives' entreaties, Lincoln remained steadfast. After heeding some editorial suggestions from his cabinet, especially Chase's concluding sentence invoking the blessings of Almighty God, in the afternoon of 1 January 1863 he issued the proclamation.

The appearance of the Emancipation Proclamation clearly indicated the changed nature of the Civil War. It was evident that the conflict was no longer merely a campaign for the restoration of the Union but also a crusade for the eradication of slavery. In the remaining period of his life, Lincoln never wavered from this purpose. Having already said that he would rather die than retract the proclamation, he insisted on its inclusion in all plans of reunion and amnesty. His administration became ever more radical and he actively furthered the adoption of the Thirteenth Amendment. It is, therefore, with considerable justice that Lincoln has been called the Great Emancipator.

The president's calculations proved correct. Following the issuance of the Emancipation Proclamation, and owing to increased evidence of federal military prowess, neither Great Britain nor any other power recognized the Confederacy; nor did any border states desert the Union. The document thus stands as a monument to Lincoln's sense of timing, his skill in maneuvering, and his ability to compromise. The freedom of some 4 million human beings and their descendants was the result.

BIBLIOGRAPHY

Cox, LaWanda C. Fenlason. *Lincoln and Black Freedom: A Study in Presidential Leadership.* Columbia: University of South Carolina Press, 1981.

Franklin, John Hope. *The Emancipation Proclamation.* Garden City, N.Y.: Doubleday, 1963.

McPherson, James M. *Abraham Lincoln and the Second American Revolution.* New York: Oxford University Press, 1991.

Quarles, Benjamin. *Lincoln and the Negro.* New York: Oxford University Press, 1962.

Trefousse, Hans L. *Lincoln's Decision for Emancipation.* Philadelphia: Lippincott, 1975.

Hans L. Trefousse / A. R.

See also **Civil War; Colonization Movement; Slavery;** *and vol. 9:* **Emancipation Proclamation.**

EMBALMED BEEF. During the Civil War Northern soldiers often called the meat canned by Chicago packers and issued to the Union "embalmed beef." Because of the large surpluses of canned meat in the army depots at the close of that war, the soldiers in the Spanish-American War insisted that the canned meat issued to them in Florida, Cuba, and the Philippines was "embalmed beef" of Civil War issue. During World War I, immense quantities of Argentine beef were canned and issued to the Allied armies. The British soldiers called it "bully beef," but the American soldiers, accustomed to red meats, called it contemptuously "embalmed beef" or "monkey meat."

BIBLIOGRAPHY

Coppin, Clayton A., and Jack High. *The Politics of Purity: Harvey Washington Wiley and the Origins of Federal Food Policy.* Ann Arbor: University of Michigan Press, 1999.

Okun, Mitchell. *Fair Play in the Marketplace: The First Battle for Pure Food and Drugs.* Dekalb: Northern Illinois University Press, 1986.

H. A. DeWeerd / A. E.

See also **Civil War; Meat Inspection Laws; Meat Packing; Pure Food and Drug Movement; Spanish-American War; World War I.**

EMBARGO ACT. From the opening of hostilities between Great Britain and France in 1803, the United States had found it difficult to steer a neutral course. Hoping to gain economic superiority, both nations attempted to restrict neutral countries from trading with the other. The United States claimed that its official policy of neutrality allowed it to engage in unmolested trade and commerce with both countries. However, although the French and British had committed occasional infractions to American shipping, the United States offered no more than casual protest over such occurrences.

That changed in 1806 when Napoleon Bonaparte issued his Berlin Decree. It declared that the French would blockade the British Isles. In reality this meant little, given the poor condition of their navy. However, Napoleon further decreed that neutral ships carrying British-made goods were subject to seizure, thus opening the way for privateers to attack American shipping. The following year, the British government responded with the Orders in Council that established a blockade on all European ports controlled by Napoleon. In addition, these Orders mandated that all neutral vessels stop in Britain and pay a transit duty if they wished to trade with any port blockaded by Britain. Later in the year, Napoleon retaliated with his Milan Decree, which authorized the seizure of any neutral vessels submitting to the British Orders in Council. This economic warfare greatly hindered the ability of the United States to conduct any meaningful trade in Europe.

The USS *Chesapeake* incident in June 1807 further strained American relations with Britain. The crew of the British ship *Leopard* fired upon the *Chesapeake* and boarded the ship in search of British deserters. Despite calls for war by some in Congress, President Thomas Jefferson chose to retaliate with economic sanctions. The Embargo Act, passed by Congress on 22 December 1807, was designed to punish France and Britain as well as protect American shipping from any further acts of aggression by either nation. The act forbade American ships and goods from leaving American ports except for those vessels in the coastal trade. Those who traded along the eastern seaboard had to post bond double the value of their vessel and cargo as a guarantee that the cargo would be delivered to an American port. Loopholes in the initial act allowed merchants to push the limits of legal trading, resulting in additional restrictions passed by Congress over the ensuing months to enforce compliance to the act. The restrictions culminated in the passage of the Enforcement Act of 1809, also referred to as the Giles Enforcement Act, which allowed customs officials to call out the militia to help enforce the embargo.

The embargo successfully curbed American commerce abroad. In 1807, the year the embargo was passed, the total exports for the United States reached $108 million. One year later, that number had declined to just over $22 million. New England was hit hardest by the embargo since it was a region heavily involved in international commerce. Other commercial cities, such as New York and Philadelphia, also suffered from the embargo. Overall, American trade declined by up to 75 percent for exports and 50 percent for imports. The embargo had less of an impact in the middle states and the South, where loyalty was greater to Jefferson's Democratic-Republican Party. In addition, the southern economy was based more upon agricultural production than the shipping industry.

The Federalist Party, politically in control of most New England states during the years of the embargo, vigorously protested against the act on several grounds. Some accused Jefferson of exercising arbitrary powers that infringed upon the constitutional rights guaranteed to states and citizens. Many protestors harkened back to the spirit of the American Revolution, when resistance to Britain had been based upon commercial restrictions. To many Americans, the Embargo Act resembled the restrictions of trade placed upon the American colonies in the 1760s (Townsend Duties) and 1774 (Coercive Acts) by the British government. Since they and their forebears had protested those acts in the generation prior, they felt free to protest the Embargo Act as another injustice that needed repealing. Some also criticized the act for having no terminus, implying that the embargo could go on for years since the Embargo Act did not specify a termination date. Yet others suggested that only a stronger navy, not an embargo, would prevent future violations by foreign powers. Finally, many Federalists believed that Jefferson's policy had evolved out of his bias toward the French and, conversely, his distaste for the British.

By the end of 1808, resistance to the Embargo Act had grown significantly across the nation because of increasing financial loss. Some New England politicians hinted that if the embargo was not lifted, it would be the duty of states and individuals to nullify such a damaging law. Smuggling dramatically increased, particularly across the Canadian border. From a practical standpoint, the embargo appeared to be a failure because neither France nor Britain backed down from their original decrees curtailing neutral shipping. Although Jefferson continued to insist that the embargo would eventually work, Congress thought otherwise, and on 1 March 1809, the Embargo Act was replaced with the Nonintercourse Act, which reopened American ports to trade with all nations except Britain and France.

BIBLIOGRAPHY

Hickey, Donald R. *The War of 1812: The Forgotten Conflict.* Urbana: University of Illinois Press, 1989. Effectively puts the Embargo Act into greater context.

Sears, Louis. *Jefferson and the Embargo.* 1927. Reprint, New York: Octagon, 1966.

Spivak, Burton. *Jefferson's English Crisis: Commerce, Embargo, and the Republican Revolution.* Charlottesville: University Press of Virginia, 1979.

Keith Pacholl

See also **Chesapeake-Leopard Incident; Federalist Party; Nonintercourse Act.**

EMBASSIES are the official missions through which nations conduct their foreign affairs. Embassies are headed by ambassadors, the highest-ranking diplomats stationed abroad. In the United States, the president, with the consent of the Senate, appoints ambassadors. From these outposts, ambassadors and their staffs promote the interests of their nation, work to protect citizens traveling abroad, and gather information about the host country.

Since the American Revolution (1775–1783), the United States has sent diplomats to and exchanged them with other nations. By the early part of the nineteenth century, the United States had nearly two hundred overseas posts. However, none of the foreign missions was officially an embassy, since U.S. leaders did not consider their dealings with other nations important enough to warrant either the creation of embassies or the naming of ambassadors. In the late-nineteenth century, however, this attitude changed, and the United States began to aspire to the rank of a great power with a more assertive foreign policy. Consequently, in 1893, President Grover Cleveland established the first American embassies in England, France, Germany, and Italy. During World War II (1939–1945), President Franklin D. Roosevelt nearly doubled the number of ambassadors and embassies so that the United States had thirty-six embassies in 1945. But the most rapid increase in the number of embassies came in the postwar era, when the United States emerged as the dominant world power. In 2002, the United States had embassies in more than 140 nations.

An American embassy not only serves as the headquarters of the ambassador, who acts as the president's representative in the host country, but it is also a busy office for lower-ranking diplomats, U.S. Department of State employees, and officials from other foreign affairs agencies. The embassy's staff of Foreign Service officers is divided into four sections: political, economic, consular, and administrative. Political officers are responsible for keeping the ambassador and State Department informed about the political climate in the host country. They analyze developments in light of American foreign policy goals. Economic officers assess the host country's financial dealings, including exports and imports, and conduct commercial negotiations over matters such as patent rights and trade regulations. Consular officers work to ensure the safety of Americans traveling or working abroad and determine whether foreigners should receive immigrant or tourist visas to enter the United States. Administrative officers manage the day-to-day operations of the embassy. Foreign service officers normally spend two to three years serving in one embassy. They are then transferred to another foreign post or brought back to the State Department in Washington, D.C.

Most embassies include employees of other foreign affairs agencies, such as the Agency for International Development, the U.S. Information Agency, the Commerce Department, the Defense Department, and the Central Intelligence Agency. U.S. marines and other military personnel provide security for embassies. In most embassies, foreign nationals make up some of the administrative staff. An embassy's staff can be as small as the U.S. embassy in Dublin, which in 1995 had 36 employees, or as big as the Moscow embassy, which had a staff of 288.

Embassies are considered an extension of the home country's territory, so no one is permitted to enter an embassy without the ambassador's permission. However, because embassies serve as tangible representatives of the home country, they can become targets for political opposition in the host country. During the later years of the twentieth century, much attention was focused on the security of Americans working abroad. The event that precipitated such concern was the 1979 takeover of the U.S. embassy in Tehran by revolutionaries opposed to America's support for the shah of Iran. Seventy-six Americans were taken hostage, excluding the ambassador, who was on vacation. For 444 days, until the inauguration of President Ronald Reagan, 52 were held in captivity. After the Tehran debacle, Congress passed legislation to shore up the security of embassies. For example, new embassies were supposed to be set back from the property line by 100 feet. Unfortunately, attacks on embassies continued. In April 1983, the Beirut embassy was the target of a terrorist bombing. And in 1998, truck bombs devastated embassies in Dar es Salaam and Nairobi. The Nairobi attack was the worst such incident in American history as 46 embassy employees were killed, including 12 Americans. Approximately 175 more innocent bystanders outside the embassy gate were also killed in the explosion.

BIBLIOGRAPHY

"Inside a U.S. Embassy." American Foreign Service Association. Available from http://www.afsa.org.

Miller, Robert Hopkins. *Inside an Embassy: The Political Role of Diplomats Abroad.* Washington, D.C.: Congressional Quarterly, 1992.

Plischke, Elmer. *United States Diplomats and Their Missions.* Washington, D.C.: American Enterprise Institute, 1975.

"Principal Officers of the Department of State and U.S. Chiefs of Mission." U.S. Department of State. Available from http://www.state.gov.

Ellen G. Rafshoon

See also **Foreign Service.**

EMBASSY BOMBINGS. On 7 August 1998, terrorists bombed the U.S. embassies in Nairobi, Kenya, and Dar es Salaam, Tanzania, killing 224 people, including 12 American citizens, and injuring over 4,000. Federal investigators soon identified Osama bin Laden and the organization Al Qaeda as the principal suspects in the attacks. Several individuals were taken into custody.

Following a grand jury investigation, several individuals were indicted in the federal district court for the Southern District of New York. The defendants were charged with numerous offenses, including the use of a weapon of mass destruction against U.S. nationals, murder of U.S. employees, and destruction of U.S. property. Four defendants in custody challenged their indictments on various grounds, including the extraterritorial application of federal law, the extension of constitutional protections abroad, and the potential imposition of the death penalty. The courts denied each of these challenges.

After a six-month jury trial, the four defendants were convicted in May 2001, but the jury declined to impose the death penalty. On 18 October 2001, all four defendants were sentenced to life imprisonment without possibility of parole. In addition, the defendants were ordered to pay $33 million in restitution to the U.S. government and the families of the victims.

BIBLIOGRAPHY

Bergen, Peter. *Holy War, Inc.: Inside the Secret World of Osama bin Laden.* New York: Simon and Schuster, 2001.

William J. Aceves

See also ***Cole*** **Bombing; 9/11 Attack; Terrorism.**

EMERGENCY FLEET CORPORATION. Because of the need during World War I to build ships rapidly, on 16 April 1917 the U.S. Shipping Board incorporated the Emergency Fleet Corporation to build, own, and operate a merchant fleet for the U.S. government. It performed these functions until 11 February 1927, when Congress changed its name to the Merchant Fleet Corporation. In 1916 the shipbuilding industry completed only 300,000 deadweight tons of ships, whereas the United States during war needed an annual output of 6 million to 10 million deadweight tonnage. To meet this emergency the Fleet Corporation first requisitioned the 431 steel ships being built in American yards for foreign operators. Second, the corporation built three great steel shipyards and invested in many other yards. To speed up construction, yards assembled "fabricated" ships of standard design out of plates and parts made in factories as far west as Kansas.

In October 1918 the peak construction program consisted of 3,116 ships, but, by 31 October 1918, only 378 steel ships had entered service. After July 1918 the shortage of cargo tonnage was acute. World War I ended as the army general staff faced the necessity of maintaining eighty divisions in France without the prospect of adequate supply ships before July 1919.

After the armistice the 218 yards building under contract for the Fleet Corporation were almost as hard to stop as they had been to start. On 30 June 1919, only 44 percent of the ships were completed. Despite protests by shipbuilders and workers, the government canceled contracts totaling 25 percent of the original program. By 30 June 1920, 90 percent of the ships were finished, but not until 1922 did the Fleet Corporation receive the last vessel.

Shipping Board policy after World War I required the Fleet Corporation to sell its fleet to private operators but to operate it until that was possible. With a drastic postwar slump in the shipping industry, buyers were hard to find. The corporation organized its ships into a large number of cargo and passenger services and entered into contracts for their operation under trade names by private companies at government expense. Fleet operating losses, though declining, were still $13 million in 1926–1927. By 1927 the Fleet Corporation had sold 1,507 ships to private operators; many of the cargo ships went to scrappers. Nevertheless, as the Merchant Fleet Corporation, it still owned 833 steel ships. What to do with this fleet, which only another war could make profitable to the government, was the major problem of the U.S. Shipping Board. The worst effect of the stockpile was the inhibition of new construction, which allowed foreign builders to surpass the U.S. Merchant Marine in quality. In 1928, in response to this situation, Congress passed the Jones-White Act to subsidize new ships, but only thirty-one were afloat in 1936, when the Maritime Commission came into existence to rejuvenate the merchant marine. The commission started with a modest goal of fifty new ships per year, a target that was vastly expanded for World War II. With title to the aging ships, the commission began selling them to scrappers, which reduced the number to 113 within a year. Since the remaining ships had an estimated useful life of five more years, many again wore wartime gray in World War II.

BIBLIOGRAPHY

Cooling, B. Franklin. *Gray Steel and Blue Water Navy: The Formative Years of America's Military-Industrial Complex, 1881–1917.* Hamden, Conn.: Archon Books, 1979.

Kilmarx, Robert A., ed. *America's Maritime Legacy: A History of the U.S. Merchant Marine and Shipbuilding Industry Since Colonial Times.* Boulder, Colo.: Westview Press, 1979.

Morris, James Matthew. *Our Maritime Heritage: Maritime Developments and Their Impact on American Life.* Washington, D.C.: University Press of America, 1979.

Frank A. Southard Jr. / A. E.

See also **Government Ownership; Government Regulation of Business; Shipping Board, United States; World War I; World War I, Economic Mobilization for; World War I, Navy in.**

EMERSON'S *ESSAYS*. The *Essays* of Ralph Waldo Emerson (1803–1882), published in two series (1841 and 1844), were only part of a career-long infatuation with the essay form, beginning with *Nature* in 1836 and ending with the collection *Society and Solitude* in 1870. Stylistically, the two series of *Essays* epitomize the Emersonian corpus. Characterized by a prophetic yet accessible tone, replete with the arresting image and the memorable aphorism, rich in varying perspectives (within single essays, and sometimes to a dizzying degree), the essays also sustain a speech-like, rhetorical mood, perhaps because some of the pieces were derived from earlier orations. The subject matter of the essays is varied, but they provide a digest of typical Transcendentalist themes. Individuality, nonconformity, and intellectual independence are advocated; the striving for a harmonious relationship between man and nature is a constant motif; and an optimistic belief in the perfectibility of humanity is espoused.

Despite a degree of contemporary puzzlement, and notwithstanding uneasy reactions from writers such as Nathaniel Hawthorne, the impact of these *Essays*, the most notable of which include "Self Reliance," "The Poet," and "The Over-Soul," has been profound. Philosophers such as William James, John Dewey, and Friedrich Nietzsche stand in Emerson's debt, but, above all, it is American writers who have rallied to Emerson's call—expressed, for instance, in "The Poet" (Second Series)—to forge a uniquely American literature, freed from what Emerson perceived as the shackles of the European literary tradition. Robert Frost, William Carlos Williams, and preeminently Walt Whitman, who faithfully sustained an Emersonian belief in the power of the poetic idiom, were all deeply influenced by this ambition. It ought not to be forgotten, however, that, beyond the influence of the *Essays* on sophisticated poetic and philosophical discourse, they also represent a unique artifact in the broader American culture as that rarest of things—a much-loved and endlessly quoted book.

BIBLIOGRAPHY

Atwan, Robert. "'Ecstasy and Eloquence': The Method of Emerson's *Essays*." In *Essays on the Essay: Redefining the Genre.* Edited by Alexander Butrym. Athens: University of Georgia Press, 1989.

Porte, Joel, and Saundra Morris, eds. *The Cambridge Companion to Ralph Waldo Emerson.* Cambridge and New York: Cambridge University Press, 1999.

Jonathan A. Wright

See also **Transcendentalism.**

EMIGRANT AID MOVEMENT, a plan to promote free-state migration to Kansas formed at the time of the KANSAS-NEBRASKA ACT of 1854, which provided that the people of that territory should decide by POPULAR SOVEREIGNTY whether the designated territory should be free-soil or slave. The act proved a disaster, since supporters of both sides quickly moved into the territory, causing economic and political turmoil. The movement seems to have been the brainchild of Eli Thayer, who a month before the passing of the act created the Massa-

Eli Thayer. The Massachusetts legislator whose organization sent antislavery settlers to Kansas starting in 1854, in an attempt to make the territory a free state. LIBRARY OF CONGRESS

chusetts Emigrant Aid Company, which was later to become the New England Emigrant Aid Company. In the same year, the Kansas Emigrant Aid Society was founded to assist "antislavery men, temperance men and otherwise men of good character" to settle in Kansas. These companies sought to attract funds by offering stock options to the public, with which they founded a few new towns and provided supplies and mechanical equipment for settlers. Charles Robinson, an agent of the company, established a free-soil government in the city of Lawrence. Funding was meager until the end of 1855, when promoters of the scheme adopted a more aggressive policy. Tensions rose between proslavery advocates and free-soilers, and, as a result, violence erupted on several occasions. In 1856, Lawrence was sacked by proslavery forces. Events like this led journalists to write sensational articles about "Bleeding Kansas." Although less than half the violent deaths that occurred in this period were due to the slavery issue, the movement capitalized on the violence to gain support outside the state. The largest expedition to Kansas under the auspices of the movement was organized by Jefferson Buford of Alabama. In all, however, it is thought that only about 1,240 settlers were sponsored by the New England Emigrant Aid Company, whose activities were largely confined to the Northeast. Although the movement had little to do with making Kansas a free-soil state, it was bitterly resented in the South and is regarded by some as a potent cause of the Civil War. Even so, it is now recognized that the division between the proslavery and antislavery lobbies was secondary to contentions about land claims. It is also the case that the Emigrant Aid Company was insufficiently financed and incompetently run. By 1857, the movement was effectively defunct. It had done little but polarize opinions and fuel passions.

BIBLIOGRAPHY

Barry, Louise. "The Emigrant Aid Company Parties of 1854" and "The New England Aid Company Parties of 1855." *Kansas Historical Quarterly* 12 (1943): 115–125 and 227–268.

Connelley, William E. *A Standard History of Kansas and Kansans.* 5 vols. Chicago: Lewis, 1918.

Harlow, Ralph Volney. "The Rise and Fall of the Kansas Aid Movement." *American Historical Review* 41 (October 1935): 1–25.

Potter, David M. *The Impending Crisis, 1848–1861.* Completed and edited by Don E. Fehrenbacher. New York: Harper and Row, 1976.

SenGupta, Gunja. *For God and Mammon: Evangelicals and Entrepreneurs, Masters and Slaves in Territorial Kansas, 1854–1860.* Athens: University of Georgia Press, 1996.

Robert Garland

See also **Kansas; Lawrence, Sack of.**

EMIGRATION from the United States has received far less attention than the influx of immigrants attracted by the reputation of a country with a tradition of welcoming freedom-seekers from around the world. Yet there have been times when the number of emigrants surpassed that of immigrants.

Patterns of Emigration

Many nineteenth-century immigrants in the United States were male Europeans whose goal was to save the money they earned in order to return home, buy land, and improve their economic status. This goal, together with feelings of cultural dislocation, and frequent expressions of hostility on the part of native-born Americans, contributed to an exceptionally high incidence of repatriation. In the late 1800s, the departure rate for Croatians, Poles, Serbs, and Slovenes was 35 percent; for Greeks, 40 percent; and more than 50 percent for Hungarians, Slovaks, and Italians. From the 1830s to the 1920s, emigrants returning to their homelands reduced net immigration gains by 20 to 50 percent.

Since 1900, the ratio of immigration to emigration has been three to one: 30 million legal immigrants were admitted to the United States between 1900 and 1930, and 10 million emigrants left the country. A notable exception occurred during the Great Depression, from 1931 to 1940, when the emigrant flow swelled to 649,000, compared with 528,000 immigrants. Trustworthy statistics for the later twentieth century are harder to find. The Immigration and Naturalization Service (INS) stopped collecting emigrant data in 1957, and the U.S. CENSUS BUREAU no longer tallies the number of U.S. citizens living abroad. In addition, Americans living in foreign countries are under no obligation to register with American consulates, and may be unknown to local immigration authorities. For example, while the U.S. Department of State estimated that more than 500,000 U.S. citizens lived in Mexico in 2000, the Instituto Nacional de Inmigracion reported only 124,082.

Estimates of the total number of U.S. citizens living abroad at the turn of the twenty-first century range from 3.2 million to more than 6 million. According to the *United Nations Demographic Yearbook* (1989), the top ten countries to which people emigrated from the United States in the 1980s, in descending order, were: Mexico, the United Kingdom, Germany, Canada, Japan, the Philippines, Guatemala, Indonesia, Australia, and Italy. Mexico also attracted the largest group of American émigrés from 1965 to 1976, displacing Germany, formerly the primary destination of Americans settling abroad

On an annual basis, it is estimated that between 200,000 and 300,000 Americans are moving out of the country. The majority are believed to be former immigrants, although as many as 100,000 may be native-born. Yet the rate of repatriation has slowed significantly (15 percent in the 1990s, versus more than 37 percent in the first decade of the twentieth century). Other factors that make it difficult to quantify recent emigration include potentially large numbers of undocumented immigrants who return to their home countries.

Cultural, Economic, and Political Reasons for Emigration

The first emigrants were some 80,000 to 100,000 LOYALISTS, supporters of Great Britain during the American Revolution who returned to their home country, including the painter John Singleton Copley. It was not until the VIETNAM WAR that significant numbers of Americans again left the country for political reasons—in this case, to evade the military draft. Canada was the favored destination for Americans of draft age, whose numbers are said to have peaked in the early 1970s. But because many draft evaders did not immediately apply for landed emigrant status in Canada, there are no reliable statistics on the scope of this phenomenon. While the Canadian government reported a total of 24,424 immigrants from the United States in 1970, and 24,366 in 1971, estimates of the number of draft evaders who went to Canada during this period have varied wildly, from more than 50,000 to more than 100,000.

In 1816, the American Society for Colonizing the Free People of Color in the United States, founded by the Reverend Robert Finley and other well-connected and well-meaning white men, sought to offer better opportunities to freed slaves, relieve racial tension in the United States, and encourage the liberation of more slaves. In 1822 the first group of freed slaves arrived in the settlement of Monrovia (named for President James Monroe), on Africa's west coast. Liberia, with Monrovia as its capital, became an independent republic in 1847. By 1870, it had attracted some 13,000 U.S. immigrants. The best-known back-to-Africa movement was led in the 1920s by Jamaican-born, New York-based Marcus Moziah Garvey, who founded the Black Star Line steamship company to transport black Americans to Africa (see BLACK NATIONALISM).

From the 1940s through the 1960s, individual African Americans weary of the struggle against racism in the United States—including prominent figures in the arts, such as the novelist James Baldwin—found havens in European cities where their color was no bar to acceptance. Popular destinations included Paris, Rome, Berlin, and Stockholm. Since the eighteenth century, Europe—particularly France, Italy, and England—has been a favored destination of American writers and artists, who initially sought training unavailable in the United States. The roster of pre-twentieth-century cultural expatriates includes painters Benjamin West and Mary Cassat, and novelists Washington Irving, James Fenimore Cooper, Nathaniel Hawthorne, and Henry James. By the 1920s—the most celebrated era of U.S. cultural expatriates—the roster included novelists Ernest Hemingway, F. Scott Fitzgerald, and Katherine Anne Porter (who settled in Mexico); poets Ezra Pound and T. S. Eliot; and art patron Gertrude Stein.

In the early 1950s—after the passage of the McCarran Internal Security and MCCARRAN-WALTER ACTS, which denied suspected "subversives" the right to apply for or renew passports and permitted deportation of naturalized citizens suspected of subversive allegiances—some Americans found a haven in Mexico. With no passport requirements for U.S. citizens, cheaper living costs, and a tradition for giving asylum to fugitives, Mexico was a popular destination for Communist Party members and sympathizers, people jailed after participation in industrial strikes, and those who refused to sign loyalty oaths.

Since the founding of the state of Israel in 1948, more than 100,000 American JEWS have emigrated there, an event known as "making aliyah." This phenomenon peaked in 1991, despite the Gulf War. Under the Law of Return established by the Israeli Knesset (parliament) in 1950 and modified in 1970, anyone born of a Jewish mother, as well as that person's spouse and children, and the spouses of their children and grandchildren (whether Jewish or not) is entitled to Israeli citizenship and residency. It has been estimated that 10 to 15 percent of these emigrants eventually return to the United States, though some move back to Israel.

Some foreign-born emigrants from developing countries, after having obtained advanced degrees from U.S. universities, return to their home countries to lend their expertise to businesses or governments. American émigrés settle overseas to work for multinational corporations and government agencies, to reconnect with their heritage, or to take advantage of tax havens. In recent years, globalization, the fall of communism in Russia and Eastern Europe, and the postwar economy of Vietnam have increased opportunities for American entrepreneurs overseas.

Americans who renounce their citizenship without acquiring citizen status in another country are considered to be stateless. Combining the intent to abandon citizenship with an act of TREASON, a formal renunciation before a consular officer, an oath of allegiance to another country, service in another country's military, or becoming a naturalized citizen of another country are legal grounds for being judged to have voluntarily relinquished U.S. citizenship.

BIBLIOGRAPHY

Anhalt, Diana. *A Gathering of Fugitives: American Political Expatriates in Mexico, 1948–1965.* Santa Maria, Calif.: Archer Books, 2001.

Dunbar, Ernest. *The Black Expatriates: A Study of American Negroes in Exile.* New York: Dutton, 1968.

Earnest, Ernest. *Expatriates and Patriots: American Artists, Scholars, and Writers in Europe.* Durham, N.C.: Duke University Press, 1968.

Hagan, John. *Northern Passage: American Vietnam War Resisters in Canada.* Cambridge, Mass.: Harvard University Press, 2001.

Ross, Ishbel. *The Expatriates.* New York: Thomas Y. Crowell Company, 1970.

Warren, Bob. "The Elusive Exodus: Emigration from the United States." *Population Trends and Public Policy*, no. 8 (March 1985).

Cathy Curtis

See also **American Colonization Society; Confederate Expatriates in Brazil; Expatriation; Immigration.**

EMILY'S LIST, a political donor network based in Washington, D.C., was formed in 1985, its name derived from the acronym "Early Money Is Like Yeast" and its mission to help elect Democratic, pro-choice women nationally. Ellen Malcolm was inspired to create a donor network for women politicians when Walter Mondale selected Representative Geraldine Ferraro of New York as a running mate in 1984. When polling results on election day suggested that Mondale lost even the women's vote 55 percent to 45 percent, feminist activists saw a need to organize in every state to counter the influence of conservative, pro-life Republicans.

Energized by Anita Hill's testimony of sexual harassment at the 1991 Senate confirmation hearings of Supreme Court Justice Clarence Thomas, several women, especially from the Midwest, were elected to Congress in 1992, which was dubbed the "year of the women." Emily's List supported Hillary Rodham Clinton in her successful 2000 Senate campaign in New York.

BIBLIOGRAPHY

Freeman, Jo. *A Room at a Time: How Women Entered Party Politics.* Lanham, Md.: Rowman and Littlefield, 2002.

Itai Sneh

See also **Campaign Financing and Resources.**

EMINENT DOMAIN is the inherent right of a sovereign power to take private property for public use without the owner's consent. The Fifth Amendment of the U.S. Constitution implicitly acknowledges this right of the national government by providing that private property shall not "be taken for public use without just compensation." By the U.S. Supreme Court's interpretation of the due process clause of the Fourteenth Amendment in *Chicago, Burlington and Quincy Railroad v. Chicago* (1897), the same right and limitation has been attributed to state governments.

The right of eminent domain is an ancient one, and the American colonies readily utilized the concept. Numerous early colonial statutes, along with English common law, carried the philosophy of eminent domain over into U.S. jurisprudence. The scope of eminent domain, however, is still unsettled. The historic conceptual debates generally focus upon one of two questions: What amounts to a "taking," in which compensation to the owner is mandated by the Constitution? What amounts to a "public use," in which the sovereign power may exercise its right to eminent domain?

Certain sovereign actions to protect health, morals, safety, or even to "promote the general welfare" are undertaken within the government's inherent police power and, as such, are not considered takings within the eminent domain power. Courts have the task of determining what is a taking as opposed to what is a regulation within the exercise of the police power. During the last two decades of the twentieth century, the U.S. Supreme Court limited the scope of the federal eminent domain power by reinvigorating the takings doctrine. In *Pennsylvania Coal Company v. Mahon* (1922), Justice Oliver Wendell Holmes established the doctrine of regulatory takings. However, this doctrine was rarely employed successfully during the period between 1950 and 1980 at the Supreme Court. But beginning in the 1980s, the Court began to take a closer look at land use regulations such as environmental controls and zoning restrictions in its effort to provide greater protections to property interests. For example, in *Lucas v. South Carolina Coastal Council* (1992) the Supreme Court determined that regulations depriving an owner of all economically viable uses of land constituted a taking notwithstanding any public use justification.

A sovereign may not take property except for public use. Until the 1950s, courts held the narrow view that public use meant literally "use by the public": taken property could not be turned over to private owners, even if the public would benefit thereby. The modern, broader view, expressed in *Berkman v. Parker* (1954), is that public use means "public advantage" or "public purpose" and permits takings even when the property is subsequently conveyed to new private owners.

BIBLIOGRAPHY

Coyle, Dennis J. *Property Rights and the Constitution: Shaping Society through Land Use Regulation.* Albany: State University of New York, 1993.

Fischel, William A. *Regulatory Takings: Law, Economics, and Politics.* Cambridge, Mass.: Harvard University Press, 1995.

R. Blake Brown
Eric L. Chase
Harold W. Chase

See also **Confiscation of Property; Police Power; Property.**

EMPIRE STATE BUILDING is on the west side of Fifth Avenue between Thirty-third and Thirty-fourth Streets in New York City, the site of the original Waldorf Astoria Hotel. In the center of Manhattan Island, it is roughly equidistant from the East and Hudson Rivers and the northern and southern tips of Manhattan. The building's 102 stories rise 1,250 feet, and the tower adds 222 feet for a total height of 1,472 feet. Primarily an office building, it has retail shops on the ground floor and observation facilities on the 86th and 102d floors.

The building was designed by Shreve, Lamb and Harmon. The financier John J. Raskob and the former New York governor Alfred E. Smith built it between 1929 and 1931. The building company of Starrett Brothers and Eken, Inc., managed the construction.

Conceived during the prosperous 1920s, the Empire State Building was intended to be the largest and most prestigious office building in New York. Originally estimated to cost $50 million, it actually cost only $24.7 million (approximately $500 million in year 2000 dollars). For forty years the Empire State Building was the tallest office building in the world, and its prominence made it a symbol of New York City. Designated a National Historic Landmark, the building has been renovated regularly for modern convenience and continued to attract prestigious tenants in the twenty-first century.

Empire State Building. Completed in 1931, this architectural landmark reigned as the tallest in the world until the 1970s.
LIBRARY OF CONGRESS

BIBLIOGRAPHY

Ellis, Edward Robb. *The Epic of New York City.* New York: Coward-McCann, 1966.

Goldberger, Paul. *The Skyscraper.* New York: Knopf, 1981.

James, Theodore, Jr. *The Empire State Building.* New York: Harper and Row, 1975.

Pacelle, Mitchell. *Empire: A Tale of Obsession, Betrayal, and the Battle for an American Icon.* New York: Wiley, 2001.

Scully, Vincent. *Architecture: The Natural and the Manmade.* New York: St. Martin's, 1991.

Tauranac, John. *The Empire State Building: The Making of a Landmark.* New York: Scribner, 1995.

Michael Carew

See also **Architecture; New York City; Skyscrapers.**

EMPLOYERS' LIABILITY LAWS. As occupational injuries increased in the nineteenth century, state courts formulated and frequently invoked three major doctrines in dealing with damage suits for work injuries: the fellow servant doctrine that the injured worker could not hold the employer liable for his coworker's negligence; the risk assumption doctrine that workers should be presumed to have assumed the intrinsic hazards of their employment; and the contributory negligence doctrine that workers who had contributed to their own injury in any degree could not recover damages. Such doctrines were intended to promote entrepreneurship and protect capital investment. But in the late nineteenth century many state legislatures challenged that common-law framework as "unjust" and "inhumane" and enacted employers' liability laws that held the employer liable for the injury suffered by employees in the course of their employment. Still, as they stood in the early years of the twentieth century, those laws had critical shortcomings. Litigation of these laws proved costly and uncertain for resourceless workers, and damages, if any, were typically meager.

The continuing injustices under the employers' liability laws became the major labor issue during the Progressive Era. While strengthening and extending employers' liability laws, such as the Federal Employers' Liability Act of 1908, broad reform coalitions—including labor unions, social and charity workers, academics, muckraking journalists, women's and consumers' clubs, social gospel ministers, and progressive politicians and labor officials—pushed workers' compensation laws through state legislatures (ten states in 1911, all the states but six by 1920) and Congress (in 1908 and 1916). These laws adjudicated work injury cases regardless of fault, with contracting out prohibited, and in most cases without litigation. Since their constitutionality was affirmed by the U.S. Supreme Court in 1917, workers' compensation laws have become the main damage recovery system for the vast majority of occupational injuries and diseases in America's workplaces.

BIBLIOGRAPHY

Park, David W. "'Compensation or Confiscation?': Workmen's Compensation and Legal Progressivism, 1898–1917." Ph.D. diss., University of Wisconsin-Madison, 2000.

Weiss, Harry. "Employers' Liability and Workmen's Compensation." In *History of Labor in the United States, 1896–1932.* John R. Commons, et al. Volume 3. New York: A. M. Kelley, 1966.

David Park

See also **Workers' Compensation.**

EMPLOYMENT ACT OF 1946 was rooted in the dismal experience of the Great Depression and the fear that remained alive during World War II that the United States might emerge victorious from the war only to confront the return of massive unemployment. Liberals especially sought to harness the newly emergent Keynesian economics and the administrative capacity built up under the New Deal to guide the economy successfully into the postwar world.

In January 1945 Senator James Murray (a Democrat from Montana) introduced the Full Employment Bill of 1945. The bill consisted of three main elements. First, it proclaimed the right of all Americans "able to work and seeking work" to regular, full-time employment. Second, it provided a Keynesian planning mechanism, the National Production and Employment Budget, to identify any pending deficiencies in expenditures and investment that might stand in the way of full employment. Third, the bill directed the federal government to address such shortfalls by encouraging private investment and if necessary by federal spending as a last resort.

Congressional consideration of the Full Employment Bill of 1945 occasioned a fierce battle between liberals and conservatives and among a variety of interest groups. The bill's backers viewed the proposed legislation as a lever of liberal reform rather than a mere technocratic tool, and its conservative opponents agreed with that assessment. The bill's supporters included Democratic staffers in Congress and the executive departments, the Union for Democratic Action, the National Planning Association, the National Farmers Union, and important segments of organized labor. The National Association of Manufacturers, the national Chamber of Commerce, and the American Farm Bureau Federation led the charge against the bill.

The final legislation, renamed the Employment Act of 1946 and signed into law by President Harry S. Truman in February 1946, was a compromise measure weighted on the conservative side. Instead of guaranteeing full employment, the Employment Act of 1946 committed the government to pursue "maximum employment, production, and purchasing power." The act dropped the explicit planning mechanism of the National Budget, replacing it with a much weaker requirement for a yearly Economic Report of the President. It also created new entities to help increase the sophistication of economic policymaking, the Council of Economic Advisers in the White House and the Joint Committee on the Economic Report (later renamed the Joint Economic Committee) in Congress.

The final product was much diluted from the initial version, but the Employment Act of 1946 was nevertheless significant. It formally recognized the federal government's new, postdepression role as the manager of national prosperity, and its organizational innovations, the Council of Economic Advisers and the Joint Economic Committee, played important roles in national economic policymaking throughout the postwar era.

BIBLIOGRAPHY

Bailey, Stephen Kemp. *Congress Makes a Law: The Story behind the Employment Act of 1946.* New York: Columbia University Press, 1950.

Collins, Robert M. *The Business Response to Keynes, 1929–1964.* New York: Columbia University Press, 1981.

Robert M. Collins

See also **Great Depression; Keynesianism.**

EMPLOYMENT RETIREMENT INCOME SECURITY ACT (ERISA) is an intricate statute that established a federal regulatory scheme for employee benefit plans in 1974. Before the act some companies promised their employees retirement or other benefits but failed to pay them, either because the benefits were not adequately funded, because the companies failed, or because the companies used the funds for other purposes. Congress passed ERISA to ensure that companies paid benefits promised to employees. ERISA covers both pension and welfare plans. Pension plans include those that provide retirement or other deferred income. Welfare plans include a variety of nonretirement benefits, including medical coverage, disability protection, vacation benefits, and day care. ERISA does not require employers to establish benefit plans. Once employers voluntarily create benefit plans for their employees, ERISA establishes high standards for the employers' management of the plans. These standards include requirements to fund the benefits promised, an obligation to disclose to employees information about the plans, and general fiduciary duties, including an obligation of truthfulness in communication to employees about the plans. Plans that meet certain requirements receive favorable tax status. Employer contributions to such "qualified" plans are tax deductible, and the earnings on the assets in the plans are tax deferred until the distributions are made to the employees.

BIBLIOGRAPHY

Domone, Dana J. *Primer on ERISA Fiduciary Duties.* Washington, D.C.: Bureau of National Affairs, 1994.

Kent Greenfield

See also **Retirement Plans.**

EMPLOYMENT SERVICE, U.S. The public employment service system in the United States evolved from a combination of city, state, and federal legislation over a period of about six decades. About 1890, individual municipalities in both the United States and Europe established the first publicly financed employment offices. These usually catered to unskilled and casual labor. The recurrent cycles of unemployment, coupled with complaints against private employment agencies and the lack of farm labor in many states, led to the development of a system of municipal offices. By the 1920s, some state employment services had come into existence. By 1923, municipal and state legislative bodies in thirty-two states had enacted public employment office laws, but many of the offices suffered from serious shortcomings. The municipal offices that continued to exist were inadequate. There was little uniformity in record keeping, and, with few exceptions, offices were inefficient and inadequately staffed. The state services were little better. Eventually, the need for improved record keeping and administrative procedures and for a closer working relationship between the public employment services and the states, became apparent.

The federal government's public employment work goes back to 1907, when the Bureau of Immigration and Naturalization became responsible for distributing immigrant labor among the states. In 1914, the Immigration Service developed the beginnings of a nationwide information system about employment opportunities. By the time the United States entered World War I, the federal government had established an employment unit in the Department of Labor—the U.S. Employment Service (USES). Reduced appropriations at the end of the war sharply curtailed the activities of this unit, and the USES ceased to exist. Nevertheless, during 1917 and 1918, the employment service made a significant contribution to mobilizing the nation's workers for the war effort. At the beginning of the Great Depression, Congress enacted a national employment service; however, President Herbert Hoover vetoed it.

The Wagner-Peyser Act of 1933, amended in 1998, re-established the USES to set minimum standards, develop uniform administrative and statistical procedures, publish employment information, and promote a system of "clearing labor" between states. During the Great Depression, the USES had a major responsibility for developing essential information about local job vacancies and job opportunities, and then seeking to match the unemployed with available positions. It also played a vital role in placing unemployed workers on the many government work projects developed during the 1930s. The Social Security Act of 1935 necessitated a state employment service since, in most cases, only a public employment office could pay unemployment insurance benefits. By the time of the American entry into World War II, state employment services operating in collaboration with the USES operated in all states.

During World War II, the nation relied heavily upon the public employment services for worker allocation. Since World War II, however, enormous changes have forced reconsideration of the role that government agencies play in combating unemployment, and of the services they provide. The expanded role of the USES now requires the federal service to make labor surveys, certify training needs, provide testing and counseling, expand job placement for trained persons, and provide information and guidance on occupational needs.

The USES has been more successful in placing unskilled and semiskilled workers than white-collar and professional employees. Most large businesses maintain extensive employment departments of their own and do not depend substantially on the public agencies. Professional societies, universities, labor unions, and fee-charging employment agencies also perform job-placement functions.

The activities of the USES are constantly under reappraisal by the Labor and Education Committee of the House of Representatives and similar committees in the Senate concerned with employment problems. As a result of that scrutiny, in the mid-1960s the federal government embarked upon a worker development and training program; in 1972 it passed the Comprehensive Employment and Training Act.

The number of persons who have been referred to or placed in jobs stands as one measure of the success or contribution of the public employment service. In the early and mid-1960s, more than 6 million placements were made. A sharp decline followed, but a reversal occurred in 1973 when the 2,500 local offices made 4.6 million nonfarm placements—a 26 percent rise over fiscal year 1972. Nonetheless, alone the number of placements made is not an adequate measure of the "productivity" of the federal and state employment service. For example, in the early 1970s, the number of short-term placements for casual labor was declining while the proportion of placements in better paid professional, technical, and managerial jobs rose from 3.5 percent in 1971 to 4.5 percent in 1973. Furthermore, the less desirable domestic service jobs declined from 8 percent to 5 percent.

BIBLIOGRAPHY

Breen, W. J. *Labor Market Politics and the Great War: The Department of Labor, the States, and the First U.S. Employment Service, 1907–1933.* Kent, Ohio: Kent State University Press, 1997.

Dubofsky, Melvyn. *The State and Labor in Modern America.* Chapel Hill: University of North Carolina Press, 1994.

Gordon, Colin. *New Deals: Business, Labor, and Politics in America, 1920–1935.* New York: Cambridge University Press, 1994.

Vittoz, Stanley. *New Deal Labor Policy and the American Industrial Economy.* Chapel Hill: University of North Carolina Press, 1987.

William Haber/A. E.

See also **Job Corps; Labor; Labor, Department of; Labor Legislation and Administration; Social Security.**

EMPRESARIO SYSTEM. After Mexican independence in 1821, the Mexican government contracted "empresarios" or land agents to aid the settlement of Texas. Each empresario agreed to settle a specific number of Catholic families on a defined land grant within six years. In return, the empresario received a land premium of just over 23,000 acres for every 100 families he settled. However, if the requisite number of families did not settle within six years, the contract was void. The empresario controlled the lands within his grant, but he owned only the lands he received as a premium.

The majority of the Texas empresario grants were effected under the national law of 18 August 1824 and the state law of 24 March 1825. Under the state law, a married man could receive 177 acres of farming land and 4,428 acres of grazing land. An unmarried man could receive one-quarter of this amount. The settler had to improve the land and pay a nominal fee to the state. By 1830, however, the Mexican government began to question the loyalty of American immigrants in Texas, who outnumbered Mexicans in the area by more than two to one. Thus, on 6 April 1830, Mexico passed a law prohibiting further American immigration and canceling existing empresario contracts.

Despite awarding numerous contracts, the empresario system failed to dramatically increase the population of Texas. The costs of obtaining a grant and surveying the land were high, and the wait for the land to become profitable was long. Although some empresarios, such as Stephen F. Austin, were successful, many others failed to fulfill their contracts.

BIBLIOGRAPHY

Cantrell, Gregg. *Stephen F. Austin: Empresario of Texas.* New Haven, Conn.: Yale University Press, 1999.

White, Richard. *"It's Your Misfortune and None of My Own:" A History of the American West.* Norman: University of Oklahoma Press, 1991.

Jennifer L. Bertolet

See also **Land Grants; Texas.**

ENABLING ACTS. The Constitution grants Congress the power to admit new states. The people of the territory desiring statehood petition Congress for such an enabling act, which authorizes holding a constitutional convention and may seek to impose conditions on the convention and on the new state. Congressional control of the admittance procedures was especially important in the 1840s and 1850s during the conflict over the expansion of slavery. In *Coyle v. Smith*, 221 U.S. 559 (1911), the Supreme Court held that restrictions were not binding when they related to matters over which the states have jurisdiction. An exception, upheld in *Ervien v. United States*, 251 U.S. 41 (1919), is when the conditions relate to the use of lands granted to a state by Congress for a specific purpose.

BIBLIOGRAPHY

Graves, W. Brooke. *American Intergovernmental Relations: Their Origins, Historical Development, and Current Status.* New York: Scribner, 1964.

W. Brooke Graves
Thomas J. Mertz

See also **Kansas-Nebraska Act; Missouri Compromise; Public Domain.**

ENCOMIENDA SYSTEM established social and racial relations as the basis for the economic and political order in the Spanish areas of the Americas. Derived from the Spanish verb *encomendar* (to entrust a mission for someone to fulfill), the mission of the encomienda was to care for and protect indigenous people by awarding part of their labor and produce to men who had served the crown—encomenderos. The encomendero was to indoctrinate his wards into the Catholic faith while acculturating them to European standards. In return, the encomendero was authorized to collect tribute and receive personal services from his wards.

The encomienda had its roots in the Spanish Reconquista (reconquest) of the Iberian Peninsula from the eighth to the fifteenth centuries. After the conquest of Granada in 1492, the Spanish crown parceled out lands as encomiendas to soldiers who were, in turn, to Christianize the Moors. Then, in 1499, a former governor of Granada introduced the encomienda to Hispaniola in the Americas, and soon all the participants in the conquests of the Caribbean, Mexico, Central America, and South America expected an encomienda as reward for their services to the crown. For example, in Mexico in 1522, the conquistador Hernán Cortés directed that his encomenderos were to receive tribute and household services from the conquered Indians in their encomiendas in return for providing food, clothing, care, and religious instruction to the Indians. Women and boys under the age of twelve were exempt from personal service and Indians were only to serve for twenty days, with at least thirty days between service requirements.

Royal fears of the encomenderos' feudal power and continuing conflict between groups of conquerors in Guatemala and particularly Peru, led to the end of personal service to the encomenderos in 1546 under the New Laws of the Indies. Encomenderos were still allowed to collect tribute from their grants but could pass them on only to the next generation. Population decline among the Indians in the later sixteenth century further weakened the encomienda by reducing the amount of Indian labor available, which prevented the encomienda from producing enough to satisfy the economic and social aspirations of the encomenderos.

Encomiendas often became a trap for early settlers, resulting in a third generation reduced to penury. However, in some central areas of the Spanish empire, especially Mexico and Peru, an encomienda sometimes became the basis for a family fortune. Some encomenderos in these regions permitted the Indians of their encomienda to sell their produce in the market reduced by population decline, accepting instead the Indians' tribute in gold currency. Encomenderos then invested this capital in other enterprises, land above all, contributing to the rise of great estates in the seventeenth century. In peripheral parts of the empire such as Paraguay, Chile, and Colombia, the encomienda survived in some fashion until the end of the colonial period. In what is now the United States, in New Mexico, Juan de Oñate granted over sixty encomiendas to reward his men and provide for military defense around 1600. These far northern encomiendas did not survive the 1680 revolt of the Pueblo Indians. By helping to establish race and ethnicity as the primary determinants of economic and political power, the encomienda system had long-reaching effects in the history of the Americas.

BIBLIOGRAPHY

Calero, Luis F. *Chiefdoms Under Siege: Spain's Rule and Native Adaptation in the Southern Colombian Andes, 1535–1700.* Albuquerque: University of New Mexico Press, 1997.

Kramer, Wendy. *Encomienda Politics in Early Colonial Guatemala, 1524–1544: Dividing the Spoils.* Boulder, Colo.: Westview Press, 1994.

Ramírez, Susan E. *Provincial Patriarchs: Land Tenure and the Economics of Power in Colonial Peru.* Albuquerque: University of New Mexico Press, 1986.

Simpson, Lesley Byrd. *The Encomienda in New Spain: The Beginning of Spanish Mexico.* Rev. ed. Berkeley: University of California Press, 1966.

Lance R. Blyth

See also **Colonial Administration, Spanish; Indian Policy, Colonial; New Mexico; Pueblo Revolt; Spanish Borderlands.**

ENCOUNTER GROUPS were nontraditional attempts at psychotherapy that offered short-term treatment for members without serious psychiatric problems. These groups were also known as sensitivity (or sensory) awareness groups and training groups (or T-groups). Encounter groups were an outgrowth of studies conducted in 1946 at the National Training Laboratories in Connecticut by Kurt Lewin. The use of continual feedback, participation, and observation by the group encouraged the analysis and interpretation of their problems. Other methods for the group dynamics included Gestalt therapy (working with one person at a time with a primary goal of increasing awareness of oneself in the moment, also known as holistic therapy) and meditation.

Encounter groups were popularized by people such as Dr. Fritz Perls and Dr. Will Schutz (of the Esalen Institute) and had their greatest impact on the general population in the 1960s and 1970s. These groups fell out of favor with the psychiatric community because of criticism that many of the group leaders at the time were not trained in traditional group therapy and that the groups could sometimes cause great harm to people with serious emotional problems.

BIBLIOGRAPHY

Corey, Gerald. *Theory and Practice of Group Counseling.* Belmont, Calif.: Brooks/Cole, 2000.

Kaplan, Harold I., and Benjamin J. Saddock, eds. *Comprehensive Textbook of Psychiatry.* Volume 2. Baltimore: Williams & Wilkins, 1995.

Lieberman, Morton A., and Irvin D. Yalom. *Encounter Groups: First Facts.* New York: Basic Books, 1973.

George R. Burkes Jr.

See also **Psychiatry; Psychology.**

ENCYCLOPEDIAS. The word "encyclopedia" comes from the Greek *enkyklios paideia*, a "circle of learning." Originally meaning a general education, it has come to signify a reference work containing information on all branches of knowledge, either in general or in a specialized field. The term is often interchanged with the word "dictionary," as in the present work.

Encyclopedias are intellectual, cultural, and commercial products and historically have had several functions. According to the eleventh edition of the *Encyclopaedia Britannica*, encyclopedias are both a "storehouse of facts" and "a systematic survey of all departments of knowledge" by expert authorities. They also are sold and thus need to be profitable. After the 1980s new information technologies dramatically changed encyclopedias, challenging at least some of those purposes.

Encyclopedias have existed for two millennia and have been organized using various methods. The philosopher Francis Bacon, for example, in 1620 proposed a systemization of all knowledge based on scientific foundations. Alphabetical schemes became prominent only in the eighteenth century. The first English general encyclopedia was John Harris's *Lexicon Technicum* (London, 1704). A fellow of the Royal Society, Harris used the advice of scientists, such as Isaac Newton, introducing a system of expert consultants. More influential was Ephraim Chambers's *Cyclopaedia; or, An Universal Dictionary of Arts and Sciences* (London, 1728), which was the model for Denis Diderot and Jean d'Alembert's *Encyclopédie* (Paris, 1751–1772).

The editors of the *Encyclopaedia Britannica* (Edinburgh, 1768–1771) sought to create a more balanced work, avoiding the polemics of the French *Encyclopédie* and seeking to overcome the fragmentation of knowledge by including comprehensive articles on principal topics along with briefer entries. The *Britannica* was quickly revised and expanded; the third edition (1788–1797) reached eighteen volumes and almost fifteen thousand pages.

Early encyclopedias in America were primarily imported, translated, or pirated from European sources. A Philadelphia publisher in 1790 "greatly improved" the third edition of the *Britannica* by deleting the dedication to King George and adding new articles more suited to the revolutionary nation. A generation later Noah Webster began a distinctly American tradition with his two-volume *American Dictionary of the English Language* (1828), which was basically an encyclopedic dictionary.

The first general encyclopedia published in America was the *Encyclopaedia Americana* (1829–1833). Edited by Francis Lieber, a German immigrant, it was based on the seventh edition of *Brockhaus' Konversations-Lexikon*, a standard German work edited by Friedrich Brockhaus. The *Americana* lapsed in 1858, and a new work under the same title was first published in 1902–1904 under the direction of Frederick C. Beach, the editor of *Scientific American*. The first encyclopedia based mainly on American contributions was the sixteen-volume *New American Cyclopaedia*, edited by George Ripley and Charles A. Dana in 1858–1863. Another innovation was the *American Annual Encyclopedia*, a one-volume work of around eight hundred pages issued annually between 1861 and 1874 and continued as *Appleton's Annual Cyclopaedia* until 1902.

The development of American scholarship led to the inclusion of a significant number of American contributors in the ninth edition of the *Britannica* (1875–1889). The famous eleventh edition (1910–1911) was an Anglo-American collaboration whose forty thousand articles were edited in London and New York. In 1920 *Britannica* was purchased by Sears, Roebuck and Company, headquartered in Chicago, and the fourteenth edition (1929) introduced a system of continuous revision. The publication of yearbooks commenced in 1938. Sears expanded its marketing, developing direct-sales methods that continued until the 1990s.

William Benton, a former advertising executive and vice president of the University of Chicago, purchased *Britannica* in 1941 and named the university's president, Robert Maynard Hutchins, as editorial board chairman. Hutchins brought with him the philosopher Mortimer J. Adler, and under Adler's direction the fifteenth edition, *Britannica Three* (1974), was drastically revised by more than four thousand contributors from more than one hundred countries at a cost of $32 million, the largest publishing venture to that point. It consisted of three parts: the *Propaedia*, a one-volume outline of all knowledge; the *Macropaedia*, which contained long, in-depth articles allowing for significant scholarly interpretation; and the *Micropaedia*, offering short articles for ready reference. The organization of *Britannica Three* marked a distinct shift. It was designed on a systematic topical outline of the whole of human knowledge, following its editor's vision that an encyclopedia should represent a single universe of discourse to overcome the fragmentation of knowledge.

The *International Encyclopedia of Unified Science* (Chicago, 1938–1962), edited by Otto Neurath, Rudolf Carnap, and Charles Morris, revealed a fundamentally different vision of the organization of knowledge. Grounded in logical empiricism, this program attempted to unify scientific knowledge through systematic method rather than topical order.

Equally important in the development of encyclopedias was the vast increase in specialized reference tools in the twentieth century, many of which summarized the collective knowledge of a specific discipline. Some fields, such as religion, have dozens of specialized encyclopedias. One of the most significant projects was the *Encyclopedia of the Social Sciences* (1930–1935), edited by Edwin Seligman and Alvin Johnson and revised in 1968 as the *International Encyclopedia of the Social Sciences*, edited by David L. Sills.

The development of encyclopedias for children and schools began in the late nineteenth century. The *Children's Encyclopaedia* (London, 1910), published in the United States as *The Book of Knowledge* (1912), was topically organized and profusely illustrated. A completely new encyclopedia, *The World Book Encyclopedia*, was published in 1917–1918 as "organized knowledge in story and picture." Frank E. Compton, a former door-to-door encyclopedia salesman, introduced *Compton's Pictured Encyclopedia* in 1922.

The commercial and cultural roles of general-purpose encyclopedias changed dramatically in the 1980s and 1990s with the introduction of personal computers, CD-ROMs, and the World Wide Web. The first electronic encyclopedias, such as *Grolier's Academic American Encyclopedia* on CD-ROM (1985), were basically digitized versions of the printed sets. But by the early 1990s publishers began adding audio, video, and Internet links, making them fully interactive multimedia platforms, and often gave them away with the purchase of a new computer. By 2002 there were several general encyclopedias available in CD-ROM format, including *World Book*, *Encarta*, *Grolier's*, and *Britannica*.

A parallel development was the advent of online encyclopedias. In 1983, before the development of the World Wide Web, Grolier Inc. licensed its product to commercial data networks. *Britannica* offered a Web version by subscription in 1994 and a simplified version for free five years later. At the beginning of the twenty-first century *Britannica Online* was the largest online encyclopedia, containing more than seventy-two thousand articles and twelve thousand images, twice the amount of competitors such as Microsoft's *Encarta*, although Microsoft updates the latter daily.

The explosion of electronic sources in many ways supplanted the "storehouse of facts" that was one of the major original functions of encyclopedias. The vast quantity of immediately accessible information made the encyclopedia's purpose of providing an authoritative "systematic survey" of knowledge even more essential in the information age.

BIBLIOGRAPHY

Collison, Robert. *Encyclopaedias: Their History throughout the Ages.* 2d ed. New York: Hafner, 1966. Collison also wrote the main article on encyclopedias in the *Encyclopaedia Britannica.*

Jacsó, Péter. "How the Reference Market Is Being Won." *Information Today* 17, no. 10 (November 2000): 54–55.

Kister, Kenneth F. *Kister's Best Encyclopedias: A Comparative Guide to General and Specialized Encyclopedias.* 2d ed. Phoenix, Ariz.: Oryx Press, 1994.

Walsh, S. Padraig. *Anglo-American General Encyclopedias: A Historical Bibliography, 1703–1967.* New York: Bowker, 1968.

Fred W. Beuttler

See also **Electronic Commerce; Publishing Industry.**

ENDANGERED SPECIES. The environmental movement reached its peak with the enactment of the Endangered Species Act of 1973. As public concern over environmental degradation heightened, Congress passed the most sweeping piece of environmental legislation in American history. When President Richard M. Nixon signed the law on 28 December 1973, he enthusiastically proclaimed that nothing is more priceless and more worthy of preservation than the wildlife with which the country had been blessed. Intent on fulfilling Nixon's mandate, the authors of the Endangered Species Act (ESA) made an unmistakably strong statement on national species protection policy. The ESA provided for the protection of ecosystems, the conservation of endangered and threatened species, and the enforcement of all treaties related to wildlife preservation.

Pre-ESA Protection Efforts

Endangered species existed long before 1973, of course. The protection of individual species was an incremental process. Rooted in the tradition of colonial law, U.S. Supreme Court decisions through the nineteenth century ensured state jurisdictional control over that of landowners. By the 1870s, the federal government made it clear that it had an interest in wildlife issues. The establishment of the U.S. Fish Commission in 1871 and Yellowstone National Park in 1872 increased the role of the federal government substantially. The tension between federal and state authority resulted in the Yellowstone Game Protection Act of 1894, which established Yellowstone as a de facto national wildlife refuge in order to protect bison.

In the first half of the twentieth century, the federal government increased its direct, national jurisdiction with such legislation as the Lacey Act (1900), the creation of the first official national wildlife refuge at Pelican Island (1903), the ratification of the Migratory Bird Treaty Act with Canada (1918), and the passage of the Bald Eagle Protection Act (1940). Yet, a comprehensive national policy on species preservation was not enacted until the 1960s. The professionalization of ecology and the dawning of the American environmental movement created the needed atmosphere for reform. Building on the political response to Rachel Carson's *Silent Spring* (1962), the Bureau of Sport Fisheries and Wildlife established the Committee on Rare and Endangered Wildlife Species in 1964. The committee of nine biologists published a prototypical list of wildlife in danger of extinction, entitled the "Redbook," listing sixty-three endangered species. Congress passed a more comprehensive Endangered Species Preservation Act in 1966, requiring all federal agencies to prohibit the taking of endangered species on national wildlife refuges and authorizing additional refuges for conservation. The follow-up Endangered Species Conservation Act of 1969 extended protection to invertebrates. It also expanded prohibitions on interstate commerce provided by the Lacey Act and called for the development of a list of globally endangered species by the secretary of the Interior. The directive to facilitate an international conservation effort resulted in the Convention on International Trade in Endangered Species of Wild Fauna and Flora in early 1973. This set the stage for the Endangered Species Act later that year.

Passage of ESA and Early Challenges

Despite a surge of environmental regulatory lawmaking in the early 1970s, including the Clean Air Act, Federal Water Pollution Control Act Amendments (Clean Water Act), Federal Environmental Pesticide Control Act, and Coastal Zone Management Act, debate continued re-

Endangered Species. The Hawaiian stilt, or ae'o, is protected in Kanaha Pond, a former royal fishpond that that is now a state-owned wildlife sanctuary within the city of Kahului on Maui. NATIONAL ARCHIVES AND RECORDS ADMINISTRATION

garding federal and state regulatory authority and the types of species warranting protection. Representative John Dingell, who introduced the bill that became the Endangered Species Act, insisted that all flora and fauna be included. Section 29a of the ESA makes this clear by stating that all "species of fish, wildlife, and plants are of aesthetic, ecological, educational, historical, recreational, and scientific value to the Nation and its people." The issue of regulation resulted in greater compromise. Section 6, which directs the secretary of the Interior to foster cooperative agreements with states while allowing them substantial involvement in species management, also provides funds for state programs. In an effort to address these issues and others, including the geographical extent of prohibitions and the location of governmental responsibility, the House worked on fourteen different versions while the Senate worked on three. The bill ultimately passed both houses of Congress almost unanimously, setting a clear mandate (with only twelve dissenting votes in the House and one in the Senate). The subsequent history of ESA was much more highly contested.

One of the first major challenges to the ESA came with the *TVA v. Hill* battle over the Tellico Dam. From its inception, the Tellico Dam project of the Tennessee Valley Authority (TVA) faced major challenges. In the early 1970s, a lawsuit charging the violation of the 1969 National Environmental Policy Act (NEPA) and an inadequate environmental impact statement delayed construction. Resuming construction in 1973, the project halted again in 1977 when a lawsuit charged Tellico with violating the Endangered Species Act. The discovery of a small fish, the snail darter, in the portion of the Little Tennessee River yet to be swallowed up by the dam, created what later became a textbook case in environmental ethics. U.S. Attorney General Griffin Bell, who argued the TVA case himself, compared the three-inch fish to the social and economic welfare of countless people. The Supreme Court response was unequivocal. With the law upheld, the project stopped in its tracks. When the ESA subsequently came up for reauthorization in 1978, a plan to provide a mechanism for dispute resolution, in cases like Tellico, resulted in the creation of the first major change in ESA. The Endangered Species Committee, dubbed the "God Squad," was given the power to decide when economic and societal interests outweighed the biological consequences. Ironically, after the committee rejected the exemption for Tellico, populations of snail darters were found in neighboring Tennessee creeks. This discovery came after the authorization for Tellico's completion squeaked through in an amendment to the 1979 Energy and Water Development Appropriations Act.

While the "God Squad" had refused the exemption for Tellico, the committee opened the door for mitigation plans by considering "alternative habitats" for endangered species. An exemption granted in 1979 to the Grayrocks Dam and Reservoir in Wyoming, which threatened whooping crane habitat downstream, became the precursor to the Habitat Conservation Plan (HCP). A 1982 amendment to ESA created HCPs as an effort to resolve alleged unequal treatment in federal and private sectors. HCPs allowed for the incidental taking of endangered species by private property owners in exchange for the creation of a plan to offset losses through separate conservation efforts. By 1990, the U.S. Fish and Wildlife Service (FWS) had formally approved seven HCPs, with twenty more under way.

Struggles between Competing Interests in the 1990s

The final extended reauthorization of ESA in 1988 allotted appropriations for five years. Amendments provided funding for state cooperative programs, encouraged the use of emergency powers to list backlogged species candidates, and strengthened the protection of endangered plants. Since 1993, however, Congress has authorized funds only in one-year increments, while bills to weaken ESA have been regularly introduced. The apparent ambivalence with respect to reauthorization reflected divisions between protagonists and antagonists for a strengthened ESA. Conservation organizations such as the World Wildlife Fund and the Nature Conservancy, along with activist oriented organizations such as the Sierra Club and the National Wildlife Federation, grew in strength and numbers during the 1990s, while demanding an expanded ESA. Meanwhile, private property advocates represented by the loose-knit but widespread "wise use" movement led efforts to stop ESA intrusion into the lives of private landowners. The National Endangered Species Act Reform Coalition was particularly effective at getting legislation introduced to modify ESA.

The widely publicized controversy over the northern spotted owl epitomized the struggle of competing interests. The U.S. Forest Service and the Bureau of Land Management advocated protection of this Pacific Northwest subspecies as early as 1977. Yet, the FWS listed the owl as threatened thirteen years later, in 1990, after years of recommendations for habitat preservation by scientific and environmental coalitions. The "God Squad" met for the third time in fourteen years, in 1993, to discuss the northern spotted owl. Amidst emotional media coverage of the plight of loggers and their families, thirteen out of forty-four tracts of land were opened up, as environmental regulations like ESA took the blame for contributing to economic hardship. While environmentalists used the spotted owl as a surrogate for old growth forests, the timber industry criticized the use of the owl to protect old growth trees. A resolution ultimately took the intervention of President Bill Clinton. The president organized a "Forest Summit" in 1993 to develop the Pacific Northwest Plan, which included a substantial reduction in timber harvesting, an ecosystem-based management plan for 25 million acres of federal land, and an economic plan for displaced loggers and their families.

The Pacific Northwest Plan signaled a shift in federal endangered species policy. In 1995 the National Research Council report on the ESA argued that an ecosystem-based approach to managing natural resources must maintain biological diversity before individual species are in dire trouble. The Clinton administration's Interagency Ecosystem Management Task Force echoed this proactive approach in their 1995 report, which called for a collaboratively developed vision of desired future conditions that integrated ecological, economic, and social factors.

The shift toward an ecosystem approach follows historical changes in the primary cause of species endangerment from overharvesting to habitat destruction to ecosystem-wide degradation. The history of ESA demonstrates that competing economic goals, political priorities, and ethical arguments have also made solutions more elusive.

BIBLIOGRAPHY

Burgess, Bonnie B. *Fate of the Wild: The Endangered Species Act and the Future of Biodiversity.* Athens: University of Georgia Press, 2001.

Clark, Tim W. *Averting Extinction: Reconstructing Endangered Species Recovery.* New Haven, Conn.: Yale University Press, 1997.

Czech, Brian, and Paul R. Krausman. *The Endangered Species Act: History, Conservation Biology, and Public Policy.* Baltimore: Johns Hopkins University Press, 2001.

Kohm, Kathryn A., ed. *Balancing on the Brink: The Endangered Species Act and Lessons for the Future.* Washington, D.C.: Island Press, 1991.

Eric William Boyle

See also **Environmental Protection Agency.**

ENEMY ALIENS IN THE WORLD WARS. Since the late nineteenth century, the United States has tried to prevent criminals, political radicals, and other "dangerous" foreigners from entering the country. In 1875, Congress passed a law excluding foreign prostitutes and convicts; in 1882, lawmakers enacted legislation banning lunatics, idiots, and potentially indigent migrants. That same year, the federal government outlawed Chinese IMMIGRATION, limited the rights of Chinese residents, and prevented them from gaining American citizenship. For the next several decades, American courts upheld congressional authority to exclude aliens. During the twentieth century, federal legislators continued passing laws that excluded a variety of aliens, particularly people who belonged to radical political organizations that advocated the violent overthrow of the government. Originally aimed at anarchists, statutes such as the Immigration Act of 1917, the Alien Registration Act (SMITH ACT) of 1940, the Internal Security Act of 1950, and the Immigration and Nationality Act (McCarran-Walter Act) of 1952, extended the country's exclusion policy to individuals supporting socialism and communism. Congress also claimed the right to deport troublesome aliens. In 1948, the Supreme Court upheld the Alien Enemies Act of 1798, which authorized the president to expel any alien whom he regards as dangerous to the public peace or safety, or whom he believes is plotting against the country. Federal lawmakers also passed legislation in 1950 and again in 1952 giving the United States Attorney General authority to hold an alien in custody without bail.

Federal officials used these powers to crack down on enemy aliens during World War I and World War II. Soon after the United States entered World War I, Congress passed the Espionage Act of 15 June 1917 to intimidate socialists, radicals, and German Americans who opposed American participation in the conflict. Proponents of the law claimed it would only prevent sabotage of the war effort at home. Yet, the act's broad provisions allowed the federal government to imprison for up to twenty years anyone who made disloyal statements or tried to interfere with recruitment and enlistment, and to fine them $10,000. Although most radical groups who opposed the war did not spy on or sabotage the government, federal officials used the Espionage Act as an excuse to suppress unruly political organizations, such as the INDUSTRIAL WORKERS OF THE WORLD. Furthermore, the president ordered enemy aliens to stay away from military camps and munitions factories, and the government prevented them from entering or leaving the United States without special permission. Although federal officials interned a comparatively small number of aliens—2,300 of the 6,300 arrested—they had few procedural limitations and sometimes arrested suspects and held them without trial. The government also seized alien property during the war. Under the Trading with the Enemy Act of 1917, Congress created the Office of the Alien Property Custodian, which maintained jurisdiction over "all money and property in the United States due or belonging to an enemy, or an ally of an enemy." Private citizens also harassed enemy aliens. Suspicious employers fired German American workers, and vigilante groups intimidated and attacked enemy aliens and political radicals around the nation. Popular hysteria reached its zenith during the war when people renamed sauerkraut "liberty cabbage," dachshunds "liberty pups," and German measles "liberty measles."

During World War II, federal officials continued to monitor the activities of enemy aliens. The government, for example, fingerprinted people of German, Italian, and Japanese descent and forced them to carry identification cards. Officials convicted few people for sedition, but the Smith Act curbed freedom of expression. Furthermore, although Postmaster General Frank Walker avoided the extremism of his predecessor, Albert S. Burleson, he rescinded the mailing privileges of Axis-sympathizer Father Charles E. Coughlin's *Social Justice* and the Trotskyist paper *The Militant*. By the middle of the war, the government had imprisoned 4,132 enemy aliens. Yet, by contrast, government and public treatment of enemy aliens, with one notorious exception, was more enlightened during World War II. Unlike World War I, federal officials rarely prosecuted citizens for criticizing the government, and vigilante action against aliens and dissenters was virtually unknown. Furthermore, German Americans never faced the same level of vehement discrimination and intimidation that they had suffered during World War I.

People of Japanese descent, however, were not so fortunate. Early in the war, deep-seated prejudice toward Asians and growing public fears convinced President Franklin Roosevelt to place Japanese Americans in internment camps. On February 19, 1942, Roosevelt issued Executive Order No. 9066, giving the secretary of war the power to restrict designated military areas. Under the auspices of this order, the federal government transferred approximately 110,000 Japanese Americans, some 70,000 of whom were American citizens, from California, Oregon, Washington, and Arizona to relocation camps in the United States interior. On March 21, 1942, Congress confirmed and ratified Roosevelt's order. Japanese internment, and the treatment of enemy aliens during war, remains one of the most troubling legacies of American history.

BIBLIOGRAPHY

Kennedy, David. *Over Here: The First World War and American Society.* Oxford, U.K.; New York: Oxford University Press, 1980; 1982.

Luebke, Frederick C. *Bonds of Loyalty: German-Americans and World War I.* Dekalb: Northern Illinois University Press, 1974.

Murphy, Paul L. *World War I and the Origin of Civil Liberties in the United States.* New York: Norton, 1979.

Preston, William. *Aliens and Dissenters: Federal Suppression of Radicals, 1903–1933.* Cambridge, Mass.: Harvard University Press, 1962; Urbana: University of Illinois Press, 1994.

Takaki, Ronald. *Strangers From a Different Shore: A History of Asian Americans.* Boston: Little, Brown, 1989; New York: Penguin Books, 1990; Boston: Little, Brown, 1998.

Joseph A. Dowling/E. M.

See also **Chinese Exclusion Act; Espionage Act; Immigration Restriction; Japanese American Incarceration.**

ENERGY, DEPARTMENT OF. The Department of Energy (DOE) became the twelfth U.S. cabinet-level agency on 1 October 1977 under the Department of Energy Organization Act. Its responsibilities fall into three broad categories: energy, research, and national security.

The agency collects data on energy production and consumption, operates the petroleum reserve, and oversees numerous research programs including energy projects and a wide array of mathematics, science, and engineering projects at the national laboratories. The DOE also oversees nuclear weapons research, production, and ultimately disposal. The energy secretary advises the president on international energy issues and nuclear nonproliferation.

Institutional Heritage

The DOE sprung primarily from the Atomic Energy Commission, the Federal Energy Administration, and the Energy Research and Development Administration. The Atomic Energy Commission was created under the Atomic Energy Act of 1946; it replaced the wartime Manhattan Engineer District, which had developed the world's first atomic weapon. The new commission primarily oversaw nuclear weapons development and testing. However research and development extended to nuclear power reactors as part of President Dwight D. Eisenhower's "Atoms for Peace" program in 1953. The oil crisis of 1973 and the increasing need for research on new forms of energy inspired passage of the Energy Reorganization Act of 1974. This act established the Energy Research and Development Administration, which assumed the Commission's research and development programs.

Before the act was passed, President Richard Nixon had established the Federal Energy Office within the Executive Office of the President to oversee fuel allocation, rationing, and prices. He wanted a cabinet-level agency to assume these roles and work on the commercial development of new energy technologies so that the United States could become energy self-sufficient by 1980.

Nixon signed into law the act creating the Federal Energy Administration (FEA) to replace the Federal Energy Office. The new agency was also made up of several offices formerly of the Department of the Interior: the offices of petroleum allocation, energy conservation, energy data and analysis, and oil and gas. For three years the FEA administered oil allocation and regulated prices. The FEA also had the task of promoting energy conservation.

The enabling legislation for the Energy Research and Development Administration (ERDA) was signed by President Gerald Ford. It came with a wave of legislation encouraging research on renewable energy. The Solar Heating and Cooling Act of 1974, the Geothermal Energy Research, Development, and Demonstration Act of 1974, and the Solar Energy Research, Development, and Demonstration Act of 1974 charged the ERDA with ambitious research goals.

The ERDA established the Solar Energy Research Institute in Golden, Colorado. It also oversaw the creation of the (then) world's largest operational solar power generator, in Albuquerque, New Mexico. In Idaho, the ERDA created pilot projects that used hydrothermal convection to generate power. It also developed a prototype wind-power system in Sandusky, Ohio, and oversaw research on conventional nuclear reactors, breeder reactors, and fusion. All of these activities were added to the responsibilities for nuclear weapons production and waste disposal that the ERDA assumed from the defunct Atomic Energy Commission.

Creation of the DOE

President Jimmy Carter requested the creation of the DOE as his first attempt at reorganizing the Federal agencies. Congress created the new agency with one major change from Carter's request. Carter wanted the authority to set wholesale interstate electricity rates and crude oil prices to rest with the DOE secretary. Congress vested this authority in an independent Federal Energy Regulatory Commission (FERC).

The enabling legislation reflected the energy and environmental concerns of the late 1970s. The DOE was to "promote maximum possible energy conservation measures" and to give the commercial use of solar, geothermal, recycling, and other renewable energy resources "the highest priority in the national energy program."

The Carter era. President Carter's National Energy Plan had two broad objectives: first, to reduce dependence on foreign oil; and, second, to develop renewable and inexhaustible sources of energy. The DOE proposed energy efficiency standards for new buildings, created the Solar Training Institute, and worked with General Motors to develop prototype electric cars and trucks.

The new agency inherited ongoing investigations into allegations that several oil companies had conspired to overcharge consumers during the 1973 oil embargo crisis. These investigations were ongoing when another oil crisis in the spring of 1979 brought new allegations of price gouging against fifteen oil companies and further DOE investigations. By the end of Carter's term in office, the DOE had collected $1.7 billion in settlements with oil companies.

During the Carter era, the DOE's weapons laboratories developed nuclear warheads for air- and land-launched cruise missiles. The agency invested heavily in nuclear weapons safety research and cleanup procedures. Underground tests of nuclear weapons continued at the Nevada Test Site.

The newly formed agency generated a substantial amount of controversy across the full range of its activities. Some lawmakers immediately attacked the renewable-energy programs because of their high costs and slow production. In the summer of 1979 the DOE revealed that it had miscalculated key oil supply figures, resulting in $9 billion overcharge in favor of the oil companies, at the expense of the consumers. A DOE official admitted that petroleum industry lobbyists had obtained access to DOE documents in advance of public release. In the first two years of the agency's existence the DOE was subjected to over two hundred investigations.

The DOE also had to deal with mismanagement problems resulting from its predecessor agencies. The DOE announced that in 1975 secret documents pertaining to the hydrogen bomb had been erroneously declassified. A DOE official also testified before Congress on the exposure of at least nine hundred people to significant doses of radiation during atmospheric nuclear weapons tests in Nevada and the South Pacific between 1951 and 1962. The DOE identified fifty sites in more than twenty states that were once used for nuclear research and still posed contamination problems for area residents.

The Reagan and Bush era. Early in his first term, Ronald Reagan sought to abolish the DOE. He cut hundreds of positions from enforcement divisions of the agency. Reagan's abolition attempt failed in Congress when a General Accounting Office study revealed that abolition of the DOE would not save any money. Reagan was still able to change the function significantly. The Reagan-era DOE placed a much stronger focus on nuclear weapons production, nuclear energy, and fossil fuels. The Reagan administration cut DOE funding for renewable energy and conservation programs by as much as 80 percent, while it pledged to speed the licensing process of new nuclear power plants. The Reagan-era DOE deregulated the gasoline market. Between 1981 and 1989 the DOE dramatically expanded its weapons production and testing activities. During the previous decade nuclear weapons had been tested once every two years. In the 1980s three nuclear tests were conducted each year. The DOE also began preparations to store high-level nuclear waste at Yucca Mountain, Nevada.

During Reagan's tenure a DOE official was convicted of accepting bribes to pass on internal documents to oil industry officials. The DOE illegally provided a $550,000 grant to a contractor to aid in a lobbying effort against Congressional attempts to constrain nuclear testing. Independent investigations by the GAO and other agencies found the DOE lacking in both security and safety measures.

President George H. Bush vowed to improve the safety and environmental record of the DOE. His agency initiated research projects on acid rain and global warming. The weapons labs oversaw the development of nuclear testing methods that did not require atmospheric or underground detonations. Nuclear weapons production fell significantly as the Cold War concluded.

The Clinton era. The new post–Cold War world enabled the Clinton administration to make significant changes in the function of the DOE. The Clinton DOE spent less on nuclear weapons production and halted all underground tests. The DOE created partnerships between the national laboratories and private industry. Where the laboratories were previously focused on weapons production, they now developed research programs on environmental modeling, supercomputing, and the human genome. The Clinton DOE also resumed the development of energy efficiency standards for appliances, which had been dropped during the Reagan administration, and started a public awareness campaign on alternative fuels for automobiles.

In 1995 the DOE published a report documenting radiation experiments conducted by its predecessor agencies from the 1930s to the 1970s that exposed 16,000 men, women, and children to significant levels of radiation. The agency also had to handle the loss of significant nuclear-weapons secrets to China. The chief suspect in this espionage case was the Los Alamos National Laboratory scientist Wen Ho Lee, who was set free after a botched investigation. This serious security lapse led to an agency reorganization in 2000 that created the Agency for Nuclear Stewardship, which now answers to an independent chief rather than to the secretary of energy.

BIBLIOGRAPHY

Fehner, Terrence R., and Jack M. Holl. *Department of Energy, 1977–1994: A Summary History.* Washington, D.C.: Department of Energy, 1994.

Fehner, Terrence R., and F. G. Gosling. "Coming in From the Cold: Regulating U.S. Department of Energy Nuclear Facilities, 1942–1996." *Environmental History* 1, no. 2 (April 1996): 5–33.

Gosling, F. G., and Terrence R. Fehner. *Closing the Circle: The Department of Energy and Environmental Management, 1942–1994.* Washington, D.C.: Department of Energy, 1994.

Hewlett, Richard G., and Oscar E. Anderson Jr. *The New World, 1939–1946.* Vol. 1 of *A History of the Atomic Energy Commission.* Berkeley: University of California Press, 1990.

Daniel John Sherman

See also **Nuclear Power; Nuclear Weapons; Oil Crises.**

ENERGY INDUSTRY. The U.S. Department of Energy recognizes and monitors eleven sources for the production of energy, including biomass, coal, electricity, geothermal energy, hydrogen, hydropower, natural gas, nuclear power, petroleum, solar power, and power wind. Not all of these sources constitute separate industries, but all contribute to the industries that dominate the supply of American energy. Chief among the major industries are those that generate power by means of fossil fuels.

The History of Fossil Fuels in the United States

The United States has always been rich in resources, but at the time of the Revolutionary War muscle power and fuel wood provided almost all of the nation's supply of energy. The land's vast stores of coal and petroleum were undiscovered. The country for the most part was energy poor, relying on water mills for local industry and sail power for its ships. Yet time would prove that America held more coal than any other fossil fuel resource, with deposits in thirty-eight of the fifty states. Still, the beginning decades of the nineteenth century saw the use of coal only in blast furnaces and coal-gas limited natural gas lighting. Experiments with battery-powered electric trains occurred in the 1840s and 1850s; however, these innovations, together with such inventions as the cotton gin and the mechanical reaper, only served to supplement human labor as the primary source of power. Not until the second half of the nineteenth century did the work output of machines surpass that of humans and work animals.

The first commercial U.S. coal production began near Richmond, Virginia, in 1748. Baltimore, Maryland, became the first city to light streets with gas made from coal in 1816. When the railroads extended into the plains and the mountains to the west, scant wood resources created a dependence on coal, which was more locally available and proved more efficient in steam locomotives. At the same time, the metals industry used increasing amounts of coal-produced coke to generate the iron and steel needed for the thousands of miles of track that led toward westward expansion, and coal became a primary resource during the latter half of the nineteenth century. With the beginning of the domestic coke industry in the later 1800s, coke soon replaced charcoal as the chief fuel for iron blast furnaces. In 1882, the first practical coal-fired electric generating station, developed by Thomas Edison, went into operation in New York City to supply electricity for household lights.

At this time, petroleum served only as a lighting fuel and as an ingredient in patent medicines. By the end of World War I coal still served the needs of 75 percent of the United States' total energy use. However, during this same interval, America began to shift to mechanical power, and the surge into the industrial age quadrupled the nation's consumption of energy between 1880 and 1918. Coal continued to feed much of this increase while electricity found a growing number of applications as well. In 1901, the discovery of the Spindletop Oil Field in Texas made petroleum a more attractive resource, particularly when mass-production automobiles reached several million by 1918.

The petrochemical industry became one of the most important of the energy businesses in just a few decades. The industry quickly grew in the 1920s and 1930s, as many of the major companies entered the field. These included—after the early success of Standard Oil of New Jersey (later Exxon) and I.G. Farben—Shell Oil, Union Carbide, and Dow. By 1936 competition was keen, and Monsanto established a petrochemical subsidiary, a move that prompted similar reactions by other large chemical companies. The petrochemical industry continued to grow through the 1940s and 1950s; and in the years following World War II petroleum replaced coal as the primary fuel in the United States. The railroad industry switched to diesel locomotives but suffered increasing losses to trucks that could run on gasoline and diesel fuel. The petroleum industry, which reached its stride in the mid-1970s, has created some of the largest chemical companies in the United States, including Exxon Chemical, OxyChem, and ARCO Chemical. As natural gas lost American favor as a fuel for light, that industry shifted to other markets, notably heating for household ranges and furnaces. The coal industry survived in large part by supplying fuel to electric utilities nationwide.

Michael Faraday invented the first electric motor in 1821, but not until 1878 did Edison Electric Light Company come into existence, followed the next year by the first commercial power station in San Francisco. At the start of the twentieth century, electric power was young but growing rapidly. Thomas Edison's work had led to the first commercial power plant for incandescent lighting and power in 1882. However, Edison's system used direct current, which could only deliver energy profitably to a limited area around the station. The work of engineers such as Nikola Tesla and Charles Steinmetz led to the successful commercialization of alternating current, which enabled transmission of high-voltage power over long distances.

Electrical power stations evolved from waterwheels to dams with a variety of turbines: reaction and hydraulic, fixed and variable blade, as well as reversible turbines that could pump water into elevated storage wells and then reverse back to generate power. In 1903, Charles Curtis pioneered the steam turbine generator, which generated 5,000 kilowatts from a plant that was the most powerful in the world at that time. Turbine generators required one-tenth the space and weighed only one-eighth as much as reciprocating engines of comparable output. Next came the world's first high-pressure steam plant, which further increased efficiency and brought substantial savings in fuel. In 1925, the Edgar Station in Boston became a model for high-pressure power plants worldwide.

Experiments continued to improve ways to adapt fuels for power generation, and the Oneida Street plant in Milwaukee began using pulverized coal in 1918. Adapting fuels to generate power was, and still is, an ongoing process. Increasing steam pressures also led the way to new materials such as chrome-molybdenum steel, which offered superior heat resistance in turbines. Power plants and improved fuel resources brought electricity to America. However, companies still focused most of their attention on urban areas, and only one in forty Americans enjoyed the benefits of electricity in the early twentieth century. Then, in 1935, the Rural Electric Administration was established, and President Franklin D. Roosevelt chose Morris Llewellyn Cooke, an engineer, to head the new agency with the charge of making electric power available across the nation. As a result, farmers soon replaced steam or gasoline power with electric motors that drove farm machinery and water pumps.

The early public works projects of the 1930s' Great Depression still provide today's electricity. Hoover Dam's hydroelectric generators, built between 1932 and 1935, supply nearly 1.5 million kilowatt-hours of electrical power per year to the people of the southwestern United States, and in 1933, the Tennessee Valley Authority was launched to bring power and flood relief to the Tennessee River basin. It currently operates numerous dams, eleven large coal-burning steam plants, and two nuclear plants in Alabama and Tennessee, producing more than 125 billion kilowatt-hours of electricity annually—about ninety times the power once generated in the region in 1933. By the 1990s, the entire country was linked into two giant grid systems, each serving a respective half of the country, and power transmission increased from 220 volts in the 1880s to 765,000 volts by 1999.

Energy Consumption in the United States

Throughout the twentieth century, fossil fuels provided most of the energy in the United States, far exceeding all other sources of energy together. Since colonial times, the United States enjoyed almost self-sufficiency in energy where supply and demand balanced until the late 1950s. Consumption began to surpass domestic production by the early 1970s, and this trend has continued since that time. In 2000 fossil fuels still accounted for 80 percent of total energy production and were valued at an estimated $148 billion. The United States at the beginning of the current millennium produced almost 72 quadrillion British thermal units (Btu) of energy and exported roughly four quadrillion Btu. Consumption totaled about 98 quadrillion Btu, and so still required imports of close to 29 quadrillion Btu, some nineteen times the level used in 1949.

The major cause of shortages results from insufficient petroleum. For example, in 1973, U.S. petroleum imports had reached 6.3 million barrels per day when Middle Eastern oil interests initiated an oil embargo. The embargo precipitated a sharp hike in oil prices followed by a two-year fall in petroleum imports. From 1979 to 1981 and again since 1986, the price of crude oil continued to climb significantly with the effect of suppressed imports. Petroleum imports to the United States in 2000 reached a yearly record level of 11 million barrels per day.

Despite the fact that electricity forms the basis of a major U.S. energy industry, it is nevertheless not an energy source per se. Electricity relies upon fossil fuels, hydroelectric power, and nuclear power for generation. Electric utilities have become large and complex in America, transmitted over long distances that span almost a half-million domestic miles. Most U.S. electricity derives from a combination of coal-burning and nuclear plants with slightly over 20 percent provided by natural gas, petroleum plants, and hydroelectric plants.

Over the years, Americans have learned to use energy more efficiently, as measured by the amount of energy used to produce a dollar's worth of gross domestic product. The result has been a 49 percent improvement between 1949 and 2000, and the amount of energy needed to generate a dollar of output has fallen from almost 21,000 Btu to just over 10,000 Btu—despite increased energy use brought on by a mounting population. The U.S. population grew 89 percent from 149 million people in 1949 to 281 million in 2000, and total energy consumption expanded by 208 percent from 32 quadrillion Btu to 98 quadrillion Btu. This translates to increased energy consumption per capita of 63 percent, from 215 million Btu in 1949 to 350 million Btu in 2000.

Energy continues to hold a key position in the economy of the United States, and energy spending keeps pace as well. Currently, American consumers spend more than half a trillion dollars on energy annually. Coal served as the leading source of energy for both residential and commercial consumers as late as 1951 but then declined rapidly. By contrast, natural gas grew strongly until 1972 and then stalled. Petroleum use grew at a slower, steadier pace but also peaked and declined around 1972. Only electricity, which was an incidental energy source in 1949, has expanded almost every year since that time, due largely to the expansion of electricity-driven appliances in U.S. households nationwide. For example, 99 percent of U.S. homes possessed a color television in 1997, and 47 percent had central air conditioning. Four-fifths of all households contained one refrigerator, and the rest had two or more. Other newer innovations such as microwave ovens and home computers have also increased residential energy use. In 1978, only 8 percent of U.S. households had a microwave, compared to 83 percent by 1997, and only 16 percent of households owned a personal computer compared to 35 percent by 1997. Home heating experienced equally large changes. One-third of all U.S. housing units used coal for heat in 1950, but only two-tenths of a percent used coal in 1999. During that same interval, home fuel oil lost half its market share (dropping from 22 percent to 10 percent), while natural gas and electricity gained as home-heating sources. Natural gas rose from one-fourth to one-half of all homes, and electricity gained, rising from only .6 percent in 1950 to 30 percent in 1999. Both electricity and natural gas have continued as the most common sources of energy used by commercial buildings as well.

Alternatives to Fossil Fuels

The America of the twentieth century has explored a number of alternatives to fossil fuels, and many of these energies are characterized as "renewable," since they do not rely on depleting finite stores of energy. In 1998, Congress increased funding for energy efficiency programs by $80 million for fiscal year 1999. That same year, President Bill Clinton issued an executive order calling for the federal government to reduce its energy use 35 percent by 2010 compared to 1985 levels—a measure that encourages alternative approaches to fossil fuel consumption.

One such alternative resource is biomass, a term that refers to plant-derived organic matter available from dedicated energy crops and trees, agricultural food and feed crops, agricultural crop wastes and residues, wood wastes and residues, aquatic plants, animal wastes, municipal wastes, and other waste materials. The resulting biopower technologies provide options for the generation of electricity in the United States, with ten gigawatts of installed capacity. Biomass fuels derive from liquid ethanol, methanol, biodiesel, Fischer-Tropsch diesel, and other gaseous fuels such as hydrogen and methane. Bio-based chemicals and materials produce so-called green chemicals, renewable plastics, natural fibers, and natural structural materials.

Another alternative industry has developed around the extraction of geothermal energy. Heat exists consistently beneath the earth's surface around the globe, where molten magma raises the temperature of hot, dry rock. This technology drills into the heated rock, injects cold water down one well to circulate through the hot, fractured rock, and then draws off the heated water from another well. In 1921, John D. Grant drilled a well into geysers just north of San Francisco, California, with the intention of generating electricity. Although this effort was unsuccessful, one year later Grant succeeded across the valley at a different site, creating the United States' first geothermal power plant.

The country's first large-scale geothermal plant for generating electricity began in 1960 at Grant's first geyser site, operated by Pacific Gas and Electric. By 2000, the plant had sixty-nine generating facilities in operation at eighteen resource sites across the country. Congress passed the Geothermal Steam Act in 1970, providing the secretary of the Interior with authority to lease public lands and other federal lands for geothermal exploration and development. By 1984, a twenty-megawatt plant began generating power at Utah's Roosevelt Hot Springs, a 1.3-megawatt binary power plant began operation in Nevada, and the Heber dual-flash power plant went online in the Imperial Valley of California with a fifty-megawatt facility. In 1994, the Department of Energy created two industry/government collaborative efforts to promote geothermal energy that reduces greenhouse gases, for both electric power generation and the accelerated use of geothermal heat pumps. In 2000, the government initiated its "GeoPowering the West" program to encourage research and development of geothermal resources in the

Alternative Energy. Large wind turbines like the ones dotting this hillside, c. 1985, are a small but growing source of clean energy in some parts of the country, such as the Great Plains and California. © GEORGE LEPP/CORBIS

western United States, with an initial group of twenty-one partnerships funded to develop new technologies.

The Atomic Energy Act of 1954 gave the civilian nuclear energy program workable access to nuclear technology, and the following year, the Atomic Energy Commission announced a cooperative program between government and industry to develop nuclear power plants. Arco, Idaho, was the first U.S. town powered by nuclear energy by using an experimental boiling water reactor. In 1957, the first power was generated by the Sodium Reactor Experiment, a civilian nuclear unit at Santa Susana, California. That same year, Congress enacted the Price-Anderson Act, designed to protect the public, utilities, and contractors financially in the event of an accident at a nuclear power plant. Also, the first full-scale nuclear power plant went into service in Shippingport, Pennsylvania.

In 1963 the Jersey Central Power and Light Company created the first nuclear plant designed as an economical alternative to a fossil-fuel plant. Following the Organization of Petroleum Exporting Countries' (OPEC) oil embargo in 1973, United States utilities ordered forty-one nuclear power plants. By 1984, nuclear power overtook hydropower to become the second-largest source of electricity, after coal. Two decades after the 1973 embargo, 109 nuclear power plants operated in the United States and provided about one-fifth of the nation's electricity. In 1996, the Nuclear Regulatory Commission granted the Tennessee Valley Authority a full-power license for its Watts Bar 1 nuclear power plant, bringing the number of operating nuclear units in the United States to 110. In 2000, the Nuclear Regulatory Commission issued the first license renewal to Constellation Energy's Calvert Cliffs Nuclear Power Plant, allowing an additional twenty years of operation. The Nuclear Regulatory Commission also approved a twenty-year extension to the operating license of Duke Energy's three-unit Oconee Nuclear Station.

A number of other alternatives to fossil fuel have undergone research and development, including wind and solar power. These technologies exist primarily in the hands of the private sector and do not constitute industries in the same sense that petrochemicals or coal, for example, have become part of the national energy resources. Rather, they contribute to individuals' power needs and in some instances, such as California's wind power stations, have contributed to the larger electrical grid.

The Future of U.S. Energy Use

The Energy Information Administration has offered certain projections of American energy use in its Annual Energy Outlook 2001, which suggests likely consumption through 2020 barring unexpected events like the 1973 oil embargo. According to these projections, energy prices are expected to increase slowly for petroleum and natural gas and may actually decline for coal and electricity. If these trends bear out, then U.S. total consumption could reach 127 quadrillion Btu by 2020, which is 29 percent higher than in 2000. The report also suggests that consumption in all areas will continue to increase, particularly in transportation because of an expected increase in travel as well as greater needs for freight carriers. Although Americans are using energy more efficiently, a higher demand for energy services will likely raise energy use per capita slightly between 2000 and 2020. Energy intensity—that is, the energy use per dollar of gross domestic product—has declined since 1970 and the projection continues to support that trend.

Long-used oil fields in the United States will produce less at the same time that America experiences a rising demand for petroleum. Imports will make up the difference, a rise from the 52 percent used in 2000 to 64 percent by 2020. Although domestic natural gas production has risen 2.1 percent each year, increasing demand will also require more gas imports. Output coal-field production within the United States will also increase to match expanding domestic demands. Renewable energy sources will likely grow by only 1.1 percent each year. Growth in production of energy from renewable sources is expected to average about 1.1 percent per year, whereas nuclear power facilities will decline at the same rate. With no strong measures to reduce emissions of carbon dioxide yet in sight, the greater use of fossil fuels, together with a relatively slow market in renewable energy sources, may well lead to higher emissions. As a result, emissions related to energy will exceed 2 billion metric tons of carbon (7.5 billion tons of gas) in 2020, up 33 percent from 2000.

BIBLIOGRAPHY

Bromley, Simon. *American Hegemony and World Oil: The Industry, the State System and the World Economy.* University Park: Pennsylvania State University Press, 1991.

Department of Energy. Home page at http://www.energy.gov/.

Ehringer, H. *Energy Conservation in Industry: Combustion, Heat Recovery and Rankine Machines.* Boston: D. Reidel, 1983.

Energy Information Annual. Home page at http://www.eia.doe.gov/emeu/aer/contents.html.

Garwin, Richard L., and Georges Charpak. *Megawatts and Megatons: A Turning Point in the Nuclear Age.* New York: Knopf, 2001.

Hirsh, Richard F. *Technology and Transformation in the American Electric Utility Industry.* Cambridge, Mass.: Cambridge University Press, 1989.

Hoover Dam National Historic Landmark. Home page at http://www.hooverdam.usbr.gov/.

Melosi, Martin V. *Effluent America: Cities, Industry, Energy, and the Environment.* Pittsburgh, Pa.: University of Pittsburgh Press, 2001.

Pratt, Joseph A. *Voice of the Marketplace: A History of the National Petroleum Council (Oil and Business History Series, 13).* College Station: Texas A&M University Press, 2002.

Redlinger, Robert Y. *Wind Energy in the 21st Century: Economics, Policy, Technology, and the Changing Electricity Industry.* New York: Macmillan, 2001.

Richards, Deanna J., and Greg Pearson, eds. *The Ecology of Industry: Sectors and Linkages.* Washington, D.C.: National Academy Press, 1998.

Saltzman, Sidney, and Richard E. Schuler, eds. *The Future of Electrical Energy: A Regional Perspective of an Industry in Transition.* Westport, Conn.: Praeger, 1986.

Stern, Jonathan P. *Natural Gas Trade in North America and Asia (Energy Papers, No. 15).* Burlington, Vt.: Ashgate, 1985.

Mark Todd

See also **Hydroelectric Power; Nuclear Power.**

ENERGY, RENEWABLE. Wood, wind, water, and sun power have been used for cooking, heating, milling, and other tasks for millennia. During the Industrial Revolution of the eighteenth and early nineteenth centuries, these forms of renewable energy were replaced by fossil fuels such as coal and petroleum. At various times throughout the nineteenth and twentieth centuries, people believed that fossil fuel reserves would be exhausted and focused their attentions on sources of renewable energy. This led to experiments with solar steam for industry and solid wood, methanol gas, or liquid biofuels for engines. Attention has refocused on renewable energy sources since the 1960s and 1970s, not only because of concern over fossil fuel depletion, but also because of apprehension over acid rain and global warming from the accumulation of carbon dioxide in the atmosphere.

Acid rain is clearly the result of the use of fossil fuels, and most authoritative climatologists also believe that these fuels are contributing to global warming. Many scientists and environmentalists have, therefore, urged a global switch to renewable energy, which derives from the sun or from processes set in motion by the sun. These energy forms include direct use of solar power along with windmills, hydroelectric dams, ocean thermal energy systems, and biomass (solid wood, methane gas, or liquid fuels). Renewable energy thus differs not only from fossil energy sources such as petroleum, gas, and coal, but also from nuclear energy, which usually involves dividing uranium atoms.

In the early 1990s, one-fifth of worldwide energy use was renewable, with by far the largest portion of this coming from fuel wood and biomass. Hydroelectric dams made up most of the rest. More than half the world's population relied on wood for cooking and heating, and although wood is generally considered to be renewable, excessive reliance has long been recognized as a cause of deforestation. Forests disappear faster than they can be renewed by natural processes. Energy "crops" —for example, fast-growing acacia or eucalyptus trees planted for fuel wood in the Third World—and more efficient wood stoves may be useful to poor, wood-reliant nations.

Solar energy is a term for many techniques and systems. The sun's energy can be trapped under glass in a greenhouse or within solar panels that heat water. It can also be concentrated in a trough or parabolic collector. In arid climates a small version of a concentrator is sometimes used to substitute for wood. Although economical, it is unreliable, hard to transport, and difficult to operate. Larger concentrators can produce steam economically for industry or for electric utilities in some climates. Another form of solar energy comes from photovoltaic cells mounted on panels. These panels are economical for all kinds of remote power needs, from cheap hand calculators to mountaintop navigational beacons to orbiting satellites. Costs have dropped dramatically since the mid-1970s, from hundreds of thousands of dollars to several thousands per installed kilowatt, and are expected to drop to under a thousand dollars early in the twenty-first century. At some point they may become competitive with nuclear and fossil energy.

Water power has been well known since its use in the Egyptian and classical Greek civilizations, and at the outset of the Industrial Revolution, it was widely used in Europe and the Americas to grind grain and run looms and in other small-scale industrial processes. Today water power is by far the cheapest of all fossil, nuclear, and renewable forms of energy for producing electricity, but the ecological disruptions caused by hydroelectric dams have caused many environmental controversies. Ocean energy takes advantage of the movement of water in tides or waves or of the temperature difference between sun-heated surface water and cold deep water. A few tidal energy projects have been built, but this form of energy production is expensive and remains largely experimental. Like tidal energy, geothermal energy is produced by continuous natural processes not directly related to solar cycles. Geothermal energy takes advantage of hot water trapped deep inside the earth to produce electricity or heat for homes and industry.

Wind power has been used for grinding grain, pumping water, and powering sawmills since the Middle Ages, and thousands of windmills once dotted coastal areas of northern Europe. Water-pumping windmills were a fixture in the American Midwest well into the twentieth century. Windmills are returning in a high-tech form in places like Altamont Pass in California, where they produce electricity. They are widely used for pumping water in the Third World.

Biomass energy involves a wide range of low and high technologies, from wood burning to use of manure, sea kelp, and farm crops to make gas and liquid biofuels. Brazil leads the world in use of pure ethyl alcohol derived from sugarcane as a replacement for petroleum. A common fuel in the United States is corn-derived ethyl alcohol, which is used as a low-pollution octane booster in a 10-percent blend with gasoline called "gasohol." Another form of renewable energy used in the rural Third World is the gas-producing biogas digester. Human and animal wastes are mixed with straw and water in an airless underground tank made of brick or cement. Methane gas is siphoned from the tank to a cooking stove. Meanwhile, the tank gets hot enough to kill disease-causing bacteria, which is an important sanitary improvement in many countries. Over the past few decades, 5 million biogas tanks have been built in China and half a million in India.

Renewable energy resources are cleaner and far more abundant than fossil resources, but they tend to be dispersed and more expensive to collect. Many of them, such as wind and solar energy, are intermittent in nature, making energy storage or distributed production systems necessary. Therefore, the direct cost of renewable energy is generally higher than the direct cost of fossil fuels. At the same time, fossil fuels have significant indirect or external costs, such as pollution, acid rain, and global warming. How to account for these external costs and assign the savings to renewable energy is a matter of continued policy debate. Another policy issue is research and development support. Conventional forms of energy, such as fossil fuels and nuclear power, receive more financial support from the federal government than does renewable energy. U.S. government policy toward renewable energy has been a roller coaster of support and neglect. By the end of President Jimmy Carter's administration in 1981, federal contributions to research in solar photovoltaics, solar thermal energy, solar buildings, biofuels, and wind energy research had soared to almost $500 million, but by 1990 the figure was only $65 million. A global transition to renewable energy will have to include developing nations, where energy use in proportion to the world total grew from 20 percent in 1970 to 31 percent in 1990.

BIBLIOGRAPHY

Berinstein, Paula. *Alternative Energy: Facts, Statistics, and Issues.* Westport, Conn.: Oryx Press, 2001.

Blackburn, John O. *The Renewable Energy Alternative: How the United States and the World Can Prosper Without Nuclear Energy or Coal.* Durham, N.C.: Duke University Press, 1987.

Butti, Ken, and John Perlin. *A Golden Thread: 2,500 Years of Solar Architecture and Technology.* New York: Van Nostrand Reinhold, 1980.

Flavin, Christopher. *Beyond the Petroleum Age: Designing a Solar Economy.* Washington, D.C.: Worldwatch Institute, 1990.

Kovarik, Bill. *Fuel Alcohol: Energy and Environment in a Hungry World.* London: International Institute for Environment and Development, 1982.

Sørensen, Bent. *Renewable Energy: Its Physics, Engineering, Use, Environmental Impact, Economy and Planning Aspects.* San Diego, Calif.: Academic Press, 2000.

Bill Kovarik / H. S.

See also **Acid Rain; Air Pollution; Conservation; Energy Policy; Energy Research and Development Administration; Global Warming; Hydroelectric Power; Nuclear Power; Water Pollution;** *and vol. 9:* **Address on Energy Crisis.**

ENERGY RESEARCH AND DEVELOPMENT ADMINISTRATION. The Energy Research and Development Administration (ERDA) was created by Congress on 11 October 1974 as part of the Energy Reorganization Act of 1974. The act created two new agencies: the Nuclear Regulatory Commission, which would regulate the nuclear power industry, and the ERDA, designed to manage the nuclear weapon, naval reactor, and energy development programs. Activated on 19 January 1975, the agency attempted to carry out President Richard M. Nixon's goal of achieving energy independence by developing plans, technologies, and conservation programs and by managing national-security activities associated with nuclear energy. Spurred on by the Arab oil embargo of 1973, the agency provided a bridge between the Atomic Energy Commission (1947–1975) and the Department of Energy (created in 1977), which absorbed the ERDA. Despite the brevity of its brief existence, ERDA represented an important step by the administration of President Gerald R. Ford in bringing together diverse energy activities across the federal government. ERDA's focus was reflected in six program areas: fossil and nuclear energy; environment and safety; solar; geothermal and advanced energy systems; conservation; and national security.

Led by Robert C. Seamans, Jr., and Robert W. Fri, the agency produced a series of national energy plans that advocated experimentation and energy leadership to stimulate private-sector commercialization. These plans stressed expanding existing resources and conservation; establishment of a synthetic-fuels industry; and long-range development of inexhaustible energy sources from breeder reactors, fusion, solar, wind, thermal, ocean thermal power, and photovoltaics. While Americans expressed some support for conservation, they responded much more enthusiastically to research into alternative energy resources. Although the agency was unsuccessful in early commercialization of synthetic fuels, it made progress in planning, mobilizing talent, and developing ties with industry and international partners. It created the Solar Energy Research Institute (which became the National Renewable Energy Laboratory in 1994). Solar power so dominated the national energy discussion in the mid-1970s that, in 1974, three of the five major bills passed by Congress involved solar and geothermal energy. The ERDA also promoted fusion and prototype wind-power demonstrations while executing its continuing responsibility for nuclear weapons production and nuclear waste disposal.

BIBLIOGRAPHY

Kash, Don E., and Robert W. Rycroft. *U.S. Energy Policy: Crisis and Complacency*. Norman: University of Oklahoma Press, 1984.

Vietor, Richard H. K. *Energy Policy in America Since 1945: A Study of Business Government Relations*. New York: Cambridge University Press, 1984.

Walsh, Roberta W., and John G. Heilman, eds. *Energizing the Energy Policy Process: The Impact of Evaluation*. Westport, Conn.: Quorum Books, 1994.

B. Franklin Cooling/s. c.

See also **Air Pollution; Conservation; Energy, Department of; Energy, Renewable; Nuclear Power; Nuclear Regulatory Commision; Oil Crises.**

ENFORCEMENT ACTS. *See* **Force Acts.**

ENGINEERING EDUCATION. Revolutionary America possessed no way to educate engineers. Millwrights and other craftsmen had solved most technical problems for colonists, but the continental army had to turn to Europeans for advice on fortifications and military engineering. After independence, early canal promoters and elected officials alike continued to rely on visiting civil engineers. The army found this situation intolerable and in 1802 established the U.S. Military Academy at West Point to train artillery and engineering officers. Sylvanus Thayer, commandant after 1817, transformed West Point into the nation's first engineering school by copying the École Polytechnique in France.

Most Americans entered the engineering profession, however, by serving an apprenticeship. Thus John Jervis began as an axeman on the Erie Canal in 1817 and rose to division engineer in 1825. Only after 1825 did additional educational opportunities become available to Americans interested in engineering careers. Partial programs, ranging from individual courses in trigonometry and surveying to year-long certificate programs, appeared at many schools, including Washington College, Princeton, New York University, and Vanderbilt. Apprenticeships then completed the training for many students. Partial programs differed in kind but not in spirit from the courses and lectures at Philadelphia's Franklin Institute and similar voluntary associations in other American cities. In keeping with Jacksonian democratic rhetoric, these were self-help programs for working people encountering new technologies.

By the 1840s informal engineering education seemed inadequate for an expanding nation that linked political independence to technology. A few schools copied the French polytechnic model, which derived technical training from a common base in mathematics and science, delivered in separate schools outside existing colleges. The Rensselaer School, started as an artisans' institute in 1824, transformed itself into the first American polytechnic in 1850. By the time the school renamed itself Rensselaer Polytechnic Institute in 1861, other polytechnics had appeared, including the Polytechnic College of Pennsylvania (1853) and Brooklyn Polytechnic (1854). All departed from liberal arts curricula to train men for careers in engineering and manufacturing.

Not all educators separated engineering from colleges. In 1847 Harvard and Yale launched undergraduate programs for engineering, albeit in separate schools outside their main colleges. But after 1850 more private institutions and state universities developed engineering programs as regular courses of study. Midwestern colleges, including Wesleyan, Denison, and Allegheny, offered engineering under general science degrees, while the universities of Illinois, North Carolina, and Iowa, and the University of Rochester added engineering degrees. The crucial step in placing engineering inside American universities was the Morrill Act of 1862, which provided federal support (initially thirty thousand acres of federal land for every congressional representative) to encourage the agricultural and mechanical arts. Land-grant colleges quickly became leading engineering schools, among them Pennsylvania State, Massachusetts Institute of Technology (MIT), and midwestern state universities in Illinois, Indiana (Purdue), Ohio State, and Wisconsin. New York's land-grant school, Cornell, was the largest and best engineering college in the country by the 1870s.

Every approach to educating American engineers shared a desire to balance theory and practice. Even as academic education became more common after 1870, hands-on training remained. Universities, land-grant schools, and polytechnics all combined lecture courses, engineering drawing, surveying, and shop classes. The basic credential for faculty was engineering experience, not advanced degrees. Indeed, some mechanical engineers were so concerned about practice they created yet another educational alternative, the technical institute. Worcester Polytechnic Institute (1868) and Stevens Institute (1870) explicitly placed machine-shop apprenticeships ahead of studies of math and science. Even Cornell's mechanical engineering program emphasized shop work until the 1880s.

But the classroom finally prevailed over practical venues for training engineers. New technologies based on electricity and chemistry required more than a common-sense knowledge base. Equally important was the desire of leading American engineers to gain the social recognition accorded other emerging professional groups. A key step was presenting engineers as college-educated gentlemen, not narrow technical specialists. The formation of the American Society for Engineering Education in 1893 symbolized the shift of engineering education from the shop to the classroom.

Balancing theory and practice remained a fundamental issue, however. Cornell's Robert Thurston led those pressing to replace shop work with math and science along the lines of French polytechnics and German universities. Other faculty emphasized training practical problem solvers for American corporations, so the University of Cincinnati introduced a cooperative education program in 1907 in which students alternated semesters working in industry and attending classes. After World War I, hints of change appeared as European émigrés demonstrated the utility of sophisticated mathematical analyses. Ukrainian-born Stephon Timoshenko, first at Westinghouse and then at the University of Michigan and at Stanford, prepared textbooks placing the strength of materials, structural mechanics, and dynamics on a mathematical footing. Hungarian-born Theodore von Kármán brought German theoretical work in fluid dynamics to the new CALIFORNIA INSTITUTE OF TECHNOLOGY. At the University of Illinois, Danish-born and German-educated Harald Westergaard connected civil engineering and theoretical mechanics through studies of bridges, pavement slabs, and dams.

Only Caltech, Harvard, and, belatedly, MIT embraced the changes introduced by this generation of European engineers in the 1930s. Developments during World War II in such areas as radar and atomic weapons confirmed the value of the European engineers' approaches. Major educational reforms followed, including greater emphasis on research and graduate study. Theory outweighed practice for the first time as engineering science replaced shop work and drawing. Driven by Cold War rhetoric and apparent challenges such as Sputnik, the Soviet satellite program, federal military funding supported this transformation and promoted hybrid interdisciplinary fields, such as materials engineering, that blurred the boundary between science and engineering. By 1960 engineering education was remarkably uniform.

Transforming engineering from a white-male preserve was much more difficult. Wartime "manpower" concerns in the 1940s and 1950s led some faculty to accept women students. But progress was slow until the social movements of the 1960s brought serious steps to recruit women and underrepresented minorities. Engineering remains, however, the least diverse profession in the United States. And by the late 1980s declining numbers of American students meant most graduate students in engineering were born outside the United States.

This demographic shift was accompanied by questions about the postwar emphasis on engineering science. Declining American competitiveness in global markets was partly connected to the lack of engineering graduates with practical problem-solving skills. New attempts to balance theory and practice in the 1990s marked a very basic continuity in the history of American engineering education.

BIBLIOGRAPHY

Emmerson, George. *Engineering Education: A Social History.* New York: Crane, Russak, 1973.

Grayson, Lawrence P. *The Making of an Engineer: An Illustrated History of Engineering Education in the United States and Canada.* New York: Wiley, 1993.

Reynolds, Terry S. "The Education of Engineers in America before the Morrill Act of 1862." *History of Education Quarterly* 32 (winter 1992): 459–482.

Seely, Bruce E. "The Other Re-engineering of Engineering Education, 1900–1965." *Journal of Engineering Education* 88, no. 3 (July 1999): 285–294.

———. "Research, Engineering, and Science in American Engineering Colleges, 1900–1960." *Technology and Culture* 34 (April 1993): 344–386.

Bruce Seely

See also **Cornell University; Sheffield Scientific School.**

ENGINEERING SOCIETIES. The appearance of professional engineering societies in the United States was symptomatic of a technological revolution—a shift from a conservative, craft tradition to a more dynamic, scientific approach to technology. Professional engineering societies played an important role in the rapid growth of technology in the nineteenth century. They became a means for developing professional spirit among engineers; and, as the sometimes-adverse effects of rapid technological change became manifest, they also became a means for expressing their members' sense of social responsibility.

The first engineering societies were local. The Boston Society of Civil Engineers (1848), the Engineers Club of Saint Louis (1868), and the Western Society of Engineers of Chicago (1869) were among the first to form. But the local societies gradually were overshadowed by national ones. The American Society of Civil Engineers was founded in 1852, although it did not become active nationally until revitalized in 1867. It set high professional standards and claimed to represent all nonmilitary engineers. This claim was disputed in 1871 with the formation of the American Institute of Mining and Metallurgical Engineers. Led by Rossiter Worthington Raymond, it made industrial service its goal rather than professional development. The increased employment of engineers in industry led to the formation of the American Society of Mechanical Engineers in 1880 and the American Institute of Electrical Engineers in 1884. In terms of professional philosophy, these two organizations stood between the societies of civil and mining engineers, combining the sometimes-antagonistic goals of industrial service and professionalism.

In theory, the four fields of civil, mining, mechanical, and electrical engineering were thought to comprise all engineering. The four societies representing these fields are called the "founder societies," and they have often served as the voice for American engineering. In practice, however, the headlong progress of technology created new technical specialties almost yearly. New societies—such as the Society of Automotive Engineers (1905), the American Institute of Chemical Engineers (1908), the American Nuclear Society (1954), and the American Academy of Environmental Engineers (1955)—were founded to meet the needs of engineers working in these new fields. In some cases, the newer fields came to overshadow traditional ones. Impelled by the spectacular growth of electronics, the Institute of Radio Engineers, founded in 1912, outpaced the American Institute of Electrical Engineers; the two merged in 1963 to form the Institute of Electrical and Electronic Engineers. Still other societies, such as the American Rocket Society (1930) and the Institute of Aerospace Sciences (1932), became more effective when they merged to become the American Institute of Aeronautics and Astronautics in 1963

While technology advances have fragmented the engineering profession, the professional spirit of the various groups has actually grown stronger and led to increased professional unity and social responsibility. One of the first organizations to express the new spirit of professional unity was the American Association of Engineers, founded in 1915. Under the leadership of Frederick Haynes Newell, the association lobbied vigorously for state licensing laws for engineers, and on other bread-and-butter issues. Internal dissension in this organization caused a rapid decline during the 1920s, but much of its program was continued by the National Society of Professional Engineers founded in 1934 by David B. Steinman. Licensing continued to be a central issue, but the society also favored professional codes of ethics, criticizing, for example, the Society of Automotive Engineers in 1965 for never having adopted a code of ethics.

Another theme in engineering unity was social responsibility. This found expression in a number of agencies sponsored by the four founder societies. The first was the Engineering Council, founded in 1917. Led by J. Parke Channing, it assisted the government in mobilizing engineering talent during World War I. It was replaced in 1920 by a more representative organization, the Federated American Engineering Societies. Herbert Hoover was the spirit behind and first president of the federation; he attempted to use it to bring the engineering viewpoint to bear on national problems, appointing committees to investigate waste in industry and the twelve-hour day. The reports from these committees were critical of business practices and antagonized powerful conservative elements within the founder societies. The American Institute of Mining Engineers withdrew from the organization in 1924; the federation was later reorganized, and its name was changed to the American Engineering Council. In its new form, it became a voice for right-wing views, sometimes criticizing Hoover's policies as president of the United States; it was abolished in 1939. In 1945, the founder societies created a new unity organization, the Engineers Joint Council, which helped secure the creation of the National Academy of Engineering in 1964 under the charter of the National Academy of Sciences. To many engineers, this represented the culmination of years of struggle to secure a permanent agency through which the engineering profession could advise the nation on public policy matters.

In the late twentieth century, a number of societies emerged to protect and further the interests of groups that traditionally faced discrimination when entering the engineering field or working as professional engineers. Groups such as the National Society of Black Engineers (1975), the Society of Mexican American Engineers and Scientists (1974), the Society of Women Engineers (1950), and the National Organization of Gay and Lesbian Scientists and Technical Professionals (1983), use their resources to expand educational and professional opportunities for their members, as well as for young people who might consider entering engineering professions but find discrimination a barrier.

BIBLIOGRAPHY

Layton, Edwin T., Jr. *The Revolt of the Engineers: Social Responsibility and the American Engineering Profession.* Cleveland, Ohio: Press of Case Western Reserve University, 1971; Baltimore: Johns Hopkins University Press, 1986.

Kirby, Richard S. *Engineering in History.* New York: McGraw-Hill, 1956; New York: Dover Publications, 1990.

Finch, James. *The Story of Engineering.* Garden City, N.Y.: Doubleday, 1960.

Mount, Ellis. *Ahead of Its Time: The Engineering Societies Library, 1913–80.* Hamden, Conn.: Linnet, 1982.

Edwin T. Layton Jr. / A. R.

See also **Electric Power and Light Industry; Electrical Workers; Industrial Relations; Industrial Revolution.**

ENGINEERS, CORPS OF. The world's largest engineering force, the U.S. Army Corps of Engineers, is the only organization of its kind that fulfills both military and civil missions. Within the army, it acts as a combat arm and a technical service; within the federal government, as a national construction agency. Older than the Republic, the corps has a proud history of service in war and peace. The breastworks at Bunker Hill, the Cumberland Road, the Panama Canal, Fort Peck Dam, and the Manhattan Project exemplify its contributions. The names of Pierre C. L'Enfant, Sylvanus Thayer, John C. Frémont, George B. McClellan, Leslie R. Groves, and Lucius D. Clay suggest the versatility of its officers.

The corps had its beginnings in the American Revolution. On 16 June 1775, the day before the Battle of Bunker Hill, the CONTINENTAL CONGRESS authorized a chief engineer and two assistants for the Grand Army. Three years later, the Congress provided for three companies of sappers and miners. Led largely by French volunteers, the infant corps helped assure the success of George Washington's Fabian strategy and the decisive siege at Yorktown. Disbanded in 1783, engineer units reappeared in 1794 as elements of the short-lived Corps of Artillerists and Engineers, which began construction of American seacoast defenses.

The present organization dates from 16 March 1802, when President Thomas Jefferson signed a bill providing for a corps of engineers to be stationed at West Point, New York, and to "constitute a military academy." The first engineering school in the United States, WEST POINT was also the leading one until the CIVIL WAR. Composed almost exclusively of top academy graduates, the Corps of Engineers formed the only sizable group of trained engineers in the country.

In the first decades of the nineteenth century, as the nation expanded, the federal government pressed the Corps of Engineers into service. Military engineers built roads, canals, piers, and lighthouses; they constructed and repaired fortifications and surveyed and explored the country. They also worked to improve the navigation of the water routes that spread people and commerce across the nation. In 1824, Congress directed the Corps of Engineers to remove the shoals, snags, and sandbars that impeded navigation on the Mississippi and Ohio Rivers. Thereafter, the corps assumed increasing responsibility for river and harbor projects. Within 150 years, the corps had spent more than $20 billion to develop thousands of miles of inland waterways and hundreds of deep-water harbors. This effort also yielded far-reaching benefits in flood control, power production, water conservation, pollution abatement, and recreation.

Although the Corps of Engineers can point to a long list of achievements, implementation of its civilian mission has not been without controversy. It has often been accused of underestimating project costs. For example, in 1887, the corps convinced Congress to authorize $10 million for 439 projects. Based upon evidence that the actual cost of the projects would be at least $200 million, President Grover Cleveland vetoed the bill. By the mid-twentieth century, critics argued that the massive dams and stream channelization projects undertaken by the corps, whatever their cost, were undesirable because they disrupted ecosystems, polluted streams, and exacerbated the effects of flooding.

Implementation of military missions by the corps generated much less criticism. American military annals are filled with the exploits of army engineers. Some 150 battle streamers adorn the corps colors. The defense of Washington in the Civil War; the siege of Santiago, Cuba, in 1898; vast port, depot, road, and railroad works in France during WORLD WAR I; the building of the Ledo Road and Alcan Highway; amphibious landings and the bridging of the Rhine during WORLD WAR II; the buildup at Pusan in Korea; and the creation of the Da Nang base in Vietnam, are instances of engineer soldiers in their traditional roles—impeding enemy advances and assisting the movement of friendly forces. On many occasions, engineer troops also fought as infantry. Engineer officers, experienced in peacetime undertakings, were well fitted for high command and staff positions. Generals Robert E. Lee and Douglas MacArthur epitomize the engineer commander. In the nation's major conflicts, the army's top logistical minds were military engineers: Montgomery C. Meigs in the Civil War, George W. Goethals in World War I, and Brehon B. Somervell in World War II.

Today, the corps is organized into eleven divisions, forty districts, and hundreds of area and project offices. Since the 1950s, it has been active in space, missile, and postal construction, as well as in its traditional fields of endeavor. And, while management of the nation's water resources remains one of its most important responsibilities, its priorities in that area—like those of the country as a whole—have shifted towards recreation; fish and wildlife conservation; pollution abatement; and small, local works to generate power and to control floods. The corps enforces the CLEAN WATER ACT, regulates activities in WETLANDS, administers hundreds of reservoirs, and manages millions of acres of federal land.

As might be expected with an agency of its size, the corps continues to face criticism from a variety of directions for the impact of its projects, its management practices, and the scope of its activities. Nevertheless, the Corps of Engineers has played a unique role in both war and peace throughout U.S. history and will continue to do so in the future.

BIBLIOGRAPHY

Fowle, Barry W., ed. *Builders and Fighters: U.S. Army Engineers in World War II.* Fort Belvoir, Va.: Office of History, U.S. Army Corps of Engineers, 1992.

Goetzmann, William H. *Army Exploration in the American West, 1803–1863.* New Haven, Conn.: Yale University Press, 1959; Lincoln: University of Nebraska Press, 1979.

Hill, Forest G. *Roads, Rails and Waterways: The Army Engineers and Early Transportation.* Norman: University of Oklahoma Press, 1957.

Shallat, Todd. *Structures in the Stream: Water, Science, and the Rise of the U.S. Army Corps of Engineers.* Austin: University of Texas Press, 1994.

Stine, Jeffrey K. *Mixing the Waters: Environment, Politics, and the Building of the Tennessee-Tombigbee Waterway.* Akron, Ohio: University of Akron Press, 1993.

Welsh, Michael. *U.S. Army Corps of Engineers: Albuquerque District, 1935–1985.* Albuquerque: University of New Mexico Press, 1987.

Lenore Fine
Jesse A. Remington / C. P.

See also **Army, United States; Explorations and Expeditions: U.S.; Mississippi River; Missouri River; Ohio River; River and Harbor Improvements; Rivers; Roads; Waterways, Inland.**

ENGLAND. *See* **Great Britain, Relations with.**

ENGLISH LANGUAGE. The English language has its origins in about the fifth century A.D., when tribes from the continent, the Jutes, the Saxons, and then the larger tribe of Angles invaded the small island we now call England (from *Angle-land*). Old English, the language of the Anglo-Saxons, is preserved in *Beowulf* (c. A.D. 800). Middle English developed following the Norman invasion of 1066, exemplified in Geoffrey Chaucer's *Canterbury Tales* (c. 1400). Modern English, dating from the sixteenth century, is exemplified in the plays of William Shakespeare (1564–1616). From the time the Pilgrims landed in America (1620), the language began to take its own course in this "New World." Expressions like "fixing to," which had never been used in England, were "cropping up" (an expression going back to Middle English) in the colonial press by 1716.

So the American Revolution (1775–1783) not only created a new nation but also divided the English language into what H. L. Mencken, author of the classic study *The American Language; An Inquiry into the Development of English in the United States*, called "two streams." These streams diverged to produce different words with the same denotation (the American "trunk" of a car is a "boot" in England), different pronunciations for the same words (the American sked-ju-el is the British shed-ju-el), and different spellings (theater vs. theatre, labor vs. labour).

By 1781, the word "Americanism" had been coined by John Witherspoon, a Scottish clergyman recruited to become president of Princeton University. These Americanisms, Witherspoon wrote, were not "worse in themselves, but merely . . . of American and not of English growth." The separation of the "two streams of English" was already noticeable. In his usual acerbic manner, Mencken applauded the American resistance to rules: "Standard [British] English must always strike an American as a bit stilted and precious" (p. 774).

Judgment by Language: The Shibboleth

Once there is any kind of "standard," people could begin passing judgment (that's spelled "judgement" in England) based on what was deemed "correct." One of the first recorded instances is the "shibboleth" test in the Old Testament. Hebrew, like all other languages, had many dialects, and the twelve tribes of Israel did not always pronounce words in the same way. Thus, when the Gileadites "seized the fords of the Jordan" (Judg. 12:5–6), it was not enough to merely ask those who wished to cross the river "Are you an Ephraimite?" They needed a test to distinguish the enemy. They used pronunciation, and those who said "sib-bo-leth" instead of "shib-bo-leth" were slain.

Americans are by and large more tolerant of language differences than the English. George Bernard Shaw (1856–1950), the Englishman who wrote *Pygmalion* (on which the musical *My Fair Lady* was based), wrote, "It is impossible for an Englishman to open his mouth without making some other Englishman hate or despise him." Shaw was, like Mencken, a great debunker and exploder of pretension. "An honest and natural slum dialect," he wrote, "is more tolerable than the attempt of a phonetically untaught person to imitate the vulgar dialect of the golf club" (Mencken, p. 775).

Dialects: The Branches of the Stream

Shaw's comment raises a point worth highlighting: we all speak a dialect. If English, in Mencken's phrase, divides into "two streams," British and American, there are within those streams many creeks and branches (two Americanisms according to Witherspoon). Both Cockney and "the Queen's English" are, after all, dialects of British English, although one carries more prestige.

Likewise, we have many dialects in the United States. Mark Twain, in his prefatory note to *Adventures of Huckleberry Finn*, tells us that there are at least seventeen distinguishable dialects in the novel. In the early twenty-first century we find many dialects of American English as we move from the New York Bronx to Charleston, or from the Midwestern plains to the San Fernando Valley (home of the "valley girls"), or from Chicago to New Orleans (is that pronounced with the stress on the first or the second syllable: ore-leans or ore-lens?) Is there such a thing today as a "standard" American language?

Guides to Correctness

Certainly there have been those willing to provide guidance to the public on "correct" usage of the language. America's most famous lexicographer, Noah Webster, published his "Blue-backed" *American Speller* soon after the Revolution, teaching not only spelling but also pronunciation, common sense, morals, and good citizenship. His first dictionary (1806) was one of several (the first in English being Samuel Johnson's in 1755), but when Webster died in 1843, the purchase of rights to his dictionary by Charles and George Merriam led to a new, one-volume edition that sold for six dollars in 1847. This edition became the standard. Except for the Bible, Webster's spelling book and dictionary were the best-selling publications in American history up to the mid-twentieth century.

Webster's spelling book (often marketed with the Bible) molded four generations of American schoolchildren, proclaiming what was "right" without apology. In contrast, *The American Heritage Dictionary* of the late twentieth century offers guidance based on a survey of its "Usage Panel," a group of respected writers and speakers who are asked what they find acceptable. In the third college edition (1997), the editors note drastic changes in the Panel's attitudes. More and more of the old shibboleths are widely accepted. For example, in 1969 most of the

Usage Panel objected to using the words "contact" and "intrigue" as verbs, but by the 1993 survey, most had no problem with either (though "hopefully" and "disinterested" remained problematic for most). Language, if it is spoken, lives and changes (in contrast to a "dead language" such as Latin, which does not evolve because it is not spoken). As with a river, so with language: you never put your tongue to the same one twice.

Lexicographers now present their dictionaries as a description of how the language looks at a particular time rather than as a prescription of what is "correct." The constant evolution of language makes new editions necessary. Many people have come to use the word "disinterested" to mean "uninterested" instead of "without bias"; therefore, despite objections of purists, it does in fact mean that. "Corruption" or change?

Likewise with pronunciation. In the 1990s, the word "harass" came into frequent use in the news. Americans had traditionally put the stress on the second syllable: he-RASS. This pronunciation, according to *The Oxford American Dictionary and Language Guide* (1999), "first occurred in American English and has gained wide acceptance over the last 50 years." But reporters on television during the 1991 Clarence Thomas hearings, in which he was accused of "sexual harassment" by Anita Hill, tended to prefer the pronunciation HAR-ess, "the older, more traditional pronunciation [which] is still preferred by those for whom British pronunciation is a guide." There are many influences on our shifting language habits.

Simplification Movement

Pragmatic Americans have often sought to simplify the language. The Simplified Spelling Board, created in 1906, sought to simplify the spelling of words like "though." "But tho their filosofy was that simpler is better, they cood not get thru to peepl as they wisht." The *Chicago Tribune* began to simplify spelling in their publication in 1935, but the American public would not send their brides down the "aile" nor transport their loved ones' caskets in a "herse," so the attempt was largely abandoned with a few exceptions, such as "tho," "thru," and "catalog." Spelling, after all, has often been used as a test of intelligence and education. It also reflects the history of the language. The word "knight" carries with it the echoes of Chaucer's Middle English pronunciation: ka-nick-te.

Another major impediment to spelling reform is the association of phonetic spelling with illiteracy: while the reformers may "ake" to "berry" those men and "wimmen" who "apose" them, those who write of the "kat's tung" open themselves to ridicule. Mencken declared, however, that "American spelling is plainly better than English spelling, and in the long run it seems sure to prevail" (p. 483).

Growing Vocabulary

One distinctive aspect of the English language is its tendency to absorb foreign words. English-speaking peoples (many of them explorers and adventurers) have adopted and adapted terms from many languages. Loanwords come from many foreign languages, sometimes directly, sometimes through other languages: dirge (Latin), history (Greek), whiskey (Celtic), fellow (Scandinavian), sergeant (French), chocolate (Spanish), umbrella (Italian), tattoo (German), sugar (Arabic), kowtow (Chinese), banana (African), moccasin (Native American).

Sometimes new words have to be created. In a survey of new words in the twentieth century, John Ayto found an interesting correlation between neologisms and the events and inventions of the times. Consider the list shown in Table 1.

TABLE 1

Trends in New Word Formation, 1900–2000

Decade	Category producing the most new words	Example
1900–1910	cars	accelerator
10s	war	flame-thrower (from the German *Flammenwerfer*)
20s	clothes	bathing beauty, threads (slang for clothes)
30s	war	decrypt, fifth column, flak
40s	war	ground zero, radar
50s	media	teleconference, Xerox
60s	computer	interface, cursor
70s	computer	hard disk, microprocessor
80s	media	cyberspace, dish (TV antenna), shock jock
90s	politics	Generation X, off-message

Promoting and Resisting One "Standard"

One of the great forces for molding a common American English since the mid-twentieth century has been the media, especially television. During the first decades of television news coverage, reporters and anchors were expected to have or to adopt a Midwestern accent, the least distinctive and most generally understandable, the most "American" as it were. This tended to promote a common "American" accent. As the century grew to a close, however, ethnic groups grew in size and multiculturalism became a potent force in society. More dialects (and more ethnicity in general) began to show up on the screen. In the 2000 presidential election, George W. Bush emphasized his ability to speak Spanish.

This increasing power of groups who spoke English as a second language or not at all led to a widespread call for "English only" laws in the 1980s and 1990s, though the movement never achieved critical mass. On the other end of the political spectrum were those who argued that teachers should use the vernacular of the pupils in order to help them learn. Great arguments swirled around the terms "Ebonics" and "bilingual education."

The International Language

English has replaced French as the international language for many reasons: the political, military, and economic dominance of the United States since World War II (1939–1945), of course, but also the influence of American culture, especially movies, television, and rock music. We were well on our way to this position before Pearl Harbor drew us into war in 1941. Mencken attributes this partly to the "dispersion of the English-speaking peoples," but in typical Mencken style goes on to say that those peoples "have been, on the whole, poor linguists, and so they have dragged their language with them, and forced it upon the human race." Robert MacNeil, in the fascinating study of the English language for the Public Broadcasting System (PBS), *The Story of English* (1986), observed that when landing in Rome, an Italian pilot flying an Italian airliner converses with the control tower in English.

The Digital Word

Just as the printing press, widely used throughout Europe by 1500, changed our use of words, leading to new written forms such as the novel and the newspaper, so the computer has created change. E-mail, chat rooms, and Web pages have made words on the screen almost as common as on the printed page. We already see changes taking place, as onscreen language becomes more informal (often creating new words, such as "online"). Words get shortened: electronic mail becomes e-mail, which in turn becomes email. Note, however, that this is not new. "Today" was spelled "to-day" in the early twentieth century.

We many need help "navigating the shifting verbal currents of the post-Gutenberg era," according to *Wired Style: Principles of English Usage in the Digital Age* (version 1.0, 1996, with 2.0 published in 1999). The online experience has spawned various means of conveying tone including acronyms (such as LOL for "laughing out loud" and IRL for "in real life"—as distinguished from the virtual world of cyberspace) and emoticons such as >:D for "demonic laughter" and >:P for "sticking tongue out at you." English continues to change with influences of all kinds.

Finding Guidance Amid the Flux

The two streams continue to evolve, of course, and the purists like William Safire and John Simon continue to preach against the "corruption" of the language. But like the river, the English language will flow whither it will. Two of the most respected guides in the midst of this flux are both in third editions.

The Elements of Style, praised as the best of its kind by professional writers for over four decades, is E. B. White's revision of his professor's book. William Strunk's "little book" (1918) so impressed White as a college freshman that decades later he revised Strunk's original (which can be found on the Internet) into this thin volume in praise of conciseness and precision in writing. It has never been out of print since 1959 when the first edition was published, is still in print and praised as the best of its kind by professional writers.

The New Fowler's Modern English Usage (1996) shows tolerance for expressions that Henry Watson Fowler (1858–1933) would have never allowed in his first edition in 1926. The third edition, unlike the first two, lists as one of three meanings for "fix": the "American expression 'to be fixing to,' meaning 'to prepare to, intend, be on the point of.'" This guide, one of the most esteemed in print, labels it "informal" and notes that it is "hardly ever encountered outside the US." American English continues to evolve and standards continue to change.

BIBLIOGRAPHY

Ayto, John. *Twentieth-Century Words.* New York: Oxford University Press, 1999.

Burchfield, R. W., ed. *The New Fowler's Modern English Usage.* New York: Oxford University Press, 1996. Widely respected guide to "correct" usage.

Hayakawa, S. I. *Language in Thought and Action.* 4th ed. New York: Harcourt Brace Jovanovich, 1978. Classic work on semantics.

Hale, Constance, and Jessie Scanlon. *Wired Style: Principles of English Usage in the Digital Age.* New York: Broadway Books, 1999. *Wired* magazine is an influential publication about computer technology.

Mencken, H. L. *The American Language; An Inquiry into the Development of English in the United States.* Raven I. McDavid, Jr., ed. New York: Alfred A. Knopf, 1963. Classic readable and influential examination of the new stream.

McCrum, Robert, William Cran, and Robert MacNeil. *The Story of English.* New York: Viking, 1986. This book is a companion to the excellent PBS television series available on videotape.

Oxford American Dictionary and Language Guide. New York: Oxford University Press, 1999.

Pyles, Thomas, and John Algeo. *The Origins and Development of the English Language.* New York: Harcourt Brace Jovanovich, 1982.

Strunk, William Jr., and E. B. White. *The Elements of Style.* 3d ed. New York: Macmillan, 1979.

William E. King

See also **Education, Bilingual; Slang.**

ENLISTMENT. Local defense in the colonial period was based on compulsory military service for all able-bodied males, but relied on volunteers for extended campaigns or assignments. During the early Republic, Americans viewed a large standing army as antithetical to their ideals of liberty and avoided instituting conscription as a method of recruitment. The early American military therefore developed a dual army tradition—a small core of regulars reinforced by local militia. In times of crisis, the militias would be supplemented by volunteers, who were enticed to enlist with promises of land grants, bounties, and other incentives. The success of the militia system (somewhat exaggerated at the time), aversion to conscription and a standing army, and the relative peace and prosperity between 1783 and southern secession in 1860 ensured the continuation of the citizen-soldier myth and the "expandable" army concept. By 1862, the manpower demands of modern, industrialized warfare forced Americans to overcome their objections to conscription, although exemptions and the hiring of substitutes were common.

As they had in the antebellum period, enlistments in the post–Civil War era continued to remain low due to insufferable military living conditions, lax training, and Americans' contemptuous attitudes toward professional military service. The nation also continued the pattern of rapid mobilization via conscription and activation of federal reserve and state-organized National Guard units during crisis, followed by rapid peacetime demobilization back to a minimal force of regulars.

In 1973, as a result of opposition to the Vietnam War, the conscription system's inherent social inequities, and economic retrenchment, the United States reduced military force levels, eliminated peacetime draft service, and created the All-Volunteer Force (AVF). Although it can be augmented by reserves and conscription, the AVF remains the foundation for U.S. armed forces and consists entirely of enlistees recruited to the service by incentives such as opportunity for adventure, occupational training, educational assistance, and financial bonuses.

BIBLIOGRAPHY

Binkin, Martin. *Who Will Fight the Next War?: The Changing Face of the American Military.* Washington, D.C.: Brookings Institution, 1993.

Chambers, John W., II. *To Raise an Army: The Draft Comes to Modern America.* New York: Free Press, 1987.

Coffman, Edward M. *The Old Army: A Portrait of the American Army in Peacetime, 1784–1898.* New York: Oxford University Press, 1986.

Fredland, J. Eric, Curtis Gilroy, Roger D. Little, and W. S. Sellman, eds. *Professionals on the Front Line: Two Decades of the All-Volunteer Force.* Washington, D.C.: Brassey's, 1996.

Segal, David R. *Recruiting for Uncle Sam: Citizenship and Military Manpower Policy.* Lawrence: University Press of Kansas, 1989.

Derek W. Frisby

See also **Conscription and Recruitment; National Guard.**

ENRON SCANDAL. Enron is an energy company that quickly grew to become one of the world's largest corporations before its financial practices caused its bankruptcy. Formed in 1985 by the merger of two gas pipeline companies, Houston Natural Gas and InterNorth, the company diversified under its manager, Kenneth Lay, into an energy trading company offering various services, including a massive e-commerce. It bought the name of the Houston Astros' ballpark and was named most innovative company of the year for five consecutive years by *Fortune* magazine. It peaked in the year 2000, with revenues of $100 billion and a share price of $90, its rapid growth attracting many investors.

In 2001, however, Enron's success appeared to be phony. The company had assigned billions of dollars of debt and risk to subsidiary companies, which then kept them off their books. Share prices began to fall precipitously. Enron's accounting firm, Arthur Anderson, was caught destroying Enron-related documents. On 2 December 2001, Enron filed for bankruptcy, along with sixty subsidiary companies. In 2002, its shares were traded at 11 cents. The company's collapse destroyed thousands of investors' savings. In July 2002, Arthur Andersen, Enron's accounting firm, was convicted of destroying evidence, although an appeal was pending at the time of this writing. Enron's officials were then undergoing further congressional hearings and criminal investigations, and numerous agencies were investigating other corporations for similar accounting and finance methods.

BIBLIOGRAPHY

Fox, Loren. *Enron: The Rise and Fall.* New York: Wiley, 2002.

Barreveld, Dirk J. *The ENRON Collapse.* New York: Universe, 2002.

Steve Sheppard

See also **Business, Big; Corporations; Scandals.**

ENSIGN. An ensign is the lowest commissioned rank in the U.S. Navy and Coast Guard. Ensign comes from the Latin word *insignia*, lending the ensign the duty of carrying emblems or banners. In British service, until 1871, an ensign carried the colors as the lowest commissioned officer of infantry. In the United States ensigns existed in the colonial militia, in the Revolution infantry, and in the regular army until 1815, as a rank lower than first, second, or third lieutenant. In the navy the rank of ensign superseded that of midshipman in 1862.

BIBLIOGRAPHY

Moskos, Charles C. *The American Enlisted Man: The Rank and File in Today's Military.* New York: Russell Sage Foundation, 1970.

Don Russell/H. S.

See also **Coast Guard, U.S.; Navy, United States.**

ENTAIL OF ESTATE limits the disposition of real property. The famous Statute of Westminster II (1285), often called *De Donis*, established the system of fee entail so that a wealthy family could retain its estates perpetually as a block inheritance. By this measure, a grantee of a feudal estate was entitled to the income from the land for life but could not sell the estate, mortgage it, or give it away. Upon the grantee's death, his eldest son inherited the estate subject to the entail. Should a grantee have no heirs, the estate went back to the grantor. The courts generally sustained this law until the fifteenth century when judges began to limit entails to one succeeding generation. Parliament abolished entails entirely in 1833.

Entailing of estates was relatively common in colonial America, especially in the agricultural sections of the southern and the middle states. Stout opposition developed, however, because of the belief that it was dangerous to perpetuate a political bloc of landed aristocrats. In several colonies, landowners resorted to devices such as common recovery and private legislative acts to gain free disposition of their land. By the time of the Revolution, colonial opinion was opposed to entail. Many of the original states followed the lead taken by Virginia in 1776 and abolished entails. Connecticut and Mississippi never recognized entail, although, in Connecticut, the common law permitted conditioned fees. Nor did the entail system emerge in Iowa, where it was held that entail was not suited to American practices, while Kansas and Delaware accepted the principle.

BIBLIOGRAPHY

Cantor, Norman F. *Imagining the Law: Common Law and the Foundations of the American Legal System.* New York: HarperCollins, 1997.

Morris, Richard B. "Primogeniture and Entailed Estates in America," *Columbia Law Review* 27 (1927): 24–51.

W. Freeman Galpin / C. P.

See also **Land Policy; Primogeniture.**

ENTANGLING ALLIANCES. Contrary to common belief, the phrase "entangling alliances" was turned by Thomas Jefferson, not George Washington. Washington advised against "permanent alliances," whereas Jefferson, in his inaugural address on 4 March 1801, declared his devotion to "peace, commerce, and honest friendship with all nations, entangling alliances with none." It is a pet phrase of isolationists warning against foreign commitments.

BIBLIOGRAPHY

Kaplan, Lawrence. *Entangling Alliances with None: American Foreign Policy in the Age of Jefferson.* Kent, Ohio: Kent State University Press, 1987.

Theodore M. Whitfield / L. T.

See also **Foreign Policy; Isolationism.**

ENTERPRISE ZONES were economically depressed districts targeted for revitalization through tax breaks and regulatory exemptions. Originating in Great Britain in the late 1970s, the concept quickly migrated across the Atlantic and was incorporated into a series of bills introduced in the U.S. Congress during the 1980s. The bills proposed to reduce corporate income taxes and eliminate capital gains taxes for businesses that located in the designated zones. Moreover, federal agencies would be authorized to suspend certain regulations and thereby attract private investment to distressed districts.

With its reliance on incentives to private enterprise rather than government grant programs, the enterprise zone concept won the backing of the Ronald Reagan administration and became the chief element of its urban policy. The Reagan administration failed to secure passage of effective enterprise zone legislation, but by 1990, thirty-seven states had enacted enterprise zone measures that established active programs in at least 400 to 500 districts. Although not magic remedies for economic decline, the state programs achieved some successes. Finally, in 1993 Congress enacted a Clinton administration proposal that provided tax incentives for investment in distressed "empowerment" zones but deviated from the pure enterprise zone concept by also targeting federal technical assistance and grants to the designated areas.

BIBLIOGRAPHY

Green, Roy E., ed. *Enterprise Zones: New Directions in Economic Development.* Newbury Park, Calif.: Sage, 1991.

Jon C. Teaford

See also **Economics.**

ENUMERATED COMMODITIES were colonial products permitted to be exported only to limited destinations, generally British colonies, England, Ireland, Wales, Berwick on Tweed, or, after 1707, Scotland. The first article enumerated was tobacco in 1621, by order in council. Parliament later enumerated other goods by specific act, including sugar, tobacco, indigo, ginger, speckle wood, and various kinds of dyewoods in 1660; rice and molasses in 1704; naval stores, including tar, pitch, rosin (omitted in 1729), turpentine, hemp, masts, yards, and bowsprits in 1705; copper ore, beaver skins, and furs in 1721; coffee, pimento, cacao, hides and skins, whale fins, raw silk, potash and pearl ash, iron, and lumber in 1764; and all other commodities in 1766–1767. Such legislation aimed to prevent important products from reaching European markets except by way of England. Enumeration did not apply to similar products from non-British possessions.

Parliament exempted direct trade to points in Europe south of Cape Finisterre for rice in 1730; sugar in 1739; and all additional enumerated products in 1766–1767. Thus, direct exportation to Europe was forbidden north of Cape Finisterre and permitted south of that point. After 1765 rice could be exported to any place south of Cape Finisterre and was not limited to Europe, giving American rice an open market in the foreign West Indies and Spanish colonies.

BIBLIOGRAPHY

Middleton, Richard. *Colonial America.* Cambridge, Mass.: Blackwell, 1996.

O. M. Dickerson / c. w.

See also **Navigation Acts; Triangular Trade.**

ENUMERATED POWERS are powers given to the federal government by the terms of the U.S. Constitution. The question whether the Constitution also should be understood to give the federal government unenumerated powers was the central issue in nineteenth century constitutional disputations. Under Article II of the Articles of Confederation, the Confederation Congress's powers were limited to those explicitly granted by that document. This limitation on the federal legislature's powers, when coupled with the extreme difficulty of changing a constitution whose amendment required the unanimous agreement of the thirteen states, stymied several nationalist initiatives in the period before the adoption of the Constitution.

The Philadelphia convention that drafted the U.S. Constitution in 1787 omitted any provision echoing Article II of the Articles of Confederation. However, several sections of the proposed constitution, particularly the list of congressional powers in Article I, section 8, gave the impression that the new federal government was to have only the powers it was expressly delegated. During the course of the ratification debates of 1787–1790, several Federalist spokesmen—most notably Governor Edmund Randolph of Virginia and Charles C. Pinckney of South Carolina—assured this principle would be followed.

When the new federal government was instituted, President George Washington found his cabinet sharply divided on the issue of unenumerated powers. Secretary of the Treasury Alexander Hamilton, who had joined with John Jay and others in offering a highly nationalist interpretation of the Constitution to the New York ratification convention, argued that both the Congress and the president could claim broad powers that, although not explicitly mentioned in the Constitution, naturally inhered in the legislative and executive branches. Secretary of State Thomas Jefferson, on the other hand, insisted on the reading of the constitution successfully offered by Attorney General Randolph in the Virginia ratification convention. Jefferson cited the Tenth Amendment to underscore his argument. A similar debate in the House pitted Federalist Representative Fisher Ames against James Madison.

Washington, whose experience in the Revolution had convinced him of the necessity of Hamilton's program, sided with Hamilton. In the following decade, Chief Justice John Marshall authored a number of Supreme Court opinions endorsing the Hamiltonian-nationalist reading of the Constitution; the most important of these, *McCulloch v. Maryland,* elicited Madison's observation that the Constitution never would have been ratified if people had seen *McCulloch* coming.

Madison's last act as president in 1817 was to veto the Bonus Bill, legislation providing for significant federal expenditures on public works. Madison instructed congressional leaders among his fellow Jeffersonians that strict construction must remain their guiding principle and that an amendment authorizing federal expenditures of this type should precede any such expenditure. President Andrew Jackson adhered to this principle, notably in his Bank Bill Veto Message, as did his Democratic successors (most of the time). Yet, while Democratic electoral success demonstrated the popular appeal of the doctrine of enumerated powers, the antebellum period saw the parallel growth of a nationalist reading of the Constitution in the Hamiltonian tradition. The divergence between these two conceptions of the federal relationship, in conjunction with the ultimate identification of each of them with a great sectional political party, formed the constitutional predicate for the Civil War.

With the triumph of the Republican Union in 1865, the doctrine of enumerated powers went into eclipse. It still figured in constitutional argumentation, but the main line of constitutional reasoning came to hold that the federal government had essentially all powers that were not explicitly denied it by the constitution. This conception was precisely that which Hamilton had offered in cabinet debate in the 1790s.

BIBLIOGRAPHY

Lenner, Andrew. *The Federal Principle in American Politics.* Lanham, Md.: Rowman and Littlefield, 2001.

McDonald, Forrest. *States' Rights and the Union: Imperium in Imperio, 1776–1876.* Lawrence: University Press of Kansas, 2000.

K. R. Constantine Gutzman

See also **Articles of Confederation; Constitution of the United States; *McCulloch v. Maryland.***

ENVIRONMENTAL BUSINESS. Since the late nineteenth century, scientists have documented how industrial production and consumption practicies have damaged the environment and human health. From early concern over coal-derived air pollution and toxins in the workplace, concern has shifted to nuclear issues, species extinction, solid waste disposal, toxic pollution, pesticides, deforestation, and global warming. As this evidence has accumulated, businesspeople, economists, environmentalists, and consumers have begun to struggle with ways to make businesses environmentally responsible. Some observers believe that "environmental business" is an oxymoron, that business by definition cannot be environmentally sound. Others maintain that business has made sufficient concessions to environmental concerns. By the 1990s, however, a growing number of consumers and businesspeople were striving to incorporate environmental, moral, and ethical concerns into business practices.

According to the U.S. Congress's Office of Technology Assessment, there are five conceptual frameworks that describe the diverse ways in which businesses and government approach the interface between business and the environment. *Frontier economics* emphasizes economic growth and unlimited resource exploitation. *Environmental protection* recognizes the environment as an economic externality that must be protected through regulations that ban or limit activities that degrade the environment. Under this view, cost-benefit analysis resolves conflicts between the economy and the environment, with the goal of reducing the quantity and toxicity of waste. *Resource management* attempts to internalize environmental costs through measures of policy and economic performance, such as green taxes or tradable pollution permits. Resource management maintains that ecological productivity is necessary to the economy and emphasizes resource conservation as well as waste reduction. *Ecodevelopment* suggests making the economy sustainable by modeling industrial production on ecological systems, which entails moving from linear production systems to closed, circular ones. It stresses designs that avoid toxic materials, replacing nonrenewable with renewable resources, and ensuring recycling of essential nonrenewable materials. Unlike the previous models, ecodevelopment does not see technology as a substitute for natural resources. Lastly, *deep ecology* calls for harmony with nature and prescribes drastic reductions in human population and the scale of human economies.

For the most part, changes in business practices during the last quarter of the twentieth century fell under the environmental-protection rubric. But as shareholders and consumers began to seek out environmentally responsible companies and regulators sought to mobilize the market to induce environmentally responsible behavior, businesses began to use resource management and ecodevelopment strategies. By 2000 more than $2 trillion had been invested in socially and environmentally screened investment funds in the United States. These investors and consumers could make decisions based upon the information companies are now required to make public such as toxic-release inventories. The requirement that companies measure their pollution and make the information public has led many businesses to adopt processes and technologies that reduce or prevent environmental degradation. In addition, for some time, many companies have been recycling waste; more and more are starting to use products made from recyled materials. A growing sector of the economy is offering products that reduce the consumers' impact on the environment. And some businesses have been developing the expertise to take advantage of emissions trading programs that are likely to be a feature of the twenty-first century marketplace.

The "greening of business" has made "green labeling" an important issue for consumers and businesses. An increasing number of consumers want to purchase products made from recycled materials, produced in environmentally sensitive ways, that help consumers reduce their own energy use or enhance their health. In some cases, such as organic produce, the federal government has assumed responsibility for defining "green products." In most cases, however, private third parties offer certification of environmental and social attributes. In the United States, the three major green labelling organizations are Green Seal, Scientific Certification Systems ("Green Cross"), and Energy Star.

At the beginning of the twenty-first century, it is clear that CEOs ignore the impact of their business practices upon the environment at their peril. It is also clear that government will continue to have a role in shaping the interface between the environment and business, especially since environmental problems do not respect state or national boundaries.

BIBLIOGRAPHY

Cairncross, Frances. *Costing the Earth: The Challenge for Governments, the Opportunities for Business.* Boston: Harvard Business School Press, 1992.

Devall, Bill, and George Sessions. *Deep Ecology.* Salt Lake City, Utah: G. M. Smith, 1985.

Greer, Jed, and Kenny Bruno. *Greenwash: The Reality Behind Corporate Environmentalism.* Penang, Malaysia: Third World Network, 1996.

Hamilton, Alice. *Exploring the Dangerous Trades: The Autobiography of Alice Hamilton, M.D.* Boston: Northeastern University Press, 1985.

Hawken, Paul. *The Ecology of Commerce: A Declaration of Sustainability.* New York: HarperBusiness, 1993.

Stradling, David. *Smokestacks and Progressives: Environmentalists, Engineers and Air Quality in America, 1881–1951.* Baltimore: Johns Hopkins University Press, 1999.

U.S. Congress, Office of Technology Assessment. *Green Products by Design: Choices for a Cleaner Environment.* Washington, D.C.: Government Printing Office, 1992.

Susan J. Cooper / C. P.

See also **Air Pollution; Conservation; Endangered Species; Energy, Renewable; Energy Industry; Global Warming; Hazardous Waste; Nuclear Power; Waste Disposal; Water Pollution.**

ENVIRONMENTAL MOVEMENT. The modern environmental movement differed from an early form of environmentalism that flourished in the first decades of the twentieth century, usually called conservationism. Led by such figures as Theodore Roosevelt and Gifford Pinchot, the conservationists focused on the wise and efficient use of natural resources. Modern environmentalism arose not out of a productionist concern for managing natural resources for future development, but as a consumer movement that demanded a clean, safe, and beautiful environment as part of a higher standard of living.

The expanding post–World War II economy raised consciousness about the environmental costs of economic progress, but it also led increasingly affluent Americans to insist upon a better quality of life. Since the demand for a cleaner, safer, and more beautiful environment that would enhance the quality of life could not be satisfied by the free market, environmentalists turned toward political action as the means to protect the earth. Still, the preservationist strand of the conservationist movement was an important precursor to the modern environmental movement. As represented by such figures as John Muir of the Sierra Club and Aldo Leopold of the Wilderness Society, the preservationists argued that natural spaces such as forests and rivers were not just raw materials for economic development, but also aesthetic resources. Thus, they stated that the government needed to protect beautiful natural spaces from development through such measures as establishing national parks. In the post–World War II era, many more Americans gained the resources to pursue outdoor recreational activities and travel to national parks. Thus, preservationist ideas came to enjoy widespread popularity. No longer simply the province of small groups led by pioneers such as Muir and Leopold, preservationism became part of a mass movement.

Yet while preservationism was an important part of the environmentalism's goals, the movement's agenda was much broader and more diverse. While preservationism focused on protecting specially designated nonresidential areas, environmentalists shifted attention to the effects of the environment on daily life. In the 1960s and 1970s, the environmental movement focused its attention on pollution and successfully pressured Congress to pass measures to promote cleaner air and water. In the late 1970s, the movement increasingly addressed environmental threats created by the disposal of toxic waste. Toward the end of the century, the environmental agenda also included such worldwide problems as ozone depletion and global warming.

Environmentalism was based on the spread of an ecological consciousness that viewed the natural world as a biological and geological system that is an interacting whole. Ecologists emphasized human responsibility for the impact of their daily living on a wider natural world, fearing that human disruption of the earth's ecosystem threatened the survival of the planet. The spread of ecological consciousness from the scientific world to the general public was reflected in popular metaphors of the planet as Spaceship Earth or Mother Earth. An ecological consciousness was evident even in works of popular culture. For instance, in his 1971 hit song "Mercy Mercy Me (The Ecology)," Marvin Gaye sang:

> Poison is the wind that blows from the north and
> south and east
> Radiation underground and in the sky, animals and
> birds who live near by all die
> What about this overcrowded land
> How much more abuse from man can she stand?

Growth of the Environmental Movement in the 1960s and 1970s

Many historians find the publication of Rachel Carson's *Silent Spring* in 1962 to be a convenient marker for the beginning of the modern American environmental movement. *Silent Spring*, which spent thirty-one weeks on the *New York Times* best-seller list, alerted Americans to the negative environmental effects of DDT, a potent insecticide that had been used in American agriculture starting in World War II. The concern about the use of DDT that the book raised led John F. Kennedy to establish a presidential advisory panel on pesticides. More significantly, however, *Silent Spring* raised concerns that the unchecked growth of industry would threaten human health and destroy animal life—the title of the work referred to Carson's fear that the continued destruction of the environment would eventually make the birds who sang outside her window extinct. Thus, *Silent Spring* conveyed the ecological message that humans were endangering their natural environment, and needed to find some way of protecting themselves from the hazards of industrial society. Along with the problem of nuclear war, Carson stated, "The central problem of our age has . . . become the contamination of man's total environment with . . . substances of incredible potential for harm."

The 1960s was a period of growth for the environmental movement. The movement began with a newfound interest in preservationist issues. In that decade, membership in former conservationist organizations like the Wilderness Society and the Sierra Club skyrocketed from 123,000 in 1960 to 819,000 in 1970. President Lyndon Johnson also took an interest in preservationist issues. Between 1963 and 1968, he signed into law almost three hundred conservation and beautification measures, supported by more than $12 billion in authorized funds. Among these laws, the most significant was the Wilderness Act of 1964, which permanently set aside certain federal lands from commercial economic development in order to preserve them in their natural state. The federal government also took a new interest in controlling pollution. Congress passed laws that served as significant precedents for future legislative action on pollution issues—for instance, the Clean Air Acts of 1963 and 1967, the Clean Water Act of 1960, and the Water Quality Act of 1965.

During the 1960s, environmentalism became a mass social movement. Drawing on a culture of political activism inspired in part by the civil rights and antiwar movements, thousands of citizens, particularly young middle-class white men and women, became involved with environmental politics. The popularity of the environmental agenda was apparent by 1970. In that year, the first Earth Day was organized on 22 April to focus the public's attention on threats to the environment. In New York City, 100,000 people thronged Fifth Avenue to show their support for protecting the earth. Organizers estimated that fifteen hundred colleges and ten thousand schools took part in Earth Day, and *Time* magazine estimated that about twenty million Americans participated in the event in some fashion.

Earth Day was organized by Wisconsin senator Gaylord Nelson, who wanted to send "a big message to the politicians—a message to tell them to wake up and do something." Thanks to widespread public support for environmental goals, the 1970s became a critical decade for the passage of federal legislation. In 1970, President Richard Nixon signed into law the National Environmental Policy Act (NEPA), which required an Environmental Impact Statement (EIS) for all "major federal actions significantly affecting the quality of the human environment." During the 1970s, twelve thousand such statements were prepared.

Along with the growth of the environmental movement, a series of well-publicized environmental crises in the late 1960s focused the nation's attention on the need to control pollution. Examples include the 1969 blowout of an oil well platform off the coast of Santa Barbara, which contaminated scenic California beaches with oil, and in the same year the bursting into flames of the Cuyahoga River near Cleveland, Ohio, because of toxic contamination. In the 1970s, Congress passed important legislation to control pollution. The most significant of these new laws included the Clear Air Act of 1970, the Pesticide Control Act of 1972, the Ocean Dumping Act of 1972, the Federal Water Pollution Control Act Amendments of 1972, the Clean Air Act of 1974, the Safe Drinking Water Act of 1974, and the Toxic Substance Control Act of 1976. These laws established national environmental quality standards to be enforced by a federally dominated regulatory process known as command and control. The Clean Air Act, for instance, established national air quality standards for major pollutants that were enforced by a federal agency.

Other significant environmental legislation passed in the 1970s included the preservationist measures of the Endangered Species Act of 1973 and the Federal Land Policy and Management Act of 1976. Another significant piece of legislation, the Comprehensive Environmental Response Compensation and Liability Act, or Superfund Act, was passed in 1980. Designed to help control toxic hazards, the act established federal "superfund" money for the cleanup of contaminated waste sites and spills.

To enforce federal regulations, the Environmental Protection Agency (EPA) was created in 1970. An independent federal agency, the EPA was given consolidated responsibility for regulating and enforcing federal programs on air and water pollution, environmental radiation, pesticides, and solid waste. In response to the flurry of environmental regulation passed by Congress in the 1970s, the EPA expanded its operations: it began with a staff of eight thousand and a budget of $455 million and by 1981 had a staff of nearly thirteen thousand and a budget of $1.35 billion. Enforcing environmental regulations proved to be a difficult and complex task, particularly as new legislation overburdened the agency with responsibilities. The enforcement process required the gathering of various types of information—scientific, economic, engineering, and political—and the agency needed to contend with vigorous adversarial efforts from industry and environmental organizations.

The flurry of federal environmental regulation resulted in part from the rise of a powerful environmental lobby. Environmental organizations continued to expand their ranks in the 1970s. Membership in the Sierra Club, for instance, rose from 113,000 in 1970 to 180,000 in 1980. During the 1970s, mainstream environmental organizations established sophisticated operations in Washington, D.C. Besides advocating new environmental legislation, these groups served a watchdog function, ensuring that environmental regulations were properly enforced by the EPA and other federal agencies. While these organizations focused on their own specific issues and employed their own individual strategies, a Group of Ten organizations met regularly to discuss political strategy. This group consisted of the National Audubon Society, Defenders of Wildlife, the Environmental Defense Fund, the Environmental Policy Institute, the Izaak Walton League, the National Wildlife Federation, the National Resources Defense Council, the National Parks Conservation Association, the Sierra Club, and the Wilderness Society. During this decade, mainstream environmental organizations became increasingly professionalized, hiring more full-time staff. They hired lobbyists to advocate for environmental legislation, lawyers to enforce environmental standards through the courts, and scientists to prove the need for environmental regulation and counter the claims of industry scientists.

In the late 1960s and early 1970s, a number of critics obtained an audience by asserting that the ecosystem placed limits on economic development and often giving a bleak outlook for the earth's future. For instance, Paul Ehrlich's 1968 work, *The Population Bomb*, which brought the issue of global overpopulation to the nation's attention, apocalyptically claimed that "the battle to feed all of humanity is over" and made a number of dire predictions that turned out to be false. The Club of Rome's best-selling *The Limits of Growth* (1972), written by a team of MIT researchers, offered a melancholy prediction of environmental degradation resulting from population pressure, resource depletion, and pollution. But while such critics reached an audience for a short period of time, their calls to address long-term threats to the earth's ecosystem, such as world population growth, went unheeded.

The 1980s: Environmental Backlash and Radical Environmentalism

In the 1970s, environmental goals enjoyed a broad bipartisan consensus in Washington. The election of Ronald Reagan in 1980 changed that. Espousing a conservative, pro-business ideology, Reagan sought to free American corporations from an expanding regulatory apparatus. Reagan capitalized on the late 1970s Sagebrush Rebellion

Earth First! Two members of the radical environmental group, demonstrating at the Lincoln Memorial on 30 September 1987, demand "Equal rights for all species. Save the rainforest."

of westerners who sought to have federal land transferred to the states in order to avoid federal environmental regulations. Reagan appointed a leader of the Sagebrush Rebellion, James Watt, as secretary of the Interior. Watt took a strong pro-development stand hostile to the traditional resource preservation orientation of the Interior Department. He used his post to portray all environmentalists as radicals outside the American mainstream. Reagan also appointed as EPA head Anne Burford, a person committed to curtailing the agency's enforcement of environmental regulations. Between 1980 and 1983, the EPA lost one-third of its budget and one-fifth of its staff. Underfunded and understaffed, these cuts had a lasting effect on the agency, leaving it without the resources to fulfill all of its functions.

Yet while Reagan was able to stalemate the environmental agenda, his anti-environmentalist posture proved unpopular. The American public still overwhelmingly supported environmental goals. Environmentalist organizations were able to expand their membership in response to Reagan's policies. Between 1980 and 1990, the Sierra Club's membership multiplied from 180,000 to 630,000, while the Wilderness Society's membership soared from 45,000 to 350,000. In 1983, Reagan was forced to replace Watt and Buford with more moderate administrators. In the mid-1980s, a number of new environmental laws were passed, including the Resource Conservation and Recovery Act Amendments of 1984, the Safe Drinking Water Act Amendments of 1986, and the Superfund Amendments and Reauthorization Act of 1986. As a testament to the continuing popularity of environmental goals, Reagan's Republican vice president, George Bush Sr., declared himself an "environmentalist" in his 1988 campaign for president. On Earth Day 1990, President Bush stated that "Every day is Earth Day" and even major industries that were the target of environmental regulation, such as oil and gas, took out advertisements in major newspapers stating, "Every day is Earth Day for us."

The 1980s saw a splintering of the environmental movement. A number of radical environmentalist groups challenged the mainstream environmental organizations, claiming that they had become centralized bureaucracies out of touch with the grassroots and were too willing to compromise the environmental agenda. One of the groups to make this challenge was Earth First!, which appeared on the national scene in 1981 espousing the slogan, "No compromise in the defense of Mother Earth." Earth First! employed a variety of radical tactics, including direct action, civil disobedience, guerilla theater, and "ecotage," the sabotage of equipment used for clearcutting, road-building, and dam construction. Two other radical environmentalist organizations were Friends of the Earth and Greenpeace—each was a global organization formed in the 1970s that had significant support in the United States. Friends of the Earth was founded by the former Sierra Club director, David Brower. It pursued activist strategies and argued that protection of the environment required fundamental political and social change. Greenpeace's aggressive campaigns against nuclear testing, whaling, sealing, nuclear power, and radioactive waste disposal received increasing attention during the 1980s. In addition, some radical environmentalists showed a new interest in deep ecology, which challenged the traditional anthropomorphism of the environmental movement.

The 1980s also saw the growth of grassroots organizations that organized to oppose threats to their local environment: a contaminated waste site, a polluting factory, or the construction of a new facility deemed to be harmful. Because their concerns were locally oriented and generally consisted of the removal of a specific environmental threat, they were referred to as NIMBY (Not in My Backyard) organizations. The threat of contaminated waste sites raised concerns throughout the country, particularly after the publicity surrounding the evacuation of Love Canal, New York, in the late 1970s after it was revealed that the town had been built on contaminated soil. National organizations arose to support local efforts, including the Citizen's Clearinghouse for Hazardous Waste, founded by former Love Canal resident Lois Gibbs, and the National Toxics Campaign. Grassroots environmental groups continued to form throughout the 1980s. While Citizen's Clearinghouse worked with 600 groups in 1984, by 1988 it was working with over 4,500. NIMBYism often limited the impact of these groups, since they frequently disbanded once their particular issue of concern was resolved. Yet participation in these organizations often raised the consciousness of participants to larger environmental issues.

The late 1980s saw the growth of the environmental justice movement, which argued that all people have a right to a safe and healthy environment. Those concerned with environmental justice argued that poor and minority Americans are subjected to disproportionate environmental risks. It concentrated on such issues as urban air pollution, lead paint, and transfer stations for municipal garbage and hazardous waste. Environmental justice organizations widened the support base for environmentalism, which had traditionally relied upon the educated white middle class. The success of the environmental justice movement in bringing the racial and class dimension of environmental dangers to the nation's attention was reflected in the creation of the Office of Environmental Justice by the EPA in 1992.

The Global Environment and the 1990s

By the end of the 1980s, the environmental movement had increasingly come to focus its attention on global issues that could only be resolved through international diplomacy. Issues such as global warming, acid rain, ozone depletion, biodiversity, marine mammals, and rain forests could not be dealt with merely on the national level. As residents in the world's largest economy, and consequently the world's largest polluter, consumer of energy, and generator of waste, American environmentalists felt a special responsibility to ensure their country's participation in international agreements to protect the earth.

While the United States was a reluctant participant in international efforts to address environmental concerns compared with other industrial nations, the federal government did take steps to address the global nature of the environmental issue. In 1987, the United States joined with 139 other nations to sign the Montreal Protocol on Substances that Deplete the Ozone Layer. The protocol pledged the signees to eliminate the production of chlorofluorocarbons, which cause destruction to the ozone layer. In 1992, representatives from 179 nations, including the United States, met in Brazil at the Conference on Environment and Development, where they drafted a document that proclaimed twenty-eight guiding principles to strengthen global environmental governance. Responding to criticism that the North American Free Trade Agreement (NAFTA) was likely to harm the North American environment, President Bill Clinton in 1993 negotiated a supplemental environmental agreement with Mexico and Canada to go along with NAFTA. While some environmental organizations endorsed that agreement, others claimed that it did not go far enough in countering the negative environmental effects of NAFTA. In 1997, Clinton committed the United States to the Kyoto Protocol, which set forth timetables and emission targets for the reduction of greenhouse gases that cause global warming. President George W. Bush, however, rescinded this commitment when he took office in 2001.

Environmentalists were an important part of an "antiglobalization" coalition that coalesced at the end of the 1990s. It argued that the expansion of the global economy was occurring without proper environmental and labor standards in place. In 1999, globalization critics gained international attention by taking to the streets of Seattle to protest a meeting of the World Trade Organization.

In 1996, environmentalists critical of mainstream politics formed a national Green Party, believing that a challenge to the two-party system was needed to push through needed environmental change. In 1996 and 2000, the Green Party ran Ralph Nader as its presidential candidate. In 2000, Nader received 2.8 million votes, or 2.7 percent of the vote. The party elected a number of candidates to local office, particularly in the western states.

Achievements and Challenges

As the twentieth century ended, American environmentalists could point to a number of significant accomplishments. The goal of protecting the planet remained a popular one among the general public. In 2000, Americans celebrated the thirty-first Earth Day. In a poll taken that day, 83 percent of Americans expressed broad agreement with the environmental movement's goals and 16 percent reported that they were active in environmental organizations. In 2000, the thirty largest environmental organizations had close to twenty million members. Meanwhile, the country had committed significant resources to environmental control. In 1996, the U.S. spent $120 billion on environmental control—approximately 2 percent of its gross domestic product.

Environmental regulations put in place in the 1960s and 1970s had led to cleaner air and water. In 1997, the EPA reported that the air was the cleanest it had been since the EPA began record keeping in 1970; the emissions of six major pollutants were down by 31 percent. In 2000, the EPA reported that releases of toxic materials into the environment had declined 42 percent since 1988. The EPA also estimated that 70 percent of major lakes, rivers, and streams were safe for swimming and fishing—twice the figure for 1970. The dramatic cleanup of formerly contaminated rivers such as the Cuyahoga and the Potomac was further evidence that antipollution efforts were having their desired effects.

Yet many environmentalists remained pessimistic about the state of the planet. Despite the nation's progress in reducing pollution, at the end of the 1990s sixty-two million Americans lived in places that did not meet federal standards for either clean air or clean water. The Superfund program to clean up toxic areas had proven both costly and ineffective. In the mid-1990s, of the thirteen hundred "priority sites of contamination" that had been identified by the EPA under the program, only seventy-nine had been cleaned up. The political stalemate on environmental legislation that persisted for much of the 1980s and 1990s stymied efforts to update outdated pollution control efforts. In addition, a number of media sources in the late 1990s reported that America's national parks were underfunded and overcrowded because of cuts in the federal budget.

A more serious problem was related to do the nation's unwillingness to address long-term threats to the environment such as global warming, population growth, and the exhaustion of fossil fuel resources. Global warming threatened to raise ocean levels and generate violent and unpredictable weather, affecting all ecosystems; unrestrained world population growth would put greater pressure on the earth's limited natural resources; and the eventual exhaustion of fossil fuel resources would require the development of new forms of energy. The administration of George W. Bush represented the United States' lack of attention to these issues: not only did Bush pull the nation out of the Kyoto Protocol designed to control global warming, but his energy policy consisted of an aggressive exploitation of existing fossil fuel resources without significant efforts to find alternate sources of energy.

By the end of the twentieth century, many environmentalists showed a new concern with the goal of sustainable development, which sought long-term planning to integrate environmental goals with social and economic ones. Yet even as environmental organizations addressed global issues such as global warming, population growth, and the exhaustion of fossil fuel resources, the American public remained more concerned with more tangible issues such as air and water pollution. Indeed, the environmental movement had been successful because it had promised a tangible increase in the everyday quality of life for Americans through a cleaner, safer, and more beautiful environment. Mobilizing popular support to combat more abstract and long-term ecological threats thus presented environmentalists with a challenge. If they proved unable to prevent future degradation of the earth's environment from these long-term threats, few environmentalists would consider their movement a real success.

BIBLIOGRAPHY

Dunlap, Riley E., and Angela G. Mertig. *American Environmentalism: The U.S. Environmental Movement, 1970–1990.* Philadelphia: Taylor and Francis, 1992.

Graham, Otis L., Jr., ed. *Environmental Politics and Policy, 1960s–1990s.* University Park: Pennsylvania State University Press, 2000.

Hays, Samuel P., and Barbara D. Hays. *Beauty, Health, and Permanence: Environmental Politics in the United States, 1955–1985.* New York: Cambridge University Press, 1987.

McCormick, John. *Reclaiming Paradise: The Global Environmental Movement.* Bloomington: Indiana University Press, 1989.

Rosenbaum, Walter A. *Environmental Politics and Policy.* 5th ed. Washington, D.C.: CQ Press, 2002.

Rothman, Hal K. *Saving the Planet: The American Response to the Environment in the Twentieth Century.* Chicago: Ivan R. Dee, 2000.

Sale, Kirkpatrick. *The Green Revolution: The American Environmental Movement, 1962–1992.* New York: Hill and Wang, 1993.

Szasz, Andrew. *EcoPopulism: Toxic Waste and the Movement for Environmental Justice.* Minneapolis: University of Minnesota Press, 1994.

Worster, Donald. *Nature's Economy: A History of Ecological Ideas.* 2d ed. New York: Cambridge University Press, 1994.

Daniel Geary

See also **Air Pollution; Audubon Society; Demography and Demographic Trends; Earth Day; Endangered Species; Environmental Protection Agency; Global Warming; Love Canal; Ozone Depletion; Sanitation, Environmental; Sierra Club; *Silent Spring*; Superfund; Toxic Substance Control Act; Water Pollution.**

ENVIRONMENTAL PROTECTION AGENCY. Following a decade of growing concern about pollution, and less than two months after the first Earth Day celebration in 1970, President Richard M. Nixon proposed creating the Environmental Protection Agency (EPA). Nixon presented the EPA proposal to Congress as a reorganization plan to consolidate the Federal Water Quality Administration, the National Air Pollution Control

Administration, the Bureau of Solid Waste Management, and the Bureau of Water Hygiene, along with certain functions of the Council on Environmental Quality, the Atomic Energy Commission, and various other agencies into one agency. The primary mission of the new agency was to research the adverse effects of pollution and to establish and enforce standards to protect human health and the environment. Congress approved, and on 2 December 1970, the EPA opened its doors.

Nixon chose thirty-eight-year-old Assistant Attorney General William D. Ruckelshaus as EPA's first administrator. Dubbed Mr. Clean, Ruckelshaus wasted no time explaining that the EPA's primary obligation was the protection of the environment, not the promotion of commerce or agriculture. Under Ruckelshaus, the EPA first attempted to establish and enforce air quality standards. It also went after water polluters. Immediately, EPA threatened Cleveland—whose Cuyahoga River was so polluted that it had recently caught fire—Detroit, and Atlanta with lawsuits if they did not clean up their waterways. The EPA warned business and local governments that it would use the power of the courts to enforce the nation's environmental laws. Initially, however, the agency's authority was limited because few strong federal environmental laws existed.

Major Environmental Legislation

This soon changed. The Clean Air Act of 1970 (CAA), signed into law only a month before the EPA began operations, gave the EPA significant new powers to establish and enforce national air quality standards and to regulate air pollution emitters from smokestacks to automobiles. To take just one of many examples, under the CAA, the EPA began phasing out leaded gasoline to reduce the amount of poisonous lead in the air. The Clean Water Act of 1972 (CWA) did for water what the CAA had done for air—it gave the agency dramatic new authority to establish and enforce national clean water standards. Under these laws, the EPA began an elaborate permitting and monitoring system that propelled the federal government—welcome or not—into almost every industry in America. The EPA promised industry a chance to make good faith efforts to implement the new standards, but warned that federal enforcement actions against violators would be swift and sure.

The EPA also took quick action under other new environmental laws. The Federal Insecticide, Fungicide, and Rodenticide Act of 1972 (FIFRA) authorized the agency to regulate a variety of chemicals found in pesticides. Under its authority, the EPA banned the use of DDT, once viewed as a miracle chemical and sprayed in neighborhoods across America to stop the spread of malaria by killing mosquitoes, but later discovered to cause cancer and kill birds. The use of DDT had driven many avian species, including the bald eagle, to the brink of extinction and had inspired Rachel Carson to write *Silent Spring* (1962), which many credit as the clarion call for the modern environmental movement. In 1974, the passage of the Safe Drinking Water Act (SDWA) supplemented the CWA by granting the EPA power to regulate the quality of public drinking water.

The EPA's regulatory powers, however, did not stop with air, water, and pesticides. In 1976, Congress passed the Resource, Conservation, and Recovery Act (RCRA), which authorized the agency to regulate the production, transportation, storage, and disposal of hazardous wastes. That same year, Congress passed the Toxic Substance Control Act (TSCA), authorizing the EPA to regulate the use of toxic substances. Under TSCA, the EPA, for example, began the phaseout of cancer-causing PCB production and use. The leaking of chemical containers discovered at Love Canal, New York, in 1978 drew the nation's attention to the problem of hazardous and toxic wastes already disposed of unsafely in sites across the country. To address this problem, Congress in 1980 enacted the Comprehensive Environmental Response, Compensation, and Recovery Act (CERCLA), which provided a federal Superfund for hazardous waste cleanup and authorized the EPA to identify contaminated sites and go after those responsible for the contamination.

The EPA's Tasks

The Superfund measure was the last major environmental law passed by Congress during the twentieth century. Although Congress passed other important environmental legislation after 1980 and added important amendments to existing laws, CAA, CWA, SDWA, FIFRA, RCRA, TSCA, and CERCLA defined the basic parameters of EPA's regulatory powers. And the agency has since had its hands full. For example, each law required the EPA to identify any substance found in air, water, drinking water, pesticides, buildings, and waste—almost any substance found in the environment—that might be harmful to human health or the environment. The EPA then has had to identify how these substances do harm and at what doses. This has involved scientific investigation of gargantuan proportions, and the EPA is far from finished with the process.

The environmental laws have also required the EPA to determine threshold levels of regulation, another colossal task, and one that has involved more than just science. Often without much guidance from Congress, the agency has had to make difficult decisions about acceptable risks. Is a single death in one million acceptable? One in 100,000? One in 10,000? Despite its mission, politics and reality have dictated that economics play an important part in the EPA's regulatory scheme. Some substances are harmful at any level, but banning them entirely would cause catastrophic economic disaster, and in some cases would require devolutionary, and generally unacceptable, changes in the structure of modern society. The EPA's science, therefore, has always been tempered by economic and political reality.

Expanding Authority

That said, the EPA's regulatory role continued to grow during the 1980s, despite the conservative administrations of Ronald Reagan and George H. W. Bush. Following a nuclear accident at Three Mile Island in 1979, the EPA began to monitor nuclear waste and fallout (though other agencies have the primary power to regulate nuclear waste). Hazardous waste leaks at Times Beach, Missouri, in 1982 accelerated the EPA's regulation of dioxins. A year later, cleanup action of the Chesapeake Bay prompted the agency to begin regulating pollution from so-called "non-point" sources, primarily urban and agricultural runoff. In 1985, scientists discovered a hole in the earth's ozone layer, and after the signing of the Montreal Protocol two years later, the EPA began regulating the phaseout of ozone-depleting chlorofluorocarbons. In 1989, the *Exxon Valdez* spilled eleven million gallons of crude oil in Alaska's Prince William Sound. The EPA fined the Exxon Corporation $1 billion, the largest criminal environmental damage settlement in history.

During the 1990s, the EPA continued its attempt to fulfill its obligations under existing laws, and responded to the requirements of new laws and to the exigencies of environmental disaster and scientific discovery. The Pollution Prevention Act of 1990 forced the EPA to focus on the prevention—not just the correction—of environmental damage. In 1991, the agency created a voluntary industry partnership for energy efficient lighting and for reducing toxic chemical emissions, and a year later the agency began the Energy Star program to help consumers identify energy efficient products. In 1994, President William Clinton ordered the EPA to make environmental justice part of its mission, meaning that it would have to be certain that its regulations did not have a disparate impact on minority and low-income groups. On an old front, the EPA launched new initiatives, battling secondhand smoke in the name of indoor air pollution and creating a market-based permit trading program to reduce the sulfur dioxide emissions that cause acid rain. By the end of the decade, it faced many new challenges, including a rapidly depleting ozone layer and global warming.

By the year 2000, the EPA had become the federal government's largest regulatory agency. It wielded a budget of nearly $8 billion and employed more than eighteen thousand people. Its ever-growing number of rules had cost the regulated community $180 billion at the twentieth century's end. The EPA's growth earned the agency many enemies in industry and among conservative politicians. It has even clashed with traditionally liberal political interests, like labor unions that fear environmental regulations will cost jobs and minority groups who resent the fact that too often environmental regulation has meant locating polluting industries and hazardous waste sites in low-income, predominantly minority communities, which have little political clout. The EPA has also received almost unending criticism from environmental groups, which believe that it has not done enough.

The Agency's Achievements

Despite its opponents and critics, the EPA has met with much success. In 2000, the air was much cleaner than it was in 1970—lead levels alone had decreased 98 percent—despite the fact that there were more cars on the road and the nation was more industrialized. Because of EPA regulations, in 2002 cars polluted 95 percent less than they did in 1970. As for water, the agency regulated pollution from 43,000 industrial facilities, preventing one billion pounds of toxics from entering the waterways each year. In 1972, one-third of the nation's waters were safe for fishing and swimming; in 2001, two-thirds were. The EPA's regulation of hazardous and toxic chemicals has saved innumerable human lives and has rescued whole species from the brink of extinction. The ban on DDT, for example, led directly to the recovery of the bald eagle, which in 1999 was removed from the endangered species list. By 2000, the EPA had led or coordinated the cleanup of half of the nation's thirteen hundred Superfund sites, and had a panoply of regulations in place to safeguard human health and the environment from hazardous wastes.

BIBLIOGRAPHY

Cannon, Jonathan Z. "EPA and Congress (1994–2000): Who's Been Yanking Whose Chain?" *Environmental Law Reporter* 31 (August 2001): 10942–10956.

Hays, Samuel P. *Beauty, Health, and Permanence: Environmental Politics, 1955–1985.* New York: Cambridge University Press, 1987.

Landy, Marc K., Marc J. Roberts, and Stephen R. Thomas. *The Environmental Protection Agency: Asking the Wrong Questions from Nixon to Clinton.* New York: Oxford University Press, 1994.

Lofton, James. "Environmental Enforcement: The Impact of Cultural Values and Attitudes on Social Regulation." *Environmental Law Reporter* 31 (August 2001): 10906–10917.

Romine, Melissa. "Politics, the Environment, and Regulatory Reform at the Environmental Protection Agency." *Environmental Law* 6 (1999): 1.

Shannon C. Petersen

See also **Air Pollution; Clean Air Act; Clean Water Act; Conservation; Endangered Species; *Exxon Valdez*; Global Warming; Insecticides and Herbicides; Love Canal; Ozone Depletion; *Silent Spring*; Superfund; Times Beach; Toxic Substance Control Act; Water Pollution.**

EPIC was an acronym for the "End Poverty in California" movement, an effort to promote left-liberal candidates within the Democratic Party in California and Washington State in 1934. Upton Sinclair formed the movement in 1933 and ran under its banner as the Democratic candidate for governor of California. Calling for "Production for Use and Not for Profit," Sinclair supported higher taxes on corporations, utilities, and the wealthy, along with a network of state factories and land colonies for the unemployed. The twelve principles of

EPIC and its twelve political planks alarmed the Democratic Party establishment but deeply appealed to factions of an electorate concerned about the contemporary economic depression. By election day there were almost two thousand EPIC clubs in California. Sinclair lost the election by a small margin, but twenty-seven EPIC candidates won seats in California's eighty-seat legislature. In Washington, EPIC backers elected a U.S. senator.

BIBLIOGRAPHY

McElvaine, Robert S. *The Great Depression: America, 1929–1941.* New York: Times Books, 1993.

McIntosh, Clarence F. "The Significance of the End-Poverty-in-California Movement." *The Pacific Historian* 27 (1983): 21–25.

Sinclair, Upton. *I, Governor of California, and How I Ended Poverty. A True Story of the Future.* New York: Farrar and Rinehard, 1933.

James Duane Squires / C. P.

See also **California; Great Depression; Share-the-Wealth Movements.**

EPIDEMICS AND PUBLIC HEALTH. In its broadest sense, public health refers to organized efforts to protect and promote the physical and mental well-being of a community. These wide-ranging efforts can include such activities as combating epidemic outbreaks of disease, controlling chronic diseases, educating the public about disease prevention and health promotion, screening and vaccinating individuals for diseases, collecting and maintaining statistics about the incidence of diseases, births, deaths, and other vital events, guarding the food and water supplies through inspections and quality standards, and enacting laws and programs to preserve health. A critical component of public health work is epidemiology, the study of the incidence, distribution, and causes of health-related events in a given population. The scope, functions, and expectations of American public health have never been fixed; rather, they have changed significantly over the course of American history, reflecting advances in science and medicine, developments in society and politics, and trends in disease incidence.

Environmental Sources of Disease

The earliest American efforts to protect public health were sporadic, organized in response to outbreaks of widespread disease, and were rooted in an understanding of the environment and climate as the leading determinants of health and illness. Miasmatism, a prevailing medical explanation for illness, attributed diseases to miasma, foul odors or effluvia that originated from the soil or decomposing organic matter. The "bad airs" could contribute to an imbalance of one or more of the body's four humors which were believed to govern physical health. Medical ideas that emphasized the role of an individual's environment influenced the measures that were deployed against epidemics of disease. Filth, foul smells, and squalor, along with climates that were warm and wet, were implicated as the features of disease-prone areas. Outbreaks of fevers, malaria, cholera, yellow fever, and smallpox, typically during the warm and wet spring and summer months, and disproportionately affecting those living in crowded, impoverished, and unsanitary conditions, reinforced the medical beliefs about environmental influences in disease causation. Before the Civil War, measures against disease were directed by local health boards that were often hastily arranged and almost always temporary, in large part because, until well into the nineteenth century, public health was seen as a responsibility of private citizens rather than the elected government. Public health measures involved sanitation: regulating privies, cleaning streets, spreading lime, and removing garbage, dead animals, and stagnant pools of water. These functions were particularly critical because growing towns and cities still lacked sewer systems, water supply systems, and other infrastructure. Measures also controlled sources of environmental pollution such as refuse from butchers, slaughterhouses, tanneries, fishmongers, bone boilers, starch makers, clothes dyers, and other nuisance industries. Other ordinances regulated the quality of the food supply and governed the sale of foodstuffs during epidemics, such as cholera when the sale and consumption of fruits, vegetables, meats, and fish were forbidden.

Although sanitary measures were the foundation of early public health efforts, public health also extended beyond cleaning the environment and regulating sources of filth. Following the experience of Europe, American port cities instituted quarantine practices beginning early in the 1700s with Charleston, South Carolina, and Boston, Massachusetts, leading the way. Arriving passengers and cargo were inspected for disease, and those passengers determined to be sick or a health threat to the community were isolated and usually returned to the country from which they arrived. As the nation expanded, towns and cities on inland waterways also followed quarantine measures, particularly during times of disease epidemics. The need for quarantine and isolation was driven by the belief that diseases were transmitted between persons by direct contact. In addition to quarantine stations used to inspect and isolate arriving passengers, many cities beginning in the early eighteenth century established pesthouses to segregate individuals whose health could threaten the health of the wider community.

Epidemics and Public Health in the Antebellum Period

Americans in the antebellum period were afflicted by two general categories of diseases. The first included such endemic ailments as fevers, malaria, respiratory afflictions, measles, mumps, dysenteries, diarrheas, and other gastrointestinal complaints which people grudgingly accepted as among the unavoidable rigors of their daily lives. The second category included the much-feared epidemic diseases of smallpox, diphtheria, yellow fever, and cholera,

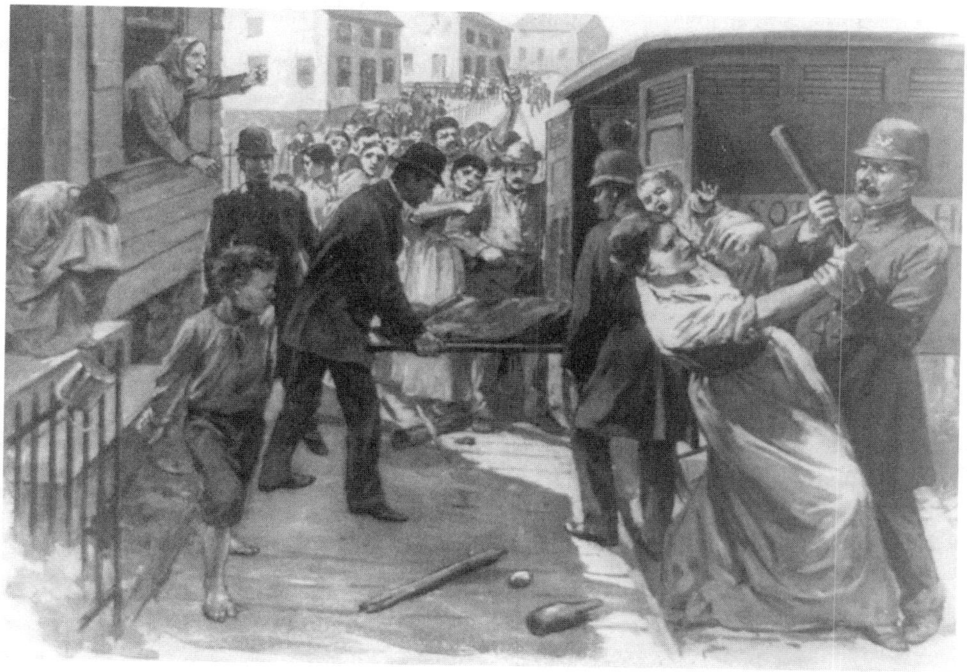

The Smallpox Troubles. This illustration, drawn by G. A. Davis from a sketch by Fred. Dougherty, depicts the resistance by foreign-born residents of Milwaukee, Wis., to the quarantining of patients in an isolation hospital. LIBRARY OF CONGRESS

which together inflicted their most punishing blows on the American population before the Civil War. Outbreaks of smallpox and yellow fever during the eighteenth century led to the passage of quarantine regulations by many cities.

Smallpox. While epidemics of yellow fever, cholera, and diphtheria were devastating but infrequent events in antebellum America, smallpox occurred much more regularly during the eighteenth century, and its harm could have been greater had it not been the first disease for which an effective prevention was devised (in the 1720s). During a smallpox outbreak in Boston in 1721, the Reverend Cotton Mather and the physician Zabdiel Boylston, following the recent practice of European physicians, inoculated their families and several hundred Bostonians, resulting in far fewer deaths among those inoculated than those who were infected during the epidemic. Inoculation, which induced a mild case of smallpox so that the person could acquire immunity against the disease, was controversial on religious and medical grounds and resisted as being dangerous because, when improperly performed, it could instigate a smallpox epidemic. Over the next half century the practice grew slowly, but by the end of the eighteenth century it was regularly practiced and accepted throughout the American colonies. Inoculation was supplanted by the much safer practice of vaccination, developed by Edward Jenner in 1798, which used cowpox vaccinia rather than active smallpox. The safety and growing acceptance of vaccination was reflected in 1813 when Congress supported a limited program of smallpox vaccination. Although state and municipal governments were generally apathetic to community health concerns in this early period, the banning of inoculation and the promotion of vaccination against smallpox were among the first state interventions into public health matters. The popularity of inoculation and the opposition to vaccination remained strong during the first half of the nineteenth century, and by 1850, most states needed to have laws forbidding inoculation.

Yellow Fever. In contrast to the regular incidence of smallpox, yellow fever appeared violently in the 1690s and then waned, only to occur occasionally during the first half of the eighteenth century. After an outbreak in 1762 in Philadelphia, the disease did not occur again for three decades, when, in 1793, it returned with overwhelming fulmination and mortality, annually wreaking fear and havoc in most American port cities until 1806. The social and medical responses to the outbreak of yellow fever in Philadelphia in August 1793 remains representative of the challenges public health efforts faced in the period. In the Philadelphia epidemic, the disease was not immediately recognized as yellow fever, in part because an outbreak had not occurred in many decades and in part because physicians disagreed about its origins and treatment. As the number of deaths rapidly climbed, nearly 20,000 of the city's 30,000 residents fled, including most federal, state, and municipal officials and civic leaders. A lack of funds, manpower, and civic leadership to enforce quarantine regulations allowed the epidemic to rage unabated, with hundreds of deaths weekly. The city's port officers and physicians did not have the funds and resources to inspect arriving ships and to isolate infected sailors and passengers, many arriving from Caribbean ports where yellow fever was epidemic. With many government officials having abandoned the city, Matthew Clarkson, Philadelphia's mayor, had to patch together emergency funds and volunteers to care for the sick and to enforce the quarantine laws. A volunteer committee of private citizens was quickly assembled by Clarkson to oversee the relief efforts, including soliciting food, money, and needed supplies from other towns. When the epidemic ended in November 1793, the death toll stood at more than 5,000, nearly one of every six residents of Philadelphia. In four months the disease had wiped out entire families, wreaking economic and social havoc on a scale never before seen in the new nation. (For comparison, 4,435 Americans died in battle over the eight years of the Revolutionary War.) Yellow fever returned to port cities along the Atlantic and Gulf coasts over the next decade, including major outbreaks in New York City in 1795 and 1798 when nearly 3,000 residents died. The responses to epidemic yellow fever did not change appreciably over the decade, and everywhere towns strengthened and enforced their quarantine regulations with hopes of avoiding local outbreaks of the disease. For much of the nineteenth century, yellow fever continued to appear in southern coastal towns but never with the severity of earlier epidemics. The yellow fever epidemics underscored the need for organized public efforts to combat epidemic diseases, although many of the measures instituted during the epidemics, particularly local health boards, were allowed to lapse after the epidemics abated.

Cholera. By the 1820s, smallpox and yellow fever continued to afflict the American population, albeit at less destructive levels than had been experienced before. But, in the early 1830s, they were joined by a third epidemic disease, cholera. After appearing in South Asia in the late 1820s, cholera spread west into Russia and eastern Europe by 1830, and despite quarantine efforts by western European countries, the pandemic spread rapidly and widely throughout Europe, appearing in England in 1831. North American newspapers carried stories of the devastation Asiatic cholera was causing in Europe, and Americans grew to fear that cholera would arrive imminently in their land. As they had with yellow fever, American cities resorted to the strict quarantine and inspection of arriving ships, passengers, and goods, but with no success. By June 1832, the first cases of cholera were reported in Quebec, Montreal, and New York. Political and civic leaders argued that cholera would not affect American cities and its peoples in the way it had in Europe. The first medical reports of cholera in New York City were dismissed by political and business leaders as unnecessarily inciting public panic and disturbing the city's economy and society. The New York City Board of Health, nevertheless, took limited actions after the first reported cases, establishing cholera hospitals to care for victims and requiring residents to remove rubbish, filth, standing water, and to generally clean the city. Cholera disproportionately affected those who were living in impoverished, crowded, squalid conditions, without proper access to clean water. Health officials promoted the widespread belief that poverty and disease were the result of immoral behaviors. In doing so, health officials were suggesting that those who contracted cholera had brought the disease upon themselves through their vices. Such a position reassured the upper classes that their social status, economic wealth, and religious beliefs made them immune from contracting the disease. Despite the city's efforts to fend off the epidemic, nearly 3,000 New Yorkers died over six weeks in June and July 1832.

Cholera continued to spread throughout the United States during 1832 and 1833. Some cities, including Boston and Charleston, were spared, but towns and cities of all sizes throughout the United States were visited by cholera during the summer of 1832. Government officials and religious leaders called for days of fasting and prayer with hopes of divine intervention against the epidemic. As in the epidemics of yellow fever, the outbreak of cholera prompted many residents, including government officers and civic leaders, to flee the towns and their duties. In the absence of permanent boards of health, the remaining population established temporary boards of health to oversee sanitation efforts, to create hospitals, dispensaries, and other medical services, to enforce quarantine and sanitation laws, and to provide social services such as burials and the care of orphans and widows. By October 1832, the epidemic reached New Orleans, killing 5,000 residents (or nearly 10 percent of the city's total population) and causing many thousands more to flee the city after the first reported cases. The deaths among those who remained in the city were very high. Occasional outbreaks of cholera continued through 1835 and then the disease disappeared, leading some Americans to believe that it would not return. However, a second major wave of cholera struck the United States between 1849 and 1854, by which time most cities had disbanded their boards of health and had returned to sanitary practices that had existed before the first wave in 1832–1833. As in the earlier epidemics, Americans saw cholera as a disease that affected classes of people who were poor, immoral, irreligious, criminal, intemperate, or lazy. During the second epidemic wave of cholera, this belief about disease susceptibility was joined with nativist, anti-immigrant attitudes, perpetuating the idea that immigrants were disease-laden and brought the diseases with them. Irish immigrants particularly, arriving in the United States after the Irish famine of 1845–1850, were treated as scapegoats for the epidemic. Immigrants were affected by cholera in overwhelming numbers, not because they were biologically susceptible or because they harbored the dis-

Spread of the Influenza Epidemic, 1918

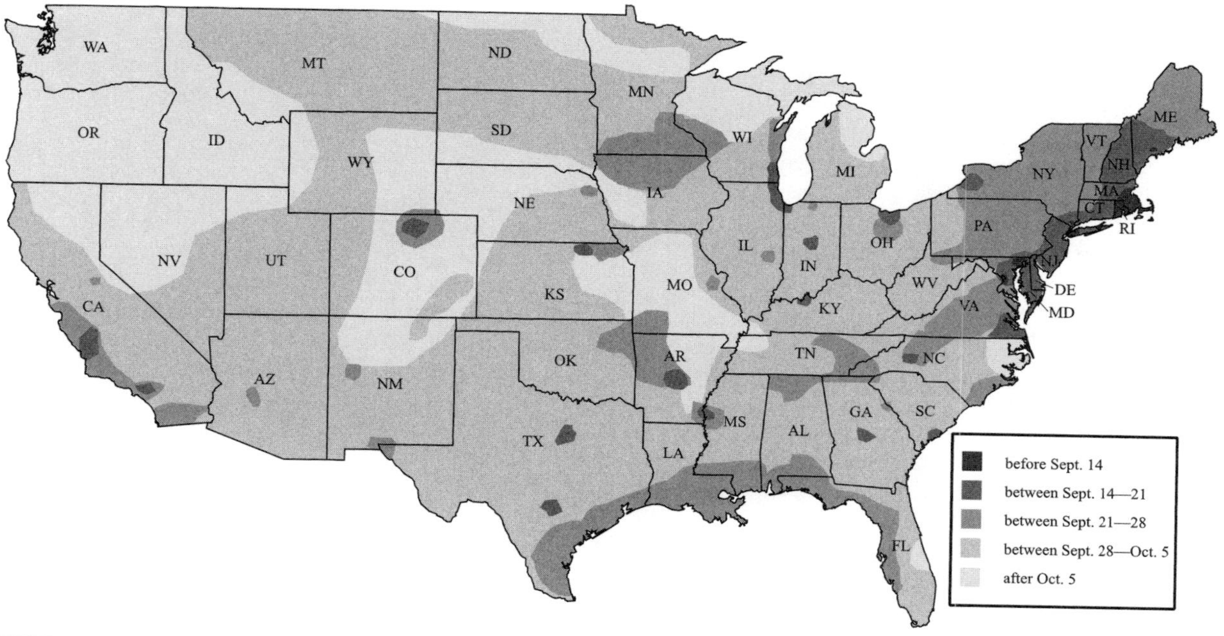

ease but because they lived in the overcrowded, squalid conditions of America's growing cities, where epidemic diseases spread rapidly.

Public Health in a Changing Nation. The cholera epidemics of 1832–1833 and 1849–1854 illustrate that the nation's towns and cities were unprepared and unable to shoulder the dual burdens of industrialization and a rapidly growing population. These population changes imposed enormous burdens on the cities' limited infrastructure and environmental resources. Many cities had antiquated or only limited systems of open sewers and gutters and lacked effective systems to remove garbage, animal waste, and rubbish from the city streets. Public water supply systems often relied on private wells that were created when the population and its needs were smaller. In short, the environmental and social conditions were rife for the rapid spread of disease when it occurred. Coupled with these conditions was the political expectation that protecting the public health was the duty of private citizens and not a government responsibility. As a result, municipal and state governments did not consistently attend to public health matters unless circumstances forced their involvement, and even then such interventions were fleeting, often consisting of private citizen groups acting in an official capacity to enforce the two measures in antebellum public health's arsenal: sanitation and quarantine.

Public Health as a Permanent State Function

The practice of public health did not change appreciably during the antebellum period, as sanitation and quarantine remained the common responses to outbreaks of disease. The epidemics of cholera, yellow fever, and diphtheria, the continuing threat posed by smallpox, malaria, and other ailments, and the growing incidence of tuberculosis during the first half of the nineteenth century highlighted the need for permanent institutions to safeguard a community's health. In the decades before the Civil War, the general health of Americans began to decline, and the rates of mortality and morbidity rose largely as a result of the consequences of urbanization and industrialization. Even smallpox, the one disease that early public health efforts made some progress in controlling through vaccination, began to occur in growing numbers by the 1840s as vaccination programs were neglected.

Calls for Sanitary Reform. During the 1830s in Europe, there was widening recognition of the relationship between the health of communities and the living conditions they enjoyed. After epidemics of influenza and typhoid in

1837 and 1838, the British government instructed Edwin Chadwick to study the problem of sanitation. Published in 1842, Chadwick's report, *The Sanitary Conditions of the Labouring Population*, argued that disease was directly tied to living conditions and that there was a dire need for public health reform. American physicians also identified appalling sanitary problems in the United States, including Benjamin McCready in an 1837 essay, "On the Influence of Trades, Professions, and Occupations in the United States in the Production of Disease," and John Griscom in his 1845 report *The Sanitary Condition of the Laboring Class of New York, With Suggestions for Its Improvement.* These studies identified the growing rates of illness among the working class and proposed public health reforms to address the problems.

The most forceful and important call for wider public health efforts by the government came from the Massachusetts physician Lemuel Shattuck in his *Report of the Sanitary Commission of Massachusetts* (1850). Its recommendations for reform were ahead of their time in light of the absence of national and state boards of health and the disorganization and transience of local boards of health. Among other things, the report called for the creation of a permanent state board of health; the collection and analysis of vital statistics and disease surveys from various localities, classes, and occupations; the creation of a smallpox vaccination program; the promotion of maternal, infant, and children's health; the protection of children's health through health education and the sanitation and ventilation of school buildings; the development of state programs to care for the mentally ill; and the instruction of physicians and nurses on matters of preventative medicine. Although highly praised, Shattuck's recommendations, like McCready's and Griscom's, were largely ignored by the medical and political communities. But they pointed to the growing realization of the need for permanent, state-sponsored public health programs.

Establishment of Public Health Boards. By the 1850s, spurred by the second wave of cholera epidemics between 1849 and 1854, cities and states began to address the grim sanitary conditions that contributed to the rapid spread of disease. Some sanitary reformers, through national conventions between 1857 and 1860, called for a national quarantine, for reform and standardization of local quarantine laws, and for greater study of cholera, yellow fever, and the effectiveness of quarantine in stemming their transmission. The conventions brought together the influential figures of the sanitary movement—Richard Arnold, Edward Barton, Jacob Bigelow, John Griscom, Edward Jarvis, Wilson Jewell, James Jones, Edwin Miller Snow, and others. John Duffy, a leading historian of American public health, has called these national conventions "the real beginning of the American sanitary revolution."

The Civil War disrupted the momentum of new sanitary efforts, but the spread of diseases by the movement of troops on both sides reiterated the needed measures for which reformers were clamoring. As in peacetime, the responsibility of caring for the sick and the wounded and rectifying the poor sanitary conditions of military camps fell on private volunteer groups, one of which evolved to become the United States Sanitary Commission. The Sanitary Commission, headed by Frederick Law Olmsted, oversaw military relief efforts, lobbied for a stronger medical corps, and succeeded in securing the appointment of the reform-minded William Hammond as surgeon general of the army.

After the war, important reforms were made in public health in the United States. Most notably, cities and states began to create permanent boards of health to oversee public health efforts. Louisiana and Providence, Rhode Island, established boards in 1855. Questions about the necessity of such bodies were answered when a third epidemic wave of cholera struck the United States during 1866 and 1867. New York City organized its Metropolitan Board of Health in 1866, and many other cities, including Cincinnati and Saint Louis, which suffered 2,000 and 3,500 deaths respectively during the cholera epidemic, quickly followed. The boards of health organized and implemented the sanitary measures and enforced the quarantine and inspection laws reformers had been urging for three decades. The tasks that had long been considered the responsibilities of private citizens were increasingly being assumed by the state. The new boards of health also expanded the reach and functions of public health in the closing decades of the nineteenth century, as an emphasis on the control of epidemic diseases declined and a greater interest in practical measures to prevent disease and preserve health emerged. New laws were passed forbidding the adulteration of milk, flour, meats, and other foods and regulating their quality. Boards demonstrated a commitment to improving infant mortality and children's health by regulating school buildings and instituting programs of health screening and vaccination. The creation of health boards also spurred the professionalization of public health as a discipline, reflected in the founding of the American Public Health Association in 1872.

Expansion of Municipal Infrastructure. On a practical level, the single greatest impediment to realizing the goals sought by the sanitary reformers was the removal of waste, garbage, standing water, and other pollution from America's crowded cities. Heavy rains and heavy use resulted in privies and sewers that would overflow, creating ideal unsanitary conditions for disease and contamination of the wells and water supply. The growing rates of typhoid, dysentery, and other enteric illnesses pointed to the need for new infrastructure. Beginning in the late 1860s and into the early twentieth century, dozens of cities initiated programs, spanning many years, to build sewers and to create a safe and protected water supply, which involved the introduction of filtration methods in the 1890s and chlorination in 1908. Health boards also enacted ordinances to curb other sources of animal pollution, which was a great concern at a time when horses were relied on for transportation and labor and when many families even in urban areas kept farm animals. Stables and manure in the streets had to be dealt with, as well as hogs and other livestock that roamed the streets. The carcasses of dead cats, dogs, and abandoned horses were common features of most large cities in the late nineteenth century. Even as late as the 1890s, New York City officials had to annually contend with removing on average 8,000 dead horses from the city's streets. Because of such circumstances, enforcing sanitation laws remained a central activity of many public health departments.

Public Health and the Federal Government. The federal government played little if any role in public health matters until the end of the nineteenth century. In 1798, the United States Marine Hospital Service was created to care for sick and injured merchant seamen, utilizing municipal and charity hospitals already in existence. Between 1830 and 1861, the federal government undertook a program of hospital construction for the Marine Hospital Service, with many of the hospitals being built along inland waterways. The system of hospitals was reorganized in 1870, placing its headquarters in Washington, D.C., and assigning as its head the newly appointed surgeon general. In 1891, the federal government conferred on the Marine Hospital Service the task of inspecting for disease newly arriving immigrants at the nation's ports. As the service's quarantine and inspection functions broadened, its name was changed in 1902 to the Public Health and Marine Hospital Service, and again in 1912 to the Public Health Service.

The second major federal foray into public health at the end of the nineteenth century was an attempt to establish a permanent National Board of Health. A devastating outbreak of yellow fever in 1878 in southern and midwestern states prompted politicians and public health leaders in the American Public Health Association to press for a federal body to oversee a national quarantine. The quarantine duties were initially vested in the existing Marine Hospital Service. After its establishment in 1879, the board pursued work in the areas of disease contagion, sanitation, and food adulteration. But, political infighting, a lack of resources, and a lack of a clear mandate led to its demise in 1883 when its funds and duties were fully transferred to the Marine Hospital Service.

Public Health after the Germ Theory of Disease

Medical and public health theory and practice were fundamentally transformed by the development of the germ theory of disease at the end of the nineteenth century. Beginning in the 1860s, Louis Pasteur, Joseph Lister, John Tyndall, Robert Koch, and other scientists offered competing versions of germ theory, which generally proposed that diseases were caused by specific microorganisms that did not propagate spontaneously. Rejecting the prevailing miasmatic explanation that diseases were the products of chemical fermentation and organic decomposition, germ theory was emblematic of the prominence held by laboratory sciences such as bacteriology and physiology in the new experimental medicine that emerged in the second half of the nineteenth century. Although the germ theory of disease was not widely accepted immediately, experimental evidence mounted in its favor, as the microorganisms responsible for tuberculosis, diphtheria, cholera, septicemia, cattle plague, and anthrax were identified.

For the public health community, which had long relied on sanitation to prevent outbreaks of disease, the germ theory of disease provided an important means of controlling diseases by identifying infected individuals. Beginning in the mid-1880s, the goals of public health work changed from sanitary measures, which were slow in realizing their benefits, to the scientific control of disease using bacteriological and epidemiological work. Germ theory allowed public health officials to identify and isolate infected individuals, to use the laboratory to diagnose diseases, and to develop vaccines against infectious diseases. Public health departments began to collect statistics about the incidence of disease, and physicians became legally obligated to report to the local health department any individual they diagnosed with a contagious disease. At the close of the nineteenth century, vaccination against smallpox was expanded, and new human vaccines were developed over the next half-century, including rabies (1885), plague (1897), diphtheria (1923), pertussis (1926), tuberculosis (1927), tetanus (1927), and yellow fever (1935). With the availability of new vaccines, many states instituted mandatory vaccination programs, which were often politically contentious and resisted by the public. Public opposition to a mandatory smallpox vaccination program in Massachusetts found its way to the United States Supreme Court in *Jacobson v. Massachusetts* (1905). In the groundbreaking case, the court's decision upheld and broadened state powers in public health matters, and declared that the state could compel private citizens to act when the health of the community was threatened.

Disease control efforts against tuberculosis and diphtheria were symbolic of public health's successes in curbing diseases using bacteriological science. Tuberculosis had been the leading cause of death in the United States during the nineteenth century and continued to afflict many Americans until the mid-twentieth century. The identification of the bacteria that causes tuberculosis allowed physicians and public health officials to definitively diagnose infected individuals and to isolate them, preventing the further spread of the disease. By the 1930s, the incidence level of tuberculosis was one-sixth of what it was in the 1870s. Diphtheria reached epidemic proportions beginning in the 1870s and killed thousands of Americans annually, particularly young children, over the next three decades. In the 1890s, the New York City Department of Health, under the leadership of Hermann Biggs, instituted a multiphase diphtheria control effort that involved diagnosing and isolating individuals with the disease, developing, testing, and distributing diphtheria antitoxin, and creating a program of screening, immunization, and public education. By the 1930s, the incidence of diphtheria in New York City was a fraction of its levels in the early 1870s. Advances in laboratory medicine, however, were not solely responsible for the success public health enjoyed at the century's turn. Rather, disease campaigns needed the participation and the support of physicians, politicians, public health officials, and the general public to succeed, and implementing disease control programs often involved complex social negotiations among these groups.

The development of a laboratory-based, quantitative public health also led to the appearance of new related disciplines including epidemiology, sanitation engineering, vital statistics, public health nursing, and preventative medicine. New schools and academic departments in epidemiology, hygiene, and public health were established, with Yale creating the first department in 1915 and Johns Hopkins (1916) and Harvard (1922) following shortly after. At the turn of the twentieth century, public health, which had long been practiced by physicians and which was regarded as a subdiscipline of medicine, emerged as a field of its own, with its exclusive professional organizations, journals, institutions, and practices.

The New Public Health and Beyond

By the 1910s, most municipal and state public health departments had established or had access to bacteriological laboratories to aid their disease control efforts. But it was also becoming clear that neither sanitation efforts nor laboratory tools alone could prevent or control disease. Public health efforts needed the participation and the cooperation of the community that they aimed to protect. The career of Charles Chapin, superintendent of health in Providence, Rhode Island, for example, reflected the transitions public health underwent in this period. During the 1880s, Chapin led Providence's efforts to eliminate privies and introduce indoor plumbing, investigated filtration and other methods to protect the public water supply, and established the nation's first municipal bacteriological laboratory in 1888. Chapin's sanitation efforts were detailed in his landmark book, *Municipal Sanitation in the United States* (1901). Even before writing his book, Chapin began to move toward a belief that public health efforts needed to be based on laboratory science. His field investigations and statistical studies concluded that general sanitary measures were not effective means of preventing diseases because diseases were spread by person-to-person contact, and therefore, personal hygiene was a critical factor in their transmission. He proposed that public health departments should be relieved of their sanitation duties, in order to focus on the diagnosis and isolation of infected individuals and on public education to promote healthy personal hygiene and practices. In articulating these views in his book, *The Sources and Modes of Infection* (1910), Chapin laid the foundation for the New Public Health movement that in the early decades of the twentieth century brought together efforts grounded in bacteriology, public health education, and social hygiene and reform. These social concerns resulted in new or expanded public health programs for the inspection of milk, the care of the mentally ill, the promotion of children's health, and the regulation of food and drug purity. There also came new laws regarding child labor and occupational health, particularly among immigrants who faced harsh, unhealthy living and working conditions.

Public health work in this period was closely associated with broader social concerns and reforms of the Progressive movement, as public health officials and social reformers advanced a relationship between individual/personal hygiene and community/social hygiene. In expanding disease control programs against tuberculosis, diphtheria, and venereal diseases, health departments engaged in public health education and took advantage of films, magazine and newspaper advertising, traveling exhibitions, and public lectures to spread their message of personal hygiene. Public health officials hoped these efforts would discourage unhealthy behaviors and practices that could spread disease and would promote such behaviors as washing hands, swatting flies, using handkerchiefs and spittoons, and avoiding common drinking cups by informing the public about how disease was spread. A newfound awareness of the presence of germs affected people's daily lives and practices, including the growing use of water closets, the removal of rugs and heavy linens in the home that could harbor germs, the use of smooth chrome, porcelain, and linoleum to protect against germs, and the raising of women's skirts so that dust and germs would not be trapped in their hems. While old products such as soap were marketed with renewed fervor, new products were developed to accommodate new hygienic practices, including disposable, one-use paper cups, clear plastic wrap to protect foods, and disinfectants for the body and home.

The expansion of public health work and the introduction of epidemiological practices grounded in bacteriology and the laboratory also raised perplexing concerns about how public health officials could best protect the community's health while preserving the civil liberties of individuals. Public protests against mandatory vaccination programs accompanied their expansion at the turn of the twentieth century, but there is no better illustration of many of the legal challenges public health officials faced than the case of Mary Mallon, an Irish immigrant cook, who was diagnosed as a carrier of the typhoid fever bacterium and was incarcerated by New York City health officials to prevent her from spreading the disease. Laboratory tests confirmed that Mallon's body harbored *salmonella typhi*, the bacterium that causes typhoid fever. As a healthy carrier, she did not manifest any of the disease's symptoms but she could communicate the bacteria to others during her cooking jobs. Derisively called "Typhoid Mary," Mallon defied orders to stop working, and New York City officials felt compelled to isolate her between 1907 and 1910 and then again permanently from 1915 until her death in 1938.

Mallon's case raised important questions about the scope and the limits of state powers in public health matters at a time when the number of governmental and private agencies and organizations addressing public health issues was growing. In the pre–World War II United States, the Rockefeller Foundation supported both national and international public health programs against hookworm, malaria, and pellagra, while the Rosenwald Fund, the Milbank Memorial Fund, the Commonwealth Fund, the W. K. Kellogg Foundation, and the Metropolitan Life Insurance Company promoted programs of public health and preventative medicine. In addition to the Public Health Service, a plethora of federal agencies, including the Communicable Disease Center (later and presently, the Center for Disease Control and Prevention), the National Institutes of Health, the Indian Health Service, the Children's Bureau, the Department of Agriculture, and various military departments undertook public health and preventative medicine work and research. During World Wars I and II, the War Department particularly sought to curb the high incidence of venereal diseases among military personnel which threatened the country's military and moral strengths.

In the years immediately after World War II, the discovery and the growing availability of new antibiotics such as penicillin, streptomycin, aureomycin, chloromycin, terramycin, and sulfonamides and new vaccines such as those against polio (1955; 1962), measles (1963), mumps (1967), and rubella (1969) contributed to further controlling infectious diseases that had long plagued the public. The incidence of and the mortality from infectious diseases had steadily declined beginning in the late nineteenth century, but the availability of powerful new vaccines and chemotherapeutic agents brought the incidence of infectious diseases to a fraction of the levels at their worst, all of which underscored the changing patterns of disease. Although a global pandemic of influenza during 1918–1919 had killed between twenty and forty million people worldwide, including 600,000 people in the United States, epidemic and infectious diseases diminished as the leading killers of Americans. During the twentieth century, chronic, noninfectious illnesses and conditions became the leading causes of death in the United States. On one hand, the increasing number of deaths from heart disease, cancers, stroke, diabetes, liver disease, arteriosclerosis, and lung diseases pointed to the fact that Americans were surviving to an older age at which they were afflicted by these degenerative conditions. But on the other hand, poor personal behaviors and conduct, such as rich, unhealthy diets, sedentary lifestyles, and addictions to alcohol, tobacco, and drugs also contributed to the incidence of these illnesses. As a result of these changes in the incidence of disease, the goals and the emphases of public health work underwent a shift from combating diseases to preventing them and to promoting sound health.

The considerable successes and confidence public health officials enjoyed in disease prevention and health promotion in the decades after World War II faced severe tests at the close of the twentieth century. Beginning in the 1980s, the global pandemic of acquired immune deficiency syndrome (AIDS) strained public health departments. Between 1981 and 2000, 774,467 cases of AIDS were reported in the United States; 448,060 people died of AIDS. Nearly one million other Americans were also infected by the human immunodeficiency virus (HIV), the virus that causes AIDS. The development of powerful antiretroviral therapies during the 1990s prolonged the lives of many Americans infected by HIV or suffering from AIDS. Further contributing to a public health crisis in which tuberculosis, malaria, sexually transmitted diseases, and other diseases again emerged as grave threats to community health were: the displacement of populations through immigration and political conflicts; the emergence of drug-resistant strains; the high rates of incarceration, homelessness, and intravenous drug use; the prevalence of mass air travel; the collapse of medical services in eastern Europe; the persistence of widespread poverty; and the progress of the AIDS pandemic, in which tuberculosis served as an opportunistic infection.

At the start of the twenty-first century, American public health officers and epidemiologists continued their work of disease prevention and health promotion in a world changed by the terrorist attacks of 11 September 2001. The outbreak of anthrax during 2001 and the threat of biological warfare and terrorism suggested that few public health departments were well-equipped or well-trained to handle a sudden, mass disease outbreak. This also raised questions about the necessity to reinstitute mass vaccination against smallpox. Globalization and commercialism continue to pose profound consequences and challenges for the American public health community in its promotion of good health for an American population beset by obesity, diabetes, stress, violence, smoking, and drug use. The still emerging threats such as Lyme disease, bovine spongiform encephalopathy (BSE, or "mad cow" disease) and infections of Ebola and West Nile viruses, point to the continuing need for American public health organizations to respond to disease threats, promote preventative measures, and above all, adapt their mission to the times.

BIBLIOGRAPHY

Brandt, Allan M. *No Magic Bullet: A Social History of Venereal Disease in the United States since 1880.* Exp. ed. New York: Oxford University Press, 1987.

Duffy, John. *The Sanitarians: A History of American Public Health.* Urbana: University of Illinois Press, 1990.

Gostin, Larry O. *Public Health Law: Power, Duty, Restraint.* Berkeley: University of California Press; New York: Milbank Memorial Fund, 2000.

Hammonds, Evelynn Maxine. *Childhood's Deadly Scourge: The Campaign to Control Diphtheria in New York City, 1880–1930.* Baltimore: Johns Hopkins University Press, 1999.

Humphreys, Margaret. *Yellow Fever and the South.* New Brunswick: Rutgers University Press, 1992.

———. *Malaria: Poverty, Race, and Public Health in the United States.* Baltimore: Johns Hopkins University Press, 2001.

Kraut, Alan M. *Silent Travelers: Germs, Genes, and the "Immigrant Menace."* New York: Basic Books, 1994.

Leavitt, Judith Walzer. *The Healthiest City: Milwaukee and the Politics of Health Reform.* Princeton, N.J.: Princeton University Press, 1982.

———. *Typhoid Mary: Captive to the Public's Health.* Boston: Beacon Press, 1996.

Markel, Howard. *Quarantine!: East European Jewish Immigrants and the New York City Epidemics of 1892.* Baltimore: Johns Hopkins University Press, 1997.

Melosi, Martin. *The Sanitary City: Urban Infrastructure in America from Colonial Times to the Present.* Baltimore: Johns Hopkins University Press, 2000.

Rogers, Naomi. *Dirt and Disease: Polio before FDR.* New Brunswick, N.J.: Rutgers University Press, 1992.

Rosen, George. *A History of Public Health.* Exp. ed. Baltimore: Johns Hopkins University Press, 1993.

Rosenberg, Charles E. *The Cholera Years: The United States in 1832, 1849, and 1866.* Chicago: University of Chicago Press, 1987.

Rosenkrantz, Barbara Gutmann. *Public Health and the State: Changing Views in Massachusetts, 1842–1936.* Cambridge, Mass.: Harvard University Press, 1972.

Rothman, Sheila M. *Living in the Shadow of Death: Tuberculosis and the Social Experience of Illness in America.* New York: Basic Books, 1994.

Shilts, Randy. *And the Band Played On: Politics, People, and the AIDS Epidemic.* New York: St. Martin's Press, 1987.

Smith, Susan Lynn. *Sick and Tired of Being Sick and Tired: Black Women's Health Activism in America, 1890–1950.* Philadelphia: University of Pennsylvania Press, 1995.

Tomes, Nancy. *The Gospel of Germs: Men, Women, and the Microbe in American Life.* Cambridge, Mass.: Harvard University Press, 1998.

D. George Joseph

See also **Cholera; Meat Inspection Laws; Poliomyelitis; Sexually Transmitted Diseases; Smallpox; Tuberculosis; Urbanization; Yellow Fever.**

EPISCOPALIANISM. The Episcopal Church, U.S.A., is the representative of the Anglican Communion in the United States. Anglicanism first came to America with the Jamestown settlement in 1607 and enjoyed establishment status in Virginia and other southern colonies. In the Middle Colonies, it competed with a variety of other denominations, while in New England, the church was viewed as an interloper that offered a high liturgical alternative to the Congregational Church. It endorsed justification by grace through faith, worship in the vernacular, the authority of Holy Scripture, and an episcopate in the Apostolic Succession. Nationally, it was the second largest denomination after Congregationalism in 1776. The coming of the American Revolution fundamentally divided the church. While laymen in the southern and lower Middle Colonies supported the Revolution, many in New England and New York did not. In Virginia, the church was disestablished after the Revolution, and the church was further weakened by the separation of the Methodists in 1784 and its clergy's growing dependence on the voluntary contributions of parishioners.

Creating an American Church

In 1782, William White responded to growing demands for a united church with historic orders of bishops, priests, and deacons by publishing *The Case of the Episcopal Churches in the United States Considered.* Two years later, the New England high church party sent the former loyalist clergyman Samuel Seabury to Scotland, where he was ordained by the nonjuring bishops. On his return, Seabury began to ordain new clergy, stressing baptismal regeneration to distinguish the church from Congregationalism and seeking to tie the Holy Spirit to the episcopate—an institution disliked in the South. Moderates from states outside New England met at Philadelphia in 1785 and resolved to send William White and Samuel Provoost to England, where they were consecrated as bishops in 1787. At the convention of 1789, the majority acknowledged Seabury's consecration, adopted an American version of the Book of Common Prayer, and endorsed a unitary church constitution with considerable local autonomy.

The High Church and the Evangelicals

During the early nineteenth century, the Episcopal Church established seminaries in New York (General Seminary) and Virginia (Virginia Theological Seminary). Increasingly, the church came to be divided into two factions. The high church party emphasized baptismal regeneration and opposed participation in transdenominational bodies and entanglement with the civil power, while the evangelical party stressed preaching and revivalism. These divisions surfaced at the 1844 General Convention, where evangelicals called for a condemnation of Roman Catholicism and the Oxford Movement, though the measure failed to pass. After the Civil War, William A. Muhlenberg led the "evangelical catholic" party, which accepted the observance of the daily office and a weekly Eucharist, but stressed personal experience and ecumenism. "Anglican catholics" led by James DeKoven rejected ecumenism and linked the doctrine of the Incarnation to the sacraments of baptism, the Eucharist, and confession, refusing to view the Episcopal Church as a part of the reformed tradition.

A National Church

The Episcopal Church grew rapidly between 1880 and 1920, and there was a strong positive response to the Social Gospel. Eleven of the thirty-eight settlement houses before 1900 had Episcopal backing. Also influential, be-

William A. Muhlenberg. The leader of the more ecumenical "evangelical catholic" party of the Episcopal Church after the Civil War. ARCHIVE PHOTOS, INC.

tween 1874 and 1934, was the Church Congress movement, which held conferences on issues of social and religious interest, the epitome of the church's openness to intellectual challenge and tolerance for diversity of thought. Many viewed the Episcopal Church as an excellent basis for a new national church because it was not divided ethnically or geographically. There was also a new openness to dialogue with other denominations, and in 1927, Bishop Charles Brent presided over the World Conference on Faith and Order. During the 1920s, the church avoided the fundamentalist-modernist schisms of other denominations, expressing a determination to uphold the creeds, if not biblical inerrancy, and arguing that clergy should not contradict the traditional statements of belief. In response, modernists launched the Modern Churchman's Union and several seminaries moved to university campuses to preserve their intellectual freedom.

Postwar Controversies

After World War II, a liturgical revival took place within the Episcopal Church, which stressed a new role for the laity. The church joined the World Council of Churches in 1948 and the National Council of Churches in 1950. After moderate growth during the 1950s, however, membership declined from 3.64 million in 1966 to 3.04 million in 1980. The church confronted severe struggles over civil rights, female ordination, and homosexuality after 1961. Black delegates had only begun to attend the General Convention in the 1940s, when southern dioceses abolished their separate colored conventions. During the civil rights era, a small group of activists formed the Episcopal Society for Cultural and Racial Unity, which took an antisegregationist stance. After the Watts riots of 1965 in Los Angeles, the presiding bishop John Hines inaugurated the $9 million General Convention Special Program to assist minority communities, but this was discontinued in 1973. In the later 1970s, the Union of Black Episcopalians achieved a larger African American presence in positions of influence. More controversial was the debate over female ordination that, in 1971, produced the Episcopal Women's Caucus. After three bishops illegally ordained eleven female deacons in 1974, the 1976 General Convention permitted the practice. The action provoked a vocal response from traditionalists, leading to the formulation of a conscience clause for dioceses opposed to female ordination; this clause was, however, later repealed by the 1997 General Convention. By far the most divisive conflict arose over the ordination of practicing homosexuals initiated by Bishop John Spong of Newark, New Jersey, which led to a rebuke of American liberals by conservative Anglican bishops from the Third World at the 1998 Lambeth Conference.

By 1998, the Episcopal Church, U.S.A., led by Presiding Bishop Frank Griswold, had 2,317,794 baptized members. Its prospects, however, were not encouraging, for membership had declined 6.7 percent between 1986 and 1996. In 2000, the church concluded a concordat with the Evangelical Lutheran Church in America, reflecting the declining size of rural congregations for both denominations. The only obvious growth was in Province IV (the South) and in the charismatic party within the church, represented by the Episcopal Charismatic Fellowship.

BIBLIOGRAPHY

Holmes, David. *A Brief History of the Episcopal Church.* Valley Forge, Pa.: Trinity Press International, 1993.

Prichard, Robert. *A History of the Episcopal Church.* Rev. ed. Harrisburg, Pa.: Morehouse, 1999.

Shattuck, Gardiner H., Jr. *Episcopalians and Race: Civil War to Civil Rights.* Lexington: University Press of Kentucky, 2000.

Spielmann, Richard M. "A Neglected Source: The Episcopal Church Congress, 1874–1934." *Anglican and Episcopal History* 58, no. 1 (March 1989): 50–80.

Sugeno, Frank. "The Establishmentarian Ideal and the Mission of the Episcopal Church." *Historical Magazine of the Protestant Episcopal Church* 53, no. 4 (December 1984): 285–292.

Jeremy Bonner

See also **Denominationalism; Protestantism; Women in Churches.**

EQUAL EMPLOYMENT OPPORTUNITY COMMISSION (EEOC) is an independent federal regulatory agency created under Title VII of the 1964 Civil Rights Act with the mission of eliminating illegal workplace discrimination. Its main function is to administer Title VII, which prohibits employment discrimination on the basis of race, color, national origin, sex, and religion.

The EEOC is composed of five commissioners—not more than three of whom may be from the same political party—appointed by the president for five-year staggered terms. The commissioners are responsible for setting EEOC policy and approving all litigation filed on the agency's behalf. The U.S. president designates one of the commissioners as chair and another as vice chair. (Franklin D. Roosevelt Jr. served as the first chair.) The president also appoints a general counsel with overall responsibility for the agency's litigation for a four-year term. The commissioners and general counsel must be confirmed by the Senate; investigative work is conducted by employees in district offices.

The history of federal efforts to create an agency to deal with discrimination goes back to 1941. Wartime manpower needs and a threat by black civil rights activists to march on Washington, D.C., in support of their demands for improved job opportunities led President Franklin D. Roosevelt to create, by executive order, the Fair Employment Practices Committee (FEPC). The FEPC was responsible for ensuring that the federal civil service and those industries essential to the war effort or holding government contracts observed fair employment practices. The committee operated until 1946. President Harry S. Truman established the Committee on Government Contract Compliance, which operated only from April 1952 to January 1953. In September 1953, President Dwight D. Eisenhower established the Committee on Government Contracts; it was replaced in April 1961 with President John F. Kennedy's Committee on Equal Employment Opportunity. In all of these cases, agency authority covered only government employment and employment in private companies doing business directly with the government. Legislative support for an agency responsible for ending discrimination in private sector employment did not exist until the passage of the CIVIL RIGHTS ACT OF 1964.

By the end of the twentieth century, the EEOC pursued its mission of equal employment opportunity in several ways: it provided technical assistance to businesses and organizations, engaged in public education, developed regulations that provided the framework for enforcement of the law, and issued enforcement guidelines that interpreted key standards within the law. Its guidelines in such areas as AFFIRMATIVE ACTION, pregnancy discrimination, fetal protection, sex-segregated advertising, and SEXUAL HARASSMENT have had an important influence on employment discrimination law and employer behavior toward employees. Also, the EEOC receives and responds to complaints of discrimination. This latter function probably receives the most public attention. However, as originally constituted, the EEOC had limited ability to respond to complaints. If it found probable cause that discrimination had occurred, the agency was empowered only to negotiate, conciliate, or attempt to persuade the employer to abandon discriminatory policies. If these efforts were unsuccessful, the commission referred the case to the Department of Justice for litigation. When the EEOC found insufficient evidence of discrimination, it issued a right-to-sue notice allowing the complainant the opportunity to file suit in federal court within ninety days.

Concerned about the limits on the agency's ability to enforce the ban on discrimination, Congress enacted the Equal Employment Opportunity Act of 1972, which authorized the EEOC to file lawsuits against employers after unsuccessful attempts at conciliation. In 1974, Congress gave the EEOC the authority to bring pattern-and-practice suits against employers in federal court—that is, suits charging discrimination on an industrywide or companywide basis. Under the direction of chairperson Eleanor Holmes Norton, appointed in 1977 by President Jimmy Carter, the EEOC began to focus most of its attention on widespread employment discrimination using class-action suits and pattern-and-practice cases as its weapons. Since receiving authority to litigate, the commission has filed many legal actions against large corporations, gaining relief for millions of employees.

Not only has Congress increased the tools available to the EEOC since 1964, it has also expanded the scope of its authority. In 1979, the EEOC became the lead agency for handing all types of employment discrimination. Congress gave it enforcement authority for complaints brought under the Age Discrimination in Employment Act, the EQUAL PAY ACT, and Title VII. Later, Congress expanded the EEOC's jurisdiction through the AMERICANS WITH DISABILITIES ACT of 1990, the Older Workers Benefit Protections Act of 1990, and the CIVIL RIGHTS ACT OF 1991.

However, not only statutory directives determine the scope of EEOC activities and powers. The enforcement philosophy and managerial concerns of its commissioners and the president of the United States are also important. In 1982, the EEOC changed direction under the leadership of Clarence Thomas, appointed by President Ronald Reagan, and began to concentrate on cases of individual discrimination. This approach, which focused on particularized fact situations involving only one or a small number of identifiable individuals, reduced the EEOC's effectiveness in combating widespread employment discrimination. In the 1990s, under the administration of President Bill Clinton, the EEOC tried to find a middle ground between an individualized and a systemic approach to law enforcement. In 1996, the commission adopted its National Enforcement Plan that emphasized voluntary resolution of disputes and provided that—when enforcement action was required—priority would be given to cases that would have the greatest impact on eliminating discrimination.

Over the years, the EEOC has influenced the direction of employment discrimination law, obtained relief for millions of discrimination victims, and educated employers and employees on their rights and responsibilities. Even so, as the agency enters the twenty-first century, it continues to face challenges. Caseloads have been growing at a record pace as a result of the commission's expanded jurisdiction and the changing nature of the workforce; it receives an increasing number of charges involving multiple or intersecting bases of discrimination; and more cases of retaliation, a problem that—if undeterred—can undermine the commission's entire mission. The EEOC must continue to use its broad array of tools—technical assistance, outreach, education, voluntary dispute resolution, and litigation—in a creative manner to promote equal employment opportunity during the twenty-first century.

BIBLIOGRAPHY

Belz, Herman. *Equality Transformed: A Quarter-Century of Affirmative Action.* Bowling Green, Ohio: Social Philosophy and Policy Center; New Brunswick, Ohio: Transaction Publishers, 1991.

Burstein, Paul. *Discrimination, Jobs, and Politics: The Struggle for Equal Employment Opportunity in the United States Since the New Deal.* Chicago: University of Chicago Press, 1985; 1998.

"The Story of the United States Equal Employment Commission: Ensuring the Promise of Opportunity for 35 Years, 1965–2000." Equal Employment Opportunity Commission. Available from http:/ /www.eeoc.gov/35th/index.html.

Graham, Hugh Davis. *The Civil Rights Era: Origins and Development of National Policy, 1960–1972.* New York: Oxford University Press, 1990.

Ruchames, Louis. *Race, Jobs and Politics: The Story of FEPC.* New York: Columbia University Press, 1953; Westport, Conn.: Negro Universities Press, 1971.

Henry N. Drewrey
Susan Gluck Mezey / C. P.

See also **Civil Rights Movement; Civil Rights Restoration Act; Discrimination: Age; Pregnancy Discrimination Act; Women's Rights Movements: The 20th Century;** *and vol. 9:* **NOW Statement of Purpose.**

EQUAL PAY ACT (1963). Legislation requiring equal pay for women was first introduced in 1945 in acknowledgment of women's war work. Business owners and labor organizations succeeded in thwarting the effort, in part because of the perceived need for women to leave the labor force to create vacancies for returning servicemen. By the end of the 1950s, policymakers were becoming concerned about insufficient use of "womanpower." Under the leadership of Esther Peterson, director of the Women's Bureau and an assistant secretary of labor in the administration of President John F. Kennedy, Congress in 1963 passed the Equal Pay Act as an amendment to the Fair Labor Standards Act of 1938 to require employers to pay equal wages to men and women doing "equal work on jobs . . . which [require] equal skill, effort, and responsibility, and are performed under similar working conditions." The Equal Pay Act was the first federal effort to bar discrimination by private employers on the basis of gender. Because the law was part of the Fair Labor Standards Act, wage and hour inspectors routinely reviewed company records and cited employers, rather than depending on complaints to alert them to violations. During the next decade 171,000 employees received $84 million in back pay. In the 1970s, however, President Jimmy Carter's administration transferred enforcement to the Equal Employment Opportunity Commission, which filed few Equal Pay Act cases. Because women and men seldom possess identical job classifications, the reach of the Equal Pay Act has been limited.

BIBLIOGRAPHY

Kessler-Harris, Alice. *A Women's Wage: Historical Meanings and Social Consequences.* Lexington: University Press of Kentucky, 1990.

Sealander, Judith. *As Minority Becomes Majority: Federal Reaction to the Phenomenon of Women in the Workforce, 1920–1963.* Westport, Conn.: Greenwood Press, 1983.

Zelman, Patricia G. *Women, Work, and National Policy: The Kennedy-Johnson Years.* Ann Arbor, Mich.: UMI Research Press, 1982.

Cynthia Harrison / T. M.

See also **Comparable Worth; Equal Employment Opportunity Commission; Fair Labor Standards Act.**

EQUAL PROTECTION OF THE LAW refers to the constitutional concept that the government should treat similar persons similarly and should not treat people of different circumstances as if they were the same. An equality principle appeared in the Declaration of Independence ("We hold these truths to be self evident: that all men are created equal . . .") but did not appear in the Constitution itself until the passage of the Fourteenth Amendment in 1868. The amendment embodied the commitment of the victorious Northern states to afford some measure of national constitutional protection for the rights of the newly emancipated slaves. The amendment's framers deliberately worded the equal protection clause more broadly, however, declaring, "No state shall . . . deny to any person within its jurisdiction the equal protection of the laws." In part because of its breadth and elasticity, this provision has become probably the single most important source of constitutional protection for individual rights.

Though the terms of the equal protection clause apply only to state and local governments, the Supreme Court has held the federal government to almost identical requirements. In *Bolling v. Sharpe,* 347 U.S. 497 (1954), the Supreme Court explained that a guarantee of equal protection was implicit in the due process clause of the Fifth Amendment, which applies to the federal government.

Problems Addressed by the Equal Protection Clause

The issue of equal protection arises when the government classifies individuals under the terms of some statute or regulation, or when government actors purposefully treat individuals differently in applying statutes that are ostensibly neutral. The analytical difficulty springs from the fact that the need for classification and different treatment is inherent in the nature of governmental activity. Even in the most benign situations, the government in pursuing social goals must "draw lines" to identify who is required to perform a particular action or who will receive a government benefit. The equal protection guarantee ensures not the absence of these classifications but the absence of impermissible criteria, such as race, in their creation or application—unless the government can show adequate justification for the criteria. The equal protection concept also protects certain "fundamental interests," such as the right to vote, from government classifications that burden those interests.

Whether specific persons are properly placed within a classification is not a matter for equal protection jurisprudence. Equal protection addresses the legitimacy of the classification itself, whether it is inherent in the law or arises during the law's application. It is the Constitution's guarantee of procedural due process that protects individuals from wrongful classification by ensuring some level of fair process in determining whether the classification is properly applied in a specific instance.

Methods of Equal Protection Analysis

Under equal protection analysis, the question of whether a law is proper turns on the legitimacy of the ends desired, the nature of the classification itself, and the "fit" between the ends and the way government has classified persons in light of that end. Traditionally, courts have described their analysis in terms of levels of scrutiny: "strict" scrutiny for particularly "suspect" classifications such as race; "intermediate" scrutiny for classifications, such as those based on sex, that require heightened attention but do not raise the exceptional problems of those in the "strict" category; and "rational basis" scrutiny for all other classifications. Some members of the Court, most notably Justice Thurgood Marshall, have periodically urged the Court to abandon these categories, and many commentators agree that a more flexible approach would allow the Court to be more sensitive to the complexities these cases present. With some exceptions, however, the Court continues to adhere to these general categories.

Strict Scrutiny. To satisfy strict scrutiny, a law must serve an extremely important, "compelling" interest. Also, the fit between the interest and classification must be very close. That is, the classification must be "narrowly tailored" to serve the goal of the law. The application of strict scrutiny is almost always fatal to the law in question.

Courts use strict scrutiny to evaluate classifications based on race, national origin, and—sometimes—status as an alien. There is much debate about why these categories should require strict scrutiny. In the famous "Footnote 4" of *United States v. Carolene Products Co.*, 304 U.S. 144 (1938), the Court explained that strict scrutiny is called for because "prejudice against discrete and insular minorities may be a special condition, which tends seriously to curtail the operation of those political processes ordinarily to be relied upon to protect minorities." Racial classifications are considered so problematic that courts apply strict scrutiny even when the classifications are intended to benefit racial minorities, such as in affirmative action programs (*Adarand Constructors, Inc. v. Pena*, 515 U.S. 200, 1995), and even when the racial classification may in fact correlate with attributes relevant to legitimate government objectives. The most famous equal protection case in the context of race is *Brown v. Board of Education*, 347 U.S. 483 (1954), which held racial segregation in public schools to be unconstitutional.

The Supreme Court has also applied strict scrutiny to laws that classify people in some way that burdens the exercise of a fundamental right, such as voting. In *Reynolds v. Sims*, 377 U.S. 533 (1964), the Supreme Court used the equal protection guarantee as the basis for the creation of the principle of "one person, one vote." While not explicitly invoking strict scrutiny, the Court in *Bush v. Gore*, 531 U.S. 98 (2000), stopped a manual recount of ballots in the contested presidential election in Florida, holding that inconsistent standards for deciding which ballots should be counted violated equal protection.

Intermediate Scrutiny. Under intermediate scrutiny, courts will not uphold a governmental classification unless it has a "substantial relationship" to an "important" government interest. While the doctrinal formulations have varied, both the "means" and the "ends" tests are less exacting than strict scrutiny and more demanding than rationality review. The Supreme Court has used intermediate scrutiny in cases involving classifications based on sex and the extramarital status of children, and sometimes in cases involving aliens.

The Court adopted the intermediate level of review for gender classifications in the case of *Craig v. Boren*, 429 U.S. 190 (1976), in which the Court struck down a statute that allowed women over age eighteen to purchase beer but allowed males to purchase beer only after age twenty-one. Applying intermediate scrutiny, the Court has invalidated gender segregation in state nursing schools (*Mississippi University for Woman v. Hogan*, 458 U.S. 718, 1982), single-sex state universities (*United States v. Virginia*, 518 U.S. 515, 1996), statutory provisions offering lower benefits to families of working women than to families of working men (*Frontiero v. Richardson*, 411 U.S. 677, 1973), and social security regulations that provided smaller survivor benefits to widowers than to widows (*Califano v. Goldfarb*, 430 U.S. 199, 1977). On the other hand, the Court has upheld a requirement that only men register for the draft (*Rostker v. Goldberg*, 453 U.S. 57, 1981) and a statutory rape law that punished only adult men for having sex with an underage individual of the opposite sex (*Michael M. v. Superior Court*, 450 U.S. 464, 1981).

Rationality Review. A classification that does not burden fundamental interests and that is not drawn on a suspect basis is subject only to low-level "rationality" review by the Court. The Court will uphold the law in question as long as the classification is a rational method of accomplishing a legitimate government interest. In *Williamson v. Lee Optical of Oklahoma*, 348 U.S. 483 (1955), the Court made clear that rationality review would sustain legislative classifications even if the basis for such classification was not obvious and even if the means-ends fit was loose. The legislature can address the problem "one step at a time" or even select one aspect of a problem and "apply a remedy there, neglecting the others."

Courts apply rational basis scrutiny to the majority of legislative enactments, including those concerning economic regulation, welfare benefits, property use, business activity, and individual conduct. Also, the Court decided in *Washington v. Davis*, 426 U.S. 229 (1976), that classifications not written in racial terms or intended to further a discriminatory purpose would be subject to rationality review even if the law in practice imposed a disparate impact on racial minorities. The Court thus upheld a qualifying test for government job applicants, even though more African American applicants failed the test than white applicants and even though the test had not been shown to provide a reliable measure of future job performance.

While rational basis review almost always results in classification being upheld, the Court in isolated situations has invalidated laws while purporting to apply rationality review. In *City of Cleburne v. Cleburne Living Center*, 473 U.S. 432 (1985), the Court used rationality review to invalidate a city's zoning ordinance that prevented the construction of a group home for the mentally retarded. Even though the Court expressly refused to declare mental retardation a suspect classification, the Court struck down the statute as based on "irrational" prejudice. The Court used a similar justification in *Romer v. Evans*, 517 U.S. 620 (1996), to invalidate an amendment to the Colorado state constitution that repealed all local ordinances banning discrimination on the basis of sexual orientation and that prohibited all state or local governmental action designed to protect homosexual persons from discrimination. The Court held that the amendment imposed special disabilities on homosexuals, that these disabilities were animated by "animosity" toward a class of people, and that animosity cannot itself be a "legitimate governmental interest."

BIBLIOGRAPHY

Bender, Leslie, and Daan Braveman. *Power, Privilege, and Law: A Civil Rights Reader.* St. Paul, Minn.: West, 1995. Anthology of readings.

Ely, John Hart. *Democracy and Distrust: A Theory of Judicial Review.* Cambridge, Mass.: Harvard University Press, 1980. Famous theoretical treatment of equal protection guarantee.

Garvey, John H., and T. Alexander Aleinikoff. *Modern Constitutional Theory: A Reader.* 4th ed. St. Paul, Minn.: West, 1999. Anthology of readings. See pp. 472–665.

Rotunda, Ronald D., and John E. Nowak. *Treatise on Constitutional Law: Substance and Procedure.* 3d ed. St. Paul, Minn.: West, 1999. Comprehensive treatise. See vol. 3, pp. 202–826.

Stone, Geoffrey R., et al. *Constitutional Law.* 4th ed. New York: Aspen, 2001. Preeminent constitutional law casebook.

Kent Greenfield

See also ***Brown v. Board of Education of Topeka; Bush v. Gore;*** **Constitution of the United States;** ***Craig v. Boren;*** **Declaration of Independence; Due Process of Law;** ***Frontiero v. Richardson; Romer v. Evans*** **(1996);** ***United States v. Virginia; Williamson v. Lee Optical;*** *and vol. 9:* **Congress Debates the Fourteenth Amendment.**

EQUAL RIGHTS AMENDMENT. Drafted by Alice Paul, a leader of the National Woman's Party, and first proposed as an addition to the U.S. CONSTITUTION in 1923, the Equal Rights Amendment (ERA) stated that "equality of rights under the law shall not be denied or abridged by the United States or by any state on account of sex." Supporters argued that the Constitution must include the principle of equality of rights for women and that such an amendment would remove sex-based discrimination. Opponents of women's rights objected, as did some women's rights advocates who feared it would jeopardize recent legislation providing female industrial workers minimum protection against exploitative working conditions. The Supreme Court had upheld protective legislation for women in *Muller v. Oregon* (1908), claiming the need to protect citizens able to bear children. Convinced that Congress would not extend labor protections to men and that the Court would therefore deny it to women if the amendment passed, organized labor opposed the ERA. It remained bottled up in the House Judiciary Committee for forty-seven years, despite efforts to secure passage.

The 1960s brought renewed attention to the amendment. Although women's roles in the economy had changed, hopes had faded that the Supreme Court would use the equal protection clause of the Fourteenth Amendment to subject laws that discriminated on the basis of sex to the same strict scrutiny applied to laws discriminating on the basis of race. Thus, when protective legislation was revealed to have harmed the very group it was intended to protect, liberal feminists had an additional reason for urging passage of the ERA. After a massive lobbying campaign, Congress, in March 1972, voted overwhelmingly to submit to the states a revised version of the ERA for ratification within seven years. Twenty-two states rushed to ratify, but, by 1975, momentum had slowed. As the ratification deadline approached, Congress extended it by three years, to 30 June 1982. Even after this extension, supporters could secure favorable votes from only thirty-five of the thirty-eight states needed for passage. Five states, meanwhile, rescinded their endorsements. In December 1981 a federal judge ruled that those rescissions were legal and that Congress had acted illegally in extending the ratification deadline. Before ERA supporters could appeal the ruling to the Supreme Court, however, the deadline for ratification expired, leaving opponents of the amendment victorious.

Opposition to the ERA in the 1970s and 1980s differed in important ways from that encountered in previous decades. Conservative legislators, mostly in southern and western states, voted against the amendment. They believed it would mean an intrusion of federal power that would diminish their ability to govern and would interfere with the right of individuals to live as they chose. Such politicians could vote according to their apprehensions and still claim to be responsive to the wishes of female constituents who opposed the amendment. Another factor was the skill with which far-right activists transformed popular perceptions of the amendment. By equating ERA and feminism, especially radical feminism, and making it appear dangerous to women, opponents succeeded in eroding the national consensus for the amendment. Although some states passed equal rights amendments to their own constitutions in the 1970s, efforts to secure congressional passage of a new federal amendment failed.

BIBLIOGRAPHY

Becker, Susan D. *Origins of the Equal Rights Amendment.* Westport, Conn.: Greenwood Press, 1981.

Berry, Mary Frances. *Why ERA Failed: Politics, Women's Rights, and the Amending Process of the Constitution.* Bloomington: Indiana University Press, 1986.

Hoff-Wilson, Joan, ed. *Rights of Passage: The Past and Future of the ERA.* Bloomington: Indiana University Press, 1986.

Mansbridge, Jane. *Why We Lost the ERA.* Chicago: University of Chicago Press, 1986.

Whitney, Sharon. *The Equal Rights Amendments.* New York: Watts, 1984.

Jane Sherron De Hart/C. P.

See also **Discrimination: Sex; *Frontiero v. Richardson*; *Muller v. Oregon*; Women's Rights Movement: The Twentieth Century; *and vol. 9:* NOW Statement of Purpose.**

EQUAL RIGHTS PARTY. The Equal Rights Party was a minor political party that supported woman's suffrage. It also advocated prohibition; uniform rights under marriage, divorce, and property law; civil service reform; and world peace. Its presidential candidate in 1884 and 1888 was Belva A. Lockwood, a leader in the woman's suffrage, peace, and temperance movements. The party failed to receive any important support, even from the suffrage organizations, and polled at most only about two thousand votes. Major feminist leaders, including Elizabeth Cady Stanton and Susan B. Anthony, opposed it on the grounds that suffrage could only be achieved by working within the existing two-party system.

BIBLIOGRAPHY

Dinkin, Robert J. *Before Equal Suffrage: Women in Partisan Politics from Colonial Times to 1920.* Westport, Conn.: Greenwood Press, 1995.

Edwards, Rebecca. *Angels in the Machinery: Gender in American Party Politics from the Civil War to the Progressive Era.* New York: Oxford University Press, 1997.

Clarence A. Berdahl/A. G.

See also **Political Parties; Prohibition; Suffrage: Woman's Suffrage; Women and the Peace Movement; Women's Rights Movement: The Nineteenth Century.**

EQUALITY, CONCEPT OF. Ancient and medieval political philosophers assumed that human beings were not merely different, but unequal in terms of their moral, political, and social worth. Since these inequalities were deemed natural, it followed that some were born to rule, and others to be ruled. The ideal regime therefore conferred power on the best sort of men and good regimes at least prevented power from falling into the wrong hands. Democracy was condemned on this account, for it inverted the natural order by making rulers of those who should be subjects, and subjects of those who should be rulers.

A modern conception of political authority was advanced by Thomas Hobbes and John Locke, two English thinkers of the seventeenth century who asserted the natural equality of human beings. Hobbes and Locke imagined human beings in a "state of nature" and explained why they would enter into a social contract with each other for their mutual benefit. Out of this contract came government, which was established for the protection of citizens and endowed with powers commensurate to that end. On this account, government derived its authority from the consent of the governed, not the natural superiority of a ruling class.

Neither Hobbes nor Locke concluded that people ought to rule themselves once government was established, however. Hobbes famously argued that people should submit to a sovereign with absolute powers, while Locke believed they would tacitly accept constitutional monarchy, reserving the right to rebel against unjust governments. Thus, each man insisted on natural equality but stopped short of recommending political equality in the sense that we understand it today.

Our understanding is summarized in the Declaration of Independence, which asserts that "all men are created equal," and that as such "they are endowed by their Creator with certain unalienable Rights," among them "Life, Liberty and the pursuit of Happiness." These revolutionary claims were put forward as self-evident truths and embraced as such by many Americans in 1776.

But there was also substantial opposition to radical notions of equality, and it resurfaced once the revolutionary ardor had cooled.

With only qualified support for the idea of equality, it proved remarkably difficult for the new nation to abolish slavery, extend the franchise, and ensure political rights and civil liberties for all. Yet it also proved impossible to resist movements aimed at combating DISCRIMINATION based on class, race, and gender. Most of these movements invoked the Declaration in support of their cause and in that sense the history of the United States after 1776 may be seen as the continuing struggle to realize what Thomas Jefferson called the self-evident truth of equality.

Equal Liberty

The concept of LIBERTY lends a particular cast to political thinking about equality in the United States. Americans understand liberty primarily in a negative sense, as freedom from unwarranted restraints on individuals' pursuit of happiness. Legal restraints are particularly suspect in this regard, reflecting the widespread assumption that government is at best a necessary evil. To be sure, some legal restraints on liberty are endorsed, and even welcomed. Few dispute the need to imprison persons who take the lives of other citizens, thereby depriving them of liberty or otherwise compromising their pursuit of happiness. Neither is there strong opposition to restrictions on the liberty of minors and adults who are mentally incompetent, since their well-being (and that of others) might be jeopardized by the exercise of too much freedom. What counts as "too much freedom" is of course a political question and reform movements regularly surface in American politics for the purpose of loosening restraints on those whose reason is suspect by conventional standards.

The aversion to arbitrary restrictions on individual freedom points in the direction of equal liberty. As Alexis de Tocqueville noted long ago (see *DEMOCRACY IN AMERICA*), Americans do not recognize privileges of rank. They certainly do not think people from different social ranks should be treated differently and they may even be reluctant to admit that social ranks or classes exist in American society. More tellingly, Americans do not think legal privileges should be conferred on individuals with superior wisdom, judgment, talents, skills, or attributes that in previous ages commanded deference from the masses. Valuable though they may be, these qualities are constitutionally irrelevant in a democratic society. No person, whatever his or her personal qualities, is formally entitled to more liberty than anyone else. Nor is anyone inclined to settle for less freedom than others enjoy.

White Americans' passion for equal liberty has only recently been extended to people of other races. The institution of chattel SLAVERY persisted for more than two hundred years, and enjoyed both legal and constitutional protection. When slavery was finally abolished after the CIVIL WAR, it was succeeded by an officially sanctioned regime of SEGREGATION that was not overturned until the 1960s. Even then there was resistance to the idea of racial equality and opposition to the use of federal power to confront discriminatory laws, policies, and practices in the South and throughout the nation. But the civil rights movement drew successfully on principles enunciated in the Declaration of Independence and the evident contradiction between racism and equality was ultimately resolved in favor of equality—in public discourse, if not always in private deeds.

Gender discrimination is similarly at odds with the commitment to equal liberty, and like racism has deep roots in American life. Indeed, this is one area in which natural differences are still held to be politically relevant by people who think biology limits women's fitness for military action, public service, and some forms of employment. The failure of the EQUAL RIGHTS AMENDMENT in the 1970s testifies to the strength of this view, just as the progress of women's liberation and feminism more generally shows the continuing power of appeals to equality. In the absence of compelling justifications, gender discrimination is politically vulnerable to challenges inspired by egalitarian sentiments. This cuts both ways, however: some remedies for discrimination, such as AFFIRMATIVE ACTION, are seen by many people as inegalitarian.

Equality under the Law

A commitment to equal liberty implies an impartial rule of law. That is, the law should be the same for everyone in both criminal and civil matters. Thus, any person who is accused of criminal conduct is entitled to due process under the Fourteenth Amendment to the Constitution. During the twentieth century, the U.S. Supreme Court's interpretations of the amendment's due process clause have substantially "nationalized" the BILL OF RIGHTS. As a result, the dispensation of justice is more uniform, which benefits all citizens, not just the victims of previous forms of discrimination. We all know our rights, and we insist on "taking our case all the way to the Supreme Court" when the need arises.

Broad interpretations of the EQUAL PROTECTION clause of the Fourteenth Amendment have generated a similar expansion of civil rights and liberties in the latter part of the twentieth century. So has the enactment of national legislation designed to combat discrimination in public schools, the workplace, and in many areas of private life. Some have called this a second American revolution, a revolution in rights for all, without regard to race, gender, or creed. The characterization is apt; there exists substantial equality under the law, and courts have become a major venue for the defense of every American's freedoms.

Equality in Making the Law

Freedom of speech, assembly, and press are valuable in their own right; the pursuit of happiness is unimaginable in the absence of these rights, and so is the enjoyment of liberty. These rights are important for another reason, too: they are the means by which people express their views on laws that govern them. The value of VOTING rights would be severely diminished by restrictions on political communication and the presentation of alternative views.

Voting rights are perhaps the ultimate test of a nation's commitment to political equality and it is instructive to note the halting expansion of the franchise in American history. Thus, in 1776, when Jefferson proclaimed equality a self-evident truth, the franchise was restricted to male property owners over the age of majority. Property qualifications were gradually removed from state constitutions in the second and third decades of the nineteenth century. After the Civil War, the Fifteenth Amendment barred racial restrictions on the franchise for adult males, but other restrictions, such as white primaries and poll taxes, effectively excluded African Americans from the polls in the South for another hundred years. The Nineteenth Amendment banned gender restrictions on suffrage in 1920, and in 1971 the Twenty-sixth Amendment lowered the voting age to eighteen.

Suffrage is now almost universal in the United States. Only convicted felons, the mentally incompetent, minors, and of course resident aliens are "second-class citizens" without voting rights. Nevertheless, many people, especially those who are ill-educated and poor, do not exercise their right to vote, so it cannot be said that equality in the making of laws has actually been achieved in the United States. Moreover, we cannot ignore the role of campaign contributions in shaping our political choices or the effect of interest groups on political decision making between elections (see CAMPAIGN FINANCING AND RESOURCES). These avenues of influence are not universally representative, and while they can be justified in terms of liberty, they may undermine equality in social life and the political arena.

Equality through the Law

Democratic politics provides the means for advancing equality through the law. That is, the law may be used to "level the playing field," thereby achieving greater equality. Thus, social programs provide minimum incomes and health care to retired workers or their families as well as to the "deserving poor." This limits inequality at the bottom of its range, while progressive forms of TAXATION, such as the graduated income tax, achieve a similar result by lowering top incomes. There is abiding political support for SOCIAL SECURITY, MEDICARE, and other spending programs in the United States, but progressive taxation is more controversial. It is seen by many as an intrusion on the success of individuals, that is, on their pursuit of happiness.

Put differently, Americans are quite prepared to accept and even defend unequal economic outcomes, so long as they result from a fair process, namely, one that is open to all. In a fair competition, there will be winners and losers, but the outcome will be decided on individual merit, or so the thinking goes. Hence it is sufficient to ensure that everyone has an equal opportunity to exercise liberty and pursue happiness as they understand it. What counts as an equal opportunity is disputed, however. Does equal opportunity merely require proscriptions against discrimination or does it demand positive measures, such as public education, to ensure that individuals can compete effectively?

The debate over equal opportunity is especially sharp where affirmative action policies are concerned. The argument in favor of affirmative action is that members of groups who have been unfairly treated in the past still suffer the lingering effects of discrimination. Hence a fair result should not be expected even though a legal framework of equal opportunities is now in place. Remedial measures are needed to overcome the legacy of discrimination and government ought to undertake these measures until such time as all are able to use their formal opportunities with equal advantage.

The argument against affirmative action is that government must go no further than combating discrimination. Preferential treatment is "reverse discrimination," and as such it unfairly expands the opportunities for some groups at the expense of others. More importantly, "group rights" come at the expense of individuals, abridging their liberties and undermining their pursuit of happiness. In this line of argument, then, a government committed to equality should, and indeed must, avoid affirmative action in favor of impartiality.

As this dispute shows, equality may be universally approved by Americans, but its meaning is not agreed upon, nor is there consensus on the role of government in promoting equality. The Declaration of Independence offers little guidance on this score; it is instead a challenge to explore the possibilities of equality in a democratic society.

BIBLIOGRAPHY

Barry, Brian. *Culture and Equality: An Egalitarian Critique of Multiculturalism.* Cambridge, Mass.: Harvard University Press, 2001.

Condit, Celeste M., and John L. Lucaites. *Crafting Equality: America's Anglo-African Word.* Chicago: University of Chicago Press, 1993.

Devins, Neal, and Davison M. Douglas, eds. *Redefining Equality.* Oxford: Oxford University Press, 1998. Scholars from a variety of disciplines discuss past and present meanings in the context of conflicts over specific issues and problems in American politics.

Ingram, David. *Group Rights: Reconciling Equality and Difference.* Lawrence: University of Kansas, 2000.

Karst, Kenneth L. *Belonging to America: Equal Citizenship and the Constitution.* New Haven, Conn.: Yale University Press, 1989.

Keyssar, Alexander. *The Right to Vote: The Contested History of Democracy in the United States.* New York: Basic Books, 2000.

Myrdal, Gunnar. *An American Dilemma: The Negro Problem and Modern Democracy.* 2 vols. New York: Harper, 1944. Explores the tension between a political creed centered on equality and cultural practices of racial discrimination.

Nelson, William E. *The Fourteenth Amendment: From Political Principle to Judicial Doctrine.* Cambridge, Mass.: Harvard University Press, 1988.

Pole, J. R. *The Pursuit of Equality in American History.* Rev. ed. Berkeley: University of California Press, 1993.

Smith, Rogers M. *Civic Ideals: Conflicting Visions of Citizenship in U.S. History.* New Haven, Conn.: Yale University Press, 1997.

Tocqueville, Alexis de. *Democracy in America.* Edited by J. P. Mayer. Translated by George Lawrence. Garden City, N.Y.: Doubleday, 1969. The classic exposition of egalitarianism and its tendencies in the United States.

Russell L. Hanson

See also **Civil Rights and Liberties; Locke's Political Philosophy; Race Relations; Women's Rights Movement;** *and vol. 9:* **The Equality of the Sexes.**

ERA OF GOOD FEELING (1817–1824), a phrase coined by the *Columbian Centinel*, a Boston newspaper, to describe the early presidency of James Monroe, whose administration found the country at peace and the economy prosperous. Monroe accepted the National Bank and protective tariff and approved further construction on the National (Cumberland) Road. Despite the economic panic of 1819, Monroe received all but one electoral vote to a second term in 1820. Despite the apparent harmony, renewed sectionalism and factionalism eroded "good feeling" during Monroe's second term and signaled the demise of the (Jeffersonian) Republican Party.

BIBLIOGRAPHY

Ammon, Harry. *James Monroe: The Quest for National Identity.* New York: McGraw-Hill, 1971.

Cummingham, Noble. *The Presidency of James Monroe.* Lawrence: University Press of Kansas, 1996.

Wait, Eugene. *America and the Monroe Years.* Huntington, N.Y.: Kroshka, 2000.

Philip Coolidge Brooks/H. S.

See also **Cumberland Road; Financial Panics; Republicans, Jeffersonian.**

ERECTOR SETS. The modernization of the Progressive Era called for engineers, the heroes of that age. In response, the toy industry released new mass-produced and nationally marketed toys aimed to shape boys into "efficient" men by teaching them to build. Inspired by seeing new girder construction on a train ride into New York City, Alfred C. Gilbert, born in Oregon in 1884, shifted from producing magic kits from his Mysto Manufacturing Co. (1909) to marketing Erector Set No. 1 or "Structural Steel and Electro-Mechanical Builder." It was patented in 1913, with accessories such as one-inch-wide metal girders, pulleys, gears, and screws to let boys, often with fathers' help, construct powered windmills, vehicles, drawbridges, skyscrapers, and elevators.

Gilbert sold larger sets in wooden boxes for more ambitious projects, and then branched out into chemistry sets. Larger sets included a DC motor to construct moveable toys. New sets marketed in 1924 with half-inch girders permitted the building of Ferris wheels, automobiles, trucks, battleships, zeppelins, and other "action models."

When metal became scarce during World War II, Gilbert produced wooden sets for a few years. He organized and became the first president of Toy Manufacturers of America in 1916, a trade association. As if echoing John Dewey, Gilbert proclaimed, "Playing is essential to learning." Today, at A. C. Gilbert's Discovery Village (1989) in Salem, Oregon, an interactive museum, children can climb the world's largest Erector Set tower.

Blanche M. G. Linden

See also ***Lincoln Logs;*** **Toys and Games.**

ERIE CANAL, a 363-mile artificial waterway connecting Buffalo to Albany, New York, was the biggest public works project in the pre–Civil War United States. Built by the State of New York between 1817 and 1825, and then enlarged between 1836 and 1862, the canal linked the Great Lakes to the Atlantic seaboard. Using locks, aqueducts, and man-made gorges, the canal overcame a combined ascent and descent of 680 feet. Celebrated for its technological achievements, the canal's practical influences were many: the waterway would hasten the displacement of New York's Iroquois Indians, quicken the westward migration of Euro-Americans, stimulate northeastern and midwestern industrialization,

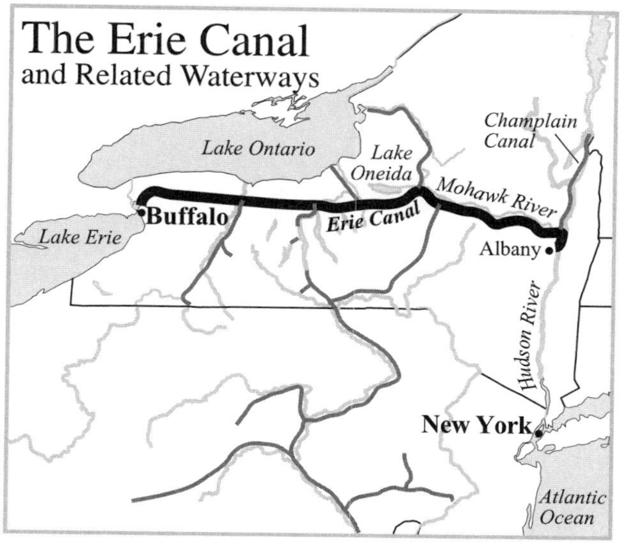

Erie Canal. This placid man-made waterway in upstate New York revolutionized early-nineteenth-century America. ARCHIVE PHOTOS, INC.

and ease commercial exchange in a growing transatlantic economy.

Early History

Ideas for building the canal dated back at least to the early eighteenth century. In the northern colonies, the only gap in the Appalachian Mountains was the one through which the Mohawk River flowed easterly from central New York to the Hudson River, which in turn ran southward into the Atlantic Ocean. While Dutch and British colonists farmed along the Mohawk and other natural rivers and lakes in central New York, they found their westward migration restrained once they reached Lake Oneida, near the head of the Mohawk. From that point, more than 150 miles east of Lake Erie, no major waterway permitted easy access to the western interior. Early efforts to improve transportation involved turnpikes and roads, and beginning in 1792, the Western Inland Lock Navigation Company and the Northern Inland Lock Navigation Company improved some of the region's natural waterways. Yet such improvements were undependable and costly. Especially with the expansion of the nation's market economy after the American Revolution, many settlers clamored for access to dependable, inexpensive transportation for trade and travel.

Building the Canal

Bringing the Erie Canal to fruition involved the support and labor of people from all strata of society. DeWitt Clinton, a leading New York politician, would become the most persistent advocate for the canal in the years after the War of 1812. Critics derided the proposed canal as "Clinton's Big Ditch." Because the longest canal in the United States was just over 27 miles long, the prospect of a 363-mile canal seemed hopelessly impractical to even some enlightened minds. Only four feet deep and forty feet wide, the original canal could in fact seem like little more than a ditch. Refused funding by the federal government, the State of New York, after much political wrangling, authorized initial funding for the Erie Canal in 1817. Work began on the Fourth of July that year; the digging, most of which was done by hand, involved thousands of workers, including local farmers, New England migrants, and foreign immigrants. (The project to deepen and enlarge the canal—to seven feet by seventy feet—coincided with the Irish potato famine, so foreign workers made up the largest share of the later construction workforce.) Working conditions were at best tedious and at worst deadly, and many workers were weakened by disease and accidents.

Canal Lock. John Collier's October 1941 photograph shows one of the locks of the Erie Canal—by then part of the New York State Barge Canal System—in operation. LIBRARY OF CONGRESS

The Canal's Influence

The original Erie Canal proved a tremendous success. In the years after its completion in 1825, the cost of transporting goods between the Midwest and New York City fell precipitously, in some cases by 95 percent. Between 1825 and 1857, New York built eight canals that, like the Champlain Canal (completed in 1823), ran north–south from the Erie. Together, these lateral canals connected much of rural New York to the main waterway. Encouraged by New York's example, other states undertook similar projects in the late 1820s and 1830s. Meanwhile, though, railroads entered the American scene and proved more economical and efficient. Most of the country's canals were financial failures, nearly crippling the economy of many northeastern states and playing an important role in the financial depression that struck the nation in 1837.

Yet New York's canal system was so successful that New York became known as the "Empire State." Farmers could now move easily to the West, and—just as important—they could market their goods in the Northeast and Europe at a fraction of the cost of the precanal era. Meanwhile, the northern industrial economy thrived due to the easy availability of inexpensive raw materials and foodstuffs and because of the creation of an enormous market of potential customers in the West. Some historians have argued that the economic connections fostered by the Erie Canal helped keep midwestern states in the Union during the Civil War.

The Canal's Legacy

In the prewar period, the Erie Canal drew mixed reactions. Many white Americans celebrated it as a symbol of "progress," a sign that humankind was fulfilling a divinely sanctioned movement to improve the physical world. It represented a triumph of "civilization" over "savagery." It represented American ingenuity and hard work. It brought settlers, luxury goods, visitors, tourists, and news to the hinterlands. But it also had its downsides: it spread its benefits unevenly; depersonalized commercial transactions; created complex economic relationships that destabilized the economy; depended on an enormous wage labor force, made up of tens of thousands of workers—men, women, and children—by the 1840s, when such labor was generally seen as a temporary evil at best; and seemed to carry disease and moral vice (often associated with coastal urban centers) to the nation's rural, supposedly "purer" interior. On balance, though, the canal's success represented the virtues of "free labor," and thus it contributed to some northerners' sense of cultural superiority over southern slave states.

The amount of freight carried on the Erie Canal peaked in the 1880s, and the waterway was enlarged once again in the early twentieth century to become part of the New York State Barge Canal System, which remained in commercial operation until the 1990s (and which continues today as a recreational resource). But the canal's role in the post–Civil War era was much less dramatic. While antebellum Americans viewed the canal as a symbol of progress and modernity, by the late nineteenth century it had come to seem antiquated and quaint. That image has been memorialized in popular culture—in Tin Pan Alley songs such as "Low Bridge, Everybody Down"—and has made the Erie Canal a cherished part of the nation's folklore.

BIBLIOGRAPHY

Carp, Roger Evan. "The Erie Canal and the Liberal Challenge to Classical Republicanism, 1785–1850." Ph.D. diss., University of North Carolina at Chapel Hill, 1986.

Miller, Nathan. *The Enterprise of a Free People: Aspects of Economic Development in New York State during the Canal Period, 1792–1838.* Ithaca, N.Y.: Cornell University Press, 1962.

Shaw, Ronald. *Erie Water West: A History of the Erie Canal.* Lexington: University of Kentucky Press, 1966.

Sheriff, Carol. *The Artificial River: The Erie Canal and the Paradox of Progress, 1817–1862.* New York: Hill and Wang, 1996.

Carol Sheriff

See also **Canals; Inland Lock Navigation; New York State; Transportation and Travel; Waterways, Inland.**

ERIE RAILROAD COMPANY V. TOMPKINS, 304 U.S. 64 (1938). The JUDICIARY ACT OF 1789 provides that in diversity-of-citizenship cases (those cases concerned with citizens of different states, and not with federal statutes or the Constitution) federal courts must apply "the laws of the several states, except where the Constitution, treaties, or statutes of the United States shall otherwise require." In 1842, in SWIFT V. TYSON, the Supreme Court held that the word "laws" meant only state statutory law; and therefore federal courts were free to ignore state common law and to fashion and apply their own, at least with regard to commercial matters. Nearly a century later, in *Erie v. Tompkins*, on dubious historical evidence, and perhaps without understanding that *Swift*'s scope was limited to the kind of commerce that was interstate in nature, the Court overruled *Swift* as both a misinterpretation of the Judiciary Act and an unconstitutional assumption of power by federal courts.

Erie now generally requires that federal courts exercising jurisdiction in diversity-of-citizenship cases apply both applicable state statutory law and common law. Justice Louis Brandeis, in his majority opinion for the Court in *Erie*, ruled as he did because of a fear of overreaching federal courts, but recent scholarship has suggested that, in overruling *Swift*, the Court may have deprived the nation of some benefits of the development of federal commercial jurisprudence.

BIBLIOGRAPHY

Freyer, Tony A. *Harmony and Dissonance: The Swift and Erie Cases in American Federalism.* New York: New York University Press, 1981.

Purcell, Edward A., Jr. *Brandeis and the Progressive Constitution: Erie, the Judicial Power, and the Politics of the Federal Courts in Twentieth-Century America.* New Haven, Conn.: Yale University Press, 2000.

Eric L. Chase
Harold W. Chase
Stephen B. Presser

ESKIMO. *See* **Inuit.**

ESPIONAGE ACT, 1917. Shortly after the United States entered World War I in April 1917, the House Committee on the Judiciary conducted public hearings regarding proposals to limit debate on administration policies. The government of President Woodrow Wilson had already sought to silence critics through proclamations restricting the movement of enemy aliens, the establishment of a loyalty-security program, and the setting up of the COMMITTEE ON PUBLIC INFORMATION for censorship purposes. Nevertheless, Department of Justice attorneys desired additional means to restrict individual conduct and quash "political agitation" during wartime. Heated debate over the proposed Espionage Act occurred in Congress during the spring of 1917. Opposition arose regarding possible prior restraint, the affording of sweeping legislative powers to the executive branch, and the treatment of critical perspectives as "seditious" or "treasonable." At the same time few expressed concerns over the part of the bill that authorized the U.S. Post Office Department to refuse to deliver radical labor or socialist publications.

On 15 June 1917 Congress passed the Espionage Act. A provision to grant the government broad powers to censor newspapers was omitted, but the legislation remained sweeping nevertheless. Title I provided a $10,000 fine and imprisonment for up to twenty years for those who "willfully" delivered "false reports or false statements" intended to impede U.S. military operations, engender disloyalty within U.S. military ranks, or obstruct recruitment or enlistment into the U.S. military. Title XII, which allowed for a $5,000 fine and a five-year prison term, authorized the postmaster general to refuse to deliver any material "advocating or urging treason, insurrection, or forcible resistance to any law of the United States." On 16 May 1918 Congress amended the Espionage Act through the passage of the Sedition Act; that measure targeted those who did "willfully utter, print, write, or publish any disloyal, profane, scurrilous, or abusive" language concerning the American government, flag, Constitution, or military. The federal government prosecuted over two thousand cases involving purported violations of the Espionage or Sedition Acts, with more than a thousand convictions obtained. Among the most celebrated individuals indicted under the Espionage Act was Socialist Party leader Eugene V. Debs; and the postmaster general declared *The Masses*, a leading publication of the World War I–era American Left, "nonmailable."

In 1919 the United States Supreme Court upheld convictions in a series of cases involving the Espionage and Sedition Acts. In the process Justices Oliver Wendell Holmes Jr. and Louis D. Brandeis began to insist that "clear and present danger" must exist to allow for a restriction of First Amendment rights. In 1921 the Sedition Act was rescinded, while the Espionage Act was amended once more with heightened penalties in 1940 after World War II had begun in Europe and Asia. The Espionage Act remained in force in the early 2000s.

BIBLIOGRAPHY

Goldstein, Robert Justin. *Political Repression in Modern America: 1870 to the Present.* New York: Schenkman, 1978.

Murphy, Paul L. *World War I and the Origin of Civil Liberties in the United States.* New York: Norton, 1979.

Rabban, David M. *Free Speech in Its Forgotten Years.* Cambridge, U.K.: Cambridge University Press, 1997.

Robert C. Cottrell

See also **Sedition Acts.**

ESPIONAGE, INDUSTRIAL. The systematic use of spies by American companies to report on their employees began after the Civil War with the rise of American industry and reached a peak during the 1930s. Employers originally recruited spies from among their workers but eventually turned to trained men from such agencies as Pinkerton, Burns, and Baldwin-Felts. Spies reported on various matters, such as inefficiency, theft, and worker unrest. Companies used spy reports to discharge union activists, and relied on state and local police to provide protection or even aid to professional strikebreakers. The use of industrial spies accelerated during the 1920s along with rising anticommunist and antiunionist sentiment, and climaxed during the heyday of the Congress of Industrial Organizations (known as the Committee on Industrial Organization until 1938), over which John L. Lewis presided after 1935. In 1937 a report by the U.S. Senate Committee on Education and Labor found that American companies employed labor spies in virtually every plant and union. By this time employer associations regularly provided professional labor spies and strikebreakers for their affiliated companies, and some large corporations employed their own private police forces to combat unionization.

The adverse publicity of the 1930s and the maturation of labor-management relations after World War II brought about the virtual cessation of professional antiunion espionage. After 1959 federal law required agents of employers reporting on the labor-management relationship to register with the U.S. Department of Labor, although few do so and not many are believed to exist. Some companies continue to spy on their employees for various reasons, but industrial espionage is now largely confined to spying by companies upon each other. Nearly universal in one form or another, the latter practice is systematic among competitive industries affected by changes in fashion or taste. Its function is to discover trade secrets. The disagreements about it center on the methods used, not on legitimacy of purpose.

As the emphasis of industrial espionage shifted after World War II from antiunionism to protecting and uncovering professional trade secrets, the Cold War context became increasingly important. Fear existed that agents from the Soviet Union and its allies would obtain sensitive technology or information from American industries that could hurt the national security of the United States. Although much information was available in scientific and technical publications, as well as through public conferences, espionage or spying proved necessary to acquire more sensitive items. No one can accurately estimate the dollar value of direct losses to U.S. industry, as well as the indirect costs of higher U.S. defense budgets, that resulted from industrial espionage during the Cold War. One authority, however, estimated that the Soviet Union had as many as 20,000 agents working as industrial spies.

The end of the Cold War failed to reduce concern about industrial espionage, however. U.S. business and political leaders had long worried about how foreign economic competition could affect national security, and shifted their attention to countries that were political allies but commercial rivals. In June 1982, for example, six executives with the Japanese firms Hitachi and Mitsubishi were arrested in Santa Clara, Calif., for trying to steal documents and computer parts from IBM. In 1993–1994 U.S. and German officials dealt with claims by General Motors that Volkswagen had obtained proprietary information from a former GM vice president who had taken a position with the German company. A former director of the French secret service publicly stated that he had instructed French agents to secure industrial information. U.S. political and business leaders were divided over whether or not U.S. intelligence organizations, such as the Central Intelligence Agency, should conduct its own counterespionage.

With U.S. businesses increasingly dependent on computer networks for relaying information, concern grew in the 1980s and 1990s about the security of their information networks. Major companies were forced to spend more money and time combating the efforts of hackers, skilled computer operators who would try on their own initiative or on behalf of others to penetrate company software programs used by companies. Ultimately, a dispute arose between U.S. private businesses, which desired sophisticated software programs to protect their information, and law enforcement and intelligence agencies, which wanted to have access to all programs and networks being used by companies operating under U.S. jurisdiction. This tension between the need to fight sophisticated means of industrial espionage and the requirements of law enforcement promised to be an increasingly contentious issue in the future global economy.

BIBLIOGRAPHY

Calkins, Clinch. *Spy Overhead: The Story of Industrial Espionage.* New York: Harcourt, Brace, 1937.

Melvern, Linda, Nick Anning, and David Hebditch. *Techno-Bandits.* Boston: Houghton Mifflin, 1984.

Schweizer, Peter. *Friendly Spies.* New York: Atlantic Monthly Press, 1993.

Winkler, Ira. *Corporate Espionage: What It Is, Why It Is Happening in Your Company, What You Must Do About It.* Rocklin, Calif.: Prima Pub., 1997.

John Hutchinson / C. W.

See also **American Federation of Labor–Congress of Industrial Organizations; Central Intelligence Agency; Cold War; Computers and Computer Industry; Intelligence, Military and Strategic; Labor; Labor, Department of; Software Industry; Strikes.**

ESSEX JUNTO is a term coined by President John Adams in the late eighteenth century for a group of Federalists he deemed his adversaries. Jeffersonians then used the term to refer to Federalist opponents they believed to be advocating secession for New England during the War of 1812. Essex Junto has become a term synonymous with secession and treason.

A number of men, natives of Essex County, Massachusetts, have been named members of this group: Fisher Ames, George Cabot, Francis Dana, Nathan Dane, Benjamin Goodhue, Stephen Higginson, Jonathan Jackson,

John Lowell, Theophilus Parsons, Timothy Pickering, Israel Thorndike, and Nathaniel Tracy. Most of the men were well educated and wealthy. They had common social and economic interests and some were related by marriage. They dominated politics in their home county during the 1770s, but in the period between the American Revolution and the early nineteenth century most relocated to Boston.

They were adversaries to John Hancock during the revolutionary period, and had opposed the Massachusetts Constitution, proposed in 1778, but from 1779 to 1780, they helped draft a new document. The members of the Essex Junto were not satisfied with the restrictions of the power of the people and did not really care for a system of checks and balances, but nonetheless they supported the Federal Constitution. They supported Alexander Hamilton and his financial program and sharply opposed Thomas Jefferson and his ideas. They were advocates of American independence, but believed in the inherent inequality of men. Disturbed by the social changes the Revolution had brought, they favored a patriarchal society and a nation ruled by an elected aristocracy of elites. They formed the nucleus of a conservative group among the Federalists, but by the turn of the century, most had withdrawn from politics. They did not have a domineering influence in Massachusetts's politics and the Federalist Party, as many historians have claimed. With the exception of Timothy Pickering, they did not support the New England secessionist movement in the aftermath of the Louisiana Purchase, which many New Englanders feared would curtail their influence in the Union.

President Jefferson, in a letter to John Melish on 13 January 1813, used the label Essex Junto when he accused a group of younger Federalists of advocating anglomany, monarchy, and separation; Federalists had vented their anger with the dire effects the Embargo Act, the Nonintercourse Act, and the War of 1812 had on New England. Early in the war, Pickering and John Lowell Jr. (son of the above mentioned John Lowell) tried to crystallize the secessionist sentiment in New England, but other members of the Junto helped to curb their plans. During the War of 1812, New England dissatisfaction was vocalized in the Hartford Convention (15 December 1814–5 January 1815) in which only two moderate members of the original Essex Junto, Dane and Cabot (the latter was chosen president of the convention) participated. Pickering opposed the convention because he did not believe it would really advocate the dissolution of the Union, as he desired.

BIBLIOGRAPHY

Fischer, David H. "The Myth of the Essex Junto." *The William and Mary Quarterly*, 3d. Series 21 (April 1964): 195–213.

Morison, Samuel Eliot. "Dissent in the War of 1812." In *Dissent in Three American Wars*. Edited by Samuel Eliot Morison, Frederick Merk, and Frank Freidel. Cambridge, Mass.: Harvard University Press, 1970.

Michael Wala

See also **Hartford Convention.**

ESSEX, ACTIONS OF THE (1812–1814). During the War of 1812 the *Essex* inflicted $6 million of damage on British whaling in the South Pacific. The *Essex*, the first American warship to round Cape Horn, attacked and captured British whalers around the Galápagos Islands between March and September 1813. On 28 March 1814, Captain David Porter was attacked by the British frigate *Phoebe* and the sloop *Cherub.* Outgunned and hampered by shifting winds and the loss of his main topmast in a squall, Porter was compelled to surrender. His losses were fifty-eight killed, sixty-five wounded, and thirty-one missing; the British had five killed and ten wounded.

BIBLIOGRAPHY

DeForest, Tim. "Fighting Ship to the Last," *Military History* 11:2 (1994): 54–61.

Long, David F. *Nothing Too Daring.* Annapolis, Md.: U.S. Naval Institute, 1970.

Walter B. Norris/A. R.

See also **Cape Horn; War of 1812; Whaling.**

ESTATE TAX LAWS. *See* **Inheritance Tax Laws.**

ETHICAL CULTURE, SOCIETY FOR. Felix Adler (1851–1933) founded the Society for Ethical Culture in New York City in 1876. The Society began as a weekly lecture program, but soon developed into a curious combination of a religious organization and a social movement. Adler was the son of an American Reform rabbi and was groomed for the pulpit, but his religious beliefs were transformed after his exposure to Kantian philosophy and the historical analysis of religion during his postgraduate study in Germany. Adler concluded that all religious principles were based upon a common set of values, and he developed a new system of belief, called "Ethical Culture," that transcended denominational boundaries. Ethical Culture was based on the intrinsic worth and goodness of the individual, the universal character of moral law, and the imperative to apply ethical principles to modern society. It rejected theological distinctions, and its adherents were unified by their performance of ethical deeds. The Society for Ethical Culture was the institutional center of the Ethical Culture movement.

Adler considered Ethical Culture to be a religion, and even developed a metaphysical explanation of its structure and ideals. The Society, however, also functioned as a vehicle for social reform and was devoted to addressing the social problems created by industrialization in late nineteenth-century America. It played an important role in the reform movements of the Progressive Era and maintained close ties to the SETTLEMENT HOUSE MOVEMENT. Many of the society's projects, such as its free kindergarten and district nursing programs, served as early models for later urban reformers.

Adler's followers created new branches of the society in many other American cities and in Europe. In 1889, the American societies were consolidated into a national organization, the American Ethical Union. The movement has endured into the twenty-first century, maintaining branches throughout the United States.

BIBLIOGRAPHY

Kraut, Benny. *From Reform Judaism to Ethical Culture: The Religious Evolution of Felix Adler.* Cincinnati: Hebrew Union College Press, 1979.

Radest, Howard B. *Toward Common Ground: The Story of the Ethical Societies in the United States.* New York: Ungar, 1969.

Mia Sara Bruch

ETHNOHISTORY. Ethnohistory is the study of cultures that combines cross-disciplinary methods of historical document research and ethnographic studies such as anthropology, linguistics, archaeology, and ecology to give as complete a picture as possible of a whole culture. It employs maps, folklore, myth, oral traditions, music, and painting. Ethnohistory usually deals with small groups that do not have written histories instead of with large societies.

First used in Vienna in the 1930s by ethnologist Fritz Röck and the Viennese Study Group for African Cultural History, ethnohistory was not utilized in the United States until the 1950s as a result of the INDIAN CLAIMS Act of 1946. Evidence used in Native American claims against the U.S. government employed both anthropological and historical reports and was presented at the Ohio Valley Historic Indian Conference. An outgrowth of the conference was the formation of the American Society for Ethnohistory, which was established in 1954 and published the first issue of its journal, *Ethnohistory*, that same year.

Ethnohistory lends itself to the study of the Indian nations in the United States. Historical documents written by European colonists, explorers, settlers, and government officials give a biased and incomplete view of Indian civilizations. Those from literate societies who originally came in contact with Native Americans interpreted Indian actions within their own limited understanding and with the intent of controlling them or even destroying them. Native American ethnohistory is an attempt to give both sides of the story and explore why people in a certain culture made the choices and took the actions they did.

Certainly, Native American histories did not begin with contact with literate individuals who could leave written records. Understanding these old cultures requires understanding the system of principles or rules that gave meaning and shared values to members of each tribe. Furthermore, defining the whole culture of a tribe requires studying various individuals within a tribe whose actions reflect their differences in gender, class, education, ancestry, and other factors.

Throughout American history, non-Indians using historical documents as their primary sources have written thousands of books. As of 2002, scholars were employing more complete records, both written and unwritten, and were producing books that revealed a more complete look at Native American cultures. Leaders in the field include William N. Fenton, James Axtell, Bruce Trigger, Richard White, Frederick E. Hoxie, Robert F. Berkhofer Jr., Francis Jennings, and Donald L. Fixico, among others.

BIBLIOGRAPHY

American Society for Ethnohistory. Home page at http://ethnohistory.org.

Fixico, Donald L., ed. *Rethinking American Indian History.* Albuquerque: University of New Mexico Press, 1997.

Veda Boyd Jones

See also **Anthropology and Ethnology; Historiography, American; Native American Studies.**

ETHNOLOGY, BUREAU OF AMERICAN. The American Bureau of Ethnology was established on 3 March 1879 as the Bureau of Ethnology, when Congress transferred to the Smithsonian Institution ethnological investigations of the American Indians, previously conducted by the Geographical and Geological Survey of the Rocky Mountain Region. Maj. John Wesley Powell, who had headed the Geological Survey's investigations, guided the new bureau until his death in 1902.

In spite of its limited resources—a scientific and supporting staff never larger than twenty and meager budgets—the bureau became recognized as the foremost center for the study of American Indians. Its publications on linguistics, ethnology, archaeology, physical anthropology, and Native American history are listed in a 130-page booklet, *List of Publications of the Bureau of American Ethnology with Index to Authors and Titles.* In addition to hundreds of sometimes massive monographs, the bureau has issued the encyclopedic *Handbook of American Indians North of Mexico*, edited by F. W. Hodge; the three-volume *Handbook of American Indian Languages*, by Franz Boas; *Handbook of the Indians of California*, by A. L. Kroeber; and the seven-volume *Handbook of South American Indians*, by Julian H. Steward. In 1964 the bureau was merged with the Department of Anthropology of the U.S. National Museum.

BIBLIOGRAPHY

Judd, Neil M. *The Bureau of American Ethnology: A Partial History.* Norman: University of Oklahoma Press, 1967.

Henry B. Collins/J. H.

See also **Anthropology and Ethnology; Smithsonian Institution.**

EUGENICS, like "pragmatism," was a new name coined in the late nineteenth century for some old ways of thinking. But while philosophers worked hard to explain what "pragmatism" meant, believers in "eugenics" were satisfied merely to use the new word to advance their varied concerns. Both parents and intellectuals had nearly always expressed hopes and anxieties about reproduction and about the health and quality of the next generation. Marriage guides, medical writings, and social reform literature in nineteenth-century America emphasized the polar terms "amelioration" and "degeneration." They anticipated that healthy, caring parents of European Protestant descent were likely to produce better children than those who were diseased, licentious, or from a less "developed" ethnoreligious group.

The English biosocial scientist Francis Galton coined the word "eugenics" to describe "the cultivation of the race" in 1883, but the term only came into general use in both England and the United States after 1900. For the first third of the twentieth century American eugenicists (also called "eugenists") promoted a variety of causes, including the encouragement of fecundity among educated women; birth control for both rich and poor; earlier marriage; easier divorce; breast-feeding; the sterilization of criminal, retarded, epileptic, insane, and sexually promiscuous people; tests for intelligence; tests for syphilis; abstinence from alcohol; the positive value of unrestricted drinking; country roads; urban parks; pacifism; military preparedness; immigration restriction; segregation of the "feeble-minded" from the general population; segregation of black Americans from white Americans; imperial expansion; and the dangers of tropical climates for European Americans.

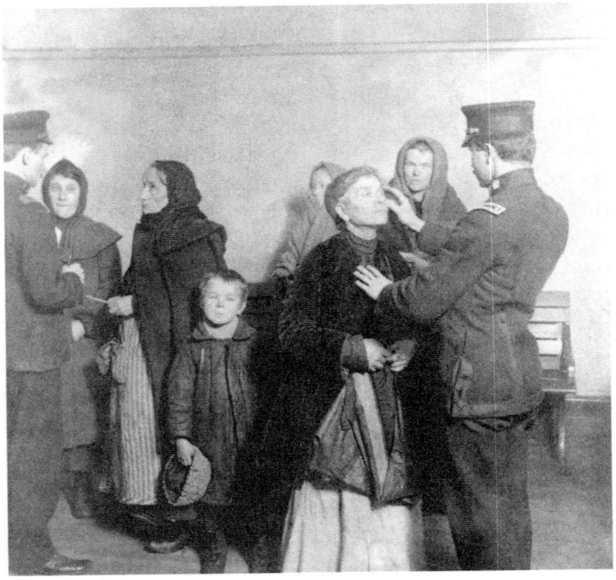

Ellis Island Examination, 1911. Among the wide range of causes promoted by some early-twentieth-century eugenicists was an attempt to keep out immigrants who belonged to ethnic groups regarded as inferior. © CORBIS

In the 1910s the biologist Charles B. Davenport, supported by the philanthropist Mary Harriman, argued that a scientifically authoritative eugenics should be grounded in the new Mendelian genetics and in a sharp distinction between influences of heredity and environment. Davenport's views, however, were inconsistent—for instance, he supported the environmental reform of alcohol prohibition as a eugenic measure—and they were never dominant. The famous 1927 opinion of Supreme Court Justice Oliver Wendell Holmes Jr. in *Buck v. Bell*, that "three generations of imbeciles are enough," owed more to the views taught by his physician father in the 1860s than to the new genetics of the Jazz Age.

Between 1925 and 1940 the tenuous cooperation among biologists, psychiatrists, sociologists, psychologists, and reformers under the big eugenics tent broke down, and the many campaigns that had for a time stood together went separate ways. After 1940 the association of the word "eugenics" with Nazi mass murder made it a term of insult. Promoters of population control, medical genetics, and reproductive therapies sought to distance themselves as much as possible from the recent past. Yet pragmatic efforts to prevent malformations and to improve the biological quality of humans have continued. It is a reasonably coherent realm of expert activity but one that remains, understandably, nameless.

BIBLIOGRAPHY

Haller, Mark H. *Eugenics: Hereditarian Attitudes in American Thought.* New Brunswick, N.J.: Rutgers University Press, 1963.

Kevles, Daniel. *In the Name of Eugenics: Genetics and the Uses of Human Heredity.* New York: Knopf, 1985.

Paul, Diane B. *Controlling Human Heredity, 1865 to the Present.* Atlantic Highlands, N.J.: Humanities Press, 1995.

Philip J. Pauly

See also **Genetics; Racial Science.**

EUROPEAN UNION (European Community). On 1 November 1993 the European Community (EC), a political and economic confederation of European countries, officially became the European Union (EU). The EU consists of three institutions: the European Coal and Steel Community (ECSC), the European Atomic Energy Community (EURATOM), and the European Economic Community (EEC). Its fifteen members are France, Germany, Italy, Belgium, the Netherlands, and Luxembourg (the original "Six" from the 1950s); Great Britain, Denmark, and Ireland (joined 1973); Greece (1981); Portugal and Spain (1986); and Austria, Finland, and Sweden (1995).

The EU's total area is about one-third the size of the United States, but its population in 2000 was 377.6 million, compared to 284.2 million for the United States. Their economies are of roughly comparable size. In 2000 the EU accounted for 18.2 percent of world imports and 17.2 percent of world exports, while its GDP totaled $7.8 trillion. The American figures were 23.9 percent and 15.7 percent with a GDP of $9.9 trillion. Both are also important economic partners. In 2000 the EU's trade with the United States was valued at $394.8 billion and made up 19.2 percent of its total imports and 24.7 percent of its total exports, while American trade with the EU was worth $385.2 billion and accounted for 18.1 and 21.1 percent, respectively. During the same year the EU also made $802.7 billion in direct investments in the United States and received $573.4 billion in return.

Institutions

The EU has four major governing organs. The European Commission, located in Brussels, proposes policies and legislation, is responsible for administration, and enforces both decisions made by European institutions and the provisions of European treaties. Including the commission president, twenty commissioners with individual portfolios serve five-year terms. They are appointed by the national governments but act independently of them. The Council of the European Union, consisting of ministers from each member state, coordinates intergovernmental policies and enacts binding legislation. Depending on the agenda, different types of national minister will attend each council meeting. Most decisions within it take place as a result of a majority vote (normally weighted to reflect the size and importance of the member state), although some issues, such as foreign policy, taxation, and the environment, still require unanimity. The council has a rotating presidency with a six-month term that ends with a meeting of all fifteen heads of state or government. It holds most of its meetings in the country that has the EU presidency. The European Parliament, which meets in Strasbourg, currently consists of 626 members elected for five-year terms. Members are seated by party group (such as Socialist, Christian Democrat, and Green) and since 1979 have been chosen in direct elections. The Parliament's key powers include approving or amending the EU budget submitted by the commission and publicly debating the work of the other governing organs. It may also censure the commission. The Court of Justice, which is located in Luxembourg and has fifteen judges, determines whether treaties in the European Union are being implemented and are in accordance with Union law. Both its judgments and EU law as a whole are binding on all member states.

European and American Perspectives on Integration

Although proposals for European integration go back as far as the Middle Ages, the origins of the present EU date from World War II. Many Europeans believed that for their continent to experience a political and economic revival, the national rivalries that characterized the past had to give way to greater international cooperation. However, ever since the 1940s there has been disagreement on what methods to utilize. "Federalists" like the Italian politician Altiero Spinelli advocated creating a unified European state as soon as possible. The Frenchman Jean Monnet and other "(neo)functionalists" believed that the consolidation of important industrial sectors across national lines would promote integration in all fields. Still another perspective, traditionally strong in Great Britain and Scandinavia but universally evident, advocated greater intergovernmental cooperation but remained wary about supranational organizations that would limit sovereignty. These divergent opinions have ensured that a mélange of approaches has characterized the road to the EU.

Since 1945 American policymakers have consistently supported European integration both publicly and privately, even if their active interest in promoting it waned dramatically starting in the 1960s. According to Geir Lundestad, several considerations informed their thinking. These include the belief that the new European institutions represented a healthy attempt to emulate the "American model" based around federalism, democracy, and free markets and also the idea that integration would promote a modernized Europe that was more efficient economically and less troubled by nationalist rivalries. More concretely, integration would reduce the burden of American military and economic commitments to Europe. Above all, a unified (Western) Europe could play an important role in containing both the Soviet Union and Germany. The United States also has promoted European integration for so long now that to some extent this policy has become traditional, irrespective of other considerations. Furthermore, the desire of Europeans themselves to work toward unity has been a tremendous influence on American policy as well.

American Support for European Integration during the 1940s and 1950s

During World War II, the Roosevelt administration feared that any moves toward European integration would contribute to a division of the world into political and economic blocs. However, the onset of the COLD WAR dramatically changed the official American attitude. Fear that communists might come to power in Western European countries due to postwar economic hardship led the Truman administration to propose the MARSHALL PLAN in 1947. This initiative led to some modest steps toward European integration, especially the establishment of the Organization for European Economic Cooperation (OEEC) to administer Marshall aid and work for the reduction of tariffs. The Marshall Plan also helped to determine the geographic limits of integration until the 1990s since the negative Soviet reaction cemented the division of the continent. To the Truman administration's frustration, little further progress came until 1950, despite the intensification of the Cold War. The major reason was that Great Britain, at the time the most important state in Western Europe politically and economically, opposed all plans for supranational organizations.

The creation of the Federal Republic of Germany in 1949 made integration seem more urgent than ever. Under pressure from Washington but also motivated by its own interests, the French government and its unofficial advisor Monnet now assumed a leading role. The "Schuman Plan" for a European Coal and Steel Community (ECSC), developed by Monnet and announced by Foreign Minister Robert Schuman on 9 May 1950, ensured that German heavy industry would be used only for peaceful purposes, significantly upgraded the international status of the Federal Republic, and marked the start of postwar Franco-German cooperation. The Truman administration greeted it with enthusiasm. The ECSC, which came into existence in 1952, also set the pattern for further initiatives. It brought together for the first time the "Six" and created the four basic governing organs that characterized later integration. After initial hesitations, the Truman administration also gave its support to Monnet's plan for a "European Defense Community" (EDC) that would prevent the creation of an independent West German army. Although in December 1953 Secretary of State John Foster Dulles even threatened an "agonizing reappraisal" of the American security commitment to Western Europe if the EDC Treaty were not ratified, the French National Assembly rejected it on 30 August 1954, largely because of misgivings about surrendering the national army. The Eisenhower administration later gave its support to the creation of the European Economic Community (EEC) and the European Atomic Energy Community (EURATOM) in 1958. These two institutions and the ECSC, at first collectively called the "European Economic Community," were officially fused into the EC in 1967. They went a long way toward fulfilling Washington's desire for integrated Western European structures that would help contain the Soviet Union and safely incorporate the Federal Republic.

Troubled Relations between the United States and the European Economic Community

Nonetheless, doubts soon arose about whether European integration was compatible with American leadership in Western Europe. Starting in 1958 French President Charles de Gaulle challenged United States political predominance by demanding a coequal role for France with it and Britain within the North Atlantic Treaty Organization (NATO). He also pursued an increasingly independent policy on issues like Berlin, the Vietnam War, relations with communist states, nuclear weapons, and British membership in the European Economic Community (which to the chagrin of American policymakers he vetoed in 1963). American leaders tried to accommodate de Gaulle while rejecting his aspirations to leadership, but already during the Kennedy administration they began to stress the Atlantic character of European-American relations. Moreover, starting in the late 1950s negative American payment balances (at first due to high levels of American foreign investment and military aid but by the late 1960s also involving trade deficits) led to increasing worries about economic competition from the "Six." Washington responded by intensifying the process of reducing tariffs between industrialized states within the General Agreement on Tariffs and Trade and in 1961 helped create an Organization for Economic Cooperation and Development with American and Canadian membership to replace the OEEC. Since the mid-1960s, the United States and the EU have been involved periodically in trade disputes involving a variety of agricultural and industrial products.

Even though National Security Advisor Henry Kissinger proclaimed 1973 the "Year of Europe," the Nixon administration reevaluated the traditional policy of American support for European integration in light of these political and economic challenges. Henceforth the United States would no longer actively promote new initiatives for supranational integration, although it would not oppose further efforts by the Europeans themselves. Although Jimmy Carter criticized the Nixon and Ford administrations' neglect of the European allies and in January 1978 became the first president to visit the European Commission in Brussels, in practice the United States' main priority had become protecting its own national interests. This became quite clear during the 1980s, when the process of European integration revived after the relative stagnation of the previous decade. The negotiations on the "Single European Act" in 1985–1986, which aimed at the creation of a fully integrated European market by 1992, led to worried speculation in the United States about a "Fortress Europe." In addition, the Reagan administration became involved in a series of disputes over commercial policy with the EC, with which the United States had run a trade deficit starting in 1984.

Relations since 1989

By 1989 an improvement in relations was in sight, however. The end of the Cold War and the reunification of Germany made expanded European structures seem the best way of providing stability for the entire continent. In addition, by 1990 the United States had a positive trade balance with the EC again but was becoming worried about economic relations with both Japan and China. President George H. W. Bush gave increased attention to the American relationship with the EC. The 1990 Transatlantic Declaration set up a mechanism for regular consultations and reaffirmed the desire of both sides to strengthen their partnership. The Bush administration reached compromises on many of the economic disputes that had arisen as a result of the Single European Act. Moreover, it strongly supported the 1992 Maastricht Treaty that created the EU in 1993 with both an Economic and Monetary Union (EMU) and a Common Foreign and Security Policy (CFSP) among its future goals. In 1995 the United States and the EU agreed on a "New Transatlantic Agenda" that committed them to active cooperation in roughly a hundred policy areas. The EMU was realized with the introduction of a common currency, the euro, on 1 January 1999, at first on an accounting basis only. Although Denmark, Great Britain, and Sweden chose not to participate for the time being, the other twelve EU states replaced their national currencies with euro banknotes and coins on 1 January 2002. The euro has the potential to rival the dollar as an international reserve currency. The United States remains sensitive to any developments toward a CFSP that might call NATO's preeminence into question, but the EU for some time will not have any capacity to conduct significant military operations outside of that alliance and also has signaled its continued desire to work within it. Moreover, the EU's attention during the first part of the twenty-first century will be devoted to its expansion into eastern Europe. In 1998 it began negotiations with six new candidates for admission (the Czech Republic, Cyprus, Estonia, Hungary, Poland, and Slovenia), with enlargement from this group not expected before the end of 2002. On 15 January 2000 it also initiated talks with six further applicants (Bulgaria, Latvia, Lithuania, Malta, Romania, and Slovakia). Ten of the twelve candidates should join around mid-decade, with Bulgarian and Romanian accession by 2009.

BIBLIOGRAPHY

Lundestad, Geir. *"Empire" by Integration: The United States and European Integration, 1945–1997.* Oxford: Oxford University Press, 1998. The standard work; also provocative with its thesis of an American "empire."

Nugent, Neill. *The Government and Politics of the European Union.* 4th ed. Durham, N.C.: Duke University Press, 1999. The standard work on how the EU functions and its policies.

Pond, Elizabeth. *The Rebirth of Europe.* Rev. ed. Washington, D.C.: Brookings Institution Press, 1999. An excellent overview of European integration and its prospects and problems since 1989.

Stirk, Peter M. R. *A History of European Integration since 1914.* London: Continuum, 1996.

Urwin, Derek W. *The Community of Europe: A History of European Integration since 1945.* 2d ed. London: Longman, 1995. Both Stirk and Urwin are good general histories, with the former paying more attention to both the Atlantic framework and the Cold War as influences on the integration process.

Thomas Maulucci

EUTAW SPRINGS, BATTLE OF (8 September 1781). General Nathanael Greene, who replaced General Horatio Gates after the crushing defeat at Camden, South Carolina, in August, lost this battle to a superior British force under Colonel Alexander Stewart. Greene was routed and lost a quarter of his 2,000 Continentals and North and South Carolina militia in the conflict. But he inflicted even heavier casualties on the British, forcing them to retreat to Charleston and preventing Stewart from aiding Lord Cornwallis, then in Virginia. Six weeks later, surrounded by Continental and French forces at Yorktown, Cornwallis surrendered.

BIBLIOGRAPHY

Lumpkin, Henry. *From Savannah to Yorktown.* Columbia: University of South Carolina Press, 1981.

Thayer, Theodore. *Nathanael Greene: Strategist of the American Revolution.* New York: Twayne, 1960.

R. L. Meriwether/A. R.

See also **Camden, Battle of; Southern Campaigns; Yorktown Campaign.**

EUTHANASIA, Greek for "good death," refers to the termination of the life of a person suffering from a painful and incurable medical condition. Also known as "mercy killing," euthanasia is distinguished from suicide by the necessary participation of a third party, typically either a physician or family member.

Twenty-first-century disputes over euthanasia are often seen as a byproduct of advances in biomedical technology capable of prolonging a person's life indefinitely. Indeed, the moral and legal aspects of euthanasia are extremely complicated, as experts distinguish between active and passive euthanasia as well as voluntary and involuntary euthanasia. Additional issues include the definition of a "terminal" illness and whether pain, an intractable disease, or both, are required to make the practice morally acceptable.

Such complexity has led to a variety of legal positions worldwide. The United States officially forbids euthanasia, while some European countries, such as Switzerland, Germany, Poland, and Norway, are more lenient, allowing for a variety of mitigating circumstances and reduced criminal penalties. In 1993 the Netherlands passed a law prescribing guidelines for medically assisted suicide; Uruguay has exempted mercy killing from criminal prosecution since 1933. To help untangle these issues and better understand euthanasia, this article will consider the history of euthanasia, the "right to die" movement, and physician-assisted suicide within an American social and legal context.

Mercy Killing

Mercy killing, practiced since antiquity, has been debated throughout history. Ancient Greek, Indian, and Asian texts describe infanticide as an acceptable solution for children physically unsuited for or incapable of living. In Plato's *Phaedo,* when Socrates drinks hemlock, a poison, he maintains his dignity in death, an action immortalized in the modern pro-euthanasia organization, the Hemlock Society.

While many other Greeks, including Aristotle and the Stoics, sanctioned euthanasia, most early Christian thinkers condemned the practice. Both Saint Augustine and Saint Thomas Aquinas prohibited active euthanasia and suicide on the grounds that it was an affront to the sanctity of life and usurped the divine right of life and death. They did, however, permit passive euthanasia—the discontinuation of life-saving treatments—even though death would then be imminent. In the seventeenth and eighteenth centuries European thinkers went even farther, as Francis Bacon, David Hume, and Immanuel Kant considered both active and passive euthanasia morally acceptable.

However, early American laws specifically forbade assisted suicide; New York enacted statutes against the practice in 1828, and both the Field Penal Code (1877) for the Dakota Territory and later the Model Penal Code followed suit. Yet the polio epidemics of the 1920s and 1930s tested these legal codes, as many protested the potential for dependence on the new Drinker tanks or "iron lungs." By the end of the decade proponents of mercy killing sought legal protection, establishing the Euthanasia Society of America in 1938 to promote the practice as well as legislation. Similar organizations formed in Great Britain and Germany, although revelations of indiscriminate and inhumane Nazi practices ultimately led to the condemnation of the movement by the Roman Catholic Church following World War II and helped defeat legislation in Connecticut (1959), Idaho (1969), Oregon (1973), and Montana (1973).

"Right to Die"

Debate over euthanasia resurfaced in the 1970s amid growing concern over individual rights, the Karen Ann Quinlan case, and the "right to die" movement. In 1975 Quinlan, a twenty-one-year-old who had accidentally overdosed on barbiturates, alcohol, and valium, slipped into a coma, and was kept alive by a respirator and other medical apparatus. The "sleeping beauty" case captivated the nation, as the public debated who was responsible for the decision to maintain or disconnect the machines and the indignity of being kept alive by medical technology.

Ultimately, Quinlan's case helped redefine "brain death" and the legal framework for voluntary and involuntary decision making. The New Jersey Supreme Court ruled in 1976 that, given her "irreversible condition" and the right to privacy guaranteed by the Constitution, her family, the appropriate surrogates, could remove her from life support. The court's approval of passive euthanasia fueled the "right to die" movement; by 1977 thirty-eight legislatures had submitted over fifty bills to enact legislation expanding the power of attorney and sanctioning living wills, precursors to "do not resuscitate" orders. At the same time, the American Medical Association renewed its opposition to euthanasia, arguing that passive euthanasia—the removal of life support—is ethically acceptable only in "terminal" cases where "extraordinary procedures" are required to maintain life in a manner inconvenient and inefficient for the patient. Remarkably, Quinlan lived in a vegetative state unassisted until 1985, by which time a "right of refusal" was generally accepted, supported by the due process clause of the Constitution giving individuals the right to make decisions free from unreasonable governmental interference.

By the 1990s, advocates of euthanasia such as the Hemlock Society (established 1980) campaigned for physician-assisted suicide or active euthanasia, reviving the debate over the limits of an individual's "right to die." Proponents argued that a painless injection or combination of drugs was far more humane than disconnecting a feeding tube and allowing the person to starve. Physicians, however, were caught in an ethical dilemma, given the Hippocratic Oath to do no harm, relieve suffering, and prolong life. For patients with intractable disease and consistent pain, the goals of relieving suffering and prolonging life are inherently contradictory. If the physician acts to end the suffering through assisted suicide, he or she violates the creed to do no harm and prolong life; if the physician refuses to act, suffering is prolonged rather than assuaged.

Physician-Assisted Suicide

Physicians, like the public, were divided over the morality of assisted suicide. The state of Washington failed to pass a "right to die" voter initiative in 1991, as did California the following year. However, in 1994, Oregon passed Measure 16, a "Death with Dignity Act" drafted by attorney Cheryl K. Smith, former legal counsel for the Hemlock Society. The act allowed physicians to prescribe and dispense, but not administer, the necessary lethal drugs. Remarkably, the bold new legislation was soon overshadowed by the figure of Dr. Jack Kevorkian, who quickly became a political lightning-rod for the "right to die" movement.

A retired pathologist, Dr. Kevorkian, or "Dr. Death" to his detractors, made headlines in the 1990s by assisting over 130 people to commit suicide. The author of *Prescription: Medicide*, Dr. Kevorkian made his reputation challenging a 1993 Michigan law prohibiting physician-assisted suicide. Backed by the American Civil Liberties Union, Kevorkian argued that the law, which had been expressly written to outlaw his practice of active euthanasia, denied individuals the right to choose how and when they died. However, Kevorkian's legal stance suffered when it was revealed that many of his patients' diseases were not terminal and were unverified. Unrepentant, the seventy-year-old physician continued his practice until a Michigan court sentenced him in 1999 to ten to twenty-five years in prison for the second-degree murder of Thomas Youk, a patient with Lou Gehrig's disease. Ultimately, Kevorkian's arrogance proved to be his downfall; the airing of Youk's suicide on the television program *60 Minutes* infuriated the court, as did his participation in another assisted suicide while released on bail.

Proponents of active euthanasia received another series of setbacks in the late 1990s as the courts, supported by a broad coalition inflamed by rumors of pressure and a lack of consent in assisted suicides in Oregon, moved to derail the movement. Although the details of Oregon's euthanasia practice remain private, fears that assisted suicide was used to reduce health care costs and that patients were pressured to accept lethal drugs rather than treatment solidified an anti-euthanasia coalition of hospice organizations, medical associations, religious organizations, and pro-life groups. In 1997 the United States Supreme Court unanimously refused to issue an assisted-suicide *Roe v. Wade* decision in the case of *Washington v. Glucksberg.* Chief Justice William Rehnquist stated that assisted suicide posed substantial harm for individuals already at risk because of their age, poverty, or lack of access to quality medical care. Months later, the Florida Supreme Court refused to consider assisted suicide a right under the privacy statute of the Florida Constitution, and a bill legalizing the practice foundered in the Maine legislature the following year.

In the early 2000s the debate over physician-assisted suicide remained contested at the state level. The Supreme Court's decision in *Washington v. Glucksberg* remanded the decision on active euthanasia to the state courts because the justices argued that each state had the right to protect its residents and thus a federal decision was inappropriate. Indeed, the Court's position in Washington is similar to one taken in an earlier ruling on passive euthanasia. In *Cruzan v. Director, Missouri Department of Health* (1990), the Supreme Court held that a state could forbid termination of treatment in the absence of "clear and convincing evidence" of the patient's own wishes. While this gave individual states the freedom to determine appropriate standards for involuntary passive euthanasia, a majority of states adhered to the precedents set by the Quinlan case in making their determination. Advocates of physician-assisted suicide hoped that responsible practices in Oregon and the Netherlands would persuade their opponents, and they downplayed the economic arguments for active euthanasia amid a social climate decrying HMO (health maintenance organization) cost-cutting operations.

BIBLIOGRAPHY

Doudera, A. Edward, and J. Douglas Peters, eds. *Legal and Ethical Aspects of Treating Critically and Terminally Ill Patients.* Ann Arbor, Mich.: AUPHA, 1982.

Humphry, Derek. *Final Exit: The Practicalities of Self-Deliverance and Assisted Suicide for the Dying.* Eugene, Ore.: Hemlock Society, 1991.

President's Commission for the Study of Ethical Problems in Medicine and Biomedical and Behavioral Research. *Deciding to Forego Life-Sustaining Treatment: A Report on the Ethical, Medical, and Legal Issues in Treatment Decisions.* Washington, D.C.: U.S. Government Printing Office, 1983.

Schneiderman, Lawrence J., and Nancy S. Jecker. *Wrong Medicine: Doctors, Patients, and Futile Treatment.* Baltimore: Johns Hopkins University Press, 1995.

Weir, Robert F. *Abating Treatment with Critically Ill Patients: Ethical and Legal Limits to the Medical Prolongation of Life.* New York: Oxford University Press, 1989.

J. G. Whitesides

See also **Assisted Suicide; Death and Dying; "Right to Die" Cases; *Washington v. Glucksberg*.**

EVANGELICAL ALLIANCE, one of the earliest attempts to bring about cooperation between the various Protestant denominations. Although founded in London in 1846, the alliance did not take root in America until Philip Schaff and Samuel S. Schmucker helped to organize a branch in 1867. Important international conferences of the alliance were held in New York in 1873; Washington, D.C., in 1887; and at the World's Fair in Chicago in 1893. By 1900, the influence of the Evangelical Alliance was waning in America and, in 1908, was replaced by the Federal Council of the Churches of Christ in America.

BIBLIOGRAPHY

Jordan, Philip D. *The Evangelical Alliance for the United States of America, 1847–1900: Ecumenism, Identity, and the Religion of the Republic.* New York: Mellen, 1982.

William W. Sweet / A. R.

See also **Evangelicalism and Revivalism; Protestantism; Religion and Religious Affiliation.**

EVANGELICALISM AND REVIVALISM are a related set of terms that label aspects of American Christianity.

Evangelism

Evangelism is the promulgation of the Christian religion among those who are not Christians. Evangelism has been a central impulse of Christianity since its beginning in the first century A.D., and is one of the main reasons the Christian religion has spread around the globe. In American history, Christians have employed an enormous variety of activities for evangelism—preaching, Sunday schools, catechism classes, music, drama, publishing, radio and television broadcasts, special interest activities, small-group meetings, person-to-person relationships—and a set of activities commonly summed up in the term "revivalism."

Revivalism

Revivalism is a set of religious practices that produce an atmosphere of spiritual intensity with two goals in mind: to convince non-Christians to convert to Christianity, and to convince Christians to revitalize their faith. Revivalism centers on vigorous preaching and audience singing of popular religious songs. The preaching and the singing aim at eliciting both rational and emotional responses from the audience.

Protestant revivalism developed out of two late seventeenth-century European movements—English Puritanism and Continental Pietism. The Puritans contributed an emphasis on visible conversion. Adults or older children were expected to be able to tell the story of how they had become aware of their sinfulness and its ultimate consequence—death—and how they had become Christians as a result. The Puritans often described the event of becoming a Christian as the "New Birth." At other times and places, it has been described as "trusting Christ," "experiencing salvation," making a "decision for Christ," or being "born again."

Pietism contributed an emphasis on personally experiencing the divine, resulting in holy living. Pietism developed in Germany in reaction against the formalism of state-church Lutheranism and the aridity of Protestant theology. The early Pietists formed small groups for prayer, Bible study, and exhortation to live by Christian principles. They emphasized the priesthood of all believers, and that true Christian faith led one to a relationship with God rather than mere knowledge about God. They avoided theological disputation, favoring instead devotional activities and charitable acts.

Puritanism and Pietism were not insulated from each other; in the late seventeenth century they mingled each other's main characteristics. They fused most dynamically in the 1740s in the Methodist movement of John and Charles Wesley and George Whitefield. Two of its most innovative elements were field preaching and popular hymnody. When Whitefield met resistance from Anglican clergy, he moved his preaching venues outside the churches to homes, meeting halls, and even pastures. Charles Wesley was the movement's songwriter, and all the Methodist preachers used his singable and memorable hymns to reinforce the movement's message. Methodism eventually became a main source for American revivalism, and open preaching-and-singing services on denominationally neutral ground became one of revivalism's hallmarks.

These fused Puritan and Pietist elements were transplanted to the English North American colonies in the 1720s and 1730s. Several colonial preachers—the best-remembered is the Congregationalist Jonathan Edwards—gained regional notoriety for effectively preaching a message of individual conversion and holy living. Then revivalism became an intercolonial phenomenon when Whitefield undertook a series of itinerant preaching tours that drew enormous crowds throughout the middle colonies and New England. Between 1740 and his death thirty years later, Whitefield may have been the most famous person in the colonies. Historians have called this upsurge of revivalism America's "First Great Awakening." It instituted the main pattern for subsequent American revivalism: nondenominational settings, the absence of social distinctions in the audience, using popular religious songs to engage audience participation and passion, and itinerant preachers exhorting people to New Birth, holy living, and "revival" of religious zeal in local churches.

Existing denominations and local churches divided sharply over whether revivalism helped or hurt them. Many revivalists, Whitefield included, antagonized local clergy by accusing them of spiritual deadness. Some leaders of Congregationalist, Presbyterian, Reformed, and Anglican churches welcomed the revivalists; others believed that revivalism undercut their authority, diluted their theology, and diminished the distinctiveness of their denomination.

Revivalism was therefore both divisive and unifying. On one hand, it split existing denominations into pro-revival and anti-revival parties; and it shepherded many of the newly awakened into pro-revival denominations. In the First Great Awakening, Presbyterians split into New Side and Old Side, Congregationalists into New Lights and Old Lights. Meanwhile, revivalism greatly expanded Baptist numbers throughout the colonies.

On the other hand, revivalism produced a common-denominator Protestantism that transcended denominational differences and stimulated ecumenical activity. The ecumenical power of revivalism became clear after the "Second Great Awakening," beginning around 1800 at several outdoor meetings in Kentucky. By the 1830s, Charles Finney had taken his highly successful mass revivals from upstate New York to Philadelphia, Boston, and New York City. There were new elements in this awakening—the American Revolution gave it a language of liberty that underwrote powerful anti-Calvinist sentiments; African Americans were for the first time Christianized in large numbers; and a genuinely new American religion, Mormonism, emerged. But in style and outcome the basic patterns repeated. Existing denominations split. Anti-revivalists—from establishment Old-School Presbyterians to immigrant groups like German Lutherans, Calvinists, and Mennonites—struggled to maintain their distinctiveness against the ecumenical, doctrinal, and liturgical corrosions of revivalism. And the ranks of pro-revival denominations—Baptists, Methodists, and Christians (Disciples of Christ)—swelled. The revivalists' success in preaching conversion and holy living prompted Protestants to cooperate across denominational lines to form societies that would convert America and make it holy. This was how the Evangelical United Front—a network of interdenominational organizations like the American Bible Society, American Sunday School Union, American Temperance Society, and others—began in the 1810s and 1820s.

The Evangelical United Front was anti-Catholic, but in spite of this, Roman Catholics in the United States had their own form of revivals called "parish missions." These originated in sixteenth-century Europe when some religious orders set out to revitalize Catholicism through itinerant preaching. When these orders immigrated to the United States, they brought parish missions along with them. The revival began in the 1850s, gained momentum in the 1860s, and did not decline until the 1890s. Like Protestant revivals, parish missions employed music and sermons aimed at conversion, the direct experience of God, and holy living (which often included signing a temperance pledge). Unlike Protestant revivals, the parish

Religious Camp Meeting. This watercolor by J. Maze Burbank, c. 1839, depicts a typical meeting—very well attended and highly emotional—during the period of revivalism known as the "Second Great Awakening." © New Bedford Whaling Museum

missions remained thoroughly Catholic, retaining ritual, sacraments, catechism, and confessional. The result was a personal religion of the heart that resembled revivalistic evangelicalism, but in form and structure remained clearly Roman Catholic.

After the Second Great Awakening, revivalism remained part of the religious landscape. The Revival of 1857–1858, centered in urban prayer meetings, was a truly national event influencing millions of people in every Protestant denomination. The holiness movement expanded rapidly after the Civil War (1861–1865), reintroducing revivalism into sectors of Methodism that had abandoned it, and spinning off a host of new denominations and institutions. Continuing revival activity within the holiness movement launched the Pentecostal movement (with its singular emphasis on "speaking in tongues") in the first decade of the twentieth century, and this has since spread around the globe.

The most important revivalist of the nineteenth century was Dwight L. Moody, a layman who led enormously successful revival meetings throughout the United States and Britain in the quarter century after 1876. The Evangelical United Front had represented a consensus that revivalism and social reform—in other words, religion and politics—traveled hand in hand. This had begun to change in the Revival of 1857–1858, and by the end of Moody's life (1899), the consensus had come apart. Moody focused his efforts on exclusively religious activities and institutions. Meanwhile, the preachers of the new Social Gospel movement (some of whom were Moody's pupils) resurrected the old Unitarian assertion that revivalism inhibited social reform. These developments, along with historical criticism of the Bible and the increased prestige of science, divided American evangelicalism into modernist and traditionalist groupings.

The Social Gospel's critique of revivalism also had a lasting impact on historical writing about revivalism. Since then, the question that has preoccupied historians has been, "To what extent has revivalism led to social reform?" In general, historians of religion whose personal roots lay outside revivalism have argued that modernism, not revivalism, most advanced social improvement, while historians with backgrounds in revivalist traditions have argued that revivalism promoted social reform. Despite the vigor of this discussion, it has had little influence on historians who write surveys of American history. They generally ignore religion when discussing social reform between the Civil War and the 1980s Reagan Revolution. When revivalism is discussed at all, it is treated as a reactionary force impeding social progress.

Moody's successor in the public eye was Billy Sunday, a professional baseball player–turned-evangelist. He began his revival career in 1896, and by the 1910s he was drawing huge crowds in Boston, Chicago, and New York City. His career peaked during the fundamentalist-modernist controversies of the 1920s, when the large northern Protestant denominations finally rejected fundamentalist demands for theological conformity. For the last ten years of his life, Sunday worked the small towns instead of the big cities, and observers interpreted this as a parable about the decline of revivalism. With the breakup of the evangelical consensus of the nineteenth century, revivalistic mass evangelism seemed doomed. Little did anyone guess that revivalism would not only survive, it would thrive; and out of the subculture of evangelicalism the greatest revivalist of all time was yet to come.

Evangelicalism

The term "evangelicalism" has multiple meanings. In the eighteenth century, it designated an insurgent Protestant religion of experience employing revivalistic methods. The Wesleys and Whitefield were the classic exemplars. In nineteenth-century America, "evangelicalism" referred to the Protestant establishment—rooted in revivalism, located in large denominations of high social standing, and cooperating in trying to embed Protestant morality into American society. Lying outside the evangelical establishment were many liturgical denominations (such as Lutherans), immigrant groups resisting revivalism (such as Mennonites), Roman Catholics, and Jews.

After the unraveling of the evangelical consensus between 1890 and 1925, "evangelicalism" came to be used in three ways. The most recent usage holds that evangelicalism consists of all Christians who hold a defining set of religious beliefs. These typically include the necessity of faith in Christ for salvation from sin, the authority of the Bible, and the importance of evangelism aimed at a conversion experience. By these criteria, at the end of the twentieth century, 20 to 30 percent of American adults were evangelicals. They can be found in every Protestant denomination, in the Roman Catholic Church, in messianic Jewish congregations, and among those who belong to no organized religious group.

Since the 1920s, the term "evangelicalism" has also been used to designate Protestant groups that retained a strong supernaturalist understanding of Christianity. Under this definition, evangelicalism is a mosaic composed of fundamentalists, the holiness movement, Pentecostals, most African American groups, Southern Baptists and Methodists, many immigrant groups, Seventh-Day Adventists, and various conservative Lutheran, Presbyterian, Congregational, Episcopalian, and Restorationist denominations. Nonevangelical denominations are the large northern Protestant groups whose leaders have de-emphasized supernaturalism—the United Methodist Church, United Church of Christ, Presbyterian Church (U.S.A.), American Baptist Convention, Evangelical Lutheran Church of America, Reformed Church of America, and Episcopal Church.

The problem with this definition is that many of the supernaturalist groups resist being called "evangelical," and many individuals within nonevangelical denominations hold supernaturalist evangelical beliefs. So it may be more helpful to think of evangelicalism as being composed of people who hold evangelical beliefs and who also identify with the transdenominational movement that calls itself evangelicalism. The institutional center of this movement is found not in denominations, but in interlocking networks of independent, special-purpose, parachurch organizations like evangelistic and missionary agencies, relief and social service organizations, publishers, broadcasters, schools, and summer camps. There are perhaps some 30,000 such organizations; the largest and best known include Campus Crusade for Christ and World Vision.

Moody was the midwife for these networks. He popularized lay leadership, entrepreneurialism, and independent nondenominational parachurch agencies. His evangelistic tours, summer conferences, and other enterprises brought together transatlantic revivalism, Keswick holiness, premillennial dispensationalism, the Student Volunteer Movement, faith missions, Bible institutes, and Princeton Seminary ideas about the inerrancy of the Bible. Moody fused these elements into a genuinely ecumenical form of Christianity that gave twentieth-century evangelicalism its characteristic texture.

The fundamentalist-modernist controversy of the 1920s was the most acrimonious moment in the unraveling of the evangelical consensus. Modernists were members of the large northern denominations who wanted to update Christianity in light of contemporary science. Underlying their program was an impulse to minimize supernaturalism and maximize concern for social issues. Fundamentalists were evangelicals who wanted to force the modernists out of the denominations. In the middle were evangelicals who believed that cooperation between modernists and evangelicals was still possible. When the fundamentalist campaign failed, some left to form their own denominations while others remained as dissenters. Over time, however, modernists and their theological descendents gradually came to dominate the leadership of the large northern denominations.

Unnoticed at the time were two shifts in the Protestant landscape that would set the direction for the development of evangelicalism. The first was that the percentage of churchgoing Protestants attending mainline churches began to decline, while the percentage attending evangelical churches began to rise. This phenomenon went unobserved partly because the mainline numbers were so much larger to begin with, and partly because the absolute numbers of mainline attendees continued to grow. Nevertheless, the trend continued, and by the 1960s, mainline denominations were experiencing declines in absolute numbers. At the end of the twentieth century, more than half of all churchgoing Protestants attended evangelical churches.

The second shift saw evangelicalism's institutional center of gravity relocate out of denominations and into its networks of parachurch organizations. After the modernists won their right to remain in the denominations, evangelicals gradually lost influence there. But for the most part, instead of creating new denominations, they poured their religious energies into building parachurch agencies, especially Bible institutes, mission agencies, and evangelism organizations. Between 1925 and 1940 the term "evangelical" received little use, but after that (the National Association of Evangelicals was founded in 1941) the term came to designate this interdenominational network.

The evangelical network's highest-profile figure was also the man who revived mass evangelism—Billy Graham. Steeped in America's revival tradition, Graham rose to prominence in the late 1940s as a traveling evangelist with the nondenominational Youth for Christ. In 1950 he formed the Billy Graham Evangelistic Association and launched a television program; in 1954 he became an international figure with a hugely successful "crusade" in England. In the twenty years after 1960 he preached to unprecedented crowds in the United States and all over the world, functioned as the unofficial chaplain of the American presidency, organized major international evangelism conferences, and was a powerful ecumenical force nearly everywhere he went.

Before Graham, interdenominational evangelicalism drew most heavily from northern Baptist and Presbyterian denominations (Graham himself was ordained a Baptist). But after Graham, the story of evangelicalism is one of steadily expanding ecumenical reach. Early on, Graham cooperated with mainline church leaders in his crusades, narrowing a gap that had opened wider since the 1920s. Pentecostal and evangelical theology had always been nearly identical, but worship practices kept the two movements apart. After World War II, however, Pentecostal and evangelical networks increasingly overlapped. Evangelical parachurch organizations began welcoming Pentecostals, and ordinary evangelicals increasingly participated in the activities of Pentecostal parachurch organizations like the Full Gospel Businessmen's Fellowship International. The widest gap of all, between evangelicalism and Catholicism, was closed considerably by Vatican II, the charismatic movement of the 1970s (which brought Pentecostal worship practices into Catholic and mainline Protestant churches), shared moral revulsion at legalized abortion, and the growing open-mindedness of key leaders in both camps. By the 1990s, many evangelical parachurch groups were treating Roman Catholicism as just another denomination, and Catholic authorities were approving evangelical literature—even evangelical versions of the Bible—for their parishioners. A formal marker of the new dispensation was the "Evangelicals and Catholics Together" statement of 1994, in which influential evangelical and Catholic leaders mutually affirmed the centrality of common elements of the faith.

Historians studying evangelicalism's social impact have tended to focus on the narrow matter of politics. During World War I, a coalition of progressives, scientists, and evangelicals capitalized on the spirit of wartime sacrifice to institute a short-lived nationwide prohibition of alcoholic beverages. Some historians argue that evangelicalism was responsible for laws that prohibited the teaching of evolution in public schools in the 1920s, while others have argued that since only southern states passed such laws, regional factors were more important. In the 1970s, the Moral Majority and the Religious Right emerged from conservative Republican efforts to mobilize apathetic evangelical voters, from opposition to legalized abortion, and from threats by the Carter administration to suppress the growing network of evangelical private schools. Some scholars have credited the Religious Right with swinging the 1980 presidential election to Ronald Reagan; but regardless, it is clear that the evangelicals who made up the bulk of the Religious Right became a powerful part of the Republican Party coalition after 1980.

However, focusing on the Religious Right distorts vision when thinking about the social impact of evangelicalism, for two reasons. First, evangelicalism is politically diverse. For every evangelical who votes Republican, there is another who votes Democratic. Second, and more importantly, politics is but a tiny aspect of evangelical activism. Of the 30,000 evangelical parachurch organizations, less than one percent are concerned with politics; and of all the money evangelicals give to parachurch organizations, less than one percent goes to political organizations. Most evangelical organizations focus on evangelism, social service, overseas relief and development, foreign missions, education, and media communication. In these areas evangelicalism's social impact has been most profound, but least understood by historians.

Evangelicalism's popularity and institutional growth stem partly from its ability to foster grass roots ecumenism. This is rooted in a few common elements shared by many Christians—faith in Christ, authority of the Bible, holy living, and spreading the faith. These were the same themes stressed by all the major revivalists, from Whitefield to Graham. By the beginning of the twenty-first century, the large number of Americans who regarded these elements as the core of Christianity, and who participated in the life of evangelical parachurch organizations, provided surface indications of the deep impact evangelicalism and revivalism have had on American society.

BIBLIOGRAPHY

Carpenter, Joel A. *Revive Us Again: The Reawakening of American Fundamentalism.* New York: Oxford University Press, 1997.

Carwarding, Richard. *Transatlantic Revivalism: Popular Evangelicalism in Britain and America 1790–1865.* Westport, Conn.: Greenwood Press, 1978.

Dayton, Donald W., and Robert K. Johnson, eds. *The Variety of American Evangelicalism.* Knoxville: University of Tennessee Press, 1991.

Dolan, Jay P. *Catholic Revivalism: The American Experience, 1830–1900.* Notre Dame, Ind.: University of Notre Dame Press, 1978.

Hatch, Nathan O. *The Democratization of American Christianity.* New Haven, Conn.: Yale University Press, 1989.

Long, Kathryn Teresa. *The Revival of 1857–58: Interpreting an American Religious Awakening*. New York: Oxford University Press, 1998.

Marsden, George M. *Fundamentalism and American Culture: The Shaping of Twentieth-Century Evangelicalism, 1870–1925*. New York: Oxford University Press, 1980.

Martin, William. *A Prophet with Honor: The Billy Graham Story*. New York: William Morrow and Company, 1991.

McLoughlin, William Gerald. *Modern Revivalism: Charles Grandison Finney to Billy Graham*. New York: Ronald Press, 1959.

Noll, Mark A. *American Evangelical Christianity: An Introduction*. Malden, Mass.: Blackwell Publishers, 2001.

Smith, Christian, et al. *American Evangelicalism: Embattled and Thriving*. Chicago: University of Chicago Press, 1998.

Stout, Harry S. *The Divine Dramatist: George Whitefield and the Rise of Modern Evangelicalism*. Grand Rapids, Mich.: William B. Eerdmans, 1991.

Michael S. Hamilton

See also **Fundamentalism; Moral Majority; Pentecostal Churches; Religion and Religious Affiliation; Televangelism.**

EVERGLADES NATIONAL PARK represents the only subtropical nature reserve in North America. The preserve in southern Florida encompasses 2,354 square miles (1,506,499 acres) of mangrove swamps, pinelands, pond apple and cypress forests, and sawgrass prairie. It supports rare species such as the Florida panther and the manatee and is the only place in the world where alligators and crocodiles coexist.

The unique ecosystem that characterizes the Everglades emerged 5,000 years ago, when decreasing sea levels and altered climatic conditions allowed plants to colonize the region. When Spanish conquistadores arrived in the 1500s, they encountered a thriving Native American culture based on hunting, fishing, and trade. War and disease signaled the demise of the indigenous population by 1763. In the early 1800s, however, Creeks and Seminoles moved to the Everglades to avoid removal from Florida. Early Euro-American visitors, such as the naturalist John James Audubon, marveled at the swampland wildlife. In 1840, Colonel William Harvey noted, "no country that I have ever seen bears any resemblance to it; it seems like a vast sea filled with grass and green trees." Interest in southern Florida burgeoned during the late 1800s, motivated by attempts to drain the land for agricultural purposes. Hunters also flocked to the Everglades, seeking to profit from the market for feathered hats.

A campaign to preserve the Everglades germinated in the 1920s. Concerned over habitat loss and declining wildlife, the Connecticut landscape architect Ernest F. Coe established the Tropic Everglades National Park Association in 1928. The same year, Senator Duncan Fletcher of Florida introduced a bill to establish Everglades National Park. In 1930, an influential commission chaired by National Park Service Director Horace Albright recommended protection. On 30 May 1934, Congress approved the Everglades Bill, and on 6 December 1947, following a lengthy process of land acquisition, the park was formally established. In preserving an area for its biological rather than geological attributes, the dedication of Everglades National Park set a precedent in national park legislation.

Everglades National Park. A mangrove swamp in southern Florida's vast, unique nature reserve. VISUALS UNLIMITED

Everglades National Park remains the only park in the Western Hemisphere to be designated an international biosphere reserve (1976) and a world heritage site (1979). As one of Florida's foremost tourist destinations, the park attracts some one million visitors each year. In 1993, the park was placed on the World Heritage in Danger list. Outside development, pollution, and Florida's expansive irrigation and flood control systems threatened the biotic integrity of the park. The National Park Service, together with state authorities, responded with a series of measures aimed at restoring the Everglades ecosystem. Under the auspices of the Everglades National Park Protection and Expansion Act (1989) and the Everglades Forever Act (1994), resource managers inaugurated long-term programs to improve water quality, increase the flow of freshwater through the park, restore wetlands habitat, and stabilize populations of native fauna.

BIBLIOGRAPHY

Douglas, Marjory Stoneman. *The Everglades: River of Grass*. Reprint. Sarasota, Fla.: Pineapple Press, 1997.

Runte, Alfred. *National Parks: The American Experience*. 2d rev. ed. Lincoln: University of Nebraska Press, 1987.

Karen Jones

See also **Florida; National Park System.**

EVOLUTIONISM. Darwin's theory of evolution by natural selection has been profoundly influential among scientists and others on both sides of the Atlantic from the time of its introduction; throughout its history, Americans have contributed to the theory's development and to its uses beyond science. An American botanist, Asa Gray, was among the select group of naturalists with whom Darwin corresponded about his work even prior to his decision to publish his theory. Copies of *On the Origin of Species* were circulating in American cities before the end of 1859, the year of its publication in Britain, and American naturalists were quick to engage in debates over the theory's meaning and implications. For the most part, working naturalists in America were enthusiastic about the general idea of organic evolution; while many wanted to maintain a place for divine influence in the case of human development, they welcomed a scientific account of the origin of species that was grounded in Darwin's careful observations and naturalistic mechanisms. Americans contributed some very significant evidence in support of Darwin's work. In addition to Gray's botanical studies, the paleontologist O. C. Marsh presented fossil discoveries of dinosaurs and of a developmental series of horse skeletons that provided Darwin's defenders with some of their favorite and most compelling arguments.

The Development of a Scientific Consensus for Natural Selection

Despite this generally enthusiastic reception of Darwin's work by American naturalists, very few if any actually embraced his theory in all its details. Darwin's proposed mechanism of evolution—natural selection—seemed even to many of his supporters to be inadequate to describe fully the development of life on earth. Some, like Asa Gray, suggested that divine intervention had guided the production of variations in individuals. Others argued that external environmental factors were the source of most variations, an idea that Darwin himself increasingly embraced, although he continued to argue that its influence was slight compared to that of natural selection. The ortho-genticists remained largely unchallenged among the community of evolutionists until the 1880s, when a more rigorous debate about the mechanisms of evolution broke out. While the ortho-geneticists sought to retain some role for the inheritance of acquired characteristics, aggressive neo-Darwinians cited laboratory experiments and other evidence to support their position that natural selection alone drove the evolution of species because the inheritance of acquired characters was impossible.

Understanding the mechanisms of evolution continued to be a difficult problem after 1900. Darwin had provided no convincing account of how characteristics passed from one generation to another, and without one, arguments against Larmackism and other variant accounts of evolution remained less than invincible. But the rediscovery of Gregor Mendel's identification of units of heredity (genes) pointed scientists in a productive direction for finally giving the theory of evolution an appropriate mechanism to support natural selection. Bringing together these two theories—evolution and genetics—was a formidable scientific challenge. American scientists were very important to the development over several decades of what came to be known as the "modern synthesis" of genetics and evolutionary theory. Among the most significant contributors to the modern synthesis were the population biologist Sewall Wright, who during a long career at the University of Chicago helped to develop a theoretical framework to integrate genetics with natural selection. Another American, the Russian-born Theodosius Dobzhansky, wrote the first widely influential book on the synthesis, *Genetics and the Origin of Species* (1937). Dobzhansky's work grew in part out of his collaboration with the pioneering genetics experiments with fruit flies undertaken at Columbia University under the leadership of Thomas Hunt Morgan. Wright and Dobzhansky were two among many important American scientists who developed and continued to refine Darwinian evolutionary theory through the twentieth century.

Social and Philosophical Applications of Evolutionary Theory

Darwin's theory of evolution by natural selection proved compelling to those studying social and philosophical developments as well. This affinity between the general Darwinian idea of evolution of life and social thought followed nearly immediately on the heels of Darwin's publication. In England, the work of Herbert Spencer on so-called Social Darwinism linked the notion of survival of the fittest to a particular model of industrialized society. In the United States, perhaps the strongest influence of evolutionism upon a field outside science can be seen in the development of pragmatism, an American philosophical movement that made great use of the insights of evolutionary theory. Pragmatism emphasized the importance of change and experience to understanding reality, in contrast with idealist accounts that emphasized eternal or essential qualities. By accepting that reality itself is plastic and malleable, the pragmatists saw knowledge as an instrument to help humans adapt to and use the world around them. Change, experience, particularity: all of these concepts came out of Darwinian evolutionary theory, as did the idea that life is a struggle of an individual within his environment. Evolutionism inspired the pragmatist philosophers to develop a philosophical system that was consonant with the leading science of the day and that promised a "modern" alternative to the static idealism of the past.

Academic philosophy was not the only area where Darwinism influenced American thought. Ideas and concepts connected, sometimes loosely, with evolutionism were incorporated into social and political agendas during the first decades of the twentieth century. One area where evolutionary concepts were abused in a policy setting was the immigration debate that took place in Congress following World War I. Opponents of immigration adopted the language of evolution to describe immigrants from eastern Europe and other unpopular regions as "unfit" and therefore a threat to the future survival of the American population should they arrive and dilute the superior resident stock. They backed up their claims with evidence from mental and physical exams that had in most cases themselves been designed with these same biases in place. Similar arguments were mounted in defense of various eugenic policies adopted in the United States during the 1920s and 1930s. For example, a number of states adopted policies legalizing the sterilization of female criminals and mental patients on the grounds that their children could only be a detriment to the population. Similarly, antimiscegenation laws were said to protect against a weakening of the races through maladaptive mixing. The idea of evolutionism and in particular the bowdlerized notion of "survival of the fittest" that so often dominated popular explanations of Darwinism were thus very influential in American social thought and policy, although the actual connections between evolutionary theory and these uses was usually quite tenuous.

Opposition to Evolutionism

While some American thinkers found the ideas of evolution irresistible and widely applicable, others found them to be frightening and dangerous. For conservative Christians, the concept of organic evolution was an unacceptable one as it contradicted the account of the origin of life given in the Bible. While many Christians found ways to read the biblical account of life's origins that could accommodate the concepts of evolution (for example, to consider that the days referred to in Genesis may have represented very long periods of actual time), fundamentalists insisted that the Bible be read literally. With no room for compromise, the conflict between fundamentalist Christians and evolutionists grew intense and has from time to time erupted into widely publicized struggles for control over the teaching of the history of life in America's schools. An early episode in the battle between "creationists" and evolutionists was the notorious Scopes trial in 1925, when a Tennessee teacher was found guilty of violating that state's new law against the teaching of evolution. For several decades creationists had little influence or respect; then, beginning in the 1970s and continuing into the next century, they discovered that by presenting creationism as being based on scientific principles (although the science was dubious), they could make some strategic progress. Concepts such as "scientific creationism," which tried to challenge the facts of evolution such as the fossil record and radiological dating practices, and "intelligent design," which resurrected the nineteenth-century argument that complex structures such as eyes could not have arisen from chance variation, were used to challenge the principle that evolutionary theory alone deserved to be presented in textbooks and classrooms. Creationists argued for balanced treatment of their theories alongside evolution, and paradoxically suggested that to do otherwise was to ignore the basic scientific practice of considering competing theories on a subject.

American scientists have been important to the development of evolutionary theory since Darwin's day, and American philosophers and social scientists have made use of the theory directly and as a model for many important developments in their own fields. On the other hand, the theory receives strangely circumspect treatment from the general public. The tenacious debates between creationists and scientists have left their mark on textbooks and classrooms, where the treatment of evolution is far less rigorous than it would be in the absence of controversy. Despite its universal endorsement by scientists, the public treats evolution skeptically, with polls showing that only about half the population accepts the theory without reservation. These numbers reveal that a reluctance to embrace evolutionism by Americans extends well beyond the community of fundamentalist Christians. More than any other scientific theory, evolutionism has invited Americans to form their own opinions about its validity—a unique and intriguing response of culture to science.

BIBLIOGRAPHY

Glick, Thomas F. *The Comparative Reception of Darwinism.* Austin: University of Texas Press, 1974.

Gould, Stephen Jay. *Ever since Darwin: Reflections in Natural History.* New York: Norton, 1977.

Moore, James R. *The Post-Darwinian Controversies: A Study of the Protestant Struggle to Come to Terms with Darwin in Great Britain and America, 1870–1900.* Cambridge, U.K.: Cambridge University Press, 1979.

Numbers, Ronald L. *Darwinism Comes to America.* Cambridge, Mass.: Harvard University Press, 1998.

Loren Butler Feffer

See also **Creationism; Genetics; Pragmatism; Scopes Trial; Social Darwinism.**

EX PARTE BOLLMAN (1807), a case in which the Supreme Court upheld its power to issue a writ of habeas corpus to review a commitment by an inferior federal court and upon hearing ordered the release of two petitioners held on charges of treason as participants in the Burr conspiracy. Justus Erich Bollman and Samuel Swartwout, by separate routes, had carried copies of a letter in cipher from Aaron Burr to General James Wilkinson at New Orleans. Wilkinson arrested them and sent them to Washington, D.C., where they were committed for trial by the circuit court for the District of Columbia. While the case was pending in the circuit court, President Thomas Jefferson attempted unsuccessfully to induce Congress to suspend the privilege of the writ of habeas corpus. In holding that the evidence had been insufficient to support a charge of treason, Chief Justice John Marshall said for the Supreme Court, "There must be an actual assembling of men for the treasonable purpose, to constitute a levying of war." But, he added, if that be proved, then a conspirator, however remote from the scene of action, would be guilty. This dictum proved embarrassing when, a few months later, Marshall presided at the trial of Burr.

BIBLIOGRAPHY

Chapin, Bradley. *The American Law of Treason, Revolutionary and Early National Origins.* Seattle: University of Washington Press, 1964.

Faulkner, Robert K. "John Marshall and the Burr Trial." *Journal of American History* 53 (1966).

McCaleb, Walter F. *The Aaron Burr Conspiracy; and a New Light on Aaron Burr.* New York: Argosy-Antiquarian, 1966.

Charles Fairman / A. R.

See also **Levy; Spanish Conspiracy; Treason.**

EX PARTE CROW DOG, 109 U.S. 556 (1883). Following the establishment of reservations in the nineteenth century, Indian groups faced new and difficult challenges. Living as "wards" of the U.S. government, Indians experienced the unprecedented intrusion of the federal government into their everyday lives. Indian families, social relations, cultural practices, and economic subsistence patterns became targeted by institutions of the state. The legal basis for state intervention into Indian community life remained unclear, however, and when one Brule Lakota, Crow Dog, was accused and convicted of murdering another, Spotted Tail, he appealed his death sentence. ("Murder" meant something different to the Lakota than to the Euro-Americans.) Arguing that the territory governments of South Dakota lacked the jurisdiction to prosecute, try, and convict members of Indian tribes, Crow Dog's case reached the Supreme Court. Since Indian affairs fall solely in the hands of the federal government, as outlined by the U.S. Constitution and nineteenth-century Court rulings, the Supreme Court overturned Crow Dog's conviction and ruled that the territory government did not have the jurisdiction to intervene into criminal matters among Indians. As Crow Dog was released, cries for additional reform measures among Indian communities arose among Indian policy advocates. A series of Indian policy reform acts followed that located Indian crimes outside the jurisdiction of state and local governments and solely in the federal judicial system. *Ex Parte Crow Dog* reinforced the supremacy of the federal government over Indian affairs.

BIBLIOGRAPHY

Price, Monroe E. *Law and the American Indian: Readings, Notes, and Cases.* New York: Bobbs-Merrill, 1973.

Ned Blackhawk

See also **Indian Policy, U.S.**

EX PARTE GARLAND, 4 Wallace 333 (1867). In December 1860, Augustus Hill Garland, who later served as an Arkansas senator in the Confederate congress, was admitted to the federal bar. Following the Civil War, Congress enacted a new IRONCLAD OATH requiring attorneys to swear that they had neither voluntarily borne arms against the United States nor held office under a hostile government. President Andrew Johnson pardoned Garland, who then petitioned the Supreme Court to readmit him to the federal bar without taking the new oath. In *Ex Parte Garland,* a 5 to 4 Court majority held that the oath constituted both a bill of ATTAINDER and an ex post facto law, violating the U.S. Constitution in either instance.

BIBLIOGRAPHY

Fairman, Charles. *Reconstruction and Reunion, 1864–88.* Vol. 1. New York: Macmillan, 1987.

R. Volney Riser
David Y. Thomas

See also ***Cummings v. Missouri;*** **Reconstruction.**

EX PARTE McCARDLE, 7 Wallace 73 U.S. 506 (1869), is the most famous judicial acquiescence in the Radical Republican punishment of the postwar South. The Southern rebellion having ended in 1865, despotic military occupation had continued across the Southern states, and military courts afforded no civil rights under the Constitution.

William McCardle, a Natchez, Mississippi, newspaper editor, had criticized Congress and General E. O. C. Ord, the military commander of Mississippi. McCardle was tried before a military commission, which convicted him of publishing inflammatory articles. He sought habeas corpus from the circuit court, which denied it, and he appealed to the U.S. Supreme Court, seeking release through habeas corpus.

The Supreme Court had issued an opinion in 1866 strongly limiting the power of military commissions over civilians, but it had refused to hear two cases brought by states against federal officials in 1867. In December of that year, it took jurisdiction over McCardle's appeal, which was brought under an 1867 law that assured that freedman and federal officials could have federal review of unlawful arrests in state court by allowing an appeal of cases seeking habeas corpus from any federal or state court. The press, and increasingly the Congress, believed that McCardle's case would lead the Court to invalidate most of the Reconstruction statutes. While McCardle's case was being argued, Congress rushed through, over President Andrew Johnson's veto, a repeal of the 1867 law that allowed McCardle's appeal.

Chief Justice Salmon P. Chase, speaking for a unanimous Supreme Court, ruled the amendment of the statute was binding upon the Court, and the effect of the repeal was to make it as if the 1867 statute had never existed. Thus, he ruled that the Court lacked jurisdiction and McCardle's appeal was dismissed. Later that same term, Chase wrote another habeas case, *Ex Parte Yerger,* 75 U.S. 85 (1869), reasserting the courts' powers of habeas corpus under the law existing prior to 1867.

The *McCardle* opinion was both immediately and repeatedly criticized for allowing Congress to determine the outcome of cases pending before the courts, as well as for allowing the military trial of civilians. The underlying policy of not allowing military jurisdiction over American civilians was clearly resolved in *Reid v. Covert* (1946). Still, several points of Chase's opinion remain the law in force, particularly that a repeal of habeas jurisdiction applies to pending cases but that it does not affect habeas jurisdiction that existed prior to that statute.

BIBLIOGRAPHY

"Ex Parte McCardle: Judicial Impotency: The Supreme Court and Reconstruction Reconsidered." *American Historical Review* 72 (1967).

Foner, Eric. *Reconstruction, 1863–1877: America's Unfinished Revolution.* New York: Harper and Row, 1988.

Kutler, Stanley I. *Judicial Power and Reconstruction Politics.* Chicago: University of Chicago Press, 1968.

Van Alstyne, William O. "A Critical Guide to Ex Parte McCardle." *Arizona Law Review* 15 (1973).

Steve Sheppard

See also **Reconstruction.**

EX PARTE MERRYMAN, Federal Cases No. 9487 (1861), involved President Abraham Lincoln's exercise of extraordinary war powers, specifically his right to suspend habeas corpus. John Merryman, a Baltimore County secessionist, was imprisoned in Fort McHenry in Baltimore harbor by military order on 25 May 1861. The commanding officer refused to comply with a writ of habeas corpus issued by Chief Justice Roger B. Taney, on the grounds that he had been authorized by the president to suspend the writ. Taney wrote an opinion, widely denounced in the North, that the writ could be suspended constitutionally only by Congress, not by the president. Lincoln did not alter his policy.

BIBLIOGRAPHY

Swisher, Carl Brent. *Roger B. Taney.* New York: Macmillan, 1935.

Warren, Charles. *The Supreme Court in United States History.* Boston: Little, Brown, 1924. Rev. ed. Littleton, Colo.: F. B. Rothman, 1987.

Shira M. Diner
Ransom E. Noble Jr.

See also **Habeas Corpus, Writ of.**

EX PARTE MILLIGAN, 71 U.S. 2 (1866) is a landmark case that drew the constitutional perimeters of the discretionary powers of the executive over the civil rights and liberties of individual citizens and also of military authority in relation to civilian authority in times of war, insurrection, or natural disaster. During the Civil War, President Abraham Lincoln—determined to preserve the Union by "taking any measure which may subdue the enemy," that is, the Confederacy—acted as commander in chief of the armed forces of the United States to proclaim martial law and suspend habeas corpus by executive action. In 1864, a civilian activist for the Confederate cause named Lambden P. Milligan was arrested at his home in Indiana by U.S. Army officials and charged with providing "aid and comfort to rebels" and inciting the people to insurrection. He was found guilty by a military commission and sentenced to death by hanging. Milligan sought release through habeas corpus from the U.S. Circuit Court in Indianapolis, claiming that he had been deprived of his constitutional right to a trial by jury. However, the two judges failed to agree on a decision and sent the case to the U.S. Supreme Court.

In 1866, the Court unanimously invalidated Milligan's conviction on grounds emanating either from the U.S. Constitution (in the opinion of the majority of five) or from the federal Habeas Corpus Act of 1863 (in the opinion of the concurring four). Speaking for the Court, Justice David Davis—an ardent supporter of Lincoln and himself a Lincoln appointee—held that as a civilian Milligan should have been tried in a civil court as the state had not been in the theater of military operations and civil courts had been fully open, and that he had been denied his right to a trial by jury as guaranteed by the Sixth Amendment. Davis also stated that Milligan had been deprived of the constitutional privilege of a writ of habeas corpus. Davis wrote emphatically that "martial law cannot arise from a threatened invasion. The necessity must be actual and present, the invasion real, such as effectually closes the [civil] courts and deposes the civil administration." The Court further held that, absent prior congressional legislation, the chief executive was not empowered to suspend habeas corpus or impose martial law even in time of war or insurrection.

After *Milligan,* the Court in *Moyer v. Peabody* (1909) upheld trials of civilians in state military tribunals during a condition of social unrest as declared by the governor. Far more infamously, during World War II the Court upheld the violation of basic civil rights and liberties of Japanese Americans in *Hirabayashi v. United States* (1943) and *Korematsu v. United States* (1944). Nevertheless, running through *Sterling v. Constantin* (1932) and *O'Callahan v. Parker* (1969), in which the Court repeatedly subjected military discretion to judicial review by the civil courts and limited the scope of military justice, the *Milligan* principle that the Constitution reigns as the law of the land not only in peacetime but also in time of war has held in large measure.

BIBLIOGRAPHY

Duker, William F. *A Constitutional History of Habeas Corpus.* Westport, Conn.: Greenwood Press, 1980.

Hyman, Harold M., and William M. Wiecek. *Equal Justice under Law: Constitutional Development, 1835–1875.* New York: Harper and Row, 1982.

Kutler, Stanley I. *Judicial Power and Reconstruction Politics*. Chicago: University of Chicago Press, 1968.

David Park

See also **Arrest, Arbitrary, During the Civil War; Habeas Corpus, Writ of; Japanese American Incarceration; Martial Law.**

EXCESS PROFITS TAX. The Excess Profits Tax, a predominantly wartime fiscal instrument, was designed primarily to capture wartime profits that exceeded normal peacetime profits. In 1863 the Confederate congress and the state of Georgia experimented with excess profits taxes. The first effective national excess profits tax was enacted in 1917, with rates graduated from 20 to 60 percent on the profits of all businesses in excess of prewar earnings but not less than 7 percent or more than 9 percent of invested capital. In 1918 a national law limited the tax to corporations and increased the rates. Concurrent with this 1918 tax, the federal government imposed, for the year 1918 only, an alternative tax, ranging up to 80 percent, with the taxpayer paying whichever was higher. In 1921 the excess profits tax was repealed despite powerful attempts to make it permanent. In 1933 and 1935 Congress enacted two mild excess profits taxes as supplements to a capital stock tax.

The crisis of World War II led Congress to pass four excess profits statutes between 1940 and 1943. The 1940 rates ranged from 25 to 50 percent and the 1941 ones from 35 to 60 percent. In 1942 a flat rate of 90 percent was adopted, with a postwar refund of 10 percent; in 1943 the rate was increased to 95 percent, with a 10 percent refund. Congress gave corporations two alternative excess profits tax credit choices: either 95 percent of average earnings for 1936–1939 or an invested capital credit, initially 8 percent of capital but later graduated from 5 to 8 percent. In 1945 Congress repealed the tax, effective 1 January 1946. The Korean War induced Congress to reimpose an excess profits tax, effective from 1 July 1950 to 31 December 1953. The tax rate was 30 percent of excess profits, with a 70 percent ceiling for the combined corporation and excess profits taxes. In 1991 some members of Congress sought unsuccessfully to pass an excess profits tax of 40 percent upon the larger oil companies as part of energy policy.

Some social reformers have championed a peacetime use of the excess profits tax, but such proposals face strong opposition from businesses and some economists, who argue that it would create a disincentive to capital investment. George W. Bush, elected president in 2000, had close ties to the energy industry and did not favor such taxes. Whatever the peacetime policy, it remains to be seen whether excess profits taxes will reappear during the "war on terrorism" that the U.S. government launched after the 11 September 2001 attacks on the United States.

BIBLIOGRAPHY

Brandes, Stuart D. *Warhogs: A History of War Profits in America*. Lexington: University Press of Kentucky, 1997.

Lent, George E. "Excess-Profits Taxation in the United States." *Journal of Political Economy* (1951).

——— "The Excess Profits Tax and Business Expenditures." *National Tax Journal* (1958).

Sidney Ratner / D. B.

See also **Capitalism; Government Regulation of Business; Keynesianism; Profiteering; Supply-Side Economics; Taxation; War Industries Board.**

EXCHANGE, BILLS OF. The most common and yet most complex form of negotiable instrument used for business transactions is known as the draft, or the bill of exchange. A bill of exchange can be used for payment, credit, or security in a financial transaction. The term comes from the English and is defined as an unconditional order in writing that is addressed by one person to another and signed by the person giving it. Bills of exchange, also referred to as commercial bills, were initially developed in inland trade by merchants who wished to resell goods before making a payment on them. Later they came to be used as a type of IOU in international trade.

In a bill of exchange transaction, a person, or the drawer, agrees to pay to another, also known as the drawee, a sum of money at a given date, usually three months ahead. In principle, the bill of exchange operates much a like a postdated check in that it can be endorsed for payment to the bearer or any other person named other than the drawee.

If the person accepts the bill of exchange by signing his name, or his name with the word "accepted," across the face of the paper, he is called an acceptor. The person to whom a bill is transferred by the acceptor's endorsement is called the endorsee. Any person in possession of a bill, whether as payee, endorsee, or bearer, is termed a holder. The basic rule applying to bills of exchange is that any signature appearing on a bill obligates the signer to pay the specified amount drawn on the bill.

The bill of exchange then must be accepted or "endorsed" by an accepting house, an institution that deals exclusively with bills of exchange, such as a bank, or a trader. Once the bill is accepted, the drawee does not have to wait for the bill to mature before receiving his funds. If he so chooses, the drawee can also sell the bill on the money market for a small discount.

A bill of exchange can also be passed beyond the drawer, drawee, and creditor. For the purposes of payment or borrowing, the creditor may transfer the bill of exchange to a fourth party, who in turn may pass it on and on through endorsement or signature of the transferor. Endorsement transfers the rights of the endorser to the new holder and also creates a liability of the endorser for payment of the amount of the draft if the drawee does not meet payment when the draft is due. A failure to pay a draft must be more or less formally recognized, and the draft holder may claim payment from any endorser whose signature appears on the instrument.

In English laws, bills of exchange were defined in the Bills of Exchange Act of 1882. The act later influenced American legislation, particularly the passage of the United States Negotiable Instruments Act, which was eventually adopted throughout the United States. However, English law of what constitutes a bill of exchange is somewhat different than bills of exchange laws in Europe and Asia. In 1988, the United Nations Commission on International Trade Law (UNCITRAL) began working to synchronize these laws through the "United Nations Convention on International Bills of Exchange and International Promissory notes." With the development of other means of credit, the use of bills of exchange has declined.

BIBLIOGRAPHY

Hedley, William. *Bills of Exchange and Bankers' Documentary Credits.* London: LLP, 1997.

Jahn, Uwe. *Bills of Exchange: A Guide to Legislation in European Countries, Asia and Oceania.* Paris: ICC Publishing, 1999.

Meg Greene Malvasi

See also **Banking: Overview; Credit.**

EXCHANGE STUDENTS. Colonial Americans (particularly those studying medicine) studied in Britain, Ireland, the Netherlands, Italy, Germany, and Sweden. During the early years of the Republic, George Washington, Thomas Jefferson, and Noah Webster—along with the Georgia and Virginia legislatures—opposed study abroad, but young Americans enrolled in European universities for medical and graduate studies nonetheless. These American exchange students and their nineteenth-century successors brought back not only German doctorates, but also German ideas for raising the standards of higher education and promoting academic freedom. Among this group were men who became influential university presidents: Henry P. Tappan (Michigan), Charles W. Eliot (Harvard), Daniel C. Gilman (Johns Hopkins), Andrew D. White (Cornell), Granville S. Hall (Clark), and Nicholas Murray Butler (Columbia). During the twentieth century, attendance by Americans in European universities increased greatly under the stimulation of the Rhodes scholarships and the Fulbright (later Fulbright-Hays) exchange program enacted by Congress in 1946.

Foreign study in American institutions began with the enrollment of Francisco Miranda, the future liberator of Venezuela, at Yale (1784). Yung Wing from China studied at Yale in the 1850s, and Jo Niishiwa from Japan at Amherst in the 1860s. In 1904, 2,673 men and women from seventy-four countries were enrolled in American higher institutions. The Boxer Indemnity Fund, established by the American government in 1908 to generate income to be used to educate Chinese youths, brought many Chinese to American universities. With the emergence of the United States on the international scene, foreign enrollment rose to 6,901 (1921) and to a high of 7,343 (1937) prior to World War II. Under the Fulbright and the Fulbright-Hays (1961) Acts, the number of foreign students in the United States increased sharply. In 1958, 47,245 students from 131 countries were in American institutions; 1972 saw 140,126 students from 175 countries enrolled in 1,650 institutions. In 1980, 311,880 foreign students studied in the United States. In 1990, that number had risen to 407,530, and, in 1999, it had risen again to 514,723. In 1972, most students came from (in descending order) India, Canada, Hong Kong, Taiwan, Iran, Thailand, Korea, and the United Kingdom. By 1980, that distribution had changed dramatically, with most students coming from (in descending order) Iran, Taiwan, Nigeria, Canada, Japan, Venezuela, Saudi Arabia, and Hong Kong. By 1999, the distribution had shifted again, with most students coming from (in descending order) China, Japan, India, Korea, Taiwan, Canada, Indonesia, Thailand, and Mexico.

BIBLIOGRAPHY

Barber, Elinor, Philip G. Altbach, and Robert G. Myers, eds. *Bridges to Knowledge: Foreign Students in Comparative Perspective.* Chicago: University of Chicago Press, 1984.

Blumenthal, Peggy, ed. *Academic Mobility in a Changing World: Regional and Global Trends.* Bristol, Pa.: Jessica Kingsley Publishers, 1996.

Dudden, Arthur P., and Russell R. Dynes, eds. *The Fulbright Experience, 1946–1986: Encounters and Transformations.* New Brunswick, N.J.: Transaction Books, 1987.

Johnson, Walter, and Francis J. Colligan. *The Fulbright Program: A History.* Chicago: University of Chicago Press, 1965.

Kraske, Gary. *Missionaries of the Book: The American Library Profession and the Origins of United States Cultural Diplomacy.* Westport, Conn.: Greenwood Press, 1985.

William W. Brickman / F. B.

See also **Education; Education, Higher: Colleges and Universities; Fulbright Act and Grants; Indemnities; Multiculturalism.**

EXCHANGES are firms that have established markets in some type of financial product. They facilitate the buying and selling of different forms of property. Financial markets have a long history beginning with informal markets during the Middle Ages. Traders often met in informal settings to buy and sell crops, clothing, and even land. Markets later expanded to include paper securities such as stocks and bonds.

The emergence of nation-states in the seventeenth and eighteenth centuries facilitated the development of exchanges. One of the earliest financial revolutions in modern Europe was created by the wartime demands of Emperor Charles V and the Habsburg Netherlands in 1542. The monarch used the Amsterdam exchange to issue and sell debt. In this fashion, governments were able to raise capital to finance wars. Secondary markets for government obligations eventually expanded to include stock and bond issues by quasi-governmental companies as well as joint-stock companies. The Dutch and British East India Companies, for example, used capital markets to finance trade around the globe and expand capitalism.

Early American Exchanges

Securities trading in the United States began with the redemption of government bonds following the American Revolution. Trading was eventually sufficient that brokers and dealers also began to specialize in buying and selling bonds and securities issued by public companies. Some of these brokers signed an agreement on 17 May 1792 in New York City to set minimum commission rates. This so-called Buttonwood Tree Agreement is generally considered to be the founding of the New York Stock Exchange.

New York City brokers established a more formal structure for trading following the War of 1812. Dealers created the New York Exchange Board in 1817 and agreed on a constitution that provided for the annual election of a president and secretary. Years later, the board changed its name to the New York Stock Exchange (NYSE) and in 1863 constructed its own building. Six years later the NYSE merged with a rival, the Open Board of Brokers. The new NYSE delegated power to a central governing committee that retained the right to discipline and expel exchange members.

The Multiplication of Exchanges

In the mid-to-late nineteenth century, stock exchanges also formed in most large American cities to raise capital for local companies. Vibrant exchanges emerged in Boston, Philadelphia, San Francisco, Los Angeles, Baltimore, and many other cities. By 1890, there were approximately one hundred regional exchanges. The scope of exchanges also expanded. The Chicago Board of Trade, formed in 1848, provided a commodity market for midwestern farmers. Produce and cotton exchanges emerged in New York City to deal exclusively in produce and cotton. Markets for sugar, coffee, and even eggs and butter emerged to trade specialized goods. The introduction of futures and options contracts on these exchanges allowed investors to hedge their risks in financial markets.

Technological advances, however, limited the growth of regional exchanges. The telegraph and telephone facilitated the flow of information, aiding in the integration of securities markets and spurring the rapid growth of national exchanges. By the late nineteenth century, the New York Stock Exchange had emerged as the leading market in American securities. The Big Board accounted for nearly 70 percent of all stock transactions carried out on organized exchanges. The curb market, which began in the 1790s and was the precursor to the American Stock Exchange (AMEX), assumed a greater roll on Wall Street in the early 1900s to provide additional trading in emerging national companies. The Chicago Board of Trade assumed a similar and dominant role in commodity markets.

Technological change also fostered competition between stock exchanges. The Consolidated Stock Exchange of New York, formed by a merger between the Mining Stock Exchange and the Petroleum Exchange, emerged as a competitor to the NYSE in 1885. The Consolidated decided to compete head-to-head with the NYSE by trading leading railroad and industrial securities. The Consolidated used the telegraph to transmit quotes from the NYSE to its own trading floor. By the early 1890s, share volume on the Consolidated averaged approximately 50 percent of NYSE volume.

The Big Board challenged the Consolidated's practice of "stealing" NYSE price quotes. A twenty-year court battle ensued between the two exchanges over ownership of price quotations in security markets. The courts ultimately decided that price quotes were private property and that the NYSE was not obligated to supply them to its competitors. The ruling affirmed the dominance of the NYSE and played an important role in the demise of the Consolidated Stock Exchange. Nevertheless, the Little Board provided the NYSE with a rivalry unprecedented in the history of American markets.

Regulation

Except for some key court decisions, securities markets were largely self-regulated before World War I. Exchanges were responsible for establishing and enforcing rules and regulations for their members as well as setting commission rates on transactions and it was generally felt that this was the way it should be. Commodity markets, however, were an exception. Concerns over insider trading, wash sales, and the manipulation of futures trading prompted the regulation of commodity exchanges. Congress passed legislation in the late 1910s and early 1920s to regulate futures trading in grain and cotton.

The stock market crash of 1929 and the Great Depression prompted regulation of the banking and financial sectors. Many felt that the close links between commercial banking and the marketing of corporate securities exacerbated the country's economic downturn. In 1933 Congress passed the GLASS-STEAGALL ACT (Banking Act), which separated the activities of commercial and investment banks. The government authorized the Federal Reserve to set margin requirements, the amount of capital required to purchase securities on credit. Congress also passed the Securities Act in 1933 and the Securities Exchange Act in 1934. The 1934 legislation created the Securities and Exchange Commission, a regulatory body that established uniform accounting standards and tighter listing requirements and monitors trading activity on registered exchanges.

Regional Exchanges versus the Principal Exchanges

Government regulation following the crash of 1929 significantly affected the role of regional exchanges. The Securities Exchange Act raised listing standards, especially for regional exchanges since relatively low-profit companies traded on local markets. Higher standards further eroded business on regional exchanges by inducing smaller firms to trade on the unregulated over-the-counter market.

Although the SEC initially drove business away from regional exchanges, subsequent legislation helped the regional stock exchanges compete for business with the NYSE. Congress amended the Securities and Exchange Act in 1936 to allow registered exchanges to trade listed securities as unlisted provided there was an active market for the security on a principal exchange, the NYSE or the AMEX. The provision allowed struggling regional exchanges to trade NYSE-listed stocks.

The amendment introduced competition between regional and national—the NYSE and AMEX—equity markets. In response, the NYSE created a special committee to investigate the practice by which its members traded on multiple exchanges. On 28 February 1940, the committee proposed that the NYSE enforce the provision of its constitution that prohibited members from multiple exchange trading on pain of expulsion or suspension. On 12 July 1940, the NYSE voted to begin enforcing the multiple trading rule after 1 September 1940.

The SEC opposed the Big Board's decision to restrict its members from engaging in multiple exchange trading. Federal regulators had requested the NYSE to rescind the rule on two separate occasions late in 1939. The NYSE refused in both instances, prompting the SEC to hold hearings in January 1941 to investigate the practice of multiple exchange trading. Presidents of several regional exchanges testified about the likely effects of such a rule. The president of the Boston Exchange argued that prohibiting multiple exchange trading would cause 25 percent of their dually listed securities with the NYSE to be without a dealer. Representatives from the Pittsburgh and Cincinnati Exchanges believed that the provision threatened their very existence. The SEC ultimately ruled in favor of the regionals and forced the NYSE to abrogate its prohibition by October 1941.

Regulatory decisions by the SEC, along with technological advances, changed the business practices of regional exchanges as they began to compete head-to-head with the Big Board for business. Listings on regional exchanges began to decline as these markets began trading NYSE-listed stocks. In 1938, regional exchanges accounted for 37 percent of listings on registered exchanges, slightly more than either the NYSE or AMEX. By 1995, regional listings represented less than 10 percent of the total listings on regional exchanges. Regional stock exchanges also introduced new business procedures and even extended trading hours. They gave rebates, expanded membership, and used other means to attract business away from the NYSE.

Head-to-head competition between regional and national markets also led to mergers among regional exchanges. The Midwest Stock Exchange was created in December 1949 following the merger of the Chicago, Cleveland, and St. Louis Stock Exchanges. New Orleans joined the Midwest Exchange in 1959. The Los Angeles and San Francisco Exchanges merged to form the Pacific Stock Exchange in January 1957. Philadelphia and Baltimore consolidated to create the Philadelphia-Baltimore Exchange in March 1948. Washington and Pittsburgh joined the merger in 1953 and 1969, respectively, making it the Philadelphia-Baltimore-Washington Exchange. From 1940 to 2001, the number of regional exchanges fell from eighteen to five. Mergers allowed regional exchanges to capture market share at the expense of the NYSE during the last half of the twentieth century. Regional market share increased from 5 percent of transactions on registered exchanges in 1934 to nearly 15 percent by the end of the century. Mergers appear to be one more example of a competitive device employed by regional markets to compete with the NYSE.

New Regulation, Technological Advances, and Internationalization

The 1970s ushered in a new era of regulation and technological advances. The Securities and Exchange Commission forced the NYSE to deregulate commissions to encourage greater competition in financial markets. Congress created the Commodities Futures Trading Commission (CFTC) to oversee the regulation of futures markets. Exchanges introduced new financial products such as derivatives and new option products to give investors greater ability to hedge their risks. A national computerized trading system was also introduced.

The last two decades of the twentieth century have seen the internationalization of securities markets. More than ever before, American exchanges operate in a global marketplace. Political and economic liberalization in many countries, along with advances in computer and telephone technology, have led to greater integration among world markets. It appears that this trend will continue as long as information costs continue to decline.

Since the American Revolution, U.S. markets have experienced tremendous changes brought on by technology, economic conditions, and political influences. Markets grew in importance during the nineteenth and early twentieth centuries with American industrialization and pathbreaking technological changes. The importance of markets waned during the interwar years and the first few decades following World War II. By the end of the twentieth century, however, American markets had reemerged and taken on a larger importance in the economy and society. Computerized trading systems and the nearly instantaneous flow of information have permanently changed the nature of markets. American exchanges operate in a global marketplace and compete for business with leading markets around the world.

BIBLIOGRAPHY

Arnold, Tom, Philip Hersch, J. Harold Mulherin, and Jeffrey Netter. "Merging Markets." *Journal of Finance* 54 (1999): 1083–1107.

Doede, Robert W. "The Monopoly Power of the New York Stock Exchange." Ph.D. diss., University of Chicago, 1967.

Garvy, George. "Rivals and Interlopers in the History of the New York Security Market." *Journal of Political Economy* 52, no. 2 (June 1944): 128–143.

Jarrell, Greg A. "Change at the Exchange: The Causes and Effects of Deregulation." *Journal of Law and Economics* 27 (1984): 273–312.

Neal, Larry. *The Rise of Financial Capitalism: International Capital Markets in the Age of Reason.* Cambridge, U.K.: Cambridge University Press, 1990.

Sobel, Robert. *Amex: A History of the American Stock Exchange, 1921–1971.* New York: Weybright and Talley, 1972.

———. *N.Y.S.E.: A History of the New York Stock Exchange.* New York: Weybright and Talley, 1975.

Stigler, George J. "Public Regulation of the Securities Markets." *Journal of Business* 37 (1964): 117–142.

Marc D. Weidenmier

See also **Commodity Exchanges; Stock Market; Stocks.**

EXECUTIVE AGENT, an individual appointed by a U.S. president to conduct negotiations with foreign countries on special terms and without Senate confirmation. Executive agents are assigned such tasks as establishing diplomatic relations with new countries, conversing with governments with which official relations have been broken, and negotiating special treaties and agreements. Usually confidantes of the presidents who appointed them, agents work outside of normal diplomatic channels and thereby give the presidents direct control of and access to the diplomatic process. Although such agents lack explicit constitutional sanction, Congress usually has acknowledged that presidents need them to conduct effective diplomacy.

President George Washington appointed the first executive agent in 1790, when he asked Gouverneur Morris to represent him personally in negotiations with Britain on trade and territorial issues. Most presidents have followed Washington's model. In 1847, for example, President James K. Polk appointed Nicholas Trist, chief clerk in the State Department, to negotiate a peace treaty with Mexico. From 1914 to 1916, President Woodrow Wilson dispatched Edward M. House to various cities in Europe to seek a settlement to World War I. In 1969–1973, President Richard M. Nixon sent National Security Adviser Henry Kissinger on secret missions to China and elsewhere to conduct diplomacy beyond the purview of the State Department and Congress.

BIBLIOGRAPHY

Plischke, Elmer. *U.S. Department of State: A Reference History.* Westport, Conn.: Greenwood Press, 1999.

Wriston, Henry M. *Executive Agents in American Foreign Relations.* Baltimore: Johns Hopkins University Press, 1967.

Peter L. Hahn

See also **Diplomacy, Secret; State, Department of.**

EXECUTIVE AGREEMENTS, a term signifying international agreements concluded by the president, as distinguished from treaties, which can be ratified by the president only with consent of the Senate. In international usage they are often called "treaties in simplified form," whether embodied in one text or in an exchange of notes. Executive agreements are as effective as formal treaties in conferring rights and obligations under international law. The Constitution mentions them obliquely as "agreements" or "compacts," without specifying limitations as to procedure, form, or substance. Early suppositions that they bind only the administration that concludes them, or that their use must be confined to routine matters, have been negated by practice. Although executive agreements are usually administrative agreements that implement policies already determined, there are many that have determined significant policies—for example, the Rush-Bagot Agreement (1817) limiting armament on the Great Lakes; the exchange of notes enunciating the Open Door policy in China (1899, 1900); the Boxer Protocol (1901); the Gentlemen's Agreement (1907) on Japanese immigration; the Lansing-Ishii Agreement (1917) on Japanese interests in China; the armistices after the Revolution, the Spanish-American War, and the two world wars; the Atlantic Charter (1941); and the Moscow, Teheran, Yalta, and Potsdam agreements during World War II (1943, 1945).

Although concluded by the president, most executive agreements have congressional authorization or approval. They can be classified according to whether they are (1) based on prior legislation; (2) implemented by subsequent legislation; (3) based on prior treaties; (4) based on prior treaties and implemented by legislation; (5) made under the president's constitutional powers; or (6) based in part on presidential powers and in part on legislation or treaty. Because of the rapid escalation of their use, critics contend that executive agreements have been employed instead of treaties to avoid submission to the Senate. Their increased use is mainly a response to expanding international administrative requirements in implementing policies otherwise determined with respect to international mail, civil aviation, mutual aid settlements and surplus property disposal ending wartime aid to allies, trade and tariff agreements, economic development, military assistance, cooperative agricultural and educational programs, international arbitration, and international telecommunications.

The debate over the president's executive authority in foreign affairs intensified in the late twentieth century, particularly in regard to the use of American military forces abroad. The controversial military intervention in

Vietnam in the 1960s and 1970s inspired Congress to take a more active role in foreign affairs, a step that increased friction with the White House. For example, during the 1980s the Reagan administration defied Congress by covertly sending aid to the Nicaraguan Contras, a policy later exposed in the Iran-Contra scandal. In the early 1990s the Bush administration committed American forces to the defense of Saudi Arabia without submitting the matter to a vote in Congress. Only on the eve of war with Iraq in January 1991 did the administration seek official congressional approval for the use of force. The ambiguous nature of presidential and congressional responsibilities in international affairs seems likely to remain a source of debate and controversy in American foreign policy.

BIBLIOGRAPHY

DeConde, Alexander. *Presidential Machismo: Executive Authority, Military Intervention, and Foreign Relations.* Boston: Northeastern University Press, 2000.

Margolis, Lawrence. *Executive Agreements and Presidential Power in Foreign Policy.* New York: Praeger, 1985.

Mayer, Kenneth R. *With the Stroke of a Pen: Executive Orders and Presidential Power.* Princeton, N.J.: Princeton University Press, 2001.

Anthony Gaughan
C. H. McLaughlin

See also **Bricker Amendment; Confirmation by the Senate; Treaties, Commercial; Treaties, Negotiation and Ratification of.**

EXECUTIVE ORDERS. Originally, executive orders based their legitimacy on Article II, Section 3 of the U.S. Constitution, which contains the phrase "he [the President of the United States] shall take Care that the Laws be faithfully executed." This phrase was interpreted as a management tool, a way for the president to enforce Congress's wishes. Almost immediately, presidents tried to widen the scope of the short phrase. For instance, George Washington proclaimed a "neutrality order" that declared that Americans must not be involved in disputes between foreign countries; this was not the execution of a law but the creation of a law.

Even though they chafed under the constitutional restriction in Article II, presidents found ways to abide by its spirit until the presidency of Andrew Jackson (1829–1837). Perhaps the most controversial of Jackson's actions was to order the forcible removal of the Cherokees from their homes in Georgia and North Carolina to the Oklahoma Territory.

At the outbreak of the U.S. Civil War in 1861, Congress granted President Abraham Lincoln wide latitude in running the government. Although Lincoln overstepped constitutional boundaries, by and large Lincoln's executive orders were upheld in federal courts because of the national crisis. It was Lincoln who began numbering executive orders, with number 1 being signed on 20 October 1862.

In the 1880s another form of executive order was created, in addition to the constitutional one: in civil service legislation, Congress said that it was up to the president to fill in the details of implementing the legislation. Thus, an executive order could depend on the president's interpretation of the legislation, and it would have the force of law. President Franklin D. Roosevelt was also allowed great latitude with executive orders during the Great Depression and World War II. By FDR's time a president could seize property and control communication. FDR used these powers to order the internment of Japanese subjects and Japanese Americans who lived in the Pacific states.

By President Richard Nixon's era (1969–1974), Congress had left enough holes in legislation for presidents to make executive orders in peacetime that had far-reaching effects on America. Nixon used executive orders to implement affirmative action, including declaring ethnic quotas on hiring and in the awarding of government contracts.

President Bill Clinton used executive orders to circumvent a hostile Congress on issues such as environmental laws. His most controversial order, with incalculable consequences, was probably Executive Order 13083 on 14 May 1998 "establishing the principles and foundations of federalism," which grants the federal government powers forbidden by the Tenth Amendment of the Constitution. Executive orders become laws when published in the FEDERAL REGISTER, as this one was on 18 May 1998.

BIBLIOGRAPHY

Clinton, Bill. "Executive Order 13083—Federalism." *Weekly Compilation of Presidential Documents* 34, no. 20 (1998): 866–869.

Mayer, Kenneth R. *With the Stroke of a Pen: Executive Orders and Presidential Power.* Princeton, NJ: Princeton University Press, 2001.

McDonald, Forrest. *The American Presidency: An Intellectual History.* Lawrence: University Press of Kansas, 1995.

Murray, Frank J. "Critics Claim Exec Orders Permit Government by Fiat." *Insight on the News* 15, no. 36 (1999): 31.

Shafroth, Frank. "Cities & States Gain Respect in Senate." *Nation's Cities Weekly* 21, no. 30 (1998): 1–2.

Kirk H. Beetz

EXECUTIVE PRIVILEGE, refers to the right of the executive branch to withhold information from Congress or the judiciary. Although presidents and executive cabinet members often assert a right to executive privilege, this right does not explicitly appear within the text of the U.S. Constitution. Nevertheless, members of the executive branch have claimed that executive privilege is an implied power under Article II and that it is consistent with the principle of SEPARATION OF POWERS.

The first assertions of executive privilege occurred during the presidency of George Washington. In 1792 the House of Representatives requested information from the Washington administration concerning the military defeat of Major General Arthur St. Clair. Even though the Washington administration did give the requested papers to the House, Washington asserted he had the right to refuse to disclose information that would be harmful to the public. Thus even though Washington cooperated, he set the precedent that at certain times presidents could withhold information.

In 1796 Washington refused to provide the House with requested information concerning the Jay Treaty, pointing out that the House does not play a constitutional role in the treaty-making process. Washington noted, however, that if the House had requested information concerning an impeachment, he would be required to supply such information to the House because of its constitutional responsibilities in the impeachment process.

The federal judiciary had its first opportunity to offer its understanding of executive privilege in *United States v. Burr* (1807). The case raised the question of whether or not a federal court could require the president to hand over documents to be used in a trial, that is, issue a subpoena. Chief Justice John Marshall ruled that federal courts had the right to issue subpoenas to presidents.

Even though the judiciary recognized that the executive branch is not above the law, Supreme Court justices noted in *United States v. Reynolds* (1953) that presidents might be able to withhold from the public information concerning military and foreign relations to protect national security. However, the Court believed a president did not possess an absolute right to executive privilege simply through the claim that national security interests were at stake.

The limited nature of executive privilege was expressed again in the landmark case of *United States v. Nixon* (1974). President Richard Nixon refused to comply with a subpoena requiring him to hand over to a federal court audiotapes that were believed to offer evidence on the executive branch's alleged involvement in the 1972 WATERGATE break-in. Nixon argued that he had the right to withhold the material to protect the privacy of his communications with his advisers. In a unanimous opinion the Supreme Court recognized that a constitutional right to executive privilege did exist. However, the Court rejected Nixon's claims and required him to produce the tapes for evidence in the investigation. Chief Justice Warren Burger explained that the president was entitled to great deference, particularly on issues of national security. Nonetheless, he emphasized that such deference was conditional and dependent on circumstance. While Nixon argued separation of powers allowed for executive privilege, the justices noted that the system of checks and balances prohibited any absolute claims of executive privilege.

BIBLIOGRAPHY

Berger, Raoul. *Executive Privilege: A Constitutional Myth.* Cambridge, Mass.: Harvard University Press, 1974.

Breckenridge, Adam Carlyle. *The Executive Privilege: Presidential Control over Information.* Lincoln: University of Nebraska Press, 1974.

Rozell, Mark J. *Executive Privilege: The Dilemma of Secrecy and Democratic Accountability.* Baltimore, Md.: Johns Hopkins University Press, 1994.

Francene M. Engel

See also **Presidents and Subpoenas.**

EXISTENTIALISM, a philosophical and literary movement identified largely with the French intellectual Jean-Paul Sartre, gained influence after World War I. The roots of existentialism are varied, found in the work of the Danish religious thinker Søren Kierkegaard, the Russian novelist Fyodor Dostoyevsky, and the German philosopher Friedrich Nietzsche. Sartre's philosophy was influenced by the German phenomenologist Edmund Husserl and philosopher Martin Heidegger. Existentialism is notoriously difficult to define. It is as much a mood or temper as it is a philosophical system. The religious existentialism of Kierkegaard, Karl Jaspers, and Gabriel Marcel differs from the resolute atheism of Sartre, Simone de Beauvoir, and Albert Camus. Nonetheless, certain essential assumptions are shared.

In existentialism, existence is both freedom and despair. In a world without apparent meaning or direction, the individual is radically free to act. Most individuals are afraid to confront the responsibility entailed by radical freedom. In Sartrean terms, bad faith and inauthenticity allow individuals to consider themselves as an essence, a fixed entity; they playact in life. In contrast, the existential individual refuses illusions. Death looms as a boundary situation, defining the limits of existence. The recognition of such limits and the responsibility for one's actions lead to an existential despair that can overwhelm the individual.

However, Sartre, Beauvoir, and religious existentialists consider despair a painful but necessary stop on the road to freedom. Since existence is prior to essence, the existential individual at every moment confronts the nothingness of existence. Transcendence occurs when the individual undertakes a project that will give meaning to his or her life. While such acts are individually subjective, they are intertwined with everyone else's reality. No act, or failure to act, is without larger meaning and context. Existentialism, initiated with the subjective despair of the individual, ends with an ethic founded upon the shared goal of human solidarity.

Religious existentialism also begins with individual anguish and despair. Men and women are radically alone, adrift in a world without apparent meaning. Religious existentialists, however, confront meaning through faith. Since existentialism is concerned with the individual and concrete experience, religious faith must be subjective and deep. Faith is less a function of religious observance than of inner transformation. But, as Kierkegaard elucidated, because of the enormous distance between the profane and the sacred, existential religious faith can never be complacent or confident. For existential men and women, whether religious or secular, life is a difficult process of becoming, of choosing to make themselves under the sign of their own demise. Life is lived on the edge.

Sartre and Beauvoir believed that existentialism would fail to catch hold in the United States, because it was a nation marked by optimism, confidence, and faith in progress. They were mistaken. Existentialism not only became significant in the postwar years, but it had been an important theme earlier. This is hardly surprising, because an existential perspective transcends national or historical boundaries. It is, as many existentialists have argued, part of the human condition.

American Existentialism: Before the Fact

An existential mood or perspective has long been important in America. Kierkegaard's theology of despair was anticipated in the Puritan's anguished religious sensibility. The distance between the individual and God that defined Puritanism has existential echoes, as the historian Perry Miller noted in his study of Jonathan Edwards's theology. Herman Melville's character Captain Ahab in *Moby-Dick* (1851) personifies the existential individual battling to create meaning in a universe abandoned by God. Radical alienation and the search for meaning in an absurd world are common themes in the work of the late-nineteenth-century writer Stephen Crane. William James, professor of philosophy at Harvard University, posited a pluralistic and wild universe. His vision promoted both radical freedom and anguish of responsibility. For James, much like Sartre later, consciousness is an active agent rather than an essence. Therefore, the individual must impose order on the universe or confront a life without depth or meaning. Similarly, turn-of-the-century dissenters from American optimism and progress, such as James, Henry Adams, and Oliver Wendell Holmes Jr., developed an existential perspective that appreciated the tragic elements in modern life and that upheld a heroically skeptical stance in the face of the absurd nature of existence. In the 1920s, novelists from the Lost Generation, such as Ernest Hemingway and F. Scott Fitzgerald, spiritually wounded survivors of World War I, presented characters adrift, searching for existential meaning in their lives.

Kierkegaard in America

Beginning in the late 1920s, largely through the efforts of the retired minister Walter Lowrie, Kierkegaard's existential theology entered into American intellectual life. By the late 1940s, most of Kierkegaard's writings had been translated by Lowrie. For Lowrie and the theologian Reinhold Niebuhr, Kierkegaard's impassioned Christian perspective, with its emphasis on how the reality of death granted meaning to life, questioned the complacency of mainstream Protestantism. Kierkegaard offered a tragic vision of life based on faith rather than church dogma. The Kierkegaardian focus on the inner life, on the individual wrestling with God, fit well with the perspective of many intellectuals and artists in America who were filled with anxiety and in search of transcendence. By the 1940s, and well into the 1960s, Kierkegaardian ideas appeared in the Pulitzer Prize–winning poem *The Age of Anxiety* (1947) by W. H. Auden, in a symphony based on that work by Leonard Bernstein, in the paintings of Mark Rothko and Barnett Newman, and in the novels of Walker Percy. The political implications of Kierkegaardian existentialism were generally conservative. The former communist agent Whittaker Chambers found a refuge from radical politics in Kierkegaard; others discovered that Kierkegaardian concerns about anxiety and salvation led them away from political engagement and toward an inward despair or religious sanctuary.

French Existentialism in America

In the wake of the economic and physical destruction caused by World War II in Europe and the dawning of the Cold War and nuclear age, French existentialism became a worldwide vogue. It seemed to be a philosophy appropriate for the postwar world. Sartre, Beauvoir, and Camus triumphantly visited the United States in the late 1940s. Their writings were quickly translated and reached wide audiences. Sartre's philosophical opus, *Being and Nothingness* (1943), was translated by Hazel E. Barnes in 1956. In that same year, the Princeton University professor Walter Kaufmann's important anthology of existentialist writings appeared. In this work, and in many other popularizations and collections of existentialism, the existential canon was narrowly presumed to be thoroughly European, in origin and current expression.

By the 1950s, existentialism fit neatly into the general sense of alienation and tragedy popular among American intellectuals. Existentialism's emphasis on the sanctity of the individual, his or her rejection of absolutes, and comprehension of the alienating nature of modern existence fed into postwar examinations of the totalitarian temper. For the African American writers Richard Wright and Ralph Ellison, existential ideals allowed them to critique both Marxism and American racism. Each of them sought in the late 1940s and early 1950s, with the help of existentialism, to ground their characters within the concrete experiences of racism while relating problems to the human condition. The novelist Norman Mailer's existentialism presented the battle between good and evil as at the heart of the human condition. The art critic Harold Rosenberg's concept of action art defined abstract expressionist painting with the vocabulary of existentialism. Although many intellectuals associated with the *Partisan Review* rejected existentialism because of Sartre and Beauvoir's radical politics, they nevertheless shared basic assumptions about the tragic responsibility that came with freedom.

Existentialism in the 1960s

For a younger generation, coming of age in the 1960s, the left-wing political associations of Sartrean existentialism were celebrated rather than rejected. Existentialism had become entrenched in the university curriculum by the early 1960s. Student radicals embraced existential commitment and rejected inauthenticity. Existentialism gave students a language to question the complacent assumptions of American society. It placed all questions in the realm of choice; passivity was a choice not to act. For Robert Moses, the decision to go to Mississippi in the early 1960s to organize voting campaigns for disfranchised blacks was an existential commitment. The repression that he faced was part of the absurd nature of existence. His ability to continue, despite the violence, was testimony to his existential beliefs. The ideas of Beauvoir in her *The Second Sex* (U.S. translation, 1953) influenced the American women's liberation movement of the late 1960s and early 1970s. Employing the terminology that she and Sartre had developed, Beauvoir's famous words that "One is not born, but rather becomes, a woman" signaled the existential fact that woman existed not as an essence but as a being with the choice to create her own existence. Betty Friedan, most famously, used many of Beauvoir's concepts in her own influential book, *The Feminine Mystique* (1963).

The Fate of Existentialism

In the late 1970s, existentialism's popularity waned for a host of reasons. The existential imperative for the individual to choose, in the hands of pop psychologists, was stripped of its anguish and despair and corrupted into a rather facile expression of unlimited human potential. In academic culture, universalist ideals of the human condition and freedom conflicted with poststructural and postmodernist thought. But existentialism, like postmodernism, viewed identity as something created, albeit with a greater sense of anguish. Today, existentialism remains a symbol of alienation and a critique of confident individualism.

BIBLIOGRAPHY

Barnes, Hazel E. *An Existentialist Ethics*. New York: Knopf, 1967.

———. *The Story I Tell Myself: A Venture into Existentialist Autobiography*. Chicago: University of Chicago Press, 1997.

Barrett, William. *Irrational Man: A Study in Existential Philosophy*. Garden City, N.Y.: Doubleday/Anchor, 1958.

Cotkin, George. *Existential America*. Baltimore: Johns Hopkins University Press, 2002.

Fulton, Ann. *Apostles of Sartre: Existentialism in America, 1945–1963*. Evanston, Ill.: Northwestern University Press, 1999.

Kaufmann, Walter, ed. *Existentialism from Dostoevsky to Sartre*. New York: Meridian, 1956.

May, Rollo. *The Meaning of Anxiety*. New York: Ronald Press, 1950.

George Cotkin

See also ***Feminine Mystique, The;*** **Individualism;** ***Moby-Dick;*** **Philosophy.**

EXPATRIATION is the right of a citizen or subject to transfer allegiance from one political state to another. Under English rule, this right could be exercised only with the government's consent, but in 1868 the U.S. Congress recognized that all persons possessed this right. Later legislation set conditions under which expatriation would occur, some of which called for loss of citizenship against the wishes of the individual citizen. The Supreme Court in the 1950s and 1960s declared unconstitutional a number of such provisions, so that expatriation is now basically voluntary and cannot be imposed against a citizen's wishes, particularly as punishment, although naturalization can be canceled for fraud.

BIBLIOGRAPHY

Roche, John P. "The Expatriation Decisions: A Study in Constitutional Improvisation and the Uses of History." *American Political Science Review* (1964).

Paul C. Bartholomew
Christopher Wells

See also **Citizenship; Naturalization.**

EXPENDITURES, FEDERAL. The Constitution of the United States provides, in Article I, Section 9, that "no money shall be drawn from the Treasury, but in Consequence of Appropriations made by Law; and a regular Statement and Account of the Receipts and Expenditures of all public Money shall be published from time to time." There is no constitutional limitation on the amount of federal expenditures. Several efforts have been made to pass a balanced budget amendment, but all have failed. Although Congress is limited by the Constitution to taxing "to pay the Debts and provide for the common Defence and general Welfare of the United States," in practice it has been demonstrated that money derived by the federal government from taxation or borrowing may be spent for any purpose for which it has been made available by an act of Congress.

When the federal government began its operation under the Constitution, its functions were comparatively few and its expenditures small. As new functions were added and old functions were expanded, federal expenditures were vastly increased. Thus, in 1791—when money was spent only for the army, interest on the public debt, pensions, foreign relations, and the salaries of government personnel—the expenditures amounted to only $3,097,000. But in the fiscal year 2000—with tremendously increased amounts spent for the above purposes

TABLE

Federal Expenditures

Period	Yearly Average (in millions)
1789–1800	$5.7
1811–1820	23.9
1831–1840	24.4
1851–1860	60.1
1876–1880	255
1896–1900	457
1916–1920	8,065
1926–1930	3,182
1936–1940	10,192
1941–1945	66,037
1946–1950	42,334
Per Year	
1955	$64,569
1960	76,539
1965	96,506
1970	194,968
1975	332,332
1976	371,779
1977	409,203
1978	458,729
1979	503,464
1980	590,920
1981	678,209
1982	745,706
1983	808,327
1984	851,781
1985	946,316
1986	990,231
1987	1,003,804
1988	1,063,318
1989	1,144,020
1990	1,251,776
1991	1,323,757
1992	1,380,794
1993	1,408,532
1994	1,460,553
1995	1,515,412
1996	1,560,094
1997	1,600,911
1998	1,652,224
1999	1,704,942
2000	1,788,045
2001	1,863,039

SOURCE: World Almanac (2001).

and great sums spent as well for such items as agricultural subsidies, social security, unemployment relief, space research and exploration, veterans' benefits, and education—the net expenditures totaled $1,788,045,000,000. Whereas the per capita expenditure in 1791 was only 76 cents, in 2001 it was in excess of $6,000.

Wars have been the chief factor in causing federal expenditures to rise. The Civil War cost the federal government nearly $13 billion; World War I, $112 billion; and World War II, $664 billion. After each war in which the United States participated federal expenditures fell markedly but failed to drop even close to the prewar level. For example, federal expenditures in 1916, just before the United States entered World War I, amounted to $724,413,000. After a peak wartime output of $18,939,532,000 in fiscal year 1919, annual expenditures never again fell below $3,000,000,000, more than four times the prewar figure. During the Vietnam War (1962–1973) federal expenditures increased enormously, nearly tripling from approximately $87.8 billion in 1962 to $246.5 billion in 1973. Federal outlays increased to $268.3 billion the following year and never again fell below $300 billion.

The largest percentage of the federal budget since World War II has been allocated to national defense. However, even though the dollar output on national defense has soared ($50 billion in 1965to $281.2 billion in 2000), the percentage of total national expenditures allocated to defense began to decrease long before the end of the Cold War in 1989–1990. From a height of 41.9 percent in 1965, defense spending sank to 29.4 percent of the national budget in 1974 to 15.1% in 2000). If defense spending was gradually reduced, the cost of the nation's indebtedness rose dramatically. In 1980, the national debt was $909 billion. From the early 1980s to the mid-1990s, the U.S. ran annual deficits in excess of $100 billion. For three consecutive years from 1998 to 2000, a robust economy and spending controls sent the budget briefly into the black, and the national debt was reduced slightly. But the combined effects of a recession in 2001 and the terrorist attacks of that year returned the government to a policy of deficit spending. By 2001, the national debt had ballooned to $5.8 trillion. Simply paying the interest on that debt cost the federal government $362.1 billion—making interest payments the government's largest single expenditure of the national debt (19.4 percent of its total outlays).

BIBLIOGRAPHY

Ippolito, Dennis S. *Uncertain Legacies: Federal Budget Policy from Roosevelt through Reagan.* Charlottesville: University Press of Virginia, 1990.

Kahn, Jonathan. *Budgeting Democracy: State Building and Citizenship in America, 1890–1928.* Ithaca, N.Y.: Cornell University Press, 1997.

Ott, David J., and Attiat F. Ott, *Federal Budget Policy.* Washington, D.C.: Brookings Institution, 1977.

Savage, James D. *Balanced Budgets and American Politics.* Ithaca, N.Y.: Cornell University Press, 1988.

Harold W. Chase / A. G.; A. R.

See also **Business Cycles; Debt, Public; Defense, National; Office of Management and Budget; Reaganomics; War Costs.**

EXPLORATION OF AMERICA, EARLY

Early Developments

For centuries there were claims suggesting that the earliest voyages of exploration to North America were made by Irish monks (St. Brendan), Welshmen (Prince Madoc) and others, but these have never been supported by credible evidence. Late tenth-century Norsemen (Vikings) sailing west from Scandinavia and Iceland colonized the west coast of Greenland, and then in about 1001 moved on to Baffin Island, southern Labrador, and finally the northern tip of Newfoundland. There, at a site now known as L'Anse aux Meadows, they made an abortive effort to establish a colony which they called Vinland. Several attempts to stabilize the infant settlement followed, but the enterprise did not prosper. Repeated attacks by hostile natives (known to the Vikings as Skrellings) may have contributed to its ultimate failure.

Over the ensuing five centuries, some Europeans heard of the Norsemen's efforts, but a number of factors precluded any new attempts at exploration. Most European trade continued to center on the Mediterranean region, there was little impetus and few resources available for sailing westward into uncharted waters, and new overland trade routes to the Far East were established. But in time, a variety of factors affecting Europeans, including population growth, the gradual evolution of nation-states, innovative developments in shipbuilding and navigation, and fresh intellectual initiatives born of titanic religious quarrels, created renewed incentives for exploration.

In the 1500s, the Catholic Church's centuries-long control over religious thought and practice began to crumble. Controversies over church reform engendered by the Protestant Reformation and the Catholic Counter-Reformation inspired a new growth of learning and individual initiative. Much of the financial and political power formerly held by the Catholic Church was transferred into the hands of kings in some European nation-states, notably Spain, Portugal, France and England. Larger ships better equipped to carry their crews longer distances, coupled with new devices such as the sextant, came into general use. At the same time, much of the increasingly lucrative overland trade with Asia was controlled by merchants residing in northern Italian city-states, such as Venice, Genoa, and Florence. From the late fourteenth century, however, this commercial activity was increasingly hampered by intermittent warfare with the Ottoman Empire, and the nations bordering the Atlantic began to consider alternative routes to Asian markets.

From the early Christian era, ancient geographers had strongly influenced European thinking about distances between various points on the globe. Maps drawn by Claudius Ptolemy (A.D. c. 73–151), for example, depicted the expanse of Eurasia as being a third wider than its actual size. Other ancient writers, notably Eratosthenes, Strabo, and Marinus of Tyre, further exaggerated the distance from Western Europe to Eastern Siberia, or implied that well-supplied mariners heading west across the Atlantic from the coast of Europe might have no great difficulty reaching China or the Indies. The existence of the Americas was not then suspected.

Portuguese and Spanish Exploration

Catholic Portugal and Spain, relatively untroubled by religious strife and located on the Iberian Peninsula jutting southwest into the Atlantic, were ideally situated to explore the various avenues by sea. Religious and commercial zeal fueled much of their activity into the early modern period. Portugal's Prince Henry the Navigator (1394–1460) established a school of navigation at Cape St. Vincent, that made significant improvements in shipbuilding and navigation, including vastly better charts, compasses, and quadrants. He dispatched a number of voyages to the south down the West African coast, setting the stage for later expeditions that rounded South Africa and crossed the Indian Ocean. King John II subsequently encouraged the search for a water route to India, and Vasco da Gama (1469–1524) successfully completed the first such round-trip voyage in 1497–1498. In 1498, King John dispatched Duarte Pacheco Pereira (?–c. 1530) in a westerly direction, and Pacheco's later account suggests that he may have encountered parts of the South American continent. Pacheco's description of his voyages of exploration, *Principio do Esmeraldo de Situ Orbis*, was not released for many years by the Portuguese government because of the information it could provide rival mariners travelling to India, and because it contained much valuable geographic data. In 1500, King Emmanuel I sent Pedro Alvarez de Cabral (1460–c. 1520) to establish trade with the Indies. The long-held view that Cabral was the first to sail (or be blown) west instead of south and onto the coast of Brazil is now at least open to question. In 1500–1501, a Portuguese exploratory expedition of three vessels led by Gaspar Corte-Real (c. 1450–1501) may have seen the southern tip of Greenland en route to Labrador. It is believed that they hugged the coast of Labrador and rounded Newfoundland, continuing as far as Cape Sable, Nova Scotia. There his brother Miguel returned to Portugal with two ships, while Gaspar continued further south and was never heard from again.

Queen Isabel of Spain, having with her husband Ferdinand subjugated the Moors early in 1492, was able to turn her attention to other matters. The Genoese-born Christopher Columbus (1451–1506) had for years advocated voyaging west across the Atlantic to Asia, and Isabel provided him with money and a patent of nobility, the latter to enhance his authority when in Asia. Columbus departed Palos in August 1492 and arrived, possibly at Watling Island (one of the Bahamas) in mid-October. But as historian S. E. Morison has noted, "America was discovered by accident, not wanted when found, and early explorations were directed to finding a way through or around it." Early discoverers and explorers also sought precious metals, principally gold and silver, but few found them. For much of the next ten years, which included

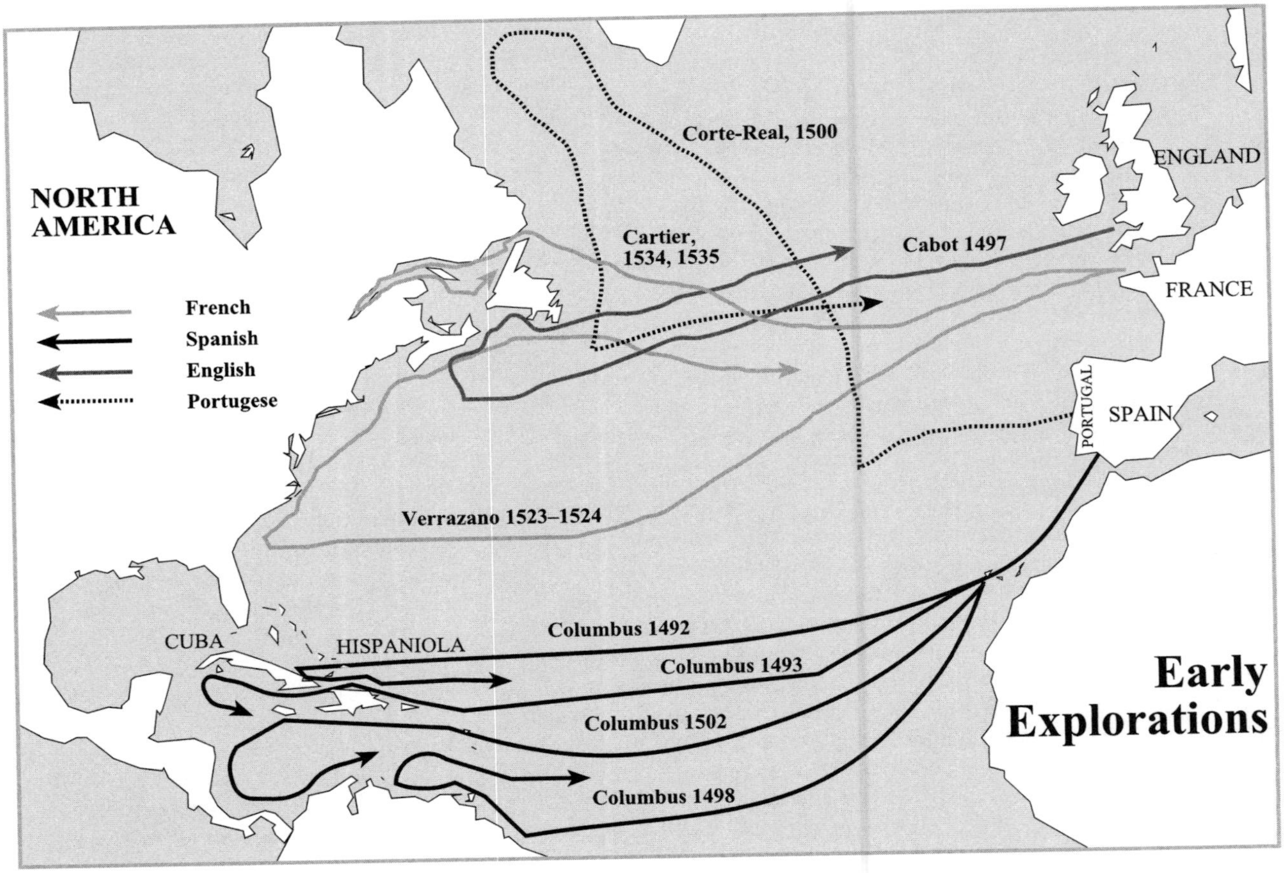

three more trips to various parts of the Caribbean region between 1494 and 1502, Columbus remained convinced that he had been navigating the Indian Ocean. Increasingly, however, many of his contemporaries did not agree, contending that a new continent had been discovered, and that the traditional view of world geography needed drastic revision.

In 1493, at the request of Spain, Pope Alexander VI established a longitudinal line one hundred leagues west of the Azores and Cape Verde Islands. Spain was granted an exclusive right to discoveries west of that line not already held by other powers as of Christmas Day, 1492. The Portuguese, unhappy with this decision, urged that this line be moved much further to the west. Some historians have reasoned that this revision was demanded because Portugal may have already been aware of the existence of Brazil, although as previously noted, its official discovery did not take place until 1500. The Treaty of Tordesillas, promulgated on 7 June 1494, established the new line 370 leagues west of the Azores. Portugal was given license to explore and settle everything in the New World east of this line, and Spain, as before, granted everything to the west.

Florentine-born Amerigo Vespucci (1454–1512), who by 1495 was directing the Seville branch of a Florentine banking and ship chandlery firm, helped to outfit Columbus's third voyage in 1498. Vespucci subsequently participated in several voyages during which he reconnoitered portions of the Brazilian coast. Vespucci's *Lettera* to his friend Piero Soderini, and his *Mundus Novus*, a briefer document printed in 1506, prompted Martin Waldseemüller, a young cartographer at the cloister of Saint-Dié, Lorraine, to designate the southern portion of the New World as "America" in a book and map published in 1507. This designation was later extended to both North and South America. In 1508, Vespucci was appointed Pilot Major of Spain, with responsibilities for opening a school of navigation and preparing charts for navigators. He held this post until his death in 1512.

In 1513 and 1521, Juan Ponce de Leon (1460–1521) discovered and explored Florida. In 1513, Vasco Nuñez de Balboa (1475–1519) discovered the Pacific Ocean by crossing the Isthmus of Panama. Between 1519 and 1521, Hernán Cortéz (1485–1547), landing on Mexico's east coast, marched inland with several hundred soldiers, and, allying himself with many smaller groups of indigenous Central Mexican peoples, brought about the destruction of the Aztec Empire. He later (1530) discovered lower California. In 1535, Álvar Nuñez Cabeza de Vaca (1490–c. 1557) explored what is now the American Southwest, and five years later, Francisco Vázquez de Coronado (1510–1554) discovered the Grand Canyon. Other Spaniards, notably Portuguese-born Juan Rodríguez Cabrillo (?–1543), explored the California coast as far north as Monterey Bay. His chief pilot, Bartoleme Ferrelo, continued north to what is now the southwest coast of Oregon in February 1543. Other Spanish ship captains subsequently investigated the North Pacific coast, reaching the southern shores of Alaska in the eighteenth century.

The Catholic priests who accompanied Spanish conquistadors felt justified in converting Native Americans wherever possible, and in their view, this imperative warranted the slaughter of many of those who resisted Christianity. In addition, numerous natives died from the introduction of unfamiliar European diseases, and from being compelled to work on Spanish colonial estates (haciendas) or to mine for precious metals.

British Exploration

The first British-sponsored explorer to visit the New World in the late fifteenth century was probably Genoese-born Giovanni Caboto, also known as John Cabot (1450–c. 1498). He was commissioned by King Henry VII to make several voyages in 1497 and 1498, during which he reached the Cape Breton and Baffin Islands, Newfoundland, and Greenland, though Cabot was lost at sea during his second voyage. Cabot's expeditions revealed that the waters off Newfoundland and New England were alive with marketable fish. Various authorities have suggested that vessels based in Bristol, England, possibly captained by Cabot or others, may have reached some land mass west of the Azores as early as 1480 or 1481, though the available evidence needs verification through further research. What is known is that dynastic and religious quarrels largely prevented the English Crown from again pursuing any American ventures until the late sixteenth century.

Queen Elizabeth I (1533–1603) encouraged mariners such as Sir Martin Frobisher (1535–1594) and John Davis (1550–1605) to explore the islands north of Canada for a Northwest Passage in the 1570s and 1580s. Sir Humphrey Gilbert (1539–1583), half-brother to Sir Walter Raleigh, made several voyages to explore and colonize eastern Canada. His first effort failed in 1579, but on his second attempt in 1583, he established St. John's, Newfoundland, the first British colony in North America.

An expedition authorized by the Queen and sent out by Sir Walter Raleigh (1552–1618) in 1583 explored the coast of North Carolina and Florida. A second initiative established the Roanoke Colony in 1585, but war with Spain prevented Raleigh from sending another expedition in support of the first, as he had planned. The colony failed, but several historians have contended that some of the colonists and their children may have intermarried with the Indians and survived with their aid until the early 1600s. The first two successful efforts at colonization in what is now the continental United States were made at Jamestown in Virginia (1607), and at Plymouth in Massachusetts Bay (1620). Thereafter, the pace of English colonization increased, fueled by various motives including adventure, greater religious freedom, and opportunities for individual economic advancement.

French Exploration

Religious wars during the sixteenth century were the principal preoccupation of France's rulers, but French mariners were not altogether inactive. Giovanni da Verrazzano (1485–1528), a Florentine, was employed to seek a Northwest Passage. Unsuccessful in that effort, he explored the Atlantic coast from North Carolina north to Cape Breton, discovering New York Harbor and Narragansett Bay. Jacques Cartier (1491–1557) made three expeditions to Canada between 1534 and 1542, discovering the St. Lawrence River and sailing up to the point where Montreal now stands. However, his attempts at colonization were unsuccessful.

In the mid-sixteenth century, France briefly competed with Spain for control of what is now the southeastern United States. Jan (or Jean) Ribault (1520–1565), sailing under a commission from the French Huguenot leader Admiral Gaspard de Coligny, established a short-lived colony at Port Royal, South Carolina in 1562, but it was soon abandoned. A second effort (1564) by Coligny was led by René Goulaine de Laudonnière, but his settlement on the St. Johns River in Florida was destroyed by the Spanish the following year. Ribault made another attempt to support French settlers in Florida, but his fleet foundered in a storm, and he was captured and killed by the Spanish late in 1565. The French then concentrated on exploring lands further to the north and west.

Louis Jolliet (1645–1700), selected by the authorities in French Canada to investigate a great river reported by Indians, went down the Wisconsin River to the Mississippi, which he first saw in June 1673. He rafted along it as far south as the mouth of the Arkansas River, reporting his findings to his superiors in Quebec in 1674. Joillet and Père Jacques Marquette (1637–1675), a Jesuit missionary-explorer, returned along the Illinois River to Lake Michigan. Marquette's journal of their travels was published six years after his death.

Sieur Robert Cavalier de La Salle (1643–1687) traveled to Canada and settled in Montreal in 1668. He may have discovered the Ohio River the next year, and then following further explorations in what is now the American Midwest, he sailed down the Mississippi River to its mouth in 1682. Named French Viceroy of North America, La Salle returned to the Caribbean in 1684, but through errors in navigation, missed the Mississippi and landed instead at Matagorda Bay in Texas. While returning east to the Mississippi, he was murdered by his men.

Samuel de Champlain (1567–1635) accompanied an expedition of explorers and fur traders to the Gulf of the St. Lawrence in 1603, then visited Port Royal and other points in Nova Scotia and New England over the next four years. Appointed lieutenant governor of the French mainland possessions, he founded Quebec in 1608, then explored to the south as far as the present Lake Champlain in 1609. He reached and explored the Great Lakes in 1615, and was named governor of New France in 1633–1635. Finding no gold or other precious metals within their new domains, the French instead developed a thriving fur trade and fishing industry. But efforts at colonization led by several private trading companies with royal charters were not as remunerative as the French crown had wished. King Louis XIV initially turned over the administration of the colony to a newly created Company of New France, but the crown subsequently exercised direct control.

Dutch Exploration

The resourceful Dutch, having finally achieved their independence from Spain, became very active in North America at the beginning of the seventeenth century. Sailing under the auspices of the Dutch East India Company, English-born Henry Hudson (c. 1565–1611) first explored Greenland (1607) and then the Arctic seas north of Russia. In 1609, in search of a sea Passage to Asia, he traveled up the river which today bears his name, as far as present-day Albany. In 1610, Hudson undertook another voyage, again in search of a Northwest Passage. He sailed through what is now Hudson Strait, spent the winter of 1610–1611 in James Bay, and then discovered Hudson's Bay. There, in June 1611, his mutinous crew marooned Hudson, his son, and six loyal crewmen and they presumably died. Because Hudson had claimed much of what is now New York, the Dutch established a settlement on Manhattan Island in 1624. It was taken over by the English four decades later.

Subsequent Efforts to Find a Northwest Passage

Following hard on Hudson's effort, the newly formed "Governor and Company of the Merchants of London" made a number of attempts to find a Northwest Passage. During two voyages between 1610 and 1616, Thomas Button (?–1634), and Robert Bylot (fl. 1610–1616) with his pilot William Baffin (1584–1622), thoroughly surveyed the previously unexplored western and northern reaches of Hudson's Bay, but without success. In 1616, Bylot and Baffin reached Smith Sound, at the northern end of what became Baffin Bay. No other mariner would get this far north again until 1853. An unsuccessful Danish effort led by Jens Munk in 1619–1620 resulted in the death of all but three of his men. In a vessel loaned by King Charles I of England, Luke Fox (1586–c. 1635) reached a point just south of the Arctic Circle in 1631, and demonstrated conclusively that sailing north from Hudson's Bay would not lead to a Northwest Passage. Thomas James (c. 1593–c. 1635) made one final attempt to find a passage in 1631–1632. Thereafter, English efforts to find the elusive passage were abandoned for nearly two centuries. Benjamin Franklin and other Philadelphia investors did mount one exploratory effort in 1753–1754, led by Charles Swaine, which had little success. It was not until 1905 that the Norwegian explorer Roald Amundsen, in his privately funded vessel, the *Gjoa*, finally succeeded in navigating a passage where so many of his predecessors had failed.

Activities of Other Nations

Colonization efforts were mounted by several Scandinavian nations. An expedition mounted by the Swedish West India Company in 1638 established a colony near the present site of Wilmington, Delaware, but this land was seized by the Dutch in 1655. A Danish West India Company settled on St. Thomas, St. John, and several of the other Virgin Islands after 1666, and the Danes maintained their presence in the Caribbean until 1917.

Russian expeditions, underwritten by several tsars and led by Danish mariner Vitus Bering (c. 1681–1741), established in 1728 that a strait existed between Siberia and Bolshaya Zemlya (now Alaska). Bering's second expedition of 1731–1741 made a grueling overland trip from St. Petersburg, and then set sail from Petropavlovsk on the Kamchatka Peninsula early in 1741. In July 1741, Bering landed on Kayak Island, east of Prince William Sound, then briefly tarried on one of the Aleutian Islands (September 1741), before turning back for Siberia. In a second vessel, Aleksey Chirkov (1703–1748), Bering's subordinate, reached a point off the Alexander Archipelago, west of what is now Ketchikan, but could not land owing to the loss of his ship's boats. On the return trip, Bering's vessel foundered on what became Bering Island, in the Komandorskyies. There, he and thirty-one of his men died during the winter of 1741–1742. Bering's survivors and leaders of later Russian expeditions reported the presence of valuable fur animals, several of which were subsequently hunted to near extinction.

BIBLIOGRAPHY

Columbus, Christopher. *Four Voyages to the New World: Letters and Selected Documents.* Edited and translated by R. H. Major. Secaucus, N. J.: Carol Publishing Group, 1992.

Francis, Daniel. *Discovery of the North: The Exploration of Canada's Arctic.* Edmonton, Canada: Hurtig, 1986.

Quinn, David B. *England and the Discovery of North America, 1481–1620.* New York: Knopf, 1974.

Quinn, David B. *Explorers and Colonies: America, 1500–1625.* London: Hambledon Press, 1990.

Mirsky, Jeannette. *To the Arctic: The Story of Northern Exploration from Earliest Times to the Present.* Chicago: University of Chicago Press, 1970.

Morison, Samuel E. *The European Discovery of America: The Northern Voyages,* A.D. *500–1600.* New York: Oxford, 1971.

Morison, Samuel E. *The European Discovery of America: The Southern Voyages,* A.D. *1492–1600.* New York: Oxford, 1974.

Skelton, R. A., Thomas E. Marston, and George D. Painter. *The Vinland Map and the Tartar Relation.* New Haven, Conn.: Yale University Press, 1964.

Steller, Georg W. *Journal of a Voyage with Bering, 1741–1742.* Edited by O. W. Frost. Stanford, Calif.: Stanford University Press, 1988.

Waldman, Carl, and Alen Wexler. *Who Was Who in World Exploration.* New York: Facts on File, 1992.

Williamson, James A. *The Cabot Voyages and Bristol Discovery Under Henry VII.* Cambridge, U.K.: The Hakluyt Society, 1962.

Keir B. Sterling

See also vol. 9: **Life and Adventures of Colonel Daniel Boon; Message on the Lewis and Clark Expedition; The Journals of the Lewis and Clark Expedition.**

EXPLORATIONS AND EXPEDITIONS

This entry includes 6 subentries:
British
Dutch
French
Russian
Spanish
U.S.

British

Great Britain ultimately was the last European nation to become a major force in the exploration and colonization of North America. Initially, however, the English were among the forerunners of New World exploration. Shortly after Christopher Columbus's discovery of the Caribbean in 1492, the English king Henry VII dispatched John Cabot (actually Giovanni Caboto), an Italian sea captain, on an expedition to find an Atlantic passage to the Orient. Cabot, like Columbus, believed the newly discovered lands in the Americas were a minor impediment to locating an ocean route to the Orient. Following an uneventful Atlantic exploration in 1495, Cabot successfully reached the coast of North America in 1497 and explored the region around Newfoundland, Canada. He failed to locate a Northwest Passage, but his return to England with news of his discovery laid the foundation for English claims to North America.

Sixteenth-Century Stagnation

The English made no meaningful efforts to capitalize on Cabot's discovery over the next century. Although Cabot's son Sebastian explored the Atlantic coast of North America in 1508–1509 and English fishermen regularly plied their trade off the Grand Banks, religious turmoil at home restricted English participation in Atlantic exploration and expansion throughout much of the sixteenth century. Following the reign of Henry VIII (1509–1547), religious contention fractured the English government. Henry VIII had initiated a Protestant reformation when he publicly renounced the Roman Catholic Church, but the fissure was not supported by the entire English population. The split with Rome had as much to do with emerging English notions of independence as it did with religious doctrine, but Henry VIII nonetheless refused to sponsor New World exploration during his reign. The king attempted to maintain cordial relations with Catholic Spain, with whom he hoped to forge a military alliance against the rising power of France. English acceptance of Protestantism quickly became a contested issue following Henry's death. His heir, the sickly Edward VI, held the throne only a short time before Mary, a Catholic, claimed the throne in 1553 and attempted to reimpose her faith upon the nation by force. After five years of bloody religious upheaval, English Protestants regained control of the government in 1558 with the ascension of Elizabeth I, the youngest child of Henry VIII.

Motivations for Expansion

Even though Henry VIII's Eurocentrism and the decade of tension following his death precluded English participation in Atlantic exploration for most of the sixteenth century, economic and social forces within the nation reignited English interest in the Americas. Throughout the first half of the seventeenth century, the enclosure movement displaced thousands of tenant farmers from the countryside, as rural landlords converted their real estate holdings into enclosed pastures in an effort to increase wool production and reap larger dividends in the escalating textile trade with the Dutch. The migrant rural population flooded into London and other urban centers, creating a large surplus workforce with little opportunity for social advancement. The unstable social situation was further complicated by increasing numbers of religious dissenters. Thousands of Catholics, Puritans, and Quakers criticized the English church along both sides of the religious axiom, while others, appropriately dubbed Separatists, advocated flight as the only means of spiritual salvation. Concurrently, English overproduction of wool brought about a significant downturn in the European textile industry, which escalated inflation and unemployment in England to almost unbearable levels.

Proposed solutions for England's problems abounded. A new economic theory, mercantilism, advocated the establishment of overseas colonies as a clearinghouse for excess industrial production and as a source of raw materials for the mother country. Two Englishmen, an uncle and his nephew, both named Richard Hakluyt, provided a theoretical foundation for mercantilism that doubled as a panacea for the ills plaguing the nation. In *A Discourse on the Western Planting* (1584), the younger Hakluyt argued that the establishment of English colonies would provide a place to send religious dissenters and the excess urban population, a market for surplus industrial production, military bases to protect English Atlantic shipping and to harass the nation's European competitors in the New World, and a foothold for Protestant missionaries in the battle to counter the spread of Catholicism among the Native peoples of the Americas.

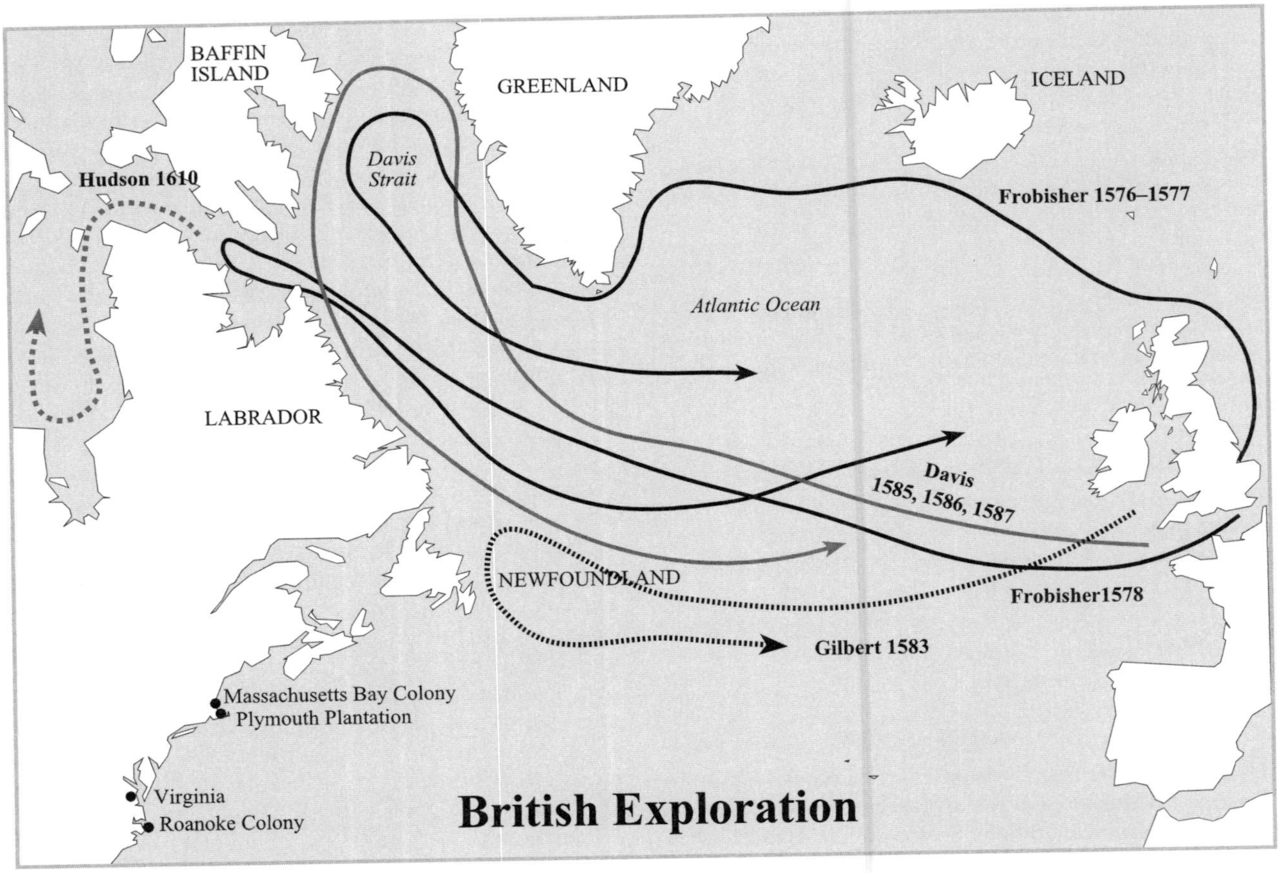

Rebirth of Exploration

These social and intellectual forces propelled a new era of English exploration, the opening phases of which occurred during the reign of Elizabeth I (1558–1603). Elizabeth did not share her father's amicable diplomatic stance toward Spain, and under her watchful gaze, the English government covertly outfitted and backed privateers, known as "sea dogs," whose sole purpose was to raid Spanish treasure ships as they crossed the Atlantic Ocean. Foremost among these English pirates was Sir Francis Drake, who circumnavigated the world in 1577–1580 on a global voyage of plunder. The activities of Drake and other privateers, such as John Hawkins and Richard Grenville, resulted in Spain's attempt to invade England and the famous defeat of the Spanish Armada in 1588.

Following the defeat of the armada, English exploration of the New World was invariably tied to colonization, although plans for overseas expansion in North America had been under way at least a decade prior to the Spanish attack. In 1578, Sir Humphrey Gilbert, an English nobleman and soldier, received a charter from Queen Elizabeth authorizing him to establish a colony in North America. Gilbert hoped to bring Hakluyt's vision of a fortified "New England" to reality. In 1583, he set out with seven ships carrying four hundred men to explore the North American coast and found a settlement. Although he succeeded Cabot in reaching Newfoundland, Gilbert, like his unfortunate predecessor, was lost at sea after his prospective colonists forced him to return to England.

Gilbert's half brother, Sir Walter Raleigh, subsequently grasped the reins of English exploration. In April 1585, Raleigh sent seven ships and six hundred men to explore the southern Atlantic coast of North America. After locating a seemingly ideal destination along the Outer Banks region of present-day North Carolina, the expedition left one hundred men to found a colony on Roanoke Island. Although reinforcements were expected to reach Roanoke the next year, the original colonists opted to return to England before the relief expedition arrived. Undaunted, Raleigh renewed his efforts in 1587, this time dispatching 110 people, including 17 women and 9 children, to found a colony on the mainland near Chesapeake Bay. Miscalculations landed the prospective colonists back at Roanoke, where they established a small fort and village. Within three years, however, the tiny community vanished without explanation. The fate of the Lost Colony, as it has come to be known, became one of the most intriguing mysteries of American history.

The failure of the Roanoke colony left Raleigh in financial ruin and illustrated to English expansionists that the challenge of overseas exploration and colonization required the consolidation of capital and resources. The next wave of English exploration of North America was carried out by joint-stock companies, business conglomerates that transformed colonization into a corporate enterprise. The colony of Virginia was founded in 1607 by adventurers employed by the London Company, a joint-stock enterprise dedicated to harvesting whatever wealth the New World had to offer. However, not all joint-stock enterprises were strictly commercial in nature. Stockholders in the Plymouth and Massachusetts Bay Companies, who were primarily religious dissenters, initially did not seek profit from their enterprises but instead pooled their resources to locate New World colonies that might serve as refuges from English persecution. The colonies of Plymouth (1621) and Massachusetts Bay (1630) thus came into being.

Northern Explorations

Although most English efforts in the New World centered upon colonization, especially following the successful establishment of Virginia and New England, the exploration of North America continued, returning to efforts to locate a Northwest Passage to China. Martin Frobisher made three voyages of discovery into the Arctic waters north of the continent beginning in 1576, but he failed to uncover a water passage through North America. His efforts were renewed by Henry Hudson, who returned to his homeland following his explorations for the Dutch. In 1610, Hudson sailed around the northern reaches of North America and reached the expansive bay of water that bears his name. After extensive efforts to locate a passage beyond Hudson's Bay failed, English efforts again turned to commercial exploitation. The Hudson's Bay Company, founded in 1670 with a monopoly over mineral rights and the fur trade, established several profitable trading posts but declined to aggressively pursue colonization due to the inhospitable climate of the region.

BIBLIOGRAPHY

Andrews, Kenneth R. *Trade, Plunder, and Settlement: Maritime Enterprise and the Genesis of the British Empire, 1480–1630.* New York: Cambridge University Press, 1984.

Loades, David. *England's Maritime Empire: Seapower, Commerce, and Policy, 1490–1690.* New York: Longman, 2000.

Mancall, Peter C., ed. *Envisioning America: English Plans for the Colonization of North America, 1580–1640.* Boston: Bedford Books, 1995.

Quinn, David B. *England and the Discovery of America, 1481–1620, from the Bristol Voyages of the Fifteenth Century to the Pilgrim Settlement at Plymouth.* New York: Knopf, 1973.

Rabb, Theodore K. *Enterprise and Empire: Merchant and Gentry Investment in the Expansion of England, 1575–1630.* Cambridge, Mass.: Harvard University Press, 1967.

Williams, Neville. *The Sea Dogs: Privateers, Plunder, and Piracy in the Elizabethan Age.* London: Weidenfeld and Nicolson, 1975.

Daniel P. Barr

See also **Colonial Settlements; Hudson's Bay Company; Massachusetts Bay Colony; North Carolina; Northwest Passage; Plymouth Colony; Raleigh Colonies; Virginia; Virginia Company of London.**

Dutch

The Dutch came late to the European exploration of North America, having entered the process only after securing independence from Spain in the early seventeenth century. Despite its political subjugation, the Netherlands had emerged during the preceding decades as a force in the seafaring commerce of western Europe. After independence, Dutch merchants quickly cut into the Spanish and Portuguese domination of Atlantic shipping and snared a large share of the evolving textile and slave trade between Europe, Africa, and the Americas. Not content with Atlantic commerce, the Dutch increasingly sought to augment their standing in the highly competitive eastern spice trade.

In 1609 Henry Hudson, an English explorer, was hired by the Dutch East India Company to discover a water passage through North America to the Orient. Hudson explored the Atlantic coast and pushed far up the river that now bears his name, but he was unable to discover a passage. Nonetheless, Hudson claimed the lands he explored for the Netherlands and in the process established the foundation for the Dutch colonization of North America.

The Dutch West India Company took direction of Dutch explorations in the New World following Hudson's discoveries. Primarily interested in piracy against Spanish treasure ships crossing the Atlantic Ocean and the hostile takeover of Portuguese slave markets in western Africa, the company turned to colonization as a secondary endeavor to help facilitate its other objectives. The company established a colony, or military post, at New Amsterdam on the present site of New York City, to serve as a base for naval expeditions against the Spanish in the Caribbean. The move paid almost immediate dividends. Over the next two decades, Dutch fleets operating out of New Amsterdam captured numerous Spanish possessions in the Caribbean, including the islands of Curaccao, St. Martin, and St. Eustatius, and even raided the Portuguese colony of Brazil.

In mainland North America, however, the fur trade quickly took precedence as a motive for further Dutch exploration and commercial expansion. Of particular interest to the Dutch were beaver pelts, a lucrative natural resource keenly sought in Europe. In 1614, the New Netherland Company formed to exploit the fur trade and established trading posts along the Hudson River. The Dutch West India Company absorbed the posts soon after the establishment of New Amsterdam and greatly ex-

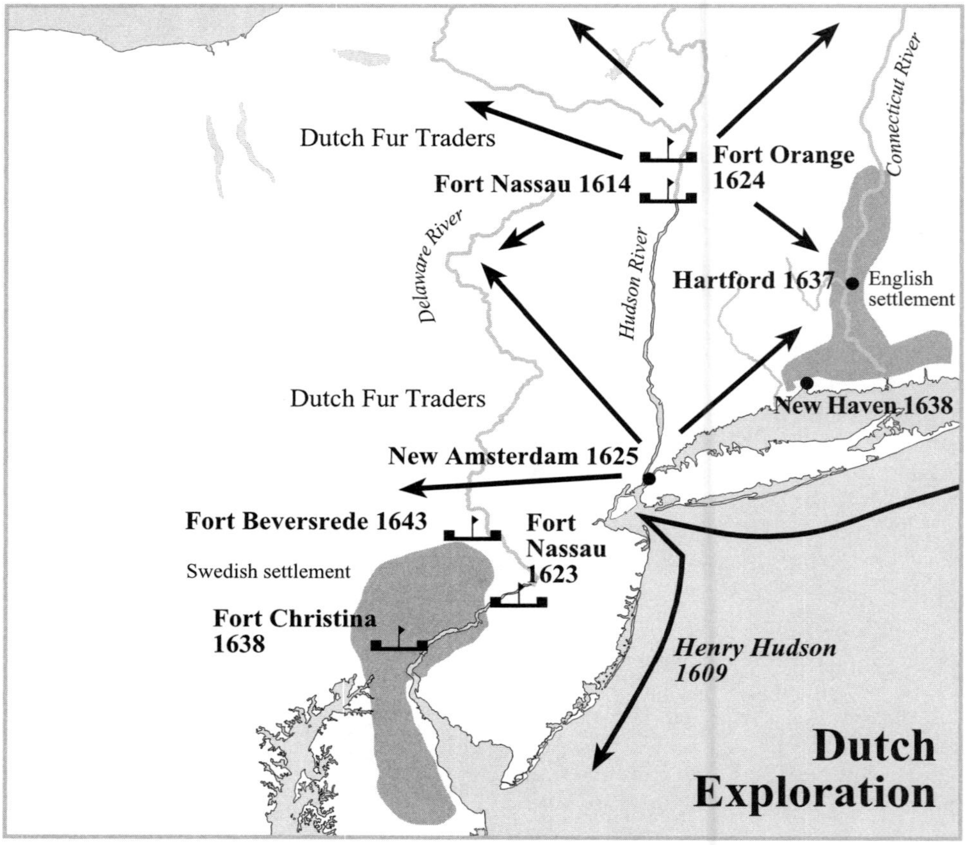

panded Dutch involvement in the fur trade. Inland exploration quickly pushed beyond the Hudson River into the Connecticut and Delaware River valleys, and led to the establishment of additional trade depots, including a significant post at Fort Orange (ALBANY, New York). By 1630, nearly 10,000 pelts passed through New Amsterdam each year on their way to markets in Europe, firmly linking the future growth and prosperity of the colony to continued exchange with their native commercial partners.

BIBLIOGRAPHY

Page, Willie F. *The Dutch Triangle: The Netherlands and the Atlantic Slave Trade, 1621–1664.* New York: Garland, 1977.

Rink, Oliver A. *Holland on the Hudson: An Economic and Social History of Dutch New York.* Ithaca, N.Y.: Cornell University Press, 1986.

Savours, Ann. *The Search for the Northwest Passage.* New York: St. Martin's Press, 1999.

Daniel P. Barr

See also **New Netherland.**

FRENCH

From about 1500 to 1763, French exploration covered an immense expanse of North America. Sixteenth-century French explorers helped improve European maps of the Atlantic coastline and gained knowledge of the people that inhabited the region. They also obtained a tantalizing view of a major waterway, the St. Lawrence. Over the next 150 years, educated Europeans learned about the heart of the continent and its inhabitants mostly owing to the efforts of French subjects. The Great Lakes basin and the water routes north to the Hudson Bay and south to the Gulf of Mexico were progressively unveiled in the seventeenth century. In the eighteenth century, travels on the Mississippi's tributaries and the western plains gave French exploration nearly continental scope.

The original North Americans influenced what explorers would see by receiving them and serving as guides. They could, if it was in their interest and power to do so, refuse them access to certain territories, routes, or neighboring peoples. Even before Natives accompanied the curious newcomers over the horizon, they shaped their expectations by describing and mapping the interior. Joined with European desires, such information could produce, for example, the mirage of the Western sea, always just out of reach.

The French no doubt covered so much ground in North America because, compared to other European colonists, they occupied little of it. Relatively few in number, the French were forced to accommodate Native interests more than the subjects of rival empires were. Even after their population and power increased, the French colonies continued to rely on Native trading partners and allies over an expanding area for commercial profit and for military assistance against the much more populous thirteen colonies. Franco-Native relations would have been well short of symbiotic even without the deadly impact of European diseases. Still, as the seventeenth century advanced, many Native people in the Great Lakes region became accustomed to dealing with French visitors or neighbors, while many of the Frenchmen, traders, missionaries, and officers acquired the basic diplomatic, social, and linguistic skills necessary for good relations with their hosts. The system tended to expand, as groups in both parties stood to benefit from establishing direct relations. Among the French, traders usually traveled the farthest into Native lands. Some of their secrets eventually reached cartographers in Quebec or Paris, and official explorers could draw on this pool of expertise in preparing for and carrying out their missions. Indeed, most of them financed their expeditions by trading with the people they were "discovering."

First Approaches

The informal geographies of both European fishermen and Native people were important in the first phase of French exploration, lasting until the founding of Quebec in 1608. To Europeans, the eastern outline of North America would emerge from the extremities inward. By 1520, two areas had come into focus: the rich fishing banks off Newfoundland and Nova Scotia; and the Caribbean and the curving, invaded continent that bounded it. Like their European rivals, the French hoped to find a direct sea route to Cathay between the two regions, 15 degrees of latitude apart. The Spanish example never far from their minds, they were also more than willing to be sidetracked by any riches they might find, generally at "Indians'" expense, along the way. In 1524, Giovanni da Verrazzano, of Florentine origin but in the French service, reconnoitered the coast between northern Florida and, probably, Cape Breton. He concluded he had seen a new continent inhabited by mostly friendly people; the land, quite narrow in places, offered no noteworthy openings to the west. Later French voyagers would take closer looks at this coastline: Jean Ribault north from the future St. Augustine (Florida) to Carolina (1562); Étienne Bellenger from Cape Breton Island to the Penobscot (1583); and Samuel de Champlain from Cape Breton to Nantucket Sound (1604–1606).

The other object of French exploration in this period was the St. Lawrence River and its gulf. On a clockwise trip around the Gulf in 1534, the mariner Jacques Cartier assembled a puzzle, the pieces of which were already known to European fishermen and Portuguese adventurers. A second voyage the following year took Cartier to Iroquoian territory in the St. Lawrence Valley. During a stay full of misunderstandings, Cartier made a lightning visit to Hochelaga, on Montreal Island, and viewed from Mount Royal the rivers extending to the western horizon, beyond which the Iroquoians had told him precious metals (probably the native copper of Lake Superior) were to be found. The conflict-ridden Cartier-Roberval enterprise of 1641–1643 seems to have gone no farther. By the 1580s, most if not all of the valley's Iroquoian inhabitants had mysteriously disappeared. It was Algonquins who would accompany Samuel de Champlain when he retraced Cartier's steps (and redrew his maps) in 1603.

The Great Lakes Region and Beyond

Within, and sometimes beyond, the framework of the developing commercial and strategic alliance between the French and Native peoples, exploration of the interior began in earnest after the foundation of Quebec in 1608. For about sixty years, few Frenchmen ventured into the interior. Champlain himself accompanied allies on military expeditions or visited their country in the years between 1609 and 1616, seeing Lake Champlain, much of southern Ontario, and parts of Iroquoia in the Finger Lakes region. The young interpreter-traders sent to live with the allied nations ranged farther westward, beyond Sault Sainte-Marie by 1623. Missionaries tended to visit regions of the country the interpreters had already seen and would publish detailed accounts of their travels. After the interpreter Jean Nicolet's inconclusive visit to Green Bay in 1634, it was largely travelling Jesuits who, by 1650, had clarified the geography of the Upper Lakes and, in the 1660s, of parts of Iroquoia and the country north of the St. Lawrence River. The Jesuit Charles Albanel also accompanied the first successful French expedition to Hudson Bay, via Lac Saint-Jean, in 1671–1672 (two further routes would be tried in the 1680s).

The expeditions to the Upper Lakes of Médard Chouart Des Groseilliers (1654–1656 and, with Pierre-Esprit Radisson, 1659–1660), an emissary of fur-trading interests, foreshadowed the reorganized trade that would soon send *coureurs de bois* and ultimately licensed traders in search of Native customers in an increasingly familiar Great Lakes region. The front of exploration now shifted south and west. In 1673, the trader Louis Jolliet and Jesuit Jacques Marquette crossed the Fox-Wisconsin portage already known to traders, and proceeded without Native guides down the Mississippi as far as the Arkansas. From the accounts of the Akamsea, the explorers concluded that the Mississippi flowed into the Gulf of Mexico, and speculated that the Missouri would lead to within hailing distance of the Pacific. Robert Cavelier de La Salle obtained exclusive trading privileges in the Illinois-Mississippi region in 1678. While La Salle's associates would investigate the upper Mississippi, the explorer himself became obsessed with the search for the river's mouth. He successfully reached it by river (1681–1682), but failed to find it by sea or overland from Matagorda Bay (from 1684 until his assassination in 1687). Pierre Le Moyne d'Iberville would make the discovery by sea in 1699. Meanwhile, trader Greysolon Dulhut was among the

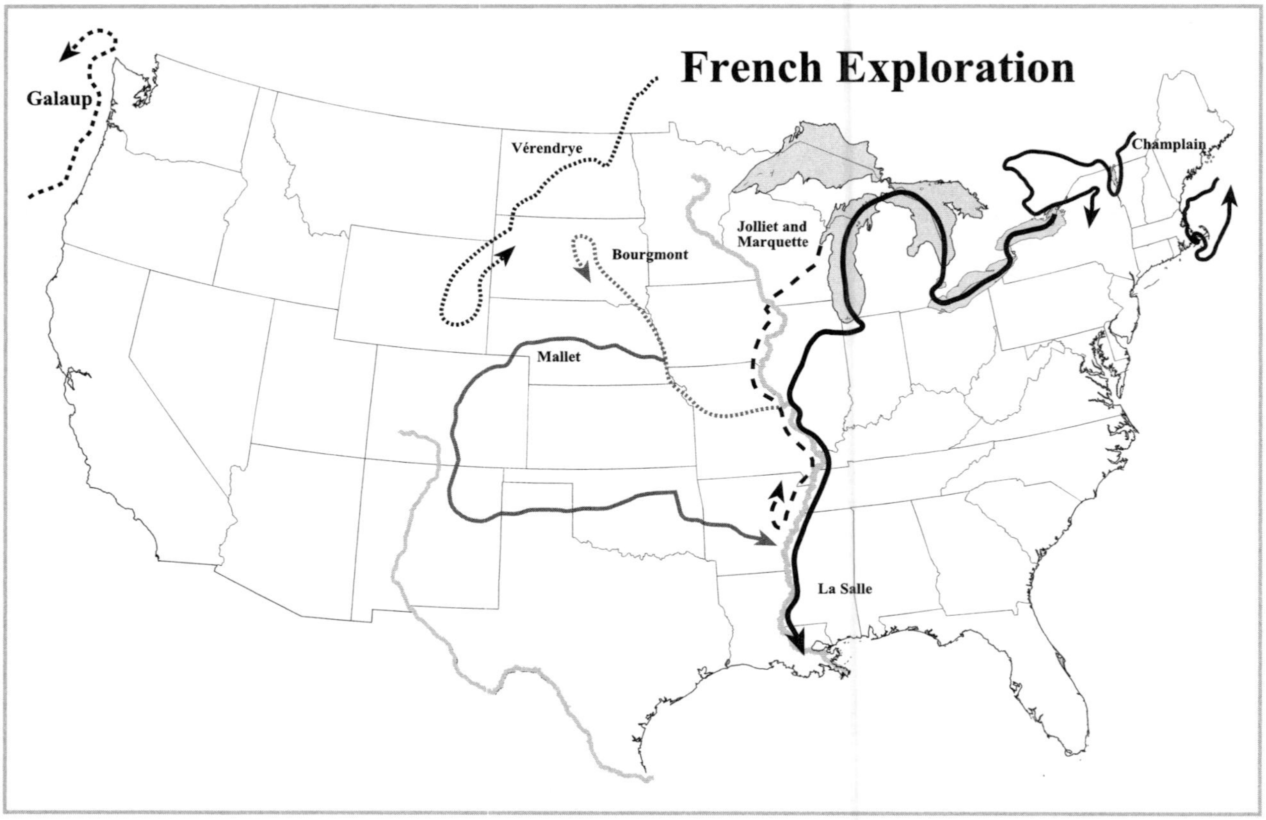

Santee Dakotas of the Mille Lacs region of Minnesota by 1679 and three of his men went considerably farther west. About 1688, Jacques de Noyon traveled from Lake Superior to Rainy Lake, where the Assiniboines told him of a river that emptied into the Western Sea.

French Exploration: The Last Phase

Slowed for a time by the effects of overproduction in the fur trade, French exploration entered a final, intense phase after 1715. Explorers were drawn westward not just from the Great Lakes but also from the new French settlements in lower Louisiana and the Illinois country. The authorities had now recognized the strategic utility of the fur trade, and it was military officers, avid for prestige but not averse to profits, if only to finance their expeditions, who did most of the official exploring during these years. West of the Mississippi, attracted by the possibilities of trade with the Spanish of Santa Fe, French explorers concentrated for a time on the Red River region. The most noteworthy expeditions of this area saw Louis Juchereau de Saint-Denis reach the Rio Grande in 1714, and Bénard de la Harpe cross from the Red to the Canadian River in 1719. Others went up the Missouri. On a thorough reconnaissance of the river and its tributaries, Véniard de Bourgmont ventured as far as the Cheyenne River in 1714–1718. Dutisné traveled into Pawnee country along the Osage River in 1719; Bourgmont went again in 1724–1725, along the Kansas River into Comanche country; and from 1739 to 1741, the two trading Mallet brothers took an epic journey up the Missouri and the (South) Platte, onward to Santa Fe, and then via the Canadian River, to New Orleans. Finally, the Saskatchewan gradually became the main focus of the official search for the Western Sea, a vast, mythical bay of the Pacific. This effort is associated with Pierre Gaultier de la Vérendrye and his sons, whose long (1727–1749) campaign of trade (in slaves as well as furs) and exploration brought them as far as the Black Hills (South Dakota, 1743) and to the Pas (Manitoba) on the Saskatchewan (1748). In the early 1750s, at least one of their successors, Joseph-Claude Boucher de Niverville, may to have come within sight of the Canadian Rockies.

The conquest of New France would place under different auspices French colonists' travels into unfamiliar parts of the interior. French exploration can be seen as 250 years of searching for a direct route to the Pacific (or, at first, the Orient). But it was just as much an encounter of geographies, as French and Native peoples discovered one another, and explorers, both official and unofficial, pieced together North America.

BIBLIOGRAPHY

Codignola, Luca. "Another Look at Verrazzano's Voyage, 1524." *Acadiensis*, 29, no. 1 (Autumn 1999): 29–42.

Eccles, W. J. "French Exploration in North America, 1700–1800." In *North American Exploration*, edited John Logan Allen. Vol. 2, *A Continent Defined.* Lincoln: University of Nebraska Press, 1997.

Heidenreich, Conrad. "Early French Exploration in the North American Interior." In *North American Exploration*, edited John Logan Allen. Vol. 2, *A Continent Defined.* Lincoln: University of Nebraska Press, 1997.

Johnson, Adrian. *America Explored. A Cartographic History of the Exploration of North America.* New York: Viking, 1974.

Kupperman, Karen Ordahl. "A Continent Revealed: Assimilation of the Shape and Possibilities of North America's East Coast, 1524–1610." In *North American Exploration*, edited John Logan Allen. Vol. 1, *A New World Disclosed.* Lincoln: University of Nebraska Press, 1997.

Lewis, G. Malcolm. "Native North Americans' Cosmological Ideas and Geographical Awareness: Their Representation and Influence on Early European Exploration and Geographical Knowledge." In *North American Exploration*, edited John Logan Allen. Vol. 1, *A New World Disclosed.* Lincoln: University of Nebraska Press, 1997.

McGhee, Robert. *Canada Rediscovered.* Montreal and Hull, Canada: Éditions Libre Expression and Canadian Museum of Civilization, 1991.

Thomas Wien

See also **Champlain, Samuel de, Explorations of; Indian Policy, Colonial; Jolliet-Marquette Explorations; La Salle Explorations.**

Russian

Russian explorations in North America centered primarily on Alaska. They were an integral part of the Russian empire's eastward expansion to Siberia and beyond. As early as the turn of the eighteenth century aggressive hunting had depleted the population of Siberian fur animals. The search for new resources of furs drove the Russians to the North Pacific Rim. The government sponsored an expedition headed by Vitus Bering and Aleksey Chirikov (1741–1742). On 26 July 1741, Chirikov "discovered" Alaska by reaching the Alexander Archipelago in southeastern Alaska. In addition, the Bering-Chirikov expedition examined and mapped Kodiak Island, the Shumagin and Commander Islands (Komandorskiye Ostrova), and a few small Aleutian Islands. Abundant flocks of sea otters discovered by this expedition aroused the appetites of eastern Siberian *promyshlenniki* (fur trappers and fur traders) and triggered Russian expansion to Alaska. Hunting sea otters or simply extracting furs by force from natives and clashing with each other, the *promyshlenniki* gradually moved eastward, "discovering" first the Andreanof Islands (P. Bashmakov, 1753–1754) and then the Alaska Peninsula (G. Pushkarev, 1760–1762). A fur trader, V. Ivanov (1792–1793) became the first European to explore Western Alaska inland: the Yukon and lower Kuskokwim Rivers. The engineer D. Tarkhanov (1796–1797)

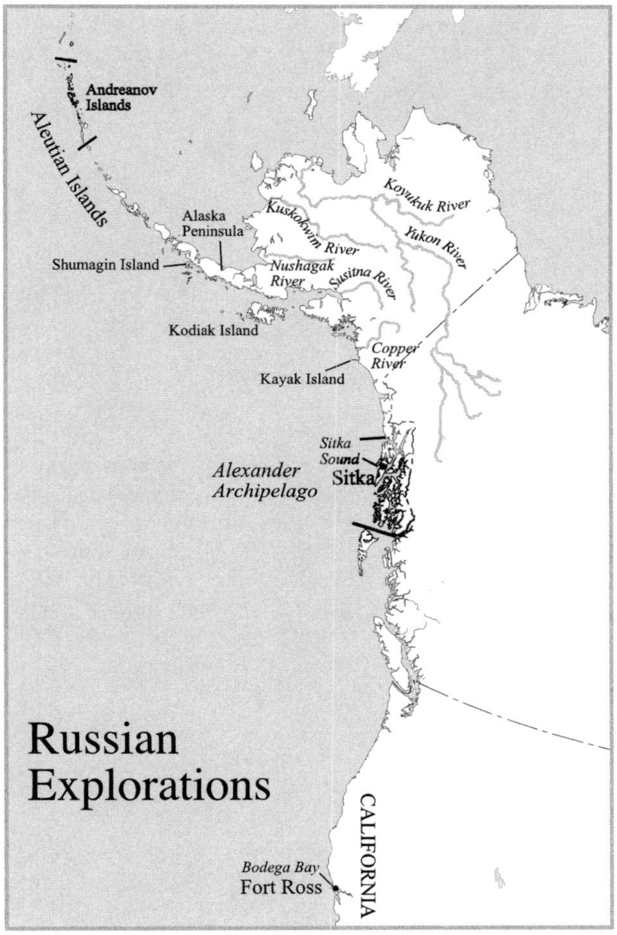

Russian Explorations

was the first to examine the lower Copper River. Governmental expeditions followed the merchants: P. K. Krenitsyn and M. D. Levashov (1766–1770), and I. I. Billins and G. A. Sarychev (1790–1792) mapped the Aleutian Islands, the Alaska Peninsula, and the Alaskan coast to Kayak Island.

In 1799 the imperial government established the Russian-American Company (RAC), a fur trade monopoly that exercised total control over Alaska. Driven by the depletion of sea otters, the RAC extended its explorations southward. In 1804, overcoming the resistance of the Tlingit, Aleksandr Baranov, the first administrator of Russian America, established New Archangel Fort in the Sitka Sound (present-day Sitka). Trying to find a better way to supply the colony, Baranov's companion Ivan Kuskov explored Bodega Bay in California and there founded Fort Ross, an agricultural settlement that existed from 1812 to 1841. In the 1820s, searching for new sources of furs, the RAC reoriented its explorations northward, sending its agents to inland and northern Alaska, to the Yupik and Athabascan tribes.

Replicating the bureaucratic semi-feudal system of imperial Russia, the RAC pursued a "closed frontier" policy in Alaska (restrictions on independent commerce and settlement). The RAC never exercised full control over native population beyond southeastern coast. Moreover, the number of "Russians" in Alaska, actually represented by people of Russian, German, Baltic German, and Finnish origin, never exceeded 823. For geographical explorations, especially in inland and northern areas of Alaska, the RAC depended heavily on its trade agents of Russian-native origin (Creoles): Andrei K. Glazunov, Petr Kolmakov, Malakhov, Ruf Serebrennikov, and Lukin. Aleksandr Kashevarov, one such explorer who headed a kayak (skin boat) expedition and mapped the northern Alaska coast in 1838, reached the rank of major general in the Russian navy.

BIBLIOGRAPHY

Chevigny, Hector. *Russian America: The Great Alaskan Venture, 1741–1867.* New York: Viking, 1965. Popular history.

Gibson, James. *Imperial Russia in Frontier America: The Changing Geography of Supply of Russian America, 1784–1867.* New York: Oxford University Press, 1976. A seminal work.

Makarova, Raisa V. *Russians on the Pacific, 1743–1799.* Kingston, Ontario: Limestone, 1975. Heavily grounded in Russian archival sources.

Smith, Barbara S., and Redmond J. Barnett, eds. *Russian America: The Forgotten Frontier.* Tacoma: Washington State Historical Society, 1990. A collection of scholarly articles, very accessible language, numerous illustrations, all about Russian exploration of and presence in Alaska.

Zagoskin, L. *Lieutenant Zagoskin's Travels in Russian America, 1842–1844.* Toronto: University of Toronto Press, 1967.

Andrei A. Znamenski

See also **Alaska.**

SPANISH

By the early sixteenth century Spain had established Caribbean bases in Hispaniola, Cuba, and Puerto Rico from which it launched further expeditions into South, Central, and North America. Later expeditions into the American Southwest were begun from Mexico, called New Spain at that time. The object of these explorations was to find glittering wealth, to Christianize natives, and to expand the Spanish Empire. The conquistadors who led the expeditions to North America expected to win land, labor, riches, and even vast realms for themselves.

To these conquerors, Spanish sovereigns granted the right to explore specified areas and rights to the fruits of their conquests. Many of the leaders of expeditions to North America were already wealthy from New World conquests and used that wealth to finance their journeys. Hernando Cortés's conquest of Mexico and Francisco Pizarro's conquest of Peru were eventually to prove lucrative beyond imagining, but in the short term the exploration and conquest of North America was frustrating, difficult, and unrewarding. Soldiers, settlers, and slaves comprised the expeditions that explored the southeast and southwest of the present-day United States.

The Southeast

Spain concentrated its first exploratory efforts on FLORIDA. Juan Ponce de León, a seasoned veteran of conquest, had sailed with Columbus on his second voyage in 1493, served in the military in Hispaniola, and from 1509 to 1512 had ruled as governor of Puerto Rico, where he amassed great wealth. Eager to gain a realm of his own, he led the first Spanish expedition into North America. In 1513, after receiving King Ferdinand's permission to explore and settle the Bahamas and places to the north, he sailed from Puerto Rico through the Bahamas and reached the east coast of Florida. Because he landed during the Easter season, Ponce named the new territory "La Florida" in honor of the Spanish term for the holiday, "Pascua Florida." After going ashore to claim "La Florida" for Spain, Ponce continued his explorations. Near the coast of Florida he discovered the powerful Gulf Stream, which would later propel Spanish treasure fleets along the Georgia and Carolina coasts before they turned east to cross the Atlantic to Spain. Indians resisted further landings so Ponce returned to Puerto Rico. Believing Florida to be extremely large, he returned to Spain to seek a contract from the king for its exploration.

In 1519, before Ponce put together his second expedition, the Alonzo Álvarez de Piñeda expedition explored and mapped the Gulf Coast from Florida to TEXAS, showing Florida to be part of a larger body of land, not an island. In 1521, with his legal rights delineated, Ponce returned to Florida with two ships, two hundred colonists, and fifty horses. He intended to found a settlement, but when he went ashore at Charlotte Harbor and built a temporary structure, Calusa Indians resisted his ingress.

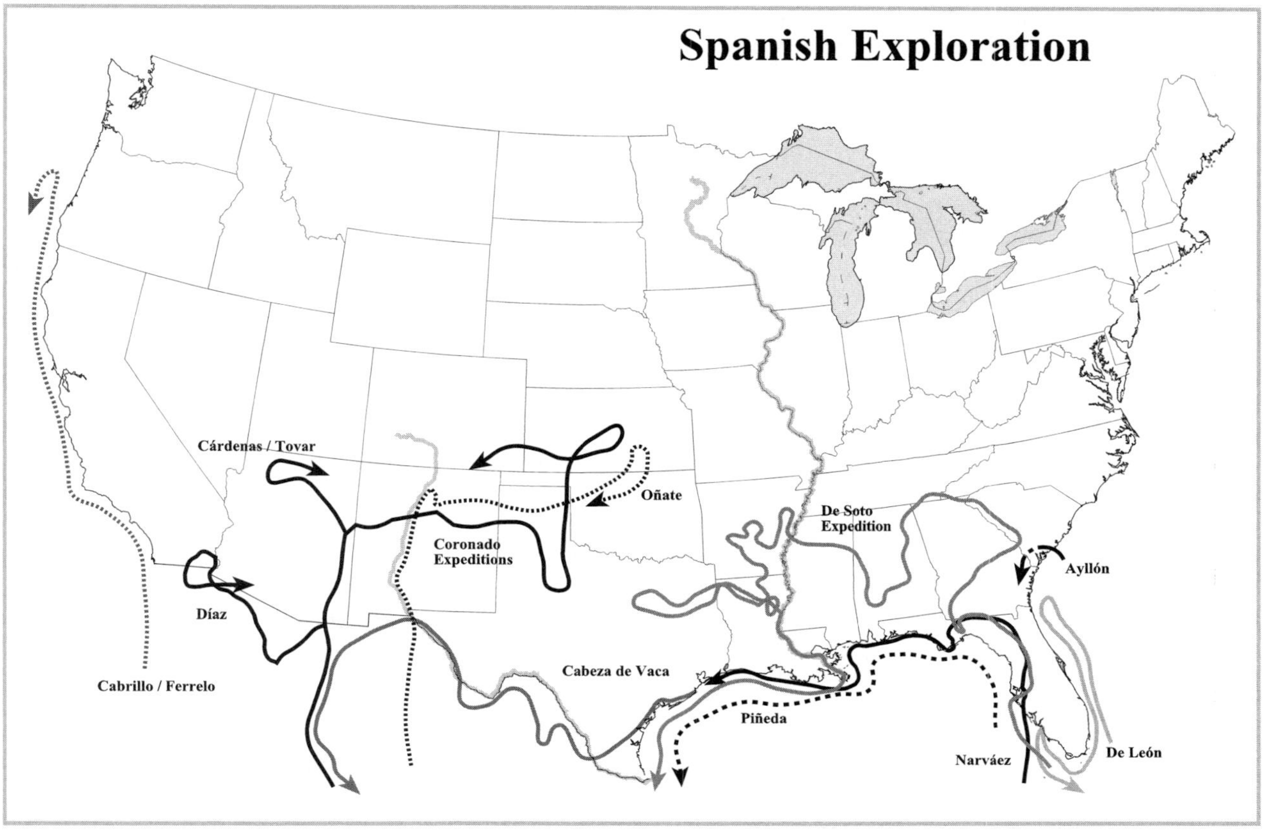

He was wounded by a poisoned arrow and forced to set sail for Cuba where he died a few days after his arrival.

Shortly after Ponce de León's failure, Lucas Vázquez de Ayllón received a charter from Charles V to colonize lands along the Atlantic coast. In 1526, Ayllón landed in South Carolina. He then moved south to Georgia where he attempted to settle his colony of San Miguel de Gualdape. Though it lasted less than two months, it was significant as the first colony established by Europeans in North America since the Vikings. Starvation and Indian resistance caused its demise, and Ayllón died along with many of his colonists. The expedition nonetheless yielded useful geographical knowledge of the Atlantic coast.

In 1528, after obtaining permission from King Charles, Pánfilo de Narváez headed an expedition with Alvar Núñez Cabeza de Vaca, the king's representative, and landed north of Tampa Bay. Narváez marched north looking for gold, but the mission was yet another failure. Having lost touch with his ships, Narváez decided to build new ones to sail back to Mexico. Battered by storms during the return voyage, many died—while others landed in Texas, where Indians took them captive. Only a handful survived their long captivity.

Hernando de Soto led the most extensive exploration of Florida and the Southeast, which lasted from 1539–1543, reaching ten states and covering 4,000 miles. De Soto was already wealthy, having participated in the conquest of Peru. In 1537 he received a charter from King Charles to conquer and settle Florida. He took hundreds of settlers and substantial supplies. After landing at Tampa Bay in 1539, he traveled north with a party—taking food from the Indians as he moved. He spent the winter of 1539–1540 in Tallahassee, Florida, then headed northeast across Georgia to the Carolinas. From there he crossed the Appalachians and moved west to Tennessee. In May 1541 he reached the Mississippi River. Though Pineda had seen the mouth of the Mississippi, de Soto is credited with its discovery. In addition, his expedition reached Arkansas, Alabama, Mississippi, Louisiana, and Texas. In 1542 he returned to the Mississippi River, where he died. The remainder of the expedition returned to Mexico in 1543. A number of accounts described the journey, though the exact route of the expedition is still disputed.

Tristán de Luna y Arellano made the next attempt at exploration and colonization of Florida in 1559. He landed at Pensacola Bay with 13 ships and 1,500 soldiers and colonists. After a cruel winter, the settlement was abandoned. At last, in 1565, Pedro Menéndez de Avilés was successful in founding a permanent settlement in St. Augustine, Florida, which remained under Spanish rule for over two centuries.

The Southwest

The first expedition to explore the Southwest was triggered by the reports of two of the refugees from the Narváez expedition, who had trod across much of the Southwest during the eight years they were missing. The king's representative Cabeza de Vaca and his former servant, Estebanico, told of the seven "golden" cities of Cíbola, where multistoried houses had windows and doors decorated with turquoise. Antonio de Mendoza, viceroy of New Spain, sent Fray Marcos de Niza and Estebanico with a small party of Pima Indians to verify these reports. Estebanico was killed when he reached the Zuni villages of New Mexico. Fray Marcos claimed the villages for Spain and then returned quickly to New Spain, still convinced of Cíbola's glory and splendor.

At nearly the same time de Soto was exploring the Southeast, Mendoza sent out a large expedition under the command of Francisco Vázquez de Coronado. In addition to hundreds of Spanish soldiers, Indians, and slaves, the expedition included two ships, under the command of Hernando de Alarcón, which were to sail up the Gulf of California to bring heavy supplies. With a small vanguard, Coronado reached one of the New Mexican villages in July of 1540, where he demanded the fealty of the Zunis. Upon their refusal, he attacked and conquered the village. Meanwhile Alarcón had sailed up the Gulf of California and had established that Lower California was a peninsula. He discovered and explored the Colorado River, but he never met up with Coronado again and so returned to Mexico.

When the greater part of the land expedition arrived at the Zuni pueblo, Coronado sent out parties to find the wealthy cities. Pedro de Tovar explored the Hopi pueblos of northeastern Arizona; García López de Cárdenas, who was following the Colorado River, was the first European to reach the Grand Canyon; Hernando de Alvarado explored twelve Pueblo villages near present-day Bernalillo, New Mexico (which the Spanish called Tiguex). Here Alvarado learned of a wealthy city called Quivira from an Indian the Spaniards named "El Turco."

In 1541 Coronado himself set out to find Quivira, which turned out to be a modest Plains Indian village in Kansas. After "El Turco" admitted his fabrication, which was designed to send the Spanish on a fruitless and wearying journey, Coronado had him executed. Coronado and his followers returned to Tiguex where they spent the winter of 1541–1542. In 1542 Coronado ordered the expedition back to Mexico. Though gilded cities were never found, Coronado laid claim to great swaths of North America from California to Kansas and his accounts gave a more realistic appraisal of the settlements to the north.

Juan Rodríquez Cabrillo and Bartolomé Ferrelo set out in 1542 to sail to Asia by following the western coastline of North America. They explored the coast of California and were credited with its discovery. Cabrillo died early in the expedition, but Ferrelo went as far north as Oregon.

Based on these explorations, the Spanish eventually sent out colonizing groups to the Southwest. Juan de Oñate took a group of settlers to New Mexico in 1598. At that time, Spain claimed a large region including present-day Arizona and New Mexico. Santa Fe became the capital of this colony in 1609. Though ousted by the Pueblo Indians in 1680, the Spanish reasserted their rule in 1692. The first missions in Texas were founded near San Antonio in the last part of the seventeenth century, while Father Junipero Serra founded the California mission system in 1769.

Spanish explorations in the southwest and southeast of the present-day United States failed to achieve their immediate goals of finding great wealth, converting Native Americans to Christianity, or locating a passage to the Far East. Rather, the conquistadors aroused the enmity of Native Americans and spread disease and disruption throughout their lands. Many Spaniards lost their lives and their personal fortunes, but they gained knowledge of a vast landscape and its inhabitants and gave Spain a claim to settle large parts of what is now the United States.

BIBLIOGRAPHY

Bedini, Silvio A., ed. *Christopher Columbus and the Age of Exploration: An Encyclopedia.* New York: Da Capo, 1998.

Cook, Jeannine, ed. *Columbus and the Land of Ayllón: The Exploration and Settlement of the Southeast.* Darien, Ga.: Lower Altamaha Historical Society, 1992.

Josephy, Alvin M., Jr. *Five Hundred Nations: An Illustrated History of North American Indians.* New York: Knopf, 1994.

Milanich, Jerald T., and Susan Milbrath, eds. *First Encounters: Spanish Explorations in the Caribbean and the United States, 1492–1570.* Gainesville: University of Florida Press, 1989.

Natella, Arthur A., Jr. *The Spanish in America 1513–1979: A Chronology and Fact Book.* Dobbs Ferry, N.Y.: Oceana, 1980.

Bonnie L. Ford

See also **Hopi; Indian Missions; Mission Indians of California; Old Southwest; Pueblo; Pueblo Revolt; Spanish Borderlands; Zuni.**

U.S.

Land Assessment and the Origins of U.S. Exploration

When the United States officially gained its independence from Great Britain in the Treaty of Paris in 1783, the new nation inherited a legacy of imperial exploration that stretched back over 250 years. East of the Appalachian Mountains, especially along river courses and the coast, the country was well-known through long settlement and cultivation. West of the mountains, however, and extending to the Mississippi River, the vast territory that had been ceded by the British to the new nation remained largely unknown to Americans. Except for land speculators like Daniel Boone in Kentucky, Revolutionary War veterans who had fought against Indian tribes along the Ohio River, and traders who had operated in the French and British fur trades, the West was only dimly known to a few government officials who were familiar with the maps and reports from earlier Spanish, French, and British explorations. As Americans came to know the region and then extended their territorial aspirations toward the Pacific Ocean, they would emulate and even compete directly with these and other European powers. In time, however, U.S. efforts to integrate new lands and resources with the more settled parts of the East would ultimately transform the nature of North American exploration from a process of colonization to one of nation building.

One of the first objectives of the federal government in the decades following the Revolutionary War was to fill the gaps in the information provided by past explorers to meet the immediate needs of the new nation. In an effort to extend agricultural settlement and gain much-needed revenue from the sale of public lands, government policy was directed toward rapidly converting Indian lands west of the Appalachian Mountains into private property. This was achieved through land cession treaties with Native peoples and the survey of these lands for sale and distribution. This did not technically constitute "exploration" or "discovery" as either Europeans or Americans would understand those words. But surveys made these lands known to Americans, and concerns about property and settlement—including the separation of Indians from their lands—became the basic motives that would distinguish U.S. exploration from its European counterparts.

Exploration in the Age of Jefferson

Following the acquisition of the Louisiana Territory in 1803, the United States embarked on a century of exploration that focused entirely on the western half of North America. Initially, these efforts involved the nation in a certain amount of diplomatic intrigue, since they situated the new nation within the broader imperial contests that had so long occupied England, Spain, France, and Russia. At the center of these various European concerns was the search for a Northwest Passage, a navigable waterway across North America that would link the commerce of the Atlantic and Pacific Oceans. While the existence of such a passage was a waning hope by 1800, the belief that whoever discovered this water route would eventually control the commerce of the continent had long been a consuming interest of President Thomas Jefferson. The success of two British explorers, namely George Vancouver's mapping of the lower Columbia River in 1792 and Alexander MacKenzie's journey across the Rocky Mountains to the Pacific Ocean via the Frasier River in 1793, gave added urgency to Jefferson's concerns and led to his support of two clandestine but unsuccessful attempts to find a land route between the Columbia and Missouri Rivers.

The fear that Great Britain might dominate the western half of North America ultimately led to the first official U.S. expedition to the West, the so-called Corps of Discovery for Northwest Exploration, under the joint command of Meriwether Lewis and William Clark. Setting out from Camp DuBois near present-day Alton, Illinois, in May 1804, the expedition traveled up the Missouri River to the villages of the Mandan Indians in what is now central North Dakota, where they spent the winter. The following spring they resumed their trek across the continent, reached the headwaters of the Missouri and crossed the Rocky Mountains, then traveled down the Clearwater, Snake, and Columbia Rivers to the Pacific Ocean, where the party's thirty-three individuals spent the winter. The following year they returned by a similar route, arriving in St. Louis in September 1806.

The Lewis and Clark expedition involved three fundamental aspects of U.S. exploration in the early nineteenth century: land assessment, Indian trade, and imperial rivalry. According to President Jefferson's instructions, the expedition surveyed two major river systems "for the purposes of commerce," sought to convince Native leaders of the "peaceful and commercial dispositions of the United States," and observed "the character" of European concerns in the vicinity of the expedition route. Jefferson also made explicit his desire that expedition members pay special attention to "the soil and face of the country, its growth and vegetable productions," and report on the potential of these lands for future commercial development and agricultural settlement.

While Jefferson had an eye on future acquisition and settlement of western lands, the more immediate interest in finding a transcontinental water route reflected a desire to make St. Louis the center of a global fur trade extending to the Pacific and the markets of the Far East. Establishing diplomatic and commercial relations with Native leaders would promote that goal by undermining the position of imperial rivals in North America's lucrative fur trade. Such relations would confirm the authority of the United States in the newly acquired Louisiana Territory and bring much-needed revenue into the fledgling nation. Lewis and Clark did not find an easy route across the continent, but they at least proved that none existed. On all other counts they succeeded, establishing American authority beyond the Mississippi River and even providing the basis for future American claims to the Pacific Northwest.

There were three other significant expeditions during Jefferson's presidency, two by Zebulon Montgomery Pike, and one under the direction of Thomas Freeman and Peter Custis. Except for the charge to find a route

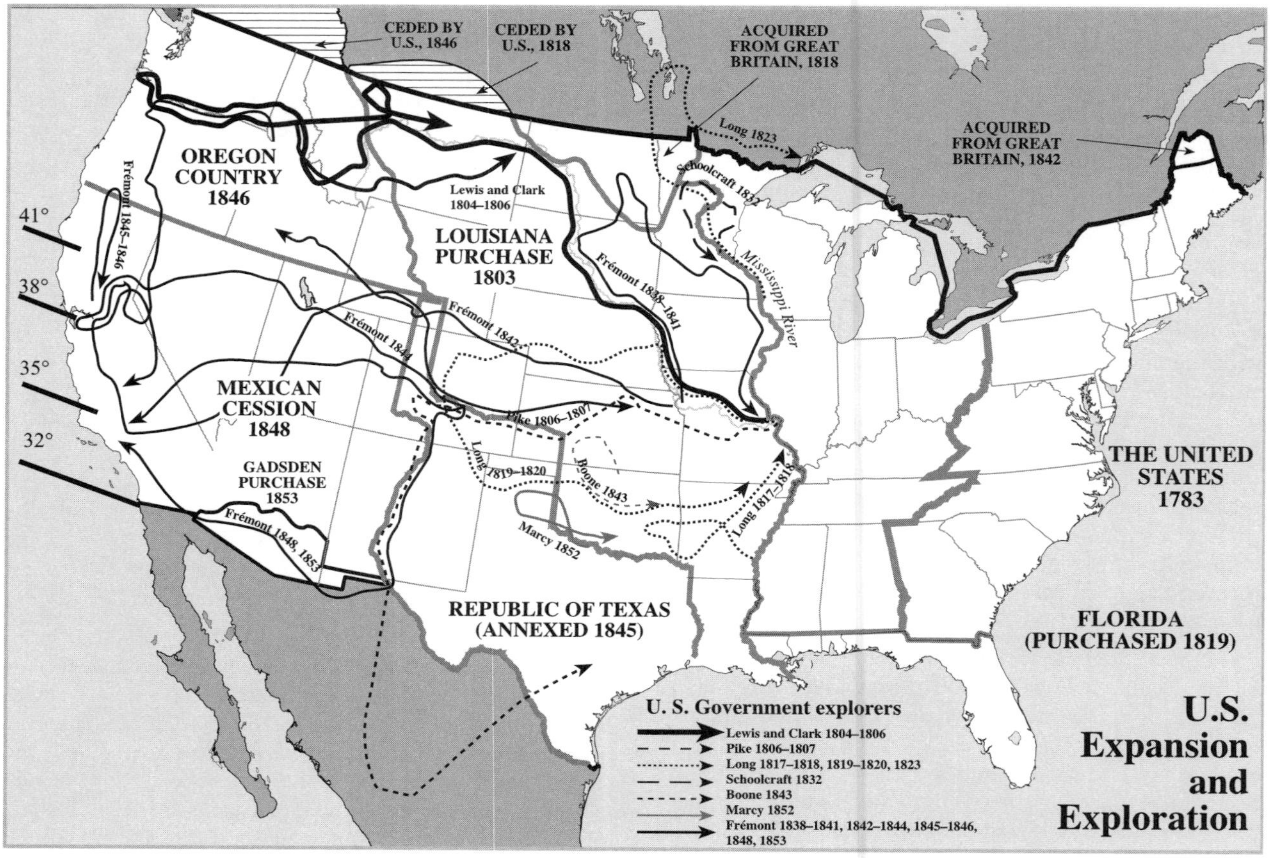

across the continent, all three mirrored the same concerns that inspired the more famous Lewis and Clark expedition. In 1805 and 1806, Pike led a small military detachment up the Mississippi River to northern Minnesota, searching for the river's northernmost source, establishing commercial relations with tribes previously involved in the French and English fur trades, and assessing promising locales for towns and forts. In the summer of 1806 he embarked on another expedition, this time to the headwaters of the Arkansas and Red Rivers, and from there to the Spanish settlements in New Mexico. Pike and his men went up the Arkansas River and through present-day Missouri, Kansas, Nebraska, and Colorado, reaching the Rocky Mountains in late November. After a brief reconnaissance to the north, Pike then traveled south to the Rio Grande. He was soon taken into custody by Spanish authorities, who brought him first to Santa Fe and then Chihuahua before releasing Pike and his small party at the border of Louisiana Territory in late June 1807. The Freeman-Custis expedition of 1806 was intended to explore the length of the Red River, and thus assess the southwesternmost bounds of the Louisiana Territory. The expedition managed to explore six hundred miles up the river, but like Pike ran afoul of Spanish authorities, who jealously guarded their colonial outposts against the new American presence to the east.

Fur Trade Exploration

While Spanish authorities effectively blocked the progress of two exploring parties and nearly intercepted the Lewis and Clark expedition (which entered lands claimed by Spain once it crossed the Continental Divide), Spain's power in North America diminished rapidly in the 1810s and 1820s. Conversely, the American presence in the West grew as a result of the fur trade, which became the primary agent of U.S. exploration in the wake of the Lewis and Clark expedition. In 1808 a former Spanish subject named Manuel Lisa formed the Missouri Fur Company, which included William Clark as a founding member. It initiated a series of trading and trapping expeditions that greatly extended American geographic knowledge of the Upper Missouri River and its headwaters. These efforts were further extended by John Jacob Astor's American Fur Company, which established operations at the mouth of the Columbia River in 1811. The strictly commercial explorations of the fur trading companies provided important information for government officials, primarily through the notes and maps of William

Clark, who served as a superintendent of Indian affairs in St. Louis from 1813 until his death in 1838.

The only government-sponsored exploration during the fur trade era was Stephen H. Long's 1820 expedition up the Platte River to the Rocky Mountains and down the Canadian River. Though not an important contribution to geographic knowledge, Long's expedition did chart a good portion of what would later become the Mormon and Oregon Trails. More significantly, Long's well-received *Account of an Expedition from Pittsburgh to the Rocky Mountains* (2 vols., 1823) presented Americans with a lasting impression of the West, first through his famous description of the Central Plains as a Great American Desert that could not support agrarian expansion, and second through the inclusion of illustrations by Samuel Seymour, an accomplished artist who accompanied the expedition and provided Americans with their first images of the Western Plains and Rocky Mountains.

The exploits of a number of individual fur traders further increased American interest in the Far West. Among these were Jedediah Strong Smith, who trekked from the Great Salt Lake across the Great Basin to southern California and back in 1826 and 1827; Joseph Walker, who traveled the length of the Humboldt River in present-day Nevada and then crossed over the Sierra Nevada to California's Central Valley in 1833 and 1834; and Jim Bridger, who explored the central and northern Rockies during the early 1830s. Artists like George Catlin, Alfred Jacob Miller, and John James Audubon often tagged along with military and fur trade expeditions, as did the famous writer Washington Irving. While none ever explored new territory, their works increased American knowledge of the West and made the exploits of western explorers into something of a national cultural event.

Exploration, Conquest, and Nation Building

Perhaps the greatest beneficiary of increased fascination with the West was John C. Frémont, whose reports for the U.S. Topographical Bureau became instant bestsellers. Following the collapse of the fur trade in the 1830s, and in the midst of a growing interest in the northern territories of Mexico, Frémont headed three major expeditions to the West in the 1840s. Never claiming to be the Pathfinder that his followers called him, Frémont relied on ex-trappers like Joseph Walker and Kit Carson, who had taken to guiding army explorers and overland migrants. In 1842 Frémont headed an expedition to the Rocky Mountains and the Wind River Range in present-day Wyoming, then embarked on a remarkable circuit of the West the following year. Setting out from Independence, Missouri, in June 1843, Frémont mapped the Oregon Trail across the Rocky Mountains to present-day Vancouver, Washington, headed south through Oregon and western Nevada, and then made a dangerous midwinter crossing of the Sierra Nevada to Sutter's Fort in California. Turning south and then east, Frémont's exploring party traveled through present-day Utah and the Colorado Rockies before returning to Independence in August 1844. By the time he set out for a new expedition to California in 1845, which would lead to his active support of a revolt against Mexican rule in Sonoma, his reports on western landscapes had made him a national hero and fanned American arguments for the conquest and annexation of northern Mexico.

The Frémont expeditions were complemented by the efforts of Lieutenant Charles Wilkes, who commanded the United States Exploring Expedition of 1838–1842 to Antarctica, Polynesia, and the Pacific Northwest. Arriving off the Oregon coast in the spring of 1841, Wilkes sent a contingent up the Columbia River to the mouth of the Snake River, while another headed south along the Willamette River, then down to northern California and San Francisco Bay. Wilkes also explored the Olympic Peninsula and the Straits of Juan de Fuca, and proposed that the U.S.-Canada border be set at the north end of Puget Sound. Although Wilkes did not actively encourage outright annexation, as Frémont would in California, the reports from his expeditions did encourage President James K. Polk (1845–1849) to take a more aggressive stance in demanding that Great Britain forfeit its claims in the Pacific Northwest. Like Frémont's reports, Wilkes's *Narrative of the United States Exploring Expedition* (5 vols., 1844) fostered great national interest in the West and together their geographic surveys updated the information of previous explorations to provide detailed maps on the trans-Mississippi West. The Wilkes expedition also took American exploration overseas for the first time and initiated a level of scientific precision that would increasingly characterize U.S. exploration for the rest of the century.

Following the Mexican War (1846–1848), and in the wake of the great migrations to Oregon and California, U.S. exploration focused on the establishment of transcontinental rail corridors and the survey of new national boundaries. To appease both southern and northern commercial interests, the U.S. Army agreed to survey four transcontinental railroad routes between 1853 and 1855. The northern survey, which approximated the future route of the Great Northern Railroad, moved from Saint Paul, Minnesota, to Puget Sound. The other surveys roughly followed the thirty-eighth, thirty-fifth, and thirty-second parallels of north latitude, with the southernmost route earning the preliminary recommendation of Secretary of War Jefferson Davis. The final reports were published between 1855 and 1860 and included illustrations and extensive scientific appendices. The Civil War prevented a final decision on the route of the first transcontinental railroad, which actually followed a route previously mapped along the forty-first parallel by Captain Howard Stansbury in 1849 and 1850. Three of the remaining four surveys also become transcontinental routes at later dates. The U.S.-Mexico boundary was surveyed in much the same manner from 1849 to 1855, with scientific reports and artistic illustrations describing whole new environments to policymakers and the eastern public.

Following the close of the Civil War in 1865, U.S. exploration was increasingly motivated by the expected consequences of railroad building and territorial administration, namely the control of Native populations and the assessment of new areas for settlement and resource development. In many respects an echo of Jefferson's instructions to Lewis and Clark, and like that earlier expedition carried out under the auspices of the U.S. Army, most explorations were conducted in the context of the Plains Indian Wars. George Armstrong Custer's expedition to the Black Hills in 1874, for instance, sought to locate a fort in the heart of Lakota territory to prevent raids on railroad construction crews and the new settlements that sprung up in their wake. The expedition, which included a photographer and university-trained scientists, also assessed the little known area's potential for gold mining and settlement. Similar objectives informed the expeditions of Major Eugene Baker in 1872 and Captain William Jones in 1873.

Science, Commerce, and the United States Geological Survey

While the inclusion of photographers and artists, as well as geologists, topographers, botanists, zoologists, and paleontologists, was commonplace on military explorations of the post–Civil War era, science and art were particularly central to the four so-called Great Surveys of the 1860s and 1870s. These included Ferdinand V. Hayden's U.S. Geological and Geographical Survey of the Territories, John Wesley Powell's U.S. Geological and Geographical Survey of the Rocky Mountain Region, Lieutenant George Wheeler's U.S. Geographical Surveys West of the One Hundredth Meridian, and Clarence King's U.S. Geological Exploration of the Fortieth Parallel.

Ferdinand V. Hayden was placed in charge of the Nebraska geological survey in 1867, but soon enlarged its purview into a more ambitious survey of the Rocky Mountains. In 1871 and 1872 he explored the Yellowstone Basin and his reports led directly to the creation of Yellowstone National Park in 1872. From 1873 to 1876 he moved his survey to Colorado, where he was the first American to describe the Mount of the Holy Cross and the Anasazi cliff dwellings of the Four Corners region, where Arizona, New Mexico, Utah, and Colorado meet. John Wesley Powell focused his attentions further south, where he explored the Colorado River region. He made the first known passage through the Grand Canyon in 1869, and repeated the feat in 1871. Powell eventually produced a systematic topographical and geological survey of the 100,000-square-mile Colorado Plateau, but his most lasting legacy came with the publication of his monumental *Report on the Lands of the Arid Region of the United States* (1878) and its call for restraint and foresight in the use of the West's scarce water resources. Like Powell, George Wheeler explored the Colorado River as well as the deserts of Arizona, California, Nevada, New Mexico, and Utah between 1869 and 1879.

After convincing Congress to fund an intensive study of the mineral resources along the route of the Union Pacific Railroad, the first transcontinental route, Clarence King embarked in 1869 on a ten-year survey that would rival those of his contemporaries in scope, significance, and adventure. Covering a one-hundred-mile wide swath along the fortieth parallel from the Rocky Mountains to the Sierra Nevada, the King survey ranged from mountain peaks to desert. Along the way King assessed the Comstock Lode, one of the richest silver deposits in history, climbed and named Mount Whitney in the southern Sierra Nevada, identified glaciers on the peaks of the Cascades, and wrote a number of popular and scholarly works. Nearing the end of his survey, King was appointed the first director of the newly formed United States Geological Survey (USGS) in 1879. Intended to consolidate the work of Powell, Hayden, Wheeler, and King under one agency, the USGS reflected King's efforts to use government-funded science to assist private mining interests.

King retired from the USGS in 1881 to work as a mining engineer and consultant. He was succeeded by Powell, who incorporated paleontology, hydrology, and the production of a national topographical map within the purview of the Survey. Following Powell's retirement in 1894, and with the acquisition of overseas colonies in the late 1890s, the USGS also turned to the exploration and mapping of American territories outside the United States. Through the twentieth century, the Survey renewed and strengthened its early focus on locating mineral resources and increasingly became involved in the evaluation of federal hydroelectric and irrigation projects as well as in marine and even lunar geology.

In the twentieth century U.S. exploration also entered a new era of competition with European interests. Some of it involved issues of national pride, as with Admiral Robert E. Peary's claim to have been the first to reach the North Pole in 1909, but most explorers focused on the location of military installations or the discovery of new mineral resources overseas. In 1958, the creation of the National Aeronautics and Space Administration (NASA) pushed these concerns into the upper atmosphere and eventually to the moon and to other planets, and NASA remains the primary governmental agency responsible for exploration. While NASA took exploration to outer space, most earth-based exploration shifted to private commercial enterprises such as United States Exploration, Inc., an oil and gas exploration company that developed into a leader in domestic and overseas exploration of energy resources. By the beginning of the twenty-first century, U.S. exploration had moved well beyond the topographical interests of early explorers yet remained closely wedded to earlier concerns about commerce, national development, and global competitors.

BIBLIOGRAPHY

Allen, John Logan, ed. *North American Exploration.* Vol. 3, *A Continent Comprehended.* Lincoln: University of Nebraska Press, 1997.

Bartlett, Richard A. *Great Surveys of the American West.* Norman: University of Oklahoma Press, 1962.

Carter, Edward C., II, ed. *Surveying the Record: North American Scientific Exploration to 1930.* Philadelphia: American Philosophical Society, 1999.

Goetzmann, William H. *Army Exploration in the American West, 1803–1863.* New Haven, Conn.: Yale University Press, 1959.

———. *Exploration and Empire: The Explorer and the Scientist in the Winning of the American West.* New York: Knopf, 1966.

Jackson, Donald Dean. *Thomas Jefferson and the Sony Mountains: Exploring the West from Monticello.* Urbana: University of Illinois Press, 1987.

Meinig, D. W. *The Shaping of America: A Geographical Perspective on 500 Years of History.* Vol. 2, *Continental America, 1800–1867.* New Haven, Conn.: Yale University Press, 1993.

———. *The Shaping of America: A Geographical Perspective on 500 Years of History.* Vol. 3, *Transcontinental America, 1850–1915.* New Haven, Conn.: Yale University Press, 1998.

Reinhartz, Dennis, and C. C. Colley, eds. *The Mapping of the American Southwest.* College Station: Texas A&M University Press, 1987.

Savage, Henry, Jr., *Discovering America 1700–1875.* New York: Harper Colophon Books, 1979.

Smith, Michael L. *Pacific Visions: California Scientist and the Environment, 1850–1915.* New Haven, Conn.: Yale University Press.

Viola, Herman J. *Exploring the West.* Washington, D.C.: Smithsonian Books, 1987.

Mark David Spence

See also **American Fur Company; Columbia River Exploration and Settlement; Freeman's Expedition; Frémont Explorations; Fur Trade and Trapping; Geological Survey, U.S.; Geophysical Explorations; Grand Canyon; Lewis and Clark Expedition; Long, Stephen H., Explorations of; National Aeronautics and Space Administration; Pike, Zebulon, Expeditions of; Transcontinental Railroad, Building of; Vancouver, Explorations; Western Exploration; Wilkes, Expedition; Yellowstone River Expeditions;** *and vol. 9:* **Life and Adventures of Colonel Daniel Boon; Message on the Lewis and Clark Expedition; The Journals of the Lewis and Clark Expedition.**

EXPLOSIVES date back to the tenth century, when the Chinese used powder, a mixture of saltpeter (potassium nitrate) and sulfur, for fireworks and signals. Europeans began using powder only in the thirteenth century, when Roger Bacon added charcoal to the saltpeter and sulfur, creating "black powder." A century after Bacon, Berthold Schwarz invented a gun by filling an iron tube with black powder and a small pebble, then setting the powder on fire. Bacon's creation was the only known explosive for several hundred years.

Explosives are also used to produce the minerals used to make everything from televisions to paper clips to toothpaste to medicines. The mining and construction industries use "low explosives," which burn at slow rates and are designed to dislodge large pieces of rock and ore. Fireworks and signaling devices are other examples of low explosives. High explosives, which burn at a much faster rate, are used primarily for warfare and can be found in bombs, torpedoes, explosive shells, and missile warheads.

Early Americans used black powder mainly for hunting game. The first powder mill was erected in Massachusetts around 1675. The first recorded blasting took place in 1773.

By the early 1770s, the American colonists were readying for war, but they did not have nearly enough black powder with which to fight. The principal supply was left over from the French and Indian War, and it had to be supplemented with imports of half a million pounds of saltpeter and 1.5 million pounds of black powder. Less than 10 percent of the powder used by the revolutionary armies up to 1778 was produced in the colonies.

Du Pont and Other Nineteenth-Century Figures

This changed with the arrival in America of Éleuthère Irénée du Pont de Nemours, who began working in a chemical lab in France at age sixteen. In 1802 he brought his expertise in manufacturing gunpowder to Delaware, building his own powder plant, Eleutherian Mills, on the Brandywine River. Two years later he was manufacturing and selling gunpowder. A year after that, his plant was exporting gunpowder to Spain. By 1811 du Pont was the largest manufacturer of gunpowder in America, producing over 200,000 pounds of powder with gross sales of $123,000.

By the early nineteenth century, Americans were no longer using powder strictly for their guns. Expanding frontiers required blasting to construct roads and canals. The discovery of coal in Virginia around 1830 increased the demand for explosives for mining.

Elsewhere in the world, refinements were being made in the process. In 1831, the Englishman William Bickford developed a "safety fuse" that really was not, since it was easily ignited, was unreliable, and sometimes caused fatalities. It was, however, the first efficient detonator, a device that goes off due to shock or heat to create a sufficient force to explode the main charge. Prior to Bickford's safety fuse, mercury fulminate served as the primary detonating compound.

In the late 1840s the Italian scientist Ascanio Sobrero mixed nitric acid and glycerin to come up with nitroglycerin, a highly unstable yet powerful explosive. Alfred Nobel and his father built a small factory in Sweden in 1861 to expand on Sobrero's experiments. In 1866 Nobel combined kieselguhr, the fossilized remains of sea animals, with nitroglycerin to create dynamite, which was significantly more stable than nitroglycerin alone. It was also much faster to ignite, making it one of the first high explosives.

In America, du Pont's grandson Lammot du Pont helped secure his family's place as the predominant manufacturer of explosives when he used the cheaper sodium nitrate instead of potassium nitrate in his powder. During the Civil War he built a plant in New Jersey and produced dynamite, which was three times more powerful than black powder.

Modern Explosives and Their Uses

From the end of the Civil War in 1865 through the end of World War II in 1945, dynamite served as the country's chief engineering tool, allowing mines to be dug deeper and more quickly; quarrying material such as limestone, cement, and concrete; deepening and widening harbors; paving the way for roads and railways; and constructing dams to store water and produce electricity. Dynamite was also instrumental in oil and gas exploration.

The DuPont Company manufactured much of this dynamite until 1911, when a U.S. circuit court found the company to be in violation of the Sherman Antitrust Act. DuPont still accounted for half the nation's total explosives for mining and heavy construction, providing U.S. industry with 840 million pounds of dynamite and blasting powder. During World War I, DuPont supplied 1.5 billion pounds of military explosives to the Allied forces.

In addition to dynamite, trinitrotoluene (TNT) was used extensively in the war effort. Amatol, a mixture of TNT and ammonium nitrate, was used as well, and between the world wars, ammonium nitrate became one of the most important ingredients used in explosives. In the 1940s it became available in an inexpensive form for mixing with fuel oil. This mixture was commonly called ANFO (ammonium nitrate-fuel oil mixtures).

By the 1970s at least 70 percent of high explosives used in the United States contained ammonium nitrate either mixed with fuel oil or in a water gel. These blasting agents are much safer than traditional agents; they produce little or no flame and explode at low temperatures, avoiding potential secondary explosions of mine gases and dust. With its low cost and relative safety, ANFO has helped revolutionize open-pit and underground mining.

Atomic and Nuclear Explosives

In 1945 a test explosion code-named Trinity ushered in the nuclear age of weaponry with the world's first atomic explosion. A plutonium sphere about the size of an orange, produced by 51,000 workers over twenty-seven months, fueled the test. The blast, equivalent to 18,600 tons of TNT, released heat four times that of the sun's interior and was seen 250 miles away.

Three weeks after the test, on 6 August 1945, the United States dropped "Little Boy," with a force of 16,000 tons of TNT, on Hiroshima, Japan. Three days later "Fat Man," equivalent to 22,000 tons of TNT, was dropped on Nagasaki, Japan, signaling the end of World War II in the Pacific theater.

The United States spent $350 billion building 70,000 nuclear warheads through the end of the Cold War in the early 1990s. Atmospheric tests had released radioactive fallout equal to 40,000 times the Hiroshima bomb. Experiments were conducted in the 1960s to find peaceful uses for nuclear explosives but met with little (or no) success.

BIBLIOGRAPHY

Brown, G. I. *The Big Bang: A History of Explosives.* Gloucestershire, U.K.: Sutton, 1998.

"The Commercial Explosives Industry." The Institute of Makers of Explosives. Available at http://www.ime.org/commercial industry.htm.

"200 Years of History." E. I. du Pont de Nemours and Co. Available at http://www.dupont.com/corp/overview/history.

T. L. Livermore
Michael Valdez

See also **Arms Race and Disarmament; Nuclear Weapons; World War II, Air War against Japan.**

EXPORT DEBENTURE PLAN. During the years 1920–1929, several bills, notably the McKinley-Adkins, the Jones-Ketcham, and the McNary-Haugen bills, sponsored an export debenture plan. The plan's essential principle was government payment of a bounty on exports of certain farm products in the form of negotiable instruments, called debentures, which could satisfy customs duties. Farm products could then be sold to domestic purchasers for no less than the export price plus the bounty, and farmers could thus sell the whole of their marketed crop at above-market prices. Opposed as futile price-fixing schemes, none of these bills became law.

BIBLIOGRAPHY

Davis, Joseph S. *The Farm Export Debenture Plan.* Palo Alto, Calif.: Stanford University Press, 1929.

Frank Parker / C. W.

See also **Agricultural Price Supports; McNary-Haugen Bill.**

EXPORT TAXES were used by the American colonies and England to raise revenue. However, some delegates at the Constitutional Convention (notably Charles Pinckney of South Carolina) disapproved of the practice because the ease with which the government could raise money by taxing exports would tempt it to select the large-scale exports of a few states for taxation, with subsequent inequity. Consequently, the power to tax exports was prohibited in the Constitution (Article I, Section 9) by a vote of 7 to 4. By Article I, Section 10, the convention also withheld this power from the individual states.

BIBLIOGRAPHY

Matson, Cathy D. *A Union of Interests: Political and Economic Thought in Revolutionary America.* Lawrence: University Press of Kansas, 1990.

Frank A. Southard Jr. / A. R.

See also **Colonial Commerce; Constitution of the United States; Taxation; Trade, Foreign.**

EXPOSITIONS. *See* **World's Fairs** *and individual expositions.*

EXPUNGING RESOLUTION. In March 1834 the United States Senate voted by 26 to 20 to censure President Andrew Jackson for removing federal deposits from the Bank of the United States. Jackson protested the censure as unconstitutional, and Thomas Hart Benton, a Democratic senator from Missouri, moved an expunging resolution to obliterate it from the Senate's official journal of proceedings.

Benton's resolution initially failed, but support for it became a defining test of Democratic Party loyalty. In January 1837, at the close of Jackson's term, Democrats captured the Senate and expunged the censure, drawing black lines around it in the original record. The episode discredited censure as a means of congressional sanction, and no president has undergone it since.

BIBLIOGRAPHY

Remini, Robert V. *Andrew Jackson and the Course of American Democracy, 1833–1845.* New York: Harper and Row, 1984.

Daniel Feller

See also **Removal of Deposits.**

EXTRA SESSIONS. Article II, Section 3, of the CONSTITUTION OF THE UNITED STATES empowers the President "on extraordinary Occasions" to "convene both Houses, [of Congress] or either of them." "Extra" or "special" sessions of Congress have been called so often that it is questionable whether these occasions are truly extraordinary. Frequently the Senate alone has been convened, often to confirm appointments made by a newly inaugurated president. Ratification of the Twentieth Amendment to the Constitution in 1933, which provides that the inauguration and the convening of the regular sessions of Congress will take place in the same month, substantially diminished the need for extra sessions.

Unlike many state governors, the president cannot limit the agenda of a special session. Furthermore, the Congress has no obligation to act upon or even consider the matters for which the president convened the session. When President Harry Truman called a special session of both houses in 1948, a contrary Congress not only refused to act on the president's recommended agenda, but it also gave its own leaders the unprecedented authorization to reconvene the legislature. With the exception of the provision involving the disability of the president (the Twenty-fifth Amendment, ratified in 1967), the national and state constitutions are silent on the question of whether legislative bodies may convene extra sessions on their own initiative.

BIBLIOGRAPHY

Bland, Randall W., Theodore T. Hindson, and Jack W. Peltason. *The President: Office and Powers, 1787–1984, by Edward S. Corwin.* 5th ed. New York: New York University Press, 1984.

Genovese, Michael A. *The Power of the American Presidency: 1789–2000.* New York: Oxford University Press, 2001.

Keefe, William J., and Morris S. Ogul. *The American Legislative Process: Congress and the States.* 10th ed. Upper Saddle River, N.J.: Prentice Hall, 2001.

Harold W. Chase
Eric L. Chase / C. P.

See also **Congress, United States; President, U.S.**

EXTRADITION is the surrendering by one state to another or by one nation to another of an individual accused of a crime in the state or nation demanding the surrender of the accused. The accused who has fled to an asylum state or nation is deemed a fugitive of the law. A state or nation makes an extradition demand in order to put the accused on trial within its jurisdiction. In the United States extradition of an accused is either interstate or international. States and nations are not required automatically to surrender a fugitive because of the sovereignty of the states and nations. Sovereignty of the states and world nations necessitates extradition laws and treaties and extradition proceedings.

Interstate extradition or interstate rendition within the United States is authorized by Article IV, Section 2 of the Constitution, which states, "A Person charged in any State with treason, felony, or other crime, who shall flee from justice, and be found in another State, shall on demand of the executive authority of the State from which he fled, be delivered up, to be removed to the State having jurisdiction of the crime." Interstate extradition is also codified in U.S. federal law. A state, acting under authority of the Constitution or federal law, may only demand the surrender of a person who is accused of committing a crime within the requesting state.

A demand from a state for the surrender of a fugitive begins extradition proceedings. Extradition proceedings are not part of the legal trial to determine the fugitive's guilt or innocence of the crime. An extradition proceeding occurs, if at all, in the asylum state to consider the merit of the demanding state's charge against the accused. After receiving a written demand and examining the facts of the charge against the accused, the governor of the asylum state may grant or deny the demand to surrender the fugitive. If denying the demand, the governor may decide to bring the accused to trial within the asylum state's jurisdiction.

If a demanding state wants to try a fugitive within the state's jurisdiction for a crime committed in the asylum state or a third state, the demanding state must rely on the authority of state legislation rather than the Constitution and federal law. Extradition of a fugitive juvenile, as opposed to a fugitive adult, from an asylum state to a requesting state occurs only if it is determined that extradition of the fugitive juvenile is in the best interests of the United States and in the best interests of the juvenile.

International extradition exists only by authority of an international treaty. The United States has the right to make an extradition demand only if a treaty with the nation providing a fugitive with asylum includes an extradition agreement. The United States has a duty to surrender an accused only if the United States has a treaty containing an extradition agreement with the nation demanding the surrender of a fugitive. Absent a treaty, neither the United States government nor the foreign government has the right to demand or the duty to deliver a criminal fugitive.

Even with a treaty, the United States and the demanding or asylum nation may place restrictions on the duty to surrender a fugitive. The use of the death penalty in many states gives reason, as authorized in the governing treaty, for a foreign asylum nation to refuse to extradite a fugitive to the United States. The foreign asylum nation may refuse to extradite a fugitive unless the United States assures the asylum country that the death penalty will not be used if the fugitive is found guilty. The United States has a "political offense exception" to extradition, which provides that the United States will not extradite to a foreign nation a fugitive accused of revolutionary activity that the offended government deems a crime. Thomas Jefferson, credited with first putting the political offense exception into international treaties, wanted to protect revolutionaries from oppressive political systems. During the 1980s U.S. courts, attempting to exempt terrorists from the political offense exception, created "wanton crimes" and "war crimes" exceptions to the U.S. political offense exception to international extradition. By 2001 the United States had treaties containing extradition agreements with 107 of the 190 nations in the world.

BIBLIOGRAPHY

Pyle, Christopher H. *Extradition, Politics, and Human Rights.* Philadelphia: Temple University Press, 2001.

United Nations Crime and Justice Information Network. Available http://www.uncjin.org/Laws/extradit/extindx.htm. Provides updated extradition information by country.

Akiba J. Covitz
Esa Lianne Sferra
Meredith L. Stewart

See also **Sovereignty, Doctrine of.**

EXTRATERRITORIALITY, RIGHT OF. The right of extraterritoriality granted immunity to prosecution under the laws of a country to the nationals of another country; under most circumstances, the foreign national is tried according to the home nation's laws and courts. The system was established to protect Western nationals from judicial systems that were considered uncivilized and barbaric. While the system was meant to protect individuals, it was often abused to the benefit of Westerners.

The United States first sought this exemption from local jurisdiction in countries where the laws, customs, and social systems differed greatly from the Western norm. The result was that extraterritorial courts were set up to administer Western law. The Turkish suzerainties of Morocco, Tripoli, and Algiers were the first to sign treaties with the United States providing for modified privileges of extraterritoriality. According to a treaty of 1830, Turkey granted U.S. citizens exemption from Islamic law, which remained in effect until 1923. U.S. citizens also enjoyed consular jurisdiction in Egypt by virtue of the same treaty. From 1873 to 1949 the United States participated with Great Britain, France, Germany, and other powers in creating the mixed courts at Alexandria and Cairo to deal with conflicts arising among foreign nationals from differing countries.

As the United States came into more contact with Asian nations, it sought to obtain extraterritorial rights in other countries. In 1844 the United States gained the right of extraterritoriality in China (see Cushing's Treaty). The United States expanded its jurisdiction in 1863, by forming the International Settlement in Shanghai in cooperation with Great Britain. In 1906 the U.S. Court for China was established and centered in Shanghai as well. Additionally, the United States obtained similar rights in Japan in 1858. The United States received consular jurisdiction in Muscat (1833), Siam (1833), and Persia (1856).

As countries that had been obliged to grant extraterritoriality grew in strength, they sought to rid themselves of the inferior position implied by the privilege. The United States took tentative steps towards revoking the privileged status its citizens enjoyed. In 1889 the American government negotiated a treaty with Japan abolishing a consular jurisdiction, but the treaty was never submitted to the Senate. Finally, following Great Britain's lead, the United States signed a treaty with Japan in 1899 abolishing extraterritoriality. The situation in China was more difficult and, at the Washington Conference (1922), the powers provided for a commission to study the Chinese legal system and make a recommendation concerning the abolishment of extraterritorial rights. The commission finally met in Peking during 1926 and went no further than recommending improvements in the administration of Chinese justice. The United States finally relinquished its right to extraterritoriality in China in 1943.

BIBLIOGRAPHY

Fishel, Wesley R. *The End of Extraterritoriality in China.* Berkeley: University of California Press, 1952.

Hinckley, Frank E. *American Consular Jurisdiction in the Orient.* Washington, D.C.: W. H. Lowdermilk, 1906.

Jones, F. C. *Extraterritoriality in Japan and the Diplomatic Relations Resulting in Its Abolition, 1853–1899.* New Haven, Conn.: Yale University Press, 1931.

Moore, J. B. *A Digest of International Law.* Washington, D.C.: Government Printing Office, 1906. Reprint, New York: AMS Press, 1970.

David R. Buck

EXXON VALDEZ. Just after midnight on 24 March 1989 the single-hulled oil tanker *Exxon Valdez* ran aground on Blight Reef in Prince William Sound. Over the next few days 11 million gallons (270,000 barrels) of North Slope crude oil spilled into the sensitive subpolar ecosystem of the Sound and the Gulf of Alaska. Caused by the negligence of the oil tanker's captain, Joseph Hazelwood—who was drunk at the time—this was the biggest oil tanker spill in United States history, and it transformed this Alaskan region into a global symbol of ecological catastrophe.

The immediate environmental impact of the spill was far-reaching: about 1,300 miles of shoreline was oiled (200 miles suffered heavy to moderate oiling and 1,100 miles light to very light oiling), while oil washed up on shores 470 miles away from Bligh Reef. An estimated 250,000 seabirds, 2,800 sea otters, 300 harbor seals, 150 bald eagles, up to 22 killer whales, and billions of salmon and herring eggs died as a direct result of the spill. Despite mechanical and bioremediation cleanup efforts between 1989 and 1992, and again in 1997, oil was still present in a large area of the Sound by 2001. Ten years after the spill, only two species (the bald eagle and the sea otter) of the original list of twenty-eight directly affected fish and wildlife species, had been declared fully recovered from the spill.

Human communities nearby also suffered, especially the native peoples who subsist on fish, plants, and wildlife. Ten years after the spill these communities have not yet fully returned to normal. The spill also cancelled the 1989 fishing season, hurting the commercial fisheries industry in the area, and commercial fishing was again cancelled from 1993 through to 1996. The aftereffects of the spill did, however, create new job opportunities for those involved in the cleanup operations, which in turn have led to the emergence of a new economic class labeled the "spillionaires."

Exxon spent more than $2 billion in cleanup efforts in the four years following the spill. On 8 October 1991 the United States District Court accepted an agreement between Exxon and the United States government, in which Exxon agreed to pay $900 million over a period of ten years as a civil settlement—$25 million for committing an environmental crime, and $100 million for criminal restitution. In 1994 a separate class action suit brought against Exxon by over 40,000 commercial fishermen and other interested parties led to a jury award of $5 billion in punitive damages. By 2001 the case was still under appeal.

Exxon Valdez. The damaged oil tanker spills millions of gallons of crude oil into Prince William Sound in Alaska, creating a long-lasting ecological catastrophe. AP/Wide World Photos

Perhaps the most significant result of the Exxon Valdez oil spill was the enactment of the Federal Oil Pollution Act of 1990. This act required faster and more aggressive cleanup operations after an oil spill, forced the responsible party to pay for a cleanup, and provided tougher penalties and more liability for oil spillers. Oil companies have also implemented changes in response to the Exxon Valdez spill, including a commitment to phase out single-hulled oil tankers in the Alaskan waters by 2015, improved techniques for loading and unloading oil, better employee training, stricter drug and alcohol screening, and faster deployment of oil spill response personnel and equipment at times of crisis.

BIBLIOGRAPHY

Exxon Valdez Oil Spill Trustee Council. *Final Environmental Impact Statement for the Exxon Valdez Oil Spill Restoration Plan.* Anchorage, Ala.: The Council, 1994.

Keeble, John. *Out of the Channel: The Exxon Valdez Oil Spill in Prince William Sound.* 2d ed. Cheney: Eastern Washington University Press, 1999.

Lebedoff, David. *Cleaning Up: The Exxon Valdez Case, the Story Behind the Biggest Legal Bonanza of Our Time.* New York: Free Press, 1997.

Owen, Brian M., et al. *The Economics of a Disaster: The Exxon Valdez Oil Spill.* Westport, Conn.: Quorum Books, 1995.

Phia Steyn

See also **Alaska; Conservation; Petroleum Industry.**

F

FAIR DEAL was the phrase adopted by President Harry S. Truman to characterize the program of domestic legislation his administration sought to pass through Congress. In September 1945 Truman sent to Congress a twenty-one point program, based in part on the Democratic platform of 1944. The Fair Deal called for a full-employment law, the permanent establishment of the Fair Employment Practices Committee, and progressive legislation on housing, health insurance, aid to education, atomic energy, and the development of the St. Lawrence Seaway. Congress passed the Employment Act of 1946, which established the Council of Economic Advisers, but Republican victories in the 1946 midterm congressional elections blocked further passage of Fair Deal legislation. In 1948 Truman defeated the Republican candidate, Governor Thomas E. Dewey of New York, and Democrats recaptured control of Congress. In his annual message to Congress in January 1949, during which he coined the phrase "Fair Deal," Truman asked for laws on housing, full employment, higher minimum wages, better price supports for farmers, more organizations like the Tennessee Valley Authority, the extension of social security, and fair employment practices. Congress responded by passing a slum clearance act, raising the minimum wage, and extending social security benefits to 10 million more people. The coming of the Korean War in June 1950 and a general prosperity lessened interest in the Fair Deal program, but many of Truman's social welfare proposals—as well as his proposals for the development of atomic energy and the St. Lawrence Seaway, for example—were legislated in subsequent administrations.

"Falsies!" Two months before Republican Dwight D. Eisenhower's victory in the election to succeed President Harry S. Truman, Fred Little Packer's cartoon in the *New York Mirror*, 6 September 1952, mocks the Democrats and Truman's Fair Deal program by claiming that the nation's economy only seems prosperous, because of inflation and spending on the Korean War. LIBRARY OF CONGRESS

BIBLIOGRAPHY

Hamby, Alonzo L. *Beyond the New Deal: Harry S. Truman and American Liberalism*. New York: Columbia University Press, 1973.

McCullough, David. *Truman*. New York: Simon and Schuster, 1992.

Vincent C. Hopkins / A. G.

See also **Minimum-Wage Legislation; Social Legislation; Social Security.**

FAIR LABOR STANDARDS ACT. During the Great Depression, many employees with little bargaining power were subjected to onerous conditions of employment and inadequate pay. In June 1938, Congress passed a bill designed to limit the maximum number of hours that could be required of employees and the minimum wages they could be paid. This legislation, known as the Fair Labor Standards Act (FLSA), or the Wages and Hours Act, was the last major piece of New Deal legislation. In general, the FLSA, administered by the U.S. Department of Labor, set minimum wages and maximum hours for all employees manufacturing products that were shipped in interstate commerce. It also established requirements for overtime and restricted child labor. Originally, the act's provisions extended to approximately one-fifth of the working population. Over the years, Congress amended the FLSA to add categories of employees to its coverage and to raise the level of the minimum wage. Effective 1 September 1997, the minimum wage became $5.15 an hour.

When first proposed the bill created controversy for a number of reasons. First, some legislators feared it would violate workers' "liberty of contract." From the 1890s through the 1930s, the Supreme Court carefully evaluated all wages and hours legislation to ensure that such laws did not infringe upon this constitutional guarantee. The liberty of contract doctrine held that in general the government should not be able to set the terms of contracts freely entered into by private parties. The Court allowed statutes designed to protect groups it considered either dependent or vulnerable but invalidated any other wages or hours legislation. For example, in *Holden v. Hardy* (1898), the Court upheld a state law limiting the working hours of miners. In *Lochner v. New York* (1905), however, the Court struck down similar legislation regulating bakers' hours on the grounds that bakers were not engaged in an inherently dangerous occupation.

For much of this period, the Court held that the freedom of contract granted to men by the Constitution did not apply to women or children. For example, in *Muller v. Oregon* (1908), the Court upheld a maximum-hours law for women. After women gained the right to vote in 1920, the Court reversed its position in *Adkins v. Children's Hospital* (1923), holding that women's new political rights made them no longer a dependent class. Freedom of contract for both sexes was largely abandoned in the late 1930s, when in *West Coast Hotel v. Parrish* (1937) the Supreme Court dramatically altered much of its constitutional jurisprudence.

At the beginning of his administration in 1933, President Franklin D. Roosevelt wished to propose legislation to guarantee minimum wages and maximum hours and to restrict child labor, but he feared constitutional challenges. In addition, he was aware that such legislation faced opposition by conservatives in Congress. Some conservatives objected to the creation of another New Deal agency. Many southern conservatives feared that the bill's requirements of minimum wages and maximum hours and abolition of child labor would eliminate the competitive advantage that the region possessed because of its generally lower wage rates. Finally, some southern congressmen did not wish to pass legislation that required that black workers receive the same wages as white workers. When the Supreme Court signaled in the *Parrish* decision that wages and hours legislation was now more likely to be found constitutional, Roosevelt encouraged members of Congress to introduce the bill that became the FLSA.

Nevertheless, some concerns remained as to whether or not the proposed law lay within the scope of congressional commerce power based on Supreme Court precedent. Congress passed the FLSA pursuant to its constitutional power to regulate interstate commerce. In *Gibbons v. Ogden* (1824), the Court interpreted the commerce power of Congress broadly. As a result, in the early twentieth century, Congress began to use its commerce power to achieve certain social purposes. For example, in 1916, Congress outlawed child labor by passing the Child Labor Act, which prohibited transportation of products made with child labor in interstate commerce. The Supreme Court, however, resisted such innovative uses of the commerce power. In *Hammer v. Dagenhart* (1918), the Court held the Child Labor Act unconstitutional as an interference with state regulatory power. The *Hammer* decision suggested that Congress lacked the power to pass legislation regulating the conditions of labor, including wages or hours. This conclusion was placed in doubt, however, by the Court's adoption in the 1930s of a more tolerant view of economic regulation. When the constitutionality of the FLSA was challenged in *United States v. Darby Lumber Company* (1941), the Court unanimously upheld the statute, stating that the decision in *Hammer v. Dagenhart* had been a departure from the Court's other holdings and should be overruled.

After Congress passed the FLSA, questions arose as to which types of work-related activities were covered by the act. One particularly difficult issue was whether or not the act should apply to the underground travel by miners to and from the "working face" of coal mines. In *Jewell Ridge Coal Corporation v. Local Number 6167, United Mine Workers of America* (1945), a closely divided Court held that the miners should be compensated for their travel time. In response, Congress in 1947 amended the FLSA by enacting the Portal-to-Portal Act, which overturned the Court's decision. Under the Portal-to-Portal Act only work deemed an integral and indispensable part of the employee's principal activities is entitled to compensation.

Congress also passed legislation that covers the federal government as both an employer and a purchaser of goods and services. The Davis-Bacon Act of 1931 requires that the federal government pay preestablished minimum wages to its employees, and the Walsh-Healey Public Contracts Act of 1936 requires that parties holding government contracts do the same. In 1963, Congress passed the Federal Equal Pay Act, which provides that men and women must receive equal pay for equal work in any industry engaged in interstate commerce.

BIBLIOGRAPHY

Hall, Kermit L. *The Magic Mirror: Law in American History*. New York: Oxford University Press, 1989.

Leslie, Douglas L. *Labor Law in a Nutshell.* 4th ed. St. Paul, Minn.: West, 2000.

Katherine M. Jones

See also ***Adkins v. Children's Hospital*; Child Labor; Commerce Clause; Equal Pay Act; *Gibbons v. Ogden*; Labor Legislation and Administration; *Lochner v. New York*; Minimum-Wage Legislation; *Muller v. Oregon*; Wages and Hours of Labor, Regulation of; *West Coast Hotel Company v. Parrish*.**

FAIR-TRADE LAWS. Fair-trade laws protect businesses and governments from companies or countries attempting to dump goods into a marketplace at low prices or with unfair subsidies. Initially, fair trade was primarily a domestic issue; after World War II, fair-trade laws developed into a key tenet of international trade relations.

The U.S. and other governments provide financial assistance, or subsidies, to companies to aid in the production, manufacture, or exportation of goods. Subsidies run the gamut from cash payments to companies to loans granted at below market rates to stimulate sales in other countries. When governments determine that an unfair subsidy has been granted, they can offset the subsidy through higher import duties, thus keeping competition open between foreign and domestic companies.

Domestic Fair Trade

In the United States, fair-trade laws were first enacted in California in 1931 to protect small retailers and druggists. Soon, most states had enacted similar legislation. These laws were frequently contested; in 1936, the U.S. Supreme Court agreed to hear *Old Dearborn Distributing Company v. Seagram Distillers Corporation.* The Court ultimately ruled that state fair-trade laws were legitimate means of protecting manufacturers. In 1937, the Miller-Tydings Amendment to the Sherman Antitrust Act of 1890 exempted fair-trade laws from antitrust legislation.

In the 1950s, fair trade was hotly contested among various corporations and in the court system, particularly at the state level. By 1956, eight state supreme courts had ruled against fair-trade statutes, making the laws meaningless in some areas. Manufacturers were no longer able to dictate the retail price at which their goods could be sold, which was at the heart of fair-trade laws. Supporters of fair trade redoubled their efforts at the state and national level in the 1950s and 1960s, but by mid-1975, fair trade had been eliminated in 25 states.

Fair-Trade in the Global Economy

Global fair-trade laws are enacted to ensure that U.S. businesses are protected in the world marketplace against unfair foreign pricing and government subsidies, which distort the flow of goods between nations. In the United States, the Import Administration (part of the International Trade Administration) within the Department of Commerce enforces laws and agreements. When a U.S. industry suspects that it is being hurt by unfair competition, either through products being dumped at a reduced cost or by an unfair subsidy, it can request that measures be taken against the offender. The process begins with a petition filed with the Import Administration and the U.S. International Trade Commission.

The General Agreement on Tariffs and Trade (GATT) governed international trade from 1948 to 1995, when it was subsumed by the World Trade Organization (WTO). The idea that global trade broke down in the 1930s as a result of the Great Depression and rise of totalitarian regimes was the impetus behind GATT. The administration of President Franklin D. Roosevelt pushed for the expansion of foreign trade and used a series of agreements to set up reciprocal trade with other nations. Initially, twenty-three nations participated in GATT. Roosevelt's successor, President Harry S. Truman, also supported global trade and forced the United States into signing GATT.

After World War II, government officials wanted to set up an international trade organization to regulate and expand world trade. After failing to win congressional ratification of such an organization in 1948, subsequent administrations adhered to GATT through executive agreement. GATT negotiations between the late 1940s and the mid-1980s lowered tariffs, reduced trade barriers, eliminated trade discrimination, and called for settling disputes through mediation. During the Uruguay Round (1986–1994), the idea for the WTO came to life. In 1996, the WTO became the first international trade organization to be ratified by the U.S. Congress. The WTO oversees international trade and has the legal authority to settle disputes between nations. At the turn of the twenty-first century, 124 nations belonged to the WTO.

Large corporations have been the strongest advocates of free trade, arguing that global competitiveness will raise wages and benefits for all workers as markets expand. In June 1991, the administration of President George H. W. Bush began talks with Canada and Mexico to achieve a trilateral trade agreement. In late 1992, the agreement was signed by Bush and later lobbied for by the administration of President Bill Clinton. The North American Free Trade Agreement (NAFTA) took effect in 1994. NAFTA eliminated tariffs for the three nations, reduced barriers to trade and investment, and exempted businesses from many state, local, and national regulations.

Many of the largest corporations in Mexico, Canada, and the United States lobbied aggressively for NAFTA. They reasoned that creating the world's largest free trade entity would bring prosperity for all three nations. Critics, however, chided NAFTA for its lack of protection for workers, small business, and the environment.

In the early twenty-first century President George W. Bush unveiled an ambitious trade agenda, including agreements with Chile and Singapore, the thirty-five democracies in the Western Hemisphere, and a global free-trade accord with the more than 140-member nations of the WTO. Bush set off a wave of protest, however, when he pushed for unilateral authority to negotiate trade agreements without amendments (known as "fast track").

Nations will continue to argue for and against free trade and protectionist policies. Since World War II, the global economy has become increasingly important for nations of all sizes. Powerful countries, like the United States, have taken steps to formalize global trade, but these issues are burdened with controversy. For example, China entered the WTO in December 2001, after fifteen years of negotiations, despite the country's poor record on human rights. The desire to gain access to the world's largest emerging economy by corporate and government officials overrode longstanding and legitimate environmental and human rights concerns.

BIBLIOGRAPHY

Eckes, Alfred E., Jr. *Opening America's Market: U.S. Foreign Trade Policy since 1776.* Chapel Hill: University of North Carolina, 1995.

Kunz, Diane B. *Butter and Guns: America's Cold War Economic Diplomacy.* New York: Free Press, 1997.

Miller, Henri, ed. *Free Trade Versus Protectionism.* New York: Wilson, 1996.

Bob Batchelor

See also **Tariff.**

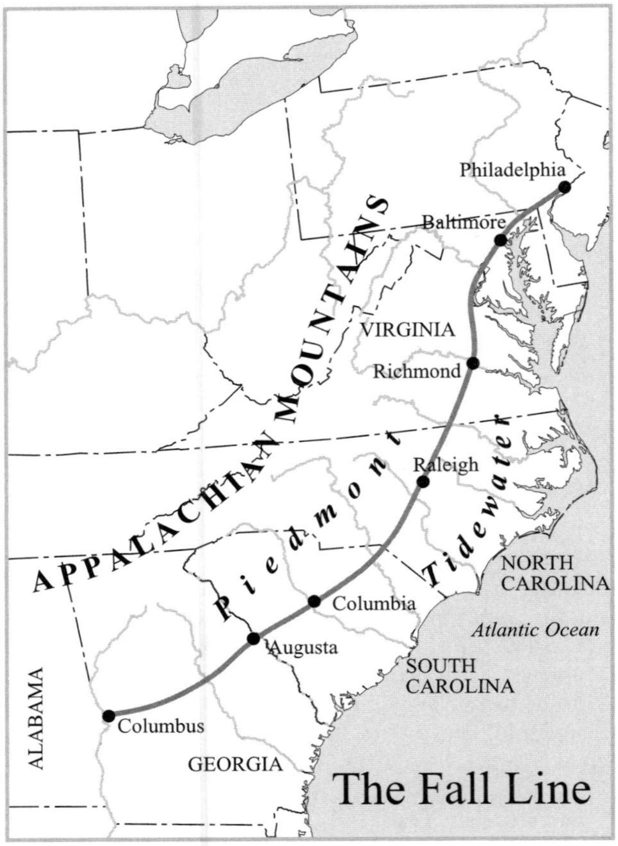

The Fall Line

FAIRS. *See* **County and State Fairs; World's Fairs.**

FALL LINE, a line running approximately parallel to the Atlantic coast and dividing the eastern Atlantic coastal plain, or tidewater, from the western Appalachian foothill region, or Piedmont. This natural boundary was created by the difference in elevation and geologic structure of the two areas. As streams flow from the slightly higher, erosion-resistant rock of the Piedmont onto the more easily eroded strata of the coastal plain, they create waterfalls or rapids—thus the name "fall line." The line, close to the sea in the North, gradually retreats inland until it is a hundred miles or more from the ocean in southern Virginia and the Carolinas. In Georgia it turns westward into central Alabama.

The falls were the head of navigation for river traffic and also provided water power. This attracted development of towns along the fall line, such as Philadelphia, Baltimore, Richmond, Raleigh, Columbia, and Augusta. Roads ran along the inland edge of the plain to connect these cities. The fall line also became associated with sectionalism, especially in the South during the colonial period. The comparatively flat tidewater area, dominated by large plantations and wealthy, influential slaveowners, contrasted starkly with the backcountry districts beyond the fall line, characterized by a small farm economy. In the colonial period, western antagonism toward the tidewater over such issues as taxation, frontier defense, ownership of land, and representation in the legislature occasionally led to mob violence. During the American Revolution some Piedmont farmers even joined the Tory side, in part because of their hostility to the tidewater planters who were opposing England. These sectional differences continued in some states until the Civil War.

BIBLIOGRAPHY

Davis, Joseph L. *Sectionalism in American Politics, 1774–1787.* Madison: University of Wisconsin Press, 1977.

Rand McNally. *Atlas of American History.* Chicago: Rand McNally, 1993.

Robert W. Twyman / c. w.

See also **Piedmont Region; Tidewater.**

FALLEN TIMBERS, BATTLE OF (20 August 1794). Frustrated by Indian raids and the slow progress of negotiations with the British, Gen. Anthony Wayne marched from Fort Greenville (in what is now Ohio) on 28 July 1794, to expel the British and their Indian allies from the Northwest Territory. In a two-hour battle on 20 August at the rapids of the Maumee River in northwest

Ohio, just two miles from the British Fort Miami, Wayne's regulars and Kentucky militiamen routed nearly 800 Indians. To secure the territory, Wayne built a stronghold and named it, appropriately, Fort DEFIANCE. This victory paved the way for white settlement in Ohio.

BIBLIOGRAPHY

Nelson, Paul David. *Anthony Wayne: Soldier of the Early Republic.* Bloomington: Indiana University Press, 1985.

Sword, Wiley. *President Washington's Indian War: The Struggle for the Old Northwest, 1790–1795.* Norman: University of Oklahoma Press, 1985.

Thomas Robson Hay / A. R.

See also **Frontier Defense; Jay's Treaty.**

FAMILY. Myths, misconceptions, and misleading generalizations distort Americans' understanding of the history of the family. Many Americans mistakenly believe that earlier families were more stable and more uniform than modern ones and that divorce, domestic violence, and single parenthood are modern developments. In fact, American family life always has been diverse and vulnerable to disruption. At the beginning of the twentieth century, the United States had the highest divorce rate in the Western world; one child in ten lived in a single-parent home; and approximately 100,000 children lived in orphanages, in many cases because their mothers and fathers could not support them.

Among the most potent myths is the notion that the traditional family in American history consisted of a breadwinner husband and a full-time mother. In fact, it was not until the 1920s that a majority of American families consisted of a breadwinner husband, a homemaker wife, and two or more children attending school.

Despite the romanticized images of family life of the past, family well-being has experienced several advances. These include the decline in the frequency with which families are broken by a member's premature death and the fact that smaller families allow parents to devote more attention and resources to each child. A lack of historical perspective nevertheless has interfered with the acceptance of families that diverge from the dominant norms.

Families in Colonial America

Since the early eighteenth century, families have undergone far-reaching changes in their roles and functions, sizes and compositions, and emotional and power dynamics. Whereas twentieth-century families primarily functioned to raise children and to provide emotional support for their members, colonial families were first and foremost productive units. Colonial families performed a wide range of functions that schools, hospitals, insurance companies, and factories subsequently assumed. Colonial families educated children in basic literacy and the rudiments of religion, transmitted occupational skills, and cared for the elderly and the infirm.

The composition of colonial families was elastic and porous, reflecting both a high mortality rate and households' expanding or contracting labor needs. Even in the most healthful regions, during the seventeenth century three children in ten died before reaching adulthood, and most children had lost at least one parent by the time they married. Consequently, a majority of colonial Americans spent some time in a stepfamily. Most children left their parental homes before puberty to work as servants or as apprentices in other households.

Colonial society attached little value to domestic privacy. Community authorities and neighbors supervised and intervened in family life. In New England selectmen oversaw ten or twelve families, removed children from "unfit" parents, and ensured that fathers exercised proper family government.

In theory, the seventeenth-century family was a hierarchical unit, in which the father held patriarchal authority. He alone sat in an armchair, his symbolic throne, while other household members sat on benches or stools. He taught children to write, led household prayers, and carried on correspondence with other family members. Domestic conduct manuals were addressed to him, not to his wife. Legally he was the primary parent. He received custody of children after divorce or separation, and in colonial New England he was authorized to correct and punish insubordinate wives, disruptive children, and unruly servants. He also was responsible for placing his children in a calling and for consenting to his children's marriages. His control over inheritance kept grown sons dependent upon him for years, while they waited for the landed property needed to establish an independent household.

In practice, gender boundaries were not as rigid as this patriarchal ideology suggests. Colonial women shouldered many duties later monopolized by men. The colonial goodwife engaged in trade and home manufacturing, supervised planting, and sometimes administered estates. Women's productive responsibilities limited the amount of time they devoted to child care, and many child-rearing tasks were delegated to servants or older daughters. Ironically, the decline of patriarchal ideology accompanied the emergence of a much more rigid gender division of labor within the home.

Themes and Variations

Profound differences existed among the family patterns in New England, the middle colonies, and the Chesapeake and southernmost colonies. In New England the patriarchal conception of family life began to break down as early as the 1670s. In the Chesapeake area and the Carolinas a more stable patriarchal structure of relationships did not emerge until the mid-eighteenth century.

Demography partly explains these regional differences. After an initial period of high mortality, life expectancy in New England rose to levels comparable to those of the twentieth century. A healthful environment contributed to a high birthrate (more than half of New England children had nine or more siblings) and the first society in history in which grandparents were common. In the Chesapeake region, in contrast, a high death rate and an unbalanced sex ratio made it impossible to establish the kind of stable, patriarchal families found in New England. In seventeenth-century Virginia, half of all marriages were broken within eight years, and most families consisted of an assortment of stepparents, stepchildren, wards, half brothers, and half sisters. Not until the late eighteenth century could a father expect to pass property directly to his sons.

Religious differences also contributed to divergent family patterns. Not nearly as anxious about infant depravity as Puritan families, Quaker families in Pennsylvania, Delaware, and New Jersey placed a greater stress on maternal nurture than did their Puritan counterparts. Quakers also emphasized early autonomy for children. They provided daughters with an early dowry and sons with sufficient land to establish a basis for early independence.

The Emergence of the "Republican" Family

During the eighteenth century, New England fathers exerted less influence than previously over their children's choices of occupations or marriage partners and over their sexual behavior. By midcentury, sons were moving further away from the parental home, fewer daughters were marrying in birth order, and rates of illegitimacy and pregnancy prior to marriage were rising markedly.

One force for change was ideological. The eighteenth century saw repeated attacks upon patriarchal authority by such popular writers as Samuel Richardson, Oliver Goldsmith, and Henry Fielding, who rejected the idea that a father should dictate a child's career or choice of a marriage partner. Popular literature also asserted that love and affection were superior to physical force in rearing children and that women were more effective than men in inducing children's obedience. Economic shifts further eroded paternal authority. Rapid population growth, which divided inherited family land into plots too small to be farmed viably, weakened paternal control over inheritance. New opportunities for nonagricultural work allowed many children to marry earlier than in the past.

By the early nineteenth century a new kind of urban middle-class family emerged as the workplace moved some distance from the household and as unmarried women working in factories assumed many of the productive tasks of married women. A new pattern of marriage based primarily on companionship and affection arose, as did a new division of domestic roles, which assigned the wife to care full time for her children and to maintain her home. At the same time a new conception of childhood emerged that viewed children as special creatures who needed attention, love, and time to mature. Spouses began to display affection more openly, and parents began to keep their children home longer than in the past. By the mid-nineteenth century a new emphasis on family privacy expelled apprentices from the middle-class home, increased the separation of servants from the family, and spawned family vacations and family-oriented celebrations, such as birthday parties and decorating the Christmas tree.

The new urban middle-class family was based on the strict segregation of sexual spheres, intense mother-child bonds, and the idea that children needed to be protected from the corruptions of the outside world. Even at its inception, however, this new family form was beset by latent tensions. Although a father might think of himself as breadwinner and household head and might consider his wife and children his dependents, in fact his connection to his family was becoming essentially economic. He might serve as disciplinarian of last resort, but his wife was now the primary parent. The courts recognized this fact by developing the "tender years" doctrine that young children should stay with their mothers following a divorce or separation.

Another source of tension in the middle-class family involved the expectation that women should sacrifice their individuality for their husband and children's sakes. During their youth, women received an unprecedented degree of freedom. Increasing numbers attended school and worked, at least temporarily, outside a family unit. After marriage they were to subordinate their needs to those of other family members. This abrupt transition led many women to experience a "marriage trauma" as they decided whether or not to marry. Women's subordinate status was partially cloaked by an ideology of separate spheres, which stressed that women were purer than men and were supreme in matters of the home and religion, but the contradiction with the ideal of equality remained.

Meanwhile, children remained home far longer than in the past, often into their late teens and their twenties. The emerging ideal was a protected childhood, in which children were shielded from knowledge of death, sex, and violence. While in theory families were training children for independence, in reality children received fewer opportunities than in the past to demonstrate their growing maturity. The result was that the transition from childhood and youth to adulthood became increasingly disjunctive and conflict riven.

These contradictions contributed to three striking developments: a sharp fall in the birthrate, a marked rise in the divorce rate, and a heightened cultural awareness of domestic violence. Nineteenth-century women rapidly reduced the birthrate. Instead of giving birth to seven to ten children, middle-class mothers by the century's end gave birth on average to only three. The decline in the birthrate did not depend on new technologies; rather, it involved the concerted use of such older methods as withdrawal and periodic abstinence, supplemented by abortions induced chemically or by trauma to the uterus. No longer were women regarded simply as childbearing chattel or were children regarded as economic assets. The new view was that children required greater parental investments in the form of education and maternal attention.

During the nineteenth century the divorce rate steadily rose, as judicial divorce replaced legislative divorce and many states allowed judges to grant divorce on any grounds they deemed fit. According to a new cultural ideal, marriage rested on mutual affection, and divorce was a safety valve for loveless and abusive marriages. In 1867 the country had 10,000 divorces, and the rate doubled between 1870 and 1900. From 3.1 divorces for every 100 marriages in 1870, the figure climbed to 7.9 in 1900.

The sensitivity toward wife beating and child abuse also grew during the nineteenth century. This sensitivity partly reflected new notions about women's purity and childhood innocence, and it also may have reflected an actual increase in assaults committed against blood relatives. Families became less subject to communal oversight; traditional assumptions about patriarchal authority were challenged; and an increasingly mobile, market-oriented society generated new kinds of stresses. All of these factors turned some families into arenas of tension, conflict, and violence.

Slave Families

No other group faced graver threats to family life than enslaved African Americans. Debt, an owner's death, or the prospects of profit could break up slave families. Between 1790 and 1860 a million slaves were transported from the Upper South to the Lower South, and another 2 million slaves were sold within states. About a third of slave marriages were broken by sale, and half of all slave children were sold away from their parents. Even in the absence of sale, spouses often resided on separate plantations or on separate units of a single plantation. On larger plantations, one husband in three had a different owner than his wife; on smaller plantations and farms the figure was two in three.

Despite the refusal of southern law to legally sanction slave marriages, most slaves married and lived with the same spouse until their deaths. Ties to the immediate family stretched outward to an involved network of extended kin. Whenever children were sold to neighboring plantations, grandparents, aunts, uncles, and cousins took on the functions of parents. When blood relatives were not present, "fictive" kin cared for and protected children. Godparenting, ritual coparenting, and informal adoption of orphans were common on slave plantations. To sustain a sense of family identity over time, slaves named children after grandparents and other kin. Slaves also passed down family names, usually the name of an ancestor's owner rather than the current owner's name.

Working-Class and Immigrant Families

While urban middle-class families emphasized a sole male breadwinner, a rigid division of gender roles, and a protected childhood, working-class and immigrant families, who made up a majority of urban families, stressed a cooperative family economy. All family members were expected to contribute to the family's well-being. Many wives performed work, such as taking in laundry or boarders, inside the home. Children were expected to defer marriage, remain at home, and contribute to the family's income.

Two distinctive types of immigrants arrived in the United States in the late nineteenth and early twentieth centuries: migrant workers, many of whom left wives and children in their home countries and who planned to return home; and immigrants who arrived in family units, often members of ethnic and religious minorities who were persecuted in their homelands. In each case, immigrants often moved for family reasons—to earn enough money to marry, acquire a home, purchase a farm, or find their family a new home offering freedom from persecution. Kinship also played an important role in helping immigrants adapt to a new environment. Much of the movement of peoples involved a process called "chain migration," in which clusters of individuals from a common kin group or place of origin moved to a common destination. The earlier migrants provided later migrants with aid and information.

It was not until the 1920s that the cooperative family economy gave way to the family wage economy, in which a male breadwinner was expected to support his family on his wages alone. The establishment of seniority systems and compulsory school attendance laws and increased real wages as a result of World War I made this possible. The New Deal further solidified the male breadwinner family by prohibiting child labor, expanding workmen's compensation, and targeting jobs programs at male workers.

Early-Twentieth-Century Families

During the late nineteenth century a moral panic gripped the country over domestic violence, divorce, infant mortality, and declining middle-class birthrates. Eleven states made desertion and nonsupport of families a felony, and three states instituted the whipping post to punish wife beaters with floggings. To combat the decline in middle-class birthrates, the 1873 Comstock Act restricted the interstate distribution of birth control information and contraceptive devices, while new state laws criminalized abortion. In a failed attempt to reduce the divorce rate, many states restricted the grounds for divorce and extended waiting periods before a divorce.

Mounting public anxiety led to increased government involvement in the family and the emergence of specialists offering expert advice about child rearing, pediatrics, and social policy. To combat exploitation and to improve the well-being of children, reformers pressed for compulsory school attendance laws, child labor restrictions, playgrounds, pure milk laws, and "widows" pensions to permit poor children to remain with their mothers. They also made concerted efforts to eliminate male-only forms of recreation, campaigns that achieved some success when red-light districts were outlawed during the 1910s and saloons became illegal following ratification of the Prohibition Amendment in 1918.

During the 1920s, in an effort to strengthen family ties, marriage counselors promoted a new ideal, the companionate family, which held that husbands and wives were to be "friends and lovers" and that parents and children should be "pals." This new ideal stressed the couple relationship and family togetherness as the primary sources of emotional satisfaction and personal happiness. Unlike the nineteenth-century family, which took in boarders, lodgers, or aging and unmarried relatives, the companionate family was envisioned as a more isolated unit.

During the Great Depression, unemployment, lower wages, and the demands of needy relatives tore at the fabric of family life. Many Americans shared living quarters with relatives, delayed marriage, and postponed having children. The divorce rate fell since fewer people could afford one, but desertions soared. By 1940, 1.5 million married couples were living apart. Many families coped by returning to a cooperative family economy. Many children took part-time jobs, and many wives supplemented the family income by taking in sewing or laundry, setting up parlor groceries, or housing lodgers.

World War II also subjected families to severe strain. During the war, families faced a severe shortage of housing, schools, and child-care facilities and prolonged separation from loved ones. Five million "war widows" ran their homes and cared for children alone, while millions of older, married women went to work in war industries. Wartime stresses contributed to an upsurge in the divorce rate. Tens of thousands of young people became latchkey children, and rates of juvenile delinquency, unwed pregnancy, and truancy all rose.

The postwar era witnessed a sharp reaction to the depression and wartime stress. The average age of marriage for women dropped to twenty, divorce rates stabilized, and the birthrate doubled. Circumstances unlikely to be duplicated, including rapidly rising real incomes; the GI Bill, which allowed many young men to purchase single-family track homes in newly built suburbs; and relatively modest expectations for personal fulfillment bred by the Great Depression contributed to the emphasis on family togetherness.

For many Americans the 1950s family represented a cultural ideal. Yet it is important to recognize that the images of family life that appeared on 1950s television were misleading. Only 60 percent of children born during that decade spent their childhoods in a male-breadwinner, female-homemaker household. The most rapid increase in unwed pregnancies took place between 1940 and 1958, not in the libertine 1960s.

The postwar family contained the seeds of its own transformation. Youthful marriages, especially by women who cut short their educations, contributed to a surge in divorces during the 1960s. The compression of childbearing into the first years of marriage meant that many wives were free of the most intense child-rearing responsibilities by their early or middle thirties. Combined with the rising costs of maintaining a middle-class standard of living, this freedom encouraged many married women to enter the workplace. As early as 1960, one-third of married middle-class women worked part or full time. Meanwhile, the expansion of schooling combined with growing affluence contributed to the emergence of a youth culture separate and apart from the family.

Late-Twentieth-Century Families

In 1960, 70 percent of American households consisted of a go-to-work dad, a stay-at-home mom, and two or more kids. By the end of the twentieth century less than 10 percent of American households fit that profile. Dual-earner families, in which both husband and wife worked; single-parent families, usually headed by a mother; reconstituted families formed after divorce; and empty nests after children left home became more common. Between 1960 and 1980 the birthrate fell by half; the divorce rate and the proportion of working mothers doubled, as did the number of single-parent homes; and the number of couples cohabitating outside of wedlock quadrupled.

By the end of the century two-thirds of all married women with children worked outside the home, compared to just 16 percent in 1950. Half of all marriages ended in divorce, twice the rate in 1966 and three times the rate in 1950, while three children in ten were born out of wedlock. Over a quarter of all children lived with only one parent, and fewer than half lived with both their biological mothers and fathers.

This "domestic revolution" produced alarm, anxiety, and apprehension. It inspired family values crusaders to condemn careerist mothers, absent fathers, single parents, and unwed parents as the root cause of such social ills as persistent poverty, drug abuse, academic failure, and juvenile crime. Many social conservatives called for enactment of "covenant" marriage laws making it more difficult to obtain divorces.

Historical perspective shows that many fears about the family's future were exaggerated. Despite upheavals in living arrangements, 90 percent of Americans married and had children, and most Americans who divorced eventually married again. In many respects family life became stronger than it was in the past. Fathers became more actively involved in child rearing than ever before; infant and child death rates fell by three-fourths in the last half of the century; and children were more likely to have living grandparents.

Nevertheless, at the beginning of the twenty-first century the family confronted unique stresses. As the proportion of single-parent and dual-earner families increased, working parents found it increasingly difficult to balance the demands of work and family. Because of increasing life spans, many parents cared for their own aging parents as well as for their children. In an attempt to deal with this "crisis of caregiving," the U.S. Congress adopted the 1993 Family and Medical Leave Act, entitling eligible employees to take up to twelve weeks of unpaid, job-protected leave in a twelve-month period for specified family and medical reasons. Despite widespread rhetoric about promoting family values, the welfare and immigration reforms of 1996 weakened social supports for families.

BIBLIOGRAPHY

Coontz, Stephanie. *The Way We Never Were: American Families and the Nostalgia Trap.* New York: Basic Books, 1992.

———. *The Way We Really Are: Coming to Terms with America's Changing Families.* New York: Basic Books, 1997.

Coontz, Stephanie, Maya Parson, and Gabrielle Raley, eds. *American Families: A Multicultural Reader.* New York: Routledge, 1998.

Degler, Carl N. *At Odds: Women and the Family in America from the Revolution to the Present.* New York: Oxford University Press, 1980.

Demos, John. *A Little Commonwealth: Family Life in Plymouth Colony.* New York: Oxford University Press, 1970.

———. *Past, Present, and Personal: The Family and the Life Course in American History.* New York: Oxford University Press, 1986.

Gordon, Linda. *Heroes of Their Own Lives: The Politics and History of Family Violence.* New York: Penguin, 1989.

Greven, Philip J., Jr. *Four Generations: Population, Land, and Family in Colonial Andover, Massachusetts.* Ithaca, N.Y.: Cornell University Press, 1970.

Grossberg, Michael. *Governing the Hearth: Law and the Family in Nineteenth-Century America.* Chapel Hill: University of North Carolina Press, 1985.

Hareven, Tamara K. *Family Time and Industrial Time: The Relationship Between the Family and Work in a New England Industrial Community.* New York: Cambridge University Press, 1982.

Hawes, Joseph M., and Elizabeth I. Nybakken, eds. *American Families: A Research Guide and Historical Handbook.* New York: Greenwood Press, 1991.

Mintz, Steven, and Susan Kellogg. *Domestic Revolutions: A Social History of American Family Life.* New York: Free Press, 1988.

Ryan, Mary P. *Cradle of the Middle Class: The Family in Oneida County, New York, 1790–1865.* New York: Cambridge University Press, 1981.

Schwartz, Marie Jenkins. *Born in Bondage: Growing Up Enslaved in the Antebellum South.* Cambridge, Mass.: Harvard University Press, 2000.

Stevenson, Brenda E. *Life in Black and White: Family and Community in the Slave South.* New York: Oxford University Press, 1996.

Steven Mintz

See also **Adolescence; Child Care; Childbirth and Reproduction; Childhood; Demography and Demographic Trends; Divorce and Marital Separation; Kinship; Sexuality; Work;** *and vol. 9:* **War and the Family.**

FAMILY AND MEDICAL LEAVE ACT (FMLA) requires employers to provide up to twelve weeks, or 480 hours, of unpaid leave annually to any employee for any serious medical condition of the employee or a member of the employee's immediate family, or for the birth or adoption of a child. The act was first introduced into Congress in 1985. It passed both houses of Congress, but was vetoed by President George Bush in 1991 and 1992 before being signed by President Bill Clinton in 1993.

The FMLA covers all public employers and private companies with more than fifty employees. A central component of FMLA is the requirement that employers who provide their workers with health insurance must maintain group health coverage for any employee while on leave. However, employers may require workers to prepay premiums or pay while on leave. The FMLA is enforced by the Wage and Hour Division of the Department of Labor. FMLA rights are in addition to paid sick leaves, but employers may force workers to use vacation or personal leaves after FMLA benefits expire. Employers are forbidden to deny benefits to or discharge those employees using FMLA benefits. Some rights coincide with the AMERICANS WITH DISABILITIES ACT of 1990, although the latter covers employers with fifteen or more workers and requires companies to provide reasonable conditions for disabled applicants.

BIBLIOGRAPHY

Elving, Ronald. *Conflict and Compromise: How Congress Makes the Law.* New York: Simon and Schuster, 1995.

Lenhoff, Donna, and Claudia Withers. "Implementation of the Family and Medical Leave Act: Toward the Family-Friendly Workplace." *American University Journal of Gender and Law* 3 (Fall 1994): 39.

"Symposium. Unbending Gender: Why Family and Work Conflict and What to Do About It." *The American University Law Review* 49 (April 2000).

Wisensale, Steven K. "The White House and Congress on Child Care and Family Leave Policy: From Carter to Clinton." *Policy Studies Journal* 25, no. 10 (1997): 75–86.

Graham Russell Hodges / C. P.

See also **Labor, Department of; Labor Legislation and Administration; Pregnancy Discrimination Act; Women's Rights Movement: The Twentieth Century.**

FAMILY EDUCATION RIGHTS AND PRIVACY ACT. This 1974 federal statute, popularly known as the Buckley Amendment, was designed primarily to protect the privacy rights of students and their parents. It authorizes the withholding of federal funds from schools that violate the act. Under the statute, information about students generally cannot be made public without the consent of parents. Further, parents have a right of access to most information about students. Private law suits for violation of the act, under the 1871 Civil Rights Act, are also possible.

In February 2002, the United States Supreme Court decided an important case relating to the Buckley Amendment (*Falvo v. Owasso Independent School District No. I-001*). The issue was whether a system under which students grade each other's work and call out the grades violated the statute. The Court held that this practice did not violate the Buckley Amendment because student-graded papers are not educational records within the meaning of the Act. The Court did not decide whether private law suits are authorized by the Buckley Amendment.

Carol Weisbrod

See also **Children's Rights.**

***FAMILY OF MAN* EXHIBITION.** After four years of preparation, Edward Steichen's *Family of Man* exhibition made its debut on 24 January 1955 at New York City's Museum of Modern Art. Steichen received more than two million photographs from professionals and amateurs from around the world. With the help of his wife, Joan, and his assistant, Wayne Miller, Steichen selected 503 pictures by 273 photographers from 68 countries and grouped them around themes relevant to all cultures: love, birth, children, death, work, play, pleasure and pain, fears and hopes, tears and laughter. Steichen aimed to show "the essential oneness of mankind throughout the world" during the Cold War. He found the title for his exhibition in a speech by Abraham Lincoln, in which Lincoln had used the expression "family of man." After leaving New York, the exhibition was shown in thirty-seven countries. It became the most popular exhibition in the history of photography, drawing more than nine million visitors from 1955 to 1964. Following the exhibit's world tour, the U.S. government gave the collection to the Grand Duchy of Luxembourg, fulfilling Steichen's wish that the "most important work of his life" be permanently housed in his country of birth.

BIBLIOGRAPHY

Brennen, Bonnie, and Hanno Hardt, eds. *Picturing the Past*. Urbana: University of Illinois Press, 1999.

Mary Anne Hansen

See also **Art: Photography.**

FAMILY VALUES became a popular and political term in the late twentieth century. While it has entailed

Family of Man. The renowned photographer Edward Steichen, director of photography at New York's Museum of Modern Art, stands amid some of the images he assembled for his newly opened, and widely acclaimed, exhibition at the museum (and then in countries around the world), 1955. © BETTMANN/CORBIS subjective meanings throughout U.S. history and contemporary usage, it can be described as a set of beliefs or morals that help provide for family unity and social interaction as well as providing for a societal view for childhood development. These beliefs have encompassed such topics as the roles of marriage, divorce, childbearing, gender roles, and sexual activity and have shaped not only the family's interaction with society, but also legislative policy.

In November 2001 the Institute for Social Research produced a report ("Four Decades of Trends in Attitudes toward Family Issues in the United States") that combined the research of five separate studies tracking family attitudes and values back to the 1960s. The study concluded that there was increased tolerance for diversity in values and behavior outside of traditional family relationships. The values discussed included attitudes towards sex roles, divorce, cohabitation without marriage, extramarital sex, and childbearing.

The results indicated an increasingly positive attitude regarding the equality of women in family relations and the decision-making process as well as the involvement of women in previously traditional male roles. The study found that paradoxically while there was a higher level of acceptance for divorce, the majority of Americans believed that marriages should be a lifetime commitment and not ended except under extreme circumstances. While unmarried cohabitation was somewhat novel in the 1960s, the study concluded it was no longer the societal stigma it once was. Americans tended to accentuate fidelity in a relationship as a desired value and extramarital sex was one moral choice that seems to have become less tolerant among the U.S. populace in the late twentieth century. While the concept that marriages "ought" to produce children had diminished considerably, most of the people interviewed believed parenthood was fulfilling.

Studies such as these have led scholars to different conclusions regarding the family and their values. Some, such as David Popenoe, indicated a decline in family values because of a weakening in parental influence of the child and the child's well-being with the loss of power to institutions such as the workplace, schools, and the state. He maintained that the seeming desirability of self-fulfillment and egalitarianism helped reduce the values of the family. Other scholars, like Stephanie Coontz, stated that "traditional families" are something of a myth and that values depended on a supportive economic and social environment.

In May 1992 Vice President Dan Quayle gave a speech to the Commonwealth Club of California regarding the strengthening of the family. The speech became famous for its attack on the television show *Murphy Brown* and the main character's decision to have a child out of wedlock. The Republican Party touted a return to "traditional family values" that propelled the discussion onto the national level in that year's presidential race. Democrats used the issue to introduce legislation that would support family leave from work in times of need. The debate from that year helped bring about several federal laws in the following years.

Previous federal laws have been passed that either directly affected the morality of the family or specifically mention the family. The Comstock Act of 1873 prohibited the mailing of information related to contraception or abortion. The Social Security Act of 1935 had in mind as one of its goals the preserving and strengthening of the family. The late twentieth century saw a profusion of federal legislation claiming to promote the well being of the family. Among the laws passed during this period were the Child Support Recovery Act of 1992 (a federal crime to willfully fail to pay past-due child support); the Family and Medical Leave Act of 1993 (allowance of up to 12 work weeks' unpaid leave to care for family member); the Violence Against Women Act of 1994 (a federal crime to cross interstate lines to kill, injure, or harass a spouse or intimate partner); the Defense of Marriage Act of 1996 (a spouse is defined as the legal union between one man and one woman); the Personal Responsibility and Work Opportunity Reconciliation Act of 1996 (welfare reform); and the Deadbeat Parents Punishment Act of 1998 (allowing the withholding of wages for child support). These laws have been enacted because of a perceived deterioration of family values that contributed to the necessity of increased governmental assistance.

The concept of family values has changed dramatically from colonial times, when the emphasis was on the notion of a household, with very few values attributed directly to families but rather to the community at large. By the twenty-first century, this evolved to values instigated and nurtured by the family in order to integrate their children into society. While there has been an increase in tolerance of once frowned-upon subjects such as divorce, single-parent families, and gender roles, idealistic reflections of family values have led to its use as a political stratagem and a sometimes scapegoat for perceived societal problems.

BIBLIOGRAPHY

Adler, Libby S. "Federalism and Family." *Columbia Journal of Gender and Law*, no. 8 (January 1999): 197–236.

Arnold, Laura W., and Herbert F. Weisberg, "Parenthood, Family Values, and the 1992 Presidential Election." *American Politics Quarterly*, no. 24 (1996): 194–220.

———. *The Way We Never Were: American Families and the Nostalgia Trap.* New York: Basic Books, 1992.

Gillis, John R. *A World of Their Own Making: Myth, Ritual, and the Quest for Family Values.* New York: Basic Books, 1996.

Popenoe, David. "American Family Decline, 1960–1990: A Review and Appraisal." *Journal of Marriage and the Family*, no. 55 (August 1993): 527–542.

Thornton, Arland, and Linda Young-DeMarco. "Four Decades of Trends in Attitudes toward Family Issues in the United States: The 1960s through the 1990s." *Journal of Marriage and the Family*, no. 63 (November 2001): 1009–1037.

George R. Burkes Jr.

See also **Divorce and Marital Separation; Gender and Gender Roles; Marriage.**

FANEUIL HALL, a historic Boston structure fondly called "The Cradle of Liberty," because of its association with American Revolutionary figures Samuel Adams and James Otis. William Lloyd Garrison and Frederick Douglass spoke in the Great Hall room, where the colossal painting *Webster's Reply to Hayne* celebrates the senator's ringing defense of the Union. Susan B. Anthony and others added luster to this treasured landmark.

The merchant Peter Faneuil gave Faneuil Hall to the town of Boston in 1742. The red brick structure was originally designed by John Smibert as a two-story building with a marketplace on the street level and a meeting room overhead. The building burned in 1761 and was replaced at public expense through a lottery. The Boston architect Charles Bulfinch designed an expanded structure in 1805–1806 adding another floor above, widening the structure, and moving the cupola forward to its present location at a cost of less than $57,000. Faneuil Hall was restored in both 1898–1899 (for nearly $105,000) and in 1992 (for six million dollars), but it continues to be topped by the distinctive copper weathervane shaped in the form of a grasshopper that Peter Faneuil had made for it. The Ancient and Honorable Artillery Company occupies the top floor of the edifice. Since its eighteenth-century use for town meetings and offices Faneuil Hall has served Bostonians as a site for civic discourse and heated debate. The first floor continues to be a marketplace, albeit one that caters to tourists, while the Great Hall maintains its status as an arena for political and community purposes.

Faneuil Hall. Rebuilt or restored several times, this historic building in Boston has been both meeting hall and marketplace since 1742. © Bettmann/corbis

BIBLIOGRAPHY

Brown, Abram E. *Faneuil Hall and Faneuil Hall Market.* Boston: Lee and Shepard, 1900.

Warden, G. B. *Boston, 1689–1776.* Boston: Little, Brown, 1970.

Whitehill, Walter Muir, and Lawrence W. Kennedy. *Boston: A Topographical History.* Cambridge, Mass.: Belknap Press of Harvard University Press, 2000.

Wilson, Susan. *Boston Sites and Insights.* Boston: Beacon Press, 1994.

Lawrence W. Kennedy

FANNIE MAE. *See* **Savings and Loan Associations.**

FAR WEST, a light-draft stern wheeler owned by the Coulson Packet Company. Commanded by Capt. Grant Marsh in 1876, it was the supply boat of the Yellowstone expedition under Gen. Alfred H. Terry, including Gen. George A. Custer's cavalry. After the Battle of the Little Bighorn, it carried Maj. Marcus A. Reno's wounded, together with the first news of the annihilation of Custer's command, to Fort Abraham Lincoln, North Dakota.

BIBLIOGRAPHY

Hanson, Joseph M. *The Conquest of the Missouri: Being the Life of Captain Grant Marsh.* Chicago: McClurg, 1909; New York, Toronto: Murray Hill Books, 1946.

Joseph Mills Hanson / A. R.

See also **Little Bighorn, Battle of; River Navigation; Steamboats; Yellowstone River Expeditions.**

FARM SECURITY ADMINISTRATION (FSA). The FSA was born in 1937 out of frustration with the failure of New Deal agricultural policy to provide help for the nation's poorest farmers. By the time the Democrats came to power in 1932, over a quarter of all farms, involving almost 8 million people, were generating less than $600 apiece in annual income, putting them on the same level as the most deprived city dwellers. Yet, despite the New Deal's announced goal of raising all farmers out of the Depression, its main program, the Agricultural Adjustment Administration (AAA), concentrated on the interests of the largest farm producers, who had irresistible

Images of Hardship. Ben Shahn's 1935 photograph of an out-of-work miner and his wife in southwestern Pennsylvania is typical of a significant depression-era project of the Farm Security Administration, resulting in films and 270,000 still pictures. LIBRARY OF CONGRESS

influence in Congress because they dominated the major farm organizations and land grant colleges.

Roosevelt responded to the situation with an executive order on 1 May 1935, setting up an independent RESETTLEMENT ADMINISTRATION (RA), headed by his close advisor on economic planning, Rexford Tugwell. The aim of the RA was to take 100 million acres of land that had been exhausted by lumbering, oil exploration, overfarming, and drought and move the 650,000 people faring badly there either to better land or into suburban communities planned by the RA. Resettlement was also offered to sharecroppers and tenant farmers who otherwise would have few prospects of escaping poverty. Congress proved reluctant to fund such a reordering of the status quo, which seemed socialistic to some and threatened to deprive influential farm owners of their tenant workforce. The RA was thus left with only enough resources to relocate a few thousand people from 9 million acres and build several greenbelt cities, which planners admired as models for a cooperative future that never arrived.

The RA project to build camps for migratory labor, especially refugees from the drought-struck DUST BOWL of the Southwest, was also resisted by Californians who did not want destitute migrants to settle in their midst. The RA managed to construct ninety-five camps that gave migrants unaccustomed clean quarters with running water and other amenities, but the 75,000 people who had the benefit of these camps were a small share of those in need and could only stay temporarily.

Concerned that criticism of him as "Rex the Red" had made him a liability, Tugwell resigned in 1936. After the triumph of the Democrats in elections later that year, Congress passed the Farm Security Act in 1937, which transformed the RA into the Farm Security Administration, with broader powers to aid poor farmers. Eventually, the staff of the FSA reached 19,000 and was deployed in nearly 2,300 county offices to aid 800,000 client families. With funds provided by the Bankhead-Jones Farm Tenant Act, some 12,000 tenant families became landowners, loans totaling $100 million reduced farm debt by nearly 25 percent, and a medical care program for borrowers grew to include clinics in thirty-one states. In order to give small farmers greater stability and control over the market, the FSA also encouraged the formation of 16,000 cooperatives with 300,000 members willing to pool their resources.

These measures, accompanied by efforts by the President's Committee on Farm Tenancy to help black farmers overcome discrimination and Secretary of Agriculture Henry Wallace's advocacy of planning to coordinate agricultural production and education, stirred up a backlash. The Farm Bureau, which had acquiesced in the creation of the RA as an emergency relief measure, denounced the FSA as "government bureaucracy gone mad"; in Congress the return of most Midwestern farmers to the Republican party by 1940 once Depression hardship had subsided emboldened critics to mount attacks on the FSA as wasteful and "un-American." By 1943 the program had lost most of its funding and three years later was revamped into a weak and short-lived Farmers' Home Administration.

Perhaps the most lasting achievement of the FSA was its image making. To convince the general public of the need for the agency's mission, Rexford Tugwell on 10 July 1935 appointed his former student Roy Stryker "Chief of the Historical Section," with the assignment of photographing the devastated land and people that were the RA's and the FSA's task to rescue. Stryker's camera crew took 270,000 pictures, and members of the team, such as Dorothea Lange, Walker Evans, Arthur Rothstein, and Ben Shahn gained reputations as leading creators of documentary photography. Alongside the photographers, Pare Lorenz made films for the FSA, most notably *The Plow that Broke the Plains* (1935) and *The River* (1937), that won fame for their artistry and the vividness with which they brought home the drastic damage inflicted by flood, drought, and careless exploitation of natural resources. These images retain an ability to evoke both the hardships of rural America during the 1930s and the New Deal conviction that the common people so beautifully photographed deserved the help that only their government could give.

BIBLIOGRAPHY

Baldwin, Sidney. *Poverty and Politics: The Rise and Decline of the Farm Security Administration.* Chapel Hill: University of North Carolina Press, 1968. The definitive work on the FSA.

Curtis, James. *Mind's Eye, Mind's Truth. FSA Photography Reconsidered.* Philadelphia: Temple University Press, 1989.

Saloutos, Theodore. *The American Farmer and the New Deal.* Ames: Iowa State University Press, 1982.

Alan Lawson

See also **Sharecroppers.**

FARM SUBSIDIES. *See* **Agricultural Price Support.**

FARMER'S LETTERS. The so-called *Farmer's Letters* constitute the most effective expression of colonial resistance to the Townshend Acts of 1767. The author of the twelve letters, John Dickinson, was a conservatively inclined lawyer from Pennsylvania who had served in the Delaware and Pennsylvania assemblies. The letters were published in newspapers across the colonies in 1767–1768, and almost immediately reprinted together as a pamphlet. Most of the letters attacked the constitutionality of the Townshend Acts, based not on the earlier distinction between internal and external taxation, but on one between duties levied to regulate trade and taxes intended to raise revenue. The former, according to Dickinson, was acceptable; the latter violated the colonists' sacred rights as Englishmen.

BIBLIOGRAPHY

Flower, Milton E. *John Dickinson, Conservative Revolutionary.* Charlottesville: University Press of Virginia, 1983.

Viola F. Barnes
Leslie J. Lindenauer

See also **Taxation.**

FARMER-LABOR PARTY OF 1920. The Farmer-Labor Party emerged from a chaotic convention held in Chicago in July 1920. It represented an amalgamation of the Labor Party of Illinois, several smaller labor parties, and radical elements in the Committee of Forty-Eight, a progressive organization containing the remnants of the "Bull Moose" Progressive Party of Theodore Roosevelt.

The party had strong support from the Chicago Federation of Labor, led by John Fitzpatrick (1871–1946), and the Illinois State Federation of Labor under the leadership of John H. Walker (1872–1955). Illinois laborites hosted a convention in Chicago in November 1919 that brought together eight hundred delegates from thirty-four states and the District of Columbia. Delegates created a national Labor Party, selected Chicago as its headquarters, and made plans to hold a July 1920 convention to draft a platform, select a presidential ticket, and unite other agrarian and progressive groups. The party's "Declaration of Principles" called for disarmament, expansion of civil rights, guarantees of civil liberties, the eight-hour day and forty-hour week, and nationalization of "all the basic industries."

The Committee of Forty-Eight gathered in St. Louis shortly afterwards. Some three hundred delegates drafted a platform calling for public ownership of most public utilities and natural resources, and full and equal civil, legal, and political rights for all regardless of sex or color. The Committee also supported the creation of a new, broadly based national political party, and made plans to attend the July 1920 convention.

Though the expressed goal of the two groups, meeting separately but advocating merger, was one of cooperation and joint action, the relationship was tense from the start, and there was mutual suspicion. Some Forty-Eight leaders feared the new party would be dominated by laborites favoring widespread economic nationalization. Ultimately, the more radical Forty-Eighters bolted their own convention and joined the Labor Party proceedings. The joint convention reconstituted itself as the Farmer-Labor Party (though little support existed from agrarian groups), drafted a platform, and sought to name Senator Robert LaFollette (1855–1925), the overwhelming choice of those in attendance, as the party's candidate for the U.S. presidency. The Wisconsin senator rejected their offer, considering the party platform too radical. The delegates then selected Parley P. Christensen (1869–1954), a little-known Utah lawyer who had chaired the Forty-Eight convention, to be their presidential candidate, and a longtime Cleveland labor leader and socialist, Max S. Hayes (1866–1945), as his vice-presidential running mate. Christensen had a long career in Utah politics. Starting as a Republican, he gradually broke with party leaders over political reforms, and affiliated with the Progressive Party in 1912. After service in the Utah legislature, where he championed a number of progressive measures, Christensen moved leftward, helped form the Utah Labor party, and served as counsel for several members of the Industrial Workers of the World incarcerated at Utah's Camp Douglas.

Despite a lack of funds, few organizers, large-scale defections by Forty-Eighters, and Eugene V. Debs's presidential campaign from prison, Christensen ran an enthusiastic effort calling for large-scale nationalization of the economy, amnesty for political prisoners, expanded civil rights for blacks, and recognition of the Soviet Union. On the ballot in only eighteen states, Christensen garnered more than a quarter million votes, primarily in Washington, South Dakota, Montana, and Illinois, though he generally ran behind state and local party candidates.

After the election, Fitzpatrick sought to assure the party's political viability. In March 1923 he called for a convention to meet in Chicago to build "a broad alliance of workers and farmers." By the time of the gathering, however, American Communists had emerged as a dominating factor; the party split, and the Communist-led Federated Farmer-Labor Party appeared as a short-lived, competing entity.

In 1924 the Farmer-Labor Party, reflecting Fitzpatrick's control, supported LaFollette's Progressive candidacy. After the disappointing outcome of the campaign, and LaFollette's death in 1925, the party shifted its headquarters to Ogden, Utah, and gradually died out, though state affiliates supported Farmer-Labor presidential candidates in 1928 and 1932.

BIBLIOGRAPHY

Draper, Theodore. *American Communism and Soviet Russia: The Formative Period.* New York: Viking, 1960.

Shapiro, Stanley P. "Hand and Brain: The Farmer-Labor Party of 1920." Ph.D. dissertation, University of California-Berkeley, 1967.

Sillito, John R. "Parley P. Christensen: A Political Biography, 1869–1954." M.A. thesis, University of Utah, 1977.

Weinstein, James. *The Decline of Socialism in America, 1919–1925.* New York: Monthly Review Press, 1967.

John R. Sillito

See also **Bull Moose Party.**

FARMER-LABOR PARTY OF MINNESOTA. The Farmer-Labor Party of Minnesota, a third party that existed between World War I and World War II, was forged from a coalition of agrarian and labor organizations. During its twenty-six-year existence, between 1918 and 1944, it achieved a remarkable record at the polls and did much to stamp Minnesota with a progressive and issue-oriented political complexion that persists today. The Farmer-Labor party inherited a large voting base among the farmers of western Minnesota from the Nonpartisan League. The league, which originated in North Dakota in 1915, entered Minnesota in 1916. It attempted to gain control of the state's dominant political party—the Republicans—in the elections of 1918 and 1920 by nominating candidates in the primary election. The Nonpartisan League reached its high point in Minnesota in 1918, when its candidate, Charles A. Lindbergh, Sr. (a progressive Republican congressman from central Minnesota), was defeated in a strong bid to win the governorship. Thereafter the league's strength declined in the state. In the general election of 1918, efforts to form a coalition with the Democrats failed, but the league-labor forces worked together and entered their candidates on the ballot under the label Farmer-Labor—the first time the name of the future third party was used.

Although it lost the election, the new farmer-labor coalition immediately displaced the Democratic party as one of the two major political forces in the state. The 1918 election also witnessed the breakup of the bipartisan political consensus that had sustained the Progressive movement of the early twentieth century. A new coalition had emerged, stemming from division over U.S. participation in World War I and over the domestic reform policies of the Nonpartisan League. The Nonpartisan League's stronghold in Minnesota had been the farmers of northwestern and west-central Minnesota—of largely Scandinavian background—and the state's socialist movement. To this voting base the Farmer-Laborites added the vote of the German-American population throughout the state, alienated by the country's entry into the war; the emerging labor vote of Minneapolis, Saint Paul, Duluth, and the iron ranges of northeastern Minnesota; and the vote of radical Progressives typified by Lindbergh.

Labor's entry into the Farmer-Labor movement was given a strong impetus at a meeting in New Ulm in July 1919, when the Minnesota State Federation of Labor established the Working People's Nonpartisan Political League as a parallel political organization to the farmer-oriented Nonpartisan League. Headed by William Mahoney, president of the Saint Paul Trades and Labor Assembly, it represented a membership of 45,000 in the state. It supported most of the same policies as the parent league: an eight-hour day; workmen's compensation; equal rights for women; and public ownership of railroads, steamships, banks, packing plants, grain terminals, and telephone and telegraph companies. On 24 March 1920, the two nonpartisan leagues held endorsing conventions in the same hotel in Saint Paul. Henrik Shipstead, a dentist from Glenwood, was selected by both organizations to head the ticket as their candidate for governor in the Republican primary. The third-party label was preserved by filing additional candidates for other offices under the "Farmer-Labor" designation. Shipstead lost to the regular Republican candidate in a close election, but two league-endorsed candidates were elected to the House of Representatives.

In 1922 the Farmer-Labor party abandoned the cautious tactics of the Nonpartisan League—that is, attempting to take control through the primary of the Republican party—and endorsed a full slate of their own candidates. A Farmer-Labor ballot appeared in the primary elections. In the general election the Farmer-Labor party's first major breakthrough for statewide office came when Shipstead defeated the incumbent senator, Frank B. Kellogg. Also elected to Congress from northwestern Minnesota was Knud Wefald. Lindbergh, Shipstead, Magnus Johnson, Ole J. Kvale, and Wefald were the political figures around whom the independent Farmer-Labor movement had rallied during its formative period, 1918–1922. Working behind the scenes were the leaders of the two nonpartisan leagues: Henry Tiegan and Mahoney.

The need for a new organization was evident. In 1923 a joint convention of the two leagues formed the Farmer-Labor Federation. In the same year, the new party captured the state's second U.S. Senate seat by getting Johnson elected in a special election. In 1924 the party failed to win the governorship and lost Johnson's Senate seat, but it won three of the state's ten congressional seats. Emboldened by their electoral successes in the early 1920s, the Farmer-Laborites committed themselves to assuming the role of a national third party. The resurgence of the Republicans during the remainder of the decade reduced Farmer-Labor strength, but the new party retained a firm grip on Shipstead's Senate seat as well as on the House seat in the Red River valley of northwestern Minnesota.

In 1930 Floyd B. Olson, the Farmer-Labor party's foremost leader, easily won the governor's race. Reelected in 1932 and 1934, he served until his unexpected death from cancer in 1936. Olson had begun his career as a Democrat but had been the Farmer-Labor party's candidate for governor in 1924. A respected trial lawyer, his dynamic personality won him public support across a broad political spectrum. In office he acted much more cautiously than his rhetoric indicated; in fact, he largely ignored the radical planks of his 1930 platform. With his reelection in 1932, he struck a political alliance with Franklin D. Roosevelt, and thereafter his policies generally reflected those of the New Deal. Despite hostile legislatures Olson secured large appropriations for unemployment relief, a two-year moratorium on farm mortgage foreclosures, old-age pensions, conservation measures, and the state's first income tax (1933). His intervention in the Minneapolis truckers' strike of 1934 succeeded in forcing employers to grant union recognition.

Olson's reelection to a third term in 1934—this time with strong backing from urban labor and reform forces—promised a more radical program. The party's 1934 platform proposed public ownership of all industry, banking, insurance, and public utilities and the formation of a "cooperative commonwealth." Toward the end of his governorship, Olson's rural support dwindled, but his strength in urban areas increased. His last term in office was turbulent, with a near deadlock in the legislature, strikes, and intraparty fights. After his death the lieutenant governor, Hjalmar Petersen, served the remaining four months of Olson's third term.

Elmer A. Benson, recently appointed by Olson to fill an unexpired term in the Senate, was elected governor in 1936 with a smashing victory—61 percent of the vote. More radical and doctrinaire than Olson, Benson lacked the skills necessary to lead a coalition of dissenting political groups. The consensus disintegrated because of internal strife and the challenge of the young Republican candidate for governor in 1938, Harold E. Stassen, who leveled charges of corruption and communism at the Benson administration. Benson was overwhelmed by Stassen in the 1938 election by as large a margin as he had won by two years earlier. The Farmer-Labor party never recovered its earlier vitality. Although it fought a rearguard action and remained one of the state's two major parties, it retained only one Senate seat until 1941, when Shipstead switched to the Republican party, and one congressional seat until 1944, when it merged with the Democratic party, forming the Democratic-Farmer-Labor party. Nationally, the party's presidential candidates were Robert M. La Follette in 1924 and Franklin D. Roosevelt in 1932, 1936, and 1940. In 1948 the Democratic-Farmer-Labor candidate Hubert Humphrey won election to the U.S. Senate. His long career in national politics owed its success in large part to the Farmer-Labor tradition in Minnesota politics.

During its existence the Farmer-Labor party of Minnesota compiled a string of victories remarkable for a third party. It won five of nine elections for the Senate, four of thirteen for governor, and twenty-six of ninety-six for the House. In all statewide elections its candidates finished lower than second only once. In congressional contests its strongholds were the northern, western, and central sections of the state. Its strongest victories came in 1932, 1934, and especially 1936, when it controlled the governorship, the state house of representatives, both seats in the U.S. Senate, and five of the state's ten House seats.

The Farmer-Labor party of Minnesota was the most successful third party in American history. It drew its strength from and enlarged upon the state's sturdy Populist tradition. It sent Shipstead, Johnson, Benson, and Ernest Lundeen to the Senate. Its foremost standard-bearer, Olson, was unquestionably one of the great leaders of radical political movements in the nation's history, holding together a tenuous coalition of political groups that together formed the Farmer-Labor party. The party brought about widespread citizen participation in political affairs and increased the public's commitment to social justice. Its legacy includes not only the name of the Democratic-Farmer-Labor party but also the strong orientation of Minnesota voters toward social concerns, progressive reforms, high taxation for a high level of public services, and, above all, the state's issue-oriented and independent political tradition.

BIBLIOGRAPHY

Leuchtenburg, William E. *Franklin D. Roosevelt and the New Deal, 1932–1940.* New York: Harper and Row, 1963.

Valelly, Richard M. *Radicalism in the States: The Minnesota Farmer-Labor Party and the American Political Economy.* Chicago: University of Chicago Press, 1989.

Russell W. Fridley / A. G.

See also **Agriculture; Democratic Party; Minnesota; Nonpartisan League, National; Political Parties; Socialist Party of America.**

FARMERS' ALLIANCE was an umbrella term for several grassroots farmers organizations active between 1877 and 1892, most prominently in the South and the Plains states. These groups sought to ameliorate debt, poverty, and low crop prices by educating and mobilizing rural men and women, engaging in cooperative economic organizing, and asserting their power in electoral politics.

Formation of the Alliances

The Alliance had its roots in the severe depression of the1870s. The so-called Southern Alliance was founded in 1877 in Lampasas County, Texas, as the Knights of Reliance. The so-called Northern Alliance had its roots in New York in the same year; founder Milton George, an editor of farm publications, moved the group to Chicago in 1880. Both began quite small but over the 1880s absorbed other local groups such as the Louisiana Farmers' Union and the Agricultural Wheel in Arkansas. The continuing decline of world cotton prices and severe drought on the Plains prompted thousands to join, and by the late 1880s Alliance influence was widespread across the South and Plains. In some states, especially Illinois, Indiana, and Iowa, similar concerns were represented through the Farmers' Mutual Benefit Association. In 1886 black farmers created a Colored Farmers' National Alliance that cooperated with, but remained separate from, the white-run groups. By 1890 Alliance organizers reached the Pacific Coast, winning particular success in California. Loosely sympathetic agrarian groups, such as the Mexican American Gorras Blancas (White Caps) in New Mexico, arose simultaneously in other states. Some groups undertook vigilante protests, destroying, for example, the barbed-wire fences of large landholders that prevented small farmers from letting their hogs and cattle range free.

The Alliances as Social, Educational, and Economic Organizations

The Alliances' work was grounded in the activities of local suballiances, where farmers met regularly to discuss their grievances and needs. Women were prominent in such

BROTHERS AND SISTERS

The time has arrived when we must have perfect harmony and unity of action throughout our entire order. If we hope for success in the demands of our just rights we must be true to our motto, "United we stand, divided we fall," for in unity lies great strength. Why are the farmers getting poorer every year? We work harder, are more economical than we have ever been.

A few years since[,] money was plentiful, the demands for labor were great; now there is very little in circulation, laborers are more numerous, begging employment but the farmers are not able to hire them. What was once the common necessities of life are now high priced luxuries. Why is it that our produce when carried to market is priced by others? Why is taxation more burdensome than during the civil war? Have we less energy? Are we more effeminate? Are we less capable of managing our affairs? Are we truly the empty-headed class we are represented to be? Why have we not been respected as a class, as a great power in the land? Is it because we failed to organize at the proper time as all other classes and occupations and organizations have done? Or is it because we failed to pledge our means and sacred honor for the advancement of our just right? Is it not because we have placed all confidence in our representatives, thinking they had the interest of the whole country at heart? Have they not sold us to the bankers, the monopolies, the trusts, the rings, to all for filthy lucre's sake? A few years since it was considered an honor to be an American citizen but we as a people have fallen into corruption and there is none so poor as to honor us.

Our country is as productive as ever. There is more money in the treasury vaults in Washington than at any previous time, but 'tis not for the laboring class to handle. 'Tis for the benefit of railroad monopolies, national banks to loan to the people at usurious interest; 'tis also for public buildings which is of very little benefit to the people, 'tis squandered by congress in appropriations but none of it goes to lighten the burdens of those who live by the sweat of their brow. There was an appeal for aid sent to congress last year for the drought stricken sufferers. Did they receive aid? Some seed in the agricultural department was bestowed upon them; congress turned a deaf ear to the cries of suffering humanity and don't forget, it is the same democratic president and congress that wants your votes next November.

SOURCE: Mrs. Anna Gray, front-page essay in the *Southern Mercury,* 19 April 1888.

groups, constituting as much as 50 percent of members in some parts of the Plains, and Alliance picnics and family socials were popular remedies for rural isolation and grinding labor. Alliance men and women wrote essays and debated such political issues as monetary policy and temperance. Alliances helped build a vibrant network of alternative newspapers that furthered the work of education and reform. Membership is difficult to determine, but at their peak in 1890 the various Alliances probably represented well over one million families. Combined membership in Kansas and Texas alone was 380,000 and the separate Colored Alliance counted 250,000.

Cooperative economic action was central to the Alliance vision. In Texas, Alliance leader Charles Macune organized the Texas Exchange, through which farmers bypassed middlemen and sold cotton directly to buyers in New England and Europe. The exchange lasted from 1887 to 1889 but failed for a lack of capital, caused by both the poverty of farmers and the hostility of banks to the cooperative venture. More successful was the jute boycott of 1889. Cotton farmers wrapped their bales in jute bagging and the monopolistic bagging manufacturer hiked prices 60 percent over two years. Outraged southern farmers created their own cotton bagging, temporarily forcing the jute cartel to reduce prices.

A Turn to Political Action

By 1890, however, many Alliancemen had concluded they must take action in electoral politics to achieve lasting change. At a convention in Ocala, Florida, in December 1890, movement leaders agreed on the "Ocala Platform," demanding a looser money supply, progressive income taxes on the wealthy, and other economic measures. In calling for "rigid" government oversight of railroads and public ownership if regulation failed to stem abuses, the Ocala demands echoed midwestern "Granger Laws" of the 1870s. Meanwhile, Kansas Alliancemen, guided by editor William A. Peffer, had joined with labor leaders in forming the Kansas People's Party, whose success in the dramatic campaign of 1890 electrified Alliance followers nationwide. The new party unseated Kansas's Republican U.S. senator, John J. Ingalls, who was hostile to Alliance goals, and replaced him with Peffer. Southern Alliancemen sought action simultaneously through the Democratic Party, telling legislators they would be judged by the "Alliance yardstick." But after legislators returned to southern state capitols, their campaign promises and flattery turned out to be largely empty and sentiment in the Southern Alliance shifted toward creation of a new party.

In February 1892 delegates from the various Alliances met in St. Louis with representatives of many labor and progressive reform groups, forming the national People's (or Populist) Party. Much of its platform echoed the Ocala Demands of 1890, set forth at a national Alliance conference in Ocala, Florida. Seeking reforms in "money, land, and transportation," Alliance leaders demanded government regulation or outright ownership of telegraphs and railroads; revocation of large land grants to railroads; various antitrust remedies; a federal progressive income tax; direct election of U.S. senators by the people; and an increased money supply to benefit borrowers rather than lenders. Some Alliance leaders, especially in the West, also called for women's suffrage. Alliance president Leonidas Polk, editor of North Carolina's *Progressive Farmer,* would have probably been the party's first presidential nominee had he not died suddenly a few weeks before the 1892 convention, dashing hopes for a farmer candidate with nationwide appeal.

The Alliance's success depended largely on political conditions in different regions. In states like Iowa and Illinois, which had already proved sympathetic to farmers' demands in passing Granger Laws in the 1870s, Democrats moved to meet farmers' demands and the People's Party never gained a foothold. In the South many Democrats resorted to violence and fraud to maintain power while playing on white racial prejudices to divide their opponents. The People's Party won its greatest victories and endured longest in Plains states such as Kansas and Nebraska, but even there it was forced to compromise with Democrats in order to retain power. The severe depression of the 1890s was a blow to both the Alliance and the new party and the Alliances had largely disappeared by 1900. Nonetheless, the political agenda of the agrarian movement endured. Southern and western farm states provided crucial support for much of the landmark reform legislation of the Progressive era, particularly in the areas of antitrust, railroad regulation, taxation, banking, credit, monetary policy, and protection of labor.

BIBLIOGRAPHY

Goodwyn, Lawrence. *Democratic Promise: The Populist Moment in America.* New York: Oxford University Press, 1976.

Hicks, John D. *The Populist Revolt: A History of the Farmers' Alliance and the People's Party.* Minneapolis: University of Minnesota Press, 1931.

Jeffrey, Julie Roy. "Women in the Southern Farmers' Alliance: A Reconsideration of the Role and Status of Women in the Late Nineteenth-Century South." *Feminist Studies* 3 (1975): 72–91.

McMath, Robert C., Jr. *Populist Vanguard: A History of the Southern Farmers' Alliance.* Chapel Hill, N.C.: University of North Carolina Press, 1975.

———. *American Populism: A Social History, 1877–1898.* New York: Hill and Wang, 1993.

Ostler, Jeffrey. *Prairie Populism: The Fate of Agrarian* Radicalism *in Kansas, Nebraska, and Iowa, 1880–1892.* Lawrence, Kans.: University of Kansas Press, 1993.

Sanders, Elizabeth. *Roots of Reform: Farmers, Workers, and the American State, 1877–1917.* Chicago: University of Chicago Press, 1999.

Rebecca Edwards

See also **Cooperatives, Farmers'; Populism;** *and vol. 9:* **Women in the Farmers' Alliance.**

FARMERS INSTITUTES were modeled on the teachers institute in order to carry agricultural knowledge to farmers. The idea was broached as early as 1853, but the first genuine example of an institute was held at Yale under the direction of Samuel William Johnson, an agricultural chemist, in 1860. The Civil War postponed further progress until the late 1860s, and, by 1870, many state farm organizations made some provision for lecturers to hold meetings of farmers. The classic form of the farmers institute took shape during the 1880s. By 1885, the plan was systematized and state appropriations granted for carrying it out; by 1889, the movement was in full swing.

At that time, W. O. Atwater, federal director of agricultural experiment stations, hailed the institute as a refinement of the work that had previously been done haphazardly by agricultural boards, colleges, societies, clubs, conventions, and experiment stations. Atwater viewed the institute as the best device thus far tried for carrying agricultural knowledge to farmers. Farm periodicals, agricultural colleges, and especially the agricultural experiment stations were steadily bringing advanced farming techniques to light. Local farmers institutes soon emerged to convey this material directly to practicing farmers. Sponsored by a county agricultural society, county grange, or farmers club, farmers institutes were directed by state lecturers and attended by leading local farmers. The programs were commonly arranged for a two-day meeting in winter. Organizers advertised the meetings widely; many of the entertainment features common to granges and county fairs—music, dramatics, declamations—were employed to add interest; and good storytellers among the lecture staff were featured. Farm problems were discussed in the light of the most recent scientific research. Discussion of household economy and the "domestic sciences" were added for the special benefit of farm women. Political partisanship was shunned, but questions of public policy affecting agriculture received attention. The attendance of farmers at the institutes held in the several states sometimes numbered as high as 4 million.

While agricultural science continued to play a vital role in the twentieth century, the farmers institutes themselves were soon incorporated into the widened municipal sphere of the Progressive Movement. With the promotion of agricultural extension on a national scale through both state and federal appropriations—which began about 1914 after the passage of the Smith-Lever Act—farmers institutes of the older type had their functions gradually absorbed by the newer agricultural extension activity.

BIBLIOGRAPHY

Rossiter, Margaret W. *The Emergence of Agricultural Science: Justus Liebig and the Americans, 1840–1880.* New Haven, Conn.: Yale University Press, 1975.

Scott, Roy Vernon. *The Reluctant Farmer: The Rise of Agricultural Extension to 1914.* Urbana, Ill.; London: University of Illinois Press, 1970).

Joseph Schafer / A. R.

See also **Agriculture; Granger Movement; Progressive Movement; Rural Life.**

FARMHAND, a term prevalent in the nineteenth and early twentieth centuries in the northern United States, referred to farm wageworkers and generally was equivalent to "hired man." Now, however, the more common designation is "agricultural worker," which includes all who labor on the land manually regardless of region, structure of enterprise, or status.

Early in colonial America, distinctive patterns among agricultural workers emerged. Landowners who wanted workers to help them paid the passage from the British Isles and western Europe for indentured servants, bound on arrival to serve for several years. Upon conclusion of this apprenticeship, servants "out of their time" ascended the agricultural ladder by settling as farmers on land of their own. Indenture, which brought an estimated half of the whites who came to colonial America, faded out by the 1830s. Waves of free immigrants also seeking land of their own, available until World War I, soon followed.

A disadvantage of indentured servitude from the master's viewpoint was the replacement cost of rapid labor turnover. Many grasped at the alternative offered early in the seventeenth century by slavery, which spread mainly southward from Virginia. The imposition of lifelong bondage eliminated workforce turnover and stimulated the spread of plantation agriculture. Prior to the American Revolution, a few Indians became enslaved, but slave laborers were of preponderantly African origin. African Americans numbered 700,000 by 1790 and 4 million by 1860. In the South, masters numbered one-thirtieth of the total population, whereas slaves numbered one-third of it. In 1860 one-quarter of all slaves in the American south were in holdings of less than ten, one-half in holdings between ten and fifty, and one-quarter in holdings of more than fifty.

Following emancipation in 1865, sharecropping, a system that remunerated laborers with a share of the crop, largely replaced slavery. At their peak in 1930, sharecroppers' farms numbered 750,000. By 1964, overwhelmed by mechanization, they had fallen to 112,000. As the decline continued, the 1969 census ceased separate tabulation.

Hired wageworkers, of which there were very few in the South prior to emancipation, date from earliest colonial times in the North. They served either seasonally or year-round. If the latter, they typically received room and board and cash and lived with the farmer's family. Competing opportunities to settle on western land or to enter fishing and shipping industries kept the numbers of wageworkers low and encouraged the exchange of labor

Filipino Farmhands. Dorothea Lange's 1939 photograph shows migrant workers bent over to pick lettuce in California. © CORBIS

between farmers and labor by the farmer's own family. By 1870 agricultural laborers and farmers were approximately equal in number: 2.9 million and 3 million, respectively. Thirteen percent of the former and 0.8 percent of the latter were women. After increasing in the early twentieth century, the numbers of each fell rapidly from 1940 on, until by 1970 laborers numbered only 1.6 or 1.1 million and farmers only 2.4 or 1.7 million, as reported by the Bureau of the Census and the Bureau of Labor Statistics, respectively. Of these, 24 and 3.7 percent, respectively, were women. Some 19 percent of the laborers and 0.8 percent of the farmers were below twenty years of age. By 1997 hired agricultural laborers accounted for less than 1 percent of the American workforce; about 17 percent of those workers were women. The era of the hired man closed shortly after World War I, with the decline in availability of cheap land and the growing mechanization of agriculture.

Over the second half of the twentieth century, the number of hired workers residing on farms fell dramatically. Advances in mechanization and technology had given an advantage to large-scale agribusiness and put thousands of small family farms out of business. Large-scale corporate farms needed abundant supplies of laborers only at harvest time. In the 1930s drought, depression, and mechanization dislodged large numbers of farmworkers from their homes to follow the crops for a living. During the Dust Bowl disaster that hit parts of OKLAHOMA and TEXAS in the 1930s, many sought better soil and higher wages in CALIFORNIA. Some labeled them "Okies," a term that has since entered American lore through the photographs of Dorothea Lange and John Steinbeck's novel *The Grapes of Wrath* (1939).

The growing separation between employer and employed on farms engendered attempts at forming TRADE UNIONS among agricultural wageworkers. Such efforts, which date from before World War I, gained footholds against great odds, mainly in the 1960s. Cesar Chavez's United Farm Workers union, using civil protest techniques learned from the black CIVIL RIGHTS MOVEMENT, gained significant concessions from agribusinesses in California and the Southwest.

Formal importation of Mexicans, a major source of the specialty-crop seasonal workers from outside the United States, ended in 1965. By 2002 nearly 10 percent of farmworkers were migratory, up from 8 percent in 1970. Migrant agricultural laborers in the United States face especially difficult working and living conditions. The abundant supply of immigrant laborers, combined with linguistic and cultural barriers, keeps wages artificially low. The workers' ambiguous residency status often

Mexican Farmhands. Migrant workers harvest lettuce, before moving on to another farm, another state. © UPI/CORBIS-BETTMANN

prevents them from taking advantage of basic health and education services. The number of agricultural workers of all classes reached a peak of 13.6 million in 1916. By 1950 the total had fallen to 9.9 million, by 1969 to 4 million, and by 2002 to just over 1 million. Full-time hired farm workers are more likely than other American wage earners to be young, single, male, and Latino. More than half have never finished high school, and over one-third are not citizens of the United States. By 2000 there was a wide gap between owners and well-paid machine operators, on the one hand, and poorly paid illegal aliens and recent immigrants on the other.

BIBLIOGRAPHY

Garcia, Matt. *A World of Its Own: Race, Labor, and Citrus in the Making of Greater Los Angeles, 1900–1970.* Chapel Hill: University of North Carolina Press, 2001.

Griffith, David Craig, et al. *Working Poor: Farmworkers in the United States.* Philadelphia: Temple University Press, 1995.

Morgan, Kenneth. *Slavery and Servitude in North America: A Short History.* Washington Square, N.Y.: New York University Press, 2001.

Murphy, Arthur D., Colleen Blanchard, and Jennifer A. Hill, eds. *Latino Workers in the Contemporary South.* Athens: University of Georgia Press, 2001.

Steinfeld, Robert J. *The Invention of Free Labor: The Employment Relation in English and American Law and Culture, 1350–1870.* Chapel Hill: University of North Carolina Press, 1991.

Whayne, Jeannie M. *A New Plantation South: Land, Labor, and Federal Favor in Twentieth-Century Arkansas.* Charlottesville: University Press of Virginia, 1996.

Paul S. Taylor / A. R.

See also **Agriculture; Dust Bowl; Great Depression; Indentured Servants; Labor; Land Policy; Mexican Americans; Migration, African American; Plantation System of the South; Rural Life; Sharecroppers; Slavery.**

FARMS AND FARMING. *See* **Agriculture.**

FASCISM, AMERICAN. The Great Depression produced numerous political groups that, in some respects, resembled contemporary European fascist movements, including those that had triumphed in Germany and Italy. The degree of resemblance between American and European fascists and the prospects of such groups achieving power in the United States was a significant part of the ideological debate of the era. These questions remain central to any historical consideration of American fascism. Liberals and radicals in the 1930s rarely doubted the significance of the transatlantic affinities and connections. The left also feared that the prospects for American fascist victory were good.

Typically, groups that were designated as American fascists—either by their contemporary opponents or by later historians—differed dramatically in leadership, worldview, and size. Until his assassination in 1935, Senator Huey Long was regarded by the left as the most promising candidate for fascist dictator. Long attracted millions of followers with a mixture of mild nationalism and a promise to "share our wealth." Father Charles Coughlin, a flamboyant "radio priest," had an equally large following, a greater fondness for ungrounded conspiracy theories, a less distributive economic program, and a propensity to anti-Semitism. In 1936, Coughlin and Long's former aide Gerald L. K. Smith sponsored the Union Party presidential candidacy of Representative William Lemke, who received less than 2 percent of the vote. Reverend Gerald B. Winrod, leader of the fundamentalist Defenders of the Christian Faith, recruited a large following in Kansas while denouncing an alleged Jewish conspiracy that stretched from the crucifixion of Jesus to the New Deal. The anti-Semitic pamphleteer Elizabeth Dilling traced a "red network" undermining every aspect of American life. Emulating Adolf Hitler, William Dudley Pelley of the Silver Shirts wanted to strip Jews of their rights. Countless lesser agitators and publicists also enjoyed brief notoriety. Adherents to this domestic far right were more deeply influenced by orthodox Christianity, usually evangelical Protestantism or conservative Catholicism, and were less prone to paramilitary organization than their European counterparts. In addition, there were German Americans and Italian Americans who formed groups celebrating the regimes of Hitler and Benito

Mussolini. At its peak, the foremost of these groups, the GERMAN-AMERICAN BUND, attracted roughly 25,000 members, most of them foreign born.

During 1939–1941, the specter of subversion by American fascists influenced the debate over U.S. entry into World War II. Most of the so-called fascists accused President Franklin D. Roosevelt of secretly maneuvering the country toward war and warned that intervention abroad would destroy democracy at home. To these standard noninterventionist arguments they typically added the charge that Roosevelt was acting on behalf of an international Jewish conspiracy. Several, including Coughlin and Pelley, printed German propaganda in their magazines. Roosevelt responded not only by publicly denouncing a native fascist menace and increasing Federal Bureau of Investigation surveillance, but also by stigmatizing respectable noninterventionists as willing collaborators or dupes of European fascists. During World War II, Roosevelt personally ordered the prosecution of native fascists for sedition. The resulting case, *United States v. McWilliams*, ended in a mistrial after seven raucous months in 1944 when the trial judge died suddenly. Coughlin avoided joining Pelley, Winrod, and Dilling as a defendant in the McWilliams case only because the Vatican had silenced him in 1942. Thus, Gerald L. K. Smith, the shrewdest politician among far right leaders, emerged during the war as the premier personification of native fascism. Smith attracted a large radio audience and ran a strong race for U.S. senator from Michigan in 1942, before his embrace of sweeping, anti-Semitic conspiracy theories led to his ostracism from mainstream politics shortly after the war. By 1946, the exaggerated fear of a native fascist menace—a "brown scare" broadly analogous to the red scare of 1919–1920—had run its course. Brown scare legacies include prosecutions and FBI surveillance that set precedents for undermining civil liberties generally, countless lurid exposes of far right groups, and two good novels about native fascism: Nathanael West's *A Cool Million* (1934) and Sinclair Lewis's *It Can't Happen Here* (1935).

The resurgence of American fascism that many liberals and radicals feared in the late 1940s never occurred, and the label itself sounded increasingly anachronistic. During the next half-century, however, numerous small groups either emulated German Nazism or drew inspiration from the so-called native fascists of the 1930s and 1940s. George Lincoln Rockwell, who claimed to have been influenced by Gerald L. K. Smith, founded the minuscule American Nazi Party in 1958. Much more significant were the virulently anti-Semitic organizations, including the Aryan Nations, the Order, and the Posse Comitatus (founded by a former Silver Shirt), which found a predominantly western following during the recession of the early 1980s. Some members of these organizations robbed banks, engaged in shootouts with law enforcement officers, and beat or killed African Americans, Jews, and Asian Americans. *The Turner Diaries* (1978), a novel written by the avowed neo-Nazi William Pierce, was popular reading among such groups. Pierce envisioned an "Aryan" war against racial minorities, gays, and the "Zionist Occupation Government." Influenced by *The Turner Diaries*, Timothy McVeigh in 1994 blew up the Alfred P. Murrah Federal Building in Oklahoma City, Oklahoma.

BIBLIOGRAPHY

Brinkley, Alan. *Voices of Protest: Huey Long, Father Coughlin, and the Great Depression.* Reprint, New York: Knopf, 1983.

Ribuffo, Leo P. *The Old Christian Right: The Protestant Far Right, from the Great Depression to the Cold War.* Philadelphia: Temple University Press, 1983.

Smith, Geoffrey S. *To Save a Nation: American Extremism, the New Deal, and the Coming of World War II.* Rev. ed. Chicago: Elephant Paperbacks, 1992.

Leo P. Ribuffo

See also **Anti-Semitism; Oklahoma City Bombing.**

FASHION. *See* **Clothing and Fashion.**

FAST DAYS, or days of humiliation and days of thanksgiving, were, in colonial NEW ENGLAND, officially dedicated to seeking the forgiveness of or expressing gratitude to God. Puritans opposed not only saints' days, but also all regular observances outside the Sabbath, such as CHRISTMAS and Easter, because of their highly developed sense of divine providence. They saw every event as an immediate act of God, where His will was continually manifesting itself either in adversities (punishments of sin) or advantages (blessings upon His people). In this theological context, no annual feast could bear any relation to His unpredictable dispensations or express true repentance or joy.

Puritan theory invested the power to designate such days in the churches, but, in the colonies, the churches asked the sanction of the legislature to enforce universal attendance at their services. The civil authorities soon assumed the initiative in proclaiming the days. The governors and councils were given legal power to name days in the absence of the general courts, while the courts determined them during their sittings. Meanwhile, individually or collectively, churches kept local or cooperative fasts and thanksgivings at will.

Both fast days and thanksgiving days were celebrated with a sermon. On a THANKSGIVING DAY, the service was followed by feasting, but a fast day did not necessarily mean entire abstinence from food, although abstinence from secular pursuits was called for.

Days of humiliation were given legendary consecration in New England by the startling experience of Plymouth in 1622: after two months of drought the church called for a fast, and the day after the fast rain fell. The church then ordered a day of thanksgiving. Similar apparent instances of divine response did occur, but there were also times when a fast was followed by affliction, particularly during KING PHILIP'S WAR. The clergy explained such failures on the ground that God was still offended, and urged for the reformation of manners. Fasts were appointed upon any public loss or affliction, such as plague, earthquake, crop failure, or drought. They were also decreed during social or political commotions, as during the ANTINOMIAN CONTROVERSY.

In the latter half of the century, ministers tried every means to awaken the languishing zeal of the people. They held fasts in the churches and persuaded the governments to order repeated public days of fasting and prayer for specific abuses. In the 1670s, the clergy began "renewing" the church covenant at such fasts, a custom that became common in community life and contributed to the growth of revivalism.

Although the original colonists abhorred fixed solemnities as an abomination of Satan, they generally held a fast in the spring before the planting and a thanksgiving after the harvest. These days gradually became annual events—the thanksgiving feast in Connecticut by the 1650s, and Massachusetts by 1660. The spring fast took a little longer—in Connecticut in the 1660s and in Massachusetts by 1694. Throughout the eighteenth century, public days were proclaimed by the governors, as were local ceremonies by particular churches. At critical moments preceding the Revolution and during the war, fasts were appointed by the clergy, by the states, or by the CONTINENTAL CONGRESS, and were used to rally the people and spread propaganda.

BIBLIOGRAPHY

Hall, David D. *Worlds of Wonder, Days of Judgment: Popular Religious Belief in Early New England.* Cambridge, Mass.: Harvard University Press, 1989.

Love, William DeLoss. *The Fast and Thanksgiving Days of New England.* Boston: Houghton, Mifflin and Co., 1895.

Perry Miller / A. R.

See also **Divine Providences; Holidays and Festivals; Puritans and Puritanism; Religion and Religious Affiliation.**

FATHER'S DAY. *See* **Mother's Day and Father's Day.**

FAX MACHINE. The transmission by wire of facsimiles of text messages or images originated in 1843 when an English inventor, Alexander Bain (1818–1903), announced a device that could reproduce writing at a distance. There were numerous subsequent variations on the theme of tele-writing, but a key invention was Edouard Belin's "Belinograph" of 1925. This device scanned an image using a photocell to detect light reflected off the image. In 1934, the Associated Press news agency introduced the first regular commercial facsimile service, which it used for many years, primarily to transmit photographs.

Although the Radio Corporation of America, various newspapers, the wire services, and others attempted to expand the use of facsimile services, there was little public demand until the late twentieth century. In the 1980s, however, facsimile machine usage exploded. The reasons are not entirely clear. The concerted effort by Japanese electronics companies to develop smaller, less expensive facsimile machines certainly offered the potential of more widespread ownership of the devices. These firms also promoted the establishment of communication standards, which made it possible for machines made by different manufacturers to receive messages from one another. Coupled with this were changes in American business practices, such as the growing number of home offices and the breakup of AT&T, which removed restrictions on the use of the telephone network. Nearly ubiquitous in offices by 1990, the fax machine then became a household appliance, with consumers spending nearly $900 million that year to buy them.

BIBLIOGRAPHY

Coopersmith, Jonathan. "The Failure of Fax: When a Vision Is Not Enough." *Business and Economic History* 23: 1 (Fall 1994): 272–282.

David Morton

FEDERAL AGENCIES. Federal agencies fall under the executive branch of the American government. Collectively, federal agencies are often referred to as "the administration" or "the bureaucracy." The latter term has developed a less favorable connotation than the former, but both terms identify the essence of federal agencies, which are part of an organizational scheme to divide government labor and expertise among a hierarchy of specialized offices. Legally, according to the Federal Administrative Procedure Act, which governs administrative law, an "agency" is any governmental authority besides Congress and the courts. This includes 98 percent of the government workforce.

The *United States Government Manual* provides an organizational chart that details all the divisions and subdivisions of this expansive category of government. The president, vice president, White House staff, and Executive Office of the President (EOP) sit at the top of a massive hierarchical structure. Beneath them are the fourteen CABINET agencies. Beneath the cabinet agencies are fifty-seven independent establishments and government corporations. However, even this chart does not capture all of the important substrata of federal agencies. For example, within the cabinet agency of the Department of Agriculture are numerous agencies like the Forest Service, the Food Safety and Inspection Service, and the Rural Utilities Service. The OFFICE OF MANAGEMENT AND BUDGET has put together tables tracking the bureaucratic workforce. In the early 2000s, government agencies employed 2.78 million civilian employees and 1.47 million military employees. This was down from a peak in the late sixties of 2.9 million civilian employees and 3.6 million military employees. Political appointees made up about 3 percent of the civilian employees. The remaining employees were hired through a merit system.

Executive Office of the President

President Franklin D. Roosevelt created the EOP in 1939 to manage a dramatic expansion in the size and responsibility of the executive branch. The EOP established agencies to perform highly specialized services for the president. Each president has altered the composition of the EOP to some extent. Some standard agencies within the EOP include the White House Office, Office of the Vice President, Council of Economic Advisors (CEA), Council on Environmental Quality (CEQ), National Security Council, Office of Administration, Office of Management and Budget (OMB), Office of National Drug Control Policy, Office of Policy Development, Office of Science and Technology Policy, and Office of the U.S. Trade Representative.

The two largest and most important agencies are the OMB and the NSC. The OMB has its roots in the Bureau of the Budget, which was created as part of the Treasury Department in 1921 and transferred to the EOP in 1939. The OMB was reorganized and given its name and form by President Richard M. Nixon in 1970. The OMB prepares the national budget, which also implies designing the president's program priorities. The OMB must exercise extensive communication with Congress and each federal agency.

The NSC was established under the National Security Act of 1947, and was placed within the EOP in 1949. The NSC is designed to advise the president on national security and foreign policy concerns and to coordinate the various agencies involved with these policy areas. The original membership of the NSC consisted of the president, vice president, secretary of state, secretary of defense, and the assistant to the president for national security affairs. Numerous other officials advise the NSC, such as the chairman of the Joint Chiefs of Staff (a military adviser), and the director of the Central Intelligence Agency. The NSC also has a large and permanent specialized staff of analysts.

Various presidents have run the NSC differently. Harry S. Truman had the secretary of state dominate the NSC, while Dwight D. Eisenhower allowed military officials to take control. Ronald Reagan invited his chief of staff to play an important role on the NSC. Bill Clinton added the secretary of the Treasury, U.S. representative to the United Nations, and the assistant to the president for economic policy to the NSC.

Smaller agencies in the EOP include the CEA, the President's Foreign Intelligence Advisory Board (PFIAB), and the CEQ. The CEA was created under the Employment Act of 1946 to advise the president on economic policy. The CEA prepares the president's economic report, furnishes other reports upon request, gathers economic data, and provides economic analysis of other federal agencies. The CEA is run by a three-member board appointed by the president with approval by the Senate.

The PFIAB was established by President Eisenhower in 1956 to provide the president with information on the quality and adequacy of intelligence collection. The PFIAB is a sixteen-member board and has been employed by every president since Eisenhower except Jimmy Carter.

The CEQ was established under the National Environmental Policy Act of 1970. The CEQ chair is appointed by the president with Senate approval and serves as the primary environmental adviser to the president. The CEQ prepares an annual report on the state of the environment, oversees the environmental-impact assessment process, coordinates all agency activities involving the environment, and presents environmental policy initiatives.

President Clinton added the Domestic Policy Council (DPC), National Economic Council, and Office of National AIDS Policy to the EOP. The DPC coordinates domestic policy-making process and ensures that all domestic-policy efforts are consistent across the many federal agencies. Clinton established the National Economic Council to advise on domestic and international economic issues and to ensure that all policies are consistent with the president's economic goals. The Office of National AIDS Policy monitors and gives advice on the AIDS epidemic.

President George W. Bush added the Office of Faith-Based Community Initiatives to the EOP. The office works with state and local governments, businesses, and the nonprofit sector to encourage faith-based community service. Bush also established several Centers for Faith-Based and Community Initiatives in the Departments of Health and Human Services, Housing and Urban Development, Justice, and Education. The agency in the EOP coordinates efforts across these cabinet agencies.

In the wake of the terrorist attacks of 11 September 2001, President Bush added the Office of Homeland Security to the EOP. This agency was charged with developing a national strategy to protect the United States against future terrorist attacks. This involves extensive coordination efforts across federal agencies as well as state and local law enforcement agencies.

The Office of Administration was established in 1977 to manage the many and changing agencies of the EOP. The Office of Administration provides financial management, information support, human-resource management, research assistants, facilities management, procurement, printing, and security for the EOP. The Office of Administration also prepares the annual budget request of the EOP and handles Freedom of Information Act requests for documents.

Cabinet Agencies and Subagencies

The U.S. Cabinet has no special Constitutional status. Unlike cabinets in parliamentary systems, it does not act collectively. Each cabinet agency oversees a portion of the bureaucracy. The cabinet secretaries are appointed by the president and approved by the Senate.

The most established cabinet agencies are the Department of State, Department of Justice (DOJ), Department of the Treasury, Department of the Interior (DOI), and Department of Agriculture. The Department of State is best known as the diplomatic arm of American activity abroad. The secretary of state is often an important figure in negotiating treaties, executive agreements, and other international agreements between the United States and other countries, and among countries other than the United States. Ambassadorships are most often "plum" political appointments offered to campaign contributors, but State Department foreign-service officers are highly trained diplomats who occupy the various regional bureaus and embassies worldwide.

The Department of Justice is headed by the U.S. attorney general. The DOJ mission is to enforce federal law. The solicitor general works under the attorney general as the top government lawyer in cases before the appellate courts where government is a party. The solicitor general plays a major role in more than half of the cases that come before the Supreme Court. In addition, the solicitor general has considerable influence in the determination of which cases deserve consideration. The DOJ contains divisions for many areas of the law, including taxes, civil rights, antitrust, and the environment. The agency also contains some powerful law-enforcement agencies such as the Federal Bureau of Investigation (FBI), Drug Enforcement Agency (DEA), Immigration and Naturalization Service (INS), and U.S. Marshals.

The Department of Treasury manages the national debt, prints currency through the U.S. Mint, and polices tax collection with the Internal Revenue Service (IRS). The Department of Treasury also houses the Secret Service, the U.S. Customs Service, and the Bureau of Alcohol Tobacco and Firearms (ATF), a law-enforcement agency. The ATF is often at the forefront of controversial conflicts involving the acquisition of illegal weapons and explosives, arson, and organized-crime activities.

President Abraham Lincoln established the Department of Agriculture in 1862. The department does not merely oversee the nation's farming sector. Although the department does contain the Farm Service Agency, and farm loan and rural development programs, it also runs the U.S. National Forest system, and oversees the Food Safety and Inspection Service and the Food Stamp Program.

While the Department of Agriculture contains the Forest Service, the DOI administers the many other public lands under the Bureau of Land Management, U.S. Fish and Wildlife Service, and the National Park Service. The DOI charts the land through the U.S. Geological Service (USGS), it administers public works projects such as dams through the Bureau of Reclamation, and oversees extractive industries through the Minerals Management Service and the Office of Surface Mining. The agency also contains the Bureau of Indian Affairs (BIA).

The DOI and the Department of Agriculture reflect the rural and expansive nature of the nation in the nineteenth century. The first two cabinet agencies established in the twentieth century reflect the increasingly industrial character of the nation. The Department of Commerce was established in 1903 as the Department of Commerce and Labor. This agency contained a Bureau of Corporations, Bureau of Manufacturers, and the Bureau of the Census among other subagencies. Over time, the agency gathered up the Patent Office and the Bureau of Mines from the Department of the Interior and many transportation agencies such as the Bureaus of Air Commerce, Lighthouses, Marine Inspection, and Public Roads. The Department of Commerce also oversaw the development of the Saint Lawrence Seaway. Newer cabinet agencies have taken back many former responsibilities of the Department of Commerce. The most notable subagencies within the department include the Department of the Census, the Economic Development Administration, the Patent and Trademark Administration, and the Technology Administration.

In 1913, President William H. Taft successfully created a spot in the cabinet for labor apart from the Department of Commerce. The new department inherited several responsibilities including the Bureau of Labor Statistics. The Department of Labor also added the Occupational Safety and Health Administration (OSHA). The Department of Labor houses the Office of Administrative Law Judges, which act as a major check on the power of all federal agencies.

After World War II (1939–1945), the expanded military capability of the United States prompted an overarching reorganization of the cabinet. The military has existed as long as the United States itself. The army was the first branch established and it became housed in the cabinet under the War Department in 1789. The navy and marine corps gained their own Naval Department. The air force was formally established after World War II. All branches were combined in the newly created Department of Defense in 1949. The Joint Chiefs of Staff and the secretary of defense coordinate the military branches and advise the president.

In the 1960s, the Department of Housing and Urban Development (HUD) and the Department of Transportation (DOT) were also added to the cabinet. HUD was created in 1965 to ensure fair housing practices, monitor housing safety issues, and help finance home ownership. The DOT assumed agencies in the Department of Commerce such as the Federal Highway Administration (FHWA), Federal Aviation Administration (FAA), and also the railroad, transit, and maritime administrations. This agency also contains the U.S. Coast Guard.

The Carter administration added three new cabinet agencies between 1977 and 1980. The Department of Education (ED) was elevated to the cabinet in 1977 and operates offices on many levels of education, civil rights, and student loans. In the same year, the Department of Energy (DOE) cobbled together a diverse array of energy research programs, fuel-price regulating agencies, and nuclear weapons programs into a single agency. The DOE oversees the country's national laboratories, which conduct programs on a wide range of scientific endeavors including nuclear weapons research. The DOE also contains the Federal Energy Regulatory Commission (FERC) and the Solar Energy Research Institute (SERI).

The Department of Health and Human Services (HHS) joined the cabinet in 1980. This agency was previously the Department of Health, Education, and Welfare, created in 1953. HHS contains several important research departments including the Centers for Disease Control and Prevention (CDC), the Food and Drug Administration (FDA), and the National Institutes of Health (NIH). HHS also administers welfare programs such as Temporary Assistance for Needy Families (TANF), Head Start, and Medicaid. The scope of the HHS also includes care for the elderly with such programs as Medicare.

The Department of Veterans Affairs (VA) was added to the cabinet in 1989. This agency provides federal benefits to veterans and their dependents. The VA runs the Veterans Hospitals and administers education and home loan programs. The agency also oversees veterans' pensions and military cemeteries.

Independent Establishments and Government Corporations

There is a dizzying array of agencies outside of the cabinet that the *United States Government Manual* calls independent establishments and government corporations. Government corporations are government-run businesses such as the U.S. Postal Service (which provides mail service), Amtrak (which provides rail service), and the Tennessee Valley Authority (which provides electricity). Other countries that have privatized a range of public services often call such agencies state-owned industries. The category of independent establishment is much less clearly demarcated. Many agencies in this category are extremely important regulatory agencies such as the Federal Reserve, the Environmental Protection Agency (EPA), the Nuclear Regulatory Commission (NRC), and the Federal Election Commission (FEC). Regulatory agencies were intended in their creation by Congress to be independent and nonpartisan powers that monitor and even clarify federal regulations across environmental, economic, and social policy areas.

The Federal Reserve, created in 1913, is the central bank of the United States. It is one of the most powerful arms of the U.S. government because it dictates monetary policy. The Federal Reserve regulates money supply and credit conditions. It also regulates the banking industry. The EPA sets and enforces environmental regulations. The NRC regulates the nuclear power industry and nuclear waste disposal. The FEC enforces election laws. Other agencies in the independent establishment category are not regulatory at all. Agencies like the Peace Corps and the Central Intelligence Agency (CIA) are not easily categorized in the bureaucratic hierarchy.

Making Sense of Federal Agencies

Trying to understand and compare agencies according to their place on the organizational chart of the executive branch can be extremely confusing. Political scientist Theodore J. Lowi developed a useful way to categorize federal agencies that does not rely on the hierarchy or the issue area of the agency. He identifies four broad kinds of agencies: regulatory, redistributive, distributive, and constituent. Regulatory agencies impose obligations and sanctions and then enforce compliance. Redistributive agencies create nonvoluntary classification schemes and dispense benefits to those that fit the scheme. Distributive agencies attempt to promote socially desirable activities by providing subsidies. Constituent agencies make rules about the scope of authority of other powers. The benefit of this classification scheme is that there are more similarities in the politics of federal agencies that share a category in this fourfold scheme than there are in their place on the formal organizational chart or similarity in issue area. For example, two agencies like the Environmental Protection Agency and the Food and Drug Agency, which are concerned with different policy areas and are on different levels of the executive hierarchy, have very similar politics and processes. This is because they are both regulatory agencies.

Modern Presidents Confronting "Big Government"

When politicians and pundits refer to "big government," they are almost certainly referring to the size and scope of federal agencies. "Big" in this context is of course a political term that is wielded differently by various parties and interests depending on the types of government services favored or disdained. Typically, the Democratic Party is considered progrowth for federal agencies and the Republican Party is typically perceived as the party for shrinking the number and influence of federal agencies. The presidents that presided over the most significant growth in the federal bureaucracy were Democrats Franklin D. Roosevelt, John F. Kennedy, and Lyndon B. Johnson. Ronald Reagan, a Republican, campaigned on a promise to reduce the size of the federal government. Early in his term he made serious cuts in agency personnel and made unsuccessful attempts to eliminate the Department of Energy and the Department of Education.

Ironically, Democratic President Bill Clinton conducted the most significant reform of federal agencies. Even skeptical Republicans regarded Clinton's National Performance Review, or Reinventing Government Program, as a highly successful effort to limit the size of the bureaucracy. Clinton eliminated nearly 300,000 federal jobs or 12 percent of the federal workforce in his first term of office. He had saved $80 billion by 1995 and eliminated 16,000 pages of federal regulations.

Agency Accountability: Congressional Oversight and Administrative Law

Although the president is usually the official held responsible for federal agencies, Congress has the most fundamental control over government agencies because it creates the legislation that enables each agency. Ideally, this legislation is a clear set of guidelines that instruct the agency on the ends and means of the policy mission. The more vague the legislation, the more discretion the executive branch is allowed.

Congress has significant powers of oversight as well. Congressional committees and subcommittees can hold public hearings at which agency officials are called to account for their actions. Congressional committees and subcommittees are not directly parallel with the division of labor in the executive branch. It is common for multiple hearings to be held on one agency across more than one Congressional Committee. Congress also has significant research capabilities within each Congressperson's office and in the Congressional Budget Office, Congressional Research Service, and General Accounting Office. This research capability is often employed to ensure bureaucratic accountability. The number of congressional hearings has increased significantly since World War II, as has the size of congressional staff to keep pace with an expanding executive branch.

Administrative law is another tool employed to ensure agency accountability. The United States is unique in the world in its adjudicatory approach toward the bureaucracy. American law dictates that the delegation of power to administrative agencies must be limited by legislative guidance on ends, means, and scope. Agencies are subject to judicial review when an agency is thought to overstep its legal bounds. In such cases, the court will interpret the enabling statute of the agency to determine legislative intent as to the authority of the agency. If Congress has created a clear statute, its intent must be followed. However, if Congress has created an ambiguous statute, the administrative agency, not the court, has the responsibility of clarifying the meaning of the statute. This is known as the Chevron doctrine, as it was determined in *Chevron v. NRDC* (1984). The court then holds the agency to a "reasonable" interpretation of the statute.

Administrative law also holds agencies accountable by adjudicating adherence to rules and procedural requirements. Agencies create rules and standards that clarify details of legislation. These rules are binding, like law, not only on the public, but also on the agency itself. The Federal Administrative Procedure Act, enacted in 1946, imposed notice and comment procedures that ensure some degree of public awareness prior to rule making. The courts ensure that public notice is given by agencies, and that agencies follow their own rules once they are established.

Finally, any administrative decision that adversely affects private individuals can lead to a formal adversarial hearing before an administrative judge. These hearings are called evidentiary hearings and they are based on the Constitutional right to "due process." These hearings are akin to trials, complete with formal public notice, the presentation of evidence, witnesses, arguments, cross-examination, and a complete public record. The right to a full hearing does not mean that all administrative decisions result in such a trial. In most cases, the right to a hearing is waived. Less than 5 percent of such decisions result in a hearing. However, this accountability provision is a powerful check on the actions of federal agencies.

BIBLIOGRAPHY

Arnold, Peri E. *Making the Managerial Presidency: Comprehensive Reorganization Planning, 1905–1996.* 2d ed. Lawrence: University Press of Kansas, 1998.

Fesler, James W., and Donald F. Kettl. *The Politics of the Administrative Process.* Chatham, N.J.: Chatham House, 1991.

Lowi, Theodore J. "The State in Politics: The Relation between Policy and Administration." In *Regulatory Policy and the Social Sciences.* Edited by Roger G. Noll. Los Angeles: University of California Press, 1985.

Ripley, Randall B., and Grace A. Franklin. *Congress, the Bureaucracy, and Public Policy.* 5th ed. Pacific Grove, Calif.: Brooks and Cole, 1991.

Schwartz, Bernard. *Administrative Law: A Casebook.* 3d ed. Boston: Little, Brown, 1988.

Skowronek, Stephen. *Building a New American State: The Expansion of National Administrative Capacities, 1877–1920.* New York: Cambridge University Press, 1982.

United States Government Manual, 2000–2001. Washington, D.C.: Office of the Federal Register, 2000.

Wilson, James Q. *The Politics of Regulation.* New York: Basic Books, 1980.

———. *Bureaucracy: What Government Agencies Do and Why They Do It.* New York: Basic Books, 1989.

Daniel John Sherman

See also **Administrative Discretion, Delegation of; Administrative Justice; Agriculture, Department of; Bureaucracy; Checks and Balances; Commerce, Department of; Congress, United States; Defense, Department of; Education, Department of; Energy, Department of; Federal Reserve System; Health and Human Services, Department of; Housing and Urban Development, Department of; Interior, Department of the; Justice, Department of; Labor, Department of; State, Department of; Transportation, Department of; Treasury, Department of the; Veterans Affairs, Department of.**

FEDERAL AID, the granting of financial assistance to the states by the federal government for a variety of reasons. Federal aid is often confused with federal SUB-

SIDIES. If subsidies are considered deliberate governmental interference with market processes for the direct benefit of a particular group—usually producers—then all subsidies are aids. On the other hand, not all aids are subsidies. Thus, the school lunch program is designed to benefit a particular group in the population, but its effect on food production and prices is secondary, like that of other welfare subventions. Furthermore, outright subsidies are often justified—sometimes remotely—because of their advantages to the public.

The granting of federal aid can be divided into two periods. Prior to the GREAT DEPRESSION of the 1930s, grants to the states of land, and money for canals, railroads, education, and roads, powerfully supplemented private enterprise and state resources for developments judged to be economically and socially desirable. During and following the Great Depression, the initial incentive was to relieve the distress of every segment of the population, and the assistance took on unprecedented variety and magnitude. Early instances of private philanthropy proved insufficient for the relief of mass unemployment, and then municipal capacity was exhausted, followed by the draining of state funds. Only national rescue prevented the hunger and homelessness of roughly one-fifth of the population and the collapse of agriculture, industry, and credit. Federal aid thereafter continued and grew in complexity and scale, often meeting needs that were hitherto untreated and leading to the reshaping of important sectors of American life. The expanded federal aid and all of its manifestations became associated with the notion of a welfare state.

Increased dependence by states and local governments upon the central government for assistance in many forms had several causes, but the primary one was the closer contact—physical, economic, and political—between all parts of the country. Mass production, as well as extended and faster transportation and communication, reduced regional differences. At the same time, federal revenue resources outran those of states, cities, and counties; large cities, in particular, had disproportionate demands for public expenditures. State and local taxes were on property and sales, and only occasionally income, which had been commandeered earlier by the federal treasury. The borrowing capacity of states and cities was limited, even with the creation of ostensibly autonomous administrative agencies, while the financial ability of the national government received no restraint from their mounting deficits.

Federal assistance takes the forms of cash payments, tax credits, payments in kind, and loans below the market interest rate. The objective may be to persuade recipients to take certain actions (for example, make capital investments) or to refrain from others (overproduction in agriculture, emission of industrial pollutants). Other aims are income redistribution, economic growth, price stability, employment increases, foreign trade balance, slum clearance and decent low-cost housing, health care, education, and efficient means of travel and transport.

The official estimate of federal grants-in-aid to state and local governments and shared revenue for 1974 was $48,293,000,000. Some particular items familiar to the public were medical assistance, $5,827,000,000; Office of Economic Opportunity and community action programs, $687,000,000; food stamps, $2,932,000,000; child nutrition (including school lunches), $905,000,000; vocational rehabilitation, $865,000,000; waste treatment and pollution control, $2,085,000,000; and Appalachian development, $291,000,000. In 1972, state and local governments received from the federal government $31,253,000,000, or 16.5 percent of their total revenue.

In 1973, President Richard M. Nixon, alleging that some of the welfare programs were wastefully administered, proposed cutting them off from federal support, referring them to state and local maintenance where he believed they belonged. Congressional opposition and the Watergate scandal derailed Nixon's plans, but efforts to reduce federal aid and increase local and state control over spending prerogatives continued for the remainder of the twentieth century. The Republican Party, in particular, attacked federal aid as a wasteful and counterproductive governmental intervention in the economy. Many Republicans believed that Ronald Reagan's election to the presidency in 1980 would reign in federal spending and lead to massive cuts in federal aid programs. During the 1980s, however, federal spending on aid programs actually accelerated, and the federal budget deficit reached record highs.

Because federal aid disproportionately benefited the middle class, a critical constituency for both Republicans and Democrats, neither major party made a serious effort to roll back middle-class entitlement programs in the 1980s. Consequently, the welfare system, which benefited low-income citizens, became the foremost target of efforts to cut federal aid. During the 1980s, the Reagan administration attempted to cut dramatically the size of welfare programs, but encountered stiff resistance from congressional Democrats. Many state governments, however, implemented welfare cutbacks on their own, and, by 1992, the issue of welfare reform had become so popular that all the major presidential candidates endorsed it. In 1996, President Bill Clinton signed a welfare reform bill that reduced benefits and established a maximum of two years for recipients. Although the bill passed Congress with bipartisan support, its controversial nature set off an intense national debate over the role and extent of federal aid in general, and federal welfare programs in particular.

By the close of the twentieth century, the debate over federal aid remained unresolved. Indeed, despite welfare reform, the federal government continued to fund massive aid programs, the majority of which benefited the middle class. For example, federal student aid grew to unprecedented levels in the 1980s and 1990s. The relatively easy accessibility of federal loans for undergraduate students played a major role in the record number of Americans attending colleges and universities. Likewise, federal expenditures on Social Security and Medicare, the two largest federal aid programs, continued to grow at an enormous rate. For example, while the Food Stamp Program received $19,005,000,000 in 1999, that same year the Social Security Administration received $419,790,000,000 in federal outlays. Moreover, by 1999 federal grants-in-aid to state and local governments amounted to $229,300,000,000, a sum nearly five times as large as in 1974.

BIBLIOGRAPHY

Bryner, Gary C. *Politics and Public Morality: The Great American Welfare Reform Debate.* New York: Norton, 1998.

Gunther, John J. *Federal-City Relations in the United States: The Role of Mayors in Federal Aid to Cities.* Newark: University of Delaware Press; London: Associated University Presses, 1990.

Malone, Laurence J. *Opening the West: Federal Internal Improvements before 1860.* Westport, Conn.: Greenwood, 1998.

Broadus Mitchell/A. G.

See also **Agricultural Price Support; Expenditures, Federal; Federal-Aid Highway Program; Medicare and Medicaid; Taxation; Welfare System.**

FEDERAL-AID HIGHWAY PROGRAM. Although the development and maintenance of public roads in the United States were, through much of the nation's history, within the authority of state and local governments, after the 1920s there was a steadily mounting participation by the federal government in highway construction and management, culminating in the building of the 44,328-mile interstate highway system between 1956 and the 1990s. The interstate highways were built largely at federal expense in order to ensure the completion of expensive urban highways and an integrated national highway system. States had to contribute only 10 percent of the total cost of construction. In addition, as of 2000, more than 155,000 miles of primary and secondary roads were maintained on a 50-50 cost-share basis by the federal government and the states acting jointly.

The Federal Highway Administration

The Bureau of Public Roads, from which the Federal Highway Administration evolved in 1970, had its origin in the Office of Road Inquiry, established within the Department of Agriculture in 1893. Following the passage of the Federal Aid Road Act of 1916 and the Federal Highway Act of 1921, the bureau became the chief agency for promoting a national network of highways. Successive administrative changes placed the bureau in the Federal Works Agency; in the Department of Commerce; and finally, in 1967, in the newly created Department of Transportation. This department was established to improve urban transportation planning, a national objective that was first listed in the Highway Act of 1962. At the time, both the department and the integration of transportation planning were opposed by rural states. They feared there would be a reduction in funds for rural roads and state influence over highway spending.

The Federal Highway Administration is charged with the administration of the Federal-Aid Highway Construction Program. In cooperation with the states, it administers the financial aid given to the states for highway construction. The administration works closely with state highway departments in correcting dangerous stretches on existing roads and in promoting safe, well-planned, well-built highways through a vigorous inspection program. It also seeks to improve the efficiency of inter- and intra-urban road systems, as well as to preserve the natural beauty along the roadways. The National Highway Traffic Safety Administration, also within the Department of Transportation, is responsible for promoting safe and efficient travel on the nation's highways.

With the authorization and planning of the interstate system in the 1950s and 1960s, the main terms of the debates over highway legislation in the 1970s shifted to the use of highway trust funds for nonhighway uses. These included mass transit, highway beautification, and relocation assistance for those who were dislocated by highway construction. With the completion of the interstate system in the 1990s, influential members of the House and Senate committees that were responsible for highway and transportation spending sought funds for special highway and transportation projects in their states.

A National Speed Limit

Of particular note in the administration of the highway program were efforts by public safety advocates who sought to use highway funds to achieve their goals on the federal level to reduce state speed limits and drunk driving. In so doing, they sought to renegotiate the relationship between the national government and the states. A mandatory maximum speed limit of 55 miles per hour (mph) was approved by Congress in 1973. It was passed as a short-term effort to conserve fuel during a national energy emergency. This temporary speed limit was made permanent in 1974 when the focus shifted to the lack of speed limit enforcement in the states. Highway legislation in 1978 required states to certify that they were enforcing the 55-mph speed limit or face penalties. The penalties for not doing so consisted of a reduction in the state's apportionment of highway funds by up to 5 percent for fiscal year 1980–1982 and up to 10 percent for fiscal year 1983 and beyond. In addition, incentive grants of up to 10 percent of the state's annual apportionment of highway safety funds were made available to states that further stepped up their enforcement efforts. The issue then moved off the formal agenda until 1986, when Senate lawmakers (primarily from the West) began suggesting that a 65-mph speed limit was appropriate for western rural interstate highways, which were far more lightly traveled than those in the eastern part of the country and were considered quite safe, given new safety features in roads and automobiles. President Ronald Reagan supported states' rights arguments that the power to set speed limits should rest with the state—not the federal—government. The federally mandated speed limit was repealed in its entirety in 1995.

A National Drinking Age

The issue of drunk driving was first attached to highway legislation in 1982. At that time, Congress offered incentives to the states by making those that cracked down on drunk driving eligible for extra highway safety funds. In 1984, the issue came up with more ferocity. The main focus was now on efforts to encourage states to raise their minimum drinking age to twenty-one. To achieve this goal, the government required withholding a portion of federal highway funds from any state that did not enact a minimum drinking age of twenty-one by 1987. Further, financial incentives were offered to states that instituted mandatory minimum sentences for drunk driving. The legislation became a states' rights issue. The Energy and Commerce Committee of the U.S. House of Representatives proposed separate legislation that would make it a federal crime under certain circumstances to sell alcoholic beverages to anyone under twenty-one. This legislation was advocated by Mothers Against Drunk Drivers (MADD). However, the proposed law never reached the floor of the House. Instead, incentives for compliance were added to the highway bill. In 1986, the legislation was strengthened: it said that funds that were withheld from states for failing to enact the minimum drinking age could not be recovered. Furthermore, all funds for fiscal year 1989 and beyond would be withheld for states that did not pass such a law. Beginning in 1988 and running through fiscal year 1991, grants totaling $125 million were offered to help states defray the costs of administering new drunk driving programs.

From Highway to Transportation Planning

Part of the impetus for the increasing role of the federal government in highway construction was to integrate highway construction and reconstruction to meet the objective of comprehensive transportation planning in states and metropolitan areas. Therefore, with the interstate highway system nearing completion in the 1990s, Congress passed the Intermodal Surface Transportation Efficiency Act (ISTEA) in 1991 and the Transportation Equity Act for the 21st Century (TEA-21) in 1998. These bills signified a new era. Senator Daniel Patrick Moynihan of New York, the leading sponsor, said, "This is the first transportation legislation of the post-Interstate era. . . . It marks the transition from system building to system performance" (*Congress and the Nation VIII, 1989–1992*, p. 437). As such, the focus of ISTEA was largely on giving states more freedom to spend funds as needed and on supporting mass transit as well as highways. TEA-21 made few major changes to ISTEA. It gave state and local governments even more flexibility and, thanks to a budget surplus, included huge increases in funding for both highways and mass transit. A focus on system performance meant that the federal government would allow more local control. The objective was to secure agreement from state transportation departments and urban planning agencies on proposals to ensure the most efficient use of highway trust fund dollars. Funds could be spent on repaving and redesigning roads and bridges or on providing mass transit in cities where creating more rights of ways for roads was opposed by citizens.

BIBLIOGRAPHY

Comeau, Clifford, and David Smallen. "Highways and Bridges on the Brink of the New Century." *Public Roads* 64, no. 1 (July/August 2000): 43–47.

"Highway Authorization." In *Congress and the Nation VIII, 1989–1992.* Washington, D.C.: Congressional Quarterly Press, 1993: 436–442.

Kahn, Ronald. "Political Change in America: Highway Politics and Reactive Policy-making." In *Public Values & Private Power in American Politics.* Edited by J. David Greenstone. Chicago: The University of Chicago Press, 1982.

Kadlec, Kevin, "Note, The National Minimum Drinking Age Act of 1984: Once Again Congress Mails Home Another Fist." *Cleveland State Law Review* 34 (1986): 637–663.

Lewis, Tom. *Divided Highways: Building the Interstate Highways, Transforming American Life.* New York: Viking, 1997.

Mazur, George D. "Federal Highway Funding—All the Basics." *Transportation Quarterly* 53 (Fall 1998): 19–32.

Mertins, Herman, Jr. *National Transportation Policy in Transition.* Lexington, Mass.: D.C. Heath, 1972.

Ronald Kahn

See also **Interstate Highway System; Roads; Transportation and Travel.**

FEDERAL AVIATION ADMINISTRATION (FAA). The FAA was established by the Federal Aviation Act of 1958, though its origins began with the Air Commerce Act of 1926. Air Traffic Control (ATC) is the FAA's most visible function. The FAA also provides airport construction grants and, through the Federal Aviation Regulations, regulates many aspects of aviation, including airport safety and security; the design, manufacture, and maintenance of aircraft and spare parts; and airline operations, minimum equipment, crew qualifications, training, flight schools, and repair stations.

Air Traffic Control ensures that aircraft are safely separated from each other and from obstacles. Some 400 ATC towers handle aircraft on takeoff and initial climb until about five miles out. Approach control then handles transition to higher altitude, where en route centers handle line-haul flight. As aircraft descend toward their destinations, approach control again handles the transition, and towers handle about the last five miles to landing.

The FAA does not prescribe how aircraft are designed or built. Instead, the FAA requires aircraft to meet certain criteria, such as handling characteristics, stability, and backup systems. Manufacturers submit designs to the FAA. If the FAA approves a design, a "finding of compliance" authorizes production of prototype aircraft. Extensive test flights are then conducted to identify unanticipated problems and demonstrate that the design actually works as intended. If test flights eventually are successful, the FAA issues a type certificate to the manufacturer, who then must develop processes to ensure that production will precisely replicate the approved prototype. Only then, with a production certificate, can production begin—with continued FAA oversight as long as the aircraft is manufactured. If problems emerge later, the FAA issues airworthiness directives, which require specific corrections.

Prospective airlines submit detailed manuals for operations, maintenance, and training to show precisely how they will operate safely, and must document how their manuals satisfy every safety regulation. If the manuals are approved, airlines still must conduct "proving flights" before receiving a FAA operating certificate. The FAA also regulates minimum initial qualifications and recurrent training for pilots, flight attendants, maintenance technicians, and dispatchers; requires certain equipment on aircraft; sets weather and equipment standards for different types of landings; and so on. Airline pilots are "rated" (licensed) for each type of aircraft they fly.

The FAA assures continued airline safety by assigning a principal operations inspector, a principal maintenance inspector, and a principal avionics inspector to each air carrier. Within their respective domains, principal inspectors must know everything about their carrier. FAA safety inspectors around the country support principal inspectors with daily oversight.

BIBLIOGRAPHY

Komons, Nick A. *Bonfires to Beacons.* Washington, D.C.: U.S. Government Printing Office, 1978. A detailed history of early government involvement in aviation safety.

Rochester, Stuart I. *Takeoff At Mid-Century.* Washington, D.C.: U.S. Government Printing Office, 1976. A history of the Federal Aviation Act of 1958.

Robert Matthews

See also **Air Transportation and Travel; Aircraft Industry; Airline Deregulation Act.**

FEDERAL BUREAU OF INVESTIGATION (FBI) was established in 1908 as the Bureau of Investigation (the word "federal" was added in 1935) by Attorney General Charles Bonaparte to serve as the investigative arm of the United States Department of Justice. The FBI quickly developed a two-track mission, as its special agents simultaneously engaged in legitimate federal law enforcement operations and unlawful domestic political surveillance activities. The latter were highly controversial throughout most of the twentieth century, and by the early twenty-first century, the FBI's competence and integrity on law-enforcement matters had also been called into question. On both fronts—law enforcement and surveillance—the FBI was a major historical force for the simple reason that its highly politicized officials were always at the center of three perplexing national issues: crime, communism, and civil rights.

During the Progressive Era presidencies of Theodore Roosevelt (1901–1909) and William Howard Taft (1909–1913), the FBI remained an obscure federal bureaucracy. FBI activities escalated following American entry into World War I in 1917, however, due to the Woodrow Wilson administration policy of suppressing antiwar dissidents. Bureau agents compiled massive files on anarchists, socialists, labor organizers, civil rights activists, and virtually every racial and ethnic group in the nation—all under the supervision of the Justice Department's General Intelligence Division and its young chief, J. Edgar Hoover. This continued after the war, with Hoover helping Attorney General A. Mitchell Palmer to organize the infamous PALMER RAIDS of 1919–1920.

Surveillance came to a halt in the early 1920s, when the FBI became embroiled in the Warren G. Harding administration scandals. In 1924, Attorney General Harlan Fiske Stone appointed Hoover director, with a mission to rid the FBI of corruption and confine investigations to violations of federal law. Hoover quickly purged corrupt agents and replaced them with men who held degrees in law and accounting. He also modernized crime-fighting techniques, chiefly through development of centralized fingerprinting records and a crime laboratory. But he never completely ended domestic political surveillance; throughout the 1920s and early 1930s, the FBI continued to track communist groups, as well as the AMERICAN CIVIL LIBERTIES UNION and the NATIONAL ASSOCIATION FOR THE ADVANCEMENT OF COLORED PEOPLE (NAACP).

Hoover spent most of his first ten years as FBI director laboring in relative obscurity. Following the LINDBERGH KIDNAPPING CASE and the brazen exploits of John Dillinger and other bank robbers, the FBI quickly emerged as one of the federal government's most prominent and powerful bureaucracies. In large part, this was the result of three Franklin D. Roosevelt administration decisions.

First, beginning in 1933, the Roosevelt administration federalized crime control to an unprecedented degree, giving the FBI what seemed like unlimited jurisdiction. For example, NEW DEAL reforms enabled the FBI to investigate a crime committed at any bank covered by the Federal Deposit Insurance Corporation. However, the FBI ignored organized crime, as those cases were simply too hard to make. In addition, Hoover had no intention of placing his agents in a position where they would be tempted by organized crime dollars.

Second, Roosevelt's New Deal decided to make heroes out of Hoover and his special agents ("G-Men") to counter the romantic notions that too often surrounded depression-era criminals. By the mid-1930s, Hoover emerged as a full-blown celebrity with an entire division devoted to publicity. The FBI cultivated favorable coverage, chiefly by performing services for anyone who might be in a position to advance the bureau's image, such as leaking information from confidential files to columnists and sending off agents to perform private detective work. Eventually, this broadened beyond the media to include politicians and virtually any prominent person.

Finally, with the nation creeping toward World War II, President Roosevelt did the FBI a service on a third front in 1939 by reviving its surveillance mission. If the White House was principally concerned with the activities of native fascists, Hoover was principally concerned with Communist activities—and he defined the latter broadly enough to encompass his New Deal benefactors. The FBI even held files on First Lady Eleanor Roosevelt. At the same time, Hoover ingratiated himself with the president by providing derogatory information on the administration's political opponents. This service included reports on such isolationists as Herbert Hoover. Ironically, during Herbert Hoover's own White House years, the FBI had performed the same service for the president by providing derogatory information on his interventionist critics.

During World War II, FBI accomplishments included investigation of the so-called Frederick Duquesne spy ring, which led to the arrest and conviction of thirty-three persons working to advance German interests. Six months after the attack on PEARL HARBOR, the FBI broke the Nazi sabotage operation with the help of George Dasch, one of eight men dropped off by German submarines at Amagansette, Long Island, and Ponte Vedra Beach, Florida. On the nation's key civil liberties issue—the decision to intern Japanese nationals and citizens of Japanese descent—Hoover put his bureau on record as opposing that policy (see JAPANESE AMERICAN INCARCERATION). Abroad, FBI agents served in the Special Intelligence Service, which gathered information on and conducted counterintelligence operations against Axis activities in South America.

During the COLD WAR years, the FBI emerged as perhaps the central player in the political phenomenon known as MCCARTHYISM. Bureau agents and officials were deeply involved in both the day-to-day workings and broader political strategies of the Federal Employee Loyalty Program; the Attorney General's list of subversive organizations; SMITH ACT prosecutions of domestic Communist Party leadership; the so-called Hollywood blacklists; pursuit of the Congress of Industrial Organizations (or CIO) left-wing labor unions; and the principal Red-hunting committees in Congress. These included the HOUSE COMMITTEE ON UN-AMERICAN ACTIVITIES, the Senate Internal Security Subcommittee, and Senator Joseph R. McCarthy's Permanent Subcommittee on Investigations. In 1951, the FBI launched a secret Responsibilities Program to purge left-wing public school teachers and university professors. Five years later, the FBI opened the Counterintelligence Program (COINTELPRO) against the American Communist Party.

In the early 1960s, pressure from Attorney General Robert F. Kennedy led the FBI to move against organized criminals and persons who violated federal civil rights law. Hoover fiercely resisted this pressure but gradually gave ground as the decade wore on. The FBI needed no pressure to move on the surveillance front. The civil rights, black power, and anti–Vietnam War movements led Hoover to approve additional COINTELPRO activities against a full spectrum of dissident groups and individuals. Following American withdrawal from Vietnam and the nearly concurrent WATERGATE collapse of the Richard M. Nixon administration, congressional committee investigations in 1975–1976 revealed the extent of the FBI's domestic political surveillance empire. In a manner vaguely similar to Harlan Stone's reforms a half century earlier, Attorney General Edward Levi issued domestic security investigations guidelines to prevent future abuse of civil rights and liberties by the nation's only national police force.

The FBI made substantial headway against organized crime with help from the Racketeer Influenced and Corrupt Organization Act of 1970. Bureau authority and operations also increased under the Ronald Reagan administration's war on drugs. High-profile Special Weapons and Tactics (SWAT) teams and hostage rescue teams were organized in 1973 and 1983, respectively, to combat domestic terrorists. The equally high-profile Behavioral Science Unit helped track down several serial killers, including Wayne B. Williams, convicted in 1980 in the Atlanta child-murders case. Nonetheless, with an almost daily release of files under the FREEDOM OF INFORMATION ACT of 1966 (as amended in 1974), the FBI has remained controversial in nearly every area of its operations.

On the civil rights front, FBI officials have endured periodic charges that their predecessors were involved in the assassination of Martin Luther King Jr. At the same time, FBI officials faced civil actions brought by their own black, female, and gay agents, alleging widespread patterns of discrimination and harassment. FBI law enforcement methods, particularly "sting" operations, were widely questioned as well. The most notable of these were the ABSCAM anti–public corruption effort, targeting members of Congress (1978–1980); the Operation Greylord effort of the 1980s in Chicago, which led to the conviction of fifteen judges and more than fifty attorneys; and the 1990 crack cocaine baiting of Washington, D.C., mayor Marion Barry.

Charges of continuing domestic surveillance abuse, though less prevalent, continued during the Reagan years; the FBI compiled dossiers on critics of the administration's Latin American policy and opened the Library

Awareness Program to monitor reading habits of dissidents. The Internet age has found the FBI keeping pace with its Carnivore Diagnostic Tool, an incredibly powerful software program capable of wiping out any notion of privacy on the Internet. Unnecessary use of deadly force was yet another area of concern, given the actions of the FBI snipers at RUBY RIDGE, Idaho, in 1992, and the FBI role a year later against the Branch Davidian Sect in Waco, Texas (see WACO SIEGE).

Perhaps most telling, the FBI's basic competence has been systematically called into question since the mid-1990s. Bureau handling of the 1996 Atlanta Olympic bombing case and its investigation of Richard Jewell represented a gross violation of any reasonable standard of fair play. Meanwhile, credible allegations of sloppy work, and what some might consider evidence tampering, plagued the FBI crime laboratory. Revelations regarding evidence withheld from defense attorneys in the OKLAHOMA CITY BOMBING case on the eve of Timothy McVeigh's execution also proved a major embarrassment, as did the discovery that longtime special agent Robert Hanssen was a Russian spy (see HANSSEN ESPIONAGE CASE).

The FBI was again roundly criticized following the 11 September 2001 terrorist attacks on the World Trade Center and the Pentagon and the anthrax mailings of that same year. This time, the principal issue was a bureaucratic culture trained to resist any sharing of intelligence with other agencies, from local police to the FEDERAL AVIATION ADMINISTRATION. Still, FBI authority was expanded once more when Attorney General John Ashcroft called for a wartime restructuring of federal anti-terrorist efforts, and by the electronic surveillance authority provided by the U.S. Patriot Act of 2001. Ashcroft also rescinded the Levi guidelines.

BIBLIOGRAPHY

Federal Bureau of Investigation. "Freedom of Information Act Reading Room Index." Compiled 20 June 2001. Available from http://foia.fbi.gov/foiaindex.htm.

Jeffreys, Diarmuid. *The Bureau: Inside the Modern FBI.* Boston: Houghton Mifflin, 1995.

Kelly, John F., and Phillip K. Wearne. *Tainting Evidence: Inside the Scandals at the FBI Crime Lab.* New York: Free Press, 1998.

Kessler, Ronald. *The FBI: Inside the World's Most Powerful Law Enforcement Agency.* New York: Pocket Books, 1973.

O'Reilly, Kenneth. *Hoover and the Un-Americans: The FBI, HUAC, and the Red Menace.* Philadelphia: Temple University Press, 1983.

———. *Racial Matters: The FBI's Secret File on Black America, 1960–1972.* New York: Free Press, 1989.

Theoharis, Athan, et al., eds. *The FBI: A Comprehensive Reference Guide.* New York: Checkmark Books, 2000.

Ungar, Sanford J. *FBI.* Boston: Little, Brown, 1976.

Whitehead, Don. *The FBI Story: A Report to the People.* New York: Random House, 1956.

Kenneth O'Reilly

See also **Anticommunism; Civil Rights and Liberties; Crime, Organized; Electronic Surveillance; Intelligence, Military and Strategic; 9/11 Attack; Police Power.**

FEDERAL COMMUNICATIONS COMMISSION. As the radio spectrum became increasingly crowded during the mid-1920s, it became necessary to regulate its frequency allocations. The Post Office and Commerce Departments and the Interstate Commerce Commission had initiated some regulation, and in 1927, Congress created the Federal Radio Commission (FRC). Its purpose was to regulate all forms of interstate and foreign radio transmissions and communications. FRC roles included assigning the frequencies and power of each station and revoking a station's license when the station violated the Radio Act of 1927 or the Commission's guidelines.

On 19 June 1934, the Communications Act became the latest addition to Roosevelt's New Deal. Introduced for the purpose of regulating interstate and foreign commerce in communication by wire and radio, it created the Federal Communications Commission (FCC). The task before the FCC was to make available a rapid, efficient, national and worldwide wire and radio communication service.

Agency Structure

The FCC is an independent U.S. government agency with jurisdiction over communications in all the states, the District of Columbia, Guam, Puerto Rico, and the Virgin Islands. Originally intended to regulate only radio, telephone, and telegraph industries, today the agency is charged with regulating interstate and international communications by radio, television, wire, satellite, and cable. It is not that the agency exceeded its charter; rather, the Act's flexibility and a sympathetic Supreme Court have allowed the agency to regulate additional communication media and related industries as they develop. However, when these modifications became too complex, Congress stepped in and passed additional amendments and acts, such as the 1962 Communications Satellite Act, to guarantee that the FCC could keep up with the pace. Congress's changing views on regulation and the market found their way into the agency and its guidelines, as reflected in the Telecommunications Act of 1996.

The agency is directed by five commissioners—appointed by the president and confirmed by the Senate—and they serve five-year terms. To avoid political bias, only three commissioners can be members of the same political party, and none of them may have a financial interest in any FCC-related business. The chairperson, assigned by the president, is responsible for setting the agency's agenda and, with the aid of the executive director, of running the Commission. By 2002, the FCC had almost 2,000 full-time employees and an annual budget of $245,071,000, about 90 percent of which comes from fees paid by the regulated industries—not from taxpayers.

The FCC, with its seven bureaus and ten offices, has a functional division of labor. The bureaus deal with the main communications sectors—processing their licenses, conducting investigations, looking into complaints, developing and implementing regulatory programs, and taking part in hearings. The offices provide the bureaus with support services. The Cable Services Bureau, originally established in 1993 to implement the Cable Television Consumer Protection and Competition Act of 1992, ensures competition among cable and satellite companies and regulates the distribution of multichannel video programming. The Common Carrier Bureau is responsible for policies regarding long distance and local service telephone companies (called "common carriers"); its primary focus is affordable, efficient, national and worldwide telephone service. Similarly, the Wireless Telecommunications Bureau is responsible for the licensing, enforcement, and regulation of all wireless telecommunications, except satellite and broadcasting; these include cellular telephone, paging, personal communications services, and amateur radio services. It is also responsible for public safety and the efficient use of the frequency spectrum in these areas.

The Mass Media Bureau regulates over 25,000 broadcast stations throughout the United States (television, radio, translators, and boosters). A station found in violation of FCC rules may be asked to rectify the situation and pay a fine; in extreme cases the bureau may revoke a station's license or refuse to renew it. The International Bureau is responsible for worldwide communications. In addition to advising and representing the FCC on all international communication matters, the bureau is concerned with the development of efficient, available, and reliable domestic and international communications services and with administering the Commission's international telecommunications policies and obligations. The Consumer Information Bureau is the FCC's link to the public. It is also charged with overseeing disability mandates. Finally, the Enforcement Bureau is responsible for enforcing most of the provisions of the Communications Act as well as the Commission's rules, orders, and authorizations.

Industry Regulation

During its early days, radio industry practices demonstrated that regulating the spectrum was necessary. In 1926, a federal district court ruled in *U.S. v. Zenith Radio Corp. et al.* that the Commerce Department had no authority to establish radio regulations. Left to the forces of the market, stations decided to set their own frequencies and transmission power, thus crowding the spectrum and filling the airwaves with interference. Following that ruling and its negative effects on the industry, Congress passed the Radio Act, making a clear statement that the frequency spectrum was a public domain and that public broadcasting was a national interest. The 1934 Communications Act gave the FCC the power to regulate all wire and radio communication. This was later interpreted by the Supreme Court to include other industries, such as cable TV. (See *U.S. v. Southwestern Cable Co.* [1968].) Ever since, the FCC has been responsible for allocating all frequencies and making sure that one industry or station does not interfere with another.

While the FCC's emphasis during its first few decades was on securing the existence of communication services, since the mid-1970s, as the public has become more antagonistic toward "big government," the agency has initiated more deregulation than regulation. After various pieces of legislation in the 1980s and early 1990s, and some deregulation by the agency itself during this period, Congress passed the Telecommunications Act of 1996, the most significant piece of communications legislation since the Act of 1934. By lifting various limitations, such as cross and multiple ownership restrictions, the act opened all telecommunications markets to competition. While the Commission argues that competition will benefit the public, as more service providers and cheaper prices become available, consumer advocates maintain that it will only lead to mergers of communication corporations, creating media empires that will drive prices up and service quality down.

Content Regulation

The FCC faces a far more difficult job than other independent regulatory agencies, for it must regulate an industry as well as its content. The First Amendment guarantees freedom of speech, and Title III of the Communications Act prohibits censorship by the FCC, yet the Commission and the courts have made it clear that speech may be limited when it does not serve the law's "public interest" requirement. "It was not that the speech of broadcasters was to be protected, as much as it was the right of the radio audience to be protected from certain forms of speech" (Creech, p. 68). This protection mainly refers to the broadcasting of obscene and indecent material; the former is completely prohibited, while the latter is only regulated.

Concerned about children's exposure to violent programming, Congress passed the Telecommunications Act of 1996, which required all TV sets with screens larger than 13 inches to be equipped with V-chip technology. When the chip is used with a voluntary TV rating system created by the television industry, this technology allows parents to program their TV sets to block programs that carry any sexual, violent, or other material they believe may be inappropriate for their children. A similar attempt to block such materials over the Internet was found to be unconstitutional in *ACLU v. Reno* (1996), when the court argued that the Internet deserves the broadest constitutional protection because it more closely resembles newspapers than a limited-spectrum broadcast.

Limitations placed on multiple ownership to promote diversity of ideas were relaxed in 1985 and significantly changed in 1992, as Congress favored promoting the availability of diverse views and information through the marketplace. Yet, even in an era of multiple ownership, stations must serve the needs of their own communities by covering local issues. While the FCC provided some guidance as to what it saw as adequate public service (in its 1960 Blue Book), it was always up to individual stations to determine how they could best serve their communities.

As part of that public service, the Communications Act forced any station allocated airtime to any political candidate to afford other candidates equal opportunities. Later, in *Red Lion Broadcasting Co. v. FCC.* (1969), the Supreme Court affirmed the "fairness doctrine," arguing that the right of the people to a marketplace of ideas has precedence over the rights of broadcasters. By 1985, however, in its Fairness Report, the Commission argued that diversity of opinion was being served by the multiplicity of voices in the marketplace. Following some criticism from the courts, the FCC abolished the doctrine in 1987.

It was Supreme Court justice Felix Frankfurter who argued in *National Broadcasting Co. v. U.S.* (1943) that Congress's lack of technical knowledge required it to delegate some of its legislative powers to the FCC. Today, as media content breaks its traditional borders (TV and radio broadcasting over the web, cell phones providing web content, digital radio transmissions via satellite) and as demand for more information and stations reaches new levels, Congress continues to lack the ability to keep up with technical advancements. Whether the FCC will be able to fill this void without being transformed into a semi-legislature for all communication issues remains to be seen.

BIBLIOGRAPHY

Creech, Kenneth C. *Electronic Media Law and Regulation.* 3d ed. Boston: Focal, 2000.

Federal Communications Commission. *FCC Handbook.* Available from http://www.fcc.gov/cgb/.

Federal Communications Commission. *The Public and Broadcasting.* Available from http://www.fcc.gov/mb/.

Lowi, Theodore J. *The End of Liberalism: The Second Republic of the United States.* 2d ed. New York: Norton, 1979.

Messere, Fritz. "Regulation." In *Encyclopedia of Radio.* Edited by Christopher H. Sterling. Chicago: Fitzroy Dearborn, 2002.

Napoli, Philip. *Foundations of Communication Policy: Principles and Process in the Regulation of Electronic Media.* Creskill, N.J.: Hampton, 2001.

Israel Waismel-Manor

FEDERAL GOVERNMENT is divided into three main branches: the legislative, the judicial, and the executive. These branches have the same basic shape and perform the same basic roles defined for them when the Constitution was written in 1787. Congress, the legislative branch, is divided into two chambers: the Senate and the House of Representatives. Representation in the chambers is carried out by the formula set forth in 1787: by population in the House and by state in the Senate. The president is the elected chief executive officer and is charged with faithful execution of the laws. The Supreme Court and all other federal courts have the judicial authority vested in them by the Constitution and by subsequent legislation. A system of checks and balances prevents power from being concentrated in any one of the three branches. Power is divided on a territorial basis between the states and national government.

Evolution

During the centuries since the Constitution first defined the federal system, the federal government has grown and evolved in response to social and political events that the members of the original Constitutional Convention could not have anticipated. The federal government's powers have increased in scope, the relationship among the branches of the federal government has changed, and the division of power between the states and the federal government has shifted. Some of these changes have occurred in accordance with the amendment process described in Article V of the Constitution. However, the vast majority of the changes to the federal system have been through such informal means as the use of precedent and the interpretation of the Constitution.

Because of their nature, foreign relations, defense, the monetary system, and foreign and interstate commerce are clearly areas where a national policy is required, and the Constitution grants the federal government the authority to exercise power in these areas. However, other areas once thought to be in the domain of state government or the private sector have become national concerns and have required federal intervention. For example, by extending its right to regulate interstate commerce, the federal government legislated the Pure Food and Drug Act in 1906 and created a national standard for the sale and manufacture of these products. In 1954, the Supreme Court's decision in *Brown v. Board of Education of Topeka* extended the scope of the equal protection clause of the Fourteenth Amendment to end state systems of segregation. Ten years later the Civil Rights Act of 1964 and the Voting Rights Act of 1965 further strengthened the federal government's role in providing equal protection as well as in enforcing the Fifteenth Amendment's guarantee of voting rights for citizens of any race or color.

Only twenty-seven amendments have been made to the Constitution in more than 200 years. Still, they have had a significant effect on the federal system. The first ten amendments, ratified in 1791, have become known as the Bill of Rights. They afford such basic civil liberties as freedom of speech and religion. Slavery was abolished with the Thirteenth Amendment. The Fourteenth Amendment strengthened the Bill of Rights by ensuring all citizens' equal protection under the law. The Fifteenth, Nineteenth and Twenty-sixth Amendments extended voting rights to citizens of all colors and races, to women, and to adults 18 years and older, respectively. The Sixteenth Amendment legalized the federal income tax. The Twenty-second and Twenty-fifth Amendments limited a president to two terms in office and established presidential succession. These amendments have brought important changes; nevertheless, how the federal government interprets the Constitution and uses precedent has institutionalized even greater change.

Interpreting Power

Each branch of the federal government shares equally in the power to interpret the Constitution. Congress, for example, has interpreted its power under the commerce clause to establish such regulatory agencies as the Federal Communications Commission, the National Labor Relations Board, and the Securities and Exchange Commission. These regulatory agencies are often viewed as the fourth branch of the federal government because they exercise powers that are legislative, administrative, and judicial. Yet, unlike the three main branches, these agencies were created and given power by ordinary legislation and not by constitutional amendment. Similarly, Congress has used implied power, derived from the Constitution's necessary and proper clause, to regulate such matters as minimum wages, social security, welfare, and Medicare; to prohibit discrimination on the basis of race, religion, sex, or physical handicap in employment, public accommodations, and housing; and to define as federal offenses certain criminal activities carried on across state lines.

The president has interpreted the Constitution by claiming the authority to deal directly with internal and international situations. Through the State of the Union message, the power to veto legislation, and Congress's vesting in the executive branch the responsibility for preparing the annual budget, the president has, in effect, become the chief legislator. The president's role as chief executive officer has been broadened to include the duties of chief peace officer. By claiming constitutional authority, presidents have used U.S. troops, federal marshals, or state national guards to quell labor disputes and racial riots and to ensure national, state, and local security after the terrorist attacks of 11 September 2001.

The Supreme Court has the power to declare whether an act or action of Congress or the executive branch violates the Constitution. In making these decisions it applies the text of the Constitution to the circumstances of the act or action and examines precedent set by past federal laws and previous Court rulings. During its more than 200 years, the Court has had occasion to reverse its own rulings. For example, *Brown v. Board of Education* overturned the Court's 1896 ruling in *Plessy v. Ferguson*, which allowed separate public facilities based on race. Although the Court cited the Fourteenth Amendment in this reversal, other reversals have been due to the Court's accepting constitutional interpretations rendered by Congress or the president. Unlike the other two branches of the federal government, the Supreme Court has developed the reputation of not involving politics in its decision-making process. However, this reputation was severely challenged by the controversy surrounding the Court's actions in the highly contested presidential election of 2000. By stopping the recount of legal votes cast in Florida, the Court's majority of conservative justices appeared to follow their political leanings and favor Republican candidate George W. Bush.

Custom and usage are other means by which the federal government reshapes itself. The frequent use of precedents leads to their becoming institutionalized features of the government, although the Constitution may not explicitly sanction them. Such features include the president's cabinet, political parties and the two-party system, and the president's use of executive agreements in lieu of treaties. Interpretation and precedent are also the bases upon which the president commits troops to hostilities without a formal declaration of war, which requires the approval of Congress. This practice can be traced to U.S. military involvement in the Korean Conflict (1950–1953) and was subsequently used to commit military personnel to combat in Vietnam (1956–1973), the military invasions of Grenada (1983) and Panama (1989), and more recently the U.S. military action in Afghanistan (2001–). This practice has also been extended to using the military to prevent illegal drug trafficking and provide internal security following the terrorist attacks of 11 September 2001.

Late-Twentieth-Century Changes

Because of the federal government's increased role in domestic and foreign affairs, its authority and responsibilities have grown tremendously. This growth is reflected in the number of federal civilian employees, which increased from 239,476 in 1901 to 2,697,602 in 2001. However, only 8 percent of this increase occurred during the past fifty years. This yearly increase of less than .01 percent is indicative of the recent trend to decrease the size and scope of the federal government.

This trend began with the Carter Administration's (1977–1981) deregulation of several key industries such as telecommunications, trucking, and air travel. Because of fiscal and political motives, it continued with following administrations, which among other actions, restructured the federal welfare system by turning most of its administration and funding over to the states. In the 1990s the Supreme Court aggressively pursued a legal agenda that asserted states' rights over federal authority. An example of this agenda was the Court's interpretation of the Eleventh Amendment, which prohibits private individuals from using the federal judiciary to sue a state. In 1990 the Court interpreted the amendment to bar private lawsuits against states that may have violated federal law. To the astonishment of many states' rights advocates, the Court extended this interpretation in 2002 to bar federal regulatory agencies from suing states on behalf of private individuals, although the federal government clearly has the right to sue a state. Many legal experts believe that this ruling will impede the federal government from effectively enforcing its regulations on a broad range of issues from environmental protection to worker safety.

BIBLIOGRAPHY

DeGregorio, William A. *The Complete Book of U.S. Presidents.* Ft. Lee, N.J.: Barricade Books, 2001.

Lieberman, Jethro K. *A Practical Companion to the Constitution.* Berkeley: University of California Press, 1999.

Mayhew, David R. *America's Congress.* New Haven, Conn.: Yale University Press, 2000.

P. Allan Dionisopoulos
John Wyzalek

FEDERAL MEDIATION AND CONCILIATION SERVICE. The Federal Mediation and Conciliation Service (FMCS) was created by the National Labor Relations Act of 1947 (better known as the TAFT-HARTLEY ACT) as an independent agency to preserve labor-management peace. The law was a response to the intense labor unrest that followed World War II. Intended primarily to reduce confrontational labor relations, the act also removed labor mediation from the Department of Labor.

The FMCS was granted less power than its predecessor. Intervention was limited to disputes affecting interstate commerce, which eliminated most state and local disputes. Railroad and airline disputes were also out of its purview.

President Harry S. Truman chose experienced labor relations expert Cyrus Ching, a Republican, as first FMCS director. The service handled 15,273 disputes and 1,296 strikes in its first year. Ching instituted Preventive Mediation (PM), a long-term program whereby mediators worked with unions and companies to improve human relations and contract administration.

During the Eisenhower administration, Director David Cole, an unconfirmed Truman holdover, was pressured by Congress to make political appointments to the mediator corps. He refused and set a precedent for nonpartisan appointment of mediation personnel. In 1955 Joseph Finnegan was appointed director of FMCS; he viewed the FMCS primarily as a mediation body, not a labor relations policy leader. Finnegan focused on broadening the PM program.

Director William Simkin (1961–1969) collaborated with the secretaries of labor and handled many labor disputes himself. He also developed a corps of mediator "paratroopers" to respond quickly to crises.

During the administrations of Richard M. Nixon and Gerald R. Ford, Secretary of Labor George Shultz asserted his authority. When Shultz left the department in 1970, Assistant Secretary W. J. Usery, a savvy mediator with roots in the labor movement, began to function as the labor adviser. Usery was named FMCS director in 1973 and served until 1976. Usery reinvigorated the agency, expanding its budget and staff and moving it out of the Labor Department's headquarters.

An unusually large number of labor disputes during the administration of James Earl Carter and the continued broadening of the FMCS's role put greater demands on a limited staff and budget. Director Wayne Horvitz (1977–1981) established an Office of Special Services; he also reached an understanding with Secretary of Labor Ray Marshall under which the FMCS retained preeminence in dispute intervention while emphasizing promotion of cooperative labor relations.

Throughout the 1970s the FMCS scope expanded. The Health Care Amendments of 1974 gave the service more authority to handle labor disputes in the rapidly growing health-care field. The agency's leadership pushed the FMCS's legal boundaries by providing mediation services in increasingly unionized state and local governments. The service began to mediate cases under the Age Discrimination Act. This was the beginning of FMCS's application of labor relations processes to the nontraditional mediating approach that eventually became known as Alternative Dispute Resolution (ADR).

The Reagan administration ordered large budget cuts, slashing the staff by 27 percent. Nevertheless, the FMCS managed to expand its ADR role through involvement in the regulatory negotiations process whereby federal agencies and interested parties jointly developed new regulations in a nonadversarial way.

During the administrations of George H. W. Bush, William Jefferson Clinton, and George W. Bush, the service recovered and maintained its stature. The Administrative Dispute Resolution Act of 1990 gave the FMCS broad responsibilities to apply ADR principles to a widened range of public disputes. In implementing Clinton's National Performance Review of federal programs, the FMCS applied private-sector management principles to its user services. With the end of the Cold War and the increasing integration of the world economy, foreign countries frequently consulted the FMCS on dispute settlement.

BIBLIOGRAPHY

Barrett, Jerome T. *The FMCS at Age 40.* Falls Church, Va.: Friends of FMCS, 1987. Friends of FMCS maintains a private archive and produces historical research on the agency.

Federal Mediation and Conciliation Service, 1947–1997. Washington, D.C.: Government Printing Office, 1997. A brief inhouse history that is lavishly illustrated.

United States. Federal Mediation and Conciliation Service. *Annual Report.* Washington, D.C: Federal Mediation and Conciliation Service, 1949–.

Judson MacLaury

See also **Conciliation and Mediation, Labor; Labor, Department of.**

FEDERAL REGISTER, the official newspaper of the U.S. government, was authorized by Congress in 1935 after the Supreme Court complained of the lack of a complete compilation of executive and administrative orders. It contains all presidential proclamations, executive orders, and federal agency regulations and proposed rules. It informs citizens of their rights and obligations, and it includes a listing of federal benefits and funding opportunities.

People read the *Federal Register* to learn about the daily operations of the federal government and how government actions are affecting health care, education, the environment, and other major issues. The *Federal Register* is available on paper, on microfiche, and on the Internet at www.access.gpo.gov/nara.

BIBLIOGRAPHY

U.S. National Archives and Records Administration, Office of the Federal Register. Home Page at http://www.archives.gov/federal_register/index.html

U.S. National Archives and Records Administration, Office of the Federal Register, "U.S. Government Manual 2000–2001." U.S. Government, 2000.

Wickliffe, Jim and Sowada, Ernie. *The Federal Register: What It Is and How to Use It.* Washington, D.C.: Office of the Federal Register, National Archives and Records Administration, 1992.

Lynda DeWitt

See also **Executive Orders; Federal Agencies.**

FEDERAL RESERVE SYSTEM. On 23 December 1913, the Owen-Glass Act founded the Federal Reserve System—the central bank of the United States. "The Fed," as most call it, is unique in that it is not one bank but, rather, twelve regional banks coordinated by a central board in Washington, D.C. A central bank is a bank for banks. It does for banks what banks do for individuals and business firms. It holds their deposits—or legal reserves—for safekeeping; it makes loans; and it creates its own credit in the form of created deposits, or additional legal reserves, or bank notes, called Federal Reserve notes. It lends to banks only if they appear strong enough to repay the loan. It also has the responsibility of promoting economic stability, insofar as that is possible, by controlling credit.

Founded in 1781, the nation's first bank, the Bank of North America, was possibly the first central bank. Certainly, the first Bank of the United States (1791–1811), serving as fiscal agent and regulator of the currency as well as doing a commercial banking business, was a central bank in its day. So too was the second Bank of the United States (1816–1836). It performed that function badly between 1817 and 1820, but improved between 1825 and 1826. The Independent Treasury System, which existed between 1840 and 1841 and between 1846 and 1921, was in no sense a central bank. A great fault of the National Banking System (1863–1913) was its lack of a central bank. The idea, and even the name, was politically taboo, which helps explain the form and name taken by the Federal Reserve System.

The faults of the National Banking System, especially perversely elastic bank notes—the paradox of dispersed legal reserves that were unhappily drawn as if by a magnet to finance stock speculation in New York—and the lack of a central bank to deal with the panics of 1873, 1884, 1893, and 1907, pointed out the need for reform. After the 1907 panic, a foreign central banker called the United States "a great financial nuisance." J. P. Morgan was the hero of the panic, saving the nation as if he were a one-man central bank. However, in doing this, he showed that he had more financial power than it seemed safe for one man to possess in a democracy. The 1912 Pujo Money Trust investigation further underlined his control over all kinds of banks. (Congressman Arsene Pujo, who became chairman of the House Banking and Currency Committee in 1911, obtained authorization from Congress to investigate the money trust, an investigation highlighted by the sensational interrogation of Morgan.) Meanwhile, the Aldrich-Vreeland Currency Act of 30 May 1908 provided machinery to handle any near-term crisis and created the National Monetary Commission to investigate foreign banking systems and suggest reforms. In 1911, Republican Sen. Nelson Aldrich proposed a National Reserve Association that consisted of a central bank, fifteen branches, and a top board controlled by the nation's leading bankers, which critics said J. P. Morgan, in turn, dominated. The proposal never passed, and the Democrats won the 1912 election. They accepted the groundwork done by Aldrich and others, but President Woodrow Wilson insisted that the nation's president choose the top board of this quasi-public institution. Democratic Rep. Carter Glass pushed the bill through Congress.

All national banks had to immediately suscribe 3 percent of their capital and surplus for stock in the Federal Reserve System so that it had the capital to begin operations. State banks could also become "members," that is, share in the ownership and privileges of the system. The new plan superimposed the Federal Reserve System on the National Banking System, with the new law correcting the major and minor shortcomings of the old one. In addition to providing a central bank, it supplied an elastic note issue of Federal Reserve notes based on commercial paper whose supply rose and fell with the needs of business; it required member banks to keep half their legal reserves (after mid-1917 all of them) in their district Federal Reserve banks; and it improved the check-clearing system. On 10 August 1914, the seven-man board took office, and on 16 November the banks opened for business. World War I having just begun, the new system was already much needed, but some of the controversial parts of the law were so vague that only practice could provide an interpretation of them. For that to be achieved, the system needed wise and able leadership. This did not come from the board in Washington, chaired by the secretary of the treasury and often in disagreement about how much to cooperate with the Treasury, but instead from Benjamin Strong, head of the system's biggest bank—that of New York. He was largely responsible for persuading bankers to accept the Federal Reserve System and for enlarging its influence.

At first, the Federal Reserve's chief responsibilities were to create enough credit to carry on the nation's part of World War I and to process Liberty Bond sales. The system's lower reserve requirements for deposits in member banks contributed also to a sharp credit expansion by 1920, accompanied by a doubling of the price level. In 1919, out of deference to the Treasury's needs, the Federal Reserve delayed too long in raising discount rates, a step needed to discourage commodity speculation. That was a major mistake. In 1922, the system's leaders became aware of the value of open-market buying operations to promote recovery, and open-market selling operations to choke off speculative booms. Strong worked in the 1920s with Montagu Norman, head of the Bank of England, to help bring other nations back to the gold standard. To assist them, he employed open-market buying operations and lowered discount rates so that Americans would not draw off their precious funds at the crucial moment of resumption. Nonetheless, plentiful U.S. funds and other reasons promoted stock market speculation in the United States. Strong's admirers felt he might have controlled the situation had he lived, but in February 1928 he fell sick and, on 16 October, died. As in 1919, the Federal Reserve did too little too late to stop the speculative boom that culminated in the October 1929 crash. In the years 1930–1932, more than 5,000 banks failed; in 1933, 4,000 more failed. Whether the Federal Reserve should have made credit easier than it did is still debatable. Businessmen were not in a borrowing mood, and banks gave loans close scrutiny. The bank disaster, with a $1 billion loss to depositors between 1931 and 1933, brought on congressional investigations and revelations, as well as demands for reforms and measures to promote recovery. Congress subsequently overhauled the Federal Reserve System.

By the act of 27 February 1932, Congress temporarily permitted the Federal Reserve to use federal government obligations as well as gold and commercial paper to back Federal Reserve notes and deposits. A dearth of commercial paper during the depression, along with bank failures that stimulated hoarding, created a currency shortage. A new backing for the bank notes was essential. However justified at the moment, the law soon became permanent and made inflation in the future easier.

Four other measures around this time were very important. These were the Banking Act of 16 June 1933; parts of the Securities Act of 27 May 1933 and of the Securities Exchange Act of 19 June 1934; and the Banking Act of 23 August 1935. Taken together, the acts had four basic goals: (1) to restore confidence in the banks, (2) to strengthen the banks, (3) to remove temptations to speculate, and (4) to increase the powers of the Federal Reserve System, notably of the board. To restore confidence, the 1933 and 1935 banking acts set up the Federal Deposit Insurance Corporation, which first sharply reduced, and, after 1945, virtually eliminated, bank failures. To strengthen banks, the acts softened restrictions on branch banking and real estate loans, and admitted mutual savings banks and some others. It was felt that the Federal Reserve could do more to control banks if they were brought into the system. To remove temptations to speculate, the banks were forbidden to pay interest on demand deposits, forbidden to use Federal Reserve credit for speculative purposes, and obliged to dispose of their investment affiliates. To increase the system's powers, the board was reorganized, without the secretary of treasury, and given more control over member banks; the Federal Reserve bank boards were assigned a more subordinate role; and the board gained more control over open-market operations and got important new credit-regulating powers. These last included the authority to raise or lower margin requirements and also to raise member bank legal reserve requirements to as much as double the previous figures.

The board, in 1936–1937, doubled reserve requirements because reduced borrowing during the depression, huge gold inflows caused by the dollar devaluation in January 1934, and the growing threat of war in Europe, were causing member banks to have large excess reserves. Banks with excess reserves are not dependent on the Federal Reserve and so cannot be controlled by it. This action probably helped to bring on the 1937 recession.

During the Great Depression, World War II, and even afterward, the Federal Reserve, with Marriner Eccles as board chairman (1936–1948), kept interest rates low and encouraged member banks to buy government obligations. The new Keynesian economic philosophy (the theory by John Maynard Keynes, perhaps the most important figure in the history of economics, that active government intervention is the best way to assure economic growth and stability) stressed the importance of low interest rates to promote investment, employment, and recovery, with the result that—for about a decade—it became almost the duty of the Federal Reserve to keep the nation on what was sometimes called a "low interest rate standard." In World War II, as in World War I, the Federal Reserve assisted with bond drives and saw to it that the federal government and member banks had ample funds for the war effort. Demand deposits tripled between 1940 and 1945, and the price level doubled during the 1940s; there was somewhat less inflation with somewhat more provocation than during World War I. The Federal Reserve's regulation limiting consumer credit, price controls, and the depression before the war, were mainly responsible. Regulation W (selective controls on consumer credit) was in effect from 1 September 1941 to 1 November 1947, and twice briefly again before 1952. The board also kept margin requirements high, but it was unable to use its open market or discount tools to limit credit expansion. On the contrary, it had to maintain a "pattern of rates" on federal government obligations, ranging from three-eighths of 1 percent for Treasury bills to 2.5 percent for long-term bonds. That often amounted to open-market buying operations, which promoted inflation. Admittedly, it also encouraged war-bond buying by keeping bond prices at par or better.

Securities support purchases (1941–1945), executed for the system by the New York Federal Reserve Bank, raised the system's holdings of Treasury obligations from about $2 billion to about $24 billion. The rationale for the Federal Reserve continuing these purchases after the war was the Treasury's wish to hold down interest charges on the $250 billion public debt and the fear of a postwar depression, based on Keynesian economics and memory of the 1921 depression. The Federal Reserve was not fully relieved of the duty to support federal government security prices until it concluded its "accord" with the Treasury, reported on 4 March 1951. Thereafter, interest rates moved more freely, and the Federal Reserve could again use open-market selling operations and have more freedom to raise discount rates. At times, bond prices fell sharply and there were complaints of "tight money." Board chairman William McChesney Martin, who succeeded Thomas McCabe (1948–1951) on 2 April 1951, pursued a middle-of-the-road policy during the 1950s, letting interest rates find their natural level whenever possible but using credit controls to curb speculative booms in 1953, 1956–1957, and 1959–1960 and to reduce recession and unemployment in 1954, 1958, and late 1960. After the Full Employment Act of 1946, the Federal Reserve, along with many other federal agencies, was expected to play its part in promoting full employment.

For many years, the thirty member banks in New York and Chicago complained of the unfairness of legal reserve requirements that were higher for them than for other banks, and bankers generally felt they should be permitted to consider cash held in the banks as part of their legal reserves. A law of 28 July 1959 reduced member banks to two classifications: 295 reserve city banks in fifty-one cities, and about 6,000 "country" banks, starting not later than 28 July 1962. According to this law, member banks might consider their vault cash as legal reserves. Thereafter, the requirement for legal reserves against demand deposits ranged between 10 and 22 percent for member city banks and between 7 and 14 percent for member country banks.

During the period 1961–1972, stimulating economic growth, enacting social welfare reforms, and waging war in Vietnam were among the major activities of the federal government that: (1) raised annual expenditures from $97 billion in fiscal 1960 to $268 billion in fiscal 1974; (2) saw a budget deficit in all but three years of that period; (3) raised the public debt by almost 70 percent; and (4) increased the money supply (currency and demand deposits) from $144 billion on 31 December 1960 to $281 billion on 30 October 1974. As early as 1958, the nation's international balance of payments situation was draining off its gold reserves (reflected in the Federal Reserve's gold certificate holdings). These fell from $23 billion on 31 December 1957 to $15.5 billion on 31 December 1964. With only $1.4 billion free (without penalties to the Federal Reserve) for payments to foreign creditors, Congress, on 18 February 1965, repealed the 25 percent gold certificate requirement against deposits in Federal Reserve banks on the theory that this action would increase confidence in the dollar by making $3.5 billion in additional gold available to foreign central banks or for credit expansion at home. Unfortunately, the situation worsened. On 18 March 1968, Congress removed a similar 25 percent reserve requirement against Federal Reserve notes, thereby freeing up all of the nation's gold. Nevertheless, the gold drain became so alarming that, on 15 August 1971, President Richard M. Nixon announced that the United States would no longer redeem its dollars in gold.

All these developments affected, and were affected by, Federal Reserve policies. During much of the 1960s, government economists thought they had the fiscal and monetary tools to "fine tune" the economy (that is, to dampen booms and to soften depressions), but the recession of 1966 damaged that belief. During the late 1960s, the monetarist school of economists, led by Milton Friedman of the University of Chicago, which sought to increase the money supply at a modest but steady rate, had considerable influence. In general, Reserve board chairman Martin advocated a moderate rate of credit expansion, and, in late May 1965, commented on the "disquieting similarities between our present prosperity and the fabulous '20s." Regardless, Congress and President Lyndon B. Johnson continued their heavy spending policies, but the president reappointed Martin as chairman in March 1967 because his departure might have alarmed European central bankers and precipitated a monetary crisis. With Martin's retirement early in 1970 and Arthur F. Burns's appointment as board chairman, credit became somewhat easier again.

Throughout this era, restraining inflation—a vital concern of the Federal Reserve—was increasingly difficult. What did the money supply consist of? If demand deposits are money, why not readily convertible time deposits? Furthermore, if time deposits are money, as monetarists contended, then why not savings and loan association "deposits," or U.S. government E and H bonds? What of the quite unregulated Eurodollar supply? As a result of such uncontrolled increases in the money supply, consumer prices rose 66 percent in the period 1960–1974, most of it occurring after 1965.

As of 27 November 1974, members of the Federal Reserve System included 5,767 of the 14,384 banks in the

United States, and they held 77 percent of all bank deposits in the nation. Nevertheless, the Federal Reserve has changed markedly in structure, scope, and procedures since the 1970s. In the middle of that decade, it confronted what came to be known as "the attrition problem," a drop-off in the number of banks participating in the Federal Reserve System. The decrease resulted from the prevalence of unusually high interest rates that, because of the central bank's so-called reserve requirement, made membership in the system unattractive to banks. In the United States, the federal government issues bank charters to national banks while the states issue them to state banks. A federal statute required all national banks to join the Federal Reserve; membership was optional for state banks. The Fed provided many privileges to its members but required them to hold reserves in non-interest-earning accounts at one of the twelve district Federal Reserve banks or as vault cash. While many states assessed reserve requirements for nonmember banks, the amounts were usually lower than the federal reserves, and the funds could be held in an interest-earning form. As interest rates rose to historical highs in the mid-1970s, the cost of membership in the Fed began to outweigh the benefits for many banks, because their profits were reduced by the reserve requirement. State banks began to withdraw from the Federal Reserve, and some national banks took up state charters in order to be able to drop their memberships. Federal Reserve officials feared they were losing control of the national banking system as a result of the attrition in membership.

The Depository Institutions Deregulation and Monetary Control Act of 1980 addressed the attrition problem by requiring reserves for all banks and thrift institutions offering accounts on which checks could be drawn. The act phased out most ceilings on deposit interest and allowed institutions subject to Federal Reserve requirements, whether members or not, to have access to the so-called discount window, that is, to borrow from the Federal Reserve, and to use other services such as check processing and electronic funds transfer on a fee-for-service basis.

In the same decade, a period of dramatic growth began in international banking, with foreign banks setting up branches and subsidiaries within the United States. Some U.S. banks claimed to be at a competitive disadvantage because foreign banks escaped the regulations and restrictions placed on domestic banks, such as those affecting branching of banks and nonbanking activities. In addition, foreign banks were free of the reserve requirement. The International Banking Act of 1978 gave regulatory and supervisory authority over foreign banks to the Federal Reserve. Together with the Depository Institutions Act of 1980, it helped level the playing field for domestic banks.

Unlike most other countries where the central bank is closely controlled by the government, the Federal Reserve System enjoys a fair amount of independence in pursuing its principal function, the control of the nation's money supply. Since passage of the Full Employment and Balanced Growth (Humphrey-Hawkins) Act of 1978, Congress has required the Federal Reserve to report to it twice each year, in February and July, on "objectives and plans. . .with respect to the ranges of growth or diminution of the monetary and credit aggregates." The Federal Reserve System must "include an explanation of the reason for any revisions to or deviations from such objectives and plans." These reports enable Congress to monitor monetary policy and performance and to improve coordination of monetary and government fiscal policies. The independence of the Federal Reserve System and its accountability continued to be controversial issues into the 1990s.

BIBLIOGRAPHY

Broz, J. Lawrence. *The International Origins of the Federal Reserve System.* Ithaca, N.Y.: Cornell University Press, 1997.

Kettl, Donald F. *Leadership at the Fed.* New Haven, Conn.: Yale University Press, 1986.

Livingston, James. *Origins of the Federal Reserve System: Money, Class, and Corporate Capitalism, 1890–1913.* Ithaca, N.Y.: Cornell University Press, 1986.

Morris, Irwin L. *Congress, the President, and the Federal Reserve: The Politics of American Monetary Policy-Making.* Ann Arbor: University of Michigan Press, 2000.

Toma, Mark. *Competition and Monopoly in the Federal Reserve System, 1914–1951: A Microeconomics Approach to Monetary History.* Cambridge, U.K.; New York: Cambridge University Press, 1997.

Wells, Wyatt C. *Economist in an Uncertain World: Arthur F. Burns and the Federal Reserve, 1970–1978.* New York: Columbia University Press, 1994.

Wheelock, David C. *The Strategy and Consistency of Federal Reserve Monetary Policy, 1924–1933.* Cambridge, U.K.; New York: Cambridge University Press, 1991.

Earl W. Adams
Donald L. Kemmerer/A. E.

See also **Aldrich-Vreeland Act; Banking; Clearinghouses; Federal Agencies; Great Depression; Keynesianism; Open-Market Operations; Pujo Committee;** *and vol. 9:* **Fireside Chat on the Bank Crisis.**

FEDERAL TRADE COMMISSION. The Federal Trade Commission (FTC) emerged from Progressive Era reformers' search for better means to manage large-scale industrial capitalism and to combat monopoly. By 1912 reformers agreed on the need for a new government agency to regulate big business. They disagreed, however, over the purposes of such an agency. One faction, including Woodrow Wilson and Louis Brandeis, sought a trust-busting commission that would dismantle big business in order to promote a more competitive market of small firms. Another group, centered around Theodore Roosevelt, envisioned an agency that would cooperate with business to help plan economic behavior.

The Federal Trade Commission Act of 1914 fulfilled both visions. The act created a five-person commission to oversee and investigate all commerce but banking and common carriers, empowered this commission with subpoena powers and also to issue cease and desist orders against "unfair" competitive practices, and instructed the agency to report to Congress to assist in legislation. A complementary bill, the Clayton Antitrust Act of 1914, enumerated FTC jurisdiction by specifying unfair practices, among them anticompetitive mergers and acquisitions. Compromise between antitrust and cooperative reformers ensured passage of the Clayton and FTC acts, but it gave the new commission a contradictory mandate to serve as both adversary and advisor to big business. The two bills also bestowed the FTC with uncertain authority and independence by dividing antitrust enforcement between the commission and the Justice Department and by subjecting the FTC to review by the president, Congress, and the courts. In the face of ambiguities the agency proceeded with diffidence. At first the commission issued antitrust orders and prosecutions with hesitation, electing instead to hold information conferences with industry. Following America's entry into World War I the government, with the help of the FTC, suspended antitrust laws and encouraged business combination. When the FTC did seek to pursue antitrust enforcement, as in its investigation of the meatpacking industry for price-fixing and lack of competition, its congressional foes countered by weakening the commission's authority and jurisdiction.

External Search for Limits, 1919–1935

Congressional restriction of the FTC following the meatpacking investigation inaugurated an era in which the legislature, president, and courts would resolve the contradictions in the FTC's regulatory mandate by limiting the commission's antitrust activity. The Supreme Court presented the greatest challenge to the FTC. The Court's ruling in *FTC v. Gratz* 253 U.S. 421 (1920) restricted "unfair practices" to those understood at the time of the 1914 legislation, a standard that prevented the commission from innovating its tactics and resulted in a string of legal defeats for the agency. The appointment by Republican presidents Harding and Coolidge of commissioners hostile to antitrust enforcement and amenable to business interests also restrained the FTC's regulatory activities.

Responding to these limits, FTC policy became cautious and reactive during the 1920s. The commission's number of cease and desist orders and antitrust cases dropped, and the agency instead turned to fostering consensus between government and industry, and association between firms within an industry, through trade practice conferences, which promoted the planning of production costs and prices.

In the depression years prior to 1935, the Hoover and Roosevelt administrations continued the associationalist and consensual model of regulation and furthered external limits on FTC action. New Deal policies undermined the commission's antitrust efforts and codified associationalism and restraint of competition as federal policy. At the same time, the Supreme Court continued to undermine FTC jurisdiction and enforcement powers. In *FTC v. Raladam*, 283 U.S. 643 (1931), the Court raised the commission's burden of proof by requiring it to show that real injury to competitors had occurred from a suspect trade practice.

Expansion and Consolidation, 1935–1969

Shifts in court opinion sparked an expansion in the powers of the FTC. A series of Supreme Court rulings overturned restrictions placed on the agency and allowed the commission an active role in regulation. In *FTC v. Keppel & Brothers, Inc.*, 291 U.S. 304 (1934), the Court reversed *Gratz* and enabled the FTC to broadly interpret the meaning of "unfair practices." The Court's ruling in *Humphery's Executor v. United States*, 295 U.S. 602 (1935), reinforced the commission's independence from presidential coercion. And the *Schechter Poultry Corporation v. United States*, 295 U.S. 495 (1935), decision declared unconstitutional the New Deal programs that had advocated anticompetitive policies.

The FTC also benefited from a resurgence of antitrust and procompetition ideas among New Deal policymakers that favored extending the FTC's authority and oversight. The Robinson-Patman Act of 1936 increased the commission's powers over price discrimination by retailers and suppliers. The Wheeler-Lea Act of 1938 reversed the burden of proof standards established in *Raladam* and broadened the FTC's mandate to include the protection of consumers against deceptive and unfair practices. The commission's investigations now found a receptive audience in congress and spurred new regulatory legislation like the Securities Exchange Act of 1934 and the Public Utility Holding Company Act of 1935.

Although the federal government suspended antitrust enforcement during World War II, the trend of FTC expansion and consolidation continued into the postwar era. The agency won a major victory against price-fixing in the cement industry in 1948 and again in 1950 when a presidential veto defeated the industry's congressional allies. A 1949 review of the commission, chaired by former President Hoover, recommended increasing the FTC chairman's authority and restructuring the agency to facilitate enforcement efforts; Congress institutionalized these recommendations in the FTC Reorganization Act of 1950. That same year the Celler-Kefauver Act broadened the commission's jurisdiction over mergers and combined assets. In the early 1960s the FTC began issuing trade rules to entire industries and increasingly scrutinized advertisements for their effect on competition and consumer interests. FTC activity during the period of expansion reflected the commission's responsiveness to evolving economic realities and its increasing attention to structural barriers to competition.

Reform, Activism, and Reaction, 1969–1990

The consolidation and expansion of the FTC raised concern during the 1960s that the agency had become complacent and ineffective. In 1969 a report issued by consumer advocate Ralph Nader criticized the FTC for failing to fulfill its antitrust and consumer protection duties. When an American Bar Association report of that same year agreed, the Nixon administration responded by reorganizing and reorienting the commission towards more energetic regulation.

These reforms inaugurated the FTC's greatest period of activism. The commission's caseload boomed in the 1970s and included ambitious prosecutions of anticompetitive practices in the breakfast cereal and petroleum industries. Congress widened the commission's jurisdiction and enforcement powers with the Magnuson-Moss Warranty/FTC Improvement Act of 1975, which empowered the commission to issue consumer protection rules for entire industries, and the Hart-Scott-Rodino Antitrust Improvement Act of 1976, which enhanced the FTC's ability to scrutinize mergers by requiring advance notice of such action.

Support for FTC activism began to wane by the late 1970s and fell precipitously following the commission's efforts in 1978 to regulate television advertisements aimed at children. Critics of the FTC argued that the commission had become too independent, too powerful, and heedless of the public good. Congressional critics sought new limits on FTC activity, and in 1979 they temporarily shut off FTC appropriations. The FTC Improvement Act of 1980 restored the agency's funding but enacted new congressional restrictions.

The Reagan administration further targeted the FTC. Executive Order 12291, issued 17 February 1981, placed the reform of regulatory commissions under the control of the president, and the FTC's actions soon turned from aggressive regulation to cooperation with business interests. The agency abandoned cases with sweeping structural implications, emphasized consumer fraud over antitrust enforcement, and liberalized its merger guidelines. The commission's Competition Advocacy Program, for example, championed promarket, probusiness regulatory policies before other state and federal agencies.

The 1990s and Beyond

During the 1990s the FTC increased its enforcement activities in consumer protection and antitrust while attempting to recast regulation to meet the challenge of an increasingly global and technology-driven economy. Adapting quickly to the development of the Internet and computer industry, the commission tackled consumer protection issues such as online privacy, e-commerce, and intellectual property rights, and issued guidelines for advertisements on the Internet. The agency launched fact-finding studies to formulate a regulatory policy for the high-tech sector and held hearings to educate consumers and industry about new enforcement standards. The FTC also adapted its antitrust activities to the new economy: in 1997 the commission launched an investigation of Intel for anticompetitive practices, and in 2000 it arbitrated the merger of America Online with Time Warner.

The FTC's efforts outside the technology economy also displayed innovation and renewed assertiveness. The commission successfully sued the tobacco industry to end cigarette advertisements that appealed to children. And in the face of the decade's merger wave, the FTC either blocked or negotiated a number of high-profile mergers, including the successful mergers of Boeing and McDonnell Douglas in 1997 and Exxon and Mobil in 1999.

Beginning with the appointment of a new chairman in 2001, the FTC retreated from the enforcement pattern of the 1990s. The commission announced its intent to tailor antitrust enforcement to the interests of the economy by exploring the benefits, especially to the consumer, of mergers and by promoting market solutions to problems of competition.

BIBLIOGRAPHY

Davis, G. Cullom. "The Transformation of the Federal Trade Commission, 1914–1929." *Mississippi Valley Historical Review* 49 (1962): 437–455.

Hawley, Ellis W. *The New Deal and the Problem of Monopoly: A Study in Economic Ambivalence.* Princeton, N.J.: Princeton University Press, 1966.

Jaenicke, Douglas Walter. "Herbert Croly, Progressive Ideology, and the FTC Act." *Political Science Quarterly* 93 (1978): 471–493.

McCraw, Thomas K. *Prophets of Regulation: Charles Francis Adams, Louis D. Brandeis, James M. Landis, Alfred E. Kahn.* Cambridge, Mass.: Harvard University Press, Belknap Press, 1984.

Murphy, Patrick E., and William L. Wilkie, eds. *Marketing and Advertising Regulation: The Federal Trade Commission in the 1990s.* Notre Dame, Ind.: University of Notre Dame Press, 1990. Contains several noteworthy essays on the history and development of the FTC.

Wagner, Susan. *The Federal Trade Commission.* New York: Praeger, 1971.

James Tejani

FEDERALIST PAPERS. On 27 October 1787, the first essay of *The Federalist,* written under the pen name Publius, appeared in a New York City newspaper. Its author was Alexander Hamilton, who conceived the project of publishing an extended series of essays to support the ratification of the newly proposed Federal Constitution. Hamilton recruited two other prominent leaders as his co-authors: John Jay and James Madison. Together, they published seventy-seven newspaper essays by April 1788, and another eight appeared in the second volume of the first book edition. Hamilton is credited with writing fifty-one essays, Madison twenty-nine, and Jay, weakened by illness, just five. All three authors drew upon their extensive experience in national politics and the military and diplomatic struggle for independence. The two main authors also played critical roles in the maneuvers leading to the Federal Convention and the drafting of the Constitution, and they also founded the rival schools of constitutional interpretation that developed after it took effect. As a result, *The Federalist* has long been regarded as the most authoritative exposition of the original meaning of the Constitution, and the leading American contribution to Western political thought.

The division of assignments allowed the authors to tap their particular strengths. Hamilton, the more ardent nationalist, had seven years of service in the Continental Army, mostly as aide-de-camp to General Washington; he was also a close student of public finance and a successful attorney. It was therefore fitting that he wrote the essays emphasizing the necessity for an effective national union with adequate powers over national defense and revenue, as well as those examining the executive and judiciary. Madison's experience was primarily legislative; he was more engaged with basic questions of political theory, and more concerned than Hamilton with balancing the authority of the Union and the states. It was equally fitting, then, that he wrote the leading essays on Congress and federalism, as well as addressing anti-Federalist objections that the Constitution violated fundamental maxims of free government.

Two of those maxims were closely associated with one of the most celebrated works of eighteenth-century political science, Montesquieu's *The Spirit of the Laws.* One of these maxims argued that republican government could safely operate only in small, homogeneous societies where the citizens shared similar interests and the virtue to subordinate private interest to public good. The other held that liberty depended upon a rigid separation of both the functions and personnel of the different departments of government. Madison challenged these propositions in two famous essays. "Federalist 10" argued that liberty would be more secure in a large, diverse republic, where "factious majorities" would find it more difficult to gain control of the government. "Federalist 51" concluded a series of essays on the separation of powers by arguing that the task of maintaining equilibrium among the departments required giving the members of each branch the incentives and means to protect their constitutional powers. Hamilton's best-known essay is "Federalist 78," which offered an early defense of the theory of judicial review, enabling courts to measure legislative and executive acts against constitutional standards.

BIBLIOGRAPHY

Adair, Douglass. "The Tenth Federalist Revisited." *William and Mary Quarterly*, 3d ser., 8 (1951): 48–67.

———. "'That Politics May Be Reduced to a Science': David Hume, James Madison, and the Tenth Federalist." *Huntington Library Quarterly*, 20 (1957): 343–360.

Cooke, Jacob, ed. *The Federalist.* Middletown, Conn.: Wesleyan University Press, 1961.

Epstein, David F. *The Political Theory of The Federalist.* Chicago: University of Chicago Press, 1984.

Furtwangler, Albert. *The Authority of Publius: A Reading of the Federalist Papers.* Ithaca, N.Y.: Cornell University Press, 1984.

Kesler, Charles R. ed. *Saving the Revolution: The Federalist Papers and the American Founding.* New York: Free Press, 1987.

Jack Rakove

See also **United States Constitution;** *and vol. 9:* **The Call for Amendments.**

FEDERALIST PARTY. The name "Federalist Party" originated in the ratification debates over the U.S. Constitution. In 1788 the group that favored ratification and a strong central government called themselves "federalists," which at that time indicated a preference for a more consolidated government rather than a loose "confederation" of semi-sovereign states. After the Constitution was ratified, the term "federalist" came to be applied to any supporter of the Constitution and particularly to members of the Washington administration. The term received wide currency with the publication of a series of eighty-one articles by Alexander Hamilton, James Madison, and John Jay arguing for the ratification of the Constitution. Thus, in the early 1790s, not only George Washington, John Adams, and Hamilton, but even Madison, then the floor leader of the administration in the House of Representatives, were all "federalists."

The Washington administration found itself divided, however, over Hamilton's debt, banking, and manufacturing policies, all of which favored the commercial and financial interests of the Northeast over the agrarian interests of the South and West. Foreign policy questions also split Washington's cabinet in his first term, especially the problems arising from treaty obligations to the increasingly radical republicans in France. These questions deeply divided the government, and eventually caused the resignations of the secretary of state, Thomas Jefferson, and James Madison as floor leader. Nevertheless, these questions did not precipitate permanent, consistent political divisions in Congress or in the states.

The Emergence of a Party

The Federalist Party took permanent and consistent form in Washington's second term as president during the controversy over the Jay Treaty with Great Britain. John Jay negotiated a treaty that alienated the frontier interests, the commercial grain exporters of the middle states, and the slaveholders of the South. The division over foreign policy—between "Anglomen" who hoped for favorable relations with Britain and "Gallomen" who hoped for continued strong relations with France—generated a climate of distrust, paranoia, and repression that propelled these foreign policy divisions into sustained political conflict at the elite level and eventually promoted the expansion of a party press, party organizations, and strong party identification in the electorate.

Although the Federalist Party did not arise from the controversy over Hamilton's economic policies, those states and interests that had benefited from Hamiltonian policies tended to favor the Federalists from the beginning. New England and the seaboard states of New Jersey, Delaware, Maryland, and South Carolina favored the Federalists in part because each of these states was dominated by commercial interests and an entrenched social and religious elite. Similarly, the urban seaboard interests and prosperous agrarian regions of Pennsylvania and New York also favored the Federalists. In New England, federalism was closely associated with the Established Congregational church in Connecticut, Massachusetts, and New Hampshire. In the middle states, Federalists tended to be Episcopalian in New York, Presbyterian in New Jersey, and might be either of these, or Quakers, in the area around Philadelphia. In Delaware, on the other hand, Federalists were more likely to be Episcopalians from the lower part of the state, rather than Presbyterians or Quakers from Wilmington.

In the South, federalism dominated only one state, South Carolina, and that was in part the result of its benefit from the Hamiltonian funding policy of state debts. Like the northern Federalists, South Carolina Federalists formed a solid elite in the Low Country along the coast. Mostly Episcopalian and Huguenot Presbyterians, their great wealth and urban commercial interests in Charleston, the South's only significant city, led them to make common cause with Hamiltonians in New England and the middle states. Elsewhere in the South, federalism thrived in regions where the social order was more hierarchical, wealth was greater, and the inroads of evangelicalism were weakest. Thus the Eastern Shore of Maryland, once Loyalist and Anglican, was a Federalist bastion, as were the Catholic counties of southern Maryland. The Tidewater of Virginia was another Federalist stronghold, as were the Cape Fear region of North Carolina and the Lowland counties of Georgia. Outside of a few New England exiles in the Western Reserve area of Ohio, Federalists did not gather much support in the new states of the West.

With strong political support across the Union at the time of Washington's retirement, the Federalists managed to hold the presidency for their party and for their candidate, John Adams, but only by three electoral votes. Adams allowed Washington's cabinet to retain their posts into his new term. They were followers of Alexander Hamilton, arch-Federalists, and far more ideological than Adams himself.

In 1798 the Federalists reached the peak of their national popularity in the war hysteria that followed the XYZ Affair. In the congressional elections of 1798 the Federalists gained greater support in their strongholds in New England, the middle states, Delaware, and Maryland. They made significant gains in Virginia, North Carolina, South Carolina, and Georgia. North and South, the popular slogan in 1798 was "Adams and Liberty." Even as they gained strength over their Democratic Republican adversaries, however, they viewed their opponents with increasing alarm. In a time of war hysteria, extreme Federalists genuinely believed that many Jeffersonians had allied themselves with the most radical factions of Revolutionary France. At a time when the Democratic Republicans were out of favor, their criticisms of the Federalists took on a shrill, often vituperative tone.

The harsh personal criticism by the leading Democratic Republican newspapers prompted some Federalists in Congress to find a way to curb this "licentious" press, punish the opposition editors, and perhaps cripple Democratic Republican political chances in the upcoming presidential election. In Congress, Representative Robert Goodloe Harper of South Carolina and Senator William Lloyd of Maryland introduced legislation in 1798 known as the Alien and Sedition Acts. The Sedition Act, modeled on the British Sedition Act of 1795, made it unlawful to "print, utter, or publish . . . any false, scandalous, and malicious writing" against any officer of the government. Under the energetic enforcement of Secretary of State Timothy Pickering, the leading Democratic Republican newspapers in Philadelphia, Boston, New York, and Richmond, Virginia, were closed down in 1799.

The Election of 1800

The election year of 1800 was the last time an incumbent Federalist engaged himself in a contest for the presidency. Despite Thomas Jefferson's referral to the election as a "revolution," the presidential contest was in fact narrowly won. Only five states allowed for the popular vote for presidential electors, and both parties used every means available—especially legislative selection of electors—to maximize their candidate's electoral vote. This was the first and last year the Federalists and Democratic Republicans contested every single state in the congressional elections. The Republicans won 67 of the 106 seats in the House of Representatives. Despite the decisive popular vote for the Democratic Republicans in Congress, the electoral vote was not at all a clear mandate for Thomas Jefferson. In fact, Thomas Jefferson owed his victory in the Electoral College to the infamous "three-fifths" rule, which stipulated that slaves would be counted in congressional (and electoral college) apportionment as a concession to the South.

Although the contest for president was mostly conducted in the legislatures and the congressional contests were conducted at the local level, the party press of both the Federalists and the Jeffersonian Republicans played up the contrast between Jefferson and Adams. Jefferson was a "Jacobin," an "atheist," and a "hypocrite" with all his talk about equality, while keeping slaves. Adams was an "aristocrat," a "monocrat," and a defender of hereditary privileges. The religious issue played an important part in the election. The *Gazette of the United States* put this controversy in its starkest form: "God—And a Religious President; Or Jefferson—And No God!!!"

The Decline of Federalism

The Federalists lost more congressional seats in 1802 and in 1804, despite Hamilton's attempt to inject the religious issue into the former election. Their opposition to the LOUISIANA PURCHASE seemed to spell certain doom for them in the West. Thanks to the unpopularity of Jefferson's Embargo Act, however, the Federalist Party experienced a revival in New England and the middle states in 1808 at the congressional and state level. By 1812 the Federalist Party and dissident anti-war Republicans grouped together behind DeWitt Clinton and the "Friends of Peace." With the unpopularity of the war in the Northeast, the Federalists and their anti-war allies gave James Madison a close contest for his reelection. The Federalist Party gained seats in Congress in 1812 and 1814 as the fortunes of war seemed arrayed against the Americans.

Some of the more extreme Federalists, however, including Timothy Pickering and Harrison Gray Otis of Massachusetts and Oliver Wolcott of Connecticut, toyed with New England secession in the midst of this unpopular war. They met in Hartford, Connecticut, from 15 December 1814 to 5 January 1815. Although the Federalist delegates defeated a secession resolution, their party was thereafter associated with disloyalty, and even treason. The end of the war made the Hartford Convention nothing more than an embarrassing irrelevance.

The Federalist Party hung on, however, in a long twilight in the seaboard states of Delaware, Maryland, New Jersey, Connecticut, Massachusetts, and New Hampshire, and even enjoyed a modest revival in Pennsylvania and New York in the early 1820s. The Federalist Party never again held power at the national level after 1800 in the election triumph that Jefferson called a "revolution." The death of Alexander Hamilton in 1804 killed the one Federalist leader who had youth, national stature, and significant popular support.

The extended influence of the Federalist Party lay in the judiciary. With the appointment of many Federalists to the bench, John Adams ensured that the Federalists would continue to exert a dominant influence on the federal judiciary for many years to come. Federalist judges predominated until the ERA OF GOOD FEELING. Thereafter, federalism continued to have influence in the law, thanks in no small part to the intellectual authority of John Marshall, chief justice of the U.S. Supreme Court, who remained on the Court until his death in 1835.

BIBLIOGRAPHY

Banner, James M. *To the Hartford Convention: Federalists and the Origins of Party Politics in Massachusetts, 1789–1815.* New York: Harper, 1970.

Ben-Atar, Doron, and Barbara B. Oberg, eds. *Federalists Reconsidered.* Charlottesville: University Press of Virginia, 1998.

Broussard, James. *The Southern Federalists.* Baton Rouge: Louisiana State University Press, 1978.

Chambers, William Nisbet. *The First Party System.* New York: John Wiley, 1972.

Dauer, Manning J. *The Adams Federalists.* Baltimore: Johns Hopkins University Press, 1953.

Elkins, Stanley, and Eric McKittrick. *The Age of Federalism: The Early American Republic, 1788–1800.* New York: Oxford University Press, 1993.

Fischer, David Hackett. *The Revolution of American Conservatism: The Federalist Party in the Era of Jeffersonian Democracy.* New York: Harper, 1965.

Formisano, Ronald P. *The Transformation of Political Culture: Massachusetts Parties, 1790–1840.* New York: Oxford University Press, 1983.

Hofstadter, Richard. *The Idea of a Party System: The Rise of Legitimate Opposition in the United States, 1780–1840.* Berkeley: University of California Press, 1969.

Kerber, Linda. *Federalists in Dissent: Imagery and Ideology in Jeffersonian America.* Ithaca, N.Y.: Cornell University Press, 1970.

Miller, John C. *The Federalist Era, 1789–1801.* New York: Harper, 1960.

Sharpe, James Roger. *American Politics in the Early Republic: The New Nation in Crisis.* New Haven, Conn.: Yale University Press, 1993.

Andrew W. Robertson

See also **Political Parties; Republicans, Jeffersonian; Two-Party System.**

FEE PATENTING refers to Native American land held in fee by the property owner with no restrictions on alienation (sale), as opposed to Native American land held in trust by the federal government, which is not freely alienable. The DAWES GENERAL ALLOTMENT ACT of 1887 provided every Native American with a parcel of his or her reservation and restricted immediate sale by providing that the land would be held in trust for twenty-five years or longer. After twenty-five years, a fee patent would be issued to the Native American allottee who would then become a U.S. citizen. This opened the way to taxation of the property and resulted in the loss of much Native American land.

BIBLIOGRAPHY

Otis, Delos Sacket. *The Dawes Act and the Allotment of Indian Lands.* Edited by Francis P. Prucha. Norman: University of Oklahoma Press, 1973.

Prucha, Francis Paul. *The Great Father: The United States Government and the American Indians.* Lincoln: University of Nebraska Press, 1995.

Michael Wala

See also **Indian Land Cessions; Indian Policy, U.S.: 1830–1900; Indian Reservations.**

FEMININE MYSTIQUE, THE. Considered a wake-up call to women, Betty Friedan's *The Feminine Mystique*, published in 1963, resulted in a social revolution. Friedan's work introduced her readers to the nature versus nurture debate and helped some women identify what she referred to as "the problem that has no name," for which the only cure could be a source of paid employment. Friedan compared the life of a "happy housewife" living in suburbia, something that Friedan herself experienced in the 1950s, to life in a Nazi concentration camp. What is ironic, however, is that Friedan was hardly the average housewife. Due to her graduate work in psychology, Friedan's work is full of citations of academic resources, and Friedan herself was first and foremost an activist. Yet she presented *The Feminine Mystique* in a manner that suggested she was not an academic, but rather, an average American nonworking woman, writing about the miserable condition of women.

Friedan worked on *The Feminine Mystique* from the New York Public Library and her dining room table, a combination of the academic and domestic spheres. This was somewhat fitting for a work that describes the post–World War II mystique that defined women solely as wives, mothers, and housekeepers. Friedan argued that this definition would cripple wives and husbands and harm the national economy. Her book changed the face of American politics and family life for good, creating a whole generation of militant women who looked for scapegoats to denigrate. Beginning with their mothers, and then moving to the stereotype of the male obsessed with football and beer, these militant reformers challenged Friedan's original movement of "housewives" with middle class values, children, and modern conveniences.

These conveniences, however, were what made women so unhappy, Friedan argued. She compared suburban women to concentration camp inmates because the camps had promoted a loss of autonomy and forced the identification of individuals with their oppressors.

Friedan's work has been challenged by various historians and sociologists, including Daniel Horowitz, who called attention to the disparity between Friedan's role as a labor union activist and her portrayal of herself as a typical suburban housewife. However, Horowitz argued that Friedan's contributions were no less significant on account of her misrepresentation of her life. Some have questioned whether Friedan sacrificed the truth to advance her cause, and although *The Feminine Mystique* is a product of Friedan's studies and her involvement in the labor movement, the book also provides an explanation of women's dilemma in the post–World War II and Cold War environments. By giving credence to the concept that women lacked a sense of power, Friedan articulated the importance of gender in historical analysis.

BIBLIOGRAPHY

Horowitz, Daniel. *Betty Friedan and the Making of the Feminine Mystique: The American Left, the Cold War, and Modern Feminism.* Amherst: The University of Massachusetts Press, 1998.

Selle, Robert. "Feminism's Matriarch." *World and I* 13.5 (1998): 50–52.

Wolfe, Alan. "The Mystique of Betty Friedan." *The Atlantic Monthly* 284 (September 1999): 98–103.

Jennifer Harrison

FENCING AND FENCING LAWS. The fencing of land was a problem in colonial America, where unoccupied land was plentiful and cultivated acreage was rare. Virginia Colony in 1632 required crops to be fenced and in 1646 defined a legal or "sufficient" fence. Maryland adopted a similar approach, but the laws of North Carolina were more rigid.

Fencing law evolved as white settlers moved west. Settlers claimed unsold PUBLIC LAND as free range for their livestock, and as settlement increased, the demand for fenced pasture grew more acute. Planters in Virginia secured some relief in 1835, as did farmers in New Jersey in 1842. Despite the depletion of timber, laws requiring the fencing of crops were the rule by the mid-nineteenth century. In 1872 Illinois extended this general principle to livestock, passing a law requiring farmers to corral their animals.

Fencing styles varied with region and time. In the Northeast, stone fences were common. Elsewhere, the zigzag, or Virginia rail, fence was used wherever timber was available. As timber grew scarce, post and pole, picket, board, and wire fences became more widespread.

By the late nineteenth century, cattlemen controlled large swaths of the West and were driving CATTLE to the railroads. The advent of BARBED WIRE allowed homesteaders to protect their crops from these enormous herds, but this evoked bitter complaints from cattlemen and sparked violent confrontations with the settlers. Open ranching gradually gave way to stock farming, with its controlled grazing and improved breeding techniques. As cattle ranching spread northward, cattlemen fenced government land for their private use, a practice curbed by federal legislation in 1885.

BIBLIOGRAPHY

Fletcher, Robert H. *Free Grass to Fences: The Montana Cattle Range Story.* New York: University Publishers, 1960.

Russell H. Anderson / A. R.

See also **Land Policy; Public Land; Fencing of; West, American.**

FENIAN MOVEMENT was an Irish-American organization created by John O'Mahony in 1858. The movement raised money, supplied equipment, and trained leaders to help the Irish Republican, or Revolutionary, Brotherhood uprising against Great Britain. Fenian membership rose to 250,000, and in 1865 the movement established an "Irish Republic" in New York and issued bonds to finance its activities. The group focused much of its attention on the Irish cause in Canada. In 1866, for example, a dissatisfied Fenian faction broke from the organization, crossed the border at Fort Erie, defeated Canadian troops, and returned to Buffalo, New York. U.S. officials halted reinforcements and arrested the raiders, but eventually released the captives. American troops checked similar invasions from Saint Albans, Vermont, and Malone, New York.

After failing in an earlier attempt against New Brunswick, Canada, the Fenians participated in the republican revolutionary movement in Ireland and sent a vessel loaded with arms and men across the Atlantic in 1867. Fenian involvement in British affairs complicated American foreign policy during the 1860s and 1870s. The Canadian government, for example, treated imprisoned American Fenians as British subjects, which strained relations between the United States and Great Britain. Fenians captured by the British also tried to use their American citizenship to draw their adopted country into a naturalization controversy. Unsuccessful in their objectives, and under growing pressure from the federal government and the Roman Catholic church, many Fenians left the movement and joined the Land League and Home Rule movements. The Fenians held their last congress in 1876 and the movement collapsed following O'Mahony's death in 1877.

BIBLIOGRAPHY

Comerford, R. V. *The Fenians in Context.* Dublin, Ireland: Wolfhound Press, 1985.

Neidhardt, Wilfried. *Fenianism in North America.* University Park: Pennsylvania State University Press, 1975.

Senior, Hereward. *The Last Invasion of Canada: The Fenian Raids, 1866–1870.* Oxford: Dundurn Press, 1991.

Ezra H. Pieper/E. M.

See also **Canada, Relations with; Great Britain, Relations with; Immigration; Ireland, Relations with; Irish Americans.**

FERGUSON IMPEACHMENT. In 1917, James E. Ferguson, nicknamed "Pa Ferguson," was impeached and removed from the governorship of Texas. He was replaced by William P. Hobby after the Texas House of Representatives found him guilty in ten of twenty-one charges. These included misappropriation of state funds, falsification of records, unwarranted interference with the control of the University of Texas—he directed the board of regents to fire a leading educator and prominent Democrat, A. Carswell Ellis—and refusal to divulge the source of a personal loan of $156,500, a huge sum at the time.

Ferguson was first elected in 1914, and was reelected in 1916. The accusations, apparently true, were typical of the corruption, graft, and manipulations of American public life. Ferguson, a political novice, suffered from the lack of a viable power-base. This independence made him critical of existing policies, earning him sufficient popular support to win office, but also the consequent wrath of the establishment that could have protected him from investigation. Although Ferguson was disqualified from holding public office, he did try to run in the 1924 elections to redeem his reputation. He was barred, but managed to have his wife ("Ma Ferguson") elected governor; she was elected for a second term in 1932.

BIBLIOGRAPHY

Gould, Lewis L. "The University Becomes Politicized: The War with Jim Ferguson." *Southwestern Historical Quarterly* 86 (October 1982).

Itai Sneh

See also **Impeachment; Texas.**

FERRIES were used to cross all large streams in colonial days and were only gradually replaced by bridges and, in some instances, tunnels. Where automobile traffic problems grew acute, however, some ferries were brought back into service. The island position of MANHATTAN necessitated ferry connections with Staten Island, LONG ISLAND, and the west bank of the Hudson. The BROOKLYN BRIDGE and subsequent bridges obviated the ferries to Long Island. However, by the end of the twentieth century, the Staten Island ferries continued to provide a vital link to Manhattan for the community while private ferries from Fort Lee and other points in NEW JERSEY alleviated road traffic congestion.

The ferry played a similar and important role in Boston Harbor; Hampton Roads, Virginia; and across the Delaware between Philadelphia and Camden, New Jersey. All of these operations were ultimately displaced by

Ferries. Steamers are docked at Minnetonka Beach in Minnesota, c. 1905. © MINNESOTA HISTORICAL SOCIETY/CORBIS

bridges and tunnels. In the West, ferries persisted between San Francisco and the East Bay well after construction of the Bay Bridge as an adjunct of rail service out of Oakland. The Golden Gate Ferry System continues to provide an alternative to traffic congestion for thousands of commuters from Marin County and elsewhere.

The country's largest public ferry system is found in Puget Sound, Washington. The Washington State Ferries, purchased from private operators and consolidated into a single system in 1951, carry 17 million passengers a year to and from Seattle, other points on the sound, and Vancouver Island.

As an adjunct of railroad services, ferries had an important role across Lake Michigan, Lake Erie, and Lake Ontario; the Straits of Mackinac; the lower Mississippi River; the Detroit River; and Suisun Bay. Lake Michigan ferries provided a shipping route between Michigan and Wisconsin that avoided the Chicago rail terminals. By the mid-twentieth century, the vessels were old, required large crews, and had seen their capacity fall as the average rail car increased in length. Hence, the service, once a profitable extension of the trans-Michigan rail lines, had become a source of large and increasing losses, and it was dismantled in the 1970s.

The rise of tourism along America's coastlines, however, has brought a new demand for excursion ferries. In the 1980s, entrepreneurs refitted the Pere Marquette Railroad's cargo ship *City of Midland* for passenger traffic and resurrected the old lumber route between Ludington, Michigan, and Wisconsin as a popular tourist attraction. Fast tourist ferries, in the form of hydrofoil or hovercraft rather than the conventional ferryboat, link mainland towns with outlying islands. The Port Judith to Block Island ferry in Rhode Island, for example, has expanded as tourism on that island has increased.

BIBLIOGRAPHY

Wright, Sarah Bird. *Ferries of America: A Guide to Adventurous Travel.* Atlanta, Ga.: Peachtree, 1987.

Ernest W. Williams Jr. / A. R.

See also **Bridges; Great Lakes; Mackinac, Straits of, and Mackinac Island; New York City; Tourism; Transportation and Travel.**

FERRIS WHEEL. A noted feature of the World's Columbian Exposition at Chicago in 1893 was a huge upright steel wheel three hundred feet tall and thirty feet wide, with thirty-six passenger cars, each of which could hold sixty people, swinging around the wheel's rim. This was the Ferris wheel. Although not the first such contraption, it became the most famous. George W. G. Ferris, a Pittsburgh engineer, built the wheel upon hearing the lament that there was nothing planned for the fair as novel as the Eiffel Tower at the Paris Exposition of 1889.

Ferris Wheel. This attraction at most modern amusement parks has come a long way from the most famous early version, built for the 1893 Chicago world's fair.

His wheel became one of the main attractions on the exposition's Midway Plaisance.

BIBLIOGRAPHY

Adams, Judith A. *The American Amusement Park Industry: A History of Technology and Thrills.* Boston: Twayne, 1991.

Alvin F. Harlow / A. E.

See also **Amusement Parks.**

FERTILITY. *See* **Childbirth and Reproduction; Demography and Demographic Trends.**

FERTILIZERS, natural or artificial substances composed of the chemical elements that enhance plant growth and productivity by adding nutrients to soil, have been used since the earliest days of agriculture. The three major fertilizer elements are nitrogen, phosphorus, and potassium. Natural fertilizers include manures, compost, plant ashes, lime, gypsum, and grasses. Chemical fertilizers may be derived from natural sources or may be synthetic compounds.

Commercial chemical fertilizers have only been in general use since the nineteenth century. Early American colonists used natural fertilizers, but overuse and lack of crop rotation quickly depleted both the nutrient-poor coastal soil and the more fertile soil of the prairies. Eighteenth- and nineteenth-century European chemists experimented with the effects of chemical fertilization. In

1840, Justus von Liebig published *Organic Chemistry in Its Application to Agriculture and Physiology.* His research demonstrated that adding nitrogen, phosphorus, and potassium to the soil stimulated plant growth. By 1849, mixed chemical fertilizers were sold commercially in the United States, though their use did not become widespread until after 1900.

Fertilizers represent one of the largest market commodities for the chemical industry. On modern farms, machines are used to apply synthetic fertilizers in solid, gaseous, or liquid form. There is also a growing movement, dating to the 1940s, toward organic agriculture, which rejects the use of chemically formulated fertilizers, growth stimulants, antibiotics, and pesticides in favor of traditional natural fertilizers, of plant or animal origin, and crop rotation.

BIBLIOGRAPHY

Havlin, John, Samuel L. Tisdale, and James D. Beaton, eds. *Soil Fertility and Fertilizers: An Introduction to Nutrient Management.* 6th ed., Upper Saddle River, N.J.: Prentice Hall, 1999.

Deirdre Sheets

See also **Agriculture; Organic Farming.**

FEUDALISM. The origins of European feudalism are in eighth-century France, where estates were granted in exchange for military service. In England, feudalism evolved into the manorial system, in which a bound peasantry was subject to the rule of landlords. English feudalism was a system of rights and duties binding an upper class (nobility) in loyalty and responsibility to a king or lord in exchange for land (fiefs) worked by peasant labor (serfs). In exchange for their labor, peasants received the protection and rule of the landowner. This system benefited the nobility, as they essentially held public power privately, and the monarchy, to whom the nobles were bound in both civil and military capacities. The peasant class functioned as a slave labor force. Under feudalism, public authority, privilege, and power were tied to land ownership as much as lineage, and service to the state was rendered not out of duty to a throne or flag but out of individual relationships between the noble and the ruling lord.

In colonial America, feudalism began as an extension of the English manorial system. In addition to the Puritans and the Protestants, who came from England to the New World seeking religious freedom, some early colonists came to expand their estates by establishing feudal domains. While the Puritans and the Protestants established colonies in New England, the Anglicans established the proprietary colonies of Maryland, the Carolinas, and Delaware, and the Dutch brought similar systems to New Amsterdam (later New York) and New Jersey. Similar systems came to the Americas in the seigneurial system of New France (Canada) and the *encomienda* system of the Spanish colonies of Latin America.

The Dutch established a system of patroonship, closely resembling traditional feudalism, in which large tracts of land were granted by Holland's government to anyone bringing fifty or more settlers to the area. The settlers then became tenants subject to the landlord's rule. The system did not thrive, however, and eventually the English took over the Dutch colonies.

Proprietary colonies originally resembled the European feudal system only in part. New settlers were a mix of self-sufficient farmers who did not own their land and wealthy planters who brought serfs with them. These settlers brought feudalistic customs that strongly influenced the society, culture, and economy developing in the southern colonies, which, in true feudal style, were organized around a mercantile economy while the northern colonies slowly industrialized. Feudalism depends on plentiful free labor, and the southern colonies quickly began to rely on slavery. Despite the apparent conflict with America's emerging democracy, feudal elements such as local rule, a class system dictated by social customs, and an economy based on forced labor survived in the South well after the American Revolution (1775–1783). Slavery continued to be a linchpin of the U.S. economy until the Fourteenth Amendment ended the institution after the Civil War (1861–1865). Slavery was then replaced with sharecropping, a system in which former slaves and other poor farmers, though theoretically free, were still bound to landowners.

BIBLIOGRAPHY

Bloch, Marc. *Feudal Society: Social Classes and Political Organization.* Translated by L. A. Manyon. Chicago: University of Chicago Press, 1982.

Orren, Karen. *Belated Feudalism: Labor, the Law, and Liberal Development in the United States.* New York: Cambridge University Press, 1991.

Deirdre Sheets

See also **Plantation System of the South; Proprietary Colonies; Slavery;** *and vol. 9:* **The Theory of the Leisure Class.**

FEUDS, APPALACHIAN MOUNTAIN. Descendants of American pioneers populate the Appalachian Mountains. The mountainous regions of Kentucky, Tennessee, North Carolina, Virginia, and West Virginia are isolated, and, in 1860, their civilization was that of the earliest western frontier. The region especially lacked well-established law and order. Although courts and law enforcement agencies did exist, the topography of the country and the sparse population made enforcing the law difficult. Likewise, the people of the mountains distrusted the courts as institutions of justice.

Bitter disputes arose between mountaineers, even over the most trivial matters; however, livestock, women, politics, and thievery were the most common sources of strife. Straying livestock, the "wronging" of a woman, or the killing of a dog, could set friend against friend, family against family, and one part of a neighborhood against the other. Nevertheless, perhaps the greatest single cause for dispute was the division of sentiment over the Civil War. During this period, armed bands of regulators tried to intimidate people on both sides of the national issue, and attempts to disperse the raiding vandals created bad blood. Most famous of the mountain feuds were those of Hatfield-McCoy (1880–1887), Martin-Tolliver (1874–1887), French-Eversole (1885–1894), and Hargis-Callahan-Cockrell (1899–1903). These mountain wars killed many people. The bloodiest fighting generally took place in the county seat towns on court days, but there were also many killings resulting from ambush.

BIBLIOGRAPHY

Inscoe, John C., and Gordon B. McKinney. *The Heart of Confederate Appalachia: Western North Carolina in the Civil War.* Chapel Hill: University of North Carolina Press, 2000.

Rice, Otis K. *The Hatfields and the McCoys.* Lexington: University of Kentucky Press, 1978; 1982.

Waller, Altina L. *Feud: Hatfields, McCoys, and Social Change in Appalachia, 1860–1900.* Chapel Hill: University of North Carolina Press, 1988.

T. D. Clark/A. E.

See also **Appalachia; Kentucky; North Carolina; Tennessee; Violence; Virginia; West Virginia.**

FIBER OPTICS. Narinder Kapany did not believe a high school teacher who told him that light could only travel in a straight line. His fascination with the idea set off a lifetime of research into fiber optics, which involves the use of reflection to transmit light through fibers of glass or plastic. In 1954, Kapany reported in the British journal *Nature* that he had successfully transmitted images through fiber optic bundles of transparent glass or plastic rods. Kapany's research built on more than 200 years of research and investigation into sending communications over translucent devices.

The American inventor Alexander Graham Bell dreamed of sending communications signals through the air via light impulses. He patented an optical telephone system in 1880, called the Photophone, but his invention of the landline telephone was more practical, thus receiving the lion's share of his time and effort. Further innovation in fiber optics was uneven until the 1920s when Clarence W. Hansell of the United States and John Logie Baird in England patented the idea of using hollow rods to transmit images for television systems. Despite the patent, the first person that established image transmission through a bundle of optical fibers was Heinrich Lamm, a medical student in Germany, who later moved to the United States to avoid persecution by the Nazis.

In 1955, after receiving a doctorate, Kapany journeyed to the United States to teach at the University of Rochester, in New York. In 1960, he moved to California's Silicon Valley and founded Optics Technology, taking it public in 1967. Another Northern California team, this one based at Stanford University, also worked on fiber optic research. Antoni E. Karbowiak and Charles K. Kao led a team examining the properties of fiber and concluded that impurities led to loss of transmission. The team attempted to figure out why light dimmed only a few yards down fiber optic strands, called "fiber attenuation." In 1966, after Karbowiak left Stanford, Kao developed a proposal for long-distance fiber optic communications over single-mode fibers. Although skeptics doubted Kao's research, he proved that fiber could be used for communications systems.

In the 1960s, Kao continued his theoretical and practical research, receiving twenty-nine patents for ideas on manufacturing pure glass fibers to splicing fibers to form communications lines. For their important early work, many observers have dubbed either Kapany or Kao as "the father of fiber optics."

Corning Glass Works produced the first commercial fiber optic cable in 1970. Company scientists used fused silica, an extremely pure material with a high melting point, to perfect fiber optic cable. Less than a decade later, in 1978, communications giant AT&T demonstrated the first fiber communications system. From this humble beginning, several million miles of fiber have been installed around the world, both on land and undersea.

In the early 1980s, when deregulation opened the telecommunications industry, telephony carriers built the national backbone of the industry on fiber optics. Soon, the technology spread from long-distance to other applications, ultimately setting the stage for nationwide fiber systems and the Internet.

In the mid- to late-1990s, the growth of the Internet and a "New Economy" based online solidified the idea that future communications networks would be built on fiber optics, or "broadband" technology. At the height of dot-com mania, companies rushed to connect Internet users to vast broadband networks, which offered the kind of high-speed access needed to fuel the growth of the wired economy.

After the dot-com economic bubble burst, however, the fiber optics industry virtually collapsed. Many formerly solid companies, such as Lucent and Nortel, foundered and startup money for new companies vanished. The fiber optic industry successfully increased bandwidth around the world, but was spread too thin in an effort to build new systems. When an economic recession hit the United States in the early 2000s, many companies were extended beyond their means.

Fiber optic data transmissions carried over silica fiber is at the heart of worldwide communications. The high bandwidth, light-carrying medium transports voice, video, and data and is the keystone of the Internet. Since the 1980s, communications companies have placed more than 300 million miles of fiber optic cable in the ground. However, less than 10 percent of this wiring is being used, eliminating any hope for profitability among many companies. These companies overextended their credit limits to install the fiber optic lines, but could not get enough users "lit" to justify the expense.

BIBLIOGRAPHY

Hecht, Jeff. *City of Light: The Story of Fiber Optics.* New York: Oxford University Press, 1999.

Hitz, Breck, James J. Ewing, and Jeff Hecht. *Introduction to Laser Technology.* 3d ed. New York: Wiley-IEEE Press, 2001.

Palais, Joseph C. *Fiber Optic Communications.* 4th ed. Garden City, N.J.: Prentice-Hall, 1998.

Bob Batchelor

See also **Computers and Computer Industry; Telecommunications.**

FIELD V. CLARK, 143 U.S. 649 (1892), sustained the McKinley Tariff Act of 1890, in which the president was given power to take certain prescribed articles off the free list if he found that the countries exporting such products to the United States unreasonably discriminated against American agricultural products. The Supreme Court ruled that this was a delegation of discretion as to the facts, not the law, and was not, therefore, an unconstitutional delegation of power.

BIBLIOGRAPHY

Kaplan, Edward S. *Prelude to Trade Wars: American Tariff Policy, 1890–1922.* Westport, Conn.: Greenwood Press, 1994.

Harvey Pinney/A. R.

See also **Sherman Silver Purchase Act; Tariff; Trade Agreements.**

"FIFTY-FOUR FORTY OR FIGHT." In 1818 the United States and Great Britain (which controlled British Canada) established a joint claim over the Oregon Territory—the region west of the Rocky Mountains between 42° North (the northern boundary of California) and 54°40′ North (the southern boundary of Russia's Alaska Territory). By the 1840s joint control had broken down, and expansionist Democrats, including their 1844 presidential candidate, James K. Polk, claimed the entire territory for the United States. This expansionist design was expressed by Polk's famous campaign slogan, "Fifty-four Forty or Fight!" The slogan also became a rally cry of settlers into the territory. The popular phrase was picked up from Sen. William Allen of Ohio, who coined the expression in an 1844 speech on the Senate floor. The boundary dispute was settled after Polk's election by the 1846 Treaty of Oregon, which struck a compromise and roughly fixed the U.S. boundary at 49° North.

BIBLIOGRAPHY

Miles, Edwin A. "'Fifty-four Forty or Fight'—An American Political Legend." *The Mississippi Valley Historical Review* 44 (1957): 291–309.

Rakestraw, Donald A. *For Honor or Destiny: The Anglo-American Crisis over the Oregon Territory.* New York: P. Lang, 1995.

J. W. Ellison/L. T.

See also **Great Britain, Relations with; Oregon; Oregon Treaty of 1846; Westward Migration.**

FILIBUSTER, CONGRESSIONAL. Filibuster is the practice by a determined minority in the United States Senate of prolonging debate and monopolizing the floor of the Senate to prevent final action on a proposal. Although promoted as a moderating force in debate and as a means to ensure full and open debate on issues, the filibuster has generally been used simply to frustrate political majorities in their attempts to pass legislation.

The filibuster was used intermittently in the Senate from 1806 to 1917, an era when no general rule limited debate. In the House of Representatives, its use has been minimized by the early adoption of strict limits on debate.

The modern history of the filibuster began in 1917, when the Senate amended Rule 22 by adopting CLOTURE provisions for limiting debate and forcing final action. Over time, the supermajority required for cloture has changed from two-thirds of the membership, to two-thirds of those voting. Since 1975 the Senate may, upon the petition of sixteen senators and after two days' delay, act to end a filibuster or any other debate by a three-fifths vote of the senators duly chosen and sworn (normally sixty votes) except on a measure or motion to amend the Senate rules, in which case a vote by two-thirds of those present and voting is required. The longest filibuster ranged over seventy-five days in 1964. The individual record belongs to Senator J. Strom Thurmond, who in 1957 held the floor for over twenty-four hours in debate on the civil rights legislation. Post-cloture debate is now limited to a maximum of thirty hours.

With the reduction in the threshold for cloture votes, the incidence and success rates of cloture petitions have increased. From 1917 to 1975 some 100 cloture petitions were voted upon; on only 20 percent of these was the filibuster ended. In the period from 1975 until 1994, 284 cloture votes were held, and cloture supporters were successful 41 percent of the time. Cloture has been used successfully on a variety of issues, such as the Treaty of Versailles (1919), Prohibition (1927), civil rights (1964), voting rights (1965), open housing (1968), the military draft system (1971), draft-evaders' pardons (1977), capital gains tax cuts (1989), and campaign finance reform (1994).

The importance of the filibuster lies in the ability of a few senators, or even one senator, to prevent issues from coming to a vote. This protection of intense minority views threatens to thwart accomplishments by the majority. Since a filibuster brings almost all organized Senate activity to a halt, even the threat of a filibuster provides substantial pressure to amend or resist bringing the controversial measure to the floor.

On the whole, while filibusters usually add little either to the knowledge of senators or to public awareness, they may provide some restraint on precipitous majority action. In the last analysis the filibuster remains a potentially powerful weapon by a determined minority. A large majority in the Senate, as evidenced in the 1964 debates on the Civil Rights Bill, can end a filibuster whatever the issue. But in the diverse American society, it is frequently difficult to create such a majority.

BIBLIOGRAPHY

Binder, Sarah A., and Steven S. Smith. *Politics or Principle: Filibustering in the United States Senate.* Washington, D.C.: Brookings Institution Press, 1997.

Congressional Quarterly's Guide to the Congress of the United States. Washington, D.C.: Congressional Quarterly Press, 2000.

Morris S. Ogul
Brian D. Posler

FILIBUSTERING. To Americans of the 1840s and 50s, the term filibusters referred to irregular armies of U.S. "adventurers" and the individuals who comprised them. Such bands often claimed to be acting on behalf of U.S. interests. But in most cases, filibusters acted without U.S. government authorization and sought conflicts with nations with which the United States was at peace. While some filibuster armies targeted Canada, most marched or sailed toward Latin America.

"Filibusters" derives from the Dutch word Vrijbuiter, itself descended from the English term "freebooter." During the seventeenth and eighteenth centuries, filibusters referred to English buccaneers, maritime pirates who plied the Caribbean hunting for Spanish quarry. The term did not become associated with private clandestine armies until the late 1840s, but historians have retroactively applied it to earlier figures of U.S. history such as Aaron Burr and James Wilkinson. Like their later counterparts, these early filibusters worked independent of—and, in a few cases, even conspired to wrest territory from—the federal government. In other cases, early filibusters acted with the tacit approval of—in some cases, with quiet support from—the federal government.

Filibustering's heyday, however, took place during the 1840s and 50s—the era of "Manifest Destiny," a period during which U.S. policymakers spoke unapologetically of building an "American empire," and in which the nation's boundaries seemed to the general public ever fluid, ever expanding. During that era, editors of the nation's penny newspapers enlivened their pages with countless stories about such colorful filibusters as Narciso López, William Walker, Henry A. Crabb, and Joseph Morehead. To thwart filibuster armies, that era's federal government employed, at various times, presidential proclamations, spies, federal Neutrality Act indictments, and the U.S. Navy. Among the filibusters, López and Walker achieved the greatest notoriety.

The son of a prosperous plantation owner, Narciso López was born in Venezuela in 1797. After fighting there in the Spanish army during its unsuccessful campaign to defeat rebel José Martí, López fled to Cuba. During the 1830s he rose to high positions in civil and political offices in both Spain and Cuba. In the late 1840s, disaffected with Spain in the wake of personal, political, and business reversals, López conspired to overthrow Cuba's colonial government.

In the wake of that insurgency's collapse, López fled in July 1848 to the United States, where he plotted to invade Cuba. Between 1848 and 1851 López raised four successive expeditionary armies. The federal government broke up two before they could leave the United States. The other two reached Cuba and fought the Spanish garrison. The final landing, with about four hundred filibusters, reached Cuba on 12 August 1851. All of the putative conquerors were killed in skirmishes with Spanish soldiers, executed, or captured and sent to prison. López was executed on 1 September in Havana.

Born in Nashville, Tennessee, in 1824, William Walker directed his filibustering expeditions toward Latin America. In 1853, after Mexican authorities rejected his plans to establish an American colony in that nation, he led an expedition of forty-five filibusters. Sailing from San Francisco, they seized the coastal town of La Paz, at the southern tip of Baja California, which Walker soon declared an independent republic, with himself as president.

On 18 January 1854 Walker declared the annexation of the neighboring Mexican state of Sonora—a brazen declaration in light of the fact that he had yet to set foot there. His Mexican empire, however, evaporated as quickly as it had been declared. U.S. officials quickly acted to block the shipment of supplies to Walker and his loyalists, and they soon faced starvation. Furthermore, Mexican officials forced the filibusters northward, where they surrendered to federal authorities at the U.S. border. The federal government subsequently tried Walker on Neutrality Act violations, but a San Francisco jury acquitted him of all charges.

In 1855, ever determined to preside over his own empire, Walker accepted a commission from a faction in a civil war then raging in Nicaragua. Sailing from San Francisco, he and fifty-seven filibusters landed on that nation's northern coast in May and soon joined the fighting. During the conflict Cornelius Vanderbilt's Accessory Transit Company, which operated a rail line across the country, agreed to transport American reinforcements to the battle theater free of charge. When his faction triumphed, Walker became commander in chief of the army, and in May 1856 his new government won U.S. diplomatic recognition. In due course Walker was sworn in as the nation's president. He soon came into conflict with Vanderbilt, however, and the U.S. government ended relations with Walker's government and joined the opposition led by Vanderbilt. In May 1857 Walker surrendered to the U.S. Navy. Three years later, Walker led two more expeditions—one to Nicaragua and another to Honduras. The first was quickly ended by the U.S. Navy, the second by the British Navy. Walker was executed in Honduras in September 1860.

Young, white, single, native-born Americans, as well as European and Latin American immigrants, tended to dominate filibuster armies. Motives of recruits ranged from republican idealism to a quest for adventure to sheer greed—a quest for land and other material gains. Although earlier historians identified filibustering—in its mid-nineteenth-century, anti–Latin American incarnation—with Southern, Democratic Party, planter interests, recent scholarship suggests that leadership and funding for the phenomenon tapped a broader, national base, one that crossed regional, economic, and party categories.

By 1861, and the commencement of the American Civil War, the phenomenon had largely ended. By the late nineteenth century, the term filibuster—with its connotation of lawless enterprise—had been transformed into a derogatory term for protracted parliamentary debate intended to obstruct the passage of legislation.

BIBLIOGRAPHY

Brown, Charles H. *Agents of Manifest Destiny: The Lives and Times of the Filibusters.* Chapel Hill: University of North Carolina Press, 1980.

Chaffin, Tom. *Fatal Glory: Narciso López and the First Clandestine U.S. War against Cuba.* Charlottesville: University Press of Virginia, 1996.

May, Robert E. *The Southern Dream of a Caribbean Empire, 1854–1861.* Baton Rouge: Louisiana State University Press, 1973.

Owsley, Frank Lawrence, Jr., and Gene A Smith. *Filibusters and Expansionists: Jeffersonian Manifest Destiny, 1800–21.* Tuscaloosa: University of Alabama Press, 1997.

Thomas Chaffin

See also **Manifest Destiny.**

FILIPINO AMERICANS are immigrants to the United States from one of the 7,107 islands and islets that form the archipelago of the Philippines, and their U.S.-born descendants. In the United States, Filipinos are categorized as Asian Americans. This official category is used to refer to people who can trace their ancestry to the peoples of the Far East, Southeast Asia, or the Indian subcontinent. However, Filipinos are unique within the Asian groups given the strong Spanish influence in their culture in addition to Chinese and Malaysian influences.

The Philippine Islands were under Spanish colonial rule from 1565 through 1898. In 1564 Miguel López de Legazpi, acting on behalf of King Philip II of Spain, set off on an expedition to colonize and Christianize the archipelago. He landed in Cebu in 1565, and during the next seven years transformed the Philippines into a Spanish colony and the only Christian nation in Asia. About one hundred years before the arrival of the Spaniards, the religious traditions of Filipinos had been strongly influenced by Muhammadans, also known as Moors or Moros. In fact, even after the Spaniards' arrival, conversion to Christianity was not uniform; the Moors in the southern Philippines successfully resisted Spanish influence for three centuries.

American Control of the Philippines

The Philippines and the United Stated have had a long-lasting, intertwined political history. At the close of the Spanish-American War of 1898, the United States paid Spain $20 million at the close of the Treaty of Paris, wherein Spain relinquished claims on the Philippines, Cuba, and Puerto Rico. Initially, U.S. military forces controlled only Manila and surrounding geographic areas. Early in 1899, the Philippine-American War began as the United States tried to gain greater control of the archipelago, whose inhabitants had already fought for and declared a Philippine Republic headed by Emilio Aguinaldo. The war ended in 1902. President Theodore Roosevelt's peace proclamation applied to all except the "country inhabited by the Moro tribes," located in the southern lands of the archipelago. Some scholars contend that the Philippine-American War extended unofficially until 1912 or 1913. On 4 July 1946, the United States granted independence to the Philippines, marking the formation of the second Philippine Republic. However, Filipinos and Filipino Americans celebrate Independence Day on 12 June, the date when the Philippines declared independence from Spain in 1898.

There have been four identified waves of Filipino migration to the United States, each marked by a particular sociopolitical context that has shaped both Filipino and American history. The beginning of the first wave was in 1763, although Filipino migration to the United States has been documented as early as 1587, when so-called Luzon Indians landed in Morro Bay, California. The Indians were crewmembers of the Spanish galleon *Nuestra Senora de Buena Esperanza.* These early travels by the Luzon are not surprising given that their lands were among the first colonized by Spaniards in the 1560s.

Filipino Migration

In the first wave of Filipino migration, Filipino seamen (Manilamen) in Acapulco crossed the Gulf of Mexico to

Barataria Bay in Louisiana in 1763. They established a series of Philippine-style fishing villages and pioneered the dried shrimp industry in America. In 1781, Antonio Miranda Rodríguez, a Filipino, and his eleven-year-old daughter were sent by the Spanish government from Mexico to settle the Pueblo de Nuestra Señora Reina de los Angeles de Porciúncula, later known as the city of Los Angeles. The second wave of migration to America occurred between 1906 and 1935, after the United States had gained control of the islands. It brought students, scholars (*pensianados*), and workers. More than 125,000 Filipinos migrated to Hawaii to work on Hawaiian sugarcane plantations. The Filipino presence in Hawaii continues to be significant. In 1994, Ben Cayetano, Hawaii's fifth governor and the first of Filipino heritage, took office; he was reelected in 1998. Some Filipinos in the second wave of immigration went to labor in the farms of California and canneries of Alaska. This led to the prominent participation of Filipinos in the United Farm Workers, most famous for its 1965 Delano, California, grape strike.

The third and fourth waves of migration follow each other very closely. The third wave began with the end of World War II (1939–1945) and lasted through 1965. These immigrants traveled to the United States mostly to join the U.S. Navy as noncitizens. The fourth wave of migration came with the passage in 1965 of the Immigration and Nationality Act that removed the 1924 national origins quota system. This wave of migration has been characterized as the "brain drain" wave because of the high numbers of Filipino professionals moving to the United States.

Filipinos as a Component of the U.S. Population

Filipino Americans make up 2.4 million of the 11.9 million Asian Americans in the United States. They are the second largest Asian subgroup in America, closely trailing the 2.7 million Chinese Americans in the country. Filipinos provided the largest number of immigrants from any Asian group between 1981 and 1998, bringing over 927,000 new immigrants to the United States during this seventeen-year span. The majority of these immigrants settled in California (47 percent of all immigrants from the Philippines settled there in 1998). In 1999, of the 1.5 million foreign-born Filipinos living in the United States, over 61 percent were naturalized citizens. Although the information is scant, available vital and health statistics for Filipino Americans compare favorably to those for other ethnic minorities in America. In 1998, 6.2 percent of births to Filipinas were to teen mothers, 19.7 percent were to unwed mothers (a far second place among Asian Americans to Hawaii's 51.1 percent), 84.2 percent of Filipino American mothers began prenatal care in the first trimester, and 8.2 percent of their children were born in the low birth weight category. These numbers are not surprising, given that the Philippine nation of over 74 million people has similarly low rates of children born to teen mothers (3.9 percent) and born at low birth weight (9 percent) along with high rates of immunization, with anywhere between 71 percent and 91 percent of children immunized for various illnesses. Filipino Americans have higher than national average rates of participation in the workforce, high school graduation, and college graduation. Even though Filipino Americans have over twice the national proportion of three or more household members participating in the workforce, their per capita income is slightly below the national average, although they have below national average poverty rates. Filipino Americans are most notably visible in Hawaii, Alaska, California, and Nevada.

BIBLIOGRAPHY

Bautista, Veltisezar. *The Filipino Americans (1763–Present): Their History, Culture, and Traditions.* 2d ed. Naperville, Ill.: Bookhaus, 2002.

Scharlin, Craig, and Lila V. Villanueva. *Philip Vera Cruz: A Personal History of Filipino Immigrants and the Farm Workers Movement.* Seattle: University of Washington Press, 2000.

U.S. Bureau of the Census. "The Asian Population: 2000." Available from http://www.census.gov/prod/2002pubs/c2kbr01-16.pdf

Melanie Domenech-Rodríguez

See also **Asian Americans; Philippine Insurrection; Philippines; Spanish-American War.**

FILM. Thomas Edison's company copyrighted its machine-viewable *Edison Kinetoscopic Record of a Sneeze* in January 1894. Two years later the first public showings of projected Vitascope images took place on Thirty-fourth Street in New York City. These public debuts, culminating decades of technical development, mark the beginnings of American cinema. The medium was quickly extended by innovations by French filmmakers the Lumière brothers, who introduced sequences, close-ups, using directors to construct scenes. French film artist, Georges Méliès introduced concepts of repeatable time, rather than progressive movement toward the future. Edison was, in fact, only presenting on screen materials that had been available in Kinetoscope viewing machines for several years. The Edison Corporation soon added footage on Coney Island, and further benefited by an embargo placed on Lumière Productions by the U.S. Customs Service. Although Edison attempted to monopolize the new industry, other companies circumvented his patent and challenged his hegemony in court. Edison attempted a further monopoly in 1907 by requiring royalties for use of his machines. That year Edison made a pact with a number of film studios that created the Motion Picture Patents Company in another attempt to secure a monopoly.

After several years of shakeups in the fledgling industry, companies such as Biograph began producing spectacles, *Photographing a Female Crook* (1904) among them, or full scale literary adaptations, for example, Edwin S. Porter's version of Harriet Beecher Stowe's *Uncle*

Tom's Cabin (1903). Porter also introduced popular concepts of romance and sexuality in *The Gay Shoe Clerk* (1903), of violence in *The Ex-Convict* (1904), and crime in *The Kleptomaniac* (1905). His *Great Train Robbery* (1903) gave audiences western settings and stories, and demonstrated film's powerful special effects such as constructing audience vision through perspective, narration, and space.

By the first decade of the twentieth century, audiences were clearly choosing fiction over documentary footage. Film presentation moved from vaudeville houses into permanent motion picture houses (NICKELODEONS) that offered amenities to attract women. Construction of motion picture houses also allowed for rental of film prints, to the great benefit of studio profits. Movie production companies became more complex; ancillary organizations such as fan magazines and professional criticism emerged. With the focus on a middle-class, family-oriented audience, companies began to be more careful about sexual content, although the rapid spread of theaters made self-policing untenable. Studio production moved from sites in Astoria (in New York City) and Ithaca, New York, to the sunny hills of Hollywood, California, which allowed for constant filming and varied sets to film on location.

Rise of Production Companies

Others, many of them immigrants, soon extended the field of film production. Adolph Zukor invested in a series of nickelodeons, then developed partnerships with Marcus Loew, William A. Brady, and the Shubert Brothers. One of their first projects was the purchase of the French Pathé film *Queen Elizabeth*, starring Sarah Bernhardt, for showing in New York City in 1912. Zukor used the movie business to transform himself creatively and financially with longer films. The use of Bernhardt coincided with public fascination with actors. Zukor's Famous Players is noted for introducing Mary Pickford, who became the biggest star of the 1910s, especially after her marriage to actor Douglas Fairbanks Sr. Fairbanks exemplified the industry's healthy, tanned, sports personality; Pickford extended an older American myth about the rise of a talented, beautiful woman to success. In 1919, the couple aligned themselves with director David Wark Griffith and comedian Charlie Chaplin to create United Artists, a move that at least partly loosened the studios' grip on film production and distribution. Griffith is important for his extraordinary energy (he directed one hundred and forty movies in 1909 alone), creative innovation of running shots, narrative, intertitles (which made up for lack of the human voice), and epic films. The best known of these was the controversial *BIRTH OF A NATION* (1915), which set forth a southern vision of the Civil War and the South's saving of the nation through racism. Immediately denounced by the National Association for the Advancement of Colored People, the film marries America's technical achievement and racial intolerance.

Still, many films were romantic fiction, such as the serial *Perils of Pauline*, which ran many episodes before 1915. The serial inspired young girls such as Anna May Wong, a Chinese American teenager, who decided upon a film career after many viewings. Her exposure was part of the mixed ethnic legacy of early film. While film helped Jews and Italians assimilate into American culture, it drew a sharp line for Asians and African Americans, who either had to develop their own cinema or endure the racism of Hollywood productions. Beginning in the 1910s some of the most famous productions—such as Cecil B. DeMille's *The Cheat* (1915), with its Asian villain, and Griffith's *Birth of a Nation*—included strongly racist messages.

Hollywood Triumphant

World War I had less impact on films in the United States than in European nations; by 1918, American studios had emerged as the world leaders because they could spend more money for sets and costumes than could European studios. Money and exoticism combined in the construction of new theaters, many of them, such as the famous Grauman Chinese Theater, designed in a style of art deco orientalism. The splendor of these palaces of cinema reflected the global power of Hollywood by the mid-1920s.

Hollywood not only took over the world, but had also wrested away the final shreds of studio power from New York City by 1925. Hollywood meant industry consolidation, specific modes of production, and directorial independence. During the classic era of silent film in the 1920s, a host of European immigrant directors, including Erich von Stroheim and Joseph von Sternberg, introduced expressionism to American audiences.

Hollywood studios offered several genres. The woman's film featured newer stars such as Gloria Swanson, Joan Crawford, and Anna May Wong; comedies had Charlie Chaplin, Harold Lloyd, W. C. Fields, and Buster Keaton. Lon Chaney, the man of a thousand faces, was the master of horror. Robert Flaherty produced outstanding documentary films. The milieu of the 1920s produced the gangster movie. Fans of each genre could follow their favorites through glossy magazines.

Hollywood did not accurately portray all Americans. Generally excluded were blacks, who, of necessity, formed their own production companies. Oscar Micheaux produced dozens of films including his classic *Body and Soul* (1924), starring Paul Robeson. Hollywood continued to use racist stereotypes; Al Jolson's film *The Jazz Singer* (1927) revived the discredited minstrel tradition.

Sound and Talent

Sound was by far the greatest innovation of the late 1920s. Filmmakers had experimented in color, most notably in *The Toll of the Sea* (1922), starring Anna May Wong, but the results were inconclusive. Silent films were always accompanied by music; the introduction of the human voice was revolutionary. Awkward or squeaky voices cost such stars as John Gilbert their careers. Hollywood was a magnet for the world's talent. As the studios perfected a "dream machine" in which mass appeal films dominated,

Europe's stars came to California attracted by promises of wealth and fame: Greta Garbo of Sweden, Anna Sten of Russia, and, most famously, Marlene Dietrich of Germany. Talking films ("talkies") promoted Nordic women as the paradigms of female beauty. This emphasis, joined with the star system, made standard a type of beauty. Hollywood's choices had a powerful impact on the nation's concept of female beauty and appropriate behavior.

Hollywood was concerned with profits and popularity; studios kept their ears to the ground to learn about public concerns about crime and then pumped out more gangster films. During the depression of the 1930s, musicals with elaborate dance productions and optimistic songs distracted audiences; comedy, now featuring assimilated Yiddish humor through the Marx Brothers, helped in the hard times. However, sexual innuendo of the films of the 1920s was eventually tempered, as were any hints of interracial love, by a rigid Production Code (implemented in 1930) and state licensing system. After a film passed the Production Code Administration office, it still might run afoul of state licensing boards. Their power in New York State, for example, could profoundly alter a script. Interracial kissing remained an informal taboo until the 1960s and beyond.

Hollywood's influence upon the nation was not limited to adults. Animation, accompanied by brilliant color, made Walt Disney a success in the 1930s. Mickey and Minnie Mouse, Snow White, and Pinocchio fascinated children. As experiments with color became more successful, narrative films began to use color. The 240-minute epic *Gone with the Wind* (1939), with its evocation of the slave South, used color to highlight its racial fantasies. *The Wizard of Oz* (1939) employed color to differentiate between "reality" and dream.

Black-and-white films still offered innovation, however. Orson Welles with *Citizen Kane* (1941) pushed lighting, angle shots, overlapping dissolves, and narrative construction to new levels.

One of the "Hollywood Ten." The director Edward Dmytryk was one of the group of mostly screenwriters jailed—and unable to find work in this country—for defying the anticommunist House Committee on Un-American Activities in 1947; in 1951, like many others fearful of the industry blacklist, Dmytryk named supposed Communist Party members and found work again. AP/Wide World Photos

Spreading the News

Theaters became organs of the news. Between Saturday afternoon features, audiences watched *The March of Time* (1935–1951), sponsored by *Time* magazine. As the nation geared up for World War II, the newsreels kept audiences informed. Most wartime films were B productions, inexpensive efforts relying on older cinematic methods; many were little more than propaganda. Films asked and answered who African Americans or Asians should fight for, showed how women could support the war, and gave reports of successful campaigns. Occasionally this could result in high art as in *Casablanca* (1942), with Ingrid Bergman and Humphrey Bogart.

Postwar Hollywood confronted major political challenges. Right-wing campaigns against alleged communist influence in Hollywood (often thinly disguised anti-Semitism), declining audiences, and postwar cutbacks influenced studio choices. The decade also evoked a new genre, eventually dubbed *film noir* by postwar French critics. In films like *The Maltese Falcon* (1942), *Double Indemnity* (1944), and *Out of the Past* (1947), American hard-boiled crime fiction and a German-inspired expressionist sensibility combined to produce a bleak vision of limited human choices. The genre's themes of paranoia, betrayal, corruption, and greed seemed to speak for the American subconscious. Women in film noir, for example, often had the role of femme fatale, and their increased social and sexual freedom was negatively depicted. Other genres, however, supported an American agenda. Westerns remained popular and represented white racial powers over weaker, "evil" races. Former football player John Wayne epitomized the masculine myth of the cowboy. More middle-of-the-road were the portrayal of the bourgeois male in *It's a Wonderful Life* (1946), starring James Stewart, and the optimistic social criticism of *The Best Years of Our Lives* (1946). Hollywood also recycled older genres and started its own revisionism in *Sunset Boulevard* (1950) and *Singin' in the Rain* (1952).

Technology

The 1950s boasted technical innovations such as three dimension (3-D) and widescreen films. While the 3-D film *House of Wax* was a big hit for Warner Brothers in 1953 and Americans were thrilled to put on special glasses for viewing, its time was short. Similarly, CinemaScope and Panavision briefly bolstered box office receipts for spectacles like *The Robe* (1953) and the *Ten Commandments* (1956), but by 1957, audiences were a quarter of the total they had been twenty years earlier. Television was a primary reason for the decline, as were such lifestyle changes as the deification of the nuclear family and sports activities. Still, powerful movies that affected American social styles continued to be made. Marlon Brando's performances in *A Streetcar Named Desire* (1951) and *On the Waterfront* (1954) prescribed dress and behavior patterns for generations of American males, as did James Dean in *Rebel without a Cause* (1955). Older genres such as the Western (*The Searchers* [1956]) and musical (*West Side Story* [1961]) showed stamina throughout the decade. The most innovative works of the late 1960s and early 1970s were done outside Hollywood. Rock music was a great influence. Documentary work such as D. A. Pennebaker's *Don't Look Back* (1967), on a Bob Dylan tour, the Maysles Brothers' production of *Gimme Shelter* (1970), on the ill-fated Altamonte Concert of the Rolling Stones, and *Woodstock* (1970), chronicling the famous concert, charted the world of the new music. Frederick Wiseman's sober investigation of insane asylums (*Titicut Follies* [1967]) and several films on the Vietnam War showed the new political power of documentaries. Never interested in political movements in the past, Hollywood responded to the tumultuous 1960s with films on racial issues such as *In the Heat of the Night* (1967) and *Guess Who's Coming to Dinner* (1967), both starring Sidney Poitier. The conflict between the generations was covered in *The Graduate* (1967) with Dustin Hoffman, who also starred in the gritty urban drama *Midnight Cowboy* (1969), with Jon Voight. The Western explored more favorable portrayals of Native Americans in *Little Big Man* (1970).

Experimental cinema captured the interest of intellectuals and college students. The work of Stan Brakhage, the Kuchar Brothers, Jack Smith, Kenneth Anger, and Maya Deren extended the possibilities of no-narrative film. Jonas Mekas worked to create an experimental archive in New York City. Some of the strangest, but ultimately successful, films were made by artist Andy Warhol, whose efforts included a twenty-four hour film of the Empire State Building, eight hours of a man sleeping, and films about the antics of his Factory crew.

The artistic challenges of Warhol and the influence of the French auteur theory manifested in the rise of a new generation of directors. The careers of such directors as Francis Ford Coppola with his highly successful *Godfather* series, George Lucas with *American Graffiti* (1973), Martin Scorsese with *Taxi Driver* (1976), and Steven Spielberg, whose biggest achievements came in the 1980s, showed the resilience of Hollywood. The 1970s have come to be considered a new Golden Age for personal cinema. Woody Allen, who strove to personify the New York intellectual in *Manhattan* (1979), Roman Polanski with the revival of film noir in *Chinatown* (1974), and Robert Altman with *Nashville* (1975), all achieved major success.

Special Effects

Artistry was not the biggest success, however, but rather special-effects spectaculars. Digitalization, improved special effects, and computer graphics helped such films as *Star Wars* (1977), the Indiana Jones series with Harrison Ford, and Spielberg's *E.T.: The Extra-Terrestrial* (1982) to reinvent the concept of the "blockbuster" with extraordinary budgets and profits. Only with collapse of the hugely expensive *Heaven's Gate* in 1979 were the perils of this approach apparent. Its failure did not prevent Hollywood studios from plowing new cash into blockbuster comedies such as *National Lampoon's Animal House* (1978), starring John Belushi, and the *Beverly Hills Cop* series starring Eddie Murphy. Murphy and Whoopi Goldberg became the first black actors since Sidney Poitier in the 1960s to get star status and paved the way for similar success for Denzel Washington, Morgan Freeman, Hallie Berry, and Samuel L. Jackson. The awarding of Oscars for best performances to Washington and Berry in 2002, and the lifetime achievement award to Poitier, seemed to mark a historic integration of the film industry. Such integration owed much to the efforts of director Spike Lee, whose films always took on the big issues. While blacks seem to have become part of the regular Hollywood crowd, the same cannot be said for Asians, none of whom have gained the prominence of Anna May Wong before 1940. Generally, the feminist movement made little other than stylistic improvements in Hollywood, which grudgingly accepted a few female directors after 1980. The same can be said for the gay movement, whose principal achievements have been limited to films about the AIDS crisis, although gay characters became more common in films in the late 1990s. Its biggest hit to date was *Boys Don't Cry* (1999) about the murder of a crossdresser in a small town in the Midwest.

Independents

The cinematic radicalism and independence of the previous twenty years rubbed off on new filmmakers in the 1990s. Quentin Tarantino, a film scholar turned director, scored with *Pulp Fiction* in 1994. *Pulp Fiction* went on to become a phenomenon on the Internet after 1996, with constant discussion of the film through chat-rooms and Web sites. More consistent in their quirky achievements were Joel and Ethan Coen, who regularly scored with off-beat melodramas such as *Fargo* (1996).

Despite the successes of independent visions, Hollywood still relied on the blockbuster, which it produced in series according to the season and age group. New technologies helped enliven *Jurassic Park* (1993), the mass appeal of Tom Hanks sparked *Forrest Gump* (1994), while computer graphics were the stars of *Toy Story* (1995). More traditional and successful were *Independence Day* (1996) and *Titanic* (1997). Computer graphics also greatly enhanced *The Matrix* (1999). All of these films again demonstrated American hegemony of world cinema, despite the rise of national filmmaking around the globe. Only occasionally have foreign-language films like Akira Kurosawa's *Rashomon* (1950), Ingmar Bergman's *The Seventh Seal* (1957), Federico Fellini's *La Dolce Vita* (1960), and Ang Lee's *Crouching Tiger, Hidden Dragon* (2000) penetrated the U.S. market.

BIBLIOGRAPHY

Berry, Sarah. *Screen Style: Fashion and Femininity in 1930s Hollywood.* Minneapolis: University of Minnesota Press, 2000.

Charney, Leo, and Vanessa R. Schwartz, eds. *Cinema and the Invention of Modern Life.* Berkeley: University of California Press, 1995.

Cohen, Paula Marantz. *Silent Film and the Triumph of the American Myth.* New York: Oxford University Press, 2001.

Harpole, Charles, ed. *History of the American Cinema.* 10 vols. New York: Charles Scribner's Sons, 1990–2003.

Kindem, Gorham. *The American Movie Industry: The Business of Motion Pictures.* Carbondale: University of Southern Illinois Press, 1982.

Koppes, Clayton R., and Gregory D. Black. *Hollywood Goes to War: How Politics, Profits and Propaganda Shaped World War II Movies.* New York: Free Press, 1987.

Rose, Steven J. *Working-Class Hollywood: Silent Film and the Shaping of Class in America.* Princeton, N.J.: Princeton University Press, 1997.

Sarris, Andrew. *"You Ain't Heard Nothing Yet": The American Talking Film, History and Memory, 1927–1949.* New York: Oxford University Press, 1998.

Schatz, Thomas. *The Genius of the System: Hollywood Film-Making in the Studio Era.* New York: Pantheon, 1988.

Segrave, Kerry. *American Films Abroad: Hollywood's Domination of the World's Movie Screens.* Jefferson, N.C.: McFarland, 1997.

Sklar, Robert. *A World History of Film.* 2d ed. New York: Abrams, 2002.

Graham Russell Hodges

See also **Cartoons; Disney Corporation; Hollywood; Mass Media.**

FINANCIAL PANICS, events during which bank depositors attempt to withdraw their deposits, equity holders sell stock, and market participants in general seek to liquefy their assets.

Panic of 1785

The panic of 1785, which lasted until 1788, ended the business boom that followed the American Revolution. The causes of the crisis lay in the overexpansion and debts incurred after the victory at Yorktown, a postwar deflation, competition in the manufacturing sector from Britain, and lack of adequate credit and a sound currency. The downturn was exacerbated by the absence of any significant interstate trade. Other factors were the British refusal to conclude a commercial treaty, and actual and pending defaults among debtor groups. The panic among business and propertied groups led to the demand for a stronger federal government.

Panic of 1792

The panic of 1792 arose from speculative activity following the adoption of the Federal Constitution, the founding of the First Bank of the United States (BUS), and the emergence of securities markets for bank shares and other government securities in New York City. Almost immediately after its establishment in 1791, the BUS overextended notes and discounts, and then sharply reversed its course. Speculators in the bank's shares quickly sold their holdings, which had risen markedly over previous months, and the nation's first true securities market panic took hold.

Panic of 1819

The Second Bank of the United States, seeking to curb speculation in commodities and western lands following the War of 1812, sharply contracted its extension of credit, provoking the panic of 1819. The downturn hit the southern and western states hardest, and many banks suspended specie (coin money) payments or closed their doors. The BUS went through a period of recrimination, congressional investigation, and financial rehabilitation. Commodity prices declined, manufacturers clamored for more protection, and debtors demanded relief legislation, which was enacted in several western states. The economic picture had improved by 1823.

Panic of 1837

A series of events led to the panic of 1837: On 11 July 1836, President Andrew Jackson issued an executive order (the Specie Circular) that attempted to end speculation in western lands by requiring specie for their purchase; the Deposit Act, passed on 23 June 1836, ordered that the more than $34 million in surplus that had accumulated in the Treasury be redistributed to the states, in proportion to their relative populations; the Second Bank of the United States dissolved following Jackson's veto of an act to recharter in 1832; and England introduced a tightened monetary policy designed to "recover" specie presumed lost to the United States. By early 1837, these factors had dislocated the nation's specie reserves out of New York City and into the interior and the hands of the public. With its specie base depleted by more than 80 percent over a six-month period, the public lost confidence in the New York banks and withdrew their deposits. Within two weeks, all of the nation's banks had suspended specie payments. This first general suspension in the nation's history started a six-year economic downturn that was the most severe of the nineteenth century.

Panic of 1857

The failure of the Ohio Life Insurance Company in August 1857 was the catalyst that initiated the panic of 1857, which spread quickly from the Ohio Valley to the eastern money centers. Unemployment grew, breadlines formed, and ominous signs of social unrest appeared. The depression was most serious in the industrial northeast and in the western wheat belt, where the new Republican Party saw increasing support. The cotton belt was less affected by the panic: cotton crops were good, prices were high, and banks were sound. These factors brought overconfidence in the South, an impulse to protection in the East, and a drive for free land in the West. Economic conditions became as potent an issue as slavery in the subsequent election of 1860.

Panic of 1873

The failure of several important eastern firms in September 1873—including the New York Warehouse and Securities Company; Kenyon, Cox and Company; and the famous banking house, Jay Cooke and Company—precipitated this panic. The stock exchange closed for ten days, and bankruptcy overtook a host of other companies and individuals. Some causes of the panic and ensuing depression were international, including a series of wars and excessive railroad construction in central Europe, Russia, South America, and the United States. Domestic factors included currency and credit inflation, losses from fires in Boston and Chicago, an adverse trade balance, and overinvestment in railroads, factories, and buildings. In the following depression, 18,000 firms failed during 1876 and 1877, a majority of the American railroads declined into bankruptcy, and more than two-thirds of the nation's iron mills and furnaces fell idle. Wage reductions led to strikes among Pennsylvania coal miners and New England textile workers, and to a railroad walkout in 1877. In 1878 the depression began to lift.

Panic of 1893

The panic of 1893 originated in the usual factors of the business cycle, including overinvestment and falling prices in the 1880s. The uneasy state of British securities markets in 1890—culminating in the liquidation of the banking house of Baring Brothers and Company—stopped the flow of foreign capital into American enterprise, and the sale of European-held securities caused a stock market collapse in New York, accompanied by substantial gold exports. The financial crisis was postponed, however, by strong exports of agricultural staples over the next two years that reestablished gold imports. Uncertainty returned in the winter of 1892–1893 as renewed gold exports raised the possibility that the nation would be forced off the gold standard by a decline in the U.S. Treasury's holdings. The nation also suffered with decreased federal revenues and heavy expenditures, including the purchases of silver under the Sherman Silver Purchase Act of 1890.

The gold reserve had fallen below the accepted minimum of $100 million by April 1893, and the failure of the National Cordage Company in May touched off a stock market panic. By the end of 1893, about 4,000 banks and 14,000 businesses had failed. President Grover Cleveland sought a repeal of the Silver Purchase Act as the one absolute cure for the depression. By 30 October the repeal had passed both houses of Congress. In the meantime, imports of gold had stabilized the monetary situation in New York somewhat. The depression did not lift substantially, however, until the poor European crops of 1897 stimulated American exports and the importation of gold.

Panic of 1907

Sometimes called the "rich man's panic," the panic of 1907 was preceded by speculative excesses in life insurance, railroad and coastal shipping combines, mining stocks, and inadequately regulated trust companies. Several profit-dampening reforms were enacted in 1906, such as the Hepburn Act (giving the Interstate Commerce Commission power to set maximum railroad rates) and the Pure Food and Drug Act, yet the economy seemed healthy in January 1907. In fact, most financiers believed that improved banking controls made it impossible for panics like those of 1873 and 1893 to recur.

In early 1907, when Henry H. Rogers of Standard Oil had to pay 8 percent interest to float a $20 million bond issue, the stock market dropped sharply—the so-called silent panic. The economy seemed to recover, but failure of the United Copper Company in the summer of 1907 precipitated runs on the Heinze and Morse chain of banks. When the Knickerbocker Trust Company closed in October, runs on the Trust Company of America and several others followed, and there was panic on the stock market. To halt the panic, Secretary of the Treasury George B. Cortelyou authorized large deposits in several banks. Investment banker J. P. Morgan headed a banking group that used a borrowed emergency fund of nearly $40 million to rescue banks and firms they deemed savable, and whose survival was crucial. To rescue the brokerage house of Moore and Schley, Morgan arranged to have the United States Steel Corporation buy the brokers' holdings of the stock of a major rival, the Tennessee Coal, Iron, and Railroad Company. This arrangement strengthened the steel trust. By the end of the year, the financial situation was normal again.

Although the panic did not lead to heavy unemployment or a wave of bankruptcies, it seriously damaged the image of the big financiers. It also had repercussions overseas, as the United States temporarily imported a large amount of gold, and interest rates abroad rose. On 30 March 1908, Congress passed the Aldrich-Vreeland Currency Act, which provided for contingency bank currency in the event of another stringency. The act also created the National Monetary Commission, which produced the Aldrich Report of 1911. This was a major step in setting up the Federal Reserve System in 1913–1914.

Panic of 1929

The panic of 1929 had many causes, most importantly annual private and corporate savings in excess of the demand for real capital formation, a large export trade in manufactured goods supported by foreign lending, a low discount Federal Reserve policy designed to support the British pound, and increasing use of stock-exchange securities rather than commercial paper for bank loans. The period of prosperity from 1924 to late 1926 had been largely aided by buying consumer durables in installments, particularly automobiles, real estate, and construction. When the automobile industry became temporarily saturated in 1927, a downturn was to be expected, but the construction boom showed surprising vitality until mid-1929. The Federal Reserve pursued a relatively easy monetary policy, and exports continued to be buoyed up by foreign lending. When opportunities for real investment sagged after 1926, top-income investors poured cash into the stock, bond, and mortgage markets. Banks made large loans on the security of blocks of the common stock of a single company to keep their depositors' money employed.

By June of 1929, some bankers had become alarmed by the continued rise of the stock market, and in August the Federal Reserve raised the discount rate. This move attracted more domestic and foreign capital into the call loan market, thus applying a final lash of the whip to the runaway boom in security prices. The stock market peaked right after Labor Day, but on Friday, 18 October, it began to decline rapidly; 29 October was the most devastating day in the history of the stock exchange. Yet during the month-long decline, the Standard and Poor Index fell by less than 40 percent, and public statements held that no harm had been done to normal business. Unseen factors that led to the nation's deepest depression, however, were large bank loans that could not be liquidated and the accompanying pressure of failed banks on healthy ones, the collapse of European finance in 1931, a monetary policy by the Federal Reserve that vacillated between meeting domestic and foreign needs, and the lack of any large capital-consuming technological development to re-stimulate private investment.

BIBLIOGRAPHY

Cowen, David J. "The First Bank of the United States and the Securities Market Crash of 1792." *Journal of Economic History* 60, no. 4 (December 2000): 1041–1060.

Friedman, Milton, and Anna Jacobson Schwartz. *A Monetary History of the United States, 1867–1960.* Princeton, N.J.: Princeton University Press, 1963.

Galbraith, John Kenneth. *The Great Crash.* Boston: Houghton Mifflin, 1961.

Hammond, Bray. *Banks and Politics in America, from the Revolution to the Civil War.* Princeton, N.J.: Princeton University Press, 1957.

Kindleberger, Charles Poor. *Manias, Panics, and Crashes: A History of Financial Crises.* 4th ed. New York: Wiley, 2000.

McGrane, Reginald C. *The Panic of 1837: Some Financial Problems of the Jacksonian Era.* Chicago: University of Chicago Press, 1924.

Nettels, Curtis P. *The Emergence of a National Economy, 1775–1815.* Armonk, N.Y.: Sharpe, 1989. The original edition was published in 1962.

Rousseau, Peter L. "Jacksonian Monetary Policy, Specie Flows, and the Panic of 1837." *Journal of Economic History* 62, no. 2 (June 2002): 457–488.

Sprague, Oliver Mitchell Wentworth. *History of Crises under the National Banking System.* Washington, D.C.: GPO, 1910.

Temin, Peter. *The Jacksonian Economy.* New York: Norton, 1969.

———. *Lessons from the Great Depression.* Cambridge, Mass.: MIT Press, 1989.

Elmer Ellis, L. C. Helderman, Donald L. Kemmerer, Reginald C. McGrane, Allan Nevins, Samuel Rezneck, Peter L. Rousseau

FINANCIAL SERVICES INDUSTRY. Until the 1970s, the financial services industry consisted of a few well-defined and separate industries that dealt in money. These included banks and savings and loan associations for personal savings, checking accounts, and mortgages; brokerage houses, such as Merrill Lynch, for investment in stocks, bonds, and mutual funds; and credit card companies, such as Visa USA or MasterCard International, for consumer credit.

The Decline of Banks

Beginning in the 1970s, the profitability of banks declined due in large part to federal regulations that restricted banks from offering the variety of products, such as insurance, mutual funds, and stocks, that their less strictly controlled competitors offered. The gradual shift away from banks as the center of the American financial services industry occurred between 1973 and 1979, when the Organization of the Petroleum Exporting Countries (OPEC) dramatically increased oil prices, leading to double-digit inflation by the end of the decade. As a result, investors with savings accounts receiving the federally imposed 5.25 percent interest rate were losing money. Coupled with inflation was the emergence of investment companies offering consumers money market mutual funds, which enabled the average investor to earn market-rate interest. Mutual funds were also a safe instrument, as they were invested primarily in high-interest federal securities and certificates of deposit (CDs). Mutual funds grew as small investors, lured by huge gains in the stock market during the 1980s, sought ways to earn returns greater than the rate of inflation. The shift to mutual funds hit American banks hard. In the years between 1977 and 1981, consumers went from investing \$3.9 billion to investing \$181.9 billion in mutual funds rather than putting their money in the bank.

Still, many Americans used their local banks for routine checking and savings. But bank assets continued to decline; in 1960 banks held 34 percent of the total assets of Americans. By 1989 that figure had declined to 26 percent. In the meantime, consumers had a number of alternatives to conventional savings accounts, including CDs and money market funds, both of which yielded higher interest than standard savings accounts.

Despite the approximately 1,295 bank failures between 1985 and 1992, banking advocates stated that the industry was competing effectively in the newly competitive financial services market. Although the traditional business of banks, taking deposits and making loans, had declined, other services more than made up for the loss, resulting in record profits in 1992 and 1993. To remain competitive, banks exploited loopholes in the Glass-Steagall Banking Act of 1933, which sharply restricted their activities. During the 1980s and 1990s, banks responded to competition by selling money market and mutual funds, creating mortgage and financing subsidiaries, and fashioning a huge network of automatic teller machines (ATMs).

The Diversification of the Financial Services Industry

By the mid-1990s, many observers believed that the banking industry and other companies offering financial services were no longer clearly defined, separate entities. Now banks, insurance companies, and brokerage houses converged. Insurance giant Prudential acquired brokerage houses to form Prudential-Bache, and such traditional Wall Street players as Merrill Lynch began to offer accounts that allowed customers to do their banking.

Analysts disagree about the effects these changes have had on the American finance scene. By the early 1990s, some believed that the United States was becoming a bankless society, with such corporations as the Ford Motor Company, General Electric, and General Motors able to offer loans to businesses and credit to consumers, all financial services previously reserved for banks and savings and loans.

Credit Cards

By 1995, Americans faced a bewildering array of choices for even the most routine financial transactions. Credit cards became increasingly popular, with $480 billion in purchases made in 1993 alone. Credit cards offered by an ever-growing number of companies and associations granted premiums and bonuses if consumers used their cards. Those who used the GM MasterCard or Visa, for example, could get credit toward their next auto purchase from General Motors; Exxon Visa cardholders could get back 3 percent of every gasoline purchase made at an Exxon station. Other credit cards offered frequent flyer miles and donations to charities. Other companies issuing credit cards included Sears, AT&T, Chrysler, and Ford Motor Company. Credit cards account for 25 percent of all profits at the ten largest banks in the United States, but with only 14 percent of all merchandise purchased via credit card, there is still room for growth.

Since the early 1970s, the use of credit cards has expanded from infrequent large purchases to include such everyday purchases as groceries, fast food, and telephone calls. Thanks to less stringent underwriting criteria at major credit card companies, credit cards are also more easily available than ever before. In 1989, 56 percent of American families had at least one general use credit card such as MasterCard or Visa. By 1998, that number had climbed to 67.5 percent. Credit card companies have also targeted new groups for their product. Offering cards to students on many college and university campuses has led to easier access to credit for those who may not yet have established a credit history. For credit card companies, this persistence has paid off: Americans charged more than $1 trillion in purchases with their credit cards in the year 2000, more than they spent in cash.

Industry Convergence

The convergence of companies offering financial services has blurred the conventional boundaries that once separated banks, brokerages, and insurance companies. This trend has now become global. As a result, the convergence of financial services has created a new class of financial provider. These financial services conglomerates strive to provide customers with a vast portfolio of integrated financial services.

Perhaps the most significant example of convergence came in April 1998 with the announcement of the merger of Citicorp and Travelers Insurance. The creation of Citigroup, already a financial giant with a presence in 100 countries across six continents, offered a glimpse of a new business model in the financial services industry: a full-service provider with formidable assets in banking, insurance, stockbrokerage, mutual funds, and more. With assets valued at $697.5 billion, Citigroup became the largest financial services company in the world. A week later, on 13 April, Banc One announced its merger with First Chicago NBD Corporation, with the new company's value now estimated at $116 billion. That very same day, NationsBank joined with BankAmerica, creating a new corporation with deposits of $346 billion, making it the second largest bank in the United States and the fifth largest in the world.

It was clear that through these mergers a complex and ongoing revolution was transforming the very nature of the financial services industry. At the very center of this revolution, however, was a conflict between what banking experts called "consolidation" and the process called "disintermediation," which meant the removal of intermediaries such as banks from financial transactions. Proponents of disintermediation, such as the software giant Microsoft, believed that the future belonged to those companies who mastered the new technology, which in turn, would give customers and investors almost complete control over their finances.

Turbulent Times

Despite its growth and its profits, the financial services industry has not escaped crises or disasters. On 19 October 1987, the New York Stock Exchange experienced the largest single-day drop in its history, losing 508.32 points, or 22.6 percent of its value. Although many factors accounted for this huge decline, a major concern was the impact of computerized trading programs, which bought and sold huge blocks of securities automatically. The market quickly rebounded from Black Monday, but the Securities and Exchange Commission enacted rules that limited the ability of computerized programs to affect the market.

One of the defining moments in the financial services industry came during the 1980s with the failure of hundreds of savings and loan (S&L) institutions. Unlike the fall of the stock market, the S&L disaster produced much more enduring consequences. A partial explanation for the failures came from the debt burden that the S&Ls carried as the result of offering low-interest mortgages, in some cases as low as 3 percent, during the 1970s when inflation was high and interest payments to depositors were as much as 12 percent. Fraud and corruption also played a role in approximately half of the failures. A government bailout costing an estimated $500 billion to $1 trillion implemented over a period of thirty years was required to pay insured depositors of failed institutions.

Like much of the United States, the financial services industry suffered a terrible tragedy in 2001 when terrorists attacked the World Trade Center (WTC) in New York City and the Pentagon in Washington, D.C. The assault had a profound and lasting impact on the financial services industry because the WTC was home to dozens of banks, insurance companies, brokerages, and securities firms. Many companies with offices in the WTC lost dozens of key personnel. Some companies were virtually wiped out, losing all their documents and records. As of 2002, other companies have recovered from effects of 11 September, but are still experiencing cash flow problems because of the interruption of normal business.

The industry felt the effects of the attacks in other ways as well. In addition to their own financial losses, they suffered from the further general contraction of an already languishing American economy. The events of 11 September have led the financial service industry to re-evaluate how the industry will function in the future. Many foresee a move toward electronic and virtual markets.

The Financial Services Industry and the Law

In 1999, Congress passed the Gramm-Leach-Bliley Act (GLBA), or the Financial Modernization Act, the most sweeping legislation directed at banks and other financial institutions since the Great Depression. Intended to monitor cross-industry mergers and affiliations, customer privacy, and lending to lower-income communities, the GLBA created opportunities for financial institutions to engage in a broader spectrum of activities. The legislation also placed additional burdens on financial institutions, such as new consumer privacy safeguards and disclosure requirements.

The law permits the convergence of the banking, insurance, and securities industries as long as appropriate safeguards are in place to protect the consumer and guarantee the solvency of the institution. At the same time, the law almost completely eliminated the legal barriers that once separated the various components of the financial services industry. Although superseding state legislation, the GLBA also recognized the importance of state regulation of financial services companies and so endorsed the "functional regulation" of institutional activities by both state and federal regulatory agencies. State laws could not discriminate against banks in licensing or authorizing securities and insurance activities, but a state could impose reasonable and necessary licensing and consumer protection requirements consistent with federal regulations.

The law also limited the extent to which financial institutions could share personal information about customers, stating that individuals must be informed about the privacy policies and practices of financial institutions. The law also gave consumers limited control over how financial institutions used and shared personal information.

Three years after the law was enacted, the freedom that the GLBA granted was in jeopardy. In 2002, the financial services industry became the subject of federal scrutiny as Congress debated new legislation that would more closely regulate the industry. The inquiries came amid scandals involving such high-profile financial firms as J. P. Morgan Chase and Company and Merrill Lynch, with accusations that company executives were guilty of deception and fraud with regard to the financial collapse of the Enron Corporation. Once willing to keep government out of the way, legislators now called for tougher laws that would mandate keener overseeing of corporate finances. Additional legislation would overhaul the Financial Accounting Standards Board.

The USA Patriot Act, also passed in 2001, will require mutual fund companies, operators of credit card systems, registered broker-dealers, futures merchants, and money services businesses to adopt programs similar to those that banks have been required to use since 1987. This piece of legislation law is aimed at curbing money-laundering activities, including those that help fund terrorism. As of 2002, some sectors of the financial services industry, such as insurance, finance, and non-mutual fund companies, remained exempt from the law.

The Future Is Now

As the financial services industry becomes more fast-paced and competitive, technology will be an even more important component of success. Probably more than any other sector of the American economy, financial services rides the crest of technological innovation. Finance is increasingly a twenty-four-hour, seven-day-a-week global activity with vast sums flashing between markets over the electronic communications web. The ability to instantaneously interpret the financial markets and anticipate their movement can bring huge profits or avoid disastrous losses. With large sums committed in the markets, financial organizations need to calculate how much risk they are accepting.

The sheer speed and complexity of financial markets has compelled banks and other financial institutions to look beyond conventional analytical techniques and computer systems. A bank's technological stockpile can include object-oriented technology, neural networks, data visualization, and virtual reality. The Citibank Corporation, for instance, files its annual report with its regulator by sending the document electronically; the physical copy is posted later merely to satisfy the requirements of law. The Federal Reserve Board, which functions as the central bank of the United States, posts complete information on bond and money markets each day on a computer bulletin board.

As more financial information is disseminated electronically, the ability to manipulate it is also growing. Advertisements on electronic bulletin boards match buyers with sellers, and borrowers with lenders. Transactions are instantly verified and settled through a global, real-time payment system. Innovations in self-service delivery, such as ATMs, telephone transactions, kiosks, and more recently, Web-enabled services through Internet "portals," have forever altered consumer expectations. Technology has also enabled new and often nontraditional competition to enter the market space of traditional providers. In response, many financial services companies are currently deploying new technologies to support an integrated product approach, wagering that their customers will find value and convenience in getting all their financial services from a single institution.

Thanks to the growing electronic market, many analysts believe that this diversification will dampen both inflation and, possibly, speculation. Bankers may also become an endangered species. At present, they control payment systems, assess creditworthiness, and transform short-term deposits into long-term loans. In the future, some experts say, many, if not all, of these functions will be performed either by individual customers or by more specialized firms, removing whatever influence banks still have over other financial service companies. If they are to survive and prosper, banks will need to find different niches, such as credit card processing, asset management, or, as in the case of Bankers Trust, the pricing and management of financial and other types of risk. Securities houses may also find themselves in jeopardy. As the costs of doing business begin to virtually disappear, consumers will have even greater opportunities to bypass financial firms all together. Finally, one of the most provocative of the claims that financial experts now put forth is that today's financial services customers could become tomorrow's rivals. Bypassing banks and securities firms, corporations might soon bid against them for financial business.

BIBLIOGRAPHY

Aspatore Books Staff, ed. *Inside the Minds: The Financial Services Industry—Industry Leaders Share Their Knowledge on the Future of the Financial Services Industry.* Boston: Aspatore Publishing, 2002.

"Bankers Trust's 2020 Vision." *The Economist* 330, no. 7856 (March 26, 1994): 91–92.

Banks, Erik. *e-Finance: The Electronic Revolution.* New York: John Wiley & Sons, 2001.

Day, Kathleen. *S&L Hell: The People and the Politics Behind the $1 Trillion Savings and Loan Scandal.* New York: Norton, 1993.

Duran, Nicole, and Barbara A. Rehm. "Policymakers GO Activist; Will They Overreach?" *American Banker* 167, no. 86 (May 6, 2002): 1–2.

Gart, Alan. *Regulation, Deregulation, Reregulation: The Future of the Banking, Thrift, Insurance, and Securities Industries.* New York: John Wiley & Sons, 1994.

Garver, Rob. "Launder Rules Will Apply Across Financial Services." *American Banker* 67, no. 77 (April 23, 2002): 1–2.

Kirsch, Clifford E., ed. *The Financial Services Revolution: Understanding the Changing Roles of Banks, Mutual Funds, and Insurance Companies.* Chicago: Irwin Professional Publishing, 1997.

Mayer, Martin. *The Money Bazaars: Understanding the Banking Revolution Around Us.* New York: E. P. Dutton, 1984.

Ratner, Ellis, and Mark Coler. *Financial Services: Insider's Views of the Future.* New York: New York Institute of Finance, 1987.

Wendel, Charles B., and Elaine S. Svensson, eds. *The New Financiers: Profiles of the Leaders Who Are Reshaping the Financial Services Industry.* Chicago: Irwin Professional Publishers, 1996.

Meg Greene Malvasi

FINNEY REVIVALS began under the preaching of the evangelist Charles G. Finney in central New York about 1825. During the height of the revivals, from 1827 to 1835, thousands of people were converted to Finney's brand of evangelical PROTESTANTISM in enormous open-air meetings held in most large cities around the country. Although supported by such wealthy philanthropists as Lewis and Arthur Tappan and Anson G. Phelps, the revivals aroused staunch opposition because of Finney's sentimental style of persuasion and reliance on emotion as a measure of conversion. His appeal spanned the social classes, but his urban, middle-class converts furnished a large proportion of the leadership for the many reform movements of the antebellum era.

BIBLIOGRAPHY

Hardman, Keith. *Charles Grandison Finney, 1792–1875: Revivalist and Reformer.* Syracuse, N.Y.: Syracuse University Press, 1987.

Johnson, Paul E. *A Shopkeeper's Millennium: Society and Revivals in Rochester, New York, 1815–1837.* New York: Hill and Wang, 1978.

William W. Sweet / A. R.

See also **Anti-Masonic Movements; Antislavery; Circuit Riders; Evangelicalism and Revivalism; Religious Thought and Writings; South, the: The Antebellum South.**

FIRE-EATERS. An outspoken group of Southern, proslavery extremists, the Fire-Eaters advocated secession from the Union and the formation of an independent confederacy as early as the 1840s. The group included a number of well-known champions of Southern sovereignty, including South Carolina newspaper editor Robert Barnwell Rhett, Virginia planter Edmund Ruffin, and William Lowndes Yancey, a radical Democrat from Alabama. Although Rhett, Ruffin, Yancey, and other Fire-Eaters were the chief spokesmen for confederacy, many moderate southerners who supported secession continued to distrust them and they seldom acquired responsible positions within the Confederate government.

BIBLIOGRAPHY

Allmendinger, David F. *Ruffin: Family and Reform in the Old South.* New York: Oxford University Press, 1990.

Dew, Charles B. *Apostles of Disunion.* Charlottesville: University Press of Virginia, 2001.

Ford, Lacy K. *Origins of Southern Radicalism.* New York: Oxford University Press, 1988.

Wendell H. Stephenson / E. M.

See also **Secession; Southern Rights Movement.**

FIRE FIGHTING. After a major fire in Boston in 1631, the first fire regulations in America were established. In 1648, fire wardens were appointed in New Amsterdam (later New York City), thereby initiating the first public fire department in North America. In 1736, Ben Franklin formed the first volunteer fire-fighting company in Philadelphia. Fire fighting was not an easy feat. Firefighters numbering up from fifty to one hundred men labored arduously at heavy pumpers of limited effectiveness. The enthusiastic but amateur volunteers were badly organized. Curious onlookers got in the way and looters stole whatever they could. Nearby buildings were often drenched or even pulled down with ropes to stop the fire from spreading; in the 1800s, firefighters also used dynamite to blow up buildings to save cities from complete destruction from a raging fire.

By the 1700s, independent volunteer fire companies began receiving payment for their services from the insurance company or the property owner. Property owners displayed fire markers outside the building to indicate that they were insured; in some cases, no marker meant no effort would be made to fight the fire. In other cases, only the first arriving companies got paid, which led to fierce competition. Volunteers sabotaged each other's equipment and fought off later-arriving companies, often using fire-fighting equipment as weapons. Often, the building burned down while the firemen brawled.

Fire-Fighting Organizations

Early in 1853 the Cincinnati, Ohio, Fire Department Committee formulated a plan that would entirely change the way fires were fought in America. To end the frequently violent competition between companies, the plan called for full-time, paid city employees to fight fires using a horse-drawn steam engine. The steam pumper would allow four or five men to spray more water on a fire than hundreds of volunteers using hand pumpers. The City Council on 16 March 1853 authorized the plan and the creation of a Fire Department, effective 1 April. At the beginning of the twenty-first century, fire department personnel are either volunteer (nonsalaried) or career (salaried). Volunteer firefighters are found mainly in smaller communities, career firefighters in cities. The modern department, with salaried personnel and standardized equipment, became an integral part of municipal administration only late in the nineteenth century. In some cities, a fire commissioner administers the department. Other cities have a board of fire commissioners with a fire chief as executive officer and head of the uniformed force. In still other cities a safety director may be in charge of both police and fire departments. The basic operating unit of the fire department is the company, commanded by a captain. A captain may be on duty on each shift, although in some fire departments, lieutenants and sergeants command companies when the captain is off duty. Fire companies are usually organized by types of apparatus: engine companies; ladder companies; and squad or rescue companies.

Boston installed the first fire-alarm systems, which used the telegraph and Morse code, in 1852. Many communities are still served either with the telegraph-alarm system or with telephone call boxes. Most fires, however, are reported from private telephones. Many large cities have removed all or many of their street alarm boxes because of false alarms and maintenance problems. Alarms are received at a central dispatch office and then transmitted to fire stations, frequently with the use of mobile teleprinters and computers.

Apparatus is dispatched according to the nature of the alarm and location of the fire. Many modern departments are now equipped with computer-aided dispatch systems that track the status of all units and provide vital information about the buildings where fires occur. Typically, on a first alarm, more apparatus is sent to industrial areas, schools and other institutions, and theaters than to private residences. Additional personnel, volunteer or off duty, is called as needed. Fires that cannot be brought under control by the apparatus responding to the first alarm are called multiple-alarm fires, with each additional alarm bringing more firefighters and equipment to the

Horse-Drawn Fire Engine. Until the 1920s, dogs were not the only animals found in many firehouses. LIBRARY OF CONGRESS

scene. Special calls are sent for specific types of equipment. Mutual aid and regional mobilization plans are in effect among adjacent fire departments for assisting each other in fighting fires. A superior example of this was exhibited with the 11 September 2001 attack on New York City's World Trade Center, when fire companies from all over Manhattan and from neighboring boroughs responded to the catastrophe.

Fire-Fighting Equipment

Early on, pioneer firefighters fought fires with bucket lines. Men usually formed a line to convey water from the nearest source to the scene of destruction, while the women and children formed a second line to pass empty buckets back to the water source. The first fire engines were developed in the seventeenth century. They were merely tubs carried on runners, long poles, or wheels. The tub functioned as a reservoir and sometimes housed a hand-operated pump that forced water through a pipe or nozzle to waiting buckets. The invention of a hand-stitched leather hosepipe in the Netherlands around 1672 made it possible for firefighters to move nearer to the fire without risking damage to the engine. During the same period, the creation of pumpers made it possible for firefighters to use water from rivers and ponds.

In the early 1900s, stitching on hoses gave way to copper rivets and fifty-foot lengths coupled with brass fittings that enabled firefighters to convey water through narrow passages, up stairways, and into buildings while the pumps operated in the street. The pumper threw a stream of water up to 133 feet while twelve men pumped for a few exhausting moments at a time. In about 1870, rubber hoses covered by cotton came into use. The steam-pump fire engine, introduced in London in 1829, gained popularity in many large cities in the 1850s. Most steam pumpers were equipped with reciprocating piston pumps, although a few rotary pumps were used. Some were self-propelled, but most used horses for propulsion, conserving steam pressure for the pump.

After establishing the first professional fire-fighting force, Cincinnati also briefly led the way in technological developments. Cincinnati inventors Able Shawk and Alexander Latta developed "Uncle Joe Ross," the first successful steam fire engine in America. First deployed in 1853, the fire engine had the capacity of the six biggest double-engine hand pumpers and needed only three men to operate it. It could supply three hand companies with water while at the same time shooting a powerful spray of water 225 feet onto the fire. The Ahrens-Fox Manufacturing Company of Cincinnati, an early leader in developing steam engines, replaced the horses with motorized tractors, and produced compressed-air aerial ladders to reach windows of tall buildings. By the 1920s, the last of the horse-drawn engines had disappeared.

With the development of the internal combustion engine in the early twentieth century, pumpers became motorized. Because of problems in adapting gear rotary gasoline engines to pumps, the first gasoline-powered fire engines had two motors, one to drive the pump and the other to propel the vehicle. The first pumper using a single engine for pumping and propulsion was manufactured in the United States in 1907. Motorized pumpers had almost entirely displaced steam pumpers by 1925. The pumps were originally of the piston or reciprocating type, but these were gradually replaced by rotary pumps and finally by centrifugal pumps, which are used by most modern pumpers. Modern pumpers consist of a powerful pump that can supply water in a large range of volumes and pressures; several thousand feet of fire hose, attached to a hydrant by a short segment of wide hose; and a water tank to be used in places lacking a water supply or to enable firefighters to begin their work while the hose is being attached to a hydrant. In the countryside, pumpers are used along with suction hoses to obtain water from rivers and ponds.

The late nineteenth century saw other innovations in fire fighting including the chemical fire extinguisher. The first was a glass fire extinguisher, the Harden Hand Grenade Extinguisher. The extinguisher, or grenade, contained carbon tetrachloride, later banned because at high temperatures it emitted a hazardous phosphene gas. The grenade, when tossed into the fire, broke open and released the carbon tetrachloride. The sprinkling system also came into use at this time and fireproof construction materials were developed as well. Several catastrophic blazes in the early history of San Francisco, California, led to other innovations. San Francisco's Fire Department Maintenance Shop Supervisors developed the Hayes Aerial Ladder in 1868 and the Gorter Nozzle in 1886, both of which were adopted by fire departments worldwide. The department was among the first to employ fireboats and to place water towers on many roofs. It also recommended sixty-foot height limits for buildings and fire escapes and standpipes on all multistory edifices.

Beginning in the late 1950s, new equipment and materials emerged on the scene: the snorkel truck, equipped with a cherry-picker boom to replace the traditional extension ladder; the super pumper, which is capable of pumping eight thousand gallons of water per minute at very high pressure (used in fighting fires in very tall structures); and foam and other chemicals to fight fires. To fight forest fires, specially equipped airplanes and helicopters are used to drop water or chemicals from the air, and to insert "smokejumpers" (firefighters who parachute in) to fight fires in remote locations. In the 1990s, fire companies began using thermal imaging cameras. Infrared technology allows firefighters to see through smoke to locate the seat of the fire and to quickly locate hazardous hotspots. With thermal imaging, large areas of land or water can be searched quickly and accurately, requiring less manpower than do conventional methods. Searches can be conducted efficiently during nighttime darkness or full sunlight, in a variety of weather conditions. Thermal imagers can be used for searches carried out on foot or from automobiles, watercraft, and aircraft.

Firefighter. This fire in Miami resulted from riots—creating yet another hazard for arriving firefighters; sometimes rioters target firefighters themselves for attack. Bettmann Newsphotos

BIBLIOGRAPHY

Ditzel, Paul C. *Fire Engines, Fire Fighters: The Men, Equipment, and Machines, from Colonial Days to the Present.* New York: Bonanza Books, 1984.

Ingram, Arthur. *A History of Fire-Fighting and Equipment.* London: New English Library, 1978.

Loeper, John J. *By Hook and Ladder: The Story of Fire Fighting in America.* New York: Atheneum, 1981.

Marston, Hope Irvin. *Fire Trucks.* New York: Dodd, Mead, 1984.

Smith, Dennis. *Dennis Smith's History of Firefighting in America: 300 Years of Courage.* New York: Dial Press, 1978.

James G. Lewis

See also **Chicago Fire; Disasters; 9/11 Attack; Wildfires.**

FIRES. *See* **Disasters; Wildfires.**

FIRST AMENDMENT. The First Amendment of the U.S. Constitution protects several essential rights, against congressional infringements: freedom of speech, freedom of the press, free exercise of religion, and the right of assembly and to petition the government for a redress of grievances. It also forbids the "establishment of religion." Beginning in 1925, in *Gitlow v. New York*, the

Supreme Court began applying the clauses against the actions of state and local governments as well.

Though these rights constitute distinct jurisprudential claims, their common denominator is freedom of thought and conscience. As the Court wrote in *West Virginia State Board of Education v. Barnette* (1943), striking down West Virginia's law requiring students to salute the American flag, "If there is any fixed star in our constitutional constellation, it is that no official, high or petty, can prescribe what shall be orthodox in politics, nationalism, religion, or other matters of opinion."

First Amendment freedoms have become considerably more extensive than when the Bill of Rights was ratified. Most scholars agree that the free speech and press clauses originally prohibited only "prior restraints" of publications, allowing for the criminal punishment of seditious libel (criticism of the government). Establishment meant primarily state support of an official church or favoritism among sects, while free exercise applied simply to beliefs, not to actions attendant to the practice of religion.

In 1798, seven years after the ratification of the Bill of Rights, the Federalist Congress passed the Sedition Act, which included punishment for any "false, scandalous and malicious" writing against the government. The Supreme Court never dealt with the act, but lower federal courts consistently upheld severe punishments meted out in its name. Over the next 150 years courts generally allowed governments to punish expression if it had a "natural tendency" to harm a legitimate state interest (the "bad tendency" test). Courts consistently upheld convictions for printing material that authorities construed as a threat to moral order, as well as writings or statements that were believed to go beyond the pale of acceptable criticism of authority. Though Justices Oliver Wendell Holmes and Louis Brandeis strove to establish the more protective "clear and present danger test" in the 1920s and 1930s, courts continued for the most part to adhere to the bad tendency test, sanctioning widespread restriction of political dissent and morally offensive expression.

With the demise of McCarthyism in the mid-1950s and the rise of the civil rights movement and political dissent in the 1960s, the Court, under Chief Justice Earl Warren, began to craft the modern doctrine of speech. The Court established the principle that government must remain "viewpoint neutral" toward all speech and significantly narrowed the definitions of such traditional exceptions to free speech as obscenity, libel, fighting words, and offensive expression. The Court ruled in *Brandenburg v. Ohio* (1969) that advocacy of violence or revolution may be proscribed only if it constitutes a "direct incitement to imminent lawless action that is likely to occur." The Court declared in *The New York Times v. Sullivan* (1964) that public officials could not recover civil damages for libel unless they prove the libel was committed intentionally or recklessly. In so holding, the Court declared that making seditious libel a crime conflicted with the "central meaning" of the First Amendment. New claims for censorship in the twentieth century involved protecting women and minorities from pornography and hate speech and shielding children from exposure to "indecent" material on the Internet. Overall the Burger and Rehnquist Courts continued to protect the modern doctrine of free speech, for example, in *Reno v. American Civil Liberties Union* (1997).

The jurisprudence of the religion clauses has developed differently from that of free speech. Following the McCarthy era, the Warren Court held that some actions pursuant to religious beliefs embrace free exercise and are constitutionally protected unless they harm a compelling state interest. Accordingly, government could not deny unemployment benefits to individuals who quit their jobs because of their religious beliefs (*Sherbert v. Verner*, 1963). The Burger Court continued this logic. But the Rehnquist Court drew a different line in *Employment Division v. Smith* in 1990, which upheld Oregon's refusal to pay unemployment benefits to two Native Americans who had been fired from their jobs in a drug rehabilitation organization for smoking peyote in a religious ceremony. The free exercise clause does not protect acts that violate a criminal law that is "a valid and neutral law of general applicability." Applying the neutrality principle in *Church of the Lukumi Babalu Aye, Inc. v. Hialeah* (1993), the Court struck down a Florida ordinance barring the ritualistic sacrifice of animals because the city allowed the killing of animals for other purposes.

Establishment clause jurisprudence has been even more convoluted. The Warren Court built up a relatively high wall of separation between church and state, most prominently in cases prohibiting state aid to religious schools and prayer in public schools, such as *Engle v. Vitale* (1962). After the 1971 *Lemon v. Kurtzman* decision, the Burger Court became more accommodating toward state involvement with religion, upholding prayers by legislative chaplains, a "moment of silence" in public schools, equal access to religious groups in schools, and tax deductions for religious school expenses. Construing religious expression as one voice in a culturally pluralistic society, the Rehnquist Court went even further in accommodating religion, especially in the areas of direct state aid in *Agostini v. Felton* (1997) and equal access in *Rosenberger v. University of Virginia* (1995). The Rehnquist Court, however, found school-sponsored prayer at official school events unconstitutional in *Santa Fe Independent School District v. Doe* (2000).

BIBLIOGRAPHY

Choper, Jesse H. *Securing Religious Liberty: Principles for Judicial Interpretation of the Religion Clauses.* Chicago: University of Chicago Press, 1995.

Haiman, Franklyn S. *Speech and Law in a Free Society.* Chicago: University of Chicago Press, 1981.

Tedford, Thomas L. *Freedom of Speech in the United States.* 2d ed. New York: McGraw-Hill, 1993.

Donald A. Downs
Martin J. Sweet

See also **Bill of Rights in U.S. Constitution; Constitution of the United States; Sedition Acts; Supreme Court.**

FIRST LADIES. The wife of the President of the United States is commonly called the First Lady. The term, like the position, is undefined, improvised, and extra-Constitutional. Nevertheless, the role of First Lady of the United States has evolved and developed certain boundaries over the years. Today, each First Lady is one of the most famous and most scrutinized women in America, for better and worse. The position offers the president's spouse a platform to address important issues. Yet, placing a modern woman in an anachronistic, derivative, and amorphous position, playing to a public with mixed emotions about the role of women, the nature of family, and the centrality of government, has made this unpaid task "the second toughest job in America."

Origins of the Term

The first "First Lady," Martha Washington, was often known as "Lady Washington." Then, as now, Americans were ambivalent. Proximity to the Revolutionary experience, and pride in their frontier independence, made Americans wary of bestowing monarchical touches on the presidency, or creating a family-based court around the chief executive. Yet a weakness for pomp and a yearning for majesty persisted. Abigail Adams was sometimes called "Mrs. President" or even "Her Majesty." Other early first ladies were addressed as "Presidentress."

The origins of the term "First Lady" are murky. In 1849, President Zachary Taylor eulogized Dolley Madison, saying, "She will never be forgotten, because she was truly our First Lady for a half-century." The British war correspondent William Howard Russell noted in his published Civil War diary in 1863 the gossip about "the first Lady in the Land." This is the first recorded reference to an incumbent First Lady, in this case Mary Todd Lincoln. A reporter and novelist, Mary Clemmer Ames, applied the same phrase to Lucy Webb Hayes in 1877, and the term was bandied about when the bachelor President Grover Cleveland married young Frances Folsom in the White House in 1886. The term became popular after Charles Nirdlinger's 1911 play about Dolley Madison, "The First Lady in the Land." Still, not all modern First Ladies have appreciated the title. Jackie Kennedy preferred the more democratic designation, "Mrs. Kennedy," grumbling that "First Lady" was more suited to "a saddle horse."

A State Prisoner? The First "First Ladies"

As all her successors would, Martha Washington balanced the informal and the formal, her private needs with public demands. George Washington decided that he and Martha would host a weekly drawing room on Friday evenings, and dinner parties on Thursday evenings. They would accept no private invitations. Mrs. Washington was miserable. "I am more like a state prisoner than anything else," she wrote, "there is certain bounds set for me which I must not depart from—and as I can not doe as I like I am obstinate and stay at home a great deal."

Many of Martha Washington's successors would resent the "bounds set" for them—by their husbands or the public. Traditional proprieties circumscribed First Ladies' behavior, well into the modern era. The ideology of domesticity constrained all wives, especially the President's wife. The one consistent duty was that of the President's hostess. Not all White House hostesses, however, were First Ladies. The widowed Thomas Jefferson relied on Dolley Madison. James Buchanan, a bachelor, relied on his niece Harriet Lane, while the widowed Andrew Jackson relied on two nieces. During John Tyler's one term four women hosted: his ailing wife Letitia, his daughter-in-law Priscilla, his daughter Letitia Semple, and after Letitia Tyler's death, his second wife Julia Gardiner Tyler.

First Ladies of the New Republic: Washington Society's Grand Dames

Still, throughout the nineteenth and early twentieth centuries, First Ladies had considerable latitude in defining their broader roles and most enjoyed a low public profile. With the president himself removed from most Americans' daily lives, the First Lady rarely made the newspapers. However, in presiding over the White House social life, all First Ladies were the titular heads of Washington society. Some, like Dolley Madison, relished the role. Others hated it. Some, like Julia Tyler, plunged into politics, lobbying at White House social events. Most did not. Some, like Sarah Polk, were effective behind-the-scenes advisers, true political partners. Most were not.

Some nineteenth-century First Ladies did attract public attention. Dolley Madison was the *grande dame* of Washington, dominating the social scene, and capturing the public's imagination, for almost half a century. The vivacious Lucy Webb Hayes and the young Frances Folsom Cleveland also charmed the public, foreshadowing the modern role of First Lady as celebrity. Mary Todd Lincoln, by contrast, was the black sheep of the Lincoln Administration, distrusted as a Southerner, despised for her extravagances, and demonized for her individuality.

Just as Theodore Roosevelt helped usher the presidency into the twentieth century, his wife, Edith Kermit Roosevelt, helped institutionalize the First Ladyship. In 1902, Mrs. Roosevelt hired the first social secretary to a First Lady. A century later, the Office of the First Lady has a multimillion-dollar budget, and usually at least one dozen employees, including a social secretary, a press secretary, and a chief of staff.

Americans' longstanding republican fears of schemers subverting the presidency made the First Lady's position even more delicate. When Ulysses S. Grant proved to be inscrutable as president in the 1870s, Washington wags decided that his wife, Julia, was manipulating him. In fact, Mrs. Grant had little interest in policy issues. Half a century later, when Woodrow Wilson suffered a stroke in late 1919, his second wife, Edith Wilson, did get involved. Mrs. Wilson functioned as a virtual chief of staff—some said as a virtual president—and suppressed information about the President's illness. Historians still debate how incapacitated Woodrow Wilson was, and how much input Mrs. Wilson had. Still, the charges that "Mrs. President" became "the first woman president," and instituted "petticoat government" offered a cautionary tale to activist First Ladies. Those who do seem too interested in power attract opprobrium.

Edith Wilson's three Republican successors reverted to the more traditional role. Although none were as passive as the public believed, they attracted less flak. Florence Harding helped orchestrate her husband's career; Grace Coolidge brought a touch of glamour to her staid husband's administration; and Lou Henry Hoover became the first First Lady to address the nation on the radio.

Modern Challenges: Eleanor Roosevelt and her Successors

The great divide in the history of First Ladies comes with Eleanor Roosevelt's tenure. Eleanor Roosevelt was more political, more engaged, more public, and more influential than her predecessors. Her activism was systematic not sporadic. She wrote an ongoing newspaper column, held frequent press conferences, lobbied Congress directly, and regularly served as Franklin Roosevelt's emissary to liberals, laborers, blacks, Jews, and other oft-forgotten men and women. In demonstrating the First Lady's great potential, Mrs. Roosevelt renegotiated the terms of the relationship between the First Lady and the public. All of Mrs. Roosevelt's successors, including the supposedly passive Bess Truman and Mamie Eisenhower, would be operating as modern First Ladies, on the political stage, and in the public eye.

Since Eleanor Roosevelt, all First Ladies have felt compelled to project a public persona; all First Ladies have tended to advance at least one pet cause, from Jackie Kennedy's White House renovation to Lady Bird Johnson's beautification of the capital, from Nancy Reagan's "Just Say No to Drugs" campaign, to Hillary Rodham Clinton's say yes to national health care crusade. The Roosevelt revolution was furthered by the expansion of the presidency and the government, the emergence of a national media, and the feminist rebellion. All these forces combined have shifted the First Ladies' priorities, making her role more public and more political.

Furthermore, in this celebrity age, First Ladies can generate excitement. Jackie Kennedy's charm and grace demonstrated First Ladies' political potential in the television age. Mrs. Kennedy became instrumental in setting the tone of her husband's "New Frontier," and perpetuating his legend.

And yet, the transformation had its limits. While First Ladies have struggled with modern demands, Americans have looked to First Ladies to embody tradition in a changing republic. First Ladies who seem too aggressive, too modern, often generate controversy, as do First Ladies who seem too powerful and too political. When Lady Bird Johnson's beautification campaign shifted from fundraising and uplift to a Highway Beautification Act in 1965, her project no longer seemed so innocuous. Nancy Reagan effectively rehabilitated her own reputation by shifting from seeming too concerned with redecorating the White House, to emphasizing her longstanding commitment to encouraging foster grandparents and discouraging drug use. But, by 1986, during Reagan's second term, as she clashed with presidential advisers, she, too, was attacked for being power-hungry. And after Barbara Bush's smooth term, wherein she avoided most political issues, Hillary Rodham Clinton's more activist stance thrilled some, and infuriated others.

Even today, in the twenty-first century, the First Lady struggles with gossamer shackles. First Ladies have a national podium, as Betty Ford discovered when she discussed her breast cancer in public in 1974. But it remains, as Nancy Reagan said, a "white-glove pulpit," a modern forum, suffused with the celebrity glow, still restrained by an American yearning for tradition, ambivalence about the role of modern women, and fear of someone, anyone, but especially his wife, getting too close to the President of the United States of America.

BIBLIOGRAPHY

Black, Allida. *Casting Her Own Shadow: Eleanor Roosevelt and the Shaping of Postwar Liberalism.* New York: Columbia University Press, 1996. Helpful in seeing Eleanor Roosevelt in her broadest context.

Caroli, Betty Boyd. *First Ladies.* New York: Oxford University Press, 1987.

Gould, Lewis L., ed. *American First Ladies: Their Lives and Their Legacy.* New York: Garland Publishing, 1996. Excellent and authoritative.

Troy, Gil. *Mr. and Mrs. President: From the Trumans to the Clintons.* Lawrence: University Press of Kansas, 2000.

Gil Troy

FISH AND MARINE LIFE, STUDY OF. *See* **Marine Biology.**

FISHING BOUNTIES in the United States were not at first true bounties. To aid domestic fisheries, from 1789 until 1807 the federal government levied duties on imported salt and paid allowances on fish and meat cured with foreign salt and then exported. This allowance, or bounty, primarily affected the cod fisheries, which used large quantities of imported salt. The bounty as revived in 1813 applied only to the fisheries. Beginning in 1828 the duty was lowered while the bounty remained unchanged. The bounty was continued in 1866 to support northeastern fisheries, considered training grounds for seamen.

BIBLIOGRAPHY

Innis, Harold A. *The Cod Fisheries: The History of an International Economy.* Toronto: University of Toronto Press, 1978.

F. Hardee Allen / A. R.

See also **Bounties, Commercial; Cod Fisheries; Hamilton's Economic Policies; Tariff; Taxation; Trade, Foreign.**

FISK EXPEDITIONS (1862–1866). The discovery of gold in the Montana and Idaho regions led prospectors to push Congress to open a new route across the northern Plains. In 1862, the army promoted private James Liberty Fisk of a Minnesota regiment to captain and put him in command of an emigrant wagon train from Fort Abercrombie to Fort Salmon. Fisk received $5,000 to open the route that became known as the Minnesota-Montana Road. Fisk was a tough frontiersman and a capable leader and followed closely the 1853 route of the John F. Stevens expedition across northern Dakota and Montana. The expedition left in July and made a pleasant and unremarkable passage to Fort Benton. Learning the Salmon River mines were overcrowded, most of the immigrants settled in the Prickly Pear Creek Valley and Bannack.

Fisk led three more expeditions into Montana, including accompanying General Alfred Sully's punitive expedition in 1864 against the Indians. Fisk separated from Sully and approached the Bighorn River when he was attacked by the Sioux. A detachment of Sully's army rescued the party and returned them to Fort Rice on the Missouri River. In 1866, Fisk led a party of miners and settlers to Helena, Montana.

The army was dissatisfied with the Minnesota-Montana Road, and in 1864, abandoned it in favor of their own program to open and protect the immigrants to Montana. However, the Great Northern Railroad revived the route and followed it to the Montana mines.

BIBLIOGRAPHY

Bancroft, Hubert Howe. *History of Washington, Idaho, and Montana, Volume 1845–1849.* San Francisco: History Company, 1890.

Malone, Michael P., Richard B. Roeder, and William L. Lang. *Montana: A History of Two Centuries.* Rev. ed. Seattle: University of Washington Press, 1991.

McElroy, Harold. "Mercurial Military: A Study of the Central Montana Frontier Army Policy." *Montana Magazine of Western History* 4, no. 4 (1954): 9–23.

Raymer, Robert George. *Montana: The Land and the People.* Chicago: Lewis Publishing, 1930.

Jerry L. Parker

See also **Explorations and Expeditions: U.S.; Montana.**

FIVE-POWER NAVAL TREATY, one of seven treaties negotiated at the Washington Conference on Limitation of Armaments (1921–1922). Settlement of Far Eastern questions, principally through the Four-Power and Nine-Power treaties, made possible the 1922 Naval Treaty of Washington, which placed limitations upon capital ships, aircraft carriers, and Far Eastern naval bases. Aggregate battleship tonnage was restricted to 525,000 for the United States and Great Britain, 315,000 for Japan, and 175,000 for France and Italy. This quota required the United States to scrap twenty-eight capital ships then under construction or completed. Competitive building of cruisers, destroyers, and submarines continued until the 1930 London Treaty.

BIBLIOGRAPHY

Buckley, Thomas H. *The United States and the Washington Conference, 1921–1922.* Knoxville: University of Tennessee Press, 1970.

Hogan, Michael J. *Informal Entente: The Private Structure of Cooperation in Anglo-American Economic Diplomacy, 1918–1928.* Columbia: University of Missouri Press, 1977; Chicago: Imprint, 1991.

Dudley W. Knox / A. G.

See also **Great Britain, Relations with; Japan, Relations with; Treaties with Foreign Nations; Washington Naval Conference.**

FLAG DAY, 14 June, marks the anniversary of the adoption by Congress in 1777 of the Stars and Stripes as emblem of the nation. Celebrations of the flag began in local communities throughout the country during the nineteenth century, largely for the purpose of educating children in history. In 1916, President Woodrow Wilson, and later, in 1927, President Calvin Coolidge, suggested that 14 June be observed as Flag Day. It was not until 3 August 1949 that the National Flag Day Bill became law, giving official recognition to 14 June to celebrate the flag.

BIBLIOGRAPHY

Furlong, William Rea, and Byron McCandless. *So Proudly We Hail: The History of the United States Flag.* Washington, D.C.: Smithsonian Institution Press, 1981.

Guenter, Scot M. *The American Flag, 1777–1924: Cultural Shifts from Creation to Codification.* Rutherford, N.J.: Fairleigh Dickinson University Press, 1990.

Mastai, Boleslaw, and Marie-Louise D'Otrange Mastai. *The Stars and the Stripes: The American Flag as Art and as History from the Birth of the Republic to the Present.* New York: Knopf, 1973.

Leland P. Lovette/H. S.

See also **Holidays and Festivals; Nationalism.**

FLAG OF THE UNITED STATES. The current form of the American flag, with its thirteen red and white stripes, blue field, and fifty white stars, has an evolutionary history. On 14 June 1777, the CONTINENTAL CONGRESS passed the first Flag Act, which reads, "Resolved, That the flag of the United States be made of thirteen stripes, alternate red and white; that the union be thirteen stars, white in a blue field, representing a new Constellation." The overall flag size, proportions, and arrangements of the stars and stripes were not fixed until President William Taft's administration in 1912. For one hundred and thirty-five years, the flag had no prescribed appearance, and many variations were designed and sewn.

There have been two other Flag Acts since, the first one in 1777, and three executive orders affecting the appearance of the flag. The Act of 13 January 1794 provided for fifteen stars and fifteen stripes after May 1795. The Act of 4 April 1818 provided for thirteen stripes with a star for each state, added to flag on the first July fourth after statehood signed by President James Monroe. President Taft, by Executive Order on 24 June 1912, designated proportions for the flag with six horizontal rows of eight stars each, with one point of each star pointing upward. President Dwight Eisenhower, by Executive Order on 3 January 1959, provided for an arrangement of stars in seven rows of seven stars each, staggered both horizontally and vertically. Again, on 21 August 1959, President Eisenhower signed an Executive Order that arranged the stars in rows of nine stars staggered horizontally and eleven rows of stars staggered vertically.

The basic design of the flag—one canton, or area similar to but smaller than a quandrant, and an open field—may be said to originate with the "red ensign," a British flag from the reign of Queen Elizabeth I. The red ensign is believed to be the first known example of a flag that borrowed the design of a canton and field from heraldic shields. The red ensign was red with a white canton crisscrossed by a red Cross of St. George. The Puritans adapted the red ensign for their own purposes by removing the cross, leaving a plain white canton and red field. Later, a small evergreen tree, representing the trees of New England, was added to the white canton. It is believed that the "Green Tree Flag" was flown at the battle Bunker Hill. Later, American patriots designed their own flags, and many varieties appeared that signified the leader in command of each regiment. With so many different flags, many of the designs became cluttered and complicated with too many symbols.

Another type of flag, the so-called liberty flag, became popular during pre-Revolutionary times. Typically these flags had white fields with various symbols or depictions and the word "liberty." The secret society, the "Sons of Liberty," had a flag with thirteen red and white stripes hanging either vertically or horizontally. This flag is thought to be the precursor of the field on the current American flag. The British labeled the flag "the rebellious stripes."

Early on, it was the symbol of stripes that mattered, not the number or their colors. Early flags show green and white stripes, for example, and the numbers varied from between nine to thirteen. The number nine was significant at the time. It came from issue 45 of "The North Britain" (23 April 1763), the pamphlet published by English civil-rights activist John Wilkes, which accused George III of falsehood. Wilkes's writing was second only to Thomas Paine's "Common Sense" in inciting action against England. The issue numbers four plus five (of "issue 45") created the nine that was grounded deeply in colonists' sensitivities and was instantly recognized as a symbol of rebellion.

It was Marquis de Lafayette who coined the phrase "stars and stripes" to describe the United States. The stripes always had precedence over the stars in American thinking and flag design. Historians no longer believe that the French flag influenced the American one, but that the tricolor choice of red, white, and blue influenced the French flag through Lafayette's impressions.

Interestingly, the star design also had to evolve to the current five-point style. The six-point style star is called the heraldic star, typically used on heraldic coats of arms. The five-point variety is called the molet, and was more typically found as knight's spurs during years of Christian chivalry. Historians differ on the reason why the molet star became the version used in the American flag. While they do not believe that Betsy Ross designed or sewed the first flag as legend has it, they do believe she sewed flags for the Navy and give some credence to reports of her preference for the five-star design for its relative ease of sewing. Another theory is that Ross took the star from Washington's coat of arms, which had somehow appropriated the molet design in contrast to the heraldic, and which was kept by later flag designers to honor the "father of the country."

Well-known American flags include the garrison pennant that flew over Fort McKinley in 1814 and inspired Francis Scott Key to write the national anthem, "THE STAR-SPANGLED BANNER." Another is the flag that Neil Armstrong planted in the moon's surface at the first human lunar landing in July 1969.

Flags continue to drape the coffins of veterans and to be folded ceremoniously out of respect when they are removed from places of honor or taken down from flagpoles. During times of national mourning, such as after the assassination of President John F. Kennedy and the terrorist attacks of 11 September 2001, the flag is flown half-staff.

Recent debate has flared up again about the constitutionality of flag burning. Those who argue for an amendment banning the practice say that it is necessary to preserve the sanctity of the symbol of America. Opponents argue that flag burning is an act of free speech that is protected by the First Amendment.

BIBLIOGRAPHY

Armed Forces History Collections. "Facts About the United States Flag." Available from http://www.si.edu/resource/faq/nmah//flag.htm.

Mastai, Boleslaw, and Marie-Louise D'Otrange Mastai. *The Stars and the Stripes: The American Flag As Art and As History, from the Birth of the Republic to the Present.* New York: Knopf, 1973.

Connie Ann Kirk

See also **Flag Day; Independence; Nationalism.**

FLAGS. Flags are the most pervasive symbol of allegiance in American society. While the American Stars and Stripes is the most ubiquitous symbol of loyalty, flags exist for every state in the union, each branch of the federal government and military, and for corporations, ethnic groups, religions, and almost any other social organization. Flags, especially the American flag, embody the core myths and ideals that undergird society. Unlike monuments, flags are often inexpensive, easily portable, and adaptable into myriad forms. Known popularly as Old Glory, the American flag inspires deep reverence and perceived attacks on it have provoked powerful passions. At the same time, the Stars and Stripes is used as a secular label on shopping bags, articles of clothing, car bumper stickers, and dozens of other consumer items and advertisements. Although displaying the flag epitomizes patriotism, Americans have long contested both flag standards and conceptions of its power. Myths surrounding the creation of the flag that are now hotly contested—including its invention by seamstress Betsy Ross—reflect the important place the Stars and Stripes holds in the imagination of the United States. This article will review the emergence of a national flag and discuss the many controversies that have attended it, with some attention paid to similar disputes over state flags.

Emergence of the Stars and Stripes

During the colonial era, Americans owed allegiance to the flags of England, France, and Spain. As the European powers gradually withdrew during the era of the American Revolution, the rebels of the thirteen colonies initially borrowed the flag of the imperialist East India Company as their own emblem. During the American Revolution the Americans used several flags, but none carried any national authority. American naval forces adapted the British Union Flag but added thirteen stripes in the field. Benjamin Franklin's cartoon of a snake divided into thirteen sections also was converted to cloth, with the motto, "Don't Tread on Me." Another reptilian image, used by the rebels after a naval victory, was a yellow cloth with a coiled rattlesnake about to strike. On 1 January 1776, General George Washington unveiled the Great Union Flag. This flag, with thirteen red and white stripes and incorporating the British Union flag, served without congressional sanction throughout the Revolutionary War and flew over Manhattan during the American occupation in the summer of 1776. But the American colonists were rebelling against the Crown, and soon rejected the Great Union Flag's crosses of St. Andrew and St. George. On 14 June 1777, the Continental Congress finally adopted a constellation of thirteen stars in place of the crosses, and thus invented the Stars and Stripes. Although the Great Union Flag fell into disuse, production of the Stars and Stripes was slow, and it was not generally available until nearly the end of the war. The new flag was most widely used at sea, where ships needed it to identify their nationality.

During the 1790s, as new states were added to the Union, there was some debate over the need to add stars. As the number of states grew to fifteen by 1794, one critic contended that in a hundred years there might be as many as one hundred stars, and that some permanence was needed. A second flag act, passed on 7 January 1794, fixed the number of stars at fifteen; Congress barely avoided passing legislation that would permanently restrict the number of stars. Congressmen at that time were far more concerned about the views of their voters than with building a national image; after all, there was no army or navy, and few Americans ever saw the Stars and Stripes. This change settled the matter for a quarter of a century.

Flag devotion increased after the siege of Fort Maher during the War of 1812 and the composition of the poem "The Star Spangled Banner" by Francis Scott Key. Using a tune borrowed from the anthem of the English Anacreontic Society (composed by John Stafford Smith), Key created a rousing patriotic song that reflected the seething anger of Americans toward the invading British. On 4 April 1818, Congress, recognizing that the old flag was now obsolete as it was five stars shy of the number of states, set the number of stripes at thirteen and agreed to add stars as needed. With this change, Congress subtly changed the meaning of the flag and recognized the march of manifest destiny across the continent. Even reflecting this imperialist consensus, the flag was not generally recognized or used. The U.S. Army had its own flag until 1834, when it determined to use the Stars and Stripes as the garrison flag and various banners of prescribed size for each regiment. Examination of textiles, china, glass, and wallpaper produced during the antebellum period shows use of the flag, but an even greater preference for the image of General Washington, personifications of Lady Liberty and Columbia, and the bald eagle. There was no full-time American flag manufacturer until the onset of the Mexican-American War in 1846.

Protecting the Flag from Challenges

The greatest challenge to the Stars and Stripes was the adoption of the red, white, and blue Stars and Bars by the seceding Confederate States during the Civil War. Variations of the Stars and Bars existed until the rebel congress passed a third Confederate Flag Act, just weeks before its final surrender in 1865. The Southern threat had the effect of making the Stars and Stripes into a popular flag, rather than one used solely by the government. After the surrender of the Stars and Stripes at Fort Sumter in the first battle of the Civil War, flags bloomed all across the North. The tattered remains of the flag from Fort Sumter were raised in a patriotic ceremony in New York City and were used as a recruiting device throughout the war. Popular magazines such as *Harper's Weekly* began publishing images of the Stars and Stripes weekly. Military songs such as the "Battle Cry of Freedom" became popular; that song used the line: "We'll rally around the flag, boys!" The war provoked angry outbursts against the flag as a symbol of the Union, and violators were harshly punished. One man, convicted of trampling on the flag, was hung in New Orleans, although President Abraham Lincoln removed the presiding general a few months later.

Patriotic fervor continued after the Civil War. With the rapid industrialization of the north and west, the Stars and Stripes was depicted in patriotic bunting and on advertising materials for bicycles, door mats, tobacconists, whiskey barrels, and porcelain spittoons and urinals. Such perceived abuses provoked the organization of the Flag Protection Movement (FPM), which flourished from 1895 to 1910. Lobbyists for the movement persuaded congressmen to back legislation describing the flag as sacred, and to attempt to ban advertising abuses. The FPM succeeded in transforming a secular symbol into a holy relic with the same status as the Bible and Christian Cross. A larger effect was to infuse patriotic loyalty to the flag with theocratic intolerance of other views. The beatification of the flag convinced its supporters—if not blacks, Mexicans, and Native Americans—that the banner had never waved in behalf of tyranny, injustice, and aggression. Backed by such racial and patriotic organizations as the Grand Army of the Republic (G.A.R.) and the Daughters of the Revolution (D.A.R.), the FPM built a national consensus that the flag needed to be protected by any means necessary. Beginning with the presidential campaign of William McKinley, politicians learned to wrap themselves in the flag and to insinuate that their opponents were not as patriotic, however doubtful such claims might be. During the campaign of 1896, a few scattered flag-desecration incidents spurred more discussion of laws to prevent them. Rather than focus on the egregious use of the flag by advertisers, legislators at the state and federal level aimed to stamp out the use of the flag by political protestors. A number of newspapers objected to this contradictory trend and pointed to vulgar political uses of the flag, such as tying a cardboard version of it to the horse that pulled a candidate's carriage. However, state courts generally upheld the use of the flag for commercial and political advertising.

Adoption of the FPM's tenets by super-patriotic groups soon led to use of the flag for racist and nativist purposes. Anti-immigrant rallies demanded that new arrivals to the United States "gather under its blessed folds." The G.A.R. began donating thousands of flags to schools and churches. Under such pressure, state lawmakers began passing bills mandating a daily salute to the flag before the start of the school day, and requiring that instruction in the salute be a part of the "melting pot schools" held for immigrants at major workplaces.

Reverence for the flag took on ugly manifestations in World War I: German Americans occasionally were forced to kiss the flag publicly, and a socialist rally in New York City in 1917 was disrupted when a mob forced marchers to kiss the flag. During the Red Scare following the war, the communist party flag was outlawed in numerous states. On 9 August 1925, the Ku Klux Klan advertised its devotion to the Stars and Stripes by marching down Pennsylvania Avenue in Washington, D.C., with a riotous display of American flags. Children who objected to the daily salute—including Jehovah's Witnesses, who objected on religious grounds—were expelled, an action upheld by the Supreme Court in June 1940 in the case of *Minersville School District v. Gobitis*. Though a number of newspapers criticized the court's decision, the case opened the way to further persecution of the children of Jehovah's Witnesses. The court affirmed what had become political reality by World War II: patriotism was synonymous with a ritualized obedience to the flag. This new patriotism was strengthened by the American military victory in World War II, with images like the raising of the American flag at Iwo Jima. Joseph Rosenthal's photographs of this event formed the basis for the Marine Court Memorial in Arlington, Virginia.

The Flag and Protest

Flags and protest became nationally visible during the Vietnam era of the 1960s and 1970s. As Americans gradually became aware of the huge contradictions between government claims and military reality, and the military draft became a specter for middle-class, college-age American males, protest against the war reached high levels of social antagonism. One means protestors used to demonstrate their anger against the war was by burning the American flag. In the year after a public flag burning in New York City's Central Park in April 1967, hundreds of laws outlawing such protests were proposed. These bills arose just as the issue of flag desecration had nearly lapsed into oblivion. The New York City incident and others like it around the country were manifestations of the immense anger many young Americans felt about the war; they defended their actions with claims of free speech for political activity. In one case, an African American defendant named Sidney Street was convicted for burning a flag in anger after the shooting of James Meredith during a civil rights march in Mississippi. The Flag Desecration Act was passed in 1968, making it illegal to mutilate, deface, or burn an American flag. Violators were subject to a fine of $1,000 or a year in jail. Fierce debate over the law and multiple prosecutions followed over the next few years, and the nation was badly divided over the issue. In a narrow decision, the Supreme Court struck down Street's conviction in 1969, based on the belief that he was convicted solely for his angry words. The Court's decision virtually nullified the Flag Desecration Act, upsetting the Court's minority, innumerable congressmen, and other political figures.

The Supreme Court revisited the flag issue only twice in the next twenty years, both times avoiding First Amendment issues by concentrating on vagaries in state laws. It did not squarely confront the issue of flag desecration until the great 1989–1990 flag burning controversy. These cases focused on the members of the Revolutionary Communist Party, a Maoist group, who had burned flags in Texas. The Court determined that flag burners were not necessarily disturbers of the peace, and that the flag did not stand for national unity nor was it a symbol of nationhood. The decision came at a time when (successful) presidential candidate George H. W. Bush was intimating that his opponent Michael Dukakis was less patriotic, and was vastly unpopular. Once elected, President Bush announced a drive for a constitutional amendment, a move seconded by former Dixie Democrat turned Republican, Senator Strom Thurmond of South Carolina. Both political parties blasted the Supreme Court decision, but legal professionals, including the American Bar Association, and an overwhelming number of newspaper editorialists supported it. Undeterred, Congress passed a Flag Protection Act of 1989; it was struck down by the Supreme Court in 1995.

Controversy over State Flags

While the American flag remained a lightning rod for controversy, state flags also came under criticism. Southern states integrated the Confederate Stars and Bars into their flags not in the Reconstruction period, but as an act of racial defiance during the Civil Rights era. A number of states adopted the symbol of the Confederacy into their state flags during the 1950s in response to the Supreme Court's *Brown v. Board of Education* decision, which outlawed public school segregation. In the late 1990s, the National Association for the Advancement of Colored People (NAACP) called for a boycott of certain southern states until they removed the Stars and Bars from their flags. In South Carolina, the Confederate flag actually flew from the state capital. After several years of controversy and financial cost to the state, a compromise lowered the flag to the capital grounds, although visitors still had to walk past it. A similar boycott in Atlanta floundered, although Mississippi's governor, Robert Khyatt, attempted to remove the Confederate flag.

Contemporary Flag Displays

The terrorist attacks of 11 September 2001 created a renewed, patriotic use of the flag. In the nation's grief, the tattered flag found on the site of the destroyed World Trade Center in New York City became a symbol of national unity, and was flown at innumerable gatherings in the aftermath of the attacks.

BIBLIOGRAPHY

Boime, Albert. *The Unveiling of the National Icons: A Plea for Patriotic Iconoclasm in a Nationalist Era.* New York: Cambridge University Press, 1998.

Goldstein, Robert Justin. *Burning the Flag: The Great 1989–1990 American Flag Desecration Controversy.* Kent, Ohio: Kent State University Press, 1996.

———. *Flag Burning and Free Speech: The Case of Texas v. Johnson.* Lawrence: University of Kansas Press, 2000.

———. *Saving Old Glory: The History of the American Flag Desecration Controversy.* Boulder, Colo.: Westview Press, 1993.

Marvin, Carolyn, and David W. Ingle. *Blood Sacrifice and the Nation: Totem Rituals and the American Flag.* New York: Cambridge University Press, 1999.

Quaife, Milo Milton. *The Flag of the United States.* New York: Grosset and Dunlap, 1942.

Graham Russell Hodges

FLAPPER. The nickname of the new female urbanites in America during the 1920s, "flapper" literally made reference to the unstrapped buckles of their shoes. While society appealed for "normalcy," the flapper practiced anything but as she sported makeup, a bob hairdo, and a tight-fitting dress to frequent the nightlife offered in the speakeasies of the big cities. Her behavior drew as much attention as her taboo attire, and a defining element of her womanhood became drinking, smoking, and a forward demeanor that included premarital intercourse, as the flapper strove to reshape gender roles in the Roaring Twenties. This entailed an assault on the Gibson Girl, the ideal of femininity in the Gilded Age. Measuring the flapper's success at overturning this convention depends on recognizing that leaders of the burgeoning woman's movement, such as Carrie Chapman Catt and Margaret Sanger, did not consider themselves flappers. This fact highlights the "new woman's" upper-class status more than her pervasiveness in society, and a penchant for comfortable living more than a desire to make a social statement. No matter, the flapper's symbolism outlasted her flare.

BIBLIOGRAPHY

Latham, Angela J. *Posing a Threat: Flappers, Chorus Girls, and Other Brazen Performers of the American 1920s.* Hanover, N.H.: University Press of New England, 2000.

Matthew J. Flynn

See also **Clothing and Fashion;** *and picture (overleaf).*

FLATBOATMEN worked on roughly made rafts that carried goods downstream, especially on the Mississippi. The occupation dates from the invention of flatboats in

Flappers. In this 1926 photograph taken with the U.S. Capitol as a backdrop, Representative Thomas Sanders McMillan of Charleston, S.C., stands near two flappers, Ruth Bennett and Sylvia Clavins, as they demonstrate the dance, named for his home city, that became a nationwide sensation after it was featured in a 1923 Broadway revue. LIBRARY OF CONGRESS

1750. Flatboating was an occasional rather than a full-time job. Flatboatmen were often farmers or laborers out to see the country or on their way to dispose of the products of their farms. Wages varied greatly but were usually about fifty dollars for the voyage.

All river cities were important terminals for flatboat commerce, but the most important was NEW ORLEANS. Many flatboatmen often made annual voyages there. They bore a reputation for thievery, debauchery, and belligerence, which may be largely undeserved, but their battles with keelboatmen are infamous. Many flatboatmen died from disease, violence, or the perils of the downstream voyage. It was common for those who made the voyage and returned home to migrate southward and westward with their families to the new areas they had visited.

Besides the flatboatmen, there were immigrant families traveling downstream on flatboats, and all of these river travelers shared a distrust of the shore dwellers. Another class of flatboat people made annual voyages on boats fitted up as stores, outfitted with goods for sale to farmers and to settlers.

BIBLIOGRAPHY

Baldwin, Leland D. *Keelboat Age on Western Waters.* 1941. Reprint, Pittsburgh, Pa.: University of Pittsburgh Press, 1980.

Ellis, David M., ed. *The Frontier in American Development.* Ithaca, N.Y.: Cornell University Press, 1969.

Leland D. Baldwin / T. D.

See also **Bargemen; Keelboat; Mississippi River; Rafts and Rafting; River Navigation.**

FLETCHER V. PECK, 6 Cranch 87 (1810), was the first opinion issued by the Supreme Court of the United States in which a state law was invalidated as contrary to the U.S. Constitution. Through various fraudulent activities, including bribery of state officials, the Georgia legislature was persuaded in 1795 to authorize the issuance of grants of certain state-owned land in what were then known as the "Yazoo lands," which encompassed much of the states of Alabama and Mississippi. In 1796 a newly elected legislature passed an act annulling these grants on the ground of fraud.

Meanwhile a parcel of the land, some 600,000 acres, had passed to John Peck, who in turn sold part of his land to Robert Fletcher with a written understanding that the title had not been impaired by the annulment of the land grants by the Georgia state legislature. Fletcher sued Peck for breach of this covenant, but in essence Fletcher was testing whether the act of the Georgia legislature that impaired the original sale and its contract was valid. Fletcher and Peck were business associates and appear to have been using this collusive case to test the legality of the annulment of the land grants.

Thus the question before the Supreme Court was whether or not the original land grant by Georgia, despite its fraudulence, was binding. Landholders argued that the CONTRACT CLAUSE of Article I, Section 10 of the Constitution and the constitutional prohibition against ex post facto laws barred the state from rescinding, by its subsequent legislative action in 1796, the original legislative contract granting the land. Attorneys for the state of Georgia contended that the state was permitted to declare the contracts void because the original legislative contract of 1795 was based on fraud and thus, they argued, the private contracts based on that act were also fraudulent. They also argued that the contract clause was intended to protect against the annulment of private contracts and was not applicable to the states.

Writing for the unanimous Court, Chief Justice John Marshall recognized the fraud involved in the original contract entered into by the state of Georgia but nevertheless held that the state was bound by the contracts selling the land. By holding that contracts are binding upon states as well as individuals, Marshall's opinion increased the force and importance of the contract clause and of the federal judiciary in relation to the states.

BIBLIOGRAPHY

Ackerman, Bruce A. *Private Property and the Constitution.* New Haven, Conn.: Yale University Press, 1977.

Magrath, C. Peter. *Yazoo: Law and Politics in the New Republic.* Providence, R.I.: Brown University Press, 1966.

Akiba J. Covitz
Esa Lianne Sferra
Meredith L. Stewart

See also **Judicial Review.**

FLOGGING refers to a common form of punishment used against criminals and military personnel to maintain good order. Its popularity lasted until the end of the colonial period, when the Quakers began agitation against its use. By the end of the American Revolution (1775–1783), the practice of flogging had significantly declined. In 1799, federal law limited a commander to the application of no more than twelve lashes with a whip of knotted rawhide or a cat-of-nine-tails (several bound leather strips) to a seaman's back except in cases of court-martial. But abuse of this practice was common. In Delaware, flogging could be administered as punishment for twenty-five different crimes. Flogging with whipping posts continued in penal institutions until 1900. The navy and merchant marine maintained the policy in the name of good maritime discipline and order.

In *Two Years Before the Mast* (1840), Richard Henry Dana Jr. realistically depicted the wretched conditions at sea and significantly contributed to reforms. While Dana had a distinguished legal and reform career, he reached the zenith of his influence with this book. In 1850, an antiflogging clause was added to the Naval Appropriations Bill for 1851, though the Navy Department lobbied against its passage. Three years later, Senator Robert Field Stockton of California was instrumental in implementing further restrictions on military flogging. On 17 July 1862, Congress completely abolished the practice.

BIBLIOGRAPHY

Colvin, Mark. *Penitentiaries, Reformatories, and Chain Gangs: Social Theory and the History of Punishment in Nineteenth-Century America.* New York: St. Martin's Press, 1997. A grim examination of the historical context of control and manipulation.

Hathaway, Jane, ed. *Rebellion, Repression, Reinvention: Mutiny in Comparative Perspective.* Westport, Conn.: Praeger, 2001. Historical analysis of the fear of mutiny and the quest for authority and order.

Donald K. Pickens

FLOODS AND FLOOD CONTROL. Floods are caused by the excessive accumulation of water over a short time in a specific area and may arise naturally or because of human factors. In the United States, floods can occur in any season and geographic region, and can be destructive to human property and life.

Types of Floods

Floods in the United States are of several types. Regional floods occur when winter or spring rains, often with snowmelt, inundate river basins over large areas. Heavy precipitation, snowmelt, and impervious frozen soils caused the March 1936 New England flood and the January 1996 winter flood in the northeastern United States. Flash floods are rapid rises in water of high velocity associated with intense or extended rainfall. Desert arroyos, along with urban and mountainous areas with steep topography and impervious surfaces, are prone to flash floods. A flash flood in Willow Creek, Oregon, destroyed the town of Heppner on 14 June 1903, resulting in 225 fatalities; in June 1972, rain in excess of fifteen inches in five hours caused flash floods in Rapid City, South Dakota, causing 237 deaths. Ice-jam floods occur on frozen rivers. Rising river water produces ice floes that create dams in shallow channels, causing water to back up; ice-dam failure releases a torrent of water downstream. Destructive ice-jam floods occurred in February 1981 in the Delaware River of New York and Pennsylvania and at the confluence of the Mississippi and Missouri Rivers in Illinois and Missouri in December 1989.

Storm-surge floods occur when water is pushed ashore by winds generated by severe storms. Extensive storm surge was caused by Hurricane Camille along the Gulf Coast in August 1969 and Hurricanes Dennis and Floyd in North Carolina in September 1999. Dam- and levee-failure floods occur when a structure is overtopped or destroyed by heavy flows, causing a flash flood. The infamous Johnstown Flood of 31 May–1 June 1889, a major nineteenth-century flood, occurred when an earthen dam on the Little Conemaugh River in Pennsylvania gave way, unleashing a torrent that caused twenty-two hundred deaths. Debris, landslide, and mudflow floods occur when mud, rocks, or logs dam a river channel; flash flooding occurs when the dam is breached. The eruption of Mount St. Helens caused a mudflow flood on 18 May 1980 that resulted in sixty deaths and untold property destruction along the Toutle and Cowlitz Rivers in Washington State.

Property and Human Losses

Property damage from floods in the United States averaged an estimated $5.9 billion yearly from 1955 to 1999. The most costly flood in U.S. history was the Great Flood of 1993, involving the Mississippi and Missouri Rivers, which caused economic losses of around $20 billion in nine states. Other costly floods of the twentieth century include the eastern North Carolina flood (Hurricanes Floyd and Dennis) in September 1999 ($6 billion); Red River Flood in North Dakota and Minnesota in April and May 1997 ($2 billion); May 1995 floods in south-central states (from $6 billion to $8 billion); floods from January to March 1995 in California ($3 billion); floods from December 1996 to January 1997 in the Pacific Northwest

Evacuation. In this 1998 photograph by David J. Phillip, members of the National Guard drive through heavily flooded streets of Wharton, Texas, to help residents evacuate safely. Despite their efforts, more than two dozen died. AP/Wide World Photos

($2–3 billion); and June 1972 floods (Hurricane Agnes) in the northeastern states ($3.2 billion). Five states led the nation in average estimated yearly flood losses from 1955 thorough 1999: Pennsylvania ($682 million), California ($521 million), Louisiana ($320 million), Iowa ($312 million), and Texas ($276 million). Pennsylvania alone sustained over $2.1 billion in damages from Hurricane Agnes in 1972, making it the worst natural disaster in the state's history.

The United States averaged 110 flood-related deaths yearly from 1940 though 1999. The greatest flood-related loss of life occurred in September 1900 when a storm-surge flood devastated Galveston Island, Texas, causing six thousand deaths. Other fatal floods of the twentieth century include the statewide flood of March and April 1913 in Ohio, resulting in 467 deaths, and the storm-surge flood of September 1938 in the Northeast, causing 494 deaths. Storm-surge floods have historically caused the greatest flood-related fatalities in the United States because of storm ferocity and the large population densities in coastal zones. Vehicle-related flood fatalities, usually caused by flash floods, have increased sharply in recent years. Of the 320 flood-caused deaths recorded in 1998–2001, 177 (55 percent) were vehicle-related.

Flood Control Measures

Human fatalities and property losses prompted extensive flood control efforts in the United States during the nineteenth and twentieth centuries. Artificial levees were first built to contain floodwaters in New Orleans in 1726 and became the favored flood control method along the Mississippi River in the 1800s. Recognizing both the economic potential and destructive force of the Mississippi River, Congress established the Mississippi River Commission on 28 June 1879 to formulate flood control and navigation policies for the river. The Army Corps of Engineers, dominant on the commission, favored a levee-based policy of flood control for the Mississippi, and by 1895, the federal government was sponsoring levee construction along the river. During the Great Flood of March though June 1927, the Mississippi overflowed its banks and destroyed levees in 170 counties, causing an estimated $230 million in damage and more than three hundred fatalities. This event renewed congressional efforts to control Mississippi River floods, resulting in the Federal Flood Control Acts of 1928 and 1936. These acts authorized construction of a system of levees, dams, and reservoirs to confine the river to a single channel. Between 1932 and 1955, channelization efforts straightened the normally meandering Mississippi River by 146 miles, and by 1990, twenty-six dams and thousands of miles of dikes and levees hemmed the river. An extensive effort was made to control river flows and floods nationwide in the twentieth century, often in conjunction with hydroelectric development. By 1990, only forty-two free-flowing rivers longer than 125 miles, out of an original total of 3.2 million miles, occurred in the conterminous United States.

In the twenty-first century, floods are pragmatically viewed as both beneficial and destructive. Floods can be used to restore fish and wildlife habitat degraded by flood control projects. In March 1996, the first artificial flood in the United States was conducted on the Colorado River (dammed in 1963) to rebuild sandbars and restore habitat for endangered fishes. Though the effort was considered a success, studies done in 2002 show that the river has returned to its pre-flood state, prompting calls for additional floods.

BIBLIOGRAPHY

Barry, John M. *Rising Tide: The Great Mississippi Flood of 1927 and How It Changed America.* New York: Simon and Schuster, 1998.

Lauber, Patricia. *Flood: Wrestling with the Mississippi.* Washington, D.C.: National Geographic Society, 1996.

McCullough, David. *The Johnstown Flood.* New York: Simon and Schuster, 1987.

McNeill, J. R. *Something New under the Sun: An Environmental History of the Twentieth-Century World.* New York: Norton, 2000.

McPhee, John. *The Control of Nature.* New York: Farrar, Straus, and Giroux, 1989.

Charles E. Williams

See also **Disasters; Engineers, Corps of; Johnstown Flood; River and Harbor Improvements.**

FLOOR LEADER. Floor leaders are senators and representatives elected at the beginning of each Congress by their respective parties. They champion party positions, drive legislative strategy, rally support and orchestrate roll call votes. Although key members of Congress were referred to by the press as party leaders in the nineteenth century, the Democrats did not formally designate floor leaders until 1920, the Republicans in 1925.

The ruling party's selection becomes the majority leader. This person establishes the daily legislative schedule. When several members seek to address the chamber, the majority leader has the right of first recognition. This power allows the leader to propose amendments, substitutes, and motions before any other.

BIBLIOGRAPHY

Ardis, Lawrence, ed. *Party Leaders in Congress, 1789–2002: Vital Statistics and Biographical Sketches.* New York: Nova Science Publishers, 2002.

Christine M. Roane

FLORIDA. The state of Florida consists of a peninsula and a strip of mainland at the southeastern corner of the United States. It is bounded on the west by the Gulf of Mexico and on the east by the Atlantic Ocean. The Gulf Stream runs only a few miles off the southeastern coast. Low-lying barrier islands and mangrove swamps fringe the long, flat coastline. Lake Okeechobee lies near the center of the peninsula. The Everglades, a grassy waterland, once extended over nearly all of southern Florida but is now restricted to the southwestern tip of the peninsula.

The first humans reached Florida at least twelve thousand years ago, at the end of the last Ice Age. Because sea level was lower then, Florida was much larger, with the Gulf coast some 100 miles west of its current position. The first people found a drier, cooler climate than today, in which they hunted and gathered edible plants, collected shellfish, and used the fibers of palms and saw palmetto to make rope and mats. As the glaciers melted and the sea level rose, Florida shrank, and the climate grew wetter and hotter. The human population grew, with major centers at the present-day Saint Johns River, Tampa Bay, and Belle Glade. By 2000 B.C. people were living in villages and making pottery; by 750 A.D. they were growing corn.

European Exploration and Settlement

Juan Ponce de León sailed along the eastern coast of the peninsula in 1513 and named it La Florida because of its lush beauty and because it was the season of Pascua Florida, the Easter feast of flowers. In 1521 Ponce de León tried to establish a settlement in southern Florida but the local Indians quickly drove him off. In 1528 Pánfilo de Narváez landed at Tampa Bay with three hundred men and forty horses and disappeared into the wilderness. Eight years later the last four survivors of his expedition stumbled back to Mexico. Landing somewhere on Florida's Gulf coast in 1539, Hernando de Soto marched north on an unsuccessful trek that covered four thousand miles in four years.

The next European attempt to settle Florida came from French Huguenots, who built Fort Caroline on the Saint Johns River in 1564. Alarmed, Spain sent Pedro Menéndez de Avilés in 1565 to wipe out Fort Caroline and establish a permanent Spanish presence. This settlement, Saint Augustine, remains the oldest continually inhabited European settlement in North America. As French and English interests grew in North America, Saint Augustine anchored the Spanish hold on the Caribbean. But during the Seven Years' War, Spain joined the French against the English, who seized Havana. To recover the Cuban city, the Spanish surrendered Florida in 1763. Diseases introduced by Europeans had already decimated the natives, and the last few indigenous Floridians joined the Spanish exodus to Cuba when the British took over.

British Rule

The British divided Florida at the Apalachicola River. West Florida extended as far as the Mississippi. With the Spanish gone, there were almost no whites in either territory. Peninsular Florida was still a wilderness of mangrove swamp, sawgrass, and everglades. The SEMINOLES, who had moved south into Florida beginning around 1700, maintained peaceful relations with the British.

The British crown offered settlers free land in Florida, often in tracts of thousands of acres. At first landholders used free labor and indentured servants, who balked at the brutal work. Therefore plantation owners began to import slaves. Since Indians could escape, and suffered terribly from European-borne diseases, the new owners brought in enslaved Africans. Under the Spanish, slavery had been relatively humane, and many free blacks thrived in Florida. The British brought the much harsher chattel slavery to Florida.

Coastal Florida was infertile, the cost of living high, the tropical fevers lethal. Nonetheless, the British began to squeeze profits from the new territories. Besides producing timber for the treeless West Indies, tar and pitch for ships, and furs and deerskins, West Florida maintained a vigorous clandestine trade with Spanish-controlled New Orleans. East Florida, where the plantations were larger, produced indigo and naval stores, and carried out an embryonic commerce in oranges, which the Spanish had introduced.

Florida remained loyalist throughout the American Revolution. American forces invaded Florida on several raids but the greatest danger came from Spain, eager to recover its old colony. A vigorous Spanish campaign took back West Florida, and when the British finally settled the issue with the Americans in the Treaty of Paris in 1783, they ceded Florida back to Spain, which was in no position to enjoy the recovery. The infant United States of America wanted Florida, and European troubles allowed her to take the territories piecemeal. In 1810 local people west of the Perdido proclaimed a Republic of West Florida, which the United States absorbed in 1812. Over the next several years, the pro-British Seminoles raided Alabama and Georgia, culminating in the first Seminole War (1817–1818). Andrew Jackson invaded West Florida in 1818 and took Pensacola. Although he eventually with-

drew, the Spanish grip on Florida was clearly failing. Spain entered into negotiations with the United States, ceded Florida to the United States through the Adams-Onís Treaty in 1819, and on 17 July 1821 the American flag went up.

U.S. Territory and State

Florida was organized as a territory in 1822, and Jackson became its first governor. In 1824 Tallahassee became the capital, and the surrounding area rapidly became the dominant region. The cotton-growing counties surrounding Tallahassee produced 80 percent of the territory's crop. In 1830 Florida's census recorded a total population of more than 33,000, of whom 16,000 lived in the area around Tallahassee, so-called Middle Florida. In 1845 Florida was granted admission to the Union as a slave state.

Throughout this period, small farmers from Georgia and the Carolinas, often called crackers, were migrating to Florida. While the Tallahassee planters grew their cotton and the large landowners south of Saint Augustine turned to sugar cane, the crackers built small farms to raise cattle, corn, vegetables, tobacco, and citrus fruit. These newcomers quickly came into conflict with the Seminoles. Tensions between white settlers and the Indians grew, and white landowners pressed the government to wipe out or remove the Indians. The federal government's efforts to do so led to the second Seminole War (1835–1842), following which only a few hundred Seminoles remained in Florida. These isolated, outnumbered bands fought a third Seminole War (1855–1858), after which attempts to remove the few remaining Seminoles ceased.

At the beginning of the Civil War, the Union seized Saint Augustine, and the small Union garrison at Pensacola managed to hold on against a much larger Confederate force under Braxton Bragg. Conscription gangs roamed the countryside forcing men into the Confederate Army; more than 16,000 Florida men (from a total white population of about 77,746 in the 1860 Census) went north to fight for the Confederacy. Left behind to fend for themselves were women, old men, and children, and more than sixty thousand slaves, all trapped inside the Union blockade. Most lived in direst poverty. Florida's civic structure collapsed.

After the Civil War, Federal troops occupied the state to enforce RECONSTRUCTION. Radical Republicans, composed of Unionist Floridians (scalawags), newly arrived Northerners (carpetbaggers), and recently enfranchised blacks, dominated the constitutional convention of 1868; but a white conservative faction managed to lock the radicals out and ram through its own constitution. However odd its inception, this document allowed the army to give Florida back to civil government, and the battle for control heated up in earnest. White Democrats were devoted to restoring Florida to the same social order it had known before the war. Republican Harrison Reed of Massachusetts was elected the first postwar governor in 1868, but he spent his nearly five years in office fighting off impeachment efforts.

Meanwhile, white conservatives worked to undermine the Republican base by intimidating black voters. Even during the war, occupying Federal authorities had broken up confiscated lands and distributed them to blacks, but after Lincoln's murder Federal policy reversed, the lands were returned to their original owners, and the blacks were kicked off. Discriminatory local laws, the Ku Klux Klan, and even cavalry charges into lines of voters terrorized former slaves. By 1881 the Democratic Party was in charge of the government, and a new constitution in 1885 imposed segregation and a poll tax. For the next eighty years all state elections were decided within the Democratic Party. Florida was still largely a frontier state, isolated and wretchedly poor. Sharecropping and tenant farming dominated agriculture. The state government was largely insolvent. With the lowest literacy rate in the south, the governor in 1876 nonetheless proposed eliminating public high schools.

Still, the seeds of modern Florida were germinating. The balmy climate had attracted tourists as early as the 1840s. By 1873, 50,000 people a year were boating up the Saint Johns River. New railroads, used at first to transport lumber, made other areas of the state accessible; economic troubles in the north encouraged people to move down into peninsular Florida. In 1880 the population was 269,493, of whom 126,690 were black. Beginning in 1883 Henry Flagler, an associate of John D. Rockefeller, developed resorts on Florida's Atlantic coast, starting at

Saint Augustine. His East Coast Railroad reached West Palm Beach in 1894, bringing tourists and supplies to the extravagant resort hotels Flagler built there. The 1894–1895 freezes, which destroyed the citrus crop in the north, convinced Flagler to build on into Miami, where heiress Julia Tuttle had founded an ambitious but empty city. The Spanish-American War, with its bases in Tampa and Key West, further stimulated the economy. By 1912 Flagler's railroad had reached Key West, then a sleepy fishing and cigar-making community. The railroad linked Florida from its southernmost tip to the continental United States. The opening of the Panama Canal brought a steady increase in commerce to the area. Nonetheless, political power remained with North Florida.

Ongoing political dissension split the dominant Democratic Party, pitting "wool hats" (farmers and small businessmen) against "silk hats" (wealthy businessmen and landowners). Farmers black and white found common ground in the Florida Farmers Alliance, whose Ocala Demands formed the basis for the platform of the national Populist Party formed in 1891. The threat of empowerment of black Floridians led to a savage backlash among whites; new laws segregated blacks and locked them into poverty and powerlessness. Yet blacks kept striving for equality, and whites resorted to increasing force to keep them down, including lynchings and the burning of black towns.

The Rise of South Florida

The Panama Canal brought another boon to Florida: weapons against the dreaded yellow fever. Terrifying epidemics of the "black vomit" had swept the state for years; the techniques that cleared the steaming jungles of Panama soon tamed the disease in Florida as well. Nonetheless, the state remained too poor to attract investors. Napoleon Bonaparte Broward, elected governor in 1904, was a wool hat liberal; he began the reclamation of the Everglades, building canals to drain off the water. In 1900 the census counted 528,542 people in Florida; 1910, there were 752,619.

The Progressive movement sweeping the nation influenced Florida as well. Progressives demanded socially responsible government; May Mann Jennings, the wife of Governor William Sherman Jennings, promoted conservation, Seminole reservations, education, and public libraries. In 1905 the Buckman Act established the University of Florida for white men, the Florida Female College for women, and the Colored Normal School for blacks.

World War I brought a new boom to Florida. Flying schools took advantage of the consistent good weather and Key West was the site of a major submarine base. Toward Prohibition Florida exhibited the same fractured sensibility as the rest of the nation. Much of the state had passed local dry laws even before the Volstead Act of 1919; yet the long coastline and steady high demand made Florida a major nexus of liquor smuggling.

During the 1920s Florida experienced a spectacular land boom, especially in Miami Beach, Dade County, up and down both coasts, and into central Florida. Speculators designed and sold whole communities, like Coral Gables and Boca Raton. Between 1922 and 1925, 300,000 people arrived in Florida. The 1930 census showed a population of 1,468,211 (29 percent black). Many people arrived in cars, feeding the motel industry. Land values soared.

In 1926, like a harbinger of bad times to come, a terrible hurricane killed four hundred people and left five thousand homeless. The great boom was fizzling out. Undermined by speculation, banks began to fail; Florida was in a depression before the rest of the nation followed in 1930. The railroads went bankrupt; there was no money and no work. The state had no funds for relief, and no inclination to deliver it anyway. Local agencies took over as best they could. By 1932, 36 percent of blacks and 22 percent of whites were on relief.

In the 1932 presidential election Franklin Delano Roosevelt won Florida with 74 percent of the vote. The index of industrial production continued to drop, Prohibition was repealed in 1933, and Roosevelt's New Deal steadied the banks and provided employment through public works. In 1931 Florida had legalized pari-mutuel gambling, and thoroughbreds, greyhounds, and jai alai become major revenue producers. By 1934 tourism was making a comeback.

The New Deal stabilized Florida's economy but World War II ended the Great Depression. After Pearl Harbor, military bases opened around the state and the shipbuilding industry boomed. This resulted in a labor shortage, which authorities in some areas dealt with by rounding up "vagrants," mostly black, and putting them into peonage. The sugar industry, booming after the fall of the Philippines, was especially bad, with labor conditions like prison camps.

In 1940 the population of Florida was 1,897,414, making it the least populated state in the Southeast. Between 1940 and 1990 an average of 1.8 million people entered Florida each decade. Air conditioning and mosquito controls made South Florida livable in the summer. Key West, nearly bankrupt in the 1930s, got a new water pipeline from the federal government in 1942, and its population tripled by the end of the war. Miami and the Gold Coast above it was transformed as new military recruits came there to train, many stationed in luxury hotels because of the severe housing shortage. These recruits included blacks, who fought with distinction in the war, and chafed angrily under Jim Crow laws at home.

After the war Florida was clearly divided into two camps: the north, which clung to Jim Crow, and the south, which, flooded with newcomers, felt no attachment to customary norms and practices. Still the north controlled the state government: less than 20 percent of the population elected more than half the legislature. The stage was set for a major confrontation between Jim Crow and the civil rights movement.

Modern Florida

In 1954, when the U.S. Supreme Court struck down segregated education in *Brown v. Board of Education,* white supremacists struggled to hold the color line, but blacks now had the federal government on their side. In 1949, five black students challenged the segregation of the University of Florida, and in 1959 the courts finally ordered the institution open to African Americans. Martin Luther King went to Saint Augustine in 1964 to preach and lead protest marches that drew national news attention. At the same time flourishing industries were realizing that race riots were bad for business. In 1968 another state constitution shifted legislative control to the south and modernized the government. Claude Kirk (1967–1971) became the first Republican governor since Reconstruction and in 1992 the first black Floridians in over a hundred years went to the House of Representatives. Leander Shaw in 1990 became the first black chief justice of the Florida supreme court.

Liberated from the long race war, which had sucked up the energies and suppressed the aspirations of so many, Florida transformed itself. No longer part of the Deep South, it now belonged to the Sunbelt, affluent and modern. Its business-friendly politics and balmy climate attracted growth industries. Starting in 1950, rockets from Cape Canaveral sent people into space and to the moon. Housing construction, high technology, and tourism pushed agriculture into the background of the economy. Disney World, opened in Orlando in 1965, drew millions of tourists a year, feeding the hotel and airline industries.

Florida's population was diversifying as it grew. In the thirty years after Fidel Castro seized power in Cuba in 1959, more than 800,000 Cubans moved to the Miami area. Haitians and Nicaraguans also fled to Florida from oppressive regimes in their homelands. People from all over Latin America and beyond came seeking jobs and advancement. From the northern states, retirees flooded into the sunshine and warmth. By 1990, 25 percent of the population was elderly. In 1990 the census counted 12,937,926 people, only 30 percent of them native Floridians.

This human tidal wave devastated Florida's natural environment. Starting at the turn of the twentieth century, developers drained the Everglades, diked Lake Okeechobee, and built high-rise hotels and condominiums on beaches and barrier islands—communities built not to exploit a local resource or serve local needs but simply to provide people a place to go that was not home. Rapid development strained water and energy supplies. The danger of such development in a hurricane zone was amply illustrated in August 1992, when Hurricane Andrew leveled extreme south Florida, killing more than 20 people and causing $20 billion in damage.

In 2000 Florida decided a presidential election. With the presidency in the balance, Democrat Albert Gore contested election results in Florida (where the governor was the brother of the Republican candidate, George W. Bush), demanding a recount; the subsequent confusion finally ended up in the U.S. Supreme Court, which stopped the recount and awarded the election to Bush.

In fifty years Florida evolved from the poorest and most isolated part of the South to a cosmopolitan, multicultural society, a winter playground for millions from the icy north, and a tourist mecca for the entire world. In 2000 the population was 15,982,378, and still growing.

BIBLIOGRAPHY

Gannon, Michael, ed. *The New History of Florida.* Gainesville: University Press of Florida, 1996.

Newton, Michael. *The Invisible Empire: The Ku Klux Klan in Florida.* Gainesville: University Press of Florida, 2001.

Storter, Rob. *Crackers in the Glade: Life and Times in the Old Everglades.* Edited and compiled by Betty Savidge Briggs. Athens: University of Georgia Press, 2000.

Williams, Joy. *The Florida Keys: A History and Guide.* 9th ed. New York: Random House, 2000.

Cecelia Holland

See also **Everglades National Park; Jim Crow Laws; Removal Act of 1830; Seminole Wars;** *and vol. 9:* **Maya in Exile: Guatemalans in Florida.**

FLORIDA, STRAITS OF, also called the New Bahama Channel and the Gulf of Florida, connect the Gulf of Mexico with the Atlantic Ocean and separate Florida from Cuba. Through them flows a part of the Gulf Stream, past the Great Bahama and Little Bahama banks. The total length of the straits exceeds 300 miles. The width varies from 60 to 100 miles. The main channel has been sounded to a depth of 6,000 feet. Traffic through the straits, beginning with the passage of Spanish treasure fleets, has always been heavy and significant. Until early in the nineteenth century, this region was also a site of extensive piracy.

BIBLIOGRAPHY

Buker, George E. *Blockaders, Refugees, and Contrabands: Civil War on Florida's Gulf Coast, 1861–1865.* Tuscaloosa: University of Alabama Press, 1993.

A. J. Hanna / H. S.

See also **Mexico, Gulf of; Piracy.**

FLOUR MILLING

Technology

American colonists in the seventeenth century introduced European grains along the eastern seaboard from Virginia to Massachusetts, built the first windmills and water mills, and developed New York as a milling and marketing center for flour. Until the mid-eighteenth century there was

Crossing the Straits of Florida. Cuban refugees packed into the freighter *Red Diamond* head for the United States on 2 June 1980. © CORBIS

little reason for colonial mills to produce for other than local consumption.

England manipulated colonial trade with bounties, tariffs, and regulated markets that favored production of goods other than flour. The export trade was also limited by food needs in the colonies and the difficulties presented by transportation. Maryland, for example, feared famine and prohibited wheat and flour exports until 1740. After 1750 markets developed in the West Indies—particularly Barbados, Jamaica, and the Leeward Islands—because profitable sugar production there excluded almost all other husbandry. Between 1763 and 1766, Philadelphia exported 350,000 barrels of flour, mostly to the West Indies.

Colonial milling, whether by wind- or waterpower, involved much human labor. Stonedressing and millwrighting required skill, but carrying sacks of grain and flour called for constant heavy work. Since millers' tolls were usually fixed by law, the cost of labor figured importantly in profit and loss. Oliver Evans deserves credit for first engineering a mill in which grain and meal moved mechanically (completed 1785). His *Young Mill-Wright and Miller's Guide*, published in Philadelphia in 1795, described a continuous system of elevators, conveyors, and other automatic devices to process wheat "from wagon to wagon again." Evans's milling machinery constituted the beginning of automation in industry.

After the Revolution and until about 1830, Baltimore was the leading flour trade center in America. Its resources were abundant waterpower on the fall line, boat access to wheat lands in both the Chesapeake Coastal Plain and the Virginia Piedmont, millers who quickly adopted Evans's automatic machinery, and merchants who concentrated on the exchange of flour and grain for European manufactured goods. The wars of the French Revolution and Napoleon opened Britain's Atlantic ports to American goods. Baltimore merchants sold flour in England, the West Indies, and to the Duke of Wellington's army fighting in the Iberian Peninsula. This trade, and the resulting milling prosperity, lasted until 1814, when the British Corn Laws virtually shut off these markets.

While South American sales accounted for most American flour shipments from 1815 to 1860, the limited extent of the market justified little expansion in merchant milling. Important technological developments in farming, transportation, and grain storage, however, established the potential for rapid growth during and after the Civil War. Inventions of agricultural machinery allowed farmers to grow and handle grain in greater amounts: Cyrus McCormick's reaper (1831); John Deere's plow (1837); the Pitts brothers'—Hiram and John—thresher (1837); and William Pennock's grain drill (1841). The Erie Canal, opened in 1825, cut freight costs between the Genesee Valley and New York by 90 percent per ton. Railroads, from 1830 onward, tapped new agricultural lands. Improved transportation created a surplus of agricultural products that forced some farmers to specialize in wheat and others in dairy, vegetables, or livestock. Joseph Dart installed automatic machinery in his mills at Buffalo and applied steam power to operate grain storage elevators in 1843.

Before 1860 American millers ground soft winter wheat between millstones set close together. "Low" milling extracted as much meal as was possible from one grinding. Necessarily, the close grinding pulverized the wheat berry—bran, flour, germ, and all. Wheat germ enzymes and bran moisture impaired the flour's durability. By 1870, millers, particularly in Minneapolis, were experimenting with a European technique of "high" grinding and gradual reduction. This "new process" involved several (usually from three to five) grindings with the stones set progressively closer. The initial breaks stripped off the outermost bran covering and granulated the middlings (that part of the kernel between the inner endosperm and the outer pericarp layers). Bolting between grindings helped separate the bran from the flour. High grinding and gradual reduction produced a finer flour and more flour per bushel of wheat. Cadwallader C. Washburn, Charles A. Pillsbury, and George H. Christian took the lead in installing this most important advancement since Evans's automatic mill. Minneapolis flour shipments rose from 1 million to 5 million barrels between 1876 and 1884.

Hard spring wheat, grown increasingly in the Dakotas and Minnesota after 1865, required certain improvements in the gradual-reduction system. Besides its different growing habit, hard spring wheat had both a higher gluten content and a more easily shattered bran than the soft winter variety. Better grinding and separating methods were therefore necessary. In 1873 Edmund La Croix and George T. Smith, both in Minneapolis, patented middlings purifiers that separated the dust, bran, middlings, and flour more completely by blowing air through screens so meshed as to sort the different particles. Middlings purifiers actually date from well before 1873, but La Croix's patent improved the middlings grading arrangement while introducing the machine to America.

Chilled iron corrugated rollers began to replace millstones for grinding at about the same time the middlings purifier was introduced. Roller breaking, perfected in Hungary, twisted the grain rather than crushing or shearing it. It allowed more precise spacing between the grinding surfaces and more even stock-feeding than burrstones. The result was a more refined chop at each step in reduction. The first important American mill to use rollers was Washburn's in 1878. The main Pillsbury mill, in 1884, had a daily flour capacity of 5,000 barrels, using a steam-powered, automatic, all-roller, gradual-reduction system. Minneapolis flour shipments rose from 5 million to 10 million barrels between 1884 and 1894.

Several other inventions and adaptations improved overall plant operation. Germ scalpers—machines that sifted off wheat germ after flattening it out—came into use after R. L. Downton's invention in 1875. Carl Haggenmacher, a Hungarian, patented a plansifter in 1888 that improved the separation of the chop between grindings. O. M. Morse invented a "cyclone" dust collector in 1886 that reduced the hazard of explosions in mills. Electric power came into use in the operation of mills as early as 1887, in Laramie, Wyo., but steam- and waterpower predominated until about 1920.

The economies brought about by the automatic, all-roller, gradual-reduction system favored those companies that adopted it first and on a large scale. Washburn, Crosby and Company; the Pillsbury Company; Northwestern Consolidated Milling; and Minneapolis Flour Manufacturing Company became leaders in plant efficiency and productive capacity. The large companies invested in projects supplying them with wheat: Pillsbury operated a string of grain elevators; Washburn helped project the Minneapolis–Saint Louis Railroad. Smaller mills could hardly compete with the industry's giants. During the depression of the 1870s many less efficient mills went out of business. The movement toward concentration created the "flour trust" in the 1890s. Thomas A. McIntyre organized the trust, the United States Flour Milling Company, in 1898, after acquiring mills and elevators in New York and Minnesota. Trusts, as management manipulations, more often brought excesses in unfair competition, price fixing, overcapitalization, and speculation than in improved products. The Sherman and Clayton antitrust laws helped curb the monopoly trend.

A decline in demand for flour in foreign markets and the growth of southwestern and Pacific Coast wheat regions geographically decentralized the milling industry. Europeans had developed their milling operations to the extent that they required more wheat and less flour from the United States. Between 1889 and 1899, wheat exports rose from 46 million to 139 million bushels. Kansas, Oklahoma, and Texas produced enormous quantities of hard winter wheat, while California and Washington grew large amounts of white wheat. Kansas City, Dallas, Seattle, and San Francisco developed as milling centers as well as grain markets. Buffalo, on the Great Lakes, took the lead from Minneapolis as the largest milling center after 1920. The Chicago Board of Trade became a major institution in the grain exchange. Wheat production continued to rise until shortly after World War I; during the

Great Depression, both wheat production and flour consumption fell.

The development of quality-control procedures allowed product standardization, no matter where flour was manufactured or sold. Testing flour for strength and quality became standard procedure after A. W. Howard set up the first testing laboratory in Minneapolis in 1886. By the early twentieth century the major milling companies operated scientific laboratories not only to test the baking qualities of flour but to find industrial uses for wheat derivatives. Fabric sizing, dye thickeners, and paper adhesives derived from the starch, while low-grade gluten proved useful in waxes and paints.

Besides general-purpose flour, mills after 1900 manufactured breakfast cereals and special pastry, cake, and pancake flours—some including leavening ingredients. Marketing specialists realized that the best way to sell flour was to make it easy to use. General Mills introduced "Bisquick" in 1930 and followed with a variety of boxed, ready-to-use flour mixes. During World War II the National Research Council recommended that flour for military use be vitamin-enriched. Thereafter millers commonly added thiamine, riboflavin, niacin, and iron to household flour. The introduction of enriched flour reduced the incidence of some vitamin-deficiency diseases and eliminated others.

The most significant new advance in milling technology since the 1870s was made after World War II when engineers devised a mechanical system for refining flour, beyond ordinary milling, using airflow dynamics. Turbogrinders, introduced by Pillsbury Mills in 1959, generate high-velocity air vortices in which flour particles become smaller as they rub against each other. Air classifiers then separate the micron-sized particles into protein and starch fractions. With air grinding and classification, millers can process flours of two or three times the normal protein content.

Airflow systems have also been used in conveying and storing flour since the mid-1960s. Pneumatic conveyors have largely replaced bucket elevators, eliminating certain dust and insect problems, while making one-floor mill layouts possible. The pneumatic lines connect to storage bins and from there to Air-Slide railroad cars to facilitate bulk flour transportation.

Industry

Industrial history is in many respects typified by the history of American flour milling. Significant changes in market, in techniques of production, and in business organization, complicated by the rapid westward expansion of agricultural production and the relative uncertainty of the yearly amount and quality of the wheat crop, have marked the industry. Its dynamism is revealed by its rapid and wide changes of centers of production; its frequent shifting of equipment, capital, and labor; and its continuous and broad search for improved supplies of raw material.

The earliest English settlers brought small hand mills to America, but the growth of population and the expansion of wheat crops soon necessitated the construction of larger mills. After 1700, mills supplied with an abundance of wheat from the rich farmlands of the Middle Atlantic region met domestic needs as well as the demands of markets in Europe and in the West Indies. By 1750 Philadelphia was a leading flour center. Trade-conscious merchants purchased the products of nearby mills, hoping either to ship the barreled staple worldwide or to speculate on the domestic grain market, which in the 1750s became lucrative for the first time. By 1780 a combination of new technology, geography, waterpower, grain supply, and entrepreneurial skill had produced American milling centers of unusual capacity, such as the Brandywine Mills on Brandywine Creek near Wilmington, Del. This group of twelve "merchant mills" (so called because they ground specifically for export, as opposed to "custom mills," which supplied local needs) ground annually more than 50,000 barrels of flour of all grades—superfine, common, middling, ship stuff, and cornmeal. One-half of the total production was superfine flour.

Large-scale milling began with the growth of Baltimore and Richmond as milling centers in the first half of the nineteenth century. By 1860 Rochester, N.Y., supplied with the fine white wheat of the Genesee Valley, and Saint Louis and Milwaukee, supplied with the surrounding region's soft red winter wheat, were the leading flour-manufacturing centers. After 1870 the mills in Minneapolis burgeoned, aided by the concentration of wheat growing in Minnesota and the Dakotas, a ready source of waterpower in Saint Anthony Falls, and the invention of the middlings purifier, which made possible the milling of superior flour from spring wheat. C. A. Pillsbury and Company was organized in Minneapolis in 1874. In 1880, Minneapolis produced more than 2 million barrels of flour, and the local millers combined to form the Pillsbury-Washburn Flour Mills Company, the Northwestern Consolidated Milling Company, and the United States Flour Milling Company in an attempt to organize a monopoly of milling from hard spring wheat. The rapid spread of hard red winter wheat in Kansas and the Southwest encouraged the growth of milling in Kansas City in the 1890s.

Changes in the locations of wheat-growing areas and transportation, the introduction of the Alsop process of artificial bleaching in 1904, and the beginning of large-scale commercial baking have influenced milling since 1900. Cheap power, ready access to the great consumer markets, the opportunity to mill Canadian wheat in bond for export, and the relatively low freight rates for wheat on the Great Lakes speeded the rise of Buffalo, N.Y., as the leading milling center in the twentieth century. The growth of competition in flour marketing and changes in flour consumption stimulated the formation of such regional and national combinations as Pillsbury Flour Mills

(1923), General Mills (1928), and Gold Dust Corporation (1929) and its subsidiaries.

Flour millers played an important role in conditioning public acceptance of the assembly line and the standardization of a dietary staple. It is not accidental that public attitudes concerning cleanliness, whiteness, color, and smell were conditioned by the improvement of milling techniques as they advanced from querns (primitive hand mills) to rollers and changed flour from an oily brown home-ground substance to a snowy-white one, mass manufactured by giant corporations.

BIBLIOGRAPHY

Giedion, Siegfried. *Mechanization Takes Command.* New York: Oxford University Press, 1948.

Lockwood, J. F. *Flour Milling.* Liverpool, New York: Northern Publishing, 1952.

Matz, Samuel. *Cereal Technology.* Westport, Conn.: AVI, 1970.

Storck, John, and Walter Teague. *Flour for Man's Bread: A History of Milling.* Minneapolis: University of Minnesota Press, 1952.

Welsh, Peter C. "The Brandywine Mills: A Chronicle of an Industry, 1762–1816." *Delaware History,* vol. 7 (1956).

G. Terry Sharrer
Peter C. Welsh / C. W.

See also **Cereal Grains; Cereals, Manufacture of; Clayton Act, Labor Provisions; McCormick Reaper; Sherman Antitrust Act; Waterpower; Wheat; Windmills.**

FLYING THE HUMP. American officials in 1941 saw a vital need to keep China in World War II, yet Japan's early conquests had cut off all land routes to China. Only one air route, a very dangerous flight from airfields in eastern Assam across the High Himalayas to K'unming in China's Yunnan province, remained open. The five-hundred-mile route posed several dangers for planes of the period. It required flying at very high altitudes, adding to the dangers of violent turbulence and severe icing the dangers of enemy aircraft and frequent monsoons, which pilots encountered at any altitude. Yet, through nearly three years of war, the U.S. Army Air Forces Air Transport Command used this route as the sole means for transporting supplies and passengers to China. Begun in 1942, the airlift delivered a total of 650,000 tons, with a monthly maximum of 71,042 tons reached in July 1945. The Hump was the proving ground of massive strategic airlift, demonstrating that large amounts of material could be delivered by air and presaging the BERLIN AIRLIFT of 1948–49 and emergency deliveries to Korea in 1950.

BIBLIOGRAPHY

Craven, Wesley F., and James L. Cate, eds. *The Army Air Forces in World War II.* Volume 2. 1949. Reprint, Chicago: University of Chicago Press, 1949.

Ford, Daniel. *Flying Tigers: Claire Chennault and the American Volunteer Group.* Washington, D.C.: Smithsonian Institution Press, 1991.

Warner Stark / T. D.

See also **World War II, Air War against Japan.**

FLYING TIGERS. Throughout the 1930s and 1940s, the U.S. government was deeply involved in developing and managing Nationalist China's aviation. The most ambitious and famous undertaking to promote China's air effort against Japan entailed furnishing China with American military pilots, American-made fighter planes, and aircraft support personnel. This expedition, first called the American Volunteer Group (AVG), but later popularly known as the Flying Tigers, was surreptitiously launched by agents of China with the sanction of President Franklin D. Roosevelt and other key officials. The scheme represented the culmination of America's policy of gradual entanglement with China's cause.

The plan was conceived in large measure by Claire L. Chennault, an American military aviator, who in 1937 retired to accept employment as an adviser to the Chinese. After strenuous training under Chennault's tutelage, AVG forces divided between Rangoon and the skies over K'un-ming, which was the terminus of the Burma Road. The Flying Tigers first engaged the Japanese on 20 December 1941, over K'un-ming, and on succeeding days over Rangoon. Chennault's AVG attracted propagandists who aimed to present favorable accounts about the Pacific war. Although the Chinese technically owned and controlled the group, they allowed the AVG to operate under American auspices as the China Air Task Force. During seven months of fighting over Burma, China, Thailand, and French Indochina, the AVG destroyed approximately 300 Japanese aircraft and recorded a like number of prob-

Flying Tigers. A Chinese soldier guards American P-40 fighter planes painted with the emblem of the Flying Tigers. LIBRARY OF CONGRESS able kills, while itself never having more than fifty planes in flying condition at any given time.

BIBLIOGRAPHY

Chennault, Anna. *Chennault and the Flying Tigers.* New York: Eriksson, 1963.

Ford, Daniel. *Flying Tigers: Claire Chennault and the American Volunteer Group.* Washington, D.C.: Smithsonian Institution Press, 1991.

Schultz, Duane P. *The Maverick of War: Chennault and the Flying Tigers.* New York: St. Martin's Press, 1987.

Gordon K. Pickler
Honor Sachs

See also **Burma Road and Ledo Road; China, U.S. Armed Forces in; World War II, Air War against Japan.**

FOLGER SHAKESPEARE LIBRARY. The Folger Shakespeare Library, opened in 1932, houses the world's largest collection of Shakespearean manuscripts. Henry Clay Folger and his wife Emily Jordan Folger, both avid manuscript collectors, established the library as a repository for their collection that would be open to the American public. The Folgers chose Washington, D.C., as the place to house their collection. It took them nine years to purchase the property adjacent to the Library of Congress, one block from the U.S. capitol, and gain permission to build on it.

Henry Clay Folger, a lifelong Shakespeare collector and oil magnate (he worked for Standard Oil under John D. Rockefeller), left sufficient endowment to insure that the Folger Library and his collection would grow. Folger died two weeks after the cornerstone of the building was laid in June 1930. Emily Clay Folger presided at the opening in 1932. The library is now administered by Henry Folger's alma mater, Amherst College, as an institute of Amherst.

The collection of Shakespearean manuscripts at the library contains 229 Quarto editions of the plays and poems; 79 First Folios, 118 Second, Third, and Fourth Folios, and about 7,000 other editions of Shakespeare's works. In addition to its original Shakespeare collection, holdings now include the largest collection of pre-eighteenth century English books. The Library's Special Collections focus on the Renaissance period and include playbills, artworks, and other materials illustrative of the theater. It also holds strong collections of Early Protestant religious tracts and books of the Humanist period.

The Folger provides fellowships for a number of scholars each year to enable them to come to Washington and work daily in the Library's research rooms. In addition, the Folger sponsors several seminars each year taught by visiting faculty that are open to independent scholars and researchers. Free tours of the library are given to the public daily. As part of an extensive Education and Outreach Program, the Library sponsors free lectures and learning opportunities throughout the school year that are aimed at students from kindergarten to twelfth grade. The Folger also sponsors numerous exhibitions in its museum and gallery spaces. In 1970, the Folger made changes in its Shakespearean Theatre to allow it to sponsor a theater group and stage public performances. Additionally, the Folger supports readings by the PEN/Faulkner winners and by noted poets, as well as concerts by the Folger Consort chamber music ensemble.

The Folger building houses the 250-seat Elizabethan theatre, the museum galleries, the magnificent reading rooms, and the library space. It has been featured in architectural magazines.

BIBLIOGRAPHY

Folger Shakespeare Library. Home page at http://www.folger.edu.

Schoenbaum, S. "The World's Finest Shakespeare Library Is This Side of the Atlantic." *Smithsonian* 13, no.1 (1982): 118–127.

Susan L. Malbin

See also **Libraries; Philanthropy.**

FOLK ART. *See* **Art: Self-Taught Artists.**

FOLK MUSIC. *See* **Music: Early American, Folk Revival.**

FOLKLORE. In spite of its relatively short history, the United States has developed a rich seam of folklore that reflects both the nation's rapid transformation from agrarian to industrial and the multicultural society which has emerged from that transformation. Whether it be Mormons in Utah, Pennsylvania Amish, Cajuns from Louisiana, Appalachian mountaineers, African Americans from the Mississippi Delta, Mexican Americans in California and Texas, Minnesotans of Scandinavian extraction, New England Yankees, Chinese Americans in San Francisco, or Jews, Italians, and Irish from New York, Chicago, and Boston, America's heterogeneity, its geography, and its regional characteristics ensure that a diverse and constantly evolving culture contains a folk tradition that renders the United States unique among the industrialized nations. Whereas European countries can situate folk traditions within medieval time spheres, and Japan, for example, possesses ancient customs that represent a purism that links all of its people, America's folk heritage, its unwritten voice, has been aided, if not configured, by a cultural cross-fertilization that has seen different groups borrow from and interact with each other. Although in relative terms the United States can be seen as a young nation, it is also the world's oldest existing fully fledged democracy, and the vigorous nature of America's accelerated metamorphosis has ensured a vibrant folk culture that has manifested itself through various mediums including art and popular culture. It is therefore fitting that the convergent forces existing within a country of extremes should emanate from the "folk" themselves, promoting a national identity that continues to resonate throughout the globe.

American Folk Culture in the Nineteenth Century

The term "folklore" was first coined in 1846 by an Englishman, William John Thoms, and was a phrase used to describe the study of the ancient system of customs and beliefs practiced by common people. Subsequently in other nations, folklore became a means of establishing a unified national culture that also included language, music, and literature. To an extent these criteria applied to the United States in the nineteenth century as it began to forge an identity of its own. In contrast, though, to some nations in Europe where aristocrats sought proof of their own nationhood through the customs and language of the peasant class, America's literate population, already accustomed to a communicative spirit generated by newspapers, periodicals, and books, rejected the concept of an autocratic ruling elite. This is not to say that there was not already a burgeoning folkloric element rooted in Old World mythology such as the witch tales of New England and Appalachia. In general, though, tales and ballads about trappers, hunters, explorers, adventurers, and a myriad of liminal American characters that had experienced captivity, revolution, and the wilderness meant that folklore had taken on an American guise which embodied the country's exceptionalism.

There were also existing aboriginal cultures predicated almost entirely on the oral tradition. However, it was the Native Americans themselves who became objectified within the wider society while their culture remained firmly enclosed within the tribal environment. Subsequently, their myths and traditions remained, and still remain, detached and ethically different from the main body of the nation's folk traditions.

By the mid-nineteenth century, it was increasingly clear that the divisions perceived to exist between folk culture and mass culture were beginning to be blurred. American folk characters of that time embodied the principles of individualism and liberty while perpetuating ideas of nationhood and anti-elitism. All-American heroes such as Davy Crockett and Kit Carson were mythologized through almanacs, newspapers, and dime novels that anticipated the Superman comic boom a century later. The frontier and the West continued to be a source of fascination well into the twentieth century as Crockett and Carson plus a plethora of Western characters from Jesse James to Calamity Jane were, through the medium of the moving picture, ensconced forever within the nation's consciousness.

As well as influencing the course of popular culture, folklore was, during the latter part of the nineteenth century, a topic that required intellectual pursuit. As anthropologists, ethnologists, and historians attempted to situate an unwritten past through songs, myths, yarns, aphorisms, games, and numerous oral histories, folklore became very much a product of modernity. By the time the American Folklore Society (AFS) was founded in 1888, the United States had suffered a civil war and an economic slump; it had also undergone an accelerated industrial revolution that had seen its cities grow from cow towns and industrial ports to sprawling urban landscapes where immigrants and refugees from southern and eastern Europe brought their own folk traditions. The AFS's membership was drawn from mainly middle-class professionals who saw an opportunity for scientific research that reached outside the university curriculum. By the 1890s, the AFS had branches in cities across the United States, eclipsing by far similar organizations in Europe. It would be easy to view such an institution as emblematic of a subliminal yearning for a simpler, preindustrial America idealized through the rose-tinted spectacles of a socially and economically privileged, predominantly eastern, professional class. However, prominent folklorists of the late nineteenth century, for example T. F. Crane and Lee J. Vance, would offer the unearthing of "primitive" materials as valid evidence of humanity's advancement. In this sense, it could be argued, folklore was intrinsic to the modernizing process as folk specialists set about researching isolated communities in order to promote the benefits of what came to be known as the Gilded Age.

African American Folklore

Collectors and folklorists such as the first president of the AFS, Francis James Child, who compiled an extensive catalogue of British-based folk songs the final volume of which was published in 1898; Cecil Sharpe, an Englishman who made several trips to the Appalachians between 1916 and 1918 to document the "Elizabethan" ballads of Kentucky; and Vance Randolph, who initially visited the Ozarks of Arkansas during 1920 and discovered a powerful British influence within the local folk culture, provided a case for those who insisted there was no such thing as a quintessentially American folk heritage. Thus, even in those environments relatively unaffected by mass culture and industrialization, extant folk traditions were unequivocally linked to Great Britain, suggesting a regional homogeneity that was untypical of America as a whole. In this context, how does one assess African American culture and its contribution to an identifiable American folklore?

The unavoidable fact that African Americans were denied, through slavery, the educational and economic advantages enjoyed by the majority of U.S. society provided the conditions for the birth of a vibrant and inventive folk culture. Although informed by both African and European elements, in essence what emerged from the plantations of the South resembled conventional notions of folklore inasmuch that it was a mythology steeped in an oral tradition of trickster tales, animal stories, and work songs. Fundamentally, whereas the rest of America had an already-established written tradition, most slaves were never allowed the opportunity to achieve any adequate level of literacy. Of course there are exceptions, given the proliferation of written slave narratives, but such instances are relatively rare.

In contrast to Native Americans, whose traditions and myths were never allowed to enter into the dominant realm, African Americans, partly because of language and Christian belief, possessed cultural traits that were instantly recognizable to whites. As the songs of Stephen Foster and the blackface minstrelsy craze that proved to be the nation's most popular form of entertainment for the best part of a hundred years would help to testify, there was a long-held fascination with black America. Though distorted by sentimentalism, parody, and racist caricature, it was a fascination which allowed for a certain amount of cultural cross-fertilization.

Beginning with the publication in 1867 of William F. Allen, Charles P. Ware, and Lucy M. Garrison's *Slave Songs*, there would be a steady flow of African American–oriented folk material that would be absorbed into white society through various mediums including music, literature, and the pages of the *Journal of American Folklore.* In 1871 the Fisk Jubilee Singers were first assembled to perform Negro spirituals. The Fisks, who refined the spiritual to make it acceptable as a serious art form to white audiences, would subsequently travel to England, appearing before Queen Victoria. Mark Twain and the Czech composer Antonín Dvořák, who embellished his New World Symphony (1893) with the sacred folk melodies of former slaves, admired the Negro spirituals as truly great American music.

In popular fiction, Joel Chandler Harris's chronicling of slave folk tales, *Uncle Remus: His Songs and His Sayings*, published in 1880, provided a predominantly white readership with an amusing foray into the world of the plantation. In writing the Uncle Remus stories, Harris incorporated the dialect of the Gullah islanders, an isolated community that resided off the coast of South Carolina. Believed to have retained many African oral inflections, the islanders were of some interest to folklorists. Years later, George Gershwin would live among the Gullah people while researching his 1934 "folk opera" *Porgy and Bess*, a musical version of DuBose and Dorothy Heyward's *Porgy*. Dubose Heyward, incidentally, was a white southerner who spent years observing the folk characteristics of the Gullah community in Charleston.

Although white novelists were initially responsible for illustrating the folkways of black America, it would be African American authors who would successfully combine the oral traditions surfacing from the nineteenth century with modernist literary forms. Although Paul Laurence Dunbar's dialect verse drew national acclaim in the early 1900s, it would be those black writers and poets who rose to prominence in the wake of the 1920s Harlem Renaissance who would successfully intertextualize trickster tales, folk songs, and other folkloric elements into their art. Langston Hughes, Jean Toomer, Sterling Brown, Zora Neale Hurston, and latterly Ralph Ellison, Alice Walker, and Toni Morrison are all examples of African Americans who would evoke black oral traditions in their written work. Thus, African American literature has taken from folklore in order to give historical license to a people whose past had hitherto only been written through the eyes of the enslaver.

The interchange between the black folk tradition and the white literary tradition suggests a synthesis that transcends racial barriers. To an extent, this is often repeated in American folk music. In the South, historically the most racially segregated region in the United States, there was (and is) a huge public domain of folk songs that have continually traversed the color line. Songs that seem to typify an America undergoing industrialization and urbanization, such as "Casey Jones," "Stagolee," "Frankie and Johnny," and "John Henry," have passed back and forth between the races only to be claimed by both. The South has produced white blues singers and black hillbilly groups, while jazz emerged from its African American folk roots in New Orleans to become a quintessentially American art form. White country music owes much to African American blues. In 1926, one of the first artists to perform on the Grand Ole Opry was a black harmonica player called DeFord Bailey, who improvised nineteenth-century folk tunes such as "Fox Chase" which he had learned from his father, a former slave from East Tennessee. White hillbilly's first million-selling artist, Jimmie Rodgers, who developed his musical style working with African Americans on the railroad, produced a number of highly successful blues sides between 1927 and 1933, while African American blues singers like Huddie Ledbetter (Leadbelly) and Blind Lemon Jefferson would include traditional white forms in their repertoires.

Put in this context, one could certainly argue that the interchange between southern black and white folk traditions, especially in folk song, produced a synthesis of sorts which could almost be defined as a single southern folk culture.

Folklore, Mass Culture, and Multiculturalism

The blurring of folklore and popular culture that was hinted at during the nineteenth century through the depiction of folk characters in dime novels, almanacs, and newspapers took on another dimension with the technological advancement that succeeded World War I. Radio, the phonograph, and the cinema all provided a facility for mass communication in an era when the unfettered consumerism of the postwar Jazz Age was followed by the Wall Street Crash and the Great Depression. During this period, America was becoming a more fluid society, with African Americans and rural whites from the South migrating to the urban centers of the North and the Midwest. Of course, these migrants brought their folk customs and their traditions with them. Ironically, as many Americans became effectively displaced, they developed a keener sense of their own regional heritage. For example, blues artists who migrated to Chicago during the 1920s would, in many of their songs, express a yearning for their southern homeland—a yearning that reflected the feelings of many whites as well as African Americans.

As southerners moved north, the children of those immigrants that had poured into the United States over the previous fifty years were gradually being assimilated into the wider society. The first-ever jazz phonograph recording, "Livery Stable Blues," was performed by the Original Dixieland Jazz Band, a white ensemble led by the son of Italian immigrant Nick La Rocca. With the expansion of the entertainment industry and Tin Pan Alley, songwriters such as Irving Berlin and George Gershwin, Jews from New York's Lower East Side, were composing ditties portraying an idyllic America that evoked Stephen Foster's sentimentalized version of a pastoral South. Gershwin and Berlin, blues singers from Chicago, white jazz bands from New Orleans: none of these were creating folklore; they were instead helping to produce commodities for the mass market. However, they were also prompting an idea of a common folk heritage that was rooted in the pastoral. Similarly, cinema portrayals of western heroes from the previous century added to the illusion of a rural America that predated mass immigration and urbanization. So, even for the children of immigrants, a perception of an American past was constructed that was all-inclusive.

The New Deal epoch and the ascendancy of the Popular Front during the 1930s produced a celebration of the people that was reflected in the photography of Dorothea Lange, whose "Migrant Mother" signified the stabilizing effect of the family and the dignifying presence of women at a time when many men were forced to travel the length and breadth of America searching for work. Lange was employed by the Works Progress Administration (WPA), a federal agency that was, between 1935 and 1943, responsible for sending folklorists, writers, and photographers out on field trips to observe the cultural mores, oral histories, education, political views, and medical needs of families in case studies that spanned twenty-four states. The work of the WPA marked a trend that had witnessed folklorists and collectors set out to explore the treasures that existed within America's cultural undergrowth.

Prompted by the anthropologist Franz Boas at Columbia University, Zora Neale Hurston made several exploratory journeys to the South to unearth a wealth of African American folktales, rhymes, and jokes which would find the light of day in her groundbreaking chronicle of African American folklore *Mules and Men*, published in 1935. For folk music, under the auspices of the Library of Congress folk song archive, John and Alan Lomax first went to the South in 1933 recording folk songs, reels, and obscure country blues by performers, some of whom had never left their locality. John Lomax was also responsible for bringing Huddie Ledbetter out of Angola State Penitentiary and to the attention of folk music. Lomax also conducted several notable interviews for the Library of Congress including Leadbelly, the now-legendary Oklahoma folk poet Woody Guthrie, and the Georgia blues singer Blind Willie McTell. To complement the Lomaxes' field recordings, the maverick avant-garde filmmaker-artist and part-time anthropologist Harry Smith uncovered dozens of vinyl recordings from between 1927 and 1932, a time when record sales plummeted. Smith's collection, which covered southern traditional music from Appalachia to Texas, found its way to Folkways Records and was eventually released as the *Anthology of American Folk Music* in 1952. The anthology would have a huge effect on the folk boom of the early 1960s, a time when folk music had become firmly entrenched as a vehicle for political protest.

Quite clearly the celebrating of a people's culture was a concept held dear by the political left. In 1968, the organizers for Martin Luther King Jr.'s Poor People's March set up folklore workshops for African American, poor white, and Hispanic participants. This notion of unity through diversity was evident in folk festivals that were first staged in the 1930s, a time when institutions such as Tennessee's Highlander Folk School took sharecroppers and trained them to be union organizers. One of the tactics employed by Highlander to attract both blacks and whites into workers' collectives was the conversion of Negro spirituals and traditional folk songs into songs of solidarity. "We Shall Not Be Moved," for example, became a rallying cry on the picket line.

Seemingly, the whole political climate of the 1930s and 1940s lent itself to the reinterpretation of folk songs as propaganda. Woody Guthrie rewrote countless traditional folk songs so as to convey a political message. "John Henry" became "Tom Joad," "The Ballad of Jesse James" became "Jesus Christ," and Leadbelly's "Good Night Irene"—itself based on a traditional melody—became "Roll On Columbia." Guthrie came from a generation that was influenced by phonograph recordings. By listening to the Carter Family and Jimmie Rodgers as a young man, he was inheriting an oral tradition, but one which had become universalized by twentieth-century technology. The radio, in particular, furnished a network that spanned the country. The fireside chats of President Franklin D. Roosevelt epitomized the "folksy" or homespun quality that has characterized many American heads of state from Abraham Lincoln to Ronald Reagan.

The radio then, whether regional or national, engendered a spirit of community that encouraged a perception of American identity among its listeners. The fact that commercial interests became interwoven with folklore established a trend that carried on into television. From the early sponsorship of the Grand Ole Opry and the 1930s King Biscuit Flour blues broadcasts in Helena, Arkansas, to present-day television commercials advertising beer that evoke rural Mississippi and the Delta blues, the business community has promoted folk culture as an exemplar for American identity in order to sell its own product.

In spite of the view that folklore has become more of a commodity than a people's culture, there is still much to suggest that oral traditions, folktales, and songs will continue to flourish in an age of spiraling technology and global communication. The Internet and the World Wide Web now provide access to the Library of Congress, the Smithsonian Institute, and any number of folklore centers, all of which contain elaborate chronicles of migrant narratives, field recordings, blues songs, and transcriptions of WPA interviews. American folklore is not static and there is still an immense amount of material that remains unrecorded and underresearched. Events, disasters, and wars all produce their unwritten histories though technology has helped to preserve those histories. Who is not to say that rap music represents an extension of the African American oral tradition, or that the AIDS memorial quilt signifies a folk heritage which predates the industrial age? The revival in American "roots" music, the boom in handicraft sales, and the success of television shows like *The Beverly Hillbillies* are all examples of how folklore, commercial interests, and popular culture blend into one another. In this respect, folklore allows the past and the present to meet head on and interacts with popular culture and the commercial world in a way that has almost become an American tradition in itself.

BIBLIOGRAPHY

Anderson, Benedict. *Imagined Communities: Reflections on the Origins and Spread of Nationalism.* London: Verso, 1983.

Bronner, Simon J. *Following Tradition: Folklore in the Discourse of American Culture.* Logan: Utah State University Press, 1998.

Brunvand, Jan Harold. *The Study of American Folklore; An Introduction.* New York: Norton, 1968.

Denning, Michael. *The Cultural Front: The Laboring of American Culture in the Twentieth Century.* New York: Verso, 1996.

Dorson, Richard M. *American Folklore.* Chicago: The University of Chicago Press, 1959.

Eagleton, Terry. *The Idea of Culture.* Oxford: Blackwell Publishers, 2000.

Filene, Benjamin. "'Our Singing Country': John and Alan Lomax, Leadbelly, and the Construction of the American Past." *American Quarterly* (December 1991): 602–624.

Grundy, Pamela. "'We Always Tried to be Good People': Respectability, Crazy Water Crystals, and Hillbilly Music on the Air, 1933–1935." *Journal of American History* 81, no. 4 (March 1995): 1591–1620.

Kelley, Robin D. G. "Notes on Deconstructing 'The Folk'." *American Historical Review* 97, no. 5 (December 1992): 1400–1408.

Levine, Lawrence W. "The Folklore of Industrial Society: Popular Culture and Its Audiences." In Levine, *The Unpredictable Past: Explorations in American Cultural History.* New York: Oxford University Press, 1993.

Malone, Bill C. *Country Music U.S.A.* Austin: University of Texas Press, 1985.

Michaels, Walter Benn. *Our America: Nativism, Modernism, and Pluralism.* Durham, N.C.: Duke University Press, 1995.

Peter Hammond

Fast Food Stand. A historical photograph of the sort of eatery where the most appetizing feature might have been the building; the menu here includes tamales, ice cream, chili—and presumably hot dogs. © UPI/CORBIS-BETTMANN

FOOD, FAST. Fast food is what one eats in the vast majority of America's restaurants. The term denotes speed in both food preparation and customer service, as well as speed in customer eating habits. The restaurant industry, however, has traditionally preferred the designation "quick service." For hourly wage earners—whether factory hands or store clerks—take-out lunch wagons and sit-down lunch counters appeared at factory gates, streetcar stops, and throughout downtown districts in the late nineteenth century. For travelers, lunch counters also appeared in railroad stations nationwide. Fried food prevailed for its speed of preparation, as did sandwich fare and other fixings that could be held in the hand and rapidly eaten, quite literally, "on the run." Novelty foods, such as hot dogs, hamburgers, french fries, came to dominate, first popularized at various world's fairs and at the nation's resorts. Soft drinks and ice cream desserts also became a mainstay. Thus, "fast food" also came to imply diets high in fat and caloric intake. By the end of the twentieth century, the typical American consumed some three hamburgers and four orders of french fries a week. Roughly a quarter of all Americans bought fast food every day.

The rise of automobile ownership in the United States brought profound change to the restaurant industry, with fast food being offered in a variety of "drive-in" restaurant formats. Mom-and-pop enterprise was harnessed, largely through franchising, in the building of regional and national restaurant chains: Howard Johnson's, Dairy Queen, Burger King, Kentucky Fried Chicken, Pizza Hut, and Taco Tico. Place-product-packaging was brought forcefully to the fore; each restaurant in a chain variously shares the same logo, color scheme, architectural design motif, and point-of-purchase advertising, all configured in attention-getting, signlike buildings. Typically, fast food restaurants were located at the "roadside," complete with driveways, parking lots, and, later, drive-through windows for those who preferred to eat elsewhere, including those who ate in their cars as "dashboard diners." Critical to industry success was the development of paper and plastic containers that kept food hot and facilitated "carry-out." Such packaging, because of the volume of largely nonbiodegradable waste it creates, has become a substantial environmental problem.

In 2000, McDonalds—the largest quick-service chain—operated at some 13,755 locations in the United States and Canada. The company's distinctive "golden arches" have spread worldwide, well beyond North America. Abroad, fast food came to stand as an important symbol of American cultural, if not economic, prowess. And, just as it did at home, fast food became, as well, a clear icon of modernity. Historically, fast food merchandising contributed substantially to the quickening pace of American life through standardization. By the beginning of the twenty-first century, it fully embraced mass production and mass marketing techniques, reduced to the scale of a restaurant. Chains of restaurants, in turn, became fully rationalized within standardized purchasing, marketing, and management systems. Such a system depends on a pool of cheap, largely unskilled labor, the quick service restaurant industry being notorious for its low wages and, accordingly, its rapid turnover of personnel.

BIBLIOGRAPHY

Jakle, John A., and Keith A. Sculle. *Fast Food: Roadside Restaurants in the Automobile Age.* Baltimore: Johns Hopkins University Press, 1999.

Pillsbury, Richard. *No Foreign Food: The American Diet and Place.* Boulder, Colo.: Westview Press, 1998.

Schlosser, Eric. *Fast Food Nation: The Dark Side of the All-American Meal.* New York: HarperCollins, 2002.

John A. Jakle

FOOD AND CUISINES. If there is a recurring theme in the history of Americans and their food it is abundance. From the earliest days of the new republic, foreign visitors and immigrants remarked on how well endowed Americans were with regard to food. This was reflected in their stature, which is closely linked to diet. During the American Revolution the average American soldier was much taller than his British foe. Even the poorly fed African slaves in the United States seem to have eaten better than most of their counterparts in Spanish, Portuguese, and French America.

Yet the triumph over Britain on the battlefield was not mirrored by independence from British-style cuisine. The British immigrants, like most arrivals from abroad, had tried to import the foods of the homeland to their new abodes in North America. For the most part the environment cooperated, allowing them to reproduce many of the grains, meats, and vegetables that had formed the core of their diets back home. Indeed, at first they had even disdained the Native Americans' maize, which they called Indian corn after the word for staple food in Britain. It was only after maize and the potato, which was native to South America, gained approval back in Britain that they became important parts of the British immigrants' diet as well. For the most part their foods, seasonings, and methods of preparation remained similar to those of the old country throughout the colonial period. Only in the South, where the climate was warmer and African slaves played a major role in food preparation, did significant variations arise, and these were mainly in the form of the seasonings that slaves brought with them from Africa and the West Indies.

The main gustatory problem for most Americans in the first years of the Republic was seasonality. About 90 percent of them lived in rural areas, and during the winter and spring, when the earth produced little, they and poorer city dwellers fell back on monotonous diets based on root vegetables, beans, corn or rye breads, and preserved meats. However, a transportation revolution was already beginning as roads and canals pushed into the hinterland. Increasingly, farms that had been largely self-sufficient could sell products for cash, which farmers used to purchase goods and foods they had previously produced themselves. The opening of the Erie Canal in 1825 created a cheap water route from the Midwest to the East Coast. Midwestern wheat then poured into the rest of the country (as well as into foreign markets), bringing markedly lower prices for flour. White bread, which only the better-off had been able to afford on a regular basis, now became commonplace. The nation's cities and towns also enjoyed ample supplies of corn-fattened pork, salted and packed in barrels, that were shipped from growing midwestern centers such as Cincinnati, which proudly called itself Porkopolis.

At the same time, cooking over open fires in fireplaces, on spits, or in iron pots was being replaced by cooking on iron stoves. These enabled cooks to have much more control over the amount of heat applied to foods and contributed to the development of more precise and complex methods of cooking. Recipe books that took advantage of these innovations came onto the market, often as part of housekeeping manuals that helped codify middle-class standards of cooking and serving food for insecure women whose husbands' rising incomes were thrusting them into the new middle class.

Class Distinctions

The recipe books were also a sign that, although the transportation and market revolutions did provide many people with previously unaffordable foods, there were still important class differences in cooking and eating. It was mainly the rising middle and upper classes who could afford houses with iron stoves, as well as many of the foods the transportation revolution and new overseas sources were making available. The story was quite different for the poorer classes. Many of them were impoverished immigrants residing in crowded cities or on poor farms who could afford neither housing with stoves nor a variety of foods to cook on them. For much of the year their diets were still based mainly on salted meats, cabbage, potatoes, other root vegetables, and beans. Although adequate in quantity, evidence that the average stature of white Americans declined from about 1800 to 1850 would indicate that their diets lacked much in terms of quality and variety. Most African American slaves, whose diets were based on vitamin- and protein-deficient corn meal, were worse off, even though defenders of slavery claimed that their immunity from the severe food shortages that still plagued parts of rural Europe meant that their lives were better than those of free European peasants.

At the other end of the scale, those in the upper class were beginning to adopt the French style of cooking that was becoming the fashion among the upper classes throughout the Western world. At first, most of the American elite had been reluctant to join in, for French haute cuisine's aristocratic connotations seemed at odds with the values of the egalitarian new Republic. Moreover, like the British, Americans prized plainly prepared meats and were suspicious that French sauces camouflaged either inferior meats or repulsive ingredients, such as the legendary frogs' legs. However, from the 1820s on, increasing numbers of well-off Americans followed in Thomas Jefferson's footsteps and, like him, returned from visits to France enamored with French cuisine. Delmonico's French restaurant, which opened in New York City in 1832, helped further popularize it among that city's elite. By the 1840s and 1850s, the United States ranked high on the list of countries to which French chefs brought their skills. French-style menus were the norm in the grand celebratory public dinners that were popular at that time. Prospectors who struck it rich in the western mining frontiers celebrated by feasting on French food, often at the fine French restaurants that sprang up in mining towns such as Denver, Colorado.

In the decades following the Civil War, new cohorts of nouveaux riches either joined or displaced the older elites as arbiters of style and taste. They built huge mansions in whose vast kitchens French chefs supervised brigades of workers turning out elaborate French haute cuisine for large dinner parties and other food-consuming entertainments. They also flocked to expensive restaurants, such as the still-flourishing Delmonico's and new luxury hotels for nine- or ten-course French dinners where champagne and other fine French wines flowed endlessly.

Normally, in societies of abundance food tastes tend to filter down the class ladder. However, in this case the upper middle class was quite unable to emulate the gustatory feats of those above them. The problem was not so much the expense of the ingredients involved as the unavailability of servants able to carry it off. Because they could afford neither the quantity nor the quality of servants involved in this kind of cooking, the middle classes were forced back on the simpler British American culinary heritage. They now extolled the cooking of New England, home of the Pilgrims and other revered founders of the nation. Cookbooks and cooking schools offered advice on how to cook this straightforward cuisine, which commonly revolved around a main course of meat, poultry, or fish with two boiled or baked vegetables, covered with some kind of white sauce. Visual qualities, particularly ones that bespoke daintiness, often took precedence over taste, especially since strong tastes and seasonings were thought to stimulate a degenerate craving for alcohol.

Immigrants and Cuisine

This kind of cuisine not only marked the middle class off from the class above; it also differentiated it from those below, particularly the immigrants who were flooding into the country in ever-greater numbers. By the 1880s most of these newcomers were headed for the cities rather the farms, and it was there in urban America, with its proliferating department stores, dance halls, saloons, and other entertainments that a new kind of culture—materialistic, hedonistic, and heterogeneous—seemed to be threatening the moral values and gender roles of the older, simpler America. As middle-class Protestants in particular sought ways to protect their traditional value system from this double threat of immigrant and urban cultures, they turned the dining rooms of their substantial new homes into deeply symbolic bastions. There, the entire family would gather, with the father sitting at what was significantly called the head of the table. He would lead in saying grace, carve the meats, and perform other acts that would symbolize the durability of the patriarchal family hierarchy. The religious solemnity of the occasions would be emphasized by filling the dining rooms with furniture of a Gothic, church-like style.

By the end of the century, the nation seemed to be taking an even worse turn as the character of immigrants changed markedly. They now came mainly from southern and eastern, rather than northern and central Europe. Many were short, dark people who dressed differently and had domestic habits that seemed completely at odds with British American ones. They were packed into smelly, overcrowded housing and cooked highly seasoned mélanges of foods that most middle-class Americans regarded as unpalatable stimulants to drunkenness.

Many native-born Americans clamored for cutting off immigration, but others—fearing this would dry up the supply of unskilled labor—supported the Americanization of the immigrants. By 1910, many social work agencies were actively engaged in trying to teach immigrant women how to cook the American way. Home economics courses for girls in slum public schools were redirected from training cooks and servants for wealthier families to training young immigrant girls how to cook in the approved fashion for their own families.

The American way, of course, meant the British American way, as perfected by such successful cooking schoolteachers as Fanny Farmer, head of the Boston Cooking School. Her emphasis on the exact measurement of ingredients helped give this kind of cooking the kind of scientific and technological aura that impressed early-twentieth-century Americans, who were already struck by the improvements that science and technology were bringing to their lives.

Cleanliness

Many of these improvements could be seen on dinner tables. In the 1870s and 1880s, public health authorities concentrated on preventing epidemic disease by cleaning up public places and exposing them to fresh air. In the 1890s the discovery of bacteria changed perceptions of the causes of illness but continued to spur concerns over cleanliness, especially in the food supply. One result was the passage in 1906 of the federal Pure Food and Drug Act, which sought to protect consumers against contaminated foods. Another was to spur the rise of large food-producing companies whose widely advertised brand names instilled consumer confidence in the cleanliness of their products. Neatly packaged Uneeda crackers rapidly replaced the traditional cracker barrel, which was pawed over by countless bacteria-laden hands. Canning companies, which had existed on a relatively small scale since before the Civil War, used efficient new canning techniques to begin turning out large quantities of foods sanitized through the application of high heat. The Heinz Company built an international empire by showcasing its spotless facilities in Pittsburgh, where teams of white-clad young ladies, looking much like nurses, stuffed pickles and other condiments into see-through bottles for bacteria-killing heating. In urban centers, sparkling lunchrooms with white tile walls and counters replaced dingy wooden ones serving the growing clientele of sanitation-conscious office and store workers.

Abundance, Anxiety, and Amalgamation

One of the most important breakthroughs affecting how people ate came on the heels of the post–Civil War expansion of the railroad network. In the West, vast tracts of land were opened to the production of cattle, whose flesh had always been highly regarded by British American and European diners. Live steers could now be transported to such centers as Chicago and Kansas City to be fattened on midwestern corn before being slaughtered. In the 1870s and 1880s, the introduction of refrigerated railway cars allowed the carcasses of steer to be shipped to the growing cities of the East, where fresh beef soon became affordable to large numbers of people. Chop houses and steak houses proliferated and Americans took pride in the size and quality of their beefsteaks. The railroads also spurred the growth of market gardening and dairy farming in East Coast states such as New York and New Jersey, where agriculture had previously suffered in the face of competition from the Midwest. Trains brought tons of fresh peaches from Georgia, carloads of fresh oysters from Maryland, and piles of Central American bananas from New Orleans to the industrial North. Soon, entrepreneurs were planting oranges for the national market in remote Southern California, beginning a process that would ultimately see the center of gravity of the country's fruit and vegetable production shift dramatically toward the Southwest.

The resulting plethora of affordable foods evoked a variety of responses. Immigrant workers were generally delighted by it, citing the regularity with which they ate beef (and drank coffee) as proof of the wisdom of their move to America. In 1906 the German sociologist Werner Sombart observed that the hopes for socialist revolution in America had been "wrecked on the reefs of roast beef and apple pie." The middle classes also welcomed the new food choices, but new anxieties began to manifest themselves. In the 1890s the discovery that foods were composed of proteins, carbohydrates, and fats and that their energy could be measured in calories added to their worries over the healthfulness of their diets. Nutritional scientists and home economists now warned that people should calibrate the intake of these substances according to the actual needs of the body. Eating more than was necessary was said to be wasteful, while eating less than necessary was dangerous to one's health. This nutritional awareness became widespread during World War I, when the government used it to explain its food conservation program, which revolved around substituting vegetable proteins for animal ones and certain kinds of grains for others.

In the mid-1920s food industries entered a remarkable period of conglomeration as giant enterprises came to dominate the production of such foods as flour, bread, shortening, dairy and pork products, breakfast cereals, canned goods, and citrus fruits. Some of this was the result of their applying the mass production techniques of other industries to the production of food. However, conglomeration was also based on the creation of widely advertised brand names that helped assuage the anxieties that consumers naturally felt as food production grew ever more remote from them. Food producers hired hundreds of home economists to create and distribute millions of copies of recipes, usually of the British American kind, to promote the use of their products. By the end of the decade, their foods and recipes were penetrating the remotest reaches of the nation, causing the first, but by no means the last, warnings that distinctive regional cuisines were being replaced by a homogeneous national one.

The mechanization of food production was matched by the mechanization of housework. Gas and electric stoves with regulated ovens replaced monstrous wood- or coal-burning ones; canning raised hopes—and fears—

that much of food preparation would be reduced to using a can opener and a few pots. The middle-class "servant problem" literally disappeared during the war, when most servants left domestic work for jobs, mostly in industry, with better pay and better hours. Also, activities such as movies, dances, spectator sports, and drives in the country by automobile came to compete directly for leisure time with family dinners. As a result, middle-class housewives now aimed at speed and simplicity in food preparation. By the mid-1920s the complaint that would resound among the middle class for the rest of the century—that families no longer ate together—was already commonplace.

Dieting and Food Supplements

A remarkable shift in attitudes toward body image contributed its share of anxiety to the mix. Before the war, a man's ample stomach was generally regarded as a sign of prosperity and stability and the reigning female beauties were decidedly hefty, particularly by later standards. The stage star Lillian Russell, the turn-of-the-century American Beauty, stood just a little more than five feet tall and is said to have weighed close to two hundred pounds. By 1920, however, ideals of attractiveness in both men and women were undergoing a sea change, as slimness became the ideal. In the movies, slim males such as Rudolph Valentino and petite females such as Mary Pickford became superstars. For women the "flapper" look, which reduced skirt lengths and did away with the old-style corsets and undergarments, made it very difficult to hide fleshy parts of the body. The result was the first wave of dieting for weight loss as the middle class began counting calories and buying bathroom scales.

In the wealthiest classes, the turn toward simplicity in eating was also spurred by Prohibition, which banned the sale of alcoholic beverages from January 1920 until it was repealed in 1933. It put an end to most luxury restaurants by depriving them of the profit margins from alcohol sales that underwrote the expenses of running a fine restaurant. Changing fashions in upper-class leisure activities also led the wealthy to reorient their social lives away from spectacular dinner parties and downsize their kitchen staffs.

Yet many Americans still did not have the luxury of picking and choosing what they ate. In depressed rural areas in particular, food supplies remained tied to the seasons and variety remained a problem. In large parts of the rural South, for example, poor people tied to cotton growing subsisted for much of the year on a diet based on little more than corn meal and salted pork. As a result, many suffered the scourge of pellagra, a debilitating, often deadly disease brought about by a deficiency of vitamin B.

Consciousness of the importance of vitamins increased quite slowly from the discovery of the first one in 1911. The understanding of their importance was spurred in the early 1920s, however, when newspapers and magazines carried striking photos of vitamin-deprived white mice that had lost their furry coats and gone blind. Food marketers seized on this to emphasize the importance of the vitamins in their products, particularly for children's health. By the mid-1930s producers of many foodstuffs, including yeast cakes, cocoa, and chewing gum, were taking advantage of the still-vague knowledge of the functions of vitamins and of the human need for them to promote unwarranted fears of vitamin deficiencies among consumers.

The Great Depression brought to the fore once again the idea that America was the land of food abundance, but now it was in the form of outrage that mountains of unsold grain were in the countryside while long lines of people waited in breadlines and went to soup kitchens. Despite the uncertainty over the actual human requirements for vitamins and minerals, government dietary surveys aroused concern over widespread malnutrition, not just among the poor, but of "hidden malnutrition" among the apparently well-fed middle class as well. Still, dieting for weight loss continued to be popular, particularly among middle-class women, who followed such fads as the grapefruit diet. Pulling them in yet another direction, however, was a renewed emphasis in the media on the importance, in the crisis time of the 1930s, of women preparing the ample, wholesome, British American–style family meal.

The Decline of Immigrant Food

The continuing hegemony of this kind of cooking was reinforced by the Americanization of immigrants' eating habits. The virtual cutoff of immigration from much of Europe and the Americas in the 1920s had deprived immigrant communities of new infusions of demand for old country foods. The children of immigrants attended public schools dominated by American-born teachers and administrators whose disapproval of their families' eating habits was manifest. Other students ridiculed them, reinforcing the lesson that their food was held in contempt in the wider community. As a result, children threw away their homemade ethnic lunches and demanded that their mothers prepare sandwiches made of Wonder Bread or allow them to eat in school cafeterias. Home economics classes, which taught British American cooking, reinforced this lesson for girls. These messages were often capped by marriage to someone of a different background. All of these factors ultimately led to the relegation of the immigrant food of the parents to nostalgic occasions. Of the major immigrant groups only Italian Americans, for whom food was extraordinarily important in family life, were able to resist these pressures. This was in part because they were able to adapt their cooking to American products and tastes and produce a distinctive Italian American cuisine whose signature dish, pasta and tomato sauce, become accepted into the American culinary pantheon.

War Rationing and Postwar Prosperity

The advent of World War II brought full employment, handsome paychecks, and the appropriation of a large portion of the food supply to the armed forces. The question of how to share equitably the rest of the food became paramount. The government's answer was to control food prices and use rationing to limit purchases of a number of foods that were in short supply, including sugar and meat. Although compliance with rationing was high, many Americans remained unconvinced that food shortages could exist in the land of abundance. There were recurring rumors that abundant supplies of the rationed foods existed, but that either government bungling or farmers' greed had caused the food to be destroyed or withheld from the market.

Still, rationing brought about a certain democratization of food consumption, since it enabled those at the bottom to eat better and put social pressure on those at the top to eat less luxuriously. This tendency of food to become more classless continued after the war as abundance again became the watchword. American farmers ratcheted up production as government subsidies financed mechanization, irrigation, and fertilization. The results were seen in more affordable foodstuffs. Beef prices declined and thick steaks sizzling on the backyard barbecues in the growing suburbs symbolized the achievement of the American Dream by large numbers of people. New poultry-raising techniques turned chicken from a special Sunday dish into an everyday one. Government officials and food industry leaders now boasted that Americans were the best-fed people on earth.

Government and industry officials also took pride in the great industrial strides that seemed to be making food preparation easier. Electric refrigerators, stoves, toasters, mixers, and other small appliances were hailed as easing the housewife's labors. Processed foods such as frozen vegetables and orange juice, TV dinners, processed cheeses, new kinds of canned goods, dried foods, and instant coffee were regarded as symbolizing the superiority of the American way of life. When Vice President Richard Nixon engaged the Soviet leader Nikita Khrushchev in a much-publicized debate over the merits of their respective systems during Nixon's 1959 visit to Moscow, the vice president chose the model kitchen at an American exhibition as its venue.

Food Protest and Fast Food, and Foreign Cuisines

In the 1960s, however, faith in both the American system and American food began to be shaken. Even in the 1950s, questions were raised about the alleged carcinogenic qualities of some of the chemicals that were added to foods to help them survive the various new processes to which they were subjected. Then came fears that crop pesticides, especially DDT, were not only killing wildlife but were also tainting mothers' breast milk. Charges that processing robbed foods of their essential nutrients and that processed foods such as breakfast cereals were devoid of vitamins helped send millions of Americans flocking to vendors of vitamin supplements.

This rising skepticism dovetailed with the impact of the protest movements of the 1960s. By the late 1960s, doubts about the trustworthiness of government and the giant corporations that were thought to exert undue influence upon it were widespread, particularly among the young. The New Left blamed the giant corporations for problems ranging from the Vietnam War to America's "plastic" foods. The adherents of the counterculture, who extolled the natural over the artificial, rejected the products of large agro-industries and processed foods and tried to turn to the unadulterated products of the land for their food. The food industries responded quite adeptly to these challenges by reformulating and repackaging foods to make them seem more "natural," additive-free, and artisanal in origin. Still, although the New Left and the counterculture faded away in the 1970s, their critiques of American food helped make the public receptive to a continuing litany of complaints about the food supply. Charges were made that sugar was dangerous and addictive and that pesticide residues on apples were killers. Most lasting were charges that cholesterol in foods was responsible for Americans' high rates of heart disease, criticisms that vegetable oil and margarine producers ensured were widely publicized. Egg producers, dairy interests, and especially the beef industry reeled as health experts called for limited consumption of their products.

Beef producers emerged relatively unscathed, thanks in large part to the spectacular rise of fast-food restaurant chains, the largest of which sold hamburgers. These enterprises were part of a much broader trend that saw food preparation and consumption move out of the home at perhaps the fastest pace ever. A major reason was the steadily increasing proportion of middle-class mothers who remained in or returned to the workforce after their children were born. With little time for their traditional role of preparing family meals, they relied very much on all kinds of foods prepared outside the home.

The turn from the traditional way of preparing foods was accompanied by a drift away from traditional cuisine itself. In the 1960s food tastes again became significant signs of class and status, as an appreciation for a succession of foreign foods became a sign of distinction within the upper middle class. First, there was a revival of French food, followed by vogues of northern Italian and regional Chinese food. Then, in the late 1960s and the 1970s, the jet age brought a boom in foreign travel that helped make a somewhat adventurous approach to food a sign of distinction among the middle classes. Liberalized immigration laws brought in new waves of non-European people, some of whom were ready to cater to these new tastes. This, plus the continuing globalization of the trade in foods, gave Americans access to an impressive choice of previously exotic cuisines and foods.

The Persistence of Food Anxiety

Yet the abundance of choice did little to quell persisting anxiety over food. Concerns over weight became more extreme than ever as ideal body images became impossible to achieve for all but a very small minority of women. Dangerous eating disorders became common among the young. The cholesterol scare became increasingly confusing and disturbing as Americans were told that there was both "good" and "bad" cholesterol, and that millions of them had been inadvertently eating the bad variety in forms such as margarine that they had previously been told were good. As the population aged, more people became ripe for messages promising that certain foods and diets would head off life-threatening ailments. They consumed more olive oil and red wine and tried to follow a Mediterranean diet not dissimilar to the kind that millions of immigrants had fled at the turn of the century. They tried to follow new government dietary guidelines that called for drastic increases in the consumption of foods thought to promote longevity and reductions in those thought to reduce it. New regulations permitted advertisements for such foods as ketchup to imply they promoted longevity. The English wag who observed that "Americans like to think that death is optional" did not seem far off base.

Anxiety about harmful ingredients contained in food continued, with the most serious concern directed at the most obvious product of abundance: calories. Americans recoiled at ever-more-alarming statistics on rising rates of obesity and their fearful health consequences. The major culprits were said to be the most distinctive of the foods produced by the modern food conglomerates: crispy snack foods, soda pop, and the fare in fast-food restaurants. As they had from the outset, Europeans still looked in wonder at America as the land of abundance, but now it was one of abundant waistlines. Only increasing indications that they themselves might be headed down the same path gave them pause.

BIBLIOGRAPHY

Belasco, Warren. *Appetite for Change: How the Counterculture Took On the Food Industry, 1966–1988.* New York: Pantheon, 1989.

Bentley, Amy. *Eating for Victory: Food Rationing and the Politics of Domesticity.* Urbana: University of Illinois Press, 1998.

Conlin, Joseph. *Beans, Bacon, and Galantines: Food and Foodways on the Western Mining Frontier.* Reno: University of Nevada Press, 1986.

Cummings, Richard Osborn. *The American and His Food: A History of Food Habits in the United States.* Chicago: University of Chicago Press, 1940.

Gabbaccia, Donna R. *We Are What We Eat: Ethnic Food in the Making of Americans.* Cambridge, Mass.: Harvard University Press, 1998.

Hooker, Richard J. *Food and Drink in America: A History.* Indianapolis, Ind.: Bobbs-Merrill, 1981.

Levenstein, Harvey A. *Revolution at the Table: The Transformation of the American Diet.* New York: Oxford University Press, 1988.

———. *Paradox of Plenty: The Social History of Eating in Modern America.* New York: Oxford University Press, 1993.

Oliver, Sandra. *Saltwater Foodways.* Mystic, Conn.: Mystic Seaport Museum, 1995.

Shapiro, Laura. *Perfection Salad: Women and Cooking at the Turn of the Century.* New York: Farrar, Straus, and Giroux, 1986.

Stearns, Peter. *Fat History: Bodies and Beauty in the Modern West.* New York: New York University Press, 1997.

Williams, Susan. *Savory Suppers and Fashionable Feasts: Dining in Victorian America.* New York: Pantheon, 1985.

Harvey Levenstein

See also **Agriculture; Diets and Dieting; Immigration; Insecticides and Herbicides; Kitchens; Nutrition and Vitamins;** *and vol. 9:* **Conditions in Meatpacking Plants, 1906.**

FOOD AND DRUG ADMINISTRATION. The Food and Drug Administration (FDA) was the first regulatory agency established in the United States with consumer protection as its principal mission. Arguably, it is the only federal regulatory agency today whose basic charge has not been substantially altered in nearly one hundred years. Although the agency's responsibilities have grown enormously since Congress first defined food and drug adulterations as a danger to health and as consumer fraud in 1906, FDA remains a science-based regulatory agency responsible for protecting the public health through the regulation of foods, drugs, biological therapeutic products (i.e., vaccines), medical devices, cosmetics, animal feed, and radiation-emitting consumer products.

FDA began as a small, analytical chemistry unit in the U.S. Department of Agriculture, created after the Civil War to promote agriculture and assist farmers. A single chemist, whose job it had been to analyze fertilizers and agricultural chemicals for the Patent Office, was transferred to the new department in 1862 to continue his work on behalf of farmers and state agricultural extension services. In 1880, the chief chemist in the Bureau of Chemistry endorsed passage of a federal food and drug law, and his successor in 1883, Harvey W. Wiley, actively campaigned for the law. When it was finally enacted by Congress in 1906, the Pure Food and Drugs Act was often referred to as the Wiley Act.

Wiley led the bureau in an era in which the transforming trilogy of industrialization, immigration, and urbanization changed America from a nation of farmers into a nation dominated by business. The earliest successful commercial foods were either new altogether—like crackers—or tasty but time-consuming to prepare at home. Condiments such as mustard, catsup, relishes, jams, and jellies, and, later, tinned fruits, meats, and vegetables, were all newly available from a burgeoning prepared foods industry. Likewise, medicines for the inevitable indigestion (dyspepsia) and other ills stemming from a poor diet were some of the most successful patent medicines. Consumers, however, had little way of telling good products from bad. State laws were frequently inconsistent and ineffective. Meanwhile, canned foods exploded, patent medicines and standard drugs were often equally unreliable, catsups fermented, and mustards were often watered down. Even products labeled "pure" were often counterfeits; most "pure Vermont maple syrup," for instance, was made from Iowa corn syrup.

The Bureau of Chemistry found its niche in the Department of Agriculture by using its analytical chemical expertise to improve the U.S. marketplace. Wiley and the bureau chemists turned their attention to the food and drug products on the market, testing them for ingredient substitutions, omissions, or additions that would be defined as "adulteration" and "misbranding," under the 1906 act. Wiley's pioneering work on the safety of food preservatives led Congress to increase his bureau's budget and include special funds for human testing of early food additives (salicylic acid, benzoate of soda, boric acid, copper salts, saccharin). As it became clear that some producers would always take shortcuts to reduce costs (so long as the consumer could not detect the difference), support for a national food and drug law began to emerge and grow, supported by national women's groups, muckraking journalists, state food and drug officials, and analytic chemists. Wiley's prowess as a "crusading chemist" became legendary. At a convention of hostile canners, for example, he single-handedly changed their minds about regulation by reminding them that what they made they should also be willing to eat.

At the height of Progressive-era politics, during the heyday of analytical chemistry, and in the midst of the bacteriological revolution, Congress transformed the Bureau of Chemistry into a regulatory agency, fully expecting that science would be the arbiter of both health and commercial issues. Signed on 30 June 1906 by Theodore Roosevelt, along with the MEAT INSPECTION ACT, which put inspectors into all of the nation's slaughterhouses, the 1906 Pure Food and Drugs Act is still considered by historians to be one of the most significant pieces of Progressive-era legislation. In 1927, the regulatory component of the Bureau of Chemistry became the Food, Drug, and Insecticide Administration, renamed the Food and Drug Administration in 1930.

Within the decade following passage of the 1906 Pure Food and Drugs Act, the consumer marketplace was transformed. Wiley felt strongly about certain issues, and highly contentious and even more highly publicized legal cases were fought over them. But it was the routine enforcement of the simplest adulteration and misbranding portions of the law that transformed the commercial landscape of the country. New federal food and drug inspectors worked with businesses, factories, and trade organizations to update equipment, institute basic sanitary procedures, and apply insights gained from the burgeoning science of bacteriology to safeguarding the nation's food and drug supply. Added to initial concerns about food additives, and in the wake of Pasteur's discovery of the microorganisms responsible for food fermentation as well as some diseases, came increasing concerns about microorganisms in food as a cause of disease. Under Wiley's leadership, the Bureau of Chemistry continued to identify products and pathogens that moved food safety from abstract speculation to concrete action. Wiley began to hire expert microbiologists who, in turn, helped transform the canning and egg industries and shape the new refrigeration industry, helping to insure safer food for all Americans. By the time Wiley left office, in 1912, many known commonplace dangers had been eliminated from interstate commerce, though threats such as botulism, mycotoxins, and e-coli were soon to be discovered. Improvements in the drug trade as well paved the way for extraordinary future advances in therapeutics.

By the 1930s, the 1906 act had become seriously outdated. A new multimillion dollar cosmetic industry, new food products and pesticides, new drugs and new classes of drugs including barbiturates and sulfa drugs, and changes in the field of advertising all made deficiencies in the Wiley Act increasingly apparent. With the active support of consumer advocates such as Consumer's Research and Consumer's Union, so-called "guinea-pig" muckraking journalists, women's organizations, and Eleanor Roosevelt herself, the old law was replaced during the New Deal with the 1938 Food, Drug, and Cosmetic Act. Propelling the new legislation through Congress and onto President Franklin Roosevelt's desk was a 1937 drug disaster. "Elixir sulfanilamide," which contained a poisonous solvent, diethylene glycol, killed over 100 people before the entire field force of the FDA could be dispatched to retrieve every ounce of the product. This episode generated support for an important new provision in the 1938 act requiring companies to perform pre-market safety testing of all new drugs and gain FDA approval before marketing them.

In 1940, the Food and Drug Administration left the Department of Agriculture to become part of a new Federal Security Agency; and in 1953, it was transferred to the Department of Health, Education and Welfare (DHEW). In 1968, FDA became a component of the Public Health Service (PHS). In 1980, education was removed from the DHEW's responsibilities, and it was renamed the Department of Health and Human Services (DHHS). During the 1960s, 1970s, and 1980s, the Drug Enforcement Administration, the Consumer Product Safety Commission, and parts of the ENVIRONMENTAL PROTECTION AGENCY and FEDERAL TRADE COMMISSION were all created to extend consumer protection procedures pioneered by the Food and Drug Administration to stop illegal drug sales, recall dangerous consumer durable goods, set tolerances for agricultural chemicals, and control drug advertising.

Significant pieces of legislation broadening and extending FDA's premarket activities were enacted between 1958 and 1976. In the Food Additives Amendment of 1958 and the Color Additives Amendment of 1960, a premarket approval system was established for food and color additives, requiring that such substances be shown to be safe, suitable, and non-carcinogenic. In 1961, a worldwide scandal erupted over the teratogenic drug thalidomide, responsible for thousands of birth defects in Europe and a few in the United States, where the drug was never approved for sale. In 1962, Congress significantly strengthened FDA's authority over drugs, charging it with assessing both the safety and efficacy of new drugs prior to approval. In 1976, medical devices were subjected to premarket regulatory assessment, and a system devised to assess such devices in accordance with their perceived risks—three separate risk categories representing high, moderate, and low risks were established. In 1971, the PHS Bureau of Radiological Health was transferred to FDA, bringing with it responsibility for ensuring the safety of radiation-emitting consumer products such as televisions and microwave ovens. In 1972, regulation of biologic products, including serums, vaccines, and blood products, was transferred from the NATIONAL INSTITUTES OF HEALTH (NIH) to FDA.

FDA currently regulates approximately $1 trillion worth of products each year (including both domestic and imported goods), representing about 25 cents of every dollar spent by consumers each year. The agency's fiscal year 2002 budget is $1.553 billion, including $184 million in industry-assessed user fees. The FDA employs about 10,000 personnel in the Washington area and in 167 field offices throughout the United States and Puerto Rico. Included in the fiscal year 2002 budget is an increase of $151.1 million and 832 full-time employees for activities related to bioterrorism and emergency preparedness following the tragic events on 11 September 2001.

BIBLIOGRAPHY

Goodwin, Lorine Swainston. *The Pure Food, Drink, and Drug Crusaders, 1879–1914.* Jefferson N.C.: McFarland, 1999.

Junod, Suzanne White. "Food Standards in the United States: The Case of the Peanut Butter and Jelly Sandwich." In *Food, Science, Policy and Regulation in the Twentieth Century.* Edited by David F. Smith and Jim Phillips. London: Routledge, 2000.

Maeder, Thomas. *Adverse Reactions.* New York: Morrow, 1994.

Marcus, Alan I. *Cancer from Beef: DES, Federal Food Regulation, and Consumer Confidence.* Baltimore: Johns Hopkins University Press, 1994.

Marks, Harry M. *The Progress of Experiment: Science and Therapeutic Reform in the United States, 1900–1990.* Cambridge: Cambridge University Press, 1997.

Okun, Mitchell. *Fair Play in the Marketplace: The First Battle for Pure Food and Drugs.* Dekalb, Ill.: Northern Illinois University Press, 1986.

Swann, John P. "Sure Cure: Public Policy on Drug Efficacy before 1962." In *The Inside Story of Medicines: A Symposium,* Madison, Wis.: American Institute of the History of Pharmacy, 1997.

White, Suzanne. "The Chemogastric Revolution and the Regulation of Food Chemicals." In *Chemical Sciences in the Modern World.* Edited by Seymour H. Mauskopf. Philadelphia: University of Pennsylvania Press, 1993.

Young, James Harvey. *Pure Food: Securing the Federal Food and Drugs Act of 1906.* Princeton, N.J.: Princeton University Press, 1989.

Suzanne White Junod

See also ***Jungle, The;*** **Pure Food and Drug Movement.**

FOOD PRESERVATION, protecting food from deterioration and decay so that it will be available for future consumption.

Natural Processes

Human beings learned to gather naturally preserved foods and to assist nature in the preserving process about 10,000 years ago, before the dawn of agriculture and animal husbandry. Human beings in the Stone Age stored nuts and seeds for winter use and discovered that meat and fish could be preserved by drying in the sun. After the discovery of fire, cooking made food more appetizing and was an aid to preservation, since heating killed some of the microorganisms and enzymes that caused spoilage. Smoking meat and fish as a means of preservation grew out of cooking. After farming developed—the Neolithic Period, or New Stone Age—human beings had more dependable surpluses for preservation. Native Americans subsisted on dry corn and beans that they had stored for winter use; Plains Indians cut buffalo meat into thin strips and dried it in the sun on wooden frames.

Salt was used for flavoring before it was learned that meat soaked in salt brine or rubbed with salt would keep for weeks or months. Brining, later called "pickling," became a favorite way to keep fruits and vegetables for winter use. Sugar was used as a preservative in ancient times, and making jam and marmalade was widely practiced. While spices were thought to preserve food, they mainly served to cover up unpleasant flavors.

Fermentation, the natural process of chemical change in food, was observed, probably by chance, and used thousands of years ago. Fermented fruit juices resulted in wine, a safe beverage in areas of uncertain water supply. Brewing came later. Another product of fermentation, vinegar, was useful for pickling meats, fish, fruits, and vegetables. The Chinese, and later the Germans and other Europeans, fermented cabbage or sauerkraut. About three thousand years ago milk, which does not keep well, was first fermented into cheese. About the same time, Egyptians developed raised sourdough bread, another result of fermentation. In some areas and during some parts of the year, people preserved food by freezing it, but thousands of years passed before freezing became available through man-made processes in all parts of the world throughout the year.

Processes Created by Humans

Canning. Until the nineteenth century human beings were dependent on the natural processes of drying, cook-

Frozen and Home-Canned Goods. Donna Choate, also known for her quilts, shows off her deep-freeze unit, under her glass jars of preserved foods. LIBRARY OF CONGRESS

ing, salting, pickling, fermenting, and freezing for food preservation. These had been only slightly modified over the ages. Then, in the early 1800s a French chemist and confectioner, Nicolas Appert, developed canning, for which he was awarded a prize by his government in 1809. Although a theoretical understanding of the benefits of canning did not come until Louis Pasteur observed the relationships between microorganisms and food spoilage some fifty years later, Appert's ideas were still valid. He placed wholesome food in clean metal containers, which were then sealed and boiled long enough to kill the spoilage-causing microorganisms.

Canning spread rapidly. In 1810 an Englishman, Peter Durand, patented a can of iron coated with tin. Today's cans are primarily steel, with a thin coating of tin and, usually, an enamel lining. Commercial canning began in the United States with pickles and ketchup in Boston in 1819 and seafood in Baltimore in 1820. The cooking in boiling water took five or six hours in the early days, but this was sharply reduced in 1860 when Isaac Solomon added calcium chloride to the water, raising its boiling point. The introduction of the pressure cooker, or retort, in 1874 was an even more important step, permitting much more rapid processing. Commercial canners then turned to machines that would do many of the tasks formerly done by hand, such as shelling peas, cutting corn from the cob, and cleaning salmon.

After 1900, enthusiasts of domestic science, agents of agricultural extensions, and others encouraged home canning of all types of food, mainly in glass jars, as a means of utilizing home garden products, providing better diets, and reducing the cost of living on farms. By the early 2000s the decline of the family farm, the low cost of commercially canned foods, and the widespread use of freezers had made home canning rare.

Drying. A sizable dried-fruit industry flourished in the United States long before the arrival of mechanical refrigeration. In colonial times great quantities of apples were dried in the sun and by artificial means. Prior to 1795 drying and the use of salt and sugar were the principal methods of preserving foods. In 1854, it was estimated, Maine could furnish the nation's supply of dried apples. The perfection of fruit evaporators in 1870–1875 increased exports of dried-fruit products. Thirty million pounds of dried apples were exported in 1880. Of nearly a half-billion pounds of dried apples exported in 1909, 83 percent came from California. Later, new drying processes and machinery enlarged outputs for domestic and foreign markets. Meanwhile, refrigeration and canning developed vastly to aid drying in preserving fruit, vegetables, meat, and other foods for human consumption. New methods of preserving foods in their fresh state reduced the need for dried foods, which became high-priced delicacies, served as appetizers or candied.

Refrigeration and freezing. As a means of commercial food preservation, refrigeration preceded freezing. In 1803 Thomas Moore, a Maryland dairy farmer who lived about twenty miles from Washington, D.C., began transporting butter to the new capital city in an icebox of his own design, getting a premium price for his product. Moore patented his refrigerator and published a pamphlet describing it. By the 1840s, American families were beginning to use iceboxes for food storage and preservation. One of the first recorded refrigerated rail shipments was a load of butter, packed in ice and shipped from Ogdensburg, N.Y., to New York City in 1851. In 1868 William Davis patented a refrigerator car with metal tanks along the sides that were filled with ice from the top.

Beginning in the 1830s, various systems of mechanical refrigeration were patented in the United States. Eventually both freight cars and trucks with mechanical refrigeration were developed. In the home the mechanical refrigerator began to replace the icebox in the 1920s. Mechanical refrigeration made possible another major advance in food preservation—freezing. This process decentralized storage and improved the taste and nutritive value of storable foods. In 1912 Clarence Birdseye, a graduate of Amherst College, was in Labrador and noticed that freshly caught fish pulled through the ice quickly froze solid. When thawed, the fish might revive because quick freezing prevented large ice crystals from forming and thus avoided the breakage of cell walls. The physical character of the tissue, and incidentally its taste, remained the same. After much experimentation, Birdseye invented a machine for quick-freezing food products. The machine froze by conduction—that is, by pressing the food directly between very cold metal plates. In 1923 Birdseye established a frozen seafood company that was eventually successful.

Frozen concentrated orange juice, based on a process developed in the U.S. Department of Agriculture, became widely used after World War II. The freezing process also permitted the marketing of precooked food, sold ready to heat and serve. As frozen foods became more prevalent, deep-freeze compartments were included in many home refrigerators. Central frozen-food lockers became popular in many small towns and were widely used to preserve meat. After World War II frozen foods became even more popular and many families began purchasing separate deep-freeze units. These could be used for freezing home-produced foods or for storing commercially prepared products. By 1973 one household in three had its own deep-freeze unit; by the end of the century virtually all full-size domestic refrigerators included freezers.

Refrigeration. A woman stores food in a 1950s-model electric refrigerator. © CORBIS

Quick freezing led to the development of another means for preserving food—freeze drying. World War II supplied a strong impetus to the development of improved methods of drying food. In general the problem was to dry quickly without heat damage. Spray drying was particularly helpful in improving the quality of dried eggs and powdered milk. Other methods of drying produced potatoes, soup mixes, fruit juices, and other items that could be conveniently shipped and stored before being reconstituted for consumption. Freeze drying developed after World War II. In this process the product is frozen and the moisture is then removed as a vapor by sublimation. The resulting food, after reconstitution, retains much of its original flavor, color, and texture. By the 1970s freeze drying was widely used for coffee, soup mixes, and other dehydrated convenience foods. Some meat was freeze dried, and other developments kept meats edible for prolonged periods of time. Antibiotics introduced into chilling tanks, for example, prolonged the freshness of poultry.

Irradiation. The late–twentieth century saw the emergence of irradiation, or radurization, a pasteurization method in which food is exposed to low levels of high-energy ionizing radiation in an effort to kill microbial contaminants. If properly refrigerated and packaged, irradiated meat, fruit, and vegetable products enjoyed a significantly extended storage life. However, because of inherent concerns about radiation, and the tendency of irradiated foods to lose some of their nutritional value, irradiation was used only sparingly. Scientists, consumer

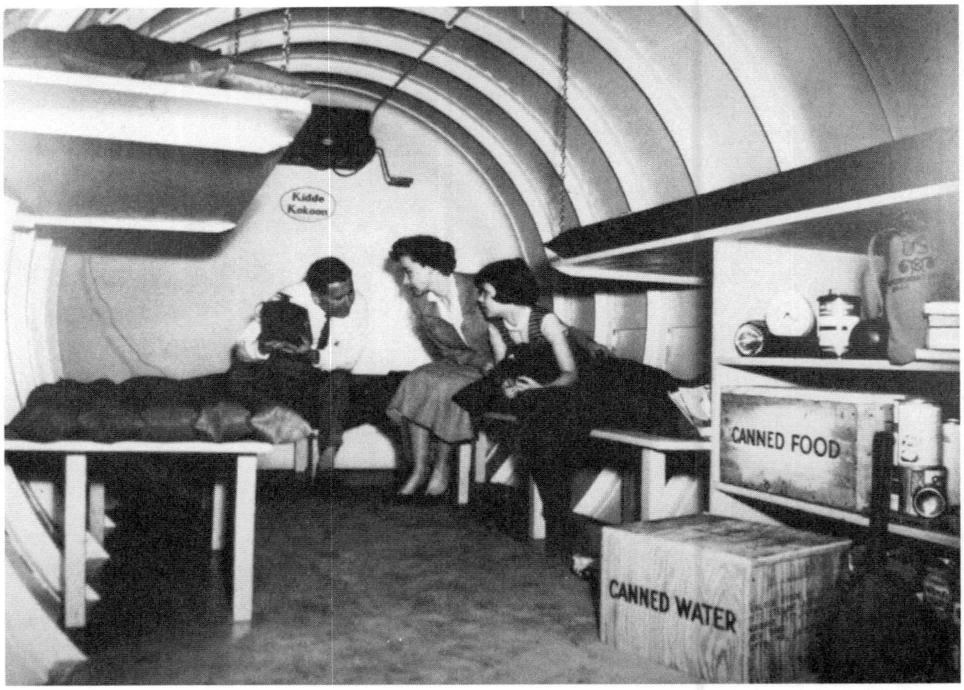

Food in Cans, Just in Case. Three people sit in a Cold War bomb shelter amid boxes of canned food and water.

groups, and the food industry continued to debate its effectiveness.

BIBLIOGRAPHY

Anderson, Oscar E. *Refrigeration in America.* Port Washington, N.Y.: Kennikat Press, 1972.

David, Elizabeth. *Harvest of the Cold Months: The Social History of Ice and Ices.* Edited by Jill Norman. New York: Viking, 1994.

Woolrich, Willis R. *The Men Who Created Cold: A History of Refrigeration.* New York: Exposition Press, 1967.

Louis Pelzer
Wayne D. Rasmussen/A. R.

See also **Canning Industry; Food and Cuisines; Pure Food and Drug Movement; Refrigeration; World War II.**

FOOD STAMP PROGRAM. The food stamp program originated in federal efforts to combat overproduction during the Great Depression by raising the consumption of agricultural products. The Department of Agriculture conceived the program as a means to assist the nation's farmers while also feeding the hungry and out-of-work. The first food stamp program began in May 1939 in Rochester, New York, and eventually spread to 1,500 counties before ending in 1943 as the wartime economic boom dampened concern about hunger and overproduction.

Despite the efforts of a number of proponents, the federal government did not reestablish the food stamp program for nearly twenty years. President John F. Kennedy, after witnessing Appalachian poverty during the 1960 campaign, instructed the Department of Agriculture to create food stamp pilot programs. The first of these began in McDowell County, West Virginia, on 29 May 1961. Its success brought program expansion, and the Food Stamp Act, enacted 31 August 1964, established a permanent program.

Like its predecessor, the second food stamp program served farmers as its primary clientele while assisting the needy through increased purchasing power and food consumption. Participants purchased stamps at prices and at an allotment level determined by their income and received bonus coupons to exchange for food deemed surplus by the government. The program's emphasis on agricultural production, consumption, and consumer choice combined, as President Lyndon B. Johnson observed, America's "humanitarian instincts" with "the free enterprise system."

In the decade following the 1964 legislation, the food stamp program expanded rapidly and transformed from a program of relief and surplus disposal into a welfare program. The Department of Agriculture adapted food stamps to serve the urban poor, liberalized benefits and eligibility to meet nutritional needs, decreased the purchase price of coupons, and increased coupon allotments. The Food

Stamp Reform Bill of 1970 codified these reforms and established national standards for nutrition and eligibility. Reforms in 1973 secured food stamps as an entitlement program, required of states and counties by the federal government and guaranteed to all who were eligible. In 1975, the program reached 17.1 million people and received a budget of $4.6 billion. This expansion resulted from the work of hunger advocacy groups, the Senate's Select Committee on Nutrition and Human Needs chaired by George McGovern, and the Nixon administration. It reflected a broad political and social consensus as to the program's necessity, effectiveness, and affordability.

Economic decline in the mid-1970s, however, triggered mounting criticism of the food stamp program. Charges of fraud and abuse, which had worried observers since the creation of the first program, emerged again. New concerns developed from the program's expansion and success. Opponents assailed food stamp benefits and eligibility requirements as too generous and as disincentives for the poor to find work. Conservatives charged that the program had expanded beyond taxpayers' ability to pay for it and represented an outsized federal government. Together, these political attacks brought increased congressional scrutiny and the first turn of public opinion against the program. The Food Stamp Act of 1977 reflected this new mood in stricter eligibility standards and stricter administrative guidelines.

In the 1980s, the Reagan administration and congressional opponents of the food stamp program stepped up efforts to trim the program and dramatically reduced program expenditure. In the course of the decade, the program faced new criticism that blamed food stamps and other welfare programs for enticing illegal and nonworking legal immigrants to the United States. Yet while subjected to budget cuts and redesigned benefits, the program's basic structure and purpose remained unchanged through the 1980s and participation continued to rise. The program reached its peak level of enrollment of 28 million individuals in March 1994.

The mounting hostility of Congress and the public toward food stamps coalesced in the bipartisan Welfare Reform Act of 1996. The legislation cut stamp allotments and eligibility and changed the formula for calculating benefits. While food stamps continued as an entitlement program, the law reduced the federal government's role in funding and administration. It placed a three-month cap on the participation of able-bodied, childless adults who remained unemployed, and it denied benefits to illegal immigrants and to many legal immigrants. The 1996 legislation successfully decreased both the program's cost and its participation levels, but seemed to have shifted much of the difference to private food charities.

The food stamp program remained a significant part of America's struggle against poverty and hunger. In fiscal year 2000, the program served 17.2 million individuals in 7.3 million households and received a budget of $21.1 billion. The Department of Agriculture's Food and Nutrition Service oversaw the program, and state public assistance agencies administered it through their local offices. The program continued to evolve. Electronic benefits systems were replacing the use of stamps, while electoral politics and concerns about access once again seemed to favor program expansion—the restoration of some legal immigrants' benefits, in particular.

BIBLIOGRAPHY

Berry, Jeffrey M. *Feeding Hungry People: Rulemaking in the Food Stamp Program.* New Brunswick, N.J.: Rutgers University Press, 1984. Focuses on federal administration of food stamps yet provides a detailed history of the program's origins and early years.

MacDonald, Maurice. "Food Stamps: An Analytical History." *Social Service Review* 51 (Dec. 1977): 642–658.

Patterson, James T. *America's Struggle against Poverty, 1900–1994.* Cambridge, Mass.: Harvard University Press, 1994.

Department of Agriculture. Food Stamp Program Web site. http://www.fns.usda.gov/fsp. Provides current information and statistics on the program.

James Tejani

See also **Welfare System.**

FOOTBALL. The game of American football as played today by high school, college, and professional teams grew out of rugby-style football which in the mid-1870s replaced a largely kicking game known as association football. Although initially played on village greens and on college fields, the first intercollegiate game took place on 6 November 1869 when Rutgers defeated Princeton 6–4 in a soccer-style game. Five years later, Montreal's McGill University playing at Harvard introduced rugby football, which would be rapidly adopted by eastern teams.

Collegiate Development

For the first fifty years of football, college teams enjoyed a virtual monopoly of what they called the gridiron (the term applied to the football field because of the lines drawn at five-yard intervals). In 1876, students at Harvard, Princeton, Columbia, and Yale met to form the Intercollegiate Football Association, all agreeing to play by rugby rules. Of the four schools, only Yale chose to remain an independent. Nevertheless, Yale continued to meet with the other schools and played a crucial role in the adoption of new rules and in the popularization of American football. Beginning in the 1880s, the eastern institutions led by Yale played "big games" before large crowds in the New York and Boston areas. From 1880 to 1888, changes in the intercollegiate rules led to the transformation of British rugby into American football. The possession rule of 1880, which decreed that the team with the ball would keep possession if tackled, led to a series of further changes. The result was a game of physical contact and deception that had progressively less in common with rugby and association football.

The possession rule and the changes that accompanied it were associated with Walter Camp, a player for Yale in the late 1870s. A gifted strategist and promoter, Camp served as a coach or adviser to the Yale team from 1879 to 1910 and as the key figure on various rules committees. Through devices such as his All-America teams, he was also instrumental in making football a nationwide intercollegiate sport. Led by Camp, the handful of youthful rules-makers enacted the yards and downs rule (three downs to gain five yards), numerical scoring, interference in front of the ball carrier, and tackling between the waist and the knees (rather than above the waist). Players could move forward before the snap of the ball (momentum plays), and push and pull the ball carrier through the defense (mass play). As a result of these rules changes, football became noticeably rougher and by the late 1800s was criticized by clergy, newspaper editors, and some older college faculty and administrators for its dangers and brutality.

In the 1890s, football spread rapidly to colleges in every part of the country. Spearheaded by former players or "missionary coaches," the teams closely followed the rules and rituals of eastern colleges, including Thanksgiving Day rivalries such as Michigan and Chicago or Stanford and California. As football gained in popularity with students and alumni, criticism of the game among faculty, college presidents, and crusading journalists grew more shrill, especially at a time when several players were killed or seriously injured each year.

On 9 October 1905, just after the beginning of the football season, President Theodore Roosevelt met with six alumni gridiron advisers from Yale, Harvard, and Princeton, including Camp and Coach Bill Reid of Harvard. Roosevelt secured their pledge to draw up a statement in which they would agree to eliminate brutal and unsportsmanlike play. Contrary to a widely held belief, Roosevelt did not issue an edict to the colleges, nor did he have a direct role in reforming the rules. In October and November 1905, football at all levels had eighteen fatalities—three in college play—and 159 serious injuries.

Following the death of a Union College player in a game against New York University, Chancellor Henry MacCracken of NYU called a meeting of nineteen colleges to consider the evils of football. That gathering in early December 1905 of twenty-four delegates led to a second, larger conference, which met in New York late in the same month. The more than sixty colleges represented appointed a reform rules committee. In addition, they organized themselves into the Intercollegiate Athletic Association of the United States (ICAA), predecessor of the National Collegiate Athletic Association (NCAA), to challenge the older, big-college football committee. Meeting together, the two committees agreed to sweeping gridiron reforms, including the ten-yard rule (ten yards to be gained in three downs), six men on the line of scrimmage and a defined neutral zone between the teams, stiffer penalties, and the forward pass. Although the number of injuries declined under the new rules, another round of deaths and injuries in 1909 led to the enactment of more comprehensive rules between 1910 to 1912.

Football in the 1920s and 1930s

After World War I, both college football and the fledgling professional version of the game prospered as a result of the booming economy and the remarkable popularity of major sports. Thousands of gridiron enthusiasts flocked to the newly constructed stadiums modeled after the Harvard, Yale, and Princeton stadiums. In October 1924, Harold "Red" Grange of Illinois became football's best-known player when he ran for five touchdowns and passed for a sixth in a game against Michigan. After his final college game, Grange signed a contract with the professional Chicago Bears of the National Football League (NFL). He immediately played to overflow crowds in Chicago and New York and agreed to lucrative deals for endorsements and movie appearances. The highly publicized and profitable entry of the "Galloping Ghost" into pro football was a precursor to the wealth of NFL players later in the twentieth century.

Just as football grew at the college level, it also took hold in the high schools. Football had been played at private secondary schools since the 1880s, and some public schools fielded teams in the 1890s and early 1900s. Promising players at private schools and high schools became the object of fierce recruiting struggles by the colleges. In the early 1900s, the emergence of the larger consolidated high schools created a need for football as a means of forging loyalties among large and diverse student bodies. Even before World War I, some coaches became known in high school football before moving up to the college level.

Football was also widely played as an unorganized, sandlot sport, or as a supervised playground recreation. By 1929, many of the serious injuries and occasional deaths in the first three decades of the twentieth century occurred during unsupervised play. Because of the need for protective equipment and adult supervision, youth leagues gradually evolved. What became the Pop Warner Leagues began as a local Philadelphia area football club in 1929. The organization was later renamed for Glenn Scobie "Pop" Warner, best known as a college coach at Carlisle Indian School, the University of Pittsburgh, and Stanford University. Beginning in 1947, the Pop Warner Leagues initiated their own national championship modeled after college and professional competitions in football and other sports.

Professional football had originated in the towns of western Pennsylvania and taken root in the smaller cities of Ohio. In 1920, a group of midwestern teams met to form the American Professional Football Association, changed the next year to the National Football League. In the 1920s and 1930s, NFL teams often went bankrupt or moved and changed names, and professional football ranked a distant second to college football in popularity

Pro Football Grows. Back in the 1930s, college football was far more popular than professional football in America, as fans preferred to see the younger players battle it out in support of their alma mater. However, professional football was gaining in popularity and continued to grow each decade until, by 2002, it had nearly surpassed baseball as America's Game. Here, Slingin' Sammy Baugh of the Washington Redskins tries to evade a tackler after completing a pass in a 1937 National Football League game. © AP/Wide World Photos

and prestige. Only after World War II, with the advent of television and air travel, did the NFL and other leagues challenge the college game.

Post–World War II Football

Television, a medium that rapidly expanded in the 1940s and 1950s, proved well-suited to the gridiron game. After setting records in the first years after World War II, attendance at college football games began to slump from 1949 on. The alarmed NCAA members ceded to their TV committee the right to control or even to ban college football telecasts. In 1951, the NCAA contracted with Westinghouse (CBS) television network to televise one game each Saturday, later broadening the agreements to include several regional games. This cartel would help to strengthen the power of the NCAA, but it would also lead to near rebellion within the association in the 1980s.

Although college football attendance revived, professional football rapidly surpassed its collegiate parent. A national audience watched a gripping telecast of the NFL championship game in 1958 when the Baltimore Colts won a dramatic sudden-death overtime victory against the New York Giants. Frustrated by the NFL's cautious approach toward expansion, the oil billionaires Lamar Hunt and Bud Adams began the American Football League (AFL) in 1959, with its first game in 1960. Bolstered by a network contract, the AFL challenged the NFL for blue-chip draft choices and TV audiences. In 1966, the AFL and NFL agreed to merge, and an annual championship known as the Super Bowl was played between the two leagues after the following season, though they would not become one league with two conferences until 1970. That year, ABC Sports innovator Roone Arledge teamed up with NFL commissioner Pete Rozelle to launch "Monday Night Football," an instant hit on prime-time evening television. Professional football franchises, which had once struggled for attendance, became businesses worth millions of dollars.

Although the players' salaries rose, they would not reach the levels achieved by major league baseball until the 1990s. Strikes in 1974 and 1987 led to victories by the owners, who effectively blocked the free agency that had resulted in soaring salaries in major league baseball. Attempts to found new professional leagues—the World Football League in 1974–1975, the United States Football League in 1983–1985, and the XFL in the winter of 2000—failed to breach the NFL cartel. Only the Canadian Football League (CFL), arena football played indoors, the World League of American Football (an NFL minor league with teams mainly in Europe), and the

Women's Professional Football League (WPFL) offered an outlet for players who could not play in the NFL.

Following World War II, African American players appeared in rapidly growing numbers both in college and professional ranks. In college football, a handful of black players had participated since the 1890s in the East, Midwest, and West. In addition to being subjected to harassment and brutality, these players were by mutual consent "held out" of games with southern teams. In the postwar years, colleges outside the South refused to accept these "gentlemen's agreements" that kept blacks out of games. Except in the South, the number of African American players grew steadily in the 1950s. Southern teams were not integrated until the late 1960s and early 1970s. In 1961, Ernie Davis of Syracuse became the first African American Heisman Trophy winner.

African Americans had played professional football in the early 1900s. A handful played in the early years of the NFL. In 1934, the league's last players, Jack Lilliard and Ray Kemp, were forced out of pro football. After World War II, the Cleveland Browns of the new All America Football League (AAFL) and the Los Angeles Rams of the NFL both integrated their teams, and the number of black professional players would show a steady increase after 1950.

College Football in the Age of the NFL

In the 1960s, college football enjoyed a brief period of prosperity and relative calm. In the fall of 1966, 33 million viewers watched a fierce struggle between Michigan State and Notre Dame, the college game's version of the Giants-Colts showdown in 1958. ABC's innovations in telecasting and the advent of color television brought more revenue and recognition to big-time teams and their coaches.

Following World War II, many teams adopted two-platoon football in which teams had separate defensive and offensive units (the innovation doubled the need for scholarships and players). Unnerved by rising costs and wedded to past practice, the NCAA football rules committee attempted in the 1950s to banish two-platoon football but returned to unlimited substitution by the end of the decade. (Unlike the colleges, the NFL never tried to abolish separate offensive and defensive teams.)

In 1951, nearly fifty institutions dropped football because of rising costs and dwindling attendance (some of these such as Georgetown, Fordham, and Detroit were ranked in the top twenty in the 1920s and 1930s). In the East, eight Ivy League institutions adopted joint rules deemphasizing football. They began less costly round-robin play in 1956 and eliminated spring practice, football scholarships, and postseason contests.

After World War II, the NCAA failed in its first attempt to regulate subsidies for supposedly amateur players. The subsequent scandals created support both for deemphasis of big-time football and for a nationwide system to enforce athletic codes of conduct. Other scandals involved booster clubs that funneled illicit payments to players and recruits. Beginning in 1956, a series of pay-for-play schemes were uncovered at five institutions in the Pacific Coast Conference, contributing to the conference's demise in 1959. Stepping into the vacuum, the NCAA levied stiff penalties against offenders, including bans on TV appearances. The commercial model pursued by many college football conferences led to charges that colleges had become the minor leagues for professional football. To some extent, the charges were true. Not only did the colleges supply the training for NFL recruits, but coaches also moved easily between the professional and collegiate ranks.

The quest for revenues in college football proved both a motivator for top teams and a cause of internecine quarrels. Faced with rising expenditures in the 1970s, big-time college teams opposed sharing TV revenues with NCAA members who had smaller football teams or no teams at all. Formed in 1976 as a lobbying group within the NCAA, the College Football Association (CFA) proposed to negotiate their own TV contracts. In 1984, two CFA members, Georgia and Oklahoma, won a Supreme Court decision against the NCAA, thereby ending the association cartel. Institutions and conferences within the association would now be responsible for their own TV contracts.

Unlike professional football, Division I-A football, comprising the most prominent intercollegiate football institutions, had no playoff championship. Beginning in 1998, the NCAA initiated the bowl championship system to replace the mythical champion chosen by sportswriters and coaches. Using a variety of methods, including computer ratings, the NCAA chose the top two teams to play in one of the major bowl games, the designations of which rotated from year to year. Critics pointed out that college football still was the only college or professional sport that did not choose the champion by playoffs.

Conclusion

Beginning in the late nineteenth century, American football developed far differently from rugby football and association football (soccer, as it is referred to in the United States). Unlike baseball and basketball, American football has been largely confined to the United States and Canada. It has remained a predominantly male game, though a women's professional league has fielded teams, and female place kickers have competed at the high school and college levels. Whereas baseball was once clearly the American pastime, football has gained preeminence at the high school, college, and professional levels. In addition, football has developed a distinctive fan culture. Tailgating or picknicking in the parking lot, participating in booster clubs, and traveling vast distances for Bowl games or intersectional rivalries have become part of the football culture of dedicated spectators. Moreover, the availability of football through cable and network TV has transformed millions of television viewers who seldom attend a major contest into knowledgeable and enthusiastic football fans.

BIBLIOGRAPHY

Davis, Parke H. *Football, the American Intercollegiate Game.* New York: Scribners, 1911.

Harris, David. *The League: The Rise and Decline of the NFL.* New York: Bantam, 1986.

Lester, Robin. *Stagg's University: The Rise, Decline, and Fall of Big-Time Football at Chicago.* Urbana: University of Illinois Press, 1995.

Nelson, David M. *Anatomy of a Game: Football, the Rules, and the Men Who Made the Game.* London and Cranbury, N.J.: Associated University Presses, 1994; Newark: University of Delaware Press, 1996.

Oriard, Michael. *King Football: Sport and Spectacle in the Golden Age of Radio and Newsreels, Movies and Magazines, the Weekly and the Daily Press.* Chapel Hill: University of North Carolina Press, 2001.

Peterson, Robert W. *Pigskin, the Early Years of Pro Football.* New York: Oxford University Press, 1997.

Roberts, Randy, and James Olson. *Winning Is the Only Thing: Sports in America since 1945.* Baltimore: Johns Hopkins University Press, 1989.

Ross, Charles K. *Outside the Lines: African-Americans and the Integration of the National Football League.* New York: New York University Press, 1999.

Smith, Ronald A. *Sports and Freedom: The Rise of Big-Time Athletics.* New York: Oxford University Press, 1988.

———. *Play-by-Play: Radio, TV, and Big-Time College Sport.* Baltimore: Johns Hopkins University Press, 2001.

Watterson, John Sayle. *College Football: History, Spectacle, Controversy.* Baltimore: Johns Hopkins University Press, 2000.

Weyand, Alexander M. *The Saga of American Football.* New York: Macmillan, 1955.

John Sayle Watterson

FORAKER ACT. The act set up the government of Puerto Rico, annexed from Spain at the conclusion of the Spanish-American War. Passed in April 1900, it provided that the executive department was to be composed of a council of eleven members appointed by the president of the United States. Legislative authority was vested in this council and in an elective house of delegates. The island's inhabitants were to be considered "citizens of Puerto Rico," not U.S. citizens. A special reduced tariff was levied on all goods moving between the United States and Puerto Rico. Congress took the view that Puerto Rico was not incorporated in the United States and therefore the clauses of the Constitution concerning citizenship and taxation need not be in force. This interpretation was upheld and refined in a series of Supreme Court decisions known as the Insular Cases.

BIBLIOGRAPHY

Argüelles, María del Pilar. *Morality and Power: The U.S. Colonial Experience in Puerto Rico from 1898 to 1948.* Lanham, Md.: University Press of America, 1995.

Montalvo-Barbot, Alfredo. *Political Conflict and Constitutional Change in Puerto Rico, 1898–1952.* Lanham, Md.: University Press of America, 1997.

Torruella, Juan R. *The Supreme Court and Puerto Rico.* Río Piedras: University of Puerto Rico Press, 1985.

William Spence Robertson / T. M.

See also **Insular Cases; Puerto Rico.**

FORCE ACTS, also known as Force Bills, refers to Congressional legislation enacted during the early 1830s and 1870s, intended to compel Southern compliance with particular federal legislation.

The first Force Act—passed by Congress, at the urging of President Andrew Jackson, on 2 March 1833—was designed to compel the state of South Carolina's compliance with a series of federal tariffs, opposed by John C. Calhoun and other leading South Carolinians. Among other things, the legislation stipulated that the president could, if he deemed it necessary, deploy the U.S. Army to force South Carolina to comply with the law.

In reality, Jackson, under the U.S. Constitution, already enjoyed that power. Indeed, by that March, he had already dispatched U.S. military forces to Charleston, with orders to make sure that the tariffs were enforced before visiting cargo ships were allowed to land. The confrontation between Jackson and South Carolina, years in the making, turned on a widespread belief among states rights advocates that many of the economic woes then bedeviling South Carolina arose from protective federal tariffs enacted in 1828 and 1832. Reacting to such fears, Calhoun and other South Carolinians had promulgated a "doctrine of nullification," which—stopping just short of claming the state's right to secede from the Union—maintained that states enjoyed a right to disobey federal statutes, which they adjudged violated states' rights under the U.S. Constitution. The Force Act of 1833 had, for the most part, a merely symbolic value, for, by the time of its passage, the dispute that gave rise to the legislation had been resolved through compromise. To wit, on the same day that Congress passed the Force Act, it also passed, with Jackson's blessings, a bill modifying the offending tariffs. South Carolina, in a face-saving gesture, was then allowed to "nullify" the Force Act—an empty gesture since the controversy had already been resolved.

The term Force Acts also refers to a series of federal statutes, enacted between 1870 and 1875, that sought to secure the compliance of recalcitrant Southerners with various Reconstruction-era reforms. An 1870 Force Bill sought to force compliance with the Civil Rights Act of 1866, which reconfirmed various political rights of African Americans. An 1871 bill, designed to protect voting

Ford Blazes a Trail. Instead of making cars one at a time by hand, Henry Ford utilized the moving assembly line, on which a stream of cars moved continuously past workers, each of whom had a specific part to attach to the car—and at the end, a finished car would roll off the line, ready for sale. To this end, Ford made only one kind of car, the Model T, and then sold it at a price far below his competition. By 1921, Ford accounted for 62 percent of all new car sales. Here an early version of the Model T rolls down a Ford assembly line. © AP/Wide World Photos

rights, mandated federally appointed election supervisors. Another 1871 Force Bill, designed to strengthen enforcement of the Fourteenth Amendment, sought to curtail voter intimidation by the Ku Klux Klan and other groups opposed to black enfranchisement. The final Force Bill, passed in 1875—just before Republicans lost control of the Congress—sought to give African Americans equal access to hotels, trains, and other public facilities. In the end, all four of that era's Force Bills fell victim to the forces of southern white supremacy that gathered resurgent powers during the 1870s. Not until the mid-twentieth century were the rights sought for African Americans in the South by the Force Bills' authors fully secured.

BIBLIOGRAPHY

Foner, Eric. *Reconstruction: America's Unfinished Revolution, 1863–1877.* New York: Harper and Row, 1998.

Freehling, William W. *The Road to Disunion: Secessionists at Bay, 1776–1854.* New York: Oxford University Press, 1990.

Tom Chaffin

See also **Civil Rights Act of 1875; Reconstruction; Tariff.**

FORD MOTOR COMPANY. Founded in 1903 by Henry Ford, and based in the Detroit suburb of Dearborn, Michigan, the Ford Motor Company quickly revolutionized the market for cars. After several years of making a range of autos, in 1908 Ford decided to concentrate on producing only one car, the Model T. His goal was to compete on the basis of price not product variety. Crucial to this strategy was his adroit use of the moving assembly line, where workers specialized in one minor part of the car-assembly process. As prices fell, sales of the Model T rose from 10,607 in 1909 to 472,350 in 1916. By 1921 Ford accounted for 62 percent of all car sales. As the 1920s wore on, however, many consumers demanded greater product variety in addition to low prices. As sales of the Model T fell, Ford Motor replaced it with the Model A, which sold 4.5 million units from 1927 to 1931.

During World War II, Ford Motor Company played an active role in the war effort. It produced a wide range of military hardware, including tanks, trucks, jeeps, engines, and airplanes. Edsel Ford, who had assumed the presidency of the company from his father in 1918, died in 1943. Henry Ford reassumed formal control of the company after his son's death, and helped position his grandson Henry Ford II to become president in 1945. Henry Ford died in 1947.

Ford Motor Company regained its place as America's number two car producer in 1950, overtaking Chrysler, which had supplanted it in the early 1930s. In 1963 Ford unveiled one of its most popular cars, the Mustang, which registered more than 500,000 sales in its first eighteen months. In 1971 Ford introduced another model, the Pinto, which was designed to compete in the sub-compact market. Despite the Pinto's potential, it generated a good deal of negative publicity for the company after the gas tanks in several cars exploded in rear-end collisions.

In 1979 Philip Caldwell replaced Henry Ford II as CEO, and within five years had helped Ford register record sales and profits. Donald Petersen succeeded Caldwell as CEO in 1985, and under his direction Ford acquired the British luxury car producer Jaguar and introduced the Taurus, a model that proved very popular with consumers. As the twentieth century drew to a close, Ford was comfortably positioned as America's second largest car producer, trailing only General Motors.

BIBLIOGRAPHY

McGraw, Thomas. *American Business, 1920–2000: How It Worked.* Wheeling, Ill.: Harlan Davidson, 2000.

Nevins, Allan. *Ford.* New York: Scribners, 1954.

Scherer, F. M. *Industry Structure, Strategy, and Public Policy.* New York: HarperCollins, 1996.

Martin H. Stack

See also **Assembly Line; Automobile;** *and vol. 9:* **Ford Men Beat and Rout Lewis.**

FOREIGN AID. Foreign aid only emerged as a significant and institutionalized aspect of U.S. diplomacy and international relations during the Cold War. After 1945 the United States and the Soviet Union presided over expanding alliance systems and increasingly disbursed large quantities of economic as well as military aid to the developing nations of the emerging Third World. During the Cold War, the International Monetary Fund (IMF), the International Bank for Reconstruction and Development (the World Bank), and the United Nations also played growing roles in distributing foreign aid and promoting economic development. The IMF and the World Bank have been heavily financed and influenced by the United States and, prior to the end of the Cold War, the governments of the Soviet bloc generally refused to participate in those organizations. While most observers acknowledge that the disbursement of foreign aid by the United States has been driven by the interaction of politico-strategic and economic interests, the relative importance of these factors has been a subject of ongoing debate. There are also commentators who emphasize the importance of humanitarian impulses in the distribution of foreign aid.

The Truman Doctrine, the Marshall Plan, and the Point Four Program

One of the first indications of the role that foreign aid was to play in the Cold War came with the announcement of the Truman Doctrine on 12 March 1947 by President Harry S. Truman. The Truman Doctrine was a response to the growing influence of Communist parties in Greece and Turkey and included the extension of $400 million in economic and military aid to the Greek and Turkish governments. This was soon followed by the implementation of the European Recovery Plan, known as the Marshall Plan, which was launched on 6 June 1947. The Marshall Plan sought to protect Western Europe from any further worsening of the post-1945 economic and political crisis. It was driven by a concern that a destabilized Western Europe would result in a power vacuum, providing an opportunity for the Soviet Union to expand its influence westward. The United States made it clear that the Marshall Plan was aimed at preventing or containing the appearance in Europe of governments, or groupings of governments, that would threaten the security interests of the United States. Washington also insisted that it have complete information as to how the aid money was used and that it had to be used to help build "free and democratic institutions." Although the plan was initially offered to the USSR and Eastern Europe, Moscow and its client regimes rejected it.

The Marshall Plan involved the disbursement of $12.5 billion towards the reconstruction of Western Europe over a four-year period. By 1952 the Marshall Plan was a key factor in increasing industrial production to 35 percent and agricultural production to 18 percent above the levels they had been at in Western Europe before World War II. The Marshall Plan also drew attention to the benefits of foreign aid for the U.S. economy. One of the requirements of the Marshall Plan was that the bulk of the aid money be used to purchase U.S. exports, which provided an important push to the U.S. economy and bolstered trade linkages that favored U.S. manufacturers. The Organization for European Economic Cooperation (OEEC) was set up to coordinate the Marshall Plan. With the cessation of aid in the 1950s, the OEEC continued to operate as a focus of economic cooperation amongst the governments of Europe. In 1960 it changed its name to the Organization for Economic Cooperation and Development (OECD). The U.S. and Canada joined the OECD, which also began to act as a vehicle for the distribution of foreign aid from North America and Western Europe to the so-called developing nations of the Third World.

More broadly, from the outset the Marshall Plan demonstrated U.S. economic prowess, and it represented an important precedent for subsequent U.S. aid to Asia, Latin America, the Middle East, and Africa. In the late 1940s, the Truman administration became increasingly concerned about political and economic turmoil in the emerging nations of the Third World. It was hoped that an extension of U.S. foreign aid to them would help to undercut the influence of the Soviet Union and "international communism." On 20 January 1949 Truman delivered his Inaugural Address at the start of his second term as president. In it he sketched out an expanded foreign aid policy that became known as the Point Four

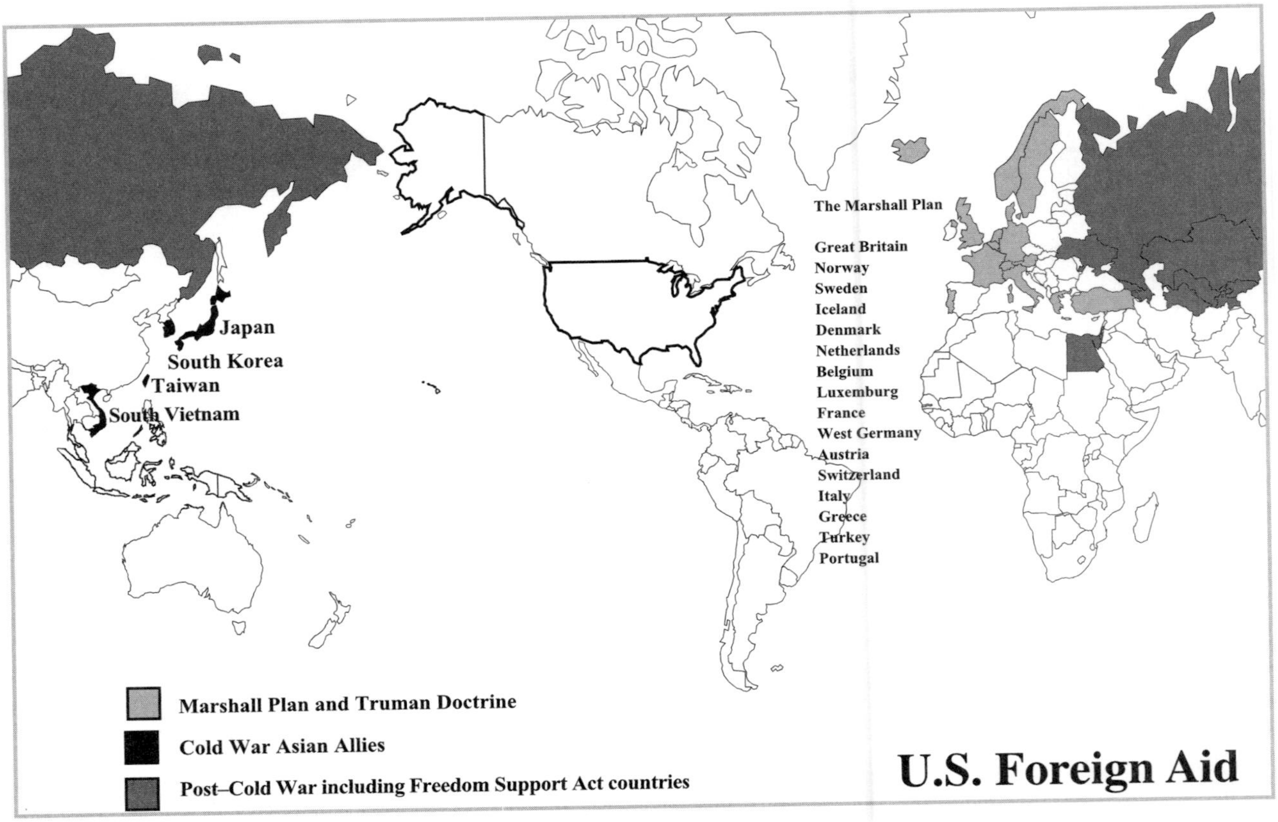

program (enacted as the International Development Act). Point one pledged continuing U.S. support for the United Nations. Point two emphasized U.S. support for world economic recovery, while point three reiterated the U.S. commitment to supporting "freedom-loving nations." Point four set out a U.S. commitment to providing American technical and scientific expertise and capital to "underdeveloped" nations in an effort to improve their living standards. The program started with a budget of $45 million. By early 1951, 350 technicians working under U.S. auspices were engaged in over one hundred cooperation projects in almost thirty countries. In 1953 Congress increased the budget of the Point Four program to $155 million.

Foreign Aid and the Cold War in the 1950s and 1960s

Apart from Western and Southern Europe, a major focus of Washington's foreign policy and its foreign aid strategy immediately after 1945 was northeast Asia. By the late 1940s foreign aid was important to the U.S. effort to turn Japan, South Korea, and Taiwan into capitalist bulwarks against the Soviet Union and Maoist China. After the Korean War the sustained American economic and military aid that went to South Korea and Taiwan in the 1950s and 1960s played an important role in strengthening the capabilities of their emergent national security states. Between 1945 and 1973 U.S. economic aid to South Korea was $5.5 billion, while U.S. military aid was $7 billion. The economic assistance to South Korea was more than all U.S. economic aid to sub-Saharan Africa and half the figure for all of Latin America over the same period. In the 1950s more than 80 percent of South Korean imports were financed by U.S. economic assistance.

Southeast Asia, by contrast, did not attract as much sustained attention in the early years of the Cold War. Washington also took a limited interest in South Asia. However, the United States began to change its assessment of Southeast and South Asia in the 1950s. For example, following the onset of the Korean War, it began participating in the Colombo Plan, which coordinated the disbursement of development aid to governments in those regions and the Pacific. This initiative was spearheaded by the British government and supported by other governments of the Commonwealth. While America was not involved in the immediate establishment of the Colombo Plan in 1950, much of the financing over the years came from the United States. A total of $72 billion was disbursed via the Colombo Plan between 1950 and 1983, with over 50 percent of that amount ($41.2 billion) coming from the United States.

By the end of 1950, meanwhile, the United States had already disbursed at least $133 million to the French colonial authorities in Indochina in support of their war effort. U.S. assistance went on by late 1952 to make up 40 percent of the overall cost of the French government's war in Indochina, while by the beginning of 1954 the U.S. contribution had risen to 80 percent. For the administration of Dwight D. Eisenhower and its immediate successor, the regime of Ngo Dinh Diem (1955–1963) was to be a "showcase for democracy" and the site for a definitive nation-building effort. Between the collapse of French colonial power in 1954 and the end of Eisenhower's presidency at the beginning of 1961, Washington disbursed over $2 billion worth of military and economic aid to the government of South Vietnam. As the 1960s began, the Diem regime was the fifth-highest recipient of U.S. foreign aid worldwide (and the third-highest recipient—after South Korea and Taiwan—among non-NATO countries). When President John F. Kennedy entered the White House in 1961, Saigon had already become the site of the biggest U.S. economic aid program worldwide.

Kennedy and influential advisers such as Walt Whitman Rostow—who served as chair of the Policy Planning Council in the State Department—increasingly advocated a shift in U.S. foreign policy towards taking the initiative in Asia and Latin America (and the Third World more generally) via infusions of economic and military aid as part of an increasingly ambitious set of national development and counterinsurgency programs. In a West Point address on 18 April 1963, Rostow declared that the key to winning the guerrilla war in South Vietnam was to "create at forced-draft the bone structure of a modern nation." In the early 1960s the Strategic Hamlet Program became the focus of Washington's wider aid and counterinsurgency strategy in South Vietnam. Drawing on previous French colonial initiatives and earlier efforts by the Diem regime, as well as British counterinsurgency programs in Malaya in the 1950s, the Kennedy administration encouraged and facilitated the removing of peasants from widely dispersed villages and the placing of them in concentrated settlements that could be controlled more directly by the government in Saigon. The State Department scheduled almost $90 million to be spent on the Strategic Hamlet Program for fiscal year 1963. Employing this approach the U.S. Military Assistance Command Vietnam (MACV) and the AGENCY FOR INTERNATIONAL DEVELOPMENT (USAID) sought to undermine the National Liberation Front's ability to get intelligence, food, and other supplies as well as recruits from the population. The National Liberation Front (NLF) quickly responded by promising the peasants that following the revolution they would be allowed to return to their old villages. The NLF also intensified its military attacks on, and its recruitment activities in, the strategic hamlets.

Despite the apparent failure of the Strategic Hamlet Program by the end of 1963, subsequent efforts to resettle and control the rural population did little but rework the basic approach while excising the term "strategic hamlet" from the counterinsurgency lexicon. Meanwhile, following the overthrow and assassination of Diem and his brother, Ngo Dinh Nhu, in a military coup in late 1963, the successor programs to the Strategic Hamlet Program were increasingly overshadowed by full-scale warfare. The United States had hoped that the overthrow of the Diem regime would improve the stability of South Vietnam; however, the deterioration in the military situation following the coup paved the way for the escalation of U.S. involvement and direct military intervention by 1965. That led, in turn, to immense human, material, and environmental destruction, but failed to solve the fundamental political problems of the Saigon regime and the fragile nation-state of South Vietnam. The pervasive reliance on U.S. aid generated growing possibilities for government and private corruption. With the Tet offensive in early 1968, any idea that U.S. power could turn South Vietnam into a viable capitalist nation-state and achieve military victory against the North disappeared. With the election of Richard Nixon as U.S. president at the end of 1968, the United States began to look for ways to withdraw "with honor," placing growing emphasis on what was called the Vietnamization of the war.

As part of its wider emphasis on foreign aid, the Kennedy administration also set up the USAID in 1961 to coordinate government foreign aid initiatives. Established as a semi-autonomous body operating in the State Department, it was responsible for disbursing and administering aid in South Vietnam and around the world. Apart from South Vietnam, a large percentage of the aid this new body disbursed initially went to the ALLIANCE FOR PROGRESS, another ambitious modernizing initiative that the Kennedy administration hoped would contain the "communist threat" to Latin America following the revolution in Cuba in 1959. The Alliance for Progress began as a decade-long program of land and economic reform that was expected to cost $100 billion and was aimed at bringing about an annual growth rate for the region of at least 2.5 percent. It also sought to achieve greater productivity in the agricultural sector, eradicate illiteracy, stimulate trade diversification, generate improvements in housing and bring about a more even income distribution in the region.

However, its major, if unstated, goal was the protection of North American investments in Latin America at the same time as many of the Alliance's proposed reforms endangered those investments. Trade diversification would undermine the monopoly of primary agricultural products and mineral extraction enjoyed by a number of U.S.-based corporations. Meanwhile, land reform threatened the power of the still largely land-based ruling elites in Latin America. This contradiction was apparent in the way that Kennedy's reformism went hand in hand with Washington's ever-deepening commitment to military and police aid and counterinsurgency to defeat peasant-based rebellions in the region. There were sixteen military coups within eight years of the launch of the Alliance for Progress. By the late 1960s high rates of economic growth in many Latin American countries had been achieved. However, high growth rates exacerbated social inequality while politics, instead of becoming more democratic, moved increasingly towards authoritarianism. American support for counterrevolutionary military and political activity in Latin America grew in the 1960s in the form of U.S. military, CIA, and civilian advisers and U.S. military aid and economic and technical assistance for counterinsurgency programs.

New Directions, the New Cold War, and Foreign Aid after the Cold War, from the 1970s to the 1990s

By the Nixon era, U.S. foreign aid policy was in disarray. In the context of the U.S. defeat in Vietnam and the wider critique of U.S. foreign policy that emerged, a growing movement to reform American economic assistance programs resulted in the passage of various reformist pieces of legislation under the heading of what was called New Directions. This led briefly to an emphasis on both the basic needs of the poor and direct grassroots participation in the process of development. At the same time the Foreign Assistance Act (1961), which had been central to the Kennedy administration's approach to foreign aid, was amended significantly between 1973 and 1978 to provide for an increased focus on human rights in the disbursement of foreign aid. However, by the late 1970s influential free-market critics of New Directions were in the ascendant. Their views were consolidated during the administration of President Ronald Reagan. In the 1980s USAID's main focus was the Private Enterprise Initiative (PEI), which promoted private-sector development and encouraged market-oriented reform. Furthermore, U.S. foreign assistance policy in the 1980s, as in earlier periods, was still firmly grounded in strategic interests. The 1980s actually saw the percentage of foreign assistance going to development-related programs decline and the amount spent on security-related projects rise.

This trend was readily apparent in the approach to Central America taken by the Reagan administration. Central America was the object of more American economic and military aid during Reagan's first term than in the entire period from 1950 to 1980. For example, between 1981 and 1984 inclusive, the El Salvadoran government received $758 million in economic aid and $396 million in military aid, compared to only $6 million in military aid in 1980. El Salvador had emerged as the recipient of more U.S. aid than any other country in Latin America by the middle of Reagan's first term. In fact, during this period El Salvador (with a total population of less than 5 million by the end of the 1980s) was the third-largest U.S. aid recipient worldwide, behind only Israel and Egypt. (Reflecting the ongoing strategic significance of the Middle East, Israel and Egypt received about one-third of all U.S. foreign aid disbursed in the 1980s.) The level of foreign aid for El Salvador in the 1980s was on a scale reminiscent of the U.S. nation-building effort in South Vietnam in the 1960s, minus the direct American military intervention. By the end of the 1980s the U.S. had disbursed upwards of $3 billion in economic and military aid to El Salvador, the equivalent of about $800,000 a day for ten years.

With the end of the Cold War, the direction of U.S. foreign assistance policy again shifted. The administration of President William Jefferson Clinton introduced a range of reforms that were again (as in the 1970s) aimed at displacing security as the key focus of foreign aid as reflected in the Cold War–era Foreign Assistance Act. The Clinton administration outlined four overall goals for U.S. foreign aid in the post–Cold War era. While USAID was still expected to promote economic development via market-oriented reform and the encouragement of trade and investment, it was also enjoined to set up programs oriented towards building democratic political institutions. A greater emphasis was also placed on humanitarian assistance and sustainable development. Ultimately, however, the foreign aid bill passed by Congress in 1994 was a major compromise and for many observers appeared to reflect a continued commitment to geostrategic concerns. In the year the bill was passed, Israel and Egypt continued to receive over one-third of all U.S. foreign aid. The figure for Israel was $3 billion and for Egypt it was $2.1 billion, while the amount for sub-Saharan Africa as a whole was $800 million. Foreign aid was also directed increasingly at the former Soviet bloc, again for security reasons. For example, more than $2.2 billion of foreign aid was disbursed to Russia between 1992 and 1997 under the Freedom Support Act (FSA). Over the same period more than $2.6 billion was also disbursed to Russia via programs not covered by the FSA. The figures for the Ukraine were over $1 billion in FSA funds and $652 million in non-FSA funds, while the former Soviet republics in the Caucasus and Central Asia together received over $1.9 billion in FSA funds and $2.4 billion in non-FSA funds between 1992 and 1997 inclusive. While there have been many changes and adjustments, the disbursement of U.S. foreign aid continues to be closely connected to wider strategic and economic objectives. In the context of the "war on terrorism" initiated in 2001, and the reorientation and increase in foreign aid that has followed, this pattern appeared set to continue.

BIBLIOGRAPHY

Adams, Francis. *Dollar Diplomacy: United States Economic Assistance to Latin America.* Aldershot, U.K.: Ashgate, 2000.

Dacy, Douglas C. *Foreign Aid, War, and Economic Development: South Vietnam, 1953–1975.* Cambridge,U.K.: Cambridge University Press, 1986.

Hogan, Michael J. *The Marshall Plan: America, Britain, and the Reconstruction of Western Europe, 1947–1952.* Cambridge, U.K.: Cambridge University Press, 1987.

Lancaster, Carol. *Transforming Foreign Aid: United States Assistance in the 21st Century.* Washington, D.C.: Institute for International Economics, 2000.

Latham, Michael E. *Modernization As Ideology: American Social Science and "Nation Building" in the Kennedy Era.* Chapel Hill: University of North Carolina Press, 2000.

LeoGrande, William M. *Our Own Backyard: The United States in Central America, 1977–1992.* Chapel Hill: University of North Carolina Press, 1998.

Rabe, Stephen G. *The Most Dangerous Area in the World: John F. Kennedy Confronts Communist Revolution in Latin America.* Chapel Hill: University of North Carolina Press, 1999.

Ruttan, Vernon W. *United States Development Assistance Policy: The Domestic Politics of Foreign Economic Aid.* Baltimore: Johns Hopkins University Press, 1996.

Wedel, Janine R. *Collision and Collusion: The Strange Case of Western Aid to Eastern Europe, 1989–1998.* New York: St. Martin's Press, 1998.

Wiegersma, Nan, and Joseph E. Medley. *US Economic Development Policies Towards the Pacific Rim: Successes and Failures of US Aid.* London: Macmillan, 2000.

Mark T. Berger

See also **Africa, Relations with; Egypt, Relations with; El Salvador, Relations with; Israel, Relations with; Korea, Relations with; Latin America, Relations with; Vietnam, Relations with.**

FOREIGN INVESTMENT IN THE UNITED STATES. From colonial times to the early 2000s, investments from abroad contributed to the economic life of the American nation. The earliest investment was that of the Virginia Company, which in 1607 provided the basis for the English settlement in Jamestown, Virginia. The company's stockholders remained in London and hoped that the settlers would enrich them by discovering gold and silver. After several reorganizations, the Virginia Company came to an end in 1623 and was formally dissolved the next year. It was replaced by a Crown colony.

The years between the settlement of Jamestown and the Declaration of Independence witnessed many other transatlantic investments, made by chartered trading companies, merchant investors, and investors in land, mining, and even manufacturing. On the eve of the Revolution, British mercantile houses played an important role in American trade. British nonresident or temporarily resident owners dominated shipping except from New England. British navigation laws notwithstanding, Dutch and French traders also had outlets in America and engaged in commerce. British absentee land ownership was substantial. By 1776, however, most infant industries in America were small-scale and domestic, despite some large British involvements in the iron industry.

During the Revolution the assets of British loyalists (resident and nonresident) were confiscated. Later there were two sets of compensation, one for British direct investments in land and other assets and the second for commercial debts. The latter were far larger in monetary value. Excluding the commercial debts, investments from abroad came to roughly £1.1 million. If the aggregate physical wealth of the thirteen colonies is estimated at £110 million, this would equal a mere 1 percent of colonial wealth. Were the commercial debt included, the sum would rise to under 4 percent. Investments from abroad would rise in percentage, as well as in absolute terms, in the postcolonial era.

Prior to the revolution, British investments were all "direct investments," using modern terminology. "Direct investments" are those that carry with them some influence or element of control. These are to be differentiated from "portfolio investments," which are purely financial interests. Foreign investment always refers to investment by nonresident foreigners.

Pre-Civil War Investments from Abroad

The American Revolution brought political but not economic independence. To finance the Revolution, Americans turned to France, Spain, and Holland. By 1789, "foreign debt" (denominated in foreign currencies) came to 22 percent of the total federal debt. If domestic debt (denominated in U.S. dollars) and debt held abroad are included, 29 percent of U.S. federal government obligations was to foreign investors. In addition, substantial foreign investments existed in state debts, as well as in equity interests in certain American businesses (for example, in the Bank of North America, the nation's first bank).

In 1789, Dutch investment in the United States was the largest of any single nationality. This would not be true for long. By 1803, if not earlier, British investment in the United States exceeded Dutch. From this point on, British investment in the United States remained the largest of any single nationality. In 1803, some 56 percent of the U.S. federal government debt was in foreign hands, up substantially from 1789, and now with sizable British holdings. Although British investments were the greatest, there continued to be investments in varying amounts from the European continent, particularly Dutch and, to a lesser extent, French holdings.

There exist detailed estimates of 1803 foreign investments in the United States (provided by Samuel Blodget, writing in 1806). These show that 62 percent of the stock of the Bank of the United States and 35 percent of stock in state banks were held by foreigners in 1803. Roughly 5 to 6 percent of the stock in insurance, turnpike, and canal companies was owned by nonresident foreigners. These were "portfolio" investments—that is, financial interests. In addition, nonresident foreigners invested in trading activities, as merchant investors, as well as in land. Thus, in the decades after the Declaration of Independence, foreign investors were especially important in financing the Revolution, providing a market for federal debt, and aiding in the establishment of nation's banking institutions.

As the American nation took shape, the contribution made by foreign investment took on new characteristics. Whereas in 1803, 56 percent of the U.S. federal debt was held abroad, by 1853 this was down to 46 percent; and the federal debt itself was much smaller. The proportion of debt held abroad ebbed and flowed, but by 1853, foreign investment in the U.S. federal debt represented only about 12 percent of the total inward foreign investment.

Far more significant were the foreign holdings of state government debts. There had been a dramatic surge in foreign investment in state debt starting in the late 1820s, and peaking in the late 1830s, before the major defaults of the early 1840s. In an era when communications were still slow, foreign investors were highly reluctant to invest in private companies of which they knew little. They were more willing to invest in state government securities. As a result, American state governments turned abroad to fund their banking and transportation industries. In the early 1840s, with many of these state debts in default, there were cries of outrage abroad at American perfidy. Nonetheless, in 1853, the largest foreign investments in the United States remained in state debts. That year, state debts constituted about half of the total foreign investments in the United States. Some 58 percent of American state government debt was held abroad. Foreign investment in land, banking, and transportation continued. When Andrew Jackson vetoed the renewal of the charter of the Second Bank of the United States, one reason was the heavy foreign investment. The veto changed American banking history. In the 1830s, railroads began to attract a growing amount of funding from abroad. By the early 1850s, railroad bonds had already become a substantial part of the foreign investment in the United States. These bonds were backed by mortgages on the railroads themselves. British companies had arranged to sell iron rails in the United States, but because the railroads would not earn money until they became operational, the rail sellers accepted bonds as payment. British merchant bankers created a market for the bonds. The bonds were sold not only in Britain, but in Holland and, to a lesser extent, elsewhere on the European continent. In 1853, a survey indicated that some 26 percent of American railroad bonds issued were held abroad. That year railroads represented about a quarter of the inward foreign investment in the United States.

The investments in federal, state, and railroad bonds, as well as in the Second Bank of the United States, were all "portfolio" investments (financial interests). At the same time foreigners also made direct investments, those that carried management and control. Throughout the first half of the nineteenth century, there were trade related foreign investments, by trading firms. In the 1820s Scottish and English manufacturers began to appoint their own agents for the first time and even sent salaried men to sell in the United States. Yet not until the 1850s were there significant sales networks by foreign manufacturers in the United States. From the early nineteenth century onward, British insurance companies made direct investments in the United States, typically in providing fire and marine insurance.

The discovery of gold in California in 1848 turned new foreign attention to the United States and influenced foreign investment patterns, stimulating new investments from Europe in everything from gold mining companies to transportation facilities. By the 1850s Americans were talking about (although not yet building) transcontinental railroads.

From the Civil War to World War I

During the Civil War, the South was able to float a large loan to the Confederacy, backed by investors in England and on the European continent. By contrast, the North depended mainly on domestic finance. Banking houses in the North developed expertise while raising large sums to finance the war. This expertise was later used in cooperation with British and other foreign financial institutions to draw huge sums of foreign capital to American railroads. After the war, some of the Northern federal government debt also drifted abroad. In fact, until roughly 1875, public sector securities—state as well as federal—got the largest share of inward foreign investment. Thereafter, the bulk of the foreign investment in the United States went to the private sector.

Foreign capital poured into the United States in the period from the mid-1870s to 1914, the so-called first time of globalization. As the world's largest recipient of foreign capital, the United States was the world's greatest "debtor nation." Foreign capital contributed in a very positive fashion to the economic growth of the country. The greatest part went into building American railroads. The investments were no longer linked with the import of iron rails. Now, there was a market in London and Amsterdam (and in Paris and Frankfurt) for American railroad securities. The foreign investments were both in new issues and traded securities. The amounts were awesome. In London, a section of the stock market was set aside for American "rails." The huge amount of funding required to construct the American transcontinental railroad system was provided by international sources. Every student of economic development reads of "capital shortages," but this was not an issue in American economic growth. Readily available foreign capital complemented domestic capital. American entrepreneurs established the railroad systems using foreign finance.

There were also inward portfolio investments in other corporate securities, especially in such giant enterprises as United States Steel Corporation. As of 14 June 1914, one quarter of U.S. Steel's shares were held abroad; but these securities were widely held and did not represent in any way "foreign control" over America's largest steel company.

More important than the portfolio investments in America's new and big businesses were the many inward foreign direct investments (FDI). In the late nineteenth and early twentieth centuries, inward FDIs were prevalent. The FDI took two forms. First, there were "free-standing companies," companies set up in a source of capital country (such as Britain, France, or Holland) that invested abroad and transferred management with the investment. In the United States, these numerous companies were involved in mining, cattle raising, meatpacking, breweries, and mortgage lending. Second, there were the companies headquartered in Britain, Germany, Switzerland, and elsewhere that did business at home, developed new products and processes and unique trademarks, and integrated economic activities. Then with their internalized knowledge and advantages they moved abroad not only to the United States but to other countries as well. Companies such as Lever Brothers, the big German chemical companies, Nestlé, Shell, and many others established themselves in the United States before the start of World War I.

Although American industry developed principally as a domestic activity, it was far from exclusively domestic. Indeed, in a few industries, from thread to rayon, foreign companies were the first movers. Rayon, the pioneer synthetic fabric, was a new "high tech" industry before World War I and the British company Courtaulds was the only significant producer in the U.S. domestic market. German dyestuffs companies sold and to a small extent manufactured in the United States; they took out numerous significant U.S. patents and registered their trademarks. The British Marconi company led in wireless telegraphy in the United States and worldwide. The German Telefunken built radio towers in America. Foreign multinational enterprises had a significant presence in "high tech" innovative activities. They presented branded, trademarked goods.

World War I, the Inter-War Years, and World War II
During World War I, America was transformed from a "debtor" to a "creditor" nation. On the eve of World War I, some $7 billion in foreign investment was present in the United States, while U.S. investments abroad totaled $3.5 billion. This meant that the United States had larger obligations to foreigners than foreigners had to it, the definition of a debtor nation. At the end of World War I inward foreign investment was actually lower than in 1914, while U.S. investments abroad had surged. America had become a creditor nation—a status it would continue to hold until the late 1980s. Yet all the time the United States was a creditor nation, inward foreign investment was present, following an uneven course.

During the war years, inward foreign investment dropped for a number of reasons. First, Europeans sold American securities to finance their own war effort. Second, after U.S. entry, an Alien Property Custodian took over "enemy" (principally German) assets in the United States. Nonetheless, many inward foreign investments remained. British direct investments in the United States were untouched by the British government mobilization of "American securities." British insurance companies continued as significant participants in providing American fire and marine insurance.

In the immediate aftermath of World War I, the United States placed new restraints on foreign direct investment. Americans believed it was inappropriate to have the new radio industry under foreign control. The U.S. government encouraged the formation of Radio Corporation of America to take over the assets of Marconi, the British controlled company that had innovated in radio communications. With Prohibition, the large British investments in breweries came to an end. The Mineral Lands Leasing Act of 1920 put restrictions on the ability of foreign oil companies to lease public land if their nations did not give Americans reciprocal rights.

After 1923, inward foreign investment in the United States rose. And as American lending and outward foreign direct investments expanded globally, inward foreign portfolio and direct investments also mounted. Inward investments were far overshadowed by the large outward U.S. foreign investments. The crash of 1929 meant sizable losses for foreign, as well as domestic, investors in Wall Street. As the world economy collapsed after the panic of 1929, capital export restrictions multiplied in Europe. But by 1933 liquid monies from all over the world flowed into America for safety from the unsettled conditions around the world. The monies went into corporate securities, equities rather than bonds. Railroads were passé and the position of railroad securities in the portfolios of foreigners shrunk. The new monies coming into the United States during the 1930s alarmed Americans, who feared that monies that flowed in would just as rapidly flow out, upsetting a fragile stock market and the fragile recovery path of the American economy. Investments were no longer associated with "new issues." Instead they were typically traded securities.

Throughout the inter-war period foreign multinational enterprises regularly entered and exited the United States. Some German direct investors restored operations that had been taken over during World War I. By 1929 some German companies were taking on a more impressive role in America than before the war, introducing new technology and developing vast multiproduct, multiproduction, and distribution networks. Some foreign investors disguised their transfer of capital into the United States. They did this for tax reasons, to avoid their home nations' capital export restrictions, and to be able to escape U.S. takeover in the event of another war. This last reason was applicable specifically to German investments. Some multinational companies that had started to manufacture in the United States before World War I persisted through the war and the 1920s, but could not survive the adverse conditions following the 1929 crash. Michelin, for example, exited in 1930. On the other hand, Dunlop, a newcomer to tire manufacture in the United States in the 1920s, managed to stay on (losses notwithstanding). In the 1930s, with adverse political and economic conditions in Europe, in relative terms Canadian investors became more important in the United States. Canadian brokers had long traded on behalf of their nationals on the New York Stock Exchange. With the end of Prohibition in 1933, the Canadian company, Seagrams was able to enter the United States, becoming by 1937 the leading whiskey producer in the country.

With the outbreak of war in Europe in 1939, the British once again sought to mobilize American securities to obtain dollars. Under U.S. pressure, British direct investment also became vulnerable. During 1940 and 1941, Americans introduced foreign fund control regulations, freezing a large portion of the sizable foreign assets in the country (British and Canadian assets were exempted). In 1941 a U.S. Treasury Department census of foreign investment in the United States was conducted. The size of foreign direct investments was far larger than the U.S. Department of Commerce, which had been reporting on the subject, had estimated.

During the period that the United States was at war, German direct investments were once again sequestered by the Alien Property Custodian. British investments in the United States declined further. At war's end, however, there still remained foreign investments in the United States.

1945–1973

From the end of World War II through the 1960s, U.S. investment abroad far surpassed foreign investment in the United States. America led the world in investment abroad. The aftermath of the war saw the final exit of some of the nineteenth century inward foreign investments that had been linked with the opening up of the West (gone were the cattle ranches and the mortgage lenders). On the other hand, British investment trusts gradually resumed their American investments. The British insurance companies survived intact and continued on. Lever, Shell, and Seagrams maintained their business, as did Swiss multinational enterprises such as Ciba, Sandoz, Geigy (as of 1996 combined into Novartis), and Hoffmann-La Roche.

In the 1960s, as the American balance of payments worried American public policymakers, the United States began to consider encouraging inward foreign investment.

1973–1990

Between 1973 and 1989, inward foreign investments in the United States (both portfolio and direct investments) rose steadily and rapidly. In 1973 and 1974, the Organization of Petroleum Exporting Countries (OPEC) raised the price of oil. The result was "a transfer of wealth," and surpluses were reinvested in the United States. Americans expressed alarm that the Arabs were taking over America. Likewise, Japan, which had witnessed spectacular growth rates at home in the 1950s and 1960s, emerged as a major actor on the world stage in the 1970s and 1980s, precipitating serious debates in the United States over a Japanese economic invasion. Foreign investment in the United States suddenly became a subject of major consequence with a proliferation of government hearings, books and articles attempting to reevaluate the position of the United States in the international economy.

The Arab investment was mainly of a portfolio nature. While unprecedented, it never represented more than a small portion of the inward foreign investment. The first wave of Japanese investments were direct investments. Then, in December 1980 the Japanese passed a Foreign Exchange Control Law that sharply reduced Japanese restraints on capital outflows. After this occurred, and when the yen strengthened against the dollar, there were sizable Japanese portfolio as well as the direct investments in the United States. The Japanese had long invested in the United States, but in small amounts. As late as 1976, Japanese direct investment in the United States never exceeded 4 percent of the total inward foreign direct investment. After 1976 the share rose annually. Soon Japanese direct investment in the United States was second only to that of the British. By 1989, Japanese direct investment represented roughly 17 percent of the total foreign direct investment in the United States. Japanese investments flowed into the electronics industry—into consumer products (TV production, for example) and producer ones (semiconductor manufacturing, for instance). By 1989 and 1990, Sony and its rival, Matsushita, were participants in $4.8 to $6.6 billion takeovers of American icons in Hollywood. This was all without precedent. And then there were the Japanese car companies: Honda built its first car at Marysville, Ohio, in 1982. Nissans, Toyotas, Mazdas came to be made in America, with production methods different from those used by the top three U.S. auto manufacturers. Ultimately, the American consumer got better quality cars not only from the Japanese, but from American producers as well. The Japanese also entered into American banking. By 1988, U.S. affiliates of Japanese banks and bank holding companies held 10.1 percent of U.S. banking assets. The Japanese became active in American government securities markets. The Japanese companies Nomura Securities, Daiwa Securities, Nikko Securities, and Yamaichi Securities served as primary dealers in the buying and selling of U.S. Treasury bonds.

The Japanese investments were large and conspicuous, and to many Americans seemed threatening. Yet they never surpassed those of the long-standing and also growing British investments. The Dutch were also important investors. But the relative position of Canadian investors shrunk as European and Japanese investment in America soared. With the vast influx of foreign investment in the late 1980s, the United States once again became a debtor nation in world accounts. It had been in this role before 1914, when foreign investment contributed mightily to American prosperity.

From 1990

The United States continued to be a debtor nation in world accounts, attracting more long term inward investments than it made outward investments. Both inward foreign portfolio and direct investments continued to grow, in an uneven manner to be sure. America's debtor nation status was not identical to that of many developing nations. By this time all America's foreign obligations were in its own currency, the dollar.

With some rare exceptions, America's foreign obligations were denominated in U.S. dollars throughout the post–World War II decades. The nature of America's foreign obligations in the 1990s, however, contrasted sharply with that of the period 1973 to 1990. In the 1990s foreign portfolio investments flowed into the United States on three streams, one that took advantage of rising stock market prices, another that went into federal government securities, and a third that blended with the easy movement of monies over borders. Mutual funds and investment companies multiplied, providing advice to foreigners on U.S. investments. Foreign pension funds invested in America. The American government imposed no barriers to foreign capital inflows into U.S. securities (there had never been any previously, but now it was much easier to make investments). Around the world restrictions on capital flows fell and the United States seemed an immensely attractive place to make investments. Prosperity in America in turn attracted further inward foreign portfolio investments.

As for foreign direct investment, foreign multinational enterprises in the early 1990s absorbed and rationalized their new businesses after the surge of mergers and acquisitions in the late 1980s. Many bad investments had been made but the United States was too critical a locale for foreign multinationals to neglect. After a brief slowdown, inward foreign direct investment resumed. Foreign direct investments stimulated changes in the domestic banking sector, opening the way to interstate banking. With deregulation, other long-standing barriers to foreign direct investments came tumbling down. The Federal Communications Commission's decision in April 2001 to allow Deutsche Telekom's takeover of VoiceStream represented an openness and a legal interpretation very much at variance with past policies.

Poor returns and bad investments by foreigners did not deter new entries in the 1990s and 2000–2001; by the late 1990s huge cross border mergers and acquisitions were occurring, with dollar sums that staggered the imagination. The new investments were different from prior ones. In the 1990s, with Internet and electronic transfers, the world economy became truly "global." Many authors pointed out that it was globalization comparable to that before 1914. Yet the speed with which new technologies allowed monies to move from one stock market to another was without precedent. As the computer came of age, multinational enterprises restructured, down-sized, and then expanded, and new products and processes proliferated.

At the start of the twenty-first century, the promise of new telecommunications and Internet industries, the "dot-com bubble," brought foreign capital to the United States in large amounts. In the 1990s, the Japanese economy had faltered; the Japanese "Big Bang" (its much heralded financial deregulation in April 1998) did little to aid its economy. The Japanese had not invested wisely in America. This was particularly true of their spectacular investments in the movie business, in California golf courses, and in Rockefeller Center in New York, but it was also true of a range of other investments. By 2000, Japanese investment in the United States was no longer at front stage. Yet, as a consequence of Japanese entries in the 1970s and 1980s, American industry had become more competitive and stronger. In the late 1990s, U.S. affiliates of foreign companies accounted for roughly 6 percent of U.S. private industry gross product and slightly less than 4 percent of civilian employment; on the other hand, they accounted for about 20 percent of American exports and 30 percent of America's foreign trade.

When the long-standing U.S. budget deficit turned to a surplus at the advent of the twenty-first century, the International Monetary Fund examined the global financial implications of a shrinking supply of U.S. Treasury securities. Throughout the years foreign investors bought these U.S. obligations, confident that in a high risk world they would never go into default. The inward investments in U.S. Treasury bonds had fluctuated over the years, but throughout the 1970s, 1980s, and 1990s, they were attractive to investors from around the world. In April 2001, some 22 percent of U.S. Treasury securities were held abroad.

At the start of the twenty-first century, the United States was deeply involved in the world economy. Foreign financial institutions had large commitments in the country and mergers of companies outside the United States affected conditions at home. Business was thoroughly international. As the North American Free Trade Agreement (NAFTA) and the European Union evolved, and as the euro was introduced, foreign multinational enterprises engaged in sizable amounts of truly international intracompany trade. Such trade within multinational enterprises was far more important than arms length transactions, trade between otherwise independent buyers and sellers. When the dot-com bubble burst, foreign investors (along with domestic ones) were affected.

Conclusion

Throughout its history the United States has attracted investments from abroad—both financial ones (portfolio investments) and direct investments (investments by multinational enterprises). The nation has had restrictions of various sorts on the inward foreign investments; overall, however, the United States allowed inward foreign investments. Exceptions that had long existed in sectors such as wireless communication were disappearing in 2001.

Not only have foreign investors been attracted by American prosperity, they have also contributed to it, not only with capital, but more importantly, by being conduits for new technologies and ideas, and by stimulating a competitive vigor within the United States. The impact of foreign multinational enterprises has been far greater than the macroeconomic percentages suggest. Indeed, it is hard to imagine that the 1990s would have been so prosperous for the United States without this global competition, which was expressed not so much in trade, but in foreign direct investment. Globalization has perils; it creates vulnerabilities. American stock markets have experienced extraordinary volatility. Yet both inward foreign direct and portfolio investments had more benefits than costs.

BIBLIOGRAPHY

Adler, Dorothy R. *British Investment in American Railways, 1834–1898.* Charlottesville: University Press of Virginia, 1970.

Davis, Lance E., and Robert E. Gallman. *Evolving Financial Markets and International Capital Flows: Britain, the Americas, and Australia, 1865–1914.* Cambridge, U.K.: Cambridge University Press, 2001.

Graham, Edward M., and Paul R. Krugman. *Foreign Direct Investment in the United States.* 1st ed., 1989; 2d ed., 1991; 3d ed., Washington, D.C.: Institute for International Economics, 1995.

Faith, Nicholas. *The Infiltrators: The European Business Invasion of America.* London: Hamish Hamilton, 1971.

International Monetary Fund. *IMF Survey.* Washington, D.C.: International Monetary Fund, 1972–2002.

Jackson, W. Turrentine. *The Enterprising Scot: Investors in the American West after 1873.* Edinburgh: Edinburgh University Press, 1968.

Jenks, Leland H. *The Migration of British Capital to 1875.* New York: Barnes and Noble, 1973.

Jones, Geoffrey, and Lina Gálvez-Muñoz, eds. *Foreign Multinationals in the United States.* London: Routledge, 2002.

Kerr, William G. *Scottish Capital on the American Credit Frontier.* Austin: Texas State Historical Association, 1976.

Lewis, Cleona. *America's Stake in International Investments.* Washington, D.C.: Brookings Institution, 1938.

Lipsey, Robert. "Foreign Direct Investment in the United States: Changes over Three Decades." In *Foreign Direct Investment.* Edited by Kenneth A. Froot. Chicago: University of Chicago Press, 1993.

Spence, Clark C. *British Investments and the American Mining Frontier, 1860–1901.* Ithaca, N.Y.: Cornell University Press, 1958.

Veenendaal, Augustus J., Jr. *Slow Train to Paradise: How Dutch Investment Helped Build American Railroads.* Stanford, Calif.: Stanford University Press, 1996.

U.S. Department of the Treasury. *Census of Foreign-Owned Assets in the United States.* Washington, D.C.: U.S. Department of the Treasury, Office of the Secretary, 1945.

Wilkins, Mira. "The Free-Standing Company, 1870–1914: An Important Type of British Foreign Direct Investment." Economic History Review, 2d ser., 41 (May 1988): 259–282.

———. *The History of Foreign Investment in the United States to 1914.* Cambridge, Mass.: Harvard University Press, 1989.

———. "Japanese Multinationals in the United States: Continuity and Change, 1879–1990." *Business History Review* 64 (Winter 1990): 585–629.

———. *The History of Foreign Investment in the United States 1914–1945.* Cambridge, Mass.: Harvard University Press, forthcoming.

———, ed. *Foreign Investments in the United States: Department of Commerce and Department of Treasury Estimates.* New York: Arno Press, 1977.

Mira Wilkins

See also **Banking.**

FOREIGN POLICY, broadly defined, is the course set at given times determining the relationships, policies, and actions of the United States with or toward other states and international entities. Its legitimacy derives ultimately from popular will, but formally and immediately from the Constitution, which divides authority among the executive, legislative, and judicial branches of government. In practice it is mostly formulated in the White House and the Departments of State and Defense and executed by diverse diplomatic, economic, and military agencies. The guiding principle of foreign policy is always stated to be the national interest, but interpretations of this are often controversial. Religious and ethnic groups, corporations, and the media are influential, and expressions of public opinion, variously mediated, are often politically decisive in what is, overall, a remarkably effusive, democratic culture.

The persistent domestic influence in American foreign policy has been further encouraged by the nation's immunity through most of its history (especially 1815–1941) from mortal threat. Its diplomacy, therefore, proceeding from choice rather than necessity, tends to invite debates that often devolve to arguments about moral values. Presidential administrations tend to navigate cautiously, hemmed in by strong constitutional constraints and often introspective but volatile public opinion. American foreign policy has sometimes been remarkably vigorous (especially since 1941), supportive in the nineteenth century of expansionary territorial impulses and, more recently, of broader economic extensions. Yet it has nevertheless tended historically to be managerial in character and moralistic in tone, often expressing itself in congenially concise formulas (Monroe Doctrine, Manifest Destiny, Good Neighbor Policy) rather than in geopolitical initiatives of the kind familiar to students of state practice in the more contentious European arena.

Among historians two general viewpoints predominate. A mainstream outlook posits a well-intentioned if sometimes flawed American diplomacy that oscillates between international engagement and detachment but is mostly guided by a desire for peace, stability, and progressive development. A more critical revisionist view typically portrays an essentially expansionist, hegemonic state. Between these two outlooks a wide range of other scholarly assessments, most notably a more conservative "realist" critique of perceived liberal tendencies, invigorates the field intellectually.

Establishment and Consolidation, 1776–1815

The American diplomatic tradition arguably begins in the colonial period. The revolutionaries were heir to a well-informed, politically self-conscious citizenry. Their initial concern was survival. The Continental Congress secured the indispensable alliance with France (1778) that eventually helped bring independence. But it preferred to stress economic rather than political relations, presenting prospective partners with the so-called Model Treaty (1776) emphasizing commerce. After the Treaty of Peace, 1783, and the creation of the Constitution, the administration of President George Washington restored trade with Britain through Jay's Treaty (1794). Pinckney's Treaty (1795) recorded a southern boundary agreement with Spain. Washington's Farewell Address (1796) also stressed trade and warned against "entangling alliances." But European politics persistently intruded, inspiring Congress to break with revolutionary France over the XYZ Affair (1798), which led to the termination of the alliance and to a naval "quasi-war" in 1798–1800 (see France, Quasi-War with). The Francophile President Thomas Jefferson, similarly beset, responded to French and British violations of America's neutral rights at sea with a trade embargo (1807) and the Nonintercourse Act (1809). These neoisolationist policies failed, and ensuing maritime and continental tensions led to the inconclusive War of 1812 with Britain (1812–1815). The agreement signed by the two countries in 1814 (see Ghent, Treaty of) registered the resulting stalemate and closed this first era of intense but finally profitable political engagement with a Europe that was conveniently preoccupied with the French revolutionary and Napoleonic wars.

Continental Expansion, 1803–1867

This period of dramatic enlargement is framed by the Louisiana Purchase (1803)—bought for $15 million from Napoleon and allowing a westward leap that doubled the size of the United States—and by the purchase of Alaska in 1867. It saw the acquisition of West Florida from Spain (1810) and the Adams-Onís Treaty (1819), which brought in East Florida, Spanish confirmation of the Louisiana Purchase, and a first window on the Pacific by cession of Spain's claims in the Northwest. The Rush-Bagot Treaty (1817) and other subsequent boundary agreements with Britain consolidated a demilitarized northern border. The Monroe Doctrine (1823) declared against both further European colonization in the Americas and any renewed projection of the European system in the Western Hemisphere. While this reflected rising American self-confidence, the doctrine's nineteenth-century viability rested with British naval power.

In the 1840s the Manifest Destiny concept expressed an intensified impulse toward western expansion. After the incorporation of Texas (1845), President James Polk's administration negotiated a favorable Oregon boundary settlement with Britain (1846) and, after a shrewdly manipulated crisis led to a successful war with Mexico, the 1848 peace agreement (see Guadalupe Hidalgo, Treaty of) brought California and a vast southwestern domain into the union. The Gadsen Purchase in Arizona (1853) and the later Alaska purchase completed the continental framework.

The impression of success in all these accomplishments is real; the appearance of inevitability is not. European machinations, Mexican resistance, and divisions at home had to all be surmounted or finessed. The desire for incorporation of larger parts of Mexico and Canada, and of certain Caribbean territories coveted by the southern slave states, were all frustrated for various reasons.

The Rise and Maturation of a World Power, 1860–1941

The Civil War inspired a vigorous diplomacy. The Confederacy tried to translate British and French establishment sympathy (not shared by the European working classes, which favored the Union) into recognition and support. President Abraham Lincoln and Secretary of State William Seward successfully prevented this. Northern wheat and sea power trumped Southern cotton in European calculations.

The rapid industrialization of the late-nineteenth-century United States produced at first a self-absorbed politics. Seward, a visionary, Pacific-focused expansionist, acquired Alaska and Midway Island. He called for an isthmian canal, but various executive initiatives in the Caribbean failed to gain support. In the early 1890s, Admiral Alfred Thayer Mahan's propagation of an imperial vision based on sea power heralded a revived expansionary mood. But it took the triumphant 1898 war with Spain, arising more directly out of the long Cuban rebellion, to propel the United States into world politics with subsequent control of the Philippines, Puerto Rico, and Guam, new positions in the Caribbean, and the formal acquisition of Hawaii. Substantial domestic opposition to this new American "empire" was overcome, and Secretary of State John Hay's Open Door notes to other powers in 1899–1900 signified a fresh American determination to share commercial opportunities and, by implication, political influence in China (see Open Door Policy).

President Theodore Roosevelt (1901–1909), an ardent nationalist, embodied the new activist tendency. In the Caribbean region, always a primary American interest, he created political conditions for the future Panama Canal at Columbia's expense, and closed the area to European military action by undertaking in the so-called Roosevelt Corollary to the Monroe Doctrine to be their self-appointed debt collector. He sent marines to quell various regional disturbances. More widely he mediated the Russo-Japanese peace settlement of 1905 and the Franco-German dispute over Morocco in 1907. His advocacy of a stronger navy and of an extended international law signified a commitment to both power and moral order, reflecting the self-confidence of the Progressive era.

The fuller implications emerged in the presidency of Woodrow Wilson. A supposed "idealist," the high-minded Wilson is perhaps better described as a passionate moralist and visionary. His multiple Caribbean interventions (most dramatically in the Mexican civil war), suggest continuity. He responded to the outbreak of World War I in Europe (August 1914) with two dangerously contradictory policies: neutrality but also, behind a show of legal impartiality, an opportunistically profitable economic relationship with Britain and France. The eventual German response of unrestricted submarine warfare forced America into the war. Wilson championed a rational, just peace. His FOURTEEN POINTS (1918) called inter alia for freedom of the seas, free trade, a wide degree of self-determination in Europe, and a postwar LEAGUE OF NATIONS. Having successfully orchestrated the armistice, he personally attended the 1919 Paris Peace Conference. His rigidly principled diplomatic style and his failure to collaborate with the resurgent Republicans at home or to win a liberal settlement from the war-embittered Allies contributed to a flawed peace agreement (see VERSAILLES, TREATY OF) and subsequently a failed campaign to secure congressional approval of American participation in the League. Wilson, incapacitated by illness during the final struggle with the Republican-dominated Senate, had nonetheless set a course for future American liberal internationalism.

During the Republican ascendancy (1921–1933), economic impulses (notably government retrenchment and active trade promotion) dominated foreign policy. War debt and reparations prolonged international tensions until the stabilizing United States–sponsored DAWES PLAN (1924) and YOUNG PLAN (1929) effected a short-term recovery. Politically the United States remained detached. The Washington Treaties of 1921–1922 fashioned a new Pacific geopolitics, but the real spur was the prospect of reduced naval spending. The illusory KELLOGG-BRIAND PACT (1928) supposedly outlawing war, the largely rhetorical Stimson Doctrine (1931) denying recognition of Japanese conquests in China, and the spasmodic interest in joining the World Court were all characteristically gestural initiatives. After 1929 the deep and widespread economic depression produced dislocation, protectionism, and a politically radicalizing international system. But although President Franklin D. Roosevelt was comparatively active from 1933—announcing a GOOD NEIGHBOR POLICY toward Latin America, recognizing the Soviet Union, pushing through a RECIPROCAL TRADE AGREEMENTS ACT—his freedom to act in the developing European crisis was inhibited by encumbering neutrality legislation that reflected congressional and public opinion. The quasi-isolationist mood persisted after the outbreak of war in Europe (September 1939), but internationalist sentiment strengthened after the shocking fall of France, the encouraging survival of Britain, and the reelection of Roosevelt. American LEND-LEASE to Britain (later to the Soviet Union and other countries) was followed by intensified economic pressure on Japan and a policy of naval harassment against Germany in the Atlantic. Roosevelt's proclamation with British prime minister Winston Churchill of the ATLANTIC CHARTER (August 1941), emphasizing freedom and democracy, reflected a growing sense of engagement that crystallized when the Japanese attack on PEARL HARBOR on 7 December 1941, and Adolf Hitler's soon thereafter declaration of war, brought the United States into World War II.

From Great Power to Superpower, 1941–1991

The United States supported Britain materially during their successful military-strategic wartime partnership, while steadily committing it to open postwar imperial markets and to permit currency convertibility. Relations with the Soviet Union (also receiving American aid) were distantly collaborative but were undermined by the United States' resentment at delays in creating a second front and, as victory neared, the Soviet Union's increasingly exclusionary policies in eastern Europe, which clashed with Roosevelt's more universalistic visions. The crucial YALTA CONFERENCE (February 1945) left basic misunderstandings over Poland and eastern Europe, though the following POTSDAM CONFERENCE produced tentative agreements over German administration and reparations. But in early 1946, persisting differences—intensified after the Hiroshima atom bomb led to the end of the Pacific war and by fresh Soviet expansionary political thrusts threatening Turkey and Iran—led to a confrontation between the United States and the Soviet Union in the United Nations. What came to be known as the "containment" policy, maintained throughout the Cold War, was inspired by the American diplomat George F. Kennan (who formulated it) and more generally by Churchill in his March 1946 IRON CURTAIN speech. The containment policy aimed to quell Russia's expansive tendencies, and it developed institutionally through the TRUMAN DOCTRINE of 1947 promising aid to Greece and Turkey; the MARSHALL PLAN of the same year offering aid for European economic recovery; and, finally, after a series of crises in 1948, through the formation of the NORTH ATLANTIC TREATY ORGANIZATION in 1949, committing the United States to protecting western Europe.

The containment policy endured as the Cold War enlarged to east Asia with the communist victory in China (1949) and the KOREAN WAR (1950–1953), which brought American commitments to protect South Korea, Japan, and Taiwan and to support France against nationalist and communist insurgency in Indochina. During Dwight D. Eisenhower's presidency, the Cold War expanded globally. From 1953 to 1954 the United States effectively deposed communist-supported governments in Iran and Guatemala. It declined to participate in the international Indochina settlement (see GENEVA ACCORDS OF 1954) and launched an anticommunist regime in South Vietnam. New multilateral treaties—SEATO in 1954 covering Southeast Asia, and CENTO in 1959 focusing on the Middle East—completed the "containment" chain around the largely communist Eurasia.

Eisenhower proclaimed "liberation" but actually practiced containment. His "New Look" strategy, emphasizing nuclear rather than conventional weaponry, led to epidemic testing and a vastly enlarged arsenal. It helped prompt a nuclear arms race with the Soviets who responded in kind. U.S.–Soviet relations were erratic. Ameliorations after Stalin's death (1953), during the 1955 Geneva summit, and again with Soviet leader Nikita Khrushchev's 1959 visit to the United States, had their counterpoints in tensions over German membership in NATO, the SUEZ CRISIS in 1956, the Cuban revolution in 1959, and the U-2 spy plane affair in 1960.

The brief but significant presidency of John F. Kennedy brought generational change, the Alliance for Progress (in Latin America), and the PEACE CORPS. A new "flexible response" based on augmented conventional forces replaced the atomic strategic emphasis. A crisis developed over Berlin, culminating in the creation of the BERLIN WALL in 1961. In Cuba, after the failed BAY OF PIGS INVASION in 1961 came the CUBAN MISSILE CRISIS, the dramatic confrontation of October 1962 between the Soviet Union and the United States over Soviet nuclear weapons in Cuba. The successfully resolved crisis led to the NUCLEAR TEST BAN TREATY (1963) and, arguably, to a more assertive policy in Indochina, with troop levels reaching approximately 16,000 by November 1963 when Kennedy was assassinated.

President Lyndon B. Johnson enlarged the Vietnam War commitment in early 1965 to about 200,000 troops (later to nearly 550,000). The escalation, reinforced by systematic bombing, probably prevented a communist victory and was initially popular at home. But as troop levels and casualties rose from 1965 to 1968 without visible improvement, Americans became divided. The politically successful communist TET OFFENSIVE in January 1968 forced profound reconsiderations. Peace talks began and continued sporadically under President Richard M. Nixon as fighting persisted. Nixon's VIETNAMIZATION policy allowed the steady extrication of American troops balanced by intensified bombing. The American withdrawal in 1973 and the communist victory in 1975 registered this regional failure.

Meanwhile, Nixon and his chief diplomatic adviser, Henry Kissinger, had developed an innovative triangular political strategy of détente with China and the Soviet Union. Groundbreaking agreements were signed in Moscow on strategic arms limitation and a range of economic, political, and cultural accords. The containment framework continued but was tempered now by increasing acceptance of Soviet legitimacy, manifest in further summits and in the HELSINKI ACCORDS (1975) accepting the dominant Soviet role in eastern Europe in exchange for commitments to enhanced human rights. This set the stage for the "human rights" foreign policy orientation from 1977 of President Jimmy Carter, a rationally oriented idealist who began with a treaty ceding the Panama Canal to Panama at a later date (with qualifying safeguards); Carter hoped to move American diplomacy from Cold War preoccupations toward broader socioeconomic global issues. He successfully brokered the CAMP DAVID PEACE ACCORDS between Israel and Egypt and intervened effectively in several Latin American issues. He negotiated a second strategic arms limitation treaty with Soviet leader Leonid Brezhnev. But the provocative Soviet invasion of Afghanistan in December 1979 ended détente. Carter responded with economic sanctions and plans for a rapid military buildup. But the revived tension, together with domestic economic problems largely caused by steeply higher oil prices and an Islamic revolution in Iran that led to the incarceration of American hostages, brought Republican Ronald Reagan to power in 1981.

In the 1980s we see two distinct phases. Within the context of renewed Cold War tensions, the primary emphasis was on refurbishing American military strength and morale. The comprehensive buildup was accompanied by a successful campaign to place Pershing missiles in Europe (countering Soviet targeting there) and low-risk but significant resistance to perceived Soviet or other communist expansion in Africa, Central Asia, and (especially) Central America. In that region, active subversion of the radical Sandinista regime in Nicaragua, support for conservative elements in El Salvador, and the GRENADA INVASION of 1983 signified the new militance.

The 1985 emergence of Mikhail Gorbachev, a new Soviet leader, had profound consequences. Bent on diverting resources to domestic change, he engaged a steadily more receptive Reagan in a series of summit meetings from 1985 to 1989. Slowed by Reagan's insistence on developing a defensive nuclear shield (see STRATEGIC DEFENSE INITIATIVE), these meetings produced a treaty in 1987 banning intermediate-range missiles, and another in 1989 looking to strategic arms reductions. Meanwhile, Gorbachev reduced conventional force levels in eastern Europe and permitted, during 1989, a remarkable series of political transformations to democratic rule in the region. He also allowed German reunification and continuing membership in NATO in exchange for economic assistance. The United States supported these moves, which ended the Cold War on a successful note. The Soviet Union dissolved in 1991.

The Post–Cold War Search for Definition, 1991–2001

The first post–Cold War decade brought widespread political democracy and market capitalism but produced no striking new American conceptual or policy definition. President George H. W. Bush, successful in the Persian Gulf War of 1991 against Iraq, anticipated a "new world order." The Muslim revival inspired notions of cultural-political confrontation. Subsequent references to "modernization" and "globalization" were similarly resonant but diffuse.

New political problems forced policy improvisations. Much of eastern Europe developed ties with NATO and the European Union. But Russia, still nuclear-armed, and undermined by weak leadership and corruption, was a principal object of American concern. The collapse of Yugoslavia and ensuing violence prompted President Bill Clinton's administration to intervene effectively in Bosnia and later in Kosovo. Diplomatic initiatives in the Middle East and Colombia were less successful. The principal emphasis was on the creation of enlarged, liberal trading regimes, notably through the NORTH AMERICAN FREE TRADE AGREEMENT (1994), the World Trade Organization (1995), and the United States–China agreement (2000). President George W. Bush's initially more unilateralist approach (a nuclear defensive shield, suspicion of international environmentalism) was transformed by the terrorist assaults upon New York City and Washington, D.C., on 11 September 2001 into actively coalitional diplomacy and a commitment to "war on terrorism."

BIBLIOGRAPHY

Combs, Jerald A. *American Diplomatic History: Two Centuries of Changing Interpretations.* Berkeley: University of California Press, 1983.

Graebner, Norman A. *Ideas and Diplomacy.* New York: Oxford University Press, 1964.

Hogan, Michael J., and Thomas G. Paterson. *Explaining the History of American Foreign Relations.* Cambridge, U.K., and New York: Cambridge University Press, 1991.

Hunt, Michael H. *Ideology and U.S. Foreign Policy.* New Haven, Conn.: Yale University Press, 1987.

Fraser Harbutt

See also vol. 9: **American Diplomacy; The Monroe Doctrine and the Roosevelt Corollary.**

FOREIGN SERVICE. Diplomacy was critically important to the success of the American Revolution (1775–1783) and the founding and early growth of the United States. Because most citizens of the young republic looked with suspicion on the European monarchies, official governmental relations were kept to a minimum until well into the nineteenth century. The American diplomatic service, made up of a very few citizens appointed by the president, expanded slowly. In 1790, the United States sent ministers plenipotentiary to only two countries: France and Great Britain. In 1830, there were still only fifteen U.S. foreign missions; the number increased to thirty-three by 1860 and forty-two by 1900. Isolationism was the prevailing foreign policy of the United States throughout these decades. Congress kept tight control over the expansion of diplomatic relations, authorizing only minimal resources for representation abroad.

Diplomacy became increasingly important during the Civil War (1861–1865) when both sides sought the support of the European powers. It was also vital in securing European acceptance of U.S. leadership under the Monroe Doctrine in the western hemisphere as the nation completed its territorial expansion to the Pacific. Presidents used appointments to overseas diplomatic missions as rewards for political support. A corps of career diplomats—a Diplomatic Service—was slow to emerge. Lower level diplomats were rare throughout the nineteenth century. In a major reform in 1856, Congress agreed to provide for a limited number of secretaries of legation to assist chiefs of mission. But as late as 1881, Congress allowed public funding for secretaries at only twelve of thirty legations. Most appointed ministers provided their own assistants. In 1893, however, Congress finally acknowledged that the United States had come of age diplomatically when it authorized the appointment of ambassadorial rank representatives to Great Britain and other major powers. The need for staff support was grudgingly acknowledged.

While a small Diplomatic Service began to emerge in the last decades of the nineteenth century, the Consular Service—including consuls, consular agents, and commercial agents whose mission it was to protect American ships and crews abroad and promote American commerce—had become an important instrument in the search for export markets for America's booming industries. In 1860, there were 480 U.S. consulates, commercial agencies, and consular agencies abroad, and by 1890 this number had risen to 760. In 1895, at a time when reforms were strengthening the expanding civil service in Washington, D.C., President Grover Cleveland issued regulations requiring the filling of vacancies on the basis of written examinations, including language tests. Other measures were adopted to deal with salaries and inspections of consular posts. The need for greater efficiency in the Consular Service resulted in a combination of Congressional and presidential actions in the first decade of the twentieth century to blunt the politics of appointments and move the Consular Service and, to a lesser extent the Diplomatic Service, toward a full merit system.

A Modern Foreign Service Develops

Expanding U.S. international responsibilities and interests after World War I (1914–1918) precipitated the establishment of a modern Foreign Service. The small Diplomatic Service, which in 1924 numbered 122 men serving mostly in Europe, was an exclusive group, scarcely dependent upon token salaries, whose standards of behavior and performance were drawn from upper-class educations. In contrast, the 511 (in 1924) members of the Consular Service in 256 overseas posts served under professional regulations and enjoyed a generous pay scale. The State Department closely oversaw the Consular Service but had little real control over the Diplomatic Service; the two systems were quite separate and there were only rare cases of interchange between them. The Foreign Service Act of 1924 amalgamated the Diplomatic and Consular Services into a new Foreign Service; established pay and retirement to make the service attractive and accessible to a much broader portion of the population; professionalized the oversight, recruitment, and training of officers; and instituted interchangeability between diplomatic and consular assignments as well as between assignments abroad and at home in the State Department. The establishment of the Foreign Service opened the way for the appointment of career officers as Chiefs of Mission. But the importance of political appointments to such positions persisted for the remainder of the twentieth century, and career officers rarely made up more than half of the total.

The United States emerged from World War II (1939–1945) as the most powerful nation in the world, with expanding economic and security interests around the globe. Diplomacy became far more vital to the nation than it ever had been. In many places around the world, U.S. Foreign Service officers became the principal agents of American presence and interests. The Foreign Service was expanded substantially to meet the diplomatic aspects of the nation's growing global responsibilities. From a mere 840 officers in 1940, the service numbered more than 1,300 in 1953 and 3,400 in 1957 after the integration of many Civil Service officers into the Foreign Service.

U.S. Interests Abroad Become More Complex

The Cold War and the revolution in international relations gave rise to a series of international crises during the latter half of the twentieth century as well as the growing globalization of politics, economics, and culture. The global scope of American interests and commitments made the representation of American interests abroad increasingly complex. As the boundaries of traditional diplomacy faded, the Foreign Service soon had many rivals. Other federal agencies became deeply involved in the preparation and execution of foreign policy. A conglomerate "foreign affairs community" came to dominate the formulation and execution of foreign policy: the NATIONAL SECURITY COUNCIL, the DEFENSE Department, the CENTRAL INTELLIGENCE AGENCY and other intelligence agencies, the U.S. Information Agency, and various foreign assistance agencies.

To improve its performance with the growing scope and complexity of foreign affairs, the Foreign Service underwent a series of reforms and studies. The Foreign Service Act of 1946 established the structure for a modern, efficient service with a consolidated classification system, promotion and retirement programs, and improved allowances and assignment policies. The Foreign Service Institute was established and sought to provide officers throughout their careers with a variety of specialized training, particularly area and language training. The Senior Seminar program, begun in 1958, gave small groups of the most promising mid-level officers, as well as some military officers and officials of other agencies, an extended experience in advanced professional development. The 1954 Wriston Report mandated the merger of the Foreign Service with many of the specialists in the State Department. The rotation between overseas posts and the government in Washington was accelerated, and by 1959, more than 1,500 Foreign Service officers held positions in the State Department. The 1962 Herter Report, the 1968 American Foreign Service Association Report, and the 1970 State Department Task Force Report sought to find management and personnel solutions that would ensure a Foreign Service equal to its challenges. As anti-American terrorism abroad intensified toward the end of the twentieth century, the danger of Foreign Service life grew and prompted new programs and procedures to protect U.S. diplomatic and consular establishments.

The New Face of the Foreign Service

In the last twenty-five years of the twentieth century, new generations of Foreign Service officers served in Washington, D.C. and around the world. These officers were different from the elite corps that existed before World War II. Recruited from around the nation, the new generations of Foreign Service officers reflected more closely the general makeup of the American population in terms of the proportions of women and minorities. Overcoming longstanding racial, sexual, and religious prejudice and discrimination in the State Department and the Foreign Service was a difficult process. As early as the 1920s, a few women and African Americans entered the Foreign Service. World War II contributed to more open recruitment and promotion, but it was not until the 1950s that purposeful recruitment of women and minorities began to alter the profile of the service. Only persistent resort to the courts by dissatisfied officers brought greater fairness in promotions and appointment to leadership positions by the 1980s. The Foreign Service Act of 1980 sought to establish more rigorous standards for recruitment and promotion, improve the rewards of service, and deal with the problems that were sapping the once high morale of the service.

The Foreign Service not only gained a leading role in America's wide-ranging activities abroad, but it was also drawn into the often intense domestic battles over the direction of foreign policy. Ideologues in high positions in government often complained about the liberal tendencies of some American diplomats, and other political leaders regarded the Foreign Service as unwilling to adapt to political agendas. The Cold War emphasis on security and loyalty had poisonous side effects that threatened the effectiveness of the Foreign Service and compromised its morale. Accusations of treasonous activity leveled against the State Department and many distinguished Foreign Service officers in the late 1940s and in the 1950s by Senator Joseph McCarthy and other members of Congress caused dismissals and needlessly destroyed promising careers. Policies pursued during the Vietnam War (1955–1975, American involvement 1964–1975) caused stresses between the Department leadership and many junior officers. Secretary of State Dean Rusk's Open Forum was begun in 1967 to enable Foreign Service and Department officers to generate alternative policy ideas, and differences with official policy came from the field in a special "dissent channel."

By the last decades of the twentieth century, the Foreign Service had lost its leadership role in representing the United States abroad. The measures of success of the Foreign Service grew more elusive as Americans, through electronic media, came to have heightened concerns and expectations about U.S. interests and citizens abroad. Terrorism, nuclear proliferation, international crime, nationalistic conflicts, and economic competition and crises appeared to be beyond diplomatic solution. Frequent attempts at reform of the conduct of American diplomacy and reorganization of the Foreign Service were vitiated by recurrent budget cuts and resource reductions. State Department resources were reduced by 50 percent during this period, despite steadily increasing responsibilities, especially after the fall of the Soviet Union and the emergence of new post-communist states in Eastern Europe. The State Department and the Foreign Service grew little after 1960, when there were about 7,000 domestic and 6,000 overseas American personnel. In the emerging global economy of the twenty-first century, the role of diplomats tended to be increasingly overshadowed by the representatives of other government agencies, individual states, and, above all, multinational corporations and international organizations. Some observers wondered if the Foreign Service had a future nearly as impressive or extensive as its history.

BIBLIOGRAPHY

Barnes, William, and John Heath Morgan. *The Foreign Service of the United States.* Washington, D.C.: Department of State, Historical Office, Bureau of Foreign Affairs, 1961.

Herz, Martin F., ed. *The Modern Ambassador: The Challenge and the Search.* Washington, D.C.: Institute for the Study of Diplomacy, Edmund A. Walsh School of Foreign Service, Georgetown University, 1983.

Ilchman, Warren F. *Professional Diplomacy in the United States, 1779–1939.* Chicago: University of Chicago Press, 1961, 1974.

Mayer, Martin. *The Diplomats.* Garden City, New York: Doubleday, 1983.

Plischke, Elmer. *Conduct of American Diplomacy.* Princeton, N.J.: Van Nostrand, 1967.

Rubin, Barry. *Secrets of State: The State Department and the Struggle Over U.S. Foreign Policy.* New York: Oxford University Press, 1985.

Stuart, Graham H. *The Department of State: A History of its Organization, Procedure, and Personnel.* New York: Macmillan, 1949.

William Z. Slany

See also **Diplomatic Missions; State, Department of.**

FOREST SERVICE. The U.S. Forest Service is the largest agency within the United States Department of Agriculture (USDA). It manages public lands in national forests and grasslands, and provides technical and financial assistance to state and private forestry agencies.

History

The history of the Forest Service dates back to the passage of a general appropriations bill in Congress on 15 August 1876, that authorized the commissioner of agriculture to appoint a forestry agent to study and report on forest supplies and conditions in the United States. Franklin B. Hough, a physician, historian, and statistician with a great passion for forestry and who had been working tirelessly for the passage of the bill, was appointed as the first forestry agent. He presented his *Report upon Forestry* in slightly more than a year's time to the commissioner of agriculture, as directed by the enabling legislation. His report discussed relevant land laws, planting and transplanting trees, soil types, use of wood by railroads and iron manufactures, problems of insects and fire, meteorology and effects of forests on climate, and the forestry resources in the United States and overseas. He also pointed out the destructive practices occurring on private lands and the need for publicly owned land for reforestation. Although federal forestlands were not set aside until fifteen years after passage of the appropriations bill, a Division of Forestry was established in 1881 and Hough was named chief. Hough was succeeded by Nathaniel Egleston in 1883 and by Bernhard E. Fernow, a professional forester from Germany, in 1886. On June 30, 1886, Congress gave full statutory recognition to the Division of Forestry. Fernow continued as the chief until Gifford Pinchot, America's first native professionally trained forester, succeeded him in 1898.

The appointment of the energetic Pinchot marked the beginning of a new era in federal policy. The changes that took place during his tenure have shaped the administration and jurisdiction of federal forestry ever since. Congress advanced the Division of Forestry to bureau status three years later, which strengthened the agency's position in the Department of Agriculture. Then, in 1905, 63 million acres of federal forestland were transferred from the Department of the Interior to the Department of Agriculture. In recognition of the dramatic increase in the bureau's responsibility, it was renamed the Forest Service in July 1905 and Pinchot became the first chief.

Pinchot and his close friend President Theodore Roosevelt provided national leadership to the forest conservation movement in the United States. They oriented the Forest Service to focus on the wise use of forests so as to provide the greatest good for the greatest number over the long run. Although the initial mandate for the Forest Service was to provide quality water and timber for the nation's benefit, the expectations of goods and services from national forests and grasslands have changed over the years. The modern Forest Service manages national forests for multiple uses and benefits and for the sustained yield of renewable resources such as water, forage, wildlife, wood, and recreation. The multiple use and sustained yield principles stress the need to balance the uses that are made of the major resources and benefits of the forests—timber, water supplies, recreation, livestock forage, wildlife and fish, and minerals—in the best public interest while ensuring the productivity of the land and protecting the quality of the environment.

The National Forest System

The public lands managed by the Forest Service are collectively called the National Forest System. It is defined as federally owned units of forest, range, and related land consisting of national forests, purchase units, national grasslands, land utilization project areas, experimental forest areas, experimental range areas, designated experimental areas, other land areas, water areas, and interests in lands that are administered by the Forest Service or designated for administration through the Forest Service.

The National Forest System grew significantly from its modest beginning in 1891 when President Benjamin Harrison signed the Forest Reserve Act following two decades of congressional debates over the nation's forests. In 1897, President William McKinley signed the Forest Management Act, or the Organic Act, which determined the purposes of the national forests—predictable supplies of water and timber. And, it was not until 1960 that Congress expanded the definition of national forest purposes with the Multiple Use–Sustained Yield Act. A significant degree of prescription was added sixteen years later with the National Forest Management Act of 1976, which reorganized, expanded, and amended the Forest and Rangeland Renewable Resources Planning Act of 1974. The National Forest Management Act requires the Secretary of Agriculture to assess forestlands, develop a management program based on multiple-use, sustained-yield principles, and implement a resource management plan for each unit of the National Forest System. It is the primary statute governing the administration of national forests. Ecosystem management, an ecological approach to forest management to assure productive, healthy ecosystems by integrating the ecological, economic, and social needs and values, has become the cornerstone of national forest management in recent years.

The National Forest System encompasses 155 national forests and 20 grasslands located among 44 states, Puerto Rico, and the Virgin Islands, comprising 191 million acres (77.3 million hectares) of land, or 8.5 percent of the total land area in the United States. The natural resources on these lands are some of the nation's greatest assets and have major socioeconomic and environmental significance. Each national forest is managed by a forest supervisor and consists of several ranger districts. Overall, the Forest Service employs approximately 30,000 people who reflect the full range of diversity of the American population.

Forest Service Lands

Approximately 73 percent of the 191 million acres owned by the Forest Service is considered forested. Of that forested land, 35 percent is available for regularly scheduled timber harvesting and about half a percentage of those trees are harvested in any given year. The remaining 65 percent of the forested land is designated for nontimber uses, such as wilderness and other areas set aside for recreation, or cannot be harvested due to environmental conditions, such as steep slopes and fragile soils. Timber harvesting has remained the most controversial of all Forest Service activities in the last three decades. Clearcutting, a regeneration method that harvests all trees, has become a symbol of the public's displeasure with national forest management. A Forest Service estimate in the early twenty-first century showed that harvesting from national forests was down to nearly 4 billion board feet of timber in 2000 (less than 5 percent of the domestic timber production), compared to 12 billion board feet per year in the 1960s and 1970s.

With more and more people living in urban areas, national forests have become more valuable for ecotourism or nature-based recreational activities. Under the Land and Water Fund Conservation Act of 1965, the agency has been able to acquire land specifically for public outdoor recreation in national forests. In 1996, the national forests received 341 million visitor days of recreational use, including activities such as hiking, fishing, camping, hunting, horseback riding, off-road vehicle use, and driving for pleasure. The announcement of the protection of 58.5 million acres of roadless areas in national forests—one of the most sweeping conservation measures in American history—by President Bill Clinton in 2001 and a subsequent bill, "The National Forest Roadless Area Conservation Act of 2002," are intended to set aside undeveloped areas of the national forests for nontimber amenity values, including recreation.

The Forest Service motto, "Caring for the Land and Serving People," summarizes the spirit of its mission, which is accomplished through five main activities: (1) protection and management of natural resources on National Forest System lands; (2) research on all aspects of forestry rangeland management, and forest resource utilization; (3) community assistance and cooperation with state and local governments, forest industries, and private landowners to help protect and manage nonfederal forest and associated range and watershed lands to improve conditions in rural areas; (4) achieving and supporting an effective workforce that reflects the full range of diversity of the American people; and (5) international assistance in formulating policy and coordinating United States support for the protection and sound management of the world's forest resources.

Challenges and Changes

In its existence, the Forest Service has been faced with a plethora of problems encompassing economic, ecological, and social concerns. Some of the most serious problems throughout the history of the Forest Service have been fires, overgrazing by cattle and sheep, soil disturbance and stream pollution caused by these forces and by mining, insect and disease epidemics of forest trees, and public opposition to timber harvesting. Following devastating fires in Idaho and Montana in 1910, the Forest Service began to set its fire policy. A new national policy was established by Congress through passage of the Weeks Law in 1911 that enabled federal purchase of forestlands damaged by farming, reckless logging, and repeated fires. Most of the national forestland in the East has been acquired under this law, which also set up a program for cooperation between the Forest Service and the states in fire protection. The General Exchange Act of 1922 allowed federal land to be exchanged for parcels of privately owned land within the boundaries of national forests. The Clarke-McNary Act of 1924 expanded the Weeks Law by allowing for the purchase of lands needed for the production of timber and by providing for agreements with the states to protect state-owned and private forestlands against fire, with the latter paying at least half the costs. Since the early days, the Forest Service has been developing ways to forecast fire behavior, inform citizens about fire prevention, extinguish the flames, and provide federal aid to state and private landowners for fire protection. The history of Smokey Bear is synonymous with the fire prevention education programs developed by the Forest Service. Since 1944, Smokey Bear has remained the forest fire and, later, wildfire prevention campaign symbol of the agency.

In addition to fire protection assistance, the Clarke-McNary Act, for the first time, offered substantial assistance to small farm and woodlot owners for planting tree seedlings. It also gave a strong impetus to the establishment of state forestry agencies. Although the Smith-Lever Act of 1914 permitted large-scale federal-state cooperation in agricultural extension work, including private forestry, it was not until the Clarke-McNary Act that private forestry received considerable attention. Further boost for private forestry was provided by the Cooperative Forest Management Act of 1950, which authorized the secretary of agriculture to cooperate with state foresters in assisting private landowners. The Cooperative Forestry Assistance Act of 1978 guided the federal-state cooperative forestry activities for many years. The National Forest-Dependent Rural Communities Economic Diversification Act of 1990 considerably enhanced the Forest Service's formal authority to work with rural communities in proximity to national forests. In 1999, Congress modified the 1990 act to include communities in proximity to national grasslands as well. Cooperative forestry provides technical and financial assistance to help rural and urban citizens, including private landowners, care for forests and sustain their communities. Several economic action programs (such as Rural Community Assistance Program, Forests Products Conservation and Recycling, and Market Development and Expansion), landowner assistance programs (such as Forest Legacy Program, Forest Stewardship Program, Stewardship Incentive Program), and urban and community forestry programs are in place.

Reforestation of national forests gained momentum in the 1930s under the Knutson-Vandenberg Act of 1930. The Forest Service operated more than 1,300 Civilian Conservation Corps (CCC) camps in national forests during the 1930s. More than 2 million unemployed young men in the CCC program performed a vast amount of forest protection, watershed restoration, erosion control, and other improvement work, including the planting of 2.25 billion tree seedlings. Another program begun around the same time was the shelterbelt tree-planting program in the Great Plains during the dust bowl. The Pest Control Act of 1947 provided for federal-state action to detect and suppress severe outbreaks of forest insects and diseases. The Multiple-Use Mining Law of 1955 curbed mining abuses and interference with management of the national forests.

Policies for wildlife management in the Forest Service have evolved over time. Aldo Leopold laid the foundation for wildlife management while working for the agency in the Southwest Region, from 1909 to 1924. The 1964 Wilderness Act verified many years of Forest Service reservations of such lands. Under the Endangered Species Preservation Act of 1966, the Forest Service has expanded its protection of rare wildlife, and under the Environmental Quality Act of 1969, it has taken special steps to minimize undesirable impacts of forest uses on land, water, wildlife, recreation, and aesthetics. The northern spotted owl in the Pacific Northwest and the red cockaded woodpecker in the South are examples of endangered species that have changed the face of forestry practices in these regions.

As the world's largest research agency, the Forest Service provides the scientific and technical knowledge necessary to protect and sustain the nation's natural resources on all lands. The biggest breakthrough for forestry research was the McSweeney-McNary Act of 1928, which authorized a broad permanent program of research and the first comprehensive nationwide survey of forest resources on all public and private lands. The first experiment station was established near Flagstaff, Arizona, in 1908, for the study of range conditions; and others followed throughout the West, and later in the East and South, for range and forest studies. The world-famous Forest Products Laboratory was established in cooperation with the University of Wisconsin at Madison in 1910. In 1908, Congress provided for states in which national forests are located to receive 25 percent of the receipts from sale of timber, grazing permits, and other special fees; such funds are to be used for schools and roads in counties containing national forestland.

Overall, the Forest Service manages the National Forest System to provide a variety of harmonious uses and to produce continuous yields of timber and other renewable resources without reducing their productive capacity and with careful regard for aesthetic, recreational, and environmental values. Each national forest and grassland is governed by a management plan prepared according to the National Forest Management Act. The Forest Service implements or revises these plans following an environmental assessment (Environmental Impact Statements or Environmental Analysis) or Categorical Exclusion in compliance with the National Environmental Policy Act of 1969 (as amended).

The headquarters of the Forest Service is in Washington, D.C., with a chief overseeing the entire Forest Service operation. The chief is a federal employee who reports to the Under Secretary for Natural Resources and Environment in the U.S. Department of Agriculture. The chief's staff provides broad policy and direction for the agency, works with the President's administration to develop a budget to submit to Congress, provides information to Congress on accomplishments, and monitors activities of the agency. The nine regional headquarters are in Atlanta, Milwaukee, Lakewood (Colorado), Albuquerque, Missoula (Montana), Ogden (Utah), San Francisco, Portland, Oregon, and Juneau (Alaska). The regional office staff coordinates activities between national forests, monitors activities on national forests to ensure quality operations, provides guidance for forest plans, and allocates budgets to the forests. Research projects are coordinated by six experiment station headquarters: Saint Paul, Newton Square (Pennsylvania), Portland (Oregon), Berkeley, Fort Collins (Colorado), and Asheville (North Carolina). Wood product research is centralized at the Forest Products Laboratory. There is an Institute of Tropical Forestry in Rio Piedras, Puerto Rico, and an Institute of Pacific Islands Forestry in Honolulu.

BIBLIOGRAPHY

Clary, D. A. *Timber and the Forest Service.* Lawrence: University Press of Kansas, 1986.

National Forest Timber Harvest. Forest Management Staff, USDA. Forest Service, 1998. Available at http:www.fs.fed.us/land/fm/salefact/salefact.htm.

Robbins, W. G. *American Forestry: A History of National, State, and Private Cooperation.* Lincoln: University of Nebraska Press, 1985.

Southern Forest Resource Assessment. Southern Research Station, USDA Forest Service, 2002.

Steen, Harold K. 1976. *The U.S. Forest Service: A History.* Seattle: University of Washington Press.

———. *The Beginning of the National Forest System.* USDA Forest Service FS-488, 1991.

Shibu Jose

See also **Agriculture, Department of; Conservation; Environmental Movement; Federal Agencies; Lumber Industry; Wildfires.**

FORESTRY. Forestry is the scientific management of forests for the production of lumber and other resources. Although concern about the depletion of forest resources dates back to the colonial period, it was not until the 1890s that forestry came into its own in the United States. The development of the science of silviculture (tree growing) in Europe, widespread fears of unsustainable cutting of forests, and the expansion of the powers of the federal government allowed for professional foresters to seek, and in some ways to gain, significant influence over the nation's woodlands.

Gifford Pinchot exercised enormous influence over the early development of American forestry. Born into a prosperous Connecticut family and educated at Yale, Pinchot attended forestry school in Nancy, France, because there were no such institutions in the United States. He had difficulty securing employment as a professional forester upon his return in the 1890s, and took a job managing the forests of Biltmore, the Vanderbilt family's large estate in North Carolina. Soon enough, however, the federal government had need of Pinchot's expertise. In the Forest Reserve Act of 1891, Congress authorized presidents to set aside forested lands for protection from overgrazing and logging. In 1891–1892, President Benjamin Harrison set aside 16 million acres, and President Grover Cleveland added 21 million acres to the reserves. The National Forest Management Act of 1897 charged the government to "protect and preserve" forests to ensure predictable supplies of timber and water. A year later the Cornell and Biltmore forestry schools were established, and Pinchot became head of the Division of Forestry in the Department of Agriculture. His influence only grew during the presidency of his friend Theodore Roosevelt. In 1905, Roosevelt replaced the Division of Forestry with the United States Forest Service, also located in the Agriculture Department. Pinchot served as its head until 1910, overseeing its dramatic expansion to some 175 million acres from only 51 million at the opening of the decade.

For Pinchot and his fellow conservationists, forestry was the centerpiece of conservation, the development of natural resources to bring, as Pinchot famously put it, "greatest good to the greatest number for the longest time." Professionally trained foresters, backed by the power of the federal government, would ensure that the nation's timber and watersheds were protected from rapacious, wasteful, and monopolistic private industry as well as from corrupt political interests. Nationalism suffused this marriage of scientific expertise and federal power. As Pinchot wrote in 1900 when he persuaded his family to found the Yale School of Forestry, "What we wanted was American foresters trained by Americans in American ways for the work ahead in American forests." Forestry was as much a crusade as a scientific discipline.

Early Conservationists

If the establishment of forestry schools and the federal public lands bureaucracies signaled that forestry had come into its own, then at the same time Progressives such as Pinchot built on an older legacy of concern with forested lands. As the rapid cutting of eastern forests that began in the colonial period continued in the early Re-

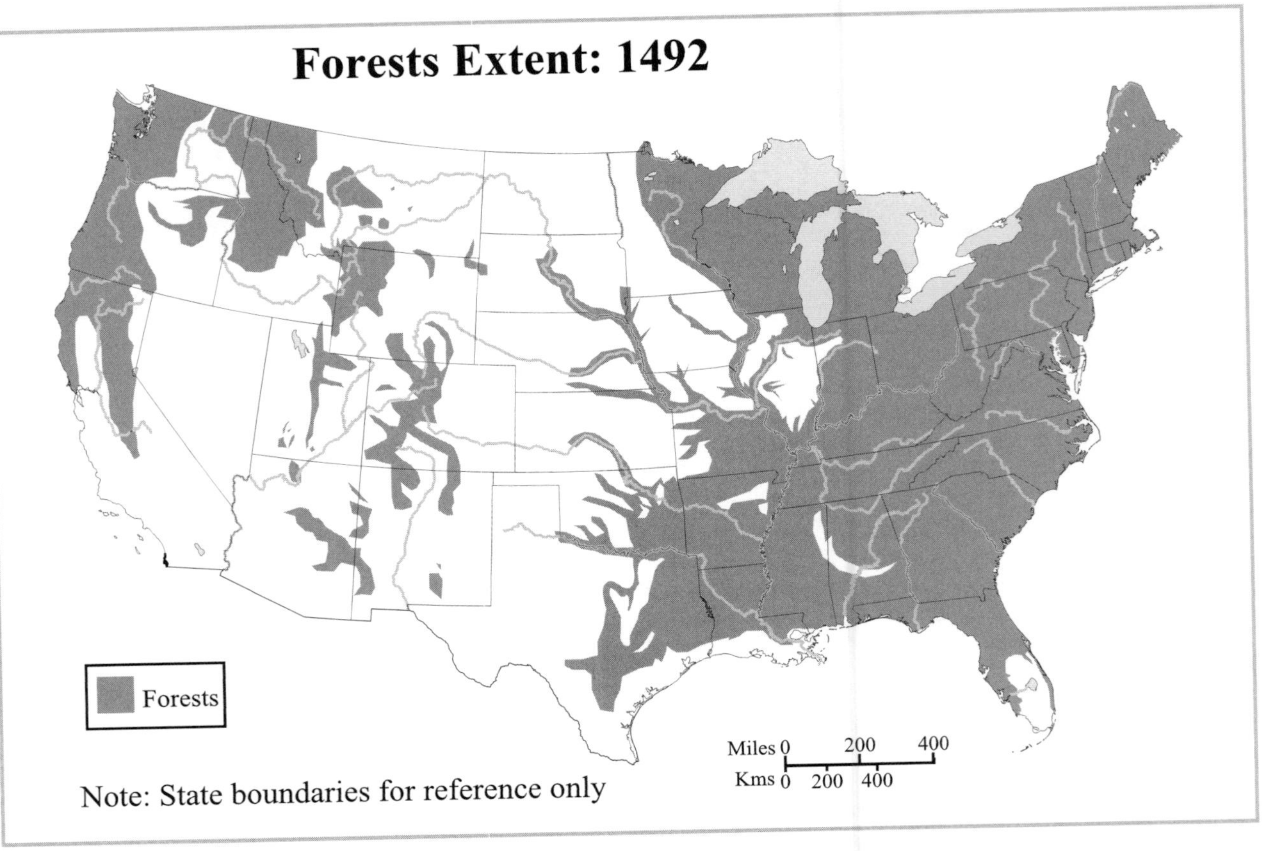

public, some began to forecast a national timber shortage. In James Fenimore Cooper's 1823 novel, *The Pioneers*, for example, one character warns of "felling the forests as if no end could be found to their treasures, nor any limits to their extent. If we go on this way, twenty years hence we shall want fuel." Foreign travelers and some domestic journalists reported exceptionally high firewood prices and the difficulty of locating timber for building construction in the urbanized Northeast. Such warnings began to influence policymakers. The 1865 annual report of the federal agriculture commissioner cast deforestation as "an impending national danger, beyond the power of figures to estimate, and beyond the province of words to express." In 1877 the secretary of the interior Carl Schurz presaged later conservation measures by calling for the establishment of federally owned forests to relieve what he thought was an impending wood shortage. Three years later, the census surveyed national forest resources for the first time.

George Perkins Marsh catalyzed this growing concern, helping to pave the way for the subsequent rise of a conservation movement. A peripatetic schoolteacher, newspaperman, and lawyer early in life, Marsh served as a Whig U.S. representative from Vermont. In 1849, President Zachary Taylor appointed him minister to Turkey and twelve years later President Abraham Lincoln chose him as minister to Italy. Struck by the contrast between classical accounts of a heavily wooded and very fertile Mediterranean and the unproductive and scrubby grasslands that he encountered, Marsh became convinced that the region was heir to an environmental catastrophe. In 1864 he published *Man and Nature*, where he used the story of Mediterranean deforestation to warn that what happened in Europe could happen in the United States as well.

Marsh deeply shaped the creation of American forestry not only because he made already familiar predictions of timber shortage, but also because he gave them an apocalyptic cast and offered a well-articulated solution. Deforestation, he warned, was not a simple matter of resource scarcity, but risked causing the collapse and disappearance of entire civilizations, as had happened with classical Greece and Rome. "The earth is fast becoming an unfit home for its noblest inhabitant," he wrote, and "another era of equal human improvidence would reduce it to such a condition of shattered surface as to threaten barbarism and perhaps even the extinction of the species." *Man and Nature* presented the state control of forests as a solution to this prospective disaster. While individual owners were motivated by short-term gain, as Marsh insisted in long passages detailing the "improvident habits of the backwoodsman," the government could deploy scientific knowledge in the best long-term interests of the nation. Although the existence of large tracts of federal-

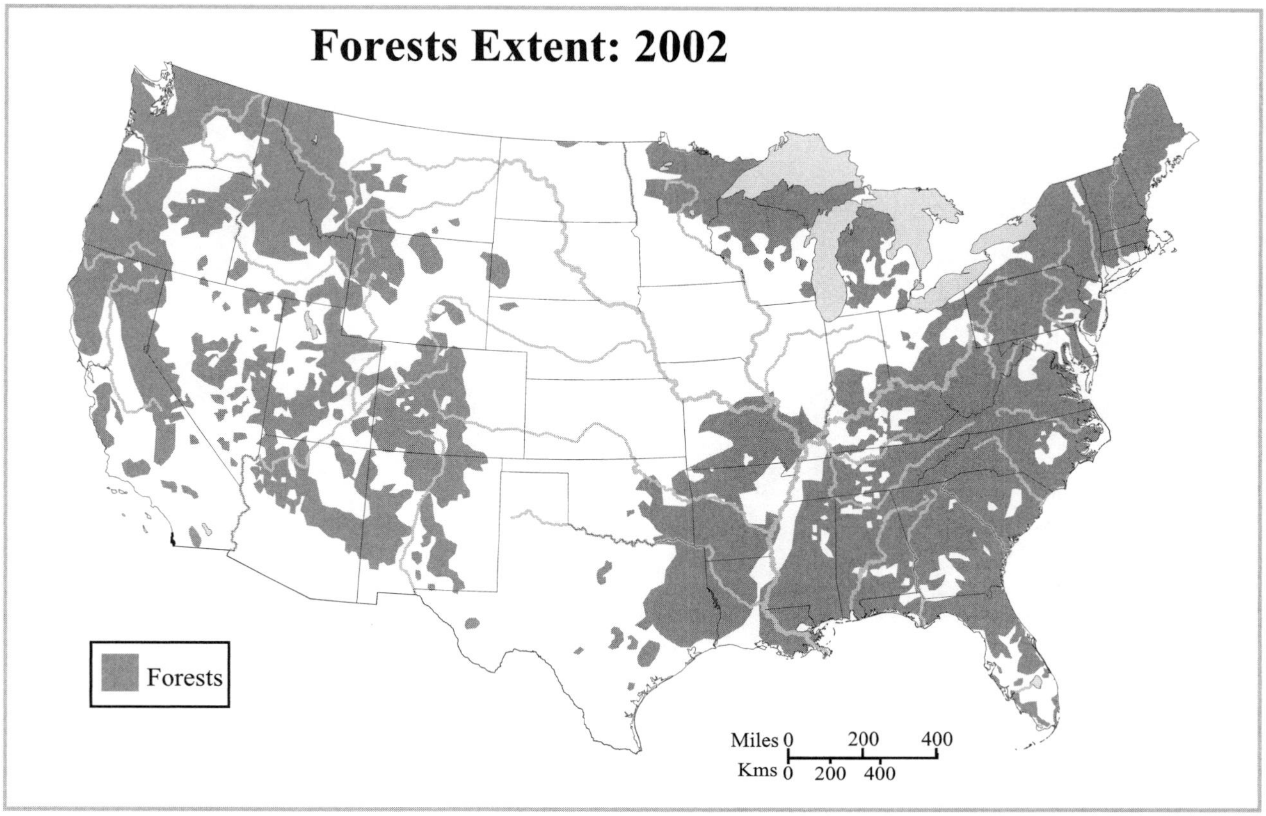

and state-owned lands came to seem commonplace in the twentieth century, at the time Marsh's proposal was truly radical. American land policy, epitomized in the Homestead Act of 1862, was still designed to convert all of the public domain into private property holdings for the burgeoning nation and its land-hungry farmers.

Early Twentieth-Century Foresters

The first generation of American foresters responded to these early nineteenth-century warnings and embodied Marsh's call for the deployment of scientific expertise to regulate the chaos of the private sector. Progressive Era foresters, however, operated with much greater confidence and ambition than did their predecessors. Where Marsh warned, for example, that "Man is everywhere a disturbing agent . . . wherever he plants his foot, the harmonies of nature are turned to discords," Pinchot breezily asserted that "the first duty of the human race . . . is to control the use of the earth and all that therein is." Where the earlier writers had hoped to avoid crippling timber shortages and the catastrophe of mass deforestation, early twentieth-century foresters saw themselves as contributing to the United States's position as an industrial power of global proportions.

The outlook of Pinchot and his peers had important and lasting practical implications for subsequent forestry and federal lands management. Above all, they insisted that economic productivity was the leading purpose of foresters and the national forests. The forests were an essential part of a modern economy in which each segment of society performed a specialized role. As one typical forest administrator stated in 1911:

> The radiating influence of the standing forests is repeated when they are cut and utilized. The *producers* of the raw materials which supply the *factories*, which sell to the *wholesalers*, distributing to the *retailers*, who sell their wares to the *wage-earners* in forest and mill—are, with their employees, and the lumber companies and their employees, all more or less dependent upon the forests.

Accordingly, although more romantic thinkers such as the naturalist and author John Muir hoped that the expanding federal land system would protect distinctive landscapes as scenic refuges from an increasingly artificial urban life, Pinchot and his peers subordinated such goals to the provision of timber and reliable water supplies. Thus, in the early 1900s, Pinchot sided with the city of San Francisco in its fight to make a reservoir of the Hetch Hetchy Valley, previously part of YELLOWSTONE NATIONAL PARK. Early forest managers also sought to curtail the extensive subsistence practices of those who lived near federal lands, devoting significant resources to ending illegal hunting and "timber poaching" for fear that they interfered with their mission to make the forests pay.

Douglas Fir. Trees twenty to forty years old are in the foreground and mature ones behind them in this 1973 photograph taken in timberland near Olympic National Park, Wash. NATIONAL ARCHIVES AND RECORDS ADMINISTRATION

The foresters' belief in state-led economic modernization led them to practice a highly interventionist form of land management. They sought to increase dramatically the rate of timber harvest, not only because the nation needed more wood products, but also because scientific forestry seemed to demand younger forests. Older forests, which dominated the heavily timbered West, lost more wood to tree death, insect infestation, and fires than they gained from new growth. Extensive cutting of old growth would thus replace "decadent" or "overmature" forests with younger woods, ensuring that they created more new annual growth than they lost. The net growth could be harvested each year without diminishing the total amount of forest resources. If done properly, heavy cutting could thus best serve Pinchot's dictum that natural resources must produce "the greatest good to the greatest number for the longest time."

Fighting fire was another important part of securing maximum forest productivity. Just as the federal government gave professional foresters substantial control over the nation's forested lands for the first time, a series of tremendous fires swept through them. Increased Euro-American settlement of the heavily forested portions of the West and Midwest and extensive logging, which left behind large amounts of extremely flammable downed trees, caused a rapid increase in forest fires in the early twentieth century. In 1910, the worse year, fire consumed more than five million acres of national forest, killing seventy-eight firefighters in the process. These fires not only took lives, destroyed entire towns, and reduced millions of potentially valuable trees, but they also seemed to threaten the Forest Service itself. What good did it do to turn over the nation's woods to professional foresters if they were just going to go up in smoke? Suppressing fires thus became one of the Forest Service's primary goals, and indeed many of the early reports of national forest supervisors were devoted almost entirely to fire control. Foresters' insistence that fires were unnatural events caused by human carelessness seemed to be borne out by their remarkable achievements in reducing the instance of forest fires. By 1935 fewer than 300,000 acres burned annually, and by 1980 the territory that regularly burned had been reduced by 95 percent. The Forest Service extended its fire fighting to most of the nation's private lands as well, beginning with a 1927 decision to withhold funds from states that failed to cooperate with the service's measures.

The Depression, World War II, and the Postwar Era

Just as the Progressive Era provided the opportunity for the creation of professional forestry, the New Deal created public works programs that expanded the reach of forestry. Nearly half of those employed by the CIVILIAN CONSERVATION CORPS, created in 1933 to provide jobs in conservation projects, worked in reforestation and forest protection projects. Some programs of other New Deal agencies, such as the Soil Conservation Service, the Tennessee Valley Authority, and the National Recovery Administration, also stressed reforestation as part of the nation's recovery effort. In response to the DUST BOWL, nearly 217 million trees were planted under the auspices of the Prairie States Forestry Project. Foresters also intensified their fire fighting program and enjoyed greater success in extending it to lands not encompassed by the national forests. In 1935 the head of the Forest Service felt confident enough to promulgate the "10 A.M. Policy," which declared that all fires should be brought under control by ten in the morning of the day following their initial discovery. Smokey Bear, the government's ubiquitous antifire mascot, was introduced to the public in 1945.

The production demands of World War II and the postwar economic boom led to a much more vigorous implementation of foresters' long-standing management goals. Declining timber yields from private forest lands in the face of the nation's incredible economic growth prompted the Forest Service to increase massively its cutting levels. In 1944 the service contracted for 3.3 billion board feet (the standard measure of timber harvest, one square foot of wood an inch thick) to be cut from its lands, a more than threefold increase over traditional levels. By

1966 the annual cut had reached 12.1 billion board feet. From 1950 to 1966 twice as much timber was cut from national forests as had been from 1905 to 1949. Clear-cutting, the cutting of all trees in a given area, replaced more selective harvesting techniques, despite the Forest Service's previous vehement criticism of the practice. The roads built to enable high harvest levels—some 310,000 miles of actively maintained roadways by the end of the twentieth century—made the United States Forest Service the owner and manager of the largest road system in the world.

At the same time, however, important changes in postwar America created deep conflicts over the meaning and purposes of forestry. The construction of the interstate highway system and economic prosperity allowed for the development of a truly mass outdoor tourism. Drawn by lures as diverse as skiing, car camping, wilderness backpacking, hunting, and fishing, millions of tourists flocked to the national forests. By 1976, recreational visits to the forests had increased nearly twentyfold from prewar levels. For the first time, millions of ordinary Americans had direct experiences with the nation's forests and felt that they had a personal stake in their future management. Many of these tourists were displeased by what they considered unsightly roads and clear-cuts. The Forest Service acknowledged these changes and cooperated in the passage of the Multiple-Use Sustained-Yield Act of 1960, which gave official sanction to outdoor recreation as a management goal for the first time. But growing public environmental sentiment still conflicted with intensive timber harvesting.

Scotch Pine. W. H. Shaffer's 1933 photo shows a grove of trees with their lower limbs removed by federal workers in the Civilian Conservation Corps. LIBRARY OF CONGRESS

The Late Twentieth Century: Ecological Forestry

Other problems challenged the traditional emphasis of foresters on intensive management. In some forests, fire suppression and extensive harvesting led to dramatic shifts in the relative abundance of tree species. Often the large expanses of even-aged trees produced by clear-cutting were more vulnerable to disease and insect infestation than were the previous multi-aged stands. After decades of relative success, fire suppression struck its critics as not only ecologically suspect but also as ineffective in preventing fires. Before the full implementation of fire suppression, wildfires were frequent but generally smaller affairs that left many of the older trees alive. By the 1980s and 1990s, however, the heavy accumulations of highly flammable dead and down woods helped to create massive conflagrations that killed almost all plants in their paths. Even enormous efforts to stop and put out fires, as in a large 1988 blaze in Yellowstone National Park, could fail. In 1992 the federal government spent nearly $11 billion to suppress forest fires across the country, losing thirty-two firefighters in the process. Gifford Pinchot's confidence that "forest fires are wholly within the control of men" was in shambles.

By the 1980s, some foresters responded to these developments by articulating a different vision of the purposes and techniques of their discipline. As articulated by the ecologist Jerry F. Franklin, the New Forestry asserted the need to manage land to preserve biodiversity and complex ecosystems rather than to maximize timber production. From this perspective, forestry was more the respectful emulation of natural patterns than the application of scientific expertise to ensure economic efficiency. The training of foresters began to incorporate these new views. By the 1990s, the science of ecology had come to replace silviculture as the bedrock of the profession at many forestry schools. Within the Forest Service, advocates of this shift in management formed the Association of Forest Service Employees for Environmental Ethics in 1989. Although the organization remained a dissident group within the bureaucracy, the Forest Service as a whole responded to the ecological critique of traditional forestry, shifting some of its resources away from timber production and toward recreation and habitat protection. In 1995, in a clear reversal of the thrust of a century of policy, the Department of Agriculture and the Interior Department announced their intention to let more wildfires burn and even actively to restore small-scale fires to some regions.

At the end of the twentieth century, the forests covered nearly one-third of the nation's land area. Dominant tree species varied significantly by region. Douglas fir dominated the western portions of Washington and Oregon, joined by redwoods and mixed coniferous forests in California. East of these coastal woods, ponderosa pine, white pine, larch, lodgepole pine, fir, and spruce were the most heavily represented species. Hardwoods and pine are the most common trees in the generally open Plains states. The pine-dominated South was separated from the maple, birch, and beech forests of the Northeast by a large belt of oak and hickory. Alaska contained huge expanses of birch and coniferous woods.

In the year 2000, the national forests comprised 191 million acres, about one-tenth of the nation's surface. These forests never produced more than one-fifth of the nation's timber production. Some 393 million acres of forests were owned by the private sector, fully 232 million of them in individual hands. Corporations owned just over 100 million acres of forests. Although professional forestry has been closely associated with the public lands systems, private forest lands may become the object of similar debates over the purposes and techniques of the discipline.

BIBLIOGRAPHY

Cox, Thomas R. *This Well-Wooded Land: Americans and Their Forests from Colonial Times to the Present.* Lincoln: University of Nebraska Press, 1985.

Hirt, Paul. *A Conspiracy of Optimism: Management of the National Forests Since World War Two.* Lincoln: University of Nebraska Press, 1994.

Jacoby, Karl. *Crimes Against Nature: Squatters, Poachers, Thieves, and the Hidden History of American Conservation.* Berkeley: University of California Press, 2001.

Langston, Nancy. *Forest Dreams, Forest Nightmares: The Paradox of Old Growth in the Inland West.* Seattle: University of Washington Press, 1995.

Lowenthal, David. *George Perkins Marsh: Prophet of Conservation.* Seattle: University of Washington Press, 2000.

Miller, Char, ed. *American Forests: Nature, Culture, and Politics.* Lawrence: University of Kansas Press, 1997.

Pinchot, Gifford. *The Fight for Conservation.* New York: Harcourt, Brace, 1910.

Pyne, Stephen J. *Fire in America: A Cultural History of Wildland and Rural Fire.* Princeton, N.J.: Princeton University Press, 1982.

Robbins, William G. *American Forestry: A History of National, State, and Private Cooperation.* Lincoln: University of Nebraska Press, 1985.

Wilkinson, Charles F. *Crossing the Next Meridian: Land, Water, and the Future of the West.* Washington, D.C.: Island Press, 1992.

Benjamin H. Johnson

See also **Agriculture, Department of; Conservation; Lumber Industry; National Park System.**

"FORGOTTEN MAN" was the title of a public lecture delivered by William Graham Sumner of Yale University in 1883. Sumner, a leading social Darwinist, was critical of those who favored social improvement schemes that took money from or imposed restrictions upon this "honest, industrious, economical" working man in order to help his negligent neighbor. In Sumner's view, such efforts as philanthropy, guild restrictions, and temperance legislation inhibited competition among workers by which worthy individuals might succeed and thereby contribute to the general prosperity. On 18 May 1932 Franklin D. Roosevelt revived the term in an address at Warms Springs, Georgia. However, he used the term to refer to the underprivileged, those whom he wanted to help with government programs.

BIBLIOGRAPHY

Curtis, Bruce. *William Graham Sumner.* Boston: Twayne, 1981.

Sumner, William Graham, *What Social Classes Owe to Each Other.* New York: Harper and Brothers, 1883. Reprint, New York: Arno Press, 1972.

Wiebe, Robert H. *The Search for Order 1877–1920.* New York: Hill and Wang, 1967.

Alvin F. Harlow / C. P.

See also **Laissez-Faire; Philanthropy; Social Legislation.**

FORT WORTH is located in the north-central area of Texas. Recognized as where the West begins, Fort Worth has maintained its reputation as a frontier cow town. Established originally as an army fort along the Trinity River in 1849, Fort Worth represented the farthest point west of the settled frontier. Although its population continued to grow, it was not until after the Civil War that Fort Worth began to prosper. The cattle industry was a major part of the local economy, from the cattle drives of the 1870s to the meat-packing businesses of Armour and Swift in the 1900s. Just as important was the Texas and Pacific Railroad, which reached Fort Worth in 1876. With the discovery of oil in Texas, Fort Worth became the "wildcat center" at the turn of the twentieth century, serving as a railroad crossroads for pipeline and refinery companies. During World War II, Fort Worth became a center of aviation, with Carswell Air Force Base, General Dynamics, and Dallas–Fort Worth Airport. In the 1980s, Fort Worth began renovation and renewal of the city's downtown and north side in an effort to preserve and retain its Old West heritage.

BIBLIOGRAPHY

Knight, Oliver. *Outpost on the Trinity.* Fort Worth: Texas Christian University Press, 1990.

Sanders, Leonard. *How Fort Worth Became the Texasmost City, 1849–1920.* Fort Worth: Texas Christian University Press, 1986.

Schmelzer, Janet. *Where the West Begins: Fort Worth and Tarrant County.* Northridge, Calif.: Windsor, 1985.

Janet Schmelzer

See also **Dallas; Texas.**

FORTIFICATIONS. Throughout the colonial period, fortifications in the Western Hemisphere strongly reflected the origins of the various European settlers. Col-

Atlanta. A small segment of the fortifications ringing this major Confederate city, which helped to prevent a direct attack by General William T. Sherman's Union forces from 22 July 1864 until the besieged defenders evacuated on 1 September. LIBRARY OF CONGRESS

onists of many countries—including Spain, France, England, Holland, Sweden, and Russia—erected defensive structures ranging from small, improvised earthworks and palisaded stockades to masonry works of substantial size.

As a young nation, the United States faced defensive requirements quite different from those of most European countries, whose chief concern was protection of inland cities against mobilized land forces. The United States, instead, needed to protect frontier settlements and outposts and to secure coastal harbors and river mouths against foreign naval forces.

Americans established frontier forts in large numbers until about the end of the nineteenth century. Built to resist Indians equipped with nothing heavier than small arms, these forts generally consisted of timber or adobe construction. Many modern communities trace their roots back to such frontier posts, which have become crucial to the folklore and romantic history of the American West.

The army, however, directed its principal engineering efforts toward the defense of harbors and river mouths. From the 1790s until after WORLD WAR II, constructing fortifications for protection against naval attack constituted a major item in the nation's defense expenditures—and the principal representation of the country's military architecture. Among the best known of these fortifications, all completed before the CIVIL WAR, were Fort Monroe, Virginia; Fort SUMTER, South Carolina; Fort Pulaski, Georgia; Fort Morgan, Alabama; and Fort Jackson, Louisiana.

The appearance of rifled artillery, which had its first widespread test in the Civil War, ended the construction of these massive, vertical-walled masonry forts. The wartime defenses for both North and South were simple, low-profile earthwork forts revested by timber or sandbags. Hundreds of such forts sprang up, in a few cases to ring large cities such as Atlanta, Georgia, and Washington—the one instance in American history of fortifying cities against land attack, somewhat in the fashion of continental Europe.

Following the Civil War, construction of fortifications was limited for a time to new earthwork defenses of a more durable style, although fort armaments developed markedly. In the 1890s a new era of fortification began with the installation of powerful 10- and 12-inch breechloading rifles, mounted on disappearing carriages that lowered the guns after each firing to protected positions behind many feet of earth and concrete. Along with several hundred 12-inch mortars, which fired projectiles in high arcs to descend onto the decks of naval targets, such armament arrived between 1893 and 1918 in forts along both continental coasts, in the Philippines and the Hawaiian Islands, and at both entrances to the Panama Canal.

Between 1937 and 1945, the country carried out a final fortification effort, characterized by concrete and steel emplacements that provided overhead cover for even more powerful guns of up to 16-inch caliber. Included in the program were defenses for several points in Alaska and in the Caribbean area, as well as for the Atlantic bases acquired from Great Britain in exchange for destroyers. Within five years of the end of World War II, however, the country disarmed and abandoned all such fortifications, which were replaced by newer defense systems utilizing aircraft and guided missiles.

BIBLIOGRAPHY

Lewis, Emanuel R. *Seacoast Fortifications of the United States.* Washington, D.C.: Smithsonian Institution Press, 1970.

Peterson, Harold. *Forts in America.* New York: Scribners, 1964.

Robinson, Willard B. *American Forts.* Urbana: University of Illinois Press, 1976.

Emanuel Raymond Lewis / c.w.

See also **Air Defense; Army on the Frontier; French Frontier Forts; Frontier Defense;** *and names of individual forts.*

"FORTY ACRES AND A MULE," a phrase echoed throughout the South in the aftermath of the Civil War, asserting the right of newly freed African Americans to redistributed lands—particularly those plantations confiscated by U.S. troops during the war—as compensation for unpaid labor during slavery. Many historians trace the phrase to General William T. Sherman's Special Field Order Number 15, issued on 16 January 1865, which set aside a thirty-mile tract of land along the South Carolina and Georgia coasts for former slaves and promised the army's help securing loaned mules. In addition, the Freedmen's Bureau initially was authorized to divide abandoned and confiscated lands into forty-acre tracts for rental and eventual sale to refugees and former slaves. Despite the efforts of RADICAL REPUBLICANS during the Reconstruction period, however, significant land redistribution measures ultimately were abandoned, and virtually all southern lands were returned to white owners. The resulting sharecropping system left the social and economic structures of slavery essentially intact in the South.

The phrase itself continued to live vividly in the minds of most African Americans throughout the twentieth century, symbolizing to many the "unfinished business" of the Civil War. It thus was used to advocate the affirmative action programs that developed from the civil rights movements of the 1960s. As the twenty-first century began, moreover, a group of prominent defense attorneys and civil rights advocates used the phrase in making proposals for class-action lawsuits and other measures designed to secure financial reparations for the descendents of African American slaves.

BIBLIOGRAPHY

Donald, David Herbert, Jean H. Baker, and Michael F. Holt. *The Civil War and Reconstruction.* New York: Norton, 2001.

Foner, Eric. *Reconstruction: America's Unfinished Revolution, 1863–1877.* New York: Harper and Row, 1988.

Oubre, Claude F. *Forty Acres and a Mule: The Freedmen's Bureau and Black Land Ownership.* Baton Rouge: Louisiana State University Press, 1978.

Lori Askeland

See also **Freedmen's Bureau; Reconstruction; Sharecroppers.**

FORTY-EIGHTERS were a group of four thousand to ten thousand Germans who immigrated to the United States as political refugees following the failed revolutions and social reform movements of 1848. Although their numbers were not large, their impact on the organizational, cultural, and political lives of German Americans and Americans in general was tremendous. They tended to be liberal if not radical, agnostic, and intellectual. They were instrumental in the proliferation of German-American organizations, such as the Turnvereine, or the Turners as they became known. The Turners were gymnastic clubs and remained so into the twenty-first century. They were initially established in Germany in 1811 to promote well-being through exercise and to advocate a kind of nationalism thought necessary to defend the fatherland against Napoleon. In the United States they served largely as social and recreational organizations that brought together the heterogeneous German-speaking population. The Forty-Eighters also played leadership roles in other national organizations, such as the Nord-Amerikanischer Saengerbund, established in 1849.

The Forty-Eighters contributed to the development of German-American cultural life in the German-language press, theater, and music. This was especially evident in cities where German numbers were greatest, like Cincinnati, St. Louis, Chicago, and Milwaukee. In Milwaukee the circulation of the German-language press was twice that of the English-language press by the late nineteenth century. In the area of education, they strongly supported German bilingual instruction as well as physical education. They advocated for public, secular educational systems and played a role in establishing the first kindergartens in the United States. Margarethe Meyer Shurz opened the first kindergarten in the United States in Watertown, Wisconsin, in 1856.

In politics the Forty-Eighters were instrumental in solidifying a "German vote" that could not be overlooked in the national political arena. Numerous leaders emerged from their ranks, but Carl Shurz, husband of Magarethe Meyer Shurz, stands out. Shurz has been described by some historians as the most influential U.S. citizen of German birth. Shurz fled to Watertown, Wisconsin, via Switzerland following the failed revolution. He was instrumental in helping Abraham Lincoln gain the presidency and also in helping abolish slavery. He served as a Union brigadier general during the Civil War and as the first U.S. senator of German birth. In the latter role he fought U.S. expansion in the Caribbean, corruption in government, and unfair treatment of Native Americans.

Carl Schurz. German-born American general and reform-minded U.S. senator and cabinet member—a standout among the Forty-Eighters. LIBRARY OF CONGRESS

He continued to champion those causes as secretary of the interior in President Rutherford B. Hayes's cabinet. Overall the Forty-Eighters played a pivotal role in creating a German identity among German immigrants in the United States and contributed to the cultural and political lives of the nation during some of its most formative years.

BIBLIOGRAPHY

Brancaforte, Charlotte L., ed. *The German Forty-Eighters in the United States.* New York: Lang, 1989.

Galicich, Anne. *The German Americans.* New York: Chelsea House, 1989.

Tolzmann, Don Heinrich, ed. *The German-American Forty-Eighters: 1848–1998.* Indianapolis: Max Kade German–American Center, Indiana University–Purdue University at Indianapolis: Indiana German Heritage Society, 1998.

Timothy Bawden

See also **German Americans.**

FORTY-MILE DESERT, a large desert area between the sink of the Humboldt River and the Carson or Truckee River routes. It was the most difficult and dangerous stretch of the entire journey for the goldseekers and westward-bound immigrants who traveled through Nevada to California. In its entire forty-mile distance, neither water nor grass was to be found, and the loss of life, both human and livestock, was excessively high among those trying to cross it.

BIBLIOGRAPHY

Koenig, George. *Beyond This Place There Be Dragons.* Glendale, Calif.: Clark, 1984.

Carl L. Cannon / c. w.

See also **Deserts; Westward Migration.**

FORTY-NINERS. The discovery of gold in the Sierra in January 1848 brought hundreds of thousands of fortune hunters to California over the next few years: the forty-niners. The first to find gold tried to keep it secret, but the strike was too huge to conceal. News of the strike reached Yerba Buena, on San Francisco Bay, in May 1848. Immediately, two-thirds of the population dropped whatever they were doing and headed for the gold fields. As the word spread over the world, people from Europe, Chile, Hawaii, China, Mexico, Australia, and especially from the eastern United States converged on California. Ninety percent were men, but women also joined the gold rush.

Thousands traveled overland, in covered wagons, pushing wheelbarrows, on horseback and on foot, a journey of 3,000 miles that took three to seven months. In 1849 some 15,597 more reached San Francisco by sailing around Cape Horn, 15,000 miles requiring four to eight months. A quicker route lay through the Isthmus of Panama, half the distance and taking only two to three months.

Once in California the forty-niners found themselves in a wild, roaring country. Gold there was but finding it required backbreaking work, in competition with thousands of other increasingly desperate fortune seekers. No infrastructure existed to support so many people. Towns like Hangtown, Skunk Gulch, and Murderers Bar were clumps of tents and shacks, and the most ordinary commodities cost their weight in gold. Far from home, the forty-niners joined together in clubs for companionship and support and for the promise of a proper burial. In many California towns the oldest building is the Odd Fellows Hall, dating from the gold rush.

Few of the forty-niners got rich. Some went home. Most stayed on and settled down, in a place utterly changed. Like a human tidal wave, the gold rush demolished the old California, swept aside the Californios and the native peoples alike, and thrust the state from its quiet backwater onto the world stage, all in less than eight years.

BIBLIOGRAPHY

Bancroft, Hubert Howe. *History of California.* San Francisco: History Company, 1884–1890.

Digging for Gold. A handful of the hundreds of thousands of forty-niners who completely changed California in just a few years. LIBRARY OF CONGRESS

Holliday, J. S. *Rush for Riches: Gold Fever and the Making of California.* Berkeley: Oakland Museum of California and University of California Press, 1999.

Levy, JoAnn. *They Saw the Elephant: Women in the California Gold Rush.* Hamden, Conn.: Archon Books, 1990.

Cecelia Holland

See also **California; Gold Rush, California.**

FOSTER CARE. Approximately three million reports of child maltreatment (physical abuse, sexual abuse, neglect, and abandonment) come to the attention of public child welfare agencies in the United States every year. Hundreds of thousands of these reports are considered serious enough to be investigated, and about one-third are substantiated or proven. Of the cases that are substantiated, approximately 175,000 to 200,000 are placed into foster care.

Health care professionals refer to foster care as the temporary out-of-home placement for abused and neglected children. Typically, such placements are made in the homes of families specifically recruited and trained to care for troubled children or, increasingly, in the homes of relatives. However, about 20 percent of these children are placed in group homes or residential treatment centers. The placements are supposed to be for as short a period of time as possible, with the primary goal being to return the child to his or her birth parent or parents as soon as it is safe to do so. If the child cannot be returned home within a reasonable period of time, other permanent plans must be made for him or her, particularly adoption.

In the United States, foster care programs are usually administered and delivered by state and local public child welfare agencies. However, public child welfare agencies often contract with private not-for-profit and, to a much lesser extent, private for-profit organizations to provide foster care services.

Although public child welfare agencies are creatures of state governments, the federal government has played an increasingly larger role in child welfare. For example, federal laws have been enacted that provide fiscal incentives to states, in order to encourage them to adopt certain child welfare policies and practices. Also, the federal government has made available increasing amounts of funding, usually on a matching basis, for foster care and adoptions services. In addition, the federal government collects, archives, and disseminates child welfare data and information and provides a modest amount of funding for research.

There were two major pieces of federal child welfare legislation enacted in the late twentieth century. The first was the Adoptions Assistance and Child Welfare Act of 1980, more popularly known as P.L. 96-272. This legislation grew out of more than six years of congressional hearings into the problems confronting the child welfare system in the United States. The act placed greater emphasis on strengthening and preserving families and, in fact, placed as much emphasis on this new policy thrust as it did on protecting and caring for abused and neglected children. Consistent with this, one of the major priorities of the legislation was to increase services to prevent the out-of-home placement of children and to reduce the numbers of children being placed into foster care. Lawmakers also hoped that the act would result in shorter lengths of stay in placement, the elimination of foster care "drift" or the "bouncing" of children from one placement to another, improved training and supervision of foster parents, improved training for child welfare workers, and the delivery of more effective services to children in placement.

The law mandated that individualized treatment plans be developed for each child placed into foster care. It required that each child in placement had to have his or her case reviewed every six months to examine the status of the case and to determine whether the placement needed to be continued or if other permanent plans needed to be made.

Unfortunately, despite the hopes and expectations of reformers, the law had relatively little impact on the child welfare system. Beginning in the mid-1980s, the numbers and rates of children placed into foster care increased dramatically. This trend continued well into the 1990s. In fact, the best available data suggests the foster care population more than doubled between 1985 and 1999. Although significant amounts of money were spent on placement prevention services, there is virtually no credible scientific evidence that they had the desired impact. Even more disturbing is the fact that many class action lawsuits were filed against state and local public child welfare systems for abusive, unprofessional, and unconstitutional practices after P.L. 96-272 was passed. This statistic suggests that many public child welfare systems may have deteriorated during this period when policymakers and reformers expected them to improve.

In 1997 Congress passed the Adoptions and Safe Families Act, or ASFA. In sharp contrast to P.L. 96-272, this legislation places more emphasis on protecting children and makes it easier to remove them from dangerous home environments. The legislation calls for placing more of the burden on abusive and neglectful parents to demonstrate that they can properly care for their children before they will be returned to them. It also reduces the amount of time children have to stay in foster care from eighteen months to twelve months before permanent plans have to be made for them.

By 2002 most child welfare officials felt it was too soon to make any definitive statements about the impact of ASFA. Preliminary data suggest that increasing numbers of children are being adopted, although the numbers may be leveling off. Also, there are signs that the size of the foster care population may be stabilizing, or even declining. However, the length of stay in foster care for children awaiting adoption continues to average three years. For these children it can be said that the state has virtually become their parent, even if by default.

BIBLIOGRAPHY

Schwartz, Ira M., and Gideon Fishman. *Kids Raised by the Government.* Westport, Conn.: Praeger, 1999.

United States Department of Health and Human Services. *The AFCARS Report.* Washington, D.C.: Administration for Children and Families, 2000.

Ira M. Schwartz

FOUNDATIONS, ENDOWED. Organized in America either as charitable trusts or nonprofit corporations, philanthropic foundations are nongovernmental, nonprofit organizations, having funds and a program managed by trustees, established to aid social, educational, charitable, religious, or other activities serving the common welfare. In 2000 there were around 50,000 foundations in America, with combined assets totaling almost $450 billion; over fifty foundations have endowments over $1 billion, with the largest, Lilly Endowment and the Gates Foundation, over $15 billion. Grant-making foundations distributed around $27 billion to nonprofit organizations in 2000.

While the modern philanthropic foundation is an American invention, dating from the early twentieth century, special-purpose endowments have existed in most civilizations for centuries. Queen Elizabeth's "Statute of Charitable Uses" (1601) provided for trustee supervision of charitable bequests and listed legitimate objects of charity, including poor relief, education, medical treatment, and the care of widows and orphans. Typical of some of the earliest trusts in America was the William Carter fund (1739) for support of an alms house in Philadelphia. In his will of 1791, Benjamin Franklin established a trust for apprentices in Boston and Philadelphia, to borrow $300 at 5 percent interest. Like Franklin's, however, most early charitable endowments were local in scope and narrow of purpose.

The first modern foundation was established by the financier George Peabody in 1867, to "aid the stricken South," although it exhausted its capital by 1914. The real beginning of the modern foundation can be traced to the philanthropic work of two great industrialists of the nineteenth century, Andrew Carnegie and John D. Rockefeller. Seeking to move beyond "retail" philanthropy, Carnegie and Rockefeller experimented with several forms before applying the business corporation model to the creation of "general purpose" foundations. These were governed by self-perpetuating boards, with professional staffs and permanent endowments, and a wide mandate, such as Rockefeller's, "to promote the well-being of mankind throughout the world."

The early foundations, such as the Russell Sage Foundation (1907), the Carnegie Corporation (1911), and the Rockefeller Foundation (1913), each sought to develop scientific principles for philanthropic giving, avoiding charitable relief and instead focusing upon underlying causes. Grants were the venture capital of philanthropy, to experiment with programs before passing successful models along to governmental agencies, such as the successful public health campaign against hookworm of the Rockefeller Sanitary Commission.

These major foundations were designed to be perpetual, with investment strategies to provide significant income for grants but also to maintain capital. For example, the Rockefeller Foundation was capitalized in 1913 with around $182 million, and after giving away almost $2 billion, its endowment in 2000 approached $4 billion. Critics of perpetual endowments have come from both sides of the political spectrum, and at least one critic, the Sears executive Julius Rosenwald, established a fund himself. Rosenwald, who helped build over 5,300 schools and teachers' homes in the South, insisted that "all of the principle of this fund must be expended within twenty-five years" of his death. Few donors or trustees have followed Rosenwald's advice, however.

Foundations have their own life cycles. Control of assets and grant making is initially under the founder's control, but after the donor's death, control passes to family and trusted business associates. Within a generation the board often becomes composed of public service trustees, who soon defer to the expertise of a bureaucratized and professional staff. The number of foundations increased dramatically over the course of the twentieth century. With less than 20 established by 1910, by the end of the 1920s there were almost 300. By 1950, there were around 2,000 endowed foundations, and between 1980 and 2000 the number of foundations doubled, to around 50,000.

Foundations came under serious scrutiny several times in the twentieth century, especially due to their tax-exempt status. The first inquiry was Senator Frank Walsh's Commission on Industrial Relations in 1915, which criticized foundations as dominated by reactionary business interests. By the late 1940s, some businesses were using corporate foundations as tax shelters, leading to the Revenue Act of 1950, which prohibited self-dealing, taxed profits unrelated to tax-exempt status, and prohibited unreasonable accumulations of assets. This soon led to the largest single grant, the Ford Foundation's of $500 million for private universities in 1955.

Two major investigations took place during the McCarthy era. In 1952 the Cox Committee investigated whether foundations were undermining "existing capitalistic structure." While endorsing foundations, the Cox Committee called for increased public accounting of activities. The following year the Reece Committee attacked foundations as subversive. Starting in 1962, the Texas congressman Wright Patman began eleven years of investigations into foundation activity, mostly from a populist direction.

The Patman investigations, along with increased economic difficulties, led to the Tax Reform Act of 1969. A historic turning point, for the first time foundations were defined in law. The IRS tax code section for tax-exempt entities, 501(c)3, created two major divisions: "public charities," which include hospitals, museums, private schools, and even public television stations; and "private foundations." Private foundations are based on a single source of funding and use income from investments to make grants to other nonprofit organizations. Restrictions were placed on political activity and excess business holdings, and foundations were prohibited from self-dealing. They were required to pay an excise tax on income, and also had a minimum payout, eventually set at 5 percent. Corporate or company-sponsored foundations also fell under this category. While historically similar to private foundations, community foundations, like the Cleveland Foundation (1914), pool the resources of many donors and are treated more liberally, as "public charities."

Since the 1969 Tax Act, while a small undercurrent of criticism has continued from left and right, there have been no major investigations of foundation activity, suggesting wide public acceptance. Much of this is due to increased public disclosure and published studies. The Foundation Center was established in 1956 to provide information about philanthropy, and the Ford Foundation began funding scholarship on the field's public activity. Two private commissions in the 1970s, most importantly the Filer Commission on Private Philanthropy and Public Needs (1973–1977), increased public awareness of the newly named "third sector." By the end of the century over seventy universities had centers or courses for the study of philanthropic foundations, and there were several lobbying organizations.

The general-purpose philanthropic foundation is a distinctive American invention, and, over the course of a century, it has developed into a necessary countervailing force in an era of big government, contributing to an American style of public/private partnerships that have helped provide for democratic pluralism and public welfare both in America and abroad.

BIBLIOGRAPHY

Dowie, Mark. *American Foundations: An Investigative History.* Cambridge, Mass.: MIT Press, 2001.

"Foundation Yearbook: Facts and Figures on Private and Community Foundations." Part of the Foundation Center's *Foundations Today* series, available at http://www.fdcenter.org.

Hammack, David, ed. *Making the Nonprofit Sector in the United States.* Bloomington: Indiana University Press, 1998.

Kiger, Joseph C. *Philanthropic Foundations in the Twentieth Century.* Westport, Conn: Greenwood Press, 2000. Kiger was the research director of the Cox Committee.

Lagemann, Ellen Condliffe. *Philanthropic Foundations: New Scholarship, New Possibilities.* Bloomington: Indiana University Press, 1999.

O'Connell, Brian, ed. *America's Voluntary Spirit.* New York: Foundation Center, 1983.

Fred W. Beuttler

See also **Carnegie Corporation of New York; Philanthropy; Rockefeller Foundation.**

401(K) PLANS. *See* **Retirement Plans.**

FOUR FREEDOMS. After his election to a third term in 1940, President Franklin D. Roosevelt began to espouse more strongly the cause of Great Britain and its allies in World War II. An indication of this came in a major speech before Congress on 6 January 1941. In that speech, he urged a world founded upon four essential human freedoms: (1) freedom of speech and expression, (2) freedom of every person to worship God in his own way, (3) freedom from want, and (4) freedom from fear. Two of these freedoms—from fear and want—are mentioned as desirable objectives in the ATLANTIC CHARTER.

Charles S. Campbell/A. G.

See also **Foreign Policy; International Law; World War II.**

FOUR HUNDRED. In the late nineteenth century Caroline Webster Schermerhorn Astor, the wife of William Astor, used her position as the heir and wife of a wealthy man to become the arbiter of New York high society and the protector of the status of family and old wealth against the claims of the nouveau rich. Her annual January ball was the social event of the year. In 1892 Mrs. Astor, finding that her list of guests exceeded her ballroom's capacity, asked Ward McAllister, a well-known socialite, to reduce it to four hundred. McAllister afterward boasted that "there were about four hundred people in New York society." The number had no significance because new millionaires soon received the social recognition to which, by American standards of conspicuous spending, they were entitled. Rather, "The Four Hundred" became a cliché denoting social exclusivity.

BIBLIOGRAPHY

Allen, Frederick Lewis. *The Lords of Creation.* New York: Harper and Brothers, 1935.

Cable, Mary. *Top Drawer: American High Society from the Gilded Age to the Roaring Twenties.* New York: Atheneum, 1984.

Harvey L. Carter/C. P.

See also **Class; Gilded Age; Industrial Revolution.**

4-H CLUBS. The 4-H Clubs, which began as a rural youth movement in the early twentieth century, have developed into one of the largest youth organizations in the United States, helping suburban and urban as well as rural youth and adults "learn, grow, and work together as catalysts for positive change," in the words of the 4-H Council. The program coordinates cooperative efforts by youth, volunteer leaders, state land-grant universities, state and local governments, 4-H Foundations, as well as the Cooperative State Research and Educational and Extension Services of the U.S. Department of Agriculture. The movement uses a variety of methods, including clubs, school enrichment groups, camps, individual study programs, child care programs, and instructional television programs. The name "4-H" came into general use after World War I; the *H*'s stand for *head*, *heart*, *hands*, and *health*. The 4-H movement receives federal money through the Smith-Lever Act of 1914 (which supports all extension programs) and private support from the National 4-H Service Committee, founded in 1921, and the National 4-H Club Foundation, founded in 1948. The U.S. Department of Agriculture and the Cooperative Extension Service of the state land-grant universities share administrative responsibilities for 4-H.

The 4-H movement originally sought to encourage rural students to incorporate farm experimentation into their studies. A variety of corn production contests offering prizes for the most impressive yields on an acre of land encouraged students to join the corn clubs, or experiment clubs, as they became known. Youthful contestants often grew more than a hundred bushels of corn on their plots; a South Carolina boy raised 228.7 bushels of corn on an acre in 1910, nearly ten times the nationwide average that year (27.4 bushels per acre). In addition to corn clubs, tomato-canning clubs, cotton clubs, and even pig clubs started up in the Midwest and South. The national clover emblem associated with 4-H dates back to 1908, when it it was designed by O. H. Benson. In 1910 Iowa used three-leaf and four-leaf clover pins to recognize achievement among club members. In 1911 the clover emblem appeared on labels marking 4-H brand tomatoes, salmon, corn, potatoes, and apples that members had grown, picked, caught, preserved, and marketed. The 4-H emblem was patented in 1924, and a 1939 law protects the use of both the 4-H name and the emblem.

After World War II, 4-H expanded beyond its traditional work in plant and animal science, nutrition, and clothing and began sending alumni abroad to encourage similar work internationally. By the early twenty-first century, more than 6.8 million people were participating in

American 4-H, and millions more in international work. The program has produced more than 50 million alumni.

BIBLIOGRAPHY

McCormick, Robert W., and Virginia E. McCormick. "4-H: A. B. Graham's Dream." *Timeline* 13 (1996).

Rasmussen, Wayne David. *Taking the University To the People: Seventy-five Years of Cooperative Extension.* Ames: Iowa State University Press, 1989.

Wessel, Thomas R., and Marilyn Wessel. *4-H, an American Idea: 1900–1980.* Chevy Chase, Md.: National 4-H Council, 1982.

Marilyn F. Wessel / D. B.

See also **Agriculture; Agriculture, Department of; Child Care; County and State Fairs; Education, Cooperative; Land Grants: Land Grants for Education; Rural Life; Science Education; Smith-Lever Act.**

FOUR-POWER TREATY, signed on 13 December 1921 by the United States, Great Britain, France, and Japan. It was one of seven treaties that emerged from the Conference on Limitation of Armaments held in Washington from 12 November 1921 to 6 February 1922. U.S. Secretary of State Charles Evans Hughes had opened the conference by dramatically calling for steep reductions in the battleship fleets of the attending nations, a surprising challenge that set the tone for a highly productive conference. The Four-Power Treaty sought to eliminate the development of rival blocs in East Asia, as well as to preserve the territorial sovereignty of the signatories' holdings in the Pacific. The treaty acted as a substitute for the Anglo-Japanese alliance that, under pressure from the dominions and the United States, Great Britain had allowed to expire in 1921, and as the necessary preliminary to the other treaties and resolutions of the conference. The signatories bound themselves to respect each others' "rights in relation to their insular possessions and insular dominions in the region of the Pacific Ocean," to go into conference for the consideration and adjustment of any controversy "arising out of any Pacific question and involving their said rights which is not satisfactorily settled by diplomacy," and to "communicate with one another fully and frankly in order to arrive at an understanding as to the most efficient measures to be taken, jointly or separately" in the event of "the aggressive action of any other Power." The treaty was to run for ten years, and thereafter until denounced by one of the signatories. A declaration of the same date applied the treaty to the mandated islands of the Pacific, but without signifying the assent of the United States to the mandates or preventing it from negotiating about the mandates. The Senate ratified the treaty with the reservation that there was "no commitment to armed force, no alliance, and no obligation to join in any defense."

By a supplementary treaty of 6 February 1922, the signatories declared that "insular possessions and insular dominions," when applied to Japan, included only Korafuto (the southern portion of Sakhalin), Formosa, the Pescadores, and the islands under the mandate of Japan. The same powers also signed the Nine-Power Treaty, which declared their collective commitment to the **Open Door Policy** and Chinese territorial sovereignty. Taken as a whole, the seven treaties negotiated at the Washington conference established a peaceful status quo in the Far East that would last until the 1930s.

BIBLIOGRAPHY

Buckley, Thomas H. *The United States and the Washington Conference, 1921–1922.* Knoxville: University of Tennessee, 1970.

Hogan, Michael J. *The Private Structure of Cooperation in Anglo-American Economic Diplomacy, 1918–1928.* Columbia: University of Missouri Press, 1977; Chicago: Imprint, 1991.

LaFeber, Walter. *The Clash: A History of U.S.–Japanese Relations.* New York: Norton, 1997.

Bernadotte E. Schmitt / A. G.

See also **France, Relations with; Great Britain, Relations with; Japan, Relations with; League of Nations; Treaties with Foreign Nations; Washington Naval Conference.**

FOURIERISM takes its name from Charles Fourier (1772–1837), a pioneering French socialist. Fourier based his idea of a harmonious society on the assumption that human nature is unchangeable and that society must therefore be adapted to the individual. His idea of an ideal community, first published in 1808, consisted of 1,600 persons living on a self-supporting estate of several thousand acres. Out of the common gain, subsistence would be provided and surpluses equitably distributed among the three groups: labor, capital, and talent.

In 1834 Albert Brisbane, a young humanitarian, returned to the United States from France, where he had studied under Fourier. He introduced Fourierism into the United States by lecturing, writing books, and contributing to newspapers. Forty poorly financed experiments sprang up as a result of the excitement, although Brisbane himself did not organize them. Brook Farm was one of the more impressive experiments; its failure in 1846 marked the end of the association movement in the United States.

BIBLIOGRAPHY

Fellman, Michael. *The Unbounded Frame: Freedom and Community in Nineteenth-Century American Utopianism.* Westport, Conn.: Greenwood Press, 1973.

Guarneri, Carl. *The Utopian Alternative: Fourierism in Nineteenth-Century America.* Ithaca, N.Y.: Cornell University Press, 1991.

Kolmerten, Carol A. *Women in Utopia: The Ideology of Gender in the American Owenite Communities.* Bloomington: Indiana University Press, 1990.

John Colbert Cochrane / A. G.

See also **Laissez Faire; "New England Way"; Pacifism; Pragmatism; Share-the-Wealth Movements; Socialist Party of America.**

FOURTEEN POINTS. Nine months after the American declaration of war on Germany, President Woodrow Wilson addressed Congress on 8 January 1918, to declare America's terms of peace. Briefly, they were as follows: (1) "open covenants of peace openly arrived at"; (2) freedom of the seas; (3) freedom from trade barriers; (4) reduction of armaments; (5) impartial adjustment of colonial claims; (6) evacuation of Russian territory and Russian self-determination; (7) evacuation and restoration of Belgium; (8) evacuation of France and restoration of Alsace-Lorraine to France; (9) readjustment of Italian frontiers; (10) autonomous development for the peoples of Austria-Hungary; (11) readjustments in the Balkans; (12) autonomous development for the non-Turkish nationalities of the Ottoman Empire and the opening of the Dardanelles; (13) restoration of an independent Poland with access to the sea; and (14) establishment of a general association of nations. The Allied Powers refused to agree to Wilson's terms until the German government began peace negotiations on the basis of the fourteen points in October 1918. After Col. Edward M. House, Wilson's chief foreign policy adviser, warned Britain and France that the United States might make a separate peace with Germany, the Allies accepted the fourteen points on 4 November 1918—with the reservation that they did not accept a blanket principle of freedom of the seas and with the further caveat that they demanded financial compensation from Germany for wartime damages. After Germany's formal surrender one week later, the fourteen points became the legal basis for the ensuing treaty of peace.

Woodrow Wilson. The American president during World War I, whose terms of peace included his idealistic proposal for the establishment of what became the League of Nations, forerunner of the United Nations. LIBRARY OF CONGRESS

BIBLIOGRAPHY

Clements, Kendrick A. *The Presidency of Woodrow Wilson.* Lawrence: University Press of Kansas, 1992.

Knock, Thomas J. *To End All Wars: Woodrow Wilson and the Quest for a New World Order.* New York: Oxford University Press, 1992.

Bernadotte E. Schmitt / A. G.

See also **Germany, Relations with; House-Grey Memorandum; League of Nations; Treaties with Foreign Nations; World War I;** *and vol. 9:* **The Fourteen Points.**

FOURTH OF JULY. *See* **Independence Day.**

FOX. *See* **Mesquakie.**

FOX WAR. The Fox, or Mesquakie, peoples dominated the Mississippi and its tributaries in northern Illinois, eastern Iowa, and southern Wisconsin throughout much of the French colonial period. Loosely tied to the expanding French empire by the Great Lakes fur trade, beginning in the first decades of the eighteenth century the Fox resisted New France's attempts to incorporate them into the evolving French–Algonquin alliance of the Great Lakes. Fearful that their trading advantages and communities would be jeopardized by expanding French–Algonquin hegemony, the Fox became bitterly embroiled in a war with the French and their Indian allies. The Fox's attempt to remain independent of French political control threatened the precarious stability of the entire region's French–Indian alliance system. French officials accordingly mobilized large military campaigns to subjugate Fox communities. After a series of indecisive battles beginning at Detroit in 1712, the Fox attempted to form alliances with the region's other Indian groups, including the Winnebagos (Ho-Chunks) and Kickapoos. Fearful that they might lose not only their trading advantages throughout the region but also their entire political and military alliance system in the Great Lakes, the French responded with a campaign of extermination. Fox communities were besieged and terrorized throughout the 1730s. Eventually driven west of the Mississippi, Fox refugees resettled in Iowa but maintained close allegiances to their former homelands and with traditional allies, particularly the Saux.

BIBLIOGRAPHY

Edmunds, R. David, and Joseph L. Peyser. *The Fox Wars: The Mesquakie Challenge to New France.* Norman: University of Oklahoma Press, 1993.

White, Richard. *The Middle Ground: Indians, Empires, and Republics in the Great Lakes Region, 1650–1815.* New York: Cambridge University Press, 1991.

Ned Blackhawk

See also **Mesquakie; Wars with Indian Nations.**

FOX-WISCONSIN WATERWAY. The Wisconsin River originates in northern Wisconsin near the state's border with Michigan's Upper Peninsula. It flows south through the northern forests, central sand plains, and picturesque gorges of the Wisconsin Dells. The river then curves around the Baraboo Range before heading west and emptying into the Mississippi near Prairie du Chien. The Fox River originates in south-central Wisconsin, where it passes close to the southerly flowing Wisconsin River before flowing northeast into Lake Winnebago at Oshkosh. This portion of the river is known as the upper Fox. The lower Fox flows north out of Lake Winnebago in a postglacial course, with the old valley buried in glacial drift. As the river crosses the walls of its old valley it descends at a steep grade before eventually emptying into Green Bay. Hence, the two rivers belong to two different continental drainage systems—the Wisconsin River to the Mississippi watershed and the Fox River to the Great Lakes–St. Lawrence watershed—yet are separated by only a swampy, one-and-one-half-mile plain near the present day city of Portage. This geographical arrangement has been called the most important topographic feature of Wisconsin in relation to its history, particularly when water transportation reigned supreme.

Native Americans, European explorers, voyageurs, and early settlers all used the Fox-Wisconsin waterway to travel from Lake Michigan to the Mississippi. Sometimes the area separating the two rivers flooded and a small boat could travel from one system to the other. Most of the time, however, boats had to be carried, or portaged. This obstruction, along with the fact that the lower Fox contained a series of rapids, made the waterway unsuitable for large boats and commercial traffic. During the mid-nineteenth century several companies and various levels of government worked to develop the waterway by digging a canal at the portage and building locks along the lower Fox. The chief promoter in its early development was Morgan Martin, a lawyer who moved to Green Bay in 1827 at the encouragement of his cousin and Wisconsin's future territorial governor, James Doty. Martin first proposed the idea of a canal in 1829 and lobbied to bring it to fruition in 1831, when he was elected to the legislative council of the Michigan Territory. His efforts resulted in the founding of the Portage Canal Company, incorporated with a capital stock of $50,000. A crude ditch was dug between the two rivers but additional funding was required.

Beginning in 1836 the Wisconsin territorial legislature requested help from the United States Congress, but the project received little attention until Martin was elected as the territorial delegate to Congress in 1845. He was successful. In 1846 the Fox-Wisconsin bill was passed. It granted the state the right to sell the odd-numbered sections of land on each side of the Fox River, the lakes, and the portage canal, with the stipulation that the proceeds be used only for the improvement of the waterway. When Wisconsin became a state in 1848 the legislature accepted the grant and set up the Board of Public Works to oversee the project. Although land sales were high by 1850, the Board's treasury was empty. The canal was completed in 1851, but large boats were still restricted because the lower Fox had not been dredged and locks had not been built. The state's governor became skeptical and urged the project be turned over to private parties. Martin and a group of investors incorporated the Fox and Wisconsin Improvement Company and received all of the rights of the state in the improvement and all the unsold lands.

Finally, in 1856 the *Aquila* was the first steamboat to make its way from the Mississippi to Green Bay. By 1866 the Fox and Wisconsin Improvement Company fell into financial trouble from which it never recovered, and the improvements and remaining lands were sold to the Green Bay and Mississippi Canal Company. Financial problems continued, however, and in 1872 Congress purchased the improvements and took control of the waterway. The channel was never developed to accommodate the large steamboats initially envisioned because the era of water-powered transportation waned with the arrival of the railroads.

BIBLIOGRAPHY

Martin, Lawrence. *The Physical Geography of Wisconsin.* 3d ed. Madison: University of Wisconsin Press, 1965. The original edition was published in 1916.

Martin, Samuel. *The Fox-Wisconsin Rivers Improvement: An Historical Study in Legal Institutions and Political Economy.* Madison: University Extension Department of Law, University of Wisconsin, 1968.

Wenslaff, Ruth Ann. "The Fox-Wisconsin Waterway." *Wisconsin Then and Now* 13, no. 1 (1966): 1–3.

Timothy Bawden

See also **Portages and Water Routes; Waterways, Inland.**

FRANCE, QUASI-WAR WITH. The Quasi-War, or naval war, with France, included a series of battles and diplomatic tensions between the U.S. government and the French as a result of attacks against American merchants shipping off the Barbary Coast and in the Caribbean. The brief undeclared war that occurred between 1798 and 1801 was one of the main catalysts for the building and support of the U.S. Navy. Under the Articles of Confederation, Congress lacked the power to maintain more than a token naval force. Furthermore, American suspicion of a standing army prohibited plans for organized forces. As a result of French pillaging and the demands of American merchants for protection, Congress found an increased naval force a necessity.

In consequence of the Franco-American misunderstanding of 1798–1800, the French, with no declaration of war, began to seize and plunder American merchant vessels. Despite U.S. attempts to settle the matter diplomatically, no solution could be reached. From March through July of 1798, Congress passed acts empowering the U.S. merchant marine to "repel by force any assault," to commission privateers, and to order the navy to seize all armed French craft found along the U.S. coast or molesting trade. George Washington was recalled from retirement and appointed commander in chief of the army. The American navy, consisting of only three ships, was rapidly enlarged by construction, purchase, and gifts to fifty-five vessels. The first went to sea on 24 May 1798. France sent no heavy vessels to the western Atlantic, because it was occupied with European wars. Rather, knowing the weakness of the untrained American navy, the French relied on privateers supported by a few frigates and sloops of war.

As American vessels were commissioned, they organized into small squadrons to guard the chief trade areas in the East and West Indies. The small American navy faced few engagements and mostly guarded against numerous privateers. Despite the hasty organization of the U.S. Navy, however, each of their three engagements against French forces resulted in victory. Those battles involved the *Insurgente*, 40 guns, and the *Constellation*, 36 guns; the *Vengeance*, 50 guns; and the *Constellation*, 36 guns, the *Berceau*, 24 guns, and the *Boston*, 32 guns. Congress presented Captain Thomas Truxtun, commander of the *Constellation* in both engagements, with two gold medals. Two vessels, the schooners *Enterprise* and *Experiment*, had especially notable careers—the former taking thirteen prizes on one cruise. Although the United States made no attempt to seize the French islands, on 23 September 1800, Captain Henry Geddes, with the ship *Patapsco*, successfully dislodged the French forces that had taken possession of the Dutch island of Curaçao. About eighty-five French vessels were captured, not including recaptures of American craft and small boats. Although the French took only one American naval vessel, the schooner *Retaliation*, France seized several hundred American merchant vessels both abroad and in home waters. These were condemned at farcical admiralty trials, and in most instances the crews were imprisoned and brutally treated.

On 30 September 1800, France and the United States concluded a convention of peace, commerce, and navigation, and shortly thereafter, hostilities ceased.

BIBLIOGRAPHY

De Conde, Alexander. *The Quasi-War: The Politics and Diplomacy of the Undeclared War with France, 1797–1801.* New York: Scribner, 1966.

Fowler, William M. *Jack Tars and Commodores: The American Navy, 1783–1815.* Boston: Houghton Mifflin, 1984.

Nash, Howard Pervear. *The Forgotten Wars: The Role of the U.S. Navy in the Quasi War with France and the Barbary Wars, 1798–1805.* South Brunswick, N.J.: Barnes, 1968.

Palmer, Michael A. *Stoddert's War: Naval Operations during the Quasi-War with France, 1798–1801.* Columbia: University of South Carolina Press, 1987.

Marion V. Brewington/H. S.

See also **Convention of 1800; France, Relations with; French Decrees.**

FRANCE, RELATIONS WITH. In the seventeenth century the French explored and colonized much of the future United States. They claimed an area stretching from Canada to the Gulf of Mexico and from the Appalachians to the Rocky Mountains and named it Louisiana in honor of their king, Louis XIV, who had established French supremacy on the European continent. France was soon contending directly with England for dominance in the New World. They fought a long series of European wars, many of which, beginning in 1689, were extended to American ground. At the end of the French and Indian War (1754–1763), the decisive struggle between the French and the British for control of the North American continent, France had been defeated by the British and their colonists. By the Treaty of Paris of 1763, all of the French lands east of the Mississippi became British, and the French possessions west of the Mississippi were ceded to Spain.

Two Revolutions

Eager to gain revenge for this defeat, France became the strongest ally of the American colonies in their war for independence. A number of prominent Americans traveled to Paris to enlist help from the French. Benjamin Franklin, the U.S. minister in Paris and very popular in France, was instrumental in obtaining arms, ammunition, and food for the American army and in bringing about the 1778 French-American alliance.

The Marquis de Lafayette, a nineteen-year-old officer in the French cavalry, who was among the young French aristocrats and intellectuals inspired by republican idealism and the American cause, arranged with Silas

Deane, the American agent in Paris, to enter service on the side of the revolutionaries as a major general. Because the war was going badly for the Americans, the French king forbade Lafayette to leave the country. A determined Lafayette departed anyway, escaping British efforts to seize him.

Lafayette served General George Washington and the American Revolution well. After fighting in a number of important battles, he joined Washington and the French military officer, the Comte de Rochambeau, to overcome the British general, Lord Cornwallis, in the climactic Battle of Yorktown in 1781. The French navy also played a crucial part in that battle by keeping the British navy at bay, thereby preventing any reinforcements from reaching Cornwallis, who was forced to surrender.

The American Revolution became the model for the French Revolution. When Lafayette returned to Paris he became active in politics and on 11 July 1789, as vice president of the National Assembly, he presented a declaration of rights based on the American Declaration of Independence. He participated in the early stages of the French Revolution but resisted the chaos into which it deteriorated. While the Americans had sought a democracy under an orderly government with the power to protect the rights of the majority, the French sought an absolute democracy with no limits on individual liberty. The failure of French democracy lead to the Napoleonic Wars and rule by an emperor.

The Jay Treaty and the Quasi-War

The United States, a fledgling nation trying to pursue a policy of neutrality, came perilously close to war, first with Britain and then with France, in the last decade of the eighteenth century. War erupted between France and Britain in 1793. Despite the American Revolution, old bonds with the British, based on a common language and culture and bloodlines, endured—especially in the North, which was also heavily dependent on the British mercantile system. Pro-French feeling was strongest in the South and among Jefferson's Republicans. The United States preferred to trade with both nations, but the British blockaded France and her colonies and began seizing American ships transporting goods to French ports. War with Britain was averted as a result of the Jay Treaty (1795), but war with France then became the problem.

France denounced the Jay Treaty as a violation of the French-American alliance of 1778 and began full-scale attacks on American merchant ships. By the summer of 1797 the French had seized more than three hundred. When President John Adams sent Charles Cotesworth Pinckney, John Marshall, and Elbridge Gerry to Paris, the French minister of foreign affairs, the Duc de Talleyrand, refused to negotiate with them. Instead, he designated three agents, whom the Americans called X, Y, and Z. The Americans were shocked when these three demanded a large bribe before they would negotiate. The Americans refused. War fever seized the country with rumors circulating of an imminent French attack. The Republicans blamed Adams for insulting the French in the past and thus causing the impasse, but they ceased wearing the tricolor cockade of France in their hats. Adams increased American military strength. Napoleon, however, did not want to fight the United States, and Talleyrand sent word in 1799 that American envoys would be welcomed in Paris. An 1800 treaty ended the Quasi-War, and the French-American alliance was nullified.

The Nineteenth Century: Relations with Imperial and Republican France

Peace with France made the Louisiana Purchase of 1803 possible. After France reacquired Louisiana from Spain in 1800, Thomas Jefferson became alarmed at the threat of powerful France on the United States's western border. Jefferson sent Robert R. Livingston, the American minister in Paris, to buy West Florida and New Orleans from France for $10 million. Napoleon, who now realized that Britain could easily seize any French colony in the Americas, offered to sell all of Louisiana for $15 million. The United States agreed and acquired with its purchase from France a doubling of its land area, control of the Mississippi River, and a new dominance on the North American continent.

The war between Britain and France resumed in 1803, and after 1805, the United States became involved in the hostilities. The British announced a blockade of the lands held by Napoleon, which they partly carried out by seizing American ships, cargoes, and sailors just outside of American ports. Britain's primary aim was the defeat of Napoleon, and it was willing to risk war with the United States to do so. Napoleon in turn sent privateers to seize any neutral ships that obeyed the British blockade, and after 1807 Napoleon captured more American ships than the British. The United States declared war on Britain in 1812, and when the war was settled in 1814, little had been gained by either side.

Lafayette returned to the United States for a yearlong triumphal tour in 1824. Wherever Lafayette went, he was met by large crowds and great public acclaim as Americans recalled the debt they owed to France for its help in the American Revolution. Another democratic French aristocrat, Alexis de Tocqueville, came to the United States in 1831 to observe America's democratic institutions. In 1835 and 1840, he published volumes one and two of *Democracy in America*, which has endured as a highly respected work of political analysis.

Relations between the United States and France were strained by the actions of Napoleon III during the American Civil War (1861–1865). The emperor sought to acquire territory in Central and South America while the United States was not in a position to enforce the Monroe Doctrine. He installed the Archduke Maximilian of Austria as emperor of Mexico. The American government withheld recognition of this puppet government, at the same time informing France that there was no threat of

Benjamin Franklin. The very popular U.S. minister is shown at the court of King Louis XVI, who would become the crucial ally of the Americans. GETTY IMAGES

war in this action. When the Civil War ended, French troops left Mexico and Maximilian was executed.

Napoleon III's government having been overthrown, in the early 1870s a group of French republican partisans conceived the idea of a gift to the United States of a large statue of liberty as a republican symbol, its purposes being to show respect for American democracy and to encourage Americans to support the republican form of government in France. The sculptor Frederic Auguste Bartholdi was commissioned to make the giant statue and Congress authorized Bedloe's Island (later Liberty Island) in New York Harbor as its site. The Statue of Liberty, dedicated in 1886, is a primary symbol of American freedom.

The Twentieth Century: A Sometimes Uneasy Alliance

In 1914 Germany declared war on France and Russia, and England declared war on Germany. France took up the battle with enthusiasm and a strong desire for revenge for the humiliating French defeat at Germany's hands in the Franco-Prussian War of 1870. From its inception, World War I produced staggering losses of life and was at an impasse in April 1917, when the United States—abandoning its neutral position—declared war on Germany. The spring offensive of the French had ended in failure and mutiny. Their new commander, Henri Philippe Petain, was at the end of his resources. As American troops began pouring into France Colonel Charles E. Stanton announced upon his arrival: "Lafayette, we are here." The Germans launched their last offensive in March 1918. The Allies, in a united effort under French marshall Ferdinand Foch, slowly drove the Germans out of France.

President Woodrow Wilson reduced France's demands for the subjugation of Germany after World War I by agreeing, with Great Britain, to guarantee French security against any future German invasion. The U.S. Senate refused to uphold this guarantee when it declined to ratify the Treaty of Versailles in 1918; consequently, Britain was also released from its obligation. The relations between France and the United States continued to be strained in the 1920s as the latter demanded that the French pay war debts to her that they could not afford. The British mostly ignored France's problems in the interwar years, and with the United States retreating into isolationism, France was left to stand alone against possible German aggression.

France's fears became a nightmarish reality when Hitler rapidly conquered France in June 1940. Germany took Alsace-Lorraine and occupied northern and western France. Unoccupied France, with its capital at Vichy, became an ally of Germany. The French general Charles de Gaulle formed a government in exile based in London while underground Resistance fighters harassed the Germans in France. The United States brought its economic and military strength to bear against European fascism and Japanese imperialism between 1942 and 1945 and with the Soviet Union and the United Kingdom and its dominions, defeated Germany and its allies, Japan and Italy.

After World War II, France was in economic crisis, and its voters turned to socialism and even communism for solutions to its problems. The Marshall Plan was created by the Truman administration to help the countries of Western Europe. As the economy of France recovered with the help of American aid, the influence of communism declined.

Jean-Paul Sartre, a French intellectual who championed the working classes and who was part of the French Resistance during World War II, was influential in encouraging anti-Americanism in France in the period after the war. Sartre hated the preeminence of the middle class in the United States. Like de Gaulle, he was strongly opposed to American political, military, and cultural hegemony in Europe. He accused the United States of deploying germ warfare in the Korean War and joined Bertrand Russell in investigating alleged American war crimes in the Vietnam War. Sartre's anti-Americanism was echoed by other postwar French intellectuals, who feared the loss of France's integrity in the face of American economic and industrial strength.

The nationalist policies of Charles de Gaulle, who served as president of France from 1959 to 1969, challenged American hegemony in world power. De Gaulle envisioned France in a new role as the head of a third force that would stand between the United States and the Soviet Union. In 1959 de Gaulle began removing French troops from NATO and by 1967 had withdrawn all of them. He then demanded that all other NATO forces, including those controlling American nuclear weapons, leave France. De Gaulle initiated a French nuclear development program, and in 1960 France conducted its first atomic bomb test.

De Gaulle also resisted the influence of the United States within the European Common Market, where he blocked the entry of Britain, the United States' closest ally. Gaullism lived on in France after 1969. François Mitterand, who was president from 1981 to 1995, refused in 1986 to allow U.S. planes based in Britain to fly over France to bomb Libya. While this refusal provoked a surge of anti-French sentiment in the United States, Gaullism allowed the French to recover their shattered pride, preserve their unique qualities, and become stronger and more independent.

When the Socialist Party lost its parliamentary majority in France in 1986, the conservative Jacques Chirac became prime minister and then was elected president in 1995 and again in 2002. By the early 1990s France had become much more closely tied to the United States and NATO and had begun cooperating with American foreign policy. Also, France was moving away from Gaullism by becoming an integral part of the European Union. In the late twentieth century a rightward political shift occurred in France, as evidenced by the surprising popularity of Jean-Marie Le Pen's fascistic Front National, which espoused withdrawal from the European Union, closing France's borders to immigration, deporting all nonnaturalized immigrants, and eliminating the income tax.

The French have continued to resist incursions of American culture such as fast food restaurants and Disneyland, and they dislike any Americanization of their language. Nevertheless, there have always been many cultural connections between France and the United States. American writers, jazz musicians, and performing artists have often taken their talents to Paris and other parts of France, where they have found receptive audiences. There has been a lively and ongoing mutual admiration of each other's film industries and Americans admire and emulate French culture's many facets but particularly its cuisine, fashion, and art. And although it acted long after the American Revolution, the United States Congress in July 2002 voted to make the Marquis de La Fayette an honorary U.S. citizen. Lafayette is only the sixth person in the history of the country to receive this special recognition.

BIBLIOGRAPHY

Bernstein, Richard. *Fragile Glory: A Portrait of France and the French.* New York: Knopf, 1990.

Bernier, Olivier. *Words of Fire, Deeds of Blood: The Mob, the Monarchy, and the French Revolution.* Boston: Little, Brown, 1989.

Judt, Tony. *Past Imperfect: French Intellectuals, 1944–1956.* Berkeley: University of California Press, 1992.

Kennedy, Paul. *The Rise and Fall of the Great Powers: Economic Change and Military Conflict from 1500 to 2000.* New York: Random House, 1987.

McCullough, David. *John Adams.* New York: Simon and Schuster, 2001.

Rosenblum, Mort. *Mission to Civilize: The French Way.* New York: Doubleday, 1988.

Zeldin, Theodore. *France 1848–1945: Intellect and Pride.* Oxford: Oxford University Press, 1980.

Judith Reynolds

See also **Democracy in America (Tocqueville); France, Quasi-War with; French in the American Revolution; French Decrees; Louisiana Purchase; Marshall Plan; Mexico, French in; North Atlantic Treaty Organization; Statue of Liberty; Versailles, Treaty of; World War I; World War II; XYZ Affair.**

FRANCHISE. *See* **Suffrage.**

FRANCISCANS. In 1209 Saint Francis of Assisi founded the Order of Friars Minor, more commonly known as the Franciscans. Despite the wishes of his wealthy father, Francis abandoned his privileged lifestyle and devoted himself to a life of poverty and preaching in the vernacular to the masses. His mendicant order soon gained the support of powerful patrons, including Pope Innocent III, who approved of the Franciscans' respect for church authority and orthodox doctrine in a time of rampant popular heresy. Soon after, Francis's childhood friend Clare founded a female counterpart to the Franciscans, called the Poor Clares, who also lived in voluntary poverty but remained cloistered rather than wandering and begging as did the Franciscans.

In colonial times, the Franciscans were preeminent in the discovery, exploration, and settlement of Spanish North America. In the SPANISH BORDERLANDS of the colonies, that is, Florida, Texas, New Mexico, Arizona, and California, they were the only missionaries to spend significant time among the Indians and to cover substantial territory. Many old missions still bear witness to the zeal and success that marked their activity. The work of bishop-elect Juan Juáres, who in 1528 journeyed to Florida with Pánfilo de Narváez's expedition, and Father José Sánchez, who in 1884 died at San Gabriel Mission, California, stand as well-known examples of Franciscan achievement.

In the sections of North America that belonged to France, where they were known as the Recollects, the Franciscans were less active. They cast their lot with Robert Cavelier, Sieur de La Salle, in the Illinois country and on the Texas coast between 1675 and 1687. Thereafter, until 1763, when French North America became English territory, the Franciscans labored in upper Louisiana, at Cahokia on the Mississippi River, at Detroit in Michigan, and at the French forts in northern Ohio, Pennsylvania (DUQUESNE), and New York (Niagara, Crown Point, and Saint Frédéric). In the English colony of Maryland, they joined the JESUITS in 1672 and were active there until 1720, when the last of their group died. It is probable that from Maryland they forayed into Pennsylvania.

During the half-century following the American Revolution, various provinces in Europe sent Franciscans to the United States, usually with immigrant groups. These Franciscans labored chiefly in the "new" West and Northwest. Among them, Father Michael Egan in 1810 became the first bishop of Philadelphia. Unfortunately, scholars have yet to trace and to write the history of these isolated Franciscans.

The present era of Franciscan activity in the United States, which has taken place chiefly in parishes and schools, began in about the 1850s. Since then, regularly organized into juridical entities, Franciscans have advanced steadily in both membership and foundations. At the end of the twentieth century, the Franciscan order boasted almost eighteen thousand members worldwide, with just under twelve thousand of those members serving as priests and the rest as scholastics and lay brothers. Working both in the United States and in foreign areas such as Bolivia, Brazil, Central America, Japan, Peru, and the Philipines, American Franciscans have focused their efforts on friaries, schools, and Indian missions.

BIBLIOGRAPHY

Galloway, Patricia K., ed. *La Salle and His Legacy: Frenchmen and Indians in the Lower Mississippi Valley.* Jackson: University Press of Mississippi, 1982.

Hann, John, and Bonnie G. McEwan. *The Apalachee Indians and Mission San Luis.* Gainesville: University Press of Florida, 1998.

Rabasa, Jose. *Writing Violence on the Northern Frontier: The Historiography of Sixteenth-Century New Mexico and Florida and the Legacy of Conquest.* Durham, N.C.: Duke University Press, 2000.

Antonine S. Tibesar / A. E.

See also **Colorado River Explorations; Exploration of America, Early; French Frontier Forts; Hennepin, Louis, Narratives of; Indian Missions.**

FRANK, LEO, LYNCHING OF. The prosecution and conviction of Leo Frank in 1913, and his murder by a lynch mob two years later, constitute the South's most notorious episode of anti-Semitism. Born in 1884, Frank was reared in Brooklyn, New York, and served as superintendent of the National Pencil Factory in Atlanta, Georgia. On 26 April 1913, a thirteen-year-old employee, Mary Phagan, was murdered. The superintendent's trial, which began on 28 July, was conducted in an atmosphere inflamed by press sensationalism. The testimony of Jim Conley, a black janitor, seemed conclusive enough to warrant a death sentence. Unsuccessful appeals launched on Frank's behalf may only have deepened the xenophobia among white Georgians. Governor John M. Slaton commuted the sentence to life imprisonment but was forced to flee the state under mob threats. Frank was abducted by two dozen men, calling themselves the Knights of Mary Phagan, who hanged him near her birthplace on 17 August 1915.

A New York Jew and a factory manager in an agrarian order succumbing to modernization, Frank had personified a challenge to regional tradition. From the Knights of Mary Phagan, the nucleus of the second Ku Klux Klan in American history was created in 1915, two years after the B'nai B'rith had established the Anti-Defamation League to combat such bigotry.

BIBLIOGRAPHY

Dinnerstein, Leonard. *The Leo Frank Case.* New York: Columbia University Press, 1968.

Stephen J. Whitfield

See also **Anti-Semitism; Lynching.**

Herbert Marcuse. A member of the Frankfurt School and an influential Marxist philosopher, especially on the New Left in the 1960s. © CORBIS

FRANKFURT SCHOOL. Although founded in Frankfurt, Germany, in 1923, the Institute for Social Research (or Frankfurt School) established itself at Columbia University in New York City in 1934 in response to the Nazi seizure of power in Germany. The Frankfurt School's principal members included the institute's director Max Horkheimer, Theodor Adorno, Walter Benjamin, Erich Fromm, Leo Lowenthal, and Herbert Marcuse. The institute reestablished itself in Frankfurt in the early 1950s, though several of its members—including Fromm, Lowenthal, and Marcuse—remained in the United States.

The diverse intellectual contributions of the Frankfurt School were linked by a common attempt to develop what they called "critical theory." Critical theory was an ambitious attempt to understand modern society through an interdisciplinary approach integrating philosophy, political economy, history, psychoanalysis, sociology, and cultural theory. Frankfurt School members were revisionist Marxists who sought both to understand society and to make it more rational and just. However, with the rise of fascism and Stalinism, they became increasingly disillusioned with the prospects for progressive social change. Thus, for the Frankfurt School, critical theory represented an intellectual challenge to the social order when a political one failed to materialize.

At the heart of critical theory was a trenchant critique of the modern "totally administered society." The Frankfurt School's analysis of fascism stressed its parallels with contemporary capitalism. Its influential critique of the "culture industry" claimed that commercialized mass culture produces conformity and political passivity, thus upholding the repressive capitalist social order.

Ironically, the influence of critical theory on American intellectuals was greater after the institute moved back to Germany. The most recognized work by a Frankfurt School member during its American exile was *The Authoritarian Personality*, a sociological study conducted by Adorno and a team of American researchers that rated its subjects on an "f" scale to determine the potential for fascism in America. But *The Authoritarian Personality* was not the most representative expression of the distinctive approach of the Frankfurt School. The full weight of critical theory's political critique was not felt in the United States until the publication of Herbert Marcuse's *One-Dimensional Man* in 1964, which found a receptive audience among the growing New Left student movement.

Not until the 1970s did many American intellectuals discover the important theoretical works of critical theory. An English translation of Horkheimer and Adorno's crucial book *Dialectic of Enlightenment*, though written in the United States in the early 1940s, did not appear until 1972. Later, American intellectuals were much influenced by the work of Jürgen Habermas, a second-generation member of the Frankfurt School who made significant contributions to understanding the public sphere, the social sciences, the nature of language, and postmodernism. Thus, the insights of the Frankfurt School continued to make their way across the Atlantic.

BIBLIOGRAPHY

Bronner, Stephen Eric, and Douglas McCay Kellner, eds. *Critical Theory and Society: A Reader.* New York: Routledge, 1989.

Jay, Martin. *The Dialectical Imagination: A History of the Frankfurt School and the Institute of Social Research, 1923–1950.* Berkeley: University of California Press, 1973.

———. *Permanent Exiles: Essays on the Intellectual Migration from Germany to America.* New York: Columbia University Press, 1985.

Daniel Geary

See also **Philosophy; Sociology.**

FRANKLIN, STATE OF. In 1784 North Carolina ceded its western lands to the United States to avoid the expenses of protecting the western settlements and to protect the investments of land speculators who had acquired large holdings under the state's land acts of 1782–1783. Residents of the eastern part of the ceded region, known as Wataugans, favored the formation of a new state. Encouraged by separatists in southwest Virginia and by Congress's adoption of ordinances authorizing the establishment of new commonwealths in the West, the Wataugans assembled in what is now Jonesboro, Tennessee, in 1784 and organized the state of Franklin. They considered the action necessary to maintain orderly government, defend themselves from Indian attacks, and protect land titles. North Carolina immediately repented the action, repealed the cession act, and attempted to woo back the westerners. Fearing the effects of separation on their land dealings in the Tennessee country and along the Tennessee River in present-day Alabama, John Sevier and other western leaders advised reconciliation. Unable to check the Franklin movement, they decided to seize power instead and adopted a constitution that validated North Carolina land titles. With Sevier as governor, the state of Franklin maintained a precarious existence for four years, characterized by Indian troubles, intrigues with the Spanish, and ineffectual efforts to obtain recognition from Congress and North Carolina. The chief cause of failure was the opposition of a rival faction led by John Tipton, which contributed materially to North Carolina's success in reestablishing jurisdiction by 1789.

BIBLIOGRAPHY

Abernethy, Thomas Perkins. *From Frontier to Plantation in Tennessee: A Study in Frontier Democracy.* University: University of Alabama Press, 1967.

Driver, Carl Samuel. *John Sevier, Pioneer of the Old Southwest.* Chapel Hill: University of North Carolina Press, 1932.

Gerson, Noel Bertram. *Franklin: America's "Lost State."* New York: Crowell-Collier, 1968.

Williams, Samuel Cole. *History of the Lost State of Franklin.* New York: The Press of the Pioneers, 1933.

S. J. Folmsbee / H. S.

See also **Ordinances of 1784, 1785, and 1787; Tennessee.**

FRANKLIN INSTITUTE, the most prominent of American mechanics institutes, was established in Philadelphia in 1824 primarily through the efforts of Samuel Merrick, who later served as first president of the Pennsylvania Railroad, and William H. Keating, professor of chemistry and mineralogy at the University of Pennsylvania. In common with the LYCEUM MOVEMENT and with other voluntary associations of the same era, the organization reflected a widespread interest in educational reform as a means of actualizing America's self-image as the chosen heir of classical democracy. It further expressed the Enlightenment conviction (a philosophical eighteenth-century movement that rejected traditional social, religious, and political ideas, and emphasized rationalism) that America's future depended on technology's promise of limitless prosperity and mastery over nature.

The institute began a series of evening lectures in March 1824 on the principles and applications of science and, in the same year, established a school of mechanical and architectural drawing, which was conducted annually until 1923. In later efforts to broaden its educational program, the institute experimented with several different kinds of schools, notably a high school for boys and an industrial design school for women. Although its educational activities carried out its initial aims, the institute was better known for its exhibitions of American industry, its *Journal of the Franklin Institute,* and its experimental research.

Exhibitions were begun in October 1824 to stimulate interest in industrial development. Continued at varying intervals throughout the century, these industrial fairs were highly popular and widely imitated. At an abstract level, they became a symbol of economic independence from Europe. More immediately, they functioned as a guide to consumers, and some, such as the Electrical Exhibition of 1884, served as the basis for the organization of new technologies. The *Journal of the Franklin Institute,* most long-lived of America's technical periodicals, began publication in 1826 as the *Franklin Journal and American Mechanics' Magazine.* It soon became an important medium for the emerging professional interests of American scientists and engineers and a vehicle for transmitting knowledge of significant advances in European technology.

The institute's experimental investigations and dramatic discoveries gave it wide reputation. The first such investigation was a set of experiments in 1830 to determine the most efficient industrial use of water power. In 1831, the institute commenced an even more sophisticated inquiry to discover the causes of steamboat boiler explosions, a problem of national consequence. Other investigations included an inquiry into the causes of the 1844 U.S.S. *Princeton* disaster, a search for a standard for American screw threads, and an 1877 series of dynamo tests.

The prominence of the institute in the nineteenth century rested mainly on its ability to identify critical problems in emerging technologies. Ironically, research demonstrated that technical advances depended less on evening lectures for working men than on specialized and rigorous engineering training. As universities and trade schools had largely taken over the institute's original function as the disseminator of useful technical knowledge, in 1932 it redirected its educational program by opening a museum of technology. Experimental investigations did not figure prominently again in its efforts until WORLD WAR II, when defense research led to the establishment of a peacetime INDUSTRIAL RESEARCH laboratory. In addition to the museum, the institute administers grants to promising researchers and continues to publish scientific papers.

BIBLIOGRAPHY

Rorabaugh, W. J. *The Craft Apprentice: From Franklin to the Machine Age in America.* New York: Oxford University Press, 1986.

Sinclair, Bruce. *Philadelphia's Philosopher Mechanics: A History of the Franklin Institute, 1824–1865.* Baltimore: Johns Hopkins University Press, 1974.

Bruce Sinclair / A. R.

See also **Engineering Education; Mechanics' Institutes; *Princeton*, Explosion on the; Science Education; Science Museums.**

FRANKLIN STOVE, invented in 1742 by Benjamin Franklin, was a device for giving greater warmth, more comfort, and cleaner heating at a lower fuel cost. Franklin's idea, drafted in cooperation with his friend Robert Grace, consisted of a low stove equipped with loosely fitting iron plates through which air might circulate and be warmed before passing into the room. This "New Pennsylvania Fireplace" avoided drafts, gave more even temperatures throughout the room, and checked loss of heat through the chimney. Designed to be used in an already existing hearth, it did not resemble what are now called Franklin stoves. The plan was probably a development of an earlier ten-plate stove and was, in turn, supplanted by the newer cannon-stove invented at Lancaster a decade later.

BIBLIOGRAPHY

Brewer, Priscilla J. *From Fireplace to Cookstove: Technology and the Domestic Ideal in America.* Syracuse, N.Y.: Syracuse University Press, 2000.

Harry Emerson Wildes / A. R.

See also **Heating.**

FRATERNAL AND SERVICE ORGANIZATIONS. Men's business lunches and women's afternoon teas blossomed into national voluntary associations for public service around 1900. The need to do public good combined with private camaraderie to change these social occasions into local clubs, which then federated with a national organization. Service clubs flourished especially in smaller cities and towns. Their typical monthly meetings involved ninety minutes of socializing over food and thirty minutes of civic uplift. Local women's clubs mostly joined the General Federation of Women's Clubs, incorporated in 1901 in Washington, D.C., by Ella Dietz Clymer. Their public service focused on schools, libraries, and parks.

Businessmen's clubs initiated the national Rotary in 1905 in Chicago and founded by Paul Harris, the Exchange in 1911 in Detroit and founded by Charles Berkey, the Kiwanis in 1915, also founded in Detroit, by Allen S. Browne, the Lions in 1917 in Chicago and started by Melvin Jones, and the Optimist in 1919 in Lexington, Kentucky, founded by William Henry Harrison. Each men's service club eventually specialized its public service. The Rotary became linked with polio, the Lions with blindness, and the Exchange with child abuse, for example. In 1931, fifteen major men's service clubs and six major women's service clubs had a total of one million members. By 1964, twenty-six major men's clubs counted four million members and eight women's clubs had fifteen million members. Although the Civil Rights Act of 1964 exempted private clubs from integration by race or gender, the U.S. Supreme Court negated this exception in *Rotary International v. Rotary Club of Duarte* in 1987. By 2000, women's service clubs had shrunk to fewer than one million members, while the men's service clubs' membership remained static in the late twentieth century.

BIBLIOGRAPHY

Charles, Jeffrey A. *Service Clubs in American Society.* Urbana: University of Illinois Press, 1993.

Sheets, Tara, ed. *Encyclopedia of Associations.* 36th ed. Detroit: Gale Group, 2000.

Bill Olbrich

FRATERNITIES AND SORORITIES. Most fraternities and sororities came into existence after the Civil War. The initial discriminatory practices of white-run fraternities and sororities encouraged African American and Jewish students to form their own "Greek" organizations. The Greek system reached its heyday in the 1920s, as college attendance levels soared, and declined during the nonconformist 1960s. Despite negative publicity over deaths and injuries during hazing, the system revived in the 1980s, but it failed to regain its former importance on most campuses. Greek organizations are the center of social life at some campuses, but by the early twenty-first century, increasing numbers of colleges and universities were banning them from campus.

BIBLIOGRAPHY

Fass, Paula S. *The Damned and the Beautiful: American Youth in the 1920s.* New York: Oxford University Press, 1977.

Giddings, Paula. *In Search of Sisterhood: Delta Sigma Theta and the Challenge of the Black Sorority Movement.* New York: Morrow, 1988.

Horowitz, Helen Lefkowitz. *Campus Life: Undergraduate Cultures from the End of the Eighteenth Century to the Present.* Chicago: University of Chicago Press, 1988.

Winston, Roger B., Jr., William R. Nettles III, and John H. Opper, Jr., eds. *Fraternities and Sororities on the Contemporary College Campus.* San Francisco: Jossey-Bass, 1987.

Lynn Dumenil / D. B.

See also **Anti-Semitism; Discrimination: Race, Religion; Education, Higher: African American Colleges, Colleges and Universities; Fraternal and Service Organizations; Phi Beta Kappa Society.**

FRAUNCES TAVERN, at the southeast corner of Broad and Pearl Streets in New York City, is a recon-

Fraunces Tavern. A view, c. 1900, of the landmark building. LIBRARY OF CONGRESS

structed eighteenth-century house originally built by Stephen De Lancey in 1719. It was opened as a tavern by Samuel Fraunces, a black West Indian man, in 1762 and became a popular gathering place. In the Long Room, on 4 December 1783, Gen. George Washington said farewell to his officers. The Sons of the Revolution purchased the tavern in 1904. Designated a landmark in 1965, the building contains, besides the Long Room, a museum and library devoted to revolutionary war history and culture.

BIBLIOGRAPHY

Drowne, Henry R. *A Sketch of Fraunces Tavern and Those Connected with Its History.* New York: Fraunces Tavern, 1919; 1925.

Rice, Kym S. *Early American Taverns: For the Entertainment of Friends and Strangers.* Chicago: Regnery Gateway, 1983.

Stanley R. Pillsbury/A. R.

See also **Colonial Society; Museums; New York City; Revolution, American: Political History; Taverns and Saloons.**

FRAZIER-LEMKE FARM BANKRUPTCY ACT represented an effort by agrarian reformers to solve the problems of the agricultural depression that began during the 1920s. Sponsored by North Dakota Senator Lynn Frazier and North Dakota Representative William Lemke, it allowed the federal courts to scale down a farmer's debt to a level commensurate with the existing value of his property. If the farmer was able to retire this scaled-down debt, no further demands could be made upon him. The bill was enacted by Congress on 28 June 1934 and authorized the courts, under certain conditions, to grant such farmers a five-year moratorium. The Supreme Court, on 27 May 1935, unanimously ruled this act to be a violation of the due process clause of the Fifth Amendment.

On 29 August 1935, Congress passed the Frazier-Lemke Farm Mortgage Moratorium Act, modifying the terms of the moratorium and limiting it to a three-year period. The law was unanimously sustained by the Supreme Court on 29 March 1937.

BIBLIOGRAPHY

Blackorby, Edward C. *Prairie Rebel: The Public Life of William Lemke.* Lincoln: University of Nebraska Press, 1963.

Jeremy Bonner
Erik McKinley Eriksson

See also **Bankruptcy Laws; Mortgage Relief Legislation.**

FREDDIE MAC. *See* **Savings and Loan Associations.**

FREDERICKSBURG, BATTLE OF (13 December 1862), the scene of a decisive Southern victory against great odds. After the defeat of Union General George B. McClellan at Sharpsburg, Maryland, command of the Army of the Potomac was given to General Ambrose E. Burnside, who made Richmond, Virginia—instead of the Army of Northern Virginia—his objective. General Robert E. Lee outmarched him to Fredericksburg and placed his army of about 78,000 on the high ground from one to two miles south of the Rappahannock River. Lee's lines roughly paralleled the river for more than six miles. Burnside slowly concentrated his 122,000 troops on the northern bank, with difficulty drove the Confederate sharpshooters out of Fredericksburg, and crossed to the southern bank, where he drew his lines for battle on 13 December. The Confederate right flank was unprotected by any natural obstacle, but Burnside launched only one major assault on the exposed line during the entire day, and this was repulsed. The main battle was fought at the base of Marye's Heights, where a sunken road provided a natural breastwork for the Confederates. Wave after wave of Union infantry was broken and rolled back by the devastating fire from this road. Nightfall ended the battle along the entire line, with 10,208 Unionists and 5,209 Confederates killed or wounded. Burnside planned to renew the attack on 14 December but was dissuaded by his commanders. His plans frustrated by his defeat, Burnside withdrew his demoralized army north of the Rappahannock during the night of 15 December, and on 25 January 1863 he was relieved of his command, which was given to General Joseph Hooker.

BIBLIOGRAPHY

Gallagher, Gary W. ed. *The Fredericksburg Campaign: Decision on the Rappahannock.* Chapel Hill: University of North Carolina Press, 1995.

McPherson, James M. *Battle Cry of Freedom: The Civil War Era.* New York: Oxford University Press, 1988.

Sutherland, Daniel E. *Fredericksbsurg and Chancellorsville: The Dare Mark Campaign.* Lincoln: University of Nebraska Press, 1998.

George Frederick Ashworth / A. R.

See also **Antietam, Battle of; Army of Northern Virginia; Chancellorsville, Battle of; Civil War.**

FREE BANKING SYSTEM. Historically, in England and Scotland, free banking resulted from laissez-faire economic theories that called for limited government intervention into markets. The Scottish free banking system proved remarkably resilient, and when failures occurred they were handled by the "double indemnity" laws governing directors and stockholders. In the United States, the free banking movement emerged from the large demand for banking institutions during the chartering era when every new bank had to obtain a state charter (except for the BANK OF THE UNITED STATES [BUS], which had a national charter). State legislatures found themselves swamped with applications, and thus, beginning in New York in 1838, a new process was established called "free banking laws," which was later applied to all corporations under "general incorporation" laws.

The free banking laws required the owners or stockholders of banks to place on deposit with the stipulated authorities (usually the state comptroller or treasurer) designated bonds equal to the value of the bank's capital. This deposit then allowed the state to authorize the bank to issue banknotes equal to its total bond deposit. If a bank failed to redeem its notes upon demand, the state authorities would sell the securities and make redemption—whereas with a chartered bank, the institution would have to forfeit its charter. In reality, neither of these steps was taken often.

The American free banking system proved nearly as strong as the Scottish system. Many of the free banking principles, such as deposit of government bonds, were incorporated into the National Banking System of 1863, but gone was the central and most important aspect: free entry without intervention by the legislature, state or national.

BIBLIOGRAPHY

Rockoff, Hugh. *The Free Banking Era: A Re-examination.* New York: Arno Press, 1975.

Rolnick, Arthur, and Warren Weber. "Inherent Instability in Banking: The Free Banking Experience." *CATO Journal* 5 (Winter 1986): 877–890.

Larry Schweikart

See also **Banking: Overview.**

FREE SILVER, the unlimited coinage of silver by the U.S. government for anyone bringing the metal into the U.S. Mint, functioned as an important political slogan in the latter half of the nineteenth century. At that time, social unrest, political ambitions, and vested economic interests combined to cause a powerful push for legislation to increase the money supply.

From 1834 to the early 1870s silver metal had enjoyed a higher market price, in relation to gold, than the 16 to 1 ratio maintained by the U.S. Treasury, so that silver was too valuable to use as coinage. Moreover, European monetary policies varied widely. Continental conditions had long enabled France to retain BIMETALLISM, while powerful Britain was gravitating to the GOLD STANDARD. The U.S. Treasury hoped to bring the value of the wartime paper dollar—the GREENBACK—up to par by accumulating gold. This left the currency system in disarray. Congress brought some order to the monetary system with a new coinage act in 1873; the rare silver dollar was simply omitted from mention in the act, a piece of absentmindedness that shortly took on the exciting quality of a "crime" against the public welfare.

As the congressional election of 1878 approached, leaders in both major parties strove to keep their faithful from joining third parties of laborites, greenbackers, bimetallists, and groups favoring the free coinage of silver. Several senators were silver mine owners, and the producer lobby was untiring; but the "sound money" administration of President Rutherford B. Hayes would not yield. Consequently, the BLAND-ALLISON ACT of 1878 fell far short of free silver. The Treasury was required to buy monthly not less than $2 million but not more than $4 million of silver and to coin it at the 16 to 1 ratio.

As the 1870s closed, good crops helped to cool inflationary ardor, but a mild recession in the early 1880s heated it up again. Republican campaign underwriters, in particular, demanded high tariff increases in silver purchases. The SHERMAN SILVER PURCHASE ACT of 1890 enlarged the government's monthly silver purchases to 4.5 million ounces and stipulated payment for 2 million of those ounces in "Treasury notes" redeemable in "coin" on demand. The act was admirably adapted to draining off the gold supply. Democratic President Grover Cleveland forced Congress to repeal the act in 1893, amidst a serious nationwide depression.

The calls for free silver reached a crescendo in the next three years. Presidential candidate William Jennings Bryan's famous sermon, "You shall not crucify mankind upon a cross of gold!" nourished the debtor's faith in cheap money, the Populist's hope for a fiat currency of paper, and the mine owner's expectation of high silver prices. Alarmed, creditor interests seized hold of the Republican platform. Close to the election of 1896, the weather turned gold standard, improving crop prospects sufficiently to prevent farmer desertion of Republican leadership. Of nearly 14 million votes, silver got about 6.25 million and gold about 7.1 million. Although government subsidy of silver production recurred occasionally in the twentieth century, the Gold Standard Act of 1900 ended free silver as an effective implement of American politics, declaring the gold dollar to be the U.S. standard of value.

BIBLIOGRAPHY

Calomiris, Charles W. "Greenback Resumption and Silver Risk: The Economics and Politics of Monetary Regime Change in the United States, 1862–1900." In *Monetary Regimes in Transition.* Edited by Michael D. Bordo and Forrest Capie. New York: Cambridge University Press, 1994.

Friedman, Milton, and Anna Jacobson Schwartz. *A Monetary History of the United States, 1867–1960.* Princeton, N.J.: Princeton University Press, 1963.

Glad, Paul W. *McKinley, Bryan, and the People.* Philadelphia: Lippincott, 1964.

Weinstein, Allen. *Prelude to Populism: Origins of the Silver Issue, 1867–1878.* New Haven, Conn.: Yale University Press, 1970.

Jeannette P. Nichols / A. R.

See also **Crime of 1873; Cross of Gold Speech; Currency and Coinage; Greenback Movement; Populism; Silver Legislation.**

FREE SOCIETY OF TRADERS, a group of wealthy Quakers in England to whom William Penn turned for financial assistance for his Pennsylvania settlement. The society purchased 20,000 acres of land in Pennsylvania, and on 24 March 1681 received a charter granting manorial rights, exemption from all quitrents, and choice waterfront sites in Philadelphia. By June 1681, the society had capital of ten thousand pounds. Nicholas More served as president and James Claypoole as secretary. Thomas Lloyd headed the society's delegation in the Pennsylvania Provincial Council, which it dominated. From 1682 to 1683, the society organized and dispatched some fifty ships to Pennsylvania. Their claims to the choicest lands and best plots in Philadelphia and domination of consignments through their private agent in London irritated poorer Quakers and settlers. While great results were anticipated, the society's power in Pennsylvania gradually diminished, and little came of their efforts.

BIBLIOGRAPHY

Middleton, Richard. *Colonial America: A History, 1585–1775.* Malden, Mass.: Blackwell, 1996.

Wayland F. Dunaway
Jerry L. Parker

See also **Pennsylvania; Philadelphia.**

FREE SOIL PARTY. This third party took shape in the aftermath of the August 1846 through March 1847 congressional debate over the Wilmot Proviso. When the House member David Wilmot of Pennsylvania and other dissident northern Democrats attempted to amend an appropriation bill by introducing language forever banning slavery in any territory acquired from Mexico as a result of the Mexican War, they reintroduced the slavery issue into national party politics. While President James K. Polk fumed and the South Carolina senator John C. Calhoun demanded southern rights in the future territories, Whigs and Democrats struggled to hold the northern and southern wings of their parties together. In 1848, after both major parties refused to endorse the Wilmot Proviso, the antiextensionists, led by opportunistic Barnburner Democrats in New York and Ohio Liberty Party men, called for a national convention to unite proponents of the proviso: Northern Democrats, unhappy with Polk's patronage assignments and his opposition to internal improvements; Liberty Party members willing to forsake abolitionism; New York Democrats loyal to Martin Van Buren, who sought revenge for his defeat at the 1844 Democratic National Convention; and Conscience Whigs, who feared the consequences of acquiring new territory from Mexico, formed an unlikely coalition.

When representatives of these groups convened on 9 and 10 August 1848 at Buffalo, New York, the New York Barnburners secured the nomination of Van Buren for president but permitted others, notably Salmon P. Chase of Ohio, to write a platform that both demanded "No more Slave States and no more Slave Territory" and announced the new party's slogan, "Free Soil, Free Speech, Free Labor, and Free Men." Although the Free Soil Party failed to carry a single state in the presidential election of 1848, it did garner 291,263 votes nationally and elected several congressmen. By 1851 Chase, John P. Hale of New Hampshire, and Charles Sumner of Massachusetts all spoke for the new party in the U.S. Senate. The party's fortunes declined precipitously, however. The New York Barnburners quickly rejoined their state Democratic Party, and Free Soilers in several other northern states soon found themselves co-opted by the regular Democrats or Whigs. In 1852 the Free Soilers nominated Hale for president, but their lack of strong state and local organizations, together with a national sense that the Compromise of 1850 had settled the slavery issue, contributed to the party's lackluster performance in that year's elections.

Assailed as fanatics on the subject of slavery by some critics, Free Soilers were not embraced by northern blacks or by Liberty men suspicious of their reluctance to endorse the abolition of slavery. Few Free Soilers favored racial equality. Indeed their vision for free territories generally encompassed only white males, not free blacks. By 1853, however, party rhetoric emphasizing the need to contain slavery and to check the dangerous slave power had exerted a powerful influence on the northern electorate. When in January 1854 the Democratic senator Stephen A. Douglas of Illinois introduced his bill to organize the Kansas and Nebraska Territories on the principle of popular sovereignty, protests began almost immediately in northern legislatures. After Douglas's bill passed in May 1854, the antiextension position long championed by the Free Soil Party became the cornerstone of the emerging Republican Party. Former Free Soil leaders such as Chase and Sumner became Republicans. The Republican Party platforms of 1856 and 1860 closely reflected Free Soil positions not only on slavery but also regarding support for internal improvements and for homesteads for white settlers.

BIBLIOGRAPHY

Foner, Eric. *Free Soil, Free Labor, Free Men: The Ideology of the Republican Party before the Civil War.* New York: Oxford University Press, 1970.

Sewell, Richard H. *Ballots for Freedom: Antislavery Politics in the United States, 1837–1860.* New York: Oxford University Press, 1976.

Smith, Theodore Clarke. *The Liberty and Free Soil Parties in the Northwest.* 1897. Reprint Arno Press, 1969.

Julienne L. Wood

See also **Antislavery; Republican Party.**

FREE TRADE. The economic rationale for free trade lies in the principle that if trade is free, certain goods and services can be obtained at lower cost abroad than if domestic substitutes are produced in their place. The concept has each country producing for export those goods in which production is relatively efficient, thereby financing the import of goods that would be inefficiently produced at home. This comparative advantage in production between nations is expected to shift over time with changes in such factors as resource endowments and rates of technological advance. Free trade is therefore thought to facilitate the optimal use of economic resources: each country commands a higher level of consumption for a given level of resource use than would be otherwise possible. Advocates of tariff protection take exception to the doctrine on two fundamental bases: at times national goals other than maximized consumption must be served (for example, national defense), and the interests of specific groups do not parallel those of the nation as a whole. Thus, the history of tariffs and other barriers to free trade is a chronicle of shifting economic interests between industries and geographic areas.

Until 1808 the export of American farm and forest products to foreign markets was so profitable and imports were so cheap that there was little incentive to engage in manufacturing. Existing duties were low and designed for revenue rather than protection. War and embargo in the years 1808–1815 stimulated manufacturing (wool, cotton, iron); restoration of peace caused a flood of imports. Free trade then became a sectional issue, a strong protectionist movement developing in the middle and western states. Depression in 1819 and 1820 convinced workers that protection was necessary to save jobs from foreign competition, whereas farmers felt that building strong American industry would create higher demand and prices for farm goods. New England was divided between the manufacturing and the commercial interests, while the South solidly favored free trade because of its desire for cheap imports and fear of English retaliation against raw cotton imported from the United States.

By 1833 free-trade sentiment revived, as northern farmers, believing that young industries no longer needed protection, joined forces with John C. Calhoun and the South in an alliance that kept tariffs low until 1860. After the Civil War the protectionists controlled tariff policy for many years. Continued southern devotion to free trade and persistent, although wavering, low-tariff sentiment in the West produced only the short-lived horizontal duty reduction of 1872 and a few haphazard reductions in 1883. In the campaign of 1888 free-traders rallied around Grover Cleveland as the tariff for the first time became strictly a party issue. But the protectionists won again and passed the Tariff Act of 1890.

Popular hatred of monopoly—evidenced in the Sherman Antitrust Act of 1890—came to the support of free trade by implicating the tariff as "the mother of trusts." Cleveland won election in 1892 against the high-tariff Republicans, but the Democrats were torn over free silver and lost the opportunity to liberalize tariffs. However, continued antitrust feeling had bred such hostility to extreme protectionism that even the Republicans promised tariff reduction in the election of 1908. Sectional interests continued to thin the ranks of free-traders; the West and South demanded lower tariffs in general but supported the particular agricultural tariffs that served their interests in the Tariff Act of 1909.

Recurring economic crises, particularly the depressions of 1893–1897 and 1907–1908, further shook public confidence in the virtues of the "American system." Only the large industrial interests appeared to be consistently served by the cyclical pattern of economic growth (for example, Standard Oil's combining of small companies during depression, as indicated in the Sherman antitrust case of 1911). The height of tariffs, identified closely by the public with large industry, became a major political issue in 1912. The victorious Democrats promised reduction but held that no "legitimate" industry would be sacrificed. Although a considerable number of items were placed on the free list, rates were reduced, on an average, 10 percent only.

After World War I, with the Republicans in power, extreme protection held sway. Agriculture accepted any tariffs on farm products—although still grumbling about industrial tariffs—and the South found its former solid free-trade front broken by districts with a stake in tariffs on products of farm and factory. In the campaign of 1928 the tariff positions of the two major parties were scarcely distinguishable. Following a full year of debate in Congress, the Hawley-Smoot Tariff Act became law in 1930; the act constructed the highest tariff wall in the nation's history, and its contribution to the shrinkage of world trade and the severity of worldwide depression was considerable. Revulsion from the indiscriminate protectionism, distress with the worsening depression, and the leadership of Cordell Hull, an old-fashioned southern tariff liberal, again turned the country toward trade liberalization.

The Trade Agreements Act of 1934 and its twelve extensions through 1962 beat a steady retreat from the high-water mark of protection reached in 1930. Reacting to the severe decline in the volume of U.S. exports after 1930, the administration of Franklin D. Roosevelt conceived reciprocal trade concessions as an antidepression measure to generate recovery in export-related industries. Following World War II a political impetus was added; by opening its markets, the United States could assist the war-ravaged European economies in reconstruction and could similarly aid the development in poor nations. The economic implications of the Trade Agreements Act and its extensions were conflicting: there was a steady trend of tariff reduction, expedited after 1945 through the General Agreements on Tariffs and Trade (GATT) and the application of the unconditional most-favored-nation concept; but the reductions were tempered by a "no-injury" philosophy, adopted to minimize injury to domestic industry. Escape clauses, peril points, and national security regulations have hedged the U.S. commitment to agreed tariff reductions. The 1958 extension was notable in firmly establishing these concepts and the necessary enforcement machinery. Under the peril-point provision the U.S. tariff commission was to determine before negotiations the level to which a tariff rate could fall before seriously damaging the domestic industry; this estimate was to provide an effective limit to the authority extended negotiators. An industry experiencing severe injury from a tariff already reduced could petition for relief under the escape clause, which had appeared in U.S. trade agreements since 1943; if the U.S. Tariff Commission found sufficient injury, the concession could be withdrawn.

The Trade Expansion Act of 1962 made a significant departure from the reciprocal agreements in providing programs for alleviating injury caused by trade liberalization. Benefits and retraining for labor and special loans and tax treatment for industry were extended on the rationale of reallocating resources into more efficient uses. The reciprocal trade legislation had avoided this process by rescinding the tariff reduction when injury was inflicted. Administration of the provisions of the 1962 act has been difficult, however, because of the difficulty of distinguishing losses owing to increased imports from losses owing to the domestic industry's inefficiency. The 1962 act extended authority for sizable tariff reductions, to be negotiated through the offices of GATT during the five years following. Tariff reductions on items not excepted from this Kennedy Round of negotiations amounted to about 35 percent. As the U.S. trade balance worsened in the late 1960s, culminating in a trade deficit in 1971—the first in the twentieth century—the forces of protection threatened to reverse the forty-year trend of trade liberalization.

Throughout the 1970s, the executive branch resisted congressional initiatives to raise trade barriers. In 1980, Ronald Reagan's election to the presidency ushered in a new era of free trade in American foreign policy, one that would last for the remainder of the century and beyond. In the 1980s the Reagan Administration promoted a new round of GATT talks, and by the early 1990s the United States, Mexico, and Canada had agreed to create a continental free trade zone, known as the North American Free Trade Agreement (NAFTA).

The collapse of communism added momentum to the global trend toward free trade and free markets. During the 1990s governments across the world embraced free-trade policies, including countries that once belonged to the communist bloc, such as Russia, Poland, and China. By the early twenty-first century free trade had emerged as a cornerstone of the new global economy. Nevertheless, substantial opposition to free-trade policies remained an active force in global politics. In particular, environmental and labor groups condemned free trade policies on the grounds that they made it easier for multinational corporations to pollute the environment and to pay sweatshop wages without fear of government regulation. The debate over free trade showed no signs of cooling off as the twenty-first century began.

BIBLIOGRAPHY

LaFeber, Walter. *The New Empire: An Interpretation of American Expansion, 1860–1898.* Ithaca, N.Y.: Cornell University Press, 1963.

Lake, David A. *Power, Protection, and Free Trade: International Sources of U.S. Commercial Strategy, 1887–1939.* Ithaca, N.Y.: Cornell University Press, 1988.

Milner, Helen V. *Resisting Protectionism: Global Industries and the Politics of International Trade.* Princeton, N.J.: Princeton University Press, 1988.

Terrill, Thomas E. *The Tariff, Politics, and American Foreign Policy, 1874–1901.* Westport, Conn.: Greenwood Press, 1973.

Thomas L. Edwards / A. G.

See also **Commerce, Department of; Free Society of Traders; General Agreement on Tariffs and Trade; Interstate Commerce Laws; North American Free Trade Agreement; Trade Agreements; Trade with the Enemy Acts.**

FREE UNIVERSITIES. Rural communities have different needs and resources than urban areas, and nontraditional or alternative educational programs have been one response to the educational needs of rural people. Free universities are nontraditional education programs in rural communities that bring together people who want to teach or learn. Generally, the creators of such programs are both formal and informal community leaders and parents. The free university uses community resources and requires little or no money for students and volunteer teachers. It is based on the assumption that anyone can teach and anyone can learn. Free universities are open to everyone, are controlled locally, and can operate cost-effectively on small budgets. They emphasize flexible arrangements for instruction, original courses or curricula, interactive teaching, student-centered learning, and often an affirmation of rural values.

The free university movement began in 1964 at the University of California at Berkeley as an outgrowth of the Free Speech Movement. Many other free universities developed on college campuses across the country as a reaction to traditional education. They arose from a need to discuss social issues, a sense that learning should be community oriented, and a belief that students should be involved in their own education. Ironically, although free universities began on college campuses, they now are almost exclusively located in rural communities.

BIBLIOGRAPHY

Embers, Pat, et al. *The Rural and Small Town Community Education Manual.* Manhattan: Kansas State University, 1980.

Sherwood, Topper. *Nontraditional Education in Rural Districts.* Charleston, W.Va.: Clearinghouse on Rural Education and Small Schools, 1989.

Mary Deane Sorcinelli / A. R.

See also **Counterculture; Education, Cooperative; Education, Higher: Colleges and Universities; Rural Life; Schools, Community.**

FREEDMAN'S SAVINGS BANK, a bank for African Americans, was incorporated under the Freedman's Bank Act of 3 March 1865 to provide a means of savings for former black slaves and black servicemen. Headquarters were in the District of Columbia, with branches in various states. The bank had many depositors, but the depression in 1873 and mismanagement led to the bank's failure on 29 June 1874. Some of the bank's depositors received a portion of the value of their accounts from Congress, but the bank's failure led many in the African American community to distrust the American BANKING system.

BIBLIOGRAPHY

Osthaus, Carl R. *Freedmen, Philanthropy, and Fraud: A History of the Freedman's Savings Bank.* Urbana: University of Illinois Press, 1976.

Hallie Farmer / A. R.; F. B.

See also **Banking: Bank Failures; Freedmen's Bureau; Philanthropy; Reconstruction.**

FREEDMEN'S BUREAU. On 3 March 1865, Congress established the Bureau of Refugees, Freedmen, and Abandoned Lands, or the Freedmen's Bureau, to assist black Americans in their transition from slavery to freedom at the end of the CIVIL WAR. The bureau provided emergency food, shelter, and medical care to people dislocated by the war; established schools; conducted military courts to hear complaints of both former slaves and former masters; put freedmen to work on abandoned or confiscated lands; and supervised the postemancipation work arrangements made by the freedmen.

Congress assigned the Bureau to the WAR DEPARTMENT; President Johnson named Major General O. O. Howard commissioner. He also appointed assistant commissioners in the seceded states to direct the work of the Freedmen's Bureau agents, who were sent into the field. Congress did not appropriate any money for agent salaries, so army commanders detailed young officers for Bureau duty as agents. A few of them were black officers, but resentment by some powerful white people caused most of these agents to be either discharged or moved into relatively uncontroversial posts in the education division. In 1868 bureau officials numbered nine hundred.

Howard, known to some as the "Christian General," had a charitable attitute toward the freedmen. He had commanded an army in General William Tecumseh SHERMAN'S MARCH TO THE SEA and had visited the South Carolina coastal islands seized in 1861 from fleeing planters. Plantations there had been divided into small holdings and farmed successfully by former slaves. With this example in mind, Congress directed the bureau to divide similarly abandoned lands across the South into forty-acre units and award them to the freedmen. Shortly thereafter President Andrew Johnson abrogated this important precedent for land redistribution by using presidential pardons to return to white former owners nearly all the land that was to have been divided.

With the restoration of the lands to white owners, bureau agents tried to convince the freedmen to support themselves and their families by entering into contracts, either for labor to work in field gangs or for land to farm as tenants or SHARECROPPERS. In addition to encouraging and supervising these work arrangements, the bureau, during its seven years of existence, also appropriated more than $15 million for food and other aid to the freedmen. Agents distributed these funds throughout the southern and border states in which most of the nation's four million black citizens lived.

The most important continuing contribution of the Freedmen's Bureau was in the area of education. Private freedmen's aid societies supplied teachers and their salaries; the bureau supplied buildings and transportation. Howard participated enthusiastically in fundraising for the schools, particularly after the early efforts at land reform had been aborted. By 1871 eleven colleges and universities and sixty-one normal schools had been founded. Among the most important were Hampton Institute, Atlanta University, Talladega College, Straight College (later Dillard University), Fisk University, and Howard University. The bureau spent over $6 million for its schools and educational work.

Congress never intended that the Freedmen's Bureau would be a permanent agency. The original authorization was for one year. In 1866, over President Johnson's veto, Congress extended the life of the agency and enhanced its powers. The Freedmen's Bureau was closed in 1872. Its legacies were the colleges begun under its auspices and the aspirations engendered among African Americans.

BIBLIOGRAPHY

Cimbala, Paul A., and Randall M. Miller, eds. *The Freedmen's Bureau and Reconstruction: Reconsiderations.* New York: Fordham University Press, 1999.

Cox, LaWanda, "From Emancipation to Segregation: National Policy and Southern Blacks." In *Interpreting Southern History: Historiographical Essays in Honor of Sanford W. Higginbotham.* Edited by John B. Boles and Evelyn Thomas Nolan. Baton Rouge: Louisiana State University Press, 1987.

Crouch, Barry A. *The Freedmen's Bureau and Black Texans.* Austin: University of Texas Press, 1992.

McFeely, William S. *Yankee Stepfather: General O. O. Howard and the Freedmen.* New Haven, Conn.: Yale University Press, 1968.

Nieman, Donald G., ed. *The Freedmen's Bureau and Black Freedom.* Vol. 2: *African American Life in the Post-Emancipation South, 1861–1900.* New York: Garland, 1994.

William S. McFeely/C. P.

See also **Carpetbaggers; Education; Education, African American; Education, Higher: African American Colleges; Philanthropy; Radical Republicans; Reconstruction.**

FREEDOM OF INFORMATION ACT (FOIA) was passed by Congress in 1966 and became effective on 4 July 1967. Amended in 1974 in light of the Watergate scandal and again by the Freedom of Information Reform Act of 1986, FOIA provides citizen access to documents held by agencies in the federal government's executive branch, including government and government-controlled corporations. The law does not apply to elected officials or the federal judiciary. FOIA requests may be denied only if they pertain to any of the following types of information: classified national security materials; matters relating to internal personnel rules and practices; information exempt under other laws; confidential business information obtained from private sector sources; internal communications regarding the formation of policy; personnel and medical files of individuals; law enforcement investigatory records; information about government-regulated financial institutions; or geological and geophysical data on oil and natural-gas wells. A requester may file an administrative appeal for access to withheld documents and if denied, may file a judicial appeal in U.S. District Court, where the burden of justifying withholding of information lies with the government.

With the rise in the 1930s of the modern administrative state and its proliferating agencies and bureaucracies, executive responsibility expanded in an often bewildering manner. The security interests of the Cold War compounded matters. A minor freedom of information movement in Congress culminated in the 1966 legislation, but the law lacked force until the events of Vietnam and Watergate discredited claims of executive privilege based on national security or separation of powers. During the 1980s, the administration of President Ronald Reagan sought to reduce the use of FOIA. The result was a reduction of personnel responsible for reviewing documents. In 1982, Executive Order 12356 required reviewers to consider security needs more important than the public's right to know. Congressional amendments in 1986 further narrowed the scope of releasable information. In 1994, President Bill Clinton reversed the policy of nine previous presidents and declared that because the National Security Council, which advises the president on security matters, is not an agency of the federal government, its records must be considered strictly as presidential papers not subject to the FOIA and other record laws. Although FOIA has its flaws, such as its use by felons to obtain appeals, it has led to greater public access to government information. When used by journalists covering current events and scholars probing the origins and workings of laws and administrations, it has brought the nation closer to its founders' ideals. "A popular government without popular information or the means of acquiring it," wrote James Madison in 1822, "is but a Prologue to a farce or a Tragedy or perhaps both."

BIBLIOGRAPHY

Franklin, Justin D., and Robert F. Bouchard, eds. *Guidebook to the Freedom of Information and Privacy Acts.* New York: C. Boardman, 1986.

Hernon, Peter, and Charles R. McClure. *Federal Information Policies in the 1980s: Conflicts and Issues.* Norwood, N.J.: Ablex Publishing, 1987.

Shira Diner
Kenneth O'Reilly

FREEDOM OF THE PRESS. *See* **First Amendment.**

FREEDOM OF RELIGION. *See* **First Amendment.**

FREEDOM OF THE SEAS is a principle that governs unrestricted access to the high seas and to waters outside of national territory. First established by the Romans, it was challenged in the sixteenth century to secure trade and by a Papal Bull that sought to divide the oceans between Portugal and Spain. During the eighteenth century, the principle again became widely accepted when the definition of territorial waters was extended to include a three-mile zone. While the United States strongly took the position that neutral ships should be allowed to carry goods for belligerents in times of war, other nations enforced rules of contraband (mostly defined as military stores) and blockade.

This became an important issue during the wars after the French Revolution when Great Britain and France imposed maritime blockades. To force these nations to change their policies (and also to end British impressment on American ships), the United States passed the EMBARGO ACT (1807) and the NONINTERCOURSE ACT (1809). After France declared it would lift its blockade, and when Great Britain did not follow suit within a three-month period as demanded by President James Madison, the United States declared war on Great Britain in June 1812.

The United States accepted the concepts of contraband and blockade as legitimate during the Civil War but shied away from capturing Confederate diplomats off of neutral vessels during the Trent Affair. As long as the United States was a neutral during World War I and World War II, it protested the extensive blockades against Germany and very liberal British definitions of contraband. President Franklin D. Roosevelt, nonetheless, established "maritime control areas" at the beginning of World War II that extended into the high seas. In both wars, activities of German U-boats against neutrals provoked sharp American protest: by President Woodrow Wilson after the sinking of the *Lusitania* in 1915, and by Roosevelt in September 1941 after the torpedoing of American ships.

The first major challenge to the freedom of the seas principle after World War II was President Harry S. Truman's 1945 announcement extending U.S. jurisdiction to natural resources on the continental shelf. Other nations followed by extending their territorial waters, some of them as far as 200 nautical miles. A 300-mile maritime defense zone around the American continents, established by the Rio Pact of 1947, was cited by the John F. Kennedy administration to legitimize the "naval quarantine" during the Cuban Missile Crisis in 1962. The Third United Nations Conference on the Law of the Sea agreed upon a 12-mile territorial limit and a 200-mile exclusive economic zone in December 1982.

BIBLIOGRAPHY

Barnett, Roger W. "U.S. Strategy, Freedom of the Seas, Sovereignty, and Crisis Management." *Strategic Review* 20, no. 1 (Winter 1992): 32–41.

Potter, Pitman B. *The Freedom of the Seas in History, Law, and Politics.* New York: Longmans, Green, 1924.

United Nations Division for Ocean Affairs and the Law of the Sea. http://www.un.org/Depts/los/. On U.N. Convention on the Law of the Sea of 10 December 1982.

Warren, Gordon H. *Fountain of Discontent: The Trent Affair and Freedom of the Seas.* Boston: Northeastern University Press, 1981.

Michael Wala

See also ***Lusitania*, Sinking of the; Rio de Janeiro Conference; *Trent* Affair.**

FREEDOM RIDERS were African American and white protesters, many associated with the CONGRESS OF RACIAL EQUALITY. In 1961, the Freedom Riders traveled by bus through Alabama and Mississippi to challenge segregation at southern bus terminals. Freedom Riders who journeyed to Alabama and Mississippi often faced extraordinary violence from resentful white southerners. For example, infuriated whites assaulted bus riders in Birmingham, Anniston, and Montgomery, Alabama, and harassed riders in McComb, Mississippi. Although the Freedom Rides exacerbated racial tension and violence, they shed new light on the plight of African Americans and the brutal actions of white segregationists. They also forced the federal government to take protective action. U.S. government officials sent more than 400 federal marshals to Montgomery to protect the Freedom Riders, whose actions ultimately influenced monumental and long-lasting changes in federal law. Within the next two years, a series of federal rulings and lawsuits ended systematic segregation in interstate travel. Attorney General Robert F. Kennedy petitioned the INTERSTATE COMMERCE COMMISSION to outlaw segregation on trains and buses and at transportation terminals. In the wake of this ruling, the Justice Department also successfully moved to end segregation in airports. Finally, in 1964 and again in 1968, Congress passed landmark civil rights legislation that prohibited segregation in public facilities for interstate travel and fulfilled many of the Freedom Riders' dreams.

BIBLIOGRAPHY

Chappell, David L. *Inside Agitators: White Southerners in the Civil Rights Movement.* Baltimore: Johns Hopkins University Press, 1994.

Weisbrot, Robert. *Freedom Bound: A History of America's Civil Rights Movement.* New York: Norton, 1990; New York: Plume, 1991.

Sheilah R. Koeppen / E. M.

See also **African Americans; Civil Rights Movement; Desegregation; Segregation; Social Legislation.**

FREEHOLDER. A freeholder is the owner of a land or estate, either for life or with inheritance rights. Tenure of land by giving service or paying rent is the common law equivalent of absolute ownership and became the prevailing system in the colonies. The colonial laws, influenced by the county franchise system of England and Wales, attached great importance to the possession of a freehold both for suffrage and officeholding. The democratic forces released by the American Revolution soon attacked such restrictions on the right to vote, and while the freeholder retained his privileged position in a few states until the Jacksonian era, universal suffrage became dominant in American politics.

Violent Response. The first Freedom Riders manage to escape their burning bus outside Anniston, Ala., a Ku Klux Klan stronghold, after a mob shot out its tires, smashed its windows, and threw an incendiary device into it on 14 May 1961. AP/WIDE WORLD PHOTOS

BIBLIOGRAPHY

Cantor, Norman F. *Imagining the Law: Common Law and the Foundations of the American Legal System.* New York: HarperCollins, 1997.

Nelson, William Edward. *Americanization of the Common Law: The Impact of Legal Change on Massachussetts Society, 1760–1830.* Cambridge, Mass.: Harvard University Press, 1975.

W. A. Robinson / A. E.

See also **Charter of Liberties; Feudalism; Primogeniture; Republicanism; Suffrage, Colonial.**

FREEMAN'S EXPEDITION was arranged to carry out President Thomas Jefferson's orders in 1805 to explore the Red River of Louisiana and Texas. With a party of twenty-five men and three boats, Thomas Freeman left Fort Adams, Mississippi, at the mouth of Red River, in April 1806. Forty-five miles above Natchitoches, Louisiana, the party left the last white settlement behind. At a point 635 miles from the mouth of the Red River, the group was turned back by a Spanish military party, having added little to American knowledge of the new Louisiana Purchase except for an accurate map of the lower Red River.

BIBLIOGRAPHY

Flores, Dan L., ed. *Jefferson and Southwestern Exploration: The Freeman and Custis Accounts of the Red River Expedition of 1806.* Norman: University of Oklahoma Press, 1984.

Carl L. Cannon / A. R.

See also **Explorations and Expeditions: U.S.; Louisiana Purchase.**

FREEMASONS. This international quasi-religious fraternity is properly called the Ancient and Accepted Order of Freemasons. The number of freemasons in the United States crested at four million around 1960. In terms of freemasons as a percentage of the population, their popularity was greatest in the United States from after the Civil War until the 1920s. Freemasons traditionally were white, native-born, and Protestant. The primary purpose of the freemasons is to meet the social and personal needs of their members. An important activity of freemasons is the performance of various secret rituals, held within Masonic temples. Symbolizing the temple of King Solomon, the temples are usually located in prominent places within urban areas. Freemason rituals are infused with religious allegories that emphasize the omnipotence of God, the importance of a moral life, and the possibility of immortality. Over the course of the twentieth century, in an effort to respond to younger members' interests as well as reverse declining membership, freemasons have increasingly emphasized community service over religious symbolism. Today there are perhaps slightly more than three million freemasons in the United States, distributed among some fourteen thousand Grand Lodges.

The term "freemason" dates from the fourteenth century, when stonemasons in Europe bound themselves together for their mutual protection and training. During the Reformation freemasonry became open to men other than stonemasons. On 24 June 1717 a group met in London to found the first Grand Lodge. The first freemason to live in the British colonies in America was Jonathan Belcher, who joined the freemasons in England in 1704 and later became the governor of Massachusetts and New Hampshire. The first lodge in the United States was established in Philadelphia in 1731, and in 1734 Benjamin Franklin became its Grand Master.

Freemasons were prominent during the revolutionary and constitutional periods, and have held important positions in modern politics. Fourteen presidents have been freemasons, most recently Gerald R. Ford. George Washington, Alexander Hamilton, and Benedict Arnold, all generals of the Continental Army, were freemasons, and it is possible that Washington selected his generals partly on the basis of their freemason status. Before the Revolution Franklin represented colonial interests in England, and after the war he was the American minister to France, and as he undoubtedly consulted with other freemasons in both countries, his fraternal standing could have served his diplomatic purposes. Franklin's efforts to expand the U.S. Constitution's protection of religious belief also accord with his freemasonry background.

While an important principle for freemasons is the acceptance of all religions, they have been denounced by the Catholic Church, in part because at certain periods they were involved with anti-immigrant or racist causes, for instance that of the KU KLUX KLAN in the 1920s. The greatest controversy in freemason history, however, involved one William Morgan of Batavia, New York. In retaliation for the order's refusal to permit him to form a local lodge, in March 1826 Morgan contracted to publish a pamphlet that revealed the secrets of freemasonry. In September Morgan was abducted and probably drowned in the Niagara River. His pamphlet, *Illustrations of Masonry*, was published in October 1826. Because of its exclusive membership (perhaps 32,000 members in 1820) and its secrecy, freemasonry was already suspected as antidemocratic. Morgan's pamphlet, and the alleged cover-up of his abduction by judges and jurors who themselves were freemasons, greatly galvanized anti-Masonic feeling across the country. In 1828 Thurlow Weed, a prominent newspaper publisher, organized a political party known as the Anti-Masonic Party. The party was the first to hold a convention for the nomination of a presidential candidate. In 1832 William Wirt, a former U.S. attorney general, headed the ticket. Anti-Masonic political activity spread to New England and the Northwest, but by the early 1840s there was little national interest in the party's agenda.

The Masonic affiliation of Joseph Smith, founder of the Mormon Church, was perhaps the most long-lived, if incidental, legacy of this controversy. Smith, a freemason, founded his church in 1830 in Palmyra, New York, and was murdered by an anti-Mormon mob on 27 June 1844. While freemasons may have taken part in the crime, Smith's successor, Brigham Young, also a freemason, held the Order of Freemasons blameless. The influence of the rituals of freemasonry upon the ceremonies and rites of the Church of Jesus Christ of Latter-day Saints is still apparent today.

Another incidental consequence of the practice of freemasonry was the rise of Negro freemasonry. A black man named Prince Hall founded a lodge in 1775. Due to racist resistance by white freemasons, Prince Hall Masonry did not gain general acceptance as a legitimate order until the 1960s. Thus the exclusivity of white freemasons was possibly an important factor in the forging of the group self-consciousness of middle-class blacks.

Especially in the twentieth century the freemasons have undertaken important reform and charitable causes. The widespread illiteracy of American men became apparent during the World War I era. As a result freemasons began lobbying for a federal department of education, which eventually came to fruition. Over their history the freemasons have spawned close to one hundred affiliated groups that emulate the freemason's secret rituals and modern commitment to public service. The first large-scale labor organization, the KNIGHTS OF LABOR, adapted many Masonic motifs and phrases. The most prominent affiliated groups today are the Knights Templar, the Scottish Rite, and the Shriners. The last group has raised millions of dollars for medical treatment of children.

BIBLIOGRAPHY

Carnes, Mark C. *Secret Ritual and Manhood in Victorian America*. New Haven, Conn.: Yale University Press, 1989.

Demott, Bobby J. *Freemasonry in American Culture and Society*. Lanham, Md.: University Press of America, 1986. A revealing but often excessively favorable account.

Dumenil, Lynn. *Freemasonry and American Culture, 1880–1930*. Princeton, N.J.: Princeton University Press, 1984.

Kutolowski, Kathleen Smith. "Freemasonry and Community in the Early Republic: The Case for Antimasonic Anxieties." *American Quarterly* 34 (1982): 543–561.

Muraskin, William Alan. *Middle-Class Blacks in a White Society: Prince Hall Freemasonry in America*. Berkeley: University of California Press, 1975.

Additionally, various state Grand Lodges publish annual *Journals of Proceedings* that contain administrative, charitable, and historical information.

Timothy M. Roberts

Planting the Flag. This heroic and patriotic illustration, labeled "Col. Frémont planting the American standard on the Rocky Mountains," was designed to be part of John C. Frémont's 1856 Republican presidential campaign. LIBRARY OF CONGRESS

See also **Anti-Masonic Movements; Latter-day Saints, Church of Jesus Christ of.**

FREEPORT DOCTRINE was Stephen Douglas's doctrine that, in spite of the Dred Scott decision, slavery could be excluded from territories of the United States by local legislation. Although propounded earlier and elsewhere, this solution of the apparent inconsistency between popular sovereignty and the Dred Scott decision, advanced at the Lincoln-Douglas debates of 1858 in Freeport, Illinois, came to be known as the Freeport Doctrine. By thus answering Abraham Lincoln's questions on slavery, Douglas was able to hold his Illinois followers and secure reelection to the Senate, but the extensive publicity the doctrine received killed his chance of Southern support for the presidency in 1860.

BIBLIOGRAPHY

Ericson, David F. *The Shaping of American Liberalism: The Debates Over Ratification, Nullification, and Slavery.* Chicago: University of Chicago Press, 1993.

Zarefsky, David. *Lincoln, Douglas, and Slavery.* Chicago: University of Chicago Press, 1990.

Paul M. Angle / A. R.

See also **Dred Scott Case; Lincoln-Douglas Debates; Popular Sovereignty.**

FRÉMONT EXPLORATIONS. John Charles Frémont (1813–1890), Republican Party presidential candidate in 1856, became famous for leading five explorations of the American West between 1842 and 1854. Commissioned in 1838 as a second lieutenant in the Army Corps of Topographical Engineers, Frémont accompanied scientist and topographer Joseph N. Nicollet on expeditions of the upper Mississippi in 1838 and 1839. Backed by his father-in-law, Senator Thomas Hart Benton of Missouri, Frémont commanded his first major expedition in 1842, journeying up the Platte River to the South Pass and the Wind River Mountains. Topographer Charles Preuss and guide Christopher "Kit" Carson assisted Frémont on this trip, as they did on several subsequent expeditions.

In 1843–1844 Frémont made an immense journey encompassing most of the territory west of the Mississippi. Departing in May 1843 from St. Louis, Missouri, he traveled to the South Pass, made a southward loop to the Great Salt Lake, and moved north via the Snake River to Fort Vancouver. He then turned south, explored the western edge of the Great Basin, and made a risky midwinter crossing of the Sierra Nevada to California. After pausing at Sutter's Fort, Frémont moved south through the Central Valley, crossed the Tehachapi Pass and turned east. He crossed Nevada, explored Utah Lake and the Rocky Mountains en route to Bent's Fort on the Arkansas River, and arrived in St. Louis on 6 August 1844. Based on this expedition Frémont and Preuss produced the era's most accurate map of the region, clarifying the geography of the Great Salt Lake and giving the Great Basin between the Wasatch and Sierra Nevada ranges its name.

Now a national figure, Frémont departed for his third expedition in June 1845. Although ordered to make a limited reconnaissance of the Arkansas and Red Rivers, he headed across the Great Basin to California, arriving at the American River on 9 December 1845. The following spring he left California for Oregon, but for reasons that remain ambiguous returned in May 1846 to California, where he played a central role in the BEAR FLAG REVOLT. Frémont's insubordination during the revolt resulted in his 1847 court-martial, after which he resigned his commission.

With private funds, Frémont embarked on another western survey in 1848–1849. This catastrophic expedition resulted in the death of ten men due to starvation in the San Juan Mountains. Frémont spent the next few years in California, tending to his business interests and serving as a senator in 1850–1851. In 1853–1854 he made his last expedition, another privately funded railroad survey searching for a southern route to the Pacific.

Frémont's romantic and colorful reports depicted the West as a fertile land rich with opportunity. Supporters of western expansion used the reports to justify their arguments, while emigrants read them as guides to their journey. Although Frémont's explorations increased scientific knowledge of the trans-Mississippi West, his expeditions were most significant for helping to spur American emigration to and acquisition of the region.

BIBLIOGRAPHY

Herr, Pamela, and Mary Lee Spence, eds. *The Letters of Jessie Benton Frémont.* Urbana: University of Illinois Press, 1993.

Jackson, Donald, and Mary Lee Spence, eds. *The Expeditions of John Charles Frémont.* 3 vols. Urbana: University of Illinois Press, 1970–1984. Annotated edition of correspondence and reports, including two supplemental volumes and map portfolio.

Nevins, Allan. *Frémont: Pathmarker of the West.* New York: Ungar, 1962. Originally published as *Frémont: The West's Greatest Adventurer* (1928). Revised edition first published in 1939.

Richmond, Patricia Joy. *Trail to Disaster: The Route of John C. Frémont's Fourth Expedition from Big Timbers, Colorado, through the San Luis Valley, to Taos, New Mexico.* Denver: Colorado Historical Society, 1989.

Monica Rico

See also **Maps and Mapmaking; Western Exploration.**

FRENCH AND INDIAN WAR. This was the last in a series of conflicts between Great Britain and France for dominance in North America. The French and Indian War (1754–1763), sometimes referred to as the Great War for Empire, and part of the global conflict called the Seven Years' War (1756–1763) in Europe, resulted in a British victory and the end of the French empire in North America.

In the seventeenth century, the French had explored and claimed a vast amount of land in the interior of North America, ranging from the mouth of the St. Lawrence River and the Great Lakes in the north to the Mississippi River and New Orleans in the south. In order to consolidate and control this enormous region, they had established a series of forts, trading posts, missions, and settlements, all enclosed by four major cites: Montreal, Quebec, Detroit, and New Orleans. In this manner, France hoped to restrict English settlement in North America to the Atlantic seaboard east of the Appalachian Mountains.

While the English colonies were still confined to the area along the North American coast from Maine to Georgia, some of the English colonies claimed lands as far west as the Mississippi. In three wars fought between 1689 and 1748, French and English colonists had struggled inconclusively for control of the interior. Interest in these unsettled lands was primarily speculative since there were not yet enough settlers in North America to occupy the entire region, although by the 1750s the British colonials were beginning to feel the pressures of population growth. Adding to the growing tensions between the colonists on both sides were disputes over the fur trade and over fishing rights along the Grand Banks of Newfoundland.

English settlers were eager to expand westward. High birth rates and a drop in the number of infant deaths were combining to produce larger families and generally dramatic rises in population. As farmers, the settlers felt it only natural that they should expand their colonies across the Appalachian Mountains into the Ohio Valley. In his "Observations Concerning the Increase of Mankind" published in 1751, Benjamin Franklin summarized the feelings held by many of his fellow colonists. Noting that the colonial population was doubling every twenty-five years, Franklin argued that additional land for settlement was required or the colonies would begin to deteriorate. He went on to state that Britain should help acquire this land, as that nation would profit greatly from the opening of new markets that would come about as the result of expansion. Like other colonial leaders Franklin understood that expansion would involve conflict with the French.

In King George's War (1744–1748), the ambitions of some of the English colonists were fulfilled by the capture of the French fort of Louisburg on Cape Breton Island. There was also talk of conquering the rest of Canada and of driving the French out of their holdings along the Mississippi. These ambitions were disappointed when the peace agreement, negotiated in Europe, returned Louisburg to the French.

Both sides understood the importance of the original inhabitants of North America in their competition for control of the continent. England and France each worked to win the support of the various native tribes, either as trading partners or as military allies. Britain had the advantage of a more advanced economy and could therefore offer the Indians more and better goods. The French, however, with a far smaller number of settlers, could be more tolerant of Native American concerns, and when the war began France enjoyed better relations with the Indians than did the British.

The powerful Iroquois Confederacy that stood astride the colony of New York tended to keep their distance from both the British and French. The Iroquois generally remained independent of both powers by trading with both and playing them off against each other.

Between 1749 and 1754, the relations between the French and English broke down rapidly, and the Iroquois Confederation found itself caught in the middle. The Iroquois had agreed to give the English what amounted to significant trading privileges in the interior; for the first time the Iroquois had taken a side. The French, interpreting this action as the prelude to British expansion into the Ohio Valley, began to construct new forts in that area. Meanwhile, in 1749, unimpressed by French claims to that region, a group of Virginia businessmen had secured a grant of half a million acres in the Ohio Valley for settlement purposes. The French program of building forts was seen as a threat to their plans, and the English began making military plans and building their own fortifications.

The French completed a line of forts in the region extending from Presque Isle to Fort Duquesne on the Monongahela River. Finally, in the summer of 1754, Virginia's governor, Robert Dinwiddie, alarmed by the actions of the French, sent a militia force under the command of the young and inexperienced officer named George Washington to halt French encroachment on what he considered English soil. Arriving near the site of present-day Pittsburgh, Washington built a small fort, named Fort Necessity, and attacked a detachment of French troops, killing their commander and several others. The French retaliated with a strike against Fort Necessity, trapping Washington and his force. Washington surrendered and retreated to Virginia. These encounters began the French and Indian War.

Meanwhile, the London Board of Trade had arranged for a conference between delegates from Pennsylvania, New York, Maryland, and New England at Albany, New York, to deal with the question of improving relations with the Indians as well as to promote frontier defense. Meeting between June 19, 1754 and July 11, 1754, the delegates learned of Washington's defeat before the conference concluded. The conference adopted the Albany Plan of Union, which would grant a central colonial authority unprecedented powers to oversee their defense, manage Indian relations, and administer the western lands. The clash at Fort Necessity had already taken place when the plan was presented to the colonial assemblies. None of them approved the plan, as they were unwilling to surrender their autonomy to any central authority, even when threatened with war.

In 1755, the British government responded to Washington's defeat by sending two regiments of infantry to Virginia under the command of General Edward Braddock. Braddock was experienced in European warfare, but not in the type of fighting that would take place in the forests of America. In May 1755 Braddock and his men started out for the French stronghold of Fort Duquesne, arriving in early July. There, the British were surprised by the French and their Indian allies, and routed. The Indians fought in the way they were accustomed, using all available cover to conceal themselves and to fire upon the enemy, and Braddock was unable to adjust to these tactics. Braddock was mortally wounded and the British troops and colonial militia were forced to withdraw. The French now controlled a line of forts extending from Lake Champlain to Lake Erie to the mouth of the Ohio River.

The war entered a new phase when Great Britain and France formally declared war on 17 May 1756. The conflict now became international in scope. To this point, a lack of reinforcements had forced the English colonists to manage the war themselves, and things had not gone well. Now, Britain unleashed the power of the Royal Navy, which proved to be highly effective at preventing the French from reinforcing New France. Meanwhile, the fighting spread to the West Indies, India, and Europe, although North America remained the focal point.

The war was inconclusive until 1757, when William Pitt, as secretary of state, took command of the effort. He planned military strategy, appointed military leaders, and even issued orders to the colonists. Since military recruitment had dropped off significantly in the colonies, British officers were permitted to forcibly enlist or "impress" colonists into the army and navy. Colonial farmers and businessmen had supplies seized from them, usually without compensation. And the colonists were required to provide shelter for British troops, again without being paid. These measures strengthened the war effort but created resentment among the colonists. By 1758, the tensions between the mother country and its colonists threatened to paralyze Britain's war effort.

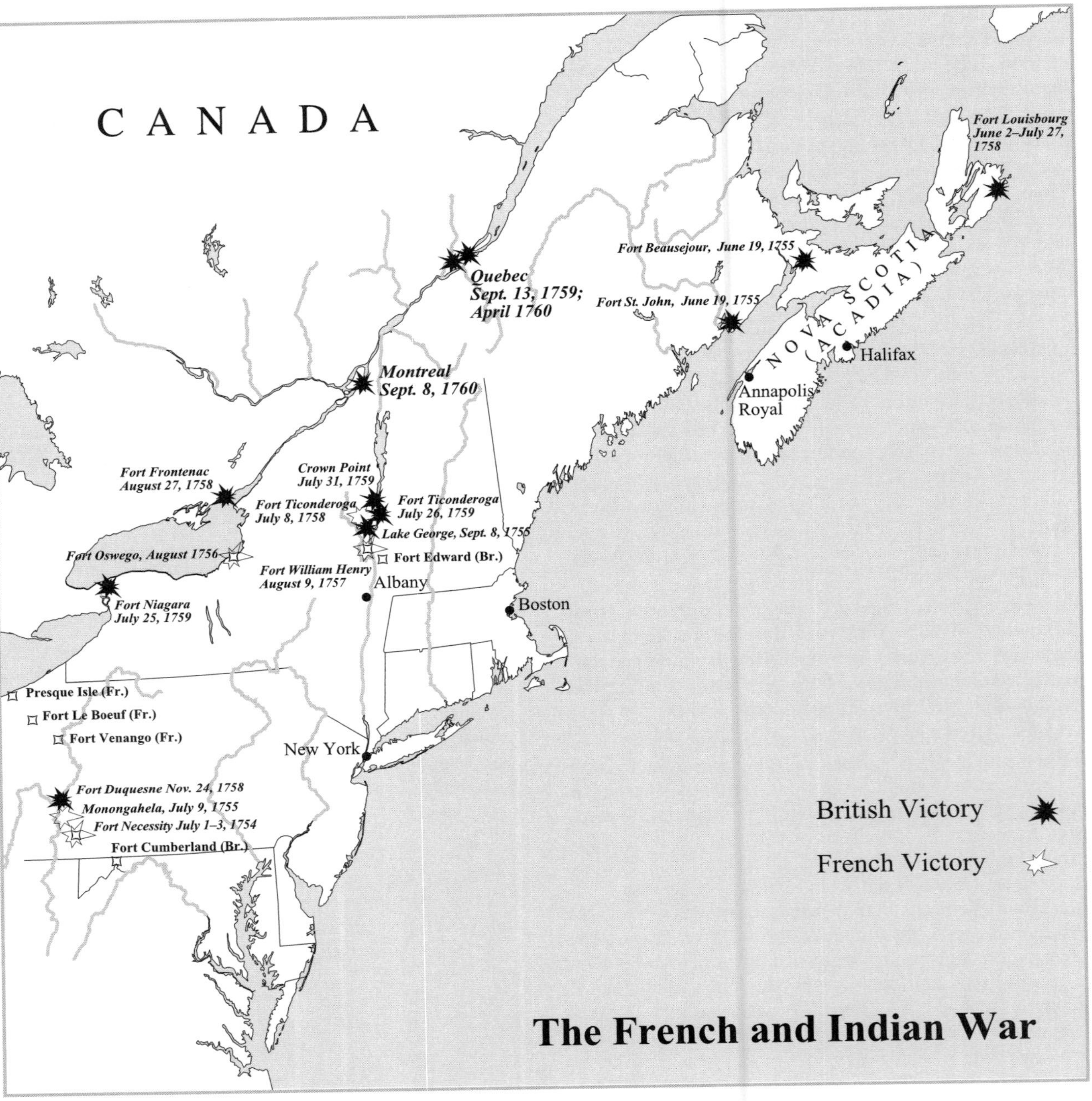

Pitt relented in 1758, easing many of the policies the Americans found objectionable. He agreed to pay back the colonists for all of the materials the army had seized, and control over recruitment was returned to the colonial assemblies. These concessions revived American support for the war, and increased militia enlistments. More important, Pitt began to send larger numbers of British regulars to North America and the tide began to turn in Britain's favor.

The French had always been significantly outnumbered by the English in North America, and after 1756, poor harvests also began to take their toll on the French. Together, the British regulars (who did most of the fighting in North America) and colonial militias began to capture important French strongholds. Pitt had developed a war plan that enabled the British to launch expeditions against the French in several areas, and the plan proved to be successful.

British forces under Jeffrey Amherst and James Wolfe took Louisburg in July of 1758. The French stronghold at Frontenac fell a month later, cutting the line of communications with the Ohio Valley. In November 1758 the French abandoned and burned Fort Duquesne just before English troops arrived.

In 1759, Quebec came under siege. Located atop a high cliff and seemingly impregnable, this century-old city was the capital of New France. But Quebec fell on 13 September 1759, after the British commander, General James Wolfe, led his men onto the Plains of Abraham, at the western edge of the city, and surprised the larger French garrison. The French commander, the Marquis de Montcalm, led his troops out of the fortress to confront the English. Both Wolfe and Montcalm were killed in the ensuing battle, but the British won the day. Montreal surrendered to Amherst nearly a year later, on 7 September 1760. This victory concluded the French and Indian War.

The French continued to struggle on other fronts until 1763, when the Peace of Paris was concluded. France gave up some of its islands in the West Indies and most of its colonial possessions in India and Canada, as well as all other French-held territory in North America. French claims west of the Mississippi and New Orleans were ceded to Spain, so that France abandoned all of its claims to territory on the North American continent.

The results of the French and Indian War were of tremendous significance to Great Britain. While England's territory in the New World more than doubled, so did the cost of maintaining this enlarged empire. The victory over France forced the British government to face a problem it had neglected to this point—how to finance and govern a vast empire. The British realized that the old colonial system, which had functioned with minimal British supervision, would no longer be adequate to administer this new realm.

The cost of the war had also enlarged England's debt and created tensions with the American colonists. These feelings were the result of what the British felt was American incompetence during the war, along with anger for what was perceived as a lack of financial support on the part of the colonies in a struggle that was being waged primarily for their benefit. For these reasons, many of Britain's political leaders believed a major reorganization of the empire was in order, and that London would have to increase its authority over its North American possessions. The colonies would now be expected to assume some of the financial burden of maintaining the empire as well.

From the American standpoint, the results of the war had a different, although equally profound, effect. For the first time, the thirteen colonies had been forced to act together to resist a common enemy, establishing a precedent for unified action against the mother country. And the hostility that had been aroused over British policies between 1756 and 1757 seemed to justify the feelings held by some of the colonials that Britain was interfering illegally in their affairs. These feelings would be intensified once Great Britain began to administer its North American empire more intensively in the years ahead.

The British victory in the French and Indian war proved to be a disaster for the Native Americans who lived in the Ohio Valley. Most of them had allied themselves with the French during the conflict, and by doing so, they were now confronted with angry Englishmen. In the century before the war, the Iroquois Confederacy had carefully played the British and the French against each other, but in the war, they had gradually moved towards an alliance with Britain. The Iroquois alliance with the English broke down soon after the war's end, and the confederation itself began to disintegrate. The Ohio Valley tribes continued to struggle with both the British and Americans for control of the region for another half century. But, outnumbered and divided among themselves, they were rarely able to confront their European opponents on equal terms. In a sense, Tecumseh's defeat, fighting with the English against the Americans near Detroit in 1813, was the Indians last battle of the Seven Years War.

BIBLIOGRAPHY

Anderson, Fred. *Crucible of War: The Seven Years' War and the Fate of Empire in British North America, 1754–1766.* New York: Knopf, 2000.

———. *A People's Army: Massachusetts Soldiers and Society in the Seven Years' War.* Chapel Hill: University of North Carolina Press, 1984.

Jennings, Francis. *Empire of Fortune: Crowns, Colonies and Tribes in the Seven Years' War in America.* New York: Norton, 1988.

Nester, William R. *The First Global War: Britain, France and the Fate of North America, 1756–1775.* Westport, Conn.: Praeger, 2000.

Rogers, Alan. *Empire and Liberty: American Resistance to British Authority, 1755–1763.* Berkley: University of California Press, 1974.

Schwartz, Seymour. *The French and Indian War, 1754–1763: The Imperial Struggle for North America.* New York: Simon & Schuster, 1994.

White, Richard. *The Middle Ground: Indians, Empires and Republics in the Great Lakes Regions, 1650–1815.* New York: Cambridge University Press, 1991.

Gregory Moore

See also **Braddock's Expedition; French Frontier Forts; Iroquois; King George's War; Louisburg Expedition; New France; Ohio Company of Virginia; Quebec, Capture of.**

FRENCH DECREES. The French decrees from 1793 to 1812 were enacted by the French government to inhibit Britain's ability to trade with other countries, including the United States. In retaliation, the British seized American ships bound for France. Thus, the United States was deprived of its two most important trading partners. A decree from France in 1794 included a threat to seize neutral ships as pirates. America gained exemption from this decree in 1795, but it was reinstated in 1796. Another decree in 1798 declared that neutral vessels carrying goods to or from Britain would be treated like British ships—as enemies. The Franco-American convention of 1800 ended French interference with American shipping, but beginning with a new decree in 1806, followed by others in 1807 and 1808, France declared a full blockade of the British Isles and authorized the seizure of neutral ships visiting Britain. Only with the outbreak of the War of 1812 between the United States and Britain did France rescind its ban on American ships.

BIBLIOGRAPHY

Sweeney, Jerry K., Stephen J. Valone, and Margaret B. Denning. *America and the World, 1776–1998: A Handbook of United States Diplomatic History.* Prospect Heights, Ill.: Waveland Press, 2000.

Kirk H. Beetz

See also **Embargo Act; France, Quasi-War with; Nonintercourse Act; XYZ Affair.**

FRENCH FRONTIER FORTS. While the Spanish, Dutch, and English struggled to establish footholds in North America, the French built a powerful domain in the Saint Lawrence River valley in the seventeenth century. By 1672, NEW FRANCE had more than five thousand colonists. Then, Jacques Marquette and Louis Joliet discovered the Mississippi River the following year. In 1682, Sieur de La Salle reached the Gulf of Mexico and claimed the Mississippi Valley for Louis XIV.

Forts figured importantly in France's imperial strategy. Bases at Kingston, Ontario (1673), and Saint Joseph, Michigan (1679), along with Fort Saint Louis and Fort Crèvecoeur in Illinois (1680–1682), safeguarded economic and military control of a growing empire. Fort Biloxi (Mississippi) was founded in 1699, Mobile in 1702, and New Orleans in 1717. Between 1701 and 1721, the French occupied strategic points at Fort Pontchartrain (Detroit), Fort Michilimackinac (Michigan), Fort de Chartres (Illinois), and Fort Niagara (New York).

As the eighteenth century progressed, the OHIO VALLEY emerged as a danger point for the French. English settlers had found routes through the Allegheny Mountains and forged competing alliances with Native Americans. In quick succession, the English established numerous forts in Pennsylvania, including Presque Isle (Erie), Le Boeuf (Waterford), Machault (near Venango), Venango, and Duquesne (Pittsburgh). The French and British rivalry quickly accelerated from protests to blows. The FRENCH AND INDIAN WAR began in this area and ended in the complete downfall of New France. French frontier forts passed into English hands or into oblivion. In the struggle for the mastery of the continent, forts had played a significant role; in many cases, great cities—Pittsburgh, Detroit, Saint Louis, New Orleans—occupy the sites of their vanished stockades.

BIBLIOGRAPHY

Eccles, William J. *The French in North America, 1500–1783.* East Lansing: Michigan State University Press, 1998.

McDermott, John F., ed. *The French in the Mississippi Valley.* Urbana: University of Illinois Press, 1965.

M. M. Quaife / A. R.

See also **Duquesne, Fort; Fur Trade and Trapping; Jolliet-Marquette Explorations.**

FRENCH IN THE AMERICAN REVOLUTION. The American Revolution, like similar upheavals, endeavored to export its ideals and secure military aid abroad. During the Revolution, the Continental Congress, the governing body of the thirteen colony-states, failed in the first respect. The Congress's appeals to French Canadians and to British settlements in the West Indies fell on deaf ears. In the second regard, Congress met with success. France, nursing grievances against Britain from the humiliating loss of its North American possessions in the Seven Years' War, provided the revolutionaries with secret military aid and eventually entered the war against its European enemy. Soon after its creation by Congress in November 1775, the Committee of Secret Correspondence met privately in Philadelphia with a French agent and agreed to secret cooperation. The French foreign minister, the Comte de Vergennes, and King Louis XVI were solely motivated by a desire to weaken Britain through the loss of its colonies and to increase France's strength in Europe.

Although proclaiming neutrality, France's involvement in the American cause deepened in 1776 and 1777. American vessels slipped in and out of French ports. Soon the Paris government regularly channeled military stores to a mercantile company, Roderigue Hortalez and Company. At intervals, the firm turned over its acquisitions to American agents, who later paid the company in tobacco. The French king accepted, while not officially recognizing, a three-man American diplomatic delegation—led by the distinguished international figure Benjamin Franklin—to lobby at the royal court. Possibly the defeat of the British general John Burgoyne near Saratoga, New York, in October 1777 gave France the incentive to enter the war on the side of the Americans. France, however, had already become so involved in the conflict that it would have been a humiliation to pull back. The two countries signed a treaty of amity and commerce as well as a treaty of alliance on 6 February 1778. By the following summer, Britain and France, the two "superpowers" of eighteenth-century Europe, were engaged in open hostilities.

Americans generally rejoiced, but the alliance was a mixed blessing to George Washington and some other revolutionary leaders. Certainly Britain became more mindful of defending the kingdom by keeping much of the fleet in home waters. The British were also forced to defend their West Indian possessions with a sizable naval complement along with some regiments previously fighting in America, while at the same time evacuating the rebel capital of Philadelphia. Yet Washington opposed the

Marquis de Lafayette's idea of a Franco-American invasion of Canada in 1778, at least partly because he feared France might wish to reclaim its former North American dominions. Moreover, two combined operations ended in failure, one at New York City in 1778 and another at Savannah in 1779, both involving the French admiral Comte d'Estaing. French diplomats won some friends and lost others by becoming involved in congressional politics concerning terms of a future peace agreement. France's wartime expenses, including substantial subsidies to America, led Vergennes to concede privately that he now waivered on his commitment to insist that American independence be part of any peace settlement.

Lord Cornwallis's surrender at Yorktown on 19 October 1781 was the only major military success of the alliance. But it was a remarkable achievement, involving luck and remarkable coordination in a day when instantaneous communication and rapid movement of armies and navies were not possible. In the early fall of 1781, two French naval squadrons, a small one off Rhode Island under the Comte de Barras and a larger one in the West Indies under the Comte de Grasse, a small French army in Rhode Island under the Comte de Rochambeau, and Washington's main army, stationed outside New York City, all converged on the Yorktown Peninsula in Virginia at approximately the same time to trap Cornwallis, who had moved his army there after failing to subdue the Carolinas. Fighting at sea continued between Britain and France for another year, but all sides seemed ready for peace, including the Netherlands and Spain, which had entered the war against Britain but had fared poorly. Preliminary articles of peace were signed in Paris late in 1782, followed by the final treaty in 1783. Tough bargaining enabled American diplomats, taking advantage of European rivalries, to gain the Mississippi River as the nation's western boundary. In time, as Washington predicted, the French alliance, which had no termination date, outlived its usefulness, and President John Adams later paid dearly to extract America from its treaty obligations. American hopes to see the post-1783 European world turn from mercantilism to free trade also met with disappointment. It was only with the conclusion of the Napoleonic Wars in 1815 that America freed itself from the ills and entanglements of the Old World.

BIBLIOGRAPHY

Dull, Jonathan R. *A Diplomatic History of the American Revolution.* New Haven, Conn.: Yale University Press, 1985.

Hutson, James H. *John Adams and the Diplomacy of the American Revolution.* Lexington: University of Kentucky Press, 1980.

Morris, Richard B. *The Peacemakers: The Great Powers and American Independence.* New York: Harper and Row, 1965.

Stinchcombe, William C. *The American Revolution and the French Alliance.* Syracuse, N.Y.: Syracuse University Press, 1969.

Don Higginbotham

See also **Diplomacy, Secret; France, Quasi-War with; France, Relations with; French and Indian War; Newport, French Army at; Revolution, American: Political History, Military History, Diplomatic Aspects; Yorktown Campaign.**

FRICK COLLECTION, at 1 East Seventieth Street in New York City, is a museum devoted to late medieval through early modern art. Founded by the industrialist Henry Clay Frick (1849–1919), it houses his collection of paintings, drawings, sculptures, and decorative arts, as well as acquisitions made after his death. They are displayed together in his mansion planned expressly for exhibiting works of art, designed and built in 1913–1914 by Thomas Hastings. Frick's widow and daughter occupied the house until Mrs. Frick's death in 1931, whereupon the building was modified; alterations have been made since then. Bequeathed to the City of New York and opened to the public in 1935, the museum offers permanent and temporary exhibitions, lectures and concerts, and, in an adjacent building at 10 East Seventy-first Street, the Frick Art Reference Library, designed by John Russell Pope and opened in 1935 at the behest of Frick's daughter, Helen; it is one of the outstanding art history libraries in North America. The Frick Collection is still supported partly by the founder's endowment, but of the $15 million annual

Henry Clay Frick. The industrialist (coal, steel, iron ore, railroads), hated by many for his strikebreaking tactics, admired by others for the art collection he bestowed on the public. LIBRARY OF CONGRESS

budget, as of 2000, more than $2 million had to be raised from outside sources.

Among the most famous paintings at the Frick Collection are three by Jan Vermeer, Giovanni Bellini's *St. Francis in Ecstasy*, a powerful self-portrait by Rembrandt, Hans Holbein's portrait of Sir Thomas More, several works by El Greco, wall panels showing *The Progress of Love* by Jean-Honoré Fragonard, Jean-Auguste-Dominique Ingres's portrait of the countess d'Haussonville, and a Gilbert Stuart portrait of George Washington. Works by Duccio, associates of Jan van Eyck, Piero della Francesca, Titian, Sir Anthony Van Dyck, Frans Hals, Velazquez, James McNeill Whistler, Edgar Degas, and Edouard Manet, among others, are displayed in rooms offering also furniture, small bronzes, sculpture, Limoges enamels, and other objects.

BIBLIOGRAPHY

The Frick Collection: An Illustrated Catalogue. New York: Princeton University Press, 1968.

Ryskamp, Charles, et al. *Art in the Frick Collection: Paintings, Sculpture, Decorative Arts*. New York: Abrams, 1996

Symington, Martha Frick. *Henry Clay Frick: An Intimate Portrait*. New York: Abbeville, 1998.

Carol Herselle Krinsky

See also **Museums.**

FRIENDS, SOCIETY OF. *See* **Quakers.**

FRIENDS OF DOMESTIC INDUSTRY was the name assumed by a convention of five hundred delegates from New England and other states, including Ohio and Virginia. The convention met at New York in 1831 to promote retaining a protective tariff. This convention's reports reveal much about early nineteenth-century American industry.

BIBLIOGRAPHY

Cochran, Thomas Childs. *Frontiers of Change: Early Industrialism in America*. New York: Oxford University Press, 1981.

Sellers, Charles Grier. *The Market Revolution: Jacksonian America, 1815–1846*. New York: Oxford University Press, 1991.

Victor S. Clark / S. B.

See also **Corporations; Labor; Manufacturing; Tariff.**

FRIES' REBELLION (1799) was the armed resistance of certain farmers in Bucks and Northampton counties in Pennsylvania to a federal tax on land and houses. The insurgents, led by John Fries, a traveling venduecrier, or auctioneer, harrassed assessors and forced the release of men imprisoned in Bethlehem for similar resistance to the tax. Federal troops were sent, and the rebellion was put down. John Fries was captured, tried twice for treason, and, along with two other men, sentenced to be hanged. The date of the execution had been set when Fries obtained a pardon from President John Adams.

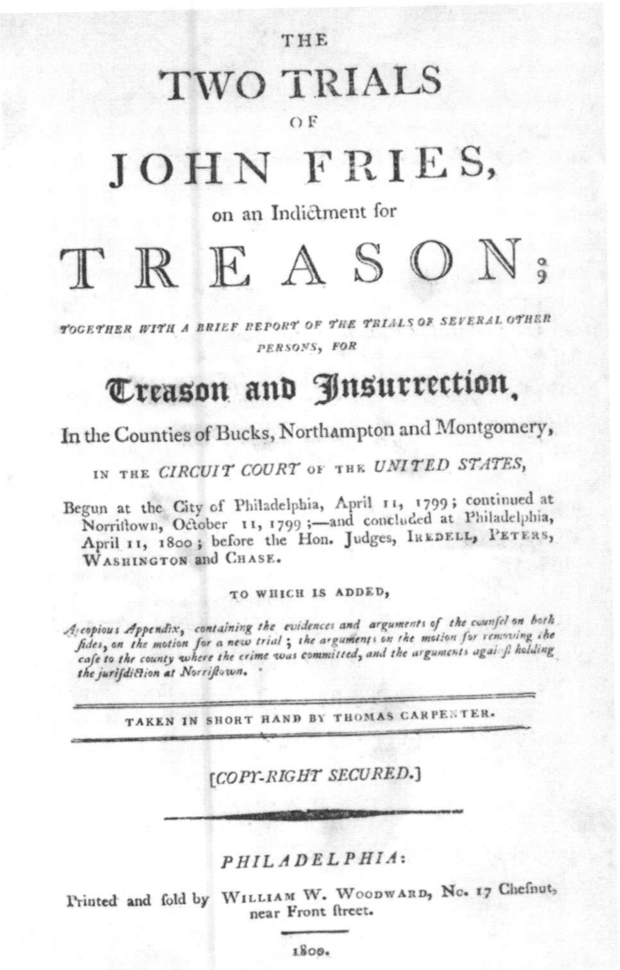
THE
TWO TRIALS
OF
JOHN FRIES,
on an Indictment for
TREASON;
TOGETHER WITH A BRIEF REPORT OF THE TRIALS OF SEVERAL OTHER PERSONS, FOR
Treason and Insurrection,
In the Counties of Bucks, Northampton and Montgomery,
IN THE CIRCUIT COURT OF THE UNITED STATES,
Begun at the City of Philadelphia, April 11, 1799; continued at Norristown, October 11, 1799;—and concluded at Philadelphia, April 11, 1800; before the Hon. Judges, IREDELL, PETERS, WASHINGTON and CHASE.
TO WHICH IS ADDED,
A copious Appendix, containing the evidences and arguments of the counsel on both sides, on the motion for a new trial; the arguments on the motion for removing the case to the county where the crime was committed, and the arguments against holding the jurisdiction at Norristown.
TAKEN IN SHORT HAND BY THOMAS CARPENTER.
[COPY-RIGHT SECURED.]
PHILADELPHIA:
Printed and sold by WILLIAM W. WOODWARD, No. 17 Chesnut, near Front street.
1800.

Fries' Rebellion. The title page from *The Two Trials of John Fries on an Indictment of Treason*, published in 1800. LIBRARY COMPANY OF PHILADELPHIA

BIBLIOGRAPHY

Davis, William W. H. *The Fries Rebellion, 1798–1799*. 1899. Reprint, New York: Arno Press, 1969.

H. H. Shenk / A. R.

See also **Insurrections, Domestic; Taxation.**

FROM THE DEEP WOODS TO CIVILIZATION. At the time when *From the Deep Woods to Civilization*, by Charles Eastman (or Ohiyesa, his name as a Santee Sioux), was published in 1916, Native Americans were no longer viewed simply as savages who deserved their fate. Instead, with the end of frontier hostilities and the growing popularity of groups like the Boy Scouts and Camp Fire Girls, both organized in 1910, the American public had come to associate Indians with noble qualities such as courage and environmental awareness. Few non-Indians understood the complex and tragic history of Native Americans, but most were curious about the continent's indigenous cultures. Charles Eastman wrote his autobiographical *From the Deep Woods to Civilization* for these curious Americans. This book sketches Eastman's life from his boyhood along the Minnesota-Canada border, through his education at mission schools, Dartmouth College, and Boston University Medical School, to his adult career as a physician, YMCA official, and Indian activist and lecturer. But the book's architecture and pleasant style are deceptive. Rather than tracing a young man's "progress" from the wilderness to civilization, Eastman's narrative grows increasingly pessimistic as the young doctor witnesses corruption at Indian agencies, the cruel killing at Wounded Knee, South Dakota, in 1890, and the hypocrisy of white society. Rather than "rising" to civilization, Eastman seems to be plunging deeper into despair. In the end, the author affirms the wisdom of his Native elders and questions the achievements of "civilization."

BIBLIOGRAPHY

Hoxie, Frederick E., ed. *Talking Back to Civilization: Indian Voices from the Progressive Era*. Boston: Bedford/St. Martin's Press, 2002.

Wilson, Raymond. *Ohiyesa: Charles Eastman, Santee Sioux*. Urbana: University of Illinois Press, 1983.

Frederick E. Hoxie

See also **Literature: Native American Literature; Wounded Knee Massacre.**

FRONTIER. Commonly regarded as the area where the settled portions of civilization meet the untamed wilderness, the frontier has persisted in American history as a topic of profound importance and intense debate. The conceptualization of the frontier has shifted greatly over time, evolving from older concepts that treated the frontier as a line of demarcation separating civilization from savagery to more modern considerations that treat the frontier as a zone of interaction and exchange between differing cultures. While numerous conceptualizations of the frontier contend for acceptance by the American public, all agree that the frontier occupies an influential position in the story of the American past.

Turner's Thesis: The Frontier as Process

Although the frontier has fascinated Americans since the colonial era, it first came to prominence as a true ideological concept late in the nineteenth century. On 12 July 1893, a young University of Wisconsin history professor named Frederick Jackson Turner, who sought to discover an antidote to the "germ theory" of history, which argued that all American institutions evolved from European precedents transplanted into the New World by the colonists, argued that the frontier was more important than any other single factor in shaping American history and culture. An influential address delivered before the American Historical Association, Turner's "The Significance of the Frontier in American History" suggests that the process of westward migration across the North American continent unleashed forces directly responsible for shaping the national character, an argument that boldly proclaimed the exceptionalism of the American experience and downplayed Europe's influence upon the development of the United States.

For Turner, the frontier was not so much a place as a reoccurring process of adaptation and change. The lure of abundant and inexpensive land brought Anglo-Europeans westward in an effort to improve their social and economic standings. As these migrants conquered the wilderness and spread across the North American continent, they experienced challenges and hardships unlike anything previously encountered in the Western world. In Turner's estimation, the process of overcoming the frontier transformed the Anglo-Europeans into a new national form, Americans. The core traits held dear by Americans, including democracy, individualism, freedom, and thrift, were generated by their experience of taming the wilderness. Turner attributed the greatest successes of American development, from the adoption of democratic self-rule to the belief in economic egalitarianism, to the indomitable national spirit created by the westering experience of the frontier populace, average people who reshaped European values and institutions in their own image. Nonetheless, Turner conceived of the frontier as a part of the past, and, based on the assertion of the 1890 census that Americans had completely filled the territorial borders of the forty-eight contiguous states, he warned that the nation was entering into a new phase in which it could no longer count upon the abundance of western land to provide the lifeblood of American culture.

The Turner thesis, as his concept of the frontier came to be known, proved extremely influential during the first half of the twentieth century. His initial essay sparked a series of test theories, conducted both by Turner and by his students, that emphasized the uniqueness of American history and the exceptionalness of the United States among the world's great nations. One Turnerian advocate, the historian Walter Prescott Webb, even expanded Turner's frontier process to include the entire Anglo-European world. The frontier experience, according to Webb, not only redefined America but also reached across the ocean to influence the modern development of Europe, giving rise to the dominant social and political institutions of the West. In a direct reversal of the European germ theory, Webb argued that democratic government, capitalist economic theory, and individualistic Protestant religion all were directly linked to the experience of westward movement and the conquering of the American frontier.

Revising Turner

Turner's grand scheme spawned a long line of criticism, ranging from petty oversimplifications of his arguments to sophisticated criticisms of his approach to the frontier. While the Turner thesis remains a formidable force in the study of the American frontier, his frontier process has some serious problems. Among the most noticeable is the racially exclusive environment created by the Turner thesis. Turner's frontier process is the triumphant story of the Anglo-American conquest of the wilderness, and it makes little mention of the diversity of peoples who played important roles in the history of the American frontier. For the most part, American Indians, African Americans, and Mexican and Asian immigrants do not merit consideration as influential players on the Turnerian frontier. Only the American Indians are afforded a place in Turner's world, and they are only an obstacle easily overcome in the advancement of the American nation. In addition, Turner's frontier does not attribute a significant role to women. His thesis gives no voice to the thousands of pioneering women who toiled alongside their husbands and fathers in the conquest of the American frontier, nor does he attempt to assess the contributions made by frontier women to the development of cherished American institutions. Finally, Turner's model allows no room for the diversity of the frontier experience in North America. His process of conquest and transformation does not lend itself favorably to the frontier history of New France, where cultural mediation and compromise prevailed, or to the Spanish frontier in America, which illustrates the construction of a frontier that existed more as a defensive perimeter for the core culture of Mexico than as a successive process of territorial conquest and acculturation.

During the 1980s, the problems inherent in the Turner thesis led to the codification of the critique under the leadership of a group of influential frontier thinkers known as the new western historians. Their concepts emphasized the frontier as a geographical region rather than as a process of westward movement, offering a more inclusive story of the American frontier than that allowed by Turner or his adherents. Focusing their attention primarily on the trans-Mississippi West, the new western historians argued that the historical diversity of the frontier must not be overlooked. All the peoples of the frontier, including American Indians, African Americans, Mexicans, Asians, and women, participated in shaping frontier America. In the estimation of the new western historians, the interaction of ethnic minorities with Anglo-American ideals, which in many instances was antagonistic, set many of the parameters for the subjugation of the frontier. New western historians also took issue with the celebratory climate invoked by Turner's seeming irresistible process of frontier transformation. Rather, they argued that taming the American wilderness was a fierce struggle, most appropriately designated by what one new western historian dubbed "the legacy of conquest." At the core of the reassessment is an understanding that all of the questions that dominate mainstream historical inquiry, including notions of conflict, race, gender, and society, provide fertile ground for studying the frontier. In addition, it is not a study bound by defined temporal limits but a legacy still at work. New western historians argue that the conquest of the frontier did not come to end in 1890, as Turner suggested, but that it continues during the modern era in the form of continuing legal and political battles over the finite resources of the American West.

New Frontiers for All

While the new western historians posed serious challenges to the Turnerian model and questioned the perspective from which the frontier should be viewed, the debate over the significance of the frontier in American history continued unabated into the twenty-first century. Turner's frontier process was perhaps deeply flawed, but it seems undeniable that the frontier played an influential role in the development of the American nation. Perhaps for this reason twenty-first-century conceptualizations of the frontier represent a delicate melding of Turner and new western history. Modern interpretations often define the frontier as a meeting place, or contact point, where differing cultures interacted on a relatively equal footing with no one group able to assert total superiority over the other. This approach to the frontier leaves no room for Turner's unstoppable process of American advancement, but what remains is Turner's suggestion that the frontier was a unique place of contact and exchange where no culture, Anglo-American or otherwise, could remain unchanged.

This concept has helped spawn a renewed interest in frontier history, not just of the western United States but of the eastern frontier as well. After the early 1990s, a new field of study, termed "backcountry history" by its adherents, applied the tenets of both Turner and new western historians to earlier frontiers, ranging from the first efforts to colonize North America through the early period of westward movement over the Appalachian Mountains. In the process, the study of the first American frontiers helped synthesize new approaches to frontier history and helped link the East to the West in a grand narrative of American westward migration.

BIBLIOGRAPHY

Cayton, Andrew R. L., and Fredrika J. Teute, eds. *Contact Points: American Frontiers from the Mohawk Valley to the Mississippi, 1750–1830.* Chapel Hill: University of North Carolina Press, 1998.

Davis, William C. *The American Frontier: Pioneers, Settlers, and Cowboys, 1800–1899.* Norman: University of Oklahoma Press, 1999.

Faragher, John Mack, ed. *Rereading Frederick Jackson Turner: "The Significance of the Frontier in American History" and Other Essays.* New York: Henry Holt, 1994.

Jones, Mary Ellen. *The American Frontier: Opposing Viewpoints.* San Diego, Calif.: Greenhaven Press, 1994.

Klein, Kerwin Lee. *Frontiers of Historical Imagination.* Berkeley: University of California Press, 1997.

Limerick, Patricia Nelson. *The Legacy of Conquest: The Unbroken Past of the American West.* New York: Norton, 1987.

Nobles, Gregory H. *American Frontiers: Cultural Encounters and Continental Conquest.* New York: Hill and Wang, 1997.

White, Richard. *"It's Your Misfortune and None of My Own": A History of the American West.* Norman: University of Oklahoma Press, 1991.

Daniel P. Barr

See also **Army on the Frontier; Frontier Thesis, Turner's; West, American;** *and vol. 9:* **Americans in Their Moral, Social and Political Relations; Half a Century (Chapter XLIII); Life and Adventures of Colonel Daniel Boon; My Army Life; Roughing It; The Vigilantes of Montana.**

FRONTIER DEFENSE required a standing army. The Continental Army had disbanded after the Revolution, but at the end of the War of 1812, Congress decided to maintain its army and establish strategic military outposts to protect the frontiers.

The theory and practice of frontier defense evolved slowly and involved attention at various times to different needs: protecting fur traders, trappers, and hunters; fortifying the irregular line of army posts; holding the outer limit of land officially acquired from the Indians; and protecting settlers on public lands that had been surveyed and opened for sale and settlement. In addition to meeting these needs, frontier defense involved a number of activities. The army surveyed rivers, lakes, and harbors; cut roads; and built bridges. It protected mail routes, ferries, government stores, immigrant trains, and trading caravans. It ejected squatters and established legal claimants. It protected surveyors and commissioners, and regulated hunters and trappers. It assisted officers of the law, protected whites and Indians from one another, and fought occasional battles, such as the campaigns of generals Josiah Harmar, Arthur St. Clair, and Anthony Wayne in western Ohio; the Seminole Wars; the Black Hawk War; the Louisiana–Texas border struggles; the Sioux outbreak in Minnesota; and George Armstrong Custer's famous battle on the Little Bighorn.

Although important, the extent and significance of Indian warfare can easily be overstated. The Indians rarely offered more than isolated and sporadic obstacles to westward expansion. Defense against the Indians was important because it led to the discovery of America in detail, to the formulation of military policy, and to the rapid conquest and settlement of the vast domain.

BIBLIOGRAPHY

Van Alstyne, Richard. *The Rising American Empire.* Oxford, U.K.: Blackwell; New York: Oxford University Press, 1960; New York: Norton, 1974.

Weeks, William E. *Building the Continental Empire: American Expansion from the Revolution to the Civil War.* Chicago: Ivan R. Dee, 1996.

Edgar B. Wesley / c. w.

See also **Army on the Frontier; Black Hawk War; Frontier; Little Bighorn, Battle of; Seminole Wars; Trading Posts, Frontier.**

FRONTIER THESIS, TURNER'S. Frederick Jackson Turner's "The Significance of the Frontier in American History" is arguably one of the most influential interpretations of the American past ever espoused. Delivered in Chicago before two hundred historians at the 1893 World's Columbian Exposition, a celebration of the four hundredth anniversary of Columbus's discovery of America, Turner's thesis discounted the then-dominant "germ theory" of American history, which argued that American political and social character evolved directly from European antecedents. Turner instead contended that Europeans had been transformed by the settlement of North America, a process that produced a distinct American mentality and culture far different from European precedents. Turner outlined progressive stages of settlement, dominated by the taming of the frontier from exploration through urban development, all the while maintaining that the experience of westward movement across the American continent was responsible for creating the independence and resourcefulness that comprised the heart of American character. The Turner thesis became the dominant interpretation of American history for the next century, although after the early 1980s "new western historians," who rejected Turner's grand theory for its lack of racial inclusiveness and overly triumphant paradigm, emphasized a more inclusive approach to frontier history. Nonetheless, the Turner thesis remained a popular albeit widely debated assessment of American development.

BIBLIOGRAPHY

Billington, Ray Allen. *The Genesis of the Frontier Thesis: A Study in Historical Creativity.* San Marino, Calif.: Huntington Library, 1971.

Faragher, John Mack, ed. *Rereading Frederick Jackson Turner: "The Significance of the Frontier in American History" and Other Essays.* New York: Henry Holt, 1994.

Limerick, Patricia Nelson, Clyde A. Milner II, and Charles E. Rankin, eds. *Trails: Toward a New Western History.* Lawrence: University Press of Kansas, 1991.

Daniel P. Barr

See also **Frontier; Historiography, American.**

FRONTIERO V. RICHARDSON, 411 U.S. 677 (1973), was a Supreme Court decision that held that the due process clause of the Fifth Amendment required the armed forces to provide equal family benefits for women and men. Sharron Frontiero, an air force lieutenant, challenged the regulation that allowed married women in the military to receive dependency benefits for their husband only if the wife paid more than half of her husband's living costs, although married men automatically received these benefits for their wife. William Frontiero was an unemployed college student, but his veterans' benefits made Sharron ineligible for a housing allowance and extra medical benefits that a man in her situation would have received. The Supreme Court had already indicated in *Reed v. Reed* (1971) that it might subject sex discrimination to more exacting scrutiny than it had in the past, but the lower court that heard *Frontiero* decided the case by the traditional rational basis test and upheld the regulation. The lower court found the discrimination on the basis of sex less important than the military's effort to cut costs by basing policy on the fact that wives were more likely to be financially dependent on their husbands than vice versa.

The Supreme Court, however, reversed the lower court's decision. Only Justice William Rehnquist voted to affirm the lower court. The other eight justices agreed that the law was unconstitutional but split on the grounds for decision. Justice William Brennan, writing for a plurality of four, argued that courts should review sex-based discrimination by the same tests used for race discrimination, meaning that sex, like race, was an inherently suspect classification. In effect, judges should presume that laws discriminating by sex were unconstitutional and subject them to strict scrutiny under the equal protection clause of the Fourteenth Amendment, upholding them only if the government could show a compelling justification. Brennan based this conclusion on three points. First, laws based on "gross, stereotyped distinctions between the sexes" had historically relegated women to a status "comparable to that of blacks under the pre–Civil War slave codes." Second, sex, like race, was "an immutable characteristic determined solely by the accident of birth"; therefore, sex was an unacceptable legal basis for imposing burdens. Third, sex was similar to "the recognized suspect criteria" because it "frequently bears no relation to ability to perform or contribute to society."

Four other justices agreed with these conclusions but dissented on the question of their applicability to the judges' task of constitutional adjudication. Both Justices Potter Stewart and Lewis Powell cited *Reed* as controlling authority. Powell, in an opinion joined by two other justices, indicated he was willing to go no further while the Equal Rights Amendment was still before the state legislatures. He chided the plurality for "reaching out to preempt a major political decision which is currently in process of resolution." In fact, the Court had come within one vote of rendering the amendment superfluous. Brennan's opinion, however, just as many dissents and concurrences, remains what one judge called an appeal to the "brooding spirit" of future generations.

BIBLIOGRAPHY

Goldstein, Leslie Friedman. *The Constitutional Rights of Women.* Madison: University of Wisconsin Press, 1988.

Hoff, Joan. *Law, Gender, and Injustice.* New York: New York University Press, 1991.

Judith A. Baer/A. R.

See also ***Craig v. Boren*; Discrimination: Sex; Equal Rights Amendment; *Reed v. Reed.***

FRUIT GROWING. Prior to the arrival of Europeans in North America, Native Americans used cranberries, concord grapes, blueberries, and wild strawberries in their diets, as dyes, and to treat illnesses. They introduced many of these fruits and their uses to Europeans, but colonists also brought fruit of their own. Fruit growing in the Americas by Europeans dates back as early as 1493. Christopher Columbus planted lemons, limes, and sweet oranges to augment the native foods unfamiliar to colonists. Other Spaniards introduced the orange to Florida with the settlement of Saint Augustine in 1565, and, by 1566, Spaniards were planting orchards of olives, dates, figs, oranges, lemons, and limes on the coast of what is now the state of Georgia. By 1769, they had planted vineyards and orchards of fruit trees all the way from Texas to California.

The earliest English settlers in North America brought with them both seed and propagating wood for European varieties of apples and other hardy fruits. Capt. John Smith reported in 1629 that residents of Jamestown were growing apples, pears, peaches, apricots, and many other fruits. In 1638, John Josselyn reported in *New England's Rarities Discovered* that all the hardy fruits were growing in New England. Large orchards quickly developed. Apples from New England were being exported to the West Indies by at least 1741; Albemarle pippins were sent from Virginia to England as early as 1759. The westward movement of settlers in North America seems to have been preceded by the distribution of apple seedlings by Indians, trappers, and itinerants. One itinerant, John Chapman,—popularly known as Johnny Appleseed—planted apple seeds extensively in what is now Ohio, Indiana, and Illinois, and gained a prominent place in American folklore.

The nineteenth century marked the beginning of commercial fruit cultivation for most fruit crops. Commercial production of most small fruit, which includes blueberries, blackberries, strawberries, dewberries, gooseberries, and cranberries, was not possible until after 1825, when most of these wild plants were domesticated. The orange did not become firmly established as a commercial crop until Florida became a state in 1821. Southern Californians began shipping table grapes to northern California in 1839, but shipments to eastern markets did not commence until 1869. In the early nineteenth century, commercial fruit growing was seldom profitable due to lack of reliable rapid transportation to population centers.

Over the late nineteenth century, the invention of the refrigerated railroad car, the spread of commercial canning, and the growing economic reach of the United States, created an explosion in commercial fruit production, especially in California. In 1871, the Department of Agriculture shipped seedless orange-tree cuttings from Brazil to California, thus starting California's navel orange industry. Florida continued to produce a majority of the nation's oranges, but California soon captured the majority of the lemon industry when a cold wave hit Florida in 1894 and 1895. In the middle of the nineteenth century, a series of events led California to be the center of wine production in the United States. In 1863, an American louse called phylloxera, which attacks the vine roots, was accidentally imported into Europe. Massive vine-growing areas were destroyed as the pest spread; nearly 2.5 million acres of land were estimated to have been ruined in France; and in Madeira and the Canary Islands, wine production came to a complete halt. The ravages were checked eventually by the importation of louse-resistant stocks from California; the older vines were grafted onto these stocks. Eventually, the louse-resistant American vines completely replaced the prephylloxera European vines. By the beginning of the twentieth century, California was exporting commercially grown oranges, lemons, strawberries, grapes, and wine.

In the mid- and late twentieth century, commercial fruit production played a central role in labor battles. By this time, migrant and immigrant laborers were picking much of the fruit in the United States, and their itinerant status and seasonal employment often left them the victims of farms that paid inadequate wages and provided substandard housing. By 1965, a group called the National Farm Workers' Organizing Committee (later the United Farm Workers) formed to protect the labor interests of migrant farm workers. By 1968—under the leadership of César Chavez—the union had convinced 17 million consumers to participate in a national boycott of table grapes. The boycott succeeded in spurring about two-thirds of grape farms to contract with the farm workers' union. Later efforts of the United Farm Workers focused on the detrimental effects of pesticides on fruit harvesters.

During the Cold War, fruit growing—particularly banana growing—also played a major role in U.S. foreign policy in Central America. Although bananas were not produced in the United States, they were imported to the U.S. from Jamaica as early as 1870. By the 1920s, Americans were eating bananas with breakfast cereal, and a U.S. company called the United Fruit Company dominated banana production in Central America and banana importation in the United States. The United Fruit Company relied heavily on railway and land concessions in Central American countries to form banana plantations, and, in 1953, the government of Guatemala announced it would expropriate United Fruit Company lands for landless peasants and pay the United Fruit Company an indemnity. The United Fruit Company objected, and U.S. Secretary of State John Foster Dulles called the indemnity unfair. When the American ambassador in Guatemala called the Guatemalan land reform policy an example of the "Marxist tentacles" spreading across Latin America, the United States joined with other Central American countries to back a successful coup in Guatemala, ending the proposed expropriation and protecting the United Fruit Company's interests. A greater number of companies participated in banana production by the close of the twentieth century, but in negotiations with European countries over banana imports, the United States continued to protect banana companies based in the United States.

By the close of the twentieth century, fruit growing continued to be a major commercial venture in the United States. In 1999, cash receipts for fruit- and nut-tree farms amounted to almost $13 billion—14 percent of sales for all U.S. agricultural crops. The United States produced about one-fourth of the world's lemons and, in 2000, the nation produced the second-largest amount of avocados in the world after Mexico. Hawaii, which had long dominated the world's production of pineapple, continued to produce the fruit for canning but lost most of the market to countries in Asia and Latin America. Florida continued to dominate citrus production, producing 76 percent of the nations navel and Valencia oranges, lemons, grapefruit, and tangerines combined. California produced 21 percent of the country's citrus fruits, and Arizona and Texas rounded out this production. Although losing out to Florida in overall citrus production, California continued to be the predominant producer of lemons. That state also produced 80 percent of the strawberries grown in the U.S. and most of the nation's wine.

BIBLIOGRAPHY

Cronon, William. *Changes in the Land: Indians, Colonists, and the Ecology of New England.* New York: Hill and Wang, 1983.

Gray, L. C. *A History of Agriculture in the Southern United States to 1860.* Washington, D.C.: The Carnegie Institution of Washington, 1933; New York: Peter Smith, 1941; Gloucester, Mass.: Peter Smith, 1958.

Stoll, Steven. *The Fruits of Natural Advantage: Making the Industrial Countryside in California.* Berkeley: University of California Press, 1998.

Wilson, David Scofield, and Angus Kress Gillespie, eds. *Rooted in America: Foodlore of Popular Fruits and Vegetables.* Knoxville: University of Tennessee Press, 1999.

Ralph T. Fulton/A. E.

See also **Agriculture; Canning Industry; Citrus Industry; Food and Cuisines; Food Preservation; Gardening;**

Nutrition and Vitamins; Refrigeration; United Farm Workers; Wine Industry.

FRUITLANDS. *See* **Utopian Communities.**

FUEL ADMINISTRATION, a World War I agency instituted 23 August 1917 under authority of the LEVER ACT. The agency exercised control over the production, distribution, and price of coal and oil. Its main activities were to (1) stimulate an increase in the production of fuel; (2) encourage voluntary economy in the private consumption of fuel; (3) restrict consumption by industries not essential to winning the war; (4) regulate the distribution of coal through a zoning system; and (5) check the inordinate rise of fuel prices by fixing maximum prices within each zone. Characteristic of its methods for inducing voluntary conservation was its appeal to people residing east of the Mississippi River to observe "gasless Sundays." The Fuel Administration ceased to function on 30 June 1919.

BIBLIOGRAPHY

Garfield, Harry A. *Final Report of the United States Fuel Administrator, 1917–1919.* Washington, D.C.: Government Printing Office, 1921.

Harries, Meirion, and Susie Harries. *The Last Days of Innocence: America At War, 1917–1918.* New York: Random House, 1997.

Cynthia R. Poe

See also **World War I, Economic Mobilization for.**

FUELS, ALTERNATIVE. The phrase "alternative fuels" is usually used to mean fuels for motor vehicles that are not gasoline. Alternative fuels can also refer to any fuel that is not a fossil fuel. Sometimes the phrase is used inaccurately to refer to alternative sources of energy or power, for example, hydroelectric dams and geothermal power plants. The search for alternative fuels has a long history in the United States. For instance, the Stanley Steamer automobile, unlike cars with internal combustion engines, could be powered with several different fuels: gasoline, raw petroleum, coal, charcoal, oil, and wood. By the mid-1920s, however, the Stanley Steamer was no longer manufactured, and gasoline was the fuel of choice for motor vehicles.

Smog created by the burning of coal, gasoline, and other petroleum derivatives created serious health hazards in American cities by the 1940s, and thereafter caused environmental damage even in remote wilderness areas by poisoning trees and other wildlife. By the 1970s, acid rain was a significant presence and poison in the nation's waters. Individual states and the federal government began enacting laws intended to limit and eventually end AIR POLLUTION. By the 1980s, manufacturers of motor vehicle engines were in a bind, because they were simultaneously required by law to lower the pollution of their fuels while increasing the mileage per gallon of their engines. Ethanol-powered vehicles were introduced for public sale in 1992 in an effort to meet the regulations of the 1990 Clean Air Act. Their fuel was a blend of 85 percent ethanol and 15 percent gasoline. Ethanol was made at first from corn but eventually many plants were used; by 2000, ethanol was generating about $5 billion per year in revenue for farmers. When the fuel additive MTBE was found to be very toxic to humans and a pollutant of water supplies, manufacturers began replacing it with ethanol, beginning with Getty Oil in 1999.

Automobile manufacturers also experimented with vehicles powered by electricity; their range was too limited, at first, and recharging them was difficult. By 2001, however, California cities were installing recharging stations in public parking lots in an attempt to comply with California laws requiring electric vehicles be available to consumers. Chrysler, Ford, General Motors, Honda, Mazda, Nissan, Toyota, Shell, and Solectra all offered assembly-line vehicles with electric engines by 2000, with the Nissan Atra EV meeting with early popular success. By 2002, manufacturers were experimenting with fuel cells that use hydrogen, thus increasing the distance a vehicle could travel on one charge. Chrysler took an early lead in the use of fuel cells with its NECAR 4, but motor vehicles powered by fuel cells were still primarily experimental in 2002.

To meet the requirements of antipollution laws, manufacturers also worked with "biodiesel,"—an alternative to traditional diesel fuel that is derived from vegetable oil. Biodiesel fuel pollutes far less than diesel oil but requires engines to be remanufactured to adjust for a different compression force. By 1999, Arizona, California, Nevada, and Utah were working on creating fuel stations for trucks that used biodiesel. A rival to biodiesel is dimethyl ether, which contains far fewer contaminants than diesel and biodiesel fuels. However, it requires methanol in its mix and by 2002 was too hard to produce on a scale large enough to meet the needs of trucks and other diesel-powered vehicles.

Methanol, derived from natural gas, has found favor with American motor vehicle manufacturers. Usually used in a mix of 85 percent methanol and 15 percent gasoline, its drawbacks include difficulty in starting cold engines and difficulty in mixing consistently with oxygen when in use. Compressed natural gas has become a popular alternative to gasoline, especially in large vehicles such as busses. A significant drawback to compressed natural gas is its expense—some bus companies and other transportation firms need government subsidies to pay for it. Even so, it pollutes far less than gasoline. In 1999, Syntroleum, in partnership with Chrysler, began working on trapping and cleaning (primarily a matter of removing sulfur) "waste" natural gas that is usually burned off at oil wells. An alternative use for natural gas is synthetic fuel, which produces hydrogen that could be used to power vehicles or in fuel cells.

Supposedly free of most pollutants, methane is a potentially an enormous source of fuel. Using methane presents technological problems, however. Manufacturers have not yet determined how to harvest enough methane to make its sale profitable. Propane, popular for heating homes, is easy for consumers to buy. Its weaknesses include difficulty in starting an engine and keeping a motor vehicle at highway speeds.

BIBLIOGRAPHY

Berinstein, Paula. *Alternative Energy: Facts, Statistics, and Issues.* Westport, Conn.: Oryx Press, 2001.

Flavin, Christopher. "Clean as a Breeze." *Time*, 15 December 1997, 60–62.

Hass, Nancy. "Alternate Fuels." *Financial World*, 19 January 1993, 50.

Hostetter, Martha, ed. *Energy Policy.* New York: H. W. Wilson. 2002.

Motavalli, Jim. *Forward Drive: The Race to Build "Clean" Cars for the Future.* San Francisco: Sierra Club Books, 2000.

U.S. Department of Energy. *Comprehensive National Energy Strategy.* Washington, D.C.: United States Department of Energy, 1998.

Yago, Jeffrey R. *Achieving Energy Independence—One Step at a Time.* Gum Spring, Va.: Dunimis Technology, 2001.

Kirk H. Beetz

See also **Clean Air Act.**

FUGITIVE-AGRARIANS. The movement that would in time become Southern Agrarianism began in 1914 when a group of amateur poets in Nashville, Tennessee, started meeting weekly to discuss their work. All were affiliated in some fashion with Vanderbilt University, with the two main figures a young English professor named John Crowe Ransom and his future colleague, Donald Davidson. World War I temporarily halted the conversations, but when they resumed in the early 1920s a pair of extraordinarily talented undergraduates, Allen Tate and Robert Penn Warren, became active participants. In April 1922, the Nashville poets launched *The Fugitive*, a magazine that would garner significant national attention during its three years of existence, due in part to the fact that much of its verse was in the advanced modernist mode—cerebral, allusive, and often experimental in form. It seemed especially striking that such writing should emerge from the South, a region long considered an intellectual backwater.

In truth, the Fugitives almost totally ignored the South, but that changed dramatically in late 1925 and 1926 when first Davidson and then Tate commenced major poems addressing their regional heritage. Within a year both had become full-fledged southern patriots, convinced that the South, with its predominantly rural life lived close to nature, was the repository of moral virtue in America. Before long their enthusiasm spread to Ransom and, to a lesser extent, Warren. Together they began planning a book of partisan essays to champion the southern cause, recruiting as contributors such notable sons of Dixie as the Arkansas poet John Gould Fletcher, the novelist Stark Young, and the historian Frank Lawrence Owsley.

When *I'll Take My Stand: The South and the Agrarian Tradition* appeared in 1930, authored by "Twelve Southerners," it produced an immediate sensation. Its introductory Statement of Principles observed defiantly that, while members of the group might differ on other issues, "all tend to support a Southern way of life against what may be called the American or prevailing way." It was the South's unique culture based on farming, they contended, that had allowed it thus far to escape the crass commercialization, impersonal cities, and polluting factories endemic to American capitalism. Subsequent articles extolled agrarian society as the perfect locale for art, religion, and education to flourish, and portrayed the region as more civilized and humane than the rest of the United States, even in regard to race relations. Previous writers of the "New South" school had labored to show that the South was rapidly catching up to the North; now members of a younger generation were insisting that Dixie was in fact superior precisely because it was so stridently old-fashioned.

The Agrarians continued their crusade for several years, but by the late 1930s the flame began to fade for all but Davidson. In different ways, Ransom, Tate, and Warren found their advocacy of the South impeding their literary careers, which now seemed more important. All three became founders of the New Criticism, by midcentury the dominant scholarly approach to understanding literature, based on an intense technical analysis of individual works. In effect, they returned to their Fugitive roots, but only after having greatly enriched the American tradition of intellectual dissent by their spirited defense of the fast-vanishing style of life of their native region.

BIBLIOGRAPHY

Conkin, Paul K. *The Southern Agrarians.* Knoxville: University of Tennessee Press, 1988.

Rubin, Louis D., Jr. *The Wary Fugitives: Four Poets and the South.* Baton Rouge: Louisiana State University Press, 1978.

Singal, Daniel Joseph. *The War Within: From Victorian to Modernist Thought in the South, 1919–1945.* Chapel Hill: University of North Carolina Press, 1982.

Daniel J. Singal

See also **Agrarianism; South, the.**

FUGITIVE SLAVE ACTS. In 1793, Congress passed an act to implement the provision in the U.S. Constitution (Article IV, Section 2) stating that "fugitives from labour" should be returned "on demand" to the person to whom they owed "service or labour." The 1793 law allowed a master to bring an alleged fugitive slave before any state or federal judge or magistrate for a summary hearing to determine if the person seized was the claimant's runaway slave. The judge could accept any evidence he found persuasive on the status of the alleged slave. He could then issue a certificate of removal, allowing the claimant to take the slave back to his home state. The law provided a $500 fine for anyone interfering with the return of a fugitive slave. In addition, a master could sue anyone helping his slave for his costs plus the actual value of any slaves actually lost.

These liberal rules, as well as blatant kidnapping of free blacks, led northern states to pass personal liberty acts to protect their black residents from illegitimate removal. In the Supreme Court case of **Prigg v. Commonwealth of Pennsylvania** (1842) Justice Joseph Story, speaking for an 8–1 majority, upheld the 1793 law, struck down all state laws that interfered with the return of a fugitive slaves, and declared that slave owners had a common law right of recaption to remove any slave without any judicial hearing, if this seizure could be accomplished without any breach of the peace. Meanwhile, in ***Jones v. Van Zandt*** (1847), the U.S. Supreme Court upheld a harsh interpretation of the 1793 law, which in effect applied to the north the southern legal presumption that all blacks were slaves until it could be proved otherwise.

Unable to protect their black residents, many free states passed new personal liberty laws withdrawing state support for enforcement of the 1793 law. Without state aid, slave owners had to rely on the tiny number of federal judges and marshals to aid them in their quest for runaway slaves.

In the wake of these new laws southerners demanded stronger federal enforcement, which led to the Fugitive Slave Law of 1850. Technically an amendment of the 1793 law, the 1850 law was in reality an entirely new approach to the problem. The 1850 law allowed for the appointment of federal commissioners throughout the nation. These commissioners would hear fugitive slave cases and were empowered to call out federal marshals, posses, or the military to aid masters in recovering runaways. Penalties for violating the law included a $1,000 fine and a six-month jail sentence. In addition, anyone helping a fugitive slave could be sued for a $1,000 penalty to compensate the master for the loss of the slave.

Hearings before the commissioners were summary affairs, with no jury present. The alleged slave was denied access to the writ of habeas corpus and could not testify at the hearing. A U.S. Commissioner hearing the case would get $5 if he decided in favor of the alleged slave, but if he held for the master he would get $10. This disparity was in theory designed to compensate commissioners for the extra work of filling out certificates of removal, but to most northerners it seemed a blatant attempt to help slavery at the expense of justice.

The law led to riots, rescues, and resistance in a number of places. In 1851 a mob stormed a courtroom in Boston to free the slave Shadrach; in Syracuse a mob rescued the slave Jerry from a jail; and in Christiana, Pennsylvania, a master was killed in a shootout with fugitive slaves. In 1854, Milwaukee citizens led by the abolitionist editor Sherman Booth freed the slave Joshua Glover from federal custody, and, in 1858, most of the students and faculty of **Oberlin College** charged a courthouse and freed a slave arrested in Wellington, Ohio. All of these cases led to prosecutions, but most were unsuccessful or led to only token penalties. In ***Ableman v. Booth*** (1859), the U.S. Supreme Court firmly upheld the 1850 law and asserted that states could interfere with the federal courts.

In the long run, the fugitive slave laws did little to help recover runaway slaves, but they did much to undermine the Union. Outrage over the 1850 law in the North helped create the constituency for the Republican Party and the election of Abraham Lincoln in 1860. Meanwhile, a number of southern states cited failure to enforce the fugitive slave laws as one of their reasons for secession (1861). In 1864, the Republican-dominated Congress repealed both fugitive slave laws.

BIBLIOGRAPHY

Campbell, Stanley W. *The Slave Catchers: Enforcement of the Fugitive Slave Law, 1850–1860.* Chapel Hill: University of North Carolina Press, 1970.

Finkelman, Paul. *Slavery in the Courtroom: An Annotated Bibliography of American Cases.* Washington, D.C.: Library of Congress, 1985.

———. "Story Telling on the Supreme Court: *Prigg v. Pennsylvania* and Justice Joseph Story's Judicial Nationalism." *Supreme Court Review* (1994): 247–294.

Morris, Thomas D. *Free Men All: The Personal Liberty Laws of the North, 1780–1861.* Baltimore: Johns Hopkins University Press, 1974.

Paul Finkelman

See also **Antislavery; Slave Insurrections; Slave Rescue Cases; Slavery; Underground Railroad.**

FULBRIGHT ACT AND GRANTS. The Fulbright Act of 1946 (Public Law 584) was sponsored by Sen. J. William Fulbright of Arkansas to initiate and finance certain international educational exchange programs. The programs used foreign currency funds accruing to the United States from the sale to other governments of property abroad that was considered surplus after World War II. Subsequent acts of Congress, including the Fulbright-Hays Act (Mutual Education and Cultural Exchange Act) of 1961, broadened the programs and authorized the use of such currencies from other sources and the appropriation of dollars if needed for the effective administration of the programs by the Department of State. By the twenty-first century, many nongovernmental organizations and participating governments provided numerous services, as well as the dollars necessary, to supplement the foreign currency grants.

Proposed as an amendment to the Surplus Property Act of 1944, the act was motivated, Fulbright stated, by the conviction "that the necessity for increasing our understanding of others and their understanding of us has an urgency that it has never had in the past." Programs were developed by executive agreements with interested, eligible nations. By 2000, these numbered more than 140 countries and territories in every region of the world. More than 84,000 Americans awarded grants had traveled abroad from every U.S. state and major dependency to study, teach, lecture, or conduct research—usually for one year. More than 146,000 foreigners with travel grants had visited the United States on similar projects. The program made possible many types of activities, among them cooperative undertakings by American and foreign specialists in journalism, the physical sciences, and social studies; and the promotion of American studies abroad and of "foreign area studies" in the United States. The act was the first to allocate to such activities foreign currency funds accruing to the United States under agreements with other governments, thus establishing a precedent for the financing of other, related programs that were to follow. It anticipated, too, the need for systematic government financing of such programs to a substantial degree. It also committed the U.S. government, for the first time, to long-term programs with global potential and on a scale more nearly commensurate with their current significance. It originated, in fact, the largest program in history consisting of international exchange grants made to individuals and thus helped demonstrate the value of such activities in increasing mutual understanding and broadening the community of interests among peoples.

BIBLIOGRAPHY

Dudden, Arthur, and Russell R. Dynes, eds. *The Fulbright Experience, 1946–1986: Encounters and Transformations.* New Brunswick, N.J.: Transaction Books, 1987.

Johnson, Walter, and Francis J. Colligan. *The Fulbright Program: A History.* Chicago: University of Chicago Press, 1965.

Woods, Randall Bennett. *Fulbright: A Biography.* Cambridge, U.K.; New York: Cambridge University Press, 1995.

Francis J. Colligan / F. B.

See also **Education; Education, Higher: Colleges and Universities; Exchange Students; Multiculturalism; Teacher Training.**

"FULL DINNER PAIL," a Republican campaign slogan in the 1900 presidential election campaign, used to emphasize the prosperity of William McKinley's first term and to appeal particularly to the labor vote. During McKinley's first term the nation pulled out of a serious depression and then waged a successful war against Spain in 1898. Despite these successes, the Republican Party's close association with big business and the growing radicalism of organized labor convinced McKinley that he needed to position himself as an ally of working-class America to be assured of reelection. His campaign strategy worked and in the November election he easily defeated William Jennings Bryan, the Democratic candidate.

BIBLIOGRAPHY

Glad, Paul W. *McKinley, Bryan, and the People.* Philadelphia: Lippincott, 1964.

Wendell H. Stephenson / A. R.

See also **"Public Be Damned"; Spanish-American War; Trust-Busting.**

FULTON'S FOLLY. In 1798, the exclusive privilege of navigating boats propelled by steam within the state of New York was given to Robert R. Livingston. In Paris, where he was minister to France, Livingston met the American painter and inventor, Robert Fulton. In 1803, they revived the monopoly, with themselves as joint beneficiaries. In 1807, Fulton built the steamboat *Clermont*, soon widely known as Fulton's Folly. The small, snub-nosed boat made the 150-mile run from New York City to Albany in 32 hours. A regular passenger service was inaugurated, and a new era in water transportation began. In 1809, Fulton applied for, and obtained, a federal patent.

The Livingston-Fulton monopoly caused much grumbling. Fulton had not invented the steamboat and had no right to a monopoly, competitors charged. The courts affirmed Fulton's monopoly but, with no way to enforce the verdict, he was forced to compromise with a rival company in Albany. During 1811, Fulton built two vessels—used along the Hudson River—and a ferryboat to shuttle travelers between New York City and New Jersey. The question of interstate ferryboats and navigation on rivers that formed boundaries between states became a source of protracted litigation and landmark Supreme Court decisions.

Spurred on by their success in New York, Livingston and Fulton attempted to gain monopolistic control of all steamboat traffic on the Ohio and Mississippi rivers. In 1811, Louisiana gave them a monopoly for a limited time on the Mississippi. Fulton accordingly built the *New Orleans*, the first steam craft to navigate the interior of the country. Litigation continued until the monopolies were broken up by the 1824 decision of Chief Justice John Marshall in the Supreme Court case of *Gibbons v. Ogden*.

BIBLIOGRAPHY

Baxter, Maurice G. *The Steamboat Monopoly: Gibbons v. Ogden, 1824.* New York: Knopf, 1972.

Haites, Erik F., James Mak, and Gary M. Walton. *Western River Transportation: The Era of Early Internal Development, 1810–1860.* Baltimore: Johns Hopkins University Press, 1975.

Jerry Falwell. The outspoken fundamentalist Baptist preacher, whose greatest influence was in the 1980s through his conservative coalition, Moral Majority. LIBRARY OF CONGRESS

Philip, Cynthia O. *Robert Fulton, A Biography.* New York: F. Watts, 1985.

A. C. Flick/A. R.

See also **Hudson River; Mississippi River; Ohio River; Steam Power and Engines; Steamboats.**

FUNDAMENTALISM is a movement within U.S. Protestantism marked by twin commitments to revivalistic evangelism and to militant defense of traditional Protestant doctrines. By the end of WORLD WAR I, a loose coalition of conservative Protestants had coalesced into a movement united in defending its evangelistic and missionary endeavors against theological, scientific, and philosophical "modernism." The threatened doctrines had recently been identified in a collaborative twelve-volume series entitled *The Fundamentals* (1910–1915). Battles over issues—most frequently biblical inerrancy (exemption from error), the virgin birth of Jesus, substitutionary atonement, bodily resurrection, and miracles—soon erupted within several leading denominations, principally among northern Baptists and Presbyterians. Many members separated from their churches to form new denominations committed to defending the fundamentals. Fundamentalists took their campaign into public education, where such organizations as the Anti-Evolution League lobbied state legislatures to prohibit the teaching of evolution in public schools. The former Democratic presidential candidate William Jennings Bryan led this effort, which culminated in his prosecution of the Dayton, Tennessee, teacher John T. Scopes, for teaching evolution. The Scopes trial of 1925 attracted national attention, and the ridicule of Bryan's views during the trial by the defense lawyer, Clarence Darrow, helped to discredit fundamentalism.

Over the next three decades the Fundamentalists' twin commitments to evangelism and doctrinal purity produced a flurry of activity that escaped much public notice but laid the groundwork for a resurgence in the late 1970s. Evangelists and missionaries began supplementing earlier revival methods with radio programs. Thousands of independent churches formed, many loosely linked in such umbrella organizations as the Independent Fundamental Churches of America. These churches sent missionaries abroad through independent mission boards. Bible colleges and seminaries trained the missionaries. Internecine squabbles (differences from within) over doctrine marked this period. The dispensational premillennialism outlined in the Scofield Reference Bible began to take on the status of another fundamental. Others formalized a doctrine of separation from the world's corruption.

Such developments prompted some leaders to forge a new evangelical movement that differed little from fundamentalism in doctrine but sought broader ecclesiastical alliances and new social and intellectual engagement with the modern world. By the late 1960s a set of institutions supported a movement centered in Baptist splinter groups and independent churches. Listener-supported Christian FM radio stations began proliferating across the country. Evangelists began television ministries. This burgeoning network reached an audience far broader than the fundamentalist core, allowing Fundamentalists, Evangelicals, and Pentecostals to identify a set of concerns that drew them together.

By the early 1970s, Fundamentalists came to believe that an array of social, judicial, and political forces threatened their beliefs. They began battling this "secular humanism" on several fronts, advocating restoration of prayer and the teaching of creationism in public schools and swelling the ranks of the prolife movement after *Roe v. Wade* (1973). In the late 1970s Fundamentalists within the Southern Baptist Convention mounted a struggle, ultimately successful, for control of the denomination's seminaries and missions. At the same time, the fundamentalist Baptist preacher Jerry Falwell mobilized a conservative religious coalition that promoted moral reform by supporting conservative candidates for public office. Many political analysts credited Ronald Reagan's presidential victory in 1980 to the support of Falwell's MORAL MAJORITY.

Falwell disbanded his organization in 1988, but activists continued to exert influence into the mid-1990s. Journalists and students tended to label this post-Falwell coalition as "fundamentalist" and applied the term to antimodernist movements within other religions. Sharp differences, however, continued to distinguish Fundamentalists from Evangelicals and Pentecostals. Indeed, Fundamentalists themselves remained divided—separationists denounced efforts to form common cause with other religious groups, and political moderates criticized alliances of groups such as the CHRISTIAN COALITION with the REPUBLICAN PARTY.

The minister, broadcaster, and one-time presidential candidate Pat Robertson founded the Christian Coalition in 1989 to promote traditional Christian values in American life. The group won a smashing victory in 1994 when it helped elect enough Republican congresspeople to give that party its first majority in both houses of Congress in four decades. Some of the measures it proposed became part of the Republicans' CONTRACT WITH AMERICA program. The "contract" called for efforts to end federal aid to the arts and humanities, restore school prayer, restrict abortion, limit pornography, and provide tax breaks for parents who send their children to private or religious schools. It also called for a "Personal Responsibility Act" to limit benefits to welfare recipients who bore children out of wedlock. Few of these measures ever made it into law. However, the Christian Coalition's political clout became abundantly clear when President Bill Clinton decided to sign a welfare reform bill called the "Personal Responsibility and Work Opportunity Reconciliation Act" in 1996.

The late 1990s brought new challenges to the political arm of American Fundamentalism. The Christian Coalition's dynamic director, Ralph Reed, left the organization in 1996 to become a political consultant. The terrorist attacks of 11 September 2001 shifted political discourse away from domestic and moral issues, which had been the Christian Coalition's strong suit, toward domestic security, military intelligence, and foreign relations. In the days after the attacks, Rev. Jerry Falwell attributed the attack on New York City to God's displeasure with homosexuals, abortionists, pagans, and civil libertarians (he later apologized for the comment). Several months later the Christian Coalition's founder, Pat Robertson, resigned from the organization. As a sign of the changed political environment facing Fundamentalists, Ralph Reed joined American Jews in pressuring the government to step up its military support for the beleaguered state of Israel.

At the start of the twenty-first century, Fundamentalists remained caught between the impulse to reform modernity and the impulse to reject and withdraw from it altogether. In some ways, the emergence of a religious marketing among a vast network of Christian publishers and television and radio stations catered to both impulses. A series of novels by Rev. Tim LaHaye depicting the Second Coming of Christ, which sold tens of millions of copies, revealed a deep understanding of a modern world even as it prophesied its destruction. The Fundamentalist movement in America continued to display great resourcefulness in adapting modern communications technology to defend its fundamentals against the modern world's ideas.

BIBLIOGRAPHY

Ammerman, Nancy T. *Bible Believers: Fundamentalists in the Modern World.* New Brunswick, N.J.: Rutgers University Press, 1987.

Armstrong, Karen. *The Battle for God: A History of Fundamentalism.* New York: Knopf, 2000.

Marsden, George. *Fundamentalism and American Culture: The Shaping of Twentieth Century Evangelicalism, 1870–1925.* New York: Oxford University Press, 1980.

Marty, Martin E., and R. Scott Appleby, eds. *Accounting for Fundamentalisms: The Dynamic Character of Movements.* Chicago: University of Chicago Press, 1994.

Watson, Justin. *The Christian Coalition: Dreams of Restoration, Demands for Recognition.* New York: St. Martin's Press, 1997.

Timothy D. Hall / A. R.

See also **Baptist Churches; Evangelicalism and Revivalism; Millennialism; Pentecostal Churches; Presbyterianism; Protestantism; Pro-Life Movement; Religion and Religious Affiliation; Scopes Trial; Televangelism; Terrorism.**

FDR's Funeral Procession. In this traditional ritual for presidents who have died in office, Franklin D. Roosevelt's casket is borne on a horse-drawn caisson in Washington, D.C., on 24 April 1945, before his burial in Hyde Park, N.Y. LIBRARY OF CONGRESS

FUNERARY TRADITIONS. Since the end of the American Revolution, funeral traditions and rituals have changed extensively in the United States. Originally, the processes of mourning and burial were based on European traditions brought to the colonies. Puritans focused on human sin and heavenly redemption, and their burial process centered on having visitations in the home, followed by religious burial in a family or church graveyard, announced by public notice and invitations. Simple headstones were locally carved and used foreboding images of skulls, weeping willows, and shrouded figures. Women and children traditionally carried out the process of mourning by dressing in black, removing themselves from social activities, and writing letters to announce the death to distant family and friends.

By the nineteenth century, traditions became more elaborate and visually oriented. Mourning continued to be the responsibility of women, who dressed in mourning garb and shrouded the household in crepe if the family could afford it. Interest in mourning jewelry containing the hair of the dead and in-death photography also developed. Postmortem photographs of loved ones, particularly children, often became the only image that the family had. Church graveyards gave way to landscaped cemeteries that provided aesthetic viewing and resolved concerns over the sanitary hazards of graveyards within growing cities. Symbolisms used in mourning art, gravestones, and jewelry became more gentle and included angels, lambs, flowers, and hands pointing toward Heaven. Families still viewed the body within the home, but undertakers were quickly developing the commercial funeral industry. Premade caskets, embalming services, and department stores specializing in mourning goods helped depersonalize death by taking it out of the home.

In twentieth-century postwar America, an increased discomfort with the subject of death resulted from a new societal focus on youth, and in response new funerary rituals evolved. The close of the century saw a trend toward personalizing funeral and burying practices. Funerals often included photos or videos of the deceased and performances of their favorite music. Caskets were sometimes personalized to reflect the interests of the deceased, or custom-built in special shapes and colors. People were also being buried with beloved objects and family mementoes. Consumers were encouraged to prepay for their funerals and plan them in advance to their personal tastes.

Methods of burial at the end of the twentieth century were changing to save space, and provide personal choice. Mummification (being embalmed, wrapped, and sealed in polyurethane), cryonics (freezing the body), and cremation were all alternatives to the traditional embalming and burial. While traditional burial with embalming was still the preferred method of disposition for the 2.3 million Americans who died in 1998, cremation was growing more popular because it is significantly cheaper than traditional embalming, and because the ashes can be disposed of in a variety of ways. Ashes can be buried in a memorial garden, spread over water, or scattered in a personally significant place; they can now even be sent into space on a commercial satellite rocket. One-half million cremations took place in the United States in 1998, and by 2010 that number was expected to double. Although funerary rituals and mourning customs have changed drastically since 1800, Americans were returning to a personalized grieving process. Global technology even had an impact on death. Online cemetery resources, memorial and obituary Web sites, and grief counseling groups were all offered on the Internet.

BIBLIOGRAPHY

Coffin, Margaret. *Death in Early America: The History and Folklore of Customs and Superstitions of Early Medicine, Funerals, Burials, and Mourning.* Nashville, Tenn.: Thomas Nelson, 1976.

Coleman, Penny. *Corpses, Coffins, and Crypts: A History of Burial.* New York: Henry Holt, 1997.

Curl, James Stevens. *The Victorian Celebration of Death.* Detroit, Mich.: Partridge Press, 1972.

Sloane, David Charles, et al. *The Last Great Necessity: Cemeteries in American History.* Baltimore: John Hopkins University Press, 1991.

Karen Rae Mehaffey

See also **Cemeteries, National; Death and Dying.**

FUR COMPANIES. The Spanish and the French entered the fur trade in the sixteenth century. The Spanish contented themselves with an annual voyage of Manila galleons between North America and the Orient, exchanging sea otter pelts harvested on the California coast for Asian luxuries. The French opened trading posts for

Fort Astoria. The Pacific Fur Company, a subsidiary of John Jacob Astor's American Fur Company, built the first permanent American trading outpost on the Pacific coast in 1811, at what is now Astoria, Oregon; the British seized it during the War of 1812 but returned it to American control in 1818. LIBRARY OF CONGRESS

the Hurons and their allies on the Saint Lawrence River. Dutch and, later, English traders pushed up the Hudson River and engaged in trade with the Iroquois.

In 1670 the British established the Hudson's Bay Company (HBC), a joint-stock, corporate monopoly enterprise. Granted a royal monopoly and backed by London financiers, the HBC controlled all furs gathered on streams flowing into Hudson Bay and erected posts throughout Canada, where American Indians brought furs to trade for manufactured goods, such as knives, hatchets, blankets, and guns. Following the French and Indian War, French *voyageurs* (boatmen), *couriers du bois* (runners of the woods), Québec Pedlars (French Canadians), and Scotsmen formed the North West Company (NWC) in 1790 to compete with the powerful British behemoth. The NWC differed from the HBC in that Montreal agents took care of the NWC logistics and supplied their trappers, who stayed in the woods, over the inland river systems. North West men, such as Alexander Mackenzie and David Thompson, explored the western half of Canada to exploit fur resources, establish trading houses, and compete with the HBC. Competition between the two rivals brought violent episodes, and the British Crown forced a merger in 1821.

Meanwhile Russian and American traders increased their fur-trading activities. The Russian-American Company (RAC) harvested sea otters from California to the Bering Sea. A royal monopoly company started in the late eighteenth century, the RAC sent out *promyshlenniks* (fur trade entrepreneurs) and adept Aleutian hunters from their bases at Kodiak and Sitka.

American fur companies started out on a more modest footing. Albany traders and Bostonians engaged in the northeastern colonial fur trade and participated in voyages to the Pacific Northwest. The United States created a factory system in 1795 to erect trading posts, supply goods to Indians at cost, stop the liquor traffic, and undermine British influence. The Lewis and Clark expedition created a rush to harvest the beavers that inhabited the Rocky Mountain streams. Individuals, including Manuel Lisa, joined the Chouteau family of Saint Louis in forming the Missouri Fur Company to expand their lower Missouri trade westward.

John Jacob Astor's American Fur Company and its subsidiaries were the most successful large-scale American venture. The AFC expanded its trading operations from the Columbia River to the Missouri River. When the government factory system ended in 1822, people like William H. Ashley and Andrew Henry entered partnerships and formed small companies to harvest furs in the northern and central Rockies, while others in Taos and Santa Fe, New Mexico, trapped in the southern Rockies.

Of all these companies, the Hudson's Bay Company endured the longest.

BIBLIOGRAPHY

Gowans, Fred R. *Rocky Mountain Rendezvous: A History of the Fur Trade Rendezvous, 1825–1840.* Provo, Utah: Brigham Young University Press, 1976.

Lavender, David. *The Fist in the Wilderness.* Garden City, N.Y.: Doubleday, 1964.

Rich, Edwin E. *The History of the Hudson's Bay Company, 1670–1870.* 2 vols. New York: Macmillian, 1960.

Robertson, R. G. *Competitive Struggle: America's Western Fur Trading Posts, 1764–1865.* Boise, Idaho: Tamarack Books, 1999.

Jay H. Buckley
Lyn S. Clayton

See also **Fur Trade and Trapping; Hudson's Bay Company.**

FUR TRADE AND TRAPPING. The North American fur trade from the sixteenth century to the late nineteenth century involved half a dozen European nations and numerous American Indian nations. European fashion drove this global economic system and resulted in cross-cultural interchanges among Europeans and Indians. Mutually beneficial liaisons created the children of the fur trade or Métis, who were bridges between Indian and white worlds. The trade superimposed itself upon and was incorporated into Native trading networks. It helped forge alliances between nations, sometimes divided tribes, and occasionally led to dependency or warfare. The harvesting of furbearing animals through hunting and trapping created zones of wildlife depletion when short-term exploitation overshadowed the wisdom of long-term yield. The trade brought Indians useful items, such as manufactured goods, tools, kettles, beads, and blankets, but also inflicted suffering through the introduction of diseases, firearms, and alcohol. Traffic in furs was an important economic and political motive in the exploration and colonization of the continent.

French Fur Trade

The Indians of North America began trading furs with Europeans upon their first encounter. Initially the fur trade was secondary to the fishing industry that brought the French to North America. In his 1534 voyage to North American waters, Captain Jacques Cartier described trading with the local Indians along the gulf of the Saint Lawrence River who held up furs on sticks to induce the French to shore. The Indians bartered all the furs they possessed to the French and promised to return with more. Cartier surmised that the way into the interior and quite possibly a water route to the Orient lay up the Saint Lawrence. On his second voyage, in 1535, he ascended the river to Hochelaga (present-day Montreal), where he found a substantial Huron (Wyandot) encampment and noticed an abundance of furbearing animals along the river.

The Hurons, a settled people who lived by fishing and agriculture, trafficked in endless quantities of furs and, to protect Huron interests, purposely hindered the French from further penetration into the continent's interior. The Hurons, Ottawas, and Algonquians acted as intermediaries between the French and the interior tribes. They exerted influence over tribes by supplying them with European trade goods and guns for hunting and defense in exchange for furs. Additionally Jesuit missionaries advised the Indians to devote more time to trapping furs. Adherence to missionaries' requests quickly resulted in the depletion of beaver in the area. Consequently Indians looked westward to distant lands and tribes to supply furs.

French penetration into the interior exacerbated and intensified the intertribal warfare between these tribes and the Iroquois (Haudenosaunees). The French formed an alliance with the Hurons and their allies and assisted them in their wars against the Iroquois. As a consequence of this union, the French traded many guns to the Hurons, who with the aid of this advanced technology gained a decisive edge over the Iroquois and drove them southward.

Franco-Indian alliances ensured a steady fur supply to Montreal. This situation remained static, except for the dealings of the *coureurs de bois* (runners of the woods), until 1608, when Samuel de Champlain embarked from Montreal and opened a canoe route up the Ottawa River to the Georgian Bay on Lake Huron. This became the major thoroughfare for furs and trade goods coming into or out of the Great Lakes region. Fur traders in the interior used European-manufactured goods as an enticement for Indian men to trap more furbearing animals than was necessary for subsistence and to trade excess furs to the French for items the Indians valued, such as guns, steel kettles, steel knives, and hatchets, or wanted, such as blankets, beads, metal objects, clothing, ammunition, jewelry, and tobacco.

Dutch Fur Traders

With the arrival of Dutch fur traders on the Hudson River in 1610 the situation became more complex. They erected Fort Orange (present-day Albany, New York) on the Hudson, and the post quickly became the fur trade center of the Iroquois. Dutch traders explored the Connecticut, Delaware, and Mohawk Rivers, established good relations with the Iroquois, and pressed westward into the Ohio River and Great Lakes region. The Iroquois armed themselves with Dutch firearms and forced a power realignment by ambushing Hurons bringing furs to Montreal and Quebec. With beaver numbers diminishing in the Northeast and the Iroquois's desire for foreign-made trade goods increasing, success against the Hurons spurred the Iroquois to extend their influence over Great Lakes tribes. This situation only compounded earlier animosities between the Iroquois and the Hurons, and by 1642 the struggle for fur trade supremacy led to warfare. The

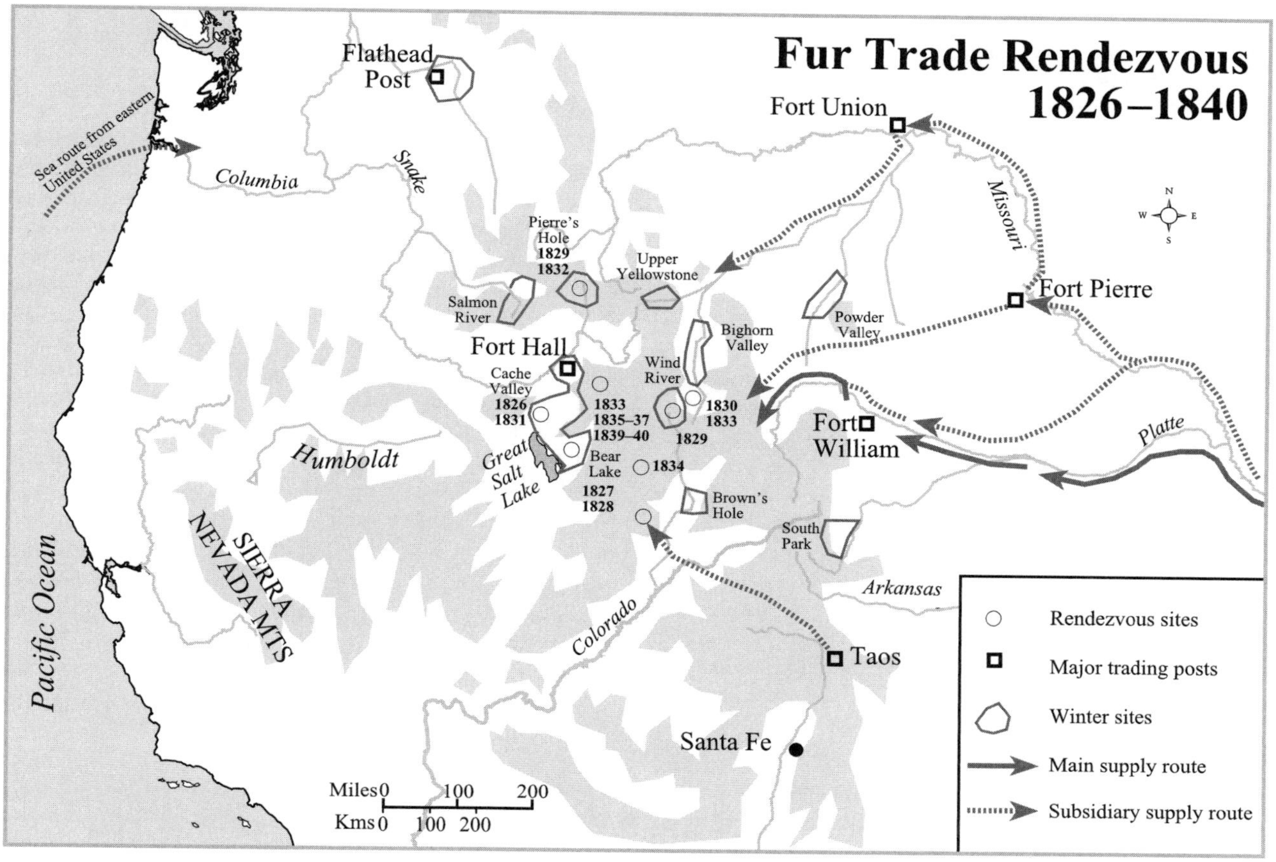

Iroquois funneled most of the northern furs to Fort Orange as Huron influence waned, although some Ottawas and Hurons resurfaced as fur trade middlemen.

The English displaced the Dutch in North America in 1664 and became the principal Iroquois suppliers. Iroquois land was too remote for England's initial settlement plans, and the Iroquois's service as fur trade intermediaries suited both nations since they became a buffer to French incursion. The five Nations—Mohawk, Oneida, Onondaga, Cayuga, and Seneca—generally sided with the English but retained their sovereignty. Armed with English guns and trade goods, Iroquois warriors penetrated into areas as far south as Virginia and as far west as Wisconsin. This combination of military power and quality English trade goods extended Iroquois influence into the rich furbearing region between the Great Lakes and the Ohio River.

Hudson's Bay Company

During the 1660s the English also gained a foothold north of New France. Ironically two Frenchmen, Medart Chouart, Sieur de Groseilliers, and Pierre Radisson, both experienced explorers and fur traders, unwittingly expanded the British Empire. Unable to interest their government in an expedition to Hudson Bay, they induced the English Crown to finance such a venture in 1668. The trading expedition into the Hudson Bay area experienced immediate economic success. In 1670 King Charles II founded and granted a royal charter to the Hudson's Bay Company (HBC). The royal charter gave the small group of London financiers a North American empire covering nearly 5 million square miles of land (called Rupert's Land after the king's cousin) drained by the rivers flowing into the bay. Additionally the HBC received a fur trade monopoly and the rights to establish local governments, make laws, and enact Indian treaties.

The imperial trading company, headquartered in London and run by a governor and committee with little fur trade acumen, nevertheless had significant financial backing that enabled it to weather market fluctuations. Most of the company's men or "servants" came from the English working class, while the "officers" were usually parsimonious Scotsmen. Officers received preferential treatment, and promotion from the lower ranks was rare. The HBC's business strategy included constructing trading forts or factories where large rivers flowed into the bay and local Indians brought their furs to barter. The bureaucracy of the HBC moved slowly in new directions over the next century, but when it did establish a policy, the company followed it relentlessly.

The company's activities and monopoly greatly reduced the influence of Indian middlemen in the French fur trade. With seashore locations, the HBC gained an advantage by obtaining English trade goods more easily, at less cost, and closer to the interior than the French, who used inland waterways to transport trade goods from Montreal. French trade goods could not compete with the quality of English-made hatchets and Caribbean tobacco, resulting in the further constriction of the French fur trade between the HBC to the north and the Anglo-Iroquois alliance to the south.

Westward Fur Trade Expansion

By the 1730s fur traders ventured down the Mississippi River, establishing trading relationships along the way. The reconnaissance of the French fur trader Pierre Gaultier de Varennes, Sieur de La Vérendrye, and his sons extended from the Lake of the Woods and the Saskatchewan River to the Missouri River and Bighorn Mountains in search of a viable western water route from the Great Lakes. As the French expanded their presence into the Great Plains, they competed with the HBC and Albany traders already established there. The French strategy involved intercepting and diverting the existing fur traffic to Montreal by relying upon the intertribal relationships of the *coureurs de bois* and the kinship ties created with their Métis offspring.

To combat these advantages, the HBC departed from its traditional business plan of allowing the Indians to come to it and actively searched for new trading partners. The company dispatched Anthony Henday from York Factory on the bay in 1754 to ascend the Saskatchewan River and entice the Blackfoot Indians to come trade at the factory. Henday and his Cree guide wintered among the Blackfeet near present-day Calgary but could not induce them to come trade at Hudson Bay. Concurrently the French constructed military forts along the Ohio and Kentucky Rivers. These actions brought the English and their Indian allies into direct conflict with the French and their Indian allies. On the forks of the Ohio River, the French and the British both tried to establish outposts, Fort Duquesne (French) and Fort Pitt (British), to control the interior. From 1756 to 1763 the French and Indian War raged, the fourth and final conflict between France and England for the North American continent. The 1763 Treaty of Ghent ended France's North American empire and helped the British gain additional Indian allies in the Old Northwest.

The French and Indian War did not curtail the fur trade for long, and soon HBC personnel moved into the interior. Independent traders—Frenchmen, Scotsmen, Englishmen, and Bostonians—began frequenting Lake Winnipeg and the Saskatchewan River, following La Vérendrye's route from Grand Portage on the northern shore of Lake Superior. They used overland and river travel to Rainy Lake, traveling upriver to Lake Winnipeg before crossing La Pas and dropping down to the Saskatchewan River. The introduction of the steel trap in the late 1790s and the use of castoreum (trapper's bait) led to the depopulation of beaver in entire watersheds and required migration to new trapping areas. This constant movement by fur traders and Indian hunters proved vital to imperial westward expansion.

The fur trade dominated Anglo-Indian interactions following the war. The two sides often found a middle ground in their dealings. The Iroquois had been trapping and trading beaver to Europeans for over 150 years, and they became an influential force in the Northeast and surrounding areas. With the expulsion of the French, the fur trade centers included the English colony at Albany, New York, which received furs collected by the Iroquois and their allies from the Great Lakes regions; the remaining French Canadians (Québec Pedlars) at Montreal, who relied on the Ottawas and *coureurs de bois* to bring in furs gathered from Crees, Ojibways, and Assiniboines on the northern Plains; and the HBC's York Factory and Fort Churchill, which garnered the northern trade.

North West Company

For the French Canadians to compete against the Hudson's Bay Company in the Old Northwest, it was necessary to commingle resources and talent to counter the HBC's powerful leadership and strong economic support in London. The North West Company (NWC) was initially established in 1784 and was modified in 1787 and 1790. Seven founders, Alexander Mackenzie, Peter Pond, Norman MacLeod, John Gregory, Peter Pangman, Simon McTavish, and Benjamin Frobisher, consolidated their different fur trade interests, creating a flexible, loosely organized company consisting of three entities. Wintering partners made up of Scotsmen and Englishmen, who had spent the greater part of their adult lives in the fur trade and knew the business, stayed in the field and traded with the Indians. Most had served as trading post clerks before becoming partners and receiving NWC shares. They made agreements with the Montreal-based financial agents, who handled the buying and selling of furs and supplies. Both groups benefited in company profits according to the number of shares they owned. The third component consisted of French-Canadian *voyageurs*, who paddled canoes, carried supplies, erected buildings, and provided the manual labor. Each August all three groups met at either the Grand Portage on the northern shore of Lake Superior or at Fort William fourteen miles to the north. Here they exchanged annual fur catches for supplies, and a Montreal-based partner brought the latest news, reported on HBC activities, and presented the NWC's plans for the coming year.

The North West Company felt it imperative to find an overland route to the Pacific Ocean. On a July evening in 1793 Mackenzie's expedition arrived at the western ocean by land. Soon thereafter NWC men journeyed from the headwaters of the Peace River across the Rocky Mountains and down to the Pacific. Mackenzie's route was not commercially viable, so the NWC decided to send an expedition to find a more favorable route across the Rockies in 1800. After his failed attempt in 1801, the fur trader David Thompson returned in 1807 and successfully completed the venture.

Enterprises in the Pacific Northwest

The Spanish explorer Juan Cabrillo first reached the Pacific Northwest and California in 1543. Spanish merchant ships used these waters to harvest sea otter and to replenish supplies for the Manila galleon trade existing between Manila and Mexico. Vitus Bering, a Dane sailing under the Russian flag, ascertained the rich fur resources along the Aleutian Islands and Alaskan coast and prompted additional Spanish voyages. The British were sailing too, and in 1778 the English sea captain James Cook initiated Vancouver Island's role as a British port of call. While there he noticed the Indians' eagerness to trade sea otter skins for European trade goods. He acquired some of the furs and set sail for China, where he found a lucrative market for the pelts. News of his successful venture spread quickly.

Spain, concerned about the lucrative China trade, sent Captain Estevan José Martínez to rectify the situation and expel the interlopers. Martínez sailed up the California coast, burning foreign trading posts wherever he found them. Upon entering Nootka Sound, a harbor on Vancouver Island, he burned the English trading house and captured an English merchant ship at anchor and sent it and its crew to Mexico. This action precipitated an international incident that almost escalated into an Anglo-Spanish war. Open hostilities were averted when Spain relinquished claim to the territory between the forty-second and fifty-fourth parallels bounded on the east by the Rocky Mountains.

The Nootka Sound Treaty of 1790 ended Spanish claims in the Pacific Northwest and prompted British, American, and Russian traders to move in. Grigorii Shelekhov's Russian-American Company (RAC), awarded monopolistic control over fur trading by Tsar Paul I in 1799, became one of Europe's major fur trading ventures. Irkutsk merchants and *promyshlenniks* (fur hunter entrepreneurs) operated from the Bering Sea to the California coast. Throughout their three districts, Unalaska, Atka, and Kodiak, the RAC employed adept Aleutian hunters to harvest sea otter pelts. Under the leadership of Alexandr Baronov, chief manager of the RAC at Kodiak and later at Sitka, the Russians expanded southward and established Fort Ross just north of San Francisco Bay to raise crops and hunt sea otters in 1812. By 1824 Russia withdrew its claim to settle south of Alaska and in 1841 sold Fort Ross to the German immigrant John Sutter.

Yankee merchants eagerly rushed in to compete with the NWC and the HBC in the lucrative Pacific Northwest trade. Bostonians frequented the Northwest coast, and in 1792 the American Robert Gray's ship the *Columbia* penetrated the river that bears that name. Mackenzie's expedition to the Pacific inspired President Thomas Jefferson to formulate plans for a similar American venture. After acquiring the Louisiana Purchase in 1803, Jefferson sent Meriwether Lewis and William Clark on their epic overland journey to establish a commercial route between the Columbia and Missouri Rivers. The Corps of Discovery ascended the Missouri during the summer of 1804 and wintered near the Mandan villages, where they found several British traders. The following year they crossed the Rocky Mountains and descended the Columbia to the Pacific, where they constructed Fort Clatsop. Not meeting a Yankee vessel for a possible return voyage, they returned overland in 1806 and arrived back in St. Louis by late summer.

Though Lewis and Clark correctly ascertained that a direct water route across North America did not exist, their friendly receptions by dozens of Indian tribes and their reports of vast quantities of beaver and river otter in Rocky Mountain streams sparked a number of fur trade ventures that established St. Louis as the gateway to the West. A number of companies and individuals who had been involved in the lower Missouri trade quickly turned their attention to the upper Missouri. In the spring of 1807 Manuel Lisa took men and trade goods up the Missouri and constructed Fort Raymond at the Bighorn River's confluence with the Yellowstone. The success of their venture prompted Lisa, Clark, and other influential Missourians, such as the Chouteau family, to form the Missouri Fur Company to exploit the Rockies' rich fur resources.

With the exception of the British-allied members of the Blackfoot Confederacy—Piegans, Bloods, Blackfeet, and Atsinas—most western tribes took advantage of and welcomed American traders and their goods. The Blackfoot Confederacy, angered by the killing of two of its warriors by Lewis in 1806, relentlessly pursued American traders, stole their horses and goods, and forcibly drove them from the upper Missouri by 1811. This hostility combined with the effects of the War of 1812 temporarily ended the interior fur trade as St. Louis merchants contented themselves with trading on the lower Missouri. Concurrently the United States began the factory system in the 1790s to provide Indians with goods at cost in exchange for furs and to undermine British influence. Though some trading houses experienced success, the system never met expectations and was discontinued in 1822.

On the Pacific coast Gray's voyage and Lewis and Clark bolstered U.S. claims to the Columbia River basin. John Jacob Astor, owner of the American Fur Company (AFC), felt that the Pacific Northwest fur trade could yield a large profit. In 1810 he founded a subsidiary, the Pacific Fur Company, that involved three former North West Company principals, Alexander McKay, Donald Mackenzie, and Duncan McDougall, plus the American partners Wilson Price Hunt, Ramsay Crooks, Robert McClellan, and Joseph Miller. They hired enterprise clerks, *voyageurs*, trappers, and hunters, and Astor owned one-half of the company's shares.

Under Attack. Moving deep into Indian lands long before most other whites, fur trappers and traders often established good relations with Natives—but not always, as depicted in this engraving showing a barge on the Missouri River coming under fire. © CORBIS

Astor established the Pacific Fur Company presence on the Columbia using a two-pronged plan. The seagoing party comprised of partners and clerks on board the *Tonquin* sailed from New York around South America and arrived at the Columbia's mouth in March 1811. After unloading the provisions and trade goods, they erected Fort Astoria. The overland Astorians, about sixty-five in number and under the command of Hunt, arrived in St. Louis, where they reoutfitted before ascending the Missouri to present-day St. Joseph. In the spring of 1811 Hunt abandoned the Lewis and Clark route and headed west, hoping to find a southern pass through the Rocky Mountains. His entourage faced numerous hardships and split into several groups before the majority finally arrived at Fort Astoria in January 1812.

The outbreak of war dashed Astor's dream of fur trade profits on the Columbia. With a British takeover probable, Astor sold Fort Astoria to the NWC, who changed the name to Fort George. Excluding Hunt, many of Astor's employees signed up with the new owners, and Robert Stuart led the returning Astorians overland back to St. Louis. The 1814 Treaty of Ghent officially ended the War of 1812, and in 1818 a joint-occupation agreement allowed private citizens of both England and the United States to enter and conduct business in this region.

During the next few years the NWC did not actively trap beaver in the Snake River country because of the availability of beaver in northern regions. In 1816 the NWC decided to supply Fort George by sea and to trap beaver itself. To expedite the latter, skilled Iroquois trappers in large brigades replaced the trading posts. Donald Mackenzie led the first Snake country expedition in 1818. These expeditions did their own trapping, traded sparingly with Indians, remained in the field for long periods of time, and experienced great success.

In 1821 excessive violence and financial competition between the NWC and the HBC caused the king and Parliament to force a merger. The Hudson's Bay Company acquired all of the NWC's assets while retaining the name and corporate structure of the HBC. As a result the Snake River area gained geopolitical significance. Of the HBC's eighteen major districts, the one wherein the Snake country resided ranked third in total fur harvest. Governor George Simpson decided to turn the region into a fur desert to discourage American encroachment from the Rockies.

Missouri and Santa Fe

Mexican independence from Spain in 1821 made it possible for Missouri merchants to openly trade with Santa Fe via the Santa Fe Trail. Traders like William Becknell set out, and soon men such as Ewing Young, Josiah Gregg, and Kit Carson were trapping in the southern Rockies. The mercantile trade incorporated and stimulated the southwestern fur trade. In addition New Mexico–based brigades and French trappers such as Étienne Provost pushed northward along the streams of present-day Utah and Colorado, while Charles Bent and William Bent constructed Bent's Fort on the Arkansas River.

The opening of the Santa Fe Trail prompted Missouri lawmakers to petition for the end of the government factory system. The end of government-sponsored trading houses in 1822 opened up new opportunities for Americans and caused a number of trading companies to enter the competition. In addition to Astor's well-organized American Fur Company, smaller companies and partnerships formed, like the partnership of Andrew Henry and William H. Ashley in 1822, intent upon extracting furs from the northern and central Rockies. Henry led a party of enterprising young men to the Yellowstone and built a fort. The trappers of this era, including James Clyman, Jedediah Smith, William Sublette, Robert Campbell, Thomas Fitzpatrick, James Beckworth, and James (Jim) Bridger, achieved legendary status.

Fortune did not smile on the partnership. In 1822 their boat loaded with $10,000 of trade goods sank in the Missouri. The following year Ashley attempted to bring additional supplies up the Missouri only to be stopped at the Arikara villages at the mouth of the Grand River. The Arikaras enjoyed their powerful position as fur trade middlemen and felt American trappers threatened their hegemony. Warriors attacked Ashley's party, killing a dozen or more, and Ashley went back to St. Louis. He returned as part of a punitive expedition under the command of Colonel Henry Leavenworth to reassert American military might on the Missouri.

Rocky Mountain Fur Trade

Ashley and Henry had been defeated on the Missouri River. Their enterprise sustained staggering losses and faced bankruptcy. They attempted to improvise by trading and trapping in the Rocky Mountains. Henry returned to Fort Henry at the mouth of the Yellowstone River, retrieved the men and trade goods there, and proceeded up the Yellowstone and Bighorn Rivers to trap beaver and trade with the Crows. Jedediah Smith left Fort Kiowa in 1823, leading another group of Ashley's men west to join those at the Crow villages near the Wind River Mountains. That winter both groups trapped and traded for large numbers of furs and learned of a nearby mountain pass that had little snow and led to a river (Green River) abounding in beaver. The area was inhabited by the friendly Eastern Shoshones, who had not engaged in trapping.

In the spring Smith traveled over South Pass into the Green River drainage, noting the feasibility of wagon travel. This rediscovery of a southern mountain pass noted by the returning Astorians in 1812 afforded easy passage over the Continental Divide. Within a few decades the pass would be utilized by those traveling the Oregon-California and Mormon Trails. Once across Smith divided his men into several brigades for the spring hunt. At the conclusion of the trapping season, Henry, Fitzpatrick, and Clyman returned to St. Louis via the Yellowstone River with the winter and spring catches. The remaining trappers stayed in the mountains for the upcoming fall hunt.

The year's returns made up Ashley's previous losses plus a substantial gain. By November 1824 Ashley organized a pack train caravan to transport supplies to the trappers in the mountains. At a preselected rendezvous site the mountain men traded furs for supplies. Ashley's departure from relying upon Indians to enterprising young men staying in the mountains year-round to procure furs worked. Annual supply caravans and the summer rendezvous replaced the need for trading posts and laborious river travel up the Missouri, saving both time and money. The men gathered in "winter quarters" for companionship and mutual protection in December, when the streams froze over, and remained until the March thaw. Sixteen annual rendezvous took place between 1825 and 1840 in Utah, Idaho, and Wyoming, the majority on tributaries of the Green. These commercial gatherings became rich social events, and the duration often depended on the availability and quantity of liquor.

Upon his return to St. Louis, Henry notified Ashley of his desire to leave the fur trade business, so Ashley needed a new partner. At the conclusion of the 1825 rendezvous on Henry's Fork of the Green, Ashley formed a partnership with Smith. Ashley taught him how to be an agent, how to buy trade goods and provisions, and how to market furs and get financial backing. In March 1826 Ashley went to the second rendezvous accompanied by Smith and Robert Campbell, a man who spent the rest of his life providing financial backing to fur trade ventures and thereby became quite prosperous. At the end of the 1826 Cache Valley rendezvous (Utah), Ashley's returns for the year exceeded $60,000, and he entered Missouri's political arena.

The American fur trade proceeded as a succession of small firms vying for control of the Rocky Mountain trade. Individual trappers did not acquire much wealth, but the St. Louis business partners generally turned a small profit. With Ashley gone, Smith asked David Jackson and William Sublette to take over Ashley's share of the business, although Ashley retained the rights to supply their trade goods and to market their furs. In 1830 Astor's American Fur Company sent trappers into the Rockies to compete head-to-head with the trio and to construct Fort Union on the upper Missouri. Smith, Jackson, and Sublette decided to sell their partnership to Fitz-

Trappers. Trapping was not just a corporate enterprise, as indicated by this 1908 photograph of two men (identified as "Crab Tree boys"), their father, dogs, and burros in Arizona Territory; their cabin was "located on Long Creek, at the entrance of Hell's Hip Pocket in Brown's Basin, between Four Peaks and Salt River." NATIONAL ARCHIVES AND RECORDS ADMINISTRATION

patrick, James Bridger, Milton Sublette, Henry Fraeb, and Jean Baptiste Gervais, who formed the Rocky Mountain Fur Company. Partnership changes, demands from creditors, fluctuating markets, and competition from the AFC made turning a profit almost impossible.

In 1834 the principal creditors and suppliers of the Rocky Mountain Fur Company (RMFC), William Sublette and Campbell, demanded payment. Unable to meet its obligations, the RMFC sold its interests and the newly constructed Fort Laramie to the AFC. By 1838 the market had declined considerably owing to the shift in fashions from beaver hats to silk hats and beaver depletion. That year the AFC decided to leave the Rocky Mountain fur trade and sold to Pierre Chouteau Jr. and Company. Most of the trappers returned to the East or traveled west to Oregon and California.

After 1840 the popularity of silk, the dominance of the AFC and the HBC, and the growing bison robe trade on the Great Plains resulted in a gradual decline of the fur trade's potent economic force. Pierre Chouteau Jr. and Company dominated the robe trade on the Missouri, though Campbell backed several rival firms. Bent, St. Vrain, and Company controlled the trade on the southern Plains. By the 1870s only the HBC remained, but the North American fur trade left a lasting legacy. The explorations and travel brought an intimate knowledge of the geography and inhabitants of the continent. The caravans to and from the rendezvous from Missouri and HBC men traveling from Oregon paved the way for later overland migration. Until the nineteenth century the fur trade was primarily an Indian trade and generally speaking engendered positive relationships that lasted until the post–Civil War era. This lifestyle has often been romanticized, but it was hard work. The men lived in fear of grizzly or Indian attacks and endured inclement weather, illness, and hunger. Images of "mountain men" historically bring to mind individual trappers in the lone wilderness. While some truth resides in this, it should be remembered that this trade was generally conducted with large brigades as part of a corporate enterprise. It is perhaps telling that only the largest one of all, the Hudson's Bay Company, remained in business at the end of the twentieth century.

BIBLIOGRAPHY

Anderson, William Marshall. *The Rocky Mountain Journals of William Marshall Anderson: The West in 1834.* Edited by Dale L. Morgan and Eleanor Towles Harris. San Marino, Calif.: The Huntington Library, 1967. Reprint Lincoln: University of Nebraska Press, 1987.

Berry, Don. *A Majority of Scoundrels: An Informal History of the Rocky Mountain Fur Company.* New York: Harper, 1961.

Cleland, Robert Glass. *This Reckless Breed of Men: The Trappers and Fur Traders of the Southwest.* New York: Knopf, 1963.

Gibson, James R. *Imperial Russia in Frontier America.* New York: Oxford University Press, 1976.

———. *Otter Skins, Boston Ships, and China Goods: The Maritime Fur Trade of the Northwest Coast, 1795–1841.* Montreal: McGill-Queen's University Press, 1992.

Gowans, Fred R. *Rocky Mountain Rendezvous: A History of the Fur Trade Rendezvous, 1825–1840.* Provo, Utah: Brigham Young University Press, 1976.

Hafen, LeRoy R., ed. *The Mountain Men and the Fur Trade of the Far West.* 10 vols. Glendale, Calif.: Arthur H. Clark, 1965–1972.

Innis, Harold A. *The Fur Trade of Canada.* Rev. ed. Toronto: University of Toronto Press, 1956.

Lavender, David. *The Fist in the Wilderness.* Garden City, N.Y.: Doubleday, 1964.

Oglesby, Richard Edward. *Manuel Lisa and the Opening of the Missouri Fur Trade.* Norman: University of Oklahoma Press, 1963.

Phillips, Paul C., and J. W. Smurr. *The Fur Trade.* 2 vols. Norman: University of Oklahoma Press, 1961.

Ray, Arthur J. *Indians in the Fur Trade: Their Role as Trappers, Hunters, and Middlemen in the Lands Southwest of Hudson Bay, 1660–1870.* Toronto: University of Toronto Press, 1974.

Rich, E. E. *The History of the Hudson's Bay Company, 1670–1870.* 2 vols. New York: Macmillan, 1960.

Robertson, R. G. *Competitive Struggle: America's Western Fur Trading Posts, 1764–1865.* Boise, Idaho: Tamarack Books, 1999.

Ronda, James P. *Astoria and Empire.* Lincoln: University of Nebraska Press, 1990.

Russell, Carl P. *Firearms, Traps, and Tools of the Mountain Men.* Albuquerque: University of New Mexico Press, 1967.

Sunder, John E. *The Fur Trade on the Upper Missouri, 1840–1865.* Norman: University of Oklahoma Press, 1965.

Van Kirk, Sylvia. *Many Tender Ties: Women in Fur-Trade Society, 1670–1870.* Norman: University of Oklahoma Press, 1983.

Washburn, Wilcomb E., ed. *History of Indian-White Relations.* Volume 4 of *Handbook of North American Indians,* edited by William C. Sturtevant et al. Washington, D.C.: Smithsonian Institution Press, 1990.

Weber, David J. *The Taos Trappers: The Fur Trade in the Far Southwest, 1540–1846.* Norman: University of Oklahoma Press, 1971.

Wishart, David J. *The Fur Trade of the American West, 1807–1840: A Geographical Synthesis.* Lincoln: University of Nebraska Press, 1979.

Jay H. Buckley
Lyn S. Clayton

See also **Fur Companies; Missouri River Fur Trade.**

FURNITURE. Far from being of a single style or culture, the first two centuries of furniture made in America reflects the transplanted tastes of many peoples, each beholden to their country of origin, and each restrained by geography and communication.

Colonial Furniture

In seventeenth- and eighteenth-century New England, and farther south along the East Coast, the predominant colonizers were English. The Hudson Valley became Dutch, while Swedes and Germans settled in parts of Pennsylvania. Production was local, mostly utilitarian, and immediate: stools, benches, small tables, and chests with drawers. Furniture construction was simple, medieval, and based on few tools. The resulting shapes were massive, boxy, and mostly without ornament, except for an occasional turning to emphasize leg, rungs, stretchers, and backs. Shallow carving, called "Kerbschnitt," formed geometric bands, leaves, and rosettes, on some flat areas. Later in the seventeenth century, Kerbschnitt became more elaborate. In all the colonies, chairs with straight backs and rush seats were common, and new decorative elements found wide acceptance. Refinements and the latest style came from the mother country and were available in very limited scope to those who could afford it. The Carver chair, a chair honored with the name of the first governor of Plymouth, is an example.

While American colonial furniture was distinctly functional, often serving more than one purpose, simple in design, and heavy looking, it was just as likely to employ Renaissance forms long outmoded in Europe as it was the more up-to-date baroque decorative elements that emphasized carving. As in Europe, the Baroque came in several variations.

As the wealth of the colonies increased, first in the South, so did the demand for quality furniture. A variety of indigenous soft and hardwoods, such as pine, birch, maple, oak, hickory, and later walnut, were easily available to colonial furniture craftsmen. With each boat, new furniture forms arrived, including cane-back, slat-back, and leather-back chairs, as well as upholstered chairs, better known as easy chairs. Counted among the new pieces of useful furniture were tall clocks, high chests with drawers, and storage boxes. Furniture was often named after its area of manufacture, such as the Hartford chests of Connecticut or the Hadley chests of Massachusetts, or it was given a broad, general style-based definition—like Restoration or William and Mary—by later scholars. Construction characteristics included thin drawer linings; dovetail construction; walnut veneers; fruitwoods such as peach, apple and cherry; and chased-brass mounts instead of iron and wooden knobs. Two-tiered cupboards became popular, utilizing carving and turned decoration in the English manner. A new domestic element was the Bible box. With a secure lid, it held a Bible, but also important papers. Where space was available, it often had its own stand. By the mid-eighteenth century, the demand for comfort had grown considerably among newly prospering merchants, resulting in finer homes, with refined interiors and elaborate furnishings. Out went simple, bulky, and functional rural furniture. In came European baroque and rococo styling—elegant urban designs in Queen Anne and Chippendale styles that fit better in the enlarged houses, which now contained a central hall, a dining room, and two parlors, including a formal one with a sofa, chairs, mirror, and several small tables. Each room required specific furniture.

Starting about 1725, the fundamental baroque qualities of the William and Mary style began to merge with the more sophisticated Queen Anne forms. With its lean and taut S-shaped cabriolet legs, pad, trifid, or pointed feet, it dominated the American British colonies for the next three decades. American Queen Anne was simpler than its English counterpart. Where the English relied on carving and gilding for decoration, Americans sought symmetry and proportion, while respecting the natural qualities of the wood. On both sides of the Atlantic, claw-and-ball feet ruled. Knees on high chests and chairs sometimes appear to buckle under the weight of scalloped shells and volutes. Whatever else it boasted, the most important element of Queen Anne was the cyma curve—the one William Hogarth called a serpentine "line of beauty." No part of a piece of furniture was spared the curve—not the solid back, the vase-shaped splats, or the bow-shaped crest. Its use went beyond decoration and into the piece of furniture itself.

In major urban centers, direct links to European craftsmen were established through royal governors, successful merchants, and immigrant craftsmen. The impact of Thomas Chippendale's *Gentleman and Cabinet-Maker's Director: Being a Large Collection of the Most Elegant and Useful Designs of Household Furniture in the Gothic, Chinese, and Modern Taste*, first published in England in 1754, did not become felt in the colonies until about 1760. It is by his name that American furniture of the Rococo is known.

While Queen Anne furniture lingered as a rival, Chippendale's pierced chair-back splats as illustrated in his pattern book and copied by skilled local craftsmen, became the rage in the British colonies of the 1760s and 1770s. While the pattern books themselves were scarce, the fundamental forms were widely current, and from them developed an indigenous style. Furniture making was one of the first trades in which American craftsmen could both match and free themselves from dependence on their English counterparts. In every urban center, mahogany, an expensive wood from the Caribbean, quickly supplanted the traditional indigenous Queen Anne favorites, walnut, maple, and cherry. Furniture was now found all over the house. Instead of gentle cyma curves, the C- and S-scrolls dominated. A notable innovation was the upholstered armchair. Widespread ownership of Chinese ceramics resulted in another new furniture form: the corner cupboard.

French-inspired bombé double chests and desk-bookcases became a specialty of Boston. Boston is also credited with introducing block-front furniture, including the widely popular blocked-front desk, an innovation by Goddard and Townsend, two Quaker cabinetmaker families in Newport, Rhode Island. The front of the chest, commode, or bureau-bookcase was divided into three vertical panels, or blocks. The middle block was mildly concave causing the blocks on either side to appear slightly projecting. Accenting this subtlety was a shell motif, carved alternately concave and convex. At this same time, the four-poster canopy bed with hangings of linen, wool, and damask became fashionable.

An elaborate French influence swept Philadelphia, the largest city in British America. Here, in the hands of William Savery, the highboy became the trophy of the Rococo in America. Philadelphia furniture craftsmen also focused on the production of the ubiquitous English Windsor chair. By far the most popular chairs inside and outside the home throughout the colonies, the Windsor—simple, utilitarian, and made of commonly available wood—quickly established itself as an American chair type. In Philadelphia, the Windsor achieved a lean elegance accented by lathe-turned legs and stretchers. Bows for the back were shaped by steam.

In the spirit of the times, American craftsmen ardently advanced technologies and, after independence, became leaders in innovative labor-saving devices used in all aspects of manufacturing. Starting in 1818 in Connecticut, Lambert Hitchcock pioneered a derivative of the Windsor chair with easy to assemble, mass-produced parts, which he shipped to the Midwest and southern locations for assemblage, painting, and stenciling. The finished chairs were distributed by the thousands around the country.

The Nineteenth Century

When publications introduced European neoclassicism to America in the 1780s and 1790s, their scholarly, archaeologically founded classical revival was taken as an appropriate expression of the young Republic, a trend that merged well with the new ideals of government. The publications of Robert Adam were indispensable, though they were known mostly through the designs in George Hepplewhite's *Cabinet-Maker and Upholsterer's Guide*, published posthumously by his wife in 1788. The Hepplewhite style is characterized by the use of Marlborough legs (a tapering leg of square section), shield-backed chairs, and a restrained application of classical ornament. Basic classical revival needs were also satisfied by Thomas Sheraton, whose *Cabinet-Maker and Upholsterer's Drawing Book*, issued in four parts (1791–1794), found immediate resonance.

At much the same time, Duncan Phyfe began to make his reputation in New York, a reputation based on a still much-admired classical style. By 1820, Phyfe employed one hundred workers, each specializing in his own craft, and all working under one roof for one employer. Specialty craftsmen, upholsterers, inlay makers, turners, carvers, and gilders working as allied artists became the staple of the urban furniture industry. Rural cabinetmakers, by contrast, could do it all.

Based on Greek and Roman forms and named after the first empire of Napoleon, the Empire style—as it was defined by the furniture designed by Charles Percier and Pierre-François-Léonard Fontaine, both of Paris—became all the vogue about 1800 in France. The main thrust of Empire furniture arrived in New York in 1803, with the émigré cabinetmaker Charles-Honoré Lannuier. It quickly spread throughout America. Bookcases became Greek temples, couches became Roman beds, consoles became ancient altars, and clocks became pyramids. Archaeological forms were often misunderstood. Adam's Pompeian delicacy became Greco-Egyptian solidity. A major characteristic of American Empire is the increased weight of all the parts. It was wildly popular.

Unconcerned with national styles and trends, uncomplicated forms of the eighteenth century dominated the furniture of the Shakers, a religious sect. Refining their style throughout the nineteenth century, the makers of Shaker furniture became a major influence on modern design from the 1880s on.

Unhampered by a rigid economic and social structure, furniture craftsmen and manufacturers in Boston, New York, and Philadelphia followed the population bubble west and set up businesses as required. Along the way, furniture craftsmen adopted and invented labor-saving machines like no other industry had before. The immediate results were acceleration in the division of labor and a significant reduction in cost, as well as constant striving for novelty combined with elegance. New Orleans, Cincinnati, and Chicago quickly developed into primary nodes of furniture production. By 1825, a steam-driven planing and grooving machine was running in Cincinnati, a city that by 1850 claimed 136 furniture-making facilities producing some $1.6 million in product and employing 1,156 hands. With the development of a national railroad distribution system after the Civil War, Chicago became the nation's center of furniture production.

The great international exhibitions in London, Paris, Vienna, Philadelphia, and Chicago sped the global diffusion of ideas in furniture design and contributed significantly to the wars of styles so evident in America in the second half of the nineteenth century. By the 1850s, as the need to represent Empire waned, American interior decorating and furniture design fell under the spell of the Gothic Revival style. Applied to any and all surfaces, its repetitive patterns were found to be especially suitable to machine production. Those aspiring to a more aristocratic elegance sought out French-inspired revivals of baroque and rococo styles.

By merging genuine historic design with machine production and innovative handcraftsmanship, in New York, John Henry Belter and the Herter Brothers emerged as inspired, independent forces in America's furniture industry. Both were much admired and copied. By combining marble with gilding and textured silk and satin, using color as pattern, and adding thin legs to thick furniture, mass produced furniture lost all semblance of tradition,

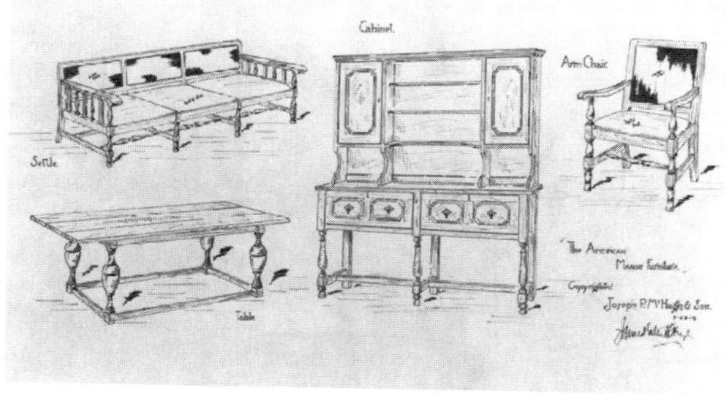

American Manor Furniture. Design drawings by James Paten McHugh of a settee (the variant spelling here, "settle," now more commonly refers to a bench with an enclosed chest under the seat), table, cabinet, and armchair, 1917. LIBRARY OF CONGRESS

while satisfying America's eclectic markets. New furniture forms, the ottoman, the lazy Susan table, and the wardrobe, joined those with a pedigree. Championing craftsmanship traditions rooted in the honesty of medieval and Renaissance construction, *Hints on Household Taste in Furniture, Upholstery and Other Details* (1868) by Charles Lock Eastlake, was catapulted into a vogue known as the Eastlake style.

Elegance may fade, but it never dies. In the 1880s, the nation fell under the spell of French academics, this time from the École des Beaux-Arts in Paris, whose support of authentic reproductions of period furnishings found broad support among America's wealthy. But American intellectuals and designers cheered strong nativism. They embraced the blossoms of the Orient that inspired forms compatible with the English Arts and Crafts style and philosophy.

Along the Arroyo Seco of Pasadena, California, the brothers Charles Sumner Green and Henry Mather Green built and exquisitely furnished a number of Japanese-influenced Craftsman-styled bungalows. The sensuous, languorous quality of California life influenced not only their style, but also that of their contemporaries Irving Gill, in San Diego, and Bernard Maybeck, in San Francisco. It was also in San Francisco that Arthur and Lucia Kleinhans Mathews founded The Furniture Shop in 1906, when the great earthquake provided a wealth of opportunity.

The Twentieth Century

In contrast, the bold lines and forthright detail characteristic of the Stickley brothers, Gustave, Leopold, and John George, are also representative of the early twentieth century. Known collectively as Craftsman or Mission, their furniture designs incorporated smooth rounded edges, elaborately pegged joints, and sometimes-intricate, sinuous inlay. In the early years of the twentieth century, Gustave Stickley sponsored furniture franchises from Los Angeles to Boston. In 1913 he opened large showrooms

Furniture Magazine. The August 1903 cover of *Grand Rapids Furniture Record* shows contemporary fashions in furniture—much of it manufactured in that Michigan city—and women's clothing. LIBRARY OF CONGRESS

in Manhattan. Two years later, he declared bankruptcy. The eccentric end of the movement is represented by Charles Rohlfs, who established his own furniture workshop in Buffalo, New York, in 1898, and soon was making entire rooms of furniture for wealthy clients throughout the United States.

By 1900, the Midwest became a hotbed of furniture design, led by such lights as Harvey Ellis, George Washington Maher, Frank Lloyd Wright, George Grant Elmslie, George Mann Niedecken, and William Gray Purcell. Two world's fairs showed off the achievements: the Chicago World's Columbian Exposition of 1893 and the Louisiana Purchase Exposition of 1904 in St. Louis. Chicago represented the apotheosis of the "American Renaissance," through Daniel Burnham's insistence on European beaux-arts influences. St. Louis presented to America the new, stylish, utilitarian modern designs of the Arts and Crafts movement. Frank Lloyd Wright is the undisputed leader. His synthesis of Louis Sullivan's organic ornament and impeccable construction, with simplified lines, forthright construction, and insistence on the totally designed environment that subjugated furnishings to architecture took the Arts and Crafts ideology to another level. While Wright never insisted on the handcrafting of furniture, he did maintain a close relationship with manufacturing firms and craftsmen who executed his designs. Foremost among them was Niedecken of Niedecken-Walbridge.

Impressed by the Stickley and Austrian exhibits at the Louisiana Purchase Exposition, Oscar Onken established The Shop of the Crafters in Cincinnati in 1904. Together with his lead employee, the Hungarian designer Paul Horti, who had worked on the Austrian exhibition at the fair, they created a distinctly European look in their furniture, distinguished by its use of inlays, applied carving, and painted designs.

Although little concerned with the theoretical foundations of the Arts and Crafts movement, Chicago-based mail-order houses like Sears Roebuck and Montgomery Ward introduced Mission-styled furnishings to a remarkably large cross-section of American society. While designers in Germany and France were successfully marketing tubular steel furniture and plate glass–topped tables, and Scandinavians were experimenting with plywood and curvilinear forms, seeking to break up mechanical regularity, some European-born American designers adopted the new rather than creating it. R. M. Schindler, Richard Neutra, Howe and Lescaze, Kem Weber, and others worked in the new idiom, but they did not make significant new contributions of their own. Meanwhile, Roebuck offered American-manufactured tubular steel chairs through its catalogs.

In startling contrast stood the mid-1920s luxurious American variants, based on the distinctly French modern furnishings created by Jacques-Emile Ruhlmann and others for the 1925 Paris Exposition Internationale des Arts Décoratifs et Industriels Modernes. While much admired, items were wildly expensive, resulting in a very limited following. Just as rare as French Deco in America were products of the Austrian Werkbund, Austria's semiofficial artists' guild, which became available in America in 1928 when Marianne Willisch began bringing annual exhibitions of modern crafts and furniture to the United States. In 1930, Willisch moved to Chicago. She was soon asked to furnish interiors, and she began to design and supervise the construction of furniture.

In 1933, the Chicago's second world's fair, Century of Progress Exposition, surpassed all previous fairs in the number of model houses on display; there were thirteen at the fair's opening, and twenty in its second season. Exceptionally popular and widely published, the twelve-sided House of Tomorrow and the all-glass Crystal House, both designed by Chicago architects George and Fred Keck, showed Bauhaus-inspired furniture designed by Leland Atwood.

Immediately after World War II, American furniture design again came into its own, based on models developed just prior to the war. In 1940, the Museum of Modern Art (MOMA) in New York inaugurated a competition for "organic Design in Home Furnishings," in which two architects, Eero Saarinen and Charles Eames, won the first prize for seating and other living room furniture. While sectional seating was not new, the MOMA prizes were revolutionary, for Saarinen and Eames united seats, back, and arm rests in a single shell made of veneer and glue and laminated in a cast iron mold. The shell was mounted on a base. This development greatly reduced the industrial process and would have immense consequences after the war. Charles and Ray Eames produced a series of furniture designs that proved to be classics. So did Eero Saarinen. Harry Bertoia's wire chairs and George Nelson's "coconut" chair and storage walls also became familiar to a broad public. Between them, Knoll and Herman Miller made available what seemed to be distinctly American modern furniture.

While wood and metal dominated American furniture design historically, plastic and fiberglass slowly became a visible furniture material by the early 1950s. Walter Papst in Germany designed the first one-piece plastic table in 1959. The following year, the first one-piece plastic chair was designed and patented by the American R. G. Reineman. By the early 1970s, plastic furniture was in the forefront of American furniture design. The introduction of vinyl and other plastic skins allowed the creation of flexible envelopes filled with beads of polystyrene, plastic foam, as in the "bean bag" chair, or filled with air for deflatable, temporary furniture. The new materials often required rounded forms to best accommodate them. Designers followed suit. In 1972, the architect Frank O. Gehry designed domestic furniture using paper—a laminated corrugated construction he named Easy Edges rocking chair.

At the same time, electronics began invading the home, dictating furniture shapes and room configurations that included not only an almost universally black-skinned television but various black electronic gadgets, each with its own specific LED lights. The introduction of these new furnishing devices were followed closely by computers, mostly beige, and large screen televisions, mostly wood finished.

These developments forced a wholly new aesthetic on American furniture design, one no longer based on construction but on casting, molding, and shaping and the color black, followed by beige, followed by pastels and primary colors. The keen interest in new materials and the exploiting of their potential in mostly rounded forms in the 1970s helped establish an interest in ergonomics and the environment. By the early 1990s, Donald Chadwick and William Stumpf designed the Aeron chair, which brought front-line radical ergonomic, anthropometric, and environmental considerations into the office. Other environmental furniture followed rapidly. While new colors and materials continued to be introduced, an aesthetic interest in retro furniture design of the 1950s, 1960s, and 1970s bloomed in the 1990s. This aesthetic continued to lead at the beginning of the twenty-first century.

BIBLIOGRAPHY

Darling, Sharon. *Chicago Furniture, Art, Craft, and History, 1833–1983.* New York: Norton, 1984.

Hanks, David A. *The Decorative Designs of Frank Lloyd Wright.* New York: Dutton, 1979.

Houston Museum of Fine Arts. *Herter Brothers: Furniture and Interiors for the Gilded Age.* Exhibition catalog, 1994.

Heckscher, Morrison H. *American Furniture in the Metropolitan Museum II: Late Colonial Period: The Queen Anne and Chippendale Styles.* New York: Metropolitan Museum of Art, 1985.

Milwaukee Museum of Art. *The Domestic Scene, 1897–1927: George M. Niedecken, Interior Architect.* Exhibition catalog, 1982. Catalog by Cheryl Robertson.

Rolf Achilles

See also **Arts and Crafts Movement.**

G

GABRIEL'S INSURRECTION, a slave uprising in Virginia in 1800. The democratic ideals expressed in the slogan of the French Revolution (1789)—"liberty, equality, fraternity"—resonated in France's Caribbean colonies. In Saint Domingue, slaveholders were slaughtered in the successful 1791 slave uprising led by the freed slave Toussaint Louverture. This led to the liberation of all slaves in that colony in 1793. Hundreds of French plantation owners fled to the United States, bringing with them thousands of slaves who had been exposed to the ideas of democracy. This made many American plantation owners nervous, including Virginians like Thomas Jefferson. Although a discourse, led by prominent Virginians, about natural rights and the duty of a regime to represent all its people had become prevalent following the American Revolution, many Virginians were increasingly fearful of slaves asserting their claim to equal human rights.

As the growing demand for cotton brought more slaves directly from Africa to Virginia, fugitive laws were tightened in order to deter and punish escaped slaves. The concomitant existence of free blacks further destabilized the social hierarchy. Furthermore, growing literacy and knowledge of the ideas that informed the American Revolution made Virginia a restive place at the turn of the nineteenth century. Ideas of democracy and freedom spread among many black urban artisans. They sought the abolition of slavery, freedom of movement, and better wages. These streams of resistance, American civic nationalism, and an emerging African American lower-middle class converged in Gabriel Prosser. He was a slave blacksmith seeking freedom by the only means he deemed plausible: violence against the merchants who oppressed laborers and the institutions of government that disenfranchised his people.

Gabriel recruited and organized a group of urban artisans and plantation workers, including his own brother and two white Frenchmen, planning to march an army on Richmond, Virginia, under the banner "Death or Liberty." He devised a military strategy to outmaneuver his enemies: they would occupy the treasury and the arsenal and capture the governor; this would unleash waves of support from poor whites, and any opponents (other than Quakers, Methodists, and Frenchmen, since they were "friendly to liberty") would be killed.

A hundred and fifty soldiers gathered near Richmond on the night of 30 August 1800, expecting hundreds of men to join their ranks. Heavy rain caused delay, and several conspirators betrayed the plan. The local militia crushed the troops. Scores, including Gabriel, were hanged; the rest were sold to slavery outside Virginia. Most memorable were the last words of a condemned man: "I have ventured my life in endeavoring to obtain the liberty of my countrymen, and I am a willing sacrifice to their cause."

Jefferson was elected president of the United States later the same year. Other sporadic insurrections heightened fears that previously docile slaves would overthrow white rule. This attitude was a setback to abolitionism, and led to a growing interest in removing blacks from U.S. soil, giving rise to various schemes by the American Colonization Society to resettle them in places such as Liberia.

BIBLIOGRAPHY

Egerton, Douglas R. *Gabriel's Rebellion: The Virginia Slave Conspiracies of 1800 and 1802.* Chapel Hill: University of North Carolina Press, 1993.

Genovese, Eugene D. *From Rebellion to Revolutionary: Afro-American Slave Revolts in the Making of the Modern World.* Baton Rouge: Louisiana State University Press, 1981.

Itai Sneh

See also **Slave Insurrections.**

GADSDEN PURCHASE. The Treaty of Guadalupe Hidalgo (1848) ended the Mexican-American War but it did not settle the so-called Mexican question. The United States was soon charged with not enforcing Article XI, which promised Mexico protection from inroads of American Indians. A boundary-line dispute also arose involving territory held necessary by some Americans for a southern railroad route to the Pacific Ocean. The activities of American speculators in Mexico increased diplomatic tension. In 1849 P. A. Hargous of New York City purchased the Garay grant, made in 1842 by the Mexican government to open a transit concession across the Isthmus of Tehuantepec. Mexico nullified this concession in 1851, but in 1853 A. G. Sloo was given an almost identical

grant. Both Hargous and Sloo demanded American protection for their concessions.

In July 1853 President Franklin Pierce instructed James Gadsden, minister to Mexico, to make a treaty not only settling the issues involved but also securing enough territory for the proposed southern railroad route. Financial needs of the administration of Antonio López de Santa Anna aided negotiation of a treaty whereby territory in northern Mexico was sold to the United States. The Gadsden Treaty, as it became known, abrogated Article XI of the Treaty of Guadalupe Hidalgo, but the United States was to aid in suppressing Indian depredations. For these concessions the United States would pay Mexico $15 million and assume all claims of its citizens against Mexico, including the Hargous claim. The United States promised to cooperate in suppressing filibustering expeditions.

The treaty met strong opposition in the Senate, where antislavery senators condemned further acquisition of slave territory. Lobbying by speculators worsened the treaty's reputation. Some senators objected to furnishing Santa Anna financial assistance. The Senate, by a narrow margin, ratified the treaty on 25 April 1854, but only after reducing the territory to be acquired to that considered essential for the railroad route. The Senate also deleted all mention of private claims and filibustering expeditions. The payment to Mexico was lowered to $10 million, and the Senate inserted an article promising American protection to the Sloo grantees. A combination of the advocates of the southern railroad route and the friends of the Sloo grant made ratification possible.

By the Gadsden Treaty the United States secured 45,535 square miles of territory. This tract became known as the Gadsden Purchase and today encompasses the southern part of Arizona and New Mexico.

BIBLIOGRAPHY

Fehrenbacher, Don E. *The Era of Expansion: 1800–1848.* New York: Wiley, 1969.

Garber, Paul Neff. *The Gadsden Treaty.* Gloucester, Mass.: Peter Smith, 1959.

Potter, David Morris. *The Impending Crisis, 1848–1861.* New York: Harper & Row, 1976.

Paul Neff Garber / A. G.

See also **Bryan-Chamorro Treaty; Compromise of 1850; Confirmation by the Senate; Indian Claims Commission; Mexican-American War; Soto, Hernando de, Explorations of.**

GAG RULE, ANTISLAVERY. In American politics the term "gag rule" refers to a series of procedural rules adopted by Congress in the 1830s and 1840s to prevent the submission of antislavery petitions. The gag rule emerged as one of the principal tools employed by the Jacksonian Democrats to silence abolitionist agitation and maintain a political coalition with slaveholders.

When the American Anti-Slavery Society formed in 1833, it launched a petition campaign as one means of encouraging opposition to slavery and identifying specific areas in which Congress could act immediately to bring slavery to an eventual end. The petitions most frequently called on Congress to abolish slavery in the District of Columbia.

As the number of antislavery petitions increased, Democrats enacted the first gag rule in 1836. It provided that petitions relating to slavery would be laid on the table without being read or referred to committee. Supporters of the gag rule argued that the drafters of the Constitution had intended that the subject of slavery should never be discussed or debated in Congress.

Serving as a Whig representative from Massachusetts, former president John Quincy Adams led the fight against the gag rule. Over nearly a decade he made opposition to and evasion of the rule a principal part of his legislative activities. Adams argued that the Democrats, in deference to the sensibilities of their slaveholding supporters, threatened to deny Americans basic civil rights since the Constitution guaranteed the right of citizens freely to petition their government. Adams's principled assault on the gag rule attracted new converts to the antislavery cause and his skillful evasions made the rule itself ineffective. In 1844 Congress lifted the rule and Adams's victory became one of the celebrated events of the abolitionist movement.

BIBLIOGRAPHY

Sewell, Richard H. *Ballots for Freedom: Antislavery Politics in the United States, 1837–1860.* New York: Oxford University Press, 1976.

Louis S. Gerteis

See also **Antislavery.**

GALÁPAGOS ISLANDS. A strategically important archipelago (group of islands), the Galápagos lie some 600 miles off the coast of Ecuador. American interest in annexing the islands began in the mid-nineteenth century and peaked half a century later. In 1906 and 1911, negotiations to build a U.S. coal station failed, largely because of popular opposition in Ecuador. During World War II, the United States established weather and signal stations on the islands. In the 1960s and 1970s, Ecuador seized a number of U.S. fishing boats in the area. In retaliation, the United States temporarily suspended military aid to Ecuador.

BIBLIOGRAPHY

Baily, Samuel L. *The United States and the Development of South America, 1945–1975.* New York: New Viewpoints, 1976.

Schoultz, Lars. *Beneath the United States: A History of U.S. Policy Toward Latin America.* Cambridge, Mass.; London: Harvard University Press, 1998.

E. T. Parks / A. G.

See also **Fishing Bounties; Guano; Latin America, Relations with; Latin American Wars of Independence.**

GALENA-DUBUQUE MINING DISTRICT is located in southwestern Wisconsin, northwestern Illinois, and Dubuque County, Iowa. Nicolas Perrot first mined lead there in 1690. Mining continued intermittently until the Fox Indians (see MESQUAKIE) granted Julien Dubuque permission to work the mines in 1788. After Dubuque died, in 1810, the Fox prevented his creditors from continuing operations. It was not until 1833 that miners returned to Dubuque.

Henry Shreve took a barge of lead to New Orleans from the Galena River mines as early as 1810. The first government leases to mine lead at the Galena River settlements were granted in 1822. Galena dominated the scene from 1822 to 1847, during which time about 472 million pounds of lead valued at approximately $14.2 million was shipped downstream.

BIBLIOGRAPHY

Libby, Orin Grant. *Significance of the Lead and Shot Trade in Early Wisconsin History.* Madison, 1895.

Wright, James E. *The Galena Lead District: Federal Policy and Practice, 1824–1847.* Madison: State Historical Society of Wisconsin, 1966.

William J. Petersen / H. S.

See also **Lead Industry; Mining Towns.**

GALLATIN'S REPORT ON MANUFACTURES, Treasury Secretary Albert Gallatin's plan for encouraging manufactures in the early nineteenth century. In 1809 the House of Representatives asked the Madison administration to prepare a report on how the federal government could best promote the development of manufactures. In April 1810 Gallatin responded with a report that suggested moderate increases in the protective duties and also suggested that the United States should issue its obligations and lend them to the manufacturers to supply capital. The significance of Gallatin's report stems from the fact that it indicated the Jeffersonians had embraced, at least in part, Hamiltonian protectionist measures on behalf of manufacturing.

BIBLIOGRAPHY

Ewing, Frank E. *America's Forgotten Statesman: Albert Gallatin.* New York: Vantage, 1959.

Kuppenheimer, L. B. *Albert Gallatin's Vision of Democratic Stability: An Interpretive Profile.* Westport, Conn.: Praeger, 1996.

Walters, Ray. *Albert Gallatin: Jeffersonian Financier and Diplomat.* New York: Macmillan, 1957.

James D. Magee / A. G.

See also **Hamilton's Economic Policies; Jeffersonian Democracy; Manufacturing; Tariff; Trade, Foreign.**

GALLATIN'S REPORT ON ROADS, CANALS, HARBORS, AND RIVERS. At its beginning the United States was so deficient in avenues of transportation—with roads in some areas practically impassable several months of the year—that political disintegration was gravely feared. So insistent were the demands for improvement that, acting on a Senate resolution of 1807, Secretary of the Treasury Albert Gallatin prepared an analysis and program, presented in 1808. He urged the national government to build a series of canals along the Atlantic seaboard from Massachusetts to the Carolinas; build interior canals and roads; and establish communication between the Atlantic and midwestern rivers and with the St. Lawrence Seaway and the Great Lakes. He thought that all of the improvements could be made for $20 million, and as the Treasury was steadily accumulating a surplus, that the debt could be paid in ten years. This proposed indebtedness, the first suggestion of the sort in U.S. history, was bitterly denounced by many, and President Thomas Jefferson did not believe the idea constitutional. While the subject was being debated, the War of 1812 approached and soon stopped all thought of the projects. After the war they were brought up again, and four roads were built, but no canals. Gallatin's report was prophetic in that most of the works he advocated were later completed either by the federal government, as was the Intracoastal Waterway, or by the states, as was the Erie Canal. The subject of internal improvements became increasingly divisive during the antebellum period, pitting Whigs, who generally supported federal funds for transportation improvements, against Democrats, who did not.

BIBLIOGRAPHY

Ewing, Frank E. *America's Forgotten Statesman: Albert Gallatin.* New York: Vantage Press, 1959.

Kuppenheimer, L. B. *Albert Gallatin's Vision of Democratic Stability: An Interpretive Profile.* Westport, Conn.: Praeger, 1996.

Walters, Ray. *Albert Gallatin: Jeffersonian Financier and Diplomat.* New York: Macmillan, 1957.

Alvin F. Harlow / A. G.

See also **Canals; River and Harbor Improvements.**

GALLAUDET UNIVERSITY. Situated in Northeast Washington, D.C., Gallaudet University is "the world's only liberal arts college for the deaf," where students are taught primarily through American Sign Language. Initially called the Columbia Institute for the Instruction of the Deaf, Dumb, and Blind, the school was founded by Amos Kendall (1789–1869) as the city's school for the deaf in 1857. Kendall, who served as postmaster general under Presidents Andrew Jackson and Martin Van Buren, established the school on his Northeast Washington estate, Kendall Green. It was later renamed for the noted nineteenth-century educator and reformer Thomas Hopkins Gallaudet (1787–1851).

Kendall hired Thomas Hopkins Gallaudet's son Edward Miner Gallaudet (1837–1917) as the first superintendent. Kendall and the younger Gallaudet lobbied Congress to permit the school to award college degrees, and the resulting bill was signed by Abraham Lincoln on 8 April 1864. The blind students were transferred to the Maryland School for the Blind, and the institution became the Columbia Institution for the Deaf and Dumb, with the collegiate division named the National Deaf-Mute College. The elementary program remained Kendall School, and in the early twenty-first century it was known as Kendall Demonstration Elementary School. Congressional funding supported the college, which held its first commencement in 1869. In 1887 women gained admittance to the college, which was redesignated Gallaudet College in 1894.

The college's importance stems from its service not only to deaf students and the American deaf community but also as a training ground for hearing graduate students in deaf education. In 1891 Gallaudet College established a teacher training program, which admitted only hearing students. Many graduates subsequently taught in and administered state residential schools for the deaf. By the twenty-first century the School of Education admitted both deaf and hearing students.

In 1986 Gallaudet College was accorded university status and became Gallaudet University. Two years later, in March 1988, a presidential search evolved into a student strike aimed at instituting a deaf president. All of Gallaudet's previous presidents had been hearing. The movement, popularly known as Deaf President Now, proved successful, and I. King Jordan, a Gallaudet professor, dean, and alumnus, was installed as Gallaudet's eighth president. The protest focused international attention on Gallaudet and sparked increased awareness of deaf issues and civil rights.

Gallaudet offers 27 majors for undergraduate students and 20 fields for graduate study. In fall 2001 attendance stood at 1,852 students, of whom 1,243 were undergraduates. The 2001–2002 budget totaled approximately $130 million, roughly 70 percent of which was direct appropriation from Congress. The remaining 30 percent derived from tuition and fees, federal grants, and other miscellaneous sources of income.

BIBLIOGRAPHY

Christiansen, John B., and Sharon N. Barnartt. *Deaf President Now!: The 1988 Revolution at Gallaudet University.* Washington, D.C.: Gallaudet University Press, 1995.

Gallaudet, Edward Miner. *History of the College for the Deaf, 1857–1907.* Washington, D.C.: Gallaudet College Press, 1983.

David S. Evans

See also **Deaf in America; Disabled, Education of the; Sign Language, American.**

GALLEY BOATS were small shiplike crafts on the Ohio River designed to use both sails and oars, known after 1800 as barges. The French and Spanish maintained galleys on the Mississippi River for military purposes. In 1782, George Rogers Clark used a large galley, the *Miami*, to prevent British and Indian parties from crossing the Ohio; it was seventy-three feet in keel and had forty oars. During the troubles with France and Spain at the close of the eighteenth century, the federal government built two galleys, the *President Adams* and the *Senator Ross.* Other gunboat galleys were built at various points in the West during the next decade.

BIBLIOGRAPHY

Baldwin, Leland D. *Keelboat Age on Western Waters.* Pittsburgh, Pa.: University of Pittsburgh Press, 1941; 1955; 1980; 1989.

Leland D. Baldwin / A. R.

See also **Keelboat; River Navigation; Waterways, Inland.**

GALLOWAY'S PLAN OF UNION. In September 1774, as the First Continental Congress debated various means of coercing Parliament toward accepting colonial sovereignty, Joseph Galloway, a Pennsylvania delegate and prominent supporter of reconciliation with Britain, devised a plan to avert the escalating crisis. Galloway rejected natural law as a basis for colonial rights, claims against Parliament, or independence. He looked instead to written and common law and sought a new imperial constitution to protect the colonies' best interests.

Galloway presented his plan to the Congress on 28 September 1774. In it, he called for the establishment of

Galveston. People stand amid the rubble of houses in the aftermath of the exceptionally destructive hurricane that pounded this island city on 8–9 September 1900. NATIONAL OCEANIC AND ATMOSPHERIC ADMINISTRATION/DEPARTMENT OF COMMERCE

an American legislature that would govern both imperial affairs in America and relations between individual colonies. The legislature would function as a branch of the British Parliament, and legislation passed by the American house would require Parliament's approval. The plan also recommended appointment, by the king and a grand council of the colonial assemblies, of a president-general to oversee the legislature. Galloway's plan for limited colonial sovereignty within unified British institutions found support among moderate delegates led by James Duane, John Jay, and John Rutledge. But the plan failed to address the crux of colonial grievances: excessive parliamentary power. Opponents of the plan, led by Patrick Henry and Richard Henry Lee, therefore assailed it as a ruse to secure England's dominance over colonial affairs. Delegates rejected the plan by a margin of one vote. Following his defeat, Galloway became an outspoken critic of the CONTINENTAL CONGRESS and popular political leaders and eventually became a Loyalist during the Revolution.

BIBLIOGRAPHY

Boyd, Julian P. *Anglo-American Union: Joseph Galloway's Plans to Preserve the British Empire, 1774–1788.* Philadelphia: University of Pennsylvania Press, 1941.

Galloway, Joseph. "Proposed Union between Great Britain and Colonies." In *Documents of the American Revolution, 1770–1783.* Eight transcripts. Edited by K. G. Davies. Shannon: Irish University Press, 1975. Text of Galloway's Plan (1774).

James Tejani

GALVANIZED YANKEES were Confederate soldiers imprisoned during the Civil War but granted their freedom in exchange for an oath of allegiance to the United States and enlistment in the Union army. About six thousand former Confederates enrolled in six regiments of U.S. volunteers during 1864 and 1865, and a few hundred others joined state volunteer units. Samuel Bowles coined the term in the *Springfield* (Mass.) *Republican* on 24 May 1865.

At General Ulysses S. Grant's insistence, the six regiments of Galvanized Yankees served in the West, manning frontier forts, guarding stagecoach routes, escorting supply trains, and rebuilding hundreds of miles of telegraph lines destroyed by Indians, thus avoiding service against former comrades-in-arms.

BIBLIOGRAPHY

Brown, Dee. *The Galvanized Yankees.* Urbana: University of Illinois Press, 1963.

Dee Brown
Christopher Wells

See also **Ironclad Oath; Loyalty Oaths.**

GALVESTON, located on the northeast part of Galveston Island, a narrow strip of land along the Gulf of Mexico roughly fifty miles southwest of Houston, is the oldest continuously settled area in Texas (since 1745). Spanish explorers named the island after the governor of Louisiana, Bernardo de Galvez, in the late 1700s. After

Gambling Saloon. A nineteenth-century photograph of a bar with gaming tables in Telluride, Colo. © CORBIS-BETTMANN

briefly serving as the capital of the Republic of Texas in 1836, much of the land was purchased by Michel B. Menard, who established a post office and customs house, platted the modern city, and incorporated it in 1839. Railroad construction arrived along with a causeway to the mainland in the 1840s, and Galveston served as the major cotton shipping point and port of entry to Texas. Disaster arrived on 8–9 September 1900, when one of the largest hurricanes on record struck, the resulting winds and storm surge obliterating much of the city and killing roughly six thousand people. The storm's aftermath brought the first commission government to the United States to manage the cleanup and to supervise the construction of a ten-mile seawall around the city. Galveston missed the 1901 Spindletop oil discovery that provided the economic boom to Houston, which eroded its neighbor's fortunes for the rest of the century despite its important port. The city has a land area of 46.2 square miles and a population of 57,247 in 2000, down from 59,070 in 1990.

BIBLIOGRAPHY

Bixel, Patricia Bellis, and Elizabeth Hayes Turner. *Galveston and the 1900 Storm: Castastrophe and Catalyst.* Austin: University of Texas Press, 2000.

Larsen, Erik. *Isaac's Storm: A Man, a Time, and the Deadliest Hurricane in History.* New York: Crown, 1999.

Weems, John Edward. *A Weekend in September.* College Station: Texas A&M Press, 1980.

Matthew L. Daley

GAMBLING. Men and women throughout history and around the world have gambled. In the early colonial days, taverns were the main meeting place—and a place to put down a bet. In addition, gamblers and those who just placed an occasional bet had gambling halls, gaming rooms, saloons, even outdoor games to wager on. Indians, judges, Mexicans, physicians, Chinese, clergymen, African Americans, salesclerks, cowboys, and professional gamblers bet their money and sometimes their possessions on games of chance. Gambling venues included logging camps, elegant steamboats, railroad cars, boxing rings, and more.

Gambling was (and is) a form of entertainment. In the early days of the nation, people worked hard and often did not live near towns, thus when they did go to town they wanted to be entertained. Gambling gave an air of fairly harmless excitement and the payoff (or loss) was immediate.

Indians and Early Gambling

The Assiniboin Indians of North Dakota had a favorite dice game. Their two-sided dice had one side granting points when it came up; the other side did not. The dice were made of pieces of broken dishes or claws from a crow, with one side painted red, the other black. Buttons or other trinkets were also used as dice. Point values for each item were agreed upon before the game began. To make the game last longer and to have more at stake, the Assiniboins often played double or nothing. They would have one round with a set object as the prize. After round one, more objects—even wives—were added to the pot as the rounds continued. Sometimes games went on two and three days and nights, breaking only for meals. The dice games continued until one of the players had lost everything. Wives were property and had no say if they were lost to another man. They just moved. But there were some men who would not bet their wives, and fatal fights sometimes ensued.

The Zuni, Papago, and Hopi Indians liked to bet on foot races. Other tribes used hand games, the equivalent of, "Button, button, who's got the button." In this hand game, a button, or other small object, was placed in a person's hand. That person then began passing the button around the circle—or at least pretended to. Whoever was, "It" had to try to discern who had the button at any given time. If he was wrong, he lost the bet. Most betting included drumming and chants that grew more enthusiastic with each round.

In the 1830s Choctaw Indians played a serious game called, "ball play" that was similar to lacrosse and involved two teams, each consisting of ten players. Sticks about two feet long with a cup fashioned on one end were used to catch and throw a ball in this competition. George Catlin, the renowned Western artist, watched such a game with close to 700 young warriors as players. Women were in charge of the betting for this particular game. At stake were mostly household items, including dogs, horses, and guns. Spectators numbered in the thousands.

On the Upper Missouri River, the Mandan Indians' favorite game was, "the game of the arrow." Each young warrior who wanted to play had to pay an entry fee of a valued possession, such as a pair of moccasins or a robe. The object was to shoot arrows as fast as possible, seeing how many arrows could be launched before the first one hit the ground. In the game that Catlin observed, one of the warriors got eight arrows off and won all the prizes ("entry fees").

Gambling on Steamboats

Initially steamboats were used only to haul freight. In January of 1812, Robert Fulton introduced his boat, the *New Orleans*, as the first steamboat to carry passengers. By 1860, western rivers had 735 passenger steamboats plying their waters; these boats carried gamblers, who often took on the air of gentlemen, wearing knee-length black coats, ruffled white shirts, vests, and fancy rings. Referred to as "dandies," these professional gamblers were frequently con men who fleeced their victims in less than honest wins.

The belief was that 99 percent of riverboat gamblers cheated and worked with an accomplice. The gambler and his partner(s) would board the boats at different points, thus covering up their collusion. A team consisted of two, three, or up to six men. Some would play cards, while the others would give them signals. Tips were specific puffs of cigar smoke, holding a cane in a certain manner, wearing a hat at various angles, or anything that would not be obvious to the other players.

Indians and Gambling. Four Paiutes gamble in southwestern Nevada, 1873, in this photograph by John K. Hillers; large-scale casino gambling on Indian reservations began a century later. NATIONAL ARCHIVES AND RECORDS ADMINISTRATION

With their lavish frescoed walls, crystal chandeliers, and flowery carpets, the riverboats were expensive to run. The *Great Republic* was sold at auction in 1871 because fuel for the round trip from St. Louis to New Orleans cost $5,000.

Gambling Women

Women also gambled. Alice Tubbs, known as Poker Alice, was born Alice Ivers in Sudbury, England, in 1851; she moved to Virginia with her family in her late teens. She married a mining engineer in Colorado; his early death left her a young widow who soon became acquainted with gambling. Poker Alice learned her craft well in Colorado, practiced it in Oklahoma, and eventually found herself working as a faro dealer in South Dakota. She was apparently the only woman faro dealer that ever lived and worked in the Black Hills, primarily in Sturgis and Deadwood. Photos of Tubbs, who never played cards with strangers, always show her with a big cigar in her mouth. In the 1880s, Tubbs sometimes made $1,000 in just one evening of cards. Also a blackjack dealer and a madam, Poker Alice marched in the 1927 parade in Deadwood, South Dakota, when the town hosted President Calvin Coolidge. She died in 1930, having outlived three husbands.

Floating Casino. Bally's *Belle of Orleans*, a four-level gambling riverboat, is launched in the Mississippi River at New Orleans on 8 April 1995. AP/Wide World Photos

Lotteries and Violence

Ironically, even though many churches frowned upon other forms of gambling, lotteries were and are accepted by nearly everyone. Many church buildings, schools, and even roads and bridges were built by proceeds from lotteries. Perhaps because the tickets did not have to be sold in the smoky saloons but could be sold by anyone, anywhere, lotteries were looked upon as a good way to raise money and were not truly considered "gambling." Some states banned them; others embraced them. States then and now, passed lottery bills, then fought over how much of the proceeds the state would receive and how they would be used.

James Monroe Pattee, a New Hampshire writing instructor, was the king of lottery sales. He migrated to California for a time then settled in Omaha, Nebraska. He created lotteries for worthy causes such as hospitals and libraries. In 1873 Nebraska outlawed lotteries and Pattee moved to Wyoming. In that state a lottery could be legally offered by buying a three-month license for $100. During his first year in Wyoming, Pattee bought a license every three months for a total of $400. He sold about $7 million worth of tickets in that year. Despite the small population of Wyoming, he was successful because he advertised in the *New York Herald* newspaper, thus getting out-of-state business.

Violence was often gambling's companion; perhaps the most famous murder was that of Wild Bill Hickok in Deadwood, Dakota Territory. Although Hickok had a strict policy of never sitting with his back to the door when he was playing cards, on 2 August 1866, for the first time, he sat with his back to the door in Saloon #10 and was shot in the back by Jack McCall. Hickok's poker hand—a pair of aces and a pair of eights—was from then on known as a "Deadman's Hand." The saloon is still operating.

Gambling on the Reservation
Large scale casino gambling on Indian reservations was allowed in 1987 when the Supreme Court ruled in *California vs. Cabazon Band of Mission Indians* that states could regulate commercial gambling on Indian reservations. Congress subsequently passed the Indian Gaming Regulatory Act (IGRA) in 1988. Proceeds of gaming operations were to be used for economic development and welfare of tribal members. Three levels, called classes, of gambling were defined. Class I: traditional tribal and social games with nominal prizes; this class is regulated solely by the tribe. Class II: in states where such games are legal and not prohibited by federal law, bingo, lotto, punch cards, and games played among individuals (not against the house) may be allowed or licensed by the tribe. Class III: casinos, which are the most highly regulated and must be legal in the state where the reservation is located; casinos are subject to state-tribal agreements. Such compacts delineate state-tribal regulatory authority; they also cover cooperative areas of criminal justice and payments to each state for enforcement and oversight.

From passage of IGRA in 1988 through the end of 1996, revenues from gambling on the reservations increased from $212 million to $6.7 billion. Of the 554 federally recognized tribes, the Bureau of Indian Affairs reports only 146 tribes with Class III gaming facilities. More than two-thirds of Indian tribes do not offer gambling; some tribes have voted not to offer gaming on their lands.

The Prairie Island Indian Community is one of eleven reservations in Minnesota and one of the smallest in that state. Prairie Island uses the revenue from its gambling operations to pay for some of its basic services and to improve the lives of tribal members. The largest Indian gambling facility in the United States, Foxwoods Casino (run by the Mashantucket Pequots) near Ledyard, Connecticut, employs about 13,000; the entire tribe has only about 500 members.

Alcohol consumption is not a given in reservation casinos; it is up to each tribe to decide if it will allow liquor to be sold on the reservation. In South Dakota, the Pine Ridge Indian Reservation is a dry reservation yet it owns and operates Prairie Wind Casino. It still draws visitors—and their dollars—to the reservation.

BIBLIOGRAPHY

Moulton,Candy Vyvey. *The Writer's Guide to Everyday Life in the Wild West From 1840–1900.* Cincinnati, Ohio: Writers Digest Books, 1999.

Sasuly, Richard. *Bookies and Bettors: Two Hundred Years of Gambling.* New York: Holt, Rinehart and Winston, 1982.

MacFarlan, Allan, and Paulette MacFarlan. *Handbook of American Indian Games.* New York: Dover, 1985.

Eadington, William. *Indian Gaming and the Law.* Reno: University of Nevada Press, 1998.

Peggy Sanders

See also **Lotteries.**

GAMES. *See* **Toys and Games.**

GARDENING. By A.D. 1000, native peoples on the American continent had developed a system of planting corn, beans, and squash together. Beans enriched the soil with nitrogen, corn provided a trellis for the bean to climb, and squash vines grew to cover the ground and discourage weeds. The effectiveness of this method was not surpassed until state agricultural stations were established in the last decades of the nineteenth century. Indigenous peoples also sowed wild rice, and cultivated sunflowers, roses, cotton, tobacco, and potatoes. The survival of many pioneering Europeans owed much to Native Americans who shared their harvests and their agricultural knowledge.

English settlers arriving in Virginia and Massachusetts in the early years of the seventeenth century brought wheat, barley, rye, oats, hay, and peas, grown as field crops. Kitchen gardens, close to the house, included vegetables, herbs, fruit trees, and berries. An integral element of the household, the garden supplied not only food, but also medicines, insect repellents, preservatives, air fresheners, dyes, and other necessities.

Such plots were laid out geometrically, with rectangles or square planting areas bordered by paths for walking between, a design familiar from Elizabethan times. Sensible housewives located sweet-smelling plants near open windows and kept those with objectionable odors, like onion or cabbage, more distant. Plants were grown in raised beds, the soil held by boards. House gardens were fenced to keep animals out.

As the colonies prospered, wealthy landowners built fine houses and fine gardens, patterned after those in Europe, based on classical ideals of symmetry and order. Pleasure gardens of the period were enclosed by a border of closely clipped hedges, often of boxwood. The interiors were laid out in elaborate geometrical patterns, sometimes tracing knots, or creating mazes against a background of colored gravel. Raised beds featured showy flowers and shrubs pruned to represent animals and other forms (topiary). Found most often in the South, this style remained popular for most of the eighteenth century. American versions of the formal garden were less fussy than their European counterparts.

The founding fathers, who so carefully planned for balance and order in the new nation, took similar care in designing their grounds and gardens. George Washington planned his Mansion House farm to include a deep border of woods, rolling meadows, serpentine walkways,

Victory Gardens. A U.S. Department of Agriculture poster, designed by Herbert Bayer in the early 1940s, promotes farm gardens as part of the war effort at home. LIBRARY OF CONGRESS

groves of trees, a pleasure garden, and a utilitarian kitchen garden. Thomas Jefferson is America's most renowned gardener of the early nineteenth century. He built on European design and imbued it with American sensibility, combining beauty and utility. Jefferson made Monticello an experimental laboratory of plants from around the world. He cultivated 250 vegetable varieties in a garden terrace and 170 fruit varieties on another eight acres. Further, he designed romantic grottoes, garden temples, and ornamental groves.

Andrew Jackson Downing began a horticultural revolution with the 1841 publication of *A Treatise on the Theory and Practice of Landscape Gardening.* Downing's idea was to unify the classical standards of European style with the irregular, raw, and picturesque beauty of America. His vision included home design and had unprecedented popular appeal. Downing advocated a free-flowing style of planting and the scattering of parts of the garden about the grounds. Public parks, even cemeteries, reflected the new naturalistic trend.

Thirty years afterward, Frank J. Scott published *The Art of Beautifying Suburban Home Grounds of Small Extent.* In his work, Scott addressed the nation's growing middle class, whose estate might be as small as an eighth of an acre. It is he who suggested that front yards be open to the street and to adjoining neighbors' properties, the look that characterizes American suburbs today.

With this guidance, Victorian gardeners decorated the outdoors with the same enthusiasm for ostentation that they demonstrated in their home interiors. Artfully placed tree specimens, groups of shrubs, and exotic ornamentals delighted the eye from an inside window or gazebo. Flowerbeds of varied shapes were cut out of the lawn and bloomed with ribbons of annuals in vivid and jarring colors. Victorians used wrought iron furniture, urns, statuary, and other decorative elements to make the garden an extension of the home.

As the twentieth century dawned, a revival of classical styles in architecture reintroduced symmetry and geometry to garden design. Flowers in softer combinations, such as white and yellow or other pastels, became the fashion. Victorian-era color and exoticism were now considered gaudy and in poor taste.

Most Americans were now more likely to be workers in offices and industry than farmers and independent tradesmen. Wages purchased food and other household needs. Gardening had been transformed from an indispensable domestic art into an interest for those with leisure time. During World War I (1914–1918) and World War II (1939–1945), the government was compelled to initiate "victory garden" campaigns to urge citizens to grow as much as possible of their family's food supply.

After World War II, a severe housing shortage caused a boom in development across the country. In the rush to build, the relationship of the house to the land, so important to earlier generations, had been forgotten. Groups of houses of identical design appeared on lots bulldozed bare and strewn with grass seed. New homeowners added trees for shade, foundation plantings or flowerbeds on whim, with no guiding aesthetic. Feeding, watering, and maintaining a flawless green expanse of lawn became the new suburban ideal.

In the 1970s, environmental awareness sparked appreciation for the natural world in a new generation of Americans. Practices that followed in later decades, including "naturalizing" with bulbs and wildflowers, adding water features and plants to attract wildlife, and selecting plants requiring less water in arid areas (xeriscape), are heirs to this new consciousness. Organic methods of growing produce also gained loyal adherents. However, the desire of many homeowners to enhance their property value by achieving "perfect" lawns and grounds continues to generate sales of grass seed, chemical fertilizers, and pesticides.

Steadily growing numbers of Americans are taking up gardening, many no doubt inspired by the ageless human desire for intimacy with nature and quiet refuge from worldly demands. The books that have been valued gardening references in American homes since colonial times have been joined by radio shows, television programs, and Internet resources. In 2001, the National Gardening Association found that eight out of ten American households regularly tend lawns and gardens. Most gardeners are homeowners, aged 35 to 54. Men and women are equally represented. In 2001, Americans spent $37.7 billion on horticultural products. The Department of Agriculture has ranked the nursery and greenhouse industry as the fastest growing segment of United States agriculture and the second most important in economic output.

BIBLIOGRAPHY

Darke, Rick. *In Harmony with Nature: Lessons from the Arts and Crafts Garden.* New York: Michael Friedman Publishing Group, 2000.

Downing, Andrew J. *A Treatise on the Theory and Practice of Landscape Gardening: Adapted to North America.* Washington, D.C.: Dumbarton Oaks Publishing Service, 1991. (Reprint)

Leighton, Ann. *Early American Gardens: "For Meate or Medicine."* Boston: Houghton Mifflin Company, 1970.

———. *American Gardens in the Eighteenth Century; "For Use or for Delight."* Amherst: University of Massachusetts Press, 1986.

———. *American Gardens of the Nineteenth Century: "For Comfort and Affluence."* Amherst: University of Massachusetts Press, 1987.

Olmsted, Frederick L. *Forty Years of Landscape Architecture: Central Park.* Cambridge, Mass.: MIT Press, 1973 (Reprint).

Weishan, Michael. *The New Traditional Garden: A Practical Guide to Creating and Restoring Authentic American Gardens for Homes of All Ages.* New York: The Ballantine Publishing Group, 1999.

Christine M. Roane

GARFIELD ASSASSINATION. *See* **Assassinations, Presidential.**

GARMENT INDUSTRY. *See* **Clothing Industry.**

GASOLINE TAXES were first used as a means to finance the American automobile highway system and have become a policy tool for environmental and foreign trade purposes. Oregon, Colorado, and New Mexico passed the first gasoline taxes, and by 1929 every state was using gasoline taxes to build highways. The tax met little opposition: it seemed fair to the public because those who used the highways paid the tax, and oil merchandisers supported highway building as a means to increase automobile use. Collected from wholesalers at very small cost to governments, the tax soon grew; by 1930, when all states had come to impose gasoline taxes, such taxes brought in $500 million ($5.385 billion in 2002 dollars) annually. By the depression of the 1930s some strong opposition had emerged. Yet the pressure for highway-building funds was so great that more than half of the nation's main highways were financed by gasoline taxes. Oil merchandisers, along with others who expected to benefit, put their effort into preventing the diversion of gas tax monies into nonhighway uses. The first federal gasoline tax dates to 1956, when the federal government took on the task of building an interstate highway system, in response to strong pressure from the public. The federal gasoline tax was one of several highway-user payments that fed the Highway Trust Fund, the federal fund for highway building.

In the postwar era lawmakers periodically turned to gas taxes to change consumer behavior, in order to reduce reliance on imported oil, or to reduce pollution. In the mid-1970s, the government began using gasoline taxes to encourage energy conservation. In that same period both state and federal governments were increasingly pressured to use gas tax monies for nonhighway purposes, particularly for mass transit. Increasing diversion suggested that the absolute hegemony of the private automobile in the United States appeared to be coming to an end.

However, the 1970s conservation policies were largely overturned in the 1980s by President Ronald Reagan, and although a gas tax remains, its size and even existence are controversial, though U.S. consumers pay only about one-fifth the gas tax that Europeans pay. In the late twentieth century, rising concern over possible links between fossil fuel use and global warming prompted environmental groups and policymakers to propose gas taxes to make gas prices more accurately reflect the real costs, including environmental impact. Arguing that the oil and gas industry is substantially subsidized through federal policy, thereby keeping gas prices artificially low, gas tax advocates argued that Americans would continue to seek "gas-guzzling" vehicles so long as fuel costs remained too low. Throughout President Clinton's adminstration, the issue was highly volatile. As fears of global warming spread, the Clinton adminstration sought policy changes so that the United States could meet its commitment to cut greenhouse gas emissions, under the United Nations Framework Convention on Climate Change. The fossil fuel industry lobbied heavily against any increase in gas taxes, arguing that fossil fuel use was not responsible for global warming. In 1993 the administration had to fight a bitter battle to raise the tax just four cents. On the other hand, at the turn of the twenty-first century, bipartisan opposition in Congress stymied some Republicans' efforts to reduce the gas tax. Some opponents argued that cutting or eliminating the gas tax would break the federal government's promise to guarantee a steady source of revenue for state construction programs.

In 2002 President George W. Bush surprised many people when his administration issued a report indicating that global warming was, indeed, a serious problem. However, he advocated solutions that involved adapting to climate change rather than trying to slow the process through cutting emissions. At the turn of the twenty-first century, the gasoline tax was about forty cents per gallon—a small fraction of the tax most European countries levy on gas.

BIBLIOGRAPHY

Burnham, John C. "The Gasoline Tax and the Automobile Revolution." *Mississippi Valley Historical Review*, 48 (1962): 435–459.

Chernick, Howard, and Andrew Reschovsky. "Who Pays the Gasoline Tax?" *National Tax Journal* (June 1997).

Fullerton, Don, and Sarah West. *Can Taxes on Cars and on Gasoline Mimic an Unavailable Tax on Emissions?* Cambridge, Mass.: National Bureau of Economic Research, 1999.

Goulder, Lawrence Herbert. *Energy Taxes: Traditional Efficiency Effects and Environmental Implications.* Cambridge, Mass.: National Bureau of Economic Research, 1993.

Kaszynski, William. *The American Highway: The History and Culture of Roads in the United States.* Jefferson, N.C.: McFarland, 2000.

John C. Burnham
Dorothea Browder/D. B.

See also **Air Pollution; Climate; Global Warming; Petroleum Industry; Taxation.**

GASPÉE, BURNING OF THE. The many waterways and islands in Narragansett Bay, Rhode Island, provided a haven for smugglers throughout the mid-1700s. Many colonial merchantmen resented imperial taxation policies; when the British government began sending revenue cutters to suppress these irregularities, anti-British sentiment grew more acute. In March 1772, HMS *Gaspée* arrived in Narragansett Bay and proceeded to stop even small market boats and to send seized property to Boston. On 9 June 1772 the *Gaspée*, while chasing the *Hannah*, a packet sloop on its way to Providence, ran ashore on Namquit (now Gaspée) Point in Warwick, Rhode Island. A group met at Sabin's Tavern in Providence and plotted to burn the ship. John Brown, a leading Providence merchant, supplied eight boats; the men armed themselves with guns, staves, and paving stones at about 10 P.M. and with muffled oars proceeded down the river. When they neared the *Gaspée*, they were hailed by the lookout and also by the captain. Captain Abraham Whipple (later a commodore in the U.S. Navy) replied, with some profanity, that he had a warrant to arrest the captain, whom Joseph Bucklin then shot. The men from the boats boarded the *Gaspée* without resistance and drove the crew below decks. The captured sailors were bound and put on shore. The *Gaspée* was set on fire and burned to the water's edge. A proclamation was issued to apprehend the participants in the raid, and although they were widely known in Providence, no substantial evidence was obtained by the commission of inquiry, and no one was brought to trial.

BIBLIOGRAPHY

Bartlett, John R. *A History of the Destruction of His Britannic Majesty's Schooner Gaspee. . . .* Providence, Rhode Island: A. Crawford Greene, 1861.

DeVaro, Lawrence J. "The Impact of the *Gaspée* Affair on the Coming of the Revolution, 1772–1773." Ph.D. diss., Case Western Reserve University, 1973.

York, Neil L. "The Uses of Law and the *Gaspée* Affair," *Rhode Island History* 50, no. 1 (1992): 2–21.

Howard M. Chapin/A. R.

See also **Navigation Acts; Townshend Acts.**

GASTONIA STRIKE. Soon after Fred E. Beal, of the National Textile Workers Union, arrived in Gastonia, North Carolina, to organize textile mill workers, a strike was called to secure union recognition. Local police frequently raided the meetings of the mill workers. On 7 June 1929 the Gastonia chief of police, O. F. Aderholt, was killed while attempting to disband a strikers' meeting, and in the fighting that followed, seven strikers were reported killed. Beal, reputedly a member of the American Communist Party, and six other men were arrested, tried, and convicted of murdering Aderholt; released on bail, all fled to Russia. Beal later returned and was arrested in 1938; he was extradited to North Carolina to serve his prison term.

BIBLIOGRAPHY

Salmond, John A. *Gastonia, 1929: The Story of the Loray Mill Strike.* Chapel Hill: University of North Carolina Press, 1995.

C. H. Hamlin/A. R.

See also **Clothing Industry; Strikes; United Textile Workers.**

GATEWAY ARCH. The Gateway Arch is located in St. Louis, Missouri on the Mississippi Riverfront. In December 1935, the Jefferson National Expansion Memorial was built to commemorate the westward expansion of the

Gateway Arch. The paddle wheeler *American Queen*, traveling along the Mississippi River, is framed by the giant tribute to westward expansion that stands in St. Louis, point of origin for countless expeditions and wagon trains. © BUDDY MAYS/CORBIS

nation. A competition was conducted in 1948 to design a monument for the memorial and architect Eero Saarinen won with his 630-foot catenary arch design. Construction began in 1963 and was completed on 28 October 1965; the cost of the entire project was less than $15 million. The National Park Service oversees the operation of the arch and the surrounding landmarks, which include the site of the 1847 and 1850 hearings of the *Dred Scott v. Sandford* case.

BIBLIOGRAPHY

Jefferson National Expansion Museum Home Page. http://www.nps.gov.jeff.

Mehrhoff, W. Arthur. *The Gateway Arch: Fact and Symbol.* Bowling Green, Ohio: Bowling Green University Popular Press, 1992.

Barbara Schwarz Wachal

See also **Architecture; Saint Louis.**

GAY AND LESBIAN MOVEMENT. The Gay and Lesbian movement in the United States refers to organized efforts to fight prejudice, discrimination, and persecution resulting from the classification of homosexuality as sin, crime, or illness. While its proponents disagree about both tactics and definitions of homosexuality, they unite around the concept of homosexuality as a component of personal and political identity. Although historians often date the movement's origin from the June 1969 riot at the Stonewall Inn, a gay bar in New York City where patrons fought with police, early manifestations of gay and lesbian activism date before World War II.

Gay Pride. Supporters assemble in front of the Stonewall Inn in lower Manhattan, thirty years after a clash during a police raid sparked the modern period of activism for gay and lesbian rights. © John-Marshall Mantel/corbis

Although distinct gay and lesbian subcultures were present in American cities for most of the twentieth century, the military deployment of World War II offered homosexuals unprecedented opportunities to meet one another, increasing the size and visibility of these subcultures and reinforcing the concept of homosexual community. Lesbians, in particular, benefited from the greater freedoms in mobility, labor, and dress that women in general experienced through wartime work. The new standards for acceptable female behavior more closely matched their own. At the same time, the greater visibility of homosexuality coincided with increasing fears of deviance. The military initiated psychiatry to define gay people as unfit for service, encouraging the belief that homosexuality was a mental illness.

In the 1950s anticommunists associated homosexuality with political danger, arguing that gay people were mentally or emotionally unstable and therefore security risks, while others simply equated homosexuality with communism. Many persons suspected of homosexuality lost their jobs, some were imprisoned, and others were subjected to "therapies" ranging from shock treatment to castration. In this atmosphere arose the homophile movement embodied in the gay men's group, the Mattachine Society, founded in 1950–1951, and the lesbian society, the Daughters of Bilitis, founded in 1955. Both groups, the first sustained organizations of their kind, sought to unite homosexuals around social and political goals and by the late 1950s emphasized accommodation to heterosexual society while seeking support from the legal and medical professions. These groups focused on normalizing homosexuality, and their publications discussed, among other issues, proper roles and dress for gay men and lesbian women. Outside of these movements, others continued to develop roles by which to define themselves in relation to each other and to straight society. Butch-femme roles became prominent among working-class lesbians, and many gay men continued to dress in drag (female attire).

The early 1960s witnessed a distinct radicalization of the gay and lesbian community, as a younger generation began to question the accommodationist stance of their elders. Homosexual organizations experienced the same tensions that characterized other movements. Coalitions such as the East Coast Homophile Organizations (ECHO) and the North American Conference of Homophile Organizations (NACHO) broadened the movement by the mid-1960s, while such groups as the Society for Individual Rights (SIR) and dissenters within older organizations advocated a more assertive stance. Leaders of gay and lesbian communities began publicly to assert their sexuality in ways inconceivable to the former generation. In 1965 gay and lesbian groups staged a march on Washington, strategically adopting conservative dress to distinguish themselves from the anti-Vietnam protesters.

By the late 1960s emerging grassroots gay and lesbian communities embraced the militance and sexual openness of the counterculture. In the wake of the Stonewall riot, "gay liberation" built upon the growing sense of identity within the general climate of revolution. From the CIVIL RIGHTS MOVEMENT and the NEW LEFT came tactics and ideas, while feminism and sexual liberation shared many goals and strategies with gay liberationists. The phrases "gay power" and "gay pride" emerged, and political organizing was revitalized. According to the historian John D'Emilio, the two features of gay liberation were "coming out" (publicly declaring oneself a homosexual) and the development of lesbian feminism and a lesbian liberation movement. The Gay Liberation Front (GLF) represented a rejection of what liberationists saw as the homophile movement's overreliance on experts and assimilation. Out of the GLF came the Gay Activists Alliance, a less radical group devoted to reform within, which produced the National Gay Task Force (later the National Gay and Lesbian Task Force).

In the 1970s the new activism reached into higher education in the form of the Gay Academic Union, caucuses within academic organizations and student groups, and the first gay and lesbian studies courses. The concept of a gay community became important socially and politically. Bars continued as the primary locus of the movement, while symbols, styles of dress, newspapers, fiction, and even music and humor arose as part of an open gay-lesbian movement. Gay-pride parades were opportunities to unite publicly. Gay and lesbian activists scored several victories. The American Psychiatric Association removed homosexuality from its diagnostic manual, and a few communities adopted antidiscrimination laws. Harvey Milk, an openly gay San Francisco supervisor, was murdered in 1978 along with Mayor George Moscone, and the light sentence given the man convicted of both shootings galvanized gay communities.

In the 1980s two factors brought setbacks for the movement: the AIDS epidemic and the hostility of conservative Christian groups. But visibility continued as the main strategy of gays and lesbians. Entertainment and sports figures came out, including the movie star Rock Hudson, who died of AIDS, the tennis champion Martina Navratilova, and the country singer k. d. lang. Gay advocates such as the Gay and Lesbian Alliance Against Defamation (GLAAD) monitored the media for tone and content, while others formed direct-action groups, such as ACT UP (AIDS Coalition to Unleash Power) and Queer Nation. After 1990 the movement focused increasingly on fighting the ban on homosexuals in the military, continuing the struggle for equal legal treatment, and promoting the idea of gay people as an economic as well as political force. In 1987 and 1993 gay people participated in marches on Washington to protest government support of discrimination in such areas as employment, housing, health care and insurance, parental rights, and adoption.

By the turn of the twenty-first century, a two-pronged effort to encourage employers to offer domestic partner benefits and governments to legalize same-sex marriage had achieved some concrete results. Vermont gave some legal sanction to same-sex unions in 2001. But despite such progress, a conservative movement, rejuvenated by the Republican victory in the 2000 presidential election, continued to promote a campaign to pass "defense of marriage" laws at every level of government. These bills, which defined marriage as a union between men and women, explicitly responded to what some conservatives viewed as an attack on traditional family values.

BIBLIOGRAPHY

Adam, Barry D. *The Rise of a Gay and Lesbian Movement.* Boston: Twayne, 1987.

Bawer, Bruce. *A Place at the Table: The Gay Individual in American Society.* New York: Poseidon Press, 1993.

Cruikshank, Margaret. *The Gay and Lesbian Liberation Movement.* New York: Routledge, 1992.

D'Emilio, John. *Sexual Politics, Sexual Communities: The Making of a Homosexual Minority in the United States, 1940–1970.* Chicago: University of Chicago Press, 1983.

D'Emilio, John, William B. Turner, and Urvashi Vaid, eds. *Creating Change: Sexuality, Public Policy, and Civil Rights.* New York: St. Martin's Press, 2000.

Duberman, Martin. *Stonewall.* New York: Dutton, 1993.

Katz, Jonathan. *Gay American History: Lesbians and Gay Men in the U.S.A.: A Documentary.* New York: Harper & Row, 1985.

Streitmatter, Rodger. *Unspeakable: The Rise of the Gay and Lesbian Press in America.* Boston: Faber and Faber, 1995.

Vicki L. Eaklor / H. S.

See also **Acquired Immune Deficiency Syndrome (AIDS); Defense of Marriage Act; Sexuality; Sexual Orientation.**

GELPCKÉ V. DUBUQUE, 6 Wallace 50 (1864). Prior to its decision in *Gelpcké v. Dubuque*, the Supreme Court of the United States stated that it would defer to the most recent state court decision when interpreting that state's constitution. In this case the city of Dubuque issued and later defaulted on bonds to finance the construction of a railroad. The city argued that it was not required to pay back the bonds because in 1862 the Iowa Supreme Court found the 1847 law authorizing the bonds unconstitutional under the state constitution.

The U.S. Supreme Court, hearing this case because Gelpcké was not a citizen of Iowa, determined that Dubuque must repay Gelpcké because the Iowa court's ruling did not impair the obligations made by the city under the law before it was found unconstitutional. In his majority opinion Justice Noah H. Swayne stated that the Court would not necessarily be bound by a state court's interpretation of that state's constitution. Preserving state court precedent was not important enough to justify "imolat[ing] truth, justice, and the law." In his dissent Justice Samuel F. Miller argued that the Court should show greater respect for the autonomy of state courts.

BIBLIOGRAPHY

Fairman, Charles. *Mr. Justice Miller and the Supreme Court, 1862–1890.* Cambridge, Mass.: Harvard University Press, 1939.

———. *Reconstruction and Reunion, 1864–88.* Volumes 6–7 of *History of the Supreme Court of the United States.* New York: Macmillan, 1987–1988.

Rehnquist, William H. *The Supreme Court.* New York: Knopf, 2001.

Akiba J. Covitz
Esa Lianne Sferra
Meredith L. Stewart

See also **Judicial Review.**

GENDER AND GENDER ROLES. As a term, "gender" refers to the social construction of sex or the psychosocial concomitants to sexed identity. Feminists, in particular, have relied on distinctions between sex as biological and gender as cultural to argue that women's oppression is historical and not inevitable. Yet at the beginning of the twenty-first century, in both feminist theory and popular discourse, "gender" has come to replace "sex" as a term referring to sexual difference in a biological sense. This shifting definition is a result, at least in part, of gender's introduction into modern discourse as a medical concept used to explain a person's felt sense of his or her lived identity as a sex. Because Western society seeks biological explanations of almost all social behaviors, distinctions between sex and gender are difficult to maintain.

Gender as a Medical Concept

"Gender," as a term, had been used for centuries as a euphemism for "sex," but never before in the sense of the social or psychosocial counterpart to biological sex. Twentieth-century treatment of intersexuality (hermaphroditism) initiated a change in perception of the sexed body, as well as a change in the linguistic usage of gender as a concept.

People whose bodies manifest anatomical signs of both femaleness and maleness have long fascinated and confounded physicians and lay people alike. Since the nineteenth century, gonadal sex (the existence of either testes or ovaries) was understood to determine sex assignment for people with intersex conditions, but in the mid-twentieth century physicians began to pay more attention to the felt sense of sex, or "psychosocial sex identity," of these patients when determining proper treatment options. The early twentieth-century development of both plastic surgery and endocrinology meant that physicians could treat patients with intersexed conditions so that their bodies would simulate the sexed anatomy and physiology of most males or females. To initiate such treatment, using plastic surgery of the genitals and hormonal preparations, doctors needed a set of protocols that would allow them to override the earlier medical truism that gonadal sex was the most important determinant for sex assignment.

A group of researchers working at Johns Hopkins University in the 1950s developed a protocol using the term "gender" as a way of designating the patient's felt sense of herself or himself as a woman or a man. These researchers, the most prominent of whom was the psychologist John Money, argued that a child's sense of herself or himself as a sex (that is, her or his gender) was not cemented as part of identity until about the age of two; before then, they hypothesized, a child's sex assignment could be changed without undue psychological damage. Money commented much later, in an interview for *Omni* magazine, that he used the term "gender" because of its prior use in philology (see Stein). In Money's initial usage, gender appeared in the context of a loose understanding of "gender role," a term that borrows from the sociologist Talcott Parsons's important term, "sex role." "Gender role" suggests the subject's enactment of behaviors in relation to role expectations, but links those expectations not to sex (and the body) but to one's felt sense of the self as a member of a sex class.

In the 1960s the psychoanalyst Robert Stoller reoriented the discourses around gender to identity, especially in the context of his work with people who identified as transsexuals. Stoller used "gender identity," however, in much the same way that Money had used "gender role"—to designate a person's sense of herself or himself as a sex. Both Stoller and Money strove to distinguish this sense of the self that develops after birth from the biological components of sex identity (gonads, hormones, internal reproductive structures, external genitalia, sex chromosomes, and secondary sex characteristics). Their emphasis on nurture—the idea that the psychodynamic constituents of the child's environment, including the parents or primary caregivers and the culture at large, were central to the development of gender as an identity—paved the way for the feminist appropriation of their ideas in the service of an examination of women's subordination as a sociocultural affair.

Gender as a Feminist Concept

Three publications from the 1970s set the stage for feminist explorations of gender as a theoretical concept in the

1980s and 1990s. Ann Oakley's 1972 book, *Sex, Gender, and Society*, inaugurated feminist attempts to theorize the relation between biological sexual difference and the social construction of gender as a historically variable system disadvantageous to women. While accepting that biological sex differences exist and may have an impact on the social behaviors of women and men, Oakley strongly asserts that culture enforces gendered meanings and maintains traditional gendered divisions in areas that might be amenable to transformation. In 1975 Gayle Rubin published her landmark essay, "The Traffic in Women: Notes on the Political Economy of Sex," which, firmly embedded in 1970s structuralist anthropology, Marxism, and psychoanalytic thinking, effectively articulates the connections between the economic, familial, and psychic registers of women's subordination. And in 1978 Suzanne Kessler and Wendy McKenna published *Gender: An Ethnomethodological Approach*, in which they demonstrate how the belief in only two sexes anchors modern perceptions of gender; bracketing off that belief reveals that assumptions about gender emerge from initial attributions of sex to each person we encounter.

Many scholars continue to use Rubin's fruitful concept of the sex/gender system, which she defines as the set of cultural mechanisms by means of which the "raw materials" of sex are made into gender. In addition, Rubin's understanding of the centrality of the exchange of women to women's subordination, as well as to their psychologically invested participation in kinship structures, remains an important contribution to feminist theorists' ideas about how women participate in the very systems that oppress them. Kessler and McKenna's insistence that all representations of sex are in fact gender (because culturally constructed) and their resistance to the "natural attitude" of binary sexual dimorphism presage later deconstructionist approaches. Other cultures recognize intermediary sexes, they argue; thus Euro-American beliefs about only two sexes are the result of the "reality" that we construct daily and therefore create as biological truth. In one example they assert that we recognize established gender identity only when children agree to the gender rules (that gender is invariant and that there are two of them) that adults understand as reality.

Following on the work of Kessler and McKenna, in 1987 the sociologists Candace West and Don Zimmerman laid out the conditions for "doing gender" as an aspect of daily experience. Bob Connell, an Australian sociologist, offered macro-oriented analyses in his book *Gender and Power* (1987), which examines how gender is produced through three social structures: labor, cathexis (sexuality and emotion), and political power. Connell shows how gender is not necessarily consistent or predictable in its effects. Also in the 1980s the impact of poststructuralist theories on feminist ideas about gender emerged. The film theorist Teresa de Lauretis published *Technologies of Gender* in 1987; in it the essay "The Technology of Gender" drew on the work of the French philosopher and historian Michel Foucault. Her work suggestively encourages the reader to consider how gender is constructed through representations, even feminist representations. The historian Joan Scott's 1988 book *Gender and the Politics of History* transformed "women's history" into a scholarly field that examines gender as an organizing framework for articulating relations of power. In "Gender: A Useful Category of Historical Analysis" (initially published in 1986), Scott argues powerfully for a discursive approach to historical study, which means, for her, a move away from "women" as the focus of feminist inquiry and toward attention to "gender" as the production of meanings about being a woman or a man.

All of these works set the stage for Judith Butler's 1990 publication, *Gender Trouble: Feminism and the Subversion of Identity*. Butler's book crystallized and advanced feminist theory's previous developments—the ethnomethodological questioning of the facticity of two sexes and the articulation of the concept of gender as a behavior that is consolidated through daily repetition ("doing gender"), poststructuralist emphases on representation and discourse as technologies that produce gender in the social world, and continued attention to gender as a variable social construction with uncertain effects.

Two ideas stand out, in terms of subsequent influence: Butler's theory of the performative and her deconstruction of the notion that a gender identity is the essence behind which gender expressions emerge socially. In terms of the former, *Gender Trouble* is somewhat equivocal, as Butler begins with a discussion of performativity as a grammatical concept derived from speech-act theory. In this sense certain kinds of linguistic articulations perform an action in the real as one says the words ("I do" in marriage is the classic example). Butler argues that gender instantiates itself as real in the same way—the social articulations of gender (bodily movements, dress, public sexual orientation; that is, its language) make gender appear to be something inhering in the body and as an identity that exists prior to its articulation, yet the articulations themselves actually create gender as we know it. Consequently, sex cannot be understood as being prior to gender, the biological ground on which gender is socially constructed, because gender as a concept is necessary to understand, to interpret, sex as a biological origin. Thomas Laqueur, in his 1990 *Making Sex: The Body and Gender from the Greeks to Freud*, argued roughly the same thing through a historical register.

Toward the end of *Gender Trouble*, Butler seems to shift toward a more theatrical understanding of performativity, which is the interpretation picked up by many radical activists and theorists who read the book. She articulates a theory of drag as emblematic of gender's alienated construction (being without identity). Ironically, it may be that this typical reading of *Gender Trouble* has been the most productive element of the text, in terms of its inauguration of a certain kind of "queer" theory that blossomed in 1990s academic and popular culture. From lesbian and gay theories to the emerging field of transgender scholarship, this notion of performativity caught fire and continues to energize both activist and academic gender projects. Thus, many of Butler's readers abandon her Foucaultian understanding of the constraining nature of social and linguistic structures—she believes they allow for some "subversive repetition," as small resistances to the normative modes of social being, but are not malleable or protean on a large scale—in favor of a celebration of postmodern possibilities of personal transformation.

Perhaps Butler's greatest contribution to the feminist theorization of gender was the way *Gender Trouble* cemented the constructionist view—that we make gender, and in that making, it makes us as well. Other scholars contributed to this discussion as well; feminist science studies scholars continued their attention to the social construction of sex as a biological category. Cultural and historical examinations of the medical treatment of intersexuality and transsexuality demonstrated how mainstream concepts of gender guided medical practice and the theories of gender authorized by biomedicine. In 1998 Suzanne Kessler published another landmark study in gender theory, *Lessons from the Intersexed*, although this text is more a study of a sociocultural phenomenon than a work of theory. Here Kessler demonstrates how rigid ideas about being a sex constrain the life choices, the social identities, and the embodied experiences of people born with intersex conditions. *Lessons* also shows us how gender, as a concept, authorizes medical practices on certain unruly bodies that not only damage those bodies in order that they will signify according to rather arbitrary standards of sexual dimorphism, but also consign those embodied subjects to silence, suffering, and marginalization.

During the 1980s and 1990s another set of influences worked to transform gender as a concept. Most of the primary texts of gender theory have been written by white feminists. As Donna Haraway states in her overview "'Gender' for a Marxist Dictionary: The Sexual Politics of a Word," feminist writers of color have long argued that the "category of gender obscured or subordinated all the other 'others'" (p. 144). Critical race theory, as it developed within legal studies and then moved on to other arenas, was linked with feminist theories to produce the hybrid "critical race feminism," in which race and gender are interrogated as connected vectors of experience. Other multicultural and interdisciplinary approaches abounded as feminist scholars attempted to account for the differences within the overarching category "women." For most feminist theorists today, gender as a category is used alongside race, class, and sexual orientation to demonstrate the complexity of any one woman's experience within intersecting oppressions. Yet "gender theory" as a field continues to be dominated by white feminists, as if gender can come into focus as a discrete category of analysis only for those women and men whose race offers them the privilege of forgetting that they have one. Indeed, Oyèrónkẹ́ Oyewùmí argues, in *The Invention of Women: Making African Sense of Western Gender Discourses* (1997), that there is something specifically Eurocentric about creating gender as a concept of such distinct importance from other markers of social relations. Oyewùmí's analysis of Yoruba social systems before and after European colonization offers cross-cultural evidence of how gender as a concept falsely universalizes experiences, social practices, and identities, an idea that had been developing in feminist theory since at least the mid-1980s.

At the beginning of the twenty-first century, gender theory is in an ambivalent position, as its focus has been, since the late 1990s at least, targeted on intersexuality, transsexuality, transgenderism, and lesbian and gay experiences. That is, the (theoretically) exemplary experiences of gender have moved from women to subjects once thought to be marginal to women's issues. In this movement, gender, as an analytical concept, has become enriched through careful articulations of its relation to other modes of being and experience, such as sexual orientation and race, but the early linkage between gender analysis and the exploration of women's subordination has at times disappeared. Indeed, the pioneer approaches of the historian Joan Scott and the philosopher Judith Butler (among others) favoring gender over women have become so entrenched that it is at times difficult to talk about women at all. (Of course, talking about women often leads to problems concerning which women, that is, problems of exclusion or privilege that go unrecognized; in addition to Butler, see Spelman.) There is also an emerging field of "masculinity studies" or "men's studies" (see Kimmel). Few feminists lament the incredibly rich and developed scholarship that has emerged from the efflorescence of "queer" approaches and critical race theory in the 1980s and 1990s, but there has been a startling dropping off, in terms of the development of gender theory, of the traditional foci of feminist inquiry: domesticity, kinship, equality, the sexual division of labor.

Joan Williams, a feminist legal theorist, has attempted to return feminist gender theory to its attention to women's experiences and subordination. In *Unbending Gender*, Williams's approach to gender theorizing is both pragmatic and theoretical, and attends to the concrete situations of domesticity that define gender in the late twentieth-century United States. In examining why so many working women "choose" to stay at home after they have children, Williams argues that domesticity operates as a "force-field" to pull women back into traditional gender norms, norms that eventually hurt women as the high rate of divorce leads to their relative impoverishment. Her multifaceted analysis includes a discussion of how gender norms articulate a language of class and race privilege and an elucidation of the ways in which divorce and custody agreements purposefully ignore the family work that women do both during and after the marriage in order to facilitate men's ideal worker status. The higher wages available to "ideal worker" men are not shared routinely with ex-spouses and children, although it is the flow of family work that makes that status possible. Williams further argues that feminists should rethink domesticity as "drag," in Butler's sense of a performance that does not mandate any particular identity as its origin. The value in this strategy is the acknowledgment, at least in the United States, that the full commodification model of feminism (outsourcing all domestic duties, including child care) has not worked as a political strategy to make women equal in the workplace, and has led to the unnecessarily antagonistic relations between those who embrace domesticity and those who repudiate it. Articulating domesticity as "drag" is one way of "unbending gender" by cutting the ties between domestic labor and women's supposed nature.

What Williams offers, then, is to take gender out of the stratospheric abstractions in which it has recently been articulated and to focus on the concrete situations in which women and men find themselves. Her conclusions around gender are equally concrete and encouraging, and she explicitly works against the notion that all women cohere around a particular gender identity or sensibility. Rather, her theory argues that women can come together through differences if they recognize how particular social structures (like the lack of well-remunerated part-time work) create circumstances negative for all women, regardless of the individual choices that women make. She articulates a theory of gender in relation to the structure of domesticity in American society, and argues that women's seemingly free choices concerning work and family must be interpreted within the constraints domesticity confers. Thus, gender, for Williams, operates as the power of domesticity; it also provides, through feminism, a way to analyze and transform women's choices by changing women's relation to domesticity and its implied origins in female identity.

Gender in American History

The history of gender in America is of a social institution that both constrains and produces womanhood and manhood throughout the centuries. Women are not only manipulated by gender norms: they create, negotiate, and transform those norms as well. The norms are racialized and linked to class status, and women, even though engaged in producing them, do not control either the economic structures or the meaning-making apparatuses that signify their power. Thus, for all their complicity with making gender, women are also disadvantaged by its operation. The specificity of that disadvantage is not stable, but its effects are enduring.

Most approaches to gender in American history examine the changing nature of women's and men's roles and relationships throughout the more than four centuries of European domination of North America. And while there may be a general story to tell about the differences between Puritan beliefs in hierarchy within community and later Enlightenment stresses on autonomous individualism, there are myriad other stories about how region, race, and religion affected how gender operated in any given historical period or geographical location. Careful attention to gender in American history demonstrates that it is produced through changing configurations of labor, kinship, racialization, and class distinction. Gender roles articulate social expectations about men's and women's proper duties and cultural practices, particularly in relation to reproduction, economic activity, and sexuality.

Men were in charge of colonial households in America, and those households were composed of family members as well as hired and indentured servants or slaves. Puritan women experienced religious equality with men, but wives were subject to the rule of their husbands. Women suffered "legal death" when they married, under the doctrine of coverture, which stipulated that women could not own property in their own right or conduct business in their own name. In the South, colonial households were generally far apart and, significantly, far from churches; women might have had more autonomy in contexts where they did not experience the direct oversight of the religious community that was common in the north. Quaker women, in addition, had more active roles in their church than women of other Protestant denominations.

Colonial white women did not experience the separation of motherhood from economic activity that became common in the domestic ideal of the nineteenth century, because the home was, in the earlier period, the center of economic life. Likewise, fathers were not estranged from the daily workings of home life, and often were responsible for the education of the children, especially sons. Linda Stone and Nancy McKee argue, in *Gender and Culture in America*, that colonial white women were able to integrate three roles of adult womanhood—economic activity, motherhood, and sexuality—in ways that are difficult for contemporary women. This is in part because the nineteenth century ushered in a set of social ideals that identified white women with self-sacrifice, nurture, and the home, and white men with autonomous individualism and the world of capitalist commerce.

Masculinity also changed over the course of the nineteenth century, from an ideal of manliness that connoted honorable character to a masculinity defined by an embodied virility associated with working-class muscularity. Femininity was defined by the "cult of true womanhood," as the historian Barbara Welter identified the interconnected ideals of domesticity, piety, submissiveness, and purity that dominated public discourses about femininity in the period. The cult of true womanhood was largely a northern, middle-class, white ideal, for southern white women were less likely to be constrained by northern notions of feminine domestic labor; slaves, of course, were unable to control their experience in order to live out the doctrine, as Harriet Jacobs explains in *Incidents in the Life of a Slave Girl.*

Jacobs demonstrates that educated female slaves, exposed to Euro-American ideals of female behavior, did try to use the cult of true womanhood to defend themselves against sexual assault and to define their lives in terms of virtue and piety, but also shows how difficult it was for black bondswomen to argue for themselves with the racialized ideals of true womanhood. Part of the difficulty here was the presumed frailty of white women, a perceived physical trait that justified their confinement to the domestic sphere, while black slave women and other working women (often not considered fully white by the middle and upper classes) could not, because of the daily expectations of bodily labor, assert this defining marker of femininity.

Yet the nineteenth century was not just about white women's confinement to the home and their submission to male authority. Married women's property acts were enacted in the mid-nineteenth century. In New York State two acts, in 1848 and 1860, made it legal for women to own property, although it was only after the second act that they had a right to their own earnings and the right of joint guardianship of their children. White women's increased moral authority in the home, concomitant to their consignment to domesticity, led many reformers to argue for their necessary involvement in public affairs. The logic was that if individual white women were to provide a softening, civilizing force against the competitive aggressivity of capitalism's effect on their menfolk, then as a group white women should bring their civilizing influence to society as a whole. This was one rationale for suffragism; the more radical rationale was that white women were citizens and were as entitled to vote as men were. The difference argument—that women constituted a special moral voice that is essential for a healthy civil society—has coexisted since the nineteenth century with the equality argument—that men and women are essentially the same politically and thus require equal rights. If in the nineteenth century the difference argument was bolstered by the cult of true womanhood and the powerful moral suasion of domestic femininity, the equality argument has dominated most of twentieth-century feminism, at least until the waning decades of the century, largely due to changing requirements of the capitalist workforce and the need for two incomes to sustain middle-class status for individual families.

The twentieth century saw an expansion of women's rights and opportunities (emblematized by the achievement of female suffrage in 1920), and thus an enlargement of their social roles as women, but many gender expectations remain. For example, as more and more women enter the workforce, women's relation to domesticity has been loosened but not cut completely. Women are still largely responsible for domestic labor, even when they work outside the home, leading to the phenomenon sociologist Arlie Hochschild calls "the second shift" (in a book of the same name). In the late nineteenth century the rise of companionate marriage and middle-class women's increasing control over their fertility seemed to indicate important advances for women. Certainly the gradual acceptance of family planning and birth control over the course of the twentieth century has been integral to the increasing freedoms that many American women experience (although variably) over their reproductive lives and, consequently, their lives in general. Yet companionate marriage and individual reproductive control have also influenced the development of new gendered expectations about women's marital sexuality and their relation to husbands (intensified) and to children (loosened, by nineteenth-century, middle-class standards). Second-wave feminism emerged in the turbulent 1960s in response, at least in part, to the stereotyped treatment of women in the student and civil rights movements. At the forefront of the early radical feminist goals was the achievement of sexual freedom for all women. Some feminists argue that women's desire for sexual freedom was exploited by men who articulated a rhetoric of freedom in the service of increased sexual access to women.

As in the antebellum period, sexual roles for women are understood culturally in relation to race and class categories, and are linked to the other main social roles for women: mothers and workers. Black women, argue Stone and McKee, have always combined work and motherhood, so white feminists' ardent desires to attain waged positions did not always define black feminist goals. Directly after emancipation, black women strove to mother their own children and be in the home as a way of resisting white oppression and the white demand that black women provide their services as underpaid domestic servants. Employment discrimination against black men made black mothers' domestic goals impossible for all but the most privileged among them, however, since black families desperately needed the wages of black women to make their households economically viable. This pattern continues in the present. But because the dominant American ideal is a domestic mother, black women have suffered socially as the economic structure, maintaining white interests, continues to mandate their absence from the home. Black women as mothers have also been treated differently from white women by welfare authorities and in public media; this differential treatment both produces and is an effect of negative views about black women as mothers and the widespread perception of black women as overly sexual (see Solinger and Roberts).

Native Americans' gender roles have also been affected by white expectations about their labor. At European conquest, native Indian women were not economically dependent on men. Tribal interactions with Europeans instituted ideas about women's necessary and natural dependence on men. For example, treaties between whites and tribal leaders often disrupted women's access to land, enforcing their dependence on men in their tribes. Men's spheres were affected as well; Stone and McKee write that the European stress on farming as a "civilized" occupation often left native men, whose gender roles were circumscribed to hunting and warfare, without distinct roles in their changing societies (pp. 78–80).

Asian Americans and Latinos or Hispanic Americans have different histories with regard to gender. Stone and McKee examine what they call the "patriarchal core" of Latino culture: domination by men, machismo, and women's sole responsibility in the domestic realm (even when they work outside the home). The Chicana lesbian feminist Cherrie Moraga writes about the entanglements of race, nationality, and sexuality in her classic essay "A Long Line of Vendidas," in which she claims, at one point, "My brother's sex was white. Mine, brown." Asian Americans are perhaps the most diverse group collected under one minority label. Immigration laws in the nineteenth and early twentieth centuries limited Asian immigration and, especially, the immigration of Chinese women. The internment of Japanese Americans and immigrant Japanese citizens during World War II affected men and women distinctly; the dislocation diminished men's authority within the family, while it tended to loosen gender roles and offer women relief from domestic burdens (Stone and McKee, p. 119). Often called the "model minority," Asian Americans struggle with a variety of stereotypes inflected by Euro-American gender expectations; in the sexual realm these include the compliant and exotic Asian woman and the emasculated Asian man.

Women of color often claim that the mainstream women's movement is oriented toward white women's experiences, perceptions, and needs; this claim demonstrates not only the way white women have dominated the discourses defining feminism but also the way in which dominant conceptions of gender apply to white, middle-class women's aspirations and situations. Lesbians and gay men have also challenged feminism's implicit privileging of heterosexual women, arguing that gender norms, expectations, and social practices do not just perpetuate sex discrimination but also operate to subordinate homosexuals. Radical feminist activists initially targeted constraining gender roles as the cause or perpetuation of oppression; however, currently some radical activism celebrates role-playing as long as it is engaged in voluntarily and is distinguished from identity or essence. Lesbian, gay, and feminist scholars continue to debate the significance of gender roles in the history of lesbianism, which in the 1950s and 1960s was comprised, at least in part, of a vibrant working-class bar culture that developed and enacted butch-femme roles. Lesbian feminists of the 1970s largely repudiated butch-femme roles in favor of an expressive politics of androgyny, although in the early 1980s the "sexuality debates" within feminism critiqued lesbian feminism for denigrating the erotic potential of earlier lesbian cultures. Annual gay pride marches that occur around the United States each June to commemorate the 1969 riots at New York City's Stonewall Inn, in which lesbian, gay, and transgender patrons protested a routine police shakedown, are testimonials to the expanding performative politics of gender disruption. Parade participants flaunt gender conventions as well as norms of sexual orientation, demonstrating the tight linkage between gender and sexuality in the construction of personhood in America.

Since the mid-1970s, as ideas about gender have proliferated, American women have experienced increasing freedom from overt discrimination and exclusion. Perhaps that is why gender as a concept has become more synonymous with sex, identifying a conservative national desire to see nature and culture in agreement on fundamental differences between women and men that explain the social subordination of female human beings. Radical emphases on alternate genders, combining or transgressing genders, may indicate increasing freedoms from the constraining binaries of historical configurations, or they may only represent utopian desires to transcend the difficulties of producing truly egalitarian, political solutions to existing inequalities of gendered power and privilege.

BIBLIOGRAPHY

Bornstein, Kate. *Gender Outlaw: On Men, Women, and the Rest of Us.* New York: Routledge, 1994.

Butler, Judith. *Gender Trouble: Feminism and the Subversion of Identity.* New York: Routledge, 1990.

Connell, R. W. *Gender and Power.* Stanford, Calif.: Stanford University Press, 1987.

Cott, Nancy F. *The Bonds of Womanhood: "Woman's Sphere" in New England, 1780–1835.* New Haven, Conn.: Yale University Press, 1977.

De Lauretis, Teresa. *Technologies of Gender: Essays on Theory, Film, and Fiction.* Bloomington: Indiana University Press, 1987.

Delgado, Richard, and Jean Stefancic, eds. *Critical Race Theory: The Cutting Edge.* 2d ed. Philadelphia: Temple University Press, 1999.

D'Emilio, John, and Estelle B. Freedman. *Intimate Matters: A History of Sexuality in America.* New York: Harper & Row, 1988.

Echols, Alice. *Daring to Be Bad: Radical Feminism in America, 1967–1975.* Minneapolis: University of Minnesota Press, 1989.

Evans, Sara M. *Born for Liberty: A History of Women in America.* New York: Free Press, 1989.

Fausto-Sterling, Anne. *Myths of Gender: Biological Theories About Women and Men.* New York: Basic Books, 1985.

Haraway, Donna J. "'Gender' for a Marxist Dictionary: The Sexual Politics of a Word." In her *Simians, Cyborgs, and Women: The Reinvention of Nature.* New York: Routledge, 1991.

Hausman, Bernice L. *Changing Sex: Transsexualism, Technology, and the Idea of Gender.* Durham, N.C.: Duke University Pres, 1995.

Hochschild, Arlie. *The Second Shift.* New York: Viking, 1989.

Jacobs, Harriet. *Incidents in the Life of a Slave Girl, Written by Herself.* Edited by L. Maria Child and Jean Fagan Yellin. Cambridge, Mass: Harvard University Press, 1987.

Kessler, Suzanne J. *Lessons from the Intersexed.* New Brunswick, N.J.: Rutgers University Press, 1998.

Kessler, Suzanne J. and Wendy McKenna. *Gender: An Ethnomethodological Approach*. New York: John Wiley, 1978. Repr. Chicago: University of Chicago Press, 1985.

Kimmel, Michael S. *Manhood in America: A Cultural History*. New York: Free Press, 1996.

Laqueur, Thomas. *Making Sex: The Body and Gender from the Greeks to Freud*. Cambridge, Mass: Harvard University Press, 1990.

Money, John, John Hampson, and Joan Hampson. "An Examination of Some Basic Sexual Concepts: The Evidence of Human Hermaphroditism." *Bulletin of the Johns Hopkins Hospital* 97, no. 4 (1955): 301–319.

———. "Hermaphroditism: Recommendations Concerning Assignment of Sex, Change of Sex, and Psychologic Management." *Bulletin of the Johns Hopkins Hospital* 97, no. 4 (1955): 284–300.

———. "Sexual Incongruity and Psychopathology: The Evidence of Human Hermaphroditism." *Bulletin of the Johns Hopkins Hospital* 91, no. 1 (1956): 43–57.

———. "Imprinting and the Establishment of Gender Role." *Archives of Neurology and Psychiatry* 77 (1957): 333–336.

Moraga, Cherrie. "A Long Line of Vendidas." In her *Loving in the War Years*. Boston: South End Press, 1983.

Oakley, Ann. *Sex, Gender, and Society*. New York: Harper & Row/Harper Colophon Books, 1972.

Oyewùmí, Oyèrónké. *The Invention of Women: Making an African Sense of Western Gender Discourses*. Minneapolis: University of Minnesota Press, 1997.

Parsons, Talcott. "Sex Roles in the American Kinship System." In *The Kinship System of the Contemporary United States: Essays in Sociological Theory*. New York: Free Press, 1954.

Roberts, Dorothy. *Killing the Black Body: Race, Reproduction, and the Meaning of Liberty*. New York: Pantheon, 1997.

Rubin, Gayle. "The Traffic in Women: Notes on the 'Political Economy' of Sex." In *Toward an Anthropology of Women*. Edited by Rayna R. Reiter. New York: Monthly Review Press, 1975.

Scott, Joan Wallach. "Gender: A Useful Category of Historical Analysis." *American Historical Review* 91, no. 5 (December 1986): 1053–1075.

———. *Gender and the Politics of History*. New York: Columbia University Press, 1988.

Solinger, Rickie. *Wake Up Little Susie: Single Pregnancy and Race Before Roe v. Wade*. 2d ed. New York: Routledge, 2000.

Spelman, Elizabeth V. *Inessential Woman: Problems of Exclusion in Feminist Thought*. Boston: Beacon, 1988.

Stein, Kathleen. "Interview: John Money." *Omni* 8, no. 7 (April 1986): 79–80, 82, 84, 86, 126, 128, 130, 131.

Stoller, Robert J. "A Contribution to the Study of Gender Identity." *Journal of the American Medical Association* 45 (1964): 220–226.

———. *Sex and Gender: On the Development of Masculinity and Femininity*. New York: Science House, 1968.

Stone, Linda and Nancy P. McKee. *Gender and Culture in America*. Upper Saddle River, N.J.: Prentice-Hall, 1999.

Welter, Barbara. "The Cult of True Womanhood." *American Quarterly* 18 (1966): 151–174.

West, Candace, and Don Zimmerman. "Doing Gender." *Gender and Society* 1, no. 2 (June 1987): 125–151.

Williams, Joan. *Unbending Gender: Why Family and Work Conflict and What to Do About It*. New York: Oxford University Press, 2000.

Wing, Adrien Katherine, ed. *Critical Race Feminism: A Reader*. New York: New York University Press, 1997.

Bernice L. Hausman

See also **Gay and Lesbian Movement; Women in Churches; Women in Military Service; Women in Public Life, Business, and Professions; Women's Rights Movement; Women's Studies;** *and vol. 9:* **Human Rights Not Founded on Sex; Letters of Abigail and John Adams; NOW Statement of Purpose; On the Equality of the Sexes; The Theory of the Leisure Class; What If I Am a Woman?**

GENEALOGY. Genealogy is an auxiliary branch of history that was first recognized as a professional field of study in 1964 with the formation of the Board for Certification of Genealogists (BCG). Celebration of the U.S. centennial heralded the beginning of solid professional genealogical research and the first amateur craze of the 1880s and 1890s. Although the National Genealogical Society (NGS) was formed in 1903, there were no prescribed standards for professional genealogists until the middle of twentieth century. During the period between World War I and World War II, New England genealogists mounted an exhaustive examination of primary sources, which ultimately led to a scientific methodology for the discipline. In 1940 Dr. Arthur Adams and John Insley Coddington moved to redress the lack of standards with the founding of the American Society of Genealogists (ASG). The ASG appointed a Committee on Standards and Ethics that functioned from the early 1940s to the early 1960s. Although several proposals were received from the committee, they were not acted upon until 1963, when Noel Stevenson recommended that an organization headquartered in Washington, D.C., the BCG, be formed for certification purposes. Dr. Jean Stephenson served as the first president and Milton Rubincam served as chair.

The four major institutes within the United States where genealogists can receive professional training are the National Institute on Genealogical Research (1950), the Samford Institute of Genealogy and Historic Research (1964), the Genealogical Institute of Mid-America (1993), and the Salt Lake Institute of Genealogy (1996). Although attending one of these institutes is highly recommended for professional genealogists, it is not required for certification purposes.

High standards were imposed not only upon the certification of genealogists but upon their research methodology as well. New genealogical research was put under a strict test of accuracy and documentation and existing genealogies were reexamined, although this new scrutiny did not greatly enhance the regard of scholarly historians for genealogical research. In his 1975 article, "The Fundamentals of Genealogy: A Neglected But Fertile New Field for Professional Historians?" Jay P. Anglin wrote that

> inadequate recognition of the contributions of genealogists unfortunately still persists among a large number of professional historians, for old views of the elite professional genealogists as merely antiquarians and of the discipline as exclusive field for silly and rich eccentrics desirous of social status by finding tenuous ancestral linkages with Europe's illustrious figures are hard to destroy.

While genealogists remain isolated from historians, a reciprocal relationship has developed in the 1990s as more university and college history departments offer introductory genealogy courses as part of their curricula.

Obtaining Certification and Doing Research

The first step toward certification is gaining the knowledge and skills imparted by the BCG Genealogical Standards Manual. Within this manual are seventy-four standards that contribute to the level of credibility in genealogy that are referred to as the Genealogical Proof Standard (GPS), which replaced a concept, "preponderance of the evidence," that BCG had once promoted. In 1997 BCG abandoned that terminology for analyzing and weighing evidence because the board's governing trustees felt that it was confusing. Originally borrowed from the legal system, the term failed genealogists because BCG standards require a higher level of proof than do legal codes. Professional genealogists are certified in three different research categories and/or two teaching categories by an examination of work samples in a portfolio submission. The research categories include Certified Genealogical Record Searcher (CGRS), Certified American Lineage Specialist (CALS), Certified American Indian Lineage Specialist (CAILS), and Certified Genealogist (CG). The teaching categories include Certified Genealogical Lecturer (CGL) and Certified Genealogical Instructor (CGI). Each application is independently evaluated by several judges. Renewal applications every five years confirm that skills are up to date.

Methodology applied in genealogical research at the turn of the twenty-first century is much improved and more sophisticated compared to the sometimes careless and inaccurate compilations of yesteryear. However, both professional and amateur genealogists begin their research with present records and documents, eventually arriving at a solution to their research question by employing reverse chronology. Essentially, genealogists investigate known information for clues that will lead them to solving the research problem. Utilizing the GPS, the researcher completes an exhaustive search of the records, documents findings with complete and accurate source citations, analyzes and correlates the findings, resolves any conflicting information, and writes a soundly reasoned conclusion to the query.

Certified genealogists abide by a Code of Ethics and Conduct that mandates high levels of truth and accuracy in their work, collegiality and honor within the discipline, adherence to the BCG's Standards of Conduct, and protection of the privacy and best interests of the client. They are also bound to protect the public, the consumer, and the profession.

Raising Standards

Donald Lines Jacobus was one of the new generation of professional genealogists who raised the status of genealogy from a hobby to a science. In 1922 Jacobus founded America's premier independent genealogical journal, *The American Genealogist* (TAG). Fondly regarded as the "dean" of genealogy, Jacobus in the 1930s dispelled the myth that America's first settlers were of prime stock with vivid statistics. He found evidence of disability and other defects among early New England settlers, while remarking that the homogeneity of the population likely resulted in birth defects associated with inbreeding. Jacobus is also noted as the founder of scientific genealogy in the United States and the first inductee to the National Genealogy Hall of Fame in 1986.

Dr. Jean Stephenson was an early proponent and supporter of genealogical education who played a major role in establishing the institutions currently serving the discipline. Although she published several genealogical works, she is remembered for her service to and membership in many organizations and societies, including the ASG, NGS, BCG, the Institute on Genealogical Research, the Samford University Institute of Genealogy and Historical Research, the National Society of the Daughters of the American Revolution (NSDAR), the American Association for State and Local History, and the Society of American Archivists, among others.

John Insley Coddington's fluency and reading knowledge of several European languages as well as his familiarity with European libraries and archives gave him a distinct edge over other American genealogists. Initially an historian, he found the development of scientific genealogy appealing. Although troubled by the lack of seriousness displayed by genealogists, Coddington—along with Arthur Adams and Meredith Colket—launched an honor society comprised of fifty fellows, the ASG. Chosen on the quality and accuracy of their research, many leading genealogists were members. Upon the death of Jacobus in 1970, Coddington acquired the title "dean" of American genealogists. Known for his advocacy of documentary evidence, he published over two hundred articles in genealogy journals, was an elected a fellow in several genealogy societies, and was a contributing editor to TAG from 1938 until his death in 1991.

James Dent Walker formed an active and viable African American genealogical community when he founded the Afro-American Historical and Genealogical Society in 1977. Employed by the National Archives and Records Administration for thirty years, he served in several positions, but was renowned for his acumen with military and pension records and exhibited an outstanding ability to uncover sources important to African American genealogists. He also aided Alex Haley with the research that became the Pulitzer Prize–winning book, *Roots* (1976), which spurred African Americans as well as other Americans to search for their ancestors. Walker's contributions are not diminished by the discrediting of Haley's work in the 1990s. Walker is most noted for his ability to uncover the inaccuracy of historical information. While doing research for the NSDAR, which estimated that only five thousand members of minorities (blacks, women, and American Indians) had served in the American Revolution, Walker identified five thousand minorities serving in the New England region alone.

BIBLIOGRAPHY

Anglin, Jay P. "The Fundamentals of Genealogy: A Neglected But Fertile New Field for Professional Historians?" *Southern Quarterly* 13 (1975): 145–150.

Carmack, Sharon DeBartolo. *The Genealogy Sourcebook.* Chicago: Contemporary Books, 1997.

Doane, Gilbert H., and James B. Bell. *Searching For Your Ancestors: The How and Why of Genealogy.* 6th ed. Minneapolis: University of Minnesota Press, 1992.

Latham, William, and Cindy Higgins. *How to Find Your Family Roots.* Rev. ed. Santa Monica, Calif.: Santa Monica Press, 2000.

Mills, Elizabeth Shown, ed. *Professional Genealogy: A Manual for Researchers, Writers, Editors, Lecturers, and Librarians.* Baltimore: Genealogical Publishing, 2001.

Stevenson, Noel C. *Genealogical Evidence: A Guide to the Standard of Proof Relating to Pedigrees, Ancestry, Heirship, and Family History.* Laguna Hills, Calif.: Aegean Park, 1989.

Wright, Raymond S. *The Genealogist's Handbook.* Chicago: American Library Association, 1995.

Rebecca Tolley-Stokes

GENERAL ACCOUNTING OFFICE. The General Accounting Office (GAO) is an independent government agency directed by the comptroller general of the United States. Congress created the office in 1921, when it passed the Budget and Accounting Act. From 1921 to 1945 the GAO functioned mainly as an auditor, checking on the legality and accuracy of federal expenditures. It also handled financial claims for and against the government, decided on bid protests on government contracts, and approved agency accounting systems. During the New Deal and World War II, the GAO expanded its jurisdiction to field sites of government programs and contract operations. After World War II, the GAO began undertaking comprehensive audits that went beyond strictly financial matters. By the 1950s its studies of federal activities in the defense, international, and civil areas combined analysis of the financial aspects of programs with an examination of their effectiveness and results. Under Comptrollers General Elmer B. Staats (1966–1981) and Charles A. Bowsher (1981–1995), the GAO focused on program evaluation.

By the 1990s, the GAO annually produced one thousand blue-cover reports, two hundred to three hundred congressional testimonies, and many oral and written briefings. By that time 80 percent of the GAO's work grew out of congressional requests, and it prepared reports on such high-profile issues as the savings and loan crisis, the Iran-Contra scandal, health care reform, the federal budget deficit, and major weapons systems. Commonly referred to as the investigative arm of Congress, the GAO, with a staff of 4,500 in 1994, was an influential force in the federal government, although its role was not widely understood by most Americans. The comptroller general, who is appointed by the president for a fifteen-year term, emerged as one of the most influential federal officials. The GAO's work has resulted in annual savings to the government of billions of dollars. For example, in 1991 GAO testimony influenced Congress to prohibit the use of funds appropriated for the Desert Shield and Desert Storm operations to pay for an indirect fuel price increase experienced by the Department of Defense outside the Persian Gulf as a result of high oil prices; this preventive measure saved the government $2.8 billion.

BIBLIOGRAPHY

Mosher, Frederick C. *The GAO: The Quest for Accountability in American Government.* Boulder, Colo.: Westview Press, 1979.

Trask, Roger R. *GAO History, 1921–1991.* Washington, D.C.: United States General Accounting Office, History Program, 1991.

Walker, Wallace Earl. *Changing Organizational Culture: Strategy, Structure, and Professionalism in the U.S. General Accounting Office.* Knoxville: University of Tennessee Press, 1986.

Roger R. Trask / c. w.

See also **Budget, Federal; Comptroller General of the United States; Congress, United States; Defense, Department of.**

GENERAL AGREEMENT ON TARIFFS AND TRADE—the world's major multinational trade agreement—and the international secretariat that oversees its operations, are both referred to as GATT. More than 100 nations are signatories, and many others pattern their trade policies on its provisions. Although Cold War tensions excluded some nations, including the Soviet Union and the Chinese governments in Taipei and Beijing, GATT served as the major international trade agreement, affecting the vast majority of world trade. In the 1990s, the end of the Cold War led to the incorporation of the former Eastern Bloc nations into GATT negotiations. The concept for such an approach to international trade policy originated in bilateral Anglo American discussions during World War II and sought to alleviate postwar economic problems. In the original plan, the Interna-

TIONAL MONETARY FUND and the WORLD BANK were to be joined by the International Trade Organization (ITO), which would regulate commerce. The general agreement that emerged from the Havana Conference in 1947 was drafted only as a temporary measure to stabilize world trade until the ITO took over. When the U.S. Senate refused to consent to the ITO charter, President Harry S. Truman decided to join GATT through an executive order. Another twenty-two nations joined the United States in endorsing the new arrangement, which incorporated many provisions in the ITO's charter but lacked envisioned enforcement powers. GATT has managed to survive and remain effective primarily because of the goodwill of member nations, the benefits they enjoy from expanded trade, and their desire to avoid retaliation from other nations that support it. Despite absence of a rigid structure and enforcement authority, GATT has played a major role in the reduction or elimination of high trade barriers among western industrialized nations, contributing factors to the GREAT DEPRESSION of the 1930s and the onset of World War II.

The agreement's goal is to encourage member nations to lower tariffs and eliminate import or other regulatory quotas. Nondiscrimination is a key principle in all of its many subagreements. That principle is carried out primarily through most-favored-nation provisions in tariff treaties, which require that no signatory shall impose greater burdens on one trading partner than on another. A second principle is that a GATT member may not rescind any TARIFF concession without compensation for trading partners adversely affected. The agreement also urges all parties to rely on negotiations and consultation to resolve trade conflicts. The arrangement is not without problems. Exceptions to its rules are permitted to accommodate the special needs of developing nations that may wish to continue relations with former colonial powers. Perhaps the most important exception to the most-favored-nation approach is one that furthers GATT's goal of reducing trade barriers. If a group of nations decides to create a free-trade zone, such as the European Community or the NORTH AMERICAN FREE TRADE AGREEMENT (NAFTA), it can do so without retaliation or sanction from other GATT members.

A series of negotiating periods, or "rounds," took place after the initial agreement in 1947: Geneva, Switzerland (1947); Annecy, France (1949); Torquay, England (1950–1951); Geneva (1955–1956); and the Dillon Round (named for U.S. Secretary of the Treasury Douglas Dillon) in Geneva (1961–1962). These first five rounds followed the pattern that had characterized negotiations under the U.S. Reciprocal Trade Agreements Act of 1934. Representatives of the primary supplier of a commodity or product would engage in talks with a major consumer, each party seeking reductions in rates. Once a bilateral bargain was struck and added to the multinational agreement, the most-favored-nation principle extended rates to all parties. In this way, world tariffs on industrial products fell to 13 percent.

The sixth round was named for President John F. Kennedy and took place in Geneva from 1964 to 1967. The United States brought in a new strategy when it offered broad, across-the-board reductions. Negotiators focused on deciding what commodities or items to exclude. The Tokyo Round (1973–1979) continued tariff reduction, leading to a general overall rate of 4 percent on industrial commodities. GATT succeeded in reducing tariffs but did not deal nearly as effectively with nontariff barriers (NTBs). The Kennedy Round was the first at which the NTBs were given serious attention, and they dominated discussions at the Tokyo Round. Negotiations led to a series of codes of conduct directed at NTBs. These attempted to lessen or eliminate such practices as dumping, government-subsidized exports, exclusionary government procurement policies, and arbitrary customs valuations. Most industrial nations agreed to abide by these codes, but developing nations did not. The Uruguay Round concluded seven years of negotiations on 15 December 1993 after a most ambitious agenda. In addition to further tariff reductions, it fashioned partial agreements on agricultural products, services, and INTELLECTUAL PROPERTY rights that earlier rounds had failed to address. As with all previous GATT negotiations, special interests in many nations were critical of the round, but prospects for international acceptance appeared positive. In the 1990s, trade policy became a major issue in American domestic politics. Protectionist and internationalist wings divided both of the two major parties. Among Democrats, President Bill Clinton's support of multinational trade agreements, such as GATT and NAFTA, placed him in direct conflict with the organized labor union constituency of his party. On the conservative side of the ideological spectrum, in 1992 and 1996, presidential candidate Pat Buchanan led a protectionist insurrection within Republican Party ranks. In both cases, however, protrade forces remained in control of the national Republican and Democratic Parties. The bulk of anti-GATT and anti-NAFTA sentiment became concentrated in the presidential campaigns of Reform Party candidate H. Ross Perot of 1992 and 1996. Internationally, in the 1990s, the GATT negotiations elicited fears that multinational trade agreements facilitated American cultural imperialism. Even countries historically friendly to the United States, such as Britain and France, expressed concern that "globalization" homogenized local cultures. The notion that global free trade promoted American cultural domination of the world remained a delicate and controversial issue at the close of the twentieth century.

BIBLIOGRAPHY

Baldwin, Robert E., and Anne O. Krueger, eds. *The Structure and Evolution of Recent U.S. Trade Policy*. Chicago: University of Chicago Press, 1984.

Evans, John W. *The Kennedy Round in American Trade Policy: The Twilight of the GATT?* Cambridge, Mass.: Harvard University Press, 1971.

John M. Dobson / A. G.

See also **Foreign Investment in the United States; Reciprocal Trade Agreements; Trade, Foreign.**

GENERAL COURT, COLONIAL. The general court, which functioned as a legislature, administrative agency, and judicial body, served as the central governing body of Massachusetts Bay from the colony's inception. By royal charter, King Charles I of England granted Puritans (Protestant dissenters against the Church of England) the right to form a company that would hold four "Greate and Generall Courts" each year where freemen would administer company business, making "wholesome and reasonable orders, lawes, statutes, and ordinances" that would not contravene English law. The court gained importance when Puritan leaders in 1629 decided to shift the Massachusetts Bay Company's whole government from London to New England. No chartered group had ever moved its entire headquarters and administrative structure to the colonies—previously, most of the important decisions about England's New World Colonies had remained in the hands of men in England. This event converted the trading company's general court into a local, not remote, body that could eventually function as a colonial assembly. In 1644, the court became a bicameral organization, with a House of Assistants (later the Senate) and a House of Deputies (later the House of Representatives) that could mutually veto each other's legislative proposals. Adopting parliamentary procedures, proposed laws were read in the general court on three separate days prior to their enactment.

Puritan leaders specifically encouraged education; their earliest initiatives through the general court created local grammar schools and a university, later known as Harvard College. The court also passed laws in many other areas, regulated certain professions (such as the practice of medicine), and served as the final court of appeal for local lawsuits.

The general court of Massachusetts Bay invited imitation and attracted controversy. Other colonies in New England, including New Haven, Connecticut, Rhode Island, and Plymouth copied the name or methods of the Massachusetts general court. Technically speaking, a general court assembled together the colonial governor, his assistants or council, and colonial freemen or their representatives. Men like John Winthrop, the first governor of Massachusetts Bay, attempted to limit who might serve in the general court by restricting the designation of "freemen" to colonists who were devout Puritan churchmen, and this religious restriction eased only after sixty years. Individuals who protested against the authority of the general court or the colony's dominant Puritan regime were banished, as in the cases of Roger Williams and Anne Hutchinson. Divisiveness did not disappear, however; the court itself fragmented into competing parties during the eighteenth century. Members of Massachusetts's general court eventually rebelled against the English monarchy in the 1770s, transforming the colonial assembly into a state legislature.

BIBLIOGRAPHY

Breen, T. H. *The Character of the Good Ruler: A Study of Puritan Political Ideas in New England, 1630–1730.* New York: Norton, 1974.

Bushman, Richard L. *King and People in Provincial Massachusetts.* Chapel Hill: University of North Carolina Press, 1985.

Dalton, Cornelius, John Wirkkala, and Anne Thomas. *Leading the Way: A History of the Massachusetts General Court, 1629–1980.* Boston: Office of the Massachusetts Secretary of State, 1984.

Sally E. Hadden

See also **Assemblies, Colonial; Assistant; Massachusetts Bay Colony;** *and vol. 9:* **Trial of Anne Hutchinson at Newton, 1637.**

GENERAL ELECTRIC COMPANY V. GILBERT, 429 U.S. 125 (1976), a Supreme Court ruling which held that employers could legally exclude conditions related to pregnancy from employee sickness and accident benefits plans. In *Geduldig v. Aiello* (1974) the Court upheld a California disability insurance program's denial of benefits for pregnancy-related disabilities. In *Gilbert* the Court fell back on *Geduldig* to rule that exclusion of pregnancy from a health plan did not violate Title VII, an equal employment opportunity provision that introduced a ban on gender discrimination into the Civil Rights Act of 1964. In deciding that such a ban did not discriminate against women, the Court reversed every appeals court that had considered the issue. Justice William Rehnquist's majority opinion pointed out that the plan in question paid out about as much money to female as to male claimants, and that pregnancy differed from other conditions not just because only women become pregnant but also because it is often "voluntarily undertaken and desired." Justice William Brennan's dissent observed that the General Electric Company did not exclude other "voluntarily undertaken" conditions, such as sports injuries, attempted suicides, elective cosmetic surgery, and vasectomies. Rehnquist relied on language from *Geduldig,* in which Justice Potter Stewart argued that when only pregnant women and nonpregnant persons (including men) were involved, there was no gender discrimination. Congress disagreed with this line of reasoning. The Pregnancy Discrimination Act of 1978 amended Title VII to prohibit employers from treating pregnancy less favorably than other conditions. The Family and Medical Leave Act of 1993 further expanded employment protections to pregnant women.

BIBLIOGRAPHY

Baer, Judith A. *Women in American Law*. Vol. 2, *The Struggle toward Equality from the New Deal to the Present*. New York: Holmes and Meier, 1991.

Hoff, Joan. *Law, Gender, and Injustice: A Legal History of U.S. Women*. New York: New York University Press, 1991.

Judith A. Baer/A. R.

See also **Family and Medical Leave Act; Pregnancy Discrimination Act; Discrimination: Sex.**

GENERAL FEDERATION OF WOMEN'S CLUBS. The GFWC was founded in 1890 at the initiative of newspaperwoman Jane ("Jennie June") Cunningham Croly at a meeting in New York City of representatives from more than sixty women's clubs from around the country. For several decades before, women in the United States had been forming voluntary organizations such as literary clubs, local and municipal improvement clubs, suffrage groups, and women's professional, religious, and ethnic organizations. The GFWC was to be an organizational umbrella under which all types of women's organizations could gather to discuss and identify common concerns and work together to implement social and political changes on the local, state, and national levels. The GFWC was chartered by Congress in 1901. By 1910 it had more than one million members in affiliated clubs on the local level and in state federations of women's clubs.

To conduct its business, the GFWC held biennial national conventions in different locales throughout the country. It established national working committees to gather information on matters of most concern to women's clubs, such as civil service reform, public education, pure food and drugs, child labor, juvenile justice, and public health. Through these national committees and publications such as the *Federation Bulletin*, the GFWC disseminated information to its member clubs and helped coordinate their activities. It also coordinated its activities with those of other women's organizations such as the National Consumers' League and the National Congress of Mothers.

Shortly after its founding, the GFWC faced controversy over whether to include African American women's clubs in the Federation or even support the membership of African American women in affiliated clubs. When the GFWC executive committee approved in 1900 admission of the Women's Era Club of Boston headed by African American activist Josephine St. Pierre Ruffin, southern women forced the convention to rescind the admission. Member clubs such as the Chicago Women's Club, which in 1894 had admitted African American clubwoman Fannie Barrier Williams, objected to the convention's decision. But African American women continued to organize themselves and work through the National Association of Colored Women (NACW) rather than the GFWC.

In the 1920s and 1930s the GFWC supported the work of the Women's Bureau within the Department of Labor, backed passage in 1921 of the federal Sheppard-Towner Infancy and Maternity Protection Act to promote the health and welfare of mothers and infants, created an Indian Welfare Committee, and protested the provisions of the New Deal's National Recovery Act that allowed lower wage rates for women workers and exempted handicapped and home workers from its protections. In the 1970s the GFWC supported the Equal Rights Amendment and at the end of the century was still engaged in women's health issues.

The GFWC expanded its work into the international arena when it supported the founding of the United Nations. At the end of the twentieth century the GFWC had affiliated clubs in twenty countries. Its international programs concentrate on issues of special concern to women and children, on literacy campaigns, and on human rights and environmental issues.

BIBLIOGRAPHY

General Federation of Women's Clubs. Home page at http://www.gfwc.org.

Scott, Anne Firor. *Natural Allies: Women's Associations in American History*. Urbana: University of Illinois Press, 1991.

Skocpol, Theda. *Protecting Soldiers and Mothers: The Political Origins of Social Policy in the United States*. Cambridge: Harvard University Press, 1992.

Maureen A. Flanagan

See also **Consumers Leagues; National Association of Colored Women; Women's Bureau; Women's Clubs.**

GENERAL MOTORS is a worldwide corporation that produces everything from microchips to locomotives. William Crapo Durant of Flint, Michigan and a small group of investors formed the General Motors Company (GM) 16 September 1908 in Trenton, New Jersey. Durant, who already owned Buick Motor Company, bought small car and parts manufacturers and incorporated them into GM. Among Durant's first acquisitions were Oldsmobile, Cadillac, and Oakland (Pontiac). By 1920 GM had purchased more than 30 companies. After World War I GM experienced a decline so severe Durant resigned his post as president. In 1923 the Board of Directors elected Alfred P. Sloan, Jr. president (10 May 1923–3 May 1937) and Chairman of the Executive Committee (3 May 1937–2 April 1956). Sloan, whose Hyatt Roller Bearing Company joined GM in 1919, utilized creative management techniques that made GM the largest car and truck manufacturer in the world. Under Sloan's leadership, GM developed a number of firsts including independent front wheel suspension and the automatic transmission. While GM participated in all U.S. war efforts, its most dramatic contribution was during World War II. From 1942 through the end of the war, GM's plants stopped all non-military production. Producing ball bearings to bombers, GM was responsible for 13,000 planes and a fourth of the engines produced for all planes. In all, GM produced 12.3 billion dollars worth of military materials. After the war GM experienced its share of the postwar boom, and by the sixties and seventies it was taking advantage of new technologies to make cars more efficient and safe even before government regulations went into effect. During the oil crisis of the 1970s GM experienced a decline in sales but responded by designing lighter and more economical autos. During the 1980s and 90s, GM continued to expand and opened plants in Germany, Brazil, Thailand, and Spain. In order to compete with an expanding import market GM developed Saturn located in Spring Hill, Tennessee, in 1990 and in 1996 it developed its own version of the electric car. GM has also been involved in various humanitarian projects such as a housing project with Habitat for Humanity for its employees in Mexico and the "Care and Share" program to collect food.

BIBLIOGRAPHY

Cray, Ed. *Chrome Colossus: General Motors and its Times.* New York: McGraw-Hill Book Co., 1980.

Madsen, Axel. *Deal Maker: How William C. Durant Made General Motors.* New York: John Wiley & Sons, 1999.

Smith, Roger B. *Building on 75 Years of Excellence: The General Motors Story.* New York: The Newcomen Society of the United States, 1984.

Lisa A. Ennis

GENERAL ORDER NO. 38, issued by Union Gen. Ambrose E. Burnside, commander of the Department of the Ohio, on 13 April 1863, forbade public expressions of sympathy for the Confederacy. Clement L. Vallandigham, a leading Ohio Democrat and a harsh critic of the Lincoln administration, denounced Burnside's order in a speech at Mount Vernon, Ohio, on 1 May 1863. Vallandigham was arrested on 5 May, tried by military commission, and, on order of President Abraham Lincoln, banished beyond the Union lines. Although some northern Democrats criticized Lincoln's action, Northern public opinion supported Vallandigham's banishment as well as the administration's broader crackdown on Confederate sympathizers.

BIBLIOGRAPHY

Klement, Frank L. *The Limits of Dissent: Clement L. Vallandigham and the Civil War.* Lexington: University Press of Kentucky, 1970.

Neely, Mark E. *The Fate of Liberty: Abraham Lincoln and Civil Liberties.* New York: Oxford University Press, 1991.

Charles H. Coleman / A. G.

See also **Blockade Runners, Confederate; Confederate Agents; Conscription and Recruitment; Military Law; New York City, Plot to Burn; Vallandigham Incident.**

GENERAL WELFARE CLAUSE. Article I, section 8 of the U.S. Constitution grants Congress the power to "lay and collect Taxes, Duties, Imposts, and Excises, to pay the Debts and provide for the common defense and general Welfare of the United States." Since the late eighteenth century this language has prompted debate over the extent to which it grants powers to Congress that exceed those powers specifically enumerated in the Constitution. The precise meaning of the clause has never been clear, in large part due to its peculiar wording and placement in the Constitution.

The confusion about its placement arises because it makes up a part of the clause related to Congress's spending power, but does not specify if or how it affects that power. For example, through use of conditional appropriations, Congress could in theory use its power to spend as a tool to regulate areas otherwise reserved to the states. This raises the issue of the extent to which Congress may achieve indirectly, through its power to "spend for the general welfare," that which it cannot legislate directly under the Congress's powers enumerated in Article I, section 8.

At the time the Constitution was adopted, some interpreted the clause as granting Congress a broad power to pass any legislation it pleased, so long as its asserted purpose was promotion of the general welfare. One of the Constitution's drafters, James Madison, objected to this reading of the clause, arguing that it was inconsistent with the concept of a government of limited powers and that it rendered the list of enumerated powers redundant. He argued that the General Welfare clause granted Congress no additional powers other than those enumerated. Thus, in their view the words themselves served no practical purpose.

In his famous *Report on Manufactures* (1791), Alexander Hamilton argued that the clause enlarged Congress's power to tax and spend by allowing it to tax and spend for the general welfare as well as for purposes falling within its enumerated powers. Thus, he argued, the General Welfare clause granted a distinct power to Congress to use its taxing and spending powers in ways not falling within its other enumerated powers.

The U.S. Supreme Court first interpreted the clause in *United States v. Butler* (1936). There, Justice Owen Roberts, in his majority opinion, agreed with Hamilton's view and held that the general welfare language in the taxing-and-spending clause constituted a separate grant of power to Congress to spend in areas over which it was not granted direct regulatory control. Nevertheless, the Court stated that this power to tax and spend was limited to spending for matters affecting the national, as opposed to the local, welfare. He also wrote that the Supreme Court should be the final arbiter of what was in fact in the national welfare. In the *Butler* decision, however, the Court shed no light on what it considered to be in the national—as opposed to local—interest, because it struck down the statute at issue on Tenth Amendment grounds.

The Court soon modified its holding in the *Butler* decision in *Helvering v. Davis* (1937). There, the Court sustained the old-age benefits provisions of the Social Security Act of 1935 and adopted an expansive view of the power of the federal government to tax and spend for the general welfare. In *Helvering*, the Court maintained that although Congress's power to tax and spend under the General Welfare clause was limited to general or national concerns, Congress itself could determine when spending constituted spending for the general welfare. To date, no legislation passed by Congress has ever been struck down because it did not serve the general welfare. Moreover, since congressional power to legislate under the Commerce clause has expanded the areas falling within Congress's enumerated powers, the General Welfare clause has decreased in importance.

BIBLIOGRAPHY

McCoy, Thomas R., and Barry Friedman. "Conditional Spending: Federalism's Trojan Horse." *1988 Supreme Court Review* 85 (1988).

Tribe, Laurence H. *American Constitutional Law.* Mineola, N.Y.: Foundation Press, 1978.

Katherine Jones

GENERATIONAL CONFLICT arises whenever the interests or ideals of one generation collide openly with those of another. A generation is defined here as a "cohort group" that is born over a span of years—typically about twenty—and that shares characteristics, including some shared childhood and coming-of-age experiences, a set of common behavioral and attitudinal traits, and a sense of common identity. Like race, class, or nationality, a generation is an abstraction that includes all kinds of individuals, but generational membership affects so many dimensions of social life that few are untouched by its influence. The history of women in the United States, for example, can hardly be told without reference to the generational waves of reformers who advanced the feminist cause—from the Seneca Falls organizers in the 1840s to the woman's suffrage crusade in the 1910s, to the women's liberation movement in the 1960s and 1970s.

Even among historically excluded minorities, the rhythm of generational conflict often echoes or inspires much that goes on in the majority society. Especially over the decades of the mid- to late 1900s, the profound minority influence on mainstream youth culture suggests that the style and outlook of each "new generation" do, indeed, transcend many ethnic and racial barriers. Sociologists argue that only modern societies—in which age-specific social roles are not prescribed by tradition—regularly give rise to different generational identities. This may help explain why the United States has a generational history of such remarkable diversity and drama. "Among democratic nations," Alexis de Tocqueville concluded after his American travels, "each generation is a new people."

Wars and economic dislocations always have been regarded as generation-defining events. Not surprisingly, Americans that came of age during a national emergency typically developed powerful collective identities, often oriented around an ethos of social discipline, secular progress, and confident public leadership. Three memorable examples are what Thomas Jefferson called his "generation of 1776" (the Revolutionary War); what Oliver Wendell Holmes, Jr., called his "generation touched with fire" (the Civil War); and what some historians call John F. Kennedy's "GI generation" (the Great Depression and World War II). Each of these generations entered public life at a conspicuously early age. With inherited institutions in disarray, their quick rise to power triggered epic struggles—which invariably unleashed generational tensions—over just how the political and economic deck would be reshuffled.

For the young Revolutionary War veterans, generational conflict emerged over their efforts to secure a more powerful yet democratic political constitution against the objections of the aging peers of Patrick Henry and John Adams. For the young Civil War veterans, it appeared when they rejected the leadership of older moralists who had recently wreaked horrible destruction. For those who came of age during the Depression of the 1930s, it surfaced in the overwhelming number of votes cast for the forward-looking and youth-favoring policies of the New Deal.

National emergencies are not the only kind of event that can trigger generational conflict. The most spectacular clashes accompany "spiritual awakenings," which ordinarily occur during eras of relative peace and prosperity. Such awakenings are marked by young people's vocal advocacy of spiritual rebirth and moral reform. According to many contemporary accounts, the Great Awakening of the late 1730s and early 1740s was largely driven by the young. Again, between the 1820s and mid-1840s, young adults dominated the ranks of the Evangelicals who spearheaded America's so-called Second Great Awakening.

The "consciousness revolution" of the late 1960s and 1970s may fit the same pattern. In this case, generational conflict was so pervasive that such terms as "generational divide" and "generation gap" were common parlance for nearly a decade. Here, the passion was fired by a (baby-boom) generation that came of age, vilifying the alleged moral complacency of an aging cadre of (GI generation) veterans. Unlike young war generations, which collide with the old over how to rebuild secular institutions, young awakening generations sometimes broadcast an institutionally subversive and spiritually antinomial message, the effects of which are felt more in the culture than in politics.

Generations raised as children during national crises typically mature into politically and culturally risk-averse young adults and thus avoid open conflict with elders. For example, Americans born from the late 1920s to the early 1940s are frequently referred to as the "silent" generation because of the reputation they earned during the 1950s for avoiding youth radicalism. Generations of this type were of special interest by the 1990s, with the coming of age of a generation of postboomers born after 1960. Variously labeled Generation X, or the Baby Bust, Scarce, New Lost, Nowhere, or Thirteenth generation, these young Americans as children in the 1970s absorbed an array of social pathologies that did not touch older generations as deeply, including post-Watergate cynicism, fragmenting families, crime and drug epidemics, schoolroom chaos, and pessimism about the nation's future. As young adults in the 1980s and early 1990s, this generation showed little of the animus that so many boomers once directed against "the establishment." Postboomers claimed in surveys to be somewhat more conservative, less interested in social change, and vastly more interested in individual survival and success.

Some generational conflicts that focused on the cultural and social ideals of youth have been followed by another—one that focuses on the political and economic interests of youth. In the late 1960s, the conflict was of the former type. By the mid-1990s, public speculation had clearly shifted toward a potential conflict of the latter type. The media, and political leaders of the mid-1990s, made routine reference to elder-imposed resource constraints on the young, including declines in living standards among young families, low rates of national savings, chronic federal deficits, mounting environmental liabilities, and public entitlement programs that directed most of their benefits to the old and were projected to impose stiff tax burdens on workers early in the twenty-first century. There was a rapidly growing academic literature on public policies that treat the young unfairly—examined under such rubrics as "generational equity" and "generational accounting." Whether this blunt economic language foretells a permanent trend toward self-preservation through material acquisition, as some have argued, is a question to be answered by the ascendant generations of the twenty-first century.

BIBLIOGRAPHY

Bagby, Meredith E. *Rational Exuberance: The Influence of Generation X on the New American Economy.* New York: Dutton, 1998.

Graubard, Stephen R., ed. *Generations.* New York: Norton, 1979.

Samuels, Richard J., ed. *Political Generations and Political Development: [Proceedings].* Lexington, Mass.: Lexington Books, 1977.

Strauss, William, and Neil Howe. *Generations: The History of American's Future, 1584 to 2069.* New York: Morrow, 1991.

Neil Howe/A. R.

See also **Demography and Demographic Trends; Family; Kinship; Marriage; Religion and Religious Affiliation; Seneca Falls Convention; Suffrage: Woman's Suffrage; Youth Movements.**

GENETIC ENGINEERING is the deliberate manipulation of an organism's genetic makeup to achieve a planned and desired result. Proponents of genetic engineering consider it an extension of the selective breeding practiced for thousands of years in the domestication of agricultural products and animals. The genesis of modern biotechnology, most scholars agree, came in the early 1970s with the advent of recombinant DNA (rDNA). Since biotechnology often refers to the use of organisms in agriculture, industry, or medicine, its origins can be traced back to the use of yeast for baking bread and the fermentation of alcohol. The impact of contemporary genetic engineering and biotechnology affects nearly every area of human activity. The introduction of rDNA engineering has revolutionized our relationship to the organic world and to ourselves, demanding a reconsideration of our values, our notion of progress, and the morality of scientific research.

The History of Genetic Engineering

Genetic engineering owes its existence to the developments in molecular genetics, virology, and cytology that culminated in the determination of the structure of DNA by James Watson and Francis Crick in 1953. Building on research involving bacteriophages (a bacterial virus), Joshua Lederberg, a geneticist at the University of Wisconsin, found that bacteria can transfer genetic information through plasmids, small mobile pieces of DNA that exist independent of the chromosomes. In the 1950s, Lederberg pioneered the earliest techniques in genetic engineering, shuffling genetic material between bacterial cells. After the identification of restriction enzymes capable of "cutting" DNA in specific locations in 1968, scientists were able to insert foreign DNA directly into bacterial cells. The discovery that the foreign DNA would naturally bond with the host DNA, made it possible to splice together genes from multiple organisms, the technique used in recombinant DNA engineering. Although highly complicated, rDNA engineering can be simply explained: genetic material from the donor source is isolated and "cut" using a restriction enzyme and then recombined or "pasted" into the genetic material of the receiver. By 1971, advanced transplantation techniques had been developed and rDNA techniques using the restriction enzyme EcoRi were operable the following year, leading to the first experiments in genetic engineering.

In 1973, Stanford biochemist Stanley Cohen undertook one of the first rDNA experiments, inserting a piece of bacterial DNA into *Escherichia coli* (*E. coli*), a bacterium found in the human intestine. However, the research soon became controversial, particularly when American molecular biologist Paul Berg designed an experiment to insert DNA from simian virus #40 (sv40)—a known cancer-causing agent—into *E. coli.* As word of the daring procedure spread, the public was captivated and fearful, afraid that a genetically engineered virus, inured to antibiotics and carried in a common bacterium, could escape and cause an epidemic. Hoping to diffuse fears of a potential biohazard and maintain control of their research, over one hundred and fifty molecular biologists and related specialists met at the Asilomar Conference Center in Monterey, California, in late February 1975. The conference represented an extraordinary moment in the history of science, as the research community, recognizing its social responsibility, officially adopted a moratorium until appropriately safe procedures and guidelines could be developed. The conference ultimately resulted in the "National Institutes of Health Guidelines for Research Involving rDNA Molecules" and an ongoing National Institute of Health rDNA Advisory Committee (RAC) founded in 1974.

Yet the guidelines only increased public concern over genetic engineering. Critics charged that attempts to splice genes together from different organisms were akin to "playing God" and could result in dangerous and immoral hybrids. Adopting the literary example of "Dr. Frankenstein's monster" as an appropriate symbol of misguided science, opponents of rDNA engineering converged on research laboratories and public meetings. An attempt to build a recombinant laboratory at Harvard University set off such a firestorm that local politicians created a review board to assess potential risks, eventually requiring more stringent controls than those set by the NIH. By 1977, protests of rDNA facilities had spread to other campuses—the University of California San Diego, the University of Wisconsin, the University of Michigan, and the University of Indiana—while the state legislatures of New York, New Jersey, and California held public hearings. However, it was the resolution of an old court case and the introduction of a new form of rDNA engineering that ultimately created the greatest controversy.

In a monumental decision handed down on 16 June 1980, the United States Supreme Court held in *Diamond v. Chakrabarty* that man-made life forms were subject to patent laws and protection. The decision resolved a long-standing issue on patents and organic material, as the case dated to 1972, when Ananda Chakrabarty, a researcher at General Electric, applied for a patent on a form of *Pseudomonas* bacteria bred (but not genetically engineered) to digest oil slicks. By a narrow five to four margin the court construed the Patent Act, originally drafted by Thomas Jefferson, so as to include all products of human invention, relying on a 1952 Senate report that recognized as patentable "anything under the sun that is made by man." More than any other single event, the ruling galvanized many mainstream religious communities and environmental groups, eventually resulting in a letter of protest to President Carter and an in-depth review by the President's Commission for the Study of Ethical Problems in Medicine and Biomedical and Behavioral Research (1980–1983). The commission's report, issued in 1982 and entitled *Splicing Life: The Social and Ethical Issues of Genetic Engineering with Human Beings*, emphasized the importance of rDNA engineering to biomedical progress and American industries, arguing that it was best that the research be conducted under the auspices of government regulation and control. However, while the study resolved anxiety over rDNA engineering and patenting, proponents of genetic engineering still had to address concerns over the development of "germ-line" engineering, a controversial procedure that allowed scientists to literally create new strains of organisms.

Germ-line engineering differs from rDNA engineering in that the donor genes are inserted into a "germ," or reproductive cell, thereby permanently altering the genetic makeup of the organism's descendants. For example, in 1982, Ralph Brinster of the University of Pennsylvania Veterinary School inserted the gene that produces rat growth hormone into mouse embryos. The resulting strain of mice, dubbed "super mice" by the press, expressed the gene and thus grew into a substantially larger and more powerful new breed of mouse. Critics of germ-line engineering quickly denounced the technique as immoral and argued it was a form of "anthropomorphic Lamarckism." Jean-Baptiste de Lamarck, a nineteenth-century French naturalist, had proposed that traits acquired during an organism's lifetime were passed on to its progeny—an idea refuted by Darwinian evolutionary theory. Yet, in germ-line engineering, traits acquired during the organism's lifetime are passed on, but only those traits deemed necessary or desirous by man. Environmental groups also denounced germ-line engineering because of "biosafety" concerns, fearing that genetically engineered species, which would possess a distinct advantage over non-engineered species, could upset the globe's finely tuned ecological systems. However, because most politicians, scientists, and manufacturers believed the potential benefits from rDNA and germ-line engineering outweighed its potential dangers, the protests were overshadowed by the development of a biotechnology industry based on genetic engineering.

Contemporary Applications of Genetic Engineering

The decision to allow patents on genetically engineered organisms, combined with the commission's sanction of rDNA engineering, and a national commitment to biomedical progress, led to tremendous growth in the biotechnology industry. In 1975, only five biotech companies participated in the Asilomar conference, by 1980 the number of similar companies had increased to one hundred. Today there are over 1,300 companies involved in genetic engineering, many of which are located in the United States, a clear indication of the rapid growth of the American biotechnology sector and the applicability of the powerful new techniques. Indeed, genetic engineering influences nearly every area of human activity, including agriculture and aquaculture, industry and environmental remediation, and the development of medicines and therapies.

Although agriculture has been one of the most successful industries in utilizing genetic engineering, the techniques have also made an impact in other areas of food production. In 1990, Chymosin, an enzyme necessary for cheese production, became the first genetically engineered food product to go to market. A few years later, in 1994, the Monsanto Company created a bovine growth hormone designed to stimulate milk production, a hormone now estimated to be given to 30 percent of dairy cows. The same year, the "Flavr-Savr" tomato developed by Calgene passed the Food and Drug Administration standards for genetically engineered foods and also went to market. Like many transgenic foods, the "Flavr-Savr" was designed to have increased shelf life and resist spoilage, although disputes regarding labeling and advertisements combined with high production costs caused the company to discontinue the product in the late 1990s. Nonetheless, genetic engineering is integrated into agriculture production; researchers estimate that as of 2001, nearly one-third of the corn and one half of the soybeans grown in the United States were transgenic. A study conducted in 2000 by the Grocery Manufacturers of America reported that the majority of processed foods sold in America contained transgenic ingredients. To help develop aquaculture, researchers at Johns Hopkins University have taken a gene from flounder and inserted it into both trout and bass in the hopes of making the fish more resistant to cold climates, thus increasing commercial and sport fishing.

Genetic engineering also has substantial applications in many other industries from plastics and energy to the new field of bioremediation. In 1993, Chris Sommerville, director of plant biology at the Carnegie Institute in Washington, D.C., successfully inserted plastic-making genes into a plant; the Monsanto Company hopes to market a cotton/polyester plant early in the twenty-first century. Scientists at numerous biotech companies are currently working on strains of *E. coli* bacteria capable of transforming agricultural refuse into ethanol, an efficient and clean source of energy. Genetic engineering is also aiding environmental clean-up through the emerging field of bioremediation—the use of organisms to reduce waste. Bacteria were employed to help with the Exxon Valdez oil spill in 1989, while scientists at the Institute for Genomic Research are among those hoping to engineer microbes that can detoxify waste, including radioactive materials. However, the fastest growing, and one of the most controversial, fields of biotechnology is applied human genetics, which includes transgenic medicines, xenotransplantation, and human gene therapy.

In 1982, Eli Lilly and Company began marketing bacterial-produced insulin, the first transgenic commercial product and an excellent marker of the industry's progress. Today, the vast majority of insulin used by Americans diabetics is genetically engineered and over 300 transgenic proteins and medicines are currently in production, many of which are made by animals. Indeed, animal "pharming" has been central to biomedical research and development since the introduction of genetic engineering; in 1988, Harvard University patented the "oncomouse," strains of mice missing or carrying specific genes and used in cancer research. In 1996, Genzyme Transgenics created a goat capable of producing antithrombin, an experimental anticancer drug; the following year PPL Therapeutics engineered a calf whose milk contains proteins necessary for nursing babies, including those born prematurely. Human hemoglobin, a protein essential for oxygen transportation in the bloodstream, can now be harvested from genetically engineered pigs. Transgenic pigs are also used in xenotransplantation, the transference of organs or parts from nonhuman species to humans. Nextran, a leading biotech company, hopes to use genetically engineered pig livers as temporary external reservoirs for patients suffering from acute liver failure. In the future, researchers hope that these transgenic medicines and proteins will help supplement human gene therapy, one of the boldest and most ethically and medically problematic areas of genetic engineering.

The history of human gene therapy is one of great promise and success mixed with controversy and stringent regulation. In the early 1980s, Martin Cline, a medical researcher at the University of California in Los Angeles, performed rDNA procedures in Italy and Israel on patients afflicted with hereditary blood disorders. Cline's unauthorized experimentation, although legal because the countries lacked genetic regulations, ultimately cost him funding and a department chairmanship. In response, the RAC established the Human Gene Therapy Subcommittee in 1984 to issue protocols and review applications. Years later, in 1990, researchers at the National Institute of Health (NIH) attempted the first approved human gene therapy for Ashanti DeSilva, a young girl forced to live inside a "bubble" because of severe combined immune deficiency, or ADA. As in most cases of human gene therapy, the researchers removed cells from the patient, genetically engineered the desired changes, and then replaced the cells. However, for ADA, as for most diseases, gene therapy offers only treatment, not a cure, as the procedure must be repeated periodically. Nonetheless, the success of Ashanti's procedure stimulated human gene therapy research; in 1992, Bernadine Healy, then director of the NIH, approved a "compassionate use exemption" to increase access to promising gene therapy trials for critically ill patients. Within a year, procedures had been approved for familial hypercholesterolemia, cystic fibrosis, and Gaucher's disease, and trials for cancer, AIDS, Parkinson's, Alzheimers, arthritis, and heart disease were being conducted. Unfortunately, the 1999 death from liver disease of Jesse Gelsinger, an eighteen-year-old student taking part in a University of Pennsylvania gene therapy trial, led to questions regarding the safety of established protocols, as the fatality resulted from a common immune reaction to the adenovirus vector (see GENETICS) that the researchers could have easily anticipated.

Although genetic engineering remains in its infancy, the rapid development of the science and its related techniques has generated considerable disagreement in the attempt to address its moral and legal implications. The birth of the sheep "Dolly" in 1997, the first cloned adult mammal, led to debates over the sanctity of life and the individual, while the advent of human gene therapy has revived fears of eugenics programs and genetically engineered "designer" children. The marketing of transgenic foods stimulated the growth of an "organic" agricultural industry and created ongoing international disputes over patent rights, truth-in-labeling claims, and restrictions on genetically engineered imports. Some critics fear that xenotransplantation will promote the transference of animal diseases to humans, while others decry the use of animals simply for the benefit of mankind. The development of stem cell research, promising because the embryonic cells can be manipulated to become nearly any type of cell in the body, has led to protests by many pro-life organizations over the use of embryonic or fetal tissue; in August 2001, President Bush declared that only a limited number of cell lines were acceptable for federal research funding. Whether involved in human gene therapy, xenotransplantation, industry, or agriculture, genetic engineering and biotechnology will no doubt continue providing astounding advancements alongside heated controversy and debate well into the future.

BIBLIOGRAPHY

Bud, Robert. *The Uses of Life: A History of Biotechnology.* New York: Cambridge University Press, 1993.

Fiechter, A., ed. *History of Modern Biotechnology.* 2 vols. Berlin: Springer Verlag, 2000.

Rifkin, Jeremy. *The Biotech Century: Harnessing the Gene and Remaking the World.* New York: Putnam, 1998.

Shannon, Thomas A., ed. *Genetic Engineering: A Documentary History.* Westport, Conn.: Greenwood Press, 1999.

Von Wartburg, Walter P., and Julian Liew. *Gene Technology and Social Acceptance.* Lanham, Md.: University Press of America, 1999.

J. G. Whitesides

See also **Microbiology; Molecular Biology.**

GENETICS, the science of heredity, includes the interrelated fields of cytology, biochemistry, evolutionary theory, and molecular biology. Today the impact of genetic research is far-reaching, affecting medical diagnosis and therapeutics, agriculture and industry, criminal prosecution, and privacy, as well as ideas regarding individuality, ethics, and responsibility. Studied since antiquity, heredity remained a puzzle until the late twentieth century even though many of its essential physical components—such as chromosomes and "nuclein" (later identified as deoxyribonucleic acid (DNA)—were known by the late nineteenth century. Indeed, genetics did not become a "science" in a contemporary empirical sense until the rediscovery of Gregor Mendel's laws in 1900. Mendel, an Austrian monk who experimented with patterns of inheritance in studies of peas and flowers, determined laws of heredity regarding the integration and assortment of inherited traits. These original principles underwent considerable refinement and expansion throughout the twentieth century as scientists uncovered the physical and chemical mechanisms of heredity. This recent history of genetics can be divided into three general periods: classical genetics, molecular genetics, and applied or modern genetics, each of which benefited greatly from American researchers and institutions.

Classical and Molecular Genetics

The rediscovery of Mendel's laws led to the flowering of classical genetics in the early twentieth century. Population studies, breeding experiments, and radiation were among the early tools in genetic research as scientists looked to uncover the patterns and basic unit of heredity as well as the causes of variation. In 1902, a mere two years after the rediscovery of Mendel's laws, the American biologist Walter S. Sutton observed similarities between Mendel's genetic "units" and chromosomes. Additional research by his Columbia University colleague Edmund Beecher Wilson confirmed the link and identified the "X" sex chromosome in butterflies, while another American, the cytologist Nettie Stevens, independently identified the "Y" chromosome in beetles. The existence of sex-linked genetic traits, such as white eyes in fruit flies (*Drosophila melanogaster*), was shown by the American biologist Thomas Hunt Morgan in 1910 in studies capable of locating a specific gene on a specific chromosome. Using light-microscope observations, Morgan and his students Alfred Henry Sturtevant, Hermann Joseph Muller, and Calvin Blackman Bridges studied the phenomenon of crossing-over, the process by which chromosomes exchange genes, and as a result were able to construct chromosome maps. Their research proceeded quickly; in 1915, the "Drosophila" group at Columbia University published *The Mechanism of Mendelian Heredity*—a seminal work that demonstrated the linear arrangement of genes in the chromosome and helped explain abnormal genetic ratios and variation. However, explanations for genetic variation remained unsatisfactory until the pioneering work of Hermann Muller at the University of Texas. Muller experimented with radiation and high temperatures to measure rates of mutation, eventually determining that genes, while generally stable, can be externally induced to mutate. (This discovery also opened the possibility of genetic engineering.) His *Artificial Transmutation of the Gene*, published in 1927, also hinted at the gene's ability to control metabolism and morphology, leading biochemists and other scientists to investigate the physical composition of the gene and the chemical basis of heredity.

Beginning in the 1940s, techniques such as bacterial vectors and X-ray diffraction analysis led to the development of both biochemical genetics and molecular genetics. In 1941, the Stanford biologist George Wells

Beadle and biochemist Edward Lawrie Tatum proposed the one gene–one enzyme theory after experimenting on the nutritional requirements of mutated bread mold, ushering in the field of biochemical genetics by providing an introductory blueprint for the chemical synthesis of enzymes. A few years later, in 1944, the American geneticists Oswald Avery, Colin MacLeod, and Maclyn McCarty transformed bacteria through the introduction of foreign DNA, thereby determining that DNA was the primary heredity material. This indicated that DNA, rather than the previously suspected class of proteins, was the actual carrier of genetic information. Further proof came in 1952 when the American geneticists Alfred D. Hershey and Martha Chase, working at the Cold Spring Harbor Biological Station in New York, demonstrated that viral DNA was responsible for replication within infected bacteria. Using a bacteriophage (a bacterial virus) as a vector, the scientists showed that it was the virus's DNA, not a protein, that infected the host bacteria. However, while DNA was clearly the molecule of heredity, questions on the structure and mechanisms of DNA remained that could only be solved by molecular biology.

By 1950, geneticists had adopted the method of X-ray diffraction analysis pioneered by the American chemist Linus Pauling at the California Institute of Technology to determine the three-dimensional structure of the DNA molecule. Pauling proposed both single- and triple-helix models, but in 1953 the American biochemist James Watson and British biophysicist Francis Crick correctly determined that the DNA molecule was a double helix. The two men proposed that DNA was transcribed into RNA, then translated or expressed as a protein, a method of genetic replication later proven by the American molecular biologists Matthew Stanley Meselson and Franklin William Stahl and now known as the "central dogma" of molecular genetics. In 1961, Crick and Sidney Brenner determined that codons, groups of three nucleotides (adenine, cytosine, guanine, uracil and thymine), were responsible for the synthesis of proteins, while the National Institutes of Health researchers Marshall W. Nirenberg and Johann H. Matthaei showed in 1965 that certain codon combinations also lead to the production of amino acids. A final piece of the genetic puzzle—the means by which genes are activated or deactivated—was resolved by the operon model of genetic regulation. Proposed by the Frenchman Jacques Monod, the operon model requires that regulatory nucleotides, which account for a substantial portion of the DNA molecule, repress the function of other genes by disrupting RNA transcription under certain conditions.

Modern Applied Genetics

The study and sophistication of genetics increased rapidly in the last quarter of the twentieth century, as scientists, aided by advances in technology and industry and government funding, concentrated on both pure and applied genetics. Recombinant DNA engineering and prenatal genetic screening for some inherited diseases became possible in the early 1970s, leading to public concern over potential misuse and eventual governmental regulation. At the same time, the central dogma expanded to include the phenomenon of reverse transcription after American virologist David Baltimore demonstrated that retroviruses were capable of reproducing themselves by copying their own RNA. Perhaps the greatest advancement in pure genetic research came in the form of the HUMAN GENOME PROJECT. Launched in 1988 by the U.S. Department of Energy and the National Institutes of Health, the Human Genome Project succeeded in sequencing a human genome in 2000 and represents the new state of "big" biology—an international partnership of government, academic, and industrial research institutions. Although researchers expect that the project will deliver remarkable medical and biological applications, some outside observers worry about the potential for genetic discrimination, genetic racial typing (see RACIAL SCIENCE), and the revitalization of EUGENICS, demonstrating both the promise and the danger of contemporary genetics.

Today genetics permeates both the biological sciences and American culture, surfacing in research laboratories, congressional hearings, and courtrooms as well as popular movies and books. Genetics has unified the biological sciences and led to the modern synthesis of evolutionary theory and biology by demonstrating that organisms share the same basic genetic materials and processes. DNA fingerprinting plays a vital role in criminal investigations and the establishment of paternity, while genetic screening and therapy provide hope for those suffering from inherited diseases like sickle-cell anemia, cystic fibrosis, or Huntington's disease. Entering the twenty-first century, transgenic crops may provide the best window into the future impact of genetics, as the rise of a transgenic agricultural industry, which produces crops with an increased pesticide resistance and shelf life, has also led to a counter industry based on organic, or non-genetically enhanced, crops.

BIBLIOGRAPHY

Caulfield, Timothy A., and Bryn Williams-Jones, eds. *The Commercialization of Genetic Research: Ethical, Legal, and Policy Issues.* New York: Kluwer, 1999.

Kohler, Robert E. *Lords of the Fly.* Chicago: University of Chicago Press, 1994.

Olby, Robert. *The Path to the Double Helix.* Seattle: University of Washington Press, 1974. Reprint, New York: Dover, 1994.

Ridley, Matt. *Genome: The Autobiography of a Species in 23 Chapters.* New York: HarperCollins, 1999.

Sarkar, Sahotra. *Genetics and Reductionism.* Cambridge, U.K., and New York: Cambridge University Press, 1998.

Sturtevant, A. H. *A History of Genetics.* New York: Cold Spring Harbor Laboratory Press, 2001.

J. G. Whitesides

See also **DNA; Genetic Engineering.**

GENEVA ACCORDS OF 1954 resulted from a conference in Geneva, Switzerland, from 26 April to 21 July 1954 that focused primarily on resolving the war between French forces and those of the Democratic Republic of Vietnam (DRV), led by the nationalist-communist Ho Chi Minh. The conference included representatives from Great Britain, France, the People's Republic of China, the Soviet Union, the United States, the DRV, Laos, Cambodia, and the State of Vietnam (later South Vietnam). Discussion of the Indochina conflict began on 8 May, the day after the defeat of the French garrison at Dien Bien Phu by DRV forces (Vietminh) underscored the futility of the French war effort.

The Vietminh expected that their defeat of France would lead to the establishment of a unified, independent Vietnamese state. However, their powerful Soviet and Chinese allies feared U.S. military intervention in Indochina and pressured the Vietminh to consent to a settlement that partitioned Vietnam. U.S. president Dwight D. Eisenhower had indeed considered military intervention to prevent a Vietminh victory, but after concluding that the merits of a unilateral strike were outweighed by the heightened risk of a global war that would preserve French colonialism in Indochina, his administration grudgingly came to accept a negotiated settlement.

The Geneva Accords consisted of separate cease-fire arrangements for Cambodia, Laos, and Vietnam as well as an unsigned final declaration. The most significant provisions temporarily divided Vietnam at the seventeenth parallel, creating a northern zone under DRV authority and a southern region dominated by the French Union. The accords called for all military forces to withdraw to their respective zones within three hundred days. In addition, neither side was to enter military alliances, establish foreign military bases, or supplement its army and armaments. The agreements called for national elections in 1956 to reunify the country and created an international commission, consisting of Canada, India, and Poland, to enforce the accords.

Since the Eisenhower administration wished to distance itself from any compromise with communist forces, Secretary of State John Foster Dulles instructed American diplomats to observe, rather than directly participate, in the Geneva negotiations. When the conference ended, the United States simply noted the existence of the accords and promised not to disturb them by force. Although conservatives in the United States quickly condemned the agreements for rewarding communist aggression, Eisenhower and Dulles reasoned that the accords provided the United States with an opportunity to build an anticommunist, capitalist bastion in Southeast Asia free of the taint of French colonialism. American officials, then, had implicitly rejected the intent of the accords that the partition be temporary well before 16 July 1955, when South Vietnamese president Ngo Dình Diem cancelled the 1956 elections with American assent.

BIBLIOGRAPHY

Anderson, David L. *Trapped by Success: The Eisenhower Administration and Vietnam, 1953–1961.* New York: Columbia University Press, 1991.

Duiker, William J. *U.S. Containment Policy and the Conflict in Indochina.* Stanford, Calif.: Stanford University Press, 1994.

Gardner, Lloyd. *Approaching Vietnam: From World War II through Dienbienphu, 1941–1954.* New York: Norton, 1988.

H. Matthew Loayza

See also **France, Relations with; Vietnam War.**

GENEVA CONFERENCES. In the twentieth century the United States participated in several diplomatic conferences held at Geneva, Switzerland. The first major one was a naval disarmament conference called by President Calvin Coolidge in 1927. It was an unsuccessful effort to extend restrictions on the construction of naval vessels to cruisers, destroyers, and submarines, none of which had been covered by the five-power treaty signed at Washington, D.C., five years earlier.

Between 1932 and 1934 the United States participated in a general disarmament conference of fifty-nine nations called by the League of Nations at Geneva. The conference concentrated on land armaments. The United States proposed the abolition of all offensive armaments, and when this did not win approval, proposed a 30 percent reduction in all armaments. Germany, Italy, and the Soviet Union welcomed this plan, but France—concerned about Germany's increasing power—rejected it. With the withdrawal of Germany from the League of Nations in October 1933, the failure of the disarmament conference became clear. It adjourned in June 1934.

In 1947 the United States participated in an international tariff conference at Geneva. This conference prepared a draft charter for a proposed international trade organization and produced a General Agreement on Tariffs and Trade. An international conference attended by the United States; the Soviet Union; Great Britain; France; the People's Republic of China; the Associated States of Vietnam, Laos, and Cambodia; the Democratic Republic of Vietnam, North Korea, and South Korea was held in Geneva in the summer of 1954. It was an effort to reach a settlement on the problems of Korea and Indochina. Talks on Korean unification became deadlocked, but the participants agreed on a cease-fire in Korea; independence for Laos and Cambodia; and a temporary partition of Indochina, pending elections there. In July 1955 the first major East-West summit conference was held at Geneva. The principal participants were President Dwight D. Eisenhower (United States), Prime Minister Anthony Eden (Great Britain), Premier Edgar Faure (France), and Premier Nikolai Bulganin along with Communist Party leader Nikita Khrushchev (Soviet Union). The term "spirit of Geneva" expressed a public expectation that the conference would lessen international tension. However, neither Eisenhower's proposal for an "open skies" inspection plan permitting Americans and Soviets to conduct aerial reconnaissance over one another's territory, nor the Soviet proposal for a mutual withdrawal of forces from Europe, made any headway.

In May 1961 a fourteen-nation conference, including the United States, convened at Geneva in an attempt to resolve the conflict in Laos between the central government and the forces of the pro-communist Pathet Lao. After prolonged discussions the conferees agreed in July 1962 to the establishment of a neutral coalition government in that country.

In December 1973 United Nations Secretary-General Kurt Waldheim convened the first ever Arab-Israeli peace conference at Geneva with foreign ministers from the United States, the Soviet Union, Egypt, Jordan, and Israel attending. Syria refused to attend, and the PLO was not invited. The initial talks were subsequently pursued through other channels, ultimately leading to the Camp David Accords in 1978.

The United States has also participated in a series of conferences on the international control of nuclear weapons that have been held at Geneva intermittently since 1958. These negotiations helped to prepare the way for the Nuclear Test Ban Treaty (1963), the Nuclear Nonproliferation Treaty (1968), and the Treaty on the Limitations of Strategic Armaments (1972). In November 1985 President Ronald Reagan and General Secretary Mikhail Gorbachev met at Geneva and declared their intention to seek a 50 percent reduction in strategic nuclear arms.

BIBLIOGRAPHY

Bischof, Günter, and Saki Dockrill, eds. *Cold War Respite: The Geneva Summit of 1955*. Baton Rouge: Louisiana State University Press, 2000.

Cable, James. *The Geneva Conference of 1954 on Indochina*. New York: St. Martin's Press, 1986.

Garthoff, Raymond L. *The Great Transition: American-Soviet Relations and the End of the Cold War*. Washington, D.C.: Brookings Institution, 1994.

Max Paul Friedman
John Lewis Gaddis

See also **Geneva Accords of 1954; Geneva Conventions; Nuclear Test Ban Treaty; Summit Conferences, U.S. and Russian.**

GENEVA CONVENTIONS, a series of international agreements drafted for the amelioration (improvement) of the treatment of the sick and wounded, in particular—but all prisoners—in land and sea warfare. The first Geneva Convention (1864) covered field armies only. Subsequent conventions extended that coverage to include the sick and wounded at sea, the treatment of prisoners of war, and the protection of noncombatants during time of war. The principles first articulated in the Geneva Conventions have become the cornerstones of international laws regulating conduct in wartime.

The first agreement resulted from the outcry that followed the publication in 1862 of *Un Souvenir de Solferino*, by Jean Henri Dunant, a cofounder of the Red Cross. His book—describing the suffering of wounded French, Italian, and Austrian soldiers in northern Italy in 1859 because of inadequate medical facilities—resulted in the convocation of an unofficial congress at Geneva in 1863 and, in the following year, of the formal sessions whose convention was ratified by the United States, most other American countries, and twelve European nations. An 1868 convention, while not ratified, expanded the earlier agreement to include naval warfare. The articles of the two conventions were observed during the Franco-Prussian (1870–1871) and Spanish-American (1898) wars.

Another conference was held in 1906 at Geneva, at which the conventions were revised; these were adopted by the Hague Peace Conference of 1907. The brutality of World War I demonstrated the need for clearer international guidelines in regard to what constituted lawful and unlawful conduct in wartime. In 1929, the conventions—signed by forty-seven nations—were widened to include provisions to improve the lot of prisoners of war. On the eastern front of the European theater, as well as in the Pacific, both the Axis and Allied powers routinely violated the protocols of the Geneva Conventions. Nazi Germany, in particular, murdered huge numbers of Soviet prisoners of war. The war crimes committed by the Nazis, coupled with their perpetration of the Holocaust, constituted the major charges levied the German government leaders during the 1946 Nuremberg Tribunal. The latest Geneva Convention—in 1949—was ratified by sixty-one countries, including the United States. Its four articles covered the amelioration of conditions of the wounded and sick in the armed forces, including those in the field and those shipwrecked at sea (articles I and II); the treatment of prisoners of war (III); and, in response to Nazi atrocities in World War II, the treatment and legal status of noncombatants in wartime (IV). The subjects of the last two articles, issues in World War II, were raised also during the Vietnam War. Since the latter was partially a guerrilla war, the distinction between armed combatants in civilian dress and noncombatants was blurred, and the applicability of the conventions to the Vietnam conflict was questioned. The United States and South Vietnam both publicly adhered to the convention, unlike North Vietnam and the National Liberation Front, which were also unwilling to allow the International Red Cross to inspect their prisoner-of-war camps.

BIBLIOGRAPHY

Ellis, L. Ethan. *Frank B. Kellogg and American Foreign Relations, 1925–1929*. New Brunswick, N.J.: Rutgers University Press, 1929; 1961.

Keegan, John. *The Second World War.* New York: Hutchinson, 1989.

Richard A. Hunt/A. G.

See also **Hague Peace Conferences; Prisoners of War; Spanish-American War; War Crimes Trials.**

GENOCIDE. International law defines genocide as acts intended to destroy a group of people defined by their nationality, ethnicity, race, or religion. The International Convention on the Prevention and Punishment of the Crime of Genocide, passed by the United Nations General Assembly in 1948 in reaction to the Nazi persecution of the Jews and other groups during World War II, lists the following prohibited acts: "killing members of the group; . . . causing serious bodily or mental harm to members of the group; . . . deliberately inflicting on the group conditions of life calculated to bring about its physical destruction in whole or in part; . . . imposing measures intended to prevent births within the group; . . . forcibly transferring children of the group to another group." States that are party to the treaty must bring individuals who have committed, conspired to commit, or incited genocide to trial, or deliver them to be tried before an international tribunal. The convention, moreover, calls for its signatories to take action to prevent genocide.

The Genocide Convention came into force after being ratified by twenty nations in 1951. Although the United States was one of the original signatories and President Harry S. Truman urged the Senate to ratify the treaty, the Senate resisted because of objections by some senators that the convention would infringe on American sovereignty. When the Senate in 1988 finally joined more than 120 governments by ratifying the treaty, it attached the conditions that the United States would not be subject to the jurisdiction of the International Court of Justice and that U.S. laws would take precedence over the convention.

Acts of genocide have a long history and they have often accompanied war, other conflicts, and colonialism. After World War II, the Nuremberg War Crimes Tribunal that tried top Nazi leaders interpreted its charter to mean that individuals could be prosecuted for crimes against humanity only if those crimes were committed during wartime. Rafael Lemkin, a Polish lawyer at Nuremberg who served the U.S. government during the war and coined the term "genocide," pressed the United Nations for an international standard that would prohibit genocide whenever it might occur. ("Genos" is a Greek word meaning race or tribe, and "cide" is from the Latin "cidium," killing.)

Since the passage of the Genocide Convention, numerous groups have sought recognition and redress by describing actions taken against them as genocidal. Because the terms of the convention can be interpreted strictly or broadly, there were a number of disputes over definitions, scale, and evidence. Native Americans have sought redress on the basis that the European settlement of the Americas led to death, displacement, and suffering, and that this outcome was the result of deliberate genocidal policies. A similar movement on behalf of aborigines recently gained momentum in Australia. Some Native American activists contend that genocidal policies have not ended, given the grim living conditions and poor health statistics on Native American reservations. Some African Americans seeking reparations for slavery invoke the Genocide Convention, which has no statute of limitations. Antiwar activists in the 1960s, 1970s, and 1980s created mock tribunals to promote their belief that U.S. military conduct in Vietnam or Soviet behavior in Afghanistan constituted genocide under international law.

Arguments remain unresolved over whether the mass killings brought about by Joseph Stalin in the Soviet Union and Pol Pot's Khmer Rouge in Cambodia qualify as genocide, since they targeted groups defined by economic and political status rather than the listed categories of race, ethnicity, nationality, and religion. These and other cases, such as Turkey's attacks on its Armenian population during World War I, further illustrate the limitations of international law to prevent mass killings undertaken by governments against their own people. The feeble international response to massacres committed in Bosnia and Rwanda in the 1990s came as some signatory governments, including that of the United States, took pains to avoid invoking the word "genocide" (using instead the euphemistic "ethnic cleansing") in order to avoid triggering the obligations called for in the Genocide Convention. After the killings ended, special international tribunals authorized by the United Nations Security Council considered charges of genocide against military and political leaders involved in both conflicts. In 1998, the International Criminal Tribunal for Rwanda convicted the former prime minister, Jean Kambanda, and other defendants of genocide and other crimes and handed down life sentences. The International Criminal Tribunal for the former Yugoslavia sought convictions for former Yugoslave president Slobodan Milosevic and Serb military commanders accused of genocide.

By the end of the twentieth century the contradictions of international law, in which the principle of respect for national sovereignty clashed with the requirement that states intervene to prevent genocidal killings, had not been resolved, nor had the United States or other nations committed themselves to an open-ended policy of undertaking the risks of military intervention to protect foreign civilians. Despite the success of legal prosecutions for genocide, the more difficult question remained of how to prevent such crimes from occurring.

BIBLIOGRAPHY

LeBlanc, Lawrence J. *The United States and the Genocide Convention.* Durham, N.C.: Duke University Press, 1991.

Power, Samantha. *"A Problem from Hell": America and the Age of Genocide.* New York: Basic Books, 2002.

Totten, Samuel, William S. Parsons, and Israel W. Charny, eds. *Genocide in the Twentieth Century: Critical Essays and Eyewitness Accounts.* New York: Garland, 1995.

Max Paul Friedman

See also **Geneva Conventions; Human Rights; International Court of Justice; United Nations; Yugoslavia, Relations with.**

GENRE PAINTING focuses on the mundane, trivial incidents of everyday life, depicting people the viewer can easily identify with employed in situations that tell a story. These anecdotal works became popular in the United States around 1830, when the country grew prosperous enough that people had the means and leisure to collect works of art. By the 1840s, the American Art Union was exhibiting and selling both paintings and print reproductions, which could be distributed at low cost to a broad audience. As a result, genre paintings such as William Sidney Mount's *Bargaining for a Horse* (1835) or George Caleb Bingham's *Jolly Flatboatmen* (1846) became widely dispersed, popular images.

Some of America's greatest genre paintings were executed by Winslow Homer and Thomas Eakins. Homer's favorite theme was the relationship of man to nature, expressed dramatically in canvases such as *Eight Bells* (1886), which pits the skill of a sailor against the awesome power of the sea. Homer's scenes of outdoor pastimes such as hunting and fishing are painted with a broad touch and vivid colors that recall the French Impressionists, without being directly influenced by them. Eakins based his genre subjects on everyday life in the area around his native Philadelphia. His paintings of rowers on the city's Schuylkill River are painted with a solid command of human anatomy and great sensitivity to sparkling atmospheric effects.

The expatriate painter James McNeill Whistler, whose works were enthusiastically collected by American art patrons, stressed the refined and exotic aspects of contemporary life in genre paintings such as *Purple and Rose: The Lange Leizen of the Six Marks* (1864), which shows a young woman in a kimono admiring a seventeenth-century Chinese jar. John Singer Sargent, another cosmopolitan artist, occasionally painted genre subjects such as *In the Luxembourg Gardens* (1879), a view of people enjoying this popular Parisian site. William Merritt Chase also portrayed scenes of genteel American society at the close of the century.

In the twentieth century, these views of polite domesticity painted in an impressionist manner continued in the work of Childe Hassam. In contrast, the grittier aspects of urban life attracted a group of artists centered in Philadelphia and New York: Robert Henri, George Luks, William J. Glackens, John Sloan, and Everett Shinn.

Snap the Whip. An 1872 genre painting of carefree childhood and one of Winslow Homer's most popular works, existing in several similar versions. © Geoffrey Clements/corbis

Their scenes of laborers and life in New York's slums reveal a social conscience and sympathy for the common lot.

Because genre painting is inherently figurative art, it survived in the twentieth century in the work of painters who stood outside the floodtide of abstraction. Charles Demuth, for example, created exquisite watercolors of circus themes or homoerotic bathhouse scenes, and George Bellows depicted the raucous night life of American cities in *Stag at Sharkey's* (1909). Several decades later, life on the middle western Plains became the subject matter for a group of artists known as "regionalists," whose work stands as a rejection of international modernism. Thomas Hart Benton's farm laborers at work or play, or Grant Wood's iconic *American Gothic* (1930), have become symbols of the American heartland. Genre painting did not survive past the 1930s, except in rare instances such as the work of Milton Avery, who represented recreational scenes of sailing or sunbathing. His simplified figures painted in flat colors manage to integrate genre subject matter with a modernist esthetic.

BIBLIOGRAPHY

Hills, Patricia. *The Painters' America: Rural and Urban Life, 1810–1910.* New York: Praeger, 1974.

Johns, Elizabeth. *American Genre Painting: The Politics of Everyday Life.* New Haven, Conn.: Yale University Press, 1991.

Victor Carlson

See also **Art: Painting; Ashcan School.**

GENTRIFICATION. In discussing renewal of cities, the term "gentrification" is rather new; yet the concept is old. Throughout the history of urban civilization, cities have grown, stagnated, and then decayed. Often the cities' residents or others have then rebuilt and revitalized the city. In the United States, by the end of the nineteenth century and throughout the twentieth century major cities faced growing slums and blighted areas in older portions. The decline included neglect and abandonment of public and private buildings and growth of poverty of the remaining residents, often recent immigrants, minorities, and the elderly.

After World War II (1939–1945), urban decline became a prominent concern, and organizations, particularly the federal government, used various programs to attack the problem. These generally were termed urban renewal projects. Large public housing structures were created in formerly blighted areas, but often there was little economic revitalization. Gradually the private sector—and perhaps local government—became interested in bringing inner cities back to life. Urban renewal became "gentrification," a term first used in England. The phenomenon has generated a great deal of attention since the 1970s in the United States and Europe.

Definition of Gentrification

Historically, the term "gentry" referred to landed people; in the twenty-first century, it usually refers to the upper middle class. As young, single professionals returned to the city to live, the English dubbed the process, "gentrification." Gentrifiers can be single or couples without children, heterosexual or homosexual; their occupations are generally professional, technical, or managerial. In the United States nearly all gentrifiers have at least some college education; in many cities, 70 to 90 percent have at least a bachelor's degree. In a few cities, such as sections of Boston or New York, gentrifiers also include college students.

Gentrification normally refers to changes in urban neighborhoods. The dictionary definition is the rehabilitation and settlement of decaying urban areas by middle- and high-income people. However, the term "gentrification" also appears in material or popular culture. For instance, studies have been done on the gentrification of blue jeans, from the durable pants for gold miners to mass-marketing in the 1960s and transformation into high fashion items.

The Gentrification Process

Gentrification begins when a deteriorated and usually partially abandoned neighborhood for some reason appeals to housing speculators. Initially, buildings may change hands several times before they are renovated. Eventually, building renovation takes place and units are usually sold for high prices, rather than rented. About the same time economic revitalization of the area begins and then the pace of gentrification and displacement of the poorer residents and the renters accelerates.

The process of gentrification is not universal in the United States, and suburban growth is still much greater than inner city gentrification. It is difficult to quantify exactly the extent of the phenomenon, but it is known that gentrification generally has occurred in the larger or older cities, initially in the East, Midwest, and South, although the process is growing in a few western cities such as San Francisco and Seattle. Some observers say that without gentrification, vibrant inner cities would cease to exist.

One of the difficulties in determining the extent and impact of gentrification is that observers define the concept differently. According to a Brookings Institution report, definitions include: the process of disinvestments and reinvestment in a neighborhood; urban revitalization commercially and residentially, physical upgrading of a low-income neighborhood; renovating housing stock and selling to newcomers (gentry); and the class and racial tensions over dislocations when new "gentrified" residents move into a neighborhood. What seems to be agreed upon is that a gentrified urban area includes some change in the neighborhood character, some displacement of older and poorer residents, and some physical upgrading of housing stock. Though gentrification may be difficult to define, it is a process of which people say, "we know it when we see it."

Factors that Encourage Gentrification

There are several factors that contribute to the gentrification process. One factor is job growth in the city, or even on its periphery, such as Silicon Valley in California, Route 128/95 in Massachusetts, or Fairfax County in Virginia. Young technical professionals move to the revitalized areas of a city for a reverse-commute. In the 1970s and 1980s, corporations reinvested in central city districts and transformed them commercially and residentially.

A second factor contributing to gentrification is the housing market. As inner cities declined in the move to the suburbs, city housing deteriorated, thus providing opportunity for housing speculators and rehabilitation. Investors sought neighborhoods with gentrification potential to find bargain housing that could be renovated and sold for great profits. Public housing was an early postwar solution to renovate or revitalize cities. Gradually these usually massive structures deteriorated and governments sought other remedies. Public housing structures have been torn down and the land sold at relatively low prices to developers for new office buildings and gentrified housing.

A third factor promoting conditions for gentrification is a preference for the cultural life of the city, that is, the easy access to diverse people and diverse entertainment which cities offer. Growth in the number of artists living in the area is generally considered a sign of coming gentrification. For example, Boston has been able to chart gentrification and predict potential for new gentrified areas by following the settlement patterns of artists over a period of years. Artists move to areas where there is plenty of space that is cheap. Cafes, bookstores, and theaters follow. The gentrifiers move in and the prices go up, forcing the artists to move on.

Government policies also affect gentrification. The federal government financially encourages demolition of large public housing and creation of less dense townhouses or condominiums with provisions for mixed income housing. State or city governments may offer tax incentives for revitalization of downtown areas. City governments may also use zoning changes to encourage an influx of new businesses and residents. Where government works in concert with the residents, such as in Lowell, Massachusetts, in the 1970s and 1980s, tensions are reduced. Where government tends to promote private investment and a laissez-faire attitude, such as on the Lower East Side of New York, conflicts with local residents may arise.

The Negatives of Gentrification

There is also a downside to gentrification. It takes an especially heavy toll on the poor and the elderly; which usually also means on minorities. Gentrification means repavement of streets, planting of trees and flowers, creation of cafes, restaurants, and new businesses, and more visible police protection and safety. However, these improvements also mean higher property values and taxes, which brings "involuntary" displacements of poor and elderly residents, especially renters, and often leads to conflicts between old and new residents. To lessen the pressure toward displacements and conflicts, many neighborhood leaders, city government, and the private sector work together to maintain income and racial diversity in gentrifying neighborhoods.

BIBLIOGRAPHY

Gale, Dennis E. *Neighborhood Revitalization and the Postindustrial City: A Multinational Perspective.* Lexington, Mass: Lexington Books. 1984.

Kennedy, Maureen, and Paul Leonard. "Dealing with Neighborhood Change: A Primer on Gentrification and Policy Choices." Brookings Institution. April, 2001. Available from http://www.brook.edu/es/urban/gentrification/gentrificationexsum.htm.

Diane Nagel Palmer

See also **City Planning; Urban Redevelopment.**

GEODESIC DOME, a type of building invented by the American engineer R. Buckminster Fuller in the late 1940s. Geodesic domes are composed of triangles of various sizes that are assembled into roughly hemispherical structures. They are exceptionally lightweight, strong, and require no interior supports. Geodesic domes first came to prominence in the 1950s, when they were used as radar shelters in the Distant Early Warning line and for exhibit pavilions in international trade fairs (most notably the Montreal Expo in 1967). These uses helped

Geodesic Dome. R. Buckminster Fuller stands alongside one of his versatile inventions, outside the Harvard Graduate School of Design. AP/Wide World Photos

solidify Fuller's reputation as a visionary yet practical thinker, and domes likewise became symbols of American ingenuity and the strength of Cold War capitalism. In the 1960s, domes were embraced by the counterculture, and thousands were built for use as homes, especially in rural communes. For these dome builders, domes were symbols of an ecologically friendly, pacifist, and anticorporate lifestyle—the rejection of precisely those values the dome embodied in the 1950s. The dome faded as countercultural architecture in the 1970s; since then, domes have principally been used in industrial applications requiring wide-span structures.

BIBLIOGRAPHY

Kahn, Lloyd, ed.. *Domebook 2.* Bolinas, Calif.: Pacific Domes, 1971.

Pang, Alex Soojung-Kim. "Whose Dome Is It, Anyway?" *American Heritage of Invention and Technology* (spring 1996), 28–31.

———. "Dome Days: Buckminster Fuller in the Cold War." In *Cultural Babbage: Technology, Time, and Invention.* Edited by Francis Spufford and Jenny Uglow. London: Faber and Faber, 1996.

Wong, Yunn Chii. "The Geodesic Works of Richard Buckminster Fuller, 1948–1968 (The Universe as a Home of Man)." Ph.D. diss. Massachusetts Institute of Technology, 1999.

Alex Soojung-Kim Pang

See also **Architecture.**

GEOGRAPHER'S LINE was established by Thomas Hutchins, geographer of the United States, according to the Ordinance of 1785. The line was to begin at the point at which the Pennsylvania boundary intersected the Ohio River and was to run due west for forty-two miles. The line is located at 40°38′ north latitude, but the inaccuracies of the survey, begun under many difficulties in 1785–86, caused it to deviate one mile to the north at its western end. The Seven Ranges, the first surveys under the ordinance, were laid out south of this line. They formed a strip six miles wide that was divided into townships six miles square.

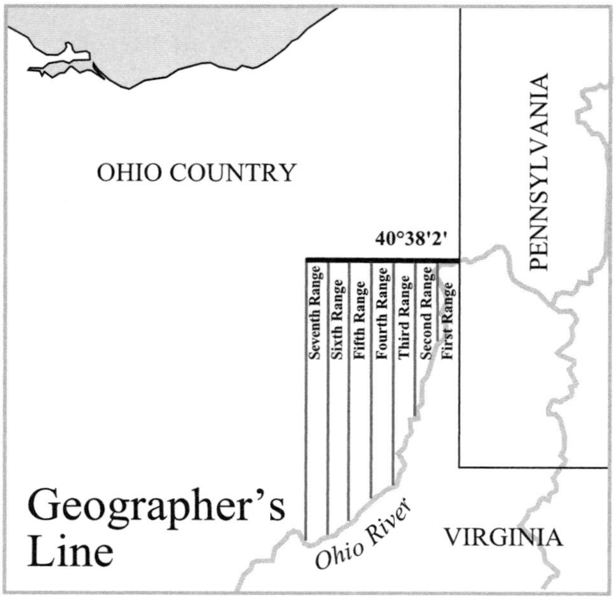

BIBLIOGRAPHY

Conzen, Michael P., ed. *The Making of the American Landscape.* Boston: Unwin Hyman, 1990.

Stilgoe, John R. *Common Landscape of America, 1580 to 1845.* New Haven, Conn.: Yale University Press, 1982.

Eugene H. Roseboom / F. B.

See also **Northwest Territory; Ordinances of 1784, 1785, and 1787; Western Lands.**

GEOGRAPHY. As the study of the earth's surface, geography is among the most concrete and accessible of all the sciences. Yet the very definition of geographical knowledge has been highly contested throughout the nineteenth and twentieth centuries. Geographers have disagreed over whether theirs is an analytic or a synthetic study, whether it deals primarily with the realm of nature or culture, and the degree to which it should be concerned with spatial relationships. Geography has also contended with a persistent reputation as simply descriptive inventory of the earth's surface, which has exacerbated its relationship with neighboring disciplines.

Institutional and Intellectual Origins

Through most of the nineteenth century geography was a broadly defined and practical field of knowledge utilized by scholars, explorers, bureaucrats, and politicians. Organizations such as the National Geographic Society and the American Geographical Society flourished in the nineteenth century as meeting grounds for men of science and government. The American Geographical Society, chartered in 1851, was devoted to the nation's growth and progress westward, especially the development of a transcontinental rail route. The organization welcomed not just geographers but also leaders in government, business, education, and science who shared their outlook. Through the society these members were exposed to the nation's exploration, surveying, and mapping efforts, primarily in the American West. Similarly, the National Geographic Society was founded in 1888 as a forum of exchange of information for the community of scientists and bureaucrats in Washington, D.C., involved in geological work. The society continued to facilitate geologically oriented research until the Spanish-American War, when it began a vigorous defense of the nation's mission abroad. In both these organizations, geographical knowledge served the state both concretely, through the supply of scientific expertise, and abstractly, in striking a nationalist posture.

Intellectually, American geography reflected a heavy European influence in the nineteenth century. Among the most influential and popular contemporary geographers were transplanted Europeans such as Karl Ritter and Alexander von Humboldt. Both elevated geography from the realm of description to that of science by considering the landscape as a unified entity to be studied as a whole, a process for which geography was uniquely suited in its stress on synthesis. Louis Agassiz, appointed at Harvard in 1848, was trained in the natural sciences and noted for his development of theories of glaciation and landforms. Arnold Guyot, appointed at the College of New Jersey (later Princeton University) in 1854, began to introduce a concept of geography not as a description of the earth's elements but rather as an observed interrelationship between land, oceans, atmosphere, and human life, all of which interacted harmoniously in a grand design. Though geography would gradually shed this teleological cast, Guyot had pushed geography from description to interpretation. George Perkins Marsh also explored this relationship in his *Man and Nature* (1864), though with a thoroughly theological bent. Into this basic framework of the relatively static view of the human and natural world, the work of Charles Darwin introduced the idea of evolution. As a result, geographers began to pay attention to the evolution of landforms over time, which eventually bolstered the study of physical geography.

By the late nineteenth century geography was no longer simply a tool of exploration, data gathering, and mapping. With the era of exploration waning, and with the coincident rise of American universities, geographers began to turn their attention toward reconceptualizing geography as an analytic, scientific body of knowledge. This was a difficult change for geographers, both intellectually and institutionally. Many worried that their field's reputation—as a broad field open to amateur armchair explorers as well as scientific experts—would taint its prospects in the newly professionalized university.

The unquestioned intellectual father of geography at this critical moment of late-century maturation was actually trained not in geography but geology, because doctoral programs in the former had yet to be developed. William Morris Davis was trained at Harvard as a geologist by Nathaniel Southgate Shaler and appointed professor of physical geography there in 1885. For Davis, the claims geographers made for their study as the "mother of all sciences" had to be halted if progress were to be made, for other scientists regarded this claim as the key indicator of geography's incoherence. Thus began a long tension within geography: What makes the field unique and worthy of its independence? How does a study that is essentially synthetic defend itself from the reach of neighboring sciences as diverse as geology, anthropology, and botany?

Together, Shaler and Davis initiated the first course of training in physical geography—the study of the surface features of the earth—and mentored the first generation of trained geographers in the United States. During the 1880s and 1890s Davis advanced an idea that applied Darwinian principles of evolution to the study of the physical landscape. The result was the science of geomorphology, in which Davis argued that different elements of the environment worked to produce change on the landscape through dynamics such as soil erosion. This concept helped legitimate geography at the university level and in the process gave geographers a tremendous source of pride. At the same time, however, geomorphology reinforced geography's identity as a subfield of geology, thereby hampering its intellectual independence.

In the late 1870s modern geography began to appear as a field of study in American universities, usually found within departments of geology or "geology and geography." Only in 1898 was an independent department of geography established at the University of California. Davis was convinced that geography's weak reputation was in part attributable to organizations such as the American Geographical Society and the National Geographic Society—especially the latter, which became an increasingly popularized and middlebrow organization after the turn of the century. These groups were irritating to Davis because they reinforced in the mind of the academic and lay communities alike the sense that geography was the pastime of leisured travelers and curious amateurs. He actively dissociated himself from these organizations at the turn of the century, and at one point even attempted to take control of the National Geographic Society in order to return it to its serious, scientific roots. Thus Davis was enthusiastic about a new organization designed exclusively for professional geographers. The Association of American Geographers was founded in 1904, toward the end of the trend toward disciplinary organizations. While geologists were initially welcomed in order to solidify the new organization's membership base, within a few years their applications were deferred in the hope that disciplinary purity might be achieved.

The Advent of Human Geography

Davis was successful in training a number of young geographers at the turn of the century who began to return to the relationship between humans and their physical environment. More specifically, this generation found itself increasingly compelled to study the human response to the physical environment. This turn toward the "causal relationship" was in part a result of the imperative to strengthen geography's position among the disciplines. This new focus had the added benefit of distinguishing geography from geology. Physiography, which linked elements of the environment with one another, and ontography, which linked the environment with its human inhabitants, were the two main areas of disciplinary focus for geography just after the turn of the century. Most early geographers conceived of their discipline as having unique power to bridge the natural and human sciences. From the mid-1890s to World War I the prospect of uniting nature and culture through geography seemed both feasible and imminent at some of the most important centers of academic geography, including Pennsylvania, Chicago, Yale, and Harvard. But it was precisely this claim to breadth that neighboring sciences began to challenge, for in the new era of university science, disciplines were legitimated not by claims of breadth and inclusiveness but rather by narrowing their focus and delimiting their boundaries.

Because of their interest in the causal relationship, theories that united the realm of humans and their environment held special appeal for geographers. For instance, natural selection, though widely misinterpreted, was used to describe the relationship between the physical and the human environments as one of inorganic control and organic response. Evolutionary concepts became central to geography's effort to explain nature's influence upon human behavior, and geography focused increasingly on the question of why certain races, societies, or groups flourished while others languished. To be sure, geographers neglected the idea of random variation and exaggerated and accelerated the process of "struggle" in order to incorporate humans into the ecological world. Yet without this causal connection—the influence of environment on human behavior—the areas of study under geography could easily be divided up among other disciplines.

Even more important than Darwin's ideas were those of Jean-Baptiste de Monet de Lamarck, who suggested that characteristics acquired through the course of a lifetime could be passed biologically to offspring. Lamarck's ideas were well suited to the needs of the new social sciences at the turn of the century because they united the study of nature and humans by linking biology with environment. Though the rediscovery of Mendel's laws concerning genetic heredity in 1900 eroded the credibility of Lamarckian thought, geographers continued to invoke this model when describing the core of their study as the relationship between humans and their natural environment. In other words, Lamarck created for geographers a process to study, and this appeal was too strong to be easily dismissed. Furthermore, Lamarckian constructions meant that geographers were now studying the progress of civilization, which vastly expanded their field of inquiry. By focusing on one's adaptation to the physical environment, the random chance of Darwinian evolution could be replaced with the strength of an individual, a culture, a race, or a nation. These assumptions were not always conceived in deterministic ways. While some geographers invoked them as evidence of an intellectual and social hierarchy in order to justify American expansionism or European imperialism, others used them to open up possibilities for social change. This indeterminacy implicit in Lamarckism allowed it to shape geography long after it had been discredited in other behavioral sciences. In fact it was the range of interpretations possible in Lamarckian expositions that made it so attractive to geographers.

Geography and the State

One of the striking characteristics of geographical thought at the turn of the twentieth century was its implicit support of American expansionism, as demonstrated in the sharp turn that the fledgling National Geographic Society made toward an aggressive defense of America's position abroad during the Spanish-American War. Two Europeans, Halford Mackinder and Friedrich Ratzel, also exercised considerable influence over American geographical thought. Ratzel, trained as a zoologist, argued that a relationship existed between human history and physical geography, in some ways similar to Davis's idea of ontography. But while Davis was relatively tentative in his formulations, Ratzel painted in broad strokes by applying the idea of Darwinian struggle to human society in order to frame the state as an organism that was forced to expand in order to survive. Known by many as the father of geopolitical thought, Ratzel fit well with the contemporary expansionist posture of Josiah Strong, Alfred Thayer Mahan, and Theodore Roosevelt, each of whom was encouraging American expansion into world affairs. Much like the work of Frederick Jackson Turner, Ratzel's ideas allowed geographers to link nature and culture. Ratzel's well-regarded *The Sea as a Source of the Greatness of a People* (1900) argued that sea power was central to national survival in the twentieth century.

Similarly, Halford Mackinder emphasized environmental influence as a key to the disciplinary identity of the new profession of geographers. His "Geographic Pivot of History" (1904) gave him an extraordinarily solid reputation in the United States; in it he laid out the geopolitical dimension of international politics. For Mackinder, the age of exploration had given way to a new era where the manipulation of information would be critical. In Mackinder's mind the human experience of geography and space had changed in fundamental ways in the late nineteenth century. As Stephen Kern has noted, the rise of geopolitics owed much to the cultural and technological changes taking place around the turn of the twentieth century, including the arrival of standardized time, the advent of flight, the expansion of the railroads, and advances in communication and radio, all of which transformed the everyday experience of space and time. Ratzel and Mackinder used geopolitical ideas in order to come to terms with this changed sense of distance resulting from these innovations. Both emphasized the relationship between geographical influence and human response.

Among the first generation of university-trained geographers who inherited these ideas of Ratzel, Mackinder, and Davis were Ellen Semple, Ellsworth Huntington, and Isaiah Bowman. Semple, a student of Ratzel's, was especially taken with environmentalist models as a way to explain American history. In works such as *American History and Its Geographic Conditions* (1903), Semple argued that living organisms evolve from simple to more complex forms through adaptation to physical environment. The larger the state, race, or people, the more certain its chance of survival relative to others competing for the same resources. Similarly, Huntington posited that the primary influence over human history was climate, and even suggested that these effects could be biologically passed on through generations. Books such as his *Civilization and Climate* (1915) were tremendously popular with the general public in the early twentieth century, though roundly criticized within geography and other social sciences.

World War I had a substantial impact on American academic geography. Most obviously, the war demonstrated the flexible nature of geographical borders in Europe and the ephemeral nature of colonial associations worldwide. The faith in European civilization was now tempered by its unparalleled capacity for destruction. In the United States, the war demonstrated the utility of geographic knowledge to the public and also advanced the careers of professional geographers called to work for the government. The geographer who benefited most from the war was Isaiah Bowman, then director of the American Geographical Society. One of Bowman's goals had been to make the society more relevant to social and political problems, and by placing its resources at the disposal of the federal government, the society's vast reserve of maps became pivotal to the construction of postwar Europe. The war also led many geographers, especially Bowman, to admit the limits of the environment over human behavior and to stress human influence over the environment. After World War I, geographers devoted tremendous energy to searching for a new relationship to unite the disparate areas under their field, prove its worth in the university, and conform to modern social scientific wisdom, which had deemed environmentalism a false and damaging approach to the study of human affairs.

Geography since Midcentury

One response to the rejection of environmentalist frameworks as the basis for research was to narrow geography's field of inquiry. The clearest indication of this was Richard Hartshorne's *The Nature of Geography* (1939), a massive statement of the field's direction written on the eve of World War II. For Hartshorne, what had historically made geography unique was its attention to systematic description of areal variation, not speculation about change over time or causal relationships between humans and their environment. The hope among earlier generations to discover laws of human behavior was dismissed by Hartshorne in favor of a focus on concrete, discrete studies.

Carl Sauer, one of the century's most influential geographers, rejected Hartshorne's treatise—and the approach of the interwar geographers generally—and characterized this period as "the great retreat" when geographers studiously avoided causal relationships between humans and their environment. Sauer thought this unacceptable: geography now conceded physiography to geology and shied away from the social sciences for fear of repeating past sins of environmental determinism. One of Sauer's alternatives was to emphasize the influence of humans over their environment rather than the reverse. In his wake, many students adopted Sauer's new approach in delving into the particularities of place and paying close attention to the development of landscape. Yet despite Sauer's attempt to discredit environmentalism, many geographers continued to grant the physical environment influence over human behavior during the interwar period, an indication of the fractured nature of the discipline at midcentury. In 1947, Harvard made the decision to dissolve its department of geography, the original locus of academic geography in the United States. In subsequent years, Stanford, Yale, Michigan, and innumerable smaller institutions closed their geography departments. Yet the overall number of geography programs rose sharply in the postwar years, a reflection of the general growth of higher education.

Geographers themselves found renewed energy in the 1950s and 1960s by turning toward quantitative analyses as the basis for a redefinition of geography. The "quantitative revolution" did not constitute a change in goals so much as in method: geographers were still searching for locational patterns, but they began to adopt mathematical models, which in some cases led a return to a more abstract, general orientation and away from the idiographic focus on discrete regions. This school of geography drew heavily from economics. But by the late 1960s the quantitative revolution left many concerned that geography was bereft of any purposive, reformist content. Some argued that the quantitative model of geography essentially operated conservatively, in defense of the status quo, and contained little critical potential. A reaction to this—in part inspired by Thomas Kuhn's *Structure of Scientific Revolutions* (1962)—brought a resurgence of political concerns to the study of geography, but this time with a radical rather than a conservative thrust.

Postmodern, or radical, geography involves first and foremost a critique of the traditional relationship between notions of space and time. For geographers such as Neil Smith and Edward Soja, for instance, Western culture has been preoccupied since the nineteenth century with a historicist focus, and this has come at the expense of an explicitly spatial orientation. They argue that this temporal bent has obscured our awareness of just how deeply the dynamics of power—especially those created by capitalism—are inscribed in spatial relations. For both Smith and Soja, to remedy this requires a critique of historicism and a turn toward spatial concerns. This goal of a more activist, self-critical form of the discipline has continued from the late 1970s forward to the beginning of the twenty-first century, and has brought special attention to the relationship between power and capitalism in the study of urban space. It has infused geography with both theoretical concerns and concrete purpose. In recent years considerable research has also been undertaken in the field of feminist geography, which explores the way gender relations are reinforced by spatial arrangements of societies. The wide influence of these new, conceptually rich areas of research extends well beyond the disciplinary bounds of geography, which suggests the trend toward a more ambitious and socially relevant scope for the subject.

BIBLIOGRAPHY

Blouet, Brian, ed. *The Origins of Academic Geography in the United States.* Hamden, Conn.: Archon, 1981.

Driver, Felix. "Geography's Empire: Histories of Geographical Knowledge." *Environment and Planning D: Society and Space* 10 (1992): 23–40.

Godlewska, Anne, and Neil Smith, eds. *Geography and Empire.* Oxford: Blackwell, 1994.

Kern, Stephen. *The Culture of Time and Space, 1880–1918.* Cambridge, Mass.: Harvard University Press, 1983.

Kirby, Andrew. "The Great Desert of the American Mind: Concepts of Space and Time and Their Historiographic Implications." In *The Estate of Social Knowledge.* Edited by JoAnne Brown and David K. van Keuren. Baltimore, Md.: Johns Hopkins University Press, 1991.

Livingstone, David N. *The Geographical Tradition: Episodes in the History of a Contested Enterprise.* Oxford: Blackwell, 1992.

Martin, Geoffrey J., and Preston E. James. *All Possible Worlds: A History of Geographical Ideas.* New York: Wiley and Sons, 1993.

Rose, Gillian. *Feminism and Geography: The Limits of Geographical Knowledge.* Cambridge, Mass.: Polity Press, 1993.

Schulten, Susan. *The Geographical Imagination in America, 1880–1950.* Chicago: University of Chicago Press, 2001.

Smith, Neil. *Uneven Development: Nature, Capital, and the Production of Space.* Oxford: Blackwell, 1984.

Soja, Edward W. *Postmodern Geographies: The Reassertion of Space in Critical Social Theory.* London and New York: Verso, 1989.

Stoddart, D. R. *On Geography and its History.* Oxford: Blackwell, 1986.

Susan Schulten

See also **Evolutionism; Geology; Maps and Mapmaking.**

GEOLOGICAL SURVEY, U.S. The United States Geological Survey is charged with the classification of the public lands and examination of the geological structure, mineral resources, and products of the national domain. It was established on 3 March 1879 in the Department of the Interior, and has been studying and mapping the land area of the United States ever since.

Origins of the Survey

Until its creation, scientific investigations were largely considered to be the responsibility of individual states or private institutions. The military had engaged in some scientific activities, but the federal government did not become involved until the 1830s. The growing realization that certain economic purposes could be advanced by science, or more accurately, that scientific activities of the federal government should serve the greater economic interests of the nation, led to change. In 1836, Congress authorized the United States Exploring Expedition to the Pacific, which had the backing of many influential scientists, as an aid to commerce. Two years later the Corps of Topographical Engineers was established to explore and map the continent. The Topographical Engineers provided geologists the opportunity to explore and study the West for the next two decades. Government support for their efforts was, however, tepid at best.

The discovery of gold changed that. The California Gold Rush of 1848 led several states in the South and the Midwest to establish state geological surveys to assess land usage and search for mineral deposits. The federal government established the Department of the Interior in 1849 in part to deal with land ownership issues. The gold rush also made the development of better communication and transportation between the eastern states and western territories more important. The Topographical Engineers explored four different routes for the transcontinental railroad and railway construction opened the West to further development and mineral exploitation. The Civil War accelerated industrial development and the demand for minerals such as iron ore and coal. The war, however, also brought an end to all but one of the state geological surveys.

The dramatic increase of demands on the nation's natural resources during and immediately following the war led Congress in 1867 to authorize western explorations in which geology would be the principal objective. It specifically called for a study of the geological and natural resources along the fortieth parallel route of the transcontinental railroad by the Army Corps of Engineers and a geological survey of the natural resources of the newest state, Nebraska, under the direction of the General Land Office. Clarence King, a member of the first class to graduate from Yale's Sheffield Scientific School in 1862, led the fortieth parallel expedition, and Ferdinand Hayden, a medical doctor by training, led the Nebraska effort. Both surveys proved successful and gained further funding. In 1870, Hayden presented plans to Congress calling for the gradual preparation of a series of geographical and geological maps of each of the territories on a uniform scale.

Meanwhile, two other surveys had gotten under way. John Wesley Powell, professor of geology at Illinois State Normal University, used private funding to explore the Rocky Mountains in Colorado and eastern Utah in 1867 and 1868. Then, in 1869, he set out by boat to travel the

Clarence King. The leader of the Fortieth Parallel Survey and the highly influential first director of the U.S. Geological Survey in the Interior Department, before becoming a mining engineer. LIBRARY OF CONGRESS

Green and Colorado Rivers and explore the Grand Canyon. Lieutenant George Wheeler of the Army Corps of Engineers received orders to scout the country south and east of White Pine, Nevada, for military purposes. In 1871, after his return, Wheeler proposed a plan for mapping the United States west of the one hundredth meridian on a scale of eight miles to the inch. Convinced that there was enough work for all four surveys, Congress continued funding both civilian and military mapping efforts until a slow economy forced it to cut costs. On the recommendation of the National Academy of Sciences, Congress consolidated all geodetic, topographic, and land-parceling surveys into the newly formed U.S. Geological Survey in the Interior Department, which would classify the public lands and study the geological and economic resources of the public domain. The survey began operations created on 1 July 1879 and Clarence King, whose Fortieth Parallel Survey had led the way in converting western exploration into an exact science, was appointed its first director.

The Early Directors

Although King remained as director for only two years—enough time to organize the work—he had such a profound impact on the organization and its mode of operation that the survey still clearly bore his imprint decades later. Geological research would no longer be a by-product as it had been on earlier expeditions, but rather the main focus. He separated the work into the Mining Geology and General Geology divisions. The legislation creating the survey did not clearly define its duties, and this gave King a great deal of latitude. He planned a series of land maps to provide information for agriculturists, miners, engineers, timbermen, and political economists, and confined operations to public lands. He gave the work of the survey a mission orientation, planned the goals, and selected the staff members while giving them the freedom to choose their own methods of work for achieving the goals. Given the lack of knowledge about precious metal resources, he focused the initial work on mining geology.

In 1881, King chose Powell as his successor. Powell, who differed greatly in his approach because of his natural history and anthropology background, immediately made the topographic work of the survey independent of geological studies. He redirected all topographic work toward the preparation of a geologic map of the entire United States. That task became the largest part of the Geological Survey's program. In 1887, an economy-minded Congress altered its method of funding the survey's work by requiring it to present itemized estimates for its funds so Congress could control expenditures.

The drought of 1886 and the severe winter that followed it on the Great Plains brought water and irrigation issues to national attention as never before. In October 1888, Congress authorized the survey to investigate the viability of irrigation in the region and to close the public domain while the survey work was conducted. Powell eagerly expanded the nature of the Geological Survey's focus into hydrography; however, that distracted the survey from its work in mineral geology. Congress quickly grew impatient waiting for results, but Powell argued that he could not offer any recommendations until all the facts were in. Congress responded by cutting off funding for the irrigation survey in 1890. Already unhappy over the irrigation survey and the Geological Survey's failure to serve directly the economic interests of the country, Congress slashed appropriations for most scientific agencies and the Senate launched an investigation of the survey's operations. Both steps were direct challenges to Powell and his policies.

Charles D. Walcott, who had begun as a paleontologist, replaced Powell in 1894. Walcott understood the problems faced by the survey and returned it to King's mission orientation while broadening it to aid all industries that could benefit from geology. The Geological Survey quickly returned to practical matters regarding mining and then cautiously began expanding its interests again. In 1894, water studies recommenced, with studies of underground water and water utilization added to the work on stream gauging. Walcott prevented the topographic work from being transferred to another agency simply by announcing that the quality of the topographic map would be improved. He also silenced some criticisms by placing the Survey under the Civil Service. The Survey

Research Ship. The U.S. Geological Survey's oceanographic research vessel *Samuel P. Lee,* used for scientific studies in Alaskan waters and various parts of the Pacific Ocean. U.S. GEOLOGICAL SURVEY PHOTOGRAPHIC LIBRARY

greatly increased the practical value of topographic maps through the placement of permanent benchmarks showing the exact location and elevation of fixed points.

The Survey As an Agent of National Policy

With federal science so vital to the economic life of the country, it inevitably became caught up in the formulation of national policy, and the Geological Survey was at the fore of the effort. Director Walcott had a hand in the passage of two key conservation measures. The Organic Act of 1897 assigned control of the newly created forest reserves (later known as national forests) to the Department of Interior, and gave the survey the task of mapping the reserves immediately. In 1902, the newly formed Reclamation Service, which was established to deal with the irrigation problems of the West, was placed within the Geological Survey. Five years later, the Reclamation Service became an independent bureau. That same year the forest reserves were transferred to the Department of Agriculture and the newly formed United States Forest Service. The increased interest in nonmetalliferous resources, including the fossil fuels, broadened the mission of the survey even more. Demand for oil and coal as fuel sources meant finding new deposits of those substances as well as formulating more efficient ways of extracting and delivering them. Eventually, the Geological Survey would become deeply involved in formulating energy policies.

The Geological Survey also started working outside the national domain. In 1897, a survey geologist and a hydrographer traveled to Nicaragua to study a proposed canal route between the Atlantic and Pacific Oceans and a few years later geologists were sent to investigate the mineral resources of Cuba and the Philippine Islands. Overseas work expanded further still during World War I as the need for new sources of minerals became critical.

Walcott's departure in 1907 signaled more than just a change in leadership. His successor, George Otis Smith, significantly altered the agency's focus. Smith was very interested in a business policy for the public domain, and believed that the work of his agency should be primarily, although not exclusively, practical. By the time he left office over twenty-three years later, nearly all of the agency's geological work was reoriented toward research. The demands placed on the Survey during World War I hastened this shift: progress in American science convinced industry of the value of research, taught scientists of different disciplines to cooperate with one another to solve problems, and introduced both public- and private-sector scientists to disciplines outside their own. The mineral shortages both during and after the war led Congress finally to appropriate funds for the classification of the public domain to determine how to handle the mineral lands.

Meanwhile, more mapping work was needed. The military demands of the war and the postwar boom in road construction revealed the critical shortage of adequate maps. Nearly 60 percent of the nation remained totally unmapped at the close of the conflict. Development of the tri-lens aerial camera and related equipment made the work easier. During his lengthy term as director, Smith oversaw the professionalization of geology as well as its diversification. The survey employed scientists in most of the scientific fields, and became involved in energy, water, topography, and mineral policy making. Despite the difficulties and the smaller budgets during the Great Depression and at the outset of World War II, Smith and his successors succeeded in maintaining a focus on the necessity of basic research.

World War II led to dramatic changes for the agency. The survey contributed to the war effort by searching out new sources of needed minerals, conducting research into making industry more efficient, and carrying on mapping work for the military both at home and abroad. The agency's expansion during the war continued well into the postwar period because of increased attention to science and the management of natural resources that resulted from Cold War politics. Topographic mapping continued, but less than 10 percent of the country had been mapped geologically, making natural resource management difficult. Geologists began adapting photogrammetric methods for mapmaking and using new devices like helicopters and electron microscopes to aid their effort.

In the 1950s and 1960s, the Geological Survey expanded its boundaries of examination still further. The nuclear arms race led to cooperation with the Atomic Energy Commission to evaluate the effects of underground nuclear testing and the environmental impacts of peaceful uses of atomic energy. Studies of geological processes led to measures for protecting the general public from natural disasters; for example, the study of volcanic activity eventually aided in the prediction of volcanic eruptions. Similar work was later undertaken on hurricanes and earthquakes. In 1959, the survey compiled a photogeologic map of the moon, and soon found itself training America's astronauts in geology. At the same time, the survey began working in Antarctica and the Trust Territory of the Pacific Islands. In 1962, the agency began marine studies of the ocean floor to identify and evaluate potential mineral resources and to aid in solving the environmental problems caused by rapid population growth, urbanization, and industrial expansion in coastal areas.

The survey also continued advising the nation on environmental and energy policies. It spearheaded fossil fuel exploration in places like Alaska and the Pacific and Atlantic Oceans and contributed to policy debates. A leaking oil well off the coast of Southern California at Santa Barbara in 1969 led to the creation of a task force, which included some survey geologists and engineers, to propose new and more stringent operating regulations to prevent or control such incidents in the future. The Santa Barbara oil spill was also a catalyst for the National Environmental Policy Act in 1970.

The next two decades saw a marked increase in multidisciplinary studies and in the diversity and complexity of agency operations, and also saw a concerted effort to make complex scientific information more easily usable in the solution of contemporary problems such as urban development or energy shortages. Technical assistance programs in Latin America, Africa, and Asia, started in 1964, were expanded and studies of the solar system were extended to Mars and other planets. The survey began using satellites to aid in its various mapping efforts. The transfer of the Alaskan Petroleum Reserve to the Department of the Interior in 1977 meant a 50 percent increase in funding and a corresponding increase in responsibility over activities on the reserve. In 1983, President Ronald Reagan's declaration of the Exclusive Economic Zone extended the jurisdiction of the United States for a distance of two hundred nautical miles seaward and thereby more than doubled the area of the national domain to be mapped and within which mineral and energy resources had to be assessed. The survey began mapping the three million square nautical miles in the zone the following year and also gathering other geological data for use by federal and state agencies.

Natural disasters such as earthquakes, hurricanes, and volcanic eruptions created new challenges for the survey, which participated in preparing for natural disasters and hazards. Research into these phenomena has helped the agency address the public's concern over the dangers from the effects of natural hazards. Addressing that concern became a paramount function of the survey in the 1980s and 1990s, and has remained such since. The work has greatly aided in reducing the loss of life.

In 2002, the agency reaffirmed that its mission is to provide reliable information to "describe and understand the Earth; minimize loss of life and property from natural disasters; manage water, biological, energy, and mineral resources; and enhance and protect [the nation's] quality of life." To meet those objectives, the survey began closer cooperation with individual states, sought to increase openness and participation in the bureau's decision-making process, and fully integrated the National Biological Service into the survey. This gave the Department of the Interior a single earth and biological science bureau consisting of four disciplines: Geological, Geographic, Water Resources, and Biological Resources. The divisions operate from the agency's headquarters in Reston, Virginia, and from regional centers in Denver, Colorado; Menlo Park, California; and other field offices.

BIBLIOGRAPHY

Bruce, Robert V. *The Launching of Modern American Science, 1846–1876.* Ithaca, N.Y.: Cornell University Press, 1987.

Dupree, A. Hunter. *Science in the Federal Government: A History of Policies and Activities to 1940.* Cambridge, Mass.: Harvard University Press, 1957.

Manning, Thomas G. *Government in Science: The U.S. Geological Survey, 1867–1894.* Lexington: University of Kentucky Press, 1967.

Rabbitt, Mary C. *The United States Geological Survey, 1879–1989.* Reston, Va.: Department of the Interior, Geological Survey, 1979. The best source for this topic.

———. *Minerals, Lands, and Geology for the Common Defence and General Welfare: A History of Public Lands, Federal Science and Mapping Policy, and Development of Mineral Resources in the United States.* 3 vols. Washington, D.C.: U.S. Geological Survey, U.S. Government Printing Office, 1979–1986.

Reisner, Marc P. *Cadillac Desert: The American West and Its Disappearing Water.* New York: Viking, 1986.

Worster, Donald. *Rivers of Empire: Water, Aridity, and the Growth of the American West.* New York: Pantheon Books, 1985.

James G. Lewis

GEOLOGICAL SURVEYS, STATE. From 1824 until about 1860, state geological surveys contributed significantly to the development of the economic and intellectual life of the American states. Even at the time they were made, these surveys were regarded as part of the nationwide campaign for internal improvements, and they were closely related to the transportation revolution. The reports of geological surveys influenced the routes of roads, canals, and railroads by describing natural features that assisted or hampered construction and by indicating valuable mineral deposits to which transportation lines could be run in anticipation of profitable business. In turn, railways and canals created cross sections of rocks for geologists to study and provided easier access to all corners of the states. Construction engineers were often hired as state geologists (and vice versa), and there was an easy two-way flow of information about topography and geological formations between engineers and state scientists.

The movement for state geological surveys began in the South. North Carolina appointed Denison Olmsted, science professor at the state university, to prosecute a survey in 1824. Elisha Mitchell inherited the geologist's job along with the professorship in 1826 and finished the survey in 1828. The survey produced four short annual reports on economical geology, and the purely scientific findings appeared in 1842 in a geological textbook written by Mitchell. South Carolina had Lardner Vanuxem, professor at South Carolina College, examine the state's minerals and strata in 1825 and 1826. Tennessee (1831–1850), Maryland (1833–1842), Virginia (1835–1842), and all the other southern states established surveys more comprehensive than the two early models.

Massachusetts fielded the first survey of a northern state from 1830 to 1833. Edward Hitchcock, its geologist, persuaded the legislature to include botany and zoology, making the survey one of natural history rather than of geology only. Massachusetts combined its geological survey with a wider effort to map the state's topography accurately; inadequate maps plagued all the state geologists, who, in addition to their other responsibilities, often made geographical discoveries. Hitchcock presented results of practical interest in his preliminary report and also published, at state expense, a heavily illustrated, seven-hundred-page final report replete with scientific data and theories to explain the state's geological history.

New York and Pennsylvania organized and financed critically important surveys beginning in 1836. Pennsylvania appointed a chief geologist and a corps of assistants who examined the coalfields in minute detail and exhaustively studied the structure of the mountains of Appalachia. New York had eight administratively independent scientists—four field geologists, a botanist, a mineralogist, a zoologist, and a paleontologist—who met annually to coordinate results. The scientists published twelve large volumes on soils, salt brines, ores, building materials (especially those relevant for canal construction), water supplies, and nearly every other practical aspect of the state's landscape in their annual reports. As in the South, so in the North and Midwest: nearly every state had a geological survey done or in progress by the beginning of the Civil War.

The surveys of the Jacksonian period fit political ideas of that era. They were decentralized away from federal control, in keeping with the then-current notions of the Democratic Party, and they signaled governmental concern for economic development, a concept usually associated with the Whigs. Both parties approved of institutions that spread information of economic and intellectual value among the whole population; private surveys would have confined such knowledge to an elite wealthy enough to finance them. American surveys differed from those of European countries partly as a result of these political premises. In England and France, learned societies and universities performed many of the functions of American state surveys. England's underfinanced effort began late (1835) relative to American surveys, and France's first survey (1766–1780) was almost purely scientific.

The work of the Jacksonian surveys marks an important chapter in American intellectual history, for state surveys trained many scientists as assistants on the job who later had distinguished careers. The surveys led to the creation of the American Association for the Advancement of Science, which grew from a meeting of the state geologists in 1840 to share field results, into the larger body by 1848. The surveys contributed also to the development of geological theory. The New York corps distinguished itself in paleontology and stratigraphy. Henry Darwin Rogers of the Pennsylvania survey (1836–1842) and his brother William Barton Rogers of the Virginia survey (1835–1842) advanced tectonics with their original and influential interpretation of the geological history of the Appalachian chain. European scientists read the reports of American state surveys and used the scientific information in them. Surveys were a significant source of employment for American scientists before the rise of universities, a focus for high-level research of both practical and theoretical benefit, and a training school functionally analogous to a modern graduate school.

Financial hard times of the late 1830s and early 1840s led the states to cut down on surveys. Thereafter, surveys had a new interest: as soils of the Atlantic and coastal area showed signs of nutrient depletion, many surveys were oriented toward scientific agriculture. The Civil War slowed activity in state surveys, and after the war several factors contributed to the eclipse of state geological surveys by other organizations. Most of the postbellum surveys began in states that had already been reported on once, if only after reconnaissance, so the sense of adventure and pioneering was missing. The four great surveys of the American West (1867–1878) sponsored by the federal government, with all of their glamour and economic significance, drew attention away from state efforts. The U.S. Geological Survey, consolidated in 1879 from these earlier federal activities, took over many operations collectively done by states, particularly problems of mapping and water supply, and also more theoretical work. Colleges and universities also gradually absorbed many of the research functions of the state surveys. By the end of the nineteenth century, state surveys were directed toward two goals that occasionally conflicted: to assist entrepreneurs in exploiting mineral resources and to promote conservation. This tension still affects state bureaus of mines and geological surveys.

BIBLIOGRAPHY

Corgan, James X., ed. *The Geological Sciences in the Antebellum South.* Tuscaloosa: University of Alabama Press, 1982.

Ferguson, Walter Keene. *Geology and Politics in Frontier Texas, 1845–1909.* Austin: University of Texas Press, 1969.

Goetzmann, William H. *Exploration and Empire: The Explorer and the Scientist in the Winning of the American West.* New York: Knopf, 1966.

Meisel, Max. *A Bibliography of American Natural History: The Pioneer Century, 1769–1865.* Brooklyn, N.Y.: Premier Publishing, 1924–1929.

Merrill, George Perkins. *Contributions to a History of American State Geological and Natural History Surveys.* Washington, D.C.: U.S. Government Printing Office, 1920.

Socolow, Arthur A., ed. *The State Geological Surveys: A History.* Tallahassee, Fl.: Association of American State Geologists, 1988.

Michele L. Aldrich / A. R.

See also **American Association for the Advancement of Science; Appalachia; Geophysical Explorations; Jacksonian Democracy; Paleontology.**

GEOLOGY. Although often sharing ground and affiliated with other natural sciences, geology at its core is the study of the earth's crust considered with respect to its rock and mineral content, its layered structure, and its dynamic transformations over time. In the United States, the science first emerged as a popular, organized pursuit around 1820, and about half a century later began to look something like the highly technical, professional discipline it is today. The crucial transition in its evolution occurred at the time of the Civil War (1861–1865), which thus serves as a boundary between the two major periods into which the history of American geology may conveniently be divided. In the first—an organizing, professionalizing stage—geologists were primarily engaged in identifying, naming, and classifying rock strata and in gathering information on mineral locations. Geology was greatly appreciated by the public for its educational value, its health benefits (claimed for the exercise and fresh air of field excursions), and its economic utility. It also attracted wide attention because of its unorthodox religious implications. In the second phase, when geology became the preserve of an enlarged corps of trained specialists, it tended to slip from public view even while it was charting paths for western expansion, unearthing the ores and energy resources needed to sustain a burgeoning economy, and performing other useful services. While geology became increasingly technical and inaccessible to the public, the plate tectonics revolution of the 1960s and 1970s made geology momentarily newsworthy, and thereafter there have been signs of the reentry of the science into the public arena as concern over global warming, water shortages, and other environmental problems has grown.

Geology in America Before the Civil War

In the early nineteenth century, geology was a fledgling science. Its practitioners were committed to avoiding the groundless speculations that had marred earlier "theories of the earth" and dedicated themselves to erecting geology on a solid foundation of observational data and well-ascertained facts. At the same time, making a pitch for public support of their endeavors, they gave assurances that geology was exceedingly useful. It could illuminate the earth's structure and chronicle its history, furnish valuable technical advice bearing on the progress of agriculture, mining, and manufacturing, and perhaps even lend confirmation to the biblical accounts of the Creation and the Flood. Receptive to these claims, the American public held geology in high esteem. In fact, during the first half of the nineteenth century it was the most popular of all the sciences. It won a place in the college curriculum, and textbooks setting forth its basic principles appeared. It was the subject of popular works and of primers, of articles in the quarterlies and the newspapers. Geology was a frequent topic for lyceum courses and public lectures, some like the Lowell Lectures in Boston, attracting thousands of auditors. In part, this high level of interest was stimulated by the ethos of "self-improvement" that Americans had adopted. Undergoing rapid growth, geology was making new discoveries in abundance, and it was the part of the educated person to keep abreast of these noteworthy advances in scientific knowledge.

But interest in geology was also stimulated by its bearing on religion. When geologists considered the rates at which geological processes like denudation and sedimentation take place, they were forced to conclude that the earth was millions of years old. How could this finding be reconciled with widely credited inferences from Old Testament history putting the age of the world at 6,000 years? And then there was the newly uncovered fossil record showing that vast stretches of time separated the first appearance on earth of the major types of plants and animals and that most of the ancient forms had become extinct before humans appeared. How could these facts be harmonized with the doctrine of the divine creation of the world in six days set forth in the book of Genesis? Benjamin Silliman Sr. and Edward Hitchcock, among other antebellum geologists, believed in the inspiration and authority of the Bible, but they were also stout champions of geology and did not want to see it succumb to biblical censorship. Certain that Genesis and geology must ultimately agree, they reconciled the two by adopting nonliteral interpretations of Scripture; Silliman, for example, subscribed to the "day-age" view, whereby the days of the Bible were interpreted as geological periods. This kind of harmonizing exegesis had an appeal for a while, but by the middle of the century it had begun to appear less convincing.

Noah's Flood was even easier to reconcile with geology, since it had long been invoked to explain the sculpting the earth's crust had undergone. As suggestive as this idea was, it did not stand up to close scrutiny, and by the mid-1830s the Flood had been abandoned as a universal, geological agency by the leading geologists. Among nonspecialists, of course, these issues were not so quickly resolved, and as long as geology appeared to bear in critical ways on the truth of Scripture, it continued to interest the public.

The perception that geology might be a source of substantial economic benefits also contributed to its popularity. To realize these benefits and join the national campaign for "internal improvements," virtually all the state legislatures authorized geological or natural history surveys. The first of these was instituted in North Carolina in 1823. By 1865, only Oregon and Louisiana had not initiated surveys. From state to state the surveys varied in scope and emphasis, but ordinarily they included a cataloging of the state's mineral deposits, an analysis of its soils for the benefit of farmers, and topographical reconnaissance to determine routes for turnpikes, railroads, and canals. Supported by annual appropriations that the geologists were obliged to justify in their annual reports, surveys would typically last a few years and conclude with the publication of "final reports." Aside from the evidence they presented of the industriousness and scientific acumen of the state geologists and their assistants, these state-funded documents served as valuable publicity for geology and gave evidence of its far-reaching utility. The public was appreciative, although occasionally there were complaints by those who did not want to hear that geological examinations of the state excluded the possibility of finding within its boundaries deposits of desirable mineral substances (coal in New York, for example).

The geologists employed in these surveys were far less specialized and professional than geologists would subsequently become. Among the approximately 500 individuals who published on earth science topics in antebellum America, few cultivated geology exclusively. Typically, their publications extended to other areas of science, notably natural history or chemistry. But whether specialists or not, they had only limited opportunities for making a living in science. Generally it was an avocational pursuit for those who found their principal work in medicine, the church, or business. Nonetheless, a living could be made in geology, and more readily than in most areas of science, since geologists could find employment in government surveys and in private consulting, as well as in college teaching. To be sure, combining the pay from two or more jobs in these different sectors might be necessary to ensure an adequate annual income.

Since as yet there were no graduate programs providing research training (these were inaugurated after the Civil War), there was no standard educational stepladder giving entry to a geological career. Apprenticing and on-the-job training as assistants in government surveys gave the best preparation. Providing not only an introduction to the practicalities of fieldwork that were essential to geology, survey work also made available through the many reports it generated a publication outlet for the aspiring geologist. The experience of the state surveys was also important in developing a collective *esprit de corps* among geologists and spurring them to organize on a national level. The year 1840 saw the founding of the Association of American Geologists, which shortly was to become the Association of American Geologists and Naturalists, and then in 1848 the American Association for the Advancement of Science. These developments bear witness to the fact that the professionalization and institutionalization of science in America was spearheaded by geologists.

As the Civil War approached, American geologists could feel they were part of a flourishing enterprise. The esteem in which geology was held by the public, the career opportunities it afforded, and the still-limited professionalism it practiced were all on the rise. There was pride in the surveying and mapping that had been accomplished in the preceding fifty years and a zest for continuing the exploration of the trans-Mississippi West. Geology was one facet of culture in which Americans no longer needed to feel they were inferior to Europeans. Textbooks now illustrated geological principles with American material, and one fundamental concept adopted by geologists everywhere, that of the geosyncline (a trough-like downwarp of the earth's crust supposed to be foundational in mountain building), had its origins in America.

Geology in America Since the Civil War

Although during the war years geological activity ground nearly to a halt, the end of the conflict launched a new and vibrant era in the cultivation of the earth sciences. Compared with its antebellum history, geology was now much more national in framework and in closer partnership with the federal government. The most expensive and highly publicized of the new projects were the federal surveys of the West. Unlike the U.S. government surveys undertaken before the Civil War, they were not primarily military in purpose nor under army direction. They were multifaceted exploring enterprises conducted by such ambitious civilian "entrepreneurs" as F. V. Hayden, Clarence King, and John Wesley Powell. The cost, competitiveness, and overlap of these surveys led in 1879 to their replacement by a consolidated bureau under the Department of the Interior, the United States Geological Survey (USGS). Initially, the USGS was especially concerned with serving the western mining industry, but subsequently its purposes broadened to include mapping the country, studying water resources, researching marine geology, and much else. In the world wars of the twentieth century it gave priority to the provision of strategic materials.

The creation of a consolidated, national framework for geological research was paralleled by the establishment in 1888 of a new association of national scope (or supranational, as it took in all of North America) dedicated to the professional growth of earth scientists. Still active in the twenty-first century and boasting a global membership in excess of 16,000, the Geological Society of America (GSA) holds an annual meeting and sponsors six regional sections that conduct their own yearly meetings. It further serves its members by publishing research papers and monographs, distributing research grants, recognizing outstanding achievements with medals and other honorific awards, and operating an employment clearinghouse. Twenty percent of GSA's members are students, and a wider participation of women in geology is encouraged by the activities of an associated society, the Association for Women Geoscientists. In seeking to achieve its aim of advancing the geosciences, the GSA, shaped by the modern culture of professionalism, has concentrated heavily on the practitioners, on the geoscientists themselves, their recruitment, development, and rewards.

This inner-directed orientation of geology's leaders, in combination with the growing technicality and inaccessibility of the science to outsiders, has opened up a gap between geology and the public that did not exist in the antebellum period. Few people are now drawn to geology because of cosmic or religious implications it is supposed to have. Nor does probing the relations between Genesis and geology currently have any cultural urgency. The GSA, to be sure, has issued a position paper (pro) on the theory of evolution, and more generally it has characterized the organization's vision as "applying geoscience knowledge and insight to human needs and aspirations and stewardship of the Earth." But getting this idealistic message to be taken seriously by an indifferent public has been difficult.

There have been signs that public awareness of geology may once again be stirring. The theory of plate tectonics established in the 1960s and 1970s has been so revolutionary and consequential that some word of it has reached almost everyone. It was a legacy of nineteenth-century geological thinking that throughout the history of the earth, continents and ocean basins have been permanently fixed (save for occasional motions upward or downward). When, starting in 1912, the German meteorologist Alfred Wegener challenged this fixist theory, arguing that continents have drifted laterally, collided, and separated, he made hardly any converts. By the late 1960s, however, continental drift had been incorporated into a new, synthetic theory that supposed the earth's crust to consist of a dozen or so rigid plates that move horizontally and interact with one another in response to heat convection patterns in the mantle. Turning back all challenges, the theory has revolutionized geology, giving it a remarkable unity and coherence and raising its explanatory power many times.

Just as the plate tectonics revolution was occurring, James Lovelock was publicizing his Gaia Hypothesis (in its biosphere the Earth functions as a single, self-regulating superorganism), the science of ecology was gaining broad recognition, and environmental alarms were registering in the public consciousness. One upshot of these developments has been a new and earnest regard for the planet, incorporating the knowledge and perspective of many fields—geology, biology, oceanography, atmospheric sciences, climatology, and so forth. If the idea is to understand how we depend on the environment and how we can keep it in balance, then help from all these sciences and others may be required. The processes to be understood are complex. They function as "systems" that only a multidisciplinary approach can unravel. Enough is at stake to suggest that geology, which is already a multidisciplinary field, will once again gain public attention.

BIBLIOGRAPHY

Aldrich, Michele L. *New York Natural History Survey, 1836–1845: A Chapter in the History of American Science.* Ithaca, N.Y.: Paleontological Research Institution, 2000.

Goetzmann, William H. *Exploration and Empire: the Explorer and the Scientist in the Winning of the American West.* New York: Knopf, 1966.

Kohlstedt, Sally Gregory. "The Geologists' Model for National Science. 1840–1847," Proceedings of the American Philosophical Society, 1974, 118: 179–195.

Manning, Thomas G. *Government in Science: The U.S. Geological Survey, 1867–1894.* Lexington: University of Kentucky Press, 1967.

Merrill, George P. *The First One Hundred Years of American Geology.* New Haven, Conn.: Yale University Press, 1924.

Newell, Julie Renee, "American Geologists and Their Geology: The Formation of the American Geological Community, 1780–1865," Ph. D. Diss., Univ. of Wisconsin-Madison, 1993.

Oreskes, Naomi. *The Rejection of Continental Drift: Theory and Method in American Earth Science.* New York and Oxford: Oxford University Press, 1999.

Schneer, Cecil J., ed. *Two Hundred Years of Geology in America: Proceedings of the New Hampshire Bicentennial Conference on the History of Geology.* Hanover, N.H.: University of New Hampshire, 1979.

Robert H. Silliman

GEOPHYSICAL EXPLORATIONS. Geophysics is a hybrid science (a combination of GEOLOGY and PHYSICS) that achieved a distinctive identity only in the mid-twentieth century, which is understandable when it is recalled that neither geology nor physics emerged as distinctive disciplines until the mid-nineteenth century. The antecedents of geophysics reach back to Isaac Newton.

The geophysical exploration of the Americas began with the French expedition of 1735–1745 to the Peruvian Andes, which was led by Charles Marie de La Condamine and included Pierre Bouguer. Paired with a simultaneous venture to northern Scandinavia, the expedition attempted to verify the Newtonian prediction that the earth would be found to bulge at the equator and narrow at the poles, and the expeditions thus inaugurated the study of geodesy (measuring the earth's surface). About sixty years later, between 1799 and 1804, Alexander von Humboldt, accompanied by Aimé Bonpland, explored the American equatorial zone. In a romantic survey of natural history, Humboldt included such broadly geophysical measurements as terrestrial magnetism, which he linked to other physical phenomena—usually meteorological. These ventures set the style of geophysical exploration in America, establishing precedents for geophysics both as the direct object of an expedition—as in the pursuit of geodesy—and as a component of a larger reconnaissance including CARTOGRAPHY, specimen collection, and geophysical measurements. For nineteenth-century America, the broader Humboldtean model was the more powerful: geophysics was rather an instrumental component of geographic surveys than a conceptual framework for geologic interpretation. After Darwin, this pattern was incorporated into an evolutionary model that supplied the theoretical context of earth science for more than a century.

Concern with applying physical theories and techniques gradually created an informal alliance between three scientific groups. Planetary ASTRONOMY, particularly as practiced by George H. Darwin, Osmond Fisher, and William Thomson (all British), addressed such problems as the formation, age, and structure of the earth. At the same time, "dynamical" geology, in contrast to historical or evolutionary geology, attempted to explain earth processes in terms of mechanics and physical laws. This group received some inspiration from such meteorologists as James Croll, who fashioned explanations for atmospheric dynamics based on physical processes; what physical chemistry and physical astronomy were to their respective disciplines, dynamical geology was to earth science. Finally, there was mining engineering, which provided technical training in metallurgy, mathematics, and physics at such schools as Columbia University and the University of California. Many of the instruments typical of geophysics, and many of the explorations that used them, stemmed from high-level prospecting, especially for oil.

In the exploration of the American West, geophysics is better understood in terms of certain themes and personalities than as a disciplinary science. Grove Karl Gilbert extended mechanics to problems in geomorphology and structural geology, framing quantitative geologic observations into rational systems of natural laws organized on the principle of dynamic equilibrium. Clarence E. Dutton, elaborating on speculations by John H. Pratt and George B. Airy, conceived the idea of isostasy, or the gravitational equilibrium of the earth's crust, and demonstrated how this pattern of vertical adjustment could become a compressive orogenic force (mountain formation, especially by the folding of the earth's crust). Dutton later made original contributions in volcanology and seismology. Samuel F. Emmons, Clarence King, and George F. Becker applied geochemical and geophysical analysis to the problems of orogeny and igneous ore formation. The latter two men were instrumental in establishing a chemistry laboratory in the U.S. Geological Survey and in applying its experimental results to geophysical phenomena. Becker explicitly attempted mathematical and mechanical models to describe ore genesis and the distribution of stress in the earth's crust. He was instrumental in the establishment of the Carnegie Institution's Geophysical Laboratory, served as the laboratory's first director, and bequeathed part of his estate to the SMITHSONIAN INSTITUTION for geophysical research. Geophysics advanced in the context of a symbiosis (mutually beneficial relationship) of field exploration and laboratory investigation. In the case of the U.S. Geological Survey, Carl Barus staffed the laboratory and Robert S. Woodward furnished field geologists with information on mathematical physics. Woodward later directed the Carnegie Institution.

Following the work of the explorers, other geologists and geodesists—among them, Bailey Willis, Joseph Barrell, and J. F. Hayford—generated quantitative models for earth structure and tectonics. But explanations developed for glacial epochs best epitomized the status of geophysics: attempts to relate glacial movements to astrophysical cycles provided a common ground for geology, geophysics, astronomy, and METEOROLOGY, but the results were rarely integrated successfully. Significantly, the most celebrated attempt at global geophysical explanation remained an unassimilated hybrid. In developing the planetesimal hypothesis in 1904, Thomas C. Chamberlin preserved a naturalistic understanding of earth geology, while F. R. Moulton supplied the mathematical physics. The earth sciences continued to subordinate their data and techniques to a broad evolutionary framework.

By the early twentieth century, geophysics was a conglomerate of pursuits promoted through federal scientific bureaus (Coast and Geodetic Survey, Geological Survey), private or university research institutes (Carnegie Institution's Geophysical Laboratory, the Smithsonian Institution), companies engaged in mineral prospecting, and exceptional individuals. Geophysics, having neither a disciplinary organization nor a unifying theory, remained more an analytic tool than a synthetic science.

This condition persisted until after WORLD WAR II. Thereafter, with new instruments and techniques developed for mining and military purposes, with additional subjects (especially OCEANOGRAPHY), and with a theoretical topic to organize its research (continental drift), geophysics developed both an identity and a distinctive exploring tradition. This was well exemplified by the INTERNATIONAL GEOPHYSICAL YEAR (IGY), planned for 1957 and 1958 but extended to 1959. In counterpoint to the space program, geophysicists proposed to drill into the interior of the earth. Although aborted in 1963, Project Mohole was superseded by other oceanic drill projects, especially the Joint Oceanographic Institute's Deep Earth Sampling Program (JOIDES) begun in 1964. The International Upper Mantle Project (1968–1972) formed a bridge between IGY and research under the multinational Geodynamics Project (1974–1979), which proposed to discover the force behind crustal movements.

In the late 1990s, geophysical exploration led to the Ocean Drilling Program. The program functioned from a ship called the JOIDES Resolution, named for the Joint Oceanographic Institutions for Deep Earth Sampling. Built to drill into the seabed for oil, the ship's high-technology laboratory was used by an international crew of scientists to conduct geophysical research. The program found evidence related to the impact of a meteorite at the end of the Cretaceous Era, evidence of ocean temperature changes in the Ice Ages, and documented changes in the earth's magnetic poles.

Geophysics is a revolution in physics, and its integrative concept, the theory of plate tectonics (formerly continental drift), rivals relativity and quantum mechanics in significance. Involving geophysical research in practically all fields of earth science, and paired with satellite surveys, plate tectonics constitutes a new inventory of natural resources and a scientific synthesis of the globe.

Geophysical exploration has, moreover, preserved its archetypal (original) forms, being international and corporate in composition, global in scale, and quantitative in data and being founded on the theoretical assumption of a steady state. It blends the styles of La Condamine and Humboldt, combining specific geophysical pursuits against a cosmic landscape. Yet the transformation is remarkable—the difference between Humboldt's surveying of sublime panoramas from the summit of the Andes, and the Earth Technology Resource Satellite (ETRS) radioing instrumental data to terrestrial computers.

BIBLIOGRAPHY

Botting, Douglas. *Humboldt and the Cosmos.* New York: Harper and Row; London: Joseph, 1973.

Fraser, Ronald. *Once Round the Sun: The Story of the International Geophysical Year.* New York: Macmillan, 1957.

Glen, William. *The Road to Jaramillo: Critical Years of the Revolution in Earth Sciences.* Stanford, Calif.: Stanford University Press, 1982.

Goetzmann, William H. *Exploration and Empire: The Explorer and the Scientist in the Winning of the American West.* New York: Knopf, 1966; New York: Norton, 1978.

Hallam, Anthony. *A Revolution in the Earth Sciences: From Continental Drift to Plate Tectonics.* Oxford: Clarendon Press, 1973.

Oreskes, Naomi. *The Rejection of Continental Drift: Theory and Method in American Earth Science.* New York: Oxford University Press, 1999.

Sullivan, Walter. *Continents in Motion: The New Earth Debate.* New York: McGraw-Hill, 1974; American Institute of Physics. 1991.

Steve Pyne / A. R.; F. B.

See also **Carnegie Institution of Washington; Climate; Geological Survey, U.S.; Geological Surveys, State; Mineralogy; Wilkes Expedition;** *and vol. 9:* **An Expedition to the Valley of the Great Salt Lake of Utah.**

GEORGE WASHINGTON BRIDGE. Spanning the Hudson River between Fort Lee, New Jersey, and 178th Street in Manhattan, the George Washington Bridge was designed by Othmar H. Ammann and constructed by the Port Authority (now Port Authority of New York and New Jersey). It was completed in October 1931, at a cost of $59 million. With a center span of 3,500 feet, twice as long as any bridge span constructed to that date, it became a symbol of the art and craft of the civil engineering profession. Between anchorages, the total length is 4,760 feet; and the deck is suspended from cables composed of galvanized steel wire, with each wire at 0.196 inches in diameter and the total length of wire at 105,000 miles. A second deck, also designed by Ammann, opened in 1962; the top level has eight lanes, and the bottom level six. The bridge towers are made of unadorned steel and rise 604 feet above the water; clearance to the Hudson River at mid-span is 212 feet. The bridge carries traffic from New England, Westchester County, New York, and New York City to connecting highways in New Jersey and from there across the nation. Typical eastbound (to New York) weekday traffic in 2000 was 153,000 vehicles and eastbound annual traffic, 54 million vehicles.

George Washington Bridge. A 1932 view from Fort Lee, N.J., looking toward New York, of what is still one of the longest suspension bridges in the world. © CORBIS

BIBLIOGRAPHY

American Society of Civil Engineers, *Transactions: George Washington Bridge.* Vol. 97. New York: American Society of Civil Engineers, 1933.

Billington, David P. *The Tower and the Bridge: The New Art of Structural Engineering.* New York: Basic Books, 1983.

Doig, Jameson W. *Empire on the Hudson: Entrepreneurial Vision and Political Power at the Port of New York Authority.* New York: Columbia University Press, 2001.

Jameson W. Doig

See also **Bridges; New Jersey; New York State.**

GEORGIA has played a pivotal role in shaping the South and the nation. Its history is one of stark contrasts,

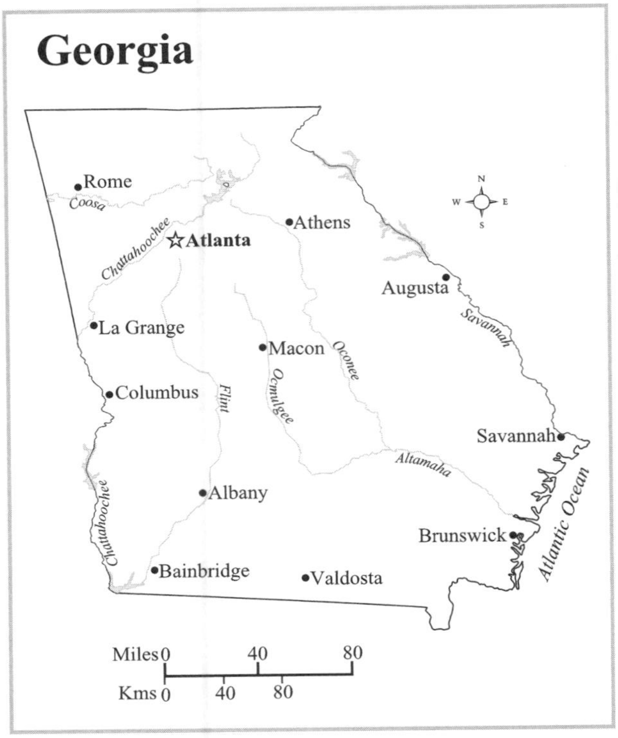

both painful and inspirational, filled with hatred and high idealism, poverty and prosperity. The landscape itself ranges from swampland in the south to mountains in the north, with the "fall line"—a topographical divide that transverses Georgia's midsection—separating the flat "lowcountry" from the hilly "upcountry." Georgia's cities have been influential: coastal Savannah; lowcountry Albany; the fall-line cities of Columbus, Macon, and Augusta; and, after the Civil War, Atlanta, which today is virtually its own state. But until recent decades, agriculture and rural life dominated the state. Tensions between rural and urban, black and white, rich and poor have characterized Georgia's economic and political developments, from the colonial era to the present.

A Contested Colony

Georgia became England's thirteenth colony in 1732, when the Crown granted a charter to reform-minded trustees, who outlawed slavery in their colony, hoping to create a yeoman's paradise for the poor. Less idealistic, the Crown wanted a defensive buffer for South Carolina's rice plantations, which suffered raids from Spanish Florida. James Edward Oglethorpe, England's well-bred champion of penal reform and religious freedom (Protestants only), arrived with the first ship and established Savannah. Although Oglethorpe wanted debtors prisons to furnish Georgia's manpower, so many middling types signed up that the prisoners never got out.

The prohibition on slavery failed, too; Carolina's wealthy plantations enticed Georgia's settlers, who illegally bought slaves. The popular Methodist revivalist George Whitefield encouraged this, preaching that God made Georgia for slavery. In 1752, the Crown reclaimed its charter and lifted Oglethorpe's ban. By 1776, Georgia's tidewater planters owned fifteen thousand slaves and controlled the colony. The Revolution gave planters a good shake. Some fled, others lost slaves to Florida's wilderness. In the war's final years, Georgia's patriots fought guerrilla campaigns in the backcountry. There, rough commoners—such as the illiterate but savvy fighter Elijah Clarke and the redcoat-killing Nancy Hart—won a place in Georgia's politics and folklore.

Early Statehood and Land

Major events between 1790 and 1810 involved land. Colonial boundaries gave Georgia vast western holdings. Greed overwhelmed Georgia's legislators, resulting in the ugly Yazoo Fraud of 1795. To save face, Georgia ceded its western lands to the federal government and set its present-day boundaries. In return, federal officials promised future support in removing Georgia's Indians, who occupied two-thirds of the state.

John Milledge, elected governor in 1802, transformed Georgia's land policies. All public lands, including Indian lands, would be surveyed into yeoman-sized lots and distributed by lottery. The system was democratic for white men; Indians and free blacks were excluded, and women had no right to own property. With the lottery, white Georgians surged upcountry, and the statehouse moved with them. In 1804, the government abandoned Savannah for the fall-line town of Milledgeville, named for the land-reform governor. The stage was set for Georgia's internal development.

The Antebellum Era

Between 1810 and 1860, three powerful trends shaped Georgia: the removal of the Creeks and Cherokees; the expansion of cotton plantations and slavery; and the rise of sectional tensions between North and South. In 1810, Indian territory still encompassed two-thirds of Georgian lands; plantation slavery was limited largely to the coast; and the southern states had no collective identity as "Dixie." By 1814, a completely new Georgia moved toward civil war.

Georgia took Creek land piecemeal over many decades. Weakened by defeat during the War of 1812, the tribe made final its cessions to Georgia in 1814, 1821, and 1825/26. The Cherokees of northwest Georgia defended themselves by adopting European ways. They enslaved blacks, developed an alphabet, and established legislative government at their capital, New Echota. But gold discovered in Dahonega, an Appalachian town, sparked the gold rush of 1829, flooding Cherokee Georgia with whites. The Indian Removal Act of 1830; Georgia's lottery for Cherokee land in 1832; and a dubious treaty in 1835 ended the Cherokee defense. In the winter of 1837–1838, federal soldiers forced them west.

White farmers plowed old Indian lands, but north and south Georgia developed differently. The upper Piedmont and Appalachian areas emerged as a yeoman stronghold. "Plain folk" settled on family farms, distant from commodity markets. They practiced subsistence farming (corn and hogs) and grew wheat or cotton for cash. Both slaves and plantations were scarce.

The lower Piedmont became a stronghold of cotton plantations. Plantations had long been fixed along the coast, where slaves could produce rice, indigo, and long-staple cotton. But improved mechanical cotton gins, produced in Savannah around 1800, facilitated cultivation of short-staple cotton in Georgia's interior. With Creek removal, aspiring whites carved sprawling plantations across the lower Piedmont. In 1800, about 60,000 slaves lived in Georgia; by 1830, some 220,000. Federal law banned slave importation in 1808, but Georgia's planters continued to smuggle slaves until the 1860s. Georgia led America in cotton production and illegal slaving.

Georgia's yeomen and planters had little need for cities in Georgia's interior, but some leaders called for modernization. Augusta, Macon, and Columbus had fall-line waterpower for industry, and, by the late antebellum period, they had textile mills, foundries, and food-processing plants. Columbus became the Deep South's manufacturing leader. Legislators sponsored railroad development, most notably the Western and Atlantic Railroad, whose construction in the mid-1840s resulted in a new railroad town—Terminus, later renamed Atlanta.

Dixie's cotton revolution made southern states different from their industrializing, free-labor neighbors up north. Sectional political conflicts and northern abolitionism made white southerners conscious of themselves as "southerners," and planters staunchly defended their "peculiar institution." When the Mexican-American War (1846–1848) opened vast western lands for Americans, sectional conflict boiled. Would the West follow the southern or the northern model? The question of slavery in the West ultimately led the North and South to war.

Civil War and Reconstruction

The Confederacy needed Georgia—economically powerful and strategically located—but opposition to secession rang across Georgia, not just among yeomen and poor whites, but also among wealthy planters; proslavery champion Benjamin Hill argued that war would bring only defeat and emancipation. When electing representatives for a state convention to rule on secession in early 1861, Georgians gave a thin majority to antisecession candidates. But at the convention, disunion sentiment reigned, and on 19 January 1861, Georgia became the fifth state to join the Confederacy.

Georgia's planters and industrialists profited from the wartime cotton prices and manufacturing needs, but they worried about rank-and-file patriotism. The Confederate legislature thus enacted a draft to fill its armies. When drafted, poor whites had no options, but large planters were exempted from military service, and small planters had buyout options. Class divisions among whites therefore flared hot, desertion rates soared, and poor women rioted for food in Columbus and Colquit. North Georgia and the Lower Chattahoochee Valley suffered recurrent guerrilla warfare.

An internally divided Georgia faced a Union onslaught in 1864 as General William T. Sherman's forces pushed into northwest Georgia. A bloodbath at Chickamauga and strong Confederate entrenchments at Kennesaw Mountain temporarily checked the Union advance. But in September 1864, Sherman took Atlanta, the Confederacy's transportation hub, ensuring Lincoln's reelection. Sherman's March to the Sea wasted Georgia and speeded Confederate surrender in 1865.

War liberated black Georgians. They fled plantations for Union camps and reveled in the Thirteenth Amendment, which outlawed slavery. "Freedmen" sought family farms or jobs in Georgia's cities, especially Atlanta, which rapidly rebuilt. Blacks supported the Republican Party, which trumpeted Lincoln and emancipation. Former Confederates championed the Democratic Party, which fought for white supremacy. Fierce political battles marked the postwar decades.

Race and Politics, 1865–1915

Reconstruction in Georgia was brief, bloody, and disastrous for African Americans. The Freedmen's Bureau met black demands for education, but proved more concerned for planter's needs. When southern Democrats passed Black Codes, virtually enslaving the freedmen, Republicans in Congress passed the Reconstruction Act of 1867, placing Dixie under military rule and enfranchising blacks. Georgia's new Republican Party—a biracial coalition of blacks and hill-country whites—formed a majority at Georgia's constitutional convention of 1867. African Americans made up 30 percent of the convention delegates. Milledgeville refused to accommodate these men and thereby lost the statehouse; the delegates met in Atlanta and made it Georgia's capital. The constitution mandated universal manhood suffrage, women's property rights, and free public schools. Georgia's legislature of 1868 included thirty-two African Americans, including civil rights activist Henry McNeal Turner. The legislature ratified the Fourteenth Amendment (black citizenship rights) in July 1868, thereby gaining Georgia's readmission to the Union.

When federal troops soon departed, the Democrat counterattack began. In Georgia's legislature, Democrats convinced white Republicans to help them purge blacks from the statehouse. This cross-party alliance expelled the black representatives, claiming that Georgia's constitution gave blacks the right to vote, not hold office. Georgia's supreme court ruled the purge unconstitutional, and Congress investigated, but Democrats resisted intervention with the help of the Ku Klux Klan (KKK). Confederate General John B. Gordon (governor, 1886–1890) led

NOTABLE GEORGIA WOMEN OF THE TWENTIETH CENTURY

Rebecca L. Felton (1835–1930), feminist, first female U.S. Senator (appointed 1922).

Juliette Gordon Low (1860–1927), founder (1912) of the Girl Scouts of America.

Gertrude "Ma" Rainey (1886–1939), pioneering blues singer.

Margaret Mitchell (1900–1949), author, winner of the Pulitzer Prize for *Gone with the Wind* (1936).

Flannery O'Connor (1925–1964), critically acclaimed writer of southern fiction.

Rosalynn Carter (b. 1927), First Lady of the United States (1977–1981), human rights activist.

Coretta Scott King (b. 1927), civil rights leader, widow of Dr. Martin Luther King Jr.

Gladys Knight (b. 1944), legendary rhythm and blues singer.

Anne Firor Scott (b. 1921), pioneering women's historian.

Alice Walker (b. 1944), author, winner of the Pulitzer Prize for *The Color Purple* (1983).

SOURCE: Georgia Politics in Transition

Georgia's Klan, which terrorized and assassinated Republicans in 1868–1869. In response, Congress expelled Georgia from the Union in 1869, crushing the Klan, reimposing military rule, and reinstalling black officials. Georgia's biracial legislature ratified the Fifteenth Amendment (voting rights), and Georgia again rejoined the Union. But in the elections of 1870, with federal troops gone, the Democrats launched a campaign of violence that effectively destroyed Georgia's Republican Party. This time Congress refused to investigate, signaling victory for Georgia's Democrats, who called themselves "Redeemers."

For the next century, Georgia's conservative Democrats would decry the long nightmare of "bayonet rule" and "Negro domination." Generations of white Georgians (and American historians) would accept this interpretation, facts notwithstanding, and use it in defense of state's rights and segregation.

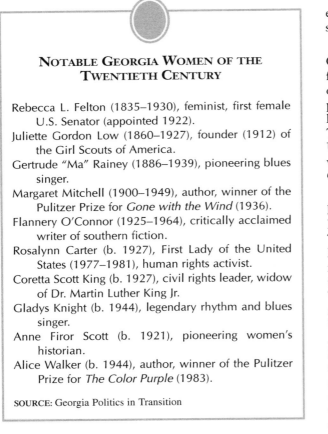

Democrats faced new challengers through the 1890s. In the 1870s, Independent Party coalitions championed reform, sometimes courting black voters. In the 1880s, the biracial Farmer's Alliance lobbied hard, but unsuccessfully, against conservative policies. In 1892, Georgia's Tom Watson led angry farmers (black and white) into the national Populist Party, seeking to empower "producers" over the planter-industrialist establishment. The presidential election of 1896 crushed the Populists and firmly established the one-party South, making Watson an outspoken racist and killing hopes for biracial insurgency.

Lowcountry planters controlled state politics through Georgia's unusual "county-unit system," which vastly inflated the value of rural votes over urban votes in Democrat primaries, the only meaningful elections in a one-party state. Sparsely settled rural counties dominated the legislature and selected rustic governors such as Eugene Talmadge, who never campaigned in any city. Only the U.S. Supreme Court's *Gray v. Sanders* (1963) decision would eliminate the county-unit system and equalize Georgia politics.

In the 1890s, Jim Crow segregation and mob violence devastated black Georgians. Without opposition, Democrat lawmakers made blacks second-class citizens. To resist was to risk lynching. Georgia led the nation in lynchings; elected officials accepted and facilitated mob rule, while northern Republicans refused to intervene. In this hostile environment, the black leader Booker T. Washington delivered his conciliatory "Atlanta Compromise" speech at Atlanta's 1895 Exposition, and Atlanta University professor W. E. B. Du Bois published *Souls of Black Folk* (1903), which launched his career as the nation's leading civil rights activist. Disenfranchisement notwithstanding, Democrats remained obsessed with race. Georgia's gubernatorial primary of 1906 featured two Democrats blasting "Negro domination" and sparking a bloody white-on-black race riot in Atlanta. As a capstone to the era, Atlanta resident William Simmons organized the second KKK at nearby Stone Mountain in 1915.

The New South Economy, 1880–1940

If planters controlled state politics and lowcountry plantations, a new urban middle class conquered the upcountry. Led by Atlanta journalist Henry Grady, boosters trumpeted a "New South Creed" of urban-industrial development. Rural transformation, as well as the creed, spurred upcountry industrialization. The plain folk's postwar poverty coupled with new railroads and fertilizers brought them into the cotton market, which destroyed them. Declining cotton prices, soaring interest rates, and a cruel crop-lien law brought perpetual debt and foreclosure; tenancy replaced small farm ownership. These events enriched small-town merchants, who invested surplus capital into the local cotton mills that arose across the southern upcountry, from Virginia to Alabama. Mills hired poor farm families, who worked for low pay and lived in "mill villages" controlled and enhanced by management. Critics and defenders of the mills clashed; industrialization proved controversial. Meanwhile, black Atlanta developed separate businesses, creating a rising black middle class to accompany its poor working class.

South of Atlanta, change moved slowly. Planters had lost their slaves but not their land. With lien laws and credit control, they controlled black sharecroppers, who experienced, instead of freedom, grinding poverty. Cotton remained king until boll-weevil damage in the 1920s forced shifts to peanuts, pecans, and dairy farms. Lowcountry pine forests fell for lumber and turpentine. With an old-money sniff at Atlanta, Savannah stagnated. World War I inaugurated a major change—the great migration of blacks from South to North. Labor shortages up North and Jim Crow down South sparked the movement; after the war, the black exodus continued.

The Great Depression and the New Deal altered Georgia's economy. President Franklin Roosevelt, a liberal Democrat who owned a "Little White House" in Warm Springs, Georgia, used unprecedented federal intervention to alleviate suffering and revive the economy. Ordinary Georgians loved Roosevelt. Georgia's conservative Democrats needed federal aid but feared for state's rights, a growing southern dilemma. Federal agricultural programs paid planters not to plant cotton; sharecroppers went uncompensated, and many were forced off land. Federal industrial policies created a code for textile production, giving approval for labor unions. Hoping to improve their working lives, thousands of mill hands joined the United Textile Workers. Labor-management conflicts sparked the General Textile Strike of 1934, which saw 400,000 southern mill hands stop work. Company guards and state troops crushed the strike and left unionism badly weakened. New Deal legislation nonetheless aided workers by mandating eight-hour days, overtime pay, minimum wages, and social security.

World War and Cold War, 1940–1960

World War II was a major turning point in Georgia's history. It brought massive federal investment in defense plants and military camps. Black outmigration soared as defense plants outside Dixie recruited workers, while rural whites moved to booming shipyards. The Progressive governor Ellis Arnall eliminated the poll tax and boosted higher education. Organized labor gained. Blacks in Atlanta spoke out for civil rights—some even began voting.

When war ended in 1945, Georgia's direction was uncertain and remained so through the 1950s, as the forces for progress and tradition clashed. The economy improved, but not without pain. Textile mills boomed until foreign imports began to undermine them. Georgia's industrial base diversified, offering higher-wage jobs. Organized labor got crushed, except in isolated upcountry mill towns. The poultry industry helped small farmers. Lowcountry plantations adopted the mechanical cotton picker, forcing hundreds of thousands of blacks off the land and speeding the black exodus.

Postwar politics exploded. Three men claimed the governor's chair after the 1946 election, prompting scandal and national embarrassment. More significant, blacks registered to vote in growing numbers. White resistance to civil rights intensified after the *Brown v. Board of Education* (1954) decision ruled against segregation. Atlanta native Martin Luther King Jr., a young Baptist preacher, led the Montgomery bus boycott (1955–1956) in Alabama, which ended segregated seating on city buses. In 1957, King helped organize the Southern Christian Leadership Conference (SCLC), a civil rights organization with its headquarters in Atlanta, while whites organized a "massive resistance" campaign against federal intervention in racial matters. Between 1955 and 1960, state legislators passed numerous laws intended to scuttle school integration and added the Confederate stars and bars to the state flag.

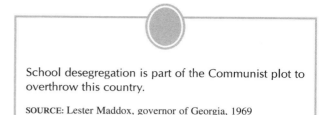

> School desegregation is part of the Communist plot to overthrow this country.
>
> SOURCE: Lester Maddox, governor of Georgia, 1969

Tensions between federal economic trends and sectional politics intensified. The Federal-Aid Highway Act of 1956 and massive defense spending helped Cold War Georgia boom. But greater federal investment in Georgia meant increased pressure for civil rights, especially after the Soviets publicized Jim Crow policies to humiliate American diplomats. Georgia's black activists brought matters to a head in the early 1960s.

The Civil Rights Movement

Martin Luther King Jr. moved back to Atlanta in 1960. Independently, black college students began lunch-counter sit-ins in southern cities, leading to the creation of the Student Nonviolent Coordinating Committee (SNCC), also headquartered in Atlanta. In 1962, the SCLC unsuccessfully battled segregation in Albany; the campaign taught activists the importance of national media attention. They got plenty in the Birmingham campaign, which helped win President John Kennedy's support for the movement. King's "I Have a Dream" speech electrified the March on Washington on 28 August 1963. Often at odds, SCLC and SNCC both participated in the climactic 1965 voting-rights campaign in Selma, Alabama, with many Georgians, including Atlanta's Hosea Williams, in the lead.

Atlanta's white leaders, eager to look progressive, tried to stave off racial conflict and bad publicity, whether they believed in the movement or not. Mayors William B. Hartsfield and Ivan Allen Jr. worked with black leaders to make the transition to desegregation. Atlanta's Georgia Institute of Technology quietly integrated in fall 1961, the first public university in the South to do so without court order. Local tensions ran high, though. When King won the Nobel Peace Prize in 1964, Atlanta's stunned elite reluctantly hosted a biracial banquet in his honor.

The Civil Rights Act of 1964 (outlawing segregation) and the Voting Rights Act of 1965 (ensuring voting rights) revolutionized Georgia society and politics, but change outside Atlanta proved slow. Black voters soon liberalized

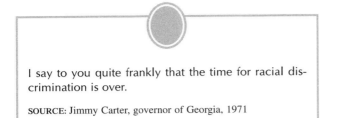

> I say to you quite frankly that the time for racial discrimination is over.
>
> SOURCE: Jimmy Carter, governor of Georgia, 1971

Georgia's Democratic Party. Civil rights stalwarts Julian Bond and Andrew Young of Atlanta won election to state and national offices. Maynard Jackson became Atlanta's first black mayor in 1974.

Angry white Democrats, mostly rural and working-class, sent arch-segregationist Lester Maddox to the governor's mansion in 1966; Atlanta's leaders cringed. Maddox was Georgia's last openly racist governor. Many white-supremacy Democrats defected to Georgia's Republican Party, which included suburban conservatives who viewed race as a secondary issue. Other Democrats, notably Jimmy Carter, forged biracial coalitions with populist undertones. These coalitions made him governor of Georgia in 1970 and president in 1976.

Prosperity and Uncertainty

After 1960, Georgia prospered as never before. Dalton became the world's "carpet capital." Civil rights victories opened doors for professional sports in Atlanta. Vietnam War production spurred industry. Gains in higher education, population, and high-tech industry boosted Georgia's reputation. Ted Turner's television network made baseball's Atlanta Braves "America's Team." Coca-Cola, invented and headquartered in Atlanta, became the world's most recognized beverage. Atlanta's selection as the location for the 1996 Olympics also marked a breakthrough.

But growth was uneven. Hard times persisted in south Georgia. Predominantly black south Atlanta suffered poverty; predominantly white north Atlanta and its suburbs boomed. Public schools declined; private schools soared. Cotton-mill closings depleted small towns. Extending prosperity to underdeveloped areas remained a key issue in the early 2000s.

Still, Georgia's relative social and economic health can be seen in the black migration back to the state. After 1970, northern and western blacks (many professionals) moved to Georgia in huge numbers, reversing the great migration and creating upper-class enclaves in Metro-Atlanta.

Georgia is no longer just black and white, however; Latino and Asian immigrants altered the ethnic mix. Traditional questions remained, but new trends intervened. Slow-growth movements, gay Atlanta, and environmental conflicts all suggested an uncertain future for a state with a deeply contested past.

BIBLIOGRAPHY

Bartley, Numan V. *The Creation of Modern Georgia.* 2d ed. Athens: University of Georgia Press, 1990.

Bayor, Ronald H. *Race and the Shaping of Twentieth-Century Atlanta.* Chapel Hill, N.C.: University of North Carolina Press, 1996.

Cobb, James C. *Georgia Odyssey.* Athens: University of Georgia Press, 1997.

Coleman, Kenneth, et al. *A History of Georgia.* 2d ed. Athens: University of Georgia Press, 1991.

DeCredico, Mary A. *Patriotism for Profit: Georgia's Urban Entrepreneurs and the Confederate War Effort.* Chapel Hill: University of North Carolina Press, 1990.

Dittmer, John. *Black Georgia in the Progressive Era, 1900–1920.* Urbana: University of Illinois Press, 1977.

Flamming, Douglas. *Creating the Modern South: Millhands and Managers in Dalton, Georgia, 1884–1984.* Chapel Hill: University of North Carolina Press, 1992.

Grant, Donald L. *The Way It Was in the South: The Black Experience in Georgia.* Secaucus, N.J.: Carol, 1993.

Shaw, Barton C. *The Wool Hat Boys: Georgia's Populist Party, 1892–1910.* Baton Rouge: Louisiana State University Press, 1984.

Stewart, Mart A. *"What Nature Suffers to Groe": Life, Labor, and Landscape on the Georgia Coast, 1680–1920.* Athens: University of Georgia Press, 1996.

Williams, David. *Rich Man's War: Class, Caste, and Confederate Defeat in the Lower Chattahoochee Valley.* Athens: University of Georgia Press, 1998.

Wood, Betty. *Gender, Race, and Rank in a Revolutionary Age: The Georgia Lowcountry, 1750–1820.* Athens: University of Georgia Press, 2000.

Douglas Flamming

See also **Atlanta; Birmingham; Civil Rights Movement; Civil War; Great Migration; Jim Crow Laws; Reconstruction; Slavery.**

GEORGIA PLATFORM, a set of resolutions written by Charles J. Jenkins and adopted in December 1850 by a convention held in Milledgeville, Georgia, to decide on the course Georgia would take regarding the Compromise of 1850. It was the sense of these resolutions that the state would accept the compromise "as a permanent adjustment of the sectional controversy." However, the platform also issued a warning that any further encroachments made on the South's rights (such as hindering the interstate slave trade or weakening the Fugitive Slave Law) what had been done, would lead to the disruption of the Union.

BIBLIOGRAPHY

Carey, Anthony G. *Parties, Slavery, and the Union in Antebellum Georgia.* Athens: University of Georgia Press, 1997.

Hubbell, John T. "Three Georgia Unionists and the Compromise of 1850." *Georgia Historical Quarterly* 51 (September 1967): 307–323.

Potter, David M. *The Impending Crisis, 1848–61.* New York: HarperCollins, 1977.

E. Merton Coulter/T. M.

See also **Civil War; Compromise of 1850; Nashville Convention; Secession; Sectionalism.**

GEORGIA V. STANTON. The United States Supreme Court in *Mississippi v. Johnson* (1867) refused to enjoin President Andrew Johnson from enforcing the Military Reconstruction Acts of 1867 on the grounds that it was a discretionary executive responsibility. Georgia sought similarly to enjoin Secretary of War Edwin M. Stanton. In *Georgia v. Stanton,* 6 Wallace (73 U.S.) 50 (1868), the Court again denied relief, on the grounds that it lacked jurisdiction to resolve a political question like that. In *Mississippi v. Stanton* (1868), an unreported decision, the justices by a vote of 4 to 4 rejected injunctive relief based on a theory of interference with private property rights. In these decisions the Court rebuffed constitutional challenges to congressional Republican Reconstruction.

BIBLIOGRAPHY

Fairman, Charles. *Reconstruction and Reunion, 1864–88.* Part I. New York: Macmillan, 1971.

Kutler, Stanley I. *Judicial Power and Reconstruction Politics.* Chicago: University of Chicago Press, 1968.

William M. Wiecek

See also ***Mississippi v. Johnson;*** **Reconstruction.**

GEORGIANA was the name chosen in 1763 for a proposed colony in honor of the king of England. It was to be established below the junction of the Mississippi and Ohio Rivers by a group of former soldiers under the leadership of General Phineas Lyman of Connecticut. In 1770, he was instead granted 20,000 acres in the vicinity of Natchez, in a less promising location farther south on the Mississippi. He led a number of families, mainly from Connecticut and Massachusetts, to that region, but after Lyman died in 1774, and with very little support during the Revolution, the colony failed.

BIBLIOGRAPHY

Clark, Delphina L. H. *Phineas Lyman, Connecticut's General.* Springfield, Mass.: Connecticut Valley Historical Museum, 1964.

Michael Wala

GERMAN AMERICANS. In the census of 1990 almost 58 million residents of the United States declared themselves to be of German ancestry, by far the largest ancestry group. The nearly continuous large-scale German migration to the United States from the late eighteenth century until the 1920s explains the size of this group.

German immigration to the United States began with the arrival of religious dissenters in Pennsylvania during the 1680s. In 1790, the U.S. Census counted 375,000 Germans in the United States. German immigration increased after the Napoleonic Wars (1793–1815). During the 1850s, more than 976,000 German immigrants arrived in the United States. Germans stood out because of their high proportion of literate and skilled newcomers, their penchant for family migration, and their dispersal throughout the rural and urban areas in the Mid-Atlantic and Midwestern states.

The peak of German immigration occurred in the 1880s, when more than 1.4 million Germans arrived. Most were craft workers and their families who streamed into the industrializing United States. Milwaukee, Chicago, and Cincinnati had the highest proportion of German Americans in the late nineteenth century, although cities such as New York and Philadelphia also numbered well over 200,000 German Americans in 1890.

The German American community reflected the diversity of Germany in a number of ways: Catholics were a slight majority, Lutherans were a significant minority, and German Jews were also a large group. German immigrants came from both cities and rural areas. People from southern, particularly southwestern Germany, predominated until the late nineteenth century, when former citizens of Prussia (present-day northern Germany and Poland) began to arrive in larger numbers.

German Americans were politically and culturally highly visible in the United States in the century before World War I (1914–1918). Their ethnic press was probably the largest and most diverse of any immigrant group; political and cultural organizations abounded, especially in urban areas. They were prominent among both Republicans and Democrats in the late nineteenth century. They formed the core of the small socialist movement and founded a number of important craft unions at the turn of the twentieth century. German Americans were heavily involved in the cultural life, especially in musical organizations, in most American metropolises.

World War I and its anti-German sentiments led German American communities to become largely invisible. While the migration of economically displaced and working-class Germans continued on a modest level after World War I (Germans received a relatively high quota allotment under the 1924 Quota Law), German American organizations dissolved or retained a low profile during most of the twentieth century.

Although more than 100,000 German Jewish refugees entered the United States as immigrants under the German quota, these newcomers were reluctant to see themselves as members of the German American community. This distance was heightened because of strong pro-fascist sentiments among some older German immigrants, even though formal membership in pro-Nazi organizations was not high. Few German Americans were interned as politically suspect or as enemy aliens during World War II (1939–1945). The end of World War II saw a modest resumption of German immigration.

In the late twentieth century, between eight and twelve thousand Germans immigrated to the United States annually. In 2002, German Americans were a group who lived almost exclusively through heritage societies and tourist sites highlighting the nineteenth-century history of German settlements.

Dorothy Schneider

See also **German-American Bund; Germany, Relations with; Immigration; Pennsylvania Germans.**

GERMAN MERCENARIES were troops hired to fight the rebellious American colonies. Given England's shortage of trained soldiers, its slow enlistments, and the political impossibility of conscription, the ministry tapped the cooperation of six German princes for the services of 29,875 German officers and men in America. Hesse-Cassel sent 16,992; Brunswick, 5,723; Hesse-Hanau, 2,422; Anspach-Bayreuth, 2,353; Waldeck, 1,225; and Anhalt-Zerbst, 1,160. For their services England paid £1,770,000 sterling to the princes alone, a small sum considering the officers' excellent training in the Seven Years' War, the troops' good discipline, and the fact that Germans constituted one-third of British land forces in North America.

German troops were organized like the British army, although the small regiments had unusually large numbers of officers, surgeons, chaplains, and musicians. They fought under three successive commanders, Leopold Philip von Heister, Baron Wilhelm von Knyphausen, and Friedrich Wilhelm von Lossberg—all Hessians, each with his own staff and rank equal to the British commanders, although they usually operated in conjunction with British troops under British command. North of Florida no major operation took place without German participation.

Initially feared by the Americans, they soon earned respect as soldiers. Congress issued several alluring proclamations urging them to desert. Of the 12,554 who did not return to Germany, many had either deserted or received permission to remain in America after the war.

BIBLIOGRAPHY

Kipping, Ernst. *The Hessian View of America, 1776–1783.* Monmouth Beach, N.J.: Philip Freneau Press, 1971.

Lowell, Edward Jackson. *The Hessians and the Other German Auxiliaries of Great Britian in the Revolutionary War.* New York: Harper & Bros., 1884.

B. A. Uhlendorf / C. W.

See also **Revolution, American: Military History; Revolution, American: Political History.**

GERMAN-AMERICAN BUND, an organization that emerged in 1936 as the successor to the Friends of the New Germany, an organization formed in 1932 to generate support for Nazism among people of German descent living in the United States. Under the leadership of Fritz Kuhn, a naturalized American citizen, the Bund gained notoriety through its use of parades and mass rallies attended by uniformed storm troopers, special training camps, and blatant racist propaganda. Membership estimates for its heyday vary from three thousand to twenty-five thousand. While publicly disavowing connection with the Bund, the German government privately supported its efforts until 1938. The movement collapsed when Kuhn was convicted in 1939 of embezzling Bund funds, but its highly publicized activities contributed to the growing American repugnance for Nazism.

BIBLIOGRAPHY

Canedy, Susan. *America's Nazis: A Democratic Dilemma.* Menlo Park, Calif.: Markgraf, 1990.

Diamond, Sander A. *The Nazi Movement in the United States, 1924–1941.* Ithaca, N.Y.: Cornell University Press, 1974.

Ludwig F. Schaefer / C. P.

GERMAN-AMERICAN DEBT AGREEMENT. The 1930 agreement (not a treaty) fixed Germany's responsibility for costs of American occupation after World War I at $247,865,645. It arranged German payment of those costs, as well as for payment of the approximately 20 percent still-unpaid awards to U.S. citizens granted by the War Settlements Act of 1928. Germany delivered to the U.S. government two sets of long-term, non-interest-bearing bonds with coupons for annual payments of principal. On the first series Germany suspended payment in 1932 after paying in annual installments a total of $65,998,512; on the second series Germany suspended payment in 1935.

BIBLIOGRAPHY

Bemis, Samuel Flagg. *Diplomatic History of the United States.* New York: Holt, Rinehart and Winston, 1965.

Samuel Flagg Bemis / C. W.

See also **Army of Occupation; World War I; World War I War Debts.**

GERMANTOWN was founded in Pennsylvania, six miles from Philadelphia, on 24 October 1683, by a band of German Quakers and Mennonites led by Francis Daniel Pastorius. He was agent for the Frankfort Land Company, which purchased twenty-five thousand acres from William Penn, whose arrival in Pennsylvania the year before ushered in a wave of Quaker immigration, mainly from England. The founding of Germantown marked the beginning of the German immigration to Pennsylvania. Germantown (also German Towne or Germanopolis) never became large, because it was a base for the distribution of Germans into the interior. Christopher Sauer's famous printing press and type foundry were established in Germantown in 1738.

BIBLIOGRAPHY

Moltmann, Gunter. "Migrations from Germany to North America: New Perspectives." *Reviews in American History* 14 (December 1986).

Wolf, Stephanie Grauman. *Urban Village: Population, Community, and Family Structure in Germantown, Pennsylvania, 1683–1800.* Princeton, N.J.: Princeton University Press, 1976.

J. Paul Selsam/A. R.

See also **Mennonites; Pennsylvania Germans; Quakers.**

GERMANY, AMERICAN OCCUPATION OF.

The American occupation of Germany began on 8 May 1945. On 5 June the Allies partitioned Germany into four occupation zones—American, British, French, and Russian. They also divided Berlin, which was located in the Soviet zone. General Dwight D. Eisenhower became the U.S. military governor in Germany and Allied troops helped rebuild its infrastructure and reestablish civilian government.

Although the American military gave up its authority on 21 September 1949, U.S. forces occupied Germany until 5 May 1955, when the Federal Republic of Germany assumed control over all of its own territory except for West Berlin. U.S. forces remained after 1955 as a part of the North Atlantic Treaty Organization's defense force.

BIBLIOGRAPHY

Gimbel, John. *The American Occupation of Germany.* Stanford, Cal.: Stanford University Press, 1968.

Merritt, Richard. *Democracy Imposed: U.S. Occupation Policy and the German Public, 1945–1949* New Haven, Conn.: Yale University Press, 1995.

James L. Collins Jr.
Eric J. Morser

See also **Cold War; Russia, Relations with; Yalta Conference.**

GERMANY, RELATIONS WITH.

The most important early contacts between Germany and the United States involved immigration. Members of various Protestant groups from Central Europe settled in colonial America for the first time in 1683 in Germantown, outside Philadelphia. In the nineteenth century political unrest, economic problems, population pressure, and famine joined religious persecution in prompting two phases of large-scale migration, first from the 1830s to the early 1850s and then from the late 1860s to the mid-1880s. Approximately 5 million Germans arrived in the United States through 1900. Nativist sentiment in the 1840s and 1850s encouraged community leaders to preserve their cultural identity through a German-language press and associations *(Vereine)*, creating a strong ethnic subculture that lasted until World War I. On the whole, though, German immigrants had a good reputation due to their education and industry. In 1869 the *New York Times* described them as "undoubtedly the healthiest element of our foreign immigration."

Until the late nineteenth century the United States enjoyed amiable official relations with the various German states. Geographic distance helped assure that the governments had few competing interests. In addition the United States had a tradition of noninterference in European affairs, and neither of the central European great powers, Prussia nor Austria, had substantial overseas concerns. Americans intensely followed the process of German unification and greeted the foundation of the German Reich in 1871. Chancellor Otto von Bismarck tried to minimize the few political disputes between the two countries and respected American predominance in the Western Hemisphere. Meanwhile, German classical music, painting, and literature, especially works by Friedrich Schiller, all found admirers in the United States by the 1860s. The German university system also attracted increasing numbers of American students in all disciplines—an estimated ten thousand through 1914—and was a model for the modern research university in the United States.

The "Great Transformation" and World War I

However, starting in the 1870s German-American relations gradually underwent a "great transformation," in the words of Manfred Jonas, from amity to hostility that culminated in World War I. Expanding industrial economies and newfound imperial ambitions drove this process. In 1879 a new German protective tariff, instituted in response to the 1873 depression, initiated a lengthy controversy about American agricultural products having access to the German market. Relations began to deteriorate seriously, however, only after William II ascended the throne in 1888. Germany's decision to build a large battleship fleet starting in 1897 gave rise to fears that it someday would try to challenge the Monroe Doctrine. Between 1898 and 1903 German activities in the Philippines and Venezuela nurtured such suspicions and alienated the American public. So too did the kaiser's occasional bellicose outbursts and inept attempts at personal diplomacy, which did little to further the German government's aspirations for American cooperation against its great naval and imperial rival Great Britain.

These developments help explain why most political and business elites in the United States favored Britain when World War I broke out in August 1914. The flow of civilian goods and loans to Europe in support of the Allied war effort through 1917 demonstrated the partisan nature of American neutrality. Woodrow Wilson's protests against the Reich's campaign of unrestricted submarine warfare led to its temporary suspension by March 1916, but with few exceptions Germany's wartime leaders did not take the United States seriously as a potential opponent. Not only did the German Foreign Office try to secure an anti-American alliance with Mexico by promising it Texas, Arizona, and New Mexico, a risky policy that backfired with the publication of the "Zimmermann telegram," but the German government resumed its submarine campaign in January 1917, knowing it would almost certainly lead to American entry in the war, which occurred on 6 April.

Alongside the effort to crush Prussian militarism in Europe, a crusade against German culture began in the United States that in some regions lasted through the early 1920s. In its wake hundreds of German-language newspapers closed, many German-American churches started conducting their services in English, German cultural associations suffered declining memberships, and countless individuals, companies, and organizations anglicized their German-sounding names. German ethnic life in the United States never recovered. In late 1918 the Reich's military and political leadership hoped for a lenient peace based on Wilson's FOURTEEN POINTS and in October even instituted a parliamentary form of government to encourage one. The kaiser's abdication on 9 November 1918, two days before the armistice, helped pave the way for the establishment of a full-fledged republic. Germany's expectations concerning Wilson were unrealistic, and Germans were bitterly disappointed with the terms of the Versailles Peace Treaty announced on 7 May 1919, especially its "war guilt clause," Article 231, which was inserted to establish Germany's obligation to pay reparations.

The Weimar Republic and the Third Reich

Nonetheless during the Weimar Republic (1918–1933) German–American relations improved markedly. The republic became the focus of Washington's stabilization policy for Europe. In 1924 the DAWES PLAN ended the Ruhr crisis by providing a new schedule for reparations payments and initiated a five-year period in which American loans and investments contributed to a brief return to prosperity in Europe, especially in Germany. Foreign Minister Gustav Stresemann, who held that position from 1923 to 1929, believed a revitalized German economy would be the most powerful tool for revising the Versailles Treaty peacefully, and he therefore placed priority on good political relations with the United States to secure capital for German reconstruction. In the 1920s American mass culture (for example, Hollywood movies) also flooded into Germany for the first time, and intense debates ensued there over "Americanization" and "Fordism." By 1929 condemnation of the YOUNG PLAN, another American-brokered reparations repayment scheme, and of the American "modern," also associated with liberalism and mass democracy, had become a standard part of the German right's political program, including that of Adolf Hitler's National Socialist German Workers' Party (NSDAP).

The Great Depression cut off American investment in Europe and thereby indirectly contributed to the NSDAP's rise to power on 30 January 1933. National Socialist attempts to establish autarky through bilateral trade treaties and aggressive export drives in Latin America and eastern Europe presented a direct threat to the open international economy deemed indispensable by the Roosevelt administration for the survival of the American way of life. Despite increasing evidence that Germany, along with Japan and Italy, was rearming for war, the American government remained inactive diplomatically before November 1938, when Franklin D. Roosevelt, already sobered by the Munich Conference, issued a sharp condemnation of Nazi anti-Semitic policies and recalled his ambassador following *Kristallnacht.* Strong isolationist sentiment at home, as expressed in the Neutrality Laws, left few weapons available other than trade policies and attempts to mobilize the Western Hemisphere against the threat of Nazi infiltration at the 1938 Lima Conference. Only the shock of France's defeat in 1940 allowed the American government to take more vigorous measures to contain German expansion, including the bases-for-destroyers deal with the United Kingdom in September 1940; the lend-lease program in March 1941; and an undeclared naval war against U-boats in the North Atlantic in the summer of 1941. Germany formally declared war on the United States on 11 December in the wake of the Japanese attack on Pearl Harbor, initiating what also became an ideological conflict. National Socialism saw "Americanism" as its enemy, while the United Sates, in Roosevelt's words, found itself locked in a struggle with a "monstrous nation."

Relations after 1945

Although the Roosevelt administration adopted a "Germany first" strategy for military campaigning during WORLD WAR II, it pursued a policy of postponement in terms of postwar planning in order to hold together the wartime alliance with the United Kingdom and the Soviet Union. By 1945 the Allies had agreed to keep Germany unified, minus territorial revisions in the east, but temporarily divided into occupation zones. Practical problems of governance and increasing differences with the Soviet Union quickly led to modifications in the initially draconian American policy for its zone, consisting of the states of Bavaria, Bremen, Hesse, and Württemberg-Baden.

Starting around 1947 the Cold War led to another "great transformation" in the German-American relationship. MARSHALL PLAN aid in 1947, relief for Berlin during the Soviet blockade of 1948–1949, CARE packages, and the daily experience with American soldiers left a generally positive view of the United States in the western zones, which in 1949 were united politically as the Federal Republic of Germany. The outbreak of the Korean War led by 1955 to West German rearmament, North Atlantic Treaty Organization (NATO) membership, and the end of occupation controls except those affecting Germany as a whole. Konrad Adenauer, chancellor from 1949 to 1963,

A Holocaust Aftermath. General Dwight Eisenhower (*standing under the gallows*) visits a deserted labor camp outside Ohrdruf, Germany, that American soldiers reached on 4 April 1945—just after Germans shot the hundreds of remaining Jews, Poles, and Russian prisoners of war there (except for four escapees); 4,000 others had been killed at the camp earlier that year.

established integration into the West as one of the cornerstones of the Federal Republic's foreign policy.

By the 1960s some strains in the West German–American relationship had arisen over issues like the Vietnam War and the onset of détente, which relegated the German question to a subordinate status internationally. In the early 1980s thousands of West Germans demonstrated against NATO's decision to station medium-range nuclear missiles there. In addition the relative decline of the American economy after 1945 compared with West German economic growth contributed to disputes over payments for the stationing of GIs in the Federal Republic through the 1970s and over trade issues with the European Community (later the European Union), which the Federal Republic had belonged to since 1958. However, these periodic differences do not detract from the fact that after 1949 the United States and West Germany had compatible political, economic, and security goals, while their citizens shared a good deal of mutual sympathy and aspects of a common culture in areas like popular music, fashion, and the love affair with the automobile. The German Democratic Republic, on the other hand, remained relatively unimportant for the United States, even after diplomatic recognition in 1974.

The George H. W. Bush administration actively promoted the cause of German unification in 1989 and 1990. After the Cold War ended the main issue facing German-American relations became whether the European Union could develop an independent identity in political and security issues that would eventually supercede the Atlantic framework based around NATO.

BIBLIOGRAPHY

Gatzke, Hans W. *Germany and the United States: A "Special Relationship?"* Cambridge, Mass.: Harvard University Press, 1980. Dated but worth reading.

Jonas, Manfred. *The United States and Germany: A Diplomatic History.* Ithaca, N.Y.: Cornell University Press, 1984. Excellent on official relations before 1945.

Junker, Detlef, ed., with the assistance of Philipp Gassert, Wilfried Mausbach, and David B. Morris. *The USA and Germany in the Era of the Cold War, 1945–1990: A Handbook.* 2 vols. Cambridge: Cambridge University Press, forthcoming. Will become the standard reference work on the post–1945 era.

Luebke, Frederick C. *Germans in the New World: Essays in the History of Immigration.* Urbana: University of Illinois Press, 1990. By the leading historian of the German community in the United States.

Schröder, Hans-Jürgen, ed. *Confrontation and Cooperation: Germany and the United States in the Era of World War I, 1900–1924*. Germany and the United States of America—The Krefeld Historical Symposia series, vol. 2. Providence, R.I.: Berg, 1993.

Trommler, Frank, and Joseph McVeigh, eds. *America and the Germans: An Assessment of a Three-Hundred-Year History*. 2 vols. Philadelphia: University of Pennsylvania Press, 1985. A good collection of essays by leading scholars.

Trommler, Frank, and Elliott Shore, eds. *The German-American Encounter: Conflict and Cooperation between Two Cultures, 1800–2000*. New York: Berghahn Books, 2001.

Thomas Maulucci

See also **Berlin Airlift; Isolationism; Neutrality; Versailles, Treaty of.**

GERRYMANDER. The word "gerrymander" was first used during Elbridge Gerry's second term as governor of Massachusetts, when a bill was passed (11 February 1812) redistricting the state in order to give the Jeffersonian Republicans an advantage in the election of state senators. The name was derived from a caricature representing a strangely shaped three-member Republican district in Essex County as a salamander, which, combined with "gerry," became "gerrymander."

Gerrymandering, the advantage obtained by a certain group through discretionary districting, has applied to congressional, state legislative, and local districts. The purpose of partisan gerrymandering is to strengthen one party by concentrating the opposing party's voters into only a few districts. The purpose of racial gerrymandering is to limit, perhaps to none, the number of districts in which the unfavored group is dominant.

Although the U.S. Supreme Court, from 1964 through the early 2000s, mandated that districts must be essentially equal in population (eliminating the "silent gerrymander," which left urban areas underrepresented as population shifted), it had yet to limit partisan gerrymandering. Even though criteria for districting, such as contiguity, compactness, and respect for subdivision boundaries, were often required, substantial leeway existed for legislators to safeguard majority party candidates or incumbents of any party. Even districts drawn by neutral commissions or judges could have differential effects. Redistricting by computer usually followed a program set to give advantage to one party.

In the late twentieth century a combination of partisan and racial gerrymandering continued to be widely practiced. This was particularly true in the South, where gerrymandering has been used to create solidly Democratic districts in predominantly African American areas and solidly Republican districts in predominantly white areas. Racial gerrymandering underwent several court challenges during the 1990s. Defenders of racial gerrymandering argued that it made possible the creation of a

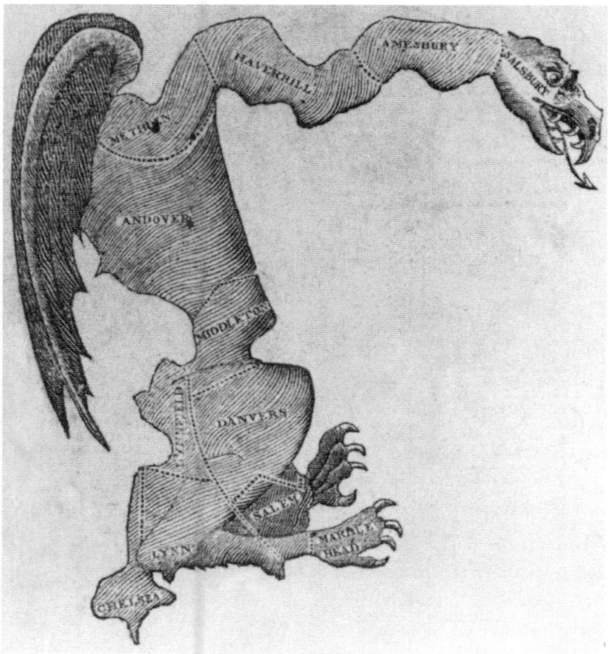

"The Gerry-Mander." The term first appeared in this 1812 political cartoon caricaturing a recently redrawn state senate district in Massachusetts as a "new species of Monster," with an eagle's claws and a dragon's head and wings. LIBRARY OF CONGRESS

black congressional delegation from the South, whereas critics maintained that it promoted a racial balkanization of American politics.

BIBLIOGRAPHY

Griffith, Elmer C. *The Rise and Development of the Gerrymander.* Chicago: Scott, Foresman, 1907. Reprint, New York: Arno Press, 1974.

Lublin, David. *The Paradox of Representation: Racial Gerrymandering and Minority Interests in Congress.* Princeton, N.J.: Princeton University Press, 1997.

Rush, Mark E. *Does Redistricting Make a Difference? Partisan Representation and Electoral Behavior.* Baltimore: Johns Hopkins University Press, 1993.

Charles H. Backstrom
Leonard Robbins/A. G.

See also **Apportionment; Congress, United States; Election Laws.**

GETTY MUSEUM. In 1954, Jean Paul Getty (1892–1976) opened a small museum in the living room and galleries of his weekend residence in Malibu, California. Writing from Kuwait, the oil magnate said that he hoped his "modest and unpretentious" museum would provide pleasure to the people from the Los Angeles region who were interested in his small, idiosyncratic collection. In 1997, the Getty Center opened its doors to what would quickly grow to be more than a million visitors a year. Designed by the international architecture star Richard Meier and constructed over thirteen years in the Brentwood section of Los Angeles, the Getty immediately assumed the status of a cultural destination for visitors from around the world.

In its earliest incarnation, the museum—open several days a week—attracted barely a thousand visitors a year. Getty was interested in antiquities, paintings, and French furniture, and he collected according to his tastes. By the late 1960s, it became clear that the collection needed larger quarters and that it could attract more visitors. The oilman had an allergy to modern architecture, but it was unclear what kind of historical building he wanted to imitate. He settled on the Villa dei Papiri, a part of the Herculaneum that had been buried since the eruption of Mount Vesuvius in A.D. 79. The resulting museum was a Roman villa in Malibu, housing a small collection with great view of the ocean. Critics saw the building as a pretentious fake, but the ever-growing number of visitors seemed to love the combination of a small museum housed in a luxurious domestic space in an extraordinary natural setting.

Getty never saw the museum, nursing an intense fear of flying as he grew older. He had left America for Europe in 1951, spending much of his time in Paris and London. He had already developed strong interests in furniture and antiquities, and with his enormous financial resources was able to acquire collections with a few star pieces. The enlarged museum in Malibu, which he planned with the architect and museum director Stephen Garrett, with intensive assistance from the archaeologist Norman Neuerburg, was to be a shiny new Roman villa. Getty spared no expense at re-creating the details of the building but was indifferent, if not downright hostile, to the basic requirements for supporting a public museum. The small staff did everything from curating shows to preparing food, and Getty insisted on personal control over all sorts of minor expenditures. It came as a shock, then, when the museum was left 4 million shares of Getty Oil stock upon the founder's death in 1976. The will was contested, but when the documents were finally authorized the bequest to the museum was valued at $1.2 billion.

Creating the Center

This was a staggering endowment in 1982, made even more impressive by the fact that almost no restrictions were set for how the money would be used. Getty asked that the funds be dedicated to "the diffusion of artistic and general knowledge." After all his micromanagement while alive, this was the only restriction in his bequest. The trustees of the museum were thinking broadly when they approached Harold M. Williams, just stepping down as head of the Securities and Exchange Commission, to be the director of the Getty Trust. This was an "operating trust," which was required to spend a certain amount of its endowment income on programs it ran. The trustees wanted to be more than a museum, to move from the arts to the "general knowledge" side of the bequest. Williams seized this opportunity to create a new kind of cultural entity: not a university or a museum, but an institution that would make a decisive contribution to research, education, and the arts while also providing its visitors with pleasure and personal enhancement through an exhibition program grounded in a strong permanent collection. In 1982, the trustees approved Williams's proposal to create institutes of art education, conservation, research, and information. Later, the Grant Program and the Leadership Institute were created to round out the programs, and the art education and information programs were consolidated with research and conservation.

Harold Williams and his staff faced stiff challenges in establishing the Getty as a cultural institution of international significance. They had the advantages of money and entrepreneurship, but in the art world they were also faced with the skepticism of older organizations that could not take seriously the idea of an art and research center in southern California (especially one whose centerpiece was a shiny new Roman villa). The different parts of the Getty had offices in Santa Monica and Malibu, with outposts in New England and Europe. Williams planned eventually to integrate the various functions in a cultural center, and he chose a site in the Santa Monica Mountains that provided extraordinary vistas of the shoreline and the city. It also provided new opportunities for criticism of the organization's detachment from the lives of the ordinary Angelenos. Richard Meier and Partners was awarded the commission to build the center in 1984.

The core of the Getty Trust's activities has been the museum, and from 1983 until 2000 John Walsh was its director. Walsh concentrated on filling out the spotty collections in antiquities and furniture, and he had enormous work to do in bringing the painting collection to an acceptable level. There has been a great deal of controversy over how the institution augmented its holdings in ancient art. As feelings of cultural patrimony have grown more intense in the Mediterranean world and elsewhere, the provenance of antiquities has come under greater scrutiny. Only after having acquired a world-class collection in this area did the Getty place a moratorium on acquiring works whose provenance was not published and clear. However, the museum has returned certain works whose histories were tainted, and has campaigned actively on behalf of cultural preservation and the rights of patrimony.

In other areas there were complaints that the large sums spent by the young California institution were distorting the art market. With astonishing rapidity, the Getty acquired paintings by Paul Cézanne, James Sydney Ensor, Fra Bartolommeo, Nicolas Poussin, Rembrandt, Joseph Turner, Vincent Van Gogh, and superb drawings by Michelangelo, Albrecht Dürer, and others. Spending hundreds of millions of dollars during the 1980s and 1990s, the museum has developed world-class collections in seventeenth- and eighteenth-century decorative arts, a manuscript collection that rivals the best in the United States for the medieval and Renaissance periods, and a photography collection that is arguably the finest in the world. In the last two areas, the museum acquired collections from other collectors, jump-starting their own efforts by successfully building on the work of earlier connoisseurs and scholars. Aside from photography, the Getty does not collect twentieth-century art.

Harold Williams stepped down as president of the trust shortly after the institution moved into the Meier's classically modernist campus in the fall of 1998. Barry Munitz, formerly the chancellor of the enormous California State University System, assumed the reins of an organization that he described as being in its adolescence. Munitz has been integrating the work of the various Getty programs and is overseeing the completion of the remodeling of the original museum in Malibu. Upon completion, the Getty Villa will house the collections and research on ancient art and artifacts.

Other Functions of the Trust

Although the museum is the part of the Getty that has received the most attention (and spent the most money), the other parts of the trust have carved out important roles in the international art world. The Conservation Institute has supported projects around the world that aim to preserve cultural heritage for future generations. Conservation scientists hired in Los Angeles have fanned out across the globe to work on projects to preserve objects, from sculptures in China to architecture in Africa. The Getty Education Institute aimed to introduce a specific art curriculum into schools across America. Although arts education remains a weak part of public education in the United States, researchers with Getty support have done much to show how an education in the arts can have important effects on many dimensions of a young person's experience. The Grant Program of the Getty has tried to complement the work of the other parts of the institution by awarding grants to organizations and individuals to enhance the study and appreciation of art in a variety of contexts.

In addition to the Grant Program's support of individual scholars and their publications, the trust has made a significant investment in developing knowledge about the visual arts through the Getty Research Institute (GRI). The GRI is the home to one of the finest art libraries in the world, containing more than 800,000 volumes, more than 2 million study photographs, and world-class archives. It also sponsors exhibitions and lectures and maintains a residency program for scholars at various stages of their careers. Getty Scholars spend anywhere from a few months to two years studying some dimension of the arts in relation to their contexts in the full range of humanities disciplines.

The Getty Center has a distinct profile among American cultural organizations. Not only does its endowment—which at the beginning of the twenty-first century stood somewhere above $4 billion—give it enormous clout anywhere it chooses to exert its influence, but the combination of an original museum in an extraordinary natural setting with collections that have gotten stronger and more interesting over time ensures that it will remain popular with the tourists who flock to southern California throughout the year. The stimulation that high-level researchers in conservation and art history provide is less easily quantified, but they deepen the programming of the institution even as they benefit from its populist agenda. Having established itself as a cultural force to be reckoned with on any number of levels, the institution can now develop partnerships (both nationally and internationally) that will allow it to pursue its mission more vigorously. The upstart from California can continue to provide pleasure to its audiences from around the world, even as it strives to be a leader in the scholarly domains related to the visual arts and their history.

BIBLIOGRAPHY

The Getty. Home page at http://www.getty.edu.

Michael S. Roth

See also **Museums.**

GETTYSBURG, BATTLE OF (1–3 July 1863), was the culmination of the Confederate invasion of Pennsylvania. The Confederate losses sustained at Gettysburg signified an end to the offensive capabilities of General Robert E. Lee's Army of Northern Virginia. The battle also forecast Southern defeat in the war, though it did not necessarily guarantee it.

Lee launched an invasion of Pennsylvania in the first week of June 1863. He hoped to relieve Virginia farmers of the burden of war and allow them to harvest crops for the Confederacy without interference. He also hoped to disrupt Union operations on the coasts of Virginia and North Carolina by forcing the Union to withdraw troops from those areas to protect Pennsylvania and the capital of Washington, D.C. Lee also hoped to encourage European intervention on the Confederacy's behalf while simultaneously encouraging the growing peace movement in the North. Lee's army was cut off from its Virginia supply base for the entire invasion but fared well, carrying all the ammunition it needed and living off the land of Pennsylvania. Major General Joseph Hooker, commanding the Army of the Potomac, slowly followed Lee into Pennsylvania but did not engage him in combat. On 28 June, President Abraham Lincoln replaced Hooker with Major General George G. Meade as commander of the Army of the Potomac. Meade's force numbered 85,000, while Lee commanded 65,000.

On the morning of 1 July, Major General Henry Heath's division from Lieutenant General A. P. Hill's

Confederate corps descended upon Gettysburg looking for shoes. Gettysburg was a prosperous town serviced by twelve roads from every direction. There the Confederates encountered the Union cavalry division of Brigadier General John Buford. Armed with breech-loading carbines, Buford's division held off Hill's superior numbers until Major General John Reynolds's I Corps arrived to drive back the Confederate assault. Lieutenant General Richard Ewell's Confederate corps arrived to push Major General Oliver O. Howard's XI Corps back to a weakened position on Cemetery Hill. Lee advised Ewell to take the high ground of Cemetery Hill "if practicable." Ewell, new to corps command and unused to the discretionary orders given by Lee, felt the position too strong to attack. Union reinforcements quickly arrived to secure a formidable position upon the high ground for the Army of the Potomac.

Robert E. Lee. The Confederacy's most important general, who lost his daring gamble to take the war into Union territory when the Union forces defeated him at Gettysburg; for the rest of the war, he was on the defensive, and the political as well as military repercussions of his loss made eventual Union victory much likelier, if not inevitable. © CORBIS

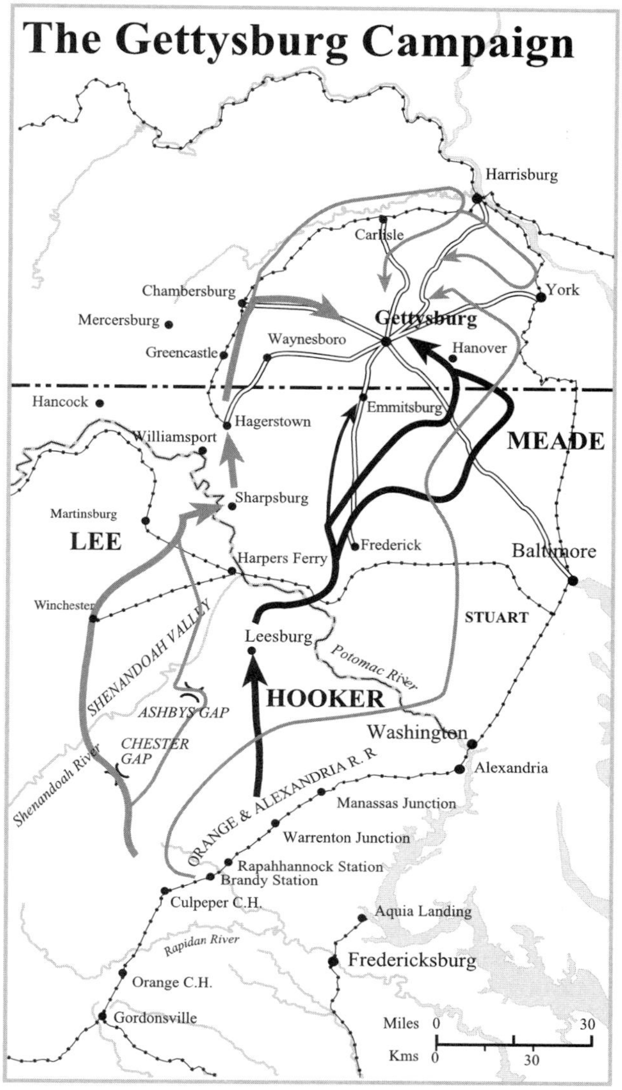

Eastward and parallel to Cemetery Hill ran Cemetery Ridge, about 1,300 yards across the Emmitsburg Road. The ridge turned eastward at Cemetery Hill toward another summit, Culp's Hill. The Union laid out a defensive line around Culp's Hill and Cemetery Hill and extending two miles south along Cemetery Ridge to a point known as Little Round Top. The Union line was not complete by the evening of 1 July, and Lee wanted to attack it on the morning of 2 July. He assigned the assault to the corps of his senior commander, Lieutenant General James Longstreet. Longstreet believed the Union position was too formidable and argued that the Confederates should turn Meade's south flank and assume a defensive position. This would force Meade to attack the Army of Northern Virginia on ground of Confederate choosing. Lee insisted on attacking the Union left holding the southern end of Cemetery Ridge.

Longstreet did not get his troops into position until 4:00 P.M. on the afternoon of 2 July, though Lee planned

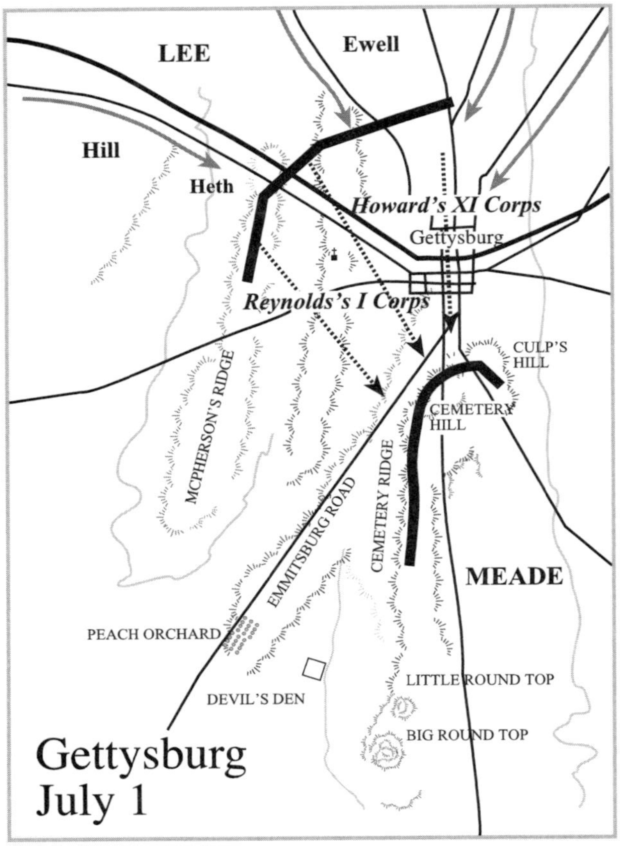

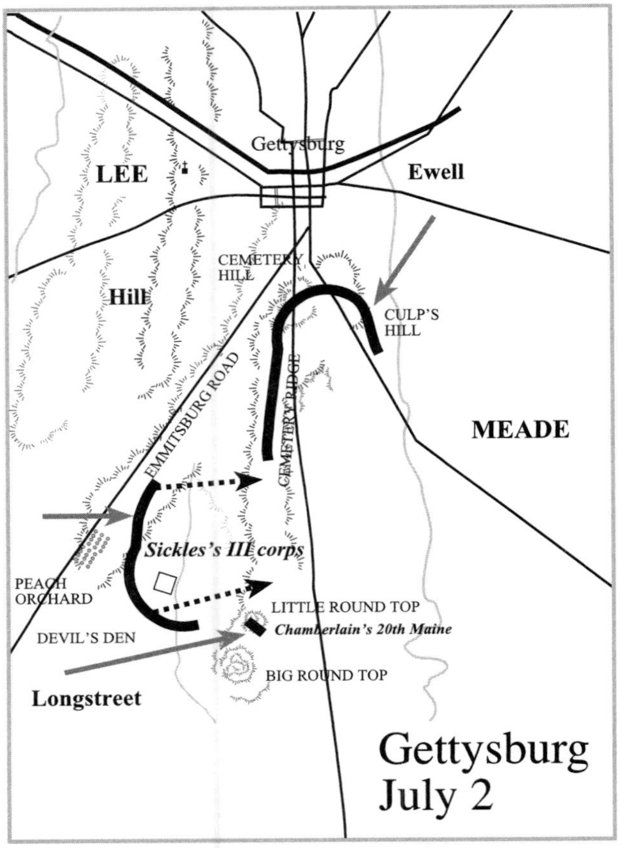

the assault for the early morning. Longstreet had good reason for the delay. His men had marched all night to reach Gettysburg, then they were forced to take a roundabout way to their attack position because Lee's guide originally led them to a road within sight of a Union signal post on Little Round Top. Historians have also speculated that Lee chafed Longstreet by rejecting his flanking plan, and the corps commander did not approach the attack with the necessary enthusiasm. Whatever the real reason behind Longstreet's delay, the general became a postwar scapegoat for the Confederate failure at Gettysburg. Southerners accused Longstreet of disobeying the infallible Lee and thus losing not only the battle but also the entire war.

When Longstreet launched his attack on the afternoon of 2 July, he ran into the Union III Corps of Major General Daniel Sickles, who had moved his troops into an unauthorized salient position in a peach orchard. Some of the war's bloodiest fighting occurred in the peach orchard, in an adjoining wheat field to the east, and in a network of boulders known as Devil's Den. Longstreet knocked holes in Sickles's line, but Meade rushed reinforcements to plug the gaps. Big and Little Round Top were unoccupied at the opening of the assault and would have given Confederate artillery control of the battlefield, but Meade's chief engineer, Gouverneur K. Warren, rushed a brigade to secure this vital high ground. The Twentieth Maine, led by Colonel Joshua L. Chamberlain, valiantly repulsed a Confederate assault despite being out of ammunition. This prevented Longstreet from turning the Army of the Potomac's left. Longstreet's only gain of the day was to drive Sickles back from his salient. On the Union right, Ewell captured Culp's Hill during a diversionary attack that turned into a full-blown assault. However, the Union line was too strong for him to go any farther.

Both sides suffered the heaviest losses of the battle on the second day. Despite this, Lee believed his assaults on both of Meade's flanks on 2 July had weakened his center, and Lee resolved that an attack on the Union center at Cemetery Ridge would break their line. Lee opened 3 July with a renewed attack by Ewell's corps on the Union right that was repulsed after hard fighting. Lee ordered Longstreet to attack the Union center with the divisions of George E. Pickett, James J. Pettigrew, and Isaac Trimble. Numbering 14,000 men, these divisions were to advance three-quarters of a mile across an open field and attack entrenched infantry supported by heavy artillery. To precede the charge, Longstreet ordered 150 pieces of artillery to bombard the Union lines for two hours, the largest Confederate artillery barrage of the war. However, the Confederate artillery was aimed too high and did little damage to the Union line.

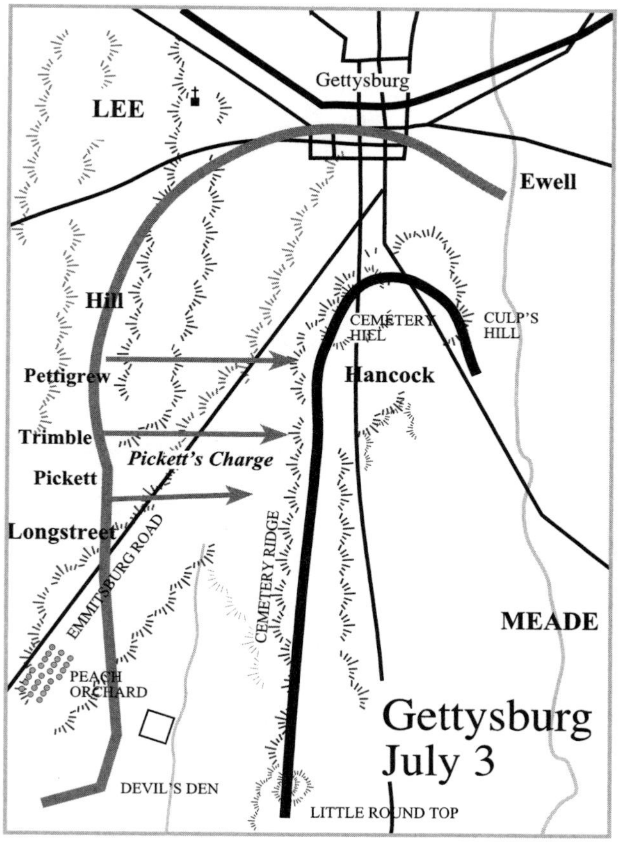

With Pickett's men in the center, the three divisions at 3:00 P.M. began the advance to Cemetery Ridge that became known as PICKETT'S CHARGE. The Union defenders, under Major General Winfield Scott Hancock, mercilessly poured rifle and artillery fire into the hapless Confederates, who were easily repulsed. Fewer than half of the 14,000 men who made the charge returned. Pickett's division suffered the most, losing two-thirds of its men, all three brigade commanders, and all thirteen colonels to either death or wounds. A small group of soldiers under Brigadier General Lewis Armistead managed to briefly penetrate the Union line before all were killed, wounded, or captured. Armistead himself fell mortally wounded, with his hat on his sword and his hand on a Union cannon in a moment glorified in the postwar years as "the high-water mark of the Confederacy." Lee withdrew from the Gettysburg area on 4 July. A combination of heavy losses, rainstorms, and uncertainty about Lee's strength prevented Meade from counterattacking.

Abraham Lincoln and the Union government hoped Meade would attack Lee and destroy the weakened Army of Northern Virginia before it escaped Pennsylvania. After much delay, Meade prepared an attack on 13 July, but overestimates of enemy strength and false intelligence reports convinced him to hold off. Lee successfully retreated back across the Potomac to Virginia on 14 July.

The losses at Gettysburg were the greatest of any battle in the Civil War. The Union lost 23,049 men, while the Confederacy lost 28,063. The Confederate population was unable to withstand such heavy casualties, and Lee's army was never able to launch another offensive invasion of Union territory. The defeat at Gettysburg, coupled with the surrender of Vicksburg on 4 July, ended Confederate hopes of European intervention in the war. The Union victory also slowed the growth of the Copperhead peace movement in the North.

BIBLIOGRAPHY

Gallagher, Gary W., ed. *The First Day at Gettysburg: Essays on Confederate and Union Leadership.* Kent, Ohio: Kent State University Press, 1992.

———. *The Second Day at Gettysburg: Essays on Confederate and Union Leadership.* Kent, Ohio: Kent State University Press, 1993.

———. *The Third Day at Gettysburg and Beyond.* Chapel Hill: University of North Carolina Press, 1994.

Hattaway, Herman, and Archer Jones. *How the North Won: A Military History of the Civil War.* Urbana: University of Illinois Press, 1983.

McPherson, James M. *Battle Cry of Freedom: The Civil War Era.* New York: Oxford University Press, 1988.

W. Scott Thomason

See also **Civil War;** *and picture (overleaf).*

GETTYSBURG ADDRESS. The Gettysburg Address was a brief oration delivered by President Abraham Lincoln on 19 November 1863 during the dedication ceremony of the Soldiers' National Cemetery in Gettysburg, Pennsylvania. The entire speech consisted of 272 words and took approximately three minutes to deliver. Its simple eloquence and evocation of transcendent themes are recognized as one of, if not the greatest, speech in American politics. Demonstrating the quintessence of Lincoln's thought concerning the sacred nature of liberty embodied in the democratic experiment, the address is heralded with transforming Northern opinion about the "unfinished work" of war before them and ultimately revolutionizing how Americans understood the nature of the Republic.

"On a Great Battle-Field of That War"

Since the opening days of July 1863, life in the town of Gettysburg and the surrounding area had been utterly transformed. During three days of battle, more than 85,000 Federals and nearly 65,000 Confederates clashed over a twenty-five-square-mile area. By the close of 3 July 1863 the number of dead, wounded, and missing from this single battle was unparalleled at the time. Nor would this level of destruction to human life be matched during the remainder of the war. Losses among the North's Army of the Potomac are conservatively estimated at more than 3,100 killed and approximately 14,500 wounded—more

Gettysburg. A detail from the popular 1880s cyclorama by Paul Philippoteaux (now at Gettysburg National Military Park) depicting Pickett's Charge on 3 July, arguably the turning point of the entire war; in the background at right, beyond the fallen tree and the wagon, General Lewis Armistead is mortally wounded (though he was not actually on a horse at the time). HULTON/ GETTY IMAGES

than 2,000 of them mortally—with about 5,400 missing. Confederate casualties rates were higher. Of the 65,000 men under General Robert E. Lee's command, one-third were killed, wounded, or missing in battle. For the nearly 2,400 residents of Gettysburg, these staggering numbers proved to be nearly overwhelming. In the weeks and months that followed, the surrounding countryside served as a makeshift hospital and morgue for the region.

An estimated eight thousand human bodies, many buried with only a scant cover of earth, were scattered throughout the battlegrounds. While thousands of rotting animal carcasses were set ablaze to help alleviate potential health risks, in late August patients at the temporary hospital in the Lutheran Seminary still complained of illnesses caused by improperly buried human remains. The often-grisly task of reinterring human remains would continue through the following spring, with nearly one thousand bodies remaining unidentified.

Amid this destruction Lincoln and his two young secretaries, John Nicolay and John Hay, stepped off the train from Washington, D.C., to prepare for the commemoration ceremonies the following day. It is hard to imagine that the president could have envisioned that his planned remarks would elicit such purpose and meaning out of the devastation witnessed around him, but Lincoln was somehow up to the task. As one scholar has observed, the transformative power of the English language has rarely achieved such heights.

"Far Above Our Poor Power to Add or Detract"

Although through time we have come to identify Lincoln's remarks as "the" Gettysburg Address, in actuality the president was but one of five scheduled speakers to address the crowd that clear November afternoon. Such a designation would have come as a surprise to the ceremony organizers, who conceived of Lincoln's "dedicatory remarks," as they were listed in the program, as secondary to those of the day's main speaker, Edward Everett. An American statesman and scholar, Everett graduated from Harvard College in 1811 and returned to the school in 1819 as a professor of Greek. He quickly established himself as a scholar, becoming editor of the *North American Review* in 1820. Four years later he was elected a member of the U.S. House of Representatives. Following a decade in the House, Everett was elected governor of Massachusetts. He briefly returned to academia as president of Harvard from 1846 to 1849. Everett returned to Washington as secretary of state in 1852. The following year he entered the U.S. Senate. As one who had been schooled at the highest levels of public oratory for years, Everett—a man praised by former students such as Ralph Waldo Emerson and one of the nation's most popular orators—seemed to be a natural selection for such an important occasion. In addition to Lincoln, those scheduled to join Everett at the podium were the Reverend T. H. Stockton, who would give the opening prayer; B. B. French, who composed a hymn for the occasion; and the Reverend H. L. Baugher, who was to deliver the benediction.

Shortly after noon on 18 November 1863, Lincoln boarded the Baltimore and Ohio Railroad from Washington. In Baltimore, the President's coach was switched to the North Central line, which made a brief stop in Hanover Junction, Pennsylvania. Arriving in Gettysburg at dusk, Lincoln was met by the principal organizers and participants of the dedication ceremonies. Coffins for the reinterrment of soldiers still lined the station platform when the president disembarked from the train. That evening the leader of the Union dined with Everett, who spoke of the somber scenes he had witnessed two days earlier on a tour of the battlefield. Later that evening the Fifth New York Artillery band serenaded the president and shortly thereafter, the commander in chief retired to his room to put the finishing touches on his speech. Late the following morning, Everett, Lincoln, and other dignitaries gathered on the small raised platform near the partially completed burial grounds. Tens of thousands of onlookers gathered that morning, many of them family members of the dead who had traveled long distances, waiting to hear words of consolation that would somehow make sense of the personal tragedies that had befallen them. Spoken among the poignant realities of war, Lincoln's remarks would soon transform this scene of despair and purposelessness into a symbol of national purpose and sacred cause.

"The World Will Little Note, Nor Long Remember What We Say Here"

Completing his speech, Lincoln purportedly returned to his seat suggesting to his bodyguard, Ward Lamon, that the remarks, like a bad plow, "won't scour." This myth, along with many others that emerged in the years following the address, suggest that Lincoln gave only scant time to prepare for his speech and subsequently was disappointed by its results. Lincoln's words, however, were not the result of his simply jotting down notes on the back of an envelope during his train ride from Washington to Pennsylvania; instead, the Gettysburg Address was the product of a gifted writer who over time had carefully crafted his message to give it a power and resonance that extended beyond the local residents, mourners, and curious spectators who gathered on that fall afternoon. With the exception of his contemporary partisan detractors, Lincoln's efforts were enormously successful on this account.

Historians have suggested that the president accomplished this objective by employing three principal literary techniques. The first was a compression of style. Lincoln's economy of the written word modeled itself after some of the great political orations of antiquity. This style, harkening to the past, appealed to Americans who were schooled in the classics. A second and related technique employed by Lincoln was a suppression of particulars. Despite what we assume to be the subjects of the Gettysburg Address, the speech never refers to Gettysburg or the battle in particular and it avoids any mention of the institution of slavery, the South, the Union, or the Emancipation Proclamation. Instead, these issues are addressed indirectly by the speech with the theme of preservation of self-government at its center. Finally, Lincoln expressed ideas about the current crisis by using polarities. The juxtaposition of themes—for example, the acts of dedication among the living contrasted with those who have died—not only engaged the audience gathered at Gettysburg that day, but speak to the essential challenges facing succeeding generations of a nation "conceived in Liberty." In this sense the Gettysburg Address retains a timeless quality, a muse for all Americans to dedicate their lives.

BIBLIOGRAPHY

McPherson, James M. *Abraham Lincoln and the Second American Revolution.* New York: Oxford University Press, 1991.

Neely, Mark E., Jr. *The Last Best Hope of Earth: Abraham Lincoln and the Promise of America.* Cambridge: Harvard University Press, 1993.

Nevins, Alan. *The War for the Union: The Organized War, 1863–1864.* New York: Scribner, 1971.

Peterson, Merrill D. *Lincoln in American Memory.* New York: Oxford University Press, 1994.

Wills, Garry. *Lincoln at Gettysburg: The Words That Remade America.* New York: Simon and Schuster, 1992. This work remains the most thorough treatment of Lincoln's address. It is an outstanding study of the literary devices Lincoln employed to draft his speech as well as the historical context in which it was delivered.

Kent A. McConnell

See also **Gettysburg, Battle of; Lincoln's Second Inaugural Address; Oratory;** *and vol. 9:* **Gettysburg Address.**

GHENT, TREATY OF. The Treaty of Ghent, ratified by the United States on 17 February 1815, marked the official end of the War of 1812 between the United States and Britain. The war was precipitated by a number of issues that were raised during the American Revolution but left unresolved at that conflict's end. Many of them, such as the precise boundary between British Canada and the United States, the failure of the British to remove all its troops from U.S. soil, and the status of Britain's former

Treaty of Ghent. This painting depicts the signing of the treaty by British and American diplomats on 24 December 1814, ending the War of 1812 (though news did not reach the United States until after the Battle of New Orleans). GRANGER COLLECTION, LTD.

Native American allies, lingered and contributed to renewed hostilities between the Americans and the British in 1812. However, on 26 June 1812, shortly after the hostilities commenced, the American government made preliminary overtures for peace. On 21 September, the Russian chancellor offered to serve as a mediator between the two warring parties. The United States presented a peace proposal through the Russians, but the British government in March 1813 quickly rejected it. However, within a few months of that failure, the British, at that point deeply committed to fighting Napoleon's army on the European continent, offered through their foreign secretary, Robert Stewart, Viscount Castlereagh, to enter into direct negotiations with the United States. This offer was accepted on 15 January 1814, and negotiations began in earnest between the two parties in Ghent, Belgium.

Issues regarding the impressment of American seamen, the status of the British-allied Indian groups, and the U.S. northern boundary with British Canada proved difficult to resolve. In the midst of these negotiations, on 27 September 1814, news reached London that the British had captured and burned Washington, D.C. Buoyed by this news, the British proposed that each party should retain its existing holdings. However, that British demand was totally abandoned when news of an American victory on Lake Champlain near British Canada reached London on 24 October. A temporary deadlock ensued.

But larger forces were at work for peace. The continental situation grew increasingly complex and dangerous as the British waged their battle against Napoleon's army. Additionally, fighting a war in two separate hemispheres strained British finances, while the Duke of Wellington, Arthur Wellesley, warned that unless the British could secure the Great Lakes, a decisive victory over the Americans was implausible. Under the weight of these considerations, the British agreed to restore the status quo that had existed between the parties prior to these recent hostilities.

Additional concessions from the United States and Great Britain were also forthcoming. The United States abandoned not only its demands regarding impressment but also demands for indemnification for commercial losses incurred as a result of the war between France and

Britain. For its part, Britain agreed to respect American rights in the Newfoundland fisheries and to abandon its demand for a permanent boundary between the United States and the Indian nations. However, the Americans did agree to an immediate cessation of hostilities against these nations after war's end and the restoration of all the possessions and privileges they had enjoyed prior to the war. Both parties also agreed to employ their best efforts to abolish the slave trade. The remaining major issue, the U.S.–British Canadian boundary, remained unresolved, and the parties agreed to turn the issue over to a boundary commission that resolved the dispute in 1822.

BIBLIOGRAPHY

Adams, Henry. *History of the United States.* 4 vols. New York: Boni, 1930.

Johnson, Paul. *A History of the American People.* New York: HarperCollins, 1998.

Faren R. Siminoff

See also **War of 1812.**

GHOST DANCE. The name Ghost Dance applies to two waves of a nativistic or messianic movement. Both originated among the Paiute Indians of Nevada in the nineteenth century.

In 1869 a prophet named Wodziwob began to predict supernatural events, claiming that the worn-out world would end, thus eliminating white men, and that all dead Indians would then return to the renewed world. Wodziwob professed to be in communication with the dead, and he instructed his followers to dance a circle dance and sing certain divinely revealed songs. The movement spread to the Indians of southern Oregon and northern California, but it gradually subsided when the promised supernatural events did not occur.

In 1889 there was a resurgence of the Ghost Dance, this time led by another Paiute messiah named Wovoka, or Jack Wilson. Wovoka claimed to have visited the spirit world while in a trance and to have seen God, who directed him to return to announce to the Indians that they should love one another and live peacefully, returning to the old Indian ways. By dancing and singing certain songs, they would hasten the end of the world and the disappearance of the whites. In the aftermath of this event, Indians would be restored to their hunting grounds and reunite with departed friends.

The revitalized Ghost Dance gained its principal strength among the tribes east of the Rockies. The movement spread rapidly to some Plains tribes, including the Lakota (Sioux), Cheyenne, Arapaho, and Comanche, who had recently been confined to reservations and were in the process of having their lands allotted. Enthusiasm for the dance, which included the wearing of "ghost shirts" that were supposedly impervious to bullets, led government officials to interpret the movement as a prelude to a militant revolt. Tensions mounted in late 1890 after Sitting Bull, a leader of the Ghost Dance at Standing Rock Reservation, was killed by Indian police attempting to arrest him. Two weeks later, more than two hundred Minniconjou Lakota Ghost Dancers who had fled the Cheyenne River Reservation after Sitting Bull's death were massacred by troops of the Seventh Cavalry at Wounded Knee, South Dakota.

Despite the tragedy, the Ghost Dance did not completely disappear after Wounded Knee. Although officially banned, Wovoka's original pacific doctrine continued to be practiced on the Pine Ridge Sioux Reservation into the early 1900s, and Ghost Dance congregations continued to function on Dakota reserves in Saskatchewan until the 1960s. Elements of the Ghost Dance were also incorporated into the revitalization of traditional cultural practices such as the Pawnee hand game and Kiowa war dance. Wovoka himself continued in his roles as shaman and healer at Walker River Reservation in Nevada until his death in 1932.

BIBLIOGRAPHY

De Mallie, Raymond. "The Lakota Ghost Dance: An Ethnohistorical Account." *Pacific Historical Review* 51 (1982): 385–405.

Hittman, Michael. *Wovoka and the Ghost Dance.* Edited by Don Lynch. Lincoln: University of Nebraska Press, 1997.

Mooney, James. "The Ghost Dance Religion and the Sioux Outbreak of 1890." In *14th Annual Report of the Bureau of American Ethnology, 1892–93, Part 2.* 1896. Reprint, Lincoln: University of Nebraska Press, 1991. A classic account.

Frank Rzeczkowski

See also **Paiute; Wounded Knee Massacre;** *and vol. 9:* **A Letter from Wovoka.**

GHOST TOWNS, the term used to identify communities that once prospered but later declined and were

Agricultural Ghost Town. A 1939 photograph by Russell Lee of the main street in Forgan, Okla.; many towns on the Great Plains were devastated by drought, dust storms, and the Great Depression, and only some recovered. Library of Congress

deserted, usually due to economic shifts and reversals. While most ghost towns are completely abandoned, small resident populations remain in some, and while many have disappeared from the landscape entirely, buildings and infrastructure remain to mark the locations of others.

Most western ghost towns were once mining towns, built—during the booms that began in California in 1849 and continued into the early twentieth century—on the promise of profits to be realized from a region's abundant mineral deposits. As mineral strikes slowed, prospectors and those providing them goods and services (merchants, saloon owners, bankers, and prostitutes) left homes and businesses so abruptly—to move on to the next strike—that towns were often left in a state of suspended animation, with displays still standing in shop windows, bottles and glasses on saloon tables, and the shelves of abandoned cabins lined with pieces of crockery. A number of mining towns—Virginia City, Nevada, and Columbia, California, among them—have been restored as tourist attractions, and provide visitors with the opportunity to relive late nineteenth-century mining days.

Some of the most interesting mining ghost towns are those that have escaped restoration efforts and remain largely unchanged from the days their mines operated at peak production. Two of the most impressive are Bodie, California, and Silver City, Idaho. Gold was discovered in 1859 in "Bad, Bad Bodie," located east of the Sierra Nevada and named for miner William S. Bodey. The town's principal mine produced over $14.5 million in gold during twenty-five years of successive mining. After the turn of the century, Bodie's mines began to close, and by the late 1940s, Bodie was officially abandoned. A California state park, it has been preserved in a state of "arrested deterioration." Silver City, Idaho, was built according to a predetermined plan in 1863, when the citizens of neighboring Ruby City decided their town was too far from their diggings, and moved it, building by building, into the canyon which became Silver City. Silver City mines produced steadily until the early 1870s and rebounded in the 1880s, but by the 1940s had become exhausted and closed one by one. In 1943, the Silver City Post Office was discontinued, making the town a true ghost town.

In addition to mining towns, deserted mill towns (Fayville, Vermont), discontinued rail stops (Everest, Kansas), stage and freight stops (Hardman, Oregon), abandoned military posts (Fort Randall, South Dakota), and dry oil-well towns (Texon, Texas) across the United States became ghost towns.

With the current interest in historic restoration and preservation, many ghost towns are being given "a second life" as adaptive reuse projects. Black Hawk, Colorado, is one of these and has been transformed into a mountain resort community with many of the original nineteenth-century buildings restored and refurbished to house hotels, restaurants, and casinos.

BIBLIOGRAPHY

Baker, T. Lindsay. *Ghost Towns of Texas.* Norman: University of Oklahoma Press, 1986.

Carter, William. *Ghost Towns of the West.* Menlo Park, Calif.: Lane Magazine and Book, 1971.

Fitzgerald, Daniel. *Ghost Towns of Kansas: A Traveler's Guide.* Lawrence: University Press of Kansas, 1988.

Silverberg, Robert. *Ghost Towns of the American West.* New York: Crowell, 1968. Reprint, Athens: Ohio University Press, 1994.

Brenda Jackson

See also **Gold Mines and Mining; Gold Rush, California.**

GI BILL OF RIGHTS. The initials "GI" originally stood for anything of "government issue." Eventually, they came to designate an enlisted soldier in the U.S. armed forces. In 1944 Congress passed the Servicemen's Readjustment Act, the so-called GI Bill of Rights, which provided government aid for veterans' hospitals and vocational rehabilitation; for the purchase by veterans of houses, farms, and businesses; and for four years of college education for veterans. Later, the act extended to veterans of the Korean War. The Readjustment Benefits Act of 1966 gave similar rights to all veterans of service in the U.S. armed forces, whether during wartime or peacetime. Subsequent acts provided for additional benefits. With the abolition of the draft in 1973, benefits were tied to length of service.

BIBLIOGRAPHY

Hyman, Harold M. *American Singularity: The 1787 Northwest Ordinance, the 1862 Homestead and Morrill Acts, and the 1944 GI Bill.* Athens: University of Georgia Press, 1986.

Christopher Lasch / A. E.

See also **Bonuses, Military; Pensions, Military and Naval; Veterans Affairs, Department of.**

G.I. JOE was developed in 1964 by Hasbro in response to the success of the BARBIE DOLL. The original G.I. Joe was fully "poseable," twelve inches tall, modeled after World War II soldiers, and came with a variety of accessories covering all branches of the military. Steeped in the victory of World War II and the impending COLD WAR, the year 1964 was an ideal time to introduce G.I. Joe. Using the phrase "action figure" instead of doll, G.I. Joe was immediately popular with young boys. As the struggle in Vietnam intensified, sales faltered with military toys, so in 1968, G.I. Joe became an adventurer. Instead of military accessories, Hasbro developed adventure accessories set in a variety of environments. In 1970, Joe came with "lifelike" hair and beards, and a new "AT" (Adventure Team) logo further distanced Joe from his military background. Sales quickened, and in 1974 designers added the famous "Kung Fu" grip allowing Joe to firmly hold accessories. Eventually Hasbro stopped the twelve-inch line and developed "Super G.I. Joe," an eight-inch figure that was more cost-effective and popular. Joe changed again in 1982 into an immensely popular three-and-three-quarter-inch figure. In the 1990s, Hasbro added another five-inch doll, developed an animated series, and even reintroduced the twelve-inch doll on a limited basis.

BIBLIOGRAPHY

Chapman, Roger. "From Vietnam to the New World Order: The G.I. Joe Action Figure as Cold War Artifact." In *The Impact of the Cold War On Popular Culture.* Carrollton: State University of West Georgia, 1999.

DePriest, Derryl. *The Collectible G.I. Joe.* Philadelphia: Courage Books, 1999.

Lisa A. Ennis

See also **Toys and Games.**

GIBBONS V. OGDEN, 9 Wheaton 1 (1824), a Supreme Court case that, for the first time since ratification of the U.S. Constitution, explicated the meaning of Article I, section 8, which gave Congress the power to regulate interstate and foreign commerce. Before the case was decided, it was common for states to legislate in matters that touched on commerce between states, and it was not clear whether navigation or transportation should be deemed "commerce." Chief Justice John Marshall, in one of his most famous decisions, made a powerful statement of the scope of Congress's power. In language that would be quoted countless times in future Supreme Court opinions, he insisted that it was wrong to "contend for that narrow construction which, in support of some theory not to be found in the Constitution, would deny to the government those powers which the words of the grant, as usually understood, import, and which are consistent with the general views and objects of the instrument." Marshall went on to state: "All America understands, and has uniformly understood, the word 'commerce' to comprehend navigation. . . . The power over commerce, including navigation, was one of the primary objects for which the people of America adopted their government, and must have been contemplated in forming it."

The dispute in the case was whether the New York legislature's grant of an exclusive monopoly to operate steamboats to Aaron Ogden could prevail over a federal law, under the authority of which Thomas Gibbons was running steamboats in competition with those of Ogden. Marshall held that the New York statute under which Ogden sought to exclude competition from Gibbons was an unconstitutional infringement of interstate commerce. Finding that a federal statute had provisions that applied to steamboats, Marshall declared New York's legislation granting Gibbons an exclusive license to operate steamboats barred. Marshall's opinion in *Gibbons* left open the question of the extent to which states could regulate interstate commerce if Congress had failed to act, and this became an important issue in future commerce clause litigation. Marshall's expansive reading in *Gibbons*, however, and his rejection of "strict construction" was frequently invoked in the late twentieth century to permit federal intrusion into many areas formerly regarded as the exclusive prerogative of state and local governments.

BIBLIOGRAPHY

Baxter, Maurice G. *The Steamboat Monopoly: Gibbons v. Ogden, 1824.* New York: Knopf, 1972.

Frankfurter, Felix. *The Commerce Clause under Marshall, Taney, and Waite.* Chapel Hill: University of North Carolina, 1937.

Kmiec, Douglas W., and Stephen B. Presser. *The American Constitutional Order: History, Cases, and Philosophy.* Cincinnati: Anderson, 1998.

Stephen B. Presser

See also **Commerce Clause; Constitution of the United States; Interstate Commerce Laws.**

GIDEON BIBLES. In 1899, Samuel Eugene Hill, John H. Nicholson, and Will J. Knights founded the Gideons, an organization for Christian commercial travelers. The organization grew so rapidly that its membership soon numbered several thousand. A few years after Hill, Nicholson, and Knights founded the society, it began the work for which it is best known: distributing Bibles to hotels, hospitals, and similar institutions. By 2002, the Gideon Society had grown to include 140,000 members in 175 countries. It claims to distribute one million copies of the Bible and New Testament in eighty different languages every week. A similar organization, the International Bible Society, also distributes Bibles.

I. Howell Kane / A. E.

See also **Religion and Religious Affiliation; Religious Thought and Writings.**

GIDEON V. WAINWRIGHT. In *Powell v. Alabama* (1932) the U.S. Supreme Court held that state prosecution of indigent defendants for a capital crime without effective appointment of defense counsel violated the due process clause of the Fourteenth Amendment to the Constitution of the United States. But in *Betts v. Brady* (1942) the Court declined to compel the states to provide counsel in noncapital cases without "special circumstances" that would render a trial without counsel "fundamentally unfair." In 1962, the year Clarence Earl Gideon was prosecuted for burglary in a Florida state court, about a dozen states, including Florida, failed to meet the minimum constitutional requirements of Betts. Gideon was forced to defend himself and was convicted, despite his insistence at trial that "the U.S. Supreme Court says I am entitled to counsel." A year later, in *Gideon v. Wainwright* (372 U.S. 335), the Supreme Court agreed with him. Overruling Betts, it held that at least in all felony cases "any person . . . too poor to hire a lawyer cannot be assured a fair trial unless counsel is provided for him."

The political reaction to Gideon was generally favorable. Many states implemented the decision by establishing public defender systems or greatly expanding existing ones. The limitation of Gideon to felony cases was rejected in 1972, when the Supreme Court held that no person may be imprisoned for any offense without representation by counsel (*Argersinger v. Hamlin*, 407 U.S. 25, 37).

BIBLIOGRAPHY

Beaney, William Merritt. *The Right to Counsel in American Courts.* Ann Arbor: University of Michigan Press, 1955.

Lewis, Anthony. *Gideon's Trumpet.* New York: Random House, 1964.

Yale Kamisar / A. R.

See also **Bill of Rights in U.S. Constitution; Constitution of the United States; Due Process of Law; Judicial Review; Supreme Court.**

GILBERT ISLANDS. In November 1943 U.S. military planners decided that the planned assault on the Marshall Islands required the capture of the Japanese-occupied Gilbert Islands, a collection of islands and atolls about two thousand miles southwest of Honolulu. After a two-hour preliminary bombardment by ships and naval planes under the command of Adm. Chester W. Nimitz and Vice Adm. Raymond A. Spruance, army troops of the Twenty-seventh Infantry Division landed on Butaritari Island in Makin Atoll on the morning of 23 November and quickly subdued the small Japanese force there with minimal casualties. The Second Marine Division's assault on the heavily defended Betio Island in Tarawa Atoll, however, cost 3,300 casualties, making Tarawa one of the bloodiest battles of the Pacific War.

BIBLIOGRAPHY

Crowl, Philip A., and Edmund G. Love. *Seizure of the Gilberts and Marshalls.* Washington, D.C.: Office of the Chief of Military History, 1955.

Gregg, Charles T. *Tarawa.* New York: Stein and Day, 1984.

Isely, Jeter A., and Philip A. Crowl. *The U.S. Marines and Amphibious War: Its Theory and Its Practice in the Pacific.* Princeton, N.J.: Princeton University Press, 1951.

Philip A. Crowl / A. R.

See also **Marine Corps, United States; Marshall Islands; Tarawa; World War II; World War II, Navy in.**

GILBERT'S PATENT. Sir Humphrey Gilbert, an English nobleman whose conduct during the imposition of Tudor rule in Ireland earned him a reputation for brutality, was by the 1570s a leading promoter of the search for a Northwest Passage through North America. In 1578 he was granted a patent by Queen Elizabeth I to plant colonies in America within a six-year period. Lands he discovered were to be held as a royal fief, and one-fifth of all gold and silver was to be reserved to the crown. Elizabeth authorized Gilbert to transport English settlers, establish one or more colonies, set up a government, grant lands, and make trade concessions "over a territory encompassing the settlement on all sides to a distance of two hundred leagues." All laws and religious policies were to conform to English practice. An expedition carefully planned in that year failed to materialize, but in June 1583 Gilbert's fleet of five ships sailed, reaching Newfoundland about the close of July. The colony failed, and Gilbert was lost at sea on his return voyage. On 25 March 1584 Gilbert's patent was renewed in the name of his half brother, Sir Walter Raleigh, whose discovery of Roanoke Island later that year was the beginning of English colonization in America. Gilbert's experience in subjugating the Irish rebellion proved useful to Raleigh in his efforts to wrest control of Virginia from Native Americans.

BIBLIOGRAPHY

Quinn, David Beers. *Set Fair for Roanoke: Voyages and Colonies, 1584–1606.* Chapel Hill: University of North Carolina Press, 1985.

Hugh T. Lefler / A. R.

See also **Explorations and Expeditions: British; Indian Policy, Colonial; Land Patents; Native Americans; Northwest Passage; Virginia.**

GILDED AGE. Named after an 1873 social satire by Mark Twain and Charles Dudley Warner, the Gilded Age encompasses the years from the 1870s to 1900. Scholars tend to see the legacies of the Civil War and Reconstruction as important contributors to the transformations that took place in the last three decades of the nineteenth century.

Congressional laws helped lay the groundwork for change. Whereas the Homestead Act (1862) opened the West for settlement by individual farmers, other laws, such as the Railroad Enabling Act (1866), the Desert Land Grant Act (1877), and the Stone and Timber Land Act (1878), transferred millions of acres of land and the resources and raw materials below ground into the hands of cattlemen, railroads, and mining and land development companies. Railroad expansion in combination with government land policies and the breaking of Native American resistance on the Plains in the 1870s and 1880s opened up the trans-Mississippi West for settlement and economic usage.

Constitutional change, too, contributed to this process. Between 1875 and 1900 the Supreme Court removed many state laws restricting interstate commerce but also blocked federal attempts at regulation. The Interstate Commerce Commission was created in 1887, but its limited powers were further circumscribed by Court decisions. Legal change helped to create a political environment in which forces of social change could unfold.

Innovations in manufacturing and communication joined by demographic changes led to a fusion of population growth, urbanization, and industrialization. Technological changes, such as the introduction of the Bessemer converter in steelmaking; the telegraph and the telephone, the latter invented in 1875 by Alexander Graham Bell; the discovery of electricity as an energy source by Thomas A. Edison; and developments in transportation and mass transit made possible the concentration of manufacturing consumption in cities. After 1880, the so-called "new immigration" from southern and southeastern Europe along with rural-urban migration within the United States provided workers and consumers for burgeoning urban marketplaces. Mass marketing companies like I. M. Singer, mail-order houses like Sears, Roebuck, and department stores like Wanamaker's catered to American consumer needs. By 1900, participation in national and urban markets was no longer a matter of choice.

Rapidly advancing industrialization led to the emergence of economies of scale. In 1850, the average capital investment in a company amounted to $700,000. In 1900, average investment had risen to $1.9 million. To remain competitive and to satisfy investors and shareholders, companies needed to increase the return on investments. Manufacturers began to replace craft techniques with routinized and segmented work processes aided by new production technologies. New technologies enabling manufacturers to produce goods and to provide services at an unprecedented scale accelerated the swings in the boom-and-bust cycle of the U.S. economy.

A cycle of global capitalist expansion begun in the 1820s came to a halt in the 1870s and crashed in the 1890s. In 1873, the Credit Mobilier scandal and the collapse of Jay Cooke's Northern Pacific Railroad resulted in a recession from which the country only recovered four years later in 1877. In May 1893, the collapse of the Pennsylvania and Reading Railroad and of the National Cordage Company led to a stock market crash and a prolonged recession. Before the year was over, five hundred banks and sixteen thousand businesses had failed. At the height of the depression four million workers lost their jobs.

What had happened? New technologies of mass production and mass distribution had consistently driven down prices. Between 1873 and the late 1890s, commodity prices had dropped by 80 percent. At the same time, "sound money" politics had kept the currency supply tight, putting the squeeze on workers and farmers especially.

Banking and monetary policies contributed to this problem. The National Banking Acts of 1863 and 1864 introduced order into banking through a federally chartered banking system but also kept the money supply tight. The Sherman Silver Purchase Act of 1890, which enabled the government to buy silver in proportion to gold, was designed to increase the money supply, but it was repealed at the most inappropriate moment, the onset of the depression in 1893. The economic policies of the presidencies from Ulysses S. Grant to William McKinley were grounded in fiscal conservatism, economic individualism, and market liberalism, which neither anticipated such problems nor adequately solved them.

Workers and farmers met such policies with some resistance. Mostly unsuccessfully, workingmen challenged railroads and manufacturers in the Great Strike of 1877, the 1886 railroad strike, the 1892 Homestead Strike, and the 1894 Pullman Strike. Workers organized in the Knights of Labor and after 1889 in the newly founded American Federation of Labor, which advocated a more cautious business unionism. Agrarian resistance gained momentum with the People's, or Populist, Party, founded in 1890. The Populists experienced a meteoric rise in political fortunes at the ballot boxes in several southern and western states. Although the Populists were successful in several state and gubernatorial elections, their attempt to take control of the presidency through a "fusion ticket" with the Democrats failed in 1896, and the party disappeared thereafter.

Economic changes may have helped undermine support for such a third party as they aided in the recovery. In the late 1890s, poor European harvests increased demand for grain and cereals, and new gold discoveries in Alaska, Colorado, South Africa, and Australia created enough inflation to raise prices out of the doldrums.

This era that experienced social and economic change on a massive scale was marked by many contradictions. Along with the beginning of the modern American labor movement and a resurgence of the movement for women's rights, the age saw the implementation of rigid race segregation in the South through so-called Jim Crow laws, sanctioned by the Supreme Court's 1896 decision in *Plessy v. Ferguson.* The Gilded Age also witnessed the emergence of the United States as an imperialist foreign power. Desire for greatness on the seas, partially spawned by Alfred Thayer Mahan's *The Influence of Sea Power upon History* (1890), led the United States into war with Spain in 1898 and into a subsequent war in the Philippines from 1899 to 1902. The Gilded Age saw the birth pangs of the United States as a global power, an urban, industrial society, and a modern, liberal corporatist state. Many problems remained unsolved, however, for the Progressive Era and New Deal reform policies to address.

BIBLIOGRAPHY

Cashman, Sean Dennis. *America in the Gilded Age: From the Death of Lincoln to the Rise of Theodore Roosevelt.* 3d ed. New York: New York University Press, 1993.

Cherny, Robert W. *American Politics in the Gilded Age, 1868–1900.* Wheeling, Ill.: Harlan Davidson, 1997.

Faulkner, Harold Underwood. *Politics, Reform, and Expansion, 1890–1900.* New York: Harper, 1959.

Garraty, John A. *The New Commonwealth, 1877–1890.* New York: Harper and Row, 1968.

Summers, Mark Wahlgren. *The Gilded Age, or, the Hazard of New Functions.* Upper Saddle River, N.J.: Prentice Hall, 1997.

Trachtenberg, Alan. *The Incorporation of America: Culture and Society in the Gilded Age.* New York: Hill and Wang, 1982.

Thomas Winter

See also **Business Cycles; Land Policy; Mass Production; Populism; Strikes; Urbanization.**

GINSENG, AMERICAN, *Panax quinquefolium,* which grew in the Hudson Valley and elsewhere, was at first regarded as a weed. It resembled a root native to Korea and northern China, to which the Chinese imputed extraordinary but wholly imaginary therapeutic and pharmacological properties. On 22 February 1784, Robert Morris dispatched to China the *Empress of China* from New York with American ginseng. The voyage netted $30,000. The owners, as Morris wrote to John Jay, hoped "to encourage others in the adventurous pursuit of commerce." Subsequent trade with China in ginseng boomed, and was restricted only by the limited quantities of American ginseng available. About 1790, the fur trade of the Pacific coast largely displaced the ginseng trade as the principal trade good that Americans used to obtain silks and teas from China, although the ginseng trade continued into the twentieth century. In the early 2000s, Wisconsin was the principal producer.

BIBLIOGRAPHY

Christman, Margaret. *Adventurous Pursuits: Americans and the China Trade, 1784–1844.* Washington, D.C.: Smithsonian Institution Press, 1984.

Dulles, Foster R. *The Old China Trade.* Boston; New York: Houghton Mifflin, 1930; New York: AMS, 1970.

Frank Edward Ross / C. W.

See also **Agriculture; China Trade; Medicine, Alternative.**